CliffsNotes®

ACT®

CliffsNotes®

ACT®

by
BTPS Testing

Contributing Authors

Joy Mondragon-Gilmore, Ph.D.

Jerry Bobrow, Ph.D.

Rebecca Carter, Ph.D.

Jean Eggenschwiler, B.A.

David A. Kay, M.S.

Mark Zegarelli, B.A.

Harold Nathan, Ph.D.

Consultants

Pitt Gilmore, B.A.

Ron Podrasky, M.S.

Kevin Nourian, M.S.

Houghton Mifflin Harcourt
Boston • New York

About the Author

BTPS Testing has presented test-preparation workshops at the California State Universities for over 35 years. The faculty at BTPS Testing has authored more than 30 national best-selling guides for the SAT, CSET, CBEST, GRE, GMAT, PPST, and RICA. Each year the authors of this study guide conduct lectures to thousands of students preparing for college-level entrance examinations.

Authors' Acknowledgments

The authors would like to thank Suzanne Snyder for her attention to detail in editing the original manuscript, and for her patience and support during the production process.

Editorial

Acquisitions Editor: Greg Tubach

Project Editor: Suzanne Snyder

Copy Editor: Kelly Henthorne

Technical Editors: Sandra McCune, Jane Burstein, Michael Yard, Tom Page

Proofreader: Betty Kish

Table of Contents

Preface xiii
    How This Book Is Organized xiii
    How to Use This Guide xiii

Introduction: An Overview of the ACT 1
    Test Format 1
    Scoring 2
        Multiple-Choice Questions. 2
        Essay Writing Section 2
        Essay Comments 3
    Frequently Asked Questions 3
    General Approaches for Multiple-Choice Questions 4
        Pace Yourself 4
        Avoid Misreading the Question 5
        Watch for Questions Containing x and y Values in Math Problems 5
        Watch for Questions with the Negative Words EXCEPT and NOT 5
        Fill in the Correct Answer 5
        The Elimination Approach. 6
        The Plus-Minus Approach 6
    Final General Tips and Helpful Hints 7

PART I: DIAGNOSTIC TEST

Chapter 1: Diagnostic Test 11
    Answer Sheets. 11
    Directions 13
    English Test. 14
    Mathematics Test 22
    Reading Test 27
    Science Test 31
    Scoring the Diagnostic Test. 36
        Answer Key for Diagnostic Test 36
        English Test 36
        Mathematics Test 36
        Reading Test. 36
        Science Test 36
        Charting and Analyzing Your Test Results 37
    Answers and Explanations 38
    English Test. 38
        Passage I 38
        Passage II. 38
        Passage III 39
    Mathematics Test 40
    Reading Test 49
        Passage I 49
        Passage II. 49
    Science Test 50
        Passage I 50
        Passage II. 50
        Passage III 51

PART II: REVIEW OF EXAM AREAS

Chapter 2: The ACT English Test **55**
  General Overview of the ACT English Test. 55
    Formation of Questions. 56
    Skills and Concepts Tested. 56
    Directions 56
    Structure 57
  General Strategies 57
  Sample Questions with Suggested Strategies. .59
    Question Type One: Usage/Mechanics Errors. 59
      Punctuation Errors. 60
      Grammar and Usage Errors 61
      Sentence Structure Errors 69
    Question Type Two: Rhetorical Skills 70
      Writing Strategy 71
      Organization Errors 71
      Style Errors 72
  Practice English Test Questions 72
    Answers and Explanations 74

Chapter 3: The ACT Mathematics Test **75**
  Format 75
  Skills and Concepts Tested. 76
    Pre-Algebra 76
    Elementary Algebra. 76
    Intermediate Algebra 76
    Coordinate Geometry 76
    Plane Geometry 76
    Trigonometry 76
  Calculator Use on the ACT 76
  Directions 77
  General Test-Taking Strategies 77
  Sample Questions with Specific Suggested Strategies 78
    Pre-Algebra Sample Questions. 78
    Elementary Algebra Sample Questions. 81
    Intermediate Algebra Sample Questions. 84
    Coordinate Geometry Sample Questions 87
    Plane Geometry Sample Questions 90
    Trigonometry Sample Questions 93

Chapter 4: The ACT Reading Test **97**
  General Overview of the ACT Reading Test 97
    Skills and Concepts Tested. 97
    Directions 98
  Identifying Question Types 98
    Indirect versus Direct Questions 99
    Question Type One: Main Point 99
    Question Type Two: Supporting Details 99
    Question Type Three: Compare/Contrast 100
    Question Type Four: Drawing Generalizations and Conclusions 100
    Question Type Five: Mood (Author's Tone or Attitude) 101
    Question Type Six: Sequence of Ideas 101
    Question Type Seven: Word Meanings 102

Four-Step Approach 102
General Tips and Suggestions. 104
Sample Passage and Questions with Mark-Ups 105
Practice Reading Question Approaches and Strategies 107
   Look for the Main Point. 108
   Look for Supporting Details. 108
   Draw Generalizations or Conclusions 109
   Look for the Mood of the Passage. .109
   Look for the Sequence of Ideas. 109
   Look for Meaning of Words or Phrases. 110
   Three "Last Resort" Strategies 110
Vocabulary Resources 111
   Memory Improvement. 111
   Power Vocabulary Words. 112
   Word Parts. 113
      Prefixes 113
      Roots 114
      Suffixes 114
      Examples of Word Parts 115

Chapter 5: The ACT Science Test **117**
General Overview of the ACT Science Test 117
   Format 117
   Skills and Concepts Tested. 117
   Directions 118
   General Strategies 118
Sample Questions with Suggested Strategies. 118
   Data Representation Passage Type 119
      Practice Data Representation 119
   Research Summary Passage Type 121
      Practice Research Summary 121
   Conflicting Viewpoints Passage Type 124
      Practice Conflicting Viewpoints .124
Glossary of Science Terms 126

Chapter 6: The ACT Plus Writing Test **137**
General Overview of the ACT Plus Writing Test 137
   Writing Test Requirements 137
   Skills and Concepts Tested. 137
   Directions 138
   Scoring 138
   Essay Comments 140
General Strategies and Tips 140
The Three-Step Writing Process 141
   Step 1: Prewriting. 141
      Brainstorming 142
      Clustering 142
      Outlining 143
   Step 2: Writing the Essay 143
      Five-Paragraph Model. 144
      The "Why Essay" Model 146
   Step 3: Proofreading. 146
Practice with Sample Topics and Essays .146
   Sample Topic 1 146
      Sample Topic 1: Two Well-Written Responses 147
      Evaluating Your Essay 148

Sample Topic 2 149
   Sample Topic 2: Two Written Responses. .149
Sample Topics for Extra Practice 150
   Extra Practice Sample Topic 1 150
   Extra Practice Sample Topic 2 151
Answers to Your Questions about the ACT Plus Writing Test 151

PART III: MATH SKILLS REVIEW

Chapter 7: Math Review Fundamentals **155**
Overview 156
   Common Math Symbols 156
   Numbers Vocabulary. 156
   ACT Common Mathematical Conventions and Terminology. 157
   Geometric Figures on the ACT 157
   Important Geometric Formulas 158
      Pythagorean Theorem 160
   Fraction-Decimal-Percent Equivalents. 160
   Customary English and Metric System Measurements 161

Chapter 8: Arithmetic (Pre-Algebra) **163**
Arithmetic Diagnostic Test 163
   Scoring the Diagnostic Test. 166
      Answer Key. 166
   Charting and Analyzing Your Diagnostic Test Results. 168
Arithmetic Review. 168
   Sets of Numbers 168
   Divisibility Rules. 169
   Grouping Symbols 170
   Order of Operations 170
   Integers. 171
      Number Line 171
      Absolute Value 172
      Addition 172
      Subtraction 173
      Multiplication and Division 173
   Fractions. 174
      Mixed Numbers. 175
      Simplified Fractions 175
      Changing the Denominator 176
   Factors 176
   Common Factors 176
   Multiples 177
   Common Multiples. 177
   Least Common Multiple 178
   Least Common Denominator 178
   Adding and Subtracting Positive and Negative Fractions 178
      Adding Mixed Numbers 179
      Subtracting Mixed Numbers 179
      Multiplying Fractions 180
      Multiplying Mixed Numbers. 181
      Dividing Fractions or Mixed Numbers. .181
      Complex Fractions. 181

Decimals 182
  Rounding Off 183
  Fractions Written in Decimal Form 183
  Adding and Subtracting Decimals 183
  Multiplying Decimals 184
  Dividing Decimals 184
  Changing a Fraction to a Decimal 185
Ratios and Proportions 185
  Cross-Products Fact 185
Percents 186
  Changing Decimals to Percents 186
  Changing Fractions to a Percent 186
  Percentage-Type Problems 187
  Equation and Proportion Methods 188
  Percent Change 189
Exponents 189
  More Exponents 189
  Negative Exponents 190
  Multiplying Two Numbers with the Same Base 190
  Dividing Two Numbers with the Same Base 190
  Base with an Exponent Raised to a Power 190
Scientific Notation 191
Square Roots 191
  Perfect Squares 191
  Simplifying a Square Root 193
Set Theory 194
Venn Diagrams 195
Factorials, Combinations, and Permutations 196
  Factorials 196
  Combinations 197
  Permutations 199
  Methods for Counting 200
Probability 201
Basic Descriptive Statistics 202
Arithmetic Practice Questions 203
  Easy to Moderate 203
  Average 205
  Above Average to Difficult 206
Answers and Explanations 208
  Easy to Moderate 208
  Average 208
  Above Average to Difficult 210

Chapter 9: Algebra 213
Algebra Diagnostic Test 214
  Scoring the Diagnostic Test 216
    Answer Key 216
  Charting and Analyzing Your Diagnostic Test Results 217
Algebra Review 218
  Algebra's Implied Multiplication 218
  Set Notations 218
  Variables and Algebraic Expressions 219
  Solving Linear Equations in One or Two Variables 220
  Solving Two Equations Involving the Same Two Variables 221

Equations Involving Absolute Value 225
Solving Linear Inequalities in One Variable. 225
Polynomials. 226
Algebraic Fractions 231
Solving Quadratic Equations in One Variable .234
Solving Equations with the Quadratic Formula 235
Logarithm Functions 236
Coordinate Geometry. 237
Functions, Function Notation, and Transformations of Functions 244
Practice Questions: Elementary Algebra, Intermediate Algebra,
and Coordinate Geometry 246
Section I: Elementary Algebra 247
Section II: Intermediate Algebra 249
Section III: Coordinate Geometry. 252
Answers and Explanations 255
Section I: Elementary Algebra 255
Section II: Intermediate Algebra 260
Section III: Coordinate Geometry. 266

Chapter 10: Geometry. 273
Geometry Diagnostic Test. 274
Scoring the Diagnostic Test. 277
Answer Key. 277
Charting and Analyzing Your Diagnostic Test Results. 278
Geometry Review 279
Lines, Segments, Rays, and Angles 279
Polygons and Their Angles 283
Triangles. 286
Exterior Angle Theorem 288
Pythagorean Theorem 288
Special Right Triangle Theorems 289
Quadrilaterals 292
Circles 295
Perimeter, Circumference, and Area of Plane Figures 297
Surface Area, Volume, and Diagonal Lengths of Three-Dimensional Figures . . .299
Congruence and Similarity 300
Geometry Practice Questions 302
Easy to Moderate 302
Average 303
Above Average to Difficult. 305
Answers and Explanations 306
Easy to Moderate 306
Average 307
Above Average to Difficult. 310

Chapter 11: Trigonometry 313
Trigonometry Diagnostic Test 313
Scoring the Diagnostic Test. 315
Answer Key. 315
Charting and Analyzing Your Diagnostic Test Results. 315
Trigonometry Review 316
Values and Properties of Trig Functions. 316
Trigonometry of Right Triangles. 322
Graphing Trig Functions 325
Graphs of the Sine and Cosine 327
Trigonometric Identities 328

Trigonometric Equations..331
Trigonometry Practice Questions..332
    Easy to Moderate...332
    Average...332
    Above Average to Difficult...333
   Answers and Explanations..333
    Easy to Moderate...333
    Average...334
    Above Average to Difficult...334

Chapter 12: Word Problems 337

Word Problems Diagnostic Test..337
   Scoring the Diagnostic Test...338
    Answer Key..338
   Charting and Analyzing Your Diagnostic Test Results...................338
Word Problems Review..339
   Motion Problems...339
   Work Problems...340
   Mixture Problems..342
   Age Problems..344
   Integer Problems..345
Word Problems Practice Questions...346
   Easy to Moderate..346
   Average...347
   Above Average to Difficult..348
   Answers and Explanations..348
    Easy to Moderate..348
    Average...349
    Above Average to Difficult..351

PART IV: THREE FULL-LENGTH ACT PRACTICE TESTS

Chapter 13: Practice Test 1 355

Answer Sheets...355
Directions..357
English Test..358
Mathematics Test..368
Reading Test..377
Science Test..385
Scoring the Practice Test...401
   Answer Key..401
Charting and Analyzing Your Test Results................................402
Practice Test 1: Answers and Explanations...............................403
   English Test..403
   Mathematics Test..407
   Reading Test..421
   Science Test..424

Chapter 14: Practice Test 2 429

Answer Sheets...429
Directions..431
English Test..432
Mathematics Test..443
Reading Test..452
Science Test..460

Scoring the Practice Test 474
   Answer Key 474
Charting and Analyzing Your Test Results 476
Practice Test 2: Answers and Explanations 476
   English Test 476
   Mathematics Test 480
   Reading Test 494
   Science Test 497

Chapter 15: Practice Test 3 501
Answer Sheets 501
Directions 503
English Test 504
Mathematics Test 515
Reading Test 524
Science Test 534
Scoring the Practice Test 548
   Answer Key 548
Charting and Analyzing Your Test Results 550
Practice Test 3: Answers and Explanations 550
   English Test 550
   Mathematics Test 556
   Reading Test 570
   Science Test 576

Final Preparation 581
One Week before the Exam 581
Exam Day 581

Preface

CliffsNotes ACT makes it easier for you to optimize your performance on the ACT. This study guide was written by teachers and educators to give you a comprehensive and easy-to-follow review while providing you with a positive, systematic learning experience. If you study the review chapters and practice regularly, you should boost your knowledge and skills in English, mathematics, reading, and science. This book is not meant to be a substitute for formal high school classroom instruction, but the enhanced subject-related teaching tools can help you improve your understanding of the test subjects and provide you with future learning opportunities in your college career. If you follow the lessons and strategies in this book and practice, you will get the best preparation possible in a reasonable amount of time.

In keeping with the fine tradition of CliffsNotes, this guide was developed by leading educational experts in the field of test preparation to meet the standards of college entrance preparation. The authors of this study guide have been successfully teaching thousands of students to prepare for college entrance exams for more than 30 years. The materials, strategies, and techniques presented in this guide have been researched, tested, and evaluated in preparation classes at leading California universities and school districts.

How This Book Is Organized

- **Introduction to the ACT:** This is a general overview of the ACT, test format, scoring, frequently asked questions, general strategies, and general tips.

- **Part I—Diagnostic Test:** An introductory diagnostic test acquaints you with ACT question types, analyzes areas where you may need to improve, and provides you with a baseline starting point.

- **Part II—Review of Exam Areas:** These review chapters focus on the core subject areas tested in English, mathematics, reading, science, and writing. Each chapter focuses on the basic skills you'll need, directions, suggested strategies with sample questions, practice questions, and additional tips.

- **Part III—Math Skills Review:** Six additional math review chapters offer you an intensive review of arithmetic/pre-algebra, elementary/intermediate algebra, coordinate geometry, plane geometry, trigonometry, and word problems. Each review area offers illustrated sample problems and practice exercises. Important symbols, terminology, and equivalents are also included.

- **Part IV—Three Full-Length ACT Practice Tests:** The full-length practice tests include answers and in-depth explanations. Practice tests are followed by analysis worksheets to assist you in evaluating your progress.

How to Use This Guide

Getting ready for the ACT requires a strategic and customized study plan, and there are as many ways to study as there are people who take the ACT. Understanding your unique learning style and applying this understanding to a customized *action plan* will aid in your success on the test.

CliffsNotes ACT includes hundreds of sample or practice problems with step-by-step explanations. They are designed to enhance many different learning styles, but before you begin reading the chapter subject reviews, start by exploring your desired college programs to gather information, set your goals, and inquire about the optional written essay requirements. Know the scores that you need for success *before* preparing for the ACT and then follow these suggested guidelines.

1. **Learn about the ACT.** Start your preparation by reading the introduction to establish a basic knowledge of the test—the test format, test directions, question types, test contents, and the scoring outlined on the official ACT website, www.actstudent.org.

2. **Assess your skills.** Before you study the ACT subjects in the review chapters, get a general sense of your starting point. Take the diagnostic test in Chapter 1 to assess your strengths and weaknesses and then compare your results with the scores you would like to attain. The areas that require the most growth are

the areas on which you want to focus the majority of your study time. Starting with a look at the growth you may desire is also a good way to guesstimate how much overall time you will need to devote to studying. Then create an *action plan* for your study time and be willing to frequently adapt and revise your goals as you evaluate your progress.

3. **Study Chapters 2 through 6.** One of the most important steps in tackling the ACT is to study each subject test separately. This is why we have divided Chapters 2 through 6 into specific subject-related tests: English, Mathematics, Reading, Science, and Writing. Each chapter presents a review of the material related to each test's format, content, question types, and strategies. Supporting sample questions and practice exercises provided in these chapters will help to strengthen your understanding of each ACT test. Work through each chapter's comprehensive material, follow the step-by-step instructions for solving problems, and work out the sample questions. Many of the problems in the practice exercises are arranged by level of difficulty. Start in sequence with the easy problems first and then work your way up to the difficult problems as you increase your ability to solve challenging problems.

4. **Study Math Test Chapters 7 through 12.** Comprehensive math review chapters aid in learning ACT mathematic concepts and skills: pre-algebra, elementary/intermediate algebra, coordinate geometry, plane geometry, and trigonometry. Each chapter provides a diagnostic test to evaluate proficiency in ACT math topics and is followed by step-by-step review material that provides valuable exam-oriented approaches, instructional tools, and practice exercises. If you follow the lessons and strategies in these chapters and practice regularly, you should be able to improve your score on the ACT Mathematics Test.

5. **Learn strategies and test directions.** Study the general strategies outlined in the introduction on pages 4–7 and study the test directions in the beginning of each review chapter. Decide which strategies work best for you and memorize the directions *before* your test day. If you plan ahead, you will be able to work quickly and efficiently on your test day.

6. **Practice, practice, practice.** Research has proven that consistent practice is a key to scoring higher on college entrance tests. This is why three full-length model practice tests are included in the final chapters. These model practice tests include answers with thorough explanations. Be sure to practice using the actual test format as often as possible.

7. **A final checklist.** Finally, the last part of this book includes a checklist on page 581 as a reminder of "things to do" before you take your exam.

An Overview of the ACT

In the United States, recognition of the ACT has increased for college admission. It is widely accepted and is required by many universities and colleges to assess your readiness for general education college coursework. The ACT is unlike other standardized tests because it places an emphasis on *achievement* in academic subjects you learned in high school, rather than an emphasis on critical thinking skills as applied to academic subjects. The ACT is a curriculum-based test that measures your knowledge of core high school academic subjects: English, mathematics, reading, and science. You are not expected to be an expert in every subject area, but a solid knowledge of high school core academic classes is expected. Although some reasoning skills help you solve problems, reasoning skills are not highlighted on the ACT.

Begin preparing for the ACT through strategic planning and preparation. Get organized and set personal goals as you read this introduction to learn more about the test format, contents, scoring, question types, and general strategies for each test on the ACT.

Test Format

Test	Content	Percentage	Number of Questions
English	Usage/mechanics Rhetorical skills **Total English Test**	53% 47% 100%	40 questions 35 questions **75 questions total** **Time: 45 minutes**
Mathematics	Pre-algebra Elementary algebra Intermediate algebra Coordinate geometry Plane geometry Trigonometry **Total Mathematics Test**	23% 17% 15% 15% 23% 7% 100%	24 questions 18 questions 14 questions 4 questions **60 questions total** **Time: 60 minutes**
Reading	Prose fiction passages Social science passages Humanities passages Natural science passages **Total Reading Test**	25% 25% 25% 25% 100%	10 questions 10 questions 10 questions 10 questions **40 questions total** **Time: 35 minutes**

Science	Biology, chemistry, earth science, physics
	    Data representation
	    Research summaries
	    Conflicting viewpoints
	Total Science Test
		
		38%
		45%
		17%
		100%
			
			15 questions
			18 questions
			7 questions
			40 questions total
			Time: 35 minutes

Totals		175 minutes (or 2 hours, 55 minutes, plus 30 minutes if taking the optional Writing Test).	**215 questions**
Writing (optional)	Essay writing prompt	1 essay	**30 minutes**

Note: Structure, scoring, and the order of tests is subject to change. Visit www.actstudent.org for updated exam information.

A short break is scheduled after the first two tests.

Scoring

The four multiple-choice ACT tests generate the following scaled scores:

- Four subject test scores in English, mathematics, reading, and science that range from 1 (low) to 36 (high).
- A composite score that averages the total of all four tests from 1 (low) to 36 (high).
- Subscores in seven areas from 1 (low) to 18 (high).

Scaled Scores

Test	Scaled Score	Subscore
English	1–36	Usage/mechanics: 1–18 Rhetorical skills: 1–18
Mathematics	1–36	Pre-algebra/elementary algebra: 1–18 Intermediate algebra/coordinate geometry: 1–18 Plan geometry/trigonometry: 1–18
Reading	1–36	Social studies/natural sciences: 1–18 Arts/literature: 1–18
Science	1–36	No subscores
Composite score	1–36 (the average of all four test scores)	

Multiple-Choice Questions

The scores for the four **multiple-choice** tests are based on the number of questions you answer correctly. Keep in mind that there is no penalty for guessing. If you are faced with a question that requires additional information or that is impossible to answer, it is to your advantage to eliminate at least one answer choice and make an educated guess.

Each question computes a *raw score* (rounded to the nearest whole number) that is based on the number of questions you answer correctly. The raw score is converted into a *scaled score* from 1 to 36 for each test. The scaled score also helps to determine your national percentile ranking that many colleges use to compare your score results with other applicants. The national *average composite score* on the ACT is 21.0, denoting that 50 percent of students score above and 50 percent of students score below 21.0.

Essay Writing Section

On the optional **ACT Plus Writing Test**, your essay is scored holistically by two independent readers who each assign a score from 1 (low) to 6 (high). The two essay scores are added together, averaged, and then rounded up to produce a single final score that represents your essay response from 2 (low) to 12 (high). If there is a discrepancy of more than one point in the assigned scores from the two readers, a third reader will read and evaluate your essay. If you take the Writing Test, scores reported to you and to the colleges you designate will include two additional scores.

- The first score is a Writing Test subscore ranging on a scale from 2 to 12.
- The second score is the *combined* essay score of English and Writing tests reported on a scale score ranging from 1 to 36.

Holistic scoring means that readers look at the *overall quality* of each essay. This means that *all aspects* of a well-written essay count toward your final score: well-developed ideas, good organization, supporting evidence, and an effective use of grammar and language. The impression that your essay makes upon the readers is important. However, keep in mind that the readers who score your essay are on your side and make every effort to focus on your writing strengths. Due to the limited time that is allotted for this task (30 minutes), readers take into consideration that even the highest scoring essay may contain some minor errors of grammar or word mechanics. Your essay is technically a "first draft" and probably will not be errorless, even with the highest score of 12. That does not mean that you should ignore the rules of standard written English in the finished essay, but remember that they are not as important to your overall score as your ideas and how you have organized them. Essays are expected to be superior in content, organization, and development.

Essay Comments

The ACT Plus Writing Test readers select comments derived from the scoring rubric to be included with the exam results. These essay comments are included to help students understand the strengths and weaknesses of their essays. See Chapter 6 for the rubric used by the ACT Plus Writing Test readers to analyze scores.

Frequently Asked Questions

Q: Who administers the ACT?

A: The ACT is administered by American College Testing (ACT Student Services), www.actstudent.org.

Q: Is the ACT the same as the SAT?

A: No. The ACT is an *achievement* test. It measures what you learned in high school core academic classes. The subjects on the ACT are English, mathematics, reading, and science (and an optional writing section). The SAT is an *abilities* test of reasoning. It measures your abilities in English, mathematics, and writing. The sections on the SAT are critical reading, mathematics, and a *required* writing section. All sections on the SAT require that you apply critical thinking, reasoning, and problem-solving skills to answer the questions.

Q: How often is the ACT administered?

A: The ACT is administered nationwide six times during the school year, depending on your location. The test is usually given in September, October, December, February, April, and June.

Q: How can I register for the ACT?

A: Most students create an ACTWeb account and register online. The ACTWeb account allows students to make registration changes and view a score report after taking the test. Online registrations accept credit card, an ACT fee waiver, or state voucher. If you are paying by check, you must register using the paper registration method. You may request "only one" mail registration packet at 2727 Scott Blvd. (minizip 46), P.O. Box 414, Iowa City, IA 52243-0414, (319) 337-1270.

Q: Can special arrangements be made if I have a disability?

A: Yes. ACT attempts to make special arrangements whenever possible. Students must complete a request for special arrangements at www.act.org/aap/pdf/arranged.pdf or call (319) 337-1510.

Q: Is standby registration available?

A: Yes, standby registration is available on a limited basis during the standby request period listed on the ACT website. If you are unable to meet regular registration deadlines, you may attempt to register online as "standby." Additional fees are required and you must arrive at the test center with a Standby Ticket.

Q: When should I take the ACT?

A: It is popular for first-time test-takers to take the ACT during the spring of their junior year, and then again in the fall of their senior year.

Q: **Can I take the test more than once?**

A: Yes. It is common for students to take the ACT more than once. ACT reports only one test score per report sent to each designated school. Statistically, retest scores can improve as much as 57 percent. Check with your high school college advisor (or counseling office) for specific recommendations based upon your personal student profile. Visit the ACT website www.actstudent.org for more information regarding your statistical chances of increasing successive test scores.

Q: **Should I guess on the ACT?**

A: Yes. The ACT score is based on the number of questions you answer correctly. There is no penalty for guessing. If you can eliminate two or more of the multiple-choice answers to a question, it is to your advantage to guess. Eliminating two or more answers increases your chance of choosing the right answer.

Q: **Where is the ACT administered?**

A: The ACT is administered at hundreds of schools within the United States, Puerto Rico, U.S. Territories, and Canada. Check online at www.actstudent.org/regist/centers for a list of test centers. When you register for the test online, you are prompted to determine which test centers have availability. Registering early will provide you with the best chance to secure your first choice. Some special administrations are given in limited locations.

Q: **When will I get my ACT test results?**

A: ACT multiple-choice test results are available through your ACTWeb account within 2.5 to 3 weeks after you take the test. Writing Plus test scores are available online about 4 weeks after your test date.

Q: **Can I request a copy of my test questions?**

A: Yes. If you take the ACT at a national test center, you can pay extra for a Test Information Release (TIR) to be sent to you with questions, answers, and a scoring rubric.

General Approaches for Multiple-Choice Questions

This section was developed as a guide to introduce general test-taking guidelines, approaches, and strategies that are useful on the ACT. Although this section is limited to general tips and strategies, specific strategies related to specific subject area question types are included in chapter reviews.

The multiple-choice questions cover a broad range of topics while considering a variety of question types. The facts and concepts on the ACT are often presented in subtle variations of selected answer choices that make it difficult for test-takers to narrow down the correct answer. Additionally, subtle variations in answer choices can distract you from choosing the right answer.

The goal in offering you strategies is for you to be able to work through problems quickly, accurately, and efficiently. As you practice problems using the strategies outlined in this section, determine whether the strategies fit with your individual learning style. What may work for some people, may not work for others. If it takes you longer to recall a strategy than to solve the problem, it's probably not a good strategy for you to adopt. And, remember, don't get stuck on any one question. Taking time to answer the most difficult question on the test correctly, but losing valuable test time, won't get you the score you deserve.

Consider the following guidelines when taking the exam:

Pace Yourself

When you begin the exam, write down the time you start to help you keep track of the time. Challenging questions can be time-consuming, so you should plan ahead to pace yourself. Try to leave a couple of minutes at the end of each individual test to quickly scan your answer sheet to look for unanswered questions, and to make sure answers are marked correctly. Depending on the individual test, never spend more than about one minute on any question. However, you must also remember not to work so quickly that you make careless errors. To help with time efficiency, some test-takers answer all of the easy questions first (within each test), and then go back to answer the more time-consuming questions later. Working through each practice test in this study guide helps you to automatically know when a problem can be solved or requires too much time to answer immediately.

Avoid Misreading the Question

Avoid careless mistakes. Do not make a hasty assumption that you know the correct answer without reading the whole question and all the possible answers. It is common to jump to conclusions and select the wrong answer choice after reading only one or two of the answer choices. Note that some of the answer choices only show a "part" of the correct answer. You must look at the entire list of answer choices.

Watch for Questions Containing *x* and *y* Values in Math Problems

Sometimes a question may have different answers depending upon what is asked.

For example: If $6y + 3x = 14$, what is the value of y?

The question may instead have asked, "What is the value of x?"

Or If $3x + x = 20$, what is the value of $x + 2$?

Notice that this question doesn't ask for the value of x, but rather the value of $x + 2$. To help you avoid misreading a question and, therefore, answering it incorrectly, simply circle what you must answer in your test booklet. For example, do you have to find x or $x + 2$?

If $6y + 3x = 14$, what is the value of $\widehat{y}$?

If $3x + x = 20$, what is the value of $\widehat{(x + 2)}$?

Reminder: These types of circles in your question booklet do not have to be erased.

Watch for Questions with the Negative Words EXCEPT and NOT

Negative questions with words like *except* and *not* can be confusing and challenge your thinking processes. You may be asked to choose an answer that is the *exception* from the list of answer choices or that is *not correct*.

To help you answer these types of questions, treat the answer choices as true or false statements and search among the answer choices for the answer that is *false*. There is always only one false answer on the list of answer choices with this type of question. Practice this type of question before your test day so that you can quickly and easily solve these types of problems.

Fill in the Correct Answer

Be very careful that your responses match your intended response. When answering questions quickly, it is common to select the wrong answer choice by mistake. Test-takers who skip questions might make the mistake of continuing to mark their answers in sequence and forget to leave blank the unanswered questions. A good idea is to mark your answer in the test booklet itself (no need to erase later) so that if you do make mistakes in transferring your answer choices to the answer sheet, you can easily correct your errors without having to reconsider the answer choices.

The Elimination Approach

Take advantage of being allowed to mark in your test booklet. When making your answer selection, try to eliminate as many of the answer choices as possible. For example, if you know that Choice C is incorrect, simply cross it out in your test booklet with a diagonal line. It takes just a few seconds to use this strategy, and helps to keep you from reconsidering impossible answer choices.

A̸

? B

C

D̸

Notice that some choices are crossed out with a diagonal line indicating that choices A and D can be eliminated. Choice B has a question mark signifying that this may be a possible answer. This technique helps you avoid reconsidering those choices you have already eliminated. It also helps you narrow down your possible answers.

Tip: The marks you make in your test booklet do not need to be erased, but the extra marks you make on your answer sheet should always be erased.

The Plus-Minus Approach

Many people who take the ACT do not get their best possible score because they spend too much time on difficult questions, leaving insufficient time to answer the easy questions. Do not let this happen to you. The Plus-Minus Approach helps you categorize problems so that you can focus your attention on problems that you are able to answer quickly (see the table that follows). Since every question is worth the same point value, making use of this approach helps you to quickly identify problems that are *solvable, possibly solvable* (+), *and difficult* (–) and be able to move quickly through the test.

Follow these three easy steps:

1. Answer easy questions immediately.
2. Place a "+" next to any problem that seems solvable but appears to be too time-consuming.
3. Place a "–" next to any problem that seems impossible to solve.

Act quickly and don't waste time deciding whether a problem is a "+" or a "–." After working all of the problems you can answer immediately, go back and work your "+" problems. If you finish them, try your "–" problems. Sometimes when you come back to a problem that seemed impossible, you may suddenly realize how to solve it.

Your answer sheet should look something like this after you finish working your easy questions:

```
   1. Ⓐ ● Ⓒ Ⓓ Ⓔ
 +2. Ⓐ Ⓑ Ⓒ Ⓓ Ⓔ
   3. Ⓐ Ⓑ ● Ⓓ Ⓔ
 −4. Ⓐ Ⓑ Ⓒ Ⓓ Ⓔ
 +5. Ⓐ Ⓑ Ⓒ Ⓓ Ⓔ
```

Tip: Make sure to erase your "+" and "–" marks before your time is up. The scoring machine may count extraneous marks as wrong answers. A word of caution: When skipping questions, be sure to mark the question so you won't accidentally lose your place.

Guidelines to Identifying Problems

	Solvable	Answer easy questions immediately. This type of question is answered with little or no difficulty, and requires little or minimal thought.
+	**Possibly Solvable**	This type of question leaves you feeling, "I can answer this question, but I need more time." A time-consuming question is one that you estimate will take you more than two minutes to answer. When you face this type of question, mark a large plus sign (+) on your answer sheet, and then move on to the next question. Go back to this type of question after you have solved all of the *solvable* problems. Remember that you can only work on one section at a time, but you can move around within a section. Do not proceed to the next section without answering all possible questions within your section.
–	**Difficult**	The difficult question appears "impossible to solve." When you come to a question that seems impossible to answer, mark a large minus sign (–) on your answer sheet, leave the question blank and move on to the next question. Don't bother with the "impossible" questions unless you have solved all of the possibly solvable (+) questions first. Rather, spend your time reviewing your work to be sure you didn't make any careless mistakes on the questions you thought were easy to answer. You should come back to review the difficult-type questions only after you have checked your work and have answered the *solvable* and *possibly solvable* questions.

Tip: Don't spend too much valuable test time deciding whether or not a question is solvable. Since you have only about a minute to answer each question, you must act quickly.

Final General Tips and Helpful Hints

This list provides general advice to review before you begin the following in-depth chapters that introduce you to the question types, subject-matter content, instructional strategies, and practice exercises.

- Set a personal goal. Remember that an average composite score is about 50 percent right.
- As you approach each chapter, master the basics and as your confidence grows, tackle the practice tests.
- Know the general directions for each question type. Memorize them if necessary.
- Answer the question that is asked. Too frequently test-takers jump to conclusions and select incorrect answers based upon their misreading the question.
- When taking the in-book practice tests, be sure to mark your answers in the right place.
- Be careful. Watch out for careless mistakes.
- When taking practice tests, don't make careless mistakes on the easy problems because you rushed to get to the challenging ones.
- Know when to skip a question.
- Don't get stuck on any one question.
- If you don't know the answer, but can eliminate one or more answers, make an educated guess.
- Don't be afraid to fill in your answer with a guess.
- Practice using the Plus-Minus and Elimination approaches. Remember to avoid misreading a question.
- When taking the in-book practice tests, get in the habit of erasing any extra marks on your answer sheet.
- If you start to feel overwhelmed and worried about difficult questions or time pressure, remember to focus on the easy questions first.

PART I

DIAGNOSTIC TEST

Chapter 1

Diagnostic Test

Answer Sheets

English Test

1 Ⓐ Ⓑ Ⓒ Ⓓ		21 Ⓐ Ⓑ Ⓒ Ⓓ
2 Ⓕ Ⓖ Ⓗ Ⓙ		22 Ⓕ Ⓖ Ⓗ Ⓙ
3 Ⓐ Ⓑ Ⓒ Ⓓ		23 Ⓐ Ⓑ Ⓒ Ⓓ
4 Ⓕ Ⓖ Ⓗ Ⓙ		24 Ⓕ Ⓖ Ⓗ Ⓙ
5 Ⓐ Ⓑ Ⓒ Ⓓ		25 Ⓐ Ⓑ Ⓒ Ⓓ
6 Ⓕ Ⓖ Ⓗ Ⓙ		26 Ⓕ Ⓖ Ⓗ Ⓙ
7 Ⓐ Ⓑ Ⓒ Ⓓ		27 Ⓐ Ⓑ Ⓒ Ⓓ
8 Ⓕ Ⓖ Ⓗ Ⓙ		28 Ⓕ Ⓖ Ⓗ Ⓙ
9 Ⓐ Ⓑ Ⓒ Ⓓ		29 Ⓐ Ⓑ Ⓒ Ⓓ
10 Ⓕ Ⓖ Ⓗ Ⓙ		30 Ⓕ Ⓖ Ⓗ Ⓙ
11 Ⓐ Ⓑ Ⓒ Ⓓ		31 Ⓐ Ⓑ Ⓒ Ⓓ
12 Ⓕ Ⓖ Ⓗ Ⓙ		32 Ⓕ Ⓖ Ⓗ Ⓙ
13 Ⓐ Ⓑ Ⓒ Ⓓ		33 Ⓐ Ⓑ Ⓒ Ⓓ
14 Ⓕ Ⓖ Ⓗ Ⓙ		34 Ⓕ Ⓖ Ⓗ Ⓙ
15 Ⓐ Ⓑ Ⓒ Ⓓ		35 Ⓐ Ⓑ Ⓒ Ⓓ
16 Ⓕ Ⓖ Ⓗ Ⓙ		36 Ⓕ Ⓖ Ⓗ Ⓙ
17 Ⓐ Ⓑ Ⓒ Ⓓ		37 Ⓐ Ⓑ Ⓒ Ⓓ
18 Ⓕ Ⓖ Ⓗ Ⓙ		38 Ⓕ Ⓖ Ⓗ Ⓙ
19 Ⓐ Ⓑ Ⓒ Ⓓ		39 Ⓐ Ⓑ Ⓒ Ⓓ
20 Ⓕ Ⓖ Ⓗ Ⓙ		40 Ⓕ Ⓖ Ⓗ Ⓙ

Mathematics Test

1 Ⓐ Ⓑ Ⓒ Ⓓ Ⓔ
2 Ⓕ Ⓖ Ⓗ Ⓙ Ⓚ
3 Ⓐ Ⓑ Ⓒ Ⓓ Ⓔ
4 Ⓕ Ⓖ Ⓗ Ⓙ Ⓚ
5 Ⓐ Ⓑ Ⓒ Ⓓ Ⓔ
6 Ⓕ Ⓖ Ⓗ Ⓙ Ⓚ
7 Ⓐ Ⓑ Ⓒ Ⓓ Ⓔ
8 Ⓕ Ⓖ Ⓗ Ⓙ Ⓚ
9 Ⓐ Ⓑ Ⓒ Ⓓ Ⓔ
10 Ⓕ Ⓖ Ⓗ Ⓙ Ⓚ
11 Ⓐ Ⓑ Ⓒ Ⓓ Ⓔ
12 Ⓕ Ⓖ Ⓗ Ⓙ Ⓚ
13 Ⓐ Ⓑ Ⓒ Ⓓ Ⓔ
14 Ⓕ Ⓖ Ⓗ Ⓙ Ⓚ
15 Ⓐ Ⓑ Ⓒ Ⓓ Ⓔ
16 Ⓕ Ⓖ Ⓗ Ⓙ Ⓚ
17 Ⓐ Ⓑ Ⓒ Ⓓ Ⓔ
18 Ⓕ Ⓖ Ⓗ Ⓙ Ⓚ
19 Ⓐ Ⓑ Ⓒ Ⓓ Ⓔ
20 Ⓕ Ⓖ Ⓗ Ⓙ Ⓚ
21 Ⓐ Ⓑ Ⓒ Ⓓ Ⓔ
22 Ⓕ Ⓖ Ⓗ Ⓙ Ⓚ
23 Ⓐ Ⓑ Ⓒ Ⓓ Ⓔ
24 Ⓕ Ⓖ Ⓗ Ⓙ Ⓚ
25 Ⓐ Ⓑ Ⓒ Ⓓ Ⓔ
26 Ⓕ Ⓖ Ⓗ Ⓙ Ⓚ
27 Ⓐ Ⓑ Ⓒ Ⓓ Ⓔ
28 Ⓕ Ⓖ Ⓗ Ⓙ Ⓚ
29 Ⓐ Ⓑ Ⓒ Ⓓ Ⓔ
30 Ⓕ Ⓖ Ⓗ Ⓙ Ⓚ

CUT HERE

Reading Test

1 Ⓐ Ⓑ Ⓒ Ⓓ
2 Ⓕ Ⓖ Ⓗ Ⓙ
3 Ⓐ Ⓑ Ⓒ Ⓓ
4 Ⓕ Ⓖ Ⓗ Ⓙ
5 Ⓐ Ⓑ Ⓒ Ⓓ
6 Ⓕ Ⓖ Ⓗ Ⓙ
7 Ⓐ Ⓑ Ⓒ Ⓓ
8 Ⓕ Ⓖ Ⓗ Ⓙ
9 Ⓐ Ⓑ Ⓒ Ⓓ
10 Ⓕ Ⓖ Ⓗ Ⓙ
11 Ⓐ Ⓑ Ⓒ Ⓓ
12 Ⓕ Ⓖ Ⓗ Ⓙ
13 Ⓐ Ⓑ Ⓒ Ⓓ
14 Ⓕ Ⓖ Ⓗ Ⓙ
15 Ⓐ Ⓑ Ⓒ Ⓓ
16 Ⓕ Ⓖ Ⓗ Ⓙ
17 Ⓐ Ⓑ Ⓒ Ⓓ
18 Ⓕ Ⓖ Ⓗ Ⓙ
19 Ⓐ Ⓑ Ⓒ Ⓓ
20 Ⓕ Ⓖ Ⓗ Ⓙ

Science Test

1 Ⓐ Ⓑ Ⓒ Ⓓ
2 Ⓕ Ⓖ Ⓗ Ⓙ
3 Ⓐ Ⓑ Ⓒ Ⓓ
4 Ⓕ Ⓖ Ⓗ Ⓙ
5 Ⓐ Ⓑ Ⓒ Ⓓ
6 Ⓕ Ⓖ Ⓗ Ⓙ
7 Ⓐ Ⓑ Ⓒ Ⓓ
8 Ⓕ Ⓖ Ⓗ Ⓙ
9 Ⓐ Ⓑ Ⓒ Ⓓ
10 Ⓕ Ⓖ Ⓗ Ⓙ
11 Ⓐ Ⓑ Ⓒ Ⓓ
12 Ⓕ Ⓖ Ⓗ Ⓙ
13 Ⓐ Ⓑ Ⓒ Ⓓ
14 Ⓕ Ⓖ Ⓗ Ⓙ
15 Ⓐ Ⓑ Ⓒ Ⓓ
16 Ⓕ Ⓖ Ⓗ Ⓙ
17 Ⓐ Ⓑ Ⓒ Ⓓ

CUT HERE

Directions

Directions: The diagnostic tests are for assessment purposes only. These tests are designed to measure skills learned in high school that are related to success in college. The diagnostic tests are NOT full-length practice tests, but three full-length practice tests are included at the end of this study guide.

- Calculators may be used on the Mathematics Test only.
- The numbered questions on each test are followed by lettered answer choices.
- After you choose an answer, carefully find the row of letters on your answer sheet that are numbered the same as the question in the diagnostic test. Mark your lettered answer selection next to the corresponding question number on the answer sheet.
- Do NOT use a ballpoint pen or a mechanical pencil. On the actual exam, you must use a soft lead pencil, and completely blacken the oval of the letter you have selected.
- Be sure to blacken only one answer to each question. If you wish to change an answer, erase your original answer thoroughly before marking in your new answer. As you mark your answers, pay special attention to make sure that your answer is marked in the right place.
- Because only your answer sheet is scored and your score is based completely on the number of questions you answer correctly in the time given, make sure to properly mark the answer you have selected. There is no penalty for guessing, so answer every question, even if you have to guess.
- You are allowed to work on only one test at a time. If you complete a test before time is up, you may go back and review questions in only that test. You may NOT go back to previous tests, and you may NOT go forward to another test. On the actual exam day, you will be disqualified from the exam if you work on another test.
- When time is up, be sure to put your pencil down immediately. After time is up, you may NOT for any reason fill in answers. This will disqualify you from the exam.
- Do not fold or tear the pages of your test booklet.

Try to simulate testing conditions and time yourself as you begin each of the following diagnostic tests:

- English Test—25 minutes
- Mathematics Test—30 minutes
- Reading Test—20 minutes
- Science Test—15 minutes

English Test

Time: 25 minutes
40 Questions

Directions: In the three passages that follow, you will find various words and phrases underlined and numbered. A set of responses corresponding to each underlined portion will follow each passage. If the underlined portion is correct standard written English, is most appropriate to the style and feeling of the passage, or best makes the intended statement, mark the letter indicating "NO CHANGE." If the underlined portion is not the best choice given, choose the one that is. For these questions, consider only the underlined portions; assume that the rest of the passage is correct as written. You will also see questions concerning parts of the passage or the whole passage. Choose the response you feel is best for these questions.

Passage I

The following paragraphs may or may not be in the most logical order. Paragraphs are numbered in brackets, and sentences in paragraphs 1 and 3 are numbered.

Plankton

[1]

[1] When people talk about life in the ocean, you usually focus on teeming fish or creatures like whales that are giant. [2] However, about 90 percent of sea life is made up of such small organisms and plants that you need an electron microscope to be capable to see its structure. [3] These organisms and plants, they are called *plankton*. [4] They are the drifters in ocean waters; they don't choose where to go but rather drift on ocean currents. [5] They do, on the other hand, fulfill a function. [6] Some plankton aren't microscopic, such as the jellyfish, whose painful sting ocean swimmers sometimes encounter. [4]

[2]

Victor Hensen a German who was a biology professor in the late 19th century gave plankton its name. But another German, Johannes Müller, collected samples of the diversity of plankton by towing a fine-meshed net earlier, in 1845, through the ocean. Then between 1872 and 1877, the HMS *Challenger* sailed around the world from the tropics to polar seas, from shallow waters to deep waters, returning home with a great many new species. It took 50 volumes to report on the expedition, and the reports were unleashing an interest in marine plankton that was worldwide.

GO ON TO THE NEXT PAGE

[3]

[1] Plankton provide the base of the food web in the sea. [2] Simple plantlike organisms called *phytoplankton* provide the raw materials on which small animal life called *zooplankton* feed. [3] In turn, zooplankton are the prey of fishes. [4] Phytoplankton also contribute between 20 and 30 percent of the world's oxygen supply. [5] They are the primary producers of the sea. [6] Like land plants, they manufacture living matter from the sun and carbon dioxide; they also produce nutrients by photosynthesis. [7] Life in the open sea can be found <u>in both neritic waters and oceanic waters,</u>₈ though neritic waters are <u>more richer in nutrients than</u>₉ <u>oceanic waters are</u>₉. [8] However, where nutrient-rich waters surface at an upswelling, the open sea can also teem with life. ⬚10

1. **A.** NO CHANGE
   B. you usually focus on teeming fish or giant whales.
   C. they usually talk about teeming fish, or whales that are giant.
   D. they usually focus on teeming fish or giant whales.

2. **F.** NO CHANGE
   G. to see their structure.
   H. to be able to see it's structure.
   J. in order to be capable of seeing their structure.

3. **A.** NO CHANGE
   B. plants, which are to be called
   C. plants are called
   D. plants, which are called

4. The writer is considering omitting sentence 6 from paragraph 1. Should this sentence be omitted?
   F. No, because it provides an example of plankton that would be familiar to most people.
   G. Yes, because it does not include enough information about jellyfish.
   H. No, because it adds a colorful detail to the paragraph.
   J. Yes, because it does not logically follow the previous sentence.

5. **A.** NO CHANGE
   B. , who was a biology professor in Germany in the late 19th century,
   C. , a German biology professor in the late 19th century,
   D. , a biology professor in Germany, late in the 19th century,

6. **F.** NO CHANGE
   G. had collected samples of diverse plankton in 1845 by towing a fine-meshed net through the ocean.
   H. collected samples of the diversity of plankton in 1845, and he did this by towing a fine-meshed net through the ocean.
   J. by towing a fine-meshed net through the ocean, samples of diverse plankton were collected in 1845.

7. **A.** NO CHANGE
   B. were unleashing, worldwide, an interest in plankton.
   C. unleashed a worldwide interest in plankton.
   D. would have unleashed an interest in plankton, worldwide.

GO ON TO THE NEXT PAGE

8. The writer should do which of the following with the underlined phrase?

    F. Delete it.
    G. Include it in the second paragraph.
    H. Provide a brief, parenthetical definition of the terms.
    J. Add it to the last sentence in the paragraph.

9. **A.** NO CHANGE
    B. richer in nutrients than oceanic waters will be.
    C. more rich, than oceanic waters, in nutrients.
    D. richer in nutrients than oceanic waters are.

Item 10 poses a question about the essay as a whole.

10. Which of the following sequences of paragraphs makes the structure of the passage most logical?

    F. NO CHANGE
    G. 2, 1, 3
    H. 1, 3, 2
    J. 3, 2, 1

Passage II

Paragraphs are numbered in brackets, and sentences in paragraph 2 are numbered.

Theater Owners and Movie Studios

[1]

According to reports from an industry trade show, theater owners are feeling optimistic again. After a period, in which their revenues dropped, they say that recently revenues have rose by 20 percent.
11 12

More movies this year are being seen in theaters by people than in their homes a spokesperson said. He also spoke of the increase in ticket sales that have taken place throughout the world.
13 13 14 14

[2]

[1] Another factor adding to the theater owner's optimistic viewpoint has been an improved relationship between they and the movie studio executives. [2] Early in the year the theater owners had been surprised (and angered) when the movie studios have announced plans to distribute movies to video-on-demand services only just a few weeks after a films theatrical release. [3] After the initial conflict, studio executives and theater owners began to be engaged in a dialogue about finding better ways to work together for the mutual benefits of both. [4] A studio executive said that the movie industry needs to find new ways to stay relevant to people who seem to have lost interest in the experience of going out to a movie. [5] He urged that the people who produce the movies and the theater owners who show them make the case that the
15 15 16 17 17 18 19 20 20 21 22 22

GO ON TO THE NEXT PAGE

movie-going experience is special, something to be savored and enjoyed. [6] He added that seeing creative, innovative films in the setting of a theater is <u>far more</u>₂₃ <u>better than to see them</u>₂₃ at home, regardless of how many big-screen television sets they possess. [7] He addressed the important issue of working with the technology industry in preventing the widespread theft of intellectual property. 24 25

11. A. NO CHANGE
    B. during which their revenues dropped
    C. , when their revenues became less
    D. that their revenues dropped

12. F. NO CHANGE
    G. revenues had rose
    H. revenues will have risen
    J. revenues have risen

13. A. NO CHANGE
    B. This year people are seeing more movies in theaters than in their homes,
    C. More movies are being seen in theaters than people are seeing in their homes this year,
    D. People, this year, are seeing more movies not in their homes but in theaters,

14. F. NO CHANGE
    G. ticket sales which have taken place worldwide
    H. worldwide ticket sales
    J. ticket sales, throughout the world

15. A. NO CHANGE
    B. optimistic viewpoint of the theater owners
    C. theater owners' optimism
    D. theater owner's optimistic point of view

16. F. NO CHANGE
    G. between movie studio executives and they
    H. between them and the movie studio executives
    J. between both the movie studio executives and them

17. A. NO CHANGE
    B. movie studios announced plans to distribute
    C. movie studios were announcing their plans of distributing
    D. movies studios announced their plans for the distribution of

18. F. NO CHANGE
    G. only just a few weeks, after a films theatrical release.
    H. only a few weeks, following the films theatrical release.
    J. just a few weeks after a film's theatrical release.

GO ON TO THE NEXT PAGE

19. A. NO CHANGE
B. began a dialogue
C. were beginning to be engaged in a dialogue
D. were engaging in a dialogue

20. F. NO CHANGE
G. the mutual benefits of both of them.
H. their mutual benefit.
J. both mutual benefits.

21. A. NO CHANGE
B. who seemed like they have lost interest
C. who appeared to have lost interest
D. whom had lost interest

22. F. NO CHANGE
G. people, who produce the movies, and the theater owners, who show them,
H. people, making the movies, and the theater owners, who show them,
J. people, who produce the movies, and the theater owners showing them

23. A. NO CHANGE
B. more better than seeing them
C. far better than seeing them
D. better than to see them

Items 24 and 25 pose questions about the paragraph as a whole.

24. If the author of the passage wanted to divide paragraph 2 into two paragraphs, the best place to make the division would be

F. between sentences 2 and 3
G. between sentences 3 and 4
H. between sentence 4 and 5
J. between sentences 5 and 6

25. Which of the following sentences should be omitted from paragraph 2?

A. sentence 3
B. sentence 4
C. sentence 6
D. sentence 7

Passage III

Paragraphs are numbered in brackets, and sentences in paragraph 3 are numbered.

University Shock

[1]

Without a doubt, Tom was the star in my high school senior class. He captained the football team, dated the prettiest girls, charmed most of the teachers, and managed to get A's and B's without studying. When he headed off to a <u>big, high-rated university that was located in the Midwest,</u> none of us was surprised.
26
But a year later, he came home on academic probation <u>and this came as a big surprise to most all of us.</u> We
27
gossiped about his return, wondering if the <u>reason was</u>
28
<u>because</u> he was having a good time and <u>just didn't</u>
28   29
<u>study hardly at all,</u> or something more serious, such as
29
taking drugs.

GO ON TO THE NEXT PAGE

[2]

Having been a close friend of Tom's, he told me
                                            30
candidly what had happened. As a freshman at the
        30   31
university, the experience was not at all like high
              31
school, where he had succeeded without having to try.
    31
The classes were so big that he didn't get to know the

professors; let alone charm them. He didn't take drugs,
              32
but he also didn't study much, and he also did poor on
                        33
exams. He said "he just didn't realize that he would
  33   34
have to work so hard."
          34

[3]

[1] Instead of giving Tom a bad time, I told him that

maybe our high school could of helped him more.
                          35
[2] Everyone had assumed that because he had always

done well, he always would. [3] Our high school was
                                              36
remiss in providing much in the way of counseling for
        36
students who succeeded in classes and had few if any

disciplinary problems. [4] After Tom's experience and

similar experiences, of other students who had troubles
                        37
their first year of college, the school made some
          37

changes in the college preparatory program. [5] If

Tom had went to a junior college first, he would of
        38
been able to make the transition from high school

more easily. 39 40

26. F.   NO CHANGE
    G.   big, highly-rated university located in the
         Midwest
    H.   big, high-rated university, which was
         located in the Midwest
    J.   big, highly rated Midwestern university

27. A.   NO CHANGE
    B.   , a big surprise to most of us.
    C.   which was a big surprise to most all of us.
    D.   ; to most all of us a big surprise.

28. F.   NO CHANGE
    G.   reason was on account of
    H.   reason might have been because of
    J.   reason was that

29. A.   NO CHANGE
    B.   just hardly wasn't studying at all
    C.   studied hardly at all
    D.   didn't hardly study at all

GO ON TO THE NEXT PAGE

30. F. NO CHANGE
  G. Tom candidly told me what had happened, having been a close friend.
  H. Because I was a close friend, Tom told me candidly what had happened.
  J. Being a close friend, candidly Tom told me what had happened.

31. A. NO CHANGE
  B. As a freshman at the university, Tom found the experience different from the one he had in high school,
  C. The experience was different for Tom than it had been in high school at the university as a freshman,
  D. Tom found his experience different from his experience in high school as a freshman at the university,

32. F. NO CHANGE
  G. professors, let alone charm them.
  H. professors. Let alone, he could not charm them.
  J. professors, so let alone it was impossible to charm them.

33. A. NO CHANGE
  B. . But also he didn't study much; and did bad on exams.
  C. , but he also didn't study much and did poorly on exams.
  D. , however, he also didn't study much and did poor on exams.

34. F. NO CHANGE
  G. "He just didn't realize that he would have had to work so hard."
  H. he just didn't realize that he would have to work so hard.
  J. , "He just didn't realize that he'd have to work so hard."

35. A. NO CHANGE
  B. could have helped him
  C. could have been of assistance to him
  D. could of been helpful to him

36. Which of the following phrases is NOT acceptable to replace the underlined phrase?
  F. neglected to provide
  G. failed to provide
  H. refused to provide
  J. overlooked providing

37. A. NO CHANGE
  B. other students' similar experiences
  C. the similar experiences of other students, whom had trouble their first year in college
  D. similar experiences of those other students, the ones who had had trouble their first year in college

GO ON TO THE NEXT PAGE

38. **F.**   NO CHANGE

      G. had first went to a junior college, he would have

      H. had gone first to a junior college, he would of

      J. had gone to a junior college first, he would have

39. The writer wants to add a sentence after sentence 4 in paragraph 3. Which of the following sentences would be the best choice?

      A. Students are now given individual counseling on choosing the best plan for their post-high-school education.

      B. Added to the curriculum has been a class covering good study habits.

      C. Many students are now discouraged from applying to large universities.

      D. A lecture series on university expectations is now being offered to seniors.

40. Of the following, which would be the best choice to follow sentence 5 in paragraph 3?

      F. No matter what, Tom is definitely still a star and will probably have a successful future.

      G. Tom, however, didn't want to go to a junior college.

      H. Going to a junior college, however, was not an option.

      J. Although Tom was a high-school star, he simply wasn't prepared to succeed in a large, impersonal university.

IF YOU FINISH BEFORE TIME IS CALLED, CHECK YOUR WORK ON THIS SECTION ONLY. DO NOT WORK ON ANY OTHER SECTION IN THE TEST.

Mathematics Test

Time: 30 Minutes

30 Questions

Directions: After solving each problem, choose the correct answer and fill in the corresponding oval on your answer sheet. Do not spend too much time on any one problem. Solve as many problems as you can and return to the problems you skipped, or recheck your work if time permits. **You are allowed to use a calculator on this test.**

Note: Unless it is otherwise stated, you can assume all of the following.

1. Figures are NOT necessarily drawn to scale.
2. Geometric figures lie in a plane.
3. The word "line" means a straight line.
4. The word "average" refers to the arithmetic mean.

---

1. The product of x and y is a constant. If the value of x is increased by 50 percent, by what percent must the value of y be decreased?

    A.   25%

    B. $33\frac{1}{3}\%$

    C.   40%

    D.   50%

    E. $66\frac{2}{3}\%$

2. One hundred students will attend a concert if tickets cost \$30 each. For each \$5 raise in the price of the ticket, 10 fewer students will attend. What price will deliver the maximum dollar sales?

    F.   \$30.00

    G.   \$35.00

    H.   \$40.00

    J.   \$45.00

    K.   \$50.00

3. Macey is 3 times as old as Mike. In 8 years, she will be twice as old as Mike. How old was Macey 3 years ago?

    A.   5

    B.   8

    C.   21

    D.   24

    E.   27

4. In the standard (x, y) coordinate plane, what is the equation of a line with slope $\frac{1}{2}$ that passes through the point (1, 2)?

    F. $x - 2y + 3 = 0$

    G. $2x - y = 0$

    H. $x + 2y - 5 = 0$

    J. $2x + y - 4 = 0$

    K. $4x - y - 2 = 0$

5. A square and a circle have equal areas. What is the circumference of the circle if the perimeter of the square is $8\sqrt{\pi}$?

    A.   4

    B. 4π

    C. $\sqrt{2}\pi$

    D. 8π

    E. $8\sqrt{\pi}$

6. Bryan is standing 2,000 feet from object A and 2,000 feet from object C. The observed angle between the objects is 48°. How far apart are objects A and C?

    F.   4000 sin 24°

    G.   2000 sin 48°

    H.   4000 sin 48°

    J.   2000 sin 24°

    K.   2000 cos 48°

GO ON TO THE NEXT PAGE

7. In a package of candies, 8 candies are green, 2 are red, and 6 are white. If the first candy chosen (and not replaced) is not a white one, what is the probability that the next one randomly chosen will be white?

A. $\dfrac{5}{16}$

B. $\dfrac{3}{8}$

C. $\dfrac{2}{5}$

D. $\dfrac{3}{5}$

E. $\dfrac{2}{3}$

8. Bryan needs 5 shelves for books. The longest shelf is to be the bottom shelf, and each shelf above is to be 4 inches shorter than the one immediately below. If the sum of the lengths of the shelves is 155 inches, what is the length, in inches, of the longest shelf?

F. 23

G. 28

H. 31

J. 36

K. 39

9. How many times does the equation $y = x^4 - x^5$ intersect the x-axis?

A. 1

B. 2

C. 3

D. 4

E. 5

10. In the standard (x, y) coordinate plane, what are the coordinates of one endpoint of a segment if the other endpoint has coordinates (x, y) and the midpoint has coordinates of $(3x, -3y)$?

F. $(2x, -y)$

G. $(-2x, y)$

H. $(5x, -7y)$

J. $(4x, -2y)$

K. $(7x, -5y)$

11. Which of the following is (are) true about the figure shown here?

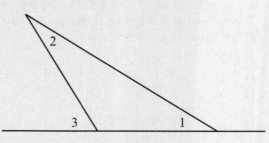

I. $\angle 1 + \angle 2 = \angle 3$

II. $\angle 2 < \angle 3$

III. $180° > \angle 2 + \angle 3$

A. I only

B. II only

C. I and II only

D. I and III only

E. II and III only

12. What is the area of the triangle below?

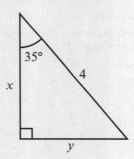

F. $8 \sin 35° \cos 35°$

G. $8 \tan 35°$

H. $\dfrac{8}{\tan 35°}$

J. $4 \sin 35° + 4 \cos 35°$

K. $8(\tan^2 35° + 1)$

13. If A is greater than B, C is less than A, and B is greater than C, then which of the following is true?

A. $A < B < C$

B. $B < A < C$

C. $B < C < A$

D. $C < A < B$

E. $C < B < A$

GO ON TO THE NEXT PAGE

14. Two hikers leave the same point and travel at right angles to each other. After 2 hours, they are 10 miles apart. If one walks 1 mile per hour faster than the other, what is the speed of the slower hiker, in miles per hour?

   F.   2
   G. 3
   H. 4
   J.   5
   K. 6

15. If $f(x) = x^2 - 2$ and $g(x) = 2x + 2$, then

$$f\left[g\left(f\left(\frac{1}{2}\right)\right)\right] =$$

   A. $\dfrac{1}{4}$

   B. $\dfrac{1}{2}$

   C. 1
   D. 2
   E. 4

16. Line A has a slope of $\frac{3}{4}$. In the standard (x, y) coordinate plane, what is the equation of a line that passes through the point $(0, 1)$ and is perpendicular to line A?

   F. $4x - 3y = 3$
   G. $3x - 4y = -4$
   H. $3x + 4y = 4$
   J. $4x - 3y = -3$
   K. $4x + 3y = 3$

17. In the figure shown here, $AB = BC$, $CD = BD$, and $\angle CAD = 70°$. What is the measure of $\angle ADC$?

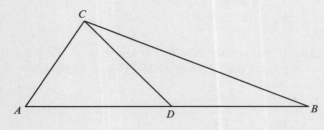

   A. 80°
   B. 70°
   C. 60°
   D. 50°
   E. 40°

18. What is the tenth term in the following sequence: 5, 6, 8, 11, 15, . . . ?

   F. 20
   G. 35
   H. 41
   J.   50
   K. 60

19. Which equation has roots that are each 4 less than the roots of $3x^2 + 2x - 4 = 0$?

   A. $3x^2 + 14x - 12 = 0$
   B. $3x^2 + 26x + 52 = 0$
   C. $6x^2 + 3x - 28 = 0$
   D. $6x^2 + 16x + 9 = 0$
   E. $3x^2 - 15x - 18 = 0$

20. Consuela biked 20 miles. If she had increased her average speed by 4 miles per hour, the trip would have taken 1 hour less. What is her average speed, in miles per hour?

   F. $2\sqrt{21} + 2$
   G. $2\sqrt{21} - 2$
   H. $2\sqrt{21} - 1$
   J. $2\sqrt{21} + 1$
   K. $\sqrt{21} - 2$

21. In the standard (x, y) coordinate plane, triangle ABC has its vertices at $(2, 8)$, $(9, 7)$, and $(4, 2)$. What is the area of triangle ABC?

   A. 20
   B. 24
   C. 24.5
   D. 28
   E. 32

22. Given rectangle $ABCD$ with diagonal $\overline{AC}$ and if $AB = 12$ and $BC = 9$, what is the ratio of the perimeter of rectangle $ABCD$ to the perimeter of triangle ACD?

   F. 2:1
   G. 6:7
   H. 1:2
   J.   7:5
   K. 7:6

GO ON TO THE NEXT PAGE

23. Which of the following is a simplified version equivalent to $3 + \cfrac{3}{3 + \cfrac{3}{3 + \cfrac{3}{3+3}}}$?

A. $3\frac{23}{27}$

B. $3\frac{7}{9}$

C. $3\frac{19}{27}$

D. $3\frac{17}{27}$

E. $3\frac{1}{3}$

24. $\dfrac{x}{x-y} - \dfrac{y}{y-x} = ?$

F. $\dfrac{x+y}{x-y}$

G. 1

H. $\dfrac{x-y}{x+y}$

J. 0

K. $x-y$

25. Machine A can do a job alone in 10 hours. Machine B can do the same job alone in 12 hours. Machine A is turned on at 6 a.m. Machine B is turned on at 9 a.m. Machine A breaks down at 10 a.m., and Machine B must finish the job alone. When will Machine B finish?

A. 2:30 p.m.

B. 3:42 p.m.

C. 4:12 p.m.

D. 4:40 p.m.

E. Cannot be determined from the given information

26. Given the circle O below, what is the measure of $\angle x$?

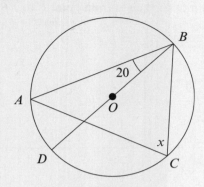

F. 40°

G. 55°

H. 70°

J. 80°

K. Cannot be determined from the given information

27. An empty fuel tank is filled with brand Z gasoline. When the tank is half empty, it is filled with brand Y gasoline. When the tank is half empty again, it is filled with brand Z gasoline. When the tank is half empty again, it is filled with brand Y gasoline. At this time, what percent of the gasoline in the tank is brand Z?

A. 50%

B. 40%

C. 37.5%

D. 25%

E. None of these

GO ON TO THE NEXT PAGE

28. In the following figure, $BC = 12$ units, $AC = 9$ units, and $\angle ACB = 90°$. How many units is the length of the height from point C to $\overline{AB}$?

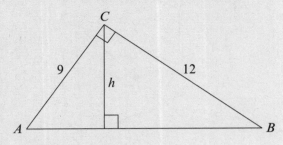

F. 5.4

G. 6.4

H. 6.8

J. 7.2

K. 8

29. How many 3-person committees can be formed in a club with 8 members?

A. 8

B. 24

C. 48

D. 56

E. 336

30. Two concentric circles have radii of 7 and 13. What is the length of a chord of the larger circle that is tangent to the smaller circle?

F. $4\sqrt{30}$

G. $2\sqrt{30}$

H. $\dfrac{\sqrt{30}}{2}$

J. $2\sqrt{162}$

K. 22

IF YOU FINISH BEFORE TIME IS CALLED, CHECK YOUR WORK ON THIS SECTION ONLY. DO NOT WORK ON ANY OTHER SECTION IN THE TEST.

STOP

Reading Test

Time: 20 Minutes

20 Questions

Directions: Each of the two passages in this test is followed by a series of multiple-choice questions. Read the passage and choose the best answer to each question. Return to the passage as often as necessary to answer the questions.

Passage I

NATURAL SCIENCE: This passage is adapted from *Universe on a T-Shirt* by Dan Falk. Reprinted by permission of Arcade Publishing, an imprint of Skyhorse Publishing, Inc.

Isaac Newton's achievements in science—his work in optics, his invention of calculus, his theories of motion and gravity—are unparalleled. In the wake of his discoveries, people began to
(5) see nature as a well-tuned machine, a clockwork governed by strict mathematical laws. That metaphor, anchored in his mammoth *Principia,* dominated scientific thought for more than two hundred years. But Newton lived at a time when
(10) the echo of the medieval world, though fading, could still be heard. He wrote treatises on ancient history, mythology, Biblical chronology, and a host of other arcane subjects; among his obsessions was an attempt to determine the date
(15) of Armageddon by a careful study of the Book of Daniel. Modern scholars talk about his work in chemistry, but it was really the ancient art of alchemy that fascinated Newton. Biographer Michael White points out that Newton had 138
(20) volumes on alchemy in his library at the time of his death, compared with 31 on what we would call chemistry.

What drove Newton—remembered today as a man of logic and rationality—into alchemy and
(25) the occult? Like today's physicists, he sought a unified, all-encompassing description of nature; unlike modern scientists, however, he was afraid to exclude ideas of ancient scholars and philosophers. According to White, Newton "was
(30) interested in a synthesis of all knowledge and was a devout seeker of some form of unified theory of the principles of the universe." Such knowledge, Newton believed, was at one time known to philosophers, but had since been lost; his great
(35) quest was to rediscover this ancient wisdom.

"Newton's *raison d'etre* was to "recover this 'frame of knowledge,'" writes White. "For this reason, on an intellectual level, he considered no avenue of research beyond his probings, no stone
(40) unimportant enough to be left unturned, no theory beyond the pale." Newton would probably have disliked being labeled as either a chemist or alchemist; he was simply a natural philosopher searching for the most elementary laws of nature,
(45) laws that would define a unified theory. He was looking for a Theory of Everything.

Newton's alchemical investigations proved futile, yet within physics his quest for unification was a spectacular success. The elliptical orbits of
(50) the planets, the rise and fall of the ocean's tides, the paths of projectiles and falling bodies, even the shape of the earth itself—all could be explained through Newton's succinct mathematical laws. Where many theories were once employed, now
(55) only two ideas were needed: Newton's laws of motion and his law of universal gravitation. He had cemented the unification of terrestrial and celestial physics begun by Galileo. Newton had constructed a mathematical framework for the
(60) physical sciences that held within it all the great advances of the previous millennium and set the stage for the progress to come.

And, like the Greeks and the scientists of the Renaissance, Newton sought simplicity. Echoing
(65) the words of William of Ockham, he wrote in his *Principia:* "Nature does nothing in vain, and more causes are in vain when fewer suffice." He believed that "Nature is simple and does not indulge in the luxury of superfluous causes."
(70) Newton may indeed have mixed reason and magic—but he was also the giant of the new scientific age, the culminating figure of the Scientific Revolution. Following Newton, science was finally weaned from philosophy and
(75) transformed into a discipline of inquiry in its

GO ON TO THE NEXT PAGE

own right. Those seeking the truth no longer needed to rely on the insights of a few learned men or the authority of a handful of dusty textbooks—instead, insight would come from (80) direct observation of nature, carried out through precise measurement and mathematical analysis. That strategy, inaugurated by Galileo and firmly established by Newton, is now called the scientific method.

1. Which of the following choices is the main point that the author makes in the opening paragraph?

   A. Newton dominated scientific thought for more than 200 years.
   B. Among Newton's greatest achievements was his introduction of the idea that the universe was governed by the laws of mathematics.
   C. The law of gravity was Newton's most important achievement.
   D. Newton introduced major changes in scientific thought but didn't reject previous scientific and philosophical ideas.

2. According to the passage, Newton studied alchemy and the occult to

   F. support his strong religious beliefs.
   G. help him in his search for a unified theory of the universe.
   H. prove their inadequacy as a scientific approach to natural law.
   J. make his work more acceptable to the church and to his contemporaries.

3. The biographer White's observation (lines 18–22) is included to show Newton's

   A. obsession solely with alchemy.
   B. commitment to the works of ancient scholars.
   C. naive belief in magic and the occult.
   D. greater interest in alchemy than in chemistry.

4. According to the passage, one important difference between Newton and modern scientists is that he

   F. believed that the principles of the universe had once been known but the knowledge had been lost.
   G. believed in God and the Bible.
   H. wasn't on a university faculty.
   J. was not concerned with his reputation among his colleagues.

5. The best definition of *arcane* (line 13) is

   A. foolish; child-like.
   B. misleading; inaccurate.
   C. mysterious; obscure.
   D. theoretical; unproven.

6. Newton's mathematical laws were successful in explaining all of the following EXCEPT the

   F. shape of the orbits of planets.
   G. errors in the theory of alchemy.
   H. cause of the ocean's tides.
   J. paths of falling bodies.

7. As evidence of Newton's belief in the importance of simplicity, the author of the passage cites which of the following?

   A. his dislike of being labeled either a chemist or an alchemist
   B. the clear language of his *Principia*
   C. his determination to study the works of the ancient philosophers in light of direct observation of phenomena
   D. the reduction of many theories to two laws joining terrestrial and celestial physics

8. The author of the passage refers to Newton as the "culminating figure of the Scientific Revolution" because he

   F. proved Galileo was right.
   G. supported the idea that laws explaining nature should be simple rather than complex.
   H. pursued science through disciplined inquiry and observation rather than philosophical conjecture.
   J. separated science from the teachings of religion.

9. By citing Newton's interest in alchemy and the occult, the author intends to

   A. question the accuracy of the current assessment of Newton.
   B. show how scientists can be negatively influenced by ancient works.
   C. illustrate the fallibility of science in every period.
   D. show Newton's connection to medieval thoughts and beliefs.

GO ON TO THE NEXT PAGE

10. This passage can best be described as a

    F. concise biography.

    G. brief summary of Newton's influences, goals, and accomplishments.

    H. fictionalized account.

    J. persuasive argument for accepting unproved theories.

Passage II

SOCIAL SCIENCE: This passage is from *Ideologies and Utopias* by Arthur A. Ekirch, Jr. (© by Arthur A. Ekirch, Jr., 1969, published by Quadrangle Books, Inc.)

The hopeful and expectant mood of watchful waiting in which intellectuals observed the aftermath of the Great Crash could not survive the evidence of growing depression. Whereas
(5) previous economic slumps had affected the agricultural or industrial population, now in the 1930s all classes and all sectors of the economy were hurt in some way. The middle class, traditionally the bulwark of American society,
(10) succumbed to the mounting unemployment and drastically reduced incomes of its white-collar workers and professional people. As stock prices rumbled to ever lower levels, doctors, lawyers, teachers, clerks and skilled laborers, writers and
(15) artists, all felt the reality of the Depression and the pangs of poverty. Authors and publishers especially found a declining market for their wares. John Steinbeck, for example, recalled later that, being without a job during the first years of
(20) the depression, he kept on writing—"books, essays, short stories. Regularly they went out and just as regularly came back. Even if they had been good, they would have come back because publishers were hardest hit of all. When people
(25) are broke, the first things they give up are books."

While the circulation of the larger metropolitan newspapers and more popular magazines held up amazingly well, the book industry experienced a severe blight. By 1933
(30) sales were only half of what they had been in 1929. Reviewing the twelve months just past, his publisher informed James Truslow Adams that "It was a very tough year and so far as we are concerned will go down as the worst so far since
(35) the firm of Little and Brown began publishing books in 1837." Although distribution of Adams' *Epic of America* had not achieved the predicted figure of a thousand copies a week, still it had enjoyed a "larger sale than any new book we
(40) published."

Americans, of course, notoriously purchased few books even in good times—about two per person in 1929, for example, with many more borrowed from libraries. With the Depression
(45) this personal buying fell off and libraries as well suffered reduced budgets. They faced the unhappy situation of having to curtail their own purchases at a time when the demand for their facilities was never higher, and when idle millions
(50) were rediscovering the public library as a kind of poor man's club, "a warm quiet place to browse or drowse." Some people merely sought escape in reading fiction, the great gainer in circulation at first, but gradually more serious interests took
(55) over. With total circulation of library books increasing by nearly 40 percent from 1920 to 1933, readers in ever greater numbers consulted educational and technical works in their often pathetic quest for jobs or self-culture. Later
(60) circulation fell off slightly, perhaps because the libraries were not acquiring enough new books or because people were again beginning to secure jobs.

Among a number of American cities that no
(65) longer cared or were unable to support their public libraries, Chicago was the greatest and the worst. There in 1932, "Through an unpremeditated bit of irony, the same year which found Chicago celebrating a century of progress by an exposition
(70) costing many millions of dollars found the Chicago Public Library for the third consecutive twelve month without a book fund." In the midst of a lavish exhibition of costly art and culture, the public library was starving for books.

11. According to the passage, the mood of many intellectuals in the United States in the immediate aftermath of the Great Crash was

    A. restrained.

    B. angry.

    C. hopeful.

    D. cynical.

12. The 1930s differed from the early years of the Depression because it

    F. primarily affected rural communities.

    G. was less severe.

    H. was not related to the stock market crash.

    J. affected all sectors of the economy.

GO ON TO THE NEXT PAGE

13. According to information in the passage, the 1930s saw

    A. increases in magazine circulation.
    B. decreases in newspaper circulation.
    C. expansion of libraries.
    D. reduction of book sales.

14. According to the quotation by John Steinbeck, during the 1930s he was

    F. forced to take menial jobs.
    G. unable to get his writing published.
    H. a chronicler of the impact of the Depression.
    J. pessimistic about the quality of his writing.

15. All of the following statements about the 1930s are supported in the passage EXCEPT:

    A. Book purchases fell to two books per person.
    B. Fiction was initially more popular than nonfiction.
    C. Libraries lost funds for buying materials.
    D. Library circulation improved 40 percent by 1933.

16. The author uses the word *pathetic* in line 59 because

    F. poverty had left many people without hope.
    G. people's attempts to make themselves more employable were often futile.
    H. libraries were unable to provide sufficient educational and technical materials to help people prepare themselves for new jobs.
    J. no jobs were available for skilled and semi-skilled workers.

17. The author uses the term "poor man's club" to describe libraries during the Depression because

    A. poor people made up the majority of library visitors.
    B. libraries offered patrons extra privileges to increase attendance.
    C. people without jobs found libraries warm, pleasant places to be.
    D. friendships between library visitors grew during that time.

18. The author suggests that library circulation fell off again late in the Depression perhaps because

    F. libraries had insufficient funds to purchase new books.
    G. people realized that reading books and magazines didn't help them get jobs.
    H. the libraries weren't able to control the numbers of indigent people who used the facilities to sleep in.
    J. many branch libraries were forced to close.

19. The term "unpremeditated bit of irony" is used in the last paragraph to characterize Chicago because

    A. although a prosperous city, Chicago closed its library to save money.
    B. Chicago had not expected to be hit so hard by the Depression.
    C. the city had always prided itself on being a center for intellectuals and possessing a number of excellent academic institutions.
    D. Chicago spent millions of dollars hosting an exposition celebrating progress but didn't find money to fund its library's purchase of new books.

20. The author's main purpose in the passage is to

    F. summarize the effects of the late Depression on books and libraries.
    G. describe the differences between the early and late years of the Depression.
    H. emphasize the importance of books, newspapers, and magazines to urban centers.
    J. criticize the lack of funding provided to libraries during the Depression.

IF YOU FINISH BEFORE TIME IS CALLED, CHECK YOUR WORK ON THIS SECTION ONLY. DO NOT WORK ON ANY OTHER SECTION IN THE TEST.

Science Test

Time: 15 Minutes

17 Questions

Directions: Each of the three passages in this test is followed by several questions. After you read each passage, select the correct choice for each of the questions that follow the passage. Refer to the passage as often as necessary to answer the questions. You may NOT use a calculator on this test.

Passage I

Global warming and climate change have been studied by scientists for decades and continue to be at the forefront of global research and debate. The debate is generally focused on whether the steady increase of the earth's surface temperature is a natural occurrence or whether it has been accelerated as a result of human activities.

Scientist 1

Future generations will inherit a world where global warming is unmanageable unless there is a significant change in energy exploitation. The planet is unstable, and more energy is being retained than is being expelled resulting in an increase of greenhouse gases at approximately 2 percent per year. To balance energy usage during this century, scientific research suggests that it is crucial to immediately reduce greenhouse emissions in the atmosphere by 6 percent per year. If immediate action is not taken and if there is a delay of another 10 years, it will be necessary to reduce emissions by more than 15 percent each subsequent year. To reduce emissions at this rate would be realistically unattainable.

Since 1920, the increasing rate at which sea levels are rising has been observed to be an effect of climate change. Most scientists agree that over the last century average sea levels have more than doubled to a rate of about 2 millimeters per year. In comparison, naturally occurring sea level changes in centuries prior to 1920 were substantially less than 1 millimeter per year. The magnitude of the current rate of rising sea levels could potentially cause coastal areas around the world to become submerged under water, displacing millions of people who reside in those regions. Necessary steps must be taken that are feasible and beneficial to human health and environmental conditions. Many scientists call for a swift and efficient utilization of clean energy combined with widespread reforestation to re-establish global energy balance.

Scientist 2

Some scientific alarmists routinely ignore possible health benefits and economic benefits of globally warming temperatures. Many health experts agree that the most significant risk to human health is a result of the impact of cold-weather stressors and freezing temperatures and are not due to higher than average warmer temperatures. Colder than normal temperatures in Europe and Russia, for example, account for approximately 100,000 people who die each year as a result of freezing temperatures during the winter months. Downturns in climatic temperatures have also hindered agricultural production, created social isolation, and caused increased health risks. Conversely, warmer climates show sizable advancements in rates of economic, technological, and societal progress. Global warming over the last 150 years has been minimal and has coincided with sizable advancements in world-wide technology and human life expectancy. Climate change is not a widespread global concern and does not demand immediate action.

1. Scientist 1 believes that greenhouse emissions should be reduced by what percentage if we are to restore the energy balance on earth?

   A. 2 percent per year starting now
   B. 2 percent per year starting now and continuing for the next fifteen years
   C. 6 percent per year starting now
   D. 15 percent per year starting now and continuing for the next ten years

GO ON TO THE NEXT PAGE

2. What connection does Scientist 2 make between global warming and technological progress?

   F. Global warming reduces technological progress.

   G. Global warming stops technological progress.

   H. Global warming and technological progress have happened concurrently.

   J. There are no connections between global warming and technological progress.

3. One of the points that Scientist 2 makes to refute the claim of Scientist 1 about the negative effects of global warming is

   A. the most significant risk to human health is cold not heat.

   B. global warming can reduce human overpopulation on the planet.

   C. rising sea levels flood prime agricultural lands and increase food production.

   D. humans will be happier living in a warmer climate.

4. What does Scientist 1 believe to be one of the major effects of climate change?

   F. Overpopulation

   G. Rising sea levels

   H. Increasing human health problems

   J. Increase in the use of fossil fuels

5. All of the following points support the belief of Scientist 2 EXCEPT:

   A. Cold temperatures can cause an increase in human mortality.

   B. Cold temperatures can cause a decrease in human mortality.

   C. Cold temperatures can cause a decrease in agricultural output.

   D. Cold temperatures can cause an increase in social disintegration.

6. In the research reported by Scientist 1, why is the rise in sea levels a major environmental concern?

   F. A continuous rise in sea levels can flood coastal areas where millions of people live.

   G. A continuous rise in sea levels can flood agricultural lands and disrupt our food supply.

   H. A continuous rise in sea levels can cause various water-borne diseases.

   J. A continuous rise in sea levels can increase the risk of malaria in many countries.

7. The argument presented by Scientist 2 would be considerably weakened if Scientist 1 was able to demonstrate that

   A. the rise in temperature is not related to the creation of greenhouse gases.

   B. technological advances, medical progress, and increase in human life expectancy are NOT direct results of the rise in temperature over the last century.

   C. a continual rise in temperature can have some positive effects on the environment.

   D. the use of automobiles, airplanes, and other forms of transportation does NOT directly cause a rise in temperature globally.

Passage II

Nearly all living organisms require oxygen to live. The amount of oxygen that aquatic animals require for survival depends upon the species, but all fish need oxygen to breathe. The water surrounding fish contains microscopic bubbles of oxygen called dissolved oxygen (DO). When water passes through the gills of fish, dissolved oxygen is absorbed and enters their blood stream. Fish and other aquatic animals are sensitive to oxygen levels in their surrounding environment. Fish will die as a result of low oxygen levels, while high oxygen levels in the surrounding waters is optimal for survival. Oxygen dissolves in water by diffusion from the atmosphere, aeration of the water as it flows, and as a byproduct of photosynthesis. The temperature of the water affects the concentration of DO. DO is measured in parts per million (ppm), which is the number of parts of oxygen per million parts of water.

GO ON TO THE NEXT PAGE

Figure 1: Range of Tolerance for
Dissolved Oxygen in Fish
PARTS PER MILLION (PPM)
DISSOLVED OXYGEN

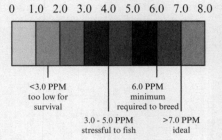

Figure 2: Temperature and Dissolved
Oxygen Analysis

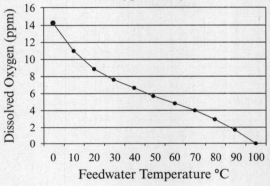

8. Which of the following statements best describes the changes observed in Figure 2?

F. As temperature increases, DO concentration decreases.

G. As temperature increases, DO concentration increases.

H. As temperature decreases, DO concentration increases.

J. The relationship between temperature and DO cannot be determined.

9. If instead of measuring the DO concentration in ppm, it is measured in parts per billion (ppb), which would be correct for a concentration of 5 ppm?

A. 50 ppb
B. 500 ppb
C. 5000 ppb
D. 50,000 ppb

10. Which of the following does NOT affect the concentration of DO in a pond of water?

F. The depth at which the DO concentration is measured

G. The temperature of the pond

H. The number of insects around the pond

J. The number of fish in the pond

11. Suppose that the concentration of oxygen in a pond was measured as 9 ppm. What would you expect the temperature of the pond water to be?

A. 25°C
B. 35°C
C. 40°C
D. 45°C

12. Which range of temperatures creates stressful conditions for fish populations?

F. 45°C–55°C
G. 65°C–75°C
H. 85°C–95°C
J. 95°C–100°C

Passage III

After a sound has been produced in an enclosed space (or room), it will be reflected by the boundaries (walls, ceilings, floors) of that enclosure. Although some energy is lost upon each reflection, several seconds may pass before the sound falls to a level that is not detectable to the human ear.

Reverberation refers to this continuation of sound after its initial production. Some reverberation adds a pleasant quality to the *acoustics* (sound design) of a room, while too much reverberation can destroy acoustics. *Reverberation time,* an important standard in architectural acoustics, refers to the time required for a specific sound to fall to one-thousandth of its initial pressure.

GO ON TO THE NEXT PAGE

Using data on the sound preferences of large groups of people, acoustical engineers have come up with curves for optimum reverberation time. Figure 1 shows optimum reverberation time (*y*-axis) as a function of sound frequency in cycles per second (cps; see *x*-axis). The optimum reverberation time is expressed as a ratio (R), relative to the optimum time for a standard sound of 500 cps. Figure 2 shows optimum reverberation time for a standard sound of 500 cps (*y*-axis) for different types of rooms and performance spaces as a function of room volume (*x*-axis).

Figure 1

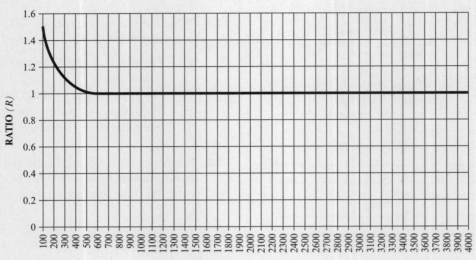

FREQUENCY *(in cycles per second)*

Figure 2

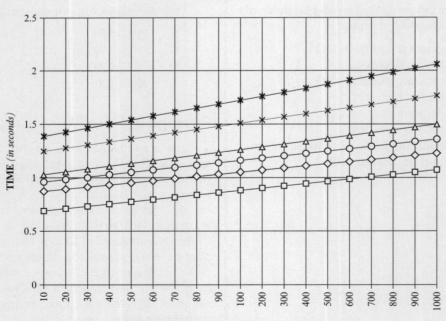

VOLUME *(in thousands of cubic feet) -- NOT TO SCALE*

—□— Speech —◇— Sound in Movie Theater —○— Chamber Music
—△— Sound in School Auditorium —✕— Average for All Music —✱— Church Music

GO ON TO THE NEXT PAGE

13. Figure 1 is a chart for computing optimum reverberation time based on sound frequency. The time at any frequency is given in terms of a ratio (R), which is then multiplied by the optimum reverberation time for a sound of 500 cps under any given conditions. Figure 2 shows the optimum reverberation time for a sound of 500 cps under different conditions. Combining the information in these two figures, what would be the optimum reverberation time for a sound of 300 cps in a 40,000 cubic foot church music room?

A.   1.1 seconds
B.   1.3 seconds
C.   1.5 seconds
D.   1.7 seconds

14. According to the data presented in Figure 2, all of the following statements about optimum reverberation times (ORT) for different sounds/ enclosures are true EXCEPT:

F.   The ORT for speech is shorter than the ORT for movie theaters.
G.   The ORT for church music is longer than the ORT for chamber music.
H.   The ORT for school auditoriums is shorter than the ORT for movie theaters.
J.   The ORT for school auditoriums is longer than the ORT for speech.

15. An architect is designing a very large college lecture hall that has a volume of 100,000 cubic feet. If the optimum reverberation time for this room is 2.0 seconds, then from the data presented, it can be inferred that the room size is

A.   just right for its intended purpose; lecturers will not have to use microphones.
B.   just right for its intended purpose, but lecturers will have to use microphones to be heard.
C.   too big for its intended purpose, so lecturers will have to use microphones to be heard.
D.   too small for its intended purpose.

16. An architect is designing a room in a historic building for use as a venue for intimate chamber music concerts. For an optimum reverberation time of 1 second, the best size room volume would be

F.   20,000 cubic feet.
G.   40,000 cubic feet.
H.   60,000 cubic feet.
J.   80,000 cubic feet.

17. An architect is designing a new high school auditorium with a projected room volume of 90,000 cubic feet. The optimum reverberation time for this enclosure is approximately

A.   0.75 seconds.
B.   1.0 seconds.
C.   1.25 seconds.
D.   1.5 seconds.

IF YOU FINISH BEFORE TIME IS CALLED, CHECK YOUR WORK ON THIS SECTION ONLY. DO NOT WORK ON ANY OTHER SECTION IN THE TEST.

Scoring the Diagnostic Test

The following section will assist you in scoring and analyzing your practice test results. Use the answer key below to score your results, then carefully review the analysis chart to identify your strengths and weakness. Finally, read through the answer explanations starting in the study guide on page 38 to clarify the solutions to the problems.

Answer Key for Diagnostic Test

English Test

1. D	**8.** H	**15.** C	**22.** F	**29.** C	**36.** H
2. G	**9.** D	**16.** H	**23.** C	**30.** H	**37.** B
3. C	**10.** H	**17.** B	**24.** G	**31.** B	**38.** J
4. J	**11.** B	**18.** J	**25.** D	**32.** G	**39.** A
5. C	**12.** J	**19.** B	**26.** J	**33.** C	**40.** J
6. G	**13.** B	**20.** H	**27.** B	**34.** H	
7. C	**14.** H	**21.** A	**28.** J	**35.** B	

Mathematics Test

1. B	**6.** F	**11.** C	**16.** K	**21.** A	**26.** H
2. H	**7.** C	**12.** F	**17.** A	**22.** K	**27.** C
3. C	**8.** K	**13.** E	**18.** J	**23.** B	**28.** J
4. F	**9.** B	**14.** G	**19.** B	**24.** F	**29.** D
5. B	**10.** H	**15.** A	**20.** G	**25.** C	**30.** F

Reading Test

1. D	**5.** C	**9.** D	**13.** D	**17.** C
2. G	**6.** G	**10.** G	**14.** G	**18.** F
3. D	**7.** D	**11.** C	**15.** A	**19.** D
4. F	**8.** H	**12.** J	**16.** G	**20.** F

Science Test

1. C	**4.** G	**7.** B	**10.** H	**13.** D	**16.** F
2. H	**5.** B	**8.** F	**11.** A	**14.** H	**17.** C
3. A	**6.** F	**9.** C	**12.** G	**15.** C	

Charting and Analyzing Your Test Results

The first step in analyzing your diagnostic test results is to chart your answers. Use the following chart to identify your strengths and areas of improvement. Complete the process of evaluating your strengths and analyzing problems in each area. Re-evaluate your results as you look for trends in the types of errors (repeated errors), and look for low scores in results in specific subject areas. This re-examination and analysis is a tremendous asset to help you maximize your best possible score. The answers and explanations following this chart will provide you clarification to help you solve these types of problems in the future.

Analysis Sheet

Topic	Number Possible	Number Correct	Number Incorrect		
			(A) Simple Mistake	(B) Misread Problem	(C) Lack of Knowledge
English Test	40				
Mathematics Test	30				
Reading Test	20				
Science Test	17				
Total Possible Explanations for Incorrect Answers: Columns A, B, and C					
Total Number of Questions	107	Add the total number of correct questions here: _____	Add columns A, B, and C for total number of incorrect questions here: _____		

Answers and Explanations

English Test

Passage I

1. **D.** The pronoun "you" should be "they" because the antecedent (the noun to which the pronoun refers) is "people." Make sure that pronouns and their antecedents are consistent. A second improvement in Choice D is shortening "whales that are giant" to "giant whales." Whenever possible without changing the meaning, choose the most concise expression.

2. **G.** This is the best choice because the possessive plural "their" refers to "organisms and plants." Choice G is better than Choice J because it is more succinct. "Its" (Choice F) is singular, not plural, and "it's" is a contraction of "it is," Choice H.

3. **C.** "They" (Choice A) should be omitted. "Plants" is the subject of the sentence, and there is no reason to use a pronoun. Choice C is the most concise expression.

4. **J.** The sentence should be omitted because it doesn't logically follow sentence 5. Choices F and H are not significant enough reasons to violate paragraph coherence. Were the sentence placed earlier (perhaps after sentence 3), it could possibly be included, but this placement is not offered as a choice.

5. **C.** The name Victor Hensen is followed by an appositive, which is a noun or pronoun—often with modifiers—that follows another noun or pronoun to identify or explain it. An appositive is enclosed in commas. Choice B is not incorrect, but Choice C is more concise.

6. **G.** Of the choices given, Choice G is best. (The placement of "in 1845" is awkward in the original version.) Using the past participle "had collected" indicates the sequence of events. "Through the ocean" is best placed without interruption next to "by towing. . . ." Choice H is not grammatically incorrect but is less efficient than Choice G, and Choice J uses the passive voice of the verb. Whenever possible, choose the active voice.

7. **C.** The simple past tense is best here; Choice A is a progressive tense, which is not appropriate. Placing the adjective "worldwide" next to the noun it modifies ("interest") is also best.

8. **H.** Of the choices, briefly defining these terms is the best. They belong here, not out of context in another location. Since "neritic" is a relatively unfamiliar term, defining both it and "oceanic" (in this context) is a good idea.

9. **D.** The comparative form of "rich" is "richer," not "more richer." "Will be" in Choice B is unnecessary.

10. **H.** Reversing paragraphs 2 and 3 is the most logical choice. Paragraph 1 ends with the point that plankton fulfill a function. Paragraph 3 is concerned with plankton providing the food web in the sea, which logically follows the idea of plankton's function. Paragraph 2 provides historical material about plankton, which can logically conclude the passage.

Passage II

11. **B.** The original version incorrectly uses a comma to set off a restrictive clause. A restrictive clause is one that is necessary to identify the noun it refers to, in this case "period." Choice B eliminates the initial comma, leaving the second comma for clarity after a long introductory clause. Choice B also correctly uses the preposition "during."

12. **J.** The present participle is appropriate in context, and "risen," not "rose," is the correct participial form of "rise."

13. **B.** This choice changes the verb from the passive to the active voice, thus avoiding wordiness and awkwardness. The speaker ("a spokesman") should be separated from the indirect quotation with a comma.

14. H. This choice is more efficient than the longer original version. Here, the adjective "worldwide" is better than the phrase "throughout the world." Also, the use of the comma in Choice J is incorrect.

15. C. "Optimism" is a perfectly good noun and a substitute for "optimistic viewpoint" or "optimistic point of view." Using the adjective "optimistic" simply adds words. Also, in Choice C, the correct plural possessive is used: theater owners'.

16. H. "Between" takes an objective ("them") not a subjective ("they") pronoun. Using subjective pronouns incorrectly with prepositions has become a common error, as in the expressions "between you and I," "for he and I," etc.

17. B. In the context of the sentence ("Early in the year"), the past tense is appropriate. Also the infinitive "plans to distribute" is idiomatic; "plans of distributing" is not. Choice D is wordier than Choice B.

18. J. There is no reason to use both the words "only" and "just." Choice J corrects this and also uses the correct possessive: "film's." The commas in choices G and H are unnecessary.

19. B. In the original version "began to be engaged" is awkward and wordy. Choice B is much more efficient and has the same meaning; only one of the two verbs ("begin," "engage") is necessary.

20. H. The original version is redundant. "Their mutual benefit" means that something benefits both parties. "Both" should be eliminated, and "benefit" should be singular.

21. A. The original version is best. Present tense is appropriate; the executive is talking about people *in the present* who have lost interest. In Choice D, "whom," the objective pronoun, is incorrect. "Who" is the subject of "had lost interest."

B is wordy and uses "like" rather than the correct "as if."

22. F. The original version is the best choice. The elements in the sentence are parallel in structure: "people who produce the movies," "theater owners who show them." Both clauses are restrictive and so, as in Choice F, shouldn't be enclosed in commas.

23. C. "More better" is incorrect; "better" is already a comparative ("good," "better," "best"), and something cannot be "more better." "Far," on the other hand, is used correctly here as an adverb to emphasize how *much* better it is.

24. G. This would be the best place to divide paragraph 2. Starting with sentence 4, the subject changes to the question of how movie producers and theater owners should encourage people to view films in theaters rather than at home. The second-best choice would be Choice F, but this choice would leave the first paragraph with only two sentences.

25. D. Sentence 7 strays from the topic of the rest of the passage. It deals with the theft of intellectual property, which has not been addressed anywhere else in the passage.

Passage III

26. J. This is the most succinct answer. Also "highly rated" is correct. In this case, an adverb ("highly") is the appropriate modifier for "rated." A hyphen shouldn't be used when the expression includes an adverb that ends in "ly." (Contrast with "hard-hitting," for example, in which the adverb does not end in "ly.")

27. B. This choice is succinct and uses the correct punctuation, which neither Choice C nor Choice D does. Also, "most all" is incorrect; use either "almost all" or "most" alone.

28. J. The use of "because" after "reason is" is common in colloquial speech, but in writing it should be avoided. "Reason is that" is correct. Choices G and H have the same kind of error as the original version.

29. C. Each of the other choices includes a double negative ("didn't," "wasn't"). "Hardly" shouldn't be used with another negative.

30. H. Only this choice corrects the dangling participle. "Having been. . ." is a phrase that modifies the speaker, not Tom. By changing the phrase to "Because I was," the problem is solved.

31. B. The original version, Choice A, is a misplaced modifier. The "experience" isn't a freshman at the university; Tom is. Choice B corrects the problem and places the modifier in its most logical position.

32. G. Choice G correctly punctuates the idiom by preceding it with a comma. The semicolon in the original creates a fragment. Choices H and J are both awkward and wordy in their use of the idiom.

33. C. This choice avoids the "strung out" sentence of Choice A and also uses the adverb "poorly" (rather than the adjective "poor") to modify the verb "did." Choices B and D incorrectly use adjectives ("bad," "poor") to modify the verb. Choice D is also a run-on sentence or comma splice. "However" should be preceded by period or semicolon.

34. H. This is the only choice that doesn't use quotation marks—and that is correct, since this is not a direct quotation but an indirect one. The writer is reporting what Tom said, not quoting him directly (notice the use of "He").

35. B. "Could have," not "could of" (as in choices A and D), is the correct conditional verb. Choice C is wordy.

36. H. Of the choices, this is the only one that would not be appropriate as a replacement. "Being remiss" is not the same as refusing. The other choices would be acceptable. Be aware of words like NOT and EXCEPT in questions.

37. B. Of the choices, this is the most concise, and it correctly uses the apostrophe ("students'"). Choice C incorrectly uses the pronoun "whom," and the comma in Choice A is incorrect. Notice that the second part of the sentence can be eliminated because by describing the other students' experiences as similar to Tom's, it is understood that the students had problems at colleges or universities.

38. J. "Had" is correct in this "if" clause; do not use "would have" in a conditional clause: And the correct participle of "go" is "gone." "Went" (Choice G) is the simple past, not the participle ("go," "went," "have gone"). Also "would of," in Choice H is incorrect; it is often mistakenly used in speech for "would have."

39. A. Both A and B are possible choices, but A is preferable because it leads from the previous sentence into the next sentence. Neither choice C nor D is as effective. Choice C is particularly implausible.

40. J. The main idea of the paragraph, and of the passage as a whole, is that Tom, while successful in high school, wasn't prepared for a large university. Choice F is a pat on Tom's back, but it isn't the best way to end the passage. Choices G and H leave the passage hanging rather than concluding it.

Mathematics Test

1. B. If x is increased by 50%, it can be represented by $\frac{3}{2}x$. This value must be multiplied by $\frac{2}{3}y$ in order to keep the product equal to xy. Since $\frac{2}{3}$ is a $\frac{1}{3}$ reduction, Choice B is the correct response.

2. H. Although the answer of $40.00 can be determined by trial and error, there is a better way.

$$\text{Maximum} = (\text{cost of ticket})(\text{number of tickets})$$
$$= (30 + 5x)(100 - 10x)$$
$$= (5)(10)(6 + x)(10 - x)$$

The roots of this symmetric curve are 10 and –6. So the line of symmetry is $x = 2$ and $(30 + 5x) = 30 + (5)(2) = 40$.

The maximum dollar sales are produced when the ticket price is $40.00.

3. C. Let x be Mike's age. Then, $3x$ is Macey's age.

Fill in a chart to help organize the given information.

Person	Current Age	Age 8 Years from Now
Mike	x	$x + 8$
Macey	$3x$	$3x + 8$

Therefore,

$$3x + 8 = 2(x + 8)$$
$$3x + 8 = 2x + 16$$
$$3x - 2x = 16 - 8$$
$$x = 8$$

So $3x = 24$, which means that Macey is now 24. Therefore, 3 years ago, she was 21.

4. F. Use the point slope form of the equation: $y = \frac{1}{2}x + b$.

Substituting the given point into this equation allows you to find b, the y-intercept.

$$2 = \frac{1}{2}(1) + b$$
$$b = \frac{3}{2}$$

Therefore, $y = \frac{1}{2}x + \frac{3}{2}$.

Multiplying both sides of the equation by 2 gives $2y = x + 3$.

Adding $-2y$ to each side gives $0 = x - 2y + 3$ or $x - 2y + 3 = 0$.

5. B. If the perimeter of the square is $8\sqrt{\pi}$ then each side is $2\sqrt{\pi}$, and the area of the square is 4π. If a circle has an area of 4π, its radius is 2, its diameter is 4, and its circumference is 4π.

6. F. From the diagram made up of one large isosceles triangle divided into two right triangles, you can see that

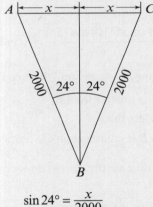

$$\sin 24° = \frac{x}{2000}$$
$$x = 2000 \sin 24°$$

Therefore, the distance between A and C is $2x$, or $4000 \sin 24°$.

7. C. The total number of candies in the package is $8 + 2 + 6 = 16$. After one candy is chosen and not replaced, 15 are left. Since there are 6 white candies out of 15 candies, the probability of getting a white candy is $\frac{6}{15}$, which equals $\frac{2}{5}$.

8. K. Because the shelf lengths are 4 inches apart, first find the average shelf length by dividing 155 by 5, which gives 31. This is the middle-length shelf. The shelf measurements are 23, 27, 31, 35, and 39. So the longest shelf is 39 inches long.

This problem can also be approached algebraically, as follows. If the longest shelf is x, the other shelves can be represented by $x - 4$, $x - 8$, $x - 12$, and $x - 16$. Add these, and you get

$$5x - 40 = 155$$
$$5x = 155 + 40$$
$$5x = 195$$
$$x = 39$$

9. B. Factoring the equation gives $y = x^4(1 - x)$.

The roots of this equation are 0 and 1, since $0 = x^4(1 - x)$ and $0 = x^4$ or $0 = 1 - x$. So the x-axis is intersected at the points 0 and 1. Thus, twice is the answer.

10. H. Since the coordinates of the midpoint are the averages of the endpoints, you have the following. Let (a, b) be the coordinates of the missing endpoint. Since no two answer choices have the same first (or second) coordinate, it is necessary to find only the first or second coordinate, but not both. If there were answer choices with the same first or second coordinate, then it would be necessary to find both missing coordinates. Use the midpoint formula to calculate the missing values. We will find both values:

$$\frac{b + y}{2} = -3y \qquad \frac{a + x}{2} = 3x$$
$$b + y = -6y \quad \text{and} \quad a + x = 6x$$
$$b = -7y \qquad\qquad a = 5x$$

Therefore, the coordinates of the missing endpoint are $(5x, -7y)$.

11. C. Statement I is the external angle theorem, which makes statement I true. Statement II follows from statement I since the total must be greater than any of its parts, therefore, it is also true. Statement III is true only some of the time. If the shape of the triangle changes, statement III could be false.

12. F. The area of a triangle is $A = \frac{bh}{2}$.

In a right triangle, the sine of an angle is the quotient of the length of the opposite side and the length of the hypotenuse, and the cosine of an angle is the quotient of the length of the adjacent side and the length of the hypotenuse. Therefore, $\sin 35° = y \div 4$ and $\cos 35° = x \div 4$. Solving for x and y gives: $y = 4 \sin 35°$ and $x = 4 \cos 35°$. Therefore, the area of the triangle is

$$A = \frac{bh}{2} = \frac{(4 \sin 35°)(4 \cos 35°)}{2} = 8 \sin 35° \cos 35°$$

13. E. Remember that the symbol "<" means *less than* and ">" means *greater than*.

$$\text{If } A \text{ is greater than } B \qquad A > B$$
$$C \text{ is less than } A \qquad\qquad C < A$$
$$\text{and } B \text{ is greater than } C \qquad B > C$$

By making use of the first and third conditions (the second does not give you any new information), $A > B > C$, or by reversing the inequality, $C < B < A$.

14. G. The information leads you to the following diagram.

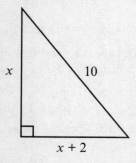

The path taken by the hikers forms a right triangle. Since the hikers hiked 2 hours, and one hiker can hike 1 mile per hour faster than the other, that hiker will be 2 miles farther than the slower one after 2 hours. Therefore, the following Pythagorean relationship exists.

$$a^2 + b^2 = c^2$$
$$x^2 + (x+2)^2 = 10^2$$
$$x^2 + x^2 + 4x + 4 = 100$$
$$2x^2 + 4x + 4 = 100$$
$$2x^2 + 4x - 96 = 0$$
$$x^2 + 2x - 48 = 0$$
$$(x+8)(x-6) = 0$$

Now, solving each one independently gives you $x + 8 = 0$, so $x = -8$, or $x - 6 = 0$, so $x = 6$.

Because distance can't be negative, x must be equal to 6. So in 2 hours, the slower hiker walked 6 miles, which is 3 miles per hour. This is an example of a problem that can be solved by working from the answers. Test each answer choice to see which one fits the given information.

Note: Another way to work this problem is to let x = speed of the slower hiker. Then $2x$ is the distance walked by the slower hiker and $2(x + 1)$ is the distance walked by the faster hiker. This representation works, but it increases the complexity of the algebra necessary to find the solution.

15. A. Work from the inside out.

$$f\left(\frac{1}{2}\right) = \left(\frac{1}{2}\right)^2 - 2$$
$$= \frac{1}{4} - 2$$
$$= -\frac{7}{4}$$

Then

$$g\left(f\left(\frac{1}{2}\right)\right) = g\left(-\frac{7}{4}\right)$$
$$= 2\left(-\frac{7}{4}\right) + 2$$
$$= -\frac{14}{4} + 2$$
$$= -\frac{14}{4} + \frac{8}{4}$$
$$= -\frac{6}{4}$$
$$= -\frac{3}{2}$$

and

$$f\left(g\left(f\left(\frac{1}{2}\right)\right)\right) = f\left(-\frac{3}{2}\right)$$
$$= \left(-\frac{3}{2}\right)^2 - 2$$
$$= \frac{9}{4} - 2$$
$$= \frac{9}{4} - \frac{8}{4}$$
$$= \frac{1}{4}$$

16. **K.** The following diagram illustrates the conditions of the problem.

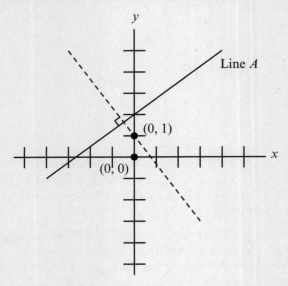

Since the line in question passes through the point (0, 1), it must have a y-intercept of 1. Since it is perpendicular to Line A, its slope must be the negative reciprocal of $\frac{3}{4}$, or $-\frac{4}{3}$. Substituting into the point-slope form of the equation of a line gives

$$y = mx + b$$
$$y = -\frac{4}{3}x + 1$$
$$3y = -4x + 3$$
$$4x + 3y = 3$$

17. **A.** Because $AB = BC$, $\angle CAD = \angle ACB$ (isosceles triangle ABC). So $\angle ACB$ is also 70°. This makes $\angle B$ equal to 40° (180 degrees in a triangle). Also, $\angle BCD$ equals 40°, for the same reason. Therefore, $\angle ADC = 80°$ (external angle theorem).

18. **J.** To determine the next numbers in the sequence, look for a relationship between the given numbers. In this case, the difference between the first and second terms is 1. The difference between the second and third terms is 2. This relationship continues as follows:

$$5 + 1 = 6$$
$$6 + 2 = 8$$
$$8 + 3 = 11$$
$$11 + 4 = 15$$
$$15 + 5 = 20$$
$$20 + 6 = 26$$
$$26 + 7 = 33$$
$$33 + 8 = 41$$
$$41 + 9 = 50$$

So the tenth term would be 50. Another method of solution would be to notice that the tenth term in this sequence would be the sum of the integers from 1 through 9, plus the starting number of 5. Using the formula for finding the sum of integers from 1 to n, you can determine the answer as follows:

$$\text{Starting number} + \frac{n(n+1)}{2} = 5 + \frac{(9)(10)}{2} = 50$$

19. B. Substitute $x + 4$ in the given equation for x.

$$3x^2 + 2x - 4 = 0$$
$$3(x+4)^2 + 2(x+4) - 4 = 0$$
$$3(x^2 + 8x + 16) + 2x + 8 - 4 = 0$$
$$3x^2 + 24x + 48 + 2x + 8 - 4 = 0$$
$$3x^2 + 26x + 52 = 0$$

20. G. Time equals distance divided by speed.

A chart can be used to organize the given information.

	Rate	Time	Distance
Slower	x	$\dfrac{20}{x}$	20
Faster	$x + 4$	$\dfrac{20}{x+4}$	20

Therefore, the difference between the two times (using the different speeds) is 1, giving

$$\frac{20}{x} - \frac{20}{x+4} = 1$$
$$(x)(x+4)\frac{20}{x} - (x)(x+4)\frac{20}{x+4} = (x)(x+4)1$$
$$20(x+4) - 20x = x^2 + 4x$$
$$20x + 80 - 20x = x^2 + 4x$$
$$x^2 + 4x - 80 = 0$$
$$x = \frac{-4 \pm \sqrt{16 + 320}}{2}$$
$$= \frac{-4 \pm \sqrt{336}}{2}$$
$$= \frac{-4 \pm 4\sqrt{21}}{2}$$
$$x = -2 \pm 2\sqrt{21}$$

Since speed must be positive, use the $+2\sqrt{21}$, which gives $-2 + 2\sqrt{21}$ or $2\sqrt{21} - 2$.

21. A. A rectangle can be drawn around the triangle as shown in the following diagram:

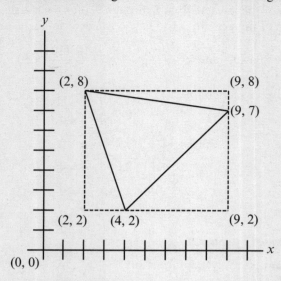

You can determine the area of the given triangle by subtracting the areas of the three right triangles from the area of the rectangle. By subtracting respective coordinates, you can determine the lengths of the required sides. The area of the given triangle is

$$A = lw - \frac{b_1 h_1}{2} - \frac{b_2 h_2}{2} - \frac{b_3 h_3}{2}$$

$$= (7)(6) - \frac{(7)(1)}{2} - \frac{(5)(5)}{2} - \frac{(2)(6)}{2}$$

$$= 42 - 3.5 - 12.5 - 6$$

$$= 20$$

22. K. From the Pythagorean Theorem, you see that the diagonal is 15. So the perimeter of the rectangle is 42, and the perimeter of the triangle is 36. Therefore, the ratio is $\frac{42}{36} = \frac{7}{6}$ or 7:6.

23. B. Start solving at the bottom right with the fraction $\frac{3}{3+3}$ and continue as follows:

$$3 + \cfrac{3}{3 + \cfrac{3}{3 + \cfrac{3}{3+3}}} = 3 + \cfrac{3}{3 + \cfrac{3}{3 + \cfrac{1}{2}}} = 3 + \cfrac{3}{3 + \cfrac{3}{\left(\frac{7}{2}\right)}} = 3 + \cfrac{3}{3 + \frac{6}{7}}$$

$$= 3 + \cfrac{3}{\left(\frac{27}{7}\right)} = 3 + \frac{21}{27} = 3\frac{21}{27} = 3\frac{7}{9}$$

24. F. You are given $\dfrac{x}{x-y} - \dfrac{y}{y-x}$.

Since $y - x = -(x - y)$, $\dfrac{y}{y-x} = \dfrac{-y}{x-y}$.

Therefore,

$$\frac{x}{x-y} - \frac{y}{y-x} = \frac{x}{x-y} + \frac{y}{x-y}$$

$$= \frac{x+y}{x-y}$$

25. C. Machine *A* works for a total of 4 hours. You can substitute what is known into the following useful formula.

$$\frac{A \text{ actual work}}{A \text{ do job alone}} + \frac{B \text{ actual work}}{B \text{ do job alone}} = 1$$

In other words, the fractional part of the job that *A* did plus the fractional part of the job that *B* did must equal one complete job. So

$$\frac{4}{10} + \frac{6}{10} = 1$$

Since $\quad \dfrac{4}{10} + \dfrac{x}{12} = 1$

Then $\quad\quad \dfrac{x}{12} = \dfrac{6}{10}$

Cross multiplying gives $10x = 72$ or $x = 7.2$.

Now, 7.2 hours = 7 hours and 12 minutes. Since *B* started at 9 a.m., *B* must finish at 4:12 p.m.

26. H. In a circle, an inscribed angle subtends (cuts off) an arc twice the angle size.

Since $\angle ABD = 20°$, $\overset{\frown}{AD} = 40°$.

Since $\overset{\frown}{BAD}$ is a semicircle, $\overset{\frown}{AB} = 180° - 40° = 140°$.

Therefore, angle *x* must be one-half of its subtended arc, or $x = 70°$.

27. C. You can tabulate the data as follows:

	Part of Tank Brand *Z*	Part of Tank Brand *Y*
After first fill-up	1	0
Before second fill-up	$\dfrac{1}{2}$	0
After second fill-up	$\dfrac{1}{2}$	$\dfrac{1}{2}$
Before third fill-up	$\dfrac{1}{4}$	$\dfrac{1}{4}$
After third fill-up	$\dfrac{3}{4}$	$\dfrac{1}{4}$
Before fourth fill-up	$\dfrac{3}{8}$	$\dfrac{1}{8}$
After fourth fill-up	$\dfrac{3}{8}$	$\dfrac{5}{8}$

Since the tank is now full, $\dfrac{3}{8}$, or 37.5%, is brand *Z*.

28. J. From the Pythagorean Theorem, you can see that *AB* is 15. (If the length of side $\overline{AB}$ is *x*, then $9^2 + 12^2 = x^2$, or $x = 15$.)

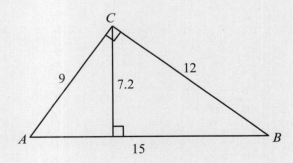

Because the height of a right triangle drawn from the right angle to the hypotenuse divides the triangle into similar triangles, you can set up the following ratio:

$$\frac{h}{9} = \frac{12}{15}$$
$$15h = 12 \times 9$$
$$h = 7.2$$

29. D. The formula for combinations of n things taken r at a time is

$$\binom{n}{r} = {}_nC_r = \frac{n!}{r!(n-r)!}$$

Therefore, $\binom{8}{3} = {}_8C_3 = \frac{8!}{3!(8-3)!} = \frac{8!}{3!5!} = \frac{8 \times 7 \times 6 \times 5 \times 4 \times 3 \times 2 \times 1}{3 \times 2 \times 1 \times 5 \times 4 \times 3 \times 2 \times 1} = 56$

Instead of using the combinations formula, you could list all 56 committees, but this is clearly a much more time-consuming process and not the preferred option.

For example: 123, 124, 125, 126, 127, 128, 134, 135, 136, 137, 138, 145, . . .

30. F. To get additional insight, you should draw the diagram.

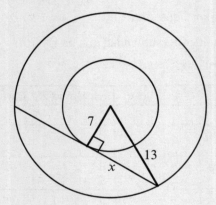

Note that a tangent to a circle is perpendicular to the radius at the point of tangency. From the Pythagorean Theorem,

$$7^2 + x^2 = 13^2$$
$$x^2 = 169 - 49$$
$$x^2 = 120$$
$$x = \sqrt{120} = 2\sqrt{30}$$

Because the length of the chord is twice the length of the leg of the right triangle:

$$2x = 4\sqrt{30}$$

Reading Test

Passage I

1. **D.** Of the choices, D is best. Although Newton's accomplishments are mentioned in the first paragraph, the main point the author makes is that Newton didn't reject the ideas and beliefs of the past. See lines 9–18.

2. **G.** According to the passage, Newton left "no stone unturned" in his search for a unified theory of the universe. He was a "devout seeker" and wouldn't exclude ideas of the ancients. No theory was "beyond the pale" to Newton when it came to his research. See lines 22–41. Choices H and J are inaccurate, and there is no evidence for Choice F.

3. **D.** More books on alchemy than on chemistry suggests Newton's greater interest in that subject. Choice A is the second best answer, but a straightforward comparison of the number of books on each subject makes D a better choice.

4. **F.** Lines 32–34 make the point. According to the passage, Newton believed his quest was to recover lost knowledge, not to discover something new. Modern scientists don't view their work as rediscovering knowledge. There is no evidence of Choice J, and although Newton did believe in God and the Bible (G), not all modern scientists are unbelievers, nor are all scientists at a university (H).

5. **C.** The best definition of *arcane* is mysterious or obscure. Newton was interested in subjects that were mysterious, such as alchemy and the date of Armageddon. This definition makes the most sense in the context of the passage.

6. **G.** Newton's efforts to prove or disprove the validity of alchemy failed. But his laws of gravity and motion did explain choices F, H, and J.

7. **D.** In lines 63–64, the passage makes it clear that Newton sought simplicity: In Newton's own words, "Nature is simple and does not indulge in the luxury of superfluous causes"; see also lines 68–69. Choices B and C may be accurate, but they don't focus on Newton's belief in simplicity, and Choice A is a supposition of the author's.

8. **H.** Newton "weaned" science from philosophy and transformed it into a disciplined inquiry, which, according to the author, made him the "culminating figure in the Scientific Revolution." His strategy for approaching science was inaugurated by Galileo, but Newton did not "prove" Galileo's theories were right (F). Choice G is true, but it was Newton's development of the scientific method, not his quest for simplicity, that made him the "culminating figure." Separating science from philosophy, not simply from religion (J), was his achievement.

9. **D.** The author's purpose is to show Newton's connection to medieval thought. Choice A is not supported in the passage. The author also is not concerned with "negative" influences (B) or the fallibility of science (C).

10. **G.** This is the best choice. The author does not go into the details of Newton's life or of his research; this passage is not a concise biography (F). Nothing suggests that it is a "fictionalized account" (H). The author is not arguing for the acceptance of unproved theories (J).

Passage II

11. **C.** Although their reaction didn't last long, according to the author, intellectuals were initially hopeful in the aftermath of the Great Crash (lines 1–4). This hopefulness is not emphasized in the passage because it quickly disappeared.

12. **J.** The Depression affected all sectors of the economy and society in the 1930s (lines 7–8), but there is no evidence that the earlier stock market crash wasn't to blame (H). Choices F and G are contradicted.

13. **D.** Book sales were greatly reduced (lines 28–31). Magazine and newspaper circulation "held up amazingly well" (lines 26–28), but the passage does not say that they increased or decreased (choices A and B). Libraries, although used by many, did not expand (C).

14. G. Although the writing that Steinbeck submitted to publishers remained unpublished during this period, he continued to write. Choices F and H are not implied. In the quotation, Steinbeck says the pieces would have been returned even if they had been good. This indicates how badly the publishing industry was doing, not that he was pessimistic about his own writing (J).

15. A. According to the author, in the 1930s book sales *fell* from two books per person, which was the figure before the stock market crash. ("Americans . . . notoriously purchased few books even in good times," the author says in lines 41–42.) All of the other choices are supported by the passage.

16. G. *Pathetic* in line 59 is used to refer to the quest for jobs—a pathetic quest because there simply weren't jobs available.

17. C. Choices A and D, while perhaps true, are not indicated in the passage. Libraries are described as "poor man's clubs" because in hard times they provided a warm haven from the effects of the Depression, just as "rich man's clubs" had always provided a haven for people with money.

18. F. The author hypothesizes that library circulation fell off later in the 1930s for two reasons: more jobs were becoming available, and libraries lacked funds to acquire new books. Although choices G and J may be accurate, they aren't indicated in the passage.

19. D. The "irony" is the incongruity (one of the definitions of irony) of a lavish, expensive exposition celebrating progress being held in a major city where the library lacked funds to buy books for three years. Choice A is inaccurate, and choices B and C aren't indicated.

20. F. The passage is a summary of the effects of the Depression on books and libraries. There is implied criticism in the final paragraph, but this criticism is not the author's main point.

Science Test

Passage I

1. C. Scientist 1 states that reducing emissions by 6 percent, starting this year, is necessary to restore energy balance during this century.

2. H. Scientist 2 states that over the past 150 years, global warming has coincided with technological progress.

3. A. Scientist 2 believes that colder temperatures contribute to sickness and the death of approximately 100,000 people each year in Europe and Russia.

4. G. Scientist 1 believes that the rise in sea levels is a result of global warming, and the rise can be one way to diagnose the effects of climate change.

5. B. Scientist 2 believes that cold temperatures INCREASE mortality, not decrease it.

6. F. Scientist 1 believes that climate change results in a rise in sea levels, potentially causing "coastal areas around the world to become submerged under water."

7. B. Scientist 2 believes that warmer climates directly influence technological and medical progress, human health, and life expectancy. A major blow to this argument would be demonstrating that there is no direct correlation between warmer temperatures and technological or medical advances or life expectancy. Choice B is the only answer that demonstrates this idea.

Passage II

8. F. Figure 2 shows a reverse relationship between temperature and dissolved oxygen (DO). Choice F is the only answer that demonstrates a reverse relationship between these two factors.

9. C. A billion is 1000 times more than a million. Therefore, if there are 5 parts in one million, there would be 5000 parts in one billion.

10. H. Depth does affect concentration of DO. DO is higher near the surface of water due to the oxygen of the air near the surface. Figure 2 shows that temperature also affects the concentration of DO. Fish use DO for respiration. Insects around the pond do not use the DO in the pond. The only answer that makes logical sense is Choice H.

11. A. Looking at Figure 2, 9 ppm corresponds to about 25°C.

12. G. Using Figure 1, we see that stressful conditions occur at dissolved oxygen levels of 3.0–5.0 ppm. Taking this information to Figure 2, we see that 3.0–5.0 ppm corresponds to temperatures of about 65–75°C.

Passage III

13. D. According to Figure 1, the ratio (R) for 300 cps is just over 1.1. According to Figure 2, a 40,000 cubic foot room for listening to church music has an optimum reverberation time of 1.5 seconds. If these are multiplied together, according to the directions in the question, the answer is just over 1.65, or about 1.7 seconds. Without doing the math, the information in the two figures shows that the answer must be larger than 1.5 seconds (because the 300 cps ratio is larger than 1), so the answer can also be found to be the only one larger than 1.5 seconds.

14. H. None of the optimum reverberation time curves for the six different sounds/enclosures overlaps. And since the slope of all the curves is positive (where values along the x-axis and the y-axis both increase), it is apparent that the sound with the shortest ORT is speech while the sound with the longest ORT is church music. The ORT for movie theaters is actually shorter than the ORT for school auditoriums. Therefore, Choice H is the correct answer. (Note the EXCEPT.)

15. C. According to Figure 2, a room that is 100,000 cubic feet in volume with an optimum reverberation time of 2.0 seconds would be better suited for church music. Speech without a microphone will not be heard in such a room, for it will be too large for its intended purpose as a lecture hall.

16. F. The point on the curve for chamber music that corresponds with a y-axis value of 1.0 seconds is an x-axis value of 20,000 cubic feet.

17. C. The point on the curve for auditorium sounds that corresponds with an x-axis value of 90,000 cubic feet is a y-axis value of approximately 1.25 seconds.

PART II

REVIEW OF EXAM AREAS

Chapter 2

The ACT English Test

The ACT English Test examines your ability to understand and identify errors in standard written English. Questions measure your knowledge of effective written communication in two main categories:

- **Usage/Mechanics** — specific grammatical errors within a sentence
- **Rhetorical Skills** — general construction errors within a sentence, a paragraph, or the whole passage.

Several sample problems in this chapter provide plenty of practice to help you reinforce your skills and your approach to English Test questions. Each section of this chapter is designed to help you improve your grammar and develop a greater understanding of written communication. You are encouraged to pace yourself and familiarize yourself with the question types by completing all the practice exercises in each section.

Repeated practice is the key to achieving the greatest success on the ACT. The final chapters of this study guide include three full-length practice tests with complete explanations and illustrations. Apply the rules, concepts, and strategies you learn in this chapter to the practice tests and review the strategies and questions regularly to maximize your chances for greater success on the actual test.

General Overview of the ACT English Test

The following table presents an overview of the English Test.

Format of the English Test

Question Type	Description	Approximate Number of Multiple-Choice Questions	Approximate Percentage of English Test
Usage/ Mechanics	**Punctuation:** Identify faulty punctuation marks in a sentence.	10	13%
	Grammar: Evaluate rules that govern how words are used together using standard written English.	12	16%
	Sentence structure: Identify mistakes in organizing words in a sentence.	18	24%
	Subtotal Usage/Mechanics	**40**	**53%**
Rhetorical Skills	**Writing strategy:** Understand a writer's choices in composing or revising a particular essay.	12	16%
	Organization: Organize thoughts to compose a logically coherent essay.	11	15%
	Style: Communicate and shape an essay through clear and concise writing, word choices, and tone.	12	16%
	Subtotal Rhetorical Skills	**35**	**47%**

Formation of Questions

Total Number of Questions: 75

Total Number of Passages: 5

Total Time: 45 minutes

Scoring: The total English Test is scored from 1 to 36, with a mean of 18, and subscores are reported in a range from 1 to 18, with a mean of 9.

Note: Students who take the writing test will receive a combined score for English and writing.

The following graph illustrates that 53 percent of English Test questions appear as usage/mechanics errors, and 47 percent of the questions appear as rhetorical skills questions. Questions can reference part of a sentence, one or more sentences, a paragraph, or the whole passage.

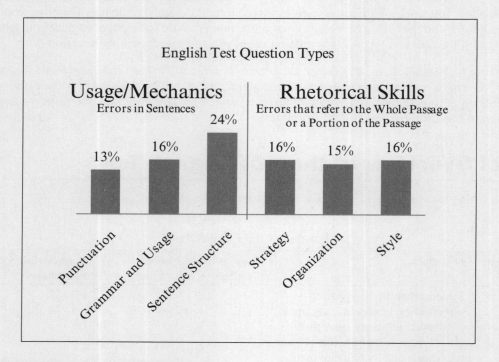

English Test Question Types

Usage/Mechanics
Errors in Sentences

Rhetorical Skills
Errors that refer to the Whole Passage
or a Portion of the Passage

13% Punctuation
16% Grammar and Usage
24% Sentence Structure
16% Strategy
15% Organization
16% Style

Skills and Concepts Tested

English Test questions assess your knowledge of effective writing (how words are combined to form meaning), as you correct errors that break the rules of standard written English in multiple-choice questions. You will be tested on how well you can demonstrate your ability to think decisively under time constraints and to correct errors that break the rules of grammar and stylistic conventions of English.

The English Test will not require you to define specific vocabulary words or know specific grammar rules. However, your knowledge of vocabulary and grammar is evaluated within the *context of a sentence*. Even though the English Test is not a test of vocabulary, you should be familiar with the obvious and subtle differences in words and their meanings. For this reason, vocabulary resources are included at the end of Chapter 4, "The ACT Reading Test," to help you expand your working vocabulary.

Directions

In each passage, you will find various words and phrases underlined and numbered. You will also find a set of four choices labeled A, B, C, D or F, G, H, J, corresponding to each underlined portion of the passage. Choose the response you feel is the best answer among the four choices.

- Sometimes the original portion is a better choice than the alternative choices. If the underlined portion is correct standard written English, is most appropriate to the style and feeling of the passage, or best makes the intended statement, mark the letter indicating "NO CHANGE."

- If the underlined portion is not the best choice given, choose one of the three remaining letter choices. For these questions, consider only the underlined portions and assume that the rest of the passage is correct as written.

The correct choice should be clear, unambiguous, and concise. Remember that your answer must be appropriate for the meaning of the passage and the writer's intended audience. Focus on grammar, word choices, sentence construction, and punctuation.

Structure

To answer English Test questions efficiently, you should become familiar with the *problem setup*. The following diagram illustrates the structure of each passage and the two categories of questions. Each problem consists of a portion of the passage (or the whole passage), a question, and four answer choices.

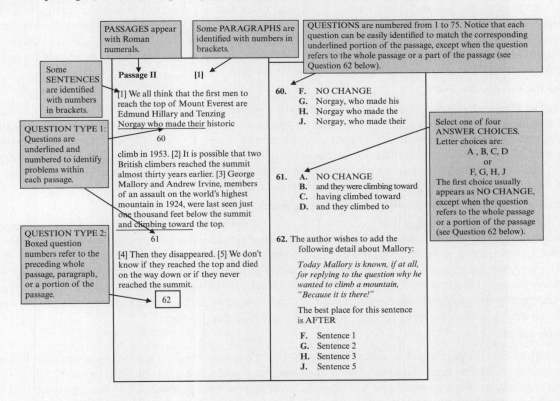

General Strategies

Test-taking strategies can accelerate your learning by teaching you time management, organizational skills, and test-taking techniques. This section describes six general "suggested" strategies to practice as you review sample questions. These proven strategies have helped hundreds of students improve their performance on the ACT by responding to questions quickly and efficiently.

As you study the general strategies in this section, pinpoint which strategies work best for your individual learning style. Strategy preferences may vary from person to person. What may work for some people may not work for others. Later in this section, we will introduce some specific strategies for different question types, but in the meantime consider these suggestions that can be applied to all types of English Test questions.

1. **Read actively**

   Take advantage of being allowed to write in your test booklets. As you read each passage and question, feel free to mark key words or relevant points, or any other items you feel are important. Key words point to specific information in the passage that help to identify errors in the sentence or the passage. As you read the passage, note the *style* and *tone* of the passage. The style and tone of the passage will often help you eliminate answer choices that "just don't sound right."

   If time permits, try to quickly reread the sentence with your answer to make sure it fits. Do not make a hasty assumption that you know the correct answer without reading the whole question and all the answer choices. The hurried test-taker commonly selects an incorrect answer by jumping to a conclusion after reading only one part of the sentence or part of the answer choices.

2. **Answer easy questions first**

   Some questions are easier than others, so if you come to a question that is difficult to understand, a good strategy to employ is to skip the question and come back to it later if time permits. With sufficient practice, you will get a feel for when a question is taking too much time and when it is time to take an educated guess.

   Be sure to mark your answer sheet correctly if you skip a question. A common mistake among test-takers is that they forget to leave blank spaces for unanswered questions and incorrectly mark their answers in the wrong spaces. A good idea is to mark your answer in the test booklet itself (no need to erase later) so that if you do make a mistake in transferring your answer choices to the answer sheet, you can easily correct your errors without having to reconsider all of the answer choices.

3. **Use the elimination strategy**

   Use the elimination strategy on page 6 to reduce the number of choices. Read all the answer choices and try to eliminate obviously wrong answers as soon as you recognize them. Eliminate choices by crossing out incorrect answers in your test booklet (not on your answer sheet). If you get stuck on any one question, take an educated guess by eliminating some of the other choices and proceed to the next question. Remember that there is no penalty for guessing so no questions should be left blank. If you can eliminate two or more of the answer choices to a question, it is always to your advantage to guess.

4. **Be on alert for the "attractive distractor" answer choices**

   Watch out for answer choices that look good but are not the best answer choice. The attractive distractor usually appears in this section as a choice that contains a subtle variation in meaning from the correct answer, thus making it more difficult for you to select the correct answer. Attractive distractors are carefully written to be *close to the best answer,* but there is never more than one right answer. The best answer is always the only correct answer choice. When you narrow your choice down to two answers, one is probably the attractive distractor. If this happens, read the question again and select the answer that fits the best *grammatically correct meaning* for the underlined portion in the passage.

5. **Don't get stuck!**

   Pace yourself and work quickly and efficiently. At first glance you might calculate that you have just over *thirty-five seconds* to read and answer each question, but challenging questions can be time-consuming for some test-takers. Pace yourself and work as efficiently as possible to answer all of the easy questions first. Don't let your concerns about time interfere with your progress. You will have only 45 minutes to complete the entire English Test, which has approximately 5 passages and 75 questions. Since all questions are weighted equally, it is recommended that you *never spend more than a minute on any one question* and answer all of the solvable questions first. Taking time to answer the most difficult question on the test correctly but losing valuable test time won't get you the score you deserve.

6. **Questions about a whole paragraph or passage**

   When reading each passage, look for numbered boxes that refer to questions about the entire passage, or a portion of the passage. If a question refers to the logical order of a paragraph or passage, it is sometimes helpful to skim the paragraph (passage) before answering the question. Determine the *context* of the written material so that you can develop a framework for the sequence of events.

In questions that mention specific sentence numbers or paragraph numbers, you will have the advantage of being able to quickly spot where the information is located. After you spot the location, be sure to read the sentences just before and the sentence after. The context of the information that comes just before and after the sentence is often helpful to put the information in the proper sequence.

Sample Questions with Suggested Strategies

Specific topics covered in this section will help you identify how to spot common errors on the ACT that break the rules of standard written English.

Start by reviewing the basic parts of speech. Knowing the parts of speech is integral to your understanding of the English Test grammar and usage question types.

Parts of Speech

Basic Parts of Speech	Definition	Examples
Noun	A word used as a person, a place, or a thing.	man, girl, Philadelphia, boat, noun
Pronoun	A word used as a substitute for a noun.	I, you, he, she, it, me, him, her, we, they, who, whom, which, what, this, that, one, none, someone, somebody, myself, anything, nothing
Verb	A word used to assert action or a state of being.	sit, clap, walk, is, are, remain, think, become
Adjective	A word used to modify a noun or pronoun. To modify is to describe, to qualify, to limit or restrict in meaning. In the phrase *a small, red rose,* both *small* and *red* are adjectives that modify the noun *rose*.	large, bitter, petite, hot, cold, old, new, sad, lucky, blue
Adverb	A word used to modify a verb, an adjective, or another adverb. In the phrase *to sing a very long song very slowly, very* and *slowly* are adverbs. The first *very* modifies an adjective (long); the second modifies an adverb (slowly); and *slowly* modifies the verb (sing).	very, rather, quickly, quite, easily, carefully

Question Type One: Usage/Mechanics Errors

Usage/mechanics questions in the English Test will never ask you to *explain* or *describe* conventions of standard written English, but it is useful to know the meaning of several of the more important grammatical rules and to recognize their distinctive features. This section targets key grammatical rules and terms to help you identify errors in punctuation, grammar, usage, and sentence structure.

The table that follows will help you keep track of the common types of mistakes found in usage/mechanics questions. Not all of these errors will appear on the exam, but many of them have appeared on previous exams. Use the table as a checklist to mark topics as you read each topic and practice the sample questions. As you evaluate your understanding of each question type, pinpoint areas that require further study by placing a check mark next to the topic. Continue to measure your progress, and refer back to this list as often as necessary.

Category	Topic Review Checklist	Page Number
Punctuation Errors	❏ Comma Errors ❏ Semicolon Errors	Page 60 Page 61
Grammar and Usage Errors	❏ Subject-Verb Agreement Errors ❏ Pronoun-Antecedent Errors ❏ Adjective-Noun Errors ❏ Adverb-Verb Errors ❏ Verb Errors ❏ Pronoun and Case Errors ❏ Idiom Errors ❏ Comparative and Superlative Modifier Errors	Page 62 Page 62 Page 63 Page 63 Page 65 Page 66 Page 67 Page 68
Sentence Structure Errors	❏ Dangling Participle or Modifier ❏ Sentence Fragments ❏ Faulty Parallelism ❏ Awkward, Run-On (Wordy) Sentences	Page 69 Page 69 Page 70 Page 70

Punctuation Errors

The proper use of punctuation is an important part of English and helps to clarify the correct meaning of a sentence. As you read a sentence, you may notice that punctuation errors can sometimes be identified if you read silently to yourself and listen for a natural pause to determine whether a punctuation mark is omitted or incorrectly inserted. On the ACT, except when a period is at the end of a sentence, suspect a punctuation error when a *comma, semicolon, colon, dash,* or *apostrophe* is part of the underlined portion. Note, however, that simply because a punctuation mark is underlined, doesn't mean that it is necessarily part of the error.

Comma Errors

Comma errors are the most common types of punctuation errors that appear on the English Test.

Comma Rule 1: Introductory clause—Use a comma to separate an introductory clause, word, or phrase that comes before the main clause. Common introductory words to look for are *if, when, after, although, because, since,* and *while.* For example, "If you exercise regularly, you will build strength and endurance."

Note: Always use a comma after a proper noun that starts a question. For example, "Michelle, did you see the solar eclipse last Sunday?"

Comma Rule 2: Nonrestrictive clause—Use a comma to set off a nonrestrictive clause. In a nonrestrictive clause, a comma is used to add a phrase (clause) to the sentence. In a way, the comma interrupts the sentence to add extra information. For example, "In 2004, when Facebook was launched, college students were eager to become socially connected."

Comma Rule 3: Series—A standard rule is to use commas to separate three or more words, phrases, or clauses in a series. For example, "Angel enjoys surfing, biking, and golfing."

Comma Rule 4: Parenthetical phrase—Use commas to set off parenthetical phrases. A parenthetical phase can be removed without changing the meaning of a sentence. Commas are used on both sides of the phrase to set it off from the sentence. For example: "Students at Franklin High School, who graduated last week, were invited to attend a concert at the Hollywood Bowl."

Comma Rule 5: Appositive–Use commas to set off nonrestrictive appositives. An appositive is a noun phrase that renames another noun and is set off by commas on each side. For example, "Russell Westbrook, a point guard for the Oklahoma City Thunder, hit a twenty-five-foot three-point basket in the fourth quarter of the NBA playoffs."

Comma Rule 6: Separate adjectives—Use a comma to separate adjectives that modify a noun. For example, "Vincent van Gogh's painting of *Starry Night* is an honest, powerful depiction of the night's sky."

Comma Rule 7: Compound sentence—Use a comma to separate two independent clauses (complete thoughts) joined by a conjunction (*and, but, or, nor, for, so,* or *yet*). For example, "Dan has three brothers, and two of them are psychologists."

Semicolon Errors

Two independent clauses may not be simply joined by a comma; they must be connected by a semicolon. This type of error is called a *comma splice* error. For example, "Each year about fifty thousand books are published in Great Britain; that is as many as in the four-times-larger United States."

Examples:

---

1. The doctor gave me <u>pain, medication after the bicycle accident</u>.

   A. NO CHANGE
   B. pain medication after the bicycle accident
   C. pain medication after, the bicycle accident
   D. pain; medication after the bicycle accident

The comma after *pain* makes no sense; the doctor gives *pain medication,* not *pain.* Removing the comma restores meaning to the sentence. The correct answer is **B.**

---

2. <u>Mr. Richards the accountant who had kept us waiting for an hour</u> finally appeared.

   F. NO CHANGE
   G. Mr. Richards the accountant who had kept us waiting, for an hour
   H. Mr. Richards: the accountant who had kept us waiting for an hour,
   J. Mr. Richards, the accountant who had kept us waiting for an hour,

---

The accountant who had kept us waiting for an hour identifies or explains the subject of the sentence (*Mr. Richards*). This group of words is called an *appositive,* and should be set off in commas, as it is in Choice J. It adds information that is not absolutely necessary to the meaning of the sentence. The correct answer is **J.**

---

3. At sunrise, we assembled <u>the climbing, gear that we had hidden</u> the night before.

   A. NO CHANGE
   B. the climbing gear that we had hidden
   C. the climbing; gear that we had hidden
   D. the climbing—gear that we had hidden

The comma following *climbing* makes the sentence unintelligible; you can't assemble a *climbing,* but you can assemble *climbing gear.* So removing the comma altogether restores meaning to the sentence. The correct answer is **B.**

Grammar and Usage Errors

A grammar error requires that the *form* of the word(s) be changed based on the conventions of grammar and usage.

Types of Agreement Errors	Types of Form Errors
Subject and verb disagreement	Incorrect verb form
Pronoun and antecedent disagreement	Incorrect pronoun and case forms
Adjective-noun or adverb-verb disagreement	Incorrect idiom
	Incorrect comparative and superlative modifiers

Subject-Verb Agreement Errors

Verbs must match the nouns they describe (in both number and gender). A subject and verb agreement error is the faulty combination of a *singular* and a *plural* in a sentence. A singular subject must agree with a singular verb, and a plural subject must agree with a plural verb. Nouns ending in *–s* are usually plural, and verbs ending in *–s* are usually singular. For example:

> The *computer runs* efficiently. (singular)
>
> The *computers run* efficiently. (plural)

As long as you know whether the subject is singular or plural, you should have no trouble with this type of problem. Be sure you can identify the subject and the verb of the sentence and do not let the intervening words distract you.

Examples:

---

4. The carton of roses and carnations <u>were</u> beautifully displayed in the window.

   F.   NO CHANGE
   G.   was
   H.   weren't
   J.   OMIT the underlined portion.

The subject (*carton*) is singular, so the verb (*was*) must be singular. Use *was* instead of *were.* The correct answer is **G.**

---

5. The <u>criteria for admission to a fine arts college includes</u> at least three pieces of original artwork in a portfolio.

   A.   NO CHANGE
   B.   criteria for admission to a fine arts college include
   C.   criterion for admission to a fine arts college include
   D.   criteria for admission to a fine arts college is

Watch for nouns with Greek or Latin endings that form plurals with an *–a.* Words like *data* (plural of *datum*), *phenomena* (plural of phenomenon), *media* (plural of *medium*), and *criteria* (plural of *criterion*) are plural forms that can cause subject agreement errors. In this case, *criteria* (plural), must match the verb *include*. Remember that even though the verb *includes* appears to be plural because it ends in an *–s,* it is singular, making Choice A incorrect. Choice C, *criterion* is singular, but *include* is plural. Choice D shows *criteria* (plural), which does not match *is* (singular). The correct answer is **B.**

---

6. His plan to find a summer job and apply for a scholarship <u>were</u> a sign of his determination.

   F.   NO CHANGE
   G.   was
   H.   weren't
   J.   have been

The subject *plan* is singular, so the verb must be the singular *was.* The correct answer is **G.**

Pronoun-Antecedent Errors

The antecedent of a pronoun (the word to which the pronoun refers) should be clear. In spoken conversation and in informal writing, we often use pronouns that have no single word as their antecedent. For example, "This happens all the time." The word *This* is problematic because it refers to a general idea of the preceding sentence, but not to a specific subject. On the ACT, you should immediately regard as an error a pronoun that does not have a specific noun (or word used as a noun) as its antecedent.

Examples:

---

7. <u>I came in 20 minutes late which</u> made the whole class difficult to understand.

    A. NO CHANGE
    B. I came in 20 minutes late, and this
    C. By coming in 20 minutes late, which
    D. My coming in 20 minutes late

The pronoun *which* has no specific antecedent here, making Choice A incorrect. Choice D eliminates the pronoun altogether and corrects the sentence. Choice B is incorrect because the change of *which* to *this* does not correct the pronoun issue, and Choice C is a sentence fragment. The correct answer is **D**.

---

8. A considerable number of California counties and cities have farmland retention policies, often as part of their general plan to develop land more efficiently, <u>which is encouraging to agricultural conservationists</u>.

    F. NO CHANGE
    G. this is one of the most encouraging practices in agricultural conservation
    H. and that is one of agricultural conservation's most encouraging practices
    J. and these policies are encouraging to agricultural conservationists

---

Sentences in which a pronoun has two or more different antecedents should be rewritten because the pronoun is ambiguous. Choice J provides a noun as the subject of the clause that replaces the pronouns *which, this,* and *that*. In choices G and H, the pronouns changing *which* to *this* or *that* do nothing to correct the ambiguity of the pronoun. The correct answer is **J**. Choice J also maintains the original *agricultural conservationists,* rather than replacing it with *agricultural conservation,* which alters the meaning.

Adjective-Noun Errors or Adverb-Verb Errors

Adjective or adverb misuse constitutes another type of error. The difference between an adjective and an adverb relates to how each functions in a sentence. Adjectives and adverbs are similar because they are both *modifiers* (words or groups of words that *describe* other words).

While **adjectives** describe nouns (*a <u>red</u> balloon, a <u>quick</u> trip*), **adverbs** describe actions, or verbs. (*the balloon sailed <u>high</u>, I traveled <u>quickly</u>*). Adverbs also describe adjectives (*the balloon was <u>very red</u>*) and other adverbs (*I traveled <u>extremely</u> <u>quickly</u>*), but their primary use is in answering questions about actions.

Several special rules apply to adjectives and adverbs.

Adjective and Adverb Rules	
Rule 1 Most adverbs end in *–ly*	Most, but not all, adverbs end in *–ly* (*quickly, happily, clearly*) and point to the place, time, or degree. Adverbs tell you: ❑ *how* an action occurred (*I traveled quickly*) ❑ *when* an action occurred (*I traveled immediately*) ❑ *where* an action occurred (*I traveled there*) ❑ *to what* extent or how much an action occurred (*I traveled long before I stopped*) On the ACT, watch for exceptions to this rule (see Rule 2).

(continued)

Adjective and Adverb Rules	
Rule 2 Some adjectives end in *–ly*	Some adjective and adverbs have the same form (*a fast ball, I ran fast*; *a straight line*), The question is not what a word <u>is</u>, but <u>how it is used</u>. Ask yourself, is the word describing a noun (such as a ball or a line) or an action (such as running)? Be aware that some adjectives end in *–ly* (*friendly* cat, *deadly* snake), but keep in mind that it is *how* the word is being used that makes it an adjective or adverb. For example, *the man treated her kindly* is an adverb, *the kindly man helped her* is an adjective. Here is another way to remember that adverbs answer the question "How?" For example, it is a common error to say, "That's real sad," but *real* modifies *sad*. Therefore, the modifier usage is incorrect because *real* is an adjective. To understand this rule, ask yourself "*How* sad is it?" The answer is, "It is *very* sad." Therefore, the phrase should use the adverb *really* to modify the adjective. The correct usage is, "That's *really* sad."
Rule 3 Use *–ly* when verbs (linking verbs) are senses	Some verbs (called linking verbs) are usually followed by an adjective rather than an adverb. Among these are verbs of the senses, such as *taste, smell, feel,* and other commonly used verbs such as forms of *to be* (*am, is, are,* etc.), *become, seem, grow, appear,* etc. Linking verbs don't express an action but rather help to make a statement by describing a state of being. The question to ask when considering whether to use an adjective or an adverb in describing a verb is, "Does the verb express an action, or is it describing a state of being or one of the senses? If the verb is used to express an action, then use *–ly*. If not, do not use *–ly*. Here are some examples: **Action: Use an adverb** **Linking: Use an adjective** *The man* looked angrily *at the girl.* *He* looked angry *when he saw her.* *The man* felt *the fabric* carefully. *He* felt bad *about his error.* *The corn* grew quickly. *He* grew sad *after their meeting.*

Examples:

9. Though the game was in Tulsa, <u>most every fan in the stands was cheering loud</u> for the Sooners.

    A. NO CHANGE
    B. almost every fan in the stands was cheering loudly
    C. almost every fan in the stands was cheering loud
    D. most fans in the stands were cheering loud

Adjectives modify nouns, and adverbs modify verbs. In this example, there are two adjective-adverb problems. *Most* is an adjective, but in this case it is meant to modify the adjective *every*, not the noun *fan*. This means it must take its adverb form *almost*. *Loud* can be used as an adjective, but here it is meant to modify a verb (*was cheering*). Therefore, it must take the form of an adverb—*loudly*. Choice B is the only choice that corrects both of these errors. The correct answer is **B**.

10. <u>The tired mechanic, happily to be finished with a hard day's work,</u> closed the hood over the newly tuned engine.

    F. NO CHANGE
    G. Happily, the tired mechanic being finished with a hard day's work
    H. Tired but happy with a hard day's work being done, the mechanic
    J. The tired mechanic, happy to be finished with a hard day's work,

Happily is used here to describe a person, the mechanic. The correct part of speech for describing a person or thing is an adjective (*happy*), rather than an adverb (*happily*), so Choice F is incorrect. Choice J is correct because it properly uses the adjective form (*happy*) to modify the noun (*mechanic*). Choices G and H are confusing and in passive voice. The correct answer is **J.**

Verb Errors

A verb is a part of speech that expresses a state of being or action. Verb tenses are formed according to person, number, voice, and tense.

- **Person** refers to the subject (or object) of the verb. The three *persons* of a verb are first (*I, we*), second (*you*), and third (*he, she, it, they*).

- **Number** simply refers to whether a verb is *singular* (she goes) or *plural* (they go).

- **Voice** refers to whether the verb is *active* or *passive*. Active (I hit the ball) and passive (The ball was hit by me) are the *voices* of verbs. If the subject of a verb performs the action of the verb, the verb is *active,* while if the subject receives the action, the verb is *passive.*

- **Tense** refers to the *time* of the action or state of being. The tenses (present, past, and future) of the verbs in a sentence must be logical and consistent. Many of the verb tense errors on the ACT occur in sentences with two verbs, and with past and past participle forms of irregular verbs. Always look carefully at the tenses of the verbs in a sentence and ask yourself, "Does the *time scheme* make logical sense?" The time scheme will determine the tense. Look carefully at the verbs and the other words in the sentence to establish the time scheme. Adverbs such as *then, subsequently, before, yesterday,* and *tomorrow,* and prepositional phrases such as *in the last decade* and *in the future,* work with verbs to make the time of the actions clearer. Commonly used verb tenses are:

  Present—Action that is happening now. (*attend*)

  Past—Action that is completed. (*attended*)

  Future—Action that will take place in the future. (*will attend*)

  Present perfect (have + verb)—Action that began in the past, and continues in the present time. (*have attended*)

  Past perfect (had + verb)—Action that began in the past, but is no longer happening. (*had attended*)

  Future perfect (will have + verb)—Action that is presently taking place, and will continuing taking place farther in the future (*will have attended*).

Examples:

---

11. Facebook users love to update their status and converse with friends, <u>but frequent changes in its privacy policies are often made by the company, which frustrates users.</u>

    A. NO CHANGE
    B. but the company has often made frequent changes to its privacy policies, which frustrates users.
    C. and frequent changes in its privacy policies are often made by the company, which frustrates users.
    D. but the company makes frequent privacy policy changes that frustrate users.

The first clause is in the preferred, active voice, in that the subjects (*Facebook users*) are acting upon the verbs (*love, update,* and *converse*). However, the second clause is in the passive voice, in that the subject (*changes*) are being acted upon by the verb (*are often made*). When possible, a passive voice is to be avoided. Choice D is the best answer because it rephrases the second clause in the active voice without introducing any additional errors. Choice B uses the active voice but changes the verb tense to past tense and is redundant. Choice C does not correct the use of the passive voice. The correct answer is **D.** Using *that* rather than *which* is preferable here, and the adjective clause should not be preceded by a comma.

12. Although he had appeared as a guest on several popular cable news shows in recent months, yesterday's interview <u>is the first time the governor has admitted</u> his interest in running for senator.

    F. NO CHANGE

    G. was the first time the governor admitted

    H. will be the first time the governor will admit

    J. had been the first time the governor had admitted

The description of the interview as *yesterday's* places the action in the past. Logically, it follows that the tense of the main verb must then be past tense—therefore, the correct answer is Choice G. Choice F uses the present tense of the verb, and Choice H uses the future tense of the verb. Choice J uses the past perfect tense of the verb, which should be used to indicate that an event preceded another event in the past. The correct answer is **G**.

Pronoun and Case Errors

Pronouns can be either singular or plural but must agree with the noun, verb, or other pronoun to which they refer. The *number* of a pronoun (i.e., whether it is singular or plural) must agree in number with its *antecedent* (the word, phrase, or clause to which it refers). Personal pronouns have distinctive singular and plural forms (he/they, his/their, him/them).

Pronouns stand for a word so that writers can avoid using the noun(s) over and over again. For example:

    Zach left *Zach's* classroom and forgot to take *Zach's* new iPad. (*without pronouns*)

    Zach left *his* classroom and forgot to take *his* new iPad. (*substituting pronouns*)

Nouns and pronouns have a *subjective* (nominative) case, a *possessive* case, and an *objective* case (see the following table). Thus, nouns and pronouns can be used as *subjects* (The *cell phone* is small. *I* am tired.), as *objects* (Danny watered the *lawn*. Danny met *him*.), and as *possessors* (*Blake's* guitar is large. *His* arm is broken.). Because the form of a noun in the subjective case is no different from the form of the same noun in the objective case (The bat hit the ball. The ball hit the bat.), errors are not a problem with nouns. However, several pronouns have different forms as subjects and objects and can sometimes be confusing.

Subjective, Possessive, and Objective Pronouns

	First Person	Second Person	Third Person
Subjective Case			
Singular	I	you	he, she, it, who
Plural	we	you	they, who
Possessive Case			
Singular	mine, my	your, yours	his, hers, its, whose
Plural	our, ours	your, yours	their, theirs, whose
Objective Case			
Singular	me	you	him, her, it, whom
Plural	us	you	them, whom

Examples:

13. The director of the animated film, along with the character designer, the 3-D rendering specialist, and the animators, <u>have made their recommendations</u> about the revision of the storyline to the screenwriter.

    A. NO CHANGE

    B. has made their recommendations

    C. had made their recommendations

    D. has made his recommendations

The subject of the sentence is the singular *director*. The phrase beginning with *along with* is parenthetical and is not the subject of the verb or the antecedent of the possessive pronoun that follows. The correct, singular verb form is *has,* and the correct, singular pronoun form is *his.* Choices A, B, and C all incorrectly use the plural pronoun *their.* The correct answer is **D.**

---

14. The wind-up toy <u>turned himself</u> around and headed straight toward the sleeping cat.

    F. NO CHANGE
    G. turned oneself
    H. turned itself
    J. is turning himself

A wind-up toy is a thing, not a person. Therefore, the correct pronoun to use is *itself.* The correct answer is **H.**

Idiom Errors

Some questions will test your ability to recognize errors of nonstandard expressions. Idioms are the usual way in which phrases or expressions are put together in a language but have not been established as standard usage. There are no general rules, but most idiom errors arise from the use of prepositions (*to, from, of, on, by, than,* and so on). For example, depending upon the sentence, you might say *agree with, agree to,* or *agree upon.* The meaning of the sentence will determine the correct usage. Here is a list of common idiom errors.

Correct	Incorrect
except for	excepting for
try to	try and
plan to	plan on
prior to	prior than
type of	type of a
by accident	on accident
on account of	on account that
fewer things	less things
ashamed of	ashamed about
amused by	amused at
at any rate	in any rate
at fault	of fault
is intent on	is intent to
in reference to	in reference of
regarded as	regarded to be
preoccupied with	preoccupied by
used to	use to
should have	should of
supposed to	suppose to

Examples:

---

15. The law prohibits passengers <u>to bring liquids in excess of 3 ounces in the plane</u>.

    A.   to bring liquids in excess of 3 ounces in the plane
    B.   from bringing liquids in excess of 3 ounces in the plane
    C.   to bring liquids in excess of 3 ounces on the plane
    D.   from bringing liquids in excess of 3 ounces onto the plane

---

The original sentence contains two idiomatic errors; first, the parallel idiom for the verb *prohibits* is *from bringing* rather than *to bring*. Second, the idiomatic preposition in this sentence should be *onto* or *on* rather than *in* or *on*. Choice D is the only choice that corrects both of these errors; the correct answer is **D.**

---

16. She refused to <u>comply to</u> the teacher's demand that she bring a signed note from home.

    F.   NO CHANGE
    G.   comply with
    H.   comply for
    J.   comply of

Comply with is the correct idiomatic usage, not *comply to*. The correct answer is **G.**

Comparative and Superlative Modifier Errors

Many of the comparatives and superlatives are formed by adding *-er* and *-est* to the adjective stem, though some words *(good, better, best; well, better, best)* change altogether, and some simply add *more* or *most (eager, more eager, most eager; quickly, more quickly, most quickly)*. Here are general rules about the three forms of adjectives and adverbs: positive, negative, comparative, and superlative.

- **Positive** is the unchanged version, and you must add *as* before (and after) the comparison. For example, "Emily is as talented as Amy."
- **Negative** is the unchanged version, but you must add *not as* or *not so* before the comparison. For example, "Emily is not as talented as Amy."
- **Comparative** is used when you are comparing *two items*. When it is clear that you are comparing two items, use a comparative and insert *more* before the adjective, or use the suffix *-er* on the end. For example, "Compared to Maryland, Washington D.C. has a <u>larger</u> population."
- **Superlative** is used when you are comparing *three or more items*. When the comparison involves *three or more* items, use a superlative and insert *most* before the adjective, or use the suffix *-est*. For example, "Alyssa has the <u>highest</u> grade in the biology class." The exception to this rule is when the superlative ends in *-y*, then you change the suffix to *-iest (happiest)*.

Example:

---

17. Dr. Bloom's comments after the lecture <u>were more clear than the lecture itself, and the students inferred</u> that he felt more comfortable when talking to a smaller group.

    A.   NO CHANGE
    B.   were more clear than the lecture itself, and the students infer
    C.   were clearer than the lecture itself, and the students inferred
    D.   was more clear than the lecture itself, and the students inferred

---

The comparative form of *clear* is *clearer,* not *more clear.* To form the comparative form of most one-syllable adjectives, such as *clear,* add *-er.* An adjective of two syllables can form the comparative with *-er (happier),* but often the comparative is formed with *more* (*more eager*). *Inferred* is correct here, and therefore, Choice B can be eliminated. Choice C is correct because *were* is in agreement with *comments* (plural). When in doubt about the comparative and superlative forms of an adjective, check a dictionary. The correct answer is **C**.

Sentence Structure Errors

Errors in sentence structure occur when (1) the parts of a sentence are not arranged in a logical order, (2) when there is an abrupt shift in clauses, or (3) when an essential part(s) has been omitted from the sentence. Questions testing for misplaced parts will usually ask you to select the answer that is not only grammatically correct but also clear and exact, free from awkwardness and ambiguity. Watch for sentences that seem odd or have an unnatural word order. Common sentence structure errors can appear as dangling participles or modifiers, fragmented sentences, awkward sentences, run-on (or wordy) sentences, or faulty parallelism (comparing two items that are not comparable).

Dangling Participle or Modifier

Examples:

---

18. A piano is for sale by a woman with walnut legs.

    F.   NO CHANGE

    G.   piano with walnut legs is for sale by a woman.

    H.   piano is for sale with walnut legs by a woman.

    J.   walnut legs piano is for sale.

The sentence seems to say that the woman has walnut legs! This confusion is corrected by placing *walnut legs* after the word that it's meant to describe, *piano*. The correct answer is **G**.

---

19. When only a child in kindergarten, my father taught me how to box.

    A.   NO CHANGE

    B.   Being only a child in kindergarten, my father taught me

    C.   When I was only a child in kindergarten, my father taught me

    D.   My father, when only a child in kindergarten, taught me

---

The sentence seems to say that *my father* was in kindergarten when he taught me how to box. By adding *I* to the opening clause, the person who was a child in kindergarten is clearly identified. Choice C corrects the confusion. The correct answer is **C**.

Sentence Fragments

Examples:

---

20. A beautiful view outside the living room window and a swimming pool in the backyard.

    F.   NO CHANGE

    G.   Both a beautiful view outside the living room window and a swimming pool in the backyard.

    H.   Looking out the window at a beautiful view and a swimming pool in the backyard.

    J.   A beautiful view outside the living room window and a swimming pool in the backyard were the house's best features.

The words are not a sentence because a verb, or predicate, is missing. Only Choice J corrects the error. The correct answer is **J**.

21. By the early eleventh century, Muslim scientists <u>knowing the rich medical literature of ancient Greece, as well as</u> arithmetic and algebra.

    A. NO CHANGE
    B. knew the rich medical literature of ancient Greece, as well as
    C. know the rich medical literature of ancient Greece, as well as
    D. having learned the rich medical literature of ancient Greece, as well as

As it stands, this is a sentence fragment with a participle (*knowing*) but no main verb. Choice B supplies the missing verb. Choice C eliminates the sentence fragment, but uses the present tense where the past tense is required. Choice D is just a participle in a different tense. The correct answer is **B**.

Faulty Parallelism

Example:

22. She loved to swim, dance, and <u>singing</u>.

    F. NO CHANGE
    G. sang
    H. a song
    J. sing

Singing isn't parallel to (doesn't have the same form as) the other verbs with which it is listed. The correct parallel structure is *swim, dance,* and *sing.* The correct answer is **J**.

Awkward or Run-On (Wordy) Sentences

Example:

23. <u>After the shipment of bananas had been unloaded, a tarantula's nest was discovered by the foreman</u> in the hold of the ship.

    A. NO CHANGE
    B. After unloading the shipment of bananas, a tarantula's nest was discovered by the foreman
    C. Having unloaded the shipment of bananas, a tarantula's nest was discovered by the foreman
    D. After the shipment of bananas had been unloaded, the foreman discovered a tarantula's nest

Both choices A and D are grammatically correct, but Choice D is the preferable option because it uses the active, rather than passive voice. Choices B and C seem to imply that the *tarantula's nest* unloaded the bananas. Keep in mind that passively phrased sentences are always wordier than actively phrased ones; you cannot rewrite an active sentence using a passive verb without using at least two additional words. When choosing between two possible correct answers, you should pick the sentence in the active voice. For example, consider:

    I hit the ball. (four words, *active*)

    The ball was hit by me. (six words, *passive*)

Also note the ambiguity in Choice A; it is unclear whether the foreman, the nest, or both are in the hold of the ship. The correct answer is **D**.

Question Type Two: Rhetorical Skills

Rhetorical errors involve evaluating passages to make decisions about effective writing composition skills. These types of questions refer to the appropriateness of a word, sentence, paragraph, or the whole passage. Questions appear with special references as illustrated here.

Problems may appear with a statement above the question.

> Question 15 asks about the
> preceding passage as a whole.

Or problems may reference a question number that appears in a box at the end of a paragraph or passage.

15

Writing Strategy

In writing strategy questions you will be required to read a passage or paragraph and decide whether the written material demonstrates a logical organization of ideas, unity of thought, development of relevant supporting details, and a focus on the intended audience.

Questions may ask you to make decisions about (1) what supporting evidence is needed to strengthen the passage's main purpose, (2) where to logically insert a transitional sentence, (3) what would be an appropriate revision (deletion or addition) to fulfill the writer's goal, or (4) they may ask you to choose the best option for an appropriate conclusion that would reinforce the essay's central focus.

Example:

[1] A dishonest newspaper may warp the day's news. [2] It may hide a story favorable to the party it opposes, or it may slant headlines for a story favorable to the party it supports. [3] Although the paper doesn't change facts, it can change the total effect of a story by placing it on an inconspicuous back page or by giving it a deliberately misleading headline. [4] Headlines are written by the paper's copyreaders, people highly skilled at their jobs. [5] In recent years, these headline writers have been accorded greater respect, easier hours, and higher pay. [6] A headline can be misleading simply by the words used. [7] "Councilwoman Bates replies to critics" gives quite a different impression from "Councilwoman Bates cracks down on critics." 24

> Question 24 asks about the
> preceding passage as a whole.

24. The writer is considering deleting two sentences from the preceding passage. Upon reviewing the passage, which of the following sentences should be omitted?

    F.   None of the sentences should be omitted.
    G.   Sentences 2 and 3
    H.   Sentences 4 and 5
    J.   Sentences 6 and 7

Sentences 4 and 5 do not develop the main topic of the paragraph, which is the way in which newspapers can manipulate stories to fit their biases. These two sentences affect the unity of the paragraph; they deal with the subject of headline writers, their skills, and their position at the newspaper. The correct answer is Choice **H.**

Organization Errors

These errors occur when sentences or paragraphs aren't arranged in a logical order.

Example:

The second act of the musical was filled with action, excitement, and great music, which members of the audience responded to immediately. <u>For example, they even stood in the aisles and danced along with the performers.</u> 25

---

25. At this point, the writer is considering adding a new paragraph. For the sake of logic and coherence, should the new paragraph be placed after the underlined portion?

    A. NO CHANGE

    B. (Begin a new paragraph) In fact,

    C. (Begin a new paragraph) For one thing,

    D. (Do NOT begin new paragraph)

No new paragraph is needed. The underlined sentence is presenting an example of the initial sentence. The correct answer is **D**.

Style Errors

Style errors test how well you can communicate and shape an essay through clear and concise writing, word choice, and tone. Watch for writing errors in diction, redundancy, wordiness, or ambiguity.

Example:

---

26. The game is played <u>with tiny, little, round balls, which in my opinion, I think are made of steel.</u>

    F. NO CHANGE

    G. with tiny balls, which I think are made of steel.

    H. with very small, tiny balls, and I think they have been manufactured out of steel.

    J. with tiny balls made of steel.

This question involves an error in redundancy. Redundancy occurs when two words or phrases say the same thing, for example, *equally the same, happy joy, exact same*. Although Choice J is the most concise version, the correct answer is Choice G. The answer retains the meaning of the original by including *I think*. When reducing wordiness, it is important not to eliminate words that affect the meaning. The sentence should include the idea that this is what the writer thinks. The correct answer is **G**.

Practice English Test Questions

Now that you have reviewed English Test topics and concepts, you can practice on your own. The answers and explanations that follow the questions will include strategies to help you understand how to solve the problems.

Directions: The following is a shorter passage than appears on the exam, but it gives examples of the kinds of questions on the ACT English Test. Most of the questions offer alternative versions or "NO CHANGE" to underlined portions of the text. Remember, you must assume that only the underlined section can be changed and that the rest of the sentence that isn't underlined is correct.

Passage I

A solar <u>plant the biggest of its kind</u> that is <u>in the</u>
                1   2
<u>process of being constructed</u> in the Mojave Desert of
            2
California will use 170,000 garage-door sized mirrors

spread over the ground to track the sun across the sky.

<u>It</u> will reflect the sun and send radiation to the <u>top of</u>
3   4

<u>three towers which are each 45-feet tall.</u> Water <u>inside</u>
                4   5
<u>the towers</u> then heats to 1,000 degrees, creating steam
  5
that is piped to a turbine that <u>generated</u> electricity.
                                     6

    Several people, including bird experts, have

expressed <u>concerns of</u> the new power plant. <u>Flying</u>
          7   8
<u>over the area, they say there is a good chance birds will</u>
                    8

die from the extreme heat reflected by the mirrors. The
8

power plant could also affect aviation. For example, a

possible hazard are the plumes of superheated air that
9

are risen skyward and may cause extreme air turbulence
10

for small planes. In addition, it is possible, but hardly
11

not certain, that interference with navigation or
11

communication of military flights from a nearby base

could occur.

Of all the concerns about the power plant being

built, mirror glare is one that, according to the experts,

can be minimized if pilots and motorists avoid staring

at the mirrors. 12

1. A. NO CHANGE
   B. plant which is the biggest of its kind
   C. plant, the biggest of its kind,
   D. plant, that is the biggest of its kind,

2. F. NO CHANGE
   G. at the stage of being constructed
   H. being built
   J. in the process of being built

3. A. NO CHANGE
   B. They
   C. It's
   D. Them

4. F. NO CHANGE
   G. tops of three 45-foot towers.
   H. top of the towers, each of them 45-feet tall.
   J. tops of the towers. Each tower is 45-feet tall.

5. A. NO CHANGE
   B. which is inside of the towers
   C. , inside the towers,
   D. which has been put inside the towers

6. F. NO CHANGE
   G. will have generated
   H. had generated
   J. generates

7. A. NO CHANGE
   B. concerns on
   C. concerns to
   D. concerns about

8. F. NO CHANGE
   G. Flying over the area, the experts say birds have a good chance that they might die, say the experts.
   H. According to experts, they say birds flying over the area have a good chance of dying
   J. Experts say that birds flying over the area have a good chance of dying

9. A. NO CHANGE
   B. hazard is the plumes
   C. hazard were the plumes
   D. hazard have been the plumes

10. F. NO CHANGE
    G. will have risen
    H. had rose
    J. rise

11. A. NO CHANGE
    B. but not certain
    C. but not hardly to be certain
    D. but hardly it will not be certain

12. The last paragraph of the passage should
    F. become the last sentence of the first paragraph.
    G. become the first sentence of the second paragraph.
    H. ·become the last sentence of the second paragraph.
    J. be left in its current position.

Answers and Explanations

1. **C.** The phrase adds information about the solar plant. The information is not necessary to the meaning of the sentence and is, therefore, set off in commas.

2. **H.** The original version takes many words to say what can be said in two words: *being built*. None of the meaning is lost. Whenever possible, use the most concise expression.

3. **B.** The pronoun refers to *mirrors* in the previous sentence and should, therefore, be plural rather than singular. Because the verb is *reflect*, the antecedent (word referred to) is *mirrors*, not sky.

4. **G.** The original version is wordy and uses the singular *top* rather than the plural (because there are three towers). Choice G is the most concise version of the phrase.

5. **A.** The underlined portion of the sentence is correct as it is. Commas should not enclose the phrase because it is necessary to identify the water. When a phrase or clause is necessary to the meaning rather than adding information, it is called *restrictive*.

6. **J.** The verb should be in the present tense to maintain consistency with the other verbs *heats* and *is piped*.

7. **D.** The idiom here is *concerned about*. One can also be *concerned for* or *concerned with,* but in this sentence, Choice J is correct. The other choices given are not idiomatic. Of the other choices, *concerns on* (B) could be used in a sentence such as "He expressed his concerns on the radio," and *concerns to* could be used in a sentence such as "He expressed his concerns to the journalist" (C). *Concerns of* could be used in a sentence such as "The concerns of the teachers were being addressed" (A).

8. **J.** The problem in this sentence is a dangling participle; it is the birds that are flying, which is not clearly indicated by the structure of the sentence. Although there are several ways to correct the problem, Choice J is the best answer here. Choice G does not correct the misplaced participle (it is the birds and not the experts that are flying), and H incorrectly follows *According to the experts* with *they say*.

9. **B.** The subject here is *hazard,* and it is singular. Therefore, the verb should be singular (*is*). Do not be misled by *plumes*.

10. **J.** The verb should be in the present tense, not a future tense. (Also, Choice H incorrectly uses the simple past *rose* as the past participle of *rise*. The correct participial form is *risen: rise, rose, have risen*.)

11. **B.** The error here is a double negative: *hardly not. Hardly* should be eliminated.

12. **H.** The last paragraph is actually a sentence, not a paragraph. Of the choices given here, the best place for the sentence would be at the end of the second paragraph, which is about the possible problems accompanying the new power plant.

Chapter 3

The ACT Mathematics Test

The Mathematics portion of the ACT test is designed to assess your math skills and level of knowledge in pre-algebra (arithmetic), elementary algebra, intermediate algebra, coordinate geometry, plane geometry, and trigonometry. This chapter reviews these fundamental skills by presenting them within specific *sample questions* that test your ability to *reason* critically and mathematically.

You are encouraged to pace yourself and become familiar with the models by completing the practice exercises in this chapter. To enhance learning, we have organized practice exercises by content areas starting with pre-algebra and ending with trigonometry. Each stage of learning builds upon your previous understanding of a math concept. As you repeat the practice questions, you will be steadily increasing your comfort level with the exam format and increasing your ability to solve more challenging questions. Take advantage of our comprehensive math review in chapters 7 to 12. These comprehensive math resource chapters help you review concepts and skills to aid in your learning ACT Mathematics problems.

Format

The ACT Mathematics Test consists of 60 questions. You will have 60 minutes to complete the test. The following table lists the content areas, along with recommended chapter reviews for the ACT Mathematics Test. Try to focus your attention on one chapter review at a time for an optimal learning experience.

ACT Mathematics Content Areas

Content Area	Test Percentage	Number of Questions	Chapter	Additional Chapters to Review
Pre-Algebra	23%	14	Chapter 8	Chapters 7 and 12
Elementary Algebra	17%	10	Chapter 9	Chapters 7, 8, and 12
Intermediate Algebra	15%	9	Chapter 9	Chapters 7 and 12
Coordinate Geometry	15%	9	Chapter 9	Chapter 7
Plane Geometry	23%	14	Chapter 10	Chapter 7
Trigonometry	7%	4	Chapter 11	Chapter 7

ACT Math Content Areas

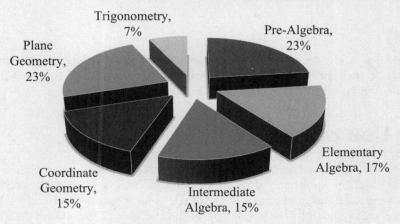

Skills and Concepts Tested

The three skill levels covered include using basic math skills, applying math skills to different situations, and analyzing when and why certain math operations will and will not yield a solution. The basic skills necessary to do well include high school math problems within the six content areas that follow.

Pre-Algebra

Questions under this content area are based on basic mathematical concepts involving whole numbers, decimals, fractions, integers, using positive exponents, square roots, approximations, percentages, ratios and proportions, multiples and factors of integers, linear equations in one variable, absolute values of and the ordering of numbers, elementary counting techniques to determine the number of ways something can happen based on given conditions, simple probability, and simple descriptive statistics and data representation using tables, charts, and graphs.

Elementary Algebra

Questions under this content area cover such topics as properties of exponents and square roots, using variables to express relationships, evaluating and using operations on polynomials, factoring polynomials, solving simple quadratic equations by factoring, and solving linear inequalities in one variable.

Intermediate Algebra

Questions under this content area are based on more advanced algebraic concepts such as the quadratic formula, inequalities and absolute value equations, systems of equations, radical expressions, sequences and series, quadratic inequalities, functions, matrices, logarithms, and complex numbers.

Coordinate Geometry

Questions under this content area involve topics such as graphing and the relationships among equations, graphing lines, points, circles, slopes of lines, perpendicular and parallel line relationships, and midpoint and distance formulas as well as transformations.

Plane Geometry

Questions under this content area are based on the relationships and properties of plane figures, lines, angles, triangles, rectangles, parallelograms, trapezoids, circles, parallel lines, perpendicular lines, rotations, translations and reflections, basic three-dimensional figures, and measurements such as perimeter, area, and volume. Simple proofs are also included under this content area.

Trigonometry

Questions in this content area involve understanding trigonometric relationships in right triangles, the graphs of trigonometric functions, values and properties of trigonometric functions, using trigonometric identities, solving trigonometric equations, and modeling using trigonometric functions.

Calculator Use on the ACT

The ACT allows you to use *approved calculators* on the exam (see the second bullet point in the following list), but all of the Mathematics problems can be solved without using a calculator. Most of the problems should be solved without a calculator, using logic and mathematical insight. Calculator-based solutions usually involve longer methods and, therefore, often constitute the wrong approach to solving problems (see the fourth bullet point in the following list).

negative. Perform the computation within the absolute value bars and then take the absolute value; this yields 2 + 7 = 9. The correct answer is **B**.

STRATEGY: Work backward from the answer choices. If you don't immediately recognize a method or formula, or if using the method or formula would take a great deal of time, try working backward—from the answer choices. Since some answer choices are clearly wrong, using a process of elimination sometimes results in just one answer choice.

---

2. Find the counting number that is less than 15 and—when divided by 3—has a remainder of 1, and—when divided by 4—has a remainder of 2.

  F. 5

  G. 8

  H. 10

  J. 12

  K. 13

By working from the answer choices, you eliminate wasting time on other numbers from 1 to 14. Choices G and J can be immediately eliminated because they are divisible by 4, leaving no remainder. Choices F and K can also be eliminated because they leave a remainder of 1 when divided by 4. The value of 10 leaves a remainder of 1 when divided by 3 and a remainder of 2 when divided by 4. Therefore, the correct answer is **H**.

STRATEGY: "Pulling" information out of a word problem's structure can often give you additional insight into the problem.

---

3. If a mixture is $\frac{3}{7}$ alcohol by volume and $\frac{4}{7}$ water by volume, what is the ratio of the volume of alcohol to the volume of water in this mixture?

  A. $\frac{3}{7}$

  B. $\frac{4}{7}$

  C. $\frac{3}{4}$

  D. $\frac{4}{3}$

  E. $\frac{7}{4}$

The first bit of information you pull out should be what you're looking for: "ratio of the volume of alcohol to the volume of water." Rewrite it as $A{:}W$ and then in its working form: $\frac{A}{W}$. Next, you should pull out the volumes of each; $A = \frac{3}{7}$ and $W = \frac{4}{7}$. Now the answer can be easily figured by inspection or substitution.

$$\frac{A}{W} = \frac{\left(\frac{3}{7}\right)}{\left(\frac{4}{7}\right)} = \frac{3}{7} \times \frac{7}{4} = \frac{3}{4}$$

When you pull out information, actually write out the numbers and/or letters to the side of the problem, putting them into some helpful form and eliminating some of the wording. The correct answer is **C**.

STRATEGY: Use 10 or 100. Some problems may deal with percent or percent change. If you don't see a simple method for working the problem, try using values of 10 or 100 and see what you get.

4. If 40% of the students in a class have blue eyes and 20% of those with blue eyes have brown hair, then what percent of the original total number have brown hair and blue eyes?

    F.   4%

    G.   8%

    H.   16%

    J.   20%

    K.   32%

First, underline or circle "percent of the original number . . . brown hair . . . blue eyes." In this problem, if you don't spot a simple method, try starting with 100 students in the class. Since 40% of them have blue eyes, then 40 students have blue eyes. Now, the problem says that 20% of those students with blue eyes have brown hair. So take 20% of 40, which gives $0.20 \times 40 = 8$.

Since the question asks what percent of the original total number have blue eyes and brown hair, and since you started with 100 students, the answer is 8 out of 100, or 8%. The correct answer is **G**.

STRATEGY: Approximate. If it appears that extensive calculations are going to be necessary to solve a problem, check to see how far apart the answer choices are and then approximate. The reason for checking the answer choices first is to give you a guide to see how freely you can approximate. If the answer choices are spread out in value, then some approximation may be used. If the answer choices are close together in value, more accuracy is needed.

5. Sam's promotion earns him a new salary that is an increase of 11% over his present salary. If his present salary is $39,400 per year, what is his new salary?

    A. $39,411

    B. $39,790

    C. $43,734

    D. $49,309

    E. $53,912

First, underline or circle "new salary." Notice that except for the first two choices, the answers are spread out. Approximate 11% as 10% and $39,400 as $40,000. Now, a quick second look tells you that choices A and B aren't sensible because if you add 10% of $40,000, you get $44,000—eliminate choices A and B. Choice C is the only answer that's close to $44,000. Since you're allowed to use a calculator on this test, this problem would be easy to check (or work) with the calculator if the answer choices were close together. But in this case, it is quicker to approximate and eliminate the possibility of calculator error. The correct answer is **C**.

STRATEGY: Draw a diagram. Sketching diagrams or simple pictures can also be very helpful in problem solving because the diagram may tip off either a simple solution or a method for solving the problem.

6. What is the maximum number of pieces of birthday cake 4 inches by 4 inches in size that can be cut from a cake 20 inches by 20 inches?

    F.   5

    G.   10

    H.   16

    J.   20

    K.   25

First, underline or circle "maximum number of pieces." Sketching the cake and marking in as follows makes this a fairly simple problem.

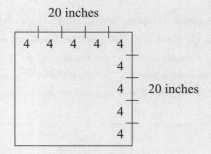

Notice that five pieces of cake will fit along each side. Therefore,

$$5 \times 5 = 25$$

Finding the total area of the cake and dividing it by the area of one of the 4-inch by 4-inch pieces would also give you the correct answer. But beware of this method because it may not work if the pieces don't fit evenly into the original area. The correct answer is **K**.

> **STRATEGY: Use your calculator. Some questions will need to be completely worked out. If you don't see a fast method but do know that you could compute the answer, use your calculator.**

7. What is the final cost of a watch that sells for $49.00 if the sales tax is 7%?

    A. $49.07
    B. $49.70
    C. $52.00
    D. $52.43
    E. $56.00

First, underline or circle "final cost." Since the sales tax is 7% of $49.00, 7% of $49.00 = (.07) ($49.00) = $3.43. The total cost of the watch is, therefore, $49.00 + $3.43 = $52.43.

Your calculator can be helpful with such calculations. The correct answer is **D**.

Elementary Algebra Sample Questions

> **STRATEGY: Answer the right question. Take advantage of being allowed to mark on the test booklet by always underlining or circling what you're looking for. Using this technique will help you ensure that you're answering the right question.**

8. If $x + 6 = 9$, then $3x + 1 =$

    F. 3
    G. 9
    H. 10
    J. 34
    K. 46

You should first circle or underline $3x + 1$ because this is what you're solving for. Solving for x leaves $x = 3$ and then substituting into $3x + 1$ gives $3(3) + 1$ or 10. The most common mistake is to solve for x, which is 3, and mistakenly choose F as your answer. But remember, you're solving for $3x + 1$, not just x. Also note that most of the other choices would all be possible answers if you made common or simple mistakes. *Make sure you're answering the right question.* The correct answer is **H**.

STRATEGY: Work backward from the answer choices. If you don't immediately recognize a method or formula, or if using the method or formula would take a great deal of time, try working backward—from the answer choices. Since the answer choices are usually given in ascending or descending order, always start by plugging in the middle answer choice first if values are given. Then you'll know whether to go up or down with your next try. (Sometimes you might want to plug in one of the simple answer choices first.)

---

9. Which of the following is a value of r for which $r^2 - r - 20 = 0$?

  A. 4
  B. 5
  C. 6
  D. 7
  E. 8

You should first underline or circle "value of r." If you've forgotten how to solve this equation, work backward by plugging in answers. Start with Choice C; plugging in 6.

$$6^2 - 6 - 20 \overset{?}{=} 0$$
$$36 - 6 - 20 \overset{?}{=} 0$$
$$10 \neq 0$$

Since this answer is too large, try Choice B, a smaller number. Plugging in 5 gives

$$5^2 - 5 - 20 \overset{?}{=} 0$$
$$25 - 5 - 20 \overset{?}{=} 0$$
$$0 = 0$$

This is a true statement. Working from the answers is a valuable technique.

You could also work this problem by factoring into $(r - 5)(r + 4) = 0$ and then setting $(r - 5) = 0$ and $(r + 4) = 0$ leaving $r = 5$ or $r = -4$.

The correct answer is **B**.

STRATEGY: Simplify. Sometimes, combining terms, performing simple operations, or simplifying the problem in some other way will give you insight and make the problem easier to solve.

---

10. If $x = -3$ and $y = 4$, then $xy^2 + 3x^2y + 4xy^2 + 2x^2y =$

  F. -420
  G. -60
  H. 60
  J. 420
  K. 4,500

Simplifying this problem means first adding the like terms $(xy^2 + 4xy^2)$ and $(3x^2y + 2x^2y)$. After simplifying this problem to $5xy^2 + 5x^2y$, plug in the value -3 for x and 4 for y, which gives you

$$(5)(-3)(4)^2 + (5)(-3)^2(4) = (5)(-3)(16) + (5)(9)(4)$$
$$= (-15)(16) + (45)(4)$$
$$= -240 + 180$$
$$= -60$$

The correct answer is **G**.

STRATEGY: Substitute numbers for variables. Substituting numbers for variables can often help in understanding a problem. Remember to substitute simple numbers, since you have to do the work.

---

11. If $x > 1$, which of the following decreases as x decreases?

    I. $x + x^2$

    II. $2x^2 - x$

    III. $\dfrac{1}{x+1}$

    A. I only

    B. II only

    C. III only

    D. I and II only

    E. II and III only

First underline or circle "decreases as x decreases." This problem is most easily solved by substituting simple numbers into each numbered alternative. For Roman numeral I, $x + x^2$, you should recognize that this expression *will* decrease as x decreases.

Trying $x = 3$ gives $3 + (3)^2 = 12$.

Trying $x = 2$ gives $2 + (2)^2 = 6$.

Notice that choices B, C, and E can be eliminated because they don't contain I. You should also realize that now you need only to try the values in II. (Since III isn't paired with I as a possible choice, III can't be one of the answers.)

    Trying $x = 3$ in the expression $2x^2 - x$ gives $2(3)^2 - 3 = 2(9) - 3 = 15$.

    Trying $x = 2$ gives $2(2)^2 - 2 = 2(4) - 2 = 6$.

This expression also decreases as x decreases, so the correct answer is **D**. Once again, notice that III shouldn't be attempted because it isn't one of the possible choices.

An alternative approach to solving this problem is to notice that II represents a parabola that opens upward with line of symmetry of $x = 0$. It should be clear that if $x > 1$, the values of II decrease as x decreases.

STRATEGY: Glance at the answer choices on procedure problems. Some problems may not ask you to solve for a numerical answer or even an answer that includes variables. Rather, you may be asked to set up the equation or expression without doing any solving. A quick glance at the answer choices will help you know what is expected.

---

12. Uli was 12 years old x years ago. In 8 years, how old will she be?

    F. $20 - x$

    G. $(12 + x) + 8$

    H. $(12 - x) + 8$

    J. $(8 + x) - 12$

    K. $(12 + 8) - x$

First, underline or circle "In 8 years, how old." Next, glance at the answer choices. Notice that none of them gives an actual numerical answer but, rather, each sets up a way to find the answer. Now set up the problem.

"12 years old x years ago" means Uli's current age can be written as $12 + x$.

"In 8 years" means you need to add 8 more, so the answer is $(12 + x) + 8$.

The correct answer is **G**.

Intermediate Algebra Sample Questions

STRATEGY: Become familiar with simple matrix manipulation rules. Working with matrices is a skill that is tested on the ACT.

13. If $A = \begin{bmatrix} 4 & -1 \\ 3 & 1 \end{bmatrix}$ and $B = \begin{bmatrix} 5 & -1 \\ -4 & 2 \end{bmatrix}$, then $A - B = ?$

A. $\begin{bmatrix} 9 & -2 \\ -3 & 3 \end{bmatrix}$

B. $\begin{bmatrix} -1 & -2 \\ 7 & 3 \end{bmatrix}$

C. $\begin{bmatrix} 9 & 0 \\ -1 & -1 \end{bmatrix}$

D. $\begin{bmatrix} -1 & 0 \\ 7 & -1 \end{bmatrix}$

E. $\begin{bmatrix} 20 & 1 \\ -12 & 2 \end{bmatrix}$

You should first underline or circle $A - B$. To find the difference of matrices A and B, subtract the corresponding entries as follows.

$$4 - 5 = -1$$
$$-1 - (-1) = 0$$
$$3 - (-4) = 7$$
$$1 - 2 = -1$$

The correct answer is **D**.

STRATEGY: Try a reasonable approach. Sometimes you'll immediately recognize the proper formula or method to solve a problem. If that's not the case, try a reasonable approach and then work from the answer choices.

14. Barney can mow the lawn in 5 hours, and Fred can mow the lawn in 4 hours. How many hours will it take them to mow the lawn together?

F. 1

G. $2\frac{2}{9}$

H. 4

J. $4\frac{1}{2}$

K. 5

First underline or circle "hours . . . mow the lawn together." Suppose that you're unfamiliar with the type of equation for this problem. Try the "reasonable" method. Since Fred can mow the lawn in 4 hours by himself, he'll take less than

4 hours if Barney helps him. Therefore, choices H, J, and K are not reasonable. Taking this method a little further, suppose that Barney could also mow the lawn in 4 hours. Then together it would take Barney and Fred 2 hours. But since Barney is a little slower than this, the total time should be a little more than 2 hours. The correct answer is $2\frac{2}{9}$ hours.

Using the information provided in the problem, in 1 hour Barney could do $\frac{1}{5}$ of the job, and in 1 hour Fred could do $\frac{1}{4}$ of the job; $\frac{1}{x}$ is that part of the job they could do together in 1 hour. Now, solving, you calculate as follows.

$$\frac{1}{5} + \frac{1}{4} = \frac{1}{x}$$
$$20x\left(\frac{1}{5}\right) + 20x\left(\frac{1}{4}\right) = 20x\left(\frac{1}{x}\right)$$
$$\frac{20x}{5} + \frac{20x}{4} = \frac{20x}{x}$$
$$4x + 5x = 20$$
$$9x = 20$$
$$x = \frac{20}{9} = 2\frac{2}{9}$$

Another algebraic approach would be to let each fraction on the left side of the equation represent the part of the total job actually done by each worker. The sum of these fractions would equal one complete job. For each fraction on the left, the denominator represents the time it would take the worker to complete the job alone and the numerator represents the time actually worked by that worker.

$$\frac{x}{5} + \frac{x}{4} = 1$$
$$20\left(\frac{x}{5}\right) + 20\left(\frac{x}{4}\right) = 20(1)$$
$$\frac{20x}{5} + \frac{20x}{4} = 20$$
$$4x + 5x = 20$$
$$9x = 20$$
$$x = \frac{20}{9} = 2\frac{2}{9}$$

The advantage to using this second method is that it is easy to vary the actual time worked by each worker. For example, if Barney had worked 1 hour longer than Fred, you would use $x + 1$ in place of the x for Barney. The correct answer is **G**. For a more complete explanation of work problems as well as other types of word problems, refer to Chapter 12, "Word Problems."

STRATEGY: Substitute simple values. If you are working with word problems and you do not recall the correct formula or procedure to use, substituting simple values often leads to a correct answer choice.

15. Let d be the distance between towns A and B. Gigi averages x miles per hour for her trip from town A to town B, and y miles per hour for her trip from town B to town A. What was her average speed for the entire trip?

A. $\dfrac{x+y}{2}$

B. $\dfrac{2(x+y)}{xy}$

C. $\dfrac{dxy}{2(x+y)}$

D. $\dfrac{2xy}{x+y}$

E. $\dfrac{dxy}{x^2+y^2}$

This problem is a challenge. The formula that relates distance, rate, and time is $d = rt$. From this relationship, you can solve for the other two variables and obtain $r = \dfrac{d}{t}$ and $t = \dfrac{d}{r}$. Since Gigi's average speed is the total distance traveled divided by the total time for the round trip, the average speed can be calculated as follows. Notice that the distance between the towns becomes unimportant. The average speed does not depend on the distance between the towns, only that it is the same distance in each direction.

$$r = \frac{\text{total distance}}{\text{total time}} = \frac{2d}{\dfrac{d}{x} + \dfrac{d}{y}} = \frac{2d}{d\left(\dfrac{1}{x} + \dfrac{1}{y}\right)} = \frac{2}{\left(\dfrac{1}{x} + \dfrac{1}{y}\right)} = \frac{2}{\dfrac{y}{xy} + \dfrac{x}{xy}} = \frac{2}{\dfrac{x+y}{xy}} = \frac{2xy}{x+y}$$

Therefore, the correct answer is **D.**

If this method is beyond your skill level, or you are running out of time to make a choice, sometimes choosing simple numeric replacements for the variables can lead to the correct answer. For example, since the given formula will work for any rates x and y, choose simple replacements. If you choose equal rates, the average would also be that rate. If you choose unequal rates, the average must be between those rates. So try replacements of $d = 1$, $x = 1$, and $y = 1$. You know that the average must be 1.

Substitute these values into the answers and determine which answer choice is equal to 1.

A. $\dfrac{x+y}{2} = \dfrac{1+1}{2} = 1$

B. $\dfrac{2(x+y)}{xy} = \dfrac{2(1+1)}{1 \times 1} = 4$

C. $\dfrac{dxy}{2(x+y)} = \dfrac{1 \times 1 \times 1}{2(1+1)} = \dfrac{1}{4}$

D. $\dfrac{2xy}{x+y} = \dfrac{2 \times 1 \times 1}{1+1} = 1$

E. $\dfrac{dxy}{x^2 + y^2} = \dfrac{1 \times 1 \times 1}{1^2 + 1^2} = \dfrac{1}{2}$

From these substitutions it is clear that you can eliminate choices B, C, and E. If you average two rates that are different, it should be clear that Gigi is not traveling the same length of time at each rate, since the distance traveled at each rate is the same. Therefore, the simple average of Choice A does not seem correct. The correct answer is **D.**

> **STRATEGY: Solving quadratic equations by factoring is the preferred method, but using the quadratic formula is necessary for some problems.**

---

16. The graph of the equation $y = x^2 + 6x + 4$ crosses the x-axis two times. What is the distance between these two points of intersection?

F. $2\sqrt{13}$
G. $2\sqrt{5}$
H. $4\sqrt{3}$
J. $3 + 4\sqrt{5}$
K. $\dfrac{6 + \sqrt{5}}{2}$

First solve the equation for the variable x. This requires using the quadratic formula with $a = 1$, $b = 6$, and $c = 4$, as follows:

$$x = \frac{-b \pm \sqrt{b^2 - 4ac}}{2a}$$

$$= \frac{-6 \pm \sqrt{36 - 16}}{2}$$

$$= \frac{-6 \pm \sqrt{20}}{2}$$

$$= \frac{-6 \pm 2\sqrt{5}}{2}$$

$$= -3 \pm \sqrt{5}$$

Therefore, the distance between these two points is

$\left(3 + \sqrt{5}\right) - \left(3 - \sqrt{5}\right) = 3 + \sqrt{5} - 3 + \sqrt{5} = 2\sqrt{5}$. The correct answer is **G**.

Coordinate Geometry Sample Questions

STRATEGY: Draw a diagram. Sketching diagrams or simple pictures can be very helpful in problem solving because the diagram may tip off either a simple solution or a method for solving the problem.

---

17. If points $P\,(1, 1)$ and $Q\,(1, 0)$ lie on the same coordinate graph, which of the following must be true?

   I. P and Q are equidistant from the origin.
   II. P is farther from the origin than P is from Q.
   III. Q is farther from the origin than Q is from P.

   A. I only
   B. II only
   C. III only
   D. I and II only
   E. I and III only

First, draw the coordinate graph, and then plot the points as follows.

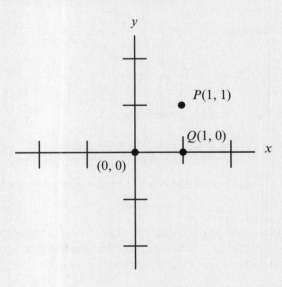

The three indicated points are the vertices of an isosceles right triangle. The distance from the origin to point Q is equal to 1, the distance between points P and Q is 1, and the distance from the origin to point P, (the length of the hypotenuse of the right triangle) is $\sqrt{2}$. Only II is true. Point P is farther from the origin than point P is from point Q. The correct answer is **B**.

> **STRATEGY: Sketches can sometimes lead to the best answer choice without spending unnecessary time on calculations.**

---

18. Triangle ABC has vertices of A (4, 3), B (–2, –3), and C (–2, 1). Line m is the perpendicular bisector of side $\overline{AB}$, and line n is the perpendicular bisector of side $\overline{AC}$. Which of the following represents the coordinates of the intersection of line m and line n?

   F. (2, –1)
   G. (1, –2)
   H. (–2, 1)
   J. (–1, 2)
   K. (–2, –1)

To solve this problem algebraically, start by finding the slopes and midpoints of $\overline{AB}$ and $\overline{AC}$. Use this information to determine the equations of the perpendicular bisectors. Solve these two equations to find the point of intersection, as follows:

$$\text{Midpoint of } \overline{AB} \text{ is} \quad \left(\frac{4+(-2)}{2}, \frac{3+(-3)}{2}\right) = (1,0)$$

$$\text{Slope of } \overline{AB} \text{ is} \quad \frac{3-(-3)}{4-(-2)} = \frac{6}{6} = 1$$

To find the equation of line m, use the negative reciprocal slope.

$$y - y_1 = m(x - x_1)$$
$$\text{Equation of line } m \text{ is} \quad y - 0 = -1(x - 1)$$
$$y = -x + 1$$

$$\text{Midpoint of } \overline{AC} \text{ is} \quad \left(\frac{4+(-2)}{2}, \frac{3+1}{2}\right) = (1,2)$$

$$\text{Slope of } \overline{AC} \text{ is} \quad \frac{3-1}{4-(-2)} = \frac{2}{6} = \frac{1}{3}$$

To find the equation of line n, use the negative reciprocal slope.

$$y - y_1 = m(x - x_1)$$
$$y - 2 = -3(x - 1)$$
$$\text{Equation of line } n \text{ is} \quad y - 2 = -3x + 3$$
$$y = -3x + 5$$

To solve for the point of intersection, solve the equations for lines m and n together. Combining the two equivalent values for y, gives $-x + 1 = -3x + 5$, or $x = 2$. Substituting back into either equation gives $y = -1$. Therefore, the point of intersection of lines m and n is (2, –1). The correct answer is **F**.

Although the numbers work out easily, this is clearly a lengthy problem. Begin by drawing a rough sketch, which can give you insight into solving this problem more directly. The one that follows is accurate; if you are careful, you should be able to be fairly accurate, even without a ruler.

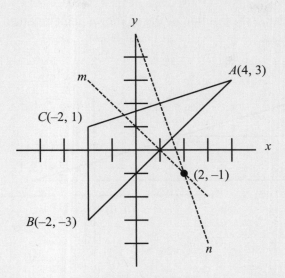

Even with a rough sketch, it should be clear that the point of intersection is in the fourth quadrant. Only answer choices F and G are in the fourth quadrant, so choices H, J, and K can be eliminated. A careful sketch will show the correct answer choice. The correct answer is **F**.

STRATEGY: Sketches often can help give clarity to coordinate geometry problems.

19. The midpoint of line segment $\overline{MN}$ is located at $(-7, 5)$. If one endpoint of line segment $\overline{MN}$ is located at $(5, 1)$, then what are the coordinates of the other endpoint of line segment $\overline{MN}$?

   A. $(17, -3)$
   B. $(-1, 3)$
   C. $(-19, 9)$
   D. $(-11, 3)$
   E. $(-13, 7)$

This problem can be solved directly using the midpoint formula. The coordinates of the midpoint are the averages of the coordinates of the endpoints. Substitute and solve for the missing endpoint. Let (x, y) represent the coordinates of the missing endpoint.

$$\left(x_m, y_m \right) = \left(\frac{x_1 + x_2}{2}, \frac{y_1 + y_2}{2} \right)$$

$$(-7, 5) = \left(\frac{x + 5}{2}, \frac{y + 1}{2} \right)$$

Two separate equation are now set up to solve for x and y.

$$-7 = \frac{x + 5}{2}$$
$$-14 = x + 5$$
$$-19 = x$$
$$5 = \frac{y + 1}{2}$$
$$10 = y + 1$$
$$9 = y$$

Solving for either coordinate would allow you to determine the correct answer choice, **C**.

Drawing a quick sketch would clarify the position of the unknown point and then the selection of answer choice **C** would be clear.

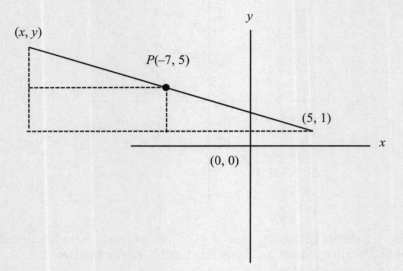

The correct answer is **C**.

Plane Geometry Sample Questions

STRATEGY: Mark in diagrams. Marking in diagrams as you read them can save you valuable time. Marking can also give you insight into how to solve a problem because you'll have the complete picture clearly in front of you.

---

20. The perimeter of the isosceles triangle shown below is 42. The two equal-length (congruent) sides, $\overline{AB}$ and $\overline{AC}$ are each three times as long as the third side. What are the lengths of each side?

    F.   21, 21, 21
    G.   6, 6, 18
    H.   18, 21, 3
    J.   18, 18, 6
    K.   4, 12, 12

Mark the equal sides on the diagram. $\overline{AB}$ and $\overline{AC}$ are each three times as long as $\overline{BC}$.

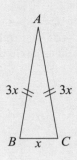

The equation for perimeter is

$$3x + 3x + x = 42$$
$$7x = 42$$
$$x = 6$$

Substituting back into the drawing gives

Note that this problem can also be solved by working directly from the answer choices. Choices F and H can be eliminated since two of the sides must be of equal length. Choice G can be eliminated since the two equal sides are shorter than the longest side. This leaves choices J and K. Choice K can be eliminated since the three sides do not add to the proper sum. The correct answer is **J.**

> **STRATEGY: Mark drawings with appropriate information. Trying to visualize all the given facts is difficult. Mark additional information as you determine it.**

21. In the triangle shown here, $\overline{CD}$ is an angle bisector, $\angle ACD = 30°$, and $\angle ABC$ is a right angle. What is the measurement of $\angle x$ in degrees?

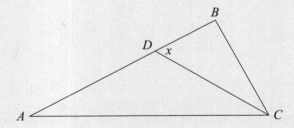

    A. 30°
    B. 45°
    C. 60°
    D. 75°
    E. 80°

First, underline or circle "measurement of $\angle x$" in the stated problem.

Next: Re-read the problem and mark in the drawing as follows. In the triangle shown here, $\overline{CD}$ is an angle bisector (**stop and mark in the drawing**), $\angle ACD = 30°$ and $\angle ABC$ is a right angle (**stop and mark in the drawing**). What is the measurement of $\angle x$ in degrees? (**Stop and mark in or circle what you're looking for in the drawing.**)

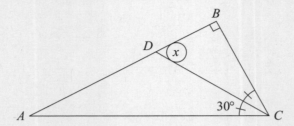

Now, with the drawing marked, it's evident that since $\angle ACD = 30°$, then $\angle BCD$ is also 30°, because they are formed by an angle bisector (divides an angle into two equal angles). Since $\angle ABC$ is 90° (a right angle) and $\angle BCD = 30°$, then $\angle x$ is 60° because there are 180° in a triangle.

$$180 - (90 + 30) = 60$$

Always mark in diagrams as you read their descriptions and information about them, including what you're looking for. The correct answer is **C**.

> **STRATEGY: Knowing the relationships between areas and linear measures of polygons is helpful in determining area/perimeter ratios.**

22. What is the best approximation for the perimeter, P, around the outside of the figure shown here? The radius of each circle is 6 units and the rectangle is twice as long as it is wide.

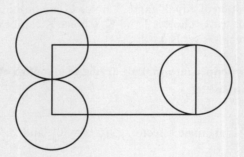

    F.   100 units
    G.   105 units
    H.   110 units
    J.   115 units
    K.   120 units

Each circle has a circumference of $2\pi r$, or 12π. The curved portion of the outside perimeter of the figure is made up of three-fourths of two circles and one-half of a third, totaling two complete circumferences, or $2(12\pi)$ or 24π. Since the radius of the circle is 6, the diameter is 12. This also represents the width of the rectangle. Therefore, the length of the rectangle is 24, 6 units of which are not included in the perimeter of the figure. So, the straight-line distances included in the figure are $18 + 18 = 36$ units. Therefore, the total perimeter of the figure is $24\pi + 36$. The approximate value of π is 3.14, so the total perimeter is approximately $24(3.14) + 36$, or about 111 units. The correct answer is **H**.

23. Given an equilateral triangle, by approximately what percent would the length of the sides have to be increased to triple the area of the triangle?

    A.   25%

    B.   50%

    C.   75%

    D.   100%

    E.   200%

Given two similar plane figures, such as equilateral triangles, the ratio of their areas is the square of the ratio of the lengths of their sides. So, doubling the length of the sides would quadruple the area, more than the triple that you need. Therefore, you can eliminate answer choices D and E as being too much. A 50 percent increase would yield a ratio of 3 to 2 for the lengths of the sides given a 9 to 4 ratio for the areas. This is just over double and clearly not enough. You can eliminate answer choices A and B as being too little. To achieve a tripling of area would require multiplying the lengths of the sides by the square root of 3, or about 1.732. This is about a 73 percent increase. The correct answer is **C**.

Trigonometry Sample Questions

STRATEGY: Know ratios. It is important to know all the basic trigonometric ratios including sine, cosine, and tangent.

24. Using the figure here, what is the sum of the tangent of $\angle A$ and the cosine of $\angle B$?

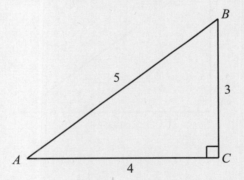

    F.   1.35

    G.   1.55

    H.   1.93

    J.   2.08

    K.   2.13

In a right triangle, the tangent of an acute angle is the ratio of the lengths of the opposite side and the adjacent side. Therefore, the tangent of $\angle A$ is $\frac{3}{4} = 0.75$. The cosine of an acute angle is the ratio of the lengths of the adjacent side and the hypotenuse. Therefore, the cosine of $\angle B$ is $\frac{3}{5} = 0.60$. The sum is $0.75 + 0.60 = 1.35$. The correct answer is **F**.

STRATEGY: Values of ratios. You will not be required to know, or even calculate, the values of trigonometric ratios of arbitrary angles. Occasionally, you will be given the values of these ratios to use in the problem.

---

25. You are standing on flat land 600 feet from the base of a building. You observe that from your vantage point the angle between the bottom and top of the building is 35°. What is the approximate height of the building? (The following approximate values may be useful in answering this question: sin 35° = 0.57, cos 35° = 0.82, tan 35° = 0.70.)

    A.   342 feet
    B.   420 feet
    C.   492 feet
    D.   857 feet
    E.   1053 feet

Using the following figure, the tangent is the correct function to use to solve this problem, as follows:

$$\tan 35° = \frac{x}{600}$$
$$600 \tan 35° = x$$
$$(600)(0.70) = x$$
$$420 = x$$

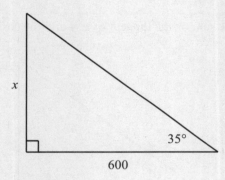

The correct answer is **B.**

STRATEGY: Sketches. It is important to know how the values of basic trigonometric ratios change as the value of the angles change. Drawing a sketch will help you visualize the given data.

---

26. Given right triangle ABC with $\angle A < \angle B < \angle C$, which of the following statement(s) is/are true?

    I.   sin $\angle A$ < sin $\angle B$.
    II.   tan $\angle A$ < sin $\angle B$.
   III.   As $\angle B$ increases, the cosine of $\angle B$ decreases.

    F.   Only one of the above statements is true.
    G.   I and II only
    H.   I and III only
    J.   II and III only
    K.   All three statements are true.

The following sketch illustrates the given information.

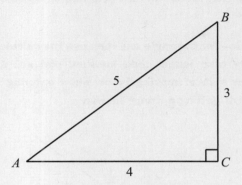

Since angle A is the smallest angle and angle C is the largest angle, the side opposite angle A is the shortest side and the side opposite the right angle C is the longest side. Using example lengths will help determine the relationships between the values of the trigonometric ratios. Using the illustrated values, $\sin A = \frac{3}{5} = 0.60$, $\sin B = \frac{4}{5} = 0.80$, $\tan A = \frac{3}{4} = 0.75$, $\cos B = \frac{3}{5} = 0.60$.

You can see that $\sin \angle A < \sin \angle B$, therefore statement I is true. Also, $\tan \angle A < \sin \angle B$, so statement II is also true. From this information, you can eliminate answer choices F, H, and J. To determine whether statement III is true or not, visualize point A moving toward the left. As point A moves to the left, $\angle B$ increases, and so does the length of the hypotenuse, while the adjacent side of $\angle B$ remains the same length. Therefore, the cosine of $\angle B$ also decreases. Thus, statement III is also true. Therefore, the correct answer is **K.**

STRATEGY: Know how to use basic trigonometric identities. Some questions involving trigonometry rely on some basic trigonometric identities. These are sometimes used to solve equations.

27. Which of the following is equivalent to $\cos \alpha + \sin \alpha \tan \alpha$?

  A. $\dfrac{1}{\sin \alpha}$

  B. $\dfrac{1}{\cos \alpha}$

  C. $\dfrac{1}{\tan \alpha}$

  D. $\dfrac{1}{\sin^2 \alpha}$

  E. $\dfrac{1}{\cos^2 \alpha}$

The faster, more direct method to solve this problem relies on knowing two trigonometric identities: $\sin^2 \alpha + \cos^2 \alpha = 1$ and $\tan \alpha = \dfrac{\sin \alpha}{\cos \alpha}$. Using these two identities, the answer can be found as follows:

$$\cos \alpha + \sin \alpha \tan \alpha = \cos \alpha \frac{\cos \alpha}{\cos \alpha} + \sin \alpha \frac{\sin \alpha}{\cos \alpha}$$

$$= \frac{\cos^2 \alpha}{\cos \alpha} + \frac{\sin^2 \alpha}{\cos \alpha}$$

$$= \frac{\cos^2 \alpha + \sin^2 \alpha}{\cos \alpha}$$

$$= \frac{1}{\cos \alpha}$$

Therefore, answer choice **B** is the correct selection.

If you do not recall these trigonometric identities, a longer alternative solution would involve drawing a diagram and calculating the various trigonometric ratios and then determining which combinations would work. The following illustrates this longer method.

TIP: Although you could enter a value for the angle and then use the calculator to find which answer choice is correct, doing so would probably take longer than knowing and using the trigonometric relationships; furthermore, it also increases the risk of making typos when entering numbers into the calculator and therefore increases the likelihood of getting a wrong answer.

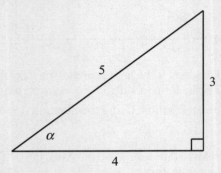

From the figure, $\sin\alpha = \frac{3}{5}$, $\cos\alpha = \frac{4}{5}$, and $\tan\alpha = \frac{3}{4}$. Substitute these values into the given relationship:

$$\cos\alpha + \sin\alpha\tan\alpha = \frac{4}{5} + \left(\frac{3}{5}\right)\left(\frac{3}{4}\right)$$
$$= \frac{4}{5} + \frac{9}{20}$$
$$= \frac{16}{20} + \frac{9}{20}$$
$$= \frac{25}{20}$$
$$= \frac{5}{4}$$
$$= \frac{1}{\left(\frac{4}{5}\right)}$$
$$= \frac{1}{\cos\alpha}$$

Remember, the questions on this test are designed to evaluate your knowledge of the subject matter and not to see how fast you can do arithmetic. The correct answer is **B.**

Chapter 4

The ACT Reading Test

The ACT Reading Test questions are designed to test your ability to read, comprehend, and interpret diverse passages that deal with a variety of subjects. Good reading skills require that you understand what you are reading so that you can derive *meaning* from written passages and then use this knowledge to answer specific questions related to the passages.

Improving reading comprehension skills is not about moving your eyes across a page more quickly. It is about forming a *mental framework* to conceptualize words and shape thought schemas. Effective reading is the conscious process of critically "thinking" about reading and is very different from passive reading. This type of reading requires your careful attention to decoding and interpreting passages. Good reading skills can be developed through consistent and structured practice and can help you with *all* subjects on the ACT.

We have developed a framework to approach questions on the Reading Test that focuses your attention on engaging in the written material as you participate in decoding passages and questions. As you study the material presented in this chapter, you will be able to apply your knowledge of reading comprehension to answer the assigned questions correctly. You are not expected to be familiar with the subject matter of the passage or with its specific content, and you will not be expected to have any prior knowledge of the subject. Everything you need to know will be provided in the passage.

General Overview of the ACT Reading Test

The following table presents an overview of the Reading Test.

Reading Test Format

Passage Category	Description	Number of Questions
Prose fiction	Excerpts from short stories or novels	10
Humanities	Excerpts from art, architecture, dance, ethics, language, literary criticism, personal essays, biographies, and philosophy	10
Social Studies	Excerpts from anthropology, archaeology, business, education, economics, history, political science, psychology, and sociology	10
Natural Sciences	Excerpts from anatomy, astronomy, biology, chemistry, environmental science, geology, medicine, physiology, physical science, and physics	10
Total Questions		40

Skills and Concepts Tested

The questions test your ability to read passages with a critical eye and to answer questions on the basis of what is directly stated or implied. The basic skills necessary to do well on the Reading Test include reading at the level of a high school graduate or college freshman. Students who have read widely and know how to read actively and efficiently tend to do well on the Reading Test, but keep in mind that it is never too late to improve your reading performance.

Common types of questions ask you to

- Identify the main idea or purpose of a paragraph or passage.
- Distinguish the main idea from significant supporting ideas.
- Make comparisons (compare and contrast) between ideas or characters.

- Draw reasonable generalizations and conclusions.
- Determine the mood (author's tone or attitude) of the passage.
- Determine the sequence of events in a passage.
- Identify the meaning of individual words and phrases from the context of the passage.

Directions

Each of the four passages will be followed by 10 questions based on its content, structure, or style (40 questions total). You can anticipate reading 600- to 800-word passages followed by questions that ask you to choose the *best* answer among the four choices. Return to the passage as often as necessary to answer the questions. Use only the information given or implied in the passage. Do not consider outside information, even if it seems more accurate than the given information.

Sample Reading Passage:

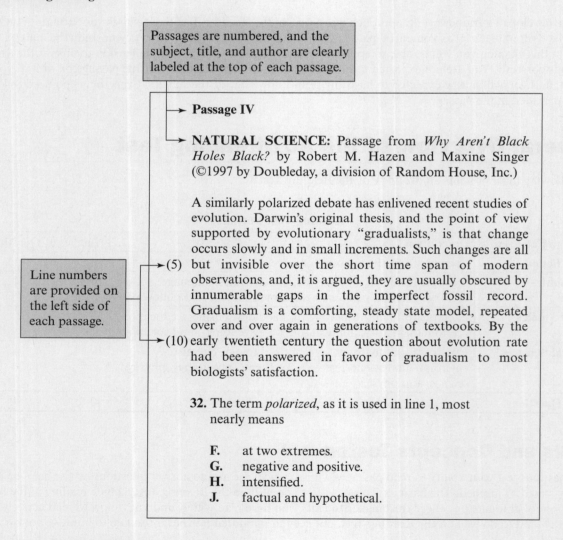

Passages are numbered, and the subject, title, and author are clearly labeled at the top of each passage.

Passage IV

NATURAL SCIENCE: Passage from *Why Aren't Black Holes Black?* by Robert M. Hazen and Maxine Singer (©1997 by Doubleday, a division of Random House, Inc.)

A similarly polarized debate has enlivened recent studies of evolution. Darwin's original thesis, and the point of view supported by evolutionary "gradualists," is that change occurs slowly and in small increments. Such changes are all (5) but invisible over the short time span of modern observations, and, it is argued, they are usually obscured by innumerable gaps in the imperfect fossil record. Gradualism is a comforting, steady state model, repeated over and over again in generations of textbooks. By the (10) early twentieth century the question about evolution rate had been answered in favor of gradualism to most biologists' satisfaction.

Line numbers are provided on the left side of each passage.

32. The term *polarized*, as it is used in line 1, most nearly means

    F.   at two extremes.
    G.   negative and positive.
    H.   intensified.
    J.   factual and hypothetical.

Identifying Question Types

This section describes the seven most common question types that appear on the ACT Reading Test. As you learn to identify the types of questions, you should be more confident in your ability to answer questions with greater ease and skill. Before we discuss specific Reading question types, let's start by explaining the general *scope* of

Reading question types—indirect and direct questions. After you have studied the question types in this section, we will walk you through a four-step process to learn how to approach Reading questions (page 102).

Indirect versus Direct Questions

All Reading questions are either indirect or direct. Reading Test questions ask you to respond to information that is *indirectly* implied (implicit) or *directly* stated (explicit). Your task is to approach each passage and question with an investigative attitude as you gather clues to help you find indirect or direct evidence to support your answer.

> **Indirect**—If a question asks you to *infer* from information presented in the passage that is not directly stated, it is an indirect question. In indirect questions, you will need to make inferences and find a flow of logic as you draw reasonable conclusions and generalizations from the passage. Look for supporting proof and evidence among the author's words. Do not overthink this type of question. The answer is never vague and is always based on evidence from the passage.

> **Direct**—If a question asks you for a specific *fact* or *detail,* it is a direct question. Direct questions always lead you to find the answer somewhere in the passage. Look for specific words, phrases, or facts that are contained in the passage and work actively back and forth between the passage and the question.

Now let's look at the seven specific indirect and direct question types: main point, supporting details, compare/contrast, drawing generalizations and conclusions, mood (author's tone or attitude), sequence of ideas, and word meanings.

Question Type One: Main Point

This type of question is listed first because it is the most common type of question. The author's main point is the *reason* why the passage was written. The most basic approach to tackling any Reading question is to understand the main point of the passage. To answer this type of question, read the whole passage carefully and look for the author's central idea and *overall message.* This question type is straightforward. After you read and take notes from the passage, try to synthesize the author's ideas. Ask yourself, "What is the author really trying to say?" or "What point is the author trying to make?" The best method of isolating the main point of the passage is to *paraphrase* the passage by summarizing and condensing the author's ideas into your own words.

Practice this type of question first before undertaking other types of questions. After developing a good command of identifying main point questions, you will be ready to tackle the slightly more challenging inference questions.

Examples:

- "What is the main point of the passage (or a paragraph)?"
- "The main idea in the second paragraph (lines 9–15) is . . ."
- "Which of the following is an accurate description of the passage?"
- "What is the primary purpose of the passage?"
- "The narrator's main argument is . . ."
- "The author claims that . . ."
- "According to the passage . . ."
- "The author's point of view is . . ."

Question Type Two: Supporting Details

After you determine the author's main point(s), make sure your answer is supported. Supporting detail questions require that you know the difference between ideas that are *clearly stated* and ideas that are *implied* by the author.

Every single answer is in the passage or can be directly inferred from the passage. Approach this type of problem like a detective looking for clues in the passage to answer the question. Look for detailed information that is directly (and sometimes indirectly) stated in the passage to answer these types of Reading questions. These questions may require you to break the passage down and examine its smaller components to find the solution. The key is that you can always find the answer somewhere in the passage.

Look for specific words, phrases, or facts that are contained in the passage and work actively back and forth between the passage and the question. To develop this skill, practice identifying supporting details on a regular basis with newspaper articles, Internet news articles, magazine articles, or excerpts from books.

Examples:

- "What details support the author's argument?"
- "What evidence supports the author's view?"
- "All of the following support the author's point, EXCEPT . . ."
- "According to the author, an important fact is . . ."
- "According to the passage, the reason that the [riverbeds] are dry is that . . ."

Question Type Three: Compare/Contrast

Compare and contrast questions make logical comparisons in the development of multiple points within the passage. These points are often interrelated with a common theme or subject and show qualities of supporting or opposing points of view. In this type of question, you are asked to recognize the similarities and differences found in the text. In other words, you will be comparing the qualities of a specific point that are *alike* and contrasting the qualities of that point that are *different*.

To distinguish information in the passage, use active reading skills and focus on finding or understanding the context clues in the passage. Use these context clues to determine the similarities and differences in the author's points of view. As you use context clues, you should notice a comparison relationship among the points of view that allows you to settle on the correct answer. Your answer should always include a solid basis for your analysis of comparisons.

Examples:

- "The distinction the narrator makes between _____ and _____ is . . ."
- "The author of the passage makes which of the following comparisons?"

Question Type Four: Drawing Generalizations and Conclusions

Drawing generalizations and conclusions from a passage involve *indirect* types of questions. These types of questions require that you gather information from the passage to make a general interpretation about the written material to formulate a general conclusion. Details must be plausible and must logically follow the circumstances presented in the passage. If you are asked to make a generalization or conclusion about the passage, you must look for *supporting proof* and *evidence* among the author's words and *tone* (see Question Type Five). "Read between the lines" as you gather evidence and mark key words to support your answer. Ask yourself, "What is not stated directly by the author?" Do not overthink this type of question. The answer is never vague and is always based on evidence from the passage. After you understand what the author is communicating in the passage, your answer should make perfect logical sense. Review the four answer choices to determine which answer is most plausible *based on the evidence* that you have gathered from the passage.

Examples:

- "It can be reasonably inferred from the passage as a whole that . . ."
- "In saying _____, the author implies that . . ."

- "Which of the following statements best summarizes . . .?"
- "Based on the passage, the author would conclude . . ."
- "Which of the following conclusions about _____ is best supported by the passage?"
- "Details in the passage suggest . . ."
- "In the context of the passage, it is most reasonable to infer . . ."
- "The narrator is most likely saying that . . ."
- "Based on the passage, it can be inferred that the author believes . . ."
- "The second paragraph (lines 29–35) suggests that . . ."
- "According to the narrator, the generalization that can be made is . . ."

Question Type Five: Mood (Author's Tone or Attitude)

Identify the mood of the passage by looking for and identifying the author's *tone* and *attitude*. The overall mood of the passage is communicated through the author's choice of language and words that help the reader feel a *sense* of connection with the written material. The words that the author uses to describe events, people, or places will help give you a clue about what and how the author wants you to feel or think. Pay careful attention to the *types* of words the author uses. For example, if you read the word *tentative,* you may feel a sense of something *unsure, cautious,* or *hesitant.* Also, look for words that stir up a subtle feeling or emotion. Punctuation marks and/or italicized words or phrases can convey the passage's mood, too. Mark key words that signal the author's tone or attitude as you read through the passage and then compare these words with the four answer choices. These types of questions can be as simple as identifying positive or negative words that set the entire mood of the passage.

Examples:

- "According to the passage, the attitude expressed by the character is . . ."
- "The tone of the passage is . . ."
- "The feeling of _____ was obtained by using . . ."
- "It is reasonable to suggest that the author believes . . ."
- "Producing color illustrations reflects a tone of . . ."
- "According to the passage when [Lauren] looks at a flower, she feels . . ."

Question Type Six: Sequence of Ideas

Every passage follows a logical pattern, a sequence of ideas that helps the reader formulate clarity and meaning. A sequence of events helps to logically develop unity of the central ideas in the passage. This type of question may ask you to determine the chronological order of events or determine the chain of events that may cause a particular outcome (cause and effect).

When answering this type of problem, it is helpful to think about the "big picture" of the passage and then to organize its components into sequential order (what happened first, second, and so forth). Refer back to the "main point" question type to understand the overall message that the author is trying to convey and then picture in your mind (or write down) the sequence of events. In cases where several choices might work as the main point, select the one that fits the *meaning* of the author's intent most exactly. After you understand the author's main point, it is easier to organize supporting points in the passage.

Look for clues to organize the author's sequence of ideas. For example, the author may use *transitional words* to guide the reader to successive events. Words and phrases like "first," "initially," and "primary" indicate the beginning of a chain of logic. Words and phrases like "another," "also," and "in addition" let the reader know that there is a continuation in the development of reasoning. Other clues that signal an impending change are found in cause and effect statements. In cause and effect statements, watch for words and phrases from the first event that signal something may happen in the next event. For example, look for signal words such as, "as a result," "since," "because," "therefore," and "so."

Examples:

- "The author identifies the cause of _____ to be . . ."
- "At the time of the story, the narrator is . . ."
- "According to the passage, when did the [economic concern] first arise?"
- "The passage states that the narrator first became aware of the _____ when . . ."

Question Type Seven: Word Meanings

Some questions test your ability to understand the meaning of certain words and phrases. To help you with these types of questions, pay close attention to the word or phrase in the *context* of the whole sentence, paragraph, or passage. Use the context to figure out the meaning, even if you're unfamiliar with the words. Sometimes you will need to read the sentence just before and after where the word is presented to understand the word's association to the surrounding text. Even if you don't know the meaning of the word, the passage will give you clues.

If you feel stuck, consider all of your options and literally plug in each answer to see which answer choice makes the most sense (or sounds the best). For suggestions about deciphering word meanings, read the "Vocabulary Resources" section at the end of this chapter.

Examples:

- "What does the author mean by . . .?"
- "When the author says [equivocation] in line 17, she most likely means . . ."
- "According to the passage, [meritorious] most accurately expresses . . ."
- "Identify the meaning of [enmity] in paragraph 1 (line 5)."
- "As it is used in line 19, the word [loquacious] most nearly means . . ."
- "An analogy made in the passage is that . . ."
- "Which of the following best explains the phrase [desultory treadmills]?"

Four-Step Approach

Successful readers use a variety of strategies to improve reading skills including the ability to visualize, pick out details, predict, decode, and summarize reading passages. For you to attain a higher score, you must *think like an investigator* to search, locate, and extract information in its given context, style, and tone so that you can accurately respond to the questions. If you do not read regularly, be confident in your ability to learn some of these reading skills. Be patient with yourself as you work through the strategies presented. Remember that repeated and consistent practice is the key to reading competency. Work through the practice questions and practice tests in this study guide, paying careful attention to the explanations. The explanations provide you with clues about the thought process of the test that help you understand how to determine the correct answer choice.

The following step-by-step approach should help you improve your reading comprehension skills. This approach has helped hundreds of students improve their overall performance on the ACT. Apply these steps to the practice questions in this chapter, but remember to avoid spending too much time on any one question. Taking a lot of time to answer the most difficult question on the test correctly, while losing valuable test time, won't get you the score you deserve.

Now, let's walk through step-by-step specific methods to improve your reading skills. The mnemonic for these methods is *The Four Reading Strategies: Review, Read, Record, and Respond.*

Review, Read, Record, and Respond

Step 1	*Review and preread the questions.*
	This proven question-driven strategy will remind you to "shop before you read." Scanning the questions before you read the passages will help you to identify what you should focus on in the passages. Mark important words and specific line numbers to give you clues about what to look for in the passages. This can be especially helpful with unfamiliar reading material. For example, highlight the line number, word, and phrase in a question that asks you to locate the meaning of a word or phrase located in the passage. If you're asked to draw a conclusion, circle the word "conclusion" to remind you what to look for as you read the passage. Allow your eyes to move quickly over the questions as you highlight the important information and key words. By scanning the questions first, you will understand the gist of what you are being asked, which, in turn, will help you to focus as you read the passage more closely. Remember to read only the questions and not the answer choices during this first step, as these may distract you. Do not spend too much time scanning the questions because you must act quickly.
Step 2	*Read actively.*
	Research shows that active reading provides the highest level of success when answering Reading questions. As you read through the passage, practice thinking like a reading detective and gather clues and specific details to help you answer the questions. Read the passage carefully to try to understand the facts, their meanings, their implications, and their logical sequence of events. As you become more mindful of the passage's content, you will be directing your attention to clues and will be able to respond with a greater sense of awareness. Use the information about the specific question types to help you know what to look for in the questions and the passages as you actively read.
Step 3	**Record important points from the passage.**
	Lessons learned from a variety of effective reading programs have shown that surveying the passage by paraphrasing, clarifying, and predicting will improve reading comprehension. After you preread the questions, you should read and actively mark the passage. This strategy helps you form visual representations of the written material. Your written notes on the passage will help trigger your memory and make mental associations to help you remember content from the passage. All students have different learning styles, but this technique helps you focus on the passage's central ideas and avoid distractions during the exam. You may be surprised at the information you can recall when writing down just a few trigger words as you link mental word associations to the context of the reading passage. It is important to mark key words and phrases and write brief notes in the margins to paraphrase, clarify, and predict important points from the passage.
	Paraphrase. Restating written material in your own words will help you concentrate as you read and untangle difficult passages. Always look for the main point of the passage and try to restate or summarize the content of the passage in your own words. When working through practice questions in this study guide, gather information to paraphrase by marking key words and phrases. Use these key words and phrases to trigger your memory so that you can summarize and restate the passage in your own words. See whether you can use your paraphrased statement to answer the question and keep in mind that getting the best answer is your only goal.
	Clarify. Some passages are difficult to understand, but the answer to every question is always stated directly within or can be inferred from the information stated in the passage. Pay attention to the written material, and if there is a word, phrase, or concept that you don't necessarily understand, write a quick note to yourself to seek further clarification. Documenting material that requires further clarification will help you complete the task at hand, and often the answer to your question may appear later in the passage. This strategy helps you to form visual representations of the written material. This technique helps you center on the passage's main ideas and avoid distractions during the exam.
	Predict. Make predictions so that your mind is continuously guessing at or anticipating what is going to come next. For example, in a passage that introduces "complex carbohydrates" in the first sentence, you might immediately predict that the passage will be a nutrition-based science topic.

Step 4	**Respond to the question.**
	After you have preread the questions, read actively through the passage, and recorded important points in the passage or in the margins by paraphrasing, clarifying, and predicting, it's time to answer the questions. Be sure that you understand exactly what you are being asked.
	Always make sure that the answer you choose agrees with the information contained in the passage and that it answers the specific question asked. Reading the questions too quickly can result in choosing the wrong answer(s)—a common mistake made by test-takers. Use the incorrect answer choices to help guide you toward the correct answer choice. Often, you can arrive at the right answer by eliminating answer choices that are not supported by the passage.
	If you get stuck on any one question, either make an educated guess by eliminating as many of the choices as you can, or leave the question blank and proceed to the next question. The *elimination strategy* is a very valuable technique that you can use for the entire test.

General Tips and Suggestions

Here are some suggestions and tips that apply to all Reading Test questions.

1. **Practice strategies.** After studying the suggested approaches outlined in this study guide, identify the strategies that are consistent with your individual learning style and practice using these strategies well *before* your exam date. Don't wait until a week before the exam to begin practicing the suggested strategies.

   For example, are you the type of person who works methodically and prefers to answer questions in the order that they appear? Or are you the type of person who prefers to answer all of the easy questions first and then come back to the difficult questions later? Remember that strategies that work well for some people may not work for others, but deciding which strategies to employ ahead of time is important for test-taking efficiency.

2. **Develop good reading habits.** Reading is a habit that develops through time and practice. Spend about 30 minutes per day, at least 6 to 10 weeks before your exam, reading faster than your normal reading speed. As you read, pay special attention to key words, transitional words, and negative words. This process will help strengthen your cognitive reading development. Developing good reading habits is similar to going to the gym to build and strengthen your muscles. You must practice reading skills frequently and consistently to build and strengthen your "brain muscles." Remember that you can read newspaper editorials, Internet news, magazine articles, or book excerpts. Don't get hooked into reading only interesting, thought-provoking articles. Try to expand your reading resources and read material that you might not normally read because you have no interest in the topic. Passages on the ACT may not be ones that you would normally choose to read.

3. **Pace yourself.** Concentrate on using your time efficiently and do not allow the reading passage and questions to slow your pace. You have 35 minutes to read four passages and answer 40 questions. This is 8 minutes and 45 seconds per passage with 10 questions. At first glance you might calculate that you have just less than 1 minute to read and answer each Reading question, but this does not include the time it takes you to read the passage. If you spend 2 to 3 minutes to read each passage, you will have only 35 seconds to answer each question. Reading Test questions can be time-consuming, so do not let the passages slow your efficiency.

4. **Read each passage actively.** As you read each passage, mark the passage when you see key words (names, definitions, places, and numbers) or any other items you feel are important. Always focus on the author's main purpose or scope of the entire passage. Do not try to memorize the passage. Instead, think of each paragraph as a "thought unit" and try to move your eyes rapidly down the passage while taking notes.

5. **Use only the information that is directly provided in the passage.** Answer all questions about the passage on the basis of what is *stated* or *implied* in that passage. The passage must support your answer. Do not consider outside information, even if it seems more accurate than the given information.

6. **Consider all passages.** Test-takers sometimes believe that the prose or humanities passages are easier to read than social studies and natural sciences, but this is not necessarily true. All passages require careful consideration and focus. Remember that you do NOT need to have knowledge about the subject to answer the questions.

7. **Refer to the line numbers in the passages.** Each passage has line numbers for easy reference. In questions that mention specific line numbers, you will have the advantage of being able to quickly spot where the information is located. After you spot the location, be sure to read the line(s) just before and after the line(s) mentioned in the question. The text information that comes before and after the line(s) in the question can be helpful in putting the information in the proper context and answering the question.

8. **Eliminate incorrect answer choices.** If you don't know the answer, try to eliminate some of the obvious wrong choices as soon as you recognize them. If you get stuck on any one question, eliminate as many of the other choices as you can and take an educated guess *before* you proceed to the next question. It is very difficult to go back to a passage and remember the details of its contents without re-reading the passage. You are not penalized for guessing, so it is in your best interest to take an educated guess to answer each question.

9. **Watch for negative questions.** You may be asked to choose an answer that is the *exception,* which can initially be confusing and challenge your thinking. Keep an eye out for the capitalized words EXCEPT or NOT in the question, as these are the most common negative question forms. Familiarize yourself by practicing these types of questions prior to taking the test. For example, a negative question can read, "All of the following are true EXCEPT . . ." To help answer this type of question, treat the answer choices as *true* or *false* statements, searching for the answer that is *mostly false.* In other words, search among the answer choices and select the *one* that is completely false. There may be more than one answer that is false, but follow the flow of logic, context clues, and key words to determine which answer is *absolutely not true,* and therefore, the correct choice.

10. **Be on alert for the "attractive distractor" answer choice.** Watch out for answers that look good, but are not the *best* answer choice. Just because an answer choice is a true statement, it does not mean that it is the best choice. Attractive distractors are usually the most common wrong answers. The facts and concepts presented on the exam are often subtle variations of selected answer choices that make it difficult for test-takers to narrow down the answer choices. Attractive distractors are carefully written to be close to the *best* answer, but there is never more than one right answer. When you narrow your choice down to two answers, one is probably the attractive distractor. If this happens, read the question again and select the answer that fits the *meaning* of the question more exactly and remember that the answer does not have to be perfect, just the *best* among the four answer choices.

Sample Passage and Questions with Mark-Ups

The following passage shows one way a test-taker might mark a passage to help understand the information. You may find that circling or bracketing works better for you, or using other marks that you personally find helpful.

Sample Passage

SOCIAL SCIENCE: This passage is from *Freedom Just Around the Corner: A New American History 1585–1828* by Walter A. McDougall (© 2004 by HarperCollins Publishers).

The imperial contest for North America began in earnest when the English settled the James River in 1607, the French founded Quebec on the St. Lawrence River in 1608, the Spaniards founded
(5) Santa Fe on the Rio Grande in 1609, and the Dutch built Fort Nassau on the Hudson River in 1614. But the Netherlands was a small nation still struggling for independence. Spain, hard-pressed to defend the vast empire it already had, lacked
(10) the population and resources to do more than plant a few forts in Florida and New Mexico and

did not reach Alta California until the 1760s. Frigid Canada's main appeal was the fur trade rather than farming, and French kings made
(15) matters worse by prohibiting religious dissenters to colonize. Even the energetic English numbered a mere 2,400 in Virginia and 1,400 in New England by 1630. Why, therefore, did the Native Americans east of the Appalachians, who numbered over
(20) 400,000 in 1600, not overwhelm the starving white beachheads on the Atlantic seaboard?

The reasons are easily stated. First, Europeans concentrated around fortified villages supported by a monopoly of sea power and firearms. To be
(25) sure, Indians quickly developed a lust for muskets, which they used to hunt game and rival tribes. But guns only made the Native Americans dependent on Europeans for ammunition, powder, and repair

(30) of weapons, while causing them to lose their skill with a weapon actually better suited to sylvan conflict, the bow. One frontier war ended in 1641 when the proud Iroquois sued for peace to regain access to French firearms. Second, colonists (35) pinned to the coasts and rivers had more incentive to fight tenaciously once there were too many of them to evacuate over a summer. Indians, by contrast, had the option to retreat inland rather than fight desperate wars with the white men. (40) Third, the English drew on inexhaustible reinforcements from a single national "tribe," whereas the Indians strewn across a thousand-mile front were more crippled by tribal feuds than the Scots and Irish.

(45) Fourth and most important were the "invisible armies" fighting on the Europeans' behalf: infectious diseases such as influenza, chickenpox, smallpox, measles, and plague against which Native Americans had no genetic immunity. (50) Upward of 90 percent of the Algonquin, Wampanoag, Massachusetts, and Pawtucket tribes on the New England coast were carried off in the years just before the Pilgrims arrived. Between 50 and 75 percent of the Hurons, Iroquois, and Mohawks in the eastern Great (55) Lakes died in the 1630s and 1640s. Perhaps 90 percent of the Powhatan, Susquehannock, and other tribes around Chesapeake Bay disappeared by 1670. The first English outposts on the Connecticut River were saved when "it pleased (60) God to visit these Indians with a great sickness and such mortality that of a thousand, above nine hundred and a half of them died, and many of them did rot above ground for want of burial." Such mortality occurred whenever Native (65) Americans first met Europeans, its effects magnified by the Indians' own low fertility (resulting in part from their habit of breast-feeding infants for three or four years) and the high death rate of children. Early Virginia (70) colonists also knew wholesale death from malaria, saline poisoning, and other maladies of the tidewater, while their birth rate was also tiny due to the sheer lack of females. But Virginians soon moved out of the fetid estuaries while being (75) supplemented by an average of 8,500 newcomers per year in the 1630s and 1649s. In comparatively healthy New England, the Puritan families were not only reinforced, but reproduced at a rate close to the biological maximum. As a result, English (80) colonists may have outnumbered all of the eastern Indians combined as early as 1690.

Examples:

The following questions show examples of ways you can mark the questions.

---

1. Which of the following best states the main point of the passage?

The words "main point" are marked here. You should always read and look for the main point, but prereading this question is a good idea. Prereading the question can give you a clue about the passage and what to look for. If you quickly scan a few of the questions before reading the passage, it may be very helpful, especially if the passage seems difficult or unfamiliar to you. After you preread the questions, read the passage actively (marking the passage), and then reread the questions and each one of the answer choices.

---

2. It can reasonably be inferred from the third paragraph that . . .

Notice that "inferred" and "third paragraph" are marked. To answer this question, you'll need to draw information from the third paragraph by "reading between the lines."

---

3. From the context of the passage, *sylvan* (line 30) most likely means . . .

Notice that *sylvan* (line 30) is marked. The marking helps you pinpoint where the answer can be found and makes you aware of looking for the meaning as the term is used in the passage.

---

4. According to the passage, in 1641 the Iroquois sought peace with the French because . . .

Notice that *1641* and *Iroquois sought peace* are marked. You need to focus on these details to answer this particular question.

Practice Reading Question Approaches and Strategies

Now let's practice the approaches and strategies you have learned. Read the passage again, but this time read actively—highlighting the main points, key words, and other items you feel are important. You can mark a passage by underlining or circling important information, but be sure you don't over mark the passage, or you'll defeat the purpose of the technique. Practice questions will follow the passage, and answers and explanations are provided at the end of each practice question.

Directions: The following reading passage is followed by several questions based on the passage's content. After reading the passage, choose the best answer among four choices to answer each question. You may refer to the passage as often as necessary.

Passage I

SOCIAL SCIENCE: This passage is from *Freedom Just Around the Corner: A New American History 1585–1828* by Walter A. McDougall (© 2004 by HarperCollins Publishers).

The imperial contest for North America begin in earnest when the English settled the James River in 1607, the French founded Quebec on the St. Lawrence River in 1608, the Spaniards founded
(5) Santa Fe on the Rio Grande in 1609, and the Dutch built Fort Nassau on the Hudson River in 1614. But the Netherlands was a small nation still struggling for independence. Spain, hard-pressed to defend the vast empire it already had, lacked the
(10) population and resources to do more than plant a few forts in Florida and New Mexico, and did not reach Alta California until the 1760s. Frigid Canada's main appeal was the fur trade rather than farming, and French kings made matters
(15) worse by prohibiting religious dissenters to colonize. Even the energetic English numbered a mere 2,400 in Virginia and 1,400 in New England by 1630. Why, therefore, did the Native Americans east of the Appalachians, who numbered over
(20) 400,000 in 1600, not overwhelm the starving white beachheads on the Atlantic seaboard?

The reasons are easily stated. First, Europeans concentrated around fortified villages supported by a monopoly of sea power and firearms. To be sure,
(25) Indians quickly developed a lust for muskets, which they used to hunt game and rival tribes. But guns only made the Native Americans dependent on Europeans for ammunition, powder, and repair of weapons, while causing them to lose their skill with
(30) a weapon actually better suited to sylvan conflict, the bow. One frontier war ended in 1641 when the proud Iroquois sued for peace to regain access to French firearms. Second, colonists pinned to the coasts and rivers had more incentive to fight
(35) tenaciously once there were too many of them to evacuate over a summer. Indians, by contrast, had the option to retreat inland rather than fight desperate wars with the white men. Third, the English drew on inexhaustible reinforcements from
(40) a single national "tribe," whereas the Indians strewn across a thousand-mile front were more crippled by tribal feuds than the Scots and Irish.

Fourth and most important were the "invisible armies" fighting on the Europeans' behalf:
(45) infectious diseases such as influenza, chickenpox, smallpox, measles, and plague against which Native Americans had no genetic immunity. Upward of 90 percent of the Algonquin, Wampanoag, Massachusetts, and Pawtucket tribes on the New
(50) England coast were carried off in the years just before the Pilgrims arrived. Between 50 and 75 percent of the Hurons, Iroquois, and Mohawks in the eastern Great Lakes died in the 1630s and 1640s. Perhaps 90 percent of the Powhatan,
(55) Susquehannock, and other tribes around Chesapeake Bay disappeared by 1670. The first English outposts on the Connecticut River were saved when "it pleased God to visit these Indians with a great sickness and such mortality that of a
(60) thousand, above nine hundred and a half of them died, and many of them did rot above ground for want of burial." Such mortality occurred whenever Native Americans first met Europeans, its effects magnified by the Indians' own low fertility (resulting
(65) in part from their habit of breast-feeding infants for three or four years) and the high death rate of children. Early Virginia colonists also knew wholesale death from malaria, saline poisoning, and other maladies of the tidewater, while their
(70) birth rate was also tiny due to the sheer lack of females. But Virginians soon moved out of the fetid estuaries while being supplemented by an average of 8,500 newcomers per year in the 1630s and 1640s. In comparatively healthy New England the Puritan
(75) families were not only reinforced, but reproduced at a rate close to the biological maximum. As a result, English colonists may have outnumbered all of the eastern Indians combined as early as 1690.

Look for the Main Point

Always look for the main point and structure of the passage. As you read the passage, try to focus on what point the author is trying to make and ask yourself questions such as, "What is the main idea that the author is trying to convey?"; "What is the author's main point?"; or "What is the author's main purpose in writing the passage?"

---

1. Which of the following best states the main point of the passage?

   A. Although the Native Americans greatly outnumbered the European settlers, the settlers had several advantages.

   B. The low fertility and high child mortality rates of Native Americans were instrumental in ensuring that they would be unsuccessful opposing the European settlers.

   C. The European settlers treated Native Americans with suspicion and hostility.

   D. By the end of the 17th century, there were more English colonists than Native Americans in New England.

The point of the entire passage is to enumerate the advantages of the European settlers over the Native Americans, so Choice A is the best answer. Both choices B and D are secondary to the main point. Choice C is an issue not addressed in the passage. The correct answer is **A.**

Look for Supporting Details

Make sure that your answer is supported by the passage. Your answer choice must be supported by information either stated or implied in the passage. Eliminate choices that the passage does not support.

---

2. It can be reasonably inferred from the third paragraph that

   F. the general health of the European settlers was significantly better than the health of the Native Americans.

   G. hygiene was important in saving the settlers lives during the spread of infectious diseases.

   H. European settlers brought many diseases to Native Americans.

   J. the fertility rate in Virginia was lower than in the other colonies.

The third paragraph states that the Native Americans had "no genetic immunity" to the diseases that decimated their numbers, and in lines 62–63 the point is made that high mortality rates of the Native Americans occurred "whenever Native Americans first met Europeans." The inference that can be made is Choice H, that the Europeans brought the diseases with them to the new country. Nothing in the passage implies choices F, G, or J. The correct answer is **H.**

---

3. According to the passage, Native Americans were not as able to reinforce their forces as English settlers were because of

   A. tribal conflicts.

   B. the inability to provide muskets.

   C. low birth rates.

   D. a lack of resources.

See lines 40–42. Unlike the English, Native Americans were made up of many tribes strewn over a large area, and these tribes often feuded, making reinforcements against the settlers difficult. Choice C is irrelevant in the context of the question. Choices B and D are not indicated as reasons for the Native Americans' inability to provide reinforcements. The correct answer is **A.**

Draw Generalizations or Conclusions

To make a generalization or draw a conclusion, you must always support your answer with information provided in the passage. If you are struggling with this type of question, plug in each answer choice to see which answer best fits the intended overall message of the passage. The word *best* is a relative term, so you may need to sort through the degrees of best before your exam (good, better, and best). Although there may be more than one good choice, the answer is always the *best* choice.

4. From information in the first paragraph, which of the following generalizations can be made about the early European settlements in North America?

   F. The search for religious freedom was the dominant motivation of the early settlers.
   G. Most of the locations chosen by the settlers were desirable because they were away from the dominant Native American tribes.
   H. Before the early settlers arrived in North America, Native Americans were free of most diseases.
   J. The relatively small number of early settlements in North America can be attributed largely to internal issues of the European countries.

The author states that most of the reasons can be attributed to events or issues in the home countries. Choice J is the best answer. Although religion was a motivation, the generalization that it was the *dominant* motivation cannot be made from the first paragraph (Choice F). Choice H is not addressed at all in the first paragraph, and Choice G is a generalization not made anywhere in the passage. The correct answer is **J**.

Look for the Mood of the Passage

Understand the passage's meaning and author's possible reason for using certain words or phrases in the passage. As you read, note the tone of the passage or portions of the passage. The structure and the words that the author uses to describe events, people, or places will help give you an understanding of how the author wants you to feel or think.

5. In the quotation in lines 58–62, the speaker implies all of the following EXCEPT

   A. the settlers believed that God was on their side.
   B. disease aided the settlers significantly by reducing the numbers of Native Americans.
   C. the settlers recognized that disease was a potent weapon.
   D. the fact that many Native American bodies remained unburied caused the Europeans great regret.

Notice the word "EXCEPT" in the question. Words such as EXCEPT or NOT should lead you to the answer choice that makes a point that is not in the passage, or that is contradicted by the *tone* of the passage. In the quotation cited, Choices A, B, and C are all implied. Although the quotation notes that many bodies "rotted above the ground," the words *reflect* no regret. On the contrary, the speaker is *relieved* that it "pleased God" to visit the disease on the Native Americans. The correct answer is **D**.

Look for the Sequence of Ideas

Use an elimination strategy to arrive at the correct answer. Watch for key words in the answer choices to help you find the main point that will lead you to the sequence of ideas. Notice that some incorrect choices are too general, too specific, irrelevant, off topic, or they contradict information given in the passage. Your answer must follow a logical sequence of ideas presented in the passage.

> **6.** According to the passage, in 1641 the Iroquois sought peace with the French because
>
>   **F.**   they feared French weaponry.
>   **G.**   they wanted to regain access to French weapons.
>   **H.**   disease had greatly reduced the numbers of their warriors.
>   **J.**   they wanted allies against the English settlers.

The Iroquois' motivation, according to the passage, was to "regain access to French firearms" (lines 32–33). Choice G is, therefore, the best answer. Choice F may or may not be true, but the passage does not make this point. There is also no evidence to support either choices H or J as the reason the Iroquois sought peace with the French in 1641. The correct answer is **G.**

Look for Meaning of Words or Phrases

This type of question tests your skills and knowledge of word meanings. To perform well, pay close attention to the word or phrase in the context of the sentence. Use the context to figure out the meaning of words, even if you're unfamiliar with them. Sometimes you will need to read the sentence just before and after where the word is presented to understand the word's association to the surrounding text. You will need to think logically and to understand subtle differences in word choices to create a coherent, meaningful passage.

> **7.** From the context of the passage, *sylvan* (line 30) most likely means
>
>   **A.**   characterized by small towns rather than large settlements.
>   **B.**   naturally beautiful.
>   **C.**   located in the woods or forests.
>   **D.**   peaceful and untouched by visitors.

Take advantage of the line numbers. All passages show the line numbering, which gives you the advantage of being able to quickly spot where the information is located. After you spot the location, be sure to read the line(s) before and after the lines mentioned, enabling you to better choose the correct answer to the question.

The best definition for *sylvan* is Choice C. As it is used in this particular context, *sylvan* should contrast with the "fortified villages" in line 23. Looking at the answers that are offered, choices B and D can be eliminated because "naturally beautiful" or "peaceful" would not necessarily make a particular area more suitable for the use of a bow as a weapon. No contrast in the passage is made between small towns and large settlements. The best definition would describe areas that the Indians would be most familiar with in their hunting—woods or forests. The correct answer is **C.**

Three "Last Resort" Strategies

If you're having real trouble with a passage or simply running out of time, try one of these "last resort" strategies.

1. **Skip a difficult passage.** You could skip a difficult passage entirely, along with the questions based on it, and come back to it later. Remember that you can return to those questions only while you're working in the Reading portion of the ACT. If you use this strategy, take care to mark your answers in the correct spaces on the answer sheet when you skip a group of questions.

2. **Skim the passage.** If you're running out of time, you might want to skim the passage and then answer the questions—referring back to the passage when necessary.

3. **Quickly scan questions and spots in the passage.** For this last-resort method, if questions on a passage refer to line numbers and you have only a few minutes left (and haven't yet read the passage), simply read the questions that refer to specific lines in the passage and read only those specific lines in the passage to try to answer the question. This final strategy may help you at least eliminate some answer choices and add one or two right answers to your score. And always remember to put down at least a guess answer for all questions.

Vocabulary Resources

Research has proven that vocabulary growth correlates with increased academic performance. An increased vocabulary can give you a greater sense of accomplishment and a greater ability to answer questions on the ACT. As you increase your vocabulary skills, you are increasing your odds of building a better score. Searching for words to study and their definitions may feel like looking for a needle in a haystack, but if you follow the word attack skills outlined in this section, you will find your vocabulary gradually expanding.

On the ACT, you will be required to know the obvious and subtle differences in words and their meanings in the context of a sentence or passage. Words are always associated with meanings, and with more than 500,000 words in the English language, even famous writers have understood the difficulty of building a rich vocabulary. While some words are used daily, others are used infrequently.

The purpose of this section is to give you a distinct learning advantage. This is done by introducing several approaches to improve your vocabulary and increase your knowledge of word meanings. The principles and methods of vocabulary improvement included in this section have been successfully researched and developed over many years. Consider using any combination of the suggested approaches presented in this section. These vocabulary development models are based on

- Memory-improvement mnemonic devices that teach you how to store, retrieve, and recall words.
- Power vocabulary words that build a solid base of commonly used words.
- Word parts: prefixes, roots, and suffixes that help you decipher the meaning of words by breaking them down into their base parts.

In studying new vocabulary words, consider the amount of time you spend memorizing words. Remember, there is no guarantee that the words you study will actually appear on the ACT. Do not let this part of the test interfere with your overall test preparation and study time. Keep in mind that vocabulary and word meanings are just a part of the overall Reading Test.

Memory Improvement

Mnemonic devices help you store, retrieve, and recall words and phrases. The principles and methods of memory improvement using mnemonics have been successfully researched and developed for many years. Memory improvement is based on techniques that integrate your physical senses (seeing, hearing, and touching) with schematic brain structures. In other words, if you can develop an association in your physical body, your brain tends to remember facts and details. You already perform this function all the time when you use your memory to recall events from your past. The three principles of memory improvement are *visual, auditory,* and *kinesthetic.*

Techniques to Improve Your Memory

| Visual encoding | The most successful mnemonic device is *visually encoding* information so that you can *associate* a word with a mental picture to form a new schematic representation of the word. As you associate a word with a mental picture, the two things communicate with one another to form *one mental representation* of the word. For example, if memorizing the word "quandary," meaning dilemma or entanglement, you might visualize two pieces of rope tied together (entangled). The trick is to form a visual image that has as much detail and clarity as possible. The more details in your visual image, the greater the possibility you will remember the word. Memory experts also report that associating bizarre visual pictures with words helps in memory retention. For example, you might visualize two snakes entangled together to remember the meaning of "quandary." Creating a visual picture is unique to your learning style. Trust whatever visual picture comes to mind. Just keep in mind that creating mental pictures has a strong link to memory improvement.

After you have mastered visual encoding, you can expand this method by *chunking* words together that have synonymous word meanings. Begin by looking up all related words for your new word. Let us say you have successfully created a visual representation for the word "quandary." Now that you know this meaning, you can chunk other synonymous words with the same visual picture. So instead of associating just one word, you can expand your vocabulary to four new related words: "quandary," "dilemma," "entanglement," and "predicament."

The process of association is especially helpful to students who are visual learners. You know you are a visual learner if you find you do not comprehend class material that was not given to you in written form (books, handouts, computer, or chalkboard). Comments from students who are visual learners typically include, "I couldn't understand what the teacher was talking about until he or she wrote it or projected it on the board." |
|---|---|
| Auditory | Another successful strategy is to use *rhymes* to trigger your auditory memory. As you associate a new word with a rhymed word, you are creating a mental representation that will aid in your memory recall. For example, the word "quandary" rhymes with "laundry." You might make up a simple phrase to help you remember, such as "It's such a quandary when I wash the laundry."

These types of word-study strategies should help you with difficult words. Try this method to see if it works for you. It may sound childish, but it works for many test-takers. This technique works especially well if you are an auditory learner, meaning that you need to repeat words or phrases to yourself before they sink in. Saying words out loud is especially helpful for auditory learners. |
| Writing (kinesthetic) | Writing is a kinesthetic action that boosts cognitive brain structures. The physical psychomotor action of writing down words is communicated through neurons to the brain to help you remember what is being written. This technique helps almost everyone. When you come across an unfamiliar word, write it down, along with its meaning. Use index cards to make flash cards to carry with you. Print the word on one side of the card and the definition on the other side of the card. This is an effective way to gain independent practice and differentiate between those words and definitions that need further memorization. The kinesthetic process of writing helps imprint words into your explicit memory. |

Power Vocabulary Words

The best way to expand your vocabulary is to read regularly. Read newspaper articles, magazines, journals, Internet news, and books. As mentioned previously, when you come across an unfamiliar word, write it down on a flash card or in a vocabulary journal. Try to read material from a wide variety of subject areas to help you with the different topics on the ACT. Repeated exposure to new words is a great tool to develop your vocabulary.

When you come across new words, try to use the words in your personal vocabulary every day and always remember to use words in context to derive the meaning of a word in question. Words on the Reading Test are always presented in the context of a sentence or a paragraph. As an example, consider the meaning of the following words in context to the phrase in which they appear. Notice that the same words have different meanings. "A farmer can *produce produce* for harvesting," "The soldier was *deserted* in the *desert*," "He was too *close* to the window to *close* the door," "I decided to *present* her with a *present* on her birthday." There are hundreds of other examples that could be used here, but the point is for you to always learn the *meaning* of words so that you can apply the words to the context of the sentence or passage.

A variety of study materials are available that list high-powered ACT vocabulary words. We recommend *The World of Words: Vocabulary for College Students* (2004) by Margaret Richek; *Name That Movie! A Painless Vocabulary Builder* (2011) by Brian Leaf; *100 Words Every High School Graduate Should Know* (2003) by the editors of *American Heritage Dictionary*; or *The Wizard of Oz Vocabulary Builder* (2003) by Mark Phillips. Some books use vocabulary lists within the context of a story or activity to help you remember the words. As you review these books, use the memory improvement techniques described in the previous section to help you remember new words.

Word Parts

When confronted with new or unusual words, use your knowledge of common word roots and prefixes to break the word down into its parts to help you understand subtle variations in words. Your knowledge of word parts can noticeably expand your ability to understand the general meaning of words.

English language developed (partially) from Latin and Greek origins, and *parts* of their words (prefixes, suffixes, and roots or stems) are shared with many languages. If you have studied other languages, you may have recognized a word or part of a word because of its similarity to a word in English. As a living language, English continues to grow daily, but the basic parts of words remain fairly consistent. One research study showed that when combining 20 prefixes and 14 root words, it is possible to learn as many as 100,000 new words.

The knowledge of word parts can dramatically improve your ability to decode, interpret, and comprehend ACT vocabulary. Most words can be broken down into their base words, and by knowing how to do this, you can skillfully make an educated guess about a word's actual meaning and, therefore, eliminate incorrect answer choices.

Prefixes

It is especially helpful to use prefixes to understand positive, negative, and neutral connotations of words. Knowing this, you can quickly assess the author's general *tone* of a reading passage. The following table contains commonly used positive and negative prefixes.

Positive and Negative Prefixes

Prefixes with Positive Connotations	Prefixes with Negative Connotations
ad- (to) ben- (well or good) con- (together) for- (front of) magni- (large, great) omni- (all, everywhere) pro- (forward, in favor of) super- (greater)	a- or an- (not or without) ab- (away from) anti-, contra-, contro-, counter- (against) de- (opposite of or away from) dis- (not or apart) dys- (bad or poor) hyper- (over or too much) hypo- (under or too little) in- (not), male- (ill) mis- or miso- (badly, wrong, hatred) of- (very), over- (extra) sub- (under or less than) un- (not)

Roots

Words are built from base words called *roots*. Root words are the second most important group of word parts, and learning these can help you pinpoint the exact meaning of the word. Unlike prefixes and suffixes, a root word is the core of a word that carries meaning. Words are made from root words and can be modified when adding a prefix at the beginning or a suffix at the end.

Suffixes

Suffixes may appear easier to remember than prefixes. Suffixes help to determine the word's part of speech. For example, the verb "establish" becomes a noun when adding the suffix "ment"—establishment. A suffix can also help determine the correct spelling of a word. The following table contains commonly used suffixes.

Common Suffixes

Suffix	Meaning	Examples
-able, -ible, -ble	able to; capable of being	viable — able to live edible — capable of being eaten
-acious, -cious	having the quality of	tenacious — holding firmly
-al	of; like	nocturnal — of the night
-ance, -ancy	the act of; a state of being	performance — the act of performing truancy — the act of being truant
-ant, -ent	one who	occupant — one who occupies
-ar, -ary	connected with; concerning	ocular — pertaining to the eye beneficiary — one who receives benefits
-ence	the act, fact, or quality of	existence — the quality of being
-er, -or	one who does	teacher — one who teaches
-ful	full of; having qualities of	fearful — full of fear masterful — having the qualities of a master
-il, -ile	pertaining to	civil — pertaining to citizens infantile — pertaining to infants
-ion	the act or condition of	correction — the act of correcting
-ism	the philosophy, act, or practice of	patriotism — support of one's country
-ist	one who does, makes, or is occupied with	artist — one who is occupied with art
-ity, -ty, -y	the state or character of	unity — the state of being one novelty — the quality of being novel or new
-ive	containing the nature of; giving or leaning toward	pensive — thoughtful
-less	without; lacking	heartless — cruel; without a heart
-logy	a kind of speaking; a study or science	eulogy — a speech or writing in praise of someone theology — the study of God and related matters
-ment	the act of; the state of	alignment — the act of aligning
-ness	the quality of	eagerness — the quality of being eager

Suffix	Meaning	Examples
-ory	having the nature of; a place or thing for	laudatory — showing praise laboratory — a place where work is done
-ous, -ose	full of; having	dangerous — full of danger verbose — wordy
-ship	the art or skill of; the state or quality of being	leadership — the ability to lead
-y	full of; somewhat; somewhat like	chilly — somewhat cold willowy — like a willow

Examples of Word Parts

Here are a few easy examples of how you can combine your knowledge of word parts to understand the meaning of a word.

- Let's look at the word "psychology." *Psych* is a root word meaning "the mind," and *ology* is a suffix meaning "the study of." Psychology is the study of the mind.
- "Biology" means the study of life. *Bio* is a root word meaning "life," and *ology* is a suffix meaning "the study of."

Now let's look at an example that incorporates all word parts:

> Wilson readily accepted the offer to run for governor of New Jersey because his position at Princeton University was becoming untenable.
>
> In the sentence above, what is the best meaning for *untenable*?
>
> **A.** Unlikely to last for years.
> **B.** Filled with considerably less tension.
> **C.** Difficult to maintain or continue.
> **D.** Filled with achievements that would appeal to voters.

Let's break "untenable" into word parts. The prefix *un* means not, the root word *ten* means to have, and *able* is a suffix that means worthiness, or an inclination toward a specified action or state. Therefore, the word untenable means unsustainable, or "difficult to maintain or continue," Choice C. Many of the answer choices may have appeared plausible, but after a careful look at word parts, you will see that the subtle differences in word meanings can make the difference between answering the question correctly and incorrectly. Notice the "attractive distractor" answer choices. Remember, it's important to look at *all* the answer choices before making your selection. Choice A appears plausible because at first glance "unlikely," appears similar to "untenable," but there is no evidence in the word parts of "untenable" that points to "lasting for years." Choice B is also plausible, because "less ten . . ." is similar to *unten . . .*, but there is no part of "untenable" that refers to tension. Choice D does not fit the context of the sentence. The skilled test-taker should make the connection to the word parts *un, ten,* and *able*. The correct answer is **C.**

Science Passage Categories

Passage Type	Description	Number of Items	Percentage
Data Representations	Information summarizing the results of a research study or experiment is presented. You will be asked to understand figures, read graphs, interpret scatter plots, and analyze information in tables. You may need to find correlations among items both *within* tables, graphs, and figures and *between* them. Familiarity with terms such as *total, average, dependent, independent, experimental,* and *control* are useful.	15	38%
Research Summaries	Descriptions of one or more experiments are presented. You will be asked questions related to the design of experiments and the interpretation of the results. You may need to find correlations between experiments and the data obtained from them. Just as with the Data Representation questions, familiarity with terms such as *total, average, dependent, independent, experimental,* and *control* are useful.	18	45%
Conflicting Viewpoints	Two or more conflicting hypotheses or views are presented. You will be asked to understand, analyze, and compare the alternative viewpoints or hypotheses. You will need to understand the underlying assumptions and the possible criticisms of each viewpoint or hypothesis.	7	17%
TOTAL		**40**	**100%**

Data Representation Passage Type

There are usually three Data Representation passages on the ACT Science Test. Each passage is typically followed by five questions. You are tested on your ability to read graphs, tables, or illustrations. Since you are frequently asked how two or more variables are related, you need to quickly determine what variables are measured, the units of measurement, and how one variable relates to another. Sometimes, you may be asked to predict where a data point will lie on a graph based on the given information. This type of passage requires the least amount of reading, so it is a good idea to do all passages of this type first.

Practice Data Representation

Table 1 shows the total weight of air pollutants for the entire United States during a recent year. The data are cross-tabulated according to both the type of pollutant and source of the material. The quantities in the chart represent millions of tons per year.

Table 1

Pollutant	Cars and Trucks	Electric Plants	Industrial Plants	Waste Disposal
Carbon monoxide	67	1	2	2
Sulfur oxides	1	14	9	1
Hydrocarbons	12	1	5	1
Nitrogen oxides	7	3	2	1
Particles	1	4	6	1
Total	88	23	24	6

1. The environmental issue referred to as "acid rain" is caused by sulfur oxide pollution. On the basis of the data presented in Table 1, which source is the major contributor to the acid rain issue?

    A. Cars and trucks
    B. Electric plants
    C. Industrial plants
    D. Waste disposal

You should first focus on understanding what information is given. You're given a table summarizing research on air pollution and asked to answer an interpretive question. Examine the table carefully to comprehend how it organizes the information. In this case, the rows show the various pollutants, and the columns display the various sources of the pollution.

The question asks about the acid rain issue, which it attributes to sulfur oxides. In the second row, the largest quantity is 14, so electric plants are the main contributors to the acid rain issue. Remember to begin by examining the table or figure to see how it organizes the information. The correct answer is Choice **B**.

2. Based on the data presented in Table 1, which of the following sources contributes the most carbon monoxide pollutant to the atmosphere?

    F. Cars and trucks
    G. Electric plants
    H. Industrial plants
    J. Waste disposal

Don't memorize the information; refer to the table or graph for each question. Table 1 indicates that cars and trucks contribute the most carbon monoxide to the atmosphere. Therefore, the correct answer is Choice **F**.

3. The data in Table 1 support which of the following combinations of pollutants as the greatest emissions problem at industrial plants?

    A. Hydrocarbons and particles
    B. Sulfur oxides and hydrocarbons
    C. Sulfur oxides and carbon monoxide
    D. Particles and sulfur oxides

Read tables, charts, and graphs carefully, looking for high points, low points, changes, and trends. Be able to work with the information given. In this case, you need to find the two highest numbers in the Industrial Plants column and then check to be sure that the combination is represented in the answer choices. Those numbers here are 9 and 6, which represent sulfur oxides and particles, respectively. The sum of these pollutants is 15 out of a total of 24, a high ratio. Therefore, the correct answer is Choice **D**.

4. An environmental regulatory agency decides on the basis of the data presented to implement some tough legislation to combat pollution. Based on the information presented in Table 1, which of the following hypothetical regulations, if passed, would be most likely to have the greatest impact on air pollution in the long run?

    F. A law requiring electric plants to be fined for sulfur oxide emissions
    G. A law requiring automobile owners to be fined for carbon monoxide emissions
    H. A law requiring car manufacturers to make cars that do not emit carbon monoxide
    J. A law requiring electric and industrial plants to be fined for all emissions

Certain questions require you to reason, or draw conclusions, from the information given. According to the data presented, carbon monoxide from cars and trucks is the single greatest contributor to air pollution. Regulation designed to reduce this particular source would, therefore, present the greatest benefit over the long run. Note also that three of the pieces of legislation involve a monetary penalty for emissions. But there is no indication of the amount of such fines or whether they would be punitive enough to ensure compliance. Choice H, however, directly mandates change to existing technology that is causing much of the problem. The correct answer is Choice **H**.

---

5. The following description is of a particular class of pollutants: "Air Pollutant *X* is emitted mainly from industrial, institutional, utility, and apartment furnaces and boilers, as well as from petroleum refineries, smelters, paper mills, and chemical plants. It is the major source of smog and can aggravate upper-respiratory disorders and cause eye and throat irritation." Based on this description and the information presented in Table 1, Air Pollutant *X* is most likely

    A. carbon monoxide.
    B. sulfur oxides.
    C. hydrocarbons.
    D. nitrogen oxides.

In general, for any graphically presented data, you should review headings, scales, factors, and/or any descriptive information given, noting the correlations between factors, items, or variables. According to the information given in Table 1, sulfur oxides are produced mainly in industrial contexts. Since the information in the question also involves primarily industrial sources of pollution, you can determine that Pollutant *X* is *most likely* sulfur oxides. The correct answer is Choice **B**.

Research Summary Passage Type

There are usually three Research Summary passages on the ACT Science Test. Each passage is typically followed by six questions. You are tested on your ability to understand one or more related experiments or studies—that is, the experiment's objective, the experimental design, and the results of the experiment. Familiarity with the scientific method is essential. Review it if you need a refresher. This type of passage may also include graphs, tables, or illustrations. These passages require more reading than the Data Representation passages.

Practice Research Summary

To investigate whether evaporation could cause a liquid to rise within a tube, a researcher placed an open glass tube in a large beaker filled with mercury. Water was then poured slowly into the tube until it was filled. Notice in Figure 1 that the weight of the water displaced the mercury in the tube slightly below its level in the beaker.

Figure 1

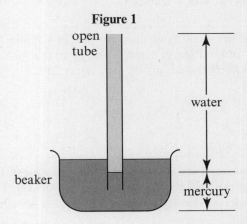

The researcher then fastened a permeable plastic membrane across the top of the tube and turned on a heat lamp to begin evaporating water through the permeable membrane. The mercury slowly rose several inches within the glass tube (see Figure 2).

Figure 2

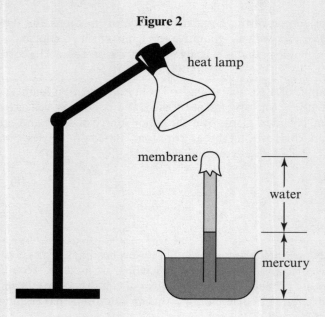

6. The rate at which the mercury rises in the tube could be accelerated by

    F.   inserting a smaller bulb in the lamp.
    G. substituting alcohol for the water.
    H. using a glass tube of smaller diameter.
    J.   using a larger beaker and more mercury.

Here you're given a detailed description of an experiment. For most of the questions in the research summary format, it's essential that you understand the reason the experiment was conducted. The first sentence of the passage usually states the purpose, so return and reread that sentence. The purpose of the experiment is to "investigate whether evaporation could cause a liquid to rise within a tube."

This question asks how one could get the mercury to rise faster. Since you know that evaporation causes the rise, to increase the rate of rising, you must increase the rate of evaporation. The correct answer is Choice G because alcohol evaporates much faster than water. Notice how an understanding of the purpose of the experiment aided in answering the question. The correct answer is Choice **G.**

7. "Density" is a measurement of the quantity of mass per unit of volume. Based on the information in the description of the experiment and in Figures 1 and 2, and given that water has a density of 1.0 at 20°C, which of the following is most likely the density of mercury at 20°C?

    A.   0.35
    B.   1.35
    C.   1.00
    D.   13.50

Pay particular attention to the methods used and the outcome of an experiment. Figure 1 indicates that when water is poured into the tube, it doesn't mix with the mercury already in the beaker. This fact suggests that the density of mercury is significantly greater than the density of water. The correct answer is Choice **D.**

8. Based on the design of the study, it can be concluded that a "liquid" is matter that has

    F.   molecules that maintain a fixed position, giving the substance a definite shape.

    G.   a definite volume but no shape, allowing it to conform to the shape of its container.

    H.   no fixed shape or volume because its molecules are always in motion.

    J.   a form that starts out as a solid and then changes shape with heat.

You should be able to draw conclusions from the study or experiment. Mercury and water are both liquids. According to the figures in the sample passage, it's apparent that the volume of mercury used in the experiment conformed to the shape of the beaker, and the volume of water used conformed to the shape of the tube. The correct answer is Choice **G.**

9. At 20°C, the densities ($\times 10^3$ kilograms/meter^3) of ethyl alcohol, chloroform, and water are 0.79, 1.49, and 1.00, respectively. Which of the following combinations and placements of liquids would best reproduce the results of the experiment described in the passage?

    A.   Water in the beaker, chloroform in the open tube

    B.   Alcohol in the beaker, water in the open tube

    C.   Water in the beaker, ethyl alcohol in the open tube

    D.   Alcohol in the beaker, chloroform in the open tube

You should always pay attention to both the design of the experiment and the reasons for the results. In the original experiment, the density of the liquid in the beaker (mercury) is higher than that of the liquid in the tube (water). To get the same experimental results with new liquids, these relative densities must be replicated—a denser liquid should be placed in the beaker, and a less dense liquid should be placed in the tube. Water has a higher density than that of ethyl alcohol, so it should be placed in the beaker. The correct answer is Choice **C.**

10. Solids, liquids, and gases have physical properties that can be observed and described as behaviors under certain given conditions. From the information provided, it can be hypothesized that

    F.   density is a property that does not depend on the amount of matter being observed.

    G.   density is a property that does depend on the amount of matter being observed.

    H.   evaporation rate is a property that is related to the boiling point of liquid matter.

    J.   evaporation rate is a property that is related to the melting point of solid matter.

Be aware of information or hypotheses not directly stated in the data that *can* or *cannot* be drawn from the experiment. This experiment doesn't specify quantities (volumes) of the matter (liquids) used. But density is an important property of the matter in this study. Melting points and boiling points are properties that are not discussed in the passage text, and nothing can be hypothesized about them from the information given or the structure of the experiment. The correct answer is Choice **F.**

11. Based on the information given, if the researcher had designed the experiment so that he placed water in the beaker and slowly continued to pour mercury into the tube, his experiment would have become impossible to complete because

    A.   the water would have evaporated before the mercury filled the tube.

    B.   the mercury would displace the water and no water would enter the tube.

    C.   the mercury would not penetrate the permeable membrane across the top of the tube.

    D.   the heat lamp could not generate enough heat to evaporate the water.

Notice conclusions that can be drawn from the design of the experiment, rather than just from the outcome of the experiment. The experiment could not have been completed because the mercury is much denser than the water, so the water would overflow the beaker and could not get into the tube. At that point, the experiment, as it stands, could not have been performed. The correct answer is Choice **B.**

Conflicting Viewpoints Passage Type

There is usually one Conflicting Viewpoint passage on the ACT Science Test. The passage is typically followed by seven questions. You are tested on your ability to answer questions about conflicting viewpoints on a scientific idea. You need to understand each viewpoint and how it agrees or disagrees with the other viewpoints. To keep your mind focused when reading the passage, read the questions first. Doing this is more important for the Conflicting Viewpoint passage than for any of the other passage types. This passage requires the most amount of reading, so it is a good idea to do the passage of this type last.

Practice Conflicting Viewpoints

What caused the extinction of the dinosaurs? Two differing views are presented in the following passage.

Scientist 1

Throughout the long Mesozoic era, hundreds of dinosaur species dominated over smaller animals. Some dinosaurs were meat eaters, and others ate only plants. Some lived in deserts, some in swamps. There were even dinosaurs swimming through the oceans and soaring through the skies. This extraordinarily successful group of reptiles all disappeared at the end of the Cretaceous period, 65 million years ago. Only a worldwide catastrophe could have simultaneously killed all dinosaurs in their diverse environmental niches (specific areas). The most probable cause of the mass extinction is a close encounter with a comet, which could have abruptly altered the earth's temperatures. Dinosaurs, like all reptiles, were cold-blooded animals and could not adapt to a great temperature change.

Scientist 2

It is almost certain that no single event killed all dinosaurs. Their record during the Mesozoic era is one of species continually evolving to new species; each old species is then said to have become extinct. The extinctions are not at all simultaneous. The early, egg-eating pelycosaurs disappeared in the Permian period. The largest dinosaur of all—Brachiosaurus—became extinct in the Jurassic. The ensuing record during the Cretaceous period is even richer and more complicated, with duck-billed hadrosaurs, predatory tyrannosaurs, and flying pterosaurs appearing and disappearing at various times. By the end of the Cretaceous, the last dinosaur species had vanished. The slow disappearance of the dinosaurs occurred as mammals evolved into more habitats. The last dinosaur and the last dinosaur egg were probably eaten by mammals.

---

12. A key point that would help settle the dispute about dinosaur extinction would be to know

    F.   whether cold-blooded animals could adapt to new temperatures slowly.

    G.   when the various dinosaur species disappeared.

    H.   whether a comet could cause a minor change of climate.

    J.   which environmental niches were occupied by dinosaurs.

You should begin by rereading the opening sentence of the passage to make sure you know the scientific issue in dispute. In this example, it's the cause of dinosaur extinction.

Then, try to perceive the main point or points of disagreement in the theories presented, since many of the questions cover these points. Try not to let the details of evidence keep you from recognizing the main points. **Circle or underline the main points of agreement and disagreement.**

In this sample passage, you should notice that Scientist 1 says that all dinosaurs were simultaneously killed, while Scientist 2 states that the different species became extinct at different times—the main point of disagreement between the two theories. You could better choose between the two theories if you definitely knew when the various dinosaur species disappeared. Understanding the main point or points of disagreement between the rival theories is your best help on the conflicting viewpoints format. The correct answer is Choice **G.**

13. One of the key differences between the views on extinction of Scientist 1 and Scientist 2 is that

    A. Scientist 1 credits sudden change; Scientist 2 credits gradual change.

    B. Scientist 1 credits environmental change; Scientist 2 credits killing by mammals.

    C. Scientist 1 credits thermal change; Scientist 2 credits deaths by natural causes.

    D. Scientist 1 credits an astronomical event; Scientist 2 credits a chemical event.

Focus on the *key* differences in the viewpoints. The perspective of Scientist 1 is that the extinctions happened suddenly, at the same time, as a result of an astronomical event. The perspective of Scientist 2 is that the extinctions happened throughout several geologic periods, spanning tens of millions of years. Choice **A** is the best answer. You might consider choosing Choice B, since Scientist 1 does suggest the astronomical event (the comet) caused an environmental change and since Scientist 2 does suggest *some* predation by mammals. It is not as good an answer as Choice A, however, because Scientist 2 doesn't necessarily suggest *only* predation as the reason for extinction. You might also consider Choice C to be a possibility, but the problem with this answer choice is that *both* scientists are speaking of deaths by "natural causes." A close encounter with a comet is just as "natural" as killing by mammals or extinction from some other environmental cause. Lastly, you might consider Choice D because Scientist 1 does suggest that a comet (an astronomical event) might have caused the extinction, however Scientist 2 does *not* credit a chemical event, so this is not the best answer.

14. Which of the following statements would most likely be made by Scientist 2 as an argument against the position taken by Scientist 1?

    F. Dinosaurs could not adapt to the sudden worldwide changes to the environment.

    G. Dinosaurs were so successful in all ecosystems that they out-competed themselves.

    H. There is no evidence for a single astronomical event at the end of the Jurassic period.

    J. There is no evidence for a single astronomical event at the end of the Cretaceous period.

Analyze each viewpoint and the argument given. Scientist 2 believes the extinctions happened gradually over long periods of time. Scientist 1 believes the extinctions happened suddenly, as a (probable) result of climate change due to an encounter with a comet. Scientist 2 would most likely cite the facts that currently known data supply. Choice F would strengthen the argument of Scientist 1, not weaken it. Choice G uses a circular logic and is not consistent with Scientist 2's argument that dinosaurs may have been outcompeted by mammals. Choice H is not relevant because the comet is hypothesized to have struck at the end of the Cretaceous period, not the Jurassic period. The correct answer is Choice **J.**

15. Which of the following lines of evidence, if true, would most seriously weaken the position of Scientist 1?

    A. Evidence that dinosaurs became extinct in different types of environments

    B. Evidence that dinosaurs became extinct in the same type of environment

    C. Evidence that species of dinosaurs became extinct in different geologic periods

    D. Evidence that all species of dinosaurs became extinct at the same time

Be aware of possible weaknesses in an argument. Scientist 1 believes the extinctions happened at generally the same time (at the end of the Cretaceous period). Evidence that dinosaurs became extinct at widely separated times (different periods) would weaken that position. Choice A is not the best answer because "types of environments" can refer to many factors, not only temperature. Choice D would strengthen the argument of Scientist 1, not weaken it. The correct answer is Choice **C.**

16. All of the following statements, if true, support the position of Scientist 2 EXCEPT:

    F. Brachiosaurs became extinct in the Jurassic period.

    G. Pelycosaurs became extinct in the Permian period.

    H. Encounters with comets can cause extreme temperature changes.

    J. Encounters with comets are uncommon on the earth.

Be aware of what might strengthen or support a viewpoint. Statements F and G contain evidence supporting the position of Scientist 2 that different dinosaurs died out at different times, so these answer choices can be eliminated. If true, the statement alleging that encounters with comets can cause extreme temperature changes would best support the position of Scientist 1 and take away from arguments made by Scientist 2. The correct answer is Choice **H**.

---

17. Recently, dinosaur extinction research has centered on a crater on the coast of the Yucatan Peninsula in Mexico. It is estimated that this crater could be the remnant of an impact crater that formed 65 million years ago. If true, this new research would lend support to the view of which scientist on dinosaur extinctions?

   A. Scientist 1
   B. Scientist 2
   C. Both Scientist 1 and Scientist 2
   D. Neither Scientist 1 nor Scientist 2

Notice how research supports or weakens an argument. Since Scientist 1 favors a belief that an encounter with a comet transformed the environment of the dinosaurs, the fact that this crater may be evidence of such an encounter would lend the most support to the position of Scientist 1. The correct answer is Choice **A**.

---

18. Current research on extinctions among mammals at the end of the Cretaceous period (65 million years ago) shows that only about 25 percent of the existing mammals became extinct then. If found to be true, this research would

   F. weaken the views of Scientist 1.
   G. undermine the views of Scientist 2.
   H. lend support to the views of Scientist 1.
   J. neither support nor undermine the views of either scientist.

Assess additional information given in a question. Since Scientist 1 believes that a comet encounter caused the extinctions of all the dinosaurs, it can be inferred that this scientist would expect this same event to have a negative impact on all other life as well. The fact that only 25 percent of the mammals died off is more supportive of the views of Scientist 2 than of the views of Scientist 1. The correct answer is Choice **F**.

Glossary of Science Terms

Absolute zero: The lowest possible temperature, equal to 0°K, –273°C, or –459°F.

Acid: A proton donor that yields hydrogen ions (H⁺) in a water solution, or an electron-pair acceptor that combines with an electron-pair donor or a base. Acids have a pH under 7 and commonly taste sour.

Adaptations: (Also called adaptive traits) The developed traits that make an organism especially suited to its environment.

Adrenaline: (Also called epinephrine) A hormone secreted by the adrenal medulla.

Algae: A very large and diverse group of simple plants, ranging from unicellular to multicellular forms. Most contain chlorophyll and are therefore photosynthetic.

The largest and most complex marine forms are called seaweeds.

Alkali metals: Members of the group of univalent metals whose hydroxides are alkalis, e.g., lithium, sodium, and potassium.

Alloy: A substance that is a mixture of two or more metals.

Amino acids: Organic compounds that are the building blocks of proteins; amino acids contain at least one amino group ($-NH_2$) and one carboxyl group (COOH).

Amphibians: A class of vertebrates capable of living both in water and on land. The larval forms have gills, and the adults have lungs; the class includes frogs and toads.

Angiosperms: The class of flowering plants, with seeds enclosed in fruits.

Antibiotic: A substance that destroys bacteria and other microorganisms or inhibits their growth.

Antibody: A substance produced by the body to combat the injurious effect of a foreign substance (antigen).

Arachnids: A class of arthropods with no antennae and four pairs of legs; includes spiders, scorpions, ticks, and mites.

Arthropods: The phylum of segmented invertebrates with jointed appendages and a chitinous exoskeleton; includes arachnids, crustaceans, and insects.

Asexual: Reproduction in one individual, without the union of gametes.

Asteroid: A minor planet or planetary fragment; most of the thousands of known asteroids are between the orbits of Mars and Jupiter.

Atmosphere: A layer of gases that surround the earth.

Atmospheric pressure: The force per unit area exerted onto the surface of the earth by the weight of the gases in the atmosphere.

Atom: The smallest component of an element that has all the characteristics of that element.

Atomic number: The number of protons in the nucleus of an atom of a given element; the different chemical elements have different atomic numbers.

Autotrophs: Organisms that are not dependent on other organisms for food and can produce their own food, usually using sunlight as energy and inorganic materials.

Bacteria: Unicellular organisms without a distinct nucleus and usually without chlorophyll.

Barometer: An instrument used to measure atmospheric pressure.

Basalt: A dark, dense igneous rock formed from lava.

Base: A proton acceptor that yields hydroxide ions (OH^-) in a water solution; or an electron-pair donor that combines with an acid (electron-pair acceptor). Bases have a pH over 7 and commonly taste bitter.

Biodiversity: The total number of types of species in a given area at a specific time.

Biome: Large ecological area primarily defined by dominant plant type, for example coniferous forest.

Boiling point: The temperature at which a liquid changes from a liquid to a vapor (gas): 212°F (100°C) for water at sea level.

Boyle's law: The volume of an ideal gas varies inversely with its pressure at constant temperature. First described in the 17th century, this rule is accurate under the relatively low pressures under which it was developed.

Calorie: The amount of heat (4.18400 joules) required to raise the temperature of 1 gram of water by 1°C.

Carbohydrates: Organic compounds that consist of carbon, hydrogen, and oxygen. These compounds are produced by photosynthetic plants and contain only carbon, hydrogen, and oxygen, usually in the ratio 1:2:1. They are a major energy source in the diet of animals.

Carbon cycle: The exchange of carbon atoms between living things and their environment.

Carbon dioxide: A colorless, noncombustible gas present in the atmosphere under normal conditions; CO_2 is formed during respiration.

Carbon monoxide (CO): A colorless, odorless, poisonous gas that results when fossil fuels are not fully combusted—that is, produced when carbon burns with insufficient air.

Carcinogen: A cancer-causing substance.

Carnivore: An animal or an insectivorous plant that feeds on flesh.

Catalyst: A substance that usually increases the rate of a reaction without being consumed in the process.

Cell: The basic structural and functional unit of all known living organisms. It is the smallest unit of life that is classified as a living thing and is often called the building block of life.

Cellular respiration: The process of converting glucose and oxygen into carbon dioxide and water, producing energy for cellular processes.

Cellulose: A chief constituent of the cell walls of plants, cellulose is the primary structural component of wood, cotton, hemp, and paper.

Centrifugal: Toward the perimeter (outward from the center).

Centripetal: Toward the center.

Chain reaction (physics): A self-sustaining reaction in which the fission of nuclei of one generation of particles produces particles that cause the fission of at least an equal number of nuclei of the succeeding generation.

Charles' law: The principle that, for relatively low pressures, the volume of an ideal gas at constant pressure varies directly with temperature.

Chemical energy: The energy stored in the bonds of atoms and molecules.

Chlorophyll: One of main pigments of plants used to capture light's energy used during photosynthesis.

Chloroplasts: The organelles in plant cells that capture the energy in light and convert carbon dioxide and water into glucose and oxygen.

Chromosome: An organized structure of DNA and protein that is the bearer of genetic information in a cell.

Climate: The prevailing weather patterns (temperature, precipitation, etc.) of a region averaged over an extended period of time (usually for at least 30 years).

Climate change: Any change in the state of the climate (e.g., temperature) that persists steadily for many years, decades, or longer.

Cloud: A collection of tiny water or ice droplets sufficiently numerous to be seen.

Coal: A rock composed of partly decayed and compressed plant material.

Coevolution: The simultaneous evolution of two organisms interacting with one another.

Coldblooded (ectothermic): An animal in which internal physiological processes minimally affect the animal's body temperature. Cold-blooded animals' body temperatures vary with their surroundings.

Combustion: Rapid oxidation that releases heat and light.

Comet: A diffuse celestial body that glows with a prominent tail when its orbit brings it near the sun. A comet consists of a central mass surrounded by an envelope of dust and gas.

Community: Multiple populations of different species in a given area.

Competition: A species interaction in which organisms vie for the same resources, resulting in one outperforming the other.

Compound: A pure chemical substance composed of two or more different chemical elements.

Concentration: The amount of a dissolved substance contained per unit of volume, especially a solution or mixture.

Condensation: The change in the phase of water from gas to liquid, usually in the form of droplets.

Conductor: A material that allows electricity, heat, or light to move through it with little resistance.

Conglomerate: A sedimentary rock consisting of pebbles cemented together.

Conservation of energy: Energy may be changed from one form to another, but it cannot be created or destroyed.

Constellation: An apparent group of stars.

Consumer: Any organism that cannot produce its own food and gets its energy and nutrients by feeding on other organisms.

Continental drift: The hypothesis of continents moving laterally from the motion of crustal plates.

Control: A scientific control is a standard of comparison designed to minimize the effects of variables other than the single independent variable. This increases the reliability of the results, through a comparison between control measurements and the other measurements.

Control variable: The one variable that must not be changed in a scientific experiment to allow the effects of the other variables to be measured.

Convection: Heat transfer in a gas or liquid by the circulation of molecules from one region to another.

Core: Dense center of the earth. It is subdivided into the solid inner and liquid outer cores.

Cross-pollination: The transfer of pollen from the flower of one plant to a flower on another plant that has a different genetic constitution.

Crust: Outermost layer of the earth and the surface on which people live (or the surface covered by ocean).

Crustaceans: The class of aquatic arthropods with gills and two pairs of antennae; includes lobsters, crabs, barnacles, and crayfish.

Cyclone: A low-pressure area around which winds blow counterclockwise in the Northern Hemisphere and clockwise in the Southern Hemisphere.

Cytoplasm: The substance of the cell outside the nucleus. It contains the cytosol, organelles, cytoskeleton, and various particles.

Decomposers: Bacteria or fungi that absorb nutrients from nonliving organic matter such as plant material, the waste of living organisms, and dead organisms.

Deforestation: The clearing of forests for other uses such as agriculture and development.

Delta: A triangular deposit of sediment at the mouth of a river.

Density: The mass per unit volume of a substance under specific pressure and temperature.

Diffusion: The movement of atoms or molecules from an area of high concentration to an area of low concentration.

Distillation: The process of purification in which an impure substance is heated to vapors, which are collected and condensed.

DNA: Deoxyribonucleic acid is a double-stranded nucleic acid that carries the genetic information for cell growth, division, and function. DNA contains the genes of an organism.

Dominant: One of two alternative genetic traits that is displayed in a heterozygous individual.

Doppler effect: The apparent change of pitch due to differing motions of the sounding source and a listener.

Eclipse: The obscuring of light from a celestial body by the passage of another body between it and the observer.

Ecology: The study of relations between organisms and their environment.

Electric current: The flow of electrons; a direct current (DC) flows in one direction, and an alternating current (AC) periodically reverses the direction of flow.

Electrical energy: Energy produced by the movement of electrons, typically moving through a wire. Usable electrical energy is produced by a generator in which coiled copper wire spins through the magnetic field, resulting in a flow of electrons.

Electrolysis: A chemical change brought about by an electric current; used to separate chemical elements.

Electromagnetic energy: Nonmechanical energy that travels in waves, including the entire electromagnetic spectrum, from low-energy radio waves, through microwaves, through ultraviolet waves, through the visible light spectrum (ROYGBIV), and through the ultraviolet waves, X-rays, and highest-energy gamma rays.

Electron: A subatomic particle with a negative charge.

Element: A pure chemical substance consisting of one type of atom.

Emissions: Common term for the gases discharged into the atmosphere from the burning of fossil fuels. The primary sources include coal and natural gas electric power plants and emissions from transportation (e.g., cars, trucks, buses, trains, and planes).

Endemic: Localized, or occurring at all times in only one location on the planet, commonly used to describe species that live in only one place. Also used to describe certain diseases or infectious agents.

Energy: The ability to perform work; kinetic energy is due to a body's motion, whereas potential energy is due to a body's position.

Enzyme: A protein that serves as an organic catalyst for metabolic reactions.

Epicenter: The point directly above the focus of an earthquake.

Equinox: The time when the sun crosses the ecliptic plane of the earth's equator, making day and night equal in length. It occurs twice a year.

Erosion: The process by which the surface of the earth is worn away by the action of wind or water.

Evaporation: Phase change of liquid or solid to gas (vapor).

Evolution: The change of a population's genetic makeup through generations via mutations, natural selection, and genetic drift.

Exoskeleton: A hard, jointed case outside the fleshy tissues of an animal.

Exponential growth: When the rate of growth is proportional to the population size, the gross rate of population growth increases.

Extrusive: Igneous rock of volcanic origin.

Fault: A planar break in rock along which displacement has occurred.

Fertilization: The union of gametes to form a zygote.

Fission: The splitting of an atomic nucleus into several lighter nuclei accompanied by the release of energy.

Food chain: A simple path of energy that flows from a producer, such as a plant, to various consumers, such as deer and wolves.

Food web: Multiple, intertwined food chains in which energy from multiple producers flows though many levels of consumers and finally through the decomposers.

Fossil: Preserved remains or traces of animals, plants, and other organisms from a past geological age.

Fossil fuel: Energy sources formed by the decomposition of plants and animals that have been compressed and heated in the earth's crust for millions of years (also from hydrocarbon deposits); they include coal, crude oil, and natural gas.

Freezing point: The temperature at which a liquid changes to a solid.

Frequency: The number of occurrences of a recurrent repeating event per unit time.

Freshwater: Naturally occurring water on the earth's surface that is low in concentrations of dissolved salts and other dissolved particles; freshwater is primarily found in glaciers, ice sheets, and ice caps, with a relatively small amount found in groundwater, ponds, lakes, rivers, and streams.

Front: The boundary between two air masses of different temperature; a common site for cloud formation and precipitation.

Fungi: Plants that lack chlorophyll; molds, mushrooms, and yeasts (usually filamentous with a chitinous cell wall and produce spores).

Fusion: Nuclear fusion is the union of atomic nuclei to form a heavier nucleus.

Galaxy: An astronomical system composed of billions of stars; galaxies are classified as spiral, elliptical, and irregular.

Gamete: A sex cell; an egg cell or sperm cell.

Gene: Any region of a chromosome that can be transcribed by the cell into a specific protein sequence.

Genetic engineering: Also called genetic modification, the creation of new organisims by changing segments of DNA.

Genetically modified organisms (GMOs): Organisms that have altered DNA as a result of genetic engineering.

Geothermal energy: Geothermal energy of hot underground rock formations, molten rock, and hot subterranean water is used to turn a water source into steam, which in turn drives turbines, creating electricity.

Germination: The stage in which a living thing starts to sprout, grow, and develop.

Global warming: The steady increase in the average temperature of the earth's surface that may be caused by man-made greenhouse emissions.

Glucose: A simple monosaccharide sugar, $C_6H_{12}O_6$. It is the major source of energy in organisms and also serves as an important metabolic substrate for most living things.

Gravitation: The force of attraction of two bodies because of their masses.

Green revolution: The advent of industrialized agriculture in the mid and late 20th century, when more effective farming techniques where combined with new methods of increasing crop production to create greater and more efficient output.

Greenhouse effect: A naturally occurring atmospheric effect trapping heat that would otherwise reflect into space, which helps warm the earth's surface temperature. Without the natural greenhouse effect, the earth's average temperature would be close to –15°C (5°F) instead of 15°C (59°F). In addition to this natural greenhouse effect, an anthropogenic greenhouse effect adds greenhouse gases to this reflective layer in the atmosphere, trapping additional heat energy and resulting in a further increase in temperature.

Greenhouse gases: Gases in the earth's troposphere that cause the greenhouse effect. Greenhouse gases include water vapor, carbon dioxide, methane, ozone, chlorofluorocarbons, nitrous oxide, carbon tetrachloride, halons, and others.

Groundwater: Water that is located beneath the ground's surface, located in the pores of soils and the fractures in rock formations.

Growth rate: The rate or speed at which the number of organisms in a population increases. Growth rate = (birth rate + immigration) – (death rate + emigration).

Gymnosperms: A class of vascular plants bearing seeds in cones.

Habitat: The environment in which an organism lives, including soil, vegetation, water supply, and many other factors.

Habitat destruction: The process of making a natural area uninhabitable for plants and animals, primarily as a result of human activities, usually by harvesting the habitat's natural resources (mining, deforestation), by agriculture, or by urbanization.

Half-life: The time it takes for half of a sample of radioactive material to decay.

Heat: Energy transferred between two objects due to a temperature difference.

Herbivores: Plant-eating organisms.

Homology: The similarity of body structures of different organisms, due to common ancestry; the structures may not have the same function. A bat's wing is homologous to a squirrel's foreleg.

Hormone: A chemical released by a cell or a gland in one part of the body that sends out messages that affect cells in other parts of the organism.

Host: The organism being invaded by a parasite.

Humidity: A measure of the amount of moisture in the air.

Hydrocarbons: Compounds of carbon and hydrogen.

Hydrolysis: Chemical decomposition of a compound by reaction with water.

Hypothesis: A proposed explanation for a phenomenon. For a hypothesis to be a scientific hypothesis, scientific method requires that one can test it.

Igneous rock: Rock formed from cooling magma or other volcanic action.

Inertia: The ability of a body to resist acceleration and continue at rest or moving with uniform velocity.

Infrared radiation: Electromagnetic radiation with longer wavelengths than those of visible light.

Inner core: Solid part of the earth's core that is mainly made up of nickel and iron.

Insulator: A substance that commonly does not conduct heat or electrical energy.

Intrusive: Igneous rock crystallized beneath the surface of the earth.

Ion: An atom or molecule in which the total number of electrons is not equal to the total number of protons, giving it a net positive or negative electrical charge.

Isotope: The version of an element that has atoms with the same number of protons but different number of neutrons.

Karst: Pitted topography due to solution of limestone.

Kinetic energy: A form of mechanical energy, kinetic energy is the energy possessed by a moving object.

Laterite: Iron-rich soil caused by tropical weathering.

Latitude: A measurement of distance from the equator, usually measured in angular degrees. The equator is 0°, the North Pole is 90° N, and the South Pole is 90° S.

Lava: Molten fluid rock extruded from a volcano or volcanic vent.

Laws of thermodynamics: Describe the transport of heat and work in the thermodynamic processes. The first law of thermodynamics states that energy is neither created nor destroyed but can change forms. The second law of thermodynamics states that in any conversion of heat energy into useful work, some of the initial energy is lost.

Light-year: The distance light travels in a vacuum in one mean solar year, about 5.9×10^{12} miles.

Limestone: Sedimentary rock composed predominantly of calcium carbonate.

Lithification: The consolidation of loose sediment via compaction or cementation.

Litmus: Paper that turns red in acid and blue in alkaline solution.

Logistic growth curve: Represents a population that grows exponentially and then levels off as it reaches environmental carrying capacity.

Longitude: The east/west location on the earth in relationship to the Prime Meridian, which runs from the poles through Greenwich, England, and is usually measured in degrees from 0° to 180°. The longitude lines are often referred to as meridian lines.

Magma: Molten rock beneath or within the earth's crust (from which igneous rock is formed).

Mammals: A class of warmblooded vertebrates, which possess hair and feed their young milk by means of mammary glands.

Mantle: The zone of the earth between the core and the crust. The mantle is 1800 miles or 2900 km thick.

Mass: The quantity of matter; the measure of inertia as determined from an object's weight or from Newton's second law of motion.

Mechanical energy: Energy possessed by moving objects (kinetic) or energy stored in objects by tension or position (potential).

Meiosis: The mode of cell division that produces gametes, each with one half the number of chromosomes of the parent cell.

Melting point: The temperature at which a solid substance changes to a liquid state (melts or fuses).

Mesosphere: The third layer of the earth's atmosphere.

Metamorphic: Rock formed by the transformation, under high temperature and pressure, of older sedimentary or igneous rock.

Metamorphic rock: Rock type formed under extreme heat and pressure, usually deep underground.

Meteor: A meteoroid that has entered the earth's atmosphere. The term may also refer to the streak of light produced by the passage of an interplanetary particle, such as a meteoroid, through the earth's atmosphere.

Meteorite: A rock from interplanetary space found on the earth's surface. A fallen meteoroid.

Methane: A naturally occurring gas with the chemical formula CH_4, methane is one of the major fossil fuels. Methane in the atmosphere is considered a greenhouse gas.

Milky Way: The spiral galaxy to which our solar system belongs.

Mineral: A naturally occurring inorganic chemical compound, having a definite composition, usually a distinct crystalline form.

Mitosis: Cell division with chromosome duplication, forming offspring cells with the same number of chromosomes as the parent cell; cell splitting.

Molecule: The smallest unit of a compound composed of two or more bonded atoms that retains the properties of that compound.

Momentum: The product of a mass and its velocity; the conservation of momentum is a fundamental law of nature.

Mutation: An inheritable change in a gene.

Mutualism: A species interaction in which all engaged species benefit (commonly confused with symbiosis).

Natural gas: A gaseous combustible fossil fuel used in the production of electricity and home uses (heating, water heaters, and cooking).

Natural selection: Process by which genetic traits that strengthen an organism's chance of survival and reproduction are passed on from generation to generation, eventually dominating less successful genetic traits.

Nebula: A cloud of gas or dust in interstellar space.

Neutron: A subatomic particle with no charge.

Nonnative species: Species that migrates into an ecosystem or is deliberately or accidentally introduced into an ecosystem by humans.

Nova: A star that suddenly becomes many times brighter than usual, then gradually fades to its original density.

Nuclear energy: The energy stored in the nuclei of atoms. It is released by the splitting (fission) or the joining (fusion) of atoms.

Nuclear fission: The process of an atom splitting into two smaller elements, releasing neutrons and heat energy. In nuclear power generation, fission is caused by bombarding unstable elements with neutrons.

Nuclear fusion: Process in which the atomic nuclei of two elements are forced together under high pressure releasing large amounts of energy.

Nucleus: The central part of an eukaryotic cell, containing the chromosomes (genetic material in the form of multiple-layer DNA molecules) and controlling cellular activities.

Organic compound: A compound with interconnected carbon atoms.

Osmosis: The movement of a liquid (solvent) through a semi-permeable membrane from an area of low solute concentration to an area of high solute concentration.

Oxidation: The addition of oxygen to a substance, forming oxide.

Paleontology: The science of fossil life.

Parasitism: A nonmutual relationship between organisms of different species where one organism, the parasite, benefits at the expense of the other, the host.

Pasteurization: The killing of microorganisms in foods, such as milk, by heating it to 145° for 30 minutes.

Petroleum: A liquid fuel from the transformation of plant and animal remains.

pH: Measures hydrogen ion concentrations on a scale of 1–14 with 7 being neutral, acidic substances ranging from 1–6.9 and alkaline (or basic) substances ranging from 7.1–14.

Photon: A particle of light energy.

Photosynthesis: The natural process in which plant chlorophyll converts carbon dioxide (CO_2) and water (H_2O) into glucose ($C_6H_{12}O_6$) and oxygen (O_2) in the presence of sunlight.

Phylum: A major group of animals or plants; the main division of a kingdom.

Pitch: The frequency of a sound wave.

Plutonic: Igneous rock that has crystallized beneath the earth's surface, as opposed to volcanic rock.

Pollination: Fertilization by the transfer of pollen from an anther to a stigma.

Population: A group of individuals of the same species living in the same area at the same time.

Population density: The number of individuals in a population per unit area.

Potential energy: A form of mechanical energy, potential energy is the energy stored in an object or system.

Precipitation: Condensation that is pulled to the earth's surface by gravity, usually in the form of rain, snow, sleet, or hail.

Predation: A species interaction in which one species hunts, captures, kills, and consumes another species.

Pressure: Measure of the force per unit area.

Prism: A triangular-based piece of glass used to disperse white light into a spectrum.

Producers: Autotrophic organisms that use solar energy (green plants) or chemical energy (cyanobacteria) to manufacture organic compounds needed for their energy and nutrition.

Protein: Any of a group of complex organic macromolecules that contain carbon, hydrogen, oxygen, nitrogen, and usually sulfur, and are composed of one or more chains of amino acids. Proteins are necessary for the proper functioning of organisms.

Proton: A subatomic particle with a positive charge.

Protoplasm: A general term for the fluid living matter of the cell, composed mainly of nucleic acids, proteins, lipids, carbohydrates, and inorganic salts.

Radioactivity: The spontaneous decay of an atomic nucleus with the emission of alpha particles, beta particles, or gamma rays.

Recessive: The one of two alternative genetic traits that is masked in a heterozygous individual.

Refraction: The bending of a light wave at the boundary between two substances.

Relativity: The principle that the laws of physics are the same for any two observers, whatever their relative motion.

Respiration: In an organism, the process that exchanges oxygen from the environment for carbon dioxide given off by cellular processes. On a cellular level, respiration refers to the conversion of nutrients into energy—a process that often uses oxygen and produces carbon dioxide as a waste product.

RNA (ribonucleic acid): A substance in the cell, similar in composition to a single-stranded form of DNA, that often acts as a template for protein production.

Sedimentary rock: Rock formed when sediment from erosion and weathering or biogenic decomposition is compressed and cemented together, or "lithified."

Solar: Energy coming from the sun.

Solstice: The date at which the sun is at its greatest distance from the celestial equator. The summer solstice is June 21st, and the winter solstice is December 21st.

Solvent: A substance that dissolves another to form a solution.

Speciation: The process through which new species are created, due to geographic, physiological, anatomical, or behavioral factors.

Species: A group of organisms that share particular characteristics and can breed and reproduce to create fertile offspring.

Spectrum: The visible spectrum is the band of colors from the dispersal of white light; the electromagnetic spectrum is the total range of frequencies for electromagnetic waves, including radio and light waves.

Stalactite: A cone of calcareous rock hanging from the roof of a cavern.

Stalagmite: A pillar of calcareous rock rising from the floor of a cavern.

Star: A large, hot, glowing body of gases.

Starch: A naturally abundant nutrient carbohydrate found in seeds, fruits, corn, potatoes, wheat, and rice.

Strata: Layers of sedimentary rock; the singular is stratum.

Stratopause: The boundary or transition layer between the stratosphere and the mesosphere.

Stratosphere: The second layer of the earth's atmosphere. The ozone layer that protects the earth from harmful UV radiation is located within the stratosphere.

Stratospheric ozone: The ozone layer that protects the earth.

Subduction: Plate boundary phenomenon resulting from tectonic plate movement, in which a denser oceanic plate is pushed below a lighter continental plate, creating a *subduction zone*.

Sublimation: The change from a solid to a gas, without an intermediate liquid phase.

Symbiosis: Close interaction between two or more different biological species that benefits both.

Syncline: The trough of a rock fold.

Synthesis: The formation of a compound by combining elements or simpler compounds.

Taxonomy: The classification of organisms.

Tectonic plates: The seven major plates and many smaller plates, all in constant motion, that make up the crust of the earth.

Temperature: The average kinetic energy of a group of molecules; it determines the direction of heat flow.

Thermal energy: Heat energy from the vibration and movement of atoms and molecules within substances.

Thermodynamics: The study of heat energy.

Thermopause: The boundary between the thermosphere and the exosphere.

Thermosphere: The fourth and deepest layer of the earth's atmosphere, above the mesosphere and below the exosphere.

Threshold dose: The minimum amount or concentration of a substance that affects an organism or population.

Tide: The rise and fall of the ocean due to gravitational attraction by the moon and sun.

Transpiration: The evaporation of water from plants, especially through the stomata.

Tropism: A growth movement in a plant in response to an environmental stimulus.

Tropopause: The boundary between the troposphere and the stratosphere.

Troposphere: The first layer of the earth's atmosphere. It contains 75 percent of the earth's atmospheric mass, but is the shallowest atmospheric level.

Tsunami: Japanese term for a giant wave generated from undersea earthquakes or volcanic eruptions.

Tundra: A cold biome of restricted tree growth, the tundra is further divided into arctic and alpine regions. The arctic tundra is located between the ice caps of the North Pole and the boreal forest and is characterized by permafrost. The alpine tundra is located in the higher elevations of the mountains around the world, above the tree line and below the permanent snow line.

Ultraviolet radiation (UV): Radiant energy with wavelengths shorter than the minimum that the human eye is designed to see.

Vapor: The gaseous state of a substance that is liquid or solid under ordinary conditions.

Vertebrates: Chordates characterized by a well-developed brain, a backbone, and usually two pairs of limbs; includes fishes, amphibians, reptiles, birds, and mammals.

Volt: The SI unit of measurement of electric potential; the amount of work necessary to move the charge.

Watt: The SI unit of measurement of electrical power, the rate at which electrical energy is dissipated.

Weathering: The physical and chemical destruction of rock by the atmosphere.

X-Ray: A form of electromagnetic energy similar to visible light, but of shorter wavelength and capable of penetrating solids and of ionizing gases.

Chapter 6

The ACT Plus Writing Test

The ACT Plus Writing Test is an optional section on the ACT that is administered after you finish the four multiple-choice tests. If you take the Writing Test, you will be required to plan and compose an original essay on an assigned topic prompt within 30 minutes. Your task will be to demonstrate an ability to write a clear and concise essay using the conventions of standard written English. In this chapter, we present scoring guidelines and criteria, general techniques and strategies, along with guidelines to approach writing your essay using a three-step process to organize, write, and proofread your essay.

A common misconception about writing is that effective writers are natural-born writers, but the process and concepts of writing can be learned by anyone. Our study guide will show you the process of effectively developing your ideas from the introduction to the conclusion and will help you learn new skills that will improve your essay score. If you are uneasy about your writing skills, remember that you already have been writing many essays and research papers for your high school classes, and now you can learn new skills to communicate and support your thoughts and ideas.

Tip: If you are taking the ACT Plus Writing Test, use the strategies and techniques presented in this chapter to prepare and write practice essays. Practice tests in Chapters 13 through 15 contain multiple-choice questions, but do not provide additional essay writing practice.

General Overview of the ACT Plus Writing Test

Writing Test Requirements

Requirements for the Writing Test vary depending upon the university or college. Even if your intended college does not require the Writing Test for admission, most colleges and universities "recommend" that applicants take the Writing Test. Because the writing assignment can reveal how well you write and think under time constraints, and you may be applying to several colleges simultaneously, it would be in your best interest to review this chapter. Taking the Writing Test does not affect subject areas scores on the ACT or the composite score. To find out which universities require the Writing Test for admission, visit the ACT official website at www.act.org/aap/writing/. The official ACT website has developed a search option to help you determine which schools "require," "recommend," or have decided that the Writing Test is "not needed" for admission.

Skills and Concepts Tested

The essay section of the exam tests your ability to carefully read a topic prompt, organize your ideas before you write, and write a clear, well-written essay. The topic prompt will contain a short paragraph featuring a specific issue relevant to high school students. You will be evaluated on your ability to communicate your perspective on the issue given while supporting your thoughts and ideas with examples from your reading, personal experiences, or observations. Good high school–level writing, reading, and reasoning skills will also help you with this portion of the test.

To demonstrate the basic skills necessary to score well on this component of the ACT, your essay must

- Take a position on an issue and provide supporting and detailed examples.
- Express your ideas clearly about the assigned topic.
- Demonstrate a logical sequence and organization of your ideas.
- Show reasoning, unity, and coherence from paragraph to paragraph to support your ideas.
- Use the conventions of English grammar and language.

Directions

The Writing Test is administered at the end of the regular ACT test. Those students taking the ACT Plus Writing Test are tested separately. You have 30 minutes to plan and write an essay on an assigned topic. Read the writing prompt topic carefully before you begin planning and writing your essay. Make sure that you understand exactly what you are being asked to do. Your essay will be evaluated on the evidence it provides to support your position on the issue and your ability to maintain focus on the topic, to organize your ideas in a logical way, and to clearly and effectively use language according to the conventions of standard written English.

Unlined pages are provided in the test booklet to plan your essay. These unlined pages will not be scored. *Your essay must be written on the lined pages in the answer folder.* Your writing on those lined pages will be scored. You may not need all the lined pages for your essay, but to make sure that you have enough room to finish, do not skip lines and avoid wide margins. Your corrections or additions should be written neatly between the lines of your essay. Do not write in the margins of the lined pages. Illegible essays cannot be scored, so write or print your essay clearly. If you finish writing your essay before time is called, you may go back and review your essay. When time is called, be sure to lay your pencil down immediately.

Scoring

Essays are scored holistically by experienced and highly trained readers. This means that *all aspects* of a well-written essay count toward your final score: well-developed ideas, good organization, supporting evidence, and an effective use of grammar and language. The impression that your essay makes upon the readers is important. However, keep in mind that the readers who score your essay are on your side and make every effort to focus on your writing strengths. Due to the limited time that is allotted for this task (30 minutes), readers take into consideration that even the highest scoring essay may contain some minor errors of grammar or word mechanics. Your essay is technically a "first draft" and will probably not be errorless, even if it receives the highest score of 12. That does not mean that you should ignore the rules of standard written English in the finished essay, but remember that they are not as important to your overall score as your ideas and your organization. Essays are expected to be superior in content, organization, and development.

Taking the Writing Test does not affect subject area scores on the ACT Assessment or the composite score. The essay generates a raw score that ranges on a scale from 2 (low) to 12 (high) from two readers. Each reader will assign a score from 1 to 6, and the sum of their combined scores will generate a total score that ranges from 2 to 12. The two readers will not know each other's scores. If their scores are more than one point apart, your essay will be scored by a third reader to resolve the disagreement.

Scores reported to you and to the colleges you designate will include two additional scores. The first additional score is the combined essay score of the English and Writing tests reported on a scale ranging from 1 to 36. The second additional score will be a Writing Test subscore ranging on a scale from 2 to 12.

Rubric for Analyzing Scores

Score of 6: Response is Effective
The highest scoring essays present a persuasive and effective response to the task with only minor errors. These essays:
• present an effective introduction and conclusion
• present a clear and insightful position that responds directly to the topic
• examine different perspectives, reasons, and implications of the issue
• provide well-developed and relevant supporting examples
• present a clear, organized sequence of connecting ideas throughout the essay
• show command of standard written English, and use a range of vocabulary and sentence variety to skillfully convey meaning

Score of 5: Response is Competent

These essays present a competent and well-developed response to the task with occasional errors. These essays:

- present a clear and generally well-developed introduction and conclusion
- present a clear position that responds directly to the task
- examine at least one perspective with implications of the issue
- elaborate most ideas with general statements, but provide logical reasons with supporting examples
- present a generally organized, but somewhat predictable analysis that connects ideas
- show competent usage of vocabulary and varied sentences to convey meaning
- demonstrate a good handling of the conventions of standard written English

Score of 4: Response is Adequate

These essays present a complete and adequately competent response to the task with occasional errors. These essays:

- present a reasonably developed introduction and conclusion
- present an expression of a position that shows the context of the issue
- provide specific and logical reasons and/or supporting examples
- present adequate sequencing and organization, although connecting ideas may be simple
- use adequate word choices and sentence variety to convey meaning
- demonstrate general control of the conventions of standard written English, but with occasional errors in grammar, spelling, and sentence structure.

Score of 3: Response is Limited

These essays show limited or marginal competence in responding to the prompt with errors that may be distracting or occasionally impede understanding. These essays:

- present a clearly evident introduction and conclusion, but are underdeveloped
- may be brief, vague, or limited in expressing a position to respond to the topic
- may use repetitious, broad, or irrelevant specific reasons and/or supporting examples
- may show a general understanding of topic, but lack focus on the specific issue
- lack organization and development of ideas
- may show little variety in vocabulary and demonstrate frequent minor errors with the conventions of standard written English

Score of 2: Response is Inconsistent

These essays show serious inconsistencies in responding to the specific directions for the task, and frequent errors impede communication. These essays:

- present a brief, underdeveloped introduction and conclusion
- may be unclear or not develop a clear position to respond to the specific issue
- may fail to show relevant reasons and/or examples to support the position
- are lacking focus and are poorly organized or misleading
- have simple or repetitious word choices and language problems that impede communication
- have major errors of grammar, word choice, and sentence structure and do not follow the conventions of standard written English

Score of 1: Response Lacks Skills

These essays show major deficiencies in responding to the task, and errors significantly impede understanding. These essays:

- fail to present a discernible introduction and conclusion
- are extremely brief and present little or no understanding of the task or issue

• fail to take a position and provide little or no evidence or support
• show no evidence of organizational structure or logical ideas
• have severe language problems that prevent communication
• have serious errors with the conventions of standard written English
Score of 0: Response is Blank or Off-Topic
These essays are often blank, do not respond to the writing task, are off topic, are not written in English, are illegible, or simply copy the issue prompt.

Essay Comments

The ACT Plus Writing Test readers will select comments derived from the scoring rubric to be included with the exam results. These essay comments are included to help students understand the strengths and weaknesses of their essays.

General Strategies and Tips

Before you read the more detailed advice about how to approach essay writing, read the general strategies described here that emphasize simple reminders about writing an ACT essay.

- **Stay focused on the assignment.** One of the primary reasons students do not perform well on the essay section is that they do not stay focused on the topic and do not respond completely to the assigned task. Because time management is critical to one's success on the ACT, the hurried test-taker frequently will read the topic and merely scan the assignment. Too often students neglect to complete all parts of the assignment, and their scores are adversely affected as a result. There is an old Buddhist saying, "The answer is contained in the question." This is important to remember when taking a standardized test like the ACT. There is always something in the question that helps to determine your response. To help you stay focused, circle or underline key words and phrases in the question as you develop your ideas.

- **Write notes in the space provided.** You have 30 minutes to plan and write an essay on one assigned topic. Use the space provided for writing notes to help you organize your thoughts. (These notes will not be read or scored by the people scoring your essay.)

- **Read and paraphrase the topic prompt.** Notice that this topic prompt features an issue to which you are asked to respond. It is written with the intent that you will be able to respond quickly regardless of your background or interests. Sometimes rephrasing the topic in your own words will help you articulate your position about the issue.

- **Use your time wisely.** Take about 5 to 7 minutes to prewrite and organize your thoughts. Take about 20 minutes to write your essay, and about 3 to 5 minutes to proofread your essay.

- **Be specific.** The assignment will ask you to take a position and give your view on a topic. Reinforce your point of view with specific reasons and supporting examples. Your readers are looking for specific details and concrete evidence of some kind to support your position.

- **Make sure your writing is legible and neat.** Don't use excessively large writing, don't leave wide margins, and don't skip any lines. Your essay must be written on the four lined pages provided. You will not be given any additional paper.

- **Avoid jargon, clichés, and slang.** Traditional, more formal writing is preferred.

- **Use the five-paragraph model.** Very short essays usually receive very low scores. Aim for a minimum of least three paragraphs, but the five-paragraph essay model described in the next section is the suggested example to follow when writing your essay. When writing an essay, it is important to remember to weave the main or unifying idea (or position) throughout your essay.

The Three-Step Writing Process

There are a number of ways to approach writing an essay, but for any timed writing task you should take three steps leading to the finished product: *prewriting, writing,* and *proofreading.* If you are able to practice the stages of the writing process, you will gain control over any writing assignment. The step-by-step guidelines that follow will help you plan and compose a well-written essay. As you practice the steps of the writing process, make a note about which strategies work best for you and use them to develop your own preferred writing style.

If you've been practicing for this part of the exam in your English class, and you and your teacher are satisfied with the way you handle a 30-minute essay, you can skip or skim this section and continue to write your essays your way. If you aren't confident with your technique or wish to review the process with a few successful techniques, then read this section carefully.

For any timed writing task, you should envision three steps leading to the finished product.

STEP 1
Prewriting
Time: 5 to 7 minutes

STEP 2
Writing
Time: 20 minutes

STEP 3
Proofreading
Time: 3 to 5 minutes

Now let's take a close look at the process using the topic and assignment that follows.

Sample Essay Topic:

Some parents encourage their high school students to get an after-school or weekend job. Other parents cite the importance of getting good grades to discourage their high school students from getting an after-school or weekend job. Which parents do you agree with?

In your essay, take a position on this question. You may write about either one of the two points of view given, or you may present a different point of view on this question. Use specific reasons and examples to support your position.

Step 1: Prewriting

One of the biggest mistakes a student can make is beginning to write an essay without first taking the time to plan it. Prewriting is when you plan your essay. The step after this, writing, is simply arranging it in the proper format. Many students believe that good writers just sit down and miraculously produce an essay. On the contrary, most experienced writers know that effective writing requires an organization and planning process. The prewriting process helps you gather information and ideas as you prepare to write a well-written essay.

Before you begin prewriting, read the topic and the assignment carefully. In the sample topic, circle or underline key words to help you focus on the assigned task. Reread the assignment. If there are several tasks given, number them and write them down. Let the nature of the assignment determine the structure of your essay.

Developing and organizing information on short notice can be difficult, unless you are ready with an effective technique. Take some time to organize your thoughts on paper before writing your essay by using the following basic prewriting techniques of *brainstorming, clustering,* or *outlining.*

Brainstorming

The technique of creating and accumulating ideas and examples is called *brainstorming.* Brainstorming is an exploration process that allows you to imagine and generate ideas about your topic. Your "imaginings" will help you to compile words and phrases about the essay topic by simply jotting down as many thoughts, ideas, and possibilities as you can remember, invent, or otherwise bring to mind to address the topic. It is important to remember that *all ideas are acceptable* during the brainstorming process and that neatness, order, and spelling do not matter at this point.

After generating as many ideas or examples as you can within a couple of minutes, evaluate and organize your notes by looking for patterns or themes so you can group your ideas into categories. Remember that development relies on specific examples. Decide which examples best support your points and your position. Cross out those you do not wish to use and number those remaining in the order in which you will want to address them in your essay response. Add any notes regarding more specific details or new thoughts that come to mind. However, do not worry about developing everything because you will be the only one using these notes. Your time will be better spent developing these points in the actual writing of your essay and not in your notes.

Remember, too, that you can change the order of your main points later. In the brainstorming stage, it is important to just consider each idea and how it might support the central purpose of your essay.

Brainstorming Examples:

Writing Simple Notes   or   **Making a Simple Chart**

List the reasons you support your position.

Learn skills	
Time management	
Enhance education	
Develop good work ethic	
Valuable experience	

Advantages	**Disadvantages**
Learn skills	*Takes time away*
Time management	*Distracting*
Enhance education	
Develop good work ethic	
Valuable experience	

Clustering

Clustering is a technique well suited to the timed essay. Use clustering as a way of organizing visual representations of your thoughts before you write. Clustering begins with a key word related to the topic. Ideas are then clustered around the key word and numbered in the order you will present them in your essay. The connecting ideas in the new clusters are thoughts and ideas that will be written in supporting sentences. They will reveal an important relationship with the original core idea. You do not have to use all the ideas in your cluster; just cross out any you decide not to use.

Clustering Example:

After you choose a topic, write it down in the prewriting area (given under the actual topic question) and draw a circle around that topic.

For
Working

For a few moments, think of all the elements of that side of the issue and connect them to the central topic cluster.

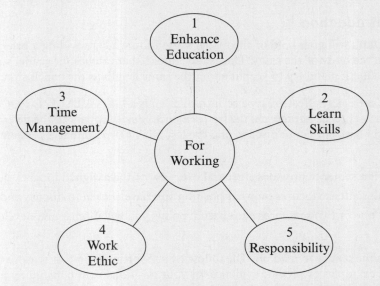

You can then number the parts of the cluster to give an order to your thoughts. You don't have to use all the elements of your cluster.

Outlining

Outlining is another, traditional, form of prewriting. Use a simple, informal outline that clearly arranges each main point and connects supporting points in the form of phrases. Your outline is meant to help you organize your thoughts in a pattern and should be kept simple so you can use it to save time when you write your essay. A formal outline (using I, II, III, A, B, C, and so on) is not recommended and is not necessary.

Outlining Example:

Introduction

    Working is beneficial

        Learn skills

        Enhance education

Body or Discussion

    Learning skills—time management

    Enhance education—develop good work ethic

Conclusion or Summary

    Working depends on student

    Students can gain a lot

Notice that this outline is informal, but the basic parts, *introduction, body,* and *conclusion* help you focus and organize your response. Remember, spend about 5 to 7 minutes prewriting and organizing your ideas before you start writing.

Step 2: Writing the Essay

The purpose of this section is to provide you with two methods that are associated with specific procedures for writing your essay. Models described in this section are

    Five-Paragraph Model

    The "Why Essay" Model

Five-Paragraph Model

Paragraph One: Introduction

A strong opening paragraph will grab hold of the reader's attention while providing a brief *preview* of the main points to be discussed in the body of the essay. This is the "hook" that catches the reader's interest in your topic. Try to avoid a long introduction and try to keep it about the same length as the conclusion.

One easy-to-master, yet extremely effective, type of introduction is a GENERALIZE-FOCUS-PREVIEW structure. In this three- to four-sentence paragraph, the first sentence *generalizes* about the given topic, the second sentence *focuses* on what you have chosen to discuss, and the last one or two sentences *preview* the particulars you intend to present.

- **Generalize**—The first sentence provides a general overview of the assigned topic or question.
- **Focus**—The second sentence focuses on what position you have chosen to discuss and states this position.
- **Preview**—The last one or two sentences cite specific points you will discuss and develop in your essay (in order).

The introduction invites the reader to read on. The following supporting points or reasons (three are usually sufficient) should reinforce examples or provide evidence for your position. Your concluding paragraph can summarize your supporting points. You may wish to tie in a restatement of your thesis sentence in the conclusion.

The five-paragraph model format looks like the following table in outline form. Remember to always connect supporting points back to the main idea, your main position, or main purpose.

Five-Paragraph Essay

Paragraph	Discussion	Sequence of Ideas
Paragraph 1	Introduction	1. Preview of main idea or purpose 2. Preview of supporting point/details #1 3. Preview of supporting point/details #2 4. Preview of supporting point/details #3
Paragraph 2	Body	Supporting point #1
Paragraph 3	Body	Supporting point #2
Paragraph 4	Body	Supporting point #3
Paragraph 5	Conclusion	1. Restate main idea, main position, or main purpose 2. Restate supporting point/details #1 3. Restate supporting point/details #2 4. Restate supporting point/details #3

Paragraphs Two, Three, and Four: Body or Discussion

Writing the body of the response involves presenting specific details and examples that relate to the aspects you introduced in the first paragraph. You should spend more time on the body than on your introduction and conclusion, but keep the writing concise and to the point. Each paragraph begins with a unifying sentence and then provides supporting evidence with specific examples from your reading, life experience, or observations. Each paragraph elaborates and provides examples (or details) of the main points briefly mentioned in paragraph one.

The body should consist of several short paragraphs, but you may choose to write a long paragraph. If you choose to break your discussion into several paragraphs, make sure that each paragraph consists of at least three sentences. Very short paragraphs may make your response appear insubstantial and scattered. Be realistic about how much you can write and provide at least one substantial example; at least one "for instance," is important for each aspect you discuss in the body of your response.

Transition Words

As you transition from one thought to another, use transition words that signal or show the relationships between ideas and bridge the paragraphs. In particular, use them between paragraphs three and four and four and five. This is not difficult to accomplish, and good transitions can make a big difference in the way your essay reads. Sequence cues such as "although," "first," "second," "however," "next," "finally," "initially," "since," "subsequently," "therefore," "thus," and "ultimately" help you clarify the hierarchy of the points being made and assist the reader in having a clear understanding of what is being said.

Some examples of transition words and phrases and their uses are in the table that follows:

Transition Words and Phrases

Uses	Examples
to add ideas	furthermore, in addition
to illustrate or demonstrate	for example, in other words
to show cause and effect	consequently, instead, regardless, therefore
to show contrast, change, opposition, negation, or limitation	conversely, however, on the other hand
to emphasize a point	above all, without a doubt
to show order	first, second, third, next, in conclusion
to summarize	in short, for these reasons
to show relationships in time	before, previously, subsequently, then

Tip: When writing the body, students sometimes digress from their original outline as they add a more personal emotional experience to their essays. Remember to stay focused on your intended topic and to keep the inclusion of additional personal material concise.

Paragraph Five: Conclusion

Having a formal conclusion to your response is unnecessary, but a conclusion should add a sense of continuity and structural integrity to your writing. Your conclusion should be about the same length as your introduction. As you prepare to write the conclusion, you should pay special attention to time. The conclusion can

- summarize the main points from your introduction (in the same order).
- complete your response to the assigned question.
- briefly clarify any points presented that may need further illumination.
- add information that you failed to discuss earlier.
- point toward the future.

Some readers comment that an essay can "start out strong but end up weak." Don't let this happen to you. Be sure to emphasize the importance of the topic (or your position) in your final paragraph.

Remember that you must allow enough time to prepare and write your conclusion and keep in mind that you should leave at least 3 to 5 minutes at the end to proofread your essay.

The "Why Essay" Model

One good way to approach an essay question that asks you to explain, analyze, or evaluate an issue is to use a *Why Essay* model format. A Why Essay is constructed around a *thesis sentence*. The thesis sentence begins with your opinion followed by the word "because" and then a list of the most important reasons *why* the opinion is valid, reasonable, or well-founded.

For example, using the "work experience" sample topic, a thesis statement could be:

> *Working while in school is beneficial to students because it provides skills that might enhance their formal education and teaches them a good work ethic.*

To use the five-paragraph essay model in conjunction with the Why Essay model, the thesis statement would come at the end of the introductory paragraph followed by paragraphs that explain each supporting point. The essay's conclusion ends with a summary of the reasons and a restatement of the thesis sentence. Each paragraph should contain approximately three to five sentences.

Step 3: Proofreading

Always allow a few minutes to proofread your essay for errors in grammar, usage, and spelling. If you detect an error, either erase it cleanly or simply line it out carefully and insert the correction neatly. Keep in mind, both while you are writing and while you are correcting, that your handwriting should be legible. Pay special attention to words you have left out. Watch the clock! Once the 30-minutes time is called, you will be unable to make any more changes.

Practice with Sample Topics and Essays

Now take a closer look at a sample topic and two sample essays.

Sample Topic 1

Directions: You have 30 minutes to plan and write an essay on the following topic. The essay is intended to give you a chance to show your writing skills. Read the writing prompt carefully before you begin planning and writing your essay. Make sure that you understand exactly what you are being asked to do. Your essay will be evaluated on the evidence it provides of your ability to express your position on an issue clearly and effectively, to maintain focus on the topic, to use logical reasoning to develop your position, to use specific supporting details, to be well organized, and to use language clearly and effectively based on the conventions of standard written English.

Unlined pages are provided in the test booklet to plan your essay. These unlined pages will not be scored. *Your essay must be written on the lined pages in the answer folder.* Your writing on those lined pages will be scored. You may not need all the lined pages for your essay, but to make sure that you have enough room to finish, do not skip lines and avoid wide margins. Your corrections or additions should be written neatly between the lines of your essay. Do not write in the margins of the lined pages. Illegible essays cannot be scored, so write or print your essay clearly. If you finish writing your essay before time is called, you may go back and review your essay. When time is called, be sure to lay your pencil down immediately.

> Some parents encourage their high school students to get an after-school or weekend job. Other parents cite the importance of getting good grades to discourage their high school students from getting an after-school or weekend job. Which parents do you agree with?
>
> In your essay, take a position on this question. You may write about either one of the two points of view given, or you may present a different point of view on this question. Use specific reasons and examples to support your position.

Essay Writing Checklist

Consider these points as you write your essay:

✔ Write naturally and try to be genuinely interested in the topic.

✔ Don't worry about the answer you think "they" want you to write.

✔ Don't be wishy-washy. Be confident as you support your position.

✔ Make sure your opening paragraph is relevant to the entire body of your essay.

✔ Ask yourself, "Are my ideas expressed clearly and coherently, and did I use suitable transition words?"

✔ Did your conclusion reiterate your essay's main points?

✔ When proofreading, remember never make an effort to radically change your entire essay. You do not have time. At this point, the best you can do is to add a few minor elements that can strengthen your work.

Now let's take a look at two well-written essays to see how they compare to your essay.

Sample Topic 1: Two Well-Written Responses

The following two essays were written by high school students. These papers are reproduced exactly as they were written, so they contain some mechanical errors and some general writing mistakes. The high school students wrote the essays within the 30 minutes allotted.

Essay 1

There is a great deal of controversy among parents as to whether or not their children should hold a paying job while in high school. Some parents believe that working while in school is a valuable experience; others believe that the importance of good grades **superceeds** any value that a job might offer. **I think that working while in school can be very beneficial to students and provide them with skills that might enhance their "formal" education.**

One of the **skills** is time management. Learning how to balance your activities and obligations is essential as an adult. It is invaluable to know what you can handle and when you are taking on too much. **When I got a job in high school, I began to realize the importance of using my time wisely since I had less of it to throw around.** I think that I gained a lot from having to make those decisions as well as earning my own money.

Another benefit is that students can **develop a work ethic** which can be applied to their academic schooling or any task that they choose to take on. **Understanding the importance of working hard, doing a good job and being responsible are skills that are assets to any endeavor.** Students often develop **confidence** from being counted on to get something done and then rising to that challenge. **Additionally, learning to take pride in your work is really important.** When you care about something your performance often reflects that. Academic success largely depends upon this same kind of pride and confidence.

Ultimately, I believe that whether a child should work while in school **depends on the child.** Some children feel that they can't handle the responsibility while others are willing to try. I think **that students stand to gain a lot from working**, but should be able to **make that choice for themselves** in the end.

This is a good first paragraph. It clearly states the writer's position, and by suggesting that work can develop nonacademic skills, it prepares for the arguments of the next three paragraphs.

Note how the repetition of the word "skills" links the second paragraph with the first.

Paragraph three moves on to another advantage (development of a work ethic). The second sentence explains fully what the writer understands a "work ethic" to be.

The last paragraph is the weakest paragraph of this essay. The writer has argued forcefully in favor of after-school work. There is no reason to weaken the argument with the trite suggestion that it will depend on the individual. What doesn't? In an argument essay like this, it is not necessary (and is usually a waste of time) to pay lip service to the opposing point of view.

A well-chosen word, but misspelled. It should be "supersede."

The writer supports her argument (that part-time work develops the ability to manage time efficiently) by referring to personal experience.

The move to a second point in this paragraph (increased confidence) would be clearer with the addition of a transitional word or phrase (such as "Further" or "Also") to begin the sentence. But, the writer rightly does include a transitional word ("Additionally") at the beginning of the next sentence.

Aside from the last paragraph, this is a very good essay, well-organized, well-supported, and specific. Its word choices, syntax, and mechanics are all competent.

Essay 2

Some parents want their high school aged children to work part-time, while other parents prefer their children not to work and instead concentrate on studies. **I agree with the parents who want their children to get good grades, although I believe that after school work, sports or other activities are helpful in establishing good study habits** and creating a well-rounded, successful student.

Life is not all study any more than it is all play. Students need to learn how to manage their time. They need to learn the organizational skills necessary to do a lot of different tasks in a timely manner. Work, sports, **and other activities are necessary to provide a break from** continual studying. **They also provide experiences that are essential to education and can lead to understanding and, therefore, better grades.**

Since my older brother was responsible for paying for his own college education, it was necessary for him to work part-time throughout his college years. He had to organize his work hours around class and study hours, so he found **a job in a grocery store** as this gave him the greatest flexibility. He organized his time and was able to work and keep up his grades.

He told me that many of his college classmates came from wealthier backgrounds. **They didn't have to work and were able to concentrate full-time on their studies and their grades.** A lot of these kids took study breaks for coffee or beers or just chatting, and didn't organize their time well. **Some did quite poorly in school even though their parents did all they could to help them focus on grades.**

From my own observations and experience **I do not feel that after-school or weekend jobs hinder a student from getting good grades.** I feel that these activities can be more helpful than harmful by providing the student with the opportunity to organize their life activities. Whether in high school or in college **a student should be encouraged to engage in many activities and to organize their time so they can succeed in all they do. I plan to get a part-time job during my senior year in high school.**

Introduction is focused and states position clearly and immediately.

The second paragraph supports the main position of the introduction—again supports the position that jobs can lead to good grades.

The fourth paragraph shows that not working in part-time jobs doesn't mean that good grades will necessarily follow. Notice the supporting example from the experience and observation of the writer.

Notice how it uses words from the counterargument, "good grades," to support the position that part-time jobs are good because they lead to good grades.

The third paragraph provides supporting details from experience as asked for — personal experience supports the position.

The conclusion:
- *again restates the essay topic*
- *uses support from observations to again support original restated position*

Note: Since the question is "What is your opinion?" it is quite permissible to write in the first person ("I") and give your opinion without saying "in my opinion" or "I believe" or "my viewpoint is." Be personal and invent supporting examples!

This essay is organized, coherent, and presents a clear position on the issue. The first line in paragraph two, "Life is not all study any more than it is all play," helps to grab the reader's interest in learning more about the topic and draws attention to the author's opinion. The author's personal story about his brother reinforces his position about working after school. The conclusion is successful in summarizing the main points and is effective in bringing together important details from the introduction.

Evaluating Your Essay

When you practice, use the following checklist to evaluate your essay.

Evaluating Your Essay

Questions	Excellent	Average	Weak
1. Does the essay focus on the topic, state your position, and complete the assigned task?			
2. Is the essay well-organized, well-developed, and consistent?			
3. Does the essay provide specific supporting details and examples?			
4. Does the essay use correct grammar, usage, punctuation, and spelling?			
5. Is the handwriting legible?			

Sample Topic 2

Directions: You have 30 minutes to plan and write an essay on the following topic. The essay is intended to give you a chance to show your writing skills. Read the writing prompt carefully before you begin planning and writing your essay. Make sure that you understand exactly what you are being asked to do. Your essay will be evaluated on the evidence it provides of your ability to express your position on an issue clearly and effectively, to maintain focus on the topic, to use logical reasoning to develop your position, to use specific supporting details, to be well organized, and to use language clearly and effectively based on the conventions of standard written English.

> Many school boards across the country have banned the selling of high calorie soft drinks and snacks, such as potato chips and candy bars, in cafeterias and vending machines on high school campuses. They argue that the easy availability of junk foods encourages poor eating habits that lead to obesity and other health problems. Opponents of the ban contend that the removal of these foods does nothing to change students' eating habits and infringes upon their right to choose. In your opinion, should high calorie–low food value soft drinks and snacks be banned from sale on high school campuses?
>
> In your essay, take a position on this question. You may write about either one of the two points of view given, or you may present a different point of view on this question. Use specific reasons and examples to support your position.

Now let's take a look at two sample essays on the preceding topic.

Sample Topic 2: Two Written Responses

Essay 1—Average-Level Score

I have mixed views about the ban of junk foods and drinks which has been in effect at my school (Walt Whitman High) for several years. The profits from the vending machines which used to sell Coke and Pepsi went to the students' activities fund. When they changed to orange juice and Snapple, the profits went way down. The cost of some sports events and other student activities like the prom and the senior play were higher. This loss of revenue is one disadvantage of the change, though the principal claims the profits from the machines improve each year.

To my unscientific eye, the health and habits of my classmates are pretty much the same. Although they can't buy junk food on campus, they still can get them at stores and machines near the school. There is no visible sign that the number of kids who are overweight has decreased.

The one success of the healthier food and drink campaign is bottled water. Bottled water (though it is way overpriced for just water) outsells the fruit juices in the machines. Why haven't the fruit juices caught on? Advertisements. TV is filled with ads showing gorgeous high school girls at parties drinking Coke or Dr. Pepper. Other ads show buff guys playing volleyball at the beach and drinking bottled waters. But there is never an oj or an apple juice in sight.

I can understand the reasons behind the ban of junk foods on campus, but I don't believe it has had much effect on what high school students eat and drink. Despite the minor success of bottled water sales, students still prefer Pepsi to cranberry juice and potato chips to raw carrots, and are willing to drive or even walk to the stores that sell what they like.

Evaluating Sample Essay 1

This essay is competent, but supporting examples are not successfully executed. Though the writer refuses to support only one side of the argument, the essay makes its position clear. Each of the four paragraphs is coherent, but the ideas from the thesis statement are not well-developed and lack a central message. The sentences are varied, but do not communicate clear transitions. The vocabulary is relaxed. Prose is straightforward and free of clichés.

Essay 2—Lower-Level Score

I agree that junk food and high calorie snacks such as candy bars and potato chips should not be sold in vending machines or in school cafeterias. These drinks and snacks encourage bad eating habits. They can lead to health problems like being overweight. It stands to reason that if these foods and drinks are not available in schools, high school students will not buy them and impair their health and become obese.

It will also save money that could have been spent on books or on foods with greater health benefits like fresh fruits. If vending machines sold fresh fruits in season such as apples and pears in fall and winter and peaches and plums in spring and summer, student's health problems would not only improve, but they would not be overweight and would look and feel better. These are good reasons for not selling junk food in high schools.

Evaluating Sample Essay 2

This essay makes the writer's position clear, but fails to support this position effectively.

In the first paragraph, the first two sentences depend almost entirely on repeating the diction of the prompt. The third sentence simply repeats the ideas of the first two.

The second paragraph does at least make one point, though it is a simple one, and does use some detail (apples, pears, and so on). Like the first, the paragraph is repetitive and bland.

Sample Topics for Extra Practice

Here are a couple of other sample essay topics for extra practice. Use the checklist on page 149 to evaluate your essay.

Extra Practice Sample Topic 1

The state legislature is debating whether or not to make physical education a required subject in all three years of high school throughout the state. If physical education classes were optional, many students who lack the natural athletic ability of their peers would be spared acute embarrassment. And in some schools, grades in physical education classes distort the academic grade point averages. On the other hand, American teenagers do not get nearly enough exercise to maintain good health. In your opinion, should physical education classes be required in all three years of high school?

In your essay, take a position on this question. You may write about either one of the two points of view given, or you may present a different point of view on this question. Use specific reasons and examples to support your position.

Extra Practice Sample Topic 2

The school board is debating whether or not to allow a series of commercially produced television programs on varied academic subjects to be shown in high school classrooms. The programs are geared for a high school audience, and have been universally praised by both students and teachers. However, all of the programs include at least 5 minutes of advertisement in each 30-minute segment. Do you think films that include commercial messages should be shown in high school classes?

In your essay, take a position on this question. You may write about either one of the two points of view given, or you may present a different point of view on this question. Use specific reasons and examples to support your position.

Answers to Your Questions about the ACT Plus Writing Test

Q. **Should I make notes or an outline before I write my essay?**

A. Prewriting is usually very helpful, but if you are a good writer and can write better essays without notes or an outline, don't change your writing habits. Your reader will be looking for good organization and development in your essay; notes or an outline (or some sort of prewriting), however brief, will help you organize your ideas. The outline itself (or any notes you make) will not be graded or counted in the scoring.

Q. **How long of an essay should I write?**

A. You will not be graded on the length of your essay, and you have only 30 minutes. Keep in mind that very short essays will probably not be sufficiently developed. Each essay is scored by two readers using a scale from 1 to 6. The highest scores are essays of four to six paragraphs and about 400 words in length. In the lower-half of the scale, the range is from two-paragraph essays of 185 words, to those at the bottom with one paragraph and 100 words.

This is not to say that the longer your essay is, the higher your score. Padding out your paper with repetition or verbose phrasing will lower your score. Before you begin to write, plan your essay to cover the topic fully with specific supporting detail.

Q. **Are spelling and punctuation important?**

A. The readers pay no attention to one or two minor spelling or punctuation errors. They understand that your essay is a first draft written in only 30 minutes. But if the mechanical errors in a paper are so numerous that they interfere with your meaning, those errors will count heavily against you.

Q. **How important is good handwriting?**

A. Readers make an effort to avoid being influenced by good or bad handwriting, but there may be an unconscious hostility toward a paper that is very hard to read. Make your writing (or printing) as legible as you can.

Q. **Is there a reward for creativity in an essay?**

A. It depends on what you mean by creativity. If you mean writing a poem or a letter or a dialogue or a diary when the question calls for an essay, the answer is an emphatic "No." If you mean writing an essay that is on the topic and has an individual voice, original ideas, wit, and style, the answer is "Yes, indeed."

Q. **How important is the use of detail or specific examples?**

A. It is crucial. The question will almost certainly ask you to give an example or specific details to support your argument. One of the most obvious differences between papers in the upper and the lower-half of the scoring scale is their use of, or their failure to use specific examples.

Q. What if I don't finish my essay?

A. The readers are told again and again to reward students for what they do well. If you have left out only a few sentences of conclusion to your essay, it may not affect your score at all. If you have written three-quarters of your essay on the topic, you will certainly get full credit for all you have written, and it may be enough to get you a good score. Do not get depressed if you haven't finished; perhaps you did not finish because what you were writing was so good.

Q. Is there any specific course required before I take the Writing Test?

A. No. Almost all students who take the exam have had one to three high school English classes, but most have not a had a course exclusively concerned with writing.

Q. How should I practice writing essays before the exam?

A. On pages 150–151 in this chapter, there are some essay topics you can use for practice. Write your practice essays seriously and pay close attention to the time so that you become accustomed to finishing your essay in the 30 minutes allowed. Be sure to write more than one paragraph. Ask your English teacher, a friend (or better yet, two friends) or any one or two people able to judge writing to read and score your essay using the evaluation checklist on page 149 and the scoring guide on pages 138–140 of this book.

You can also use the student essays printed here to refine your editorial or revising skills. The essay in the lower-half of the scale is especially likely to contain a number of mechanical errors or weaknesses of style that aren't specified in the comments. If you can find and correct these errors, you will be able to avoid similar mistakes in your own writing.

PART III

MATH SKILLS REVIEW

Chapter 7

Math Review Fundamentals

The fundamentals of math are discussed in this chapter. The next five chapters, Chapters 8 to 12, consist of important math topics with comprehensive reviews, which present effective test-taking strategies, and practice questions that reinforce your understanding of ACT mathematics concepts. ACT math concepts include topics in arithmetic (pre-algebra), algebra, geometry, trigonometry, and word problems. As you review these chapters, continue to assess your strengths and evaluate areas in which you feel you may need improvement. Even if your cumulative knowledge of math is strong, you should at least skim through the topic headings to help trigger your memory of forgotten math concepts.

Each math review chapter includes a *diagnostic test* to help you assess your knowledge of that topic and a *review section* that provides you with illustrated examples, explanations, and clarifications about solving basic math problems. After you have taken the diagnostic test and systematically reviewed each topic area, you will be ready to practice what you have learned with the *practice exercises* provided at the end of each topic area subject.

Pace yourself as you work through each chapter, and remember that the ACT Mathematics Test evaluates your ability to use your *cumulative knowledge* of mathematics. This is why it is important to focus your attention on one math concept at a time (that is, finish the arithmetic [pre-algebra] diagnostic and review before you begin the algebra diagnostic and review, etc.).

ACT Math Content Areas You Should Know

Arithmetic (pre-algebra) (Chapter 8)	Algebra and Coordinate Geometry (Chapter 9)	Plane Geometry (Chapter 10)	Trigonometry (Chapter 11)	Word Problems (Chapter 12)
Arithmetic diagnostic test	Algebra diagnostic test	Geometry diagnostic test	Trigonometry diagnostic test	Word problems diagnostic test
Sets of numbers	Set notations	Lines, segments, rays, and angles	Trigonometric functions	Motion problems
Divisibility rules	Variables	Polygons and their angles	Trigonometry of triangles	Work problems
Grouping symbols	Solving linear equations in one or two variables	Triangles	Graphs of trigonometric functions	Mixture problems
Order of operations	Solving linear inequalities in one variable	Quadrilaterals	Trigonometric identities	Age problems
Integers	Polynomials	Circles	Trigonometric equations	Integer problems
Absolute value	Algebraic fractions	Perimeter, circumference, and area of plane figures		
Fractions	Solving quadratic equations in one variable	Surface area, volume, and diagonal lengths of 3-dimensional figures		
Factors	Coordinate geometry	Congruence and similarity		
Decimals	Functions and function notation			
Ratios and proportions				
Percents				
Exponents				
Square roots				

Overview

This overview section contains basic references that you will refer to again and again during your ACT math preparation. These fundamental facts and formulas were compiled so that you can have important basic math concepts at your fingertips. As you review different topics, keep in mind that these basic references will help you solve math problems so that you don't spend valuable time trying to search for information and formulas. The math overview includes the following: common math symbols, vocabulary related to sets of numbers, common math conventions and terminology, geometric formulas (perimeter, area, and volume), important fraction-decimal-percent equivalents, and measurement equivalents (English and metric systems).

Common Math Symbols

$x = 5$	x is equal to 5.
$x \neq 5$	x is not equal to 5.
$x \approx 5$	x is approximately equal to 5.
$x \leq 5$	x is less than or equal to 5.
$x < 5$	x is less than 5.
$x \geq 5$	x is greater than or equal to 5.
$x > 5$	x is greater than 5.
$|x|$	The absolute value of x.
$\sqrt{x}$	The nonnegative square root of x when $x \geq 0$.
$-\sqrt{x}$	The nonpositive square root of x when $x \geq 0$.
$n!$	The product of the positive integers 1, 2, 3, ..., n.
$0!$	Defined to have the value of 1.
$k \parallel p$	Line k is parallel to line p.
$k \perp p$	Line k is perpendicular to line p.

Numbers Vocabulary

Natural numbers	$\{1, 2, 3, 4, ...\}$ The counting numbers.
Whole numbers	$\{0, 1, 2, 3, 4, ...\}$ The counting numbers and zero.
Integers	$\{0, \pm 1, \pm 2, \pm 3, \pm 4, ...\}$ The whole numbers and their opposites.
Positive integers	$\{1, 2, 3, 4, ...\}$ The natural numbers.
Nonnegative integers	$\{0, 1, 2, 3, 4, ...\}$ The whole numbers.
Negative integers	$\{-1, -2, -3, -4, ...\}$ The opposites of the natural numbers.
Nonpositive integers	$\{0, -1, -2, -3, -4, ...\}$ The opposites of the whole numbers.
Rational numbers	Any value that can be expressed as $\frac{p}{q}$, where p is any integer and q is any nonzero integer. In decimal form, it either terminates or has a block of repeating digits. For example, $\frac{3}{4} = 0.75$, $\frac{1}{12} = 0.08333... = 0.08\overline{3}$

Irrational numbers	Any value that exists that cannot be expressed as $\frac{p}{q}$, where p is any integer and q is any nonzero integer. In decimal form, it neither terminates nor has any block of repeating digits. For example, $\sqrt{2}$, π.
Real numbers	All the rational numbers and irrational numbers.
Prime numbers	Any integer, greater than 1, that has only 1 and itself as divisors. The first 10 prime numbers are 2, 3, 5, 7, 11, 13, 17, 19, 23, and 29.
Composite numbers	Any integer greater than 1, which is not prime. The first 10 composite numbers are 4, 6, 8, 9, 10, 12, 14, 15, 16, and 18.
Even integers	$\{0, \pm 2, \pm 4, \pm 6, \ldots\}$ Integers that are perfectly divisible by 2.
Odd integers	$\{\pm 1, \pm 3, \pm 5, \pm 7, \ldots\}$ Integers that are not perfectly divisible by 2.
Squares	$\{(\pm 1)^2, (\pm 2)^2, (\pm 3)^2, (\pm 4)^2, \ldots\} = \{1, 4, 9, 16, \ldots\}$ The squares of the nonzero integers.
Cubes	$\{(\pm 1)^3, (\pm 2)^3, (\pm 3)^3, (\pm 4)^3, \ldots\} = \{\pm 1, \pm 8, \pm 27, \pm 64, \ldots\}$ The cubes of the nonzero integers.

ACT Common Mathematical Conventions and Terminology

1. Most numbers used on the ACT are **real numbers.** Imaginary values such as $i = \sqrt{-1}$ are considered. Expressions that have no value, real or imaginary, such as $\frac{8}{0}$, $\frac{0}{0}$, 0^0, are not considered.

2. Exponents can be positive, negative, or zero. For example, $5^2 = 5 \times 5 = 25$, $5^{-2} = \frac{1}{5^2} = \frac{1}{25}$, and $5^0 = 1$.

3. When **function notation** is used on the test, it will be standard function notation. For example, $f(x) = 2x$ and $g(x) = x + 3\sqrt{x}$. Replacements for the variable are assumed to be all real numbers except for those that produce values not allowed. For the function called f, $f(x) = 2x$, all real numbers can be used for replacements. For the function called g, $g(x) = x + 3\sqrt{x}$, only nonnegative replacements are allowed for the variable. The composition of the two functions, g with f, is shown by $g(f(x))$, which requires you to evaluate $f(x)$ first, and then bring its value to the g function.

   For example, using the f and g functions described previously, $g(f(50))$ has you first find $f(50)$. Since $f(x) = 2x$, then $f(50) = 2 \times 50 = 100$. Now use this value to replace the variables in the g function. Since $g(x) = x + 3\sqrt{x}$, then $g(100) = 100 + 3\sqrt{100} = 100 + 3(10) = 130$. Hence, $g(f(50)) = 130$.

Geometric Figures on the ACT

- Lines are assumed to be straight and extend indefinitely in opposite directions.
- Triangles will have interior angle sums of 180 degrees.
- Angle measures will be assumed to be positive and less than or equal to 360 degrees.
- All closed geometrical figures are assumed to be convex.
- The area of a figure refers to the region enclosed by the figure.
- The perimeter of a figure, or circumference in the case of circles, refers to the distance around the figure.
- If A and B refer to points on a figure, AB will refer to the segment joining A and B or the distance between A and B. For example: Symbols $\overline{AB}$ and $\overleftrightarrow{AB}$ denoting line segments and lines may or may not appear on the ACT. Possibly, AB will appear instead. (You can determine which is being used through context.)
- Since figures are not necessarily drawn to scale, do not assume quantities such as lengths, angle measurements, areas, or perimeters based on appearance.

The following diagram will illustrate some things that can and cannot be assumed from a figure.

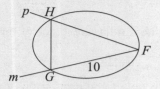 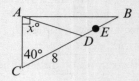

In geometric figures on the ACT, you *can assume*:

- *ABD, ACD, ABC,* and *FGH* are triangles.
- *D* lies between *C* and *E* on segment *BC, E* lies between *D* and *B* on segment *BD*.
- *CD* = 8.
- *BC* > 8.
- Angle *C* has a measure of 40 degrees.
- Angle *CAB* has a measure of 90 degrees (indicated by the small square symbol at *A*).
- *x* has a measure less than 90 degrees.
- The area of triangle *ABC* is greater than the area of triangle *ABD*.
- *F, G,* and *H* lie on the closed curve.
- *H* and *F* lie on line *p; F* and *G* lie on line *m*.
- Lines *p* and *m* intersect at *F*.
- *FG* = 10.
- The area of the closed curve region is greater than the area of triangle *FGH*.

In geometric figures on the ACT, you *cannot assume*:

- *BD* < 8.
- Angle *BAD* < *x* degrees.
- Area of triangle *ABD* < area triangle *ACD*.
- Angles *FGH, FHG,* and *HFG* are each less than 90 degrees.
- Line *HG* is parallel to line *AC*.
- Area of the region between *FH* and the closed curve > area of the region between *GH* and the closed curve.

Important Geometric Formulas

The following table is a reference with formulas of basic shapes: perimeter, area, and volume. The Pythagorean Theorem follows the table to illustrate how the lengths of the sides of a right triangle relate to one another.

Shape	Illustration	Perimeter	Area
Square	*a*	$P = 4a$	$A = a^2$
Rectangle	*h* *b*	$P = 2b + 2h$ or $P = 2(b + h)$	$A = bh$
Parallelogram	*a* *h* *b*	$P = 2a + 2b$ or $P = 2(a + b)$	$A = bh$

Shape	Illustration	Perimeter	Area
Triangle		$P = x + y + b$	$A = \dfrac{bh}{2}$ or $A = \dfrac{1}{2}bh$
Rhombus		$P = 4a$	$A = ah$
Trapezoid		$P = b_1 + b_2 + x + y$	$A = \dfrac{h(b_1 + b_2)}{2}$ or $A = \dfrac{1}{2}h(b_1 + b_2)$
Circle		$C = \pi d$ or $C = 2\pi r$	$A = \pi r^2$

Shape	Illustration	Surface Area	Volume
Cube		$SA = 6a^2$	$V = a^3$
Rectangular prism		$SA = 2(lw + lh + wh)$ or $SA = $ (Perimeter of base)h + 2(Area of base)	$V = lwh$ or $V = $ (Area of base)h
Prisms in general		$SA = $ (Perimeter of base)h + 2(Area of base)	$V = $ (Area of base)h
Cylinder		$SA = $ (Perimeter of base, or Circumference)h + 2(Area of base) or $SA = 2\pi rh + 2\pi r^2$ or $SA = 2\pi r(h + r)$	$V = $ (Area of base)h or $V = \pi r^2 h$
Sphere		$SA = 4\pi r^2$	$V = \dfrac{4}{3}\pi r^3$

Pythagorean Theorem

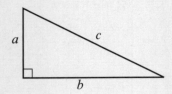

Pythagorean Theorem: The sum of the squares of the legs of a right triangle equals the square of the hypotenuse $(a^2 + b^2 = c^2)$.

Fraction-Decimal-Percent Equivalents

A time-saving tip is to try to memorize some of the following equivalents before you take the ACT to eliminate unnecessary computations on the day of the exam.

$$\frac{1}{100} = 0.01 = 1\%$$

$$\frac{1}{10} = 0.1 = 10\%$$

$$\frac{1}{5} = \frac{2}{10} = 0.2 = 0.20 = 20\%$$

$$\frac{3}{10} = 0.3 = 0.30 = 30\%$$

$$\frac{2}{5} = \frac{4}{10} = 0.4 = 0.40 = 40\%$$

$$\frac{1}{2} = \frac{5}{10} = 0.5 = 0.50 = 50\%$$

$$\frac{3}{5} = \frac{6}{10} = 0.6 = 0.60 = 60\%$$

$$\frac{7}{10} = 0.7 = 0.70 = 70\%$$

$$\frac{4}{5} = \frac{8}{10} = 0.8 = 0.80 = 80\%$$

$$\frac{9}{10} = 0.9 = 0.90 = 90\%$$

$$\frac{1}{4} = \frac{25}{100} = 0.25 = 25\%$$

$$\frac{3}{4} = \frac{75}{100} = 0.75 = 75\%$$

$$\frac{1}{3} = 0.33\frac{1}{3} = 33\frac{1}{3}\%$$

$$\frac{2}{3} = 0.66\frac{2}{3} = 66\frac{2}{3}\%$$

$$\frac{1}{8} = 0.125 = 0.12\frac{1}{2} = 12\frac{1}{2}\%$$

$$\frac{3}{8} = 0.375 = 0.37\frac{1}{2} = 37\frac{1}{2}\%$$

$$\frac{5}{8} = 0.625 = 0.62\frac{1}{2} = 62\frac{1}{2}\%$$

$$\frac{7}{8} = 0.875 = 0.87\frac{1}{2} = 87\frac{1}{2}\%$$

$$\frac{1}{6} = 0.16\frac{2}{3} = 16\frac{2}{3}\%$$

$$\frac{5}{6} = 0.83\frac{1}{3} = 83\frac{1}{3}\%$$

$$1 = 1.00 = 100\%$$

$$2 = 2.00 = 200\%$$

$$3\frac{1}{2} = 3.50 = 350\%$$

Customary English and Metric System Measurements

Length

English	Metric
12 inches (in) = 1 foot (ft)	10 millimeters (mm) = 1 centimeter (cm)
3 feet = 1 yard (yd)	10 centimeters = 1 decimeter (dm)
36 inches = 1 yard	10 decimeters = 1 meter (m)
5,280 feet = 1 mile (mi)	10 meters = 1 decameter (dam)
1,760 yards = 1 mile	10 decameters = 1 hectometer (hm)
	10 hectometers = 1 kilometer (km)
One meter is about 3 inches more than a yard.	
One kilometer is about 0.6 mile.	

Weight

English	Metric
16 ounces (oz) = 1 pound (lb)	10 milligrams (mg) = 1 centigram (cg)
2,000 pounds = 1 ton (T)	10 centigrams = 1 decigram (dg)
	10 decigrams = 1 gram (g)
	10 grams = 1 decagram (dag)
	10 decagrams = 1 hectogram (hg)
	10 hectograms = 1 kilogram (kg)
One kilogram is about 2.2 pounds.	
1,000 kilograms is a metric ton.	

Volume (capacity)

English	Metric
1 cup (cp) = 8 fluid ounces (fl oz)	10 milliliters (ml or mL) = 1 centiliter (cl or cL)
2 cups = 1 pint (pt)	10 centiliters = 1 deciliter (dl or dL)
2 pints = 1 quart (qt)	10 deciliters = 1 liter (l or L)
4 quarts = 1 gallon (gal)	10 liters = 1 decaliter (dal or daL)
	10 decaliters = 1 hectoliter (hl or hL)
	10 hectoliters = 1 kiloliter (kl or kL)
One liter is a little more than 1 quart.	

Chapter 8

Arithmetic (Pre-Algebra)

The Math Skills Review in this study guide is designed specifically to review, refresh, and reintroduce you to a variety of skill-based mathematics concepts. Since math concepts are best understood through orderly stages of learning, this chapter focuses on arithmetic concepts before presenting algebraic concepts in Chapter 9. The ACT merges arithmetic concepts with primary algebraic concepts in the same category, "pre-algebra," but this chapter purposely reviews arithmetic concepts first to emphasize the importance of understanding math basics before learning advanced topics. A solid knowledge of arithmetic is important for *all math concepts* on the ACT. Arithmetic shares the basic properties of counting (adding, subtracting, multiplying, and dividing) with all other math topics. As you become more proficient at solving arithmetic problems, you will be strengthening your ability to attempt more sophisticated and challenging problems in algebra and other math topics.

Pre-Algebra Concepts You Should Know

Arithmetic Concepts in Chapter 8	Pre-Algebra Concepts Discussed in Chapter 9
Number properties: positive and negative integers, odd and even numbers, prime numbers, factors and multiples, divisibility Order of operations Place value, number line: order, consecutive numbers Absolute value Basic problem-solving operations using whole numbers, integers: addition, subtraction, multiplication, and division Fractions Factors Decimals Ratio, proportion, and percent Exponents Scientific notation Square roots Elementary counting techniques Probability Descriptive statistics: arithmetic mean (average), mode, and median	Linear equations in one variable Properties of exponents and square roots Evaluating algebraic expressions: substitution method Functions Quadratic equations Word problems, solving for: percents, averages, rate, time, distance, interest, price per item (Chapter 12)

Now, let's get started and see what pre-algebra arithmetic skills you remember. Take the diagnostic test that follows and evaluate how familiar you are with the selected topics. The diagnostic test will give you valuable insight into the topics you will need to study.

Arithmetic Diagnostic Test

Directions: Solve each problem in this section by using the information given and your own mathematical calculations.

1. Which of the following are integers? $\frac{1}{2}$, -2, 0, 4, $\sqrt{25}$, $-\frac{15}{3}$, 7.5

2. Which of the following are rational numbers? 5.8, -4, $\sqrt{7}$, π, $2\frac{5}{8}$

3. List the prime numbers between 0 and 50.

4. List the perfect cubes between 1 and 100.

5. Which integers between 1 and 10 divide into 2,730?

6. $3[3^2 + 2(4 + 1)] =$

7. $-4 + 8 =$

8. $-12 - 6 =$

9. $(-6)(-8) =$

10. $\dfrac{-48}{3} =$

11. Change $5\dfrac{3}{4}$ to an improper fraction.

12. Change $\dfrac{59}{6}$ to a mixed number in lowest terms.

13. $\dfrac{2}{7} + \dfrac{3}{5} =$

14. $1\dfrac{3}{8} + 2\dfrac{5}{6} =$

15. $11 - \dfrac{2}{3} =$

16. $6\dfrac{1}{8} - 3\dfrac{3}{4} =$

17. $-\dfrac{7}{8} - \dfrac{5}{9} =$

18. $-\dfrac{1}{6} \times \dfrac{1}{3} =$

19. $2\dfrac{3}{8} \times 1\dfrac{5}{6} =$

20. $-\dfrac{1}{4} \div \dfrac{9}{14} =$

21. $2\dfrac{3}{7} \div 1\dfrac{1}{4} =$

22. $\dfrac{1}{3 + \dfrac{2}{1 + \dfrac{1}{3}}} =$

23. Round 4.4584 to the nearest thousandth.

24. Round -3.6 to the nearest integer.

25. $0.08 + 1.3 + 0.562 =$

26. $0.45 - 0.003 =$

27. $8.001 \times 2.4 =$

28. $0.147 \div 0.7 =$

29. Change $\frac{3}{20}$ to a decimal.

30. Change 7% to a decimal.

31. Solve the proportion for x: $\frac{4}{x} = \frac{7}{5}$

32. Change $\frac{1}{8}$ to a percent.

33. 79% of 64 =

34. 40% of what is 20?

35. What percent of 45 is 30?

36. What is the percent increase of a rise in temperature from 80° to 100°?

37. $8^3 \times 8^7 =$

38. $9^5 \div 9^{-2} =$

39. $(5^3)^2 =$

40. $\sqrt{135}$ is between what two consecutive integers and to which is it closer?

41. Simplify $\sqrt{80}$

42. $-\sqrt{9} =$

Use the spinner with 12 equally divided sections pictured here for questions 43–44.

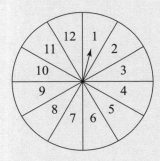

43. What is the probability of spinning a number that is both a multiple of 2 and a multiple of 3 in one spin?

44. What is the probability of *not* spinning a factor of 8 in one spin?

Use the frequency table that follows for question 45.

x	f
1	2
2	2
3	1
5	2
7	3

45. Use the frequency table to find each of the following:

    a) mean

    b) median

    c) mode

Scoring the Diagnostic Test

The following section assists you in scoring and analyzing your practice test results. Use the answer key and the analysis worksheet that follows to help you evaluate specific problem types. Corresponding topic headings can be found in the "Arithmetic Review" section following the diagnostic test.

Answer Key

Sets of Numbers

1. $-2, 0, 4, \sqrt{25}, -\dfrac{15}{3}$

2. $5.8, -4, 2\dfrac{5}{8}$

3. $2, 3, 5, 7, 11, 13, 17, 19, 23, 29, 31, 37, 41, 43, 47$

4. $8, 27, 64$

Divisibility Rules

5. $2, 3, 5, 6, 7$

Order of Operations and Grouping Symbols

6. 57

Integers

7. 4

8. -18

9. 48

10. -16

Fractions

11. $\dfrac{23}{4}$

12. $9\dfrac{5}{6}$

13. $\dfrac{31}{35}$

14. $4\dfrac{5}{24}$

15. $10\dfrac{1}{3}$

16. $2\dfrac{3}{8}$

17. $-\dfrac{103}{72} = -1\dfrac{31}{72}$

18. $-\dfrac{1}{18}$

19. $\dfrac{209}{48} = 4\dfrac{17}{48}$

20. $-\dfrac{7}{18}$

21. $\dfrac{68}{35} = 1\dfrac{33}{35}$

22. $\dfrac{2}{9}$

Decimals

23. 4.458

24. –4

25. 1.942

26. 0.447

27. 19.2024

28. 0.21

29. 0.15

30. 0.07

Ratios and Proportions

31. $x = \dfrac{20}{7}$ or $2\dfrac{6}{7}$

Percents

32. $12\dfrac{1}{2}\%$ or 12.5%

33. 50.56

34. 50

35. $66\dfrac{2}{3}\%$

36. 25%

Exponents

37. 8^{10}

38. 9^{7}

39. 5^{6}

Square Roots

40. 11 and 12, closer to 12

41. $4\sqrt{5}$

42. –3

Probability

43. $\dfrac{1}{6}$

44. $\dfrac{2}{3}$

Basic Statistics

45. **a)** mean = 4

b) median = 4

c) mode = 7

Charting and Analyzing Your Diagnostic Test Results

Record your diagnostic test results in the following chart and use these results as a guide to plan your arithmetic review goals and objectives. Mark the problems that you missed and pay particular attention to those that you missed in Column (C) because they were unfamiliar math concepts to you. These are the areas you will want to focus on as you study arithmetic topics.

Analysis Sheet

Topic	Number Possible	Number Correct	Number Incorrect		
			(A) Simple Mistake	(B) Misread Problem	(C) Unfamiliar Math Concept
Sets of numbers	4				
Divisibility rules	1				
Order of operations and grouping symbols	1				
Integers	4				
Fractions	12				
Decimals	8				
Ratios and proportions	1				
Percents	5				
Exponents	3				
Square roots	3				
Probability	2				
Basic statistics	1				
Total Possible Explanations for Incorrect Answers: Columns A, B, and C	▓▓▓▓▓▓▓	▓▓▓▓▓▓▓			
Total Number of Questions Correct and Incorrect	45	Add the total number of correct questions here: _____	Add columns A, B, and C for total number of incorrect questions here: _____		

Arithmetic Review

This section is a comprehensive arithmetic review of topics that are important for your success on the ACT. Remember to use the references in Chapter 7 as needed during your review. Pace yourself as you work through each topic area and try to focus on one concept at a time. Continue to evaluate your progress as you complete the illustrated examples that accompany each topic explanation.

Sets of Numbers

You already should be familiar with the fundamentals of addition, subtraction, multiplication, and division of sets of numbers found in the "Numbers Vocabulary" section of Chapter 7. Here are corresponding examples for your review.

Examples:

> **1.** Which of the following are integers? $\frac{1}{2}$, -2, 0, 4, $\sqrt{25}$, $-\frac{15}{3}$, 7.5

Integers are only whole numbers or their opposites. Only the numbers $-2, 0, 4, \sqrt{25} = 5$, and $-\frac{15}{3} = -5$ are integers.

> **2.** Which of the following are rational numbers? 5.8, -4, $\sqrt{7}$, π, $2\frac{5}{8}$

Any value that can be expressed as $\frac{\text{integer}}{\text{nonzero integer}}$, or as a decimal that either ends or has a repeating pattern is a rational number. Only the numbers 5.8, -4, and $2\frac{5}{8}$ are rational numbers.

> **3.** List the prime numbers between 0 and 50.

A prime number is an integer greater than 1 that can be divided only by itself or 1. Only the numbers 2, 3, 5, 7, 11, 13, 17, 19, 23, 29, 31, 37, 41, 43, and 47 satisfy this definition for integers between 1 and 50.

> **4.** List the perfect cubes between 1 and 100.

Perfect cubes are integers raised to the third power (see the "Exponents" section later in this chapter). The perfect cubes between 1 and 100 come from $2^3 = 8$, $3^3 = 27$, and $4^3 = 64$. The value 1 is not between 1 and 100, thus $1^3 = 1$ is not included in this list. The perfect cubes between 1 and 100 are 8, 27, and 64.

Divisibility Rules

The following divisibility chart will help you to quickly evaluate and rule out wrong answer choices.

If a number is divisible by	Divisibility Rule
2	it ends in 0, 2, 4, 6, or 8.
3	the sum of its digits is divisible by 3.
4	the number formed by the last two digits is divisible by 4.
5	it ends in 0 or 5.
6	it is divisible by 2 and 3 (use the rules for both).
7	N/A (no simple rule).
8	the number formed by the last three digits is divisible by 8.
9	the sum of its digits is divisible by 9.

Examples:

> **1.** Which integers between 1 and 10 divide into 2,730?

2 — 2,730 ends in a 0.

3 — The sum of the digits is 12, which is divisible by 3.

5 — 2,730 ends in a 0.

6 — The rules for 2 and 3 both work.

7 — $2{,}730 \div 7 = 390$.

Even though 2,730 is divisible by 10, 10 is not between 1 and 10.

> **2.** Which integers between 1 and 10 divide into 2,648?

2 — 2,648 ends in 8.

4 — 48, the number formed by the last two digits, is divisible by 4.

8 — 648, the number formed by the last three digits is divisible by 8.

Grouping Symbols

Parentheses ( ), brackets [ ], and braces { } are frequently needed to group numbers in mathematics. Generally parentheses are used first, followed by brackets, and then braces. Operations inside grouping symbols must be performed before any operations outside the grouping symbols.

Parentheses are used to group numbers or variables. Calculations inside parentheses take precedence and should be performed before any other operations.

$$50(2 + 6) = 50(8) = 400$$

If a parenthesis is preceded by a minus sign, the parentheses must be removed before calculations can be performed. To remove the parentheses, change the plus or minus sign of each term within the parentheses.

$$6 - (-3 + a - 2b + c) = 6 + 3 - a + 2b - c = 9 - a + 2b - c$$

Brackets and *braces* are also used to group numbers or variables. Operations inside parentheses should be performed first, then brackets, and finally braces: { [( )] }. Sometimes, instead of brackets or braces, you'll see the use of larger parentheses:

$$\left((3+4)\cdot 5\right)+2$$

An expression using all three grouping symbols might look like this:

$$2\left\{1+\left[4(2+1)+3\right]\right\}$$

This expression can be simplified as follows (notice that you work from the inside out):

$$2\left\{1+\left[4(2+1)+3\right]\right\} = 2\left\{1+\left[4(3)+3\right]\right\}$$
$$= 2\left\{1+[12+3]\right\}$$
$$= 2\left\{1+[15]\right\}$$
$$= 2\left\{16\right\}$$
$$= 32$$

Order of Operations

If multiplication, division, exponents, addition, subtraction, or parentheses are all contained in one problem, the *order of operations* is as follows:

1. Parentheses
2. Exponents
3. Multiplication or division in the order it occurs from left to right
4. Addition or subtraction in the order it occurs from left to right

An easy way to remember the order of operations is **Please Excuse My Dear Aunt Sally** (Parentheses, Exponents, Multiplication, Division, Addition, Subtraction).

Examples:

1. $3\left[3^2 + 2(4+1)\right] = 3\left[3^2 + 2(5)\right]$ (most inside parentheses first)

$3\left[3^2 + 2(5)\right] = 3\left[9 + 2(5)\right]$ (exponents next)

$3\left[9 + 2(5)\right] = 3\left[9 + 10\right]$ (mult./div. in order from left to right next)

$3\left[9 + 10\right] = 3\left[19\right]$ (add/subtract in order from left to right)

$3\left[19\right] = 57$

2. $10 - 3 \times 6 + 10^2 + (6+1) \times 4 = 10 - 3 \times 6 + 10^2 + 7 \times 4$ (parentheses first)

$10 - 3 \times 6 + 10^2 + 7 \times 4 = 10 - 3 \times 6 + 100 + 7 \times 4$ (exponents next)

$10 - 3 \times 6 + 100 + 7 \times 4 = 10 - 18 + 100 + 28$ (mult./div. in order from left to right)

$10 - 18 + 100 + 28 = -8 + 100 + 28$ (add/subtract in order from left to right)

$-8 + 100 + 28 = 92 + 28$ (add/subtract in order from left to right)

$92 + 28 = 120$

3. $-3^2 + (-2)^3 = -1(3)^2 + (-2)^3$

the exponent 2 only applies to the 3, while
the exponent 3 applies to the entire (-2)

$= -1(9) + (-8)$

$= -9 + (-8)$

$= -17$

Integers

Number Line

On a ***number line,*** the numbers to the right of 0 are *positive.* Numbers to the left of 0 are *negative* as follows:

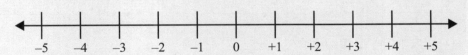

Given any two integers on a number line, the integer located farthest to the right is always larger, regardless of its sign (positive or negative). Note that fractions may also be placed on a number line and can be similarly compared.

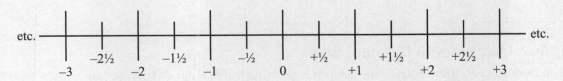

Examples:

For each pair of values, select the one with the greater value.

> **1.** −8, −3

−3 > −8 since −3 is farther to right on the number line.

> **2.** $0, -3\frac{1}{4}$

$0 > -3\frac{1}{4}$ since 0 is farther to the right on the number line.

Absolute Value

The **absolute value** of a number is its distance from 0 on a number line. It can also be interpreted as the value of the number disregarding its sign. The symbol denoting the absolute value of 5, for example, is |5|. Two vertical lines are placed around the number.

The absolute value of −5 is denoted as |−5|, and its value is 5.

Examples:

> **1.** |−12| = 12

> **2.** $\left|-3\frac{1}{2}\right| = 3\frac{1}{2}$

> **3.** −|−5| = −5

First find |−5|, which is 5; then find the negative of this result, which is −5.

Addition

Adding Two Integers with the Same Sign

To **add two integers with the same sign** (either both positive or both negative), add the absolute values of the integers and keep their same sign.

Examples:

> $\begin{array}{r} +5 \\ \textbf{1.} \ \underline{++7} \\ +12 \end{array}$ |+5| = 5, |+7| = 7, 5 + 7 = 12

> $\begin{array}{r} -8 \\ \textbf{2.} \ \underline{+-3} \\ -11 \end{array}$ |−8| = 8, |−3| = 3, 3 + 8 = 11

Adding Two Integers with Different Signs

To **add two integers with different signs** (one positive and one negative), subtract their absolute values and keep the sign of the integer with the greater absolute value.

Examples:

1. $-4 + 8 = 4$ $\qquad$ $|-4| = 4, \ |8| = 8 \qquad 8 - 4 = 4 \qquad |8| > |-4|$

2. $\begin{array}{r} +5 \\ +-7 \\ \hline -2 \end{array}$ $\qquad$ $|+5| = 5, \ |-7| = 7 \qquad 7 - 5 = 2 \qquad |-7| > |+5|$

Subtraction

Subtracting Positive and/or Negative Integers

To *subtract positive and/or negative integers,* just change the sign of the number being subtracted and then add.

Examples:

1. $-12 - 6 = -12 + -6 = -18$

2. $\begin{array}{r} +12 \\ -+4 \\ \hline \end{array}$ becomes $\begin{array}{r} +12 \\ +-4 \\ \hline +8 \ \text{or} \ 8 \end{array}$

3. $\begin{array}{r} -14 \\ --4 \\ \hline \end{array}$ becomes $\begin{array}{r} -14 \\ ++4 \\ \hline -10 \end{array}$

When number values are positive, the "+" is dropped, +5 = 5.

Minus Sign Precedes a Parenthesis

If a *minus sign precedes a parenthesis,* it means everything within the parentheses is to be subtracted. Therefore, using the same rule as in the subtraction of integers, change every sign within the parentheses to its opposite and then add.

Examples:

1. $\begin{aligned} 9 - (3 - 5 + 7 - 6) &= 9 + \left[(-3) + 5 + (-7) + 6\right] \\ &= 9 + 1 \\ &= 10 \end{aligned}$

2. $\begin{aligned} 20 - (35 - 50 + 100) &= 20 + \left[(-35) + 50 + (-100)\right] \\ &= 20 + (-85) \\ &= -65 \end{aligned}$

Multiplication and Division

Multiply or Divide Integers with Negative Signs

To *multiply or divide integers with negative signs* use these rules:

- Multiplying or dividing with an odd number of negative signs will produce a negative answer.
- Multiplying or dividing with an even number of negative signs will produce a positive answer.

Examples:

1. $(-3)(8)(-5)(-1)(-2) = 240$

2. $(-3)(8)(-1)(-2) = -48$

3. $\dfrac{-64}{-2} = 32$

4. $\dfrac{-64}{2} = -32$

Zero Times Any Number

Zero times any number equals zero.

Examples:

1. $(0)(5) = 0$

2. $(-3)(0) = 0$

3. $(8)(9)(0)(3)(-4) = 0$

Zero Divided by a Nonzero Number

Similarly, zero divided by any *nonzero* number is zero.

Examples:

1. $0 \div 5$ also written as $\dfrac{0}{5} = 0$

2. $\dfrac{0}{-3} = 0$

Important note: Dividing by zero is "undefined" and is not permitted. $\dfrac{6}{0}$ and $\dfrac{0}{0}$ are not permitted because there are no values for these expressions. The answer is not zero.

Fractions

Fractions compare two values. The **numerator** is written above the fraction bar, and the **denominator** is written below the fraction bar. The fraction bar indicates division.

$$\frac{1}{2} \quad \begin{array}{l} 1 \text{ is the numerator} \\ 2 \text{ is the denominator} \end{array}$$

All rules for the arithmetic operations involving integers also apply to fractions.

Fractions may be *negative* as well as *positive*. However, negative fractions are typically written $-\dfrac{3}{4}$, not $\dfrac{-3}{4}$ or $\dfrac{3}{-4}$ (although they are all equal): $-\dfrac{3}{4} = \dfrac{-3}{4} = \dfrac{3}{-4}$.

A fraction with a value less than 1, such as $\frac{3}{5}$, where the numerator is smaller than the denominator, is called a *proper fraction.* A fraction with a value greater than or equal to 1, such as $\frac{12}{7}$ or $\frac{6}{6}$, where the numerator is larger than or equal to the denominator, is called an *improper fraction.*

Mixed Numbers

When a term contains both a whole number and a fraction, it is called a *mixed number.* For instance, $5\frac{1}{4}$ and $290\frac{3}{4}$ are both mixed numbers. To change an improper fraction to a mixed number, you divide the denominator into the numerator to get the whole number portion and then place the remainder over the divisor to get the fraction portion.

$$\frac{18}{7} = 2\frac{4}{7} \quad \begin{array}{l} \leftarrow \text{ remainder} \\ \leftarrow \text{ divisor} \end{array} \qquad \begin{array}{r} 2 \\ 7\overline{)18} \\ \underline{14} \\ 4 \end{array}$$

To change a mixed number to an improper fraction, you multiply the denominator of the fraction portion with the whole number and then add the numerator portion to that product. Then put that total over the original denominator.

$$4\frac{1}{2} = \frac{9}{2} \qquad \frac{2\times 4 + 1}{2} = \frac{9}{2}$$

Examples:

1. Change $5\frac{3}{4}$ to an improper fraction.

$$5\frac{3}{4} = \frac{23}{4} \qquad \frac{4\times 5 + 3}{4} = \frac{23}{4}$$

2. Change $\frac{59}{6}$ to a mixed number.

$$\frac{59}{6} = 9\frac{5}{6} \qquad \begin{array}{r} 9 \\ 6\overline{)59} \\ \underline{54} \\ 5 \end{array}$$

Simplified Fractions

On the ACT, fractions should be *simplified.* This is done by dividing both the numerator and denominator by the largest number that will divide into both without a remainder.

Examples:

1. $\frac{30}{50} = \frac{30 \div 10}{50 \div 10} = \frac{3}{5}$

2. $\frac{8}{40} = \frac{8 \div 8}{40 \div 8} = \frac{1}{5}$

3. $\frac{9}{15} = \frac{9 \div 3}{15 \div 3} = \frac{3}{5}$

Changing the Denominator

The *denominator* of a fraction may be changed by multiplying both the numerator and the denominator by the same number.

Examples:

1. Change $\frac{1}{2}$ into tenths.

$$\frac{1}{2} = \frac{1 \times 5}{2 \times 5} = \frac{5}{10}$$

2. Change $\frac{3}{4}$ into fortieths.

$$\frac{3}{4} = \frac{3 \times 10}{4 \times 10} = \frac{30}{40}$$

Factors

Factors of a number are those whole numbers that divide the number with no remainder.

Examples:

1. What are the factors of 8?

$$8 = 1 \times 8 \text{ and } 8 = 2 \times 4$$

Therefore, the factors of 8 are 1, 2, 4, and 8.

2. What are the factors of 24?

$$24 = 1 \times 24, \, 24 = 2 \times 12, \, 24 = 3 \times 8, \, 24 = 4 \times 6$$

Therefore, the factors of 24 are 1, 2, 3, 4, 6, 8, 12, and 24.

Common Factors

Common factors are those factors that are the same for two or more numbers.

Examples:

1. What are the common factors of 6 and 8?

Number	List of factors
6	1 2 3 6
8	1 2 4 8

1 and 2 are common factors of 6 and 8.

Note: Some numbers may have many common factors.

2. What are the common factors of 24 and 36?

Number	List of factors
24	1 2 3 4 6 8 12 24
36	1 2 3 4 6 9 12 18 36

The common factors of 24 and 36 are 1, 2, 3, 4, 6, and 12.

Greatest Common Factor

The *greatest common factor* (GCF), also known as the greatest common divisor, is the largest factor common to two or more numbers.

Example:

1. What is the greatest common factor of 24 and 36?

Number	List of factors
24	1 2 3 4 6 8 12 24
36	1 2 3 4 6 9 12 18 36

Notice that while, 1, 2, 3, 4, 6, and 12 are all common factors of 24 and 36, 12 is the greatest common factor.

Multiples

Multiples of a number are found by multiplying that number by 1, by 2, by 3, by 4, by 5, and so on.

Examples:

1. Multiples of 3 are 3, 6, 9, 12, 15, 18, 21, and so on.

2. Multiples of 4 are 4, 8, 12, 16, 20, 24, 28, 32, and so on.

3. Multiples of 7 are 7, 14, 21, 28, 35, 42, 49, 56, and so on.

Common Multiples

Common multiples are those multiples that are the same for two or more numbers.

Example:

1. What are the common multiples of 2 and 3?

Number	Multiples
2	2 4 6 8 10 12 14 16 18 etc.
3	3 6 9 12 15 18 etc.

The common multiples of 2 and 3 are 6, 12, 18. . . . Notice that common multiples may go on indefinitely.

Least Common Multiple

The *least common multiple* (LCM) is the smallest multiple that is common to two or more numbers.

Example:

> **1.** What is the least common multiple of 2 and 3?

Number	Multiples
2	2 4 **6** 8 10 12 14 16 18 etc.
3	3 **6** 9 12 15 18 etc.

The least common multiple of 2 and 3 is 6.

Least Common Denominator

To add fractions, you must first change all denominators to their *least common denominator* (LCD). The LCD is also known as the least common multiple of the denominators. After all the denominators are the same, add fractions by adding the numerators (notice the denominator remains the same).

Examples:

> **1.** $\frac{2}{7} + \frac{3}{5} = \left(\frac{5}{5}\right)\left(\frac{2}{7}\right) + \left(\frac{7}{7}\right)\left(\frac{3}{5}\right) = \frac{10}{35} + \frac{21}{35} = \frac{31}{35}$

35 is the LCD and $\frac{2}{7} = \frac{10}{35}, \frac{3}{5} = \frac{21}{35}$.

> **2.** $\frac{3}{8} = \frac{3}{8}$ $\left\{ 8 \text{ is the LCD and } \frac{3}{8} = \frac{3}{8} \right.$
>
> $+\ \frac{1}{2} = \frac{4}{8}$ $\left\{ 8 \text{ is the LCD and } \frac{1}{2} = \frac{4}{8} \right.$
>
> $\phantom{+\ \frac{1}{2} =}\ \frac{7}{8}$

> **3.** $\frac{4}{11} + \frac{9}{11} = \frac{13}{11}$ or $1\frac{2}{11}$

Since the denominators are the same, it is not necessary to find an LCD.

Adding and Subtracting Positive and Negative Fractions

The rules for integers apply to adding or subtracting positive and negative fractions.

Examples:

> **1.** $-\frac{1}{2} + \frac{1}{3} = -\frac{3}{6} + \frac{2}{6} = \frac{-3}{6} + \frac{2}{6} = \frac{-3+2}{6} = -\frac{1}{6}$

> **2.** $\frac{3}{4} = \frac{9}{12}$
>
> $+\left(-\frac{1}{3}\right) = +\left(-\frac{4}{12}\right)$
>
> $\phantom{+\left(-\frac{1}{3}\right) =}\ \frac{5}{12}$

178

3. $-\dfrac{7}{8} - \dfrac{2}{3} = -\dfrac{7}{8} + \left(-\dfrac{2}{3}\right)$

$\qquad\qquad = \left(\dfrac{3}{3}\right)\left(\dfrac{-7}{8}\right) + \left(\dfrac{8}{8}\right)\left(\dfrac{-2}{3}\right)$

$\qquad\qquad = \dfrac{-21}{24} + \dfrac{-16}{24}$

$\qquad\qquad = \dfrac{-37}{24} \text{ or } -1\dfrac{13}{24}$

4. $\qquad \dfrac{9}{10} = \dfrac{9}{10} = \dfrac{9}{10}$

$\quad \underline{-\left(-\dfrac{1}{5}\right) = +\dfrac{1}{5} = +\dfrac{2}{10}}$

$\qquad\qquad\qquad \dfrac{11}{10} \text{ or } 1\dfrac{1}{10}$

Adding Mixed Numbers

The rules for adding and subtracting integers also apply to mixed numbers. To **add mixed numbers,** add the fraction portions together, add the whole numbers, and then combine the two results.

Example:

1. $1\dfrac{3}{8} + 2\dfrac{5}{6} = (1+2) + \left(\dfrac{3}{8} + \dfrac{5}{6}\right) \qquad \dfrac{3}{8} = \dfrac{9}{24} \text{ and } \dfrac{5}{6} = \dfrac{20}{24}$

$\qquad\qquad = 3 + \left(\dfrac{9}{24} + \dfrac{20}{24}\right)$

$\qquad\qquad = 3 + \dfrac{29}{24}$

$\qquad\qquad = 3 + 1\dfrac{5}{24}$

$\qquad\qquad = 4\dfrac{5}{24}$

Subtracting Mixed Numbers

When you subtract mixed numbers, sometimes you may have to "borrow" from the whole number, just as you sometimes borrow from the next column when subtracting ordinary numbers.

Examples:

1.
$\quad \overset{\displaystyle 3\,\overset{7}{\cancel{6}}}{\underset{\cancel{4}\,\cancel{\frac{1}{6}}}{}} \leftarrow \begin{cases} \text{borrowed 1 in the form } \dfrac{6}{6} \text{ from the 4} \\[6pt] \text{and added it to the } \dfrac{1}{6} \text{ to get } \dfrac{7}{6} \end{cases}$

$\quad \underline{-\,2\,\dfrac{5}{6}}$

$\qquad 1\dfrac{2}{6} = 1\dfrac{1}{3}$

To subtract a mixed number from a whole number, you have to "borrow" from the whole number.

2. $6 = 5\frac{5}{5} \leftarrow \left\{\text{borrow 1 in the form of } \frac{5}{5} \text{ from the 6}\right.$

$\underline{-3\frac{1}{5} = -3\frac{1}{5}}$

$2\frac{4}{5}$

---

3. $11 = 10\frac{3}{3} \leftarrow \left\{\text{borrow 1 in the form of } \frac{3}{3} \text{ from the 11}\right.$

$\underline{-\frac{2}{3} = \quad -\frac{2}{3}}$

$10\frac{1}{3}$

---

4. $6\frac{1}{8} - 3\frac{3}{4} = 6\frac{1}{8} - 3\frac{6}{8} = \overset{5}{\cancel{6}}\overset{\frac{9}{8}}{\cancel{\frac{1}{8}}} - 3\frac{6}{8} = 2\frac{3}{8}$

---

5. $-\frac{7}{8} - \frac{5}{9} = -\frac{63}{72} + \left(-\frac{40}{72}\right)$ $\frac{7}{8} = \frac{63}{72}, \frac{5}{9} = \frac{40}{72}$

$= -\frac{103}{72}$ or $-1\frac{31}{72}$

Multiplying Fractions

The rules for multiplying and dividing integers also apply to multiplying and dividing fractions. To **multiply fractions,** multiply the numerators and then multiply the denominators. Simplify if possible.

Examples:

1. $-\frac{1}{6} \times \frac{1}{3} = -\frac{1 \times 1}{6 \times 3} = -\frac{1}{18}$

---

2. $\left(-\frac{3}{4}\right)\left(-\frac{5}{7}\right) = +\frac{3 \times 5}{4 \times 7} = \frac{15}{28}$

---

3. $\frac{2}{3} \times \frac{5}{12} = \frac{10}{36}$ Simplify $\frac{10}{36}$ to $\frac{5}{18}$.

Notice the answer was simplified because $\frac{10}{36}$ was not in lowest terms.

Whole numbers can be written as fractions: $\left(3 = \frac{3}{1}, 4 = \frac{4}{1}, \text{and so on}\right)$.

4. $3 \times \frac{3}{8} = \frac{3}{1} \times \frac{3}{8} = \frac{9}{8} = 1\frac{1}{8}$

When multiplying fractions, it is often possible to simplify the problem by **canceling.** To cancel, find a number that divides into one numerator and one denominator. In the next example, 2 in the numerator and 12 in the denominator are both divisible by 2.

5. $\dfrac{\overset{1}{\cancel{2}}}{3} \times \dfrac{5}{\underset{6}{\cancel{12}}} = \dfrac{5}{18}$

Remember: You can cancel only when *multiplying* fractions.

6. $\dfrac{1}{4} \times \dfrac{2}{7} = \dfrac{1}{\overset{\cancel{4}}{2}} \times \dfrac{\overset{1}{\cancel{2}}}{7} = \dfrac{1}{14}$

7. $\left(-\dfrac{\overset{1}{\cancel{3}}}{\underset{2}{\cancel{8}}}\right) \times \left(-\dfrac{\overset{1}{\cancel{4}}}{\underset{3}{\cancel{9}}}\right) = \dfrac{1}{6}$

Multiplying Mixed Numbers

To *multiply mixed numbers,* change any mixed numbers or whole numbers to improper fractions and then multiply as previously shown.

Examples:

1. $2\dfrac{3}{8} \times 1\dfrac{5}{6} = \dfrac{19}{8} \times \dfrac{11}{6} = \dfrac{209}{48}$ or $4\dfrac{17}{48}$

2. $\left(-3\dfrac{1}{3}\right)\left(2\dfrac{1}{4}\right) = \left(-\dfrac{\overset{5}{\cancel{10}}}{\underset{1}{\cancel{3}}}\right)\left(\dfrac{\overset{3}{\cancel{9}}}{\underset{2}{\cancel{4}}}\right) = -\dfrac{15}{2}$ or $-7\dfrac{1}{2}$

Dividing Fractions or Mixed Numbers

To *divide fractions or mixed numbers* invert (turn upside down) the second fraction (the one "divided by") and multiply. Simplify where possible.

Examples:

1. $-\dfrac{1}{4} \div \dfrac{9}{14} = \left(-\dfrac{1}{\overset{\cancel{4}}{2}}\right)\left(\dfrac{\overset{7}{\cancel{14}}}{9}\right) = -\dfrac{7}{18}$

2. $6 \div 2\dfrac{1}{3} = \dfrac{6}{1} \div \dfrac{7}{3} = \dfrac{6}{1} \times \dfrac{3}{7} = \dfrac{18}{7}$ or $2\dfrac{4}{7}$

Complex Fractions

Sometimes a division-of-fractions problem may appear in the following form. Division problems in this form are called *complex fractions.*

$$\dfrac{\dfrac{3}{4}}{\dfrac{7}{8}}$$

The line separating the two fractions means "divided by." This problem may be rewritten as $\dfrac{3}{4} \div \dfrac{7}{8}$. Now follow the same procedure as previously shown.

$$\dfrac{3}{4} \div \dfrac{7}{8} = \dfrac{3}{\underset{1}{\cancel{4}}} \times \dfrac{\overset{2}{\cancel{8}}}{7} = \dfrac{6}{7}$$

Some complex fractions require applying the order of operations.

Example:

1. $\dfrac{1}{3+\dfrac{2}{1+\dfrac{1}{3}}}$

This problem can be rewritten using grouping symbols.

$$\frac{1}{3+\dfrac{2}{1+\dfrac{1}{3}}} = 1 \div \left\{ 3 + \left[2 \div \left(1 + \frac{1}{3} \right) \right] \right\} \quad \text{Start with the most inside grouping.}$$

$$= 1 \div \left\{ 3 + \left[2 \div \left(\frac{4}{3} \right) \right] \right\} \quad \text{Do the next most inside grouping.}$$

$$= 1 \div \left\{ 3 + \left[\frac{\cancel{2}}{1} \times \frac{3}{\cancel{4}} \right] \right\}$$

$$= 1 \div \left\{ 3 + \left[\frac{3}{2} \right] \right\} \quad \text{Do the next most inside grouping.}$$

$$= 1 \div \left\{ \frac{9}{2} \right\}$$

$$= 1 \times \frac{2}{9}$$

$$= \frac{2}{9}$$

Decimals

Each position in any decimal number has **place value.** For instance, in the number 485.03, the 4 is in the hundreds place, the 8 is in the tens place, the 5 is in the ones place, the 0 is in the tenths place, and the 3 is in the hundredths place. The following chart will help you identify place value.

millions	hundred thousands	ten thousands	thousands	hundreds	tens	ones	tenths	hundredths	thousandths	ten thousandths	hundred thousandths
							1/10	1/100	1/1,000	1/10,000	1/100,000
1,000,000	100,000	10,000	1,000	100	10	1	0.1	0.01	0.001	0.0001	0.00001
10^6	10^5	10^4	10^3	10^2	10^1	10^0	10^{-1}	10^{-2}	10^{-3}	10^{-4}	10^{-5}
				4	8	5	0	3			

Rounding Off

To *round off* any **positive number:**

1. Underline the place value that you're rounding off.
2. Look to the immediate right (one place) of the underlined place value.
3. Identify the number (the one to the right). If it is 5 or higher, round up the underlined place value by 1. If the number (the one to the right) is 4 or less, leave your underlined place value as it is and change all the other numbers to the right of it to zeros, or drop them if the place value is to the right of the decimal point.

To *round off* any **negative number:**

1. Take the absolute value of the number.
2. Do the three steps as previously listed.
3. Replace the negative sign on the number.

Examples:

1. Round 4.4584 to the nearest thousandth.

The 8 is in the thousandth place. To its right is a 4. Thus, the 8 is left unchanged and to its right the digits are dropped. The rounded off answer becomes 4.458.

2. Round 3456.12 to the nearest ten.

The 5 is in the tens place. To its right is a 6. Thus the 5 is increased by 1 and the digits until the decimal become zeros, then the remaining digits are dropped. The rounded off answer is 3460.

3. Round –3.6 to the nearest integer.

|–3.6| = 3.6. Rounding to the nearest integer is the same as rounding to the nearest one. The 3 is in the one's place and to its right is a 6. Thus, 3.6 rounded to the nearest one is 4. Therefore, –3.6 rounded to the nearest integer is –4.

Fractions Written in Decimal Form

Fractions and mixed numbers can be written in decimal form (**decimal fractions**) by using a *decimal point.* All numbers to the left of the decimal point are whole numbers. All numbers to the right of the decimal point are fractions with denominators of powers of 10 (10^1, 10^2, 10^3 . . .).

Examples:

1. $0.6 = \dfrac{6}{10} = \dfrac{3}{5}$

2. $3.25 = 3\dfrac{25}{100} = 3\dfrac{1}{4}$

Adding and Subtracting Decimals

To *add or subtract decimals,* line up the decimal points and then add or subtract in the same manner you would add or subtract regular numbers. Placing zeros at the right of the number can make the problem more readable.

Examples:

1. $0.08 + 1.3 + 0.562 =$ 0.080

                          1.300

                      +0.562

                          1.942

2. $0.45 - 0.003 = 0.4\overset{4}{\cancel{5}}\,\overset{10}{\cancel{0}}$

                        $-0.00\ 3$

                         $0.44\ 7$

A whole number has an understood decimal point to its right.

3. $17 - 8.43 = 1\overset{6}{\cancel{7}}.^{1}\overset{9}{\cancel{0}}\,\overset{10}{\cancel{0}}$

                       $-\ 8\ .\ 4\ 3$

                         $8\ .\ 5\ 7$

Multiplying Decimals

To *multiply decimals,* multiply as if there were no decimals in the numbers. Then place the decimal point in the answer so that the number of digits to the right of the decimal point is equal to the sum of the number of digits to the right of the decimal point in both numbers multiplied (the multiplier and multiplicand). It is sometimes necessary to insert zeros immediately to the right of the decimal point in the answer to have the correct number of digits.

Examples:

1.   8.001 ← {3 digits to the right of the decimal point

      ×   2.4 ← {1 digit to the right of the decimal point

    32004

    16002

    19.2024   {decimal point placed so there is the same number of digits to the right of the decimal point $(1 + 3 = 4)$

2.   3.02 ← {2 digits to the right of the decimal point

    × 0.004 ← {3 digit to the right of the decimal point

    0.01208   {zero inserted immediately to the right of the decimal so there is the same number of digits to the right of the decimal point $(2 + 3 = 5)$

Dividing Decimals

To *divide decimals,* divide as usual, except that if the *divisor* (the number you're dividing by) has a decimal, move it to the right as many places as necessary until it's a whole number. Then move the decimal point in the *dividend* (the number being divided into) to the right the same number of places. Sometimes you may have to insert zeros in the *dividend* (the number inside the division bracket).

Examples:

> **1.** $0.147 \div 0.7$ becomes $0.7\overline{)0.147} = 7\overline{)1.47}$ $\dfrac{0.21}{}$

The decimal point was moved to the right one place in each number.

> **2.** $0.002\overline{)26.} = 2\overline{)26000.}$ $\dfrac{13000.}{}$

The decimal point was moved three places to the right in each number. This required inserting three zeros in the dividend.

Changing a Fraction to a Decimal

To *change a fraction to a decimal,* divide the numerator by the denominator. Every fraction, when changed to a decimal, either terminates (comes to an end) or has a repeating pattern in its decimal portion.

Examples:

Change each fraction into its decimal name.

> **1.** $\dfrac{3}{20}$ becomes $20\overline{)3.00} = 0.15$ $\dfrac{0.15}{}$

> **2.** $\dfrac{5}{8}$ becomes $8\overline{)5.000} = 0.625$ $\dfrac{0.625}{}$

> **3.** $\dfrac{7}{12}$ becomes $12\overline{)7.00000} = 0.58333\ldots$ or $0.58\overline{3}$ $\dfrac{0.58333}{}$

Ratios and Proportions

A *ratio* is a comparison of two values usually written in fraction form. The ratio of 3 to 5 can be expressed as 3:5 or $\dfrac{3}{5}$. A *proportion* is a statement saying that two ratios are equal. Because $\dfrac{5}{10}$ and $\dfrac{4}{8}$ both have values of $\dfrac{1}{2}$, it can be stated that $\dfrac{5}{10} = \dfrac{4}{8}$.

Cross-Products Fact

In a proportion, the cross products (multiplying across the equal sign) always produce equal answers. In the example of $\dfrac{5}{10} = \dfrac{4}{8}$, $5 \times 8 = 10 \times 4$.

You can use this cross-products fact to solve proportions.

Examples:

> **1.** Solve for x: $\dfrac{4}{x} = \dfrac{7}{5}$.

Applying the cross-products fact, you get

$$7x = (4)(5)$$
$$7x = 20$$
$$x = \frac{20}{7} = 2\frac{6}{7}$$

2. Solve for x: $\dfrac{x}{100} = \dfrac{4}{25}$.

Applying the cross-products fact, you get

$$25x = (4)(100)$$
$$25x = 400$$
$$x = \frac{400}{25} = 16$$

Percents

The symbol for *percent* is %. The word percent means hundredths (per hundred). The expression 37% is read as 37 hundredths and can be expressed either as the fraction $\dfrac{37}{100}$ or decimal 0.37.

Changing Decimals to Percents

Decimals to Percents	Steps to Change Decimals to Percents	Examples: Changing Decimals to Percents
	1. Move the decimal point two places to the right. 2. Insert a percent sign.	1. 0.75 = 75% 2. 0.005 = 0.5% 3. 1.85 = 185% 4. 20.3 = 2,030%
Percents to Decimals	**Steps to Change Percents to Decimals**	**Examples: Changing Percents to Decimals**
	1. Eliminate the percent sign. 2. Move the decimal point two places to the left. 3. Notice that sometimes inserting zeros will be necessary as in Examples 1 and 3.	1. 7% = 0.07 2. 23% = 0.23 3. 0.2% = 0.002

Changing Fractions to a Percent

There are two methods for changing a fraction to a percent.

Method 1: Changing Fractions to a Percent

1. Change the fraction to a decimal.
2. Change the decimal to a percent.

Examples:

Change each fraction into a percent.

1. $\dfrac{1}{8}$ $\dfrac{1}{8} = 0.125 = 12.5\%$ or $12\dfrac{1}{2}\%$

2. $\dfrac{2}{5}$ $\dfrac{2}{5} = 0.4 = 40\%$

3. $\dfrac{5}{2}$ $\dfrac{5}{2} = 2.5 = 250\%$

Method 2: Changing Fractions to a Percent

1. Create a proportion that sets the fraction equal to $\frac{x}{100}$.
2. Solve the proportion for x. Place a percent sign next to the x.

Examples:

Change each fraction into a percent.

---

1. $\frac{3}{8}$

$$\frac{3}{8} = \frac{x}{100}$$
$$8x = 300$$
$$x = \frac{300}{8} = 37\frac{1}{2} \text{ or } 37.5$$
$$\frac{3}{8} = 37\frac{1}{2}\% \text{ or } 37.5\%$$

---

2. $\frac{2}{3}$

$$\frac{2}{3} = \frac{x}{100}$$
$$3x = 200$$
$$x = \frac{200}{3} = 66\frac{2}{3}$$
$$\frac{2}{3} = 66\frac{2}{3}\%$$

Tip: To eliminate many unnecessary computations and save you time, try to make time to memorize the important equivalents presented in "Fraction-Decimal-Percent Equivalents" in Chapter 7.

Percentage-Type Problems

Percentage-type problems are of the form A is $B\%$ of C. If the B and C are known, the process is simply to multiply the B-percent value with the C-value.

Examples:

---

1. What is 79% of 64?

Using fractions: 79% of $64 = \frac{79}{100} \times \frac{64}{1} = \frac{5056}{100}$ or 50.56

Using decimals: 79% of $64 = (0.79)(64) = 50.56$

---

2. What is 15% of 50?

Using fractions: 15% of $50 = \frac{\overset{3}{\cancel{15}}}{\underset{\underset{2}{20}}{\cancel{100}}} \times \frac{\overset{5}{\cancel{50}}}{1} = \frac{15}{2} = 7\frac{1}{2}$ or 7.5

Using decimals: 15% of $50 = 0.15 \times 50 = 7.5$

---

3. What is $33\frac{1}{3}\%$ of 36?

The fraction method works best in this case.

$$33\tfrac{1}{3}\% \text{ of } 36 = \frac{1}{\underset{1}{\cancel{3}}} \times \frac{\overset{12}{\cancel{36}}}{1} = \frac{12}{1} = 12$$

If the A value is known and one of the B or C values is unknown, then two methods make solving the problem easier.

Equation and Proportion Methods

Method 1: Equation Method for Percentage-Type Problems

1. Turn the question word for word into an equation. (Change percents to decimals or fractions, whichever you find easier.)
2. Solve the equation. (To review solving linear equations, see Chapter 9, "Algebra.")

Method 2: Proportion Method for Percentage-Type Problems

1. Use x to replace the unknown value.
2. Replace *is* with an *equal sign* (=) and replace *of* with *multiplication*. The proportion will look like this:

$$\frac{\%\text{-number}}{100} = \frac{\text{"is"-number}}{\text{"of "-number}}$$

Examples:

1. 40% of what is 20?

Equation method	Proportion method
$0.4(x) = 20$	$\dfrac{40}{100} = \dfrac{20}{x}$
$x = \dfrac{20}{0.4}$	$40x = 2000$
$x = 50$	$x = 50$

Therefore, 40% of 50 is 20.

2. What percent of 45 is 30?

Equation method	Proportion method
$\left(\dfrac{x}{100}\right)(45) = 30$	$\dfrac{x}{100} = \dfrac{30}{45}$
$\dfrac{45}{100}x = 30$	$45x = 3000$
$x = \left(\dfrac{\overset{2}{\cancel{30}}}{1}\right)\left(\dfrac{100}{\underset{3}{\cancel{45}}}\right)$	$x = \dfrac{3000}{45}$
$x = \dfrac{200}{3} \text{ or } 66\tfrac{2}{3}$	$x = \dfrac{200}{3} \text{ or } 66\tfrac{2}{3}$

Therefore, $66\tfrac{2}{3}\%$ of 45 is 30.

Percent Change

To find *percent change* (increase or decrease), use this formula:

$$\frac{\text{amount of change}}{\text{starting amount}} \times 100\% = \text{percent change}$$

Examples:

1. What is the percent increase of a rise in temperature from 80° to 100°?

The amount of change is the difference between 100 and 80 or 20.

$$\frac{\text{amount of change}}{\text{starting amount}} \times 100\% = \frac{\overset{1}{\cancel{20}}}{\underset{4}{\cancel{80}}} \times 100\% = 25\% \text{ increase}$$

2. What is the percent decrease of Jon's salary if it went from $150 per hour to $100 per hour?

$$\frac{\text{amount of change}}{\text{starting amount}} \times 100\% = \frac{\overset{1}{\cancel{50}}}{\underset{3}{\cancel{150}}} \times 100\% = \left(\frac{100}{3}\right)\% = 33\tfrac{1}{3}\% \text{ decrease}$$

3. What is the percent change from 2,100 to 1,890?

$$\frac{\text{amount of change}}{\text{starting amount}} \times 100\% = \frac{\overset{1}{\cancel{210}}}{\underset{10}{\cancel{2,100}}} \times 100\% = 10\% \text{ change}$$

Note: The terms *percentage rise, percentage difference,* and *percentage change* are the same as percent change.

Exponents

An *exponent* is a positive, negative, or zero number placed above and to the right of a quantity. The quantity is known as the base, and the exponent expresses the power to which the base is to be raised. In 4^3, 4 is the base and 3 is the exponent. It shows that 4 is to be used as a factor three times: $4^3 = (4)(4)(4)$, and is read as *four to the third power* or *four cubed.*

Examples:

1. $2^5 = (2)(2)(2)(2)(2) = 32$

2. $(-3)^3 = (-3)(-3)(-3) = -27$

3. $\left(-\frac{1}{4}\right)^2 = \left(-\frac{1}{4}\right)\left(-\frac{1}{4}\right) = \frac{1}{16}$

More Exponents

Remember that $x^1 = x$ for all replacements of x and $x^0 = 1$ as long as $x \neq 0$.

Examples:

1. $(-5)^0 = 1$

2. $-6^0 = -1$ (In this case, the 0 exponent is applied to only the 6 since the negative sign was not in a parentheses as in example 1.)

3. $(2.4)^0 = 1$

4. $6^1 = 6$

Negative Exponents

If the *exponent is negative*, such as 3^{-2}, then the base and its exponent may be dropped under the number 1 in a fraction to remove the negative sign.

Examples:

1. $6^{-1} = \dfrac{1}{6^1} = \dfrac{1}{6}$

2. $3^{-2} = \dfrac{1}{3^2} = \dfrac{1}{9}$

3. $(-2)^{-3} = \dfrac{1}{(-2)^3} = \dfrac{1}{-8} = -\dfrac{1}{8}$

Multiplying Two Numbers with the Same Base

To multiply two numbers with the same base, you add their exponents and keep the same base.

Examples:

1. $8^3 \times 8^7 = 8^{3+7} = 8^{10}$

2. $(-2)^6(-2)^{-3} = (-2)^{6+(-3)} = (-2)^3$

Dividing Two Numbers with the Same Base

To divide two numbers with the same base, you subtract the exponent on the dividing number from the exponent on the number being divided.

Examples:

1. $9^5 \div 9^{-2} = 9^{5-(-2)} = 9^{5+2} = 9^7$

2. $\dfrac{3^7}{3^4} = 3^{7-4} = 3^3$

Base with an Exponent Raised to a Power

To raise an expression involving a base and exponent to a power, keep the base and use the product of the exponent and the power as the new exponent.

Examples:

1. $\left(5^3\right)^2 = 5^{(2)(3)} = 5^6$

2. $\left[(-4)^{-4}\right]^{-2} = (-4)^{(-4)(-2)} = (-4)^8$

Scientific Notation

Very large or very small numbers are sometimes written in *scientific notation.* A number written in scientific notation is a number between 1 and 10 and multiplied by a power of 10.

2,100,000 written in scientific notation is 2.1×10^6. Simply place the decimal point to get a number between 1 and 10 and then count the digits to the right of the decimal to get the power of 10.

$$2\underset{6\;\;5\;\;4\;\;3\;\;2\;\;1}{1\,0\,0\,0\,0\,0}$$

0.000042 written in scientific notation is 4.2×10^{-5}. The first non-zero digit from left to right is the "4." Place the decimal point to the right of the 4 and count how many places the decimal point moved. The decimal point was moved five places. The original value was less than 1, and so the exponent on the 10 is negative.

$$0\underset{1\;\;2\;\;3\;\;4\;\;5}{0\,0\,0\,0\,4}\,2$$

Notice that numbers greater than 1 have positive exponents when expressed in scientific notation, and numbers less than 1 have negative exponents when expressed in scientific notation. That is, if a number expressed in scientific notation has a positive exponent, then its value is greater than 1, and if it has a negative exponent, then its value is less than 1.

Examples:

Change the following to scientific notation:

1. $35,000 = 3.5 \times 10^4$

2. $1,112,000,000 = 1.112 \times 10^9$

3. $0.00000000327 = 3.27 \times 10^{-9}$

Change the following from scientific notation:

4. $2.6 \times 10^4 = 26,000$

5. $3.11 \times 10^7 = 31,100,000$

Square Roots

Perfect Squares

A perfect square is a product that results from squaring a number (multiplying a number by itself).

It is useful to memorize the perfect squares found by squaring the integers 1 through 15:

$$1, 4, 9, 16, 25, 36, 49, 64, 81, 100, 121, 144, 169, 196, \text{ and } 225$$

Tip: These are also found by squaring the integers (–1) through (–15).

Square Roots of Perfect Squares

The symbol for square root is $\sqrt{}$. The square roots of *perfect squares* have exact answers. To find the square root of a number, you want to find some number that when multiplied by itself gives you the original number. In other words, to find the square root of 25, you want to find the number that when multiplied by itself gives you 25. Therefore, the square root of 25 is 5. For example:

$$\sqrt{5^2} = \sqrt{25} = 5$$

Following is a partial list of perfect (whole number) square roots.

$$\sqrt{0} = 0 \quad \sqrt{16} = 4 \quad \sqrt{64} = 8$$
$$\sqrt{1} = 1 \quad \sqrt{25} = 5 \quad \sqrt{81} = 9$$
$$\sqrt{4} = 2 \quad \sqrt{36} = 6 \quad \sqrt{100} = 10$$
$$\sqrt{9} = 3 \quad \sqrt{49} = 7$$

If a negative sign precedes a square root, the answer is the negative of the square root.

$$\sqrt{(-4)^2} = \sqrt{16} = 4$$

Example:

1. $-\sqrt{9} = -3$

2. $-\sqrt{(-4)^2} = -\sqrt{16} = -4$

Square Roots of Nonperfect Squares

To find the square root of a number that is *not a perfect square,* it is necessary to find an approximate answer by using the procedure given in the following example.

Example:

1. Between what two consecutive integers is $\sqrt{135}$ and to which is it closer?

$$\sqrt{135} \text{ is between } \sqrt{121} \text{ and } \sqrt{144}.$$
$$\sqrt{121} < \sqrt{135} < \sqrt{144}, \text{ and } \sqrt{121} = 11, \ \sqrt{144} = 12$$
$$11 < \sqrt{135} < 12$$

Since 135 is closer to 144 than 121, $\sqrt{135}$ is closer to 12 than to 11.

Tip: Use your calculator on the ACT only when necessary. All problems can be done without a calculator, although using one can save time in some situations. After calculating the square root, use your knowledge of rounding off to determine the desired place value.

Simplifying a Square Root

Sometimes you will have to *simplify square roots,* or write them in simplest form. In fractions, $\frac{2}{4}$ can be simplified to $\frac{1}{2}$. In square roots, $\sqrt{32}$ can be simplified to $4\sqrt{2}$.

Methods to Simplify a Square Root

Method 1	Method 2
Factor the number under the $\sqrt{}$ into two factors, one of which is the largest possible perfect square that divides the number. (Perfect squares are 1, 4, 9, 16, 25, 36, 49. . .)	Completely factor the number under the $\sqrt{}$ into prime factors and then simplify by bringing out any factors that came in pairs.

Examples:

1. Simplify $\sqrt{32}$.

Method 1.
$$\sqrt{32} = \sqrt{16 \times 2}$$
$$= \sqrt{16} \times \sqrt{2}$$
Take the square root of the perfect square number 16
$$= 4 \times \sqrt{2}$$
Finally, write it as a single expression.
$$= 4\sqrt{2}$$

Method 2.
$$\sqrt{32} = \sqrt{2 \times 16}$$
$$= \sqrt{2 \times 2 \times 8}$$
$$= \sqrt{2 \times 2 \times 2 \times 4}$$
$$= \sqrt{2 \times 2 \times 2 \times 2 \times 2}$$
Rewrite with pairs under the radical
$$= \sqrt{2 \times 2} \times \sqrt{2 \times 2} \times \sqrt{2}$$
$$= 2 \times 2 \times \sqrt{2}$$
$$= 4\sqrt{2}$$

In Example 1, the largest perfect square is easy to see, so Method 1 is probably the faster method to use.

2. Simplify $\sqrt{80}$.

Method 1.
$$\sqrt{80} = \sqrt{16 \times 5}$$
$$= \sqrt{16} \times \sqrt{5}$$
$$= 4\sqrt{5}$$

Method 2.
$$\sqrt{80} = \sqrt{2 \times 40}$$
$$= \sqrt{2 \times 2 \times 20}$$
$$= \sqrt{2 \times 2 \times 2 \times 10}$$
$$= \sqrt{2 \times 2 \times 2 \times 2 \times 5}$$
$$= \sqrt{2 \times 2} \times \sqrt{2 \times 2} \times \sqrt{5}$$
$$= 2 \times 2 \times \sqrt{5}$$
$$= 4\sqrt{5}$$

In Method 1, it might not be so obvious that the largest perfect square is 16, so Method 2 might be the faster method to use.

3. Simplify $\sqrt{\dfrac{384}{8}}$.

First, do the division under the square root and then proceed with the simplifying.

$$\sqrt{\frac{384}{8}} = \sqrt{48}$$

Method 1.

$$\sqrt{48} = \sqrt{16 \times 3}$$
$$= \left(\sqrt{16}\right)\left(\sqrt{3}\right)$$
$$= 4\sqrt{3}$$

Method 2.

$$\sqrt{48} = \sqrt{2 \times 24}$$
$$= \sqrt{2 \times 2 \times 12}$$
$$= \sqrt{2 \times 2 \times 2 \times 6}$$
$$= \sqrt{2 \times 2 \times 2 \times 2 \times 3}$$
$$= \left(\sqrt{2 \times 2}\right)\left(\sqrt{2 \times 2}\right)\sqrt{3}$$
$$= (2)(2)\sqrt{3}$$
$$= 4\sqrt{3}$$

Set Theory

Set theory is fundamental for most topics in modern mathematics. Sets are defined as a collection of groups of objects.

Term	Definition	Examples
Set	A set is a collection of objects that are separated by a comma and grouped in braces.	$A = \{1, 2, 3, 4, 5\}$ $B = \{a, e, i, o, u\}$
Element	The objects that make up a set are called elements (or members) of the set. The symbol used for an element is $\in$. ($\notin$ means not an element of the set.)	$4 \in A$ $h \notin B$
Subset	If a set is part of or identical to another set, it is called a subset of the set. The symbol used for subset is $\subseteq$. *Note: A proper subset $\subset$ cannot be identical to the original set.*	$\{1, 4, 5\} \subseteq \{1, 2, 3, 4, 5\}$ $\{a, e, i, o, u\} \subseteq \{a, e, i, o, u\}$
Empty or Null Set	A set with no elements is called the empty set or null set. The symbol used for the empty set is $\varnothing$ or $\{\ \}$.	$\varnothing$ or $\{\ \}$
Finite Set	A set that has a countable number of elements is called a finite set.	$\{1, 2, 3, 4, 5\}$ is a finite set with 5 elements.
Infinite Set	A set whose elements continue indefinitely is called an infinite set. Note that three dots are used to indicate a set is infinite.	$\{5, 10, 15, 20, 25, 30 \ldots\}$
Equal Sets	Sets that have exactly the same elements are called equal sets.	$\{3, 8, 10, 12\} = \{10, 8, 3, 12\}$
Equivalent Sets	Sets that have the same number of elements are called equivalent sets.	$\{1, 2, 3, 4, 5\}$ and $\{a, e, i, o, u\}$ are equivalent sets.

Term	Definition	Examples
Union	The union of two or more sets is a set that contains the elements of all the sets. The symbol used for union is ∪.	$\{1, 2, 3, 4, 5\} \cup \{2, 4, 6, 8\} = \{1, 2, 3, 4, 5, 6, 8\}$
Intersection	The intersection of two or more sets is a set that contains only those elements that are common to the sets. If the sets have no elements in common, then their intersection is the null set. The symbol used for intersection is ∩.	$\{1, 2, 3, 4, 5\} \cap \{2, 4, 6, 8\} = \{2, 4\}$ $\{1, 3, 5, 7\} \cap \{2, 4, 6, 8, 10\} = \varnothing$

Venn Diagrams

A Venn diagram is a useful method to visually represent two or more sets, and to illustrate whether or not sets have any elements in common. Diagrammed sets are generally represented as circles or ovals, but other geometric figures can be used. Sets that have elements in common will overlap, while sets that have no elements in common are shown disjointed from each other. When a number is positioned in an area of overlapping regions, that is how many objects, or the percent of objects, share the characteristics of the overlapping regions.

Questions 1–3 that follow refer to the following Venn diagram.

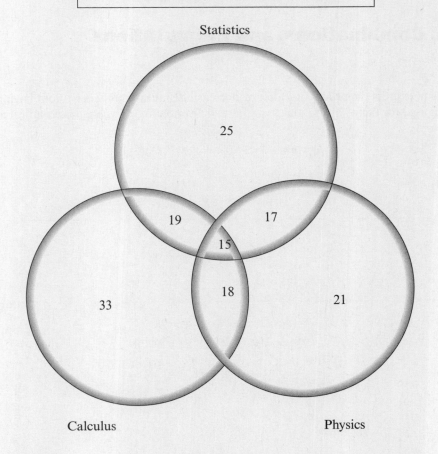

University of Las Vegas Mathematics Majors
Enrolled in Calculus, Physics, and Statistics

Examples:

> **1.** How many mathematics majors are enrolled in calculus and statistics, but not in physics?

The students enrolled in calculus and statistics, but not physics is found in the overlapping area of calculus and statistics, but outside the physics circle. This would yield an answer of 19 students.

> **2.** What percent of mathematics majors are enrolled in calculus? Give the answer to the nearest whole percent.

The number of mathematics majors enrolled in calculus is:

$$33 + 18 + 15 + 19 = 85$$

The total number of mathematics majors is:

$$33 + 18 + 15 + 19 + 21 + 17 + 25 = 148$$

The percentage of mathematics majors that are enrolled in calculus is:

$$\frac{85}{148} \approx 0.574 \approx 57.4\% \approx 57\% \text{ to the nearest whole percent.}$$

> **3.** How many mathematics majors are enrolled in at least two of the given courses?

The total number of mathematics majors enrolled in at least two of the given courses is found where any of the circles overlap or:

$$19 + 18 + 17 + 15 = 69 \text{ students}$$

Factorials, Combinations, and Permutations

Factorials

Factorials allow us to express the product of a set of decreasing natural numbers without having to write each factor. The symbol used for factorials is ! and the general definition for $n!$, where n is a natural number is:

$$n! = n(n-1)(n-2)(n-3) \ldots (3)(2)(1)$$

By definition $0! = 1$

Examples:

> **1.** (a) 4!
>
> (b) 6!
>
> (c) 9!

$$\text{(a) } 4! = 4 \cdot 3 \cdot 2 \cdot 1 = 24$$
$$\text{(b) } 6! = 6 \cdot 5 \cdot 4 \cdot 3 \cdot 2 \cdot 1 = 720$$
$$\text{(c) } 9! = 9 \cdot 8 \cdot 7 \cdot 6 \cdot 5 \cdot 4 \cdot 3 \cdot 2 \cdot 1 = 362,880$$

2. Evaluate $\frac{10!}{6!}$

$$\text{Since } 10! = 10 \bullet 9 \bullet 8 \bullet 7 \bullet (6!)$$

$$\frac{10!}{6!} = \frac{10 \bullet 9 \bullet 8 \bullet 7 \bullet 6!}{6!}$$

$$= 10 \bullet 9 \bullet 8 \bullet 7$$

$$\frac{10!}{6!} = 5040$$

3. Evaluate $\frac{13!}{10! \bullet 3!}$

$$\text{Since } 13! = 13 \bullet 12 \bullet 11 \bullet (10!)$$

$$\frac{13!}{10! \bullet 3!} = \frac{13 \bullet 12 \bullet 11 \bullet 10!}{10! \bullet 3!}$$

$$= \frac{13 \bullet \overset{2}{\cancel{12}} \bullet 11}{\cancel{3} \bullet \cancel{2} \bullet 1}$$

$$\frac{13!}{10! \bullet 3!} = 286$$

4. Simplify $\frac{(x+2)!}{(x-1)!}$

$$\text{Since } (x+2)! = (x+2)(x+1)(x)(x-1)!$$

$$\frac{(x+2)!}{(x-1)!} = \frac{(x+2)(x+1)(x)\cancel{(x-1)!}}{\cancel{(x-1)!}}$$

$$= (x+2)(x+1)(x)$$

$$\frac{(x+2)!}{(x-1)!} = x^3 + 3x^2 + 2x$$

Combinations

A selection of r objects from a set with a total of n objects without regard for the order of the selected objects is called a combination. The notation for the number of combinations of n objects taken r at a time is:

$$_nC_r \text{ or } C(n, r)$$

The total number of ways to select r objects from a set of n objects without regard for the order of the selected objects is:

$$_nC_r = C(n,r) = \frac{n!}{r!(n-r)!}$$

Examples:

1. How many different groups of 5 students can be formed by choosing from a total of 11 students?

Since the order of the students selected is not important, this is a combination of 5 students from a set of 11 students. The number of different groups possible is:

$$_{11}C_5 = C(11,5) = \frac{11!}{5!(11-5)!}$$

$$= \frac{11!}{5! \bullet 6!}$$

$$= \frac{11 \bullet 10 \bullet 9 \bullet 8 \bullet 7 \bullet \cancel{6!}}{5! \bullet \cancel{6!}}$$

$$= \frac{11 \bullet 10 \bullet 9 \bullet 8 \bullet 7}{5 \bullet 4 \bullet 3 \bullet 2 \bullet 1}$$

$$= 462 \text{ groups}$$

To illustrate that order is not important, note that a group consisting of students A, B, C, D, and E is the same as a group consisting of students B, E, A, D, and C.

2. How many different pairs of books may be selected from a shelf containing 15 books?

This is a combination of 2 books from a set of 15 books. The number of different pairs possible is:

$$_{15}C_2 = C(15,2) = \frac{15!}{2!(15-2)!}$$

$$= \frac{15!}{2! \bullet 13!}$$

$$= \frac{15 \bullet 14}{2 \bullet 1}$$

$$= 105 \text{ pairs}$$

3. How many different 5-card poker hands are possible from a deck of 52 cards?

This is a combination of 5 cards from a set of 52 cards. The number of different 5-card hands is:

$$_{52}C_5 = C(52,5) = \frac{52!}{5!(52-5)!}$$

$$= \frac{52!}{5! \bullet 47!}$$

$$= \frac{52 \bullet 51 \bullet 50 \bullet 49 \bullet 48}{5 \bullet 4 \bullet 3 \bullet 2 \bullet 1}$$

$$= 2,598,960 \text{ hands}$$

4. How many 5-person committees may be formed from a group of 6 males and 6 females if each committee must have 2 male and 3 female members?

This is a combination of 2 males from a group of 6 males and a combination of 3 females from a group of 6 females.

The number of different groups of 2 males is:

$$_6C_2 = C(6,2) = \frac{6!}{2!(6-2)!}$$

$$= \frac{6!}{2! \bullet 4!}$$

$$= \frac{6 \bullet 5}{2 \bullet 1}$$

$$= 15$$

The number of different groups of 3 females is:

$$_6C_3 = C(6,3) = \frac{6!}{3!(6-3)!}$$

$$= \frac{6!}{3! \bullet 3!}$$

$$= \frac{6 \bullet 5 \bullet 4}{3 \bullet 2 \bullet 1}$$

$$= 20$$

Hence, the number of 2-male, 3-female groups of 5-person committees is:

$$_6C_2 \bullet {_6C_3} = 15 \bullet 20$$

$$= 300 \text{ groups}$$

Permutations

A selection of r objects to be arranged in order from a set with a total of n objects is called a permutation. The primary difference between a combination and a permutation is that the order is *important* to consider in a permutation, but *not* in a combination. The notation for the number of permutations is $_nP_r$ or $P(n, r)$. The total number of ways to arrange r objects in order from a set of n objects is:

$$_nP_r = P(n,r) = \frac{n!}{(n-r)!}$$

Examples:

1. How many 4-letter words can be formed using the letters in the word *importance*?

This is a permutation of 4 letters from a set of 10 letters where the order is *important*. The number of different four-letter words is:

$$_{10}P_4 = P(10,4) = \frac{10!}{(10-4)!}$$

$$= \frac{10!}{6!}$$

$$= 10 \bullet 9 \bullet 8 \bullet 7$$

$$= 5040 \text{ four-letter words}$$

2. How many different first-, second-, and third-place finishers are possible if there are 9 competitors in the race?

This is a permutation of 3 ordered finishers from a set of 9 competitors. The number of different finishers possible is:

$$_9P_3 = P(9,3) = \frac{9!}{(9-3)!}$$

$$= \frac{9!}{6!}$$

$$= 9 \bullet 8 \bullet 7$$

$$= 504 \text{ different finishers}$$

3. Four offices—president, vice president, secretary, and treasurer—are to be selected from a 12-member committee. How many different ways can these offices be selected?

This is a permutation of 4 ordered offices to be selected from a set of 12 committee members. The number of different outcomes is:

$$_{12}P_4 = P(12,4) = \frac{12!}{(12-4)!}$$
$$= \frac{12!}{8!}$$
$$= 12 \bullet 11 \bullet 10 \bullet 9$$
$$= 11,880 \text{ outcomes}$$

4. How many numbers between 5000 and 9000 can be formed using the digits 0 through 9, if each digit may not be repeated once it is used?

The first place (thousands place) of the four-digit number may be filled by only one of four numbers: 5, 6, 7, or 8. The remaining nine numbers may be used to fill the other three place values, which is a permutation of 3 numbers from a set of 9 numbers. The total number of four-digit numbers possible is:

$$4 \bullet {}_9P_3 = 4 \bullet P(9,3) = 4 \bullet \frac{9!}{(9-3)!}$$
$$= 4 \bullet \frac{9!}{6!}$$
$$= 4 \bullet 9 \bullet 8 \bullet 7$$
$$= 2016 \text{ four-digit numbers}$$

Methods for Counting

The *counting principle,* or *multiplying principle,* states that if a number of successive choices are to be made, and the choices are independent of each other (order makes no difference), the total number of possible choices is the product of each of the choices at each stage.

Example:

1. How many different arrangements of shirts and ties are there if there are 5 shirts and 3 ties?

There are 5 choices for shirts and 3 choices for ties; therefore, there are $5 \times 3 = 15$ possible choices. The 15 choices can be illustrated. Let the 5 choices for shirts be called S1, S2, S3, S4, and S5. Let the 3 choices for ties be called T1, T2, and T3.

The 15 possible pairings are as follows:

S1–T1, S1–T2, S1–T3
S2–T1, S2–T2, S2–T3
S3–T1, S3–T2, S3–T3
S4–T1, S4–T2, S4–T3
S5–T1, S5–T2, S5–T3

Probability

Probability is the numerical measure of the chance of an outcome or event occurring. The probability is assigned a measure from 0 to 1, where 0 indicates that the outcome will never happen, while 1 indicates that the outcome is sure to occur. As a formula, the probability *P* may be expressed by:

$$\text{probability} = \frac{\text{number of favorable outcomes}}{\text{number of possible outcomes}}$$

Examples:

> **1.** The positive integers 4 through 20 are individually written on index cards and placed in a bowl. What is the probability of randomly selecting a prime number?

The integers 4 through 20 are 4, 5, 6, 7, 8, 9, 10, 11, 12, 13, 14, 15, 16, 17, 18, 19, and 20.

There are 17 integers from 4 to 20. The integers that are prime numbers are 5, 7, 11, 13, 17, and 19. There are 6 prime integers from 4 to 20.

$$\text{probability} = \frac{\#\text{favorable}}{\#\text{total}} = \frac{6}{17}$$

Use the spinner with 12 equally divided sections pictured here for questions 2–4.

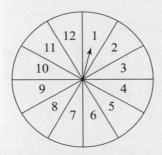

> **2.** What is the probability of spinning a number that is both a multiple of 2 and a multiple of 3 in one spin?

To be a multiple of 2 and 3 means to be a multiple of 6. Of the 12 numbers, only 6 and 12 are multiples of 6.

$$\text{probability} = \frac{\#\text{favorable}}{\#\text{total}} = \frac{2}{12} = \frac{1}{6}$$

> **3.** What is the probability of *not* spinning a factor of 8 in one spin?

The factors of 8 are 1, 2, 4, and 8. The probability of spinning a factor of 8 becomes

$$\text{probability} = \frac{\#\text{favorable}}{\#\text{total}} = \frac{4}{12} = \frac{1}{3}$$

Therefore, the probability of *not* spinning a factor of 8 is $1 - \frac{1}{3} = \frac{2}{3}$.

You could also have found the numbers that were not factors of 8, namely 3, 5, 6, 7, 9, 10, 11, and 12 (there are 8 of them), and then said the probability of *not* spinning a factor of 12 is $\frac{8}{12} = \frac{2}{3}$.

4. If the spinner is spun twice, what is the probability that the spinner will stop on the number 6 the first time and the number 2 the second time?

This problem can be solved in two ways. One way is to first find the individual probabilities and multiply them together. The probability of spinning a 6 the first time is $\frac{1}{12}$. There is only one 6, and there are 12 numbers. Similarly, the probability of spinning a 2 on the second spin is also $\frac{1}{12}$. Therefore, the probability of spinning a 6 on the first spin followed by spinning a 2 on the second spin is $\frac{1}{12} \times \frac{1}{12} = \frac{1}{144}$.

The second method is to use the counting principle to find the total number of ways of spinning a first number followed by a second number. There are 12 numbers possible for each spin; therefore, there are $12 \times 12 = 144$ possibilities. Of these, only one is a 6 followed by a 2. Therefore, the probability is $\frac{1}{144}$.

5. If a number between 1 and 100 is drawn at random, what is the probability that the number will be divisible by 5?

For a number to be divisible by 5, its last digit must be 0 or 5. There are nine numbers that end in 0 between 1 and 100 and ten numbers that end in 5 between 1 and 100. There are a total of 98 numbers between 1 and 100. Hence, the probability P that a number chosen at random will be divisible by 5 is:

$$P = \frac{9+10}{98} = \frac{19}{98}$$

Basic Descriptive Statistics

Any measure indicating a center of a distribution is called a ***measure of central tendency.*** The three basic measures of central tendency are mean (or arithmetic mean), median, and mode.

The ***mean*** (arithmetic mean) is what is usually called the *average.* To determine the arithmetic mean, find the sum of the data values and then divide by the number of data values.

The ***median*** of a set of numbers arranged in ascending or descending order is the middle number. If an odd number of data values is in the set, then one of the data values is the median and an equal number of data values will be on either side of this middle value. To find the location of the median value when there is an odd number of data values, add 1 to the number of data values and divide that number by 2. This, then, is the position of the median value. For example, if there were 15 data values in the set, then $\frac{15+1}{2} = \frac{16}{2} = 8$; the 8th data value would be the median value with 7 data values to its left and 7 data values to its right.

If an even number of data values is in the set, the median is the arithmetic mean of the middle two numbers. To find the position of the two middle numbers, take the number of data values in the set and divide by 2. That number and the next integer are the positions of the two middle values. For example, if the data set has 20 values, then $\frac{20}{2} = 10$. The 10th and 11th data values are the middle values, and the median would be the average of these two values. The median is easy to calculate and is not influenced by extreme measurements.

The ***mode*** is the data value, or values, that appears most, or whose frequency is the greatest. In order to have a mode, there must be a repetition of a data value. There can be more than one mode if there is more than one value that repeats the same (most) number of times.

The ***range*** for a set of data values is the difference between the largest and the smallest values.

When a set of data values is listed from least to greatest, the median value sometimes is referred to as the *2nd quartile* or the *50th percentile* value. To the left of the median are a set of data values called the *lower values,* and to the right of the median are a set of data values called the *upper values.* The median of the lower values is called the *1st quartile* or *25th percentile* value, and the median of the upper values is called the *3rd quartile* or the *75th percentile* value.

Arithmetic Practice Questions

Now that you have reviewed the strategies, you can practice on your own. Practice questions are an integral part of your review. This is an opportunity for you to increase your understanding of arithmetic concepts and practice all types of ACT-related topics, even those that rarely appear on the ACT.

The questions are roughly grouped into three categories: easy to moderate, average, and above average to difficult. The answers and explanations that follow the questions include strategies to help you understand how to solve the problems.

Note: Additional ACT math concepts that are not specifically covered in the math review chapters may be included in practice problems and practice tests. It is important to review *all* practice tests to get a full understanding of the math topics covered on the ACT.

Directions: Solve each problem in this section by using the information given and your own mathematical calculations.

Easy to Moderate

1. In the sequence 8, 9, 12, 17, 24. . . the next number would be

    A. 29
    B. 30
    C. 33
    D. 35
    E. 41

2. A third-grade class is composed of 16 girls and 12 boys. There are 2 teacher-aides in the class. The ratio of girls to boys to teacher-aides is

    A. 16:12:1
    B. 8:6:2
    C. 8:6:1
    D. 8:3:1
    E. 4:3:1

3. The closest approximation of $\dfrac{69.28 \times 0.004}{0.03}$ is

    A. 0.092
    B. 0.92
    C. 9.2
    D. 92
    E. 920

4. In a survey of students that was conducted at a junior high school, 30% of the students said they like broccoli and 15% of the students said they like spinach. If every one of the students who said they like spinach also said they like broccoli, what fraction of the students responding to the survey said they liked at least one of the two vegetables?

A. $\frac{3}{20}$

B. $\frac{3}{10}$

C. $\frac{9}{20}$

D. $\frac{11}{20}$

E. $\frac{7}{10}$

5. Out of 100 shoppers checking out in a supermarket, 45 of the shoppers asked for a paper bag, 60 paid by credit card, and 10 asked for a paper bag and paid by credit card. Of these 100 shoppers, what is the probability that the shopper used a credit card given that they asked for a paper bag?

A. 0.133
B. 0.167
C. 0.222
D. 0.550
E. 0.700

6. A professor has kept records of all the grades he has given to former students. He has given 18% As, 26% Bs, 34% Cs, 12% Ds, and 10% Fs. If a former student did not get a D or F, what is the probability that he/she got a B?

A. 0.220
B. 0.260
C. 0.333
D. 0.380
E. 0.780

7. Katie wants to buy a block of tickets for a play. She can spend $3500 for the tickets. Tickets for orchestra seats cost $17.50 each, and tickets for balcony seats cost $12.50 each. How many more tickets can Katie buy if she chooses to buy tickets for balcony seats instead of buying tickets for orchestra seats?

A. 65
B. 70
C. 75
D. 80
E. 85

Average

8. The average of 9 numbers is 7, and the average of 7 numbers is 9. What is the average of all 16 numbers?

A. 8

B. $7\frac{7}{8}$

C. $7\frac{1}{2}$

D. $7\frac{1}{4}$

E. $7\frac{1}{8}$

9. Mary will be y years old x years from now. How old will she be z years from now?

A. $y - x + z$
B. $y + x + z$
C. $y + x - z$
D. $y - x - z$
E. $x + z - y$

Use the following information for problems 10 and 11.

Four departments in a company, A, B, C, and D, are responsible for sales of the four different products, W, X, Y, and Z, that the company sells. The stacked bar chart that follows shows the sales records of units sold by each of the four departments. During the reporting period represented by the chart, the company sold the same number of units of each of the four products.

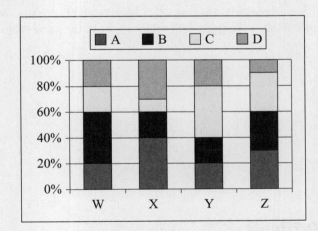

10. Which department sold 25% of all units sold by the company?

A. Department A
B. Department B
C. Department C
D. Department D
E. Cannot be determined from the information given in the chart.

11. If Department B sold 30 units of product X, how many units of product Z did Department C sell?

    A. 30

    B. 35

    C. 40

    D. 45

    E. Cannot be determined from the information given in the chart.

12. As a payment for helping at home, you have been given a choice of either a flat payment of $5, or a chance of randomly drawing a bill from a box. The box contains one $100 bill, two $20 bills, seven $10 bills, ten $5 bills, and thirty $1 bills. Which choice gives you the greatest expected payment?

    A. Flat payment because the expected value of selecting a bill from the box is less than $5.

    B. Flat payment because the expected value of selecting a bill from the box is equal to $5, and it is better to have a sure thing.

    C. Draw from the box because the expected value of selecting a bill from the box is greater than $5.

    D. Draw from the box because the expected value of selecting a bill from the box is equal to $5, so you have nothing to lose.

    E. Flat payment because the expected value of selecting from the box cannot be determined.

13. If m and n are integers and $\sqrt{mn} = 10$, which of the following CANNOT be a value of $m + n$?

    A. 25

    B. 29

    C. 50

    D. 52

    E. 101

14. A bag contains ten balls. Six of the balls are blue and four are red. Two balls are selected randomly from the bag (without replacement). What is the probability they are both the same color?

    A. $\dfrac{2}{15}$

    B. $\dfrac{1}{3}$

    C. $\dfrac{7}{15}$

    D. $\dfrac{13}{25}$

    E. $\dfrac{8}{15}$

Above Average to Difficult

15. How many times does the digit "8" appear in all the integers between 200 and 1200?

    A. 120

    B. 210

    C. 300

    D. 320

    E. 360

16. If x, y, and z are consecutive negative integers, not necessarily in that order, which of the following may be true?

   A. $x + y > z$

   B. $xy < z$

   C. $z + y = y + x$

   D. $2x = \dfrac{yz}{2}$

   E. $x + y = z$

17. Given the following two sets of data:

   Set P: $\{3, 4, 4, 4, 5, 5, 5, 6, 6, 8, 10, 10\}$

   Set Q: $\{5, 5, 8, 8, 11, 11, 11, 11, 12, 12\}$

   If one number is selected randomly from each set, what is the approximate probability that the sum of the two numbers will be an even number?

   A.   0.43

   B.   0.47

   C.   0.49

   D.   0.53

   E.   0.58

18. The product of x and y is a constant. If the value of x is increased by 50%, by what percentage must the value of y be decreased?

   A.   50%

   B.   40%

   C. $33\dfrac{1}{3}\%$

   D.   25%

   E.   20%

19. What is the sum of the 43rd, 44th, and 45th digits to the right of the decimal point in the decimal expansion of $\dfrac{4}{33}$?

   A.   2

   B.   3

   C.   4

   D.   5

   E.   6

20. How many 3-person committees can be formed from a group of 9 people?

   A.   3

   B.   27

   C.   28

   D.   56

   E.   84

Answers and Explanations

Easy to Moderate

1. C. In the sequence 8, 9, 12, 17, 24 . . .

$$9 - 8 = 1 \qquad\qquad 17 - 12 = 5$$
$$12 - 9 = 3 \qquad\qquad 24 - 17 = 7$$

The difference between successive pairs of numbers increases by 2. Hence, the difference between 24 and the next term must be 9. Therefore, the next term is 33.

2. C. Girls to boys to teacher-aides are in proportion 16 to 12 to 2. Ratios should be written in reduced form. Dividing each number by 2 gives a ratio of 8:6:1.

3. C. This problem is most easily completed by rearranging and approximating as follows:

$$\frac{69.28 \times 0.004}{0.03} = \frac{69.28}{1} \times \frac{0.004}{0.03} \cong 69 \times 0.13 \cong 9$$

Therefore, the only reasonable answer is 9.2.

4. B. Since spinach is a subset of broccoli, $P(S \cup B) = P(B) = 0.30 = \frac{3}{10}$.

5. C. You need to calculate the conditional probability of using a credit card given that they ask for a paper bag. Using a Venn diagram to organize the data will help.

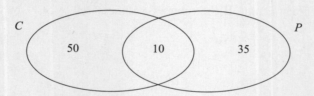

The Paper Bag oval (P) must total to 45, and the Credit Card oval (C) must total 60. Since you are asked for the probability of using a credit card given that they asked for a paper bag, you divide the credit card portion of the paper bag oval by the total in the paper bag oval. Therefore: $P(C \text{ given } P) = \frac{10}{45} = 0.222$.

6. C. Eliminate the percentages for the D and F grades. Divide the percentage for the B grade (26%) by the sum of the percentages for the A, B, and C grades (78%). Since 26 is one-third of 78, the correct answer is Choice C.

$$P(B) = \frac{0.26}{0.18 + 0.26 + 0.34} = 0.333$$

7. D. Although this problem can be done without a calculator, this is one case where use of the calculator would definitely save you time. Divide $3500 by both $17.50 and $12.50 to determine how many of each type of ticket can be purchased with the $3500. Then, subtract the two quantities. She could buy 280 balcony seat tickets or 200 orchestra seat tickets. Thus, the difference is 80, Choice D.

Average

8. B. If the average of 9 numbers is 7, then the sum of these numbers must be (9)(7) = 63. If the average of 7 numbers is 9, then the sum of these numbers must be (7)(9) = 63. The sum of all 16 numbers must be 63 + 63, or 126. Therefore, the average of all 16 numbers must be $\frac{126}{16} = \frac{63}{8} = 7\frac{7}{8}$.

9. A. Because Mary will be y years old x years from now, she is $y - x$ years old now. Hence, z years from now she will be $y - x + z$ years old.

10. C. The total number of units sold is not given, but you know that the number of units sold for each product is the same. For ease of computation, assume that 100 units of each product were sold by the company. This gives a total of 400 units for the four products. The number of units sold by each department can be calculated.

If the total units sold is 400, then:

Units sold by Department A:

$$20\% \text{ of } 100 + 40\% \text{ of } 100 + 20\% \text{ of } 100 + 30\% \text{ of } 100 = 110$$

Units sold by Department B:

$$40\% \text{ of } 100 + 20\% \text{ of } 100 + 20\% \text{ of } 100 + 30\% \text{ of } 100 = 110$$

Units sold by Department C:

$$20\% \text{ of } 100 + 10\% \text{ of } 100 + 40\% \text{ of } 100 + 30\% \text{ of } 100 = 100$$

Units sold by Department D:

$$20\% \text{ of } 100 + 30\% \text{ of } 100 + 20\% \text{ of } 100 + 10\% \text{ of } 100 = 80$$

The percentage sold by Department C is 25% of 400.

11. D. Department B sold 20% of the total units of product X. If this is 30 units, then the total number of units sold of product X must be 150. Since the total number of units sold of each product is the same, 150 units of product Z were sold by the company. Since Department C sold 30% of the units sold of product Z, Department C sold 45 units of product Z.

12. C. In order to determine which choice should be made, the average value of a bill chosen from the box must be calculated. There are 50 bills in the box. Add the products of the various bill values and their respective quantities. Then divide by 50, the total number of bills in the box.

$$Average = \frac{(100)(1)+(20)(2)+(10)(7)+(5)(10)+(1)(30)}{50} = \frac{290}{50} = 5.80$$

The average bill value is greater than 5. Notice that this is nothing more than determining the total value of the bills in the box and dividing by the number of bills.

13. C. Because $\sqrt{mn} = 10$ and $mn = 100$, the possible values for m and n are

1 and 100

2 and 50

4 and 25

5 and 20

10 and 10

Because none of these combinations yields a sum of 50, Choice C is correct.

14. C. The probability that both balls are the same color is the sum of the probabilities that they are both blue and that they are both red. (You could list all the possibilities and count to see how many satisfied the conditions, but this is clearly a time-consuming approach and should be avoided.)

$$\left(\frac{6}{10}\right)\left(\frac{5}{9}\right)+\left(\frac{4}{10}\right)\left(\frac{3}{9}\right) = \frac{30}{90} + \frac{12}{90} = \frac{42}{90} = \frac{7}{15}$$

Above Average to Difficult

15. C. Although writing out all 1001 integers from 200 through 1200 and counting the 8s would certainly work, it clearly is not the best method. One method would be to examine each digit position individually.

Ones digit: 100 groups of 10 with one 8 in each group = 100 "8"s.

Tens digit: 10 groups of 100 with ten 8s in each group = 100 "8"s.

Hundreds digit: 1 group of 100 with one hundred 8s = 100 "8"s.

Therefore, the digit 8 appears 300 times in the integers from 200 to 1200. The correct answer choice is C.

16. E. Since x, y, and z are consecutive negative integers, try plugging in values to test each choice. For example, x, y, and z could equal -1, -2, and -3 (not necessarily in that order) or, for that matter, -8, -9, and -10. Only Choice E may be true, and that will occur if $x = -1$, $y = -2$, and $z = -3$. Choice A is eliminated since the sum of any two consecutive negative integers is less than or equal to the third, not greater than. Choice B is eliminated since the product of any two of the negative integers would be positive, and therefore greater than, not less than, the third. Choice C is eliminated since x and z are of different value. Choice D is eliminated since $2x$ is negative, and $\frac{yz}{2}$ must be positive.

17. B. The sum of two numbers is even if they are either both even or both odd. First compute the probability that both selected numbers are even. Then compute the probability that both selected numbers are odd. Then add the two probabilities. In set P, 8 of the 12 numbers are even, and in set Q, 4 of the 10 numbers are even. Therefore, the probability that both selected numbers are even is $\frac{8}{12} \times \frac{4}{10} = \frac{2}{3} \times \frac{2}{5} = \frac{4}{15}$. In set P, 4 of the 12 numbers are odd, and in set Q, 6 of the 10 numbers are odd. Therefore, the probability that both selected numbers are odd is $\frac{4}{12} \times \frac{6}{10} = \frac{1}{3} \times \frac{3}{5} = \frac{3}{15}$. Adding the two probabilities gives $\frac{4}{15} + \frac{3}{15} = \frac{7}{15} \approx 0.47$. Thus, answer choice B is correct.

18. C. If x is increased by 50%, you can use $\frac{3}{2}x$ to represent it. You must multiply this by $\frac{2}{3}y$ in order to keep the product equal to xy. That is, $\left(\frac{3}{2}x\right)\left(\frac{2}{3}y\right) = xy$. Because $\frac{2}{3}y$ is a $\frac{1}{3}$ reduction from y, answer choice C is the correct response.

19. C. The decimal expansion of $\frac{4}{33}$ is: $\frac{4}{33} = 0.\overline{12}$ where the odd-numbered digits after the decimal are ones, and the even-numbered digits after the decimal are twos. Since the 43rd, 44th, and 45th digits are made up of 2 odd-numbered digits and 1 even-numbered digit, the sum must be $1 + 2 + 1 = 4$.

20. E. This is a counting problem. It is best solved using the formula for combinations of objects. In this case, you are choosing 3 objects from a group of 9 objects. Using the formula gives

$$_nC_r = {}_9C_3 = \frac{n!}{r!(n-r)!}$$

$$= \frac{9!}{3!6!} = \frac{9 \times 8 \times 7 \times 6!}{3 \times 2 \times 1 \times 6!}$$

$$= \frac{9 \times 8 \times 7}{3 \times 2 \times 1} = 3 \times 4 \times 7 = 84$$

A time-consuming alternative would be to write down all of the possible selections and count them. If person 1 is chosen, there are 28 ways of choosing the other two people. If person 2 is chosen, and without repeating any of the previous combinations, there are 21 ways of choosing the other two people. If person 3 is selected, there are 15 ways of choosing the other two people, and so on. Totaling these numbers would give $28 + 21 + 15 + 10 + 6 + 3 + 1 = 84$.

The following table, which shows how many 3-person committees can be formed from the first 7 of 9 people chosen, gives you an idea of how laborious this alternative is. It is clearly not the best strategy.

Person 1	Person 2	Person 3	Person 4	Person 5	Person 6	Person 7
123	234	345	456	567	678	789
124	235	346	457	568	679	
125	236	347	458	569	689	
126	237	348	459	578		
127	238	349	467	579		
128	239	356	468	589		
129	245	357	469			
134	246	358	478			
135	247	359	479			
136	248	367	489			
137	249	368				
138	256	369				
139	257	378				
145	258	379				
146	259	389				
147	267					
148	268					
149	269					
156	278					
157	279					
158	289					
159						
167						
168						
169						
178						
179						
189						

Chapter 9

Algebra

This chapter introduces important algebraic topics, defines key algebraic terms, and walks you through step-by-step practice examples. To solve algebra problems, you must use the basic building blocks of mathematics. Understanding *algebraic expressions* depends upon your knowledge of arithmetic operations. Algebra requires that you apply basic mathematic operations to symbols (variables) and numbers. Variables, such as the letter symbols x and y, and numbers are used to represent two or more relationships so that math operations can be performed.

Many students find learning algebra to be challenging. Algebra requires a different approach to looking at problems in order to *reason* and perform interrelated connections among variables, numbers, and their operations. If you are one of these students, pace yourself as you learn new concepts and practice step-by-step methods as often as possible. Start by taking the diagnostic test that follows. Then study and practice each of the major algebraic topics covered in this chapter.

As you review this chapter, always keep in mind that algebraic equations are like a balance scale. The relationship of symbols and numbers must be kept in balance. When you perform an operation on one side of the equal sign, you must perform the same operation on the other side of the equal sign.

Algebra Concepts You Should Know

- Evaluating algebraic expressions
- Solving linear equations in one variable or two variables
- Evaluating algebraic expressions: substitution method and elimination method
- Absolute value equations
- Inequalities
- Polynomials
- Properties of exponents and square roots
- Rational and radical expressions
- Algebraic fractions
- Quadratic equations
- Coordinate geometry
- Functions

Take the algebra diagnostic test that follows and evaluate how familiar you are with the selected topics. The diagnostic test will give you valuable insight into the topics you will need to study.

Algebra Diagnostic Test

Directions: Solve each problem in this section by using the information given and your own mathematical calculations.

1. $\{1,3,5\} \cap \{1,2,3\} =$

2. $\{2,5\} \cup \{3,4,5\} =$

3. $\{1,2,3\} \cap \{4,5\} =$

4. $\left| \{3,5,7,9\} \right| =$

5. $\left| \varnothing \right| =$

6. Evaluate the following diagram and determine which statement is correct.

$$A \cap B = C,\ A \cup B = C,\ A \cap C = B,\ A \cup C = B,\ B \cap C = A,\ B \cup C = A$$

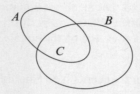

7. Express algebraically: five increased by three times x.

8. Evaluate: $-3x^2 - 4x - 6$ if $x = -5$

9. Evaluate: $\dfrac{x}{3} - \dfrac{x+2y}{y}$ if $x = 2$ and $y = 6$

10. Solve for x: $2x - 9 = 21$

11. Solve for y: $\dfrac{4}{7}y + 6 = 18$

12. Solve for x: $3x - 5 = -2x - 25$

13. Solve for x: $ax + by = c$

14. Solve for y: $\dfrac{8}{y-3} = \dfrac{2}{y+3}$

15. Solve this system for x and y: $8x + y = 4$
$\qquad\qquad\qquad\qquad\qquad\ 2x - y = 6$

16. Solve for x: $|x| = 12$

17. Solve for x: $|x - 3| = 10$

18. Solve for x: $-3x + 5 > 14$

19. Solve for x: $8x + 4 \geq 6x - 10$

20. $12x + 4x - 23x - (-3x) =$

21. $(4x - 7z) - (3x - 4z) =$

22. $6x^2y(4xy^2) =$

23. $(-2x^4y^2)^3 =$

24. $\dfrac{a^{10}b^3}{a^2b^6} =$

25. $\dfrac{-5\left(a^3b^2\right)\left(2a^2b^5\right)}{a^4b^3} =$

26. $(5^3)(2^3) =$

27. $-8(2x - y) =$

28. $(4x + 2y)(3x - y) =$

29. $\dfrac{16x^2 y + 18xy^3}{2xy} =$

30. Factor: $8x^3 - 12x^2$

31. Factor: $16a^2 - 81$

32. Factor: $x^2 - 2x - 63$

33. Factor: $3a^2 - 4a + 1$

34. Simplify: $\dfrac{x^2 - 3x + 2}{3x - 6}$

35. $\left(\dfrac{x^3}{2y}\right)\left(\dfrac{5y^2}{6x}\right) =$

36. $\left(\dfrac{x-5}{x}\right)\left(\dfrac{x+2}{x^2 - 2x - 15}\right) =$

37. $\dfrac{6x - 3}{2} \div \dfrac{2x - 1}{x} =$

38. $\dfrac{3x - 2}{x + 1} - \dfrac{2x - 1}{x + 1} =$

39. $\dfrac{5}{x} + \dfrac{7}{y} =$

40. $\dfrac{3}{a^3 b^5} + \dfrac{2}{a^4 b^2} =$

41. $\dfrac{2x}{x - 1} - \dfrac{x}{x + 2} =$

42. Solve for x: $3x^2 - 4x - 5 = 2x^2 + 4x - 17$

43. Solve for x: $9x^2 - 49 = 0$

44. Name the quadrant(s) in which points have positive x-coordinates.

45. Name the quadrant(s) in which points have negative x-coordinates and positive y-coordinates.

Use the following graph to answer questions 46–51.

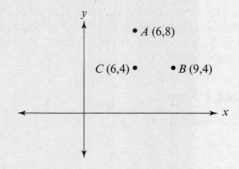

46. What is the distance between A and B?

47. What are the coordinates of the midpoint between A and B?

48. What is the slope of the line joining A and B?

49. What is the equation of the line, in slope-intercept form, joining A and B?

50. If the line joining A and B was extended, what would be its exact y-intercept?

51. Given that points A, B, and C are connected to form a triangle, what would be the area of $\triangle ABC$? What would be the perimeter of $\triangle ABC$?

52. If $f(x) = x^2 - 3x$, then $f(3) - f(1) = ?$

53. If $h(x) = |x|$, then $\dfrac{4}{h(4)} - \dfrac{-2}{h(-2)} = ?$

54. If $m(x) = 3x + 2$ and $t(x) = x^2$, then $t\big[m(-2)\big] = ?$

Scoring the Diagnostic Test

The diagnostic test explanations include topic headings that correspond with step-by-step learning tools and examples to help you solve specific problem types. Use the answer key and the analysis worksheet that follows to help you evaluate specific problem types. Topic headings can be found in the "Algebra Review" section following the diagnostic test.

Answer Key

Set Notations

1. $\{1, 3\}$
2. $\{2, 3, 4, 5\}$
3. $\varnothing$
4. 4
5. 0
6. $A \cap B = C$

Variables and Algebraic Expressions

7. $5 + 3x$
8. -61
9. $-\dfrac{5}{3}$

Solving Linear Equations in One or Two Variables

10. $x = 15$
11. $y = 21$
12. $x = -4$
13. $x = \dfrac{c - by}{a}$
14. $y = -5$
15. $x = 1, y = -4$
16. $x = 12$ or $x = -12$
17. $x = 13$ or $x = -7$

Solving Linear Inequalities in One Variable

18. $x < -3$
19. $x \geq -7$

Polynomials

20. $-4x$
21. $x - 3z$
22. $24x^3y^3$
23. $-8x^{12}y^6$
24. $\dfrac{a^8}{b^3}$

25. $-10ab^4$
26. $\left[(5)(2)\right]^3 = 10^3 = 1{,}000$
27. $-16x + 8y$
28. $12x^2 + 2xy - 2y^2$
29. $8x + 9y^2$
30. $4x^2(2x - 3)$
31. $(4a + 9)(4a - 9)$
32. $(x - 9)(x + 7)$
33. $(3a - 1)(a - 1)$

Algebraic Fractions

34. $\dfrac{x - 1}{3}$
35. $\dfrac{5x^2y}{12}$
36. $\dfrac{x + 2}{x(x + 3)}$
37. $\dfrac{3x}{2}$
38. $\dfrac{x - 1}{x + 1}$
39. $\dfrac{5y + 7x}{xy}$ or $\dfrac{7x + 5y}{xy}$
40. $\dfrac{3a + 2b^3}{a^4b^5}$
41. $\dfrac{x^2 + 5x}{(x - 1)(x + 2)}$

Solving Quadratic Equations in One Variable

42. $x = 6$ or $x = 2$
43. $x = \dfrac{7}{3}$ or $x = -\dfrac{7}{3}$

Coordinate Geometry

44. I and IV
45. II

46. 5

47. $\left(\frac{15}{2},6\right)$ or $(7.5, 6)$

48. $-\frac{4}{3}$

49. $y = -\frac{4}{3}x + 16$

50. 16 or $(0,16)$

51. Area = 6, perimeter = 12

Functions and Function Notation

52. 2

53. 2

54. 16

Charting and Analyzing Your Diagnostic Test Results

Record your diagnostic test results in the following chart and use these results as a guide to plan your algebra review goals and objectives. Mark the problems that you missed and pay particular attention to those that you missed in Column (C) because they were unfamiliar math concepts to you. These are the areas you will want to focus on as you study algebra topics.

Analysis Sheet

Topic	Number Possible	Number Correct	Number Incorrect		
			(A) Simple Mistake	(B) Misread Problem	(C) Unfamiliar Math Concept
Set notations	6				
Variables and algebraic expressions	3				
Solving linear equations in one or two variables	8				
Solving linear inequalities in one variable	2				
Polynomials	14				
Algebraic fractions	8				
Solving quadratic equations in one variable	2				
Coordinate geometry	8				
Functions and Function Notation	3				
Total Possible Explanations for Incorrect Answers: Columns A, B, and C					
Total number of questions	54	Add the total number of correct questions here: _____	Add columns A, B, and C for total number of incorrect questions here: _____		

Algebra Review

Algebra's Implied Multiplication

The operation of multiplication may be expressed in a variety of ways algebraically. For example, the product of 3 times y may be expressed as $3y$, with no operation symbol indicating the operation of multiplication. A raised dot or parentheses may also be used to indicate the operation of multiplication. For example, the product of 5 times 6 may be expressed as $5 \cdot 6 = 5(6) = (5)(6) = 5 \times 6$.

Set Notations

The *intersection* of two sets is a set containing only the members that are in each set at the same time. The symbol for finding the intersection of two sets is $\cap$. If two sets are *disjointed,* then they have no common members. The intersection of disjointed sets is called the *empty set* (or *null set*) and is indicated by the symbol $\varnothing$.

The *union* of two sets is a set containing all the members in those sets. Any duplicates are written only once. The symbol for finding the union of two sets is $\cup$.

The size or *magnitude of a set* refers to how many elements are in the set. This usually is expressed by placing absolute value symbols around the set. The magnitude of the empty set is zero.

A *Venn diagram* (or *Euler circle*) is a method of pictorially describing sets as shown in the following figure.

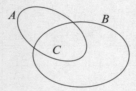

In the Venn diagram, A represents all the elements in the smaller oval, B represents all the elements in the larger oval, and C represents all the elements that are in both ovals at the same time.

Examples:

1. $\{1,3,5\} \cap \{1,2,3\} = \{1,3\}$

The intersection of the set with members 1, 3, 5 together with the set with members 1, 2, 3 is the set that has only the 1 and 3.

2. $\{2,5\} \cup \{3,4,5\} = \{2,3,4,5\}$

The union of the set with members 2, 5 together with the set with members 3, 4, 5 is the set with members 2, 3, 4, 5.

3. $\{1,2,3\} \cap \{4,5\} = \varnothing$

The intersection of disjointed sets is the empty set.

4. $|\{3,5,7,9\}| = 4$

The set consisting of the elements 3, 5, 7, and 9 has 4 elements in it.

5. $|\varnothing| = 0$

The empty set has no elements in it. The value zero indicates this.

6. $A \cap B = C$

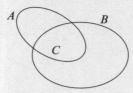

The intersection, or overlapping area, of sets A and B is C.

Variables and Algebraic Expressions

A *variable* is a symbol used to denote any element of a given set—often a letter used to stand for a number. Variables are used to change verbal expressions into ***algebraic expressions.*** A *coefficient* is the number used to multiply a variable. For example, in the expression $4x$, the 4 would be the coefficient and the x would be the variable.

Important Key Words

Addition	sum, more than, enlarge, plus
Subtraction	difference, less than, diminish, minus
Multiplication	product, times, of, twice
Division	quotient, ratio, divided by, half

Examples:

Express each of the following algebraically.

1. Five increased by three times x: $5 + 3x$

2. The sum of twice x and y: $2x + y$

3. Twice the sum of x and y: $2(x + y)$

4. The product of 6 and the difference between x and y: $6(x - y)$

5. The ratio of x and y decreased by the quotient of s and r: $\dfrac{x}{y} - \dfrac{s}{r}$

Evaluate an Expression

To ***evaluate an expression,*** replace the unknowns with grouping symbols, insert the *value* for the unknowns, and then do the arithmetic, making sure to follow the rules for the order of operations.

Examples:

1. Evaluate $-3x^2 - 4x - 6$ if $x = -5$.

$$
\begin{aligned}
-3x^2 - 4x - 6 &= -3(-5)^2 - 4(-5) - 6 \\
&= -3(25) + 20 - 6 \\
&= -75 + 20 - 6 \\
&= -61
\end{aligned}
$$

2. Evaluate $\dfrac{x}{3} - \dfrac{x+2y}{y}$ if $x = 2$ and $y = 6$.

$$\frac{x}{3} - \frac{x+2y}{y} = \frac{(2)}{3} - \frac{(2)+2(6)}{(6)}$$
$$= \frac{2}{3} - \frac{2+12}{6}$$
$$= \frac{2}{3} - \frac{14}{6}$$
$$= \frac{2}{3} - \frac{7}{3}$$
$$= -\frac{5}{3}$$

Solving Linear Equations in One or Two Variables

An equation is like a balance scale. In order to maintain the balance, the arithmetic operations you perform on one side of the equation must be performed on the other side of the equation. To solve a linear equation with one variable, cancel the numbers that are added or subtracted by using the opposite operation on both sides of the equation. Then divide by the number in front of the variable to get the variable by itself.

Examples:

1. Solve for x: $2x - 9 = 21$

$$2x - 9 = 21 \qquad (\text{Add 9 to each side.})$$
$$\underline{+9 \quad +9}$$
$$2x \quad = 30 \qquad (\text{Divide each side by 2.})$$
$$\frac{2x}{2} = \frac{30}{2}$$
$$x = 15$$

2. Solve for y: $\dfrac{4}{7}y + 6 = 18$

$$\frac{4}{7}y + 6 = 18 \qquad (\text{Subtract 6 from each side.})$$
$$\underline{-6 \quad -6}$$
$$\frac{4}{7}y \quad = 12 \qquad \left(\text{Divide each side by } \frac{4}{7}, \text{which is the same as multiplying each side by } \frac{7}{4}.\right)$$
$$\frac{\cancel{7}}{\cancel{4}}\left(\frac{\cancel{4}^{\,1}}{\cancel{7}}y\right) = \frac{7}{\cancel{4}_{1}}\left(\frac{\cancel{12}^{\,3}}{1}\right)$$
$$y = 21$$

3. Solve for x: $3x - 5 = -2x - 25$

$$3x - 5 = -2x - 25 \quad (\text{Add } 2x \text{ to each side to get all the } x\text{'s on one side.})$$

$$\underline{+2x \qquad +2x}$$

$$5x - 5 = \qquad -25 \quad (\text{Add 5 to each side.})$$

$$\underline{+5 \qquad +5}$$

$$5x = \qquad -20 \quad (\text{Divide each side by 5.})$$

$$\frac{5x}{5} = \frac{-20}{5}$$

$$x = -4$$

4. Solve for x: $ax + by = c$

$$ax + by = c \qquad (\text{Subtract } by \text{ from each side.})$$

$$\underline{-by \qquad -by}$$

$$ax = c - by \qquad (\text{Divide each side by } a.)$$

$$\frac{ax}{a} = \frac{c - by}{a}$$

$$x = \frac{c - by}{a}$$

5. Solve for y: $\dfrac{8}{y - 3} = \dfrac{2}{y + 3}$

Solve using the proportions method (refer to the proportions method discussed in Chapter 8, "Arithmetic (Pre-Algebra)").

$$\frac{8}{y - 3} = \frac{2}{y + 3} \qquad (\text{Cross multiply to clear the denominators.})$$

$$8(y + 3) = 2(y - 3) \qquad (\text{Multiply out each side.})$$

$$8y + 24 = 2y - 6 \qquad (\text{Subtract } 2y \text{ from each side to get the } y\text{'s on one side.})$$

$$\underline{-2y \qquad -2y}$$

$$6y + 24 = \qquad -6 \qquad (\text{Subtract 24 from each side.})$$

$$\underline{-24 \qquad -24}$$

$$6y = \qquad -30 \qquad (\text{Divide each side by 6.})$$

$$\frac{6y}{6} = \frac{-30}{6}$$

$$y = -5$$

Solving Two Equations Involving the Same Two Variables

To solve **two equations involving the same two variables,** you can use either of two algebraic methods: the *elimination method* or the *substitution method*.

Method 1—The Elimination Method

1. Arrange each equation so that it has all the variables on one side.
2. Multiply each side of one equation so that the numbers to the immediate left of the same variable in each equation are exact opposites. *(Note: Sometimes you need to multiply each equation by different numbers to accomplish this.)*

3. Add the two equations to eliminate one variable.

4. Solve for the remaining variable.

5. Substitute this value into one of the original equations to find the second variable.

Examples:

---

1. Solve for x and y: $3x + 3y = 24$

$2x + y = 13$

Both equations are already in the required form. Multiply each side of the bottom equation by –3. Now the y is immediately preceded by exact opposites in the two equations.

$$3x + 3y = 24 \quad \rightarrow \quad 3x + 3y = 24$$
$$-3(2x + y) = -3(13) \rightarrow \quad \underline{-6x - 3y = -39}$$

Add the equations, eliminating the y terms.

$$
\begin{aligned}
3x + 3y &= 24 \\
\underline{-6x + -3y} &= \underline{-39} \\
-3x &= -15
\end{aligned}
$$

Solve for the remaining variable.

$$\frac{-3x}{-3} = \frac{-15}{-3}$$
$$x = 5$$

Replace x with 5 in one of the original equations to solve for y:

$$
\begin{aligned}
2x + y &= 13 \\
2(5) + y &= 13 \\
10 + y &= 13 \\
\underline{-10} \quad &\underline{-10} \\
y &= 3
\end{aligned}
$$

Answer: $x = 5$ and $y = 3$

Of course, if the numbers to the immediate left of a variable are already opposites in each equation, you don't have to change either equation. Simply add the equations. See example 2.

---

2. Solve for x and y: $x + y = 7$

$x - y = 3$

$$
\begin{aligned}
x + y &= 7 \\
\underline{x - y} &= \underline{3} \\
2x &= 10 \\
\frac{2x}{2} &= \frac{10}{2} \\
x &= 5
\end{aligned}
$$

Replacing x with 5 in the first equation gives

$$\begin{array}{r} 5 + y = 7 \\ \underline{-5 \quad\quad -5} \\ y = 2 \end{array}$$

Answer: $x = 5$ and $y = 2$

Note that this method will not work when the two equations *are the same equation* but written in two different forms. See example 3.

---

3. Solve for a and b: $3a + 4b = 2$

$\quad\quad\quad\quad\quad\quad\quad 6a + 8b = 4$

The second equation is actually the first equation multiplied by 2. In this instance, the system does not have a unique solution. Any replacements for a and b that make one of the sentences true will also make the other sentence true. In this situation, the system has an infinite number of solutions for a and b.

Sometimes each equation will have to be multiplied by different numbers to get the numbers to the immediate left of one variable to be opposites of one another. See example 4.

---

4. Solve for x : $3x + 2y = 8$

$\quad\quad\quad\quad\quad\quad 2x - 5y = 18$

The equations are already in the required form. Since it is the x value desired, find a way to eliminate the y variable. The numbers to the left of the y terms are already of the opposite sign. Multiply the upper equation with the coefficient of y from the lower equation, and multiply the lower equation by the coefficient of y from the upper equation.

$$5(3x + 2y) = 5(8) \quad \rightarrow \quad 15x + 10y = 40$$
$$2(2x - 5y) = 2(18) \quad \rightarrow \quad \underline{4x - 10y = 36}$$

Add the equations.

$$\begin{array}{r} 15x + 10y = 40 \\ \underline{4x - 10y = 36} \\ 19x \quad\quad\quad = 76 \\ \dfrac{19x}{19} = \dfrac{76}{19} \\ x = 4 \end{array}$$

Answer: $x = 4$

Method 2—The Substitution Method

1. Solve one equation for one of its variables in terms of the other variable.
2. Replace this expression for that variable in the other equation.
3. Solve the equation for that variable.
4. Replace this value into one of the original equations to find the second variable.

Examples:

1. Solve for x and y: $x = y + 8$
$\qquad\qquad\qquad\qquad x + 3y = 48$

The first equation already has been solved for x in terms of y. Replace x with $(y + 8)$ in the second equation.

$$x + 3y = 48$$
$$(y + 8) + 3y = 48$$

Solve for y.

$$y + 3y + 8 = 48$$
$$4y + 8 = 48$$
$$\underline{-8 \quad -8}$$
$$4y \quad = 40$$
$$\frac{4y}{4} = \frac{40}{4}$$
$$y = 10$$

Replace y with 10 in one of the original equations and solve for x.

$$x = y + 8$$
$$x = 10 + 8$$
$$x = 18$$

Answer: $x = 18$ and $y = 10$

2. Solve for x and y: $8x + y = 4$
$\qquad\qquad\qquad\qquad 2x - y = 6$

This problem now can be solved by using the *elimination method*.

$$8x + y = 4$$
$$\underline{2x - y = 6}$$
$$10x \quad = 10$$
$$\frac{10x}{10} = \frac{10}{10}$$
$$x = 1$$

Using the top equation:

$$8x + y = \ 4$$
$$8(1) + y = \ 4$$
$$8 + y = \ 4$$
$$\underline{-8 \qquad -8}$$
$$y = -4$$

Answer: $x = 1$ and $y = -4$

Equations Involving Absolute Value

Recall that the numerical value, when the direction or sign is not considered, is called the **absolute value.** The absolute value of x is written $|x|$. If $|x| = 2$, then $x = 2$ or $x = -2$, since $|2| = 2$ and $|-2| = 2$.

Examples:

1. Solve for x: $|x| = 12$

$$x = 12 \text{ or } x = -12$$

2. Solve for x: $|x - 3| = 10$

$$
\begin{aligned}
x - 3 &= 10 &\quad \text{or} \quad& x - 3 = -10 \\
&\underline{+3 \ +3} && \underline{+3 \ +3} \\
x \ &= 13 &\quad \text{or} \quad& x \ \ = -7
\end{aligned}
$$

3. Solve for x: $|2x - 1| = 7$

$$
\begin{aligned}
2x - 1 &= 7 &\quad \text{or} \quad& 2x - 1 = -7 \\
&\underline{+1 \ +1} && \underline{+1 \ +1} \\
2x \ &= 8 &\quad \text{or} \quad& 2x \ \ = -6 \\
\frac{2x}{2} &= \frac{8}{2} &\quad \text{or} \quad& \frac{2x}{2} = \frac{-6}{2} \\
x &= 4 &\quad \text{or} \quad& x = -3
\end{aligned}
$$

4. Solve for x: $|x| = -3$

There is no solution because the absolute value of any number is never negative.

5. Solve for x: $|2x - 1| \geq 0$

The answer is all real numbers, because the absolute value of any number is always positive or zero.

Solving Linear Inequalities in One Variable

An inequality sentence is one involving $\leq$, $<$, $\geq$, or $>$ separating the two sides of the sentence. Solving an inequality sentence involves the same procedures as solving an equation, with one exception: *When you multiply or divide each side of an inequality sentence by a negative number, the direction of the inequality switches.*

Examples:

1. Solve for x: $-3x + 5 > 14$

$$
\begin{aligned}
-3x + 5 &> 14 &\quad& \text{(Subtract 5 from each side.)} \\
\underline{-5} \ &\underline{-5} && \\
-3x \ &> 9 &\quad& \text{(Divide each side by } -3 \text{, switch the direction of the inequality.)} \\
\frac{-3x}{-3} &< \frac{9}{-3} && \\
x &< -3 &&
\end{aligned}
$$

2. Solve for x: $8x + 4 \geq 6x - 10$

$$8x + 4 \geq 6x - 10 \qquad \text{(Subtract } 6x \text{ from each side to get all the } x\text{'s on one side.)}$$

$$\underline{-6x \qquad -6x}$$

$$2x + 4 \geq \qquad -10 \qquad \text{(Subtract 4 from each side.)}$$

$$\underline{-4 \qquad \qquad -4}$$

$$2x \qquad \geq \qquad -14 \qquad \text{(Divide each side by 2.)}$$

$$\frac{2x}{2} \geq \frac{-14}{2}$$

$$x \geq -7$$

3. Solve for x: $-\frac{3}{8}x - 2 < 13$

$$-\frac{3}{8}x - 2 < 13 \qquad \text{(Add 2 to each side.)}$$

$$\underline{+2 \quad +2}$$

$$-\frac{3}{8}x \quad < 15 \qquad \left(\begin{array}{l} \text{Divide each side by } -\frac{3}{8}, \text{ which is the same as multiplying each} \\ \text{side by } -\frac{8}{3}, \text{ and then switch the direction of the inequality.} \end{array} \right)$$

$$\left(-\frac{\cancel{8}}{3} \right)\left(\frac{\cancel{3}}{\cancel{8}}x \right) > \left(-\frac{8}{\cancel{3}} \right)\left(\frac{\cancel{15}}{1} \right)$$

$$x > -40$$

Polynomials

A *monomial* is an algebraic expression that consists of only one term. (A *term* is a numerical or literal expression with its own sign.) For instance, $9x$, $4a^2$, and $3mpxz^2$ are all monomials. When there are variables with exponents, the exponents must be whole numbers.

A *polynomial* consists of two or more terms. For instance, $x + y$, $y^2 - x^2$, and $x^2 + 3x + 5y^2$ are all polynomials. A *binomial* is a polynomial that consists of exactly two terms. For instance, $x + y$ is a binomial. A *trinomial* is a polynomial that consists of exactly three terms. For instance, $y^2 + 9y + 8$ is a trinomial. The number to the immediate left of the variable is called the *numerical coefficient*. In $9y$, the 9 is the numerical coefficient.

Polynomials are usually arranged in one of two ways:

- *Ascending order* is when the power of a term increases for each succeeding term. For example, $x + x^2 + x^3$ or $5x + 2x^2 - 3x^3 + x^5$ are arranged in ascending order.

- *Descending order* is when the power of a term decreases for each succeeding term. For example, $x^3 + x^2 + x$ or $2x^4 + 3x^2 + 7x$ are arranged in descending order. Descending order is more commonly used.

Adding and Subtracting Polynomials

To *add* or *subtract polynomials,* follow the same rules as with integers introduced in Chapter 8, "Arithmetic (Pre-Algebra)," provided that the terms are alike. Notice that you add or subtract the coefficients only and leave the variables the same.

Examples:

---

1. $12x + 4x - 23x - (-3x) = [12 + 4 - 23 - (-3)]x = [12 + 4 - 23 + 3]x = -4x$

---

2. $(4x - 7z) - (3x - 4z) = 4x - 7z - 3x + 4z = (4 - 3)x + (-7 + 4)z = x - 3z$

---

3. $15x^2yz$

$-18x^2yz$

$\overline{-3x^2yz}$

Multiplying and Dividing Monomials

To **multiply** or **divide monomials,** follow the rules and definitions for powers and exponents introduced in Chapter 8.

Examples:

---

1. $6x^2y(4xy^2) = (6)(4)(x^2x)(yy^2) = 24x^{2+1}y^{1+2} = 24x^3y^3$

---

2. $(-2x^4y^2)^3 = (-2)^3 \, x^{(4)(3)} \, y^{(2)(3)} = -8x^{12}y^6$

---

3. $\dfrac{a^{10}b^3}{a^2b^6} = \left(\dfrac{a^{10}}{a^2}\right)\left(\dfrac{b^3}{b^6}\right) = a^{10-2}b^{3-6} = a^8b^{-3} = a^8\left(\dfrac{1}{b^3}\right) = \dfrac{a^8}{b^3}$

Note: You might have solved example 3 quickly by recognizing that the remaining exponent ends up where the larger exponent was originally.

---

4. $\dfrac{-5\left(a^3b^2\right)\left(2a^2b^5\right)}{a^4b^3} = \dfrac{-5(2)\left(a^3a^2\right)\left(b^2b^5\right)}{a^4b^3}$

$ = \dfrac{-10}{1}\left(\dfrac{a^{3+2}}{a^4}\right)\left(\dfrac{b^{2+5}}{b^3}\right)$

$ = \dfrac{-10}{1}\left(\dfrac{a^5}{a^4}\right)\left(\dfrac{b^7}{b^3}\right)$

$ = -10a^{5-4}b^{7-3}$

$ = -10ab^4$

---

5. $(5^3)(2^3) = [(5)(2)]^3 = 10^3$ or $1,000$

Multiplying Polynomials

To **multiply polynomials,** multiply each term in one polynomial by each term in the other polynomial. Simplify if possible.

FOIL Method—Use the FOIL method to help you remember the order of multiplying terms together in a pair of binomials. The steps to the FOIL method are:

    F – *first* - multiply the *first* terms inside each set of parentheses

    O –*outside* - multiply the *outside* (outermost) terms in each set of parentheses

    I – *inside* - multiply both of the *inside* (innermost) terms in each set of parentheses

    L – *last* - multiply the *last* terms in each set of parentheses

Examples:

1. $-8(2x - y) = -8(2x) - (-8)(y)$
$$= -16x + 8y$$

2. $(4x + 2y)(3x - y) = \left[(4x)(3x)\right] + \left[(4x)(-y)\right] + \left[(2y)(3x)\right] + \left[(2y)(-y)\right]$
$$= 12x^2 - 4xy + 6xy - 2y^2$$
$$= 12x^2 + 2xy - 2y^2$$

After multiplying using the FOIL method, simplify if possible. See the following example.

$$(3x + a)(2x - 2a)$$

Multiply *first terms* from each quantity. The first terms are the "$3x$" from the left parentheses and the "$2x$" from the right parentheses.

$$\downarrow \quad \text{first} \quad \downarrow$$
$$(3x + a)(2x - 2a) = \underline{6x^2}$$

Then multiply *outside terms*. The outside terms are the "$3x$" from the left parentheses and the "$-2a$" from the right parentheses.

$$\downarrow \quad \text{outside} \quad \downarrow$$
$$(3x + a)(2x - 2a) = 6x^2 \underline{-6ax}$$

Then multiply *inside terms*. The inside terms are the "a" from the left parentheses and the "$2x$" from the right parentheses.

$$\downarrow \text{inside} \downarrow$$
$$(3x \ + \ a) \ (2x \ - \ 2a) = 6x^2 - 6ax \underline{+2ax}$$

Finally, multiply *last terms*. The last terms are the "a" from the left parentheses and the "$-2a$" from the right parentheses.

$$\downarrow \quad \text{last} \quad \downarrow$$
$$(3x + a)(2x - 2a) = 6x^2 - 6ax + 2ax \underline{-2a^2}$$

Now simplify.

$$(3x + a)(2x - 2a) = 6x^2 - 6ax + 2ax - 2a^2 = 6x^2 - 4ax - 2a^2$$

Dividing a Polynomial by a Monomial

To **divide a polynomial by a monomial,** divide each term in the polynomial by the monomial.

Examples:

1. $\dfrac{16x^2y + 18xy^3}{2xy} = \dfrac{16x^2y}{2xy} + \dfrac{18xy^3}{2xy}$

$\qquad\qquad = \left(\dfrac{16}{2}\right)\left(\dfrac{x^2}{x}\right)\left(\dfrac{y}{y}\right) + \left(\dfrac{18}{2}\right)\left(\dfrac{x}{x}\right)\left(\dfrac{y^3}{y}\right)$

$\qquad\qquad = \quad 8x \quad + \quad 9y^2$

2. $\left(6x^2 + 2x\right) \div (2x) = \dfrac{6x^2 + 2x}{2x} = \dfrac{6x^2}{2x} + \dfrac{2x}{2x} = 3x + 1$

Factoring Each Polynomial Using a Common Factor

To **factor** means to find two or more quantities whose product equals the original quantity. To **factor out a common factor:**

1. Find the largest common monomial factor of each term.
2. Divide the original polynomial by this factor to obtain the second factor. The second factor will also be a polynomial.

Examples:

1. $8x^3 - 12x^2$

The largest common factor of $8x^3$ and $12x^2$ is $4x^2$.

$$\dfrac{8x^3}{4x^2} = 2x, \quad \dfrac{12x^2}{4x^2} = 3$$

Therefore, $8x^3 - 12x^2 = 4x^2(2x - 3)$.

2. $x^5 - 4x^3 + x^2$

The largest common factor of x^5, $4x^3$, and x^2 is x^2.

$$\dfrac{x^5}{x^2} = x^3, \quad \dfrac{4x^3}{x^2} = 4x, \quad \dfrac{x^2}{x^2} = 1$$

Therefore, $x^5 - 4x^3 + x^2 = x^2(x^3 - 4x + 1)$.

Factoring Each Polynomial Using Difference of Squares

The *difference of two squares* refers to the subtraction of two expressions that are each the results of the squares of other expressions. To **factor the difference of two squares:**

1. Find the square root of the first term and the square root of the second term.
2. Express your answer as the product of the sum of the quantities from Step 1 times the difference of those quantities.

Examples:

> **1.** $16a^2 - 81$

$$\sqrt{16a^2} = 4a, \ \sqrt{81} = 9$$

Therefore, $16a^2 - 81 = (4a + 9)(4a - 9)$.

> **2.** $9y^2 - 1$

$$\sqrt{9y^2} = 3y, \ \sqrt{1} = 1$$

Therefore, $9y^2 - 1 = (3y + 1)(3y - 1)$.

Note: $x^2 + 144$ is not factorable using difference of squares. Even though both x^2 and 144 are square numbers, the expression $x^2 + 144$ (the sum of two squares) is not a difference of squares.

Factoring Polynomials that Have Three Terms of the Form $ax^2 + bx + c$ when $a = 1$

To factor polynomials having three terms of the form $ax^2 + bx + c$ when $a = 1$ (that is, the first term is simply x^2):

1. Use double parentheses and place an x at the left sides of the parentheses: $(x \quad)(x \quad)$.
2. Find two numbers that multiply to make the c value and at the same time add to make the b value.
3. Place these numbers, with their appropriate signs, in the parentheses with the x's.

Examples:

> **1.** Factor $x^2 - 2x - 63$.

This is a polynomial in the form of $ax^2 + bx + c$ with $a = 1$, $b = -2$, $c = -63$. Find two numbers that multiply to make -63 and add to make -2. Only the numbers -9 and $+7$ do that. Therefore, $x^2 - 2x - 63 = (x - 9)(x + 7)$. The two parenthetical expressions could be written in reverse order as well: $(x + 7)(x - 9)$.

> **2.** Factor $x^2 - 8x + 15$.

This is a polynomial in the form of $ax^2 + bx + c$ with $a = 1$, $b = -8$, $c = 15$. Find two numbers that multiply to make $+15$ and add to make -8. Only the numbers -3 and -5 do that. Therefore, $x^2 - 8x + 15 = (x - 3)(x - 5)$. The two parenthetical expressions could be written in reverse order as well: $(x - 5)(x - 3)$.

Factoring Polynomials that Have Three Terms of the Form $ax^2 + bx + c$ when $a \neq 1$

Factoring polynomials having three terms of the form $ax^2 + bx + c$ when $a \neq 1$ requires a trial-and-error approach. The following problems demonstrate what type of thinking is required.

Examples:

> **1.** Factor $3a^2 - 4a + 1$.

This is a polynomial in the form of $ax^2 + bx + c$ with $a = 3$, $b = -4$, $c = 1$. Set up two parenthetical expressions: $(\quad)(\quad)$. The values that are in the *first* positions must multiply to make $3a^2$. These could be $3a$ and a. The values in the *last* position need to make +1. These could either be +1 and +1 or –1 and –1. The values in the inner and outer positions need to multiply and combine to make –4*a*. Consider the possibilities:

$$(3a+1)(a+1) \qquad \text{Here, the } \textit{outer} \text{ and } \textit{inner} \text{ products combine to make } +4a.$$

$$(3a-1)(a-1) \qquad \text{Here, the } \textit{outer} \text{ and } \textit{inner} \text{ products combine to make } -4a.$$

Therefore, $3a^2 - 4a + 1 = (3a - 1)(a - 1)$.

> **2.** Factor $4x^2 + 5x + 1$.

To get $4x^2$, the *first terms* could be $2x$ and $2x$ or $4x$ and x. To get +1, the *last terms* could be +1 and +1 or –1 and –1. Experiment with $2x$ and $2x$ together with +1 and +1 and multiply.

$$(2x + 1)(2x + 1) = 4x^2 + 2x + 2x + 1 = 4x^2 + 4x + 1$$

This expression has $4x$ as the result of the *outer* and *inner* multiplications, but the original expression has $5x$ as the result of the *outer* and *inner* multiplications. Thus, $(2x + 1)(2x + 1)$ is not the correct factored form.

If the 1s were replaced with –1s, the only change would be that the result of the *inner* and *outer* multiplications would be $-4x$. Thus, $(2x - 1)(2x - 1)$ is not the correct factored form.

Experiment with $4x$ and x together with +1 and +1 and multiply.

$$(4x + 1)(x + 1) = 4x^2 + 4x + x + 1 = 4x^2 + 5x + 1$$

Therefore, $4x^2 + 5x + 1 = (4x + 1)(x + 1)$.

Some factoring problems combine one or more of the methods described:

> **3.** Factor $4a^2 + 6a + 2$.

Notice that the expression $4a^2 + 6a + 2$ has a common factor of 2. Factoring out a 2 gives $2(2a^2 + 3a + 1)$. The expression $2a^2 + 3a + 1$ can be further factored into $(2a + 1)(a + 1)$. Therefore, $4a^2 + 6a + 2 = 2(2a + 1)(a + 1)$.

> **4.** Factor $x^4 - 81$.

$\sqrt{x^4} = x^2$ and $\sqrt{81} = 9$; therefore, $x^4 - 81 = (x^2 + 9)(x^2 - 9)$. Notice that $x^2 - 9$ is a difference of squares.

$\sqrt{x^2} = x$ and $\sqrt{9} = 3$; therefore $x^2 - 9 = (x + 3)(x - 3)$. Therefore, $x^4 - 81 = (x^2 + 9)(x + 3)(x - 3)$.

Algebraic Fractions

Algebraic fractions are fractions that have a variable in the numerator, denominator, or both the numerator and denominator, such as $\frac{3}{x}$, $\frac{x+1}{2}$, or $\frac{x^2 - x - 2}{x+1}$. Since division by 0 is impossible, variables in the denominator have certain restrictions. The denominator can *never* equal 0. Therefore in $\frac{5}{x}$, $x \neq 0$; in $\frac{2}{x-3}$, $x \neq 3$; in $\frac{3}{a-b}$, $a - b \neq 0$ (which implies $a \neq b$); and in $\frac{4}{a^2 b}$, $a \neq 0$ and $b \neq 0$. Be aware of these types of restrictions.

Simplifying an Algebraic Fraction

To *simplify an algebraic fraction*, first factor the numerator and the denominator; then cancel (or divide out) common factors.

Examples:

> **1.** Simplify: $\dfrac{x^2 - 3x + 2}{3x - 6}$

$$\frac{x^2 - 3x + 2}{3x - 6} = \frac{(x-1)(x-2)}{3(x-2)} = \frac{(x-1)\cancel{(x-2)}^{1}}{3\cancel{(x-2)}_{1}} = \frac{(x-1)}{3}$$

> **2.** Simplify: $\dfrac{(3x - 3)}{(4x - 4)}$

$$\frac{(3x-3)}{(4x-4)} = \frac{3(x-1)}{4(x-1)} = \frac{3\cancel{(x-1)}^{1}}{4\cancel{(x-1)}_{1}} = \frac{3}{4}$$

Warning: Do *not* cancel through an addition or subtraction sign. The following is NOT allowed:

$$\frac{x+1}{x+2} \neq \frac{\cancel{x}+1}{\cancel{x}+2} \quad \text{or} \quad \frac{x+6}{6} \neq \frac{x+\cancel{6}}{\cancel{6}}$$

Multiplying Algebraic Fractions

To *multiply algebraic fractions,* first factor the numerators and denominators that are polynomials and then cancel where possible. Multiply the remaining numerators and denominators together. *If you've canceled properly, your answer will be in simplified form.*

Examples:

> **1.** $\left(\dfrac{x^3}{2y}\right)\left(\dfrac{5y^2}{6x}\right) = \dfrac{\cancel{x^3}^{x^2}}{2\cancel{y}_{1}} \cdot \dfrac{5\cancel{y^2}^{y}}{6\cancel{x}_{1}} = \dfrac{5x^2 y}{12}$

> **2.** $\left(\dfrac{x-5}{x}\right)\left(\dfrac{x+2}{x^2 - 2x - 15}\right) = \dfrac{\cancel{(x-5)}^{1}}{x} \cdot \dfrac{x+2}{\cancel{(x-5)}_{1}(x+3)} = \dfrac{x+2}{x(x+3)}$

Dividing Algebraic Fractions

To *divide algebraic fractions,* invert the second fraction (the divisor) and then multiply the fractions. **Remember:** You can cancel only after you invert.

Examples:

> **1.** $\dfrac{3x^2}{5} \div \dfrac{2x}{y} = \dfrac{3x^2}{5} \times \dfrac{y}{2x} = \dfrac{3\cancel{x^2}^{x}}{5} \times \dfrac{y}{2\cancel{x}_{1}} = \dfrac{3xy}{10}$

> **2.** $\dfrac{6x-3}{2} \div \dfrac{2x-1}{x} = \dfrac{6x-3}{2} \times \dfrac{x}{2x-1} = \dfrac{3\cancel{(2x-1)}^{1}}{2} \cdot \dfrac{x}{\cancel{(2x-1)}_{1}} = \dfrac{3x}{2}$

Adding or Subtracting Algebraic Fractions with a Common Denominator

To *add or subtract algebraic fractions that have a common denominator,* simply keep the denominator and combine (add or subtract) the numerators. Simplify if possible.

Examples:

1. $\dfrac{4}{x} + \dfrac{5}{x} = \dfrac{4+5}{x} = \dfrac{9}{x}$

2. $\dfrac{3x-2}{x+1} - \dfrac{2x-1}{x+1} = \dfrac{3x-2-(2x-1)}{x+1} = \dfrac{3x-2-2x+1}{x+1} = \dfrac{x-1}{x+1}$

Adding or Subtracting Algebraic Fractions with Different Denominators

To *add or subtract algebraic fractions that have different denominators,* first find the lowest common denominator (LCD), and then change each fraction to an equivalent fraction with the common denominator. Finally, combine the numerators and simplify if possible.

Examples:

1. $\dfrac{5}{x} + \dfrac{7}{y} =$

LCD $= xy$

$$\left(\dfrac{5}{x} \times \dfrac{y}{y}\right) + \left(\dfrac{7}{y} \times \dfrac{x}{x}\right) = \dfrac{5y}{xy} + \dfrac{7x}{xy} = \dfrac{5y+7x}{xy} \text{ or } \dfrac{7x+5y}{xy}$$

2. $\dfrac{3}{a^3b^5} + \dfrac{2}{a^4b^2}$

LCD $= a^4b^5$

$$\left(\dfrac{3}{a^3b^5} \times \dfrac{a}{a}\right) + \left(\dfrac{2}{a^4b^2} \times \dfrac{b^3}{b^3}\right) = \dfrac{3a}{a^4b^5} + \dfrac{2b^3}{a^4b^5} = \dfrac{3a+2b^3}{a^4b^5}$$

3. $\dfrac{2x}{x-1} - \dfrac{x}{x+2} =$

LCD $= (x-1)(x+2)$

$$\left(\dfrac{2x}{x-1} \times \dfrac{(x+2)}{(x+2)}\right) - \left(\dfrac{x}{x+2} \times \dfrac{(x-1)}{(x-1)}\right) = \dfrac{2x^2+4x}{(x-1)(x+2)} - \dfrac{x^2-x}{(x-1)(x+2)}$$

$$= \dfrac{2x^2+4x-(x^2-x)}{(x-1)(x+2)}$$

$$= \dfrac{2x^2+4x-x^2+x}{(x-1)(x+2)}$$

$$= \dfrac{x^2+5x}{(x-1)(x+2)}$$

Solving Quadratic Equations in One Variable

A *quadratic equation* is an equation that can be written as $ax^2 + bx + c$ with $a \neq 0$. Some quadratic equations can be solved quickly by *factoring,* but factoring is not always possible. Quadratic equations can also be solved by using the *quadratic formula.*

Steps to Solving a Quadratic Equation Using Factoring

1. Place all terms on one side of the equal sign, leaving zero on the other side.
2. Factor the quadratic expression.
3. Set each factor equal to zero.
4. Solve each of these equations.

Examples:

1. Solve for x by factoring: $x^2 - 6x = 16$

Following the preceding steps:

$x^2 - 6x = 16$ becomes $x^2 - 6x - 16 = 0$.

$x^2 - 6x - 16 = 0$ becomes $(x - 8)(x + 2) = 0$.

$$x - 8 = 0 \quad \text{or} \quad x + 2 = 0$$
$$x = 8 \quad \text{or} \quad x = -2$$

2. Solve for x by factoring: $3x^2 - 4x - 5 = 2x^2 + 4x - 17$

$3x^2 - 4x - 5 = 2x^2 + 4x - 17$ becomes $x^2 - 8x + 12 = 0$.

$x^2 - 8x + 12 = 0$ becomes $(x - 6)(x - 2) = 0$.

$$x - 6 = 0 \quad \text{or} \quad x - 2 = 0$$
$$x = 6 \quad \text{or} \quad x = 2$$

3. Solve for x by factoring: $9x^2 - 49 = 0$

The quadratic is already in the "= 0" form.

$9x^2 - 49 = 0$ becomes $(3x + 7)(3x - 7) = 0$.

$$3x + 7 = 0 \quad \text{or} \quad 3x - 7 = 0$$
$$3x = -7 \quad \text{or} \quad 3x = 7$$
$$x = -\frac{7}{3} \quad \text{or} \quad x = \frac{7}{3}$$

4. Solve for x by factoring: $x^2 = 6x$

$x^2 = 6x$ becomes $x^2 - 6x = 0$.

$x^2 - 6x = 0$ becomes $x(x - 6) = 0$.

$$x = 0 \quad \text{or} \quad x - 6 = 0$$
$$x = 0 \quad \text{or} \quad x = 6$$

Solving Equations with the Quadratic Formula

Frequently, even when a quadratic equation can be factored, finding the appropriate factors is difficult. When finding the appropriate factors becomes difficult, use the quadratic formula.

The **quadratic formula** is a rule that allows you to solve all quadratic problems, even the quadratic equations that are not factorable over the integers. The general quadratic equation is $ax^2 + bx + c = 0$.

The quadratic formula says $x = \dfrac{-b \pm \sqrt{b^2 - 4ac}}{2a}$. In order to use the formula, all terms must be on one side of an equation set equal to zero.

The following examples are taken from the original four examples. Each problem begins with the original problem rewritten in the "= 0" form. Notice that the answers are the same as when the problems were solved by factoring.

Examples:

1. Solve for x using the quadratic formula: $x^2 - 6x - 16 = 0$

$a = 1, b = -6, c = -16$

$$x = \frac{-(-6) \pm \sqrt{(-6)^2 - 4(1)(-16)}}{2(1)}$$
$$= \frac{6 \pm \sqrt{36 + 64}}{2}$$
$$= \frac{6 \pm \sqrt{100}}{2}$$
$$= \frac{6 \pm 10}{2}$$
$$= \frac{6 + 10}{2} = \frac{16}{2} = 8 \quad \text{or} \quad \frac{6 - 10}{2} = \frac{-4}{2} = -2$$

2. Solve for x using the quadratic formula: $x^2 - 8x + 12 = 0$

$a = 1, b = -8, c = 12$

$$x = \frac{-(-8) \pm \sqrt{(-8)^2 - 4(1)(12)}}{2(1)}$$
$$= \frac{8 \pm \sqrt{64 - 48}}{2}$$
$$= \frac{8 \pm \sqrt{16}}{2}$$
$$= \frac{8 \pm 4}{2}$$
$$= \frac{8 + 4}{2} = \frac{12}{2} = 6 \quad \text{or} \quad \frac{8 - 4}{2} = \frac{4}{2} = 2$$

3. Solve for x using the quadratic formula: $9x^2 - 49 = 0$

$a = 9, b = 0, c = -49$

$$x = \frac{-(0) \pm \sqrt{(0)^2 - 4(9)(-49)}}{2(9)}$$

$$= \frac{\pm\sqrt{4(9)(49)}}{18}$$

$$= \frac{\pm(2)(3)(7)}{18}$$

$$= \frac{\pm 42}{18}$$

$$= \frac{42}{18} = \frac{7}{3} \quad \text{or} \quad \frac{-42}{18} = -\frac{7}{3}$$

4. Solve for x using the quadratic formula: $x^2 - 6x = 0$

$a = 1, b = -6, c = 0$

$$x = \frac{-(-6) \pm \sqrt{(-6)^2 - 4(1)(0)}}{2(1)}$$

$$= \frac{6 \pm \sqrt{36 - 0}}{2}$$

$$= \frac{6 \pm \sqrt{36}}{2}$$

$$= \frac{6 \pm 6}{2}$$

$$= \frac{6+6}{2} = \frac{12}{2} = 6 \quad \text{or} \quad \frac{6-6}{2} = \frac{0}{2} = 0$$

Logarithm Functions

Logarithm questions do not frequently appear on the ACT, but you should be familiar with a basic strategy to approach this type of problem. Logarithms, abbreviated **log,** are shortcuts for exponents just as exponents are shortcuts for multiplication. Because exponential functions can increase very quickly, logarithmic functions (rules) are useful in working with very large numbers while manipulating numbers.

Logarithmic functions are the inverse (opposite) of exponential functions. For example:

The inverse of $x = 2^y$ is equal to the logarithmic equation of $y = \log_2 x$.

In other words, if $x = 2^y$, then $y = $ (the power on base 2) to equal x. This can be rewritten as $y = \log_2 x$, which is read as:

"y equals the log of x, base 2" or "y equals the log, base 2, of x."

A **logarithmic function** is a function of the form

$y = \log_b x \quad x > 0$, where $b > 0$ and $b \neq 1$

which reads "y equals the log of x, base b" or "y equals the log, base b, of x."

$$y = \log_b x \quad \text{is equivalent to} \quad x = b^y$$

the base remains
the base

Examples:

Rewrite each exponential equation in its equivalent logarithmic form.

1. $5^2 = 25$

2. $4^{-3} = \dfrac{1}{64}$

3. $\left(\dfrac{1}{2}\right)^{-4} = 16$

Answers:

$5^2 = 25$ becomes $2 = \log_5 25$
— the base remains the base —

$4^{-3} = \dfrac{1}{64}$ becomes $-3 = \log_4\left(\dfrac{1}{64}\right)$
— the base remains the base —

$\left(\dfrac{1}{2}\right)^{-4} = 16$ becomes $-4 = \log_{\frac{1}{2}} 16$
— the base remains the base —

Coordinate Geometry

Each point on a number line is assigned a number. In the same way, each point in a plane is assigned a pair of numbers. These numbers represent the placement of the point relative to two intersecting lines. In ***coordinate graphs,*** two perpendicular number lines are used and are called the *coordinate axes.* One axis is horizontal and is called the *x-axis.* The other is vertical and is called the *y-axis.* The point of intersection of the two number lines is called the *origin* and is represented by the coordinates (0, 0).

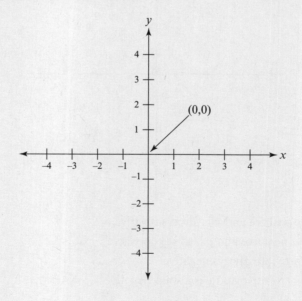

Each point on a plane is located by a unique pair of ordered numbers called the *coordinates.* Some coordinates are noted in the following figure.

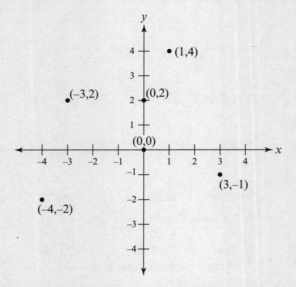

Notice that on the *x*-axis, numbers to the right of 0 are positive and numbers to the left of 0 are negative. On the *y*-axis, numbers above 0 are positive and numbers below 0 are negative. The first number in the ordered pair is called the ***x*-coordinate,** or *abscissa,* and the second number is the ***y*-coordinate,** or *ordinate.* The *x*-coordinate shows the right or left direction, and the *y*-coordinate shows the up or down direction from the origin. The coordinate graph is divided into four regions (quarters) called *quadrants.* These quadrants are labeled here.

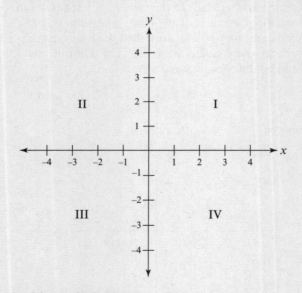

In quadrant I, *x* is always positive and *y* is always positive.

In quadrant II, *x* is always negative and *y* is always positive.

In quadrant III, *x* and *y* are both always negative.

In quadrant IV, *x* is always positive and *y* is always negative.

Examples:

> **1.** In which quadrant(s) do points have positive x-coordinates?

Points have positive x-coordinates in quadrants I and IV.

> **2.** In which quadrant(s) do points have negative x-coordinates and positive y-coordinates?

Only in quadrant II do points have negative x-coordinates and positive y-coordinates.

Distance and Midpoint

Given the coordinates of any two points, you can find the *distance* between them, the *length* of the segment, and the *midpoint* (the point that is located halfway between them) by using appropriate formulas.

Given that $A\ (x_1, y_1)$ and $B\ (x_2, y_2)$ are any two points, then:

Distance Formula

$$\text{Distance between } A \text{ and } B = \sqrt{(x_2 - x_1)^2 + (y_2 - y_1)^2} \text{ or } \sqrt{(x_1 - x_2)^2 + (y_1 - y_2)^2}$$

Midpoint Formula

$$\text{Midpoint between } A \text{ and } B = \frac{x_1 + x_2}{2}, \frac{y_1 + y_2}{2} \text{ or } \frac{x_2 + x_1}{2}, \frac{y_2 + y_1}{2}$$

Examples:

Use the following graph for example questions 1 and 2.

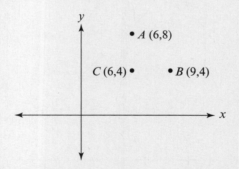

> **1.** What is the distance between A and B?

$$AB = \sqrt{(6-9)^2 + (8-4)^2} = \sqrt{(-3)^2 + (4)^2} = \sqrt{9+16} = \sqrt{25} = 5$$

> **2.** What are the coordinates of the midpoint between A and B?

$$\text{Midpoint}\ (AB) = \left(\frac{6+9}{2}, \frac{8+4}{2}\right) = \left(\frac{15}{2}, \frac{12}{2}\right) = \left(\frac{15}{2}, 6\right) \text{ or } (7.5, 6)$$

Constructing a Graph

Given the equation of a line, you can **construct the graph** of this line by finding ordered pairs that make the equation true. One method for finding the solutions begins with giving a value for one variable and solving the resulting equation for the other value. Repeat this process to find other solutions.

Tip: When giving a value for one variable, start with 0, then try 1, and so on. Then graph the solutions.

Example:

1. Graph the equation $x + y = 6$.

If x is 0, then y is 6: $(0) + y = 6$; $y = 6$

If x is 1, then y is 5: $(1) + y = 6$; $y = 5$

If x is 2, then y is 4: $(2) + y = 6$; $y = 4$

Using a simple chart is helpful.

x	y
0	6
1	5
2	4

Now plot these coordinates and connect them.

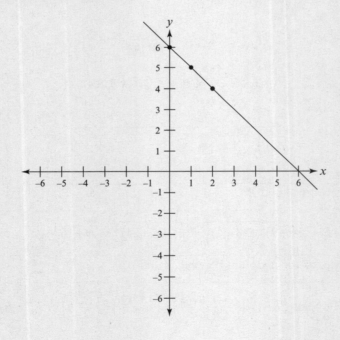

Notice that these solutions form a straight line when plotted. Equations whose solution sets form a straight line are called *linear equations.* Equations that have a variable raised to a power, show division by a variable, involve variables with square roots, or have variables multiplied together will not form straight lines when their solutions are graphed. These are called *nonlinear equations.*

Slope and y-Intercept

There are two relationships between the graph of a linear equation and the equation itself. One involves the *slope of the line,* and the other involves the point of intersection of the line with the *y*-axis, known as the *y-intercept.* When a linear equation is written in the $y = mx + b$ form, the *m* value becomes the slope of the line, and the *b* value is the location on the *y*-axis where the line intercepts the *y*-axis. Thus, the $y = mx + b$ form is called the *slope-intercept form* for the equation of a line.

Example:

> **1.** Find the slope and *y*-intercept of the line with equation $3x - 4y = 12$.

$$3x - 4y = 12 \qquad (\text{Solve for } y \text{ by first subtracting } 3x \text{ from each side.})$$
$$\underline{-3x \qquad -3x}$$
$$-4y = -3x + 12 \qquad (\text{Divide each term on each side by} - 4.)$$
$$\frac{-4y}{-4} = \frac{-3x}{-4} + \frac{12}{-4}$$
$$y = \frac{3}{4}x - 3$$

Therefore, the slope of the line is $\frac{3}{4}$, and its *y*-intercept is at –3.

Slope-Intercept

Given any two points on a line, you can locate the equation of the line that passes through these points. This will require finding the slope of the line and the *y*-intercept.

Given that $A\,(x_1, y_1)$ and $B\,(x_2, y_2)$ are any two points, then:

$$m = \frac{y_2 - y_1}{x_2 - x_1} \text{ or } \frac{y_1 - y_2}{x_1 - x_2}$$

To find an equation of a line given either two of its points (or the slope and one of its points), use the following step-by-step approach.

1. Find the slope, *m*. (Either it is given, or you need to calculate it from two given points.)
2. Find the *y*-intercept, *b* (Either it is given, or you need to use the equation $y = mx + b$ and substitute the slope value found in Step 1 and the *x*- and *y*-coordinates of any given point.)
3. Write the equation of the line in the $y = mx + b$ form using the values found in steps 1 and 2.

Examples:

Use the following graph for questions 1–3.

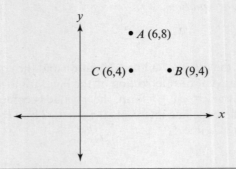

---

1. What is the slope of the line joining A and B?

$$m = \frac{4-8}{9-6} = -\frac{4}{3} \quad \left(\text{or} \quad \frac{8-4}{6-9} = -\frac{4}{3} \right)$$

---

2. What is the equation of the line, in slope-intercept form, joining A and B?

$$y = mx + b \qquad \left(\text{Replace } m \text{ with } -\frac{4}{3}. \right)$$

$$y = -\frac{4}{3}x + b \qquad \left(\begin{array}{l} \text{Use the point } (6, 8) \text{ and replace } x \text{ with 6 and } y \text{ with 8;} \\ \text{then solve the resulting equation for } b. \end{array} \right)$$

$$8 = -\frac{4}{\cancel{3}_{1}}\left(\frac{\cancel{6}^{2}}{1} \right) + b$$

$$8 = -8 + b$$

$$16 = \quad b$$

Therefore, the equation is $y = -\frac{4}{3}x + 16$.

---

3. If the line joining A and B were extended, what would be its exact y-intercept?

The b-value represents the y-intercept, thus the exact y-intercept is 16.

Quadratic Graphs

The graph of an equation in the form $y = ax^2 + bx + c$ or $x = ay^2 + by + c$ where $a \neq 0$ is a U-shaped curve called a **parabola.** If $y = ax^2 + bx + c$ with $a > 0$, the parabola will open upward. If $a < 0$, the parabola will open downward. If $x = ay^2 + by + c$ with $a > 0$, the parabola will open to the right. If $a < 0$, the parabola will open to the left.

A critical point on the graph of a parabola is its **vertex,** because this is where the U-shaped curve changes direction. If the quadratic equation is of the form $y = ax^2 + bx + c$, then the x-coordinate of the vertex is:

$$x = \frac{-b}{2a}$$

The y-coordinate can be determined by substituting this value for x in the original equation. Similarly, if the quadratic equation is of the form $x = ay^2 + by + c$, then the y-coordinate of the vertex is

$$y = \frac{-b}{2a}$$

and the x-coordinate can be determined by substituting this value for y in the original equation.

Example:

> **1.** Find the vertex of the parabola with equation $y = 2x^2 + 8x - 3$.

Since the equation is of the form $y = ax^2 + bx + c$, the x-coordinate of the vertex is:

$$x = \frac{-b}{2a}$$
$$x = \frac{-8}{2(2)}$$
$$x = \frac{-8}{4}$$
$$x = -2$$

Substituting $x = -2$ in the original equation:

$$
\begin{aligned}
y &= 2x^2 + 8x - 3 \\
  &= 2(-2)^2 + 8(-2) - 3 \\
  &= 2(4) - 16 - 3 \\
  &= 8 - 16 - 3 \\
y &= -11
\end{aligned}
$$

Hence the vertex of the parabola is the point $(-2, -11)$. Also note that the parabola will open upward from the vertex, since $a > 0$.

Finding Perimeter and Area

Once the coordinates of a figure are known, certain measurements regarding the figure can be calculated. That is, you can find its *perimeter* (distance around) and its *area.*

Examples:

Use the following graph for questions 1 and 2.

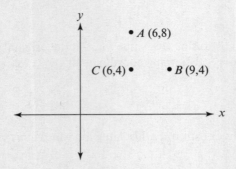

Points *A*, *B*, and *C*, when connected, form a triangle.

---

1. What is the perimeter of $\triangle ABC$?

To find the perimeter of a triangle, simply add the lengths of its sides.

$$AB = \sqrt{(6-9)^2 + (8-4)^2} = \sqrt{(-3)^2 + (4)^2} = \sqrt{9+16} = \sqrt{25} = 5$$
$$AC = \sqrt{(6-6)^2 + (8-4)^2} = \sqrt{(0)^2 + (4)^2} = \sqrt{16} = 4$$
$$BC = \sqrt{(9-6)^2 + (4-4)^2} = \sqrt{(3)^2 + (0)^2} = \sqrt{9} = 3$$

Therefore, the perimeter of $\triangle ABC = 5 + 4 + 3 = 12$.

---

2. What is the area of $\triangle ABC$?

Since point *A* is directly above point *C* and point *B* is directly to the right of point *C*, then $\triangle ABC$ is a right triangle.

Now use $\overline{BC}$ as a base and $\overline{AC}$ as a height, and find the area of $\triangle ABC$ using the following formula:

$$A = \frac{1}{2}bh, \text{ where } b \text{ is the length of the base and } h \text{ is the length of the height}$$

$$\text{Area of } \triangle ABC = \frac{1}{2}(3)(4) = \frac{1}{2}(12) = 6$$

Functions, Function Notation, and Transformations of Functions

A *function* is an equation that expresses an output for any acceptable input. Often the letters *f*, *g*, or *h* are used to denote functions. Consider the function $f(x) = x^2 - 2x$. The English phrase "find the value of the function when *x* is 6" is expressed as $f(6) = ?$

The function is then evaluated by replacing each *x* with the value 6.

$$f(x) = x^2 - 2x$$
$$f(6) = (6)^2 - 2(6)$$
$$f(6) = 36 - 12$$
$$f(6) = 24$$

Examples:

1. If $f(x) = x^2 - 3x$, then $f(3) - f(1) = ?$

First find $f(3)$ and $f(1)$. Then solve the subtractions of these results.

$$f(x) = x^2 - 3x \qquad\qquad f(x) = x^2 - 3x$$
$$f(3) = (3)^2 - 3(3) \qquad\qquad f(1) = (1)^2 - 3(1)$$
$$f(3) = 9 - 9 \qquad\qquad\qquad f(1) = 1 - 3$$
$$f(3) = 0 \qquad\qquad\qquad\quad f(1) = -2$$
$$f(3) - f(1) = 0 - (-2) = 2$$

2. If $h(x) = |x|$, then $\dfrac{4}{h(4)} - \dfrac{-2}{h(-2)} = ?$

First find $h(4)$ and $h(-2)$. Then make the appropriate replacements and evaluate the results.

$$h(x) = |x| \quad\quad h(4) = |4| \quad\quad h(-2) = |-2|$$
$$h(4) = 4 \quad\quad\quad h(-2) = 2$$
$$\frac{4}{h(4)} = \frac{4}{4} = 1 \quad\quad \frac{-2}{h(-2)} = \frac{-2}{2} = -1$$
$$\frac{4}{h(4)} - \frac{-2}{h(-2)} = 1 - (-1) = 2$$

3. If $m(x) = 3x + 2$ and $t(x) = x^2$, then $t[m(-2)] = ?$

First find $m(-2)$, then use its value to replace the x and $t(x)$ function.

$$m(x) = 3x + 2 \qquad\qquad t(x) = x^2$$
$$m(-2) = 3(-2) + 2 \qquad\qquad t[m(-2)] = [m(-2)]^2$$
$$m(-2) = -6 + 2 \qquad\qquad t[m(-2)] = [-4]^2$$
$$m(-2) = -4 \qquad\qquad\quad t[m(-2)] = 16$$

Transformations of Functions

Transformations of a function $f(x)$ change the positions of the graph of $f(x)$ but do not affect the basic shape of the graph. Three basic types of transformations are **horizontal shifts, vertical shifts,** and **reflections.** The following represent the basic transformations on the graph of $y = f(x)$:

Basic Transformations on the Graph of $y = f(x)$:

Reflection about the x-axis:	$y = -f(x)$
Reflection about the y-axis:	$y = f(-x)$
Reflection about the origin:	$y = -f(-x)$
Horizontal shift a units to the right:	$y = f(x - a)$ where $a > 0$
Horizontal shift a units to the left:	$y = f(x + a)$ where $a > 0$
Vertical shift a units upward:	$y = f(x) + a$ where $a > 0$
Vertical shift a units downward:	$y = f(x) - a$ where $a > 0$

Examples:

> **1.** If $f(x) = x^2$, how will the graph of $g(x) = x^2 - 2$ differ from the graph of $f(x)$?

Since $g(x) = f(x) - 2$, the graph of $g(x)$ will be the graph of $f(x)$ shifted vertically down 2 units.

> **2.** If $f(x) = x^3$, how will the graph of $h(x) = (x + 5)^3$ differ from the graph of $f(x)$?

Since $h(x) = f(x + 5),$ the graph of $h(x)$ will be the graph of $f(x)$ shifted horizontally 5 units to the left.

> **3.** If $f(x) = x^4$, how will the graph of $m(x) = -x^4$ differ from the graph of $f(x)$?

Since $m(x) = -f(x),$ the graph of $m(x)$ will be the graph of $f(x)$ reflected about the x-axis.

> **4.** If $f(x) = \sqrt{x}$, how will the graph of $t(x) = \sqrt{x-2} + 3$ differ from the graph of $f(x)$?

Since $t(x) = f(x - 2) + 3$ the graph of $t(x)$ will be the graph of $f(x)$ shifted horizontally to the right 2 units and shifted vertically up 3 units.

Practice Questions: Elementary Algebra, Intermediate Algebra, and Coordinate Geometry

Now that you have reviewed the strategies, you can practice on your own. Questions are grouped into the three types of ACT algebra problems: elementary algebra, intermediate algebra, and coordinate geometry. In addition, questions are roughly grouped into three categories: easy to moderate, average, and above average to difficult. The answers and explanations that follow the questions will include strategies to help you understand how to solve the problems.

- Section I: Elementary Algebra—19 questions
- Section II: Intermediate Algebra—20 questions
- Section III: Coordinate Geometry—15 questions

Note: Additional ACT math concepts that are not specifically covered in the math review chapters may be included in practice problems and practice tests. It is important to review *all* practice tests to get a full understanding of the math topics covered on the ACT.

Section I: Elementary Algebra

Easy to Moderate

1. If $3x = -9$, then $3x^3 - 2x + 4 =$

- **A.** -83
- **B.** -71
- **C.** -47
- **D.** -17
- **E.** 61

2. If the angle measures of the angles in a triangle are represented by $3x$, $x + 10$, and $2x - 40$, what is the measure of the smallest angle?

- **A.** $30°$
- **B.** $35°$
- **C.** $40°$
- **D.** $45°$
- **E.** $50°$

3. $(x + 3)(2x + 4) = ?$

- **A.** $2x^2 + 10x + 12$
- **B.** $x^2 + x + 6$
- **C.** $2x^2 + 6x + 12$
- **D.** $x^2 + 3x + 6$
- **E.** $2x^2 + 2x + 12$

4. Which of the following is a simplified form of $\dfrac{12x^6 y^4 z^2}{6x^2 y^4 z^8}$?

- **A.** $\dfrac{2x^4}{z^6}$
- **B.** $2x^8 y^8 z^{10}$
- **C.** $6x^4 z^{-6}$
- **D.** $\dfrac{2x^3}{z^4}$
- **E.** $\dfrac{2x^6}{z^4}$

5. Which of the following is a simplified version equivalent to $\dfrac{\left(x^{2y+2}\right)\left(x^{6y-1}\right)}{x^{4y-3}}$?

- **A.** x^{3y+4}
- **B.** x^{4y+4}
- **C.** x^{3y-2}
- **D.** x^{4y-2}
- **E.** x^{4y+1}

6. What is the sum of $4x^3 - 2x^2$, $-3x^3 + 3x^2$, and $-2x^3 - 4x^2$?

- **A.** $-x^3 - 3x^2$
- **B.** $x^3 + 3x^2$
- **C.** $3x^3 - 5x^2$
- **D.** $-3x^3 + 5x^2$
- **E.** $4x^5$

7. The total resistance, R, of two resistors, A and B, connected in parallel, is given by the following formula:

$$\frac{1}{R} = \frac{1}{A} + \frac{1}{B}$$

If $A = 10$ and $R = 4$, then what is the value of B?

- **A.** $7\frac{1}{4}$
- **B.** 7
- **C.** $6\frac{3}{4}$
- **D.** $6\frac{2}{3}$
- **E.** 6

8. Which of the following expressions is a simplified form of $\sqrt{\dfrac{78x^5y^7}{6x^2y^3}}$?

   A. $\dfrac{1}{3}x^2y^2\sqrt{39x}$

   B. $x^2y\sqrt{13x}$

   C. $xy^2\sqrt{13x}$

   D. $\dfrac{1}{3}xy^2\sqrt{117x}$

   E. $\dfrac{1}{3}xy^2\sqrt{13x}$

Average

9. Jane is six years older than Tom, and Tom is five years younger than Phillip. Chris is three years older than Tom. If Jane's age is expressed as J, what is the sum of the ages of Jane, Tom, Phillip, and Chris in terms of J?

   A. $4J - 10$
   B. $J - 9$
   C. $3J - 6$
   D. $4J + 12$
   E. $J + 14$

10. If $6x - 3y = 30$ and $4x = 2 - y$, what is the value of $x + y$?

   A. 2
   B. -4
   C. -6
   D. -8
   E. -10

11. If $ab \neq 0$, then $\dfrac{a+8b}{8a} - \dfrac{a+2b}{2a} =$

   A. $-\dfrac{3}{8}$

   B. $\dfrac{-3a+16b}{8a}$

   C. 0

   D. $\dfrac{3a+6b}{8a}$

   E. $\dfrac{10b}{8a}$

12. If x and y are integers such that $2 < y < 25$ and $5 < x < 13$, then the largest possible value of $\dfrac{y}{x} + \dfrac{x}{y}$ is

   A. $\dfrac{1}{2}$

   B. 4

   C. $4\dfrac{1}{4}$

   D. 8
   E. 10

13. If $3x + 2y = 14$ and $3x = 2y$, then $x + y = ?$

   A. 6

   B. $5\dfrac{5}{6}$

   C. $5\dfrac{1}{6}$

   D. $4\dfrac{5}{6}$

   E. $3\dfrac{1}{2}$

14. Marlo has a basketball court that measures 30 feet by 50 feet. She needs a grass strip around it. How wide must the strip be, in feet, to provide 900 square feet of grass?

   A. 3
   B. 4
   C. 5
   D. 6
   E. 7

15. If $x - 10 = \dfrac{-9}{x}$ and $x \neq 0$, then what is the difference between the two roots?

   A. 1
   B. 3
   C. 6
   D. 8
   E. 9

16. Which of the following is a simplified form of $\dfrac{x^2 - 7xy + 12y^2}{x^2 - 4xy + 3y^2}$?

 A. $\dfrac{x - 3y}{x - y}$

 B. $\dfrac{x - 6y}{x - y}$

 C. $\dfrac{x - 4y}{x - y}$

 D. $3xy - 4$

 E. 12

Above Average to Difficult

17. If m is an integer such that $-5 < m < 2$, and n is an integer such that $-4 < n < 5$, what is the least possible value for $3m^2 - 2n$?

 A. -85

 B. -75

 C. -10

 D. -8

 E. 0

18. Ellen can mow a lawn in 2 hours. Dave can mow the same lawn in $1\frac{1}{2}$ hours. Approximately how many minutes will it take to mow the lawn if Ellen and Dave work together?

 A. 210

 B. 90

 C. 51

 D. 48

 E. 30

19. The sum of two numbers is 25. The sum of their squares is 313. What is the value of the larger number?

 A. 10

 B. 11

 C. 12

 D. 13

 E. 14

Section II: Intermediate Algebra

Easy to Moderate

1. Which of the following could NOT be a solution for $4 - 3x < -3$?

 A. 4

 B. 3.5

 C. 3

 D. 2.5

 E. 2

2. Which of the following expressions is a simplified form of $\dfrac{2\sqrt{3} - 4}{\sqrt{3} + 2}$?

 A. $4\sqrt{3} + 7$

 B. $2\left(4\sqrt{3} - 7\right)$

 C. $2\sqrt{3} - 7$

 D. $2\left(7 - 4\sqrt{3}\right)$

 E. $2\left(4\sqrt{3} + 7\right)$

3. If $4x^2 + 2x + A = 0$, which value of A will result in a solution for x of 2 and $-\dfrac{5}{2}$?

 A. -20

 B. -10

 C. 6

 D. 12

 E. 16

Average

4. How many liters of 20-percent solution must be added to a 60-percent solution to yield 40 liters of a 50-percent solution?

 A. 32

 B. 30

 C. 20

 D. 10

 E. 8

5. A man walks from B to C, a distance of x miles, at 8 miles per hour and returns at 12 miles per hour. What is his average speed, in miles per hour?

A. 10.2
B. 10
C. 9.8
D. 9.6
E. 9

6. The length of a rectangle is 6 centimeters greater than its width. The area of the rectangle is 18 square centimeters. What is the width of the rectangle, in centimeters?

A. $3(\sqrt{3}-1)$
B. $3(\sqrt{3}+1)$
C. $3(1-\sqrt{3})$
D. $3\sqrt{3}-1$
E. $3\sqrt{3}+1$

7. Write as a single logarithm:

$$\frac{1}{2}\log(49)+3\log(y)$$

A. $\log\left(\dfrac{49+3y}{2}\right)$

B. $\log\left(7y^3\right)$

C. $\log(147y)$

D. $\log\left(\dfrac{21y}{2}\right)$

E. Cannot write as a single logarithm

8. Given $f(x) = 3x^2 - 2x - 1$ and $g(x) = 4x - 2$, find the value of $(f \circ g)(2)$.

A. 42
B. 56
C. 78
D. 95
E. 108

9. Which of the following represents the solution set for $|2x+6| < 4$?

A. x is less than 5 AND x is greater than 1.
B. x is less than 1 AND x is greater than –5.
C. x is less than –1 AND x is greater than –5.
D. x is less than –1 OR x is greater than 5.
E. x is less than –5 OR x is greater than –1.

10. Find AB if $A=\begin{bmatrix} -8 & 3 & 2 \\ 2 & 0 & -1 \end{bmatrix}$ and $B=\begin{bmatrix} 1 \\ 4 \\ 3 \end{bmatrix}$.

A. $\begin{bmatrix} -6 \\ 12 \\ 3 \end{bmatrix}$

B. $\begin{bmatrix} 16 & 0 & -6 \end{bmatrix}$

C. $\begin{bmatrix} -10 \\ 5 \end{bmatrix}$

D. $\begin{bmatrix} -24 \\ 8 \end{bmatrix}$

E. $\begin{bmatrix} 10 \\ -1 \end{bmatrix}$

11. Find AB if $A=\begin{bmatrix} 5 & 1 \\ -2 & 4 \end{bmatrix}$ and $B=\begin{bmatrix} 4 & 1 \\ -1 & -2 \end{bmatrix}$.

A. $\begin{bmatrix} 20 & 1 \\ 2 & -8 \end{bmatrix}$

B. $\begin{bmatrix} 19 & 3 \\ -12 & -10 \end{bmatrix}$

C. $\begin{bmatrix} 18 & 8 \\ -1 & -9 \end{bmatrix}$

D. $[15]$
E. $[-9]$

Above Average to Difficult

12. How many pounds of tea worth 93¢ per pound must be mixed with tea worth 75¢ per pound to produce 10 pounds worth 85¢ per pound?

  A. $2\frac{2}{9}$

  B. $3\frac{1}{2}$

  C. $4\frac{4}{9}$

  D. $5\frac{5}{9}$

  E. $9\frac{1}{2}$

13. If # is a binary operation such that $a \, \# \, b$ is defined as $\dfrac{a^2+b^2}{a^2-b^2}$ and $(a^2 - b^2 \neq 0)$, then what is the value of $a \, \# \, b$ if $2a = b$ and $a \neq 0$?

  A. $1\frac{1}{3}$

  B. $\frac{3}{5}$

  C. $-\frac{1}{2}$

  D. $-\frac{3}{5}$

  E. $-1\frac{2}{3}$

14. Tom is filling a bathtub with hot and cold water. Running by itself, the hot water tap would fill the tub in exactly 40 minutes. The cold water tap, running by itself, would fill the tub in exactly 20 minutes. With the plug out, it takes 30 minutes to empty a full tub. Tom accidentally leaves the plug out of the tub. When Tom checks on the tub 16 minutes after turning on the hot and cold water, he finds the tub

  A. empty.
  B. one-third full.
  C. one-half full.
  D. two-thirds full.
  E. overflowing.

15. The current in a river is 4 miles per hour. A boat can travel 20 miles per hour in still water. How many miles up the river and back can the boat travel if the round trip is to take 10 hours?

  A. 88
  B. 96
  C. 100
  D. 112
  E. 124

16. Solve for x: $x = \frac{1}{2}\log_3\left(\frac{1}{81}\right)$

  A. $-\frac{1}{9}$

  B. $-\frac{1}{3}$

  C. $-\frac{1}{2}$

  D. -2

  E. -3

17. Given the function $f(x) = \frac{3-2x}{4x-5}$, find $f^{-1}(x)$.

  A. $\frac{5x+3}{4x+2}$

  B. $\frac{4x+2}{5x+3}$

  C. $\frac{-5x+3}{4x-2}$

  D. $\frac{5x-3}{-4x+2}$

  E. $\frac{5x+2}{4x+3}$

18. Find a polynomial function with real coefficients that has roots of -6 and $2i$.

  A. $y = x^3 - 6x^2 - 4x - 24$
  B. $y = x^3 + 6x^2 + 4x + 24$
  C. $y = x^3 + 4x^2 + 6x + 24$
  D. $y = x^3 + 4x^2 - 6x - 24$
  E. $y = x^2 + 12x + 24$

19. Which of the following is equivalent to $\frac{4+3i}{1-2i}$?

   A. $\frac{-11i-10}{3}$

   B. $\frac{2-i}{2}$

   C. $\frac{11i+10}{3}$

   D. $\frac{i-4}{2i+3}$

   E. $\frac{11i-2}{5}$

20. Which of the following represents the solution set for $|4x+12| < |6x-2|$?

   A. $x < 1$ OR $x > 7$
   B. $x < -1$ OR $x > 7$
   C. $x < 2$ OR $x > 5$
   D. $x > -1$ AND $x < 7$
   E. $x > -2$ AND $x < 5$

Section III: Coordinate Geometry

Easy to Moderate

1. In the standard (x, y) coordinate plane, what is the slope of a line that passes through the points $(-2, 3)$ and $(3, -2)$?

   A. -2
   B. -1
   C. 0
   D. 1
   E. 2

2. Select the inequality that best represents the following graph on the number line.

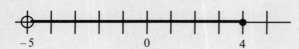

   A. $-5 < x < 4$
   B. $-5 \leq x \leq 4$
   C. $-5 \leq x < 4$
   D. $-5 < x \leq 4$
   E. None of these represents the graph accurately.

3. In the standard (x, y) coordinate plane, what is the point of intersection of the two lines with the equations of $3y + 2x = 18$ and $y = 4x - 8$?

   A. $(8, -3)$
   B. $(4, 3)$
   C. $(3, 4)$
   D. $(9, 0)$
   E. $(-3, 8)$

4. In the standard (x, y) coordinate plane, line m passes through the point $(-3, 7)$ and is parallel to a line with the equation $2y = 3x - 4$. What is the slope of line m?

   A. $-\frac{3}{2}$

   B. $-\frac{2}{3}$

   C. $\frac{2}{3}$

   D. $\frac{3}{2}$

   E. Cannot be determined from the information given.

5. A line segment has endpoints of $(-4, 12)$ and $(6, -6)$. What are the coordinates of the midpoint of the segment?

   A. $(4, 0)$
   B. $(3, 1)$
   C. $(5, -9)$
   D. $(-5, 9)$
   E. $(1, 3)$

6. In the standard (x, y) coordinate plane, two lines are perpendicular to each other. If the equation of one of the lines is $2x + 6y = 12$, what is the slope of the other line?

   A. -3

   B. $-\frac{1}{3}$

   C. $\frac{1}{3}$

   D. 1
   E. 3

Average

Use the following diagram for problem 7.

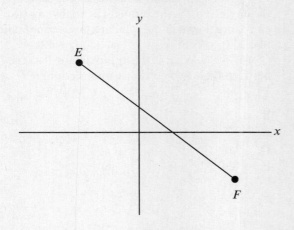

7. If point *E* has coordinates (–3, 5) and point *F* has coordinates (6, –7), then what is the length of $\overline{EF}$?

   A. 21
   B. 15
   C. 7
   D. 5
   E. 3

Use the following diagram for problem 8.

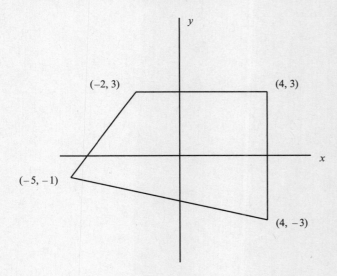

8. What is the area, in square units, of the quadrilateral shown?

   A. 24
   B. 27
   C. 39
   D. 46
   E. 54

9. In the standard (*x, y*) coordinate plane, what is the equation of the line that passes through the point (1, 1) and is perpendicular to the line with the equation $y = -\frac{1}{2}x + 3$?

   A. $y = -\frac{1}{2}x - 2$

   B. $y = -\frac{1}{2}x + \frac{3}{2}$

   C. $y = 2x + 6$
   D. $y = 2x - 1$
   E. None of these

10. In the standard (*x, y*) coordinate plane, if a line passes through the points (6, 4) and (–2, –4) what is its *y*-intercept?

   A. 1
   B. 0
   C. –1
   D. –2
   E. –3

11. In the standard (*x, y*) coordinate plane, at which of the following does the graph of the equation $y + 4 = 2x^2$ cross the graph of the equation $x = -1$?

   A. –6
   B. –2
   C. 0
   D. 2
   E. 6

12. In the standard (*x, y*) coordinate plane, a line segment has a midpoint of (–2, 5) and an endpoint located at (8, –1). Which of the following represents the length of the line segment?

   A. $2\sqrt{13}$
   B. $2\sqrt{34}$
   C. $4\sqrt{13}$
   D. $4\sqrt{34}$
   E. $8\sqrt{34}$

13. Which of the following lines pass through the third quadrant?

   I. $3x + 2y = 7$

   II. $3x - 4y = -8$

  III. $-4x = 6 + 2y$

   A.   I only

   B.   II only

   C.   III only

   D.   Exactly two of the above

   E.   All of the above

Above Average to Difficult

14. In the standard (x, y) coordinate plane, an isosceles triangle has vertices located at $(x, 6)$, $(x + 4, 10)$, and $(8, 2)$, where the vertex located at $(8, 2)$ is the common vertex for the two equal-length sides. What is the length of each of the two equal-length sides?

   A. $4\sqrt{2}$

   B. $2\sqrt{5}$

   C. $4\sqrt{5}$

   D. $8\sqrt{2}$

   E.   Cannot be determined from the information given.

15. In the standard (x, y) coordinate plane, the equation for a circle is $(x - h)^2 + (y - k)^2 = r^2$, where (h, k) are the coordinates of the center of the circle and r is the radius. The following two circles are drawn in the standard (x, y) coordinate plane: $(x - 2)^2 + (y - 4)^2 = 64$ and $(x - 12)^2 + (y - 4)^2 = 36$. What is the approximate distance between their two points of intersection?

   A.   8.4

   B.   8.8

   C.   9.2

   D.   9.6

   E.   10.0

Answers and Explanations

Section I: Elementary Algebra

Easy to Moderate

1. B. First solve $3x = -9$: $x = -3$. Now plug the value of x into $3x^3 - 2x + 4$:

$$3x^3 - 2x + 4$$
$$3(-3)^3 - 2(-3) + 4$$
$$3(-27) + 6 + 4$$
$$-81 + 6 + 4$$
$$-71$$

2. A. Since the three angles of a triangle total 180°,

$$(3x) + (x + 10) + (2x - 40) = 180$$
$$6x - 30 = 180$$
$$6x = 210$$
$$x = 35$$

Therefore, the 3 angles are 105°, 45°, and 30°, and the smallest angle is 30°, thus answer choice A is correct.

3. A. Remember to perform all four multiplications if you use the FOIL method: First, Outer, Inner, and Last. An alternate method is to line them up and multiply as follows:

$$\begin{array}{r} 2x + 4 \\ (\times) \quad x + 3 \\ \hline 6x + 12 \\ 2x^2 + 4x \quad\quad \\ \hline 2x^2 + 10x + 12 \end{array}$$

The correct answer choice is A.

4. A. When dividing numbers of the same base, subtract the exponents, canceling or dividing as follows:

$$\frac{12x^6 y^4 z^2}{6x^2 y^4 z^8} = \frac{12}{6} x^{6-2} y^{4-4} z^{2-8} = 2x^4 z^{-6} = \frac{2x^4}{z^6}$$

Therefore, answer choice A is the correct choice.

5. B. When multiplying, add exponents. When dividing, subtract exponents. Adding the exponents of the factors in the numerator and then subtracting the exponent of the factor in the denominator gives $(2y + 2) + (6y - 1) - (4y - 3) = 4y + 4$.

Therefore, $\dfrac{\left(x^{2y+2}\right)\left(x^{6y-1}\right)}{x^{4y-3}} = x^{4y+4}$. This is Choice B.

6. A. You must combine similar terms.

$$\left(4x^3 - 2x^2\right) + \left(-3x^3 + 3x^2\right) + \left(-2x^3 - 4x^2\right)$$
$$= \left(4x^3 - 3x^3 - 2x^3\right) + \left(-2x^2 + 3x^2 - 4x^2\right)$$
$$= \left(-x^3\right) + \left(-3x^2\right)$$
$$= -x^3 - 3x^2$$

Therefore, the sum is $-x^3 - 3x^2$, or Choice A.

7. D. Simply substitute in the formula.

$$\frac{1}{4} = \frac{1}{10} + \frac{1}{B}$$

Multiply through by the common denominator of $20B$ to eliminate the denominators, giving

$$5B = 2B + 20$$
$$3B = 20$$
$$B = 6\frac{2}{3}$$

8. C. Be careful to handle exponents correctly. "Pull out" perfect squares from the radical and simplify.

$$\sqrt{\frac{78x^5y^7}{6x^2y^3}} = \sqrt{13x^3y^4}$$
$$= \sqrt{13\left(x^2\right)x\left(y^4\right)}$$
$$= xy^2\sqrt{13x}$$

The correct answer choice is Choice C.

Average

9. A. *Jane:* Jane = J

Tom: Since Jane is six years older than Tom, Tom is six years younger than Jane, or Tom = $J - 6$.

Chris: Since Chris is three years older than Tom, add three to Tom's age to get Chris's age: Chris = $J - 6 + 3 = J - 3$.

Phillip: Tom is five years younger than Phillip, so Phillip is five years older than Tom. So add five to Tom's age to get Phillip's age: $J - 6 + 5 = J - 1$.

The *sum* of their ages is $J + (J - 6) + (J - 3) + (J - 1) = 4J - 10$.

10. **B.** Solve simultaneously:

$$6x - 3y = 30$$
$$4x + y = 2$$

Multiply the bottom equation by 3 and add the two equations together.

$$\begin{array}{rl} 6x - 3y &= 30 \\ 12x + 3y &= 6 \\ \hline 18x &= 36 \\ x &= 2 \end{array}$$

Substitute back into one of the original equations, and you find that $y = -6$. Thus, the sum of $x + y$ is -4.

11. **A.** Using $8a$ as a common denominator:

$$\frac{a + 8b}{8a} - \frac{a + 2b}{2a} = \frac{a + 8b}{8a} - \frac{4a + 8b}{8a} = \frac{-3a}{8a} = -\frac{3}{8}$$

12. **C.** To obtain the largest sum of $\frac{y}{x} + \frac{x}{y}$, make the numerators as large as possible and the denominators as small as possible. So, for $\frac{y}{x}$, let $y = 24$ and let $x = 6$. Therefore, $\frac{y}{x} = \frac{24}{6} = 4$. For $\frac{x}{y}$, let $x = 6$ and let $y = 24$. So, $\frac{x}{y} = \frac{6}{24} = \frac{1}{4}$. Therefore, the largest sum of both fractions is $4 + \frac{1}{4} = 4\frac{1}{4}$. You can also use the opposite extremes of $x = 12$ and $y = 3$ to get the same answer: $\frac{12}{3} + \frac{3}{12} = 4 + \frac{1}{4} = 4\frac{1}{4}$.

13. **B.** Solving by substitution solves for both x and y:

$$\begin{array}{ccc} 3x + 3x = 14 & & 2y + 2y = 14 \\ 6x = 14 & & 4y = 14 \\ x = \dfrac{14}{6} & \text{and} & y = \dfrac{14}{4} \\ x = \dfrac{7}{3} & & y = \dfrac{7}{2} \end{array}$$

Therefore,

$$\begin{aligned} x + y &= \frac{7}{3} + \frac{7}{2} \\ &= \frac{14}{6} + \frac{21}{6} \\ &= \frac{35}{6} \\ &= 5\frac{5}{6} \end{aligned}$$

The correct answer is Choice B.

14. **C.** You can sketch the following diagram.

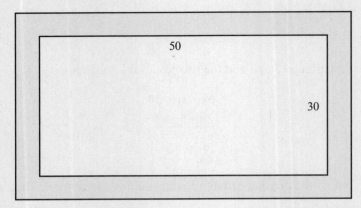

Now you can solve the problem by working from the answers. Since the answers are in order from smallest to largest, you may want to start from the middle answer and then go up or down as needed. If you use the value in Choice C, 5, the diagram looks like this.

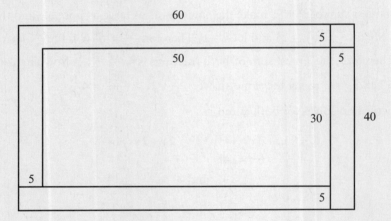

The overall area is 60 feet by 40 feet, or 2,400 square feet. The area of the court is 1,500 square feet. Subtracting the area of the court from the overall area gives the area of the grass strip, which is 900 square feet. So the strip is 5 feet wide. This is answer choice C.

An algebraic solution for the problem looks like the one that follows, although it is not the preferred method. Working from the answers sometimes yields the correct solution without doing complex arithmetic or algebra. If the width of the strip is x, then

$$(2x+50)(2x+30)-1,500 = 900$$
$$4x^2 +160x+1,500-1,500 = 900$$
$$x^2 +40x-225 = 0$$
$$(x+45)(x-5) = 0$$

Because distance cannot be negative, you're left with $x = 5$, or Choice C.

15. D. Multiplying through the equation $x - 10 = \dfrac{-9}{x}$ by x gives

$$x^2 - 10x = -9$$
$$x^2 - 10x + 9 = 0$$
$$(x-9)(x-1) = 0$$

Therefore, the roots are 9 and 1. Their difference is 8, or answer choice D.

16. C. First factor the numerator and denominator and then simplify.

$$\frac{x^2 - 7xy + 12y^2}{x^2 - 4xy + 3y^2} = \frac{(x-3y)(x-4y)}{(x-3y)(x-y)}$$
$$= \frac{x-4y}{x-y}$$

Choice C is the correct answer choice.

Above Average to Difficult

17. D. First examine what you are trying to minimize. The first term, $3m^2$, must be positive or could be zero if m is zero. To minimize the second term, $2n$, n should be as large as possible. Therefore, let $m = 0$ and $n = 4$. Therefore:

$$3m^2 - 2n = 3(0)^2 - 2(4) = 0 - 8 = -8$$

18. C. For this problem, change the hours to minutes and set up the following equation. The numerators in this "work" problem represent the time actually worked, and the denominators represent the time to do the entire job alone.

$$\frac{x}{120} + \frac{x}{90} = 1$$

Multiply both sides of this equation by 360 and solve.

$$3x + 4x = 360$$
$$7x = 360$$
$$x \approx 51$$

Therefore, the correct answer choice is C.

An alternate form of the equation is $\dfrac{1}{120} + \dfrac{1}{90} = \dfrac{1}{x}$.

19. D. You could work this problem by plugging in values from the answer choices. Choices A, B, and C are not reasonable answers because if the sum of two numbers is 25, the larger number could not be 10, 11, or 12. So, plug in choice D, 13. If 13 is the larger number, 12 is the smaller number (since the sum is 25). Now square each of them and add them together as follows:

$$12^2 + 13^2 = 144 + 169$$
$$144 + 169 = 313$$

This is the required sum. Therefore, 13 is the largest number, and the correct answer is D.

Algebraically, if x represents one number, then $(25 - x)$ can be used to represent the other number. Therefore,

$$x^2 + (25 - x)^2 = 313$$
$$x^2 + 625 - 50x + x^2 = 313$$
$$2x^2 - 50x + 312 = 0$$
$$x^2 - 25x + 156 = 0$$
$$(x - 12)(x - 13) = 0$$

So the two numbers are 12 and 13. Since 13 is the larger number, the correct answer choice is D.

Section II: Intermediate Algebra

Easy to Moderate

1. E. Solving the inequality gives

$$4 - 3x < -3$$
$$-3x < -7$$
$$x > \frac{7}{3}$$

Therefore, x is greater than $2\frac{1}{3}$. The only answer choice that is not greater than $2\frac{1}{3}$ is answer choice E.

2. B. Perform the following. To clear the radical from the denominator, multiply by a fraction with the value of one in which the numerator and denominator are the conjugate of the denominator.

$$\frac{2\sqrt{3} - 4}{\sqrt{3} + 2} \times \frac{\sqrt{3} - 2}{\sqrt{3} - 2} = \frac{(2\sqrt{3} - 4)(\sqrt{3} - 2)}{(\sqrt{3} + 2)(\sqrt{3} - 2)} = \frac{(6 - 8\sqrt{3} + 8)}{3 - 4}$$

Now simplify,

$$\frac{6 - 8\sqrt{3} + 8}{3 - 4} = \frac{14 - 8\sqrt{3}}{-1} = 8\sqrt{3} - 14 = 2(4\sqrt{3} - 7)$$

The correct answer choice is B.

3. A. Simply substitute either value into the equation and solve. For example, using the value of 2 gives

$$4x^2 + 2x + A = 0$$
$$4(2)^2 + (2)(2) + A = 0$$
$$16 + 4 + A = 0$$
$$A = -20$$

Substituting the value of $-\frac{5}{2}$ would give the same results, although choosing 2 is faster and more direct.

Average

4. **D.** To set up the following equation, let x be the number of liters of 20-percent solution and $(40 - x)$ be the number of liters of 60-percent solution. Then

$$(.20)(x) + (.60)(40 - x) = (.50)(40)$$

Simplifying and multiplying by 100 gives

$$20x + 2400 - 60x = 2000$$
$$-40x = -400$$
$$x = 10$$

Since x represents the amount of 20-percent solution needed, the correct answer choice is D.

5. **D.** First of all, the answer choice is NOT B. Choosing 10 is the most common incorrect answer. In order to simply average the two rates, 8 and 12, to get 10, would require the time spent at each speed to be equal. They are not. Since the same distance is traveled at each rate, more time is spent at the slower rate of 8 miles per hour. Therefore, 8 has more influence on the average than 12. Thus, the average must be less than 10. This eliminates answer choices A and B. To determine the correct answer, set up an equation and solve. Average speed is total distance/total time. The total distance is $2x$. The time spent going is $\frac{x}{8}$. The time coming back is $\frac{x}{12}$. So average speed is

$$\frac{2x}{\frac{x}{8} + \frac{x}{12}} = \frac{2x}{\frac{3x}{24} + \frac{2x}{24}}$$
$$= \frac{2x}{\frac{5x}{24}}$$
$$= \left(\frac{2x}{1}\right)\left(\frac{24}{5x}\right)$$
$$= \frac{48}{5}$$
$$= 9.6$$

Therefore, answer choice D is correct.

6. **A.** You can make the following drawing.

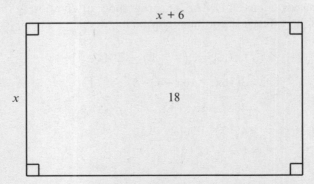

If the width of the rectangle is x, the length can be represented by $x + 6$. So

$$x(x + 6) = 18$$
$$x^2 + 6x = 18$$
$$x^2 + 6x - 18 = 0$$

Using the quadratic formula in which $a = 1$, $b = 6$, and $c = -18$ gives

$$x = \frac{-b \pm \sqrt{b^2 - 4ac}}{2a}$$
$$= \frac{-6 \pm \sqrt{36 + 72}}{2}$$
$$= \frac{-6 \pm \sqrt{108}}{2}$$
$$= \frac{-6 \pm 6\sqrt{3}}{2}$$
$$= -3 \pm 3\sqrt{3}$$

Since x must be positive, you must use $+3\sqrt{3}$; the positive value of x gives

$$x = -3 + 3\sqrt{3} = 3\sqrt{3} - 3 = 3\left(\sqrt{3} - 1\right)$$

This is answer choice A.

7. B. Using the rules to simplify logarithms, proceed as follows:

$$\frac{1}{2}\log(49) + 3\log(y)$$
$$= \log 49^{\frac{1}{2}} + \log y^3$$
$$= \log 7 + \log y^3$$
$$= \log\left(7y^3\right)$$

Therefore, the correct answer choice is B.

8. D. This is the composition of functions f and g. You can rewrite $(f \circ g)(x)$ as $f\left(g(x)\right)$. There are two approaches at this point. Compose the two functions and then evaluate at 2, or evaluate g at 2 and then substitute into f. The latter method is much faster and less prone to error: $g(2) = 4(2) - 2 = 6$.

Now substitute the value of 6 into the function f:

$$f(6) = 3(6)^2 - 2(6) - 1 = 108 - 12 - 1 = 95$$

Therefore, the correct answer choice is D. The longer method, of composing the functions first and then evaluating at 2, is shown here, but it is not the preferred method.

$$f\left(g(x)\right) = 3(4x - 2)^2 - 2(4x - 2) - 1$$
$$= 3\left(16x^2 - 16x + 4\right) - 8x + 4 - 1$$
$$= 48x^2 - 56x + 15$$
$$= 48(2)^2 - 56(2) + 15$$
$$= 192 - 112 + 15$$
$$= 95$$

9. C. To solve this inequality, set up two inequalities and solve each one.

$$2x+6<4 \qquad 2x+6>-4$$
$$2x<-2 \quad \text{and} \quad 2x>-10$$
$$x<-1 \qquad\qquad x>-5$$

In this case, all values of x that are less than -1 AND at the same time greater than -5 will satisfy the inequality. This can also be written $-5<x<-1$, or x is between -5 and -1. Therefore, answer choice C is the correct choice.

10. E. Perform this matrix multiplication as follows:

$$AB=\begin{bmatrix} -8 & 3 & 2 \\ 2 & 0 & -1 \end{bmatrix}\begin{bmatrix} 1 \\ 4 \\ 3 \end{bmatrix}=\begin{bmatrix} (-8)(1)+(3)(4)+(2)(3) \\ (2)(1)+(0)(4)+(-1)(3) \end{bmatrix}=\begin{bmatrix} 10 \\ -1 \end{bmatrix}$$

In creating the product matrix, multiply the corresponding values in each row of the matrix on the left with the values in each column of the matrix on the right. The correct answer choice is E.

11. B. Perform this matrix multiplication as follows:

$$AB=\begin{bmatrix} 5 & 1 \\ -2 & 4 \end{bmatrix}\begin{bmatrix} 4 & 1 \\ -1 & -2 \end{bmatrix}$$

$$=\begin{bmatrix} (5)(4)+(1)(-1) & (5)(1)+(1)(-2) \\ (-2)(4)+(4)(-1) & (-2)(1)+(4)(-2) \end{bmatrix}=\begin{bmatrix} 19 & 3 \\ -12 & -10 \end{bmatrix}$$

In creating the product matrix, multiply the corresponding values in each row of the matrix on the left with the values in each column of the matrix on the right. The correct answer choice is B.

Above Average to Difficult

12. D. Try looking at problems logically before diving into time-consuming algebraic computations. The only reasonable answer is $5\frac{5}{9}$, because 85¢ per pound is slightly closer to 93¢ per pound than to 75¢ per pound. Therefore, since the average of 85¢ is closer to 93¢, slightly more than half of the 10 pounds must be valued at 93¢ per pound. Thus, answer choice D is the correct one.

Algebraically, if you let x stand for the quantity in pounds of 93¢ tea, then $10-x$ can be used to represent the quantity of the 75¢ tea. This leads to the equation

$$0.93x+0.75(10-x)=0.85(10)$$
$$93x+75(10-x)=850$$
$$93x+750-75x=850$$
$$18x=100$$
$$x=\frac{100}{18}$$
$$x=5\frac{5}{9}$$

13. **E.** Since $2a = b$, substitute in the formula:

$$a \# b = \frac{a^2 + b^2}{a^2 - b^2} = \frac{a^2 + (2a)^2}{a^2 - (2a)^2} = \frac{a^2 + 4a^2}{a^2 - 4a^2} = \frac{5a^2}{-3a^2} = \frac{5}{-3} = -1\frac{2}{3}$$

14. **D.** This problem involves items that are either working with or against each other. Organizing the information is important. One method involves setting up a set of fractions, each one representing a "worker." In this case, the "workers" worked for 16 minutes. The numerator of each fraction represents the time actually worked while the denominator represents the time required to complete the entire task alone. Since the cold and hot water work together, they get added together. The drain works against, so it is subtracted, as follows:

$$\frac{16}{40} + \frac{16}{20} - \frac{16}{30} = \frac{48}{120} + \frac{96}{120} - \frac{64}{120} = \frac{80}{120} = \frac{2}{3}$$

Thus, the tub will be two-thirds full after 16 minutes.

15. **B.** You can set up the following chart: If $D = R \cdot T$, then $T = \frac{D}{R}$

	D	$=$	R	$*$	T
Up	D		$20 - 4$		$\frac{D}{16}$
Down	D		$20 + 4$		$\frac{D}{24}$

Since the time allocated for the entire trip is 10 hours,

$$\frac{D}{16} + \frac{D}{24} = 10$$

$$48\left(\frac{D}{16}\right) + 48\left(\frac{D}{24}\right) = 48(10)$$

$$3D + 2D = 480$$

$$5D = 480$$

$$D = 96$$

Therefore, the boat can travel 96 miles up the river and back in 10 hours. The correct answer choice is B.

16. **D.** First, rewrite the right half of the equation.

$$x = \frac{1}{2} \log_3\left(\frac{1}{81}\right)$$

$$x = \log_3\left(\frac{1}{81}\right)^{\frac{1}{2}} = \log_3 \sqrt{\frac{1}{81}}$$

$$x = \log_3\left(\frac{1}{9}\right)$$

Since $x = \log_b a$ is equivalent to $a = b^x$, you can rewrite this expression as $\frac{1}{9} = 3^x$. Solving for x gives $3^x = \frac{1}{9} = \frac{1}{3^2} = 3^{-2}$. Therefore, $x = -2$. This is answer choice D.

17. **A.** To find the inverse function, let $f(x) = y$, exchange the variables x and y, and solve for y as follows:

$$y = \frac{3 - 2x}{4x - 5}$$

Exchange x and y.

$$x = \frac{3 - 2y}{4y - 5}$$

$$x(4y - 5) = 3 - 2y$$

$$4xy - 5x = 3 - 2y$$

$$4xy + 2y = 3 + 5x$$

$$y(4x + 2) = 5x + 3$$

$$y = \frac{5x + 3}{4x + 2}$$

Therefore, the correct answer choice is A.

18. **B.** Whenever a polynomial with real coefficients has a root of $2i$, it must also have a root of $-2i$. Therefore, the three roots of the polynomial are -6, $2i$, and $-2i$. Write a polynomial in factored form and then multiply out.

$$y = (x + 6)(x - 2i)(x + 2i)$$

$$= (x + 6)\left(x^2 - 2ix + 2ix - 4i^2\right) \text{where } i^2 = -1$$

$$= (x + 6)\left(x^2 - 2ix + 2ix + 4\right)$$

$$= (x + 6)\left(x^2 + 4\right)$$

$$= x^3 + 6x^2 + 4x + 24$$

Therefore, the correct answer is choice B.

19. **E.** To simplify this fraction containing a complex number in the denominator, multiply both the numerator and denominator by the complex conjugate.

$$\frac{4 + 3i}{1 - 2i} = \left(\frac{4 + 3i}{1 - 2i}\right)\left(\frac{1 + 2i}{1 + 2i}\right) = \frac{(4 + 3i)(1 + 2i)}{(1 - 2i)(1 + 2i)}$$

$$\frac{4 + 3i + 8i + 6i^2}{1 - 2i + 2i - 4i^2} = \frac{4 + 11i - 6}{1 + 4} \text{ where } i^2 = -1 = \frac{-2 + 11i}{5}$$

This is answer choice E.

20. **B.** To solve this inequality, set up two *equalities* and solve each one to determine the boundary points. This will divide the number line into three parts. Test a randomly chosen value in each interval to determine which intervals satisfy this double inequality problem.

$$4x + 12 = 6x - 2$$
$$-2x = -14$$
$$x = 7$$

or

$$4x + 12 = -(6x - 2)$$
$$4x + 12 = -6x + 2$$
$$10x = -10$$
$$x = -1$$

Choose the points -2, 0, and 8 to test which intervals satisfy the inequality. If $x = -2$, you get $4 < 14$. This is true. Next, if $x = 0$, you get $12 < 2$. This is false. Next, if $x = 8$, you get $44 < 46$. This is true. Therefore, the two intervals that satisfy this inequality are $x > 7$ or $x < -1$. This is answer choice B.

Section III: Coordinate Geometry

Easy to Moderate

1. B. Drawing the following x-y graph and placing the points can be helpful.

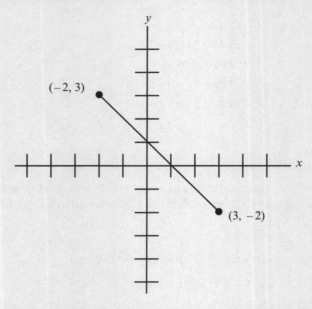

Because the line goes down from left to right, the slope is negative, so the answer is either A or B. From this drawing and using the "definition" that slope $= \dfrac{\text{rise}}{\text{run}}$, you can determine that the answer is –1, Choice B.

The formula for the slope of a line (where m = slope), given its two endpoints, is $m = \dfrac{y_2 - y_1}{x_2 - x_1}$. Therefore, $m = \dfrac{y_2 - y_1}{x_2 - x_1} = \dfrac{3 - (-2)}{(-2) - 3} = \dfrac{5}{-5} = -1$.

Thus, B is the correct answer choice.

2. D. The graph extends between –5 and 4. A closed (filled in) circle indicates that the endpoint is included and an open (not filled in) circle indicates that the endpoint is not included. The "less than" symbol does not include the endpoint and the "less than or equal to" symbol includes the endpoint. Therefore, answer choice D best represents this graph.

3. C. To solve this problem, you could either carefully draw the two lines on a graph and find the point of intersection by inspection, or you could solve these two equations simultaneously to calculate the values of x and y. Both methods are illustrated here. First, to solve simultaneously, rewrite both equations in standard form.

$$3y + 2x = 18$$
$$y - 4x = -8$$

Multiply the first equation by 2 and add it to the second equation.

$$6y + 4x = 36$$
$$\underline{y - 4x = -8}$$
$$7y = 28$$
$$y = 4$$

At this point, you can stop, since only answer choice C has a y-coordinate of 4. Solving for x would confirm the value of 3.

Drawing a quick sketch (as in the illustration that follows) would also allow you to choose the correct answer. The second equation is already written in slope-intercept form. From this form you see that the slope is 4 and the y-intercept is –8. Simply start your line at (0, 8) and move up and to the right, drawing a line with a slope of 4. Next, to sketch the first equation, simply calculate the intercepts. If $x = 0$, then $y = 6$. If $y = 0$, then $x = 9$. Simply draw a line segment between these two points (extending if necessary) to determine the approximate point of intersection. Clearly, it is in the first quadrant. This eliminates answer choices A and E. By inspection, it is clear that answer choice C is the correct one.

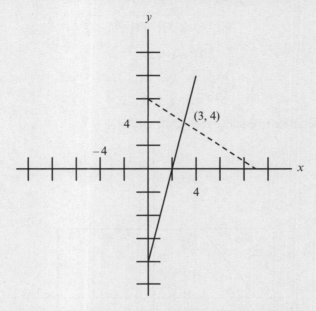

4. **D.** If two lines are parallel, they have the same slope. Solving the given equation for y yields

$$2y = 3x - 4$$
$$y = \frac{3}{2}x - 2$$

Line m has a slope equal to the slope of this line, or a slope of $\frac{3}{2}$. This is answer choice D.

5. **E.** To find the midpoint of a segment, average the two endpoints. If the coordinates of the midpoint are (x, y), the values of x and y are found as follows:

$$(x, y) = \left(\frac{(-4)+6}{2}, \frac{12+(-6)}{2} \right) = (1, 3)$$

Therefore, answer choice E is the correct one.

6. **E.** If two lines are perpendicular, their slopes are negative reciprocals of each other. First compute the slope of the given line. Rewrite in slope-intercept form.

$$2x + 6y = 12$$
$$6y = -2x + 12$$
$$y = -\frac{1}{3}x + 2$$

From this form of the equation, you see that the slope of this line is $-\frac{1}{3}$. Therefore, the slope of the other line is the negative reciprocal of $-\frac{1}{3}$, or 3. This is answer choice E.

Average

7. B. If two points have coordinates (x_1, y_1) and (x_2, y_2), the distance between these points is defined to be $D = \sqrt{(x_2 - x_1)^2 + (y_2 - y_1)^2}$. Since point E has coordinates of $(-3, 5)$ and point F has coordinates of $(6, -7)$, the distance between E and F is

$$D = \sqrt{(x_2 - x_1)^2 + (y_2 - y_1)^2}$$
$$= \sqrt{(6 - (-3))^2 + ((-7) - 5)^2}$$
$$= \sqrt{(9)^2 + (-12)^2}$$
$$= \sqrt{225}$$
$$= 15$$

8. C. Start by drawing a rectangle to enclose the quadrilateral.

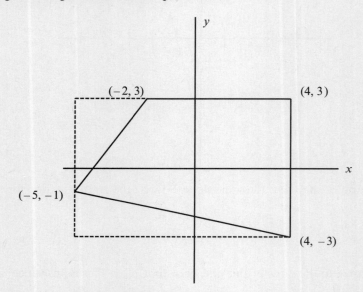

To find the area of the quadrilateral, start with the area of the large rectangle and subtract the areas of the two triangles:

The height of the large rectangle is $3 - (-3) = 6$, and the width of the large rectangle is $4 - (-5) = 9$; the area of the large rectangle is, therefore, 54 square units.

The lower triangle has a width of $4 - (-5) = 9$ and a height of $(-1) - (-3) = 2$; its area is, therefore, $\frac{(9)(2)}{2} = 9$ square units.

The upper triangle has a width of $(-2) - (-5) = 3$ and a height of $3 - (-1) = 4$; its area is, therefore, $\frac{(4)(3)}{2} = 6$ square units

The area of the quadrilateral is, therefore, $54 - 9 - 6 = 39$ square units. Thus, the correct answer choice is C.

9. D. Lines that are perpendicular to each other have slopes that are negative reciprocals of each other. So the equation must be of the form $y = 2x + b$.

If you substitute the given point $(1, 1)$ into this form, you can determine the value of b.

$$1 = (2)(1) + b$$

So $b = -1$. Therefore, $y = 2x - 1$, and Choice D is the answer.

10. **D.** You can draw the following *x-y* graph and plot the points.

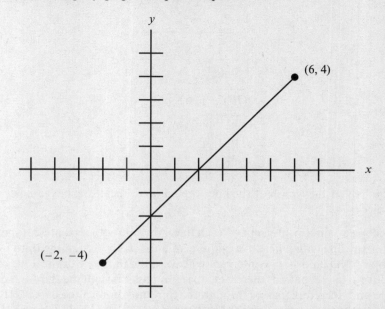

If you understand that the *y*-intercept is where the line crosses the *y*-axis, you can eliminate choices A and B, since they are positive. From the graph, the *y*-intercept will be negative. If you draw the graph fairly accurately, you can spot the answer of –2, which is answer choice D.

To solve for the *y*-intercept, first determine the slope of the line (*m* = slope of line).

$$m = \frac{y_2 - y_1}{x_2 - x_1}$$
$$= \frac{4 - (-4)}{6 - (-2)}$$
$$= \frac{8}{8}$$
$$= 1$$

You can use the point-slope formula to determine the *y*-intercept, but there is a faster way. Since the slope is 1, each unit you move to the right results in 1 unit up. So if you start with the point (–2, –4) and add 2 to each coordinate, you get (0, –2). Therefore, the *y*-intercept is –2. This is answer choice D.

11. **B.** The point of intersection of these two graphs has an *x*-coordinate of –1. Simply substitute –1 into the equation for *x* and solve for *y*.

$$y + 4 = 2x^2$$
$$y + 4 = 2(-1)^2$$
$$y + 4 = 2$$
$$y = -2$$

Therefore, the point of intersection is (–1, –2). The correct answer choice is B.

12. D. First find the distance between the given endpoint and the midpoint, and then double it. Use the distance formula.

$$d = \sqrt{(x_2 - x_1)^2 + (y_2 - y_1)^2}$$
$$= \sqrt{(8-(-2))^2 + ((-1)-5)^2}$$
$$= \sqrt{(10)^2 + (-6)^2}$$
$$= \sqrt{100 + 36}$$
$$= \sqrt{136}$$
$$= 2\sqrt{34}$$

This represents one-half of the length of the line segment and, therefore, has to be doubled to $4\sqrt{34}$. The correct answer choice is D.

13. D. Determine the slope and the y-intercept of each line. Any line with a positive slope must pass through the third quadrant. Any line with a negative y-intercept must pass through the third quadrant. Only lines with a negative slope AND a positive y-intercept will avoid the third quadrant. Line choice I has a negative slope AND a positive y-intercept and, therefore, does not pass through the third quadrant. Line choice II has a positive slope and, therefore, passes through the third quadrant. Line choice III has a negative y-intercept and, therefore, passes through the third quadrant. So line choices II and III satisfy the requirement, making answer choice D the correct one.

Above Average to Difficult

14. C. The lengths of the sides of the triangle can be determined using the distance formula.

Distance between $(x, 6)$ and $(x + 4, 10)$ is

$$d = \sqrt{(x + 4 - x)^2 + (10 - 6)^2}$$
$$= \sqrt{16 + 16} = \sqrt{32} = 4\sqrt{2}$$

Distance between $(x, 6)$ and $(8, 2)$ is

$$d = \sqrt{(x - 8)^2 + (6 - 2)^2}$$
$$= \sqrt{(x^2 - 16x + 64) + 16}$$
$$= \sqrt{x^2 - 16x + 80}$$

Distance between $(x + 4, 10)$ and $(8, 2)$ is

$$d = \sqrt{(x + 4 - 8)^2 + (10 - 2)^2}$$
$$= \sqrt{(x - 4)^2 + 8^2}$$
$$= \sqrt{(x^2 - 8x + 16) + 64}$$
$$= \sqrt{x^2 - 8x + 80}$$

Solve for x by setting the second two distance formulas equal to each other.

$$\sqrt{x^2 - 16x + 80} = \sqrt{x^2 - 8x + 80}$$
$$x^2 - 16x + 80 = x^2 - 8x + 80$$
$$-16x = -8x$$
$$x = 0$$

Substitute $x = 0$ into either the second or third radical to obtain $\sqrt{80} = 4\sqrt{5}$. This is answer choice C.

15. **D.** The centers of the two circles are (2, 4) and (12, 4), respectively. They lie on the same horizontal line and are 10 units apart. The radii of the two circles are 8 and 6, respectively. The following figures shows the distances between the centers of the circles, the lengths of their radii, and the location of the points of intersection. The figure on the right shows an enlarged portion of the figure on the left.

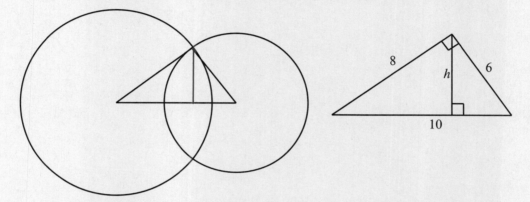

The distance between the points of intersection of the two circles is twice the height (h) shown in the triangle on the right. Since the lengths of the three sides of the triangle are 6, 8, and 10, then from the Pythagorean Theorem we see that this is a right triangle. The area of this triangle can be found by using the two perpendicular sides of the triangle (6 and 8) or by using the longest side of the triangle and h. Equate these two area formulas and solve for h. Use $A = \frac{bh}{2}$ for the area of a triangle.

$$\frac{(6)(8)}{2} = \frac{10h}{2}$$
$$48 = 10h$$
$$4.8 = h$$

The distance between the points of intersection of the two circles is $2h$, or $(2)(4.8) = 9.6$, or answer choice D.

Chapter 10

Geometry

The ACT tests your understanding of measurements as applied to numerous shapes, sizes, and dimensions. On the Mathematics Test, you will be asked to apply your knowledge of geometric shapes, angles, and other configurations in the context of mathematical logic. You likely have already started to formalize these concepts in your high school math classes.

Geometry concepts have been studied for thousands of years, and the word *geometry* literally means "measurement of the Earth." Although different types of geometry exist, ACT geometry problems primarily use *plane Euclidean geometry* (with coordinates and without coordinates) and *trigonometry*. Remember that math concepts are best learned in orderly stages, and geometry is no exception. To help you learn geometry concepts, this study guide separates the types of ACT geometry questions into three general stages of learning:

- Chapter 9—Coordinate geometry
- Chapter 10—Plane geometry (without coordinates)
- Chapter 11—Trigonometry (another branch of geometry that evaluates triangles and the relationships between their sides and angles)

On the ACT, visual illustrations of geometric figures are not necessarily drawn to scale. However, lines shown in the figures are straight, and points on the line occur in the order shown. Some shapes may appear larger, and others may appear smaller. When selecting the answer choice, you should always base your answer on geometric logic, and not on estimating or comparing quantities by sight.

Plane Geometry Concepts You Should Know

- Lines, segments, rays, angles, and congruence
- Polygons and their angles
- Triangles
- Quadrilaterals: rectangles, parallelograms, and trapezoids
- Circles
- Perimeter, circumference, and area
- Volume, surface area, and diagonal lengths of 3-D figures

To evaluate your knowledge of plane geometry, take the geometry diagnostic test that follows and analyze how familiar you are with the selected topics. The diagnostic test will give you valuable insight into the topics you will need to study.

Geometry Diagnostic Test

Directions: Solve each problem in this section by using the information given and your own mathematical calculations.

1. Lines that stay the same distance apart and never meet are called _____ lines.

2. Lines that meet to form right angles are called _____ lines.

3. A(n) _____ angle measures more than 0 degrees but less than 90 degrees.

4. A(n) _____ angle measures 90 degrees.

5. A(n) _____ angle measures more than 90 degrees but less than 180 degrees.

6. A(n) _____ angle measures 180 degrees.

7. Find the smaller angle of a pair of complementary angles such that the larger one is 30 degrees greater than twice the smaller one.

8. Find the larger of two supplementary angles such that the smaller one is half the larger one.

9. In the following diagram, find the measures of $\angle 1$, $\angle 2$, and $\angle 3$.

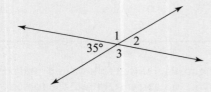

10. In the diagram that follows, find the value of x and then find the measures of all the numbered angles.

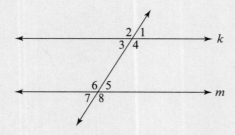

$k \| m; \angle 1 = 2x + 6$ and $\angle 6 = 10x + 30$

Questions 11 and 12 refer to the following figure.

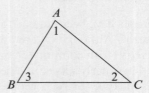

11. Name $\angle A$ of this triangle in three different ways.

12. $\angle 1 + \angle 2 + \angle 3 = $ ____°.

13. What are the generic names of polygons with 4, 5, 6, 7, 8, 9, and 10 sides?

14. What are the interior angle sums of convex polygons having 4, 5, 6, 7, 8, 9, or 10 sides?

15. What is the sum of all the exterior angles, one at each vertex, for any convex polygon?

16. What are the measures of one interior angle and one exterior angle of a regular dodecagon (12-sided polygon)?

17. In $\triangle ABC$ below,

segment BD is a(n) _____.

segment BE is a(n) _____.

segment BF is a(n) _____.

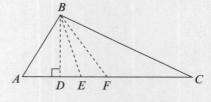

$\overline{BD} \perp \overline{AC}$, $AF = FC$, $\angle ABE = \angle CBE$

18. A(n) _____ triangle has three equal-length (congruent) sides. Therefore, each interior angle measures ____°.

19. In the following diagram, ABC is an isosceles triangle with base $\overline{BC}$ and $\angle B = 38°$. Find $\angle A$ and $\angle C$.

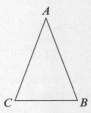

Questions 20 and 21 refer to the diagram that follows.

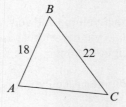

20. In $\triangle ABC$, what is the range of possible values for $\overline{AC}$?

21. In $\triangle ABC$, which angle is smaller, $\angle A$ or $\angle C$?

22. In the diagram that follows, what is the measure of $\angle RST$ if it is an exterior angle of $\triangle QRS$ and $\angle Q = 4x - 3$, $\angle R = 6x - 7$, and $\angle RST = 9x + 5$?

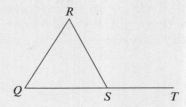

Questions 23–26 refer to the following diagram.

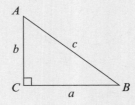

23. If $b = 8$ and $a = 15$, find c.

24. If $b = 10$ and $c = 26$, find a.

25. If $\angle A = 45°$ and $a = 9$, find $\angle B$, b, and c.

26. If $\angle B = 60°$ and $a = 12$, find $\angle A$, b, and c.

27. If in trapezoid $ABCD$ below, $\angle A = 45°$, $\angle B = 30°$, $CD = 10$, and $BC = 12$, find the exact length of $\overline{AB}$.

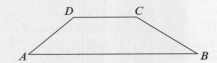

28. Examine the table of quadrilaterals that follows and place a check mark (✓) next to the statements that *must* be true.

Property Statements	Square	Rectangle	Rhombus	Parallelogram	Trapezoid
Diagonals are equal in length (congruent).					
Diagonals bisect each other.					
Diagonals are perpendicular.					
Diagonals bisect the angles.					
All sides are equal in length.					
All angles are equal in measure.					
Opposite angles are equal in measure.					
Opposite sides are equal in length.					
At least one pair of opposite sides are parallel.					
At least two pairs of consecutive angles are supplementary.					

Questions 29–36 relate to the circle with diameter of
$\overline{AC}$, *center at O; points A, B, C, and D lie on the circle;*
and segment EF is tangent to the circle at point C.

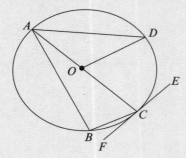

29. Name all the radii.

30. Name all the chords. What is the longest chord in a circle called?

31. Name all the central angles.

32. Name all the inscribed angles.

33. Name all the angles that *must* have a measure of 90°.

34. If $\overset{\frown}{CD} = 80°$ and $\overset{\frown}{BC} = 50°$, find $\angle DOC$ and $\angle DAB$.

35. If $AC = 12$ in, find the exact area and circumference of the circle.

36. If $\angle DOC = 40°$ and $DO = 10$ in, find the exact length of $\overset{\frown}{CD}$ and the exact area of sector DOC.

37. Find the perimeter and area of the following trapezoid.

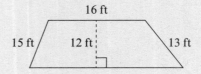

38. Find the area and perimeter of a rhombus if its diagonals have lengths of 24 in and 10 in.

39. The area of a triangle with a base of 20 in is 32 in². What is the height associated with this base?

40. Find the exact volume and surface area of a right circular cylinder with a base radius of 12 in and a height of 10 in.

41. Find the volume of a cube whose surface area is 24 in².

42. A rectangular prism has a diagonal length of $\sqrt{61}$ ft. It has a length of 4 ft and a height of 3 ft. What is its width?

43. If $\triangle ABC \cong \triangle EFG$ and $\angle A = 35°$, $\angle B = 75°$, then $\angle G =$ _____?

44. Use the following diagram to find x and y.

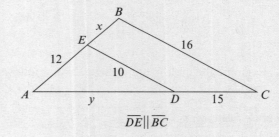

$\overline{DE} \| \overline{BC}$

Scoring the Diagnostic Test

The diagnostic test explanations listed include topic headings that correspond with step-by-step learning tools and examples to help you solve specific problem types. Use the answer key and the analysis worksheet that follows to help you evaluate specific problem types. Topic headings can be found in the "Geometry Review" section following the diagnostic test.

Answer Key

Lines, Segments, Rays, and Angles

1. parallel

2. perpendicular

3. acute

4. right

5. obtuse

6. straight

7. 20 degrees

8. 120 degrees

9. $\angle 1 = \angle 3 = 145°$, $\angle 2 = 35°$

10. $x = 12$, $\angle 1 = \angle 3 = \angle 5 = \angle 7 = 30°$, $\angle 2 = \angle 4 = \angle 6 = \angle 8 = 150°$

Polygons and Their Angles

11. $\angle BAC$, $\angle CAB$, $\angle 1$

12. 180

13. 4 sides = quadrilateral, 5 sides = pentagon, 6 sides = hexagon, 7 sides = septagon or heptagon, 8 sides = octagon, 9 sides = nonagon, 10 sides = decagon

Quadrilaterals

14. 4 sides = 360°, 5 sides = 540°, 6 sides = 720°, 7 sides = 900°, 8 sides = 1080°, 9 sides = 1260°, 10 sides = 1440°

15. 360°

16. Each interior angle is 150°; each exterior angle is 30°.

Triangles

17. $\overline{BD}$ is an altitude; $\overline{BE}$ is an angle bisector; $\overline{BF}$ is a median.

18. equilateral, 60

19. $\angle A = 104°$, $\angle C = 38°$

20. AC can be any value between 4 and 40.

21. $\angle C$

22. $\angle RST = 140°$

23. 17

24. 24

25. $\angle B = 45°$, $b = 9$, $c = 9\sqrt{2}$

26. $\angle A = 30°$, $b = 12\sqrt{3}$, $c = 24$

27. $16 + 6\sqrt{3}$

28.

Property Statements	Square	Rectangle	Rhombus	Parallelogram	Trapezoid
Diagonals are equal in length (congruent).	✓	✓			
Diagonals bisect each other.	✓	✓	✓	✓	
Diagonals are perpendicular.	✓		✓		
Diagonals bisect the angles.	✓		✓		
All sides are equal in length.	✓		✓		
All angles are equal in measure.	✓	✓			
Opposite angles are equal in measure.	✓	✓	✓	✓	
Opposite sides are equal in length.	✓	✓	✓	✓	
At least one pair of opposite sides are parallel.	✓	✓	✓	✓	✓
At least two pairs of consecutive angles are supplementary.	✓	✓	✓	✓	✓

Circles

29. $\overline{OA}$, $\overline{OC}$, $\overline{OD}$

30. $\overline{AB}$, $\overline{AC}$, $\overline{AD}$, $\overline{BC}$; diameter

31. $\angle AOD$, $\angle DOC$

32. $\angle DAC$, $\angle DAB$, $\angle CAB$, $\angle ABC$, $\angle ACB$

33. $\angle ABC$, $\angle ACE$, $\angle ACF$

34. $\angle DOC = 80°$, $\angle DAB = 65°$

Perimeter, Circumference, and Area of Plane Figures

35. area = 36π in^2, circumference = 12π in

36. $\overparen{CD} = \frac{20}{9}\pi$ in, area of sector $DOC = \frac{100}{9}\pi$ sq. in

37. perimeter = 74 ft, area = 276 ft^2

38. perimeter = 52 in, area = 120 in^2

39. height = 3.2 in or $3\frac{1}{5}$ in

Surface Area, Volume, and Diagonal Lengths

40. volume = 1440π in^3, surface area = 528π in^2

41. volume = 8 in^3

42. width = 6 ft

Congruence and Similarity

43. $\angle G = 70°$

44. $x = 7.2$ or $7\frac{1}{5}$, $y = 25$

Charting and Analyzing Your Diagnostic Test Results

Record your diagnostic test results in the following chart, and use these results as a guide to plan your geometry review goals and objectives. Mark the problems that you missed, and pay particular attention to those that you missed in Column (C) because of they were unfamiliar math concepts to you. These are the areas you will want to focus on as you study geometry topics.

Analysis Sheet

Topic	Number Possible	Number Correct	Number Incorrect		
			(A) Simple Mistake	(B) Misread Problem	(C) Unfamiliar Math Concept
Lines, segments, rays, and angles	10				
Polygons and their angles	6				
Triangles	11				
Quadrilaterals	1				
Circles	6				
Perimeter, circumferences, and area of plane figures	5				
Surface area, volume, and diagonal lengths	3				
Congruence and similarity	2				
Total Possible Explanations for Incorrect Answers: Columns A, B, and C					
Total Number of Questions	44	Add the total number of correct questions here: _____	Add columns A, B, and C for total number of incorrect questions here: _____		

Geometry Review

Lines, Segments, Rays, and Angles

A *line* always will be considered to be straight. It continues forever in opposite directions. A line consists of an infinite number of points and is named by any two points on it. A line may also be named by one lowercase letter.

The preceding line can be referred to as line *AB*, line *BA*, or line *k*.

A *line segment* is a portion of a line that contains two endpoints and all the points that are between them. A line segment is named by its two endpoints. A segment has a length and is expressed by writing the two endpoints next to one another. On the ACT, a line segment and its length could be expressed using the same expression. It is important to recognize the context of the expression that is being referenced.

The segment that has endpoints at *A* and *B* is referred to as *AB*, or $\overline{AB}$, or segment *AB*. The distance between *A* and *B*, or the length of segment *AB* is also referred to as *AB* (no bar).

A *midpoint* of a line segment is the halfway point, or the point equidistant from the endpoints.

If *AM* = *MB*, then *M* is the midpoint of $\overline{AB}$. In the previous sentence, the *AM* and *MB* are considered to be lengths, and the $\overline{AB}$ is considered to be the segment itself.

A *ray* is a portion of a line with one endpoint and continues forever in only one direction. Referring to the preceding figure, ray *AB* would be the portion of the line starting at *A*, its endpoint, passing through *B*, and continuing on in that direction. Ray *BA* would start at *B*, its endpoint, pass through *A*, and continue forever in that direction. Notice that ray *AB* and ray *BA* are not the same ray, yet ray *AB* and ray *AM* represent the same ray.

An *angle* is formed by two rays that have the same endpoint (or two lines that intersect at a point). The endpoint of intersection of an angle is called the *vertex of the angle,* and the rays are called the *sides* of the angle. An angle is measured in degrees from 0 to 360. The number of degrees indicates the size of the angle. The angle symbol ∠ is often used instead of the word "angle."

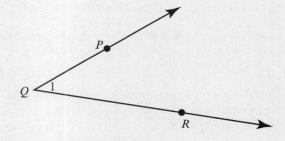

In the preceding figure, you can name the angle in several ways:

- by the letter of the vertex, ∠*Q*
- by the number in its interior, ∠1
- by three letters with the middle letter the vertex of the angle, ∠*PQR* or ∠*RQP*

A *right angle* has a measure of 90°. In the following figure, the small square symbol in the interior of an angle means a right angle. Angle *T* is a right angle.

Any angle whose measure is greater than 0° and less than 90° is called an *acute angle.* Any angle whose measure is greater than 90° but less than 180° is called an *obtuse angle. A straight angle* has a measure of 180°.

In the figure that follows, ∠*PQR* is an acute angle, ∠*PQS* is an obtuse angle, and ∠*RQS* is a straight angle.

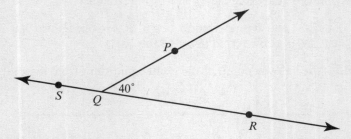

When lines intersect, four angles are formed. The angles opposite each other are called *vertical angles.* The angles sharing a common side and a common vertex are *adjacent angles.* Vertical angles are always equal in measure, and adjacent angles formed by intersecting lines will always have a sum of 180°.

In the following figure, line *n* and line *m* intersect.

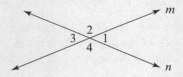

$$\angle 1 = \angle 3, \angle 2 = \angle 4, \angle 1 + \angle 2 = \angle 2 + \angle 3 = \angle 3 + \angle 4 = \angle 4 + \angle 1 = 180°$$

Two angles whose sum is 90° are called *complementary angles.* Two angles whose sum is 180° are called *supplementary angles.* Adjacent angles formed from intersecting lines are supplementary. An *angle bisector* is a ray, segment, or line from the vertex of an angle that divides the angle into two angles of equal measure.

Two lines that meet to form right angles are called *perpendicular lines.* The symbol ⊥ is used to denote perpendicular lines. Two or more lines that remain the same distance apart at all times are called *parallel lines.* Parallel lines never meet. The symbol ∥ is used to denote parallel lines.

In the figure that follows, ray *m* is an angle bisector. $k \perp n$ and $l \perp n$. $k \parallel l$.

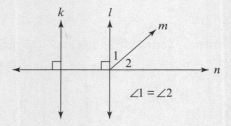

When two parallel lines are both intersected by a third line, eight angles (none of which are straight angles) are formed. Angles in the same relative positions will have equal measures. With this information—knowing any one angle, or how any two angles are related—the measures of all eight angles can be determined.

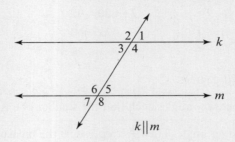

$$\angle 1 = \angle 5, \angle 3 = \angle 7 \qquad \angle 2 = \angle 6, \angle 4 = \angle 8$$
$$\text{but } \angle 1 = \angle 3 \text{ and } \angle 5 = \angle 7 \quad \text{and} \quad \angle 2 = \angle 4 \text{ and } \angle 6 = \angle 8$$
$$\text{because vertical angles are equal,}$$
$$\text{therefore,}$$
$$\angle 1 = \angle 3 = \angle 5 = \angle 7 \quad \text{and} \quad \angle 2 = \angle 4 = \angle 6 = \angle 8$$

When two parallel lines are intersected by a third line, any two angles will either have equal measures or be supplementary.

Examples:

1. Lines that stay the same distance apart and never meet are called _____ lines.

This is the definition of parallel lines.

2. Lines that meet to form right angles are called _____ lines.

This is the definition of perpendicular lines.

3. A(n) _____ angle measures greater than zero degrees and less than 90 degrees.

This is the definition of an acute angle.

4. A(n) _____ angle measures 90 degrees.

This is the definition of a right angle.

5. A(n) _____ angle measures more than 90 degrees but less than 180 degrees.

This is the definition of an obtuse angle.

6. A(n) _____ angle measures 180 degrees.

This is the definition of a straight angle.

7. Find the smaller angle of a pair of complementary angles such that the larger one is 30 degrees greater than twice the smaller one.

Let x represent the measure of the smaller angle. Then $2x + 30$ represents the measure of the larger angle. Complementary angles have a sum of 90°. Therefore,

$$x + (2x + 30) = 90$$
$$3x + 30 = 90$$
$$3x = 60$$
$$x = 20$$

The smaller angle has a measure of 20 degrees.

---

8. Find the larger of two supplementary angles such that the smaller one is half the larger one.

Let x represent the measure of the larger angle. Then $\frac{1}{2}x$ represents the measure of the smaller angle. Supplementary angles have a sum of 180°. Therefore,

$$x + \frac{1}{2}x = 180$$
$$\frac{3}{2}x = 180$$
$$x = 120$$

The larger angle has a measure of 120 degrees.

---

9. In the following diagram, find the measure of $\angle 1$, $\angle 2$, and $\angle 3$.

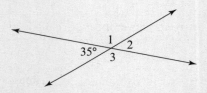

$$\angle 1 + 35° = 180°$$
$$\angle 1 = 145°$$

And since vertical angles have equal measure, $\angle 2 = 35°$, $\angle 3 = 145°$.

---

10. In the diagram that follows, find the value of x, then find the measure of all the numbered angles.

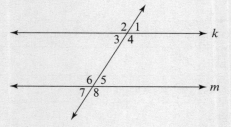

$k \| m$; $\angle 1 = 2x + 6$ and $\angle 6 = 10x + 30$

Lines k and m are parallel. Since $\angle 1$ and $\angle 6$ are not equal, then they must be supplementary. Therefore,

$$\angle 1 + \angle 6 = 180$$
$$(2x+6)+(10x+30) = 180$$
$$12x + 36 = 180$$
$$12x = 144$$
$$x = 12$$

$\angle 1 = 2x + 6 = 2(12) + 6 = 24 + 6 = 30,$ $\angle 6 = 10x + 30 = 10(12) + 30 = 120 + 30 = 150$
$\angle 1 = \angle 3 = \angle 5 = \angle 7 = 30°$ $\angle 2 = \angle 4 = \angle 6 = \angle 8 = 150°$

Polygons and Their Angles

Closed shapes, or figures in a plane, with three or more sides are called **polygons**. *Poly* means "many," and *gon* means "sides." Thus, polygon means "many sides."

Convex polygons are polygons such that a line segment joining any two points inside the figure lies completely inside the figure. A non-convex polygon is called a concave polygon. The ACT examination deals only with convex polygons. Examples of convex and concave polygons are provided here.

Convex polygon   Concave polygon

Convex polygons and their generic names are illustrated in the following figures.

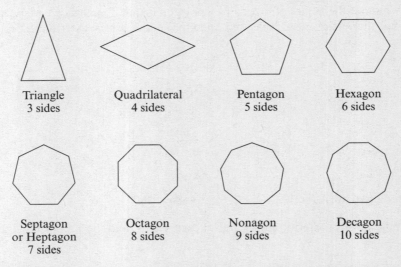

Triangle   Quadrilateral   Pentagon   Hexagon
3 sides   4 sides   5 sides   6 sides

Septagon   Octagon   Nonagon   Decagon
or Heptagon   8 sides   9 sides   10 sides
7 sides

Regular polygons are polygons that have all sides of the same length and all angles of the same measure. A regular three-sided polygon is an **equilateral triangle**. A regular four-sided polygon is a **square**. A regular five-sided polygon is a **regular pentagon**. A regular six-sided polygon is a **regular hexagon**.

A *diagonal of a polygon* is a line segment that connects one vertex with another vertex and is not itself a side.

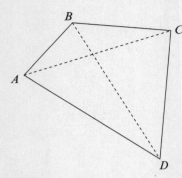

In quadrilateral *ABCD* above, $\overline{AC}$ and $\overline{BD}$ are both diagonals. If all the diagonals from one vertex of a polygon were drawn, it would divide the polygon into nonoverlapping triangles. The following figure illustrates nonoverlapping triangles in a quadrilateral, pentagon, and hexagon.

In each case, the number of triangles created is 2 less than the number of sides of the polygon. Since the sum of the angles of any triangle is 180°, you can now find the sum of the interior angles of any convex polygon by taking 2 less than the number of sides times 180°. That is, if *n* is the number of sides a polygon has, then $180°(n-2)$ is the sum of all its interior angles.

Another interesting fact about the angles of any convex polygon is that if each side was extended in one direction and the exterior angles at the vertices were measured, then the sum of all the exterior angles, one at each vertex, would equal 360°.

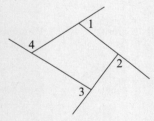

In the case of the preceding quadrilateral, $\angle 1 + \angle 2 + \angle 3 + \angle 4 = 360°$.

A 15-sided polygon would have 15 exterior angles, one at each vertex, and the sum of those 15 angles would also be 360°.

Examples:

Questions 1 and 2 refer to the following figure.

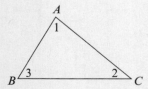

---

1. Name $\angle A$ of this triangle in three different ways.

If three letters are used, the vertex must be the middle letter. The three possible answers are $\angle BAC$, $\angle CAB$, and $\angle 1$.

---

2. $\angle 1 + \angle 2 + \angle 3 = $ ____°.

The sum of the angles of a triangle is always 180°.

---

3. What are the generic names of polygons with 4, 5, 6, 7, 8, 9, and 10 sides?

---

4 sides = quadrilateral, 5 sides = pentagon, 6 sides = hexagon, 7 sides = septagon or heptagon, 8 sides = octagon, 9 sides = nonagon, 10 sides = decagon

---

4. What are the interior angle sums of convex polygons having 4, 5, 6, 7, 8, 9, or 10 sides?

The formula for the sum of the interior angle sums is $180° (n-2)$, where n is the number of sides of the polygon.

n	$180°(n-2)$	Total (in degrees)
4	180°(2)	360°
5	180°(3)	540°
6	180°(4)	720°
7	180°(5)	900°
8	180°(6)	1080°
9	180°(7)	1260°
10	180°(8)	1440°

---

5. What is the sum of all the exterior angles, one at each vertex, for any convex polygon?

The sum is always 360°.

---

6. What are the measures of one interior angle and one exterior angle of a regular dodecagon (12-sided polygon)?

There are two methods of solving this problem.

Method 1:

Find the interior angle and then subtract that from 180° to find the exterior angle. The sum of the interior angles is $180°(12-2) = 180°(10) = 1800°$.

Since there are 12 angles in a 12-sided figure, and a regular polygon has each of its interior angles equal to one another, each angle will have a measure of $\frac{1800°}{12} = 150°$.

Then, each exterior angle has a measure of $180° - 150° = 30°$.

Method 2:

Find each exterior angle, then subtract that from 180° to find the interior angle. The sum of all the exterior angles is 360°.

Since the figure is regular, each of its exterior angles will have the same measure. There are 12 exterior angles; therefore each exterior angle has the measure $\frac{360°}{12} = 30°$, which means each interior angle has the measure $180° - 30° = 150°$.

Triangles

Triangles can be classified by the lengths of their sides.

- A triangle having all three sides equal in measure is called an ***equilateral triangle.***
- A triangle having at least two equal-length (congruent) sides is called an ***isosceles triangle.***
- A triangle having no equal-length (congruent) sides is called a ***scalene triangle.***

Triangles can also be classified by their angles.

- A triangle having all three angles equal in measure is called an ***equiangular triangle.***
- A triangle having a right angle in its interior is called a ***right triangle.***
- A triangle having an obtuse angle in its interior is called an ***obtuse triangle.***
- A triangle having all acute angles in its interior is called an ***acute triangle.***

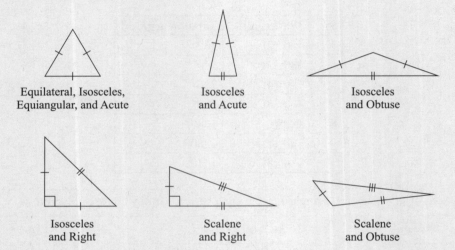

In any triangle, if two of its sides have equal length, the angles opposite those sides have equal measure; and if any two angles in a triangle have equal measure, then the sides opposite those angles have equal length. If all three sides in a triangle are equal in length, then all three angles in the triangle are equal in measure, and vice-versa. In any triangle, if one side is longer than another side, then the angle opposite the longer side will be greater than the angle opposite the shorter side, and vice-versa.

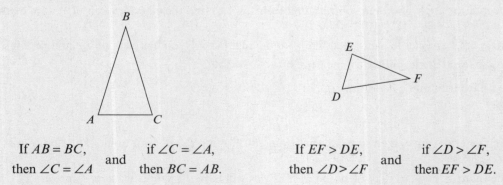

Any side of a triangle can be called a ***base.*** With each base, there is an associated ***height*** (or *altitude*). Each height segment is the perpendicular segment from a vertex to its opposite side or the extension of the opposite side. The height, ***h,*** can go inside the triangle to its associated base, ***b,*** it can be one of the sides of the triangle, or it can go outside the triangle as shown in the following diagram.

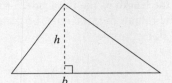
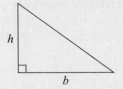
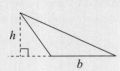

Every triangle has three medians. A **_median_** is a line segment drawn from a vertex to the midpoint of the opposite side. In the following figure, $\overline{BD}$ is a median to side $\overline{AC}$.

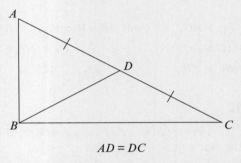

$$AD = DC$$

Every triangle has three **_angle bisectors._** The angle bisector divides an angle into two smaller angles that are equal in measure. In the following figure, $\overline{GI}$ is the angle bisector from vertex G.

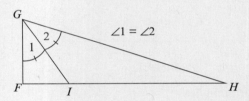

An interesting fact: In any triangle, if one segment functions as any two of the three special segments (altitude, median, angle bisector) in a triangle, then it automatically functions as the third one, and the triangle is isosceles. The vertex from which the segments are drawn becomes the vertex of the isosceles triangle, and it is at the vertex of the isosceles triangle where the equal sides meet. See the following figure.

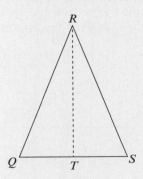

- If $\overline{RT}$ is an altitude <u>and</u> an angle bisector, or
- If $\overline{RT}$ is an altitude <u>and</u> a median, or
- If $\overline{RT}$ is an angle bisector <u>and</u> a median,
- Then $\overline{RT}$ is all three, $\triangle QRS$ is isosceles, and $QR = RS$.

The sum of the lengths of any two sides of a triangle must be larger than the length of the third side. This statement can be interpreted as, "given any two sides of a triangle, the length of the remaining side must be greater than the difference of the two lengths, but less than the sum of the two lengths." For example:

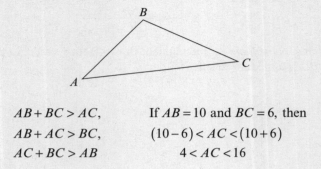

$AB + BC > AC,$ If $AB = 10$ and $BC = 6$, then

$AB + AC > BC,$ $(10 - 6) < AC < (10 + 6)$

$AC + BC > AB$ $4 < AC < 16$

Exterior Angle Theorem

If one side of a triangle is extended, the measure of the exterior angle formed by that extension is equal to the sum of the measures of the remote interior angles. For example,

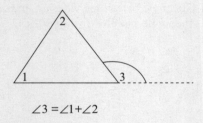

$\angle 3 = \angle 1 + \angle 2$

Note that every triangle has six exterior angles.

Pythagorean Theorem

In any right triangle, the relationship between the lengths of the sides is stated by the ***Pythagorean Theorem***. The side opposite the right angle is called the ***hypotenuse*** (side c). The hypotenuse will always be the longest side in a right triangle. The other two sides are called the ***legs*** (sides a and b). The theorem states that the square of the length of the hypotenuse equals the sum of the squares of the lengths of the legs.

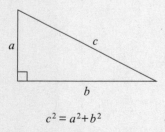

$c^2 = a^2 + b^2$

An extension of this theorem can be used to determine the type of triangle based on knowing its angle measures or the lengths of its three sides. If a, b, and c are the lengths of the sides of any triangle, with c being the longest side, then the following is true:

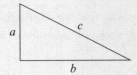 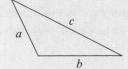

If $c^2 = a^2 + b^2$, then the triangle is a right triangle and the angle opposite c is 90°.

If $c^2 > a^2 + b^2$, then the triangle is an obtuse triangle and the angle opposite c is greater than 90°.

If $c^2 < a^2 + b^2$, then the triangle is an acute triangle and the angle opposite c is less than 90°.

If the angle opposite c is 90°, the triangle is a right triangle and $c^2 = a^2 + b^2$.

If the angle opposite c is greater than 90°, the triangle is an obtuse triangle and $c^2 > a^2 + b^2$.

If the angle opposite c is less than 90°, the triangle is an acute triangle and $c^2 < a^2 + b^2$.

Special Right Triangle Theorems

There are two very special right triangles whose side relationships you should know. One is called the **30-60-90 right triangle,** and the other is the **45-45-90 right triangle.**

The 30°-60°-90° Right Triangle Theorem

In the 30-60-90 right triangle,

- The side opposite the 30 degrees is the shortest side.
- The hypotenuse is twice as long as the shortest side.
- The side opposite the 60 degrees is the shortest side times $\sqrt{3}$.

This is shown in the following figure.

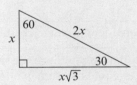

The 45°-45°-90° Right Triangle Theorem

In the 45-45-90 right triangle, the legs have equal lengths and the length of the hypotenuse is a leg times $\sqrt{2}$. This is shown in the following figure.

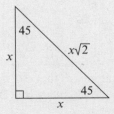

Besides these two special right triangles, right triangles with sides 3-4-5, 5-12-13, 7-24-25, and 8-15-17 are often used on tests. Triangles with side-lengths in these ratios are known as Pythagorean Triples.

It is useful to note that certain integer values work in the Pythagorean Theorem, and these integers are called Pythagorean Triples. Any multiples of these triples will also satisfy the Pythagorean Theorem as well.

For example,

1. 3, 4, 5, and any multiple of these, such as 6, 8, 10 and 9, 12, 15.

2. 5, 12, 13, and any multiple of these, such as 10, 24, 26 and 15, 36, 39.

3. 8, 15, 17, and any multiple of these, such as 16, 30, 34, and 24, 45, 51.

Examples:

---

1. In $\triangle ABC$ that follows,

segment BD is a(n) _____.

segment BE is a(n) _____.

segment BF is a(n) _____.

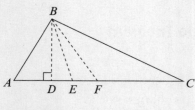

$\overline{BD} \perp \overline{AC}$, $AF = FC$, $\angle ABE = \angle CBE$

Since $\overline{BD} \perp \overline{AC}$, $\overline{BD}$ is an altitude. Since $\angle ABE = \angle CBE$, $\overline{BE}$ is an angle bisector. Since $AF = FC$, $\overline{BF}$ is a median.

---

2. A(n) _____ triangle has three equal-length sides. Therefore, each interior angle measures _____°.

An equilateral triangle has all three sides of equal length. Since the sum of the angles of any triangle is 180°, and equal-length sides means opposite angles are of equal measure in a triangle, then each angle measures 60°.

---

3. In the diagram that follows, ABC is an isosceles triangle with base $\overline{BC}$ and $\angle B = 38°$. Find $\angle A$ and $\angle C$.

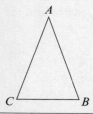

Since BC is the base of the isosceles triangle, that means that $AC = AB$, which, in turn, means $\angle B = \angle C$. Hence, $\angle C = 38°$. The sum of the angles of a triangle is 180°, thus $\angle A + 38° + 38° = 180°$, then $\angle A = 104°$.

Questions 4 and 5 refer to the following figure.

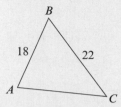

4. In $\triangle ABC$, what is the range of possible values for AC?

AC is greater than the difference of the two given lengths and less than their sum, thus $4 < AC < 40$.

5. In $\triangle ABC$, which angle is smaller, $\angle A$ or $\angle C$?

Since $BC > AB$, then $\angle A > \angle C$, which means $\angle C$ is the smaller angle.

6. In the diagram that follows, what is the measure of $\angle RST$ if it is an exterior angle of $\triangle QRS$ and $\angle Q = 4x - 3$, $\angle R = 6x - 7$, and $\angle RST = 9x + 5$?

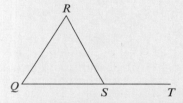

The measure of the exterior angle of a triangle equals the sum of the measures of its remote interior angles, thus

$$
\begin{aligned}
\angle RST &= \quad \angle Q \ + \ \angle R \\
9x + 5 &= (4x - 3) + (6x - 7) \\
9x + 5 &= 10x - 10 \\
5 &= x - 10 \\
15 &= x \\
\angle RST &= 9x + 5 \\
&= 9(15) + 5 \\
&= 135 + 5 \\
&= 140°
\end{aligned}
$$

Questions 7–10 refer to the following figure.

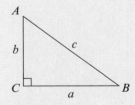

7. If $b = 8$ and $a = 15$, find c.

$$c^2 = a^2 + b^2$$
$$c^2 = (15)^2 + (8)^2$$
$$c^2 = 225 + 64$$
$$c^2 = 289$$
$$c = \sqrt{289}$$
$$c = 17$$

This is an example of the special 8-15-17 right triangle.

8. If $b = 10$ and $c = 26$, find a.

$$c^2 = a^2 + b^2$$
$$26^2 = a^2 + (10)^2$$
$$676 = a^2 + 100$$
$$576 = a^2$$
$$\sqrt{576} = a$$
$$24 = a$$

This is an example of the special 5-12-13 right triangle with each side doubled.

9. If $\angle A = 45°$ and $a = 9$, find $\angle B$, b, and c.

Since the angle at C is 90° and the sum of the angles of a triangle is always 180°, then $\angle B = 45°$. In the 45-45-90 right triangle, the legs are equal and the hypotenuse is a leg times $\sqrt{2}$. Therefore, $b = 9$ and $c = 9\sqrt{2}$.

10. If $\angle B = 60°$ and $a = 12$, find $\angle A$, b, and c.

Since the angle at C is 90° and the sum of the angles of a triangle is always 180°, then $\angle A = 30°$. In the 30-60-90 right triangle, the side opposite the 30-degree angle is the short leg, the hypotenuse is twice that value, and the long leg is the short leg times $\sqrt{3}$. Therefore, $b = 12\sqrt{3}$ and $c = 2(12) = 24$.

Quadrilaterals

A polygon having four sides is called a *quadrilateral.* There are four angles in its interior. The sum of the measures of these interior angles will always be 360°. A quadrilateral is named by using the four letters of its vertices, named in order either clockwise or counterclockwise.

A *square* is a quadrilateral with four equal-length sides and four right angles. Both pairs of opposite sides are parallel. Diagonals of a square are equal in length, bisect each other, are perpendicular to each other, and bisect the angles through which they pass. Figure $ABCD$ here is a square.

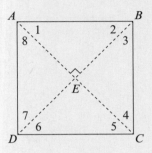

$\overline{AB} \parallel \overline{CD}, \overline{AD} \parallel \overline{BC}, AB = BC = CD = AD$

$\angle ABC = \angle BCD = \angle CDA = \angle DAB = 90°$

$AC = BD, \overline{AC} \perp \overline{BD}, AE = EC = BE = DE$

$\angle 1 = \angle 2 = \angle 3 = \angle 4 = \angle 5 = \angle 6 = \angle 7 = \angle 8 = 45°$

A *rectangle* has opposite sides of equal length and parallel and four right angles. Diagonals of a rectangle are of equal length and bisect each other. Figure $ABCD$ here is a rectangle.

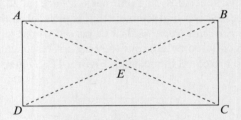

$\overline{AB} \parallel \overline{CD}, \overline{AD} \parallel \overline{BC}, AB = CD, AD = BC$

$AC = BD, AE = EC = BE = DE$

$\angle ABC = \angle BCD = \angle CDA = \angle DAB = 90°$

A *parallelogram* has opposite sides that are of equal length and parallel; its opposite angles are equal in measure, and its consecutive angles are supplementary. Diagonals of a parallelogram are not necessarily of equal length, but they do bisect each other. Figure $ABCD$ here is a parallelogram.

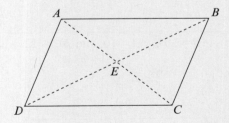

$\overline{AB} \parallel \overline{CD}, \overline{AD} \parallel \overline{BC}, AB = CD, AD = BC$

$AE = EC, BE = DE$

$\angle ABC + \angle BCD = 180°, \angle BCD + \angle CDA = 180°,$

$\angle CDA + \angle DAB = 180°, \angle DAB + \angle ABC = 180°,$

$\angle ABC = \angle CDA, \angle DAB = \angle BCD$

A *rhombus is* a parallelogram with four equal-length sides but not necessarily four angles of equal measure. Diagonals of a rhombus are not necessarily of equal length, but they do bisect each other, are perpendicular to each other, and bisect the angles through which they pass. Figure *ABCD* here is a rhombus.

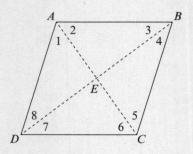

$$\overline{AB} \parallel \overline{CD}, \ \overline{AD} \parallel \overline{BC}, \ AB = CD = AD = BC$$
$$AE = EC, \ BE = DE, \ \overline{AC} \perp \overline{BD}$$
$$\angle ABC + \angle BCD = 180°, \ \angle BCD + \angle CDA = 180°$$
$$\angle CDA + \angle DAB = 180°, \ \angle DAB + \angle ABC = 180°$$
$$\angle ABC = \angle CDA, \ \angle DAB = \angle BCD$$
$$\angle 1 = \angle 2 = \angle 5 = \angle 6, \ \angle 3 = \angle 4 = \angle 7 = \angle 8$$

A *trapezoid* has at least one pair of parallel sides. The parallel sides are called the *bases.* The nonparallel sides are called the *legs.* The *median* of a trapezoid is a line segment that is parallel to the bases and bisects the legs (connects the midpoints of the legs). An *isosceles trapezoid* is a trapezoid whose legs are equal in length. Only in the isosceles trapezoid are the diagonals equal in length, but they do not bisect each other. In an isosceles trapezoid, each pair of angles on the same base are equal in measure. Figure *ABCD* here is a trapezoid with median $\overline{EF}$.

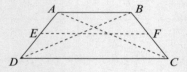

$$\overline{AB} \parallel \overline{CD} \ (\text{the bases})$$
$$AE = ED, \ BF = FC, \ \overline{EF} \parallel \overline{AB} \text{ and } \overline{EF} \parallel \overline{CD}, \ (\overline{EF} \text{ is a median})$$
$$\angle ABC + \angle BCD = 180°, \ \angle BAD + \angle CDA = 180°$$

If $AD = BC$ (an isosceles trapezoid), then $AC = BD$, $\angle DAB = \angle CBA$, $\angle ADC = \angle BCD$.

Examples:

1. In trapezoid *ABCD*, if $\angle A = 45°$, $\angle B = 30°$, $CD = 10$, and $BC = 12$, what is the exact length of *AB*?

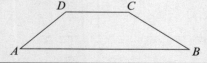

Begin by drawing a perpendicular segment to *AB* from *D* and from *C* to create two special right triangles.

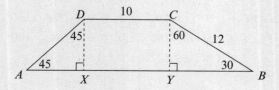

In the 30-60-90 right triangle BCY, CY will be half as long as BC, therefore $CY = 6$. BY then will be $6\sqrt{3}$. The figure $DCYX$ is a rectangle, therefore $DC = XY$ and $DX = CY$. So $XY = 10$ and $DX = 6$. In the 45-45-90 right triangle DXA, the legs are equal in length; therefore $AX = 6$. The length of AB is the sum of the lengths of AX, XY, and BY.

$$AB = AX + XY + BY$$
$$= 6 + 10 + 6\sqrt{3}$$
$$= 16 + 6\sqrt{3}$$

2. In chart form, summarize the properties of quadrilaterals.

Properties of Quadrilaterals

Property Statements	Square	Rectangle	Rhombus	Parallelogram	Trapezoid
Diagonals are equal in length.	✓	✓			
Diagonals bisect each other.	✓	✓	✓	✓	
Diagonals are perpendicular.	✓		✓		
Diagonals bisect the angles.	✓		✓		
All sides are equal in length.	✓		✓		
All angles are equal in measure.	✓	✓			
Opposite angles are equal in measure.	✓	✓	✓	✓	
Opposite sides are equal in length.	✓	✓	✓	✓	
At least one pair of opposite sides are parallel.	✓	✓	✓	✓	✓
At least two pairs of consecutive angles are supplementary.	✓	✓	✓	✓	✓

Circles

The following are some circle fundamentals:

- The *radius* of a circle can either be the segment that joins the center to any point on the circle or the length of that segment. All radii of the same circle have the same length.

- The *diameter* of a circle can either be the segment that joins any two points on a circle and passes through the center of the circle or the length of that segment. In any circle, all diameters have the same length, and a diameter equals two radii in length. A *chord* of a circle is a line segment whose endpoints lie on the circle. The *diameter* is the longest chord in any circle.

- An *arc* is the portion of a circle between any two points on the circle. Arcs are measured in degree units or in length units. In degrees, it is a portion of the 360° that is a full rotation. In length, it is a portion of the circumference, which is the distance around the circle.

- The symbol $\overset{\frown}{AB}$ is used to denote the arc between points A and B. It is written on top of the two endpoints that form the arc. It is in the context of use that you would know whether the measure is intended to be a degree measure or a length measure.

- When an arc involves half or more than half of a circle, three letters must be used with the first and third, indicating the ends of the arc and the middle letter indicating an additional point through which the arc passes.

- A *central angle* in a circle has the center as its vertex and two radii as its sides. The measure of a central angle in degrees is the same as the number of degrees in the arc it intercepts.

- An *inscribed angle* in a circle has its vertex on the circle and two chords as its sides. The measure of an inscribed angle in degrees is half the number of degrees of the arc it intercepts.

- The ***tangent*** to a circle is a line that intersects a circle at only one point. That point is referred to as *the point of tangency.* A tangent is perpendicular to both a radius and a diameter at the point of tangency; a 90° angle is formed at the intersection.

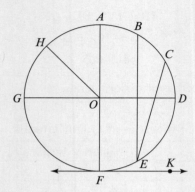

The preceding diagram is of circle *O*. (A circle is named by its center.) Points *A, B, C, D, E, F, G,* and *H* lie on the circle. The radii shown are $\overline{OA}$, $\overline{OD}$, $\overline{OF}$, $\overline{OG}$, and $\overline{OH}$. The diameters shown are $\overline{AF}$ and $\overline{DG}$. $DG = 2(OH)$. Chords shown that are not diameters are $\overline{BE}$ and $\overline{CE}$.

The shortest path along the circle from point *A* to point *E* is $\overset{\frown}{AE}$. The longest path along the circle from point *A* to point *E* can be shown by $\overset{\frown}{AFE}$. The central angles shown are $\angle AOD$, $\angle DOF$, $\angle FOG$, $\angle FOH$, $\angle GOH$, $\angle GOA$, and $\angle HOA$. In degrees, $\overset{\frown}{AH} = \angle AOH$, $\overset{\frown}{ADH} = 360° - \angle AOH$.

The inscribed angle shown is $\angle BEC$. In degrees, $\frac{1}{2}\overset{\frown}{BC} = \angle BEC$. Line *FK* is tangent to circle *O*. The point of tangency is *F*. $\angle AFK = 90°$.

Examples:

Questions 1–7 relate to the circle shown here. The diameter is $\overline{AC}$; the center is at O; points A, B, C, and D lie on the circle; and $\overline{EF}$ is tangent to the circle at point C.

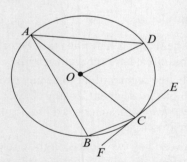

> **1.** Name all the radii.

The radii are $\overline{OA}$, $\overline{OC}$, and $\overline{OD}$.

> **2.** Name all the chords.

The chords are $\overline{AB}$, $\overline{AC}$, $\overline{AD}$, and $\overline{BC}$.

> **3.** What is the longest chord in a circle called?

The longest chord in a circle is called the diameter.

> **4.** Name all the central angles.

The central angles are $\angle AOD$ and $\angle DOC$.

> **5.** Name all the inscribed angles.

The inscribed angles are $\angle ABC$, $\angle ACB$, $\angle BAD$, $\angle CAD$, and $\angle BAC$.

> **6.** Name all the angles that must have a measure of 90°.

The 90° angles are $\angle ACE$, $\angle ACF$, and $\angle ABC$.

Where a tangent and diameter meet, they form a 90° angle. $\angle ABC$ is an inscribed angle that intercepts a half circle, so it is $\frac{1}{2}$ of 180°.

> **7.** If $\overset{\frown}{CD} = 80°$ and $\overset{\frown}{BC} = 50°$, find $\angle DOC$ and $\angle DAB$.

$$\overset{\frown}{CD} = \angle DOC, \text{ therefore, } \angle DOC = 80°.$$

$$\overset{\frown}{DB} = \overset{\frown}{DC} + \overset{\frown}{CB} \text{ and } \angle DAB = \frac{1}{2}\overset{\frown}{DB}, \text{ therefore, } \angle DAB = \frac{1}{2}(80° + 50°) = 65°.$$

Perimeter, Circumference, and Area of Plane Figures

Perimeter is the distance around the outside of a polygon. *Circumference* is the distance around a circle. *Area* is the number of square units that fill the interior of a plane figure.

For the circle, the **circumference** and **area** formulas use the symbol π. This is a value that is approximately 3.14 in decimal form or about $\frac{22}{7}$ in fraction form. See "Important Geometric Formulas" in Chapter 7 for *perimeter*, *circumference*, and *area* formulas of the most common geometric figures.

In addition to these fundamental formulas, you have formulas for the length of an arc of a circle and the area of a sector of a circle. The length of an arc is a portion of the circumference. The sector of a circle is a portion of the area of a circle between two radii. In order to calculate either of these quantities, you need to know the measure of a central angle and the length of a radius.

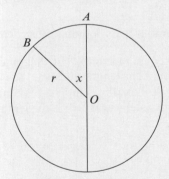

If x is the measure of the central angle and r is the length of the radius, then the length of $\overset{\frown}{AB}$ is $\overset{\frown}{AB} = \frac{x}{360}(2\pi r)$ and the area of sector $AOB = \frac{x}{360}(\pi r^2)$.

Examples:

> **1.** Find the perimeter and area of the trapezoid shown here.

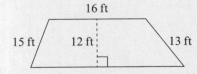

In order to make this question easier to solve, draw the perpendicular segments from the ends of the upper base to the lower base, creating two right triangles. Then use the Pythagorean Theorem to find the missing lengths.

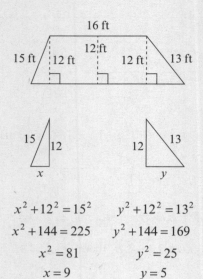

$$x^2 + 12^2 = 15^2 \qquad y^2 + 12^2 = 13^2$$
$$x^2 + 144 = 225 \qquad y^2 + 144 = 169$$
$$x^2 = 81 \qquad y^2 = 25$$
$$x = 9 \qquad y = 5$$

Now the figure can be redrawn with all the measurements indicated.

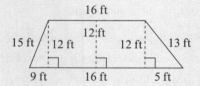

The trapezoid now can be seen as having base lengths of 16 ft and 30 ft, (9 + 16 + 5 = 30), and a height of 12 ft.

$$\text{perimeter} = \text{ sum of all the sides} = (15 + 16 + 13 + 30)\,\text{ft} = 74 \text{ ft}$$
$$\text{area} = \frac{h(b_1 + b_2)}{2} = \frac{(12)(16+30)}{2}\,\text{ft}^2 = 276 \ \text{ft}^2$$

---

2. Find the area and perimeter of a rhombus if its diagonals have lengths of 24 in and 10 in.

A rhombus is a quadrilateral with all sides equal in length. The diagonals of a rhombus are perpendicular to one another and bisect each other. If one diagonal has length of 24 in, then each half would be 12 in. If the other diagonal has a length of 10 in, then each half would be 5 in. Now you have a right triangle with legs of 5 and 12. Use the Pythagorean Theorem to find the hypotenuse, which is the length of one side of the rhombus.

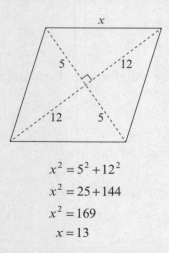

$$x^2 = 5^2 + 12^2$$
$$x^2 = 25 + 144$$
$$x^2 = 169$$
$$x = 13$$

Each side of the rhombus is 13 in, therefore its perimeter is 4(13) or 52 in.

To find the area of the rhombus, find the area of each of the identical four triangles created with the intersecting diagonals. Each is a right triangle with legs of 5 and 12. Use one of these as the height and the other as the base.

$$\text{Area triangle} = \frac{bh}{2} = \frac{(5)(12)}{2} \text{ in}^2 = 30 \text{ in}^2$$
$$\text{Area rhombus} = 4(30) \text{ in}^2 = 120 \text{ in}^2$$

3. The area of a triangle with a base of 20 in is 32 in². What is the height associated with this base?

$$\text{Area triangle} = \frac{bh}{2}$$
$$32 = \frac{(20)(h)}{2}$$
$$64 = 20h$$
$$3.2 = h$$

The height is 3.2 in or $3\frac{1}{5}$ in.

Surface Area, Volume, and Diagonal Lengths of Three-Dimensional Figures

Surface area is the sum of all the areas of the surfaces of a three-dimensional figure. *Volume* is the number of cubic units that fill the interior of a three-dimensional figure. See "Important Geometric Formulas" in Chapter 7 for the surface area and volume formulas of the most common three-dimensional geometric figures.

In a rectangular prism, besides the length, width, and height, a diagonal goes from one corner to the extreme opposite corner. Refer to the following figure.

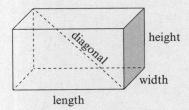

The relationship between the length (*l*), width (*w*), height (*h*), and the diagonal (*d*) of a rectangular prism is illustrated with the following formula:

$$d = \sqrt{l^2 + w^2 + h^2}$$

Examples:

1. Find the exact volume and surface area of a right circular cylinder with a base radius of 12 in and a height of 10 in.

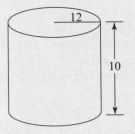

$$\text{Surface area} = 2\pi r^2 + 2\pi rh \qquad\qquad \text{Volume} = \pi r^2 h$$
$$= 2\pi(12)^2 + 2\pi(12)(10) \qquad\qquad = \pi(12)^2(10)$$
$$= 2\pi(144) + 2\pi(120) \qquad\qquad = \pi(144)(10)$$
$$= 288\pi + 240\pi \qquad\qquad = 1440\pi \ \text{in}^3$$
$$= 528\pi \ \text{in}^2$$

---

2. Find the volume of a cube whose surface area is 24 in².

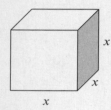

$$\text{Surface area} = 6x^2 \qquad \text{Volume} = x^3$$
$$24 \ \text{in}^2 = 6x^2 \qquad\qquad = (2)^3$$
$$4 = x^2 \qquad\qquad = 8 \ \text{in}^3$$
$$2 \ \text{in} = x$$

---

3. A rectangular prism has a diagonal length of $\sqrt{61}$ ft. It has a length of 4 ft and a height of 3 ft. What is its width?

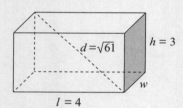

$$d = \sqrt{l^2 + w^2 + h^2}$$
$$\sqrt{61} = \sqrt{4^2 + w^2 + 3^2}$$
$$\sqrt{61} = \sqrt{16 + w^2 + 9} \qquad (\text{square both sides})$$
$$61 = w^2 + 25$$
$$36 = w^2$$
$$6 = w$$

The width is 6 ft.

Congruence and Similarity

Two figures are said to be *congruent* if they have the same shape and have exactly the same size. The symbol for "is congruent to" is ≅. When congruent figures are named, the order in which their vertices are named indicates which angles and sides have the same measure. If $\triangle ABC \cong \triangle DEF$, then $\angle A = \angle D$, $\angle B = \angle E$, $\angle C = \angle F$ and $AB = DE$, $AC = DF$, $BC = EF$.

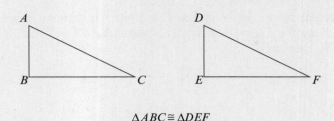

$$\triangle ABC \cong \triangle DEF$$

If two figures are *similar,* they have exactly the same shape but are not necessarily the same size. When similar figures are named, the order in which their vertices are named also indicates which angles are equal in measure and which sides are proportional in measure. The symbol for "is similar to" is ~. If $\triangle ABC \sim \triangle DEF$, then $\angle A = \angle D$, $\angle B = \angle E$, $\angle C = \angle F$ and $\dfrac{AB}{DE} = \dfrac{AC}{DF} = \dfrac{BC}{EF}$.

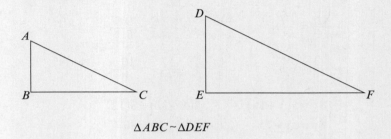

$$\triangle ABC \sim \triangle DEF$$

Triangles That Are Congruent or Similar

The easiest way to show that two triangles are congruent or similar is to show that two angles in one of them have the same measure as two angles in the other.

Examples:

1. If $\triangle ABC \cong \triangle EFG$, $\angle A = 35°$, and $\angle B = 75°$, then $\angle G = $ _____?

If $\triangle ABC \cong \triangle EFG$, then $\angle A = \angle E$, $\angle B = \angle F$, and $\angle C = \angle G$.

In any triangle, the sum of its angles is 180°. Therefore,

$$\angle A + \angle B + \angle C = 180°$$
$$35° + 75° + \angle C = 180°$$
$$110° + \angle C = 180°$$
$$\angle C = 70°$$
$$\text{but } \angle C = \angle G, \text{ therefore}$$
$$\angle G = 70°$$

2. Use the following diagram to find x and y.

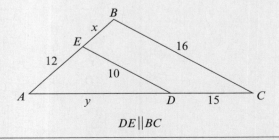

$$DE \parallel BC$$

Two triangles are in the preceding figure: $\triangle ADE$ and $\triangle ACB$. Angle A is the same measure in each triangle. Since $\overline{DE} \parallel \overline{BC}$, then $\angle ADE$ and $\angle C$ have the same measure. This makes $\triangle ADE \sim \triangle ACE$. Redraw the triangles separately with their corresponding measures.

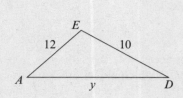
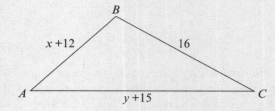

Therefore,

$$\frac{AD}{AC} = \frac{DE}{BC} \qquad \text{and} \qquad \frac{AE}{AB} = \frac{DE}{BC}$$

$$\frac{y}{y+15} = \frac{\overset{5}{\cancel{10}}}{\underset{8}{\cancel{16}}} \qquad\qquad \frac{12}{x+12} = \frac{\overset{5}{\cancel{10}}}{\underset{8}{\cancel{16}}}$$

$$8y = 5(y+15) \qquad\qquad 5(x+12) = 8(12)$$

$$8y = 5y + 75 \qquad\qquad 5x + 60 = 96$$

$$3y = 75 \qquad\qquad 5x = 36$$

$$y = 25 \qquad\qquad x = \frac{36}{5} \text{ or } 7\frac{1}{5} \text{ or } 7.2$$

Geometry Practice Questions

Now that you have reviewed the strategies, you can practice on your own. Questions are grouped roughly into three categories: easy to moderate, average, and above average to difficult. The answers and explanations that follow the questions will include strategies to help you understand how to solve the problems.

Easy to Moderate

1. What is the area of a rectangle, in in², if its length is 36 in and its diagonal is 39 in?

   A. 1,404
   B. 702
   C. 540
   D. 108
   E. 75

2. What is the measure of $\angle w$ in the figure shown here?

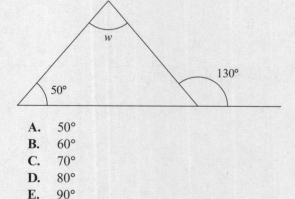

   A. 50°
   B. 60°
   C. 70°
   D. 80°
   E. 90°

3. What is the area, in square inches, of an equilateral triangle if its perimeter is 30 in?

   A. 50

   B. $50\sqrt{3}$

   C. 25

   D. $25\sqrt{3}$

   E. $10\sqrt{3}$

4. How many degrees are there in each interior angle of a regular decagon (10-sided figure)?

   A. 15

   B. 18

   C. 120

   D. 144

   E. 172

5. Let h represent the height of a trapezoid. What is the area of the trapezoid, if the height of the trapezoid is twice the average of the bases of the trapezoid?

   A. $\frac{1}{2}h$

   B. $\frac{1}{2}h^2$

   C. h^2

   D. $2h^2$

   E. $4h$

Average

Use the following diagram for problem 6.

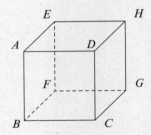

6. In the preceding figure, $\overline{AB}$ is one edge of a cube. If $\overline{AB} = 5$, what is the surface area of the cube?

   A. 25

   B. 100

   C. 125

   D. 150

   E. 300

Use the following diagram for problem 7.

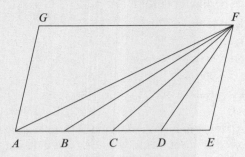

7. In parallelogram *AEFG*, if $\overline{AB} = \overline{BC} = \overline{CD} = \overline{DE}$, what is the ratio of the area of triangle *CDF* to the area of triangle *ABF*?

   A. 1:4

   B. 1:1

   C. 2:1

   D. 4:1

   E. The ratio cannot be determined from the information given.

Use the following diagram for problem 8.

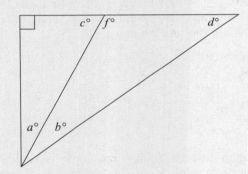

8. In the figure above, a, b, c, d, and f refer to the measure of the indicated angles where $c = 2a$ and $d > 2b$. Which of the following statements must be true?

   A. $c > b + d$

   B. $a > b$

   C. $a = b$

   D. $b > a$

   E. $d = 2a$

9. What is the area of a square in square inches if its perimeter is 10 ft?

   A. 6.25
   B. 25
   C. 400
   D. 900
   E. 1,600

10. A tank 4 in high is to be made from a square piece of sheet metal by cutting a square out of each corner and folding up the sides. The volume of the tank is to be 900 cubic inches. What is the width of the piece of sheet metal, in inches?

   (Note: $V = lwh$)

   A. 12
   B. 15
   C. 19
   D. 21
   E. 23

11. Three interior angles of a pentagon are 130°, 90°, and 80°. Of the remaining two angles, one is 30° more than twice the other. What is the sum of the smallest two angles?

   A. 140°
   B. 150°
   C. 160°
   D. 170°
   E. 180°

12. In an isosceles triangle, one angle equals 120°. If one of the legs is 6 in long, what is the length of the longest side in inches?

   A. $3\sqrt{3}$
   B. $6\sqrt{2}$
   C. $3\sqrt{6}$
   D. $3\sqrt{2}$
   E. $6\sqrt{3}$

13. What is the length, in feet, of the diagonal of a square if the area of the square is 12 ft²?

   A. $12\sqrt{2}$
   B. 6
   C. $2\sqrt{6}$
   D. $\dfrac{6\sqrt{3}}{2}$
   E. $2\sqrt{3}$

14. In the following figure, angles a, b, c, d, e, and f are formed by three intersecting lines. Express the sum of d and f in terms of e.

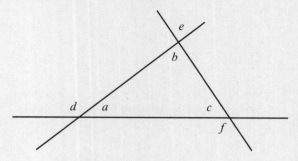

   A. $180° - e$
   B. $90° - e$
   C. $e + 90°$
   D. $e + 180°$
   E. $3e - 90°$

15. In rectangle $ABCD$ shown here, $BC = 4$, $CD = 10$, and $BE = x$. What is the area of the shaded region?

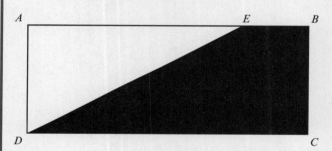

   A. $20 + 2x$
   B. $2 + 4x$
   C. $\dfrac{40 - x}{2}$
   D. $20 + x$
   E. $40 + 2x$

16. In the following figure, $\overline{AB} \perp \overline{BC}$, $\overline{BD} \perp \overline{AC}$, and each triangle is scalene. If $AD = 4$ and $BD = 8$, then what is the length of $\overline{AC}$?

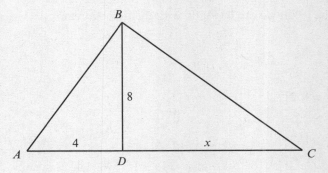

A. 12

B. 16

C. 20

D. 32

E. Cannot be determined from the information given.

Above Average to Difficult

17. The area of circle S is eight times the area of circle R. What is the radius of circle R if the circumference of circle S is x?

A. $\dfrac{x}{16\pi}$

B. $\dfrac{2x}{\pi}$

C. $\dfrac{x\sqrt{2}}{16\pi}$

D. $\dfrac{x\sqrt{2}}{8\pi}$

E. $\dfrac{x}{4\pi}$

18. In the following figure, lines m and n are parallel. What is the measure of angle a in terms of angle b and angle c?

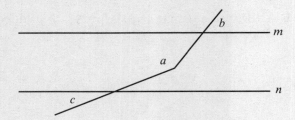

A. $180 + c - b$

B. $180 + b - c$

C. $90 + b + c$

D. $270 - b - c$

E. Cannot be determined from the information given.

19. In the following figure, $\angle w + \angle z = 170°$.

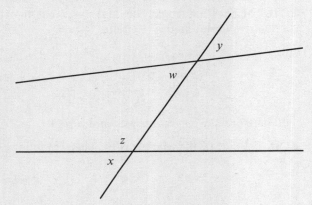

Which of the following is (are) true?

I. $\angle x > \angle y$

II. $\angle x$ and $\angle z$ are supplementary

III. $\angle x < 90°$

A. I only

B. I and II only

C. I and III only

D. II and III only

E. I, II, and III

Answers and Explanations

Easy to Moderate

1. **C.** Because a right triangle is formed, the width of the rectangle can be found with the Pythagorean Theorem.

$$w^2 + l^2 = d^2$$
$$w^2 + 36^2 = 39^2$$
$$w^2 + 1296 = 1521$$
$$w^2 = 225$$
$$w = 15$$

Since the area of a rectangle is the product of its width and length, the area is (15)(36) = 540. This is answer choice C.

You can save time and not use the Pythagorean Theorem if you note that the sides of the triangle are multiples of the "Pythagorean Triple" 5, 12, 13. Multiplying each by the factor of 3 gives the sides of 15, 36, and 39. Memorizing the basic Pythagorean Triples (3, 4, 5), (5, 12, 13), and (8, 15, 17) can save valuable time on the test.

2. **D.** The External Angle Theorem states that an exterior angle of a triangle is equal to the sum of the two remote interior angles. Therefore,

$$50 + w = 130$$
$$w = 130 - 50$$
$$w = 80$$

Therefore, the correct answer choice is D.

3. **D.** The side of the triangle is 10. The area follows from the formula for the area of an equilateral triangle.

$$A = \frac{x^2 \sqrt{3}}{4}$$
$$A = \frac{10^2 \sqrt{3}}{4}$$
$$= \frac{100\sqrt{3}}{4}$$
$$= 25\sqrt{3}$$

Therefore, answer choice D is the correct one. If you do not remember the formula for the area of an equilateral triangle given the length of one of its sides, you could divide the equilateral triangle into two 30-60-90 right triangles. Each of these right triangles has sides in the ratio of 1 to 2 to $\sqrt{3}$, where $\sqrt{3}$ is the ratio factor for the height of the right triangle. Therefore, the height of the equilateral triangle is $5\sqrt{3}$ (since 5 is half of the side length of the equilateral triangle). Using this height, the area of the equilateral triangle can be found using the standard area formula for a triangle.

$$A = \frac{1}{2} bh$$
$$= \frac{1}{2}(10)(5\sqrt{3})$$
$$= 25\sqrt{3}$$

This also provides the correct answer choice of D.

4. D. The formula for the total number of degrees of all interior angles in an n-sided polygon is $(n - 2)180°$ where n is the number of sides. Since a decagon has 10 sides, there are $(10 - 2)180° = 1440$ degrees total. Since the polygon is regular, all angles (and all sides) are the same size. Therefore, dividing by 10, $\frac{1440°}{10} = 144°$. The correct answer is Choice D.

5. B. The area of a trapezoid is the product of the height and the average of the bases. Since the height, h, is twice the average of the bases, the average of the bases can be represented by $\frac{1}{2}h$. Therefore, the area is the product of h and $\frac{1}{2}h$, or $\frac{1}{2}h^2$. This is answer choice B. You could substitute values for the height and bases to determine the relationship, but here the answer follows directly from the formula for the area.

Average

6. D. Since one edge of the cube is 5, all edges equal 5. Therefore, the area of one face of the cube is $(5)(5) = 25$. Since a cube has 6 equal faces, its surface area will be $(6)(25) = 150$.

7. B. In parallelogram $AEFG$, all the small triangles have the same base, and they all meet at F, giving them all the same height. The area formula for a triangle is $A = \frac{1}{2}bh$; therefore, all the small triangles have equal areas. The ratio of the area of triangle CDF to the area of triangle ABF is 1:1, and the correct answer is B.

8. B. In the right triangle, if $c = 2a$, then angle $a = 30°$ and angle $c = 60°$, since there are a total of $180°$ in a triangle. Because angle f is supplementary to angle c, angle f must be $120°$. If angle f is $120°$, then there are $60°$ left to be divided between angles d and b. Because $d > 2b$, b must be less than $20°$; therefore, the correct answer is B; angle a $(30°)$ is greater than angle b (less than $20°$). Notice the way you should have marked the diagram to assist you.

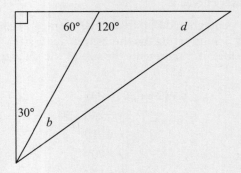

9. D. Perimeter = 10 ft = (10)(12) in = 120 in

$$\text{Perimeter} = 4s \text{ (where } s = \text{length of side)}$$
$$4s = 120, \text{ so } s = 30. \text{ Next, find the area:}$$
$$\text{Area} = s^2 = 30^2 = 900 \text{ in}^2$$

10. **E.** You can sketch a diagram similar to the following:

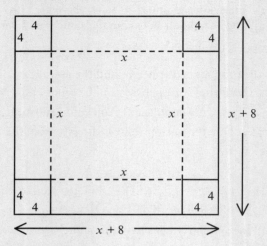

Because the square bottom of the tank can be represented by x^2,

$$4x^2 = 900$$
$$x^2 = 225$$
$$x = 15$$

Therefore, the width of the tank is 15 inches. Since the 4-in sides are folded up, you must add 8 to this figure, giving 23 in. This is answer choice E.

11. **B.** The five interior angles of a pentagon add up to 540°. (A pentagon can be partitioned into three triangles, each made up of 180°.) Subtracting the three given angle sizes from 540° leaves 240° left over for the two unknown angles. Therefore, if x represents the size of the smaller unknown angle, find the unknown angles as follows.

$$x + (2x + 30) = 240$$
$$3x = 240 - 30$$
$$3x = 210$$
$$x = 70$$
$$2x + 30 = 170$$

Therefore, the two unknown angles are 70° and 170° and the sum of the two smallest angles in the pentagon is 70° + 80° = 150°. Thus, the correct answer choice is B.

12. **E.** The drawing would look like this.

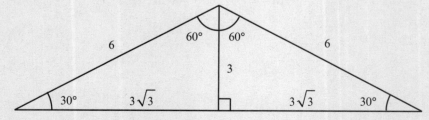

If you divide the triangle in half, you get two 30-60-90 right triangles. The longest side (hypotenuse) of each small triangle is 6. So the shortest (common) side of each small triangle is 3, and the third side of each small triangle is $3\sqrt{3}$. Therefore, the length of the longest side of the large triangle is $(2)(3\sqrt{3}) = 6\sqrt{3}$. Therefore, the correct answer choice is E.

13. C. To gain insight, you could draw a diagram such as the following.

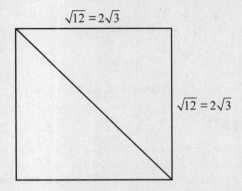

$$\sqrt{12} = 2\sqrt{3}$$

$$\sqrt{12} = 2\sqrt{3}$$

If the area of a square is 12, then each side of the square is $\sqrt{12}$ or $2\sqrt{3}$. From the relationship in the 45-45-90-degree right triangle, you know that the hypotenuse, and in this case the diagonal, is equal to the product of the length of a side (leg) and $\sqrt{2}$. Therefore,

$$d = \left(\sqrt{2}\right)\left(2\sqrt{3}\right) = 2\sqrt{6}$$

The correct answer choice is Choice C.

14. D. Angles a, b, and c are three angles of a triangle and, therefore, add up to 180°. Angles b and e are vertical angles and, therefore, are equal in size. Angles d and f are external angles and are equal in measure to the sum of the remote interior angles (External Angle Theorem). The sum of d and f can be expressed in terms of e as follows.

$$d = b + c$$
$$f = a + b$$
$$d + f = a + b + b + c$$
$$= a + 2b + c$$
$$= 2b + (a + c)$$
$$= 2b + (180 - b)$$
$$= b + 180$$
$$= e + 180$$

This is answer choice D.

15. A. The shaded region is a trapezoid. Substituting into the formula for the area of a trapezoid gives

$$A = \left(\frac{b_1 + b_2}{2}\right)h$$
$$= \left(\frac{10 + x}{2}\right)4$$
$$= 2(10 + x)$$
$$= 20 + 2x$$

Thus, the correct answer choice is A.

16. **C.** The number 8 is the geometric mean between 4 and x. Therefore,

$$\frac{4}{8} = \frac{8}{x}$$
$$4x = 64$$
$$x = 16$$

Thus, $AC = 4 + x = 4 + 16 = 20$. The correct answer choice is Choice C.

Above Average to Difficult

17. **D.** The ratio of the areas of similar figures (all circles are similar) is the square of the ratio of corresponding linear measures. Since the area of circle S is eight times the area of circle R, their areas are in the ratio of 1 to 8. Therefore, their radii are in the ratio of 1 to $\sqrt{8}$. Since the circumference of circle S is x, its diameter is $\frac{x}{\pi}$ and its radius is $\frac{x}{2\pi}$. If you use r to represent the radius of circle R, then you can set up the following proportion, allowing you to write r in terms of x.

$$\frac{1}{\sqrt{8}} = \frac{r}{\left(\dfrac{x}{2\pi}\right)}$$

$$r = \left(\frac{1}{\sqrt{8}}\right)\left(\frac{x}{2\pi}\right)$$

$$= \frac{x}{2\pi\sqrt{8}}$$

$$= \left(\frac{x}{2\pi\sqrt{8}}\right)\left(\frac{\sqrt{8}}{\sqrt{8}}\right)$$

$$= \frac{x\sqrt{8}}{16\pi}$$

$$= \frac{2x\sqrt{2}}{16\pi}$$

$$= \frac{x\sqrt{2}}{8\pi}$$

Therefore, the correct answer choice is D.

18. **A.** This problem is most easily solved by adding another line, parallel to lines m and n and passing through the vertex of angle a.

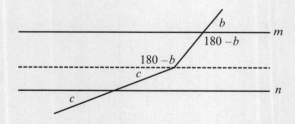

By drawing this additional line, it is clear that angle a is made up of two parts. One part is congruent to angle c (by corresponding angles), and the other part is congruent to the supplement of angle b (alternate interior angles). Thus, angle a can be expressed as the sum of c and $(180 - b)$, or $180 + c - b$. This is answer choice A.

19. B. Statement II is true since the measures of angles x and z add up to the measure of a line, or 180°. Thus, you can eliminate answer choices A and C. Angle z is the same measure as $180° - x$. Angle w has the same measure as angle y. Therefore, using the given relationship that $\angle w + \angle z = 170°$ and the previously stated substitutions gives the following.

$$w + z = 170$$
$$y + (180 - x) = 170$$
$$y + 180 - x = 170$$
$$y + 180 - 170 = x$$
$$y + 10 = x$$

You see that angle x is 10° larger than angle y. Therefore, Statement I is also true. This eliminates answer choice D. You see that if the transversal is rotated counterclockwise, statement III could be false. This eliminates answer choice E. Remember that you should always base your answer on geometric logic, and not on estimating or comparing quantities by sight. Thus, the correct answer choice is B.

Chapter 11

Trigonometry

This chapter will help ACT test-takers understand the content area of trigonometry. These questions are based on the student's understanding of trigonometric relationships in right triangles, including understanding and using the sine, cosine, and tangent functions. Also covered are the values and properties of these and other trigonometric functions and their graphs, as well as trigonometric identities and the solving of trigonometric equations.

This chapter helps to alleviate your worries about solving trigonometry problems found on the ACT. You are introduced to key terms, topics, functions, and step-by-step practice examples.

Trigonometry Concepts You Should Know

- Values and properties of trigonometric functions
- Working with right triangles
- Graphing with trigonometric functions
- Graphs with sine and cosine
- Trigonometric identities
- Trigonometric equations

Take the following trigonometry diagnostic test and evaluate how familiar you are with the selected topics. The diagnostic test will give you valuable insight into the topics you will need to study.

Trigonometry Diagnostic Test

Directions: Solve each problem in this section by using the information given and your own mathematical calculations.

1. Given $\sin\theta = \frac{1}{10}$ and $\sec\theta < 0$, find $\cos\theta$ and $\tan\theta$.

2. Find the exact value of $(\sin 60°)(\cos 60°)$. Do not use a calculator.

3. Find $\sin\theta$ and $\cos\theta$ for the acute angle θ if $\tan\theta = \frac{2}{3\sqrt{13}}$.

4. If the hypotenuse of a right triangle measures 29 units, what is the tangent of the angle that is opposite the leg that measures 20 units?

5. What is the reference angle for 687°?

6. Find the exact value of $\cos 270°$. Do not use a calculator.

7. Find the exact value of $(\cos 60°)(\cos 60°)$. Do not use a calculator.

8. Determine the sign of the following trigonometric functions: $\sin 255°$, $\tan 240°$, and $\cos (-110°)$.

9. Find $\sin\theta$ and $\cos\theta$ for the acute angle θ if $\tan\theta = \frac{1}{2\sqrt{2}}$.

Questions 10 and 11 refer to the following figure.

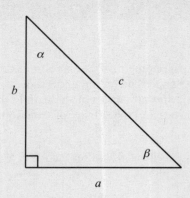

10. Given the right triangle, find β, b, and c, given that $\alpha = 20°$ and $a = 7$.

11. Given the right triangle, find α, a, and b, given that $\beta = 55°$ and $c = 10$.

12. Given the right triangle, find the value of x.

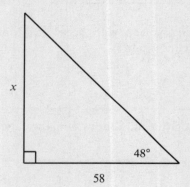

13. Find the area of a triangle with $\alpha = 68°$, $b = 8$, and $c = 8$.

14. Find the exact value of $\cos\frac{\pi}{4}\sin\frac{\pi}{4}$. Do not use a calculator.

15. Find the exact value of $\tan\frac{\pi}{6} + \cos\frac{\pi}{6}$. Do not use a calculator.

16. Find the amplitude, phase shift, and period of $y = -\frac{2}{3}\cos(4x + 3\pi)$.

17. If $f(x) = \tan x$ and $f(a) = 9$, find the exact value of $f(a) + f(a + 3\pi) + f(a - 3\pi)$.

18. Find the amplitude and period of $f(x) = -8\sin(2x)$.

19. If $\sin A = \frac{4}{7}$, $\cos B = \frac{5}{6}$, $\frac{\pi}{2} \le A \le \pi$, and $-\frac{\pi}{2} \le B \le 0$, find the exact value of $\sin(A + B)$ given that $\sin(A + B) = \sin A \cos B + \cos A \sin B$.

20. The expression $\cos\left(\theta + \frac{3\pi}{2}\right)$ forms an identity with which of the following: $\cos\theta - \cos\theta$, $\sin\theta$, or $-\sin\theta$?

21. Is $\frac{\cos x}{1 - \sin x} = \sec x + \tan x$ an identity?

22. Solve the equation $2\cos x - 1 = 0$, where $0 \le x < 2\pi$.

23. Solve the equation $\sin^2\theta + 2\sin\theta + 1 = 0$, where $0 \le x < 2\pi$.

24. Solve the equation $-\sin\theta + 1 = 2\cos^2\theta$, where $0 \le x < 2\pi$.

Scoring the Diagnostic Test

The diagnostic test explanations listed here include topic headings that correspond with step-by-step learning tools and examples to help you solve specific problem types. Use the answer key and the analysis worksheet that follows to help you evaluate specific problem types. Corresponding topic headings can be found in the "Trigonometry Review" section following the diagnostic test.

Answer Key

Values and Properties of Trigonometric Functions

1. $\cos\theta = -\frac{3\sqrt{11}}{10}$, $\tan\theta = -\frac{\sqrt{11}}{33}$

2. $\frac{\sqrt{3}}{4}$

3. $\sin\theta = \frac{2}{11}$, $\cos\theta = \frac{3\sqrt{13}}{11}$

4. $\frac{20}{21}$

5. $33°$

6. 0

7. $\frac{1}{4}$

8. negative, positive, negative

9. $\sin\theta = \frac{1}{3}$, $\cos\theta = \frac{2\sqrt{2}}{3}$

Working with Right Triangles

10. $\beta = 70°$, $b = \frac{7}{\tan 20°}$, $c = \frac{7}{\sin 20°}$

11. $\alpha = 35°$, $a = 10\cos 55°$, $b = 10\sin 55°$

12. $x = 58\tan 48°$

13. $64\sin 34° \cos 34°$

Graphing Trigonometric Functions

14. $\frac{1}{2}$

15. $\frac{5\sqrt{3}}{6}$

Graphs of the Sine and Cosine

16. amplitude $= \frac{2}{3}$, phase shift $= -\frac{3\pi}{4}$, period $= \frac{\pi}{2}$

17. 27

18. amplitude $= 8$, period $= \pi$

Trigonometric Identities

19. $\frac{20+11\sqrt{3}}{42}$ or $\frac{1}{42}\left(20+11\sqrt{3}\right)$

20. $\sin\theta$

21. Yes

Trigonometric Equations

22. $\frac{\pi}{3}$, $\frac{5\pi}{3}$

23. $\theta = \frac{3\pi}{2}$

24. $\theta = \frac{\pi}{2}$, $\theta = \frac{7\pi}{6}$, $\theta = \frac{11\pi}{6}$

Charting and Analyzing Your Diagnostic Test Results

Record your diagnostic test results in the following chart and use these results as a guide to plan your trigonometry review goals and objectives. Mark the problems that you missed and pay particular attention to those that you missed in Column (C) because they were unfamiliar math concepts to you. These are the areas you will want to focus on as you study trigonometry topics.

Analysis Sheet

Topic	Number Possible	Number Correct	Number Incorrect		
			(A) Simple Mistake	(B) Misread Problem	(C) Unfamiliar Math Concept
Values and properties of trigonometric functions	9				
Working with right triangles	4				
Graphing trigonometric functions	2				
Graphs of sine and cosine	3				
Trigonometric identities	3				
Trigonometric equations	3				
Total Possible Explanations for Incorrect Answers: Columns A, B, and C					
Total Number of Questions	24	Add the total number of correct questions here: _____	Add columns A, B, and C for total number of incorrect questions here: _____		

Trigonometry Review

Values and Properties of Trig Functions

Angles can be measured in one of two units: degrees or radians. In trigonometry, radians are used to describe units of measure for angles instead of degrees. A radian is the ratio between the length of an arc to the length of its radius. There are 360 degrees in a full circle and there are 2π radians in the full revolution of a circle. The relationship between these two measures may be expressed as follows:

$$180° = \pi \text{ radians}$$

$$1° = \frac{\pi}{180} \text{ radians}$$

$$1 \text{ radian} = \frac{180°}{\pi}$$

The following ratios are defined using a circle with the equation $x^2 + y^2 = r^2$.

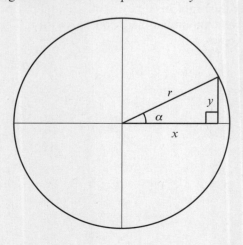

$$\text{sine of } \alpha \ = \ \sin \alpha = \frac{y}{r} = \frac{\text{length of side opposite } \alpha}{\text{length of hypotenuse}}$$

$$\text{cosine of } \alpha \ = \ \cos \alpha = \frac{x}{r} = \frac{\text{length of side adjacent to } \alpha}{\text{length of hypotenuse}}$$

$$\text{tangent of } \alpha \ = \ \tan \alpha = \frac{y}{x} = \frac{\text{length of side opposite } \alpha}{\text{length of side adjacent to } \alpha}$$

Angles are measured in a counter-clockwise direction starting at the positive x-axis. Remember, if the angles of a triangle remain the same, but the sides increase or decrease in length proportionally, these ratios remain the same.

The **cosecant, secant,** and the **cotangent** are **trigonometric functions** that are the reciprocals of the **sine, cosine,** and **tangent**, respectively.

$$\text{cosecant of } \alpha \ = \ \csc \alpha = \frac{r}{y} = \frac{\text{length of hypotenuse}}{\text{length of side opposite } \alpha}$$

$$\text{secant of } \alpha \ = \ \sec \alpha = \frac{r}{x} = \frac{\text{length of hypotenuse}}{\text{length of side adjacent to } \alpha}$$

$$\text{cotangent of } \alpha \ = \ \cot \alpha = \frac{x}{y} = \frac{\text{length of side adjacent to } \alpha}{\text{length of side opposite } \alpha}$$

Example:

> **1.** Find $\sin \theta$ and $\cos \theta$ if θ is an acute angle and $\tan \theta = 6$.

If the tangent of an angle is 6, then the ratio of the side opposite the angle and the side adjacent to the angle is 6. Since all right triangles with this ratio are similar, the hypotenuse can be found by choosing 1 and 6 as the values of the two legs of the right triangle and then applying the Pythagorean Theorem.

$$r^2 = x^2 + y^2$$
$$r^2 = 6^2 + 1^2$$
$$r^2 = 36 + 1$$
$$r^2 = 37$$
$$r = \sqrt{37}$$

$$\sin \theta = \frac{\text{length of the side opposite } \theta}{\text{hypotenuse}} = \frac{6}{\sqrt{37}}$$

$$\cos \theta = \frac{\text{length of the side adjacent to } \theta}{\text{hypotenuse}} = \frac{1}{\sqrt{37}}$$

There are three pairs of trigonometric functions that are referred to as **cofunctions.** (1) The sine and cosine are cofunctions. (2) The tangent and cotangent are cofunctions. (3) The secant and cosecant are cofunctions. By definition, a function of any angle is equal to the cofunction of its complement.

From right triangle XYZ, the following identities can be derived.

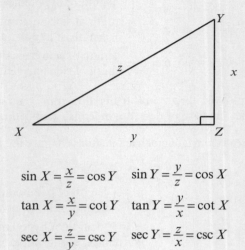

$$\sin X = \frac{x}{z} = \cos Y \quad \sin Y = \frac{y}{z} = \cos X$$

$$\tan X = \frac{x}{y} = \cot Y \quad \tan Y = \frac{y}{x} = \cot X$$

$$\sec X = \frac{z}{y} = \csc Y \quad \sec Y = \frac{z}{x} = \csc X$$

Observe that $\angle X$ and $\angle Y$ are complementary. Thus, in general:

$$\sin \alpha = \cos(90° - \alpha) \quad \cos \alpha = \sin(90° - \alpha)$$

$$\tan \alpha = \cot(90° - \alpha) \quad \cot \alpha = \tan(90° - \alpha)$$

$$\sec \alpha = \csc(90° - \alpha) \quad \csc \alpha = \sec(90° - \alpha)$$

Example:

2. What are the values of the six trigonometric functions for angles that measure 30°, 45°, and 60°?

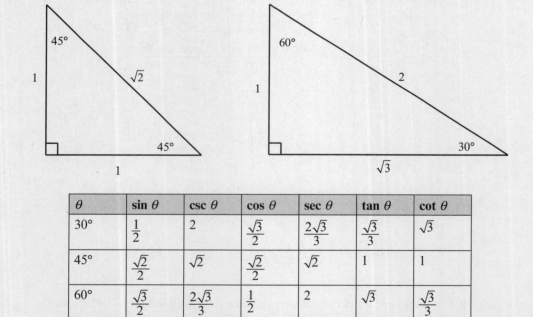

θ	$\sin \theta$	$\csc \theta$	$\cos \theta$	$\sec \theta$	$\tan \theta$	$\cot \theta$
30°	$\frac{1}{2}$	2	$\frac{\sqrt{3}}{2}$	$\frac{2\sqrt{3}}{3}$	$\frac{\sqrt{3}}{3}$	$\sqrt{3}$
45°	$\frac{\sqrt{2}}{2}$	$\sqrt{2}$	$\frac{\sqrt{2}}{2}$	$\sqrt{2}$	1	1
60°	$\frac{\sqrt{3}}{2}$	$\frac{2\sqrt{3}}{3}$	$\frac{1}{2}$	2	$\sqrt{3}$	$\frac{\sqrt{3}}{3}$

Angles in standard position have their vertex at the origin, and their initial side on the positive x-axis. Acute angles in standard position are all in the first quadrant, and all of their trigonometric functions exist and are positive in value. This is not necessarily true of angles in general. **Quadrantal angles** are angles that are in standard position and are multiples of 90°. Some of the six trigonometric functions of quadrantal angles are undefined (see the following), and some of the six trigonometric functions have negative values, depending on the size of the angle. The following four diagrams show a point $A(x,y)$ located on the terminal side of angle θ with r as the distance AO. Note that r is always positive.

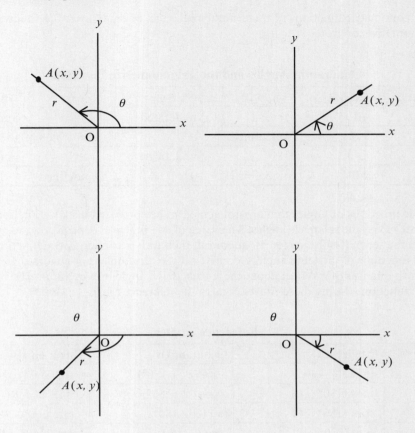

Based on these figures,

$$\sin \theta = \frac{y}{r} \qquad \csc \theta = \frac{r}{y} \; ; \; y \neq 0$$

$$\cos \theta = \frac{x}{r} \qquad \sec \theta = \frac{r}{x} \; ; \; x \neq 0$$

$$\tan \theta = \frac{y}{x} ; \; x \neq 0 \quad \cot \theta = \frac{x}{y} ; \; y \neq 0$$

If angle θ is a quadrantal angle, then either x or y will be 0, yielding the undefined values if the denominator is zero. The sign, positive or negative, of the trigonometric functions depends on the quadrant in which the point $A(x,y)$ is located. The following chart summarizes this information:

Function	Quadrant			
	I	II	III	IV
$\sin \theta$, $\csc \theta$	+	+	−	−
$\cos \theta$, $\sec \theta$	+	−	−	+
$\tan \theta$, $\cot \theta$	+	−	+	−

If you know the sign of the sine, cosine, and tangent in each of the four quadrants, then you also know the sign of their reciprocals (the cosecant, the secant, and the cotangent). One way to remember which functions are positive and which are negative in the various quadrants is to remember a simple four-letter acronym, **ASTC**. This reminds us that **A**ll are positive in quadrant I, only the **S**ine (and cosecant) is positive in quadrant II, only the

Tangent (and cotangent) is positive in quadrant III, and only the <u>C</u>osine (and secant) is positive in quadrant IV. This acronym could stand for <u>A</u>rizona <u>S</u>tate <u>T</u>eachers' <u>C</u>ollege, <u>A</u>ll <u>S</u>tudents <u>T</u>ake <u>C</u>lasses, or some other four-word expressions that will help you remember the relationships.

The values of the trigonometric functions of quadrantal angles can be summarized as follows. Note that undefined values result from division by 0.

Quadrantal Angles and the Trigonometric Functions

	$\sin \theta$	$\cos \theta$	$\tan \theta$	$\cot \theta$	$\sec \theta$	$\csc \theta$
0°	0	1	0	undefined	1	undefined
90°	1	0	undefined	0	undefined	1
180°	0	−1	0	undefined	−1	undefined
270°	−1	0	undefined	0	undefined	−1

The six trigonometric functions of angles that are not acute can be converted back to functions of acute angles. These acute angles are called the **reference angles.** The value of the function depends on the quadrant of the angle. If angle θ is in the second, third, or fourth quadrant, then the six trigonometric functions of θ can be converted to equivalent functions of an acute angle. Geometrically, if the angle is in quadrant II, reflect about the y-axis. If the angle is in quadrant IV, reflect about the x-axis. If the angle is in quadrant III, rotate 180°. Keep in mind the sign of the functions during these conversions to the reference angle.

Reference Angles

Function	Quadrant II	Quadrant III	Quadrant IV
$\sin \theta$	$\sin (180° - \theta)$	$-\sin (\theta - 180°)$	$-\sin (360° - \theta)$
$\cos \theta$	$-\cos (180° - \theta)$	$-\cos (\theta - 180°)$	$\cos (360° - \theta)$
$\tan \theta$	$-\tan (180° - \theta)$	$\tan (\theta - 180°)$	$-\tan (360° - \theta)$
$\cot \theta$	$-\cot (180° - \theta)$	$\cot (\theta - 180°)$	$-\cot (360° - \theta)$
$\sec \theta$	$-\sec (180° - \theta)$	$-\sec (\theta - 180°)$	$\sec (360° - \theta)$
$\csc \theta$	$\csc (180° - \theta)$	$-\csc (\theta - 180°)$	$-\csc (360° - \theta)$

Example:

3. Find the six trigonometric functions of an angle α that is in standard position and whose terminal side passes through the point (–5, 12).

You can use the Pythagorean Theorem to find the hypotenuse. Then the six trigonometric functions follow from the definitions.

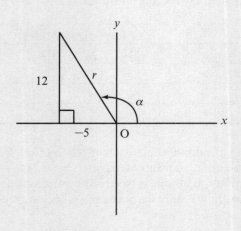

$$\sin \alpha = \frac{12}{13}$$

$$r^2 = x^2 + y^2 \qquad \cos \alpha = -\frac{5}{13}$$

$$r^2 = (-5)^2 + 12^2$$

$$r^2 = 25 + 144 \qquad \tan \alpha = -\frac{12}{5}$$

$$r^2 = 169 \qquad \cot \alpha = -\frac{5}{12}$$

$$r = \sqrt{169} = 13 \qquad \sec \alpha = -\frac{13}{5}$$

$$\csc \alpha = \frac{13}{12}$$

Example:

4. If $\sin \theta = \frac{1}{3}$, what is the value of the other five trigonometric functions if $\cos \theta$ is negative?

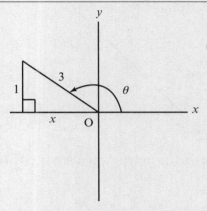

Since $\sin \theta$ is positive and $\cos \theta$ is negative, θ must be in the second quadrant. From the Pythagorean Theorem, $x^2 + 1^2 = 3^2$; $x^2 + 1 = 9$; $x^2 = 8$; $x = \sqrt{8} = 2\sqrt{2}$ and then it follows that

$$\cos \theta = -\frac{2\sqrt{2}}{3}$$

$$\tan \theta = -\frac{1}{2\sqrt{2}} = -\frac{\sqrt{2}}{4}$$

$$\cot \theta = -2\sqrt{2}$$

$$\sec \theta = -\frac{3}{2\sqrt{2}} = -\frac{3\sqrt{2}}{4}$$

$$\csc \theta = 3$$

Example:

5. What is the exact sine, cosine, and tangent of 330°?

Since 330° is in the fourth quadrant, sin 330° and tan 330° are negative and cos 330° is positive. The reference angle is 30°. Using the 30-60-90 triangle relationship, the ratio of the three sides is 1:2:$\sqrt{3}$. Therefore,

$$\sin 30° = \frac{1}{2} \qquad\qquad \sin 330° = -\frac{1}{2}$$

$$\cos 30° = \frac{\sqrt{3}}{2} \quad \text{and} \quad \cos 330° = \frac{\sqrt{3}}{2}$$

$$\tan 30° = \frac{1}{\sqrt{3}} = \frac{\sqrt{3}}{3} \qquad \tan 330° = -\frac{1}{\sqrt{3}} = -\frac{\sqrt{3}}{3}$$

Trigonometry of Right Triangles

All triangles are made up of three sides and three angles. If the three angles of the triangle are labeled $\angle A$, $\angle B$, and $\angle C$, then the three sides of the triangle should be labeled as a, b, and c. The following figures illustrate how lowercase letters are used to name the sides of the triangle that are opposite the angles named with corresponding uppercase letters. For right triangles, $\angle C$ is usually the right angle. The process of finding missing measurements in a triangle is known as **solving the triangle.** The right triangle can be solved if you are given the measures of two of the three sides or you are given the measure of one side and one of the other two angles.

Example:

> **1.** Solve the right triangle shown if $\angle B = 22°$ and $b = 16$.

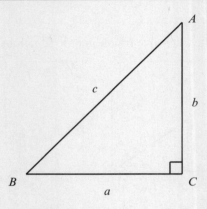

Since the three angles of a triangle must add up to 180°, $\angle A = 90° - \angle B$. Thus, $\angle A = 68°$. Find the missing measures as follows:

$$\sin B = \frac{b}{c} \qquad \tan B = \frac{b}{a}$$
$$\sin 22° = \frac{16}{c} \qquad \tan 22° = \frac{16}{a}$$
$$c = \frac{16}{\sin 22°} \qquad a = \frac{16}{\tan 22°}$$

If you were given a numeric value for the sin 22° and the value of tan 22°, you could substitute and find numeric answers. Answers are typically left in function form.

The following is an alternate way to solve for sides a and c:

$$\csc B = \frac{c}{b} \qquad \cot B = \frac{a}{b}$$
$$\csc 22° = \frac{c}{16} \qquad \cot 22° = \frac{a}{16}$$
$$c = 16(\csc 22°) \qquad a = 16(\cot 22°)$$

Similar solutions could be worked out using the 68° angle.

In many applications, certain angles are referred to by special names. Two of these special names are *angle of elevation* and *angle of depression.*

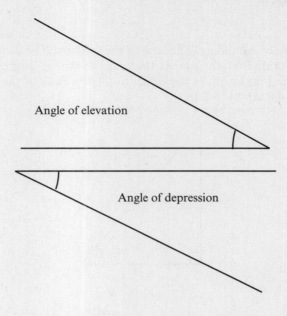

Angle of elevation

Angle of depression

Example:

2. A large airplane (plane A) flying at 26,000 feet sights a smaller plane (plane B) traveling at an altitude of 24,000 feet. The angle of depression is 40°. What is the line of sight distance (x) between the two planes?

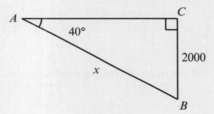

From the figure, you can see that to solve for x involves the sine of 40° as follows:

$$\sin 40° = \frac{2000'}{x}$$

$$x = \frac{2000'}{\sin 40°}$$

When you are using trigonometric functions to solve problems, the answers are usually written using the function instead of calculating the value of the function, as shown immediately above. Occasionally you will be given a specific value for the function and will be asked to compute a final answer. For example, if in the problem above you were told "If $\sin 40° = 0.643$, determine the value of x to the nearest tenth," then you would divide 2000 by 0.643 to get the final answer. Normally, this does not happen and the functions themselves are left in the answer. You will not be asked to calculate values of trigonometric functions using your calculator.

Example:

> **3.** A ladder must reach the top of a building. The base of the ladder will be 25 feet from the base of the building. The angle of elevation from the base of the ladder to the top of the building is 64°. Find the height of the building (h) and the length of the ladder (m). Use any/all of the following approximations: sin 64° = 0.90; cos 64° = 0.44; tan 64° = 2.05.

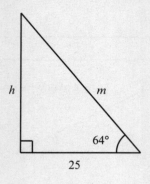

$$\tan 64° = \frac{h}{25'} \qquad \cos 64° = \frac{25'}{m}$$

$$2.05 = \frac{h}{25'} \qquad\qquad .44 = \frac{25'}{m}$$

$$h = (25')(2.05) \qquad m = \frac{25'}{.44}$$

$$h = 51.25' \qquad\qquad m = 56.82'$$

Example:

> **4.** Find the lengths of sides x and y and the area of the large triangle shown here.

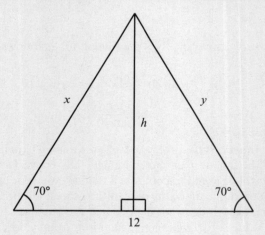

Since this is an isosceles triangle, and equal sides are opposite equal angles, the values of x and y are the same. If the triangle is divided into two right triangles, the base of each will be 6. Therefore,

$$\cos 70° = \frac{6}{x} \qquad\qquad \tan 70° = \frac{h}{6}$$

$$x = \frac{6}{\cos 70°} \qquad\qquad h = (6)(\tan 70°)$$

Since $x = y$ $\qquad\qquad$ area $= \dfrac{bh}{2}$

$$y = \frac{6}{\cos 70°} \qquad\qquad = \frac{(12)(6)(\tan 70°)}{2}$$

$$= 36\tan 70°$$

Graphing Trig Functions

The unit circle of radius 1 has a circumference of $C = 2\pi$. Therefore, if a point P travels around the unit circle for a distance of 2π, it ends up where it started. In other words, if integer multiples of 2π are added or subtracted, the coordinates of P and, therefore, the value of the trig functions remain unchanged. It follows that if k is an integer:

$$\sin(q + 2k\pi) = \sin q$$
$$\cos(q + 2k\pi) = \cos q$$

Functions that have this property are called **periodic functions.** A function, f, is periodic if there is a positive real number, q, such that $f(x + q) = f(x)$ for all x's in the domain of f. The smallest possible value for q for which this is true is called the **period** of f.

Example:

1. If $\sin y = \dfrac{3\sqrt{5}}{10}$, then what is the value of each of the following sins: $\sin(y + 8\pi)$, $\sin(y - 6\pi)$, $\sin(y + 210\pi)$?

All three have the same value of $\dfrac{3\sqrt{5}}{10}$ since the sine function is periodic and has a period of 2π.

The cosine is known as an **even function** and the sine is known as an **odd function.** In general,

$$g \text{ is an even function if } g(-x) = g(x)$$
$$g \text{ is an odd function if } g(-x) = -g(x)$$

for every value of x in the domain of g. Some functions are odd, some are even, and some are neither odd nor even.

If a function is **even,** then the graph of the function will be symmetric about the y-axis. Alternatively, for every point (x, y) on the graph, the point $(-x, y)$ will also be on the graph.

If a function is **odd,** then the graph of the function will be symmetric about the origin. Alternatively, for every point (x, y) on the graph, the point $(-x, -y)$ will also be on the graph.

The following graphs of the sine and cosine function are examples of **odd** and **even** functions.

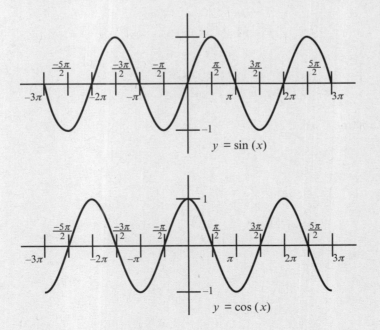

$y = \sin(x)$

$y = \cos(x)$

Example:

> **2.** Is the function $f(x) = 2x^3 + x$ even, odd, or neither?

Replacing $-x$ for x gives

$$f(-x) = 2(-x)^3 + (-x)$$
$$= -2x^3 - x$$
$$= -(2x^3 + x)$$

Since $f(-x) = -f(x)$, the function is odd.

Example:

> **3.** Is the function $f(x) = \sin x - \cos x$ even, odd, or neither?

Replacing $-x$ for x gives

$$f(-x) = \sin(-x) - \cos(-x)$$
$$= -\sin x - \cos x$$
$$= -(\sin x + \cos x)$$

Since

$$-(\sin x + \cos x) \neq -(\sin x - \cos x)$$
$$-(\sin x + \cos x) \neq \sin x - \cos x$$

this function is neither even nor odd. Note: The sum of an odd function and an even function is neither even nor odd.

Example:

> **4.** Is the function $f(x) = x \sin x \cos x$ even, odd, or neither?

Replacing $-x$ for x gives

$$f(-x) = (-x)\sin(-x)\cos(-x)$$
$$= (-x)(-\sin x)\cos x$$
$$= x \sin x \cos x$$
$$= f(x)$$

Since $f(-x) = f(x)$, this function is even.

Graphs of the Sine and Cosine

Several additional terms and factors can be added to the sine and cosine function that modify their shapes.

The additional term A in the function $y = A + \sin x$ allows for a **vertical shift** in the graph of the sine function. (This also holds for the cosine function.)

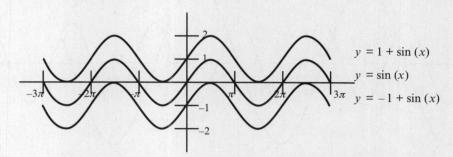

$$y = 1 + \sin (x)$$
$$y = \sin (x)$$
$$y = -1 + \sin (x)$$

The additional term B in the function $y = B \sin x$ allows for **amplitude** variation of the sine function. (This also holds for the cosine function.) The amplitude is always positive and represents one-half the vertical distance between the peak (high point of the curve) and the valley (low point of the curve). In the figure above, all three sine functions have an amplitude of 1.

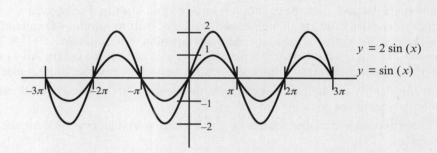

$$y = 2 \sin (x)$$
$$y = \sin (x)$$

Combining the preceding illustrations yields the functions $y = A + B \sin x$ and also $y = A + B \cos x$.

Example:

1. Graph the function $y = 1 + 2 \sin x$.

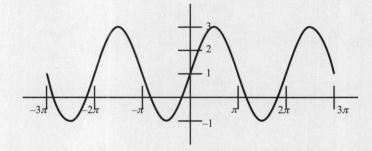

The additional factor C in the function $y = \sin Cx$ allows for **period** variation of the sin function. (This also holds for the cosine function.) The period of the function $y = \sin Cx$ is $\frac{2\pi}{|C|}$. Thus, the function $y = \sin 5x$ has a period of $\frac{2\pi}{5}$. The additional term D in the function $y = \sin (x + D)$ allows for a **phase shift** in the graph of the sine function. (This also holds for the cosine function.) The sine function is odd, and the cosine function is even. The cosine function looks exactly like the sine function, except that it is shifted $\frac{\pi}{2}$ units to the left. In other words, $\sin x = \cos\left(x - \frac{\pi}{2}\right)$ or $\cos x = \sin\left(x + \frac{\pi}{2}\right)$.

The following graph illustrates both changes in amplitude and phase shift.

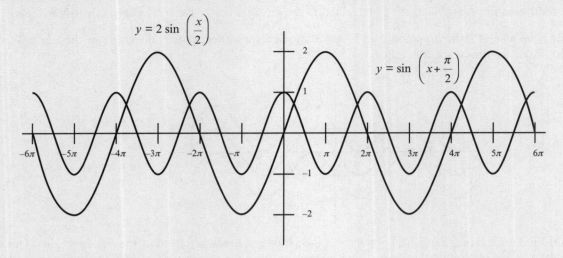

Trigonometric Identities

If an equation contains one or more variables and is valid for all replacement values of the variables for which both sides of the equation are defined, then the equation is known as an **identity.** The equation $x^2 + 2x = x(x + 2)$, for example, is an identity since it is valid for all replacement values of x. If an equation is valid only for certain replacement values of the variable, then it is called a **conditional equation.** The equation $3x + 4 = 25$, for example, is a conditional equation since it it is valid for some replacement values and not for others. An equation that is said to be an identity without stating any restrictions is, in reality, an identity only for those replacement values for which both sides of the identity are defined. For example, the identity $\frac{\sin \alpha}{\cos \alpha} = \tan \alpha$ is valid only for those values of α for which both sides of the equation are defined.

The fundamental or basic trigonometric identities can be divided into several groups. First are the **reciprocal identities.** These include

$$\cot \alpha = \frac{1}{\tan \alpha}$$

$$\sec \alpha = \frac{1}{\cos \alpha}$$

$$\csc \alpha = \frac{1}{\sin \alpha}$$

Next are the **quotient identities.** These include

$$\tan \alpha = \frac{\sin \alpha}{\cos \alpha}$$

$$\cot \alpha = \frac{\cos \alpha}{\sin \alpha}$$

Then there are the **cofunction identities.** These include

$$\sin \alpha = \cos (90° - \alpha) \quad \cot \alpha = \tan (90° - \alpha)$$
$$\cos \alpha = \sin (90° - \alpha) \quad \sec \alpha = \csc (90° - \alpha)$$
$$\tan \alpha = \cot (90° - \alpha) \quad \csc \alpha = \sec (90° - \alpha)$$

Next there are the **identities for negatives.** These include

$$\sin(-\alpha) = -\sin\alpha$$
$$\cos(-\alpha) = -\cos\alpha$$
$$\tan(-\alpha) = -\tan\alpha$$

Finally there are the **Pythagorean identities.** These include

$$\sin^2\alpha + \cos^2\alpha = 1$$
$$\tan^2\alpha + 1 = \sec^2\alpha$$
$$\cot^2\alpha + 1 = \csc^2\alpha$$

The second and third identities are obtained by dividing the first identity by $\cos^2\alpha$ and $\sin^2\alpha$, respectively.

Example:

---

1. Use the basic trigonometric identities to determine the other five values of the trigonometric functions given that $\sin\alpha = \frac{7}{8}$ and $\cos\alpha < 0$.

$$\sin^2\alpha + \cos^2\alpha = 1 \qquad \tan\alpha = \frac{\sin\alpha}{\cos\alpha}$$

$$\left(\frac{7}{8}\right)^2 + \cos^2\alpha = 1 \qquad \tan\alpha = \frac{\left(\frac{7}{8}\right)}{-\frac{\sqrt{15}}{8}}$$

$$\cos^2\alpha = 1 - \left(\frac{7}{8}\right)^2 \qquad \tan\alpha = -\frac{7}{\sqrt{15}}$$

$$\cos^2\alpha = 1 - \frac{49}{64} \qquad \tan\alpha = -\frac{7\sqrt{15}}{15}$$

$$\cos^2\alpha = \frac{15}{64}$$

Since we are given that $\cos\alpha < 0$

$$\cos\alpha = -\sqrt{\frac{15}{64}}$$

$$\cos\alpha = -\frac{\sqrt{15}}{8}$$

$$\cot\alpha = \frac{1}{\tan\alpha} \qquad \sec\alpha = \frac{1}{\cos\alpha} \qquad \csc\alpha = \frac{1}{\sin\alpha}$$

$$\cot\alpha = \frac{1}{-\left(\frac{7\sqrt{15}}{15}\right)} \qquad \sec\alpha = \frac{1}{-\left(\frac{\sqrt{15}}{8}\right)} \qquad \csc\alpha = \frac{1}{\frac{7}{8}}$$

$$\cot\alpha = -\frac{15}{7\sqrt{15}} \qquad \sec\alpha = -\frac{8}{\sqrt{15}} \qquad \csc\alpha = \frac{8}{7}$$

$$\cot\alpha = -\frac{\sqrt{15}}{7} \qquad \sec\alpha = -\frac{8\sqrt{15}}{15}$$

Example:

> **2.** Verify that the following is an identity: $\cos \alpha + \sin \alpha \tan \alpha = \sec \alpha$.

$$\cos \alpha + \sin \alpha \tan \alpha = \sec \alpha \qquad \text{Identity to be verified}$$

$$(\cos \alpha)\left(\frac{\cos \alpha}{\cos \alpha}\right) + (\sin \alpha)\left(\frac{\sin \alpha}{\cos \alpha}\right) = \sec \alpha \qquad \text{Quotient identity}$$

$$\frac{\cos^2 \alpha + \sin^2 \alpha}{\cos \alpha} = \sec \alpha \qquad \text{Algebraic manipulation}$$

$$\frac{1}{\cos \alpha} = \sec \alpha \qquad \text{Pythagorean identity}$$

$$\sec \alpha = \sec \alpha \qquad \text{Reciprocal identity}$$

Note: You will not be required to verify identities on the ACT but the preceding example serves as an example of using basic trigonometric identities to solve problems.

Note: The fundamental or basic identities discussed in the previous section involved only one variable. The following identities, involving two variables, are called **trigonometric addition identities**.

$$\sin(\alpha + \beta) = \sin \alpha \cos \beta + \cos \alpha \sin \beta$$

$$\sin(\alpha - \beta) = \sin \alpha \cos \beta - \cos \alpha \sin \beta$$

$$\cos(\alpha + \beta) = \cos \alpha \cos \beta - \sin \alpha \sin \beta$$

$$\cos(\alpha - \beta) = \cos \alpha \cos \beta + \sin \alpha \sin \beta$$

You are NOT required to know these addition identities for the ACT, but you may be asked to use one to solve a problem. The following example is much more complex than you would find on the ACT, but serves to illustrate the use of identities.

Example:

> **3.** Use the identity $\sin(\alpha + \beta) = \sin \alpha \cos \beta + \cos \alpha \sin \beta$ to find $\sin(\alpha + \beta)$ given that $\sin \alpha = -\frac{4}{5}$, $\cos \beta = \frac{15}{17}$, and α and β are fourth quadrant angles.

First find $\cos \alpha$ and $\sin \beta$. The sine is negative, and the cosine is positive in the fourth quadrant. Use the Pythagorean identity.

$$\sin^2 \alpha + \cos^2 \alpha = 1 \qquad\qquad \sin^2 \beta + \cos^2 \beta = 1$$

$$\left(-\frac{4}{5}\right)^2 + \cos^2 \alpha = 1 \qquad\qquad \sin^2 \beta + \left(\frac{15}{17}\right)^2 = 1$$

$$\cos^2 \alpha = 1 - \frac{16}{25} \qquad\qquad \sin^2 \beta = 1 - \frac{225}{289}$$

$$\cos^2 \alpha = \frac{9}{25} \qquad\qquad \sin^2 \beta = \frac{64}{289}$$

$$\cos \alpha = \frac{3}{5} \qquad\qquad \sin \beta = -\frac{8}{17}$$

Next, use the given addition identity.

$$\sin(\alpha + \beta) = \sin \alpha \cos \beta + \cos \alpha \sin \beta$$

$$\sin(\alpha + \beta) = \left(-\frac{4}{5}\right)\left(\frac{15}{17}\right) + \left(\frac{3}{5}\right)\left(-\frac{8}{17}\right)$$

$$\sin(\alpha + \beta) = \left(-\frac{60}{85}\right) + \left(-\frac{24}{85}\right)$$

$$\sin(\alpha + \beta) = -\frac{84}{85}$$

Trigonometric Equations

Trigonometric identities are true for all replacement values for the variables for which both sides of the equation are defined. **Conditional trigonometric equations** are true for only some replacement values. Solutions in a specific interval, such as $0 \le x \le 2\pi$, are usually called **primary solutions**. A **general solution** is a formula that names all possible solutions. The process of solving general trigonometric equations is not a clear-cut one. No rules exist that will always lead to a solution. The procedure usually involves the use of identities, algebraic manipulation, and trial and error. The following guidelines can help lead to a solution.

- If the equation contains more than one trigonometric function, use identities and algebraic manipulation (such as factoring) to rewrite the equation in terms of only one trigonometric function.
- Look for expressions that are in quadratic form and solve by factoring.
- Not all equations have solutions, but those that do usually can be solved using appropriate identities and algebraic manipulation.
- Look for patterns.
- There is no substitute for experience.

Example:

> **1.** Use the Pythagorean identity $\sin^2 \alpha + \cos^2 \alpha = 1$ to find the exact solution for α given that $\cos^2 \alpha = -\cos^2 \alpha + \sin^2 \alpha$ and $0° \le \alpha \le 360°$.

Use the given Pythagorean identity $\sin^2 \alpha + \cos^2 \alpha = 1$. Then solve the resulting quadratic equation.

$$\cos^2 \alpha = -\cos \alpha + \left(1 - \cos^2 \alpha\right)$$

$$2\cos^2 \alpha + \cos \alpha - 1 = 0$$

$$\left(2\cos \alpha - 1\right)\left(\cos \alpha + 1\right) = 0$$

Set each factor equal to zero and solve for α.

$$2\cos \alpha - 1 = 0$$
$$2\cos \alpha = 1 \qquad\qquad \cos \alpha + 1 = 0$$
$$\cos \alpha = \frac{1}{2} \qquad\qquad \cos \alpha = -1$$
$$\alpha = 60°, 300° \qquad\qquad \alpha = 180°$$

Therefore, $\alpha = 60°$, $180°$, and $300°$.

On the ACT, you may be asked to use other trigonometric identities to solve trigonometric equations, but you will be given the identity as part of the problem.

Trigonometry Practice Questions

Now that you have reviewed the strategies, you can practice on your own. The questions are roughly grouped into three categories: easy to moderate, average, and above average to difficult. The answers and explanations that follow the questions will include strategies to help you understand how to solve the problems.

Easy to Moderate

1. If the three sides of a right triangle measure 3 centimeters, 4 centimeters, and 5 centimeters, what is the sine of the angle opposite the side with a length of 4 centimeters?

   A. $\dfrac{3}{5}$

   B. $\dfrac{3}{4}$

   C. $\dfrac{4}{5}$

   D. $\dfrac{5}{4}$

   E. $\dfrac{5}{3}$

2. A line with a slope of $-\dfrac{2}{3}$ intercepts the x-axis at the point $(6, 0)$. What is the sine of the acute angle that the line makes with the y-axis?

   A. $\dfrac{2}{3}$

   B. $\dfrac{3}{2}$

   C. $\dfrac{2\sqrt{13}}{13}$

   D. $\dfrac{3\sqrt{13}}{13}$

   E. Cannot be determined from the information given

Average

3. As shown in the following figure, a tower casts a shadow 60 ft long. If the angle of elevation of the sun is 40°, what is the height of the tower?

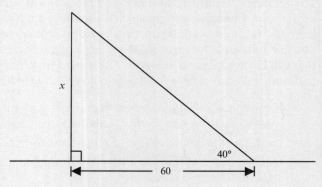

   A. 60 sin 40°

   B. 60 tan 40°

   C. 60 tan 50°

   D. 60 cot 40°

   E. 60 cos 50°

4. For all values of x where $\sin x$, $\cos x$, and $\tan x$ are defined, which of the following is equivalent to $\dfrac{\sin x \cos x}{\tan x}$?

   A. $\sin^2 x$

   B. $\cos^2 x$

   C. $\tan^2 x$

   D. $\dfrac{1}{\sin x}$

   E. $\dfrac{1}{\cos x}$

Above Average to Difficult

5. If $\sin \alpha = x$, then, in terms of x, what is the value of $\tan^2 \alpha$?

A. $\dfrac{x^2+1}{x^2}$

B. $\dfrac{1+x^2}{1-x^2}$

C. $\dfrac{x^2+1}{1-x}$

D. $\dfrac{1-x^2}{x^2}$

E. $\dfrac{x^2}{1-x^2}$

6. If $\tan \theta < -1$ and $\sin \theta > 0$, then which of the following answer choices contain two values, both of which could be the value of θ?

A. $\dfrac{\pi}{6}$ and $\dfrac{\pi}{3}$

B. $\dfrac{\pi}{3}$ and $\dfrac{2\pi}{3}$

C. $\dfrac{5\pi}{8}$ and $\dfrac{7\pi}{8}$

D. $\dfrac{5\pi}{8}$ and $\dfrac{2\pi}{3}$

E. $\dfrac{2\pi}{3}$ and $\dfrac{3\pi}{4}$

Answers and Explanations

Easy to Moderate

1. **C.** In a right triangle, the hypotenuse is the longest side, in this case 5 centimeters. The sine of an angle is defined as the quotient of the side opposite the angle and the hypotenuse. In this case, the sine is $\dfrac{4}{5}$.

2. **D.** A sketch helps illustrate the ratios used.

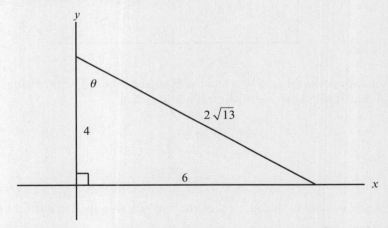

Since the given line intercepts the x-axis at 6 and the slope of the line is $-\dfrac{2}{3}$, the line intercepts the y-axis at 4. The length of the hypotenuse of the resulting triangle is calculated using the Pythagorean Theorem. The sine is the ratio of the opposite side and the hypotenuse, or $\sin\theta = \dfrac{\text{opposite}}{\text{hypotenuse}} = \dfrac{6}{2\sqrt{13}} = \dfrac{3\sqrt{13}}{13}$. This is answer choice D.

Average

3. **B.** In a right triangle, the tangent of an angle is defined as the ratio of the length of the opposite side divided by the length of the adjacent side. In this case,

$$\tan 40° = \frac{x}{60}$$
$$60 \tan 40° = x$$

Therefore, answer choice B is the correct one.

4. **B.** Simplify as follows:

$$\frac{\sin x \cos x}{\tan x} = \frac{\sin x \cos x}{\frac{\sin x}{\cos x}} = \left(\frac{\sin x \cos x}{1} \right) \left(\frac{\cos x}{\sin x} \right) = \cos^2 x$$

Therefore, answer choice B is the correct selection.

Above Average to Difficult

5. **E.** Sketching a right triangle and filling in what you know will help you visualize the given information.

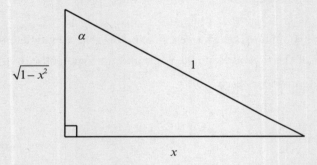

If $\sin \alpha = \frac{x}{1}$, let the side opposite angle α be x and the hypotenuse be 1. Use the Pythagorean Theorem to determine the third side. If the third side of the triangle is y, then

$$x^2 + y^2 = 1^2$$
$$y^2 = 1 - x^2$$
$$y = \sqrt{1 - x^2}$$

The tangent of an angle is equal to the quotient of the opposite side and the adjacent side.

$$\tan \alpha = \frac{x}{\sqrt{1 - x^2}}$$
$$\tan^2 \alpha = \frac{x^2}{1 - x^2}$$

This is answer choice E.

An alternative technique would be to use the quotient identity for tangent and the Pythagorean identity for sine and cosine, then substitute x for the sine, as follows:

$$\tan^2 \alpha = \frac{\sin^2 \alpha}{\cos^2 \alpha} = \frac{\sin^2 \alpha}{1 - \sin^2 \alpha} = \frac{x^2}{1 - x^2}$$

This also gives the correct answer choice of E.

6. **D.** Since the sin θ is positive, then θ must be in the first or second quadrant. Since tan θ is negative, θ must be in the second or fourth quadrant. So, this limits us to the second quadrant. In addition, since tan $\theta < -1$, $\frac{\pi}{2} < \theta < \frac{3\pi}{4}$. The correct answer choice is Choice D. Both $\frac{5\pi}{8}$ and $\frac{2\pi}{3}$ fall in the acceptable range. Note that $\frac{3\pi}{4}$ is not in the acceptable range.

Chapter 12

Word Problems

ACT Mathematics Test questions often appear as *word problems*. To solve math word problems, you must be able to translate English words that describe a situation or scenario into math equations. The key to solving these types of problems is to identify specific details about "what the question is asking." A common mistake is that the hurried test-taker quickly reads the question and rushes to a solution. Word problems can be misleading unless you carefully organize words into math symbols and numbers. Use the concepts and strategies discussed in Chapters 7 to 11 for specific types of math questions and follow these simple step-by-step strategies when approaching word problems.

Solving Word Problems

1. **Identify what you are trying to solve.** Circle or underline what the question is asking. For example, "How much **time** does it take to get to the airport **30 miles** away?," or "What is the cost of **two** cell phones at **$124.75** each, plus **one** adapter at **$36.55** ?"

2. **Watch for key words.** Circle or underline key words. For example, (a) **add**: <u>sum, total, plus, increase</u>; (b) **subtract**: <u>difference, fewer, remainder, less, reduced, decreased, minus</u>; (c) **multiply**: <u>product, of, times, at, total</u>; (d) **divide**: <u>quotient, divided by, ratio, half</u>.

3. **Order of operations.** Always follow the order of operations rules discussed in Chapter 8 when setting up your equation and perform the calculations carefully.

4. **Restate** your answer in a sentence to verify that it makes sense and that it is *reasonable*.

To evaluate your knowledge of word problems, take the following diagnostic test and analyze how familiar you are with the selected topics. The diagnostic test will give you valuable insight into the topics you will need to study.

Word Problems Diagnostic Test

Directions: Solve each problem in this section by using the information given and your own mathematical calculations.

1. Traveling from point A to point B, John averages 30 miles per hour. The return trip is along the same route, and he averages 40 miles per hour. Find John's average speed for the entire trip, to the nearest tenth of a mile per hour.

2. Jim can do a job in 8 hours by himself, but it would take Tom 12 hours to do the same job by himself. Working together, how long should it take to do the job?

3. A chemist wants to dilute 50 ml of a 40% acid solution into a 30% acid solution. How much pure water must be added?

4. Currently, Carlos is 5 years older than three times his daughter Juanita's age. Two years ago, he was 4 years older than four times her age. How many years from today will he be twice her age?

5. Find the product of three consecutive odd integers such that twice the smallest increased by the largest is 13 less than four times the middle integer.

Scoring the Diagnostic Test

The diagnostic test explanations listed here include topic headings that correspond with step-by-step learning tools and examples to help you solve specific problem types. Use the answer key and the analysis worksheet that follows to help you evaluate specific problem types. Topic headings can be found in the "Word Problems Review" section following the diagnostic test.

Answer Key

Motion Problem

   1. 34.3 miles/hour

Work Problem

   2. $4\frac{4}{5}$ hours or 4.8 hours

Mixture Problem

   3. $16\frac{2}{3}$ ml

Age Problem

   4. 12 years

Integer Problem

   5. 1,287

Charting and Analyzing Your Diagnostic Test Results

Record your diagnostic test results in the following chart and use these results as a guide to plan your word problems review. Mark the problems that you missed and pay particular attention to those that you missed in Column (C) because they were unfamiliar math concepts to you. These are the areas you will want to focus on as you study word problem topics.

Analysis Sheet

Topic	Number Possible	Number Correct	(A) Simple Mistake	(B) Misread Problem	(C) Unfamiliar Math Concept
			Number Incorrect		
Motion	1				
Work	1				
Mixture	1				
Age	1				
Integer	1				
Total Possible Explanations for Incorrect Answers: Columns A, B, and C					
Total Number of Questions	5	Add the total number of correct questions here: _____	Add columns A, B, and C for total number of incorrect questions here: _____		

Word Problems Review

Common types of word problems are motion, work, mixture, age, and integer.

Motion Problems

Motion problems all use the basic formula of (average rate)(total time) = (total distance) or more simply $r \times t = d$.

A chart that organizes the given information can help you create an equation to be solved that can answer the question. Such a chart could look like this:

	Average Rate	Total Time	Total Distance
A			
B			

Examples:

> **1.** Traveling from point A to point B, John averages 30 miles per hour. On the return trip along the same route, he averages 40 miles per hour. Find, to the nearest tenth of a mile per hour, his average speed for the entire trip.

The most common error made on this type of problem is to add the rates together and divide by 2. Average speed is found by taking the total distance traveled and dividing by the total time it took to travel that distance. To make the problem simpler, assume the distance traveled was 120 miles, a number that is easily divided by both 30 and 40.

	Average Rate	Total Time	Total Distance
A to B	30 mi/hr	x	120 mi
B to A	40 mi/hr	y	120 mi

Then

$$30x = 120 \quad \text{and} \quad 40y = 120$$
$$x = 4 \qquad\qquad y = 3$$

which means that the entire trip of 240 miles took 7 hours. Thus, the average speed becomes $\dfrac{240 \text{ miles}}{7 \text{ hours}} \approx 34.29 \text{ mi/hr}$, which—rounded off to the nearest tenth of a mile per hour—is 34.3 mi/hr.

The problem can also be solved algebraically:

Let d be the one-way distance, then $\dfrac{d \text{ mi}}{30 \text{ mi/hr}} = \dfrac{d}{30}$ hr is the time used going from A to B, and $\dfrac{d \text{ mi}}{40 \text{ mi/hr}} = \dfrac{d}{40}$ hr is the time used going from B to A.

$$\begin{aligned}
\text{average speed} &= \frac{\text{total distance}}{\text{total time}}\\[6pt]
&= \frac{2d}{\dfrac{d}{30} + \dfrac{d}{40}} =\\[6pt]
&= \frac{2d}{\dfrac{70d}{1200}}\\[6pt]
&= \frac{2d}{1} \times \frac{\overset{1}{\cancel{1200}}}{\underset{35}{\cancel{70d}}}\\[6pt]
&\approx 34.29
\end{aligned}$$

You should also be able to get an estimate before starting the problem. To travel a certain distance going 30 miles per hour will take longer than going that distance at 40 miles per hour, which means that the average speed will be closer to 30 mi/hr than to 40 mi/hr. Had this been a multiple-choice question and only one answer choice was between 30 and 35, calculations would have been unnecessary.

> **2.** If a girl can run m miles in h hours, how many hours will it take her to run k miles at the same rate?

Let x be the rate for each direction and t the time for the second run.

	Average Rate	Total Time	Total Distance
A	x mi/hr	h hr	m mi
B	x mi/hr	t hr	k mi

$$xh = m \quad \text{and} \quad xt = k$$
$$x = \frac{m}{h} \qquad\qquad x = \frac{k}{t}$$
$$\text{Therefore, } \frac{m}{h} = \frac{k}{t}$$
$$tm = hk$$
$$t = \frac{hk}{m}$$

It will take $\dfrac{hk}{m}$ hours to run k miles.

> **3.** A boat travels 30 miles against a current in 3 hours. It travels the same 30 miles with the current in 1 hour. How fast is the current, and what is the boat's speed in still water?

Let b be the boat's speed in still water, and let c be the current's speed. Going with the current, the boat's speed will be $b + c$ mi/hr. Going against the current, the boat's speed will be $b - c$ mi/hr. Use a chart to organize the information.

	Average Rate	Total Time	Total Distance
With the current	$b + c$ mi/hr	1 hr	30 mi
Against the current	$b - c$ mi/hr	3 hr	30 mi

This now translates into the following system of equations:

$$(b+c)(1) = 30 \qquad\qquad \rightarrow \qquad\qquad b + c = 30$$
$$(b-c)(3) = 30 \;\;\left(\text{divide each side by 3}\right) \qquad \underline{b - c = 10} \quad \left(\text{add the equations}\right)$$
$$2b \;\;= 40$$
$$b = 20$$

Since $b + c = 30$ and $b = 20$, then $c = 10$. The current's speed is 10 mi/hr, and the boat's speed in still water is 20 mi/hr.

Work Problems

Work problems, which usually involve how much time it takes each of two ways to complete a job or one way to complete a job and the other to undo a job, can be quickly calculated. If two methods of completing a job are given, to find the time it would take working together, take the product of the two times and divide by the sum of the two times. If one method undoes the job, then take the product of the two times and divide by the difference of the two times.

If the work problem involves more than two methods of either completing or undoing the job, then an algebraic approach to get the answer would look like this:

$$\frac{1}{\text{first person's time}} + \frac{1}{\text{second person's time}} + \frac{1}{\text{third person's time}} + \cdots = \frac{1}{\text{time together}}$$

Examples:

> **1.** Jim can do a job in 8 hours by himself that would take Tom 12 hours to do by himself. Working together, how long should it take to do the job?

Using the fast method: $\dfrac{(8)(12)}{8+12} = \dfrac{96}{20} = 4\dfrac{4}{5}$ or 4.8

Using the algebraic method, let x be the amount of time it takes together:

$$\frac{1}{8} + \frac{1}{12} = \frac{1}{x} \qquad \left(\text{multiply each side by the LCD of } 24x\right)$$

$$24x\left(\frac{1}{8} + \frac{1}{12}\right) = 24x\left(\frac{1}{x}\right)$$

$$3x + 2x = 24$$

$$5x = 24$$

$$x = \frac{24}{5} = 4\frac{4}{5} \text{ or } 4.8$$

It will take them $4\dfrac{4}{5}$ or 4.8 hours together.

> **2.** If it takes 6 hours to fill a tank with water and 15 hours to drain it, how long would it take to fill the tank if the drain was accidently left open?

Using the fast method: $\dfrac{(15)(6)}{15-6} = \dfrac{90}{9} = 10$

Using the algebraic method, let x be the amount of time it takes together:

$$\frac{1}{6} - \frac{1}{15} = \frac{1}{x} \qquad \left(\text{multiply each side by the LCD of } 30x\right)$$

$$30x\left(\frac{1}{6} - \frac{1}{15}\right) = 30x\left(\frac{1}{x}\right)$$

$$5x - 2x = 30$$

$$3x = 30$$

$$x = 10$$

With the drain open, it will take 10 hours to fill the tank.

> **3.** Working alone, Bill can do a job in 4 hours. With Fred's help, it takes only $2\dfrac{2}{9}$ hours. How long should it take Fred working alone to do the job?

Using the fast method: First change $2\dfrac{2}{9}$ to $\dfrac{20}{9}$. Let x be how long it would take Fred alone: $\dfrac{4x}{4+x} = \dfrac{20}{9}$. You can quickly see that x is 5.

Using the algebraic method:

$$\frac{1}{4} + \frac{1}{x} = \frac{1}{2\frac{2}{9}} \qquad \left(\frac{1}{2\frac{2}{9}} = \frac{1}{\frac{20}{9}} = \frac{9}{20} \right)$$

$$\frac{1}{4} + \frac{1}{x} = \frac{9}{20} \qquad \text{(multiply each side by the LCD of } 20x)$$

$$20x\left(\frac{1}{4} + \frac{1}{x}\right) = 20x\left(\frac{9}{20}\right)$$

$$5x + 20 = 9x$$

$$20 = 4x$$

$$5 = x$$

It would take Fred 5 hours to do the job alone.

Mixture Problems

Like motion problems, you can solve *mixture problems* more easily using a chart to organize the given information. Depending on the type of mixture problem, you can use different organizing charts.

Examples:

1. A chemist wants to dilute 50 ml of a 40% acid solution into a 30% acid solution. How much pure water must be added?

This problem involves acid and water. Begin with 50 ml of a solution of which 40% is acid and 60% is not acid. The chemist is adding pure water, and then the new mixture will only be 30% acid and 70% not acid.

Let x be how many ml of water is being added.

	Start	Add	Totals
Mixture	50 ml	x ml	$x + 50$ ml
Acid	(0.40)(50) ml	0 ml	(0.30)(x + 50) ml
Not acid	(0.60)(50) ml	x ml	(0.70)(x + 50) ml

There are now two different equations that can be used to find x.

$$(0.40)(50) + 0 = (0.30)(x + 50) \text{ or } (0.60)(50) + x = (0.70)(x + 50)$$

The easier one is the one on the left since the x appears on only one side of the equation.

$$(0.40)(50) + 0 = (0.30)(x + 50)$$

$$20 = 0.3x + 15$$

$$5 = 0.3x$$

$$\frac{50}{3} = x \text{ or } x = 16\frac{2}{3}$$

The chemist must add $16\frac{2}{3}$ ml of pure water.

2. One solution is 75% saltwater, and another solution is 50% saltwater. How many gallons of each should be used to make 10 gallons of a solution that is 60% saltwater?

Let x be the number of gallons of the 75% saltwater solution. Then $10 - x$ will be the number of gallons of the 50% solution since there will be a total of 10 gallons in the final mixture.

	Start	Add	Totals
Mixture	x gal	$10 - x$ gal	10 gal
Salt	$(0.75)(x)$ gal	$(0.50)(10 - x)$ gal	$(0.60)(10)$
Water	$(0.25)(x)$ gal	$(0.50)(10 - x)$ gal	$(0.40)(10)$

There are now two different equations that can be used to find x.

$$(0.75)(x) + (0.50)(10 - x) = (0.60)(10) \text{ or } (0.25)(x) + (0.50)(10 - x) = (0.40)(10)$$

Selecting the first equation:

$$(0.75)(x) + (0.50)(10 - x) = (0.60)(10)$$
$$0.75x + 5 - 0.50x = 6$$
$$0.25x + 5 = 6$$
$$0.25x = 1$$
$$x = \frac{1}{0.25}$$
$$x = 4 \quad \text{and} \quad 10 - x = 6$$

Therefore, 4 gallons of 75% saltwater solution and 6 gallons of 50% saltwater solution are used.

3. Nuts worth $1.50 per pound are mixed with nuts worth $1.75 per pound to make 20 pounds of nuts worth $1.65 per pound. How many pounds of each type are used?

Let x be the number of pounds of $1.75/lb nuts. Then $20 - x$ would be the number of pounds of $1.50/lb nuts since there will be 20 pounds in the final mixture.

A slightly different chart (with different column headings) will be used to organize the information.

	Cost/lb	# Pounds	Total Cost
Mixture	$1.65	20	$(\$1.65)(20)$
$1.75/lb	$1.75	x	$(\$1.75)(x)$
$1.50/lb	$1.50	$20 - x$	$(\$1.50)(20 - x)$

The total cost of the individual type of nuts should equal the total cost of the mixture:

$$1.75x + 1.50(20 - x) = 1.65(20)$$
$$1.75x + 30 - 1.50x = 33$$
$$0.25x + 30 = 33$$
$$0.25x = 3$$
$$x = \frac{3}{0.25}$$
$$x = 12 \quad \text{and} \quad 20 - x = 8$$

Therefore, 12 pounds of the $1.75/lb nuts and 8 pounds of the $1.50/lb nuts are used.

Age Problems

Age problems usually require a representation of ages now, ages in the past, and/or ages in the future. Use a chart to keep the information organized.

Examples:

1. Currently, Carlos is 5 years older than three times his daughter, Juanita's, age. Two years ago, he was 4 years older than four times her age. How many years from now will he be twice her age?

Let j represent Juanita's current age. Then $3j + 5$ is Carlos' current age.

Person	Current Age	Age 2 Years Ago
Juanita	j	$j - 2$
Carlos	$3j + 5$	$(3j + 5) - 2$

Translating the sentence "Two years ago, he was 4 years older than four times her age" algebraically, you get

$$\underbrace{(3j+5)-2}_{\substack{\text{Carlos' age}\\\text{2 years ago}}} = 4 \underbrace{\left(j-2 \right)}_{\substack{\text{Juanita's age}\\\text{2 years ago}}} +4$$

$$3j+5-2 = 4j-8+4$$
$$3j+3 = 4j-4$$
$$3 = j-4$$
$$7 = j$$

Therefore, currently, Juanita is 7 years old and Carlos is $3(7) + 5$ or 26 years old. The question asks when in the future he will be twice as old as his daughter.

Let t be how many years into the future this takes place and set up a new chart.

Person	Current Age	Age t Years from Now
Juanita	7	$7 + t$
Carlos	26	$26 + t$

"Carlos will be twice his daughter's age" translates into

$$26+t = 2(7+t)$$
$$26+t = 14+2t$$
$$26 = 14+t$$
$$12 = t$$

Therefore, in 12 years, Carlos will be twice his daughter's age. In 12 years he will be 38, and his daughter will be 19, hence his age will be twice hers.

2. Ed is 12 years older than Jim. Five years ago, the sum of their ages was 42. What will be the product of their ages in 5 years?

Let x be Jim's age now and $12 + x$ Ed's age now.

Person	Current Age	Age 5 Years Ago
Jim	x	$x - 5$
Ed	$12 + x$	$12 + x - 5$ or $x + 7$

Translate "Five years ago, the sum of their ages was 42" into an algebraic equation.

$$(x-5)+(12+x-5) = 42$$
$$2x + 2 = 42$$
$$2x = 40$$
$$x = 20 \quad \text{and} \quad 12 + x = 32$$

Therefore, Jim is currently 20 years old, and Ed is 32 years old. In 5 years, Jim will be 25, and Ed will be 37 years old. The product of their ages will be $(25)(37) = 925$.

Integer Problems

Integer problems usually involve consecutive integers, consecutive even integers, or consecutive odd integers. If you let x represent any integer, then $x + 1$ would represent the next larger integer, $x + 2$ would be the next larger after that, then $x + 3$, and so on.

If you let x represent either an odd or an even integer, then the next odd or even integer would be 2 more than that, or $x + 2$, and the one after that would be $x + 4$ and so on.

Examples:

1. Find the product of three consecutive odd integers such that twice the smallest increased by the largest is 13 less than four times the middle integer.

Let x be the smallest of the three consecutive odd integers. Then $x + 2$ and $x + 4$ would be the next two consecutive odd integers.

Translate "twice the smallest increased by the largest is 13 less than four times the middle integer" into

$$2x+(x+4) = 4(x+2)-13$$
$$3x+4 = 4x+8-13$$
$$3x+4 = 4x-5$$
$$4 = x-5$$
$$9 = x \quad \text{and} \quad x+2 = 11, \quad x+4 = 13$$

The integers are 9, 11, and 13, and their product is $(9)(11)(13) = 1{,}287$.

2. The sum of four consecutive even integers is 60. What is the largest integer?

Let x, $x + 2$, $x + 4$, and $x + 6$ represent the four consecutive even integers.

$$x + (x + 2) + (x + 4) + (x + 6) = 60$$
$$4x + 12 = 60$$
$$4x = 48$$
$$x = 12 \quad \text{and} \quad x + 2 = 14, \ x + 4 = 16, \ x + 6 = 18$$

Therefore, the largest integer is 18.

Word Problems Practice Questions

Now that you have reviewed the strategies, you can practice on your own. The questions are roughly grouped into three categories: easy to moderate, average, and above average to difficult. The answers and explanations that follow the questions will include strategies to help you understand how to solve the problems.

Easy to Moderate

1. Alex is 19 years older than Bruno. In 12 years, Alex will be twice as old as Bruno. How old is Alex now?

A. 6
B. 10
C. 25
D. 26
E. 27

2. Kellie mixes nuts worth $6 per pound with nuts worth $15 per pound to obtain 24 pounds of nuts worth $9 per pound. How many pounds of $6 nuts were used in the mixture?

A. 14
B. 15
C. 16
D. 17
E. 18

3. Two ports, A and B, are located 40 miles apart along the bank of a river. If there is a constant current in the river of 3 miles per hour and a boat can travel at 9 miles per hour in still water, how many hours would it take for the boat to make a round trip from port A to port B and back to port A?

A. 8
B. $8\frac{8}{9}$
C. $9\frac{1}{3}$
D. 10
E. $10\frac{2}{3}$

Average

4. Six years from now Trudie will be three times as old as Monica. If Trudie was five times as old as Monica eight years ago, what is the difference in their ages?

    A. 36
    B. 48
    C. 56
    D. 60
    E. 64

5. Working together, Ingrid and Casey can complete a job in 8 hours. If Casey can complete the job alone in 20 hours, how long would it take Ingrid to complete the job alone?

    A. 10 hours
    B. $12\frac{1}{2}$ hours
    C. 13 hours
    D. $13\frac{1}{3}$ hours
    E. 15 hours

6. Tex mixes together three different concentrations of alcohol solutions. If Tex uses twice as much 19% solution as 12% solution, how many ounces of 10% solution need to be added to the mixture to obtain 40 ounces of 14% solution?

    A. 8
    B. 16
    C. 18
    D. 24
    E. 28

7. What is the sum of the fifty odd integers between 200 and 300?

    A. 11,750
    B. 12,000
    C. 12,250
    D. 12,500
    E. 12,750

Above Average to Difficult

8. Tito, working alone, can complete a task in 18 hours. Ronnie, working alone, can complete the same task in 12 hours. Ronnie begins working on the task alone. Four hours later, Tito joins Ronnie, and they complete the task working together. How long did Ronnie work on the task?

    A.   7 hours, 24 minutes
    B.   8 hours, 12 minutes
    C.   8 hours, 48 minutes
    D.   9 hours
    E.   9 hours, 36 minutes

9. A car averages 50 miles per hour on one portion of a trip from point X to point Y and 30 miles per hour for the other portion of the trip from point Y to point X. If the distances traveled on each portion of the trip were the same, then what was the average speed for the entire trip?

    A.   37.5 miles per hour
    B.   38.75 miles per hour
    C.   40 miles per hour
    D.   41.25 miles per hour
    E.   Cannot be determined from the given information

10. Given four consecutive even numbers such that five times the smallest number is 30 less than four times the largest number. What is the value of the sum of the four numbers?

    A.   −36
    B.   −12
    C.   12
    D.   36
    E.   228

Answers and Explanations

Easy to Moderate

1. **D.** Set up a chart to help organize the given information. Let x represent Bruno's age now.

Person	Current Age	Age 12 Years From Now
Alex	$x + 19$	$x + 31$
Bruno	x	$x + 12$

Set up an equation to solve for x.

$$x + 31 = 2(x + 12)$$
$$x + 31 = 2x + 24$$
$$7 = x$$
$$x = 7$$
$$x + 19 = 26$$

Since Bruno is 7 years old, Alex must be 26 years old, or answer choice D.

2. C. You can set up a chart, such as the one that follows, to help organize the given information—although this problem is simple enough that you may be able to go straight to the equation setup without using a chart. Let x represent the number of pounds of \$6.00 nuts.

	Cost/lb	# Pounds	Total Cost
Mixture	\$9.00	24	(\$9.00)(24)
\$6.00/lb	\$6.00	x	(\$6.00)(x)
\$15.00/lb	\$15.00	$24 - x$	(\$15.00)($24 - x$)

Set up an equation that represents the given information.

$$6x + 15(24 - x) = 9(24)$$
$$6x + 360 - 15x = 216$$
$$-9x = -144$$
$$x = 16$$

There are 16 pounds of \$6 nuts, or Choice C.

3. D. You can use a chart to help organize the given information, although the times to travel each direction can be computed directly.

	Average Rate	Total Time	Total Distance
With the current	9 + 3 mi/hr	$\frac{40}{9+3}$ hr	40 mi
Against the current	9 − 3 mi/hr	$\frac{40}{9-3}$ hr	40 mi

When traveling upstream, the boat can travel $9 - 3 = 6$ miles per hour. The upstream 40-mile trip would take $\frac{40}{6} = 6\frac{2}{3}$ hours. When traveling downstream, the boat can travel $9 + 3 = 12$ miles per hour. The downstream 40-mile trip would take $\frac{40}{12} = 3\frac{1}{3}$ hours. This is a total of 10 hours, or answer choice D.

Average

4. C. A chart will help organize the given information.

Person	Age 8 Years Ago	Age in 6 Years
Trudie	$3x - 14$	$3x$
Monica	$x - 14$	x

Set up an equation and solve for the two ages. In this example, the ages are defined using "Six years from now" and the equation is set up using "Eight years ago."

$$3x - 14 = 5(x - 14)$$
$$3x - 14 = 5x - 70$$
$$56 = 2x$$
$$x = 28$$
$$3x = 84$$

The ages of 28 and 84 represent their ages six years from now. Therefore their current ages are 78 and 22. The difference in their current ages is $78 - 22 = 56$. Notice that the difference in their ages could have been computed using their ages six years from now, since the difference between 84 and 28 is also 56. The correct answer choice is C.

Their ages could have been defined using "Eight years ago" and the equation set up using "Six years from now." You would get the same answer.

Person	Age 8 Years Ago	Age in 6 Years
Trudie	$5x$	$5x + 14$
Monica	x	$x + 14$

$$5x + 14 = 3(x + 14)$$
$$5x + 14 = 3x + 42$$
$$2x = 28$$
$$x = 14$$
$$5x = 70$$

The difference in their ages is $70 - 14 = 56$. Using the second method avoids the use of negative numbers. In either case, their ages are 22 and 78 now.

5. D. If the numerators of the fractions represent the time actually worked (in this case, working together) and the denominators of the fractions represent the time required to do the job alone, you can set up the following equation.

$$\frac{8}{x} + \frac{8}{20} = 1$$
$$\frac{8}{x} = 1 - \frac{8}{20}$$
$$\frac{8}{x} = \frac{12}{20}$$
$$12x = 160$$
$$x = 13\frac{1}{3}$$

This method is quicker than multiplying through by the common denominator. You can use this quicker method because the variable appears in only one of the two fractions. This is answer choice D.

6. B. Let x represent the amount of 12% solution. You can use the following chart to help organize the given information, but when taking the test, you should be able to set up the equation without setting up the chart.

	Percentage	Quantity	Totals
Mixture	0.14	40	(0.14)(40)
12% solution	0.12	x	(0.12)(x)
19% solution	0.19	$2x$	(0.19)($2x$)
10% solution	0.10	$40 - 3x$	(0.10)(40 − 3x)

If x represents the amount of 12% solution needed, you can set up the following equation. After solving for x, the amount of 12% solution needed, calculate the amount of 10% solution needed.

$$0.19(2x) + 0.12(x) + 0.10(40 - 3x) = 0.14(40)$$
$$19(2x) + 12(x) + 10(40 - 3x) = 14(40)$$
$$38x + 12x + 400 - 30x = 560$$
$$20x = 160$$
$$x = 8$$
$$2x = 16$$
$$40 - 3x = 16$$

Therefore, Since $(40 - 3x)$ represents the quantity of 10% solution, Tex needs 16 ounces of 10% solution, or answer choice B.

7. D. Adding the numbers directly is a waste of valuable time. Look for a quicker way to solve the problem. In this case, adding the numbers *twice* allows you to set up a simple multiplication and division problem.

$$201 + 203 + 205 + \ldots + 297 + 299$$
$$\underline{299 + 297 + 295 + \ldots + 203 + 201}$$
$$500 + 500 + 500 + \ldots + 500 + 500$$

Simply multiply 500 by 50. This gives twice the required sum. Then, divide by 2. $(500)(50) \div 2 = 12{,}500$. This is answer choice D.

Above Average to Difficult

8. C. If x represents the amount of time Ronnie actually worked on the task, you can set up the following equation:

$$\frac{x - 4}{18} + \frac{x}{12} = 1$$
$$36\left(\frac{x - 4}{18} + \frac{x}{12}\right) = 36(1)$$
$$2(x - 4) + 3(x) = 36$$
$$2x - 8 + 3x = 36$$
$$5x = 44$$
$$x = 8\frac{4}{5} \text{ hours}$$
$$x = 8 \text{ hours, 48 minutes}$$

Ronnie worked 8 hours, 48 minutes on the task, or answer choice C.

9. A. This problem looks more difficult than it really is. First, no distances are given for the trip. The actual distance does not matter. Choose a distance that will simplify your calculations. For example, use 150 miles as the distance from point X to point Y. This means that the portion of the trip spent at 50 miles per hour would take 3 hours to complete and the portion of the trip spent at 30 miles per hour would take 5 hours to complete. Therefore, the entire trip of 300 miles took a total of 8 hours to complete. Divide to obtain the average speed: $300 \div 8 = 37.5$ miles per hour, or answer choice A.

10. B. Since even numbers differ by two, you can use x, $x + 2$, $x + 4$, and $x + 6$ to represent the four consecutive even numbers. Set up an equation and solve for each of the numbers. Then add to determine their sum.

$$5x = 4(x+6) - 30$$
$$5x = 4x + 24 - 30$$
$$x = -6$$
$$x + 2 = -4$$
$$x + 4 = -2$$
$$x + 6 = 0$$

Adding the four numbers gives $(-6) + (-4) + (-2) + (0) = -12$. This is answer choice B.

PART IV

THREE FULL-LENGTH ACT PRACTICE TESTS

Chapter 13

Practice Test 1

Answer Sheets

English Test

1 Ⓐ Ⓑ Ⓒ Ⓓ	26 Ⓕ Ⓖ Ⓗ Ⓙ	51 Ⓐ Ⓑ Ⓒ Ⓓ
2 Ⓕ Ⓖ Ⓗ Ⓙ	27 Ⓐ Ⓑ Ⓒ Ⓓ	52 Ⓕ Ⓖ Ⓗ Ⓙ
3 Ⓐ Ⓑ Ⓒ Ⓓ	28 Ⓕ Ⓖ Ⓗ Ⓙ	53 Ⓐ Ⓑ Ⓒ Ⓓ
4 Ⓕ Ⓖ Ⓗ Ⓙ	29 Ⓐ Ⓑ Ⓒ Ⓓ	54 Ⓕ Ⓖ Ⓗ Ⓙ
5 Ⓐ Ⓑ Ⓒ Ⓓ	30 Ⓕ Ⓖ Ⓗ Ⓙ	55 Ⓐ Ⓑ Ⓒ Ⓓ
6 Ⓕ Ⓖ Ⓗ Ⓙ	31 Ⓐ Ⓑ Ⓒ Ⓓ	56 Ⓕ Ⓖ Ⓗ Ⓙ
7 Ⓐ Ⓑ Ⓒ Ⓓ	32 Ⓕ Ⓖ Ⓗ Ⓙ	57 Ⓐ Ⓑ Ⓒ Ⓓ
8 Ⓕ Ⓖ Ⓗ Ⓙ	33 Ⓐ Ⓑ Ⓒ Ⓓ	58 Ⓕ Ⓖ Ⓗ Ⓙ
9 Ⓐ Ⓑ Ⓒ Ⓓ	34 Ⓕ Ⓖ Ⓗ Ⓙ	59 Ⓐ Ⓑ Ⓒ Ⓓ
10 Ⓕ Ⓖ Ⓗ Ⓙ	35 Ⓐ Ⓑ Ⓒ Ⓓ	60 Ⓕ Ⓖ Ⓗ Ⓙ
11 Ⓐ Ⓑ Ⓒ Ⓓ	36 Ⓕ Ⓖ Ⓗ Ⓙ	61 Ⓐ Ⓑ Ⓒ Ⓓ
12 Ⓕ Ⓖ Ⓗ Ⓙ	37 Ⓐ Ⓑ Ⓒ Ⓓ	62 Ⓕ Ⓖ Ⓗ Ⓙ
13 Ⓐ Ⓑ Ⓒ Ⓓ	38 Ⓕ Ⓖ Ⓗ Ⓙ	63 Ⓐ Ⓑ Ⓒ Ⓓ
14 Ⓕ Ⓖ Ⓗ Ⓙ	39 Ⓐ Ⓑ Ⓒ Ⓓ	64 Ⓕ Ⓖ Ⓗ Ⓙ
15 Ⓐ Ⓑ Ⓒ Ⓓ	40 Ⓕ Ⓖ Ⓗ Ⓙ	65 Ⓐ Ⓑ Ⓒ Ⓓ
16 Ⓕ Ⓖ Ⓗ Ⓙ	41 Ⓐ Ⓑ Ⓒ Ⓓ	66 Ⓕ Ⓖ Ⓗ Ⓙ
17 Ⓐ Ⓑ Ⓒ Ⓓ	42 Ⓕ Ⓖ Ⓗ Ⓙ	67 Ⓐ Ⓑ Ⓒ Ⓓ
18 Ⓕ Ⓖ Ⓗ Ⓙ	43 Ⓐ Ⓑ Ⓒ Ⓓ	68 Ⓕ Ⓖ Ⓗ Ⓙ
19 Ⓐ Ⓑ Ⓒ Ⓓ	44 Ⓕ Ⓖ Ⓗ Ⓙ	69 Ⓐ Ⓑ Ⓒ Ⓓ
20 Ⓕ Ⓖ Ⓗ Ⓙ	45 Ⓐ Ⓑ Ⓒ Ⓓ	60 Ⓕ Ⓖ Ⓗ Ⓙ
21 Ⓐ Ⓑ Ⓒ Ⓓ	46 Ⓕ Ⓖ Ⓗ Ⓙ	71 Ⓐ Ⓑ Ⓒ Ⓓ
22 Ⓕ Ⓖ Ⓗ Ⓙ	47 Ⓐ Ⓑ Ⓒ Ⓓ	72 Ⓕ Ⓖ Ⓗ Ⓙ
23 Ⓐ Ⓑ Ⓒ Ⓓ	48 Ⓕ Ⓖ Ⓗ Ⓙ	73 Ⓐ Ⓑ Ⓒ Ⓓ
24 Ⓕ Ⓖ Ⓗ Ⓙ	49 Ⓐ Ⓑ Ⓒ Ⓓ	74 Ⓕ Ⓖ Ⓗ Ⓙ
25 Ⓐ Ⓑ Ⓒ Ⓓ	50 Ⓕ Ⓖ Ⓗ Ⓙ	75 Ⓐ Ⓑ Ⓒ Ⓓ

Mathematics Test

1 Ⓐ Ⓑ Ⓒ Ⓓ Ⓔ	21 Ⓐ Ⓑ Ⓒ Ⓓ Ⓔ	41 Ⓐ Ⓑ Ⓒ Ⓓ Ⓔ
2 Ⓕ Ⓖ Ⓗ Ⓙ Ⓚ	22 Ⓕ Ⓖ Ⓗ Ⓙ Ⓚ	42 Ⓕ Ⓖ Ⓗ Ⓙ Ⓚ
3 Ⓐ Ⓑ Ⓒ Ⓓ Ⓔ	23 Ⓐ Ⓑ Ⓒ Ⓓ Ⓔ	43 Ⓐ Ⓑ Ⓒ Ⓓ Ⓔ
4 Ⓕ Ⓖ Ⓗ Ⓙ Ⓚ	24 Ⓕ Ⓖ Ⓗ Ⓙ Ⓚ	44 Ⓕ Ⓖ Ⓗ Ⓙ Ⓚ
5 Ⓐ Ⓑ Ⓒ Ⓓ Ⓔ	25 Ⓐ Ⓑ Ⓒ Ⓓ Ⓔ	45 Ⓐ Ⓑ Ⓒ Ⓓ Ⓔ
6 Ⓕ Ⓖ Ⓗ Ⓙ Ⓚ	26 Ⓕ Ⓖ Ⓗ Ⓙ Ⓚ	46 Ⓕ Ⓖ Ⓗ Ⓙ Ⓚ
7 Ⓐ Ⓑ Ⓒ Ⓓ Ⓔ	27 Ⓐ Ⓑ Ⓒ Ⓓ Ⓔ	47 Ⓐ Ⓑ Ⓒ Ⓓ Ⓔ
8 Ⓕ Ⓖ Ⓗ Ⓙ Ⓚ	28 Ⓕ Ⓖ Ⓗ Ⓙ Ⓚ	48 Ⓕ Ⓖ Ⓗ Ⓙ Ⓚ
9 Ⓐ Ⓑ Ⓒ Ⓓ Ⓔ	29 Ⓐ Ⓑ Ⓒ Ⓓ Ⓔ	49 Ⓐ Ⓑ Ⓒ Ⓓ Ⓔ
10 Ⓕ Ⓖ Ⓗ Ⓙ Ⓚ	30 Ⓕ Ⓖ Ⓗ Ⓙ Ⓚ	50 Ⓕ Ⓖ Ⓗ Ⓙ Ⓚ
11 Ⓐ Ⓑ Ⓒ Ⓓ Ⓔ	31 Ⓐ Ⓑ Ⓒ Ⓓ Ⓔ	51 Ⓐ Ⓑ Ⓒ Ⓓ Ⓔ
12 Ⓕ Ⓖ Ⓗ Ⓙ Ⓚ	32 Ⓕ Ⓖ Ⓗ Ⓙ Ⓚ	52 Ⓕ Ⓖ Ⓗ Ⓙ Ⓚ
13 Ⓐ Ⓑ Ⓒ Ⓓ Ⓔ	33 Ⓐ Ⓑ Ⓒ Ⓓ Ⓔ	53 Ⓐ Ⓑ Ⓒ Ⓓ Ⓔ
14 Ⓕ Ⓖ Ⓗ Ⓙ Ⓚ	34 Ⓕ Ⓖ Ⓗ Ⓙ Ⓚ	54 Ⓕ Ⓖ Ⓗ Ⓙ Ⓚ
15 Ⓐ Ⓑ Ⓒ Ⓓ Ⓔ	35 Ⓐ Ⓑ Ⓒ Ⓓ Ⓔ	55 Ⓐ Ⓑ Ⓒ Ⓓ Ⓔ
16 Ⓕ Ⓖ Ⓗ Ⓙ Ⓚ	36 Ⓕ Ⓖ Ⓗ Ⓙ Ⓚ	56 Ⓕ Ⓖ Ⓗ Ⓙ Ⓚ
17 Ⓐ Ⓑ Ⓒ Ⓓ Ⓔ	37 Ⓐ Ⓑ Ⓒ Ⓓ Ⓔ	57 Ⓐ Ⓑ Ⓒ Ⓓ Ⓔ
18 Ⓕ Ⓖ Ⓗ Ⓙ Ⓚ	38 Ⓕ Ⓖ Ⓗ Ⓙ Ⓚ	58 Ⓕ Ⓖ Ⓗ Ⓙ Ⓚ
19 Ⓐ Ⓑ Ⓒ Ⓓ Ⓔ	39 Ⓐ Ⓑ Ⓒ Ⓓ Ⓔ	59 Ⓐ Ⓑ Ⓒ Ⓓ Ⓔ
20 Ⓕ Ⓖ Ⓗ Ⓙ Ⓚ	40 Ⓕ Ⓖ Ⓗ Ⓙ Ⓚ	60 Ⓕ Ⓖ Ⓗ Ⓙ Ⓚ

Reading Test

1 Ⓐ Ⓑ Ⓒ Ⓓ	21 Ⓐ Ⓑ Ⓒ Ⓓ
2 Ⓕ Ⓖ Ⓗ Ⓙ	22 Ⓕ Ⓖ Ⓗ Ⓙ
3 Ⓐ Ⓑ Ⓒ Ⓓ	23 Ⓐ Ⓑ Ⓒ Ⓓ
4 Ⓕ Ⓖ Ⓗ Ⓙ	24 Ⓕ Ⓖ Ⓗ Ⓙ
5 Ⓐ Ⓑ Ⓒ Ⓓ	25 Ⓐ Ⓑ Ⓒ Ⓓ
6 Ⓕ Ⓖ Ⓗ Ⓙ	26 Ⓕ Ⓖ Ⓗ Ⓙ
7 Ⓐ Ⓑ Ⓒ Ⓓ	27 Ⓐ Ⓑ Ⓒ Ⓓ
8 Ⓕ Ⓖ Ⓗ Ⓙ	28 Ⓕ Ⓖ Ⓗ Ⓙ
9 Ⓐ Ⓑ Ⓒ Ⓓ	29 Ⓐ Ⓑ Ⓒ Ⓓ
10 Ⓕ Ⓖ Ⓗ Ⓙ	30 Ⓕ Ⓖ Ⓗ Ⓙ
11 Ⓐ Ⓑ Ⓒ Ⓓ	31 Ⓐ Ⓑ Ⓒ Ⓓ
12 Ⓕ Ⓖ Ⓗ Ⓙ	32 Ⓕ Ⓖ Ⓗ Ⓙ
13 Ⓐ Ⓑ Ⓒ Ⓓ	33 Ⓐ Ⓑ Ⓒ Ⓓ
14 Ⓕ Ⓖ Ⓗ Ⓙ	34 Ⓕ Ⓖ Ⓗ Ⓙ
15 Ⓐ Ⓑ Ⓒ Ⓓ	35 Ⓐ Ⓑ Ⓒ Ⓓ
16 Ⓕ Ⓖ Ⓗ Ⓙ	36 Ⓕ Ⓖ Ⓗ Ⓙ
17 Ⓐ Ⓑ Ⓒ Ⓓ	37 Ⓐ Ⓑ Ⓒ Ⓓ
18 Ⓕ Ⓖ Ⓗ Ⓙ	38 Ⓕ Ⓖ Ⓗ Ⓙ
19 Ⓐ Ⓑ Ⓒ Ⓓ	39 Ⓐ Ⓑ Ⓒ Ⓓ
20 Ⓕ Ⓖ Ⓗ Ⓙ	40 Ⓕ Ⓖ Ⓗ Ⓙ

Science Test

1 Ⓐ Ⓑ Ⓒ Ⓓ	21 Ⓐ Ⓑ Ⓒ Ⓓ
2 Ⓕ Ⓖ Ⓗ Ⓙ	22 Ⓕ Ⓖ Ⓗ Ⓙ
3 Ⓐ Ⓑ Ⓒ Ⓓ	23 Ⓐ Ⓑ Ⓒ Ⓓ
4 Ⓕ Ⓖ Ⓗ Ⓙ	24 Ⓕ Ⓖ Ⓗ Ⓙ
5 Ⓐ Ⓑ Ⓒ Ⓓ	25 Ⓐ Ⓑ Ⓒ Ⓓ
6 Ⓕ Ⓖ Ⓗ Ⓙ	26 Ⓕ Ⓖ Ⓗ Ⓙ
7 Ⓐ Ⓑ Ⓒ Ⓓ	27 Ⓐ Ⓑ Ⓒ Ⓓ
8 Ⓕ Ⓖ Ⓗ Ⓙ	28 Ⓕ Ⓖ Ⓗ Ⓙ
9 Ⓐ Ⓑ Ⓒ Ⓓ	29 Ⓐ Ⓑ Ⓒ Ⓓ
10 Ⓕ Ⓖ Ⓗ Ⓙ	30 Ⓕ Ⓖ Ⓗ Ⓙ
11 Ⓐ Ⓑ Ⓒ Ⓓ	31 Ⓐ Ⓑ Ⓒ Ⓓ
12 Ⓕ Ⓖ Ⓗ Ⓙ	32 Ⓕ Ⓖ Ⓗ Ⓙ
13 Ⓐ Ⓑ Ⓒ Ⓓ	33 Ⓐ Ⓑ Ⓒ Ⓓ
14 Ⓕ Ⓖ Ⓗ Ⓙ	34 Ⓕ Ⓖ Ⓗ Ⓙ
15 Ⓐ Ⓑ Ⓒ Ⓓ	35 Ⓐ Ⓑ Ⓒ Ⓓ
16 Ⓕ Ⓖ Ⓗ Ⓙ	36 Ⓕ Ⓖ Ⓗ Ⓙ
17 Ⓐ Ⓑ Ⓒ Ⓓ	37 Ⓐ Ⓑ Ⓒ Ⓓ
18 Ⓕ Ⓖ Ⓗ Ⓙ	38 Ⓕ Ⓖ Ⓗ Ⓙ
19 Ⓐ Ⓑ Ⓒ Ⓓ	39 Ⓐ Ⓑ Ⓒ Ⓓ
20 Ⓕ Ⓖ Ⓗ Ⓙ	40 Ⓕ Ⓖ Ⓗ Ⓙ

Directions

The practice tests are for assessment purposes only. These tests are designed to measure skills learned in high school that relate to success in college. Try to simulate test conditions and time yourself as you begin each of the following practice tests:

> English Test—45 minutes
>
> Mathematics Test—60 minutes
>
> Reading Test—35 minutes
>
> Science Test—35 minutes

- Calculators may be used on the mathematics test only.

- The numbered questions on each test are followed by lettered answer choices. Make sure to properly mark the answer you have selected next to the corresponding question number on the answer sheet. If you want to change an answer, erase your original answer thoroughly before marking in the new answer.

- On the actual exam, you must use a soft lead pencil and completely blacken the oval of the letter you have selected because your score is based completely on the number of questions you answer and mark correctly on the answer sheet. Do NOT use a ballpoint pen or a mechanical pencil.

- You are allowed to work on only one test at a time. If you complete a test before time is up, you may go back and review questions only in that test. You may NOT go back to previous tests, and you may NOT go forward to another test. On the actual exam day, you will be disqualified from the exam if you work on another test.

- There is no penalty for guessing, so *answer every question,* even if you need to guess.

- On the actual exam, when time is up, be sure to put your pencil down immediately. After time is up, you may NOT for any reason fill in answers. This will disqualify you from the exam.

- Do not fold or tear the pages of your test booklet.

English Test

Time: 45 Minutes
75 Questions

Directions: In the passages that follow, you will find various words and phrases underlined and numbered. A set of responses corresponding to each underlined portion will follow each passage. If the underlined portion is correct standard written English, is most appropriate to the style and feeling of the passage, and best expresses the intended idea, mark the letter indicating "NO CHANGE." If, however, the underlined portion is not the best choice given, choose the best answer to the question. For these questions, consider only the underlined portions and assume that the rest of the passage is correct as written.

You will also find questions concerning a sentence, several parts of the passage, or the whole passage. These questions do not refer to an underlined portion, but refer to the portion of the passage that is identified with the corresponding question number in a box. Choose the response you feel is best for these questions.

Passage I

The following paragraphs may or may not be in the most logical order. Paragraphs are numbered in brackets.

Feeding the Growing World Population

[1]

Estimates indicate that by 2050 our <u>worlds</u> population
₁
will increase by as much as three billion people. The
amount of food<u>, which will be needed,</u> to feed that many
₂
people is staggering. <u>Right now today</u> agriculture is
₃
taking up almost half of the <u>earth, is</u> it any wonder many
₄
experts are working on the problem <u>of how enough food</u>
₅
<u>can be grown for us in the future.</u>
₅

[2]

Water is a problem because not only will its supply
<u>not be sufficient enough</u> <u>but also it will be</u> even more
₆   ₇
contaminated than it is <u>now. Being that</u> pesticides,
₈
herbicides, and fertilizers will be used in greater amounts

to spur agricultural production. In these products,
chemicals<u>, along with other pollutants,</u> will be a danger
₉
to the environment in general. Although improved
agricultural methods over the last two decades have led to
an increased global yield of about twenty percent, that
increase is still not enough to meet the needs of a rapidly
growing population. ☐10

[3]

We must find ways <u>in which we can increase</u>
₁₁
food production to feed this expanding population<u>,</u>
<u>however devoting more land to farming is not the</u>
₁₂
<u>answer</u>. Much of the land that remains uncultivated
₁₂
<u>has been</u> made up of cities, mountains, deserts, and ice.
₁₃
The remaining frontiers are mainly in areas such as
tropical forests and savannas, which are of extreme
importance to the <u>world; especially</u> as stores of carbon
₁₄
and biodiversity. ☐15

GO ON TO THE NEXT PAGE

1. A. NO CHANGE
   B. worlds'
   C. world's
   D. World's

2. F. NO CHANGE
   G. needed
   H. which will be needed,
   J. that will be needed,

3. A. NO CHANGE
   B. Omit the underlined words
   C. Today
   D. At the present time

4. F. NO CHANGE
   G. earth: is
   H. earth. Is
   J. Earth—is

5. A. NO CHANGE
   B. of how to grow enough food for us in the future?
   C. of how it will be possible to grow enough food in the future.
   D. of growing food in the future?

6. F. NO CHANGE
   G. not be sufficient
   H. not be sufficient or be enough
   J. be insufficient

7. A. NO CHANGE
   B. but it will be also
   C. but it in addition will be
   D. but also it can be

8. F. NO CHANGE
   G. now because
   H. now; being that
   J. now: because

9. A. NO CHANGE
   B. in addition with other pollutants
   C. as well as with other pollutants;
   D. , along with other pollutants

Question 10 is the sentence preceding the boxed number 10. It poses a question about Passage I as a whole.

10. F. NO CHANGE
    G. Make this the last sentence in paragraph 1.
    H. Make this the first sentence in paragraph 3
    J. Omit this sentence.

11. A. NO CHANGE
    B. by which we can increase
    C. to increase
    D. that we can increase

12. F. NO CHANGE
    G. however, devoting more land to farming is not the answer.
    H. . However, the devotion of more land to farming is not the answer.
    J. ; however, devoting more land to farming is not the answer.

13. A. NO CHANGE
    B. will have been
    C. is
    D. should be

14. F. NO CHANGE
    G. world, especially
    H. World: especially
    J. world: especially

Question 15 poses a question about the Passage I essay as a whole.

15. Which of the following sequences of paragraphs makes the structure of the Passage I essay most logical?

    A. NO CHANGE
    B. 1, 3, 2
    C. 3, 1, 2
    D. 3, 2, 1

GO ON TO THE NEXT PAGE

Passage II

Paragraphs are numbered in brackets, and sentences in paragraphs 1 and 3 are numbered.

Identical Twins

[1]

[1] <u>As a twin, the information about similarities and</u>
₁₆
<u>differences between identical twins has always been of</u>
₁₆
<u>interest to me.</u> [2] Therefore, I was fascinated by a
₁₆
story in the *National Geographic* about twin boys in
<u>Ohio which had been separated</u> at birth in 1939. [3]
₁₇
Those two boys were adopted by different parents and,
by chance, both sets of parents named the boys "Jim."
[4] The two boys grew up in similar middle-class
homes, and neither had siblings. [5] The twins were
born in the town of Piqua. [18]

[2]

The boys had no contact until <u>each were 39 years of</u>
₁₉
<u>age,</u> when they reconnected. Since they <u>had been born</u>
₁₉   ₂₀
identical twins, maybe it's no surprise that both grew
to be six-feet tall. And maybe it's also not surprising
that <u>each was 180 pounds in weight.</u> But other
₂₁
similarities <u>cannot hardly</u> be ignored, such as that they
₂₂
both had dogs named Toy and both <u>frequently were</u>
₂₃
<u>traveling to Florida on vacation.</u> Is it also purely a
₂₃
matter of coincidence that each had first married a
woman named Linda and then, after both of them
divorced in the 1960s, each married a second time to a
woman <u>named Betty?</u> However, those are not the only
₂₄

similarities. Both <u>Jim's</u> had sons, one named James
₂₅
Alan and the other named James Allan. Both the older
Jims smoked, drank beer, and liked to work on home
carpentry projects, and, according to the researchers
who observed them, both had similar mannerisms.

[3]

[1] The example of these two men doesn't prove
anything about identical <u>twins, for example that genes</u>
₂₆
are more important than environment <u>to decide what a</u>
₂₇
<u>person</u> is going to be like. [2] The "nature versus
₂₇
nurture" argument has been going on for years, and
most scientists now believe that what a person is and
what he or she does are the result of an intricate
balance of heredity and environment. [3] These men,
however, do suggest the power of genetic inheritance.
[4] In the case of my twin sister and <u>I,</u> she works harder
₂₈
than I do in school to achieve her goals while people
say that I seem more happy-go-lucky. [5] Our genes are
definitely the same genes. [6] Even our environments
have been, for the most part, the same. [7] She believes
my parents treated us equally as we were growing up,
though I tend to believe they were actually harder on
me than they were on her. [8] Undoubtedly, researchers
will continue to study identical twins separated at birth
in an effort to understand what traits are inherited and
what traits are <u>the environment.</u> [30]
₂₉

GO ON TO THE NEXT PAGE

16. F. NO CHANGE

G. As a twin, I have always been interested in information about the similarities and differences between identical twins.

H. Information about the similarities and differences between identical twins are always of interest to me because I am a twin.

J. Being as how I am a twin, information about the similarities and differences of identical twins has always been of interest to me.

17. A. NO CHANGE

B. Ohio, which had been separated

C. Ohio, that had been separated

D. Ohio separated

18. The author of the passage wants to eliminate a sentence in this paragraph. Which sentence could be omitted without changing the main idea and direction of the passage as a whole?

F. None of the sentences should be eliminated.

G. Sentence 2

H. Sentence 3

J. Sentence 5

19. A. NO CHANGE

B. they were 39 years old,

C. they had become 39 years of age,

D. each was 39 years old,

20. F. NO CHANGE

G. are born

H. were both born

J. have been born

21. A. NO CHANGE

B. each is 180 pounds.

C. each weighed 180 pounds.

D. both weighed 180 pounds each.

22. F. NO CHANGE

G. can't hardly

H. hardly cannot

J. can hardly

23. A. NO CHANGE

B. had frequently been traveling to Florida on vacation.

C. had frequently traveled to Florida on vacation.

D. are traveling to Florida on vacation frequently.

24. F. NO CHANGE

G. named Betty.

H. who were named Betty.

J. named Betty!

25. A. NO CHANGE

B. Jims'

C. Jims

D. men named Jim

26. F. NO CHANGE

G. twins; for example that genes

H. twins, for example whose genes

J. twins. For example, that genes

27. A. NO CHANGE

B. in order to decide what a person

C. to deciding what a person

D. in deciding what a person

28. F. NO CHANGE

G. me

H. I myself

J. myself

29. A. NO CHANGE

B. the environmental ones.

C. the result of environment.

D. the environmentally based ones.

30. Which of the following would improve the unity of paragraph 3?

F. citing more case histories on the issue of "nature vs. nurture"

G. eliminating sentences 4–7

H. expanding on the experiences of the author and her sister.

J. eliminating sentence 8.

GO ON TO THE NEXT PAGE

Passage III

The National Parks

According to the British diplomat, James Bryce, establishing national parklands was the best idea America ever had. Bryce made the statement in 1912, when there were hardly any parks in the country. It wasn't until four years later that a federal agency <u>which was designed to look after them.</u> Now the National Park Service is almost a hundred years old, and we ought to celebrate <u>their</u> amazing successes. It <u>has went</u> from overseeing fourteen parks, 21 monuments, and a reservation of six million acres to overseeing 390 areas of 84 million acres located in 45 states, the District of Columbia, and islands in the Pacific and Caribbean. In the beginning, <u>there was a small amount of rangers to oversee</u> the parks while now approximately 20,000 employees are employed by the National Park Service. 36

The parks are overwhelmed by <u>visitors who, in the words of one person,</u> are <u>"Loving the parks to death."</u> Because of recent budget shortfalls, the park system has been unable to keep up with its high standards of park maintenance. And park visitors do not always do their part <u>for keeping</u> the sites in good order, <u>especially unsupervised.</u> Some parks have actually limited the number of daily visitors, a necessary but unpopular move.

With <u>less dollars but more visitors</u> wanting to come to the parks, <u>it is believed by many people</u> that the future of the National Parks System may be in danger. On the other hand, other people remain unaware of the problems that pose a threat to the parks, <u>such as maintenance projects left unfinished, repairs postponed, and programs for park visitors eliminated.</u> The parks will continue to offer beautiful vistas and memorable experiences to visitors, but unless Americans pay attention and offer support, they will have only <u>theirselves</u> to blame if John Bryce's description of the national parks as "the best idea America ever had" becomes an empty phrase. 45

31. A. NO CHANGE
B. James Bryce,
C. James Bryce
D. , whose name was James Bryce,

32. F. NO CHANGE
G. was designed to look after them.
H. which had been designed to look after them.
J. that was designed to look after them.

33. A. NO CHANGE
B. it's
C. there
D. its

34. F. NO CHANGE
G. had went
H. has gone
J. will have gone

GO ON TO THE NEXT PAGE

35. A. NO CHANGE
B. were a small amount of rangers to oversee
C. a small number of rangers oversaw
D. were a smaller number of rangers to oversee

36. Which of the following choices most effectively signals a shift from this paragraph to the next paragraph?

F. The beauty and grandeur of the national parks have inspired not only the visitors who arrive every day but also famous artists and writers.
G. Supporters of the national park system look forward to adding even more areas to the park service in the future.
H. Visitors to the many parks under the National Park System include large numbers of foreign travelers, who often remark on the parks' beauty and variety.
J. Even with the addition of personnel to the National Park Service over the years, the parks suffer today from manpower problems because of recent budget shortfalls.

37. A. NO CHANGE
B. visitors, that in the words of one person
C. visitors whom in the words of one person
D. visitors, whom in the words of one person,

38. F. NO CHANGE
G. "loving the parks to death."
H. loving the parks to death.
J. loving the parks to death!

39. A. NO CHANGE
B. to keep
C. for the maintenance of
D. for making

40. F. NO CHANGE
G. especially in the case of a lack of supervision.
H. especially when the camp sites are unsupervised.
J. at those times being unsupervised.

41. A. NO CHANGE
B. few dollars but more visitors
C. more visitors but less dollars
D. fewer dollars but more visitors

42. F. NO CHANGE
G. it is believed, by many people
H. many people, they believe
J. many people believe

43. If the writer were to delete the underlined portion from this sentence and end the sentence with a period after "parks," the paragraph would lose

A. logic and coherence.
B. the writer's tone of moral superiority.
C. details that support the need for increasing park system funds.
D. a clear notion of the responsibilities of park rangers.

44. F. NO CHANGE
G. themselfs
H. themselves
J. they theirselves

Question 45 poses a question about Passage III as a whole.

45. Which of the following would most improve the essay?

A. a personal account of the writer's experiences in a national park
B. a list of areas that have been projected as sites for new parks
C. specific details about the costs of running the National Park Service
D. comparison with the park systems that exist in other countries

GO ON TO THE NEXT PAGE

Passage IV

Paragraphs are numbered in brackets, and sentences in paragraphs 1 and 3 are numbered.

Classical Art

[1]

[1] <u>Looking at art from ancient times, it is</u>
46
<u>important for us to remember that</u> we are not
46
envisaging objects in the same way <u>as the ancients.</u> [2]
47
In Greece, statues from the archaic period <u>for example</u>
48
were not displayed in a glass <u>showcase: which is</u> the
49
way we usually view them today. [3] Even the most
beautiful artifacts were to be used rather than
<u>having people simply admire them.</u> [4] Among some of
50
the surviving pottery vessels are *amphorae* and *kraters,*
which were used for mixing wine and water, *hydria*
(water jars), and *lekythos,* bottles for oils that were
used as funeral offerings. 51 52

[2]

Modern viewers <u>who hold Greek art in high esteem</u>
53
are even fascinated by mere fragments of ancient
pottery, while the ancient Greeks would have no reason
to view their broken, everyday dishes with such
reverence. Museums today contain many ancient
Greek pieces that have been partially destroyed as well
as pieces that are intact. <u>It is a fact that</u> much of the
54
archaeological record of life in ancient Greece depends

on the existence of Greek pottery. But modern viewers
are impressed by the artistic merits of the pottery; the
ancient Greeks were interested only in its utility.

[3]

[1] The difference between the reaction of modern
viewers and the reaction of early Greeks to their own
pottery is of course understandable. [2] Much of the art
of ancient Greece had a different role <u>to that</u> of art
55
today. [3] The concept of "art appreciation" or the belief
in "art for art's sake" was unknown in ancient Greece.
[4] Neither an "art market" <u>nor did "collectors of art"</u>
56
<u>exist</u> at that time. [5] Greeks didn't even have a separate
56
word for art in our sense<u>; only craft.</u> [6] Artists were
57
considered the way shoemakers were, <u>as providing a</u>
58
<u>commodity.</u> [7] During that period, all the visual arts,
58
including sculpture, <u>was held</u> in such low regard that the
59
artists were seen as manual laborers. [8] Greek statues
were not ostentatiously displayed as art in a wealthy
man's home but were commissioned by aristocrats or
the state to serve as public memorials. 60

46. **F.** NO CHANGE
    G. Looking at art from ancient times, it
        should be remembered that
    H. To look at art from ancient times, it is
        important to remember that
    J. Looking at art from ancient times, we
        should remember that

47. **A.** NO CHANGE
    B. as the ancients did envisage them.
    C. that the ancients did.
    D. in which the ancients did envisage them.

GO ON TO THE NEXT PAGE

48.
F. NO CHANGE
G. , for example,
H. —for example
J. for example,

49.
A. NO CHANGE
B. showcase, being
C. showcase, that is
D. showcase, which is

50.
F. NO CHANGE
G. to have people simply admire them.
H. simply admired.
J. being simply admired by people.

51. Which of the following choices, if any, would be best as the last sentence of paragraph 1?

A. No sentence should be added.
B. Such pottery was created for its practicality, not for its beauty.
C. Approximately one hundred of such items have actually weathered the long period between ancient Greece and modern times.
D. Many other types of urns, identified by their unique shapes, were also produced during this period.

52. Which of the following would be the best choice for the first sentence of paragraph 2?

F. The aesthetic appreciation of early Greek pottery came centuries after its creation.
G. The names of the artists who created early Greek pottery are unknown.
H. Early Greek paintings have not withstood the centuries as well as ancient pottery.
J. The unique techniques used to decorate early Greek pottery are remarkably sophisticated.

53.
A. NO CHANGE
B. whom hold Greek art in high esteem
C. whom have held Greek art in high esteem
D. who have held Greek art in high esteem

54.
F. NO CHANGE
G. Omit the underlined section
H. It is true that
J. Interestingly,

55.
A. NO CHANGE
B. from that
C. of that
D. as that

56.
F. NO CHANGE
G. or "collectors of art" have existed
H. nor "collectors of art" had existed
J. nor "art collectors" existed

57.
A. NO CHANGE
B. , only a word for craft.
C. , only for craft.
D. but craft only.

58.
F. NO CHANGE
G. , providing a commodity that is useful to people.
H. ; as providing a commodity.
J. : providing commodities.

59.
A. NO CHANGE
B. had been held
C. were held
D. was considered with

60. The most logical position for sentence 8 of paragraph 3 is

F. its current position.
G. after sentence 4.
H. after sentence 1.
J. after sentence 6.

Passage V

Paragraphs are numbered in brackets, and sentences in paragraphs 1 and 4 are numbered.

A Blazing Memory

[1]

[1] Many years ago, when my neighborhood pal Jimmy and <u>me</u> left our houses on July 5th, we didn't
61
have a clue how the day would turn out. [2] We were seven years old, and by and large good kids, but both of us were adventurous and <u>curious; traits</u> that
62
sometimes would lead to trouble. [3] Once, for example,

GO ON TO THE NEXT PAGE

when we were five, we tried to walk by ourselves all the way downtown, five miles away. [4] This town was a small, sleepy town with few residents and fewer businesses. 63 64

[2]

The field between our two houses had dried up during the month before, and maybe this should have been a warning to us that lighting sparklers left over from the Fourth was not the best idea we <u>had ever had.</u>
₆₅
Also, it was unfortunate that Jimmy <u>would have</u>
₆₆
<u>brought</u> along a book of matches. He lit <u>one</u> and then
₆₆   ₆₇
I lit one, and then he lit another, and so on.

[3]

The sparklers produced a burst of light, followed by glowing embers. What a rush that was! I was the first to realize that the embers had <u>descended down into</u>
₆₈
the weeds and that the weeds were smoldering.
<u>Panicking, my shoe came off in a flash,</u> I threw it on
₆₉
the smoldering patch, which by now was seriously becoming a small fire. Jimmy and I looked at each other in dismay and ran as <u>quick from the spot</u> as we
₇₀
could. My burning shoe would be the evidence that would convict us.

[4]

[1] By the time we reached the road, most of the field was in flames. [2] Fortunately, a nosy woman who lived down the street called the fire department before any houses—including mine and Jimmy's—were damaged.

[3] This <u>escapade of ours or maybe crime is a better word</u>
₇₁
led our parents to ground us for what seemed an eternity and also to subject us to long and (dare I say it?) boring lectures on the danger of playing with matches. [4] I don't blame them, though. <u>In fact,</u> today I give those
₇₂
same lectures to my children, who I suspect are just as bored as I was. [5] <u>As for Jimmy and me,</u> we still get
₇₃
together once in awhile. [6] We are definitely wiser, but we haven't lost all our sense of adventure. 74 75

61. A. NO CHANGE
   B. I myself
   C. me myself
   D. I

62. F. NO CHANGE
   G. curious, traits
   H. curious; the traits
   J. curious, which are traits

63. The first paragraph could be improved by

   A. reversing the order of sentences 3 and 4.
   B. adding a brief description of the writer's neighborhood.
   C. eliminating sentence 4.
   D. including the year in which the following incident occurred.

64. Which of the following sentences links paragraph 2 most effectively to paragraph 1?

   F. On the day in question, Jimmy and I were feeling especially eager for adventure, stirred up by the excitement of the Fourth of July.
   G. Jimmy had lived next door to me for over three years, and his parents were much less strict than mine.
   H. July 5th was hotter than usual, actually setting a record, which we learned later.
   J. The following paragraphs are an account of what happened to Jimmy and me on the 5th of July.

GO ON TO THE NEXT PAGE

65. A. NO CHANGE
B. will have ever had.
C. might have ever had
D. would of ever had

66. F. NO CHANGE
G. has brought
H. is bringing
J. had brought

67. A. NO CHANGE
B. a sparkler
C. his
D. matches

68. F. NO CHANGE
G. descended into
H. descended down to
J. ascended

69. A. NO CHANGE
B. I was panicking, my shoe was taken off in a flash,
C. Panicking, I took my shoe off in a flash.
D. On account of panicking, my shoe came off in a flash,

70. F. NO CHANGE
G. quick away from the spot
H. so quick from the spot
J. quickly from the spot

71. A. NO CHANGE
B. escapade of ours; or maybe crime is a better word;
C. escapade of ours, although the word crime is maybe a better word,
D. escapade of ours, or maybe crime is a better word,

72. F. NO CHANGE
G. Omit the phrase.
H. It's a fact that
J. I find that

73. A. NO CHANGE
B. As to Jimmy and me
C. As for Jimmy and I
D. As for myself and Jimmy

74. The writer wants to add a sentence after sentence 2 in the paragraph to make the immediate results of the fire more vivid. Which of the following choices would be best to add?

F. Jimmy and I stared at the flames as if we couldn't believe the spectacular scene we had created.

G. But I'll never forget the screaming sound of the siren as the town's rickety old fire truck screeched around the corner, raced wildly down our street, and coughed to a stop in front of the field.

H. All I could think of was how my father's face would turn white and then purple when he found out that his child had been responsible for this disaster.

J. The neighbor who had called the police stood on her front porch and looked down the street, searching for the culprits responsible for the fire.

Item 75 poses a question about Passage V as a whole.

75. The language of Passage V is best described as

A. persuasive.
B. slang.
C. colloquial.
D. defensive.

IF YOU FINISH BEFORE TIME IS CALLED, CHECK YOUR WORK ON THIS SECTION ONLY. DO NOT WORK ON ANY OTHER SECTION IN THE TEST.

STOP

Mathematics Test

Time: 60 Minutes

60 Questions

Directions: After solving each problem, choose the correct answer and fill in the corresponding space on your answer sheet. Do not spend too much time on any one problem. Solve as many problems as you can and return to the others if time permits. You are allowed to use a calculator on this test.

Note: Unless it is otherwise stated, you can assume all of the following:

1. Figures are NOT necessarily drawn to scale.
2. Geometric figures lie in a plane.
3. The word "line" means a straight line.
4. The word "average" refers to the arithmetic mean.

---

1. If the following points were graphed on the standard number line, which one would be the closest to 7?

    A. $6\sqrt{2}$
    B. $2\sqrt{6}$
    C. $5\sqrt{3}$
    D. $3\sqrt{5}$
    E. $4\sqrt{4}$

2. If $wxyz \neq 0$, which of the following is equivalent to $\dfrac{w^2x}{yz^2}$?

    F. $\dfrac{xw^4y^3z}{w^2z^3x^2y^4}$

    G. $\dfrac{w^3z^2x^5y}{wz^4x^4y^2}$

    H. $\dfrac{z^6x^3y^3w^3}{w^5z^4x^4y^2}$

    J. $\dfrac{yz^2}{w^2x}$

    K. $\dfrac{(wx)^2}{(yz)^2}$

3. If $7x = 3y$, what is the ratio of x to y?

    A. $\dfrac{7}{3}$

    B. $\dfrac{7}{4}$

    C. $\dfrac{4}{3}$

    D. $\dfrac{4}{7}$

    E. $\dfrac{3}{7}$

4. What is the value of $-\left|2-\left|6-(-2)\right|\right|$?

    F. -6
    G. -4
    H. -2
    J. 2
    K. 4

5. If two sides of a triangle measure 9 inches and 12 inches, what must the length of the third side be, in inches, so that the area of the triangle is a maximum?

    A. $3\sqrt{3}$
    B. 10.5
    C. 15
    D. $9\sqrt{3}$
    E. $12\sqrt{2}$

6. Beka's only income is her Social Security check. She is currently receiving $940 per month in benefits. She has been informed that this amount will increase 5.5 percent next year. How much will her benefits be next year?

    F. $945.17
    G. $945.50
    H. $991.70
    J. $995.00
    K. $1,457.00

GO ON TO THE NEXT PAGE

7. Solve the following equation for y:
$\frac{1}{2}(y+3) = \frac{3}{2}(2y-3)$

  A. $-\frac{3}{2}$

  B. $-\frac{6}{5}$

  C. $-\frac{5}{6}$

  D. $\frac{12}{5}$

  E. $\frac{5}{2}$

8. Which of the following is equivalent to $(x^2y - xy^2)(x^2y + xy^2)$?

  F. $xy(xy^3 - x^3y)$

  G. $xy(x^3y - xy^3)$

  H. $x^2y^2(x^2 - 2xy + y^2)$

  J. $x^2y^2(x^2 - y^2)$

  K. $x^2y^2(x^2y^4 - x^4y^2)$

9. A \$4,500 computer is scheduled for a 12 percent price drop. What will be the new price?

  A. \$3,300

  B. \$3,960

  C. \$4,104

  D. \$4,446

  E. \$4,488

10. What is the distance between the x-intercepts of the two lines defined by $6x - 3y = 2$ and $5y - 4x = 8$?

  F. 1

  G. $\frac{5}{3}$

  H. $\frac{7}{3}$

  J. $\frac{11}{3}$

  K. 5

11. In the figure that follows, if $AB = 25$ then what is the length of DE?

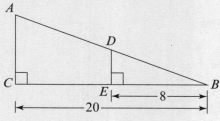

  A. 4

  B. 6

  C. 8

  D. 10

  E. 12

12. If line m is perpendicular to the line $5x - 2y = -2$, what is the slope of line m?

  F. $-\frac{5}{2}$

  G. $-\frac{2}{5}$

  H. $\frac{2}{3}$

  J. $\frac{5}{2}$

  K. -10

Use the following information to answer questions 13–15.

A political club is composed of nine members, five men and four women. Of the five men, two are Democrats and three are Republicans. Of the four women, three are Democrats and one is a Republican.

13. How many ways can the club select a committee of four members such that two are men and two are women?

  A. 4

  B. 24

  C. 48

  D. 60

  E. 90

GO ON TO THE NEXT PAGE

14. What is the ratio of the percentage of men who are Democrats to the percentage of women who are Democrats?

F. $\dfrac{7}{15}$

G. $\dfrac{8}{15}$

H. $\dfrac{2}{3}$

J. $\dfrac{4}{5}$

K. $\dfrac{5}{4}$

15. If a member of the club is chosen at random, what is the approximate probability it is a Democratic woman?

A. 0.11
B. 0.22
C. 0.25
D. 0.33
E. 0.56

16. Using the following figure, write y in terms of w, x, and z.

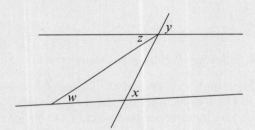

F. $y = x + w - z$
G. $y = w + z$
H. $y = x + z - w$
J. $y = 180° - (w + x - z)$
K. $y = w + z - x$

17. A bag contains seven red apples and three green apples. The average weight of the seven red apples is 190 grams, and the average weight of all ten apples is 210 grams. What is the approximate average weight of the three green apples, in grams?

A. 220
B. 230
C. 240
D. 250
E. 260

18. Given right triangle ABC shown here, which of the following is the value of $\cot B$?

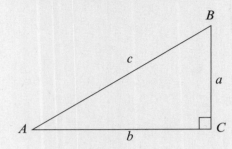

F. $\dfrac{a}{b}$

G. $\dfrac{b}{a}$

H. $\dfrac{b}{c}$

J. $\dfrac{c}{b}$

K. $\dfrac{a}{c}$

19. In the following figure, $\overline{AB}$ is tangent to circle O at point C, $\overline{CD} \parallel \overline{AO}$. If $y = 70°$, then what is the value of x?

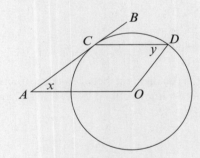

A. 15°
B. 18°
C. 20°
D. 25°
E. 35°

GO ON TO THE NEXT PAGE

20. During an average summer day, a homeowner uses 75 KWH of electricity, 35 KWH of which is peak usage, and the remaining 40 KWH is non-peak usage. The homeowner has a choice of rate plans: a flat rate plan with a charge of $0.11/KWH and a flexible rate plan with a charge of $0.07/KWH for non-peak usage and $0.20/KWH for peak usage. What would be the average daily savings by using the flat rate plan instead of the flexible rate plan?

F. $1.40
G. $1.45
H. $1.50
J. $1.55
K. $1.60

21. Three lines are graphed in the standard (x, y) coordinate plane. The equations for these three lines are $3x - 2y = -4$, $y = \frac{3}{2}x + 2$, and $2x = 3y - 4$. How many points of intersection are there for these three lines?

A. 0
B. 1
C. 2
D. 3
E. 4

22. Solve for x: $4x + \frac{13}{3} = x + \frac{19}{3}$

F. $\frac{2}{3}$
G. $\frac{3}{4}$
H. $\frac{4}{3}$
J. $\frac{3}{2}$
K. $\frac{5}{2}$

23. If $(2^x)(8^y) = 4^z$, then what is the value of z in terms of x and y?

A. $z = \frac{2x + y}{8}$
B. $z = \frac{x + 3y}{2}$
C. $z = \frac{3xy}{4}$
D. $z = \frac{3x + y}{2}$
E. $z = \frac{6x + y}{2}$

24. If $\sin X = -\frac{1}{3}$ and $\cos Y = \frac{1}{2}$, then both angle X and angle Y could be located in which quadrant?

F. First quadrant
G. Second quadrant
H. Third quadrant
J. Fourth quadrant
K. Cannot be determined from the information given

25. A baker is going to make cupcakes for a party. She has a choice of three different cake mixes, six different frostings, and four different toppings. If each cupcake uses one cake mix, one frosting, and two different toppings, how many different combinations of cupcakes can the baker make?

A. 11
B. 36
C. 72
D. 108
E. 144

Use the following information to answer questions 26–28.

A suitcase in the shape of a rectangular prism has an inside length of 20 inches, an inside width of 14 inches, and an inside height of 10 inches. If the expansion zipper is opened, the inside height increases by 2 inches.

26. What is the inside volume of the suitcase, in cubic inches, when the expansion zipper is closed?

F. 42
G. 2660
H. 2800
J. 3040
K. 3360

27. By what percent does the inside volume increase when the expansion zipper is opened?

A. 10%
B. 17%
C. 20%
D. 22%
E. 24%

GO ON TO THE NEXT PAGE

28. How many 2-inch cubes can be packed inside the suitcase with the expansion zipper open?

F. 210
G. 360
H. 400
J. 420
K. 630

29. Simplify the following: $\dfrac{\left(4\times10^{6}\right)\left(9\times10^{4}\right)}{\left(2\times10^{2}\right)\left(3\times10^{5}\right)}$

A. 6×10^{1}
B. 6×10^{3}
C. 3×10^{4}
D. 6×10^{14}
E. 3×10^{15}

30. If $6(2x-3)-4(4x-5)=7$, then what is the value of x?

F. $-2\le x<-1$
G. $-1\le x<0$
H. $0\le x<1$
J. $1\le x<2$
K. $2\le x<3$

31. What is the value of the following determinant?

$$\begin{vmatrix} -4 & 2 \\ 3 & 5 \end{vmatrix} = ?$$

A. -26
B. -14
C. 14
D. 26
E. None of these

32. One angle measures $\dfrac{3\pi}{5}$ radians, and a second angle measures $\dfrac{2\pi}{3}$ radians. What is the sum, s, of these two angles measured in degrees?

F. $30°<s\le70°$
G. $70°<s\le110°$
H. $110°<s\le150°$
J. $150°<s\le190°$
K. $190°<s\le230°$

33. What is the slope of the line $\dfrac{1}{4}x-\dfrac{1}{3}y=5$?

A. $-\dfrac{4}{3}$
B. $-\dfrac{3}{4}$
C. $\dfrac{3}{4}$
D. $\dfrac{4}{3}$
E. 12

34. In the standard (x, y) coordinate plane, what is the distance between the points $(-4, 2)$ and $(-8, -4)$?

F. $2\sqrt{5}$
G. $2\sqrt{13}$
H. $2\sqrt{37}$
J. $2\sqrt{41}$
K. $6\sqrt{5}$

35. The following four operations were performed in succession on a given value; divide by 3, multiply by 6, divide by 4, and multiply by 3. Which of the following two operations, when performed in succession would accomplish the same thing?

A. Multiply by 9 and then divide by 4.
B. Divide by 4 and then multiply by 3.
C. Multiply by 4 and then divide by 3.
D. Divide by 3 and then multiply by 2.
E. Multiply by 3 and then divide by 2.

GO ON TO THE NEXT PAGE

36. Given the right triangle is the following figure, find the value of $\dfrac{\sin P}{\tan Q \cos P}$.

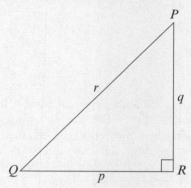

F. $\dfrac{q^2}{r^2}$

G. $\dfrac{p^2}{r^2}$

H. $\dfrac{p^2}{q^2}$

J. $\dfrac{pr^2}{q^2}$

K. $\dfrac{q}{rp}$

37. Given two numbers, x and y, such that $xy \neq 0$, if the difference between their product (xy) and their quotient $\left(\dfrac{x}{y}\right)$ is two more than the difference between their quotient and their product, then what is the value of x in terms of y?

A. $x = \dfrac{y-1}{y+1}$

B. $x = \dfrac{y^2+1}{y}$

C. $x = \dfrac{y}{y^2-1}$

D. $x = \dfrac{y^2-1}{y}$

E. $x = \dfrac{y+1}{y^2}$

38. A chord of length 8 cm is drawn in a circle that is 12 cm in diameter. How far, in cm, is the chord from the center of the circle?

F. 3

G. $2\sqrt{3}$

H. $2\sqrt{5}$

J. $3\sqrt{3}$

K. $4\sqrt{2}$

39. The depth of paint in a can that is 10 inches in diameter is 5 inches. If the paint in the can is poured into another can that has a diameter of 8 inches, approximately how deep would the paint be, in inches?

A. 6.6

B. 7.1

C. 7.4

D. 7.8

E. 8.1

40. What is the graph of the solution set of $4 - y > -2$?

F.

G.

H.

J.
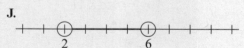

K.
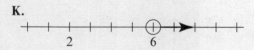

41. If $f(x) = 2x - 5$ and $g(x) = 4x - 2$, then what is the value of $f\big(g(x)\big) - g\big(f(x)\big)$?

A. 0

B. 10

C. 13

D. $16x - 31$

E. $8x + 10$

GO ON TO THE NEXT PAGE

42. In the standard (x, y) coordinate plane, point A and point B lie on the line $x = 2y$. The midpoint of $\overline{AB}$ is $(-2, -1)$. If the x-coordinate of point A is 6, then what is the y-coordinate of point B?

- **F.** −8
- **G.** −7
- **H.** −6
- **J.** −5
- **K.** −4

43. If the * of a number is defined as the sum of the square of the number and three times the number, then what is **5?

- **A.** 40
- **B.** 460
- **C.** 1040
- **D.** 1720
- **E.** 1980

44. As shown in the diagram that follows, circle O and circle P, each with a diameter of 16 inches, are drawn such that each circle passes through the center of the other circle. What is the distance, in inches, around this figure, starting at point A and passing through point B, point C, point D, and back to point A?

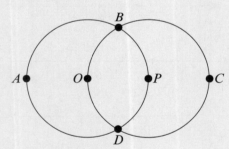

- **F.** 32π
- **G.** 24π
- **H.** $\dfrac{64\pi}{3}$
- **J.** $\dfrac{96\pi}{5}$
- **K.** 16π

45. What is the sum of the three solutions of $x^3 - 2x^2 = 24x$?

- **A.** −5
- **B.** −2
- **C.** 0
- **D.** 2
- **E.** 5

46. Point A is located on the real number line at a coordinate of (-5). Point A moves three units to the right, then one unit to the left, then three units to the right, then one unit to the left. . . . This "right 3, left 1" pattern is continued until point A arrives at a coordinate of 20. What is the total distance traveled by point A from the time it leaves (-5) until it arrives at 20?

- **F.** 46
- **G.** 47
- **H.** 48
- **J.** 49
- **K.** 50

47. How many gallons of plain water must be added to 32 gallons of a 15 percent salt solution to obtain a 12 percent salt solution?

- **A.** 4
- **B.** 6
- **C.** 8
- **D.** 10
- **E.** 12

48. What is the sum of the 25 odd integers from 13 through 61?

- **F.** 782
- **G.** 798
- **H.** 875
- **J.** 890
- **K.** 925

GO ON TO THE NEXT PAGE

49. A right pyramid with a height of 15 feet has a square base, 10 feet on each side. Each of the four faces of the pyramid are congruent isosceles triangles. What is the total surface area of the four faces of the pyramid in square feet?

A. $100\sqrt{5}$
B. $100\sqrt{10}$
C. $225\sqrt{2}$
D. 324
E. $150\sqrt{5}$

50. Four circles of equal size are inscribed in a square, as shown in the following figure below. Approximately what percent of the square's area is covered by the four circles?

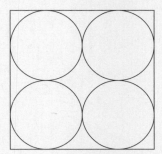

F. 76%
G. 78%
H. 80%
J. 82%
K. 84%

51. If $\dfrac{|x|}{|y|} < 1$, then which of the following could be true?

I. $x > y$
II. $x < y$
III. $x + y = 0$

A. I only
B. II only
C. III only
D. I and II only
E. II and III only

52. What is the period of the function shown in the following figure?

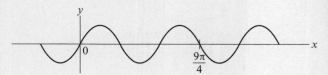

F. $\dfrac{\pi}{2}$
G. $\dfrac{3\pi}{4}$
H. π
J. $\dfrac{3\pi}{2}$
K. $\dfrac{9\pi}{4}$

53. Which of the following is equivalent to $x = \log_y z$?

A. $y^x = z$
B. $x^y = z$
C. $z^x = y$
D. $z^x = z$
E. None of these

54. A storage container is in the shape of a rectangular prism with a length of 40 feet, a width of 10 feet, and a height of 10 feet. What is the length of the main diagonal of the prism?

F. $10\sqrt{18}$
G. $20\sqrt{5}$
H. $40\sqrt{2}$
J. $25\sqrt{10}$
K. $40\sqrt{10}$

55. In the standard (x, y) coordinate plane, $\overline{XY}$ has endpoints of $(-2, 6)$ and $(6, -10)$. Which of the following are true statements about $\overline{XY}$?

I. $\overline{XY}$ intercepts the negative x-axis.
II. $\overline{XY}$ intercepts the negative y-axis.
III. The distance from the midpoint of $\overline{XY}$ to the origin is $2\sqrt{2}$.

A. None of these
B. Exactly one of these
C. I and II only
D. II and III only
E. All of these

GO ON TO THE NEXT PAGE

56. In the standard (x, y) coordinate plane, the equation of a circle is

$$\left(\frac{x-2}{2}\right)^2 + \left(\frac{y+2}{2}\right)^2 = 1$$

What is the area of the circle?

F. π
G. 2π
H. 4π
J. 8π
K. 16π

57. If $2x - y = 20$ and $y = 16 - x$, then what is the value of $x - y$?

A. 4
B. 8
C. 12
D. 16
E. 20

58. If $A = \begin{bmatrix} 3 & 4 \\ -1 & 2 \end{bmatrix}$ and $B = \begin{bmatrix} -2 & 1 \\ 3 & -1 \end{bmatrix}$, then what is the matrix product AB?

F. $\begin{bmatrix} -6 & 4 \\ -3 & -2 \end{bmatrix}$

G. $\begin{bmatrix} -6 & -1 \\ 12 & -2 \end{bmatrix}$

H. $\begin{bmatrix} 6 & -1 \\ 8 & -3 \end{bmatrix}$

J. $[-10]$
K. $[-7]$

59. If $a = 3 - 2i$ and $b = 2 - 3i$, then what is the value of $\frac{a}{b}$?

A. $-i$
B. $\frac{6-5i}{5}$
C. $\frac{5-6i}{13}$
D. $\frac{12+5i}{13}$
E. $\frac{5-5i}{6}$

60. In the following figure, $\cot \angle ABC = \frac{4}{3}$ and $\cos \angle CAD = \frac{3}{4}$. What is the value of $\frac{x}{y}$?

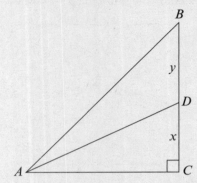

F. $\frac{4\sqrt{7}-7}{7}$

G. $\frac{4\sqrt{7}+7}{9}$

H. $\frac{9\sqrt{7}+4}{7}$

J. $\frac{9\sqrt{7}-4}{9}$

K. 1

IF YOU FINISH BEFORE TIME IS CALLED, CHECK YOUR WORK ON THIS SECTION ONLY. DO NOT WORK ON ANY OTHER SECTION IN THE TEST.

Reading Test

Time: 35 Minutes

40 Questions

Directions: Each of the four passages in this test is followed by a series of multiple-choice questions. Read the passage and choose the best answer to each question. Return to the passage as often as necessary to answer the questions.

Passage I

PROSE FICTION: This passage is from *The House of Mirth* by Edith Wharton (Scribners, 1905).

After two years of hungry roaming, Mrs. Bart had died—died of a deep disgust. She had hated dinginess, and it was her fate to be dingy. Her visions of a brilliant marriage for Lily had faded
(5) after the first year.

"People can't marry you if they don't see you— and how can they see you in these holes where we're stuck?" That was the burden of her lament; and her last adjuration to her daughter was to
(10) escape from dinginess if she could.

"Don't let it creep up on you and drag you down. Fight your way out of it somehow—you're young and can do it," she insisted.

She had died during one of their brief visits to
(15) New York and there Lily at once became the centre of a family council composed of the wealthy relatives whom she had been taught to despise for living like pigs. It may be that they had an inkling of the sentiments in which she
(20) had been brought up, for none of them manifested a very lively desire for her company; indeed, the question threatened to remain unsolved till Mrs. Peniston with a sigh announced: "I'll try her for a year."

(25) Every one was surprised, but one and all concealed their surprise lest Mrs. Peniston should be alarmed by it into reconsidering her decision.

Mrs. Peniston was Mr. Bart's widowed sister, and if she was by no means the richest of the
(30) family group, its other members nevertheless abounded in reasons why she was clearly destined by Providence to assume the charge of Lily. In the first place she was alone, and it would be charming for her to have a young companion. Then, she
(35) sometimes traveled, and Lily's familiarity with foreign customs—deplored as a misfortune by her more conservative relatives—would at least enable her to act as a kind of courier. But as a matter of fact, Mrs. Peniston had not been affected by these
(40) considerations. She had taken the girl simply because no one else would have her and because

she had the kind of moral *mauvaise honte* which makes the public display of selfishness difficult, though it does not interfere with its private
(45) indulgence. It would have been impossible for Mrs. Peniston to be heroic on a desert island, but with the eyes of her little world upon her she took a certain pleasure in her act.

She reaped the reward to which disinterestedness
(50) is entitled, and found an agreeable companion in her niece. She had expected to find Lily headstrong, critical, and "foreign"—for even Mrs. Peniston, though she occasionally went abroad, had the family dread of foreignness—but the girl
(55) showed a pliancy which, to a more penetrating mind than her aunt's, might have been less reassuring than the open selfishness of youth. Misfortune had made Lily supple instead of hardening her, and a pliable substance is less easy
(60) to break than a stiff one.

Mrs. Peniston, however, did not suffer from her niece's adaptability. Lily had no intention of taking advantage of her aunt's good nature. She was in truth grateful for the refuge offered her;
(65) Mrs. Peniston's opulent interior was at least not externally dingy. But dinginess is a quality which assumes all manner of disguises, and Lily soon found that it was as latent in the expensive routine of her aunt's life as in the makeshift
(70) existence of a continental pension.

1. From Passage I, one can infer that Lily and her mother

  A. had been deserted by Lily's father.

  B. were fortune hunters.

  C. had been living abroad.

  D. did not get along with each other.

2. Mrs. Peniston takes Lily in because she

  F. wants to appear unselfish.

  G. is lonely.

  H. plans to use Lily as a maid.

  J. is the only unselfish relative.

GO ON TO THE NEXT PAGE

3. The definition of what Mrs. Bart calls "dinginess" is most likely

    A. lack of education.
    B. ostentatious display.
    C. mediocrity and bad taste.
    D. poor judgment.

4. According to the passage, Lily's wealthy relatives were perhaps not inclined to take her in because they

    F. disapproved of her father.
    G. knew she had been taught to look down on them.
    H were miserly and unwilling to support her ambitions.
    J. disapproved of her "foreignness."

5. The circle of relatives in New York believed Mrs. Peniston was the best person to take Lily in because they

    A. thought Lily would be a good courier for Mrs Peniston when they traveled together.
    B. knew that Mrs. Peniston was a widow and needed a companion.
    C. were bitter toward Lily and her mother.
    D. didn't want to take her in themselves.

6. Which of the following can be inferred from Passage I?

    F. Mrs. Bart's marriage had been a disappointment to her.
    G. Lily distrusted men and was determined not to marry.
    H. Lily and Mrs. Bart had been abandoned in Europe.
    J. Mrs. Peniston had been estranged from her brother.

7. In lines 51–57, the author of Passage I suggests that Mrs. Peniston

    A. feared young people.
    B. wasn't particularly perceptive.
    C. felt inferior to her relatives.
    D. expected Lily to be grateful to her.

8. Which of the following best describes Lily's behavior at Mrs. Peniston's?

    F. She is grateful to have found a home but resents Mrs. Peniston's attitude toward her.
    G. Hypocritically, she pretends to do whatever Mrs. Peniston wants her to do.
    H. Although grateful to Mrs. Peniston, she disapproves of the woman's lavish life style.
    J. She enjoys her expensive surroundings and is grateful, but she realizes that money doesn't necessarily save one from "dinginess."

9. The author's presentation of Mrs. Peniston can best be described as

    A. lightly satiric.
    B. strongly critical.
    C. objective.
    D. stereotyping.

10. The best definition of a *pension* (line 70) is a

    F. stipend.
    G. boarding house.
    H. luxury hotel.
    J. spa.

Passage II

SOCIAL SCIENCE: The passage is adapted from *The Wisdom of Crowds: Why the Many are Smarter than the Few and How Collective Wisdom Shapes Business, Economies, Societies and Nations* by James Surowiecki (Doubleday, a division of Random House, 2004).

The legendary organizational theorist James G. March wrote: "The development of knowledge may depend on maintaining an influx of the naive and the ignorant, and...competitive victory does
(5) not reliably go to the properly educated." The reason, March suggested, is that groups that are too much alike find it harder to keep learning, because each member is bringing less and less new information to the table. Homogeneous groups
(10) are great at doing what they do well, but become progressively less able to investigate alternatives. Or, as March has famously argued, they spend too much time exploiting and not enough time

GO ON TO THE NEXT PAGE

exploring. Bringing new members into the (15) organization, even if they're less experienced and less capable, actually makes the group smarter simply because what little the new members do know, is not redundant with what everyone else knows. As March wrote, "[The] effect does not (20) come from the superior knowledge of the average new recruit. Recruits are, on average, less knowledgeable than the individuals they replace. The gains come from their diversity."

The fact that cognitive diversity matters does (25) not mean that if you assemble a group of thoroughly uninformed people, their collective wisdom will be smarter than an expert's. But if you can assemble a diverse group of people who possess varying degrees of knowledge and insight, (30) you're better off entrusting it with major decisions rather than leaving them in the hands of one or two people, no matter how smart these people are. If this is difficult to believe—in the same way that March's assertions are hard to believe—it's (35) because it runs counter to our basic intuitions about intelligence and business. Suggesting that the organization with the smartest people may not be the best organization is heretical, particularly in a business world caught up in a ceaseless "war (40) for talent" and governed by the assumption that a few superstars can make the difference between an excellent and a mediocre company. Heretical or not, it's the truth: the value of expertise is, in many contexts, overrated.

(45) Now experts obviously exist. The play of a great chess player is qualitatively different from the play of a merely accomplished one. The great player sees the board differently, and he recognizes meaningful patterns almost instantly. As Herbert (50) A. Simon and W. G. Chase demonstrated in the 1970s, if you show a chess expert and an amateur a board with a chess game in progress on it, the expert will be able to re-create from memory the layout of the entire game. The amateur won't. Yet (55) if you show that same expert a board with chess pieces irregularly and haphazardly placed on it, he will not be able to re-create the layout. This is impressive testimony to how thoroughly chess is imprinted on the minds of successful players. (60) But it also demonstrates how limited the scope of their expertise is.

A chess expert knows about chess, and that's it. We intuitively assume that intelligence is fungible, and that people who are excellent at (65) one intellectual pursuit would be excellent at another. But this is not the case with experts. Instead, the fundamental truth about expertise is, as Chase has said, "spectacularly narrow."

More important, there's no real evidence that (70) one can become expert in something as broad as "decision making" or "policy" or "strategy." Auto repair, piloting, skiing, perhaps even management— these are skills that yield to application, hard work, and native talent. But forecasting an uncertain (75) future and deciding the best course of action in the face of that future are much less likely to do so. And much of what we've seen so far suggests that a large group of diverse individuals will come up with better and more robust forecasts and make (80) more intelligent decisions than even the most skilled "decision maker."

11. According to James March, the success of groups in developing knowledge and finding solutions depends on

A. cooperation.
B. motivation.
C. diversity.
D. individuality.

12. The author agrees with James March that homogeneous groups "spend too much time exploiting and not enough time exploring." Which of the following is most effective in explaining this phrase?

F. When members of a group are alike, they rely too much on what they already know and don't spend enough time looking for alternative solutions to problems.
G. Members of a homogeneous group resist ideas they don't agree with and tend to make conservative judgments.
H. Members of a homogeneous group lack a broad education and are, therefore, unable to see problems from a wider perspective.
J. When members of a group are too much alike, they are reluctant to challenge each other in discussing a problem.

GO ON TO THE NEXT PAGE

13. According to Passage II, forming a group of people with the same occupation and education would likely lead to

   A. dissension.

   B. redundancy.

   C. frustration.

   D. boredom.

14. The author's theories run "counter to intuition" because he

   F. believes people of limited education usually make the best decisions.

   G. doesn't believe a group should have a leader.

   H. doubts that an organization made up of only the smartest people is the best organization.

   J. questions the validity of consulting experts when making decisions.

15. The example of an expert chess player in the third paragraph of Passage II

   A. proves that expertise is not the result of training.

   B. disproves the idea that chess experts are the best players.

   C. provides an example of an expert's limitations.

   D. rejects the idea that experts are needed in any situation.

16. The author derives which of the following conclusions in the third paragraph of Passage II?

   F. Chess is primarily a game for highly intelligent people.

   G. An amateur often performs better than an expert if chess pieces are placed randomly on the board.

   H. An expert chess player cannot rely on memory to assure success in a game.

   J. Expertise in one field doesn't lead to expertise in other fields.

17. From context, the word *fungible* in line 64 is best defined as

   A. interchangeable.

   B. irreplaceable.

   C. unimportant.

   D. invaluable.

18. It can be inferred from Passage II that the author

   F. would recommend classes that train people in decision making and forecasting.

   G. mistrusts people who consider themselves experts.

   H. believes people with real-life experience are smarter than well-educated people.

   J. would not leave business decisions to "superstars" alone.

19. In line 38 the word *heretical* is best defined as

   A. disavowing proven truths.

   B. departing from accepted beliefs.

   C. denying religious influence.

   D. refusing to comply with rules.

20. The author of Passage II would be LEAST likely to agree with which of the following?

   F. Advanced education is of no use in business organizations.

   G. Bringing new recruits into an organization is likely to improve it.

   H. Expertise in playing a musical instrument doesn't guarantee expertise in conducting an orchestra.

   J. Decisions about future actions in a business organization should not be made by the leader alone.

GO ON TO THE NEXT PAGE

Passage III

HUMANITIES: The passage is from the introduction to *Painting in Renaissance Italy* by Filippo Pedrocco and Sionetta Nava (Rizzoli Publications, 1999).

Renaissance is a term used in historiography primarily to designate the historical period from the beginning of the fifteenth to just after the middle of the sixteenth century, one marked—
(5) particularly in Italy—by an astounding flowering of artistic and literary expression.

In art criticism, the term was adopted by Giorgio Vasari, taken up in his *Lives of the Most Excellent Painters, Sculptors and Architects*,
(10) printed for the first time in Florence in 1550, a concept earlier formulated by Lorenzo Ghiberti in his *Commentaries*. Vasari placed the accent on the sharp break which he says occurred between the "rough manner" that marks the Byzantine
(15) and Gothic artists and that of Giotto, whom he considers the father of modern art, since Giotto was the one to bring about its rebirth (the original meaning of the word renaissance, *rinascimento* in Italian) by restoring it to the
(20) splendor of ancient times.

Vasari's position, in reality, arose from the intention of this painter and historian from Arezzo to exalt the production of artists like Leonardo, Raphael, and Michelangelo, as he
(25) considered himself in some ways their heir, and consequently to celebrate the epoch in which he himself lived and worked. This critical position—which enjoyed great consideration in the past, when the Renaissance was considered the true
(30) and only "golden age" of European art, and of Italian art in particular—is now obviously outdated; today no one would deny that also in Byzantine and Gothic art two great cultures reached heights of refinement in formal
(35) expression. In addition, historians agree in considering Giotto and the artists of the second half of the fourteenth century, from Simone Martini to Giovanni Pisano, not so much the initiators of the Renaissance as the interpreters
(40) of a new cultural world—that of humanism, shared with sublime poets and writers like Dante, Petrarch, and Boccaccio. These artists and writers brought about a real revolution in the meaning of art itself, involving not only its
(45) means of expression but also the tasks which it is called to accomplish in society. In other words, the artists of humanism appear different from those who preceded them because their interest is now focused—although not yet exclusively—on

(50) man, on phenomenological reality and the clear, precise narration of the events they present.

It seems evident, however, that the great protagonists of fourteenth century art should be considered—Vasari notwithstanding—only the
(55) precursors, not the protagonists of the Renaissance. It is only with the early years of the fifteenth century, in fact, that the rigid structure of medieval thought, resting solidly on theological foundations, and to which the fourteenth century
(60) artists still refer, begins progressively to fall away. It crumbles slowly under the weight of investigations ranging across all fields of human learning, which not coincidentally take the name of *Studia humanitatis*, since their exclusive object
(65) is man, protagonist and shaper of history. And it is from the grandiose project of rediscovery of the world as the dominion of the human will that the epoch indicated by modern criticism as the Renaissance begins. It is a term which is somewhat
(70) imprecise if it is limited to the concept of the "rebirth of the antique," since the knowledge and imitation of the artistic forms of classical antiquity, even in preceding centuries, had never died out. The term is certainly more convincing if
(75) understood in the sense of a new will to interpret the past in view of a full consciousness of human dignity in the present.

21. According to Passage III, Giorgio Vasari

  A. originated the concept of "renaissance."
  B. believed that Byzantine and Gothic art were the precursors of Renaissance art.
  C. wanted his epoch to be seen as heir to the period that produced Leonardo, Michelangelo, and Raphael.
  D. wrote the definitive book about Renaissance art and artists.

22. The authors of Passage III suggest which of the following points?

  F. Italian art changed at the time of the Renaissance because the view of the world changed.
  G. The "golden age" of Italian art is the fourteenth century.
  H. The Renaissance grew out of the breakdown of society.
  J. Simone Martini and Giovanni Pisano have been overlooked as Renaissance artists.

GO ON TO THE NEXT PAGE

23. According to the authors, Vasari saw the Renaissance as

  A. the culmination of "rough art."
  B. a period that showed great progress in artistic techniques.
  C. the beginning of a "human centered" view of art.
  D. a return to the splendor of ancient art.

24. It can be inferred from the passage that modern art critics

  F. value Byzantine and Gothic art more than early Renaissance art.
  G. consider Leonardo Da Vinci the father of modern art.
  H. disagree with Vasari about Giotto's place in the Renaissance.
  J. believe the art produced during the Italian Renaissance surpasses the art from the classical period.

25. The term *humanism* can best be defined as

  A. the belief in science rather than in religion.
  B. a view of the world that places man at the center.
  C. the study of human endeavor.
  D. the rejection of rigid theology.

26. The authors of Passage III describe the term *renaissance* as imprecise for this period in art because it

  F. ignores the great art of previous centuries, particularly the Gothic and Byzantine periods.
  G. does not apply to the major changes in disciplines other than art.
  H. means the "rebirth of the antique," when in fact imitation of classical antiquity had never died out.
  J. emphasizes "rebirth" and, therefore, ignores the importance of innovation.

27. According to the authors, the artists, poets, and writers of the late fourteenth century were revolutionary in that they

  A. changed the meaning of art to include its role in society.
  B. refused to be dominated by the restraints put upon them by the church.
  C. had little interest in returning to the subject matter of previous art.
  D. insisted on experimenting with new techniques and ideas.

28. As it is used in line 50, the word *phenomenological* means

  F. known by the senses rather than by thought or intuition.
  G. arrived at through imagination and fantasy.
  H. gained through a study of scholarly works.
  J. determined through the study of theological interpretation.

29. The authors' purpose in Passage III is to

  A. summarize Vasari's view of the Renaissance.
  B. identify the techniques of Renaissance painters such as Leonardo, Raphael, and Michelangelo.
  C. show that Giotto was a precursor of the Renaissance rather than a protagonist.
  D. briefly describe the change in world view occurring in the Renaissance.

30. From Passage III, one can infer that a Renaissance painting, as opposed to one from the Byzantine period, would be

  F. more abstract and colorful.
  G. less rigid and stylized
  H. more formal and subdued.
  J. less imaginative and more imitative.

GO ON TO THE NEXT PAGE

Passage IV

NATURAL SCIENCE: This passage is from *The Long Summer: How Climate Changed Civilization* by Brian Fagan (by Basic Books, a division of Harper Collins Publishers, 2004).

At first, archaeologists thought the first Americans were just big-game hunters. In 1908, a cowboy named George McJunkin unearthed some large animal bones and a sharp stone
(5) fragment in the wall of a dry gully near Folsom, New Mexico. He took them back to the ranch house, where they lay forgotten for seventeen years. In 1925, the finds landed on the desk of Jesse Figgins, director of the Colorado Museum
(10) of Natural History, who realized at once that the bones were those of large, long-extinct Plains bison. He dug into the Folsom site from 1926 to 1928. Almost immediately he found a stone spear point in direct association with the ancient bison
(15) fragments. The Folsom discovery proved once and for all that humans had lived in the Americas at the same time as long-extinct animals. Figgins estimated that the Folsom kill site was at least 10,000 years old—far earlier than the previous
(20) chronology of a mere 2,000 years.

Four years later, in 1932, two amateur collectors found some quite different, finely made stone spearheads with thinned bases alongside extinct mammal bones on the shores
(25) of long-dried up lakes at Clovis, New Mexico. Some of the points lay among broken mammoth ribs, but no one knew how old they were. Further excavations after World War II showed that these early "Clovis" points lay below a later "Folsom"
(30) layer at the same location. For years the Clovis people came to epitomize the first Americans.

At first Clovis sites were found only on the Great Plains, with their massive herds of bison and sporadic sightings of other large animals like
(35) mammoths, mastodons, and camelids. These early finds gave birth to the idea that Clovis people were expert big-game hunters and rapacious ones at that. In the late 1960s, the University archaeologist Paul Martin proclaimed that Clovis people had
(40) swept through the ice-free corridor, "old hands at hunting woolly mammoths and other large Eurasian animals." They descended on the Plains, where they found large gregarious animals and hunted them with ease. The newcomers
(45) spearheaded a blitzkrieg of voracious hunters, armed with the newly invented Clovis point, who killed all large animals on sight. Within five hundred years or so, they had colonized all of the Americas, right down to the Straits of Magellan.
(50) They had also driven most animals weighing more than 45 kilograms into extinction.

Martin's overkill theory was controversial from the beginning. His ideas ran in the face of much of what science knew about both ecology
(55) and hunter-gatherer societies. He argued the Clovis people with so much meat to eat would have reproduced rapidly, at an astounding rate of about 3–4 percent annually, far above the 0.5 percent rate of historical hunter-gatherer
(60) populations. As the archaeologist James Adovasio notes, they "would have had to be copulating machines to accomplish this" and have experienced a far lower infant mortality rate than is typical of hunter-gatherers.

(65) Archaeology also discredits the overkill theory. Clovis people did indeed hunt large animals, but archaeologists have found only twelve putative mammoth kill sites, mainly in Arizona. A further dozen locations *may* have
(70) been mammoth kills, one as far east as Michigan. If these people were habitual big-game hunters, they left remarkably few traces behind. At best, such a hunt was a rare occurrence. As the Clovis researcher James Judge once remarked, "Each
(75) Clovis generation probably killed one mammoth, then spent the rest of their lives talking about it."

31. According to Passage IV, many archaeologists originally believed that the first Americans were primarily big-game hunters because of

   A. the finding of long-extinct Plains bison bones.

   B. a discovery of stone spear points in Folsom.

   C. the theories of Jesse Figgins and George McJunkin.

   D. the discovery of spear points next to extinct large mammal bones.

32. The discoveries at Folsom proved which of the following?

   F. The first humans in America appeared in the southwestern states.

   G. Large animals such as bison had become extinct because of early hunting practices.

   H. Humans had been in America at the same time as long-extinct animals.

   J. The first humans in America dated back 2,000 years.

GO ON TO THE NEXT PAGE

33. Proof that the Clovis people preceded the period of the Folsom findings was that

   A. at the same location, the geologic layer of the Clovis findings was below the Folsom layer.

   B. the tools of the Clovis people were more sophisticated than the tools found with the Folsom bison.

   C. a greater number of the bones of large mammals, such as mammoths, mastodons, and camelids, was found at the Clovis site.

   D. only bison bones, no human bones, were found at the Folsom site.

34. From Passage IV, one can infer that current archaeology

   F. questions the theory that the first humans in America appeared as early as Figgins believed.

   G. accepts that the Clovis people were the first humans in America.

   H. doubts that the Clovis people were voracious big-game hunters.

   J. has found a large number of mammoth killing sites in the eastern states.

35. The author uses all of the following words to exaggerate or dramatize Paul Martin's theories EXCEPT

   A. "proclaimed"

   B. "blitzkrieg"

   C. "swept through"

   D. "colonized"

36. According to Passage IV, Paul Martin believed that the Clovis people would have

   F. been more warlike than other ancient peoples.

   G. reproduced rapidly.

   H. been healthier than other ancient peoples

   J. moved frequently to new killing sites.

37. The word *putative* as it is used in line 68 most nearly means

   A. ancient.

   B. discovered.

   C. presumed.

   D. unidentified.

38. Martin's theory is most likely referred to as the "overkill" theory because

   F. it sets forth the idea that the Clovis people hunted most large animals to extinction.

   G. the theory was considered extreme by other archaeologists.

   H. according to the theory, the Clovis people eliminated competing early humans.

   J. Martin himself had dubbed it with that name.

39. The comment made by James Judge in lines 74–76 of Passage IV

   A. supports the idea that the Clovis people hunted big-game animals to extinction.

   B. pokes fun at the accomplishments of the Clovis people.

   C. denounces the basis of Paul Martin's theories.

   D. refers to the absence of evidence that the Clovis people killed large numbers of big-game animals.

40. Which of the following best defines the author's main purpose in Passage IV?

   F. to briefly summarize early archaeological findings and theories about the first humans in America

   G. to prove that the Clovis people were not the first humans in America

   H. to support the theories of Paul Martin

   J. to establish that there were humans in America at the same time as now-extinct animals

IF YOU FINISH BEFORE TIME IS CALLED, CHECK YOUR WORK ON THIS SECTION ONLY. DO NOT WORK ON ANY OTHER SECTION IN THE TEST.

Science Test

Time: 35 Minutes

40 Questions

Directions: Each of the seven passages in this test is followed by several questions. After you read each passage, select the correct choice for each of the questions that follow the passage. Refer to the passage as often as necessary to answer the questions. You may NOT use a calculator on this test.

Passage I

DNA is made of a double strand of a sequence of four different nucleotides, denoted by the letters A, G, C, and T. At some loci, these nucleotides occur in a special pattern in which a short string is repeated multiple times in a row. These sequences are termed "short tandem repeats (STRs)."

An example of an STR is "TAATAATAATAATAA" in which three base-pairs—the nucleotide sequence TAA—are repeated five times in a row, creating an allele 15 base-pairs in length. If the STR at the same locus were measured and found to be 21 base-pairs long, we could assume it was a different allele of that STR, made of seven tandem repeats.

Study 1

A class is learning to use STRs to study paternity in a group of birds. The students have identified four loci where STRs occur in this species' genome and made a table of their results (Table 1). They have recorded the sequence of nucleotides that is repeated in each STR, and the total length of the STR in base-pairs.

Table 1

STR ID	Nucleotide sequence	Alleles identified (length in base-pairs)
STR-1	-TA-	50, 54, 56, 58, 60
STR-2	-GA-	102, 104, 106, 108, 110, 116, 122
STR-3	-CACAT-	15, 20, 30
STR-4	-GTT-	243, 255, 261, 264

Study 2

At each locus, the students know that each individual bird will carry two alleles: one STR from its mother on one chromosome, and another at the same locus on the matching chromosome from its father. They take a small blood sample from two adults and four chicks at a single nest and measure the length of STR-1 and STR-2 in each bird. The two alleles for each bird at each locus are shown in Table 2.

Table 2

Individual	STR-1 alleles	STR-2 alleles	Sex and/or Age
Alpha	50, 58	102, 110	Male adult
Beta	54, 56	102, 104	Female adult
Gamma	50, 54	104, 110	Juvenile
Delta	56, 58	102, 102	Juvenile
Epsilon	54, 56	102, 110	Juvenile
Zeta	50, 56	102, 104	Juvenile

GO ON TO THE NEXT PAGE

Study 3

Once the students have identified a chick with uncertain paternity, they take blood samples from other males near the nesting grounds in hopes of identifying that chick's true father. They initially identify potential fathers by measuring the length of STR-1 and STR-2 and comparing these to those of the chick.

Table 3

Individual	STR-1 alleles	STR-2 alleles	Sex and/or Age
Eta	56, 54	102, 102	Male adult
Theta	50, 56	102, 110	Male adult
Iota	50, 54	104, 110	Male adult

1. Referring to Table 1, if an allele of STR-1 is 60 base-pairs long, how many times is its short nucleotide sequence repeated?

    A. 60
    B. 30
    C. 25
    D. 20

2. According to Study 1, which of the following STRs was NOT identified in the DNA of one of the birds in the study?

    F. CACAT CACAT CACAT
    G. CACAT CACAT CACAT CACAT
    H. CACAT CACAT CACAT CACAT CACAT
    J. CACAT CACAT CACAT CACAT CACAT CACAT

3. According to Study 2, which of the chicks in the nest does not appear to be fathered by the male adult at that nest?

    A. Gamma, because both parents have an STR-2 allele 102 base-pairs long, and it does not have any alleles this length.
    B. Delta, because it has two STR-2 alleles 102 base-pairs long, instead of just one.
    C. Epsilon, because it does not share any STR-1 alleles with the male.
    D. Zeta, because it does not share both STR-1 alleles with the male.

4. Referring to Tables 2 and 3, what is the best reason for the students to conclude that the 102 base-pair allele of STR-2 is more common than the other alleles at that locus?

    F. It appears 9 times out of 18 alleles measured, more than any other STR-2 allele.
    G. It appears 5 times out of 10 alleles measured in presumably unrelated adults, more than any other STR-2 allele.
    H. It appears at least once in 7 of 9 birds tested, more than any other STR-2 allele.
    J. It appears at least once in 4 out of 5 presumably unrelated adults tested, more than any other STR-2 allele.

GO ON TO THE NEXT PAGE

5. According to Study 3, could any of the three additional males tested be the father of the chick that was not fathered by Alpha?

    A. No. None of them could be the father.
    B. Yes. Only Eta could be the father.
    C. Yes. Only Theta could be the father.
    D. Yes. Either Theta or Iota could be the father, but not Eta.

6. The students extend Study 3 and measure STR-1 and STR-2 in all the chicks and adults they can find. If the students wish to identify or exclude the potential fathers for chicks in the study with more certainty, what should they do for Study 4?

    F. Measure STR-1 and STR-2 again, double-checking their results.
    G. Measure STR-3 and STR-4 in all the chicks and parents and try to identify relationships from those data, instead of STR-1 and STR-2.
    H. Measure STR-3 and STR-4 in all the chicks and parents, and combine those data with the results of STR-1 and STR-2.
    J. Find and identify a totally different STR (STR-5), and measure it in all the chicks and parents, instead of doing any further work with STRs 1-4.

Passage II

The existence of dark matter—invisible matter in the universe that neither emits nor absorbs light—is supported by observations of gravitational anomalies that indicate the presence of matter where none is visible. Dark matter is estimated to constitute more than 80 percent of the matter of the universe.

Scientist 1

The gravitational anomalies observed by astrophysicists can be explained by objects made of normal baryonic matter (i.e., containing protons and neutrons)—a novel particle is not required to explain these phenomena.

For example, brown dwarfs, neutron stars, black holes, or even chunks of dense heavy metals that emit little to no light may go unobserved when calculating the mass of visible objects in a distant galaxy. These massive bodies—collectively referred to as MACHOs (Massive Astrophysical Compact Halo Objects)—could impose strong gravitational forces on surrounding objects or passing light, without being seen directly through our telescopes.

We detect the vast majority of large celestial bodies as they emit or interact with electromagnetic energy such as light and radio-waves. We also detect the presence of non-light-emitting bodies, such as distant planets, by the gravitational effect they have on surrounding visible matter. So-called "dark matter" is merely an instance of very large objects of the latter category—we have observed their gravitational signal and so can observe the presence of these objects, though we have failed to detect the objects' electromagnetic signals.

Scientist 2

Conservative theories that attempt to explain the observed gravitational anomalies through normal baryonic matter, such as MACHOs, do not account for even a quarter of the unseen matter in the universe. In addition, the amount of total matter in the universe far exceeds the amount of baryonic particles theorized to have been created in the Big Bang. The answer must be that dark matter represents an entirely new, non-baryonic particle.

GO ON TO THE NEXT PAGE

A leading theory is that dark matter is composed of Weakly Interacting Massive Particles (WIMPs). These particles interact very little, if at all, with the atoms and electromagnetic forces that govern our everyday experiences. WIMPs do, however, interact through gravity and the "weak force," which is responsible for phenomena such as radioactive decay.

Although we cannot see WIMPs, we can attempt to directly detect WIMPs as they pass through the earth. Although the vast majority of WIMPs will pass through our atoms with no effect whatsoever, we expect that an occasional particle may be detectable if it collides directly with an atomic nucleus. If WIMPs exist, we expect them to be arranged such that as our planet circles the sun we should pass through more and less WIMP-dense areas. At least one experiment appears to have detected a signal that matches that expected pattern, with more potential WIMP detections as we pass through some areas in our annual solar cycle, and fewer as we pass through other areas. This is evidence in favor of the WIMP model of dark matter, though these experimental results need to be replicated many more times before we can be confident of the findings.

7. What is the primary point of disagreement between these two scientists?

   A. Whether or not dark matter exists.

   B. Whether or not dark matter is made of baryonic or non-baryonic particles.

   C. Whether or not dark matter interacts with the weak or strong forces.

   D. Whether or not dark matter is made of MACHOs.

8. On what point do the two scientists appear to agree?

   F. Dark matter involves some form of radioactive decay.

   G. Dark matter is made of atoms, with protons, neutrons, and electrons.

   H. Dark matter never emits any light whatsoever.

   J. Dark matter is observable due to the gravitational anomalies it causes.

9. Which of the following statements is consistent with Scientist 1's theory?

   A. Most dark matter is in the form of objects larger than planet Earth.

   B. Earth, itself, could be made of dark matter.

   C. None of our current instruments have been able to detect anything similar to dark matter.

   D. If a celestial body stops emitting any electromagnetic energy, it becomes dark matter, by definition.

10. Which of the following statements is consistent with Scientist 2's theory?

   F. Dark matter exists only in distant galaxies.

   G. Dark matter passes around and through the earth all the time.

   H. Dark matter is radioactive.

   J. Dark matter does not interact with gravity.

11. What do the scientists' models predict about the presence of dark matter in our own solar system?

   A. Scientist 1 thinks dark matter is in our solar system; Scientist 2 does not.

   B. Scientist 2 thinks dark matter is in our solar system; Scientist 1 does not.

   C. Both scientists think dark matter is in our solar system.

   D. Neither scientist thinks dark matter is in our solar system.

GO ON TO THE NEXT PAGE

12. How do the two models describe the potentially observable size of dark matter?

   F.   The scientists describe dark matter as equally massive objects.

   G.   The scientists describe dark matter as equally tiny particles.

   H.   Scientist 1 thinks dark matter can be observed as tiny particles; Scientist 2 thinks dark matter can be observed as massive objects.

   J.   Scientist 1 thinks dark matter can be observed as massive objects; Scientist 2 thinks dark matter can be observed as tiny particles.

13. If a future observation described the discovery of numerous "black dwarfs"—theoretical collapsed stars that emit little to no electromagnetic energy—would that refute Scientist 2's theory?

   A.   No. Scientist 2 would maintain that there is not sufficient baryonic matter in the universe to account for the expected quantity of "missing" matter.

   B.   Yes. Black stars meet the criteria to be dark matter if there is a sufficient quantity of them to explain the gravitational anomalies.

   C.   No. Scientist 2 would maintain that if black stars exist, they must be made of WIMPs.

   D.   Yes. If black stars exist, WIMPs cannot exist.

Passage III

When an isotope of potassium, ^{40}K, undergoes radioactive decay, about 89 percent of the decay product is calcium (^{40}Ca), and the remaining 11 percent is argon (^{40}Ar). In this notation, the number 40—the approximate atomic weight of each element—is the sum of the protons and neutrons in the element.

Potassium-Argon (K-Ar) dating is a method used to calculate the age of volcanic deposits by comparing the relative amounts of the isotopes ^{40}K and ^{40}Ar in volcanic rock. While volcanic lava is in a liquid state, any argon gas in the material easily escapes the rock, leaving fresh lava practically devoid of argon. It can, therefore, be assumed that argon found in solid volcanic rock is the result of radioactive decay that occurred since that rock was last in a liquid state.

Table 1 and Figures 1 and 2 describe the results from K-Ar dating of samples of rock from ten volcanic islands in an archipelago spread over a 1500-mile stretch of the Pacific Ocean. Island 1 is the eastern-most and southern-most island in the chain.

Table 1

Island Number	Distance West of Island 1 (miles)	Distance North of Island 1 (miles)	Max Elevation (feet above sea level)	Quantity of ^{40}Ar per Milligram of ^{40}K (mg)	Estimated Age (millions of years)
1	0	0	7,200	0.000045	0.74
2	250	21	12,000	0.000079	1.3
3	393	32	14,000	0.00022	3.7
4	400	53	12,200	0.00021	3.5
5	555	62	8,500	0.00031	5.1
6	673	70	7,600	0.0004	6.2
7	832	98	3,400	0.00055	9.0
8	1012	110	2,000	0.0009	15.5
9	1250	124	500	0.0013	21.3
10	1535	155	1,700	0.0014	22.2

GO ON TO THE NEXT PAGE

Figure 1: Relationship between Island Age and Distance from Island 1

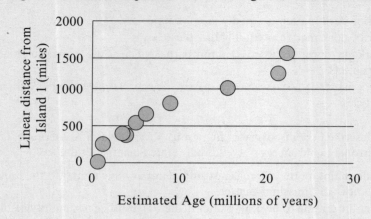

Figure 2: Relationship between Island Age and Elevation

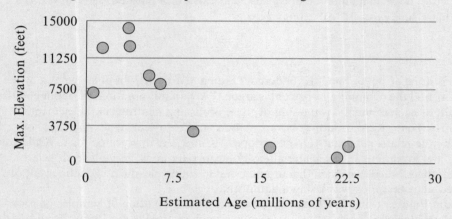

14. Referring to Passage III and Figure 1, why is ^{40}Ar the isotope that is measured to establish the age of volcanic rocks, rather than the other decay product, ^{40}Ca?

   F. Argon is a gas, and calcium is not.
   G. There is more argon in the decay product than calcium.
   H. Argon is much easier to measure.
   J. Argon has a higher atomic weight.

15. Do older volcanic rocks have more or less ^{40}Ar than younger volcanic rocks?

   A. Older volcanic rocks have more ^{40}Ar, because ancient magma used to have more ^{40}Ar than newer magma does.
   B. Older volcanic rocks have less ^{40}Ar, because the argon leaches out slowly over time.
   C. Older volcanic rocks have more ^{40}Ar, because ^{40}Ar slowly builds up in the rock due to ^{40}K decay.
   D. Older volcanic rocks have less ^{40}Ar, because the argon decays back to ^{40}K over time.

GO ON TO THE NEXT PAGE

16. According to Figure 1, which of the following statements appears to be true?

    F. As island age increases, the distance from Island 1 decreases.
    G. As island age increases, the distance from Island 1 increases.
    H. As island age decreases, the distance from Island 1 increases.
    J. As island age decreases, the distance from Island 1 decreases.

17. According to Figure 2, which of the following statements appears to be true?

    A. As islands get older, the island's elevation only increases.
    B. As islands get older, the island's elevation only decreases.
    C. As islands get older, the island's elevation decreases then increases.
    D. As islands get older, the island's elevation increases then decreases.

18. Researchers locate a large underwater mound of volcanic rock approximately 900 miles west and 100 miles north of Island 1. It will be extremely expensive to send a dive team to sample the rock of this island. Until they can get a direct sample, what assumption about the age of the underwater mound is justifiable from their data?

    F. The mound is probably less than 0.25 million years old, because it is still underwater.
    G. The mound is probably more than 9 and less than 15.5 million years old, because it is geographically between islands 7 and 8.
    H. The mound is probably more than 22 million years old because it has eroded back under the ocean.
    J. It is impossible to predict, because there is no pattern relating height or location to island age.

Passage IV

Oxidation-reduction reactions (redox reactions) involve the transfer of electrons from one atom to another. The reduction potential of an element, measured in volts, demonstrates the tendency of that element's ions to be reduced (accept electrons) in a redox reaction. Whichever element in the reaction has the highest reduction potential will be the element that accepts the electrons from the other half of the reaction.

Study 1

A student applies this knowledge of reduction potentials to build several galvanic cells. A galvanic cell (Figure 1) creates an electrical current by separating the two halves of a redox reaction and connecting the half-reactions with a wire such that the electrons in the reaction must travel through the wire to be exchanged.

Figure 1: Diagram of Galvanic Cell

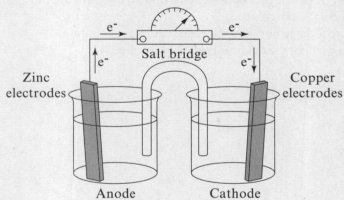

The student equips one terminal of the galvanic cell with a standard hydrogen electrode and attaches a test electrode to the other terminal. The student then measures the voltage across the cell for each of five different types of metals, and a second hydrogen standard, and records the results in Table 1.

Table 1

Test Electrode Element	Half-Reaction	Reduction Potential Relative to Hydrogen (volts)
Magnesium	$Mg^{2+} + 2e-$	−2.37
Zinc	$Zn^{2+} + 2e-$	−0.76
Lead	$Pb^{2+} + 2e-$	−0.13
Hydrogen	$2H^+ + 2e-$	0.00
Copper	$Cu^{2+} + 2e-$	+0.34
Silver	$Ag^+ + e-$	+0.80

Study 2

The student expects that the total voltage across the cell will be the sum of the reduction potential and the oxidation potential in each reaction. She confirms this expectation by pairing every element in her collection and measuring all 21 reactions. She records the resulting voltages of each reaction in Table 2.

Table 2

Cell Voltage	Mg	Zn	Pb	H	Cu	Ag
Mg	0 Volts					
Zn	1.61	0				
Pb	2.24	0.63	0			
H	2.37	0.76	0.13	0		
Cu	2.71	1.10	0.47	0.34	0	
Ag	3.17	1.56	0.93	0.80	0.46	0

19. In Study 1, why does hydrogen have zero reduction potential?

A. There is a hydrogen electrode on both terminals, so no electrons are transferred.

B. Hydrogen is not electrically charged.

C. Hydrogen ions are a single proton; they cannot attract an electron.

D. Hydrogen is a gas, but all the other test elements are metals.

GO ON TO THE NEXT PAGE

20. Which of the tested elements has the strongest tendency to accept electrons in a redox reaction?

    F.   Magnesium

    G.   Lead

    H.   Copper

    J.   Silver

21. In Study 1, how should the negative reduction potentials be interpreted?

    A.   Elements with negative reduction potentials relative to hydrogen donated electrons, and hydrogen accepted electrons in this redox reaction.

    B.   Elements with negative reduction potentials relative to hydrogen accepted electrons, and hydrogen donated electrons in this redox reaction.

    C.   Elements with negative reduction potentials relative to hydrogen will always donate electrons in redox reactions.

    D.   Elements with negative reduction potentials relative to hydrogen will always accept electrons in redox reactions.

22. In Study 2, when zinc and lead react, which is being reduced (accepting electrons) and which is being oxidized (donating electrons)?

    F.   Zinc is being reduced, and lead is being oxidized.

    G.   Zinc is being oxidized, and lead is being reduced.

    H.   They are both being oxidized because they both have negative reduction potentials.

    J.   They are both being reduced because they both have negative reduction potentials.

23. Oxidation potentials (when an element donates electrons) are the inverse of reduction potentials. Which of the following calculations best represents the summation of reduction and oxidation potentials in the redox reaction between zinc (Zn) and copper (Cu)?

    A. $0.34 + 0.76$ = total voltage

    B. $0.34 + (-0.76)$ = total voltage

    C. $(-0.76) - (-0.34)$ = total voltage

    D. $(-0.76) + (-0.34)$ = total voltage

24. The lithium (Li) half-reaction has a reduction potential of -3.05 volts when paired with a standard hydrogen electrode. If a lithium electrode were paired with a copper electrode, what would the total voltage be across the cell?

    F.   2.73 V

    G.   1.95 V

    H.   3.39 V

    J.   4.15 V

GO ON TO THE NEXT PAGE

Passage V

A veterinarian is attempting to select an effective antibiotic for a strain of *Staphylococcus* bacteria that has infected a dog and is not responding to penicillin. He cultures samples of the bacteria from the dog, applies it evenly across the agar growth medium in a petri dish, and places eight different antibiotic-impregnated disks on the agar, as shown in Figure 1.

Figure 1: Petri Dish Showing Placement of Antibiotic Disks

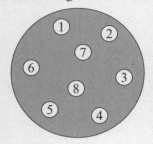

Study 1

After a period of incubation, he measures the size of the "zone of inhibition" around each disk (the area where bacteria failed to grow (Figure 2) and records the diameter of each in Table 1. He compares these measurements to standard inhibition-zone sizes for each antibiotic (Table 1) so that he can characterize the strain as "susceptible," "intermediate," or "resistant" to each antibiotic.

Figure 2: Petri Dish Showing Relative Sizes of Inhibition Zones for Dog 1

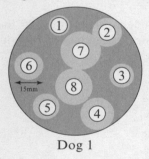

Dog 1

Table 1

Disk	Antibiotic	Dog 1 Zone of Inhibition (mm)	Zone Diameter Standards (mm) Resistant	Intermediate	Susceptible
1	Penicillin	8	≤28	–	≥29
2	Kanamycin	14	≤13	14–17	≥18
3	Gentamicin	12	≤12	13–14	≥15
4	Erythromycin	21	≤13	14–22	≥23
5	Streptomycin	12	≤11	12–14	≥15
6	Neomycin	15	≤12	13–16	≥17
7	Ampicillin	30	≤28	–	≥29
8	Novobiocin	25	≤17	18–21	≥22

GO ON TO THE NEXT PAGE

Study 2

The veterinarian examines two more dogs showing similar symptoms that also do not respond to a first round treatment of penicillin. He cultures and tests the bacteria in these dogs as in Figure 3, and records his results in Table 2.

Figure 3: Petri Dish Showing Relative Sizes of Inhibition Zones for Dogs 2 and 3

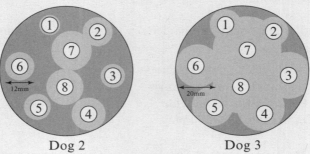

Dog 2   Dog 3

Table 2

Disk	Antibiotic	Zone of Inhibition (mm)		
		Dog 1	Dog 2	Dog 3
1	Penicillin	8	9	15
2	Kanamycin	14	15	16
3	Gentamicin	12	14	32
4	Erythromycin	21	23	32
5	Streptomycin	12	11	30
6	Neomycin	15	12	20
7	Ampicillin	30	33	50
8	Novobiocin	25	27	?

25. According to Study 1, which antibiotic(s), if any, appear effective against the bacterial strain infecting Dog 1?

A. Ampicillin and novobiocin are effective.
B. Penicillin and gentamicin are effective.
C. All of these antibiotics are effective.
D. None of these antibiotics is effective.

26. According to Table 1, how susceptible are the bacteria infecting Dog 1 to erythromycin?

F. Susceptible. The zone of inhibition is larger than the "resistant" zone size.
G. Intermediate. The zone of inhibition is smaller than the "susceptible" zone size.
H. Susceptible. The zone of inhibition is smaller than the "susceptible" zone size.
J. Intermediate. The zone of inhibition falls between the susceptible and resistant zone sizes.

27. Why is there no measurement recorded for novobiocin for the test plate for Dog 3?

A. The disk was faulty and does not appear to have contained any antibiotic.
B. Novobiocin was completely ineffective against the bacteria.
C. Of all the antibiotics in the experiment, novobiocin was the most effective.
D. Novobiocin's effectiveness could not be measured.

GO ON TO THE NEXT PAGE

28. Before beginning the experiments, the veterinarian noticed that none of the dogs' infections responded to treatment with penicillin. Was this result confirmed in the studies?

    F. It was confirmed for all three dogs.

    G. It was confirmed for Dogs 1 and 2, but not Dog 3.

    H. It was confirmed for Dog 1, but not Dogs 2 and 3.

    J. It was not confirmed for any dog.

29. Referring to Tables 1 and 2, how would you characterize the antibiotic-resistance of the bacteria infecting Dog 3?

    A. Those bacteria are susceptible to most antibiotics.

    B. Those bacteria are resistant to most antibiotics.

    C. Those bacteria are susceptible to all antibiotics.

    D. Those bacteria are resistant to all antibiotics.

30. If all three dogs were treated with erythromycin, what outcome would you expect?

    F. All of the dogs would be likely to be restored to good health.

    G. Dogs 2 and 3 would be more likely to be restored to good health than Dog 1.

    H. Dogs 1 and 2 would be more likely to be restored to good health than Dog 3.

    J. None of the dogs would be likely to be restored to good health.

Passage VI

Acidity is expressed on the pH scale, which ranges from 0 (very acidic) to 14 (very alkaline); perfectly pure water has a pH of 7.

Normal rain is impure and typically has a slightly acidic pH of approximately 5.6. Acid rain, with a pH below 5.0, frequently contains an overabundance of sulfur and nitrogen compounds that form molecules such as sulfuric acid (H_2SO_4); many of these compounds are derived from industrial sources (Figure 1).

Figure 1: Sources of Acid Rain Pollutants

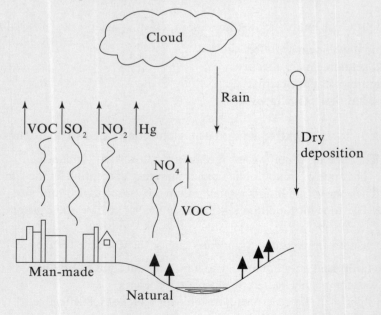

GO ON TO THE NEXT PAGE

In addition to environmental degradation, the effects of acid rain can be seen in the rapid weathering and pitting of statues and buildings made of limestone, marble, and other materials high in calcium carbonate ($CaCO_3$), due to the following reaction:

$$\text{Calcium carbonate + sulfuric acid: } CaCO_3 + H_2SO_4 \rightarrow CaSO_4 + H_2CO_3$$
$$H_2CO_3 \rightarrow CO_2 \text{ gas} + H_2O$$

The remaining calcium sulfate ($CaSO_4$) is soluble in water, and is easily washed away. The pH of rainwater is monitored at several locations across the nation (Figure 2).

Figure 2: Rainwater pH Over Time at Three Experimental Sites

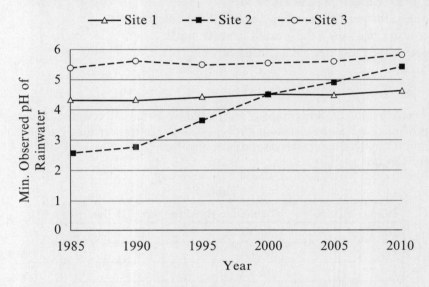

31. According to Figure 1, what are the sources of acid-rain-producing compounds?

    A. All acid-rain-producing compounds can be traced to a human source.

    B. Acid-rain-producing compounds can be traced to both human and natural environmental sources.

    C. All acid-rain-producing compounds can be traced to natural environmental sources.

    D. The sources of acid-rain-producing compounds are largely unknown.

32. According to Figure 1, in what ways are atmospheric acids deposited back to ground-level?

    F. Acids in the atmosphere can only be deposited to ground-level by rain.

    G. Sulfur compounds are deposited by rain, and nitrogen compounds are deposited through dry processes.

    H. Nitrogen compounds are deposited by rain, and sulfur compounds are deposited through dry processes.

    J. Sulfur and nitrogen compounds can both be deposited through wet or dry processes.

33. Once the reaction between calcium carbonate and sulfuric acid is complete, which molecule contains the original hydrogen ions from the acid rain?

    A. H_2O

    B. H_2SO_4

    C. H_2CO_3

    D. None, they escape back into the atmosphere.

GO ON TO THE NEXT PAGE

34. According to Figure 2, which of the three sites has NOT experienced acid rain during the monitoring period?

    F. Site 1

    G. Site 2

    H. Site 3

    J. All of the sites experienced acid rain in at least one year.

35. Referring to Figure 2, which of the three sites is likely to have the greatest observable erosion of limestone, marble, and other calcium-based stone?

    A. Site 1, because it currently has the lowest pH.

    B. Site 2, because there have been many years with extremely low pH.

    C. Site 2, because it has shown the greatest increase in pH.

    D. Site 3, because the rainwater has a consistently high pH.

Passage VII

An elevator-cable manufacturing company must build cable that can counteract the downward force of an elevator and its load, as well as the increased force caused by acceleration during normal use. Table 1 describes the thickness and strength of several elevator cables, and Table 2 and Figures 1–3 describe the characteristics of three types of elevators.

Table 1

Diameter (mm)	Minimum Breaking Strength (Newtons)
10	54,900
11	66,400
13	92,800
14	108,000
16	141,000

Table 2

Type	Elevator Weight (kg)	Maximum Load (kg)	Max Speed (m/s)	Time to Reach Max Speed (seconds)
Passenger	3,000	1,200	2.5	1
Freight	7,000	5,000	2.0	2
Construction	12,000	14,000	1.5	3

GO ON TO THE NEXT PAGE

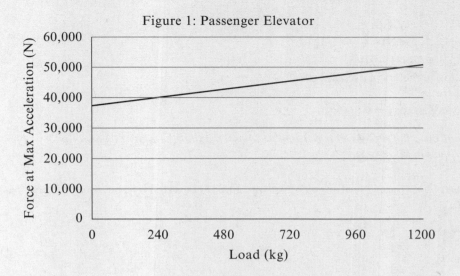

Figure 1: Passenger Elevator

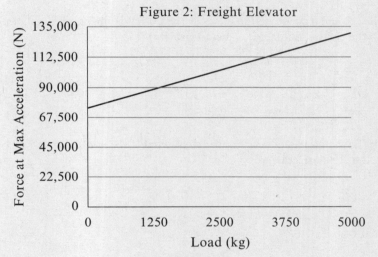

Figure 2: Freight Elevator

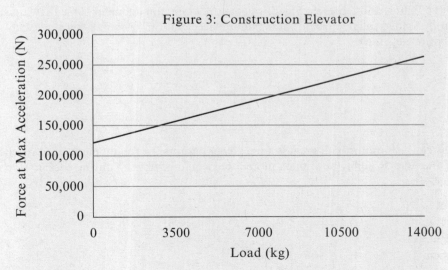

Figure 3: Construction Elevator

GO ON TO THE NEXT PAGE

$F = ma$

F: force in Newtons (N)

m: mass in kilograms (kg)

a: acceleration in meters per second per second (m/s^2)

Acceleration of gravity = 9.8m/s^2

For the purposes of questions 36–40, it is reasonable to assume that the weight of a stationary object, in kilograms, approximates its mass in kilograms.

36. Approximately how many Newtons of downward force are exerted by a stationary, empty passenger elevator?

    F.   3,000 N

    G. 15,000 N

    H. 30,000 N

    J.   40,000 N

37. According to Table 2, when a construction elevator rises, what is the approximate rate of acceleration of the elevator, relative to the earth's surface? (i.e., net of gravity)

    A. 0.5 m/s^2

    B. 1.5 m/s^2

    C. 5.0 m/s^2

    D. 10.3 m/s^2

38. According to Table 2, when a passenger elevator rises, what is the approximate rate of acceleration of the elevator, including the effect of gravity?

    F.   2.5 m/s^2

    G. 7.3 m/s^2

    H. 12.3 m/s^2

    J.   24.5 m/s^2

39. Referring to the figures and tables provided, what is the minimum diameter cable that can support the weight of a fully loaded freight elevator at maximum acceleration? (Assume any single cable must be able to support the entire elevator.)

    A. 11mm

    B. 13mm

    C. 14mm

    D. 16mm

40. Assume a new elevator motor with greater horsepower permits the freight elevator to reach its maximum speed in half the time. Roughly how much more force would be exerted during acceleration compared to the current model?

    F.   2 percent

    G. 10 percent

    H. 50 percent

    J.   100 percent

IF YOU FINISH BEFORE TIME IS CALLED, CHECK YOUR WORK ON THIS SECTION ONLY. DO NOT WORK ON ANY OTHER SECTION IN THE TEST.

Scoring the Practice Test

The following section will assist you in scoring and analyzing your practice test results. Use the following answer key to score your results, and then carefully review the analysis charts to identify your strengths and weakness. Finally, read through the answer explanations starting in the study guide on page 403 to clarify the solutions to the problems.

Answer Key

English Test

1. C	14. G	27. D	40. H	53. A	66. J
2. G	15. B	28. G	41. D	54. G	67. B
3. C	16. G	29. C	42. J	55. B	68. G
4. H	17. D	30. G	43. C	56. J	69. C
5. B	18. J	31. B	44. H	57. B	70. J
6. J	19. B	32. G	45. C	58. F	71. D
7. A	20. F	33. D	46. J	59. C	72. G
8. G	21. C	34. H	47. C	60. G	73. A
9. A	22. J	35. C	48. G	61. D	74. G
10. G	23. C	36. J	49. D	62. G	75. C
11. C	24. F	37. A	50. G	63. C	
12. J	25. C	38. G	51. B	64. F	
13. C	26. F	39. B	52. F	65. A	

Mathematics Test

1. D	12. G	23. B	34. G	45. D	56. H
2. G	13. D	24. J	35. E	46. G	57. B
3. E	14. G	25. D	36. H	47. C	58. H
4. F	15. D	26. H	37. C	48. K	59. D
5. C	16. H	27. C	38. H	49. B	60. G
6. H	17. E	28. J	39. D	50. G	
7. D	18. F	29. B	40. F	51. D	
8. J	19. C	30. F	41. C	52. J	
9. B	20. J	31. A	42. J	53. A	
10. H	21. B	32. K	43. D	54. F	
11. B	22. F	33. C	44. H	55. B	

Reading Test

1. C	8. J	15. C	22. F	29. D	36. G
2. F	9. A	16. J	23. D	30. G	37. C
3. C	10. G	17. A	24. H	31. D	38. F
4. G	11. C	18. J	25. B	32. H	39. D
5. D	12. F	19. B	26. H	33. A	40. F
6. F	13. B	20. F	27. A	34. H	
7. B	14. H	21. C	28. F	35. D	

Science Test

1. B	8. J	15. C	22. G	29. A	36. H
2. H	9. A	16. G	23. A	30. G	37. A
3. C	10. G	17. D	24. H	31. B	38. H
4. G	11. B	18. G	25. A	32. J	39. D
5. D	12. J	19. A	26. J	33. A	40. G
6. H	13. A	20. J	27. D	34. H	
7. B	14. F	21. A	28. F	35. B	

Charting and Analyzing Your Test Results

The first step in analyzing your test results is to chart your answers. Use the following chart to identify your strengths and areas of improvement. Complete the process of evaluating your strengths and analyzing problems in each area. Re-evaluate your results as you look for trends in the types of errors (repeated errors), and look for low scores in results in *specific* subject areas. This re-examination and analysis is a tremendous asset to help you maximize your best possible score. The answers and explanations following these charts will provide you clarification to help you solve these types of problems in the future.

Practice Test 1 Analysis Sheet

Test	Number Possible	Number Correct	Number Incorrect		
			(A) Simple Mistake	(B) Misread Problem	(C) Lack of Knowledge
English Test	75				
Mathematics Test	60				
Reading Test	40				
Science Test	40				
Total Possible Explanations for Incorrect Answers: Columns A, B, and C					
Total Number of Questions Correct and Incorrect	215	Add the total number of correct questions here: _____	Add columns A, B, and C for total number of incorrect questions here: _____		

Practice Test 1: Answers and Explanations

English Test

Passage I

1. **C.** The singular possessive form ("world's") is correct here, and world is not a proper noun and should not be capitalized.

2. **G.** This is the most succinct way to express the meaning. Also, the original phrase in Passage I should not be enclosed in commas because it is necessary to the meaning. When a clause or phrase is necessary to the meaning of a sentence, it is called *restrictive*. When a clause or phrase adds information that is not necessary to the meaning, it is called *nonrestrictive*.

3. **C.** The original phrase in Passage I is redundant; it repeats the idea of "today." The phrase should not be omitted entirely because it is necessary to the point being made. Choice D is wordy.

4. **H.** The original version in Passage I is a run-on sentence, or comma splice. Punctuation stronger than a comma is required between the independent clauses. A period is a better choice than a dash or colon to separate these clauses.

5. **B.** Using the active "to grow" is both more concise and more effective than "can be grown." A question mark is correct here. Choice C is wordy, and Choice D leaves out "enough," changing the meaning.

6. **J.** "Insufficient" is the best, most concise way to express the idea.

7. **A.** The original version in Passage I maintains parallel structure: "Not only will be . . . but also will be." None of the other choices does.

8. **G.** The original version in Passage I creates a fragment. Substituting "now because" is the best choice for correcting it. No comma is required between "now" and "because"; a comma is only needed when the dependent clause begins the sentence. Using a semicolon or colon (choices H and J) does not correct the fragment.

9. **A.** Setting the nonrestrictive phrase off in commas is correct, making the original version in Passage I the best. The other choices are wordy.

10. **G.** The sentence should not be omitted. It fits best as the last sentence of the first paragraph of Passage I. Since the second paragraph deals with water supply, this sentence isn't as appropriate where it is, nor is it the best opening sentence for the third paragraph, which deals with available land.

11. **C.** Once again, choosing the most direct, succinct expression is best as long as meaning is not affected.

12. **J.** This choice efficiently corrects the run-on sentence (Choice A) by using a semicolon to separate the clauses. Choice H also corrects the run-on but is wordier.

13. **C.** There is no need to use "has been" or "will have been." The verb should be in the present tense: "is."

14. **G.** A comma is the appropriate punctuation here. Semicolons (Choice F) are used to separate independent clauses. A colon is generally not used to separate a phrase from an independent clause.

15. **B.** Paragraphs 1 and 3 of Passage I are the most logical opening paragraphs and should be together because they are both dealing with food supply. Paragraph 2 is concerned with water supply.

Passage II

16. **G.** The original sentence of Passage II contains a dangling or misplaced modifier. "As a twin" doesn't refer to "information" but to "I." Choice G corrects this problem. Choice H incorrectly uses a plural verb ("are") with a singular subject ("information"). Choice J is awkward.

17. **D.** This is the most succinct expression. If a pronoun were used, however, it should be "who," not "which" or "that," choices B and C.

18. J. Sentence 5 adds little to the meaning. The town could have been included in the second sentence, but creating a separate sentence to include this information is not an effective way to end the paragraph, and the information adds nothing to the point of Passage II.

19. B. This is the best choice. The original, in addition to being wordy, uses a plural verb *"were"* with the singular *"each."* Choice C is also wordy. Also, since the men are identical twins, "each" in Choice D is unnecessary.

20. F. The original version in Passage II is correct. The past participle of the verb is the appropriate choice for an action completed in the past. Choices G and J use incorrect tenses.

21. C. This is the best choice, replacing a wordy clause and also choosing *"weighed"* as a better verb than *"is,"* as in Choice B. The past tense is consistent with the rest of Passage II.

22. J. The other choices contain double negatives. The correct expression is *"can hardly."*

23. C. The original version in Passage II is not parallel in structure: *"had dogs"* and *"traveling."* Choice C corrects this: *"both had dogs"* and *"both had frequently traveled."* This is the only choice that corrects the faulty parallelism of the original.

24. F. The original phrase in Passage II is correct. The sentence is a question that should be followed by a question mark, not a period (Choice G) or an exclamation point (Choice J).

25. C. Adding "s" to Jim creates the correct plural. An apostrophe creates a possessive, not a plural. The extra words in Choice D are unnecessary.

26. F. The original version in Passage II is correct. A comma precedes the dependent clause. (The word "that" identifies the clause as dependent.) A semicolon (Choice G) is not the correct punctuation between an independent and dependent clause, and, like Choice J, creates a sentence fragment.

27. D. "In deciding" is idiomatic here, not "to deciding." Choice B contains unnecessary words.

28. G. The correct pronoun here is "me"; it is the object of the preposition "of." Reading the sentence without *"my twin sister"* makes it clear that the pronoun should be in the objective case. The reflexive "myself" (Choice J) should only be used when referring to "I" in a sentence ("I hurt myself") or when adding emphasis ("I myself refused to sign").

29. C. The "traits" are the <u>result</u> of the environment, not the environment itself, as the original in Passage II states.

30. G. Of the choices, Choice G is best. Sentences 4–7, about the author and her twin, introduce a separate (although perhaps related) topic. Citing another case study (Choice F) is also off the topic; Passage II is concerned with one case. The last sentence (Choice J) is an appropriate (if not imaginative) conclusion to the paragraph.

Passage III

31. B. The name should not be set off in commas (Choice A) because it is *restrictive*, which means it is necessary to identify exactly which British diplomat made the statement. When a phrase or clause is *nonrestrictive*, adding information but not necessary, it should be enclosed in commas: "My sister, Jane Smith, bought the house across the street." A comma should follow Bryce, however, because the name ends an introductory phrase.

32. G. The original version in Passage III is not a complete sentence. Simply removing "which" corrects the problem. The other choices do not.

33. D. "Service" is a singular noun and requires a singular pronoun. "Its" is the correct singular possessive. Choice B is a contraction: "it is."

34. H. The correct past participle of "go" is "has gone" not "went," which is the simple past tense. The future tense (Choice J) is not called for by the rest of the sentence.

35. C. "Number" (not "amount") is correct for individual people or things. Choice C is also less wordy than the other choices. Note that it changes the verb to past tense.

36. J. This sentence is the best transition from this paragraph to the next because it introduces the subject of the National Park Service's financial position.

37. A. The sentence is correct as it is. "Who" is the correct pronoun because it is the subject of "are." Setting off the parenthetical phrase in commas is appropriate.

38. G. The quotation marks are appropriate here; this is a direct quote. However, because it is only part of the quote and not a complete sentence, "loving" should be lowercase. Also, it is better not to use an exclamation point after a sentence that is not an exclamation (Choice J).

39. B. This choice replaces "for keeping" with the infinitive "to keep," which is idiomatic here. The other choices are not idiomatic.

40. H. This choice is more precise than the original version in Passage III, although it uses more words. It makes clear, which the other choices do not, that the *sites* are unsupervised.

41. D. "Fewer" is the correct modifier for plural units. "Less" is used to refer to a quantity of one thing. Also, the comparative form "fewer" is called for by the meaning, which is that the park service has less money than previously.

42. J. This choice eliminates the wordy passive voice of the original version in Passage III. Adding a comma (Choice G) doesn't help (nor is a comma appropriate in this construction). Repeating the subject with a pronoun (Choice H) is also incorrect.

43. C. The underlined portion helpfully provides a few examples of what a reduced budget could mean to the National Park Service. It does not indicate a "morally superior tone" (Choice B) nor would its absence cause a loss of coherence and logic (Choice A). It does not provide a significant picture of the responsibilities of rangers (Choice D).

44. H. "Themselves" is the correct word and the correct spelling. There is no such word as "theirselves."

45. C. Of the choices, Choice C would be the most reasonable improvement to the Passage III essay since it is concerned with the financial needs of the National Park Service. Details about the costs of the service could strengthen the writer's point. None of the other choices is clearly related to the problems encountered by the service because of a reduced budget.

Passage IV

46. J. This choice corrects the dangling participle. The participial phrase should refer to viewers, not to "it." None of the other choices corrects the dangling participle.

47. C. This is the idiomatic choice ("that," not "as"). "Did" correctly completes the sentence construction; "envisage them" is unnecessary.

48. G. The phrase "for example" interrupts the sentence and should be set off in commas. A dash is not correct nor is a single comma.

49. D. Choice D is the correct selection for separating the dependent "which" clause from the preceding independent clause. In Choice A, the colon introduces the dependent clause, which is incorrect. The use of the participle in Choice B is awkward. In Choice C, the demonstrative pronoun "that" should not be preceded by a comma.

50. G. To maintain parallel structure, "to be used" should be followed by "simply admired." In this sentence "to be" refers to both "used" and "admired." The other choices do not use forms that are parallel.

51. B. This is the only choice that is consistent with the main idea, which is that the Greeks viewed their pottery as utilitarian. It also rounds out the paragraph rather than leaving it with a list of examples, as does Choice A. Choices C and D are off the main topic of the paragraph.

52. F. Choice F is the only sentence that introduces the topic of this paragraph. The unnamed artists are not addressed anywhere in this paragraph or in the Passage IV essay (Choice G), no comparison is made between painting and pottery (Choice H), and decorative techniques are not considered (Choice J).

53. A. The original version in Passage IV is correct. The pronoun should be in the subjective case ("who") because it is the subject of the verb "hold." "Have held" (Choice D) is not correct; the present tense is appropriate.

54. G. The underlined section should be omitted. It adds nothing to the idea of the sentence. The same point can be made about choices H and J.

55. B. "Different from" is the correct phrase. "To," "of," and "as" are not acceptable in this construction.

56. J. This is the best choice. It changes "collectors of art" to the more succinct "art collectors" and is parallel with "neither an art market" because it eliminates "did." The past tense of the verb is also correct.

57. B. In the original version in Passage IV, a semicolon is incorrectly used in place of a comma. Also, "word for craft" correctly parallels "word for art."

58. F. This is the clearest and most succinct of those that are offered. Choice G is wordy and redundant, and both choices H and J use incorrect punctuation.

59. C. "Visual arts" is plural and, therefore, requires a plural verb. The simple past, not the past participle (Choice B), is the best choice. Changing the verb doesn't help; Choice D still uses a singular form.

60. G. The sentence doesn't logically follow the point made in sentence 7 that artists were viewed as manual laborers (Choice F), nor does it logically follow the opening sentence (Choice H) of Passage IV. It also does not fit well between sentences 6 and 7. The best choice is placing the sentence after sentence 4, which makes the point that art collectors didn't exist at that time.

Passage V

61. D. The subjective pronoun "I" is needed here because it is part of the compound subject of the verb "left." It's easy to spot this if the other part of the compound subject is dropped: "I left" as opposed to "me left." Nothing is gained by following the "I" with the reflexive pronoun "myself." Avoid using reflexive pronouns except where they are actually needed, as in "I hurt myself."

62. G. The semicolon after "curious" is incorrect. Semicolons are used to separate independent clauses. Choice J is punctuated correctly, but is wordier than Choice G.

63. C. Eliminating the sentence about the town is the best choice; it doesn't add information related to the main incident described in Passage V. The example of the boys' going to town alone is sufficient to show their curiosity, and details about the town are irrelevant. Adding a description of the neighborhood and including the year when the incident happened would not improve the paragraph.

64. F. This sentence is the best choice because it returns to the ideas in sentences 1, 2, and 3 of the preceding paragraph. Choices G and H, although they deal with the boys' relationship and with the weather on July 5th, do not lead from the preceding paragraph into the event described in paragraph 2. Choice J is an awkward, mechanical introduction to the writer's account of the incident.

65. A. The original version in Passage V is correct. The word "ever" indicates that a past perfect verb tense is appropriate. The construction "would of" is ungrammatical; the correct construction is "would have."

66. J. Again, the past perfect tense is right here. Choices G and H are not consistent with the rest of Passage V. And the original version substitutes "would have" for "had."

67. B. The problem in the original version in Passage V is that the antecedent of "one" is unclear. Does "one" refer to a book of matches? It is unlikely that Jimmy lit the whole book, particularly in view of the rest of the sentence. "Sparkler" is the best choice, especially considering the next sentence.

68. G. "Descended down" is redundant. One cannot "descend up." Choice J ("ascended") is the opposite of "descended."

69. **C.** The shoe did not panic, as the original version suggests. "Panicking" refers to the speaker. The original is a good example of a dangling participle. Choice D doesn't correct the problem. Choice B is a run-on sentence (and awkwardly uses the passive voice of the verb).

70. **J.** The problem with all the other choices is that they use an adjective to modify the verb "ran." Verbs should be modified by adverbs ("quickly").

71. **D.** The problem with the original version in Passage V is that it lacks commas around the parenthetical expression "or maybe crime is a better word." The other choices are either incorrectly punctuated (Choice B) or wordy (Choice C).

72. **G.** Phrases such as this add nothing to a sentence and generally should be omitted. Choices H and J also add nothing to the sentence.

73. **A.** In this sentence the objective pronoun "me" is the object of the preposition "for." By reading the phrase without "Jimmy," you can see that "me" is correct. Choice C is not a correct use of the reflexive pronoun.

74. **G.** This sentence is the best choice, describing a detail of the scene with vivid verbs and adjectives. Choices F and H do not focus on the scene itself but on what the results will be. The detail about the neighbor (Choice J) is less lively than Choice G.

75. **C.** Passage V is neither persuasive (Choice A) nor defensive (Choice D). While casual, the piece is not written in slang. Colloquial (conversational) language is the best choice.

Mathematics Test

1. **D.** A good technique for comparing these square roots is to rewrite the square root by bringing the number on the outside of the root back under the root. The one closest to the square root of 49 is the answer.

$$6\sqrt{2} = \sqrt{36 \times 2} = \sqrt{72}$$
$$2\sqrt{6} = \sqrt{4 \times 6} = \sqrt{24}$$
$$5\sqrt{3} = \sqrt{25 \times 3} = \sqrt{75}$$
$$3\sqrt{5} = \sqrt{9 \times 5} = \sqrt{45}$$
$$4\sqrt{4} = \sqrt{16 \times 4} = \sqrt{64}$$

You can see that $3\sqrt{5}$ is the closest to the value of 7. Thus, Choice D is correct.

2. **G.** When dividing variables of the same base, subtract the exponents. Thus,

$$\frac{w^3 z^2 x^5 y}{w z^4 x^4 y^2} = \frac{w^2 x}{y z^2}$$

One way to approach this problem is to look at one variable, such as x. The given expression contains a factor of x. Inspecting the five answer choices, Choice F can be eliminated since $\frac{x}{x^2} = x^{-1}$. Choice H can be eliminated since $\frac{x^3}{x^4} = x^{-1}$. Choice J can be eliminated since $\frac{1}{x} = x^{-1}$. Choice K can be eliminated since $\frac{x^2}{1} = x^2$. This leaves Choice G.

3. **E.** To get a ratio of $\frac{x}{y}$, divide both sides of the equation by $7y$.

$$\frac{7x}{7y} = \frac{3y}{7y}$$
$$\frac{x}{y} = \frac{3}{7}$$

4. F. Start with the innermost absolute value.

$$-\left|2-\left|6-(-2)\right|\right| = -\left|2-\left|8\right|\right|$$
$$= -\left|2-8\right|$$
$$= -\left|-6\right|$$
$$= -6$$

5. C. The maximum area will occur when the triangle is a right triangle with the side of length 9 and the side of length 12 as the height and base of the triangle, respectively. So

$$c^2 = a^2 + b^2$$
$$c^2 = 9^2 + 12^2$$
$$c^2 = 81 + 144$$
$$c^2 = 225$$
$$c = 15$$

6. H. Next year's benefits can be calculated by multiplying the current benefit by 1.055. This gives the correct result of $991.70 directly. If you prefer a two-step process, first multiply the original benefit by 0.055, which gives the increase in benefits. Then add this increase to the original benefits to get the benefits for next year. This also gives the correct answer.

7. D. First, multiply both sides of the equation by 2. This will eliminate fractions. Then solve.

$$\frac{1}{2}(y+3) = \frac{3}{2}(2y-3)$$
$$y+3 = 3(2y-3)$$
$$y+3 = 6y-9$$
$$-5y = -12$$
$$y = \frac{12}{5}$$

8. J. The direct approach is simply to perform the "FOIL" multiplication.

$(x^2y - xy^2)(x^2y + xy^2)$
$x^4y^2 + x^3y^3 - x^3y^3 - x^2y^4$
$x^4y^2 - x^2y^4$
$x^2y^2(x^2 - y^2)$

This is Choice J. An alternative approach would be to factor out an xy from each factor first.

$(x^2y - xy^2)(x^2y + xy^2)$
$xy(x-y)xy(x+y)$
$x^2y^2(x-y)(x+y)$
$x^2y^2(x^2 - y^2)$

9. B. Set up an equation using the given information and solve.

$$x = 4500 - (.12)4500 = 4500 - 540 = 3960$$

10. **H.** Since the y-coordinate of the x-intercept is zero, simply substitute zero for y in each equation and solve for x.

$$6x - 3y = 2$$
$$6x - 3(0) = 2$$
$$6x = 2$$
$$x = \frac{2}{6}$$
$$x = \frac{1}{3}$$

$$5y - 4x = 8$$
$$5(0) - 4x = 8$$
$$-4x = 8$$
$$x = -2$$

To find the distance, subtract the two values of x. Remember the distance is always positive.

$$\frac{1}{3} - (-2) = \frac{1}{3} + 2 = \frac{1}{3} + \frac{6}{3} = \frac{7}{3}.$$

11. **B.** If $AB = 25$, you can use the Pythagorean Theorem to find the value of AC. Let $AC = x$.

$$x^2 + 20^2 = 25^2$$
$$x^2 + 400 = 625$$
$$x^2 = 225$$
$$x = 15$$

If you recognize that the lengths of the sides of this triangle are in the ratio of 3:4:5, you can determine the value of x directly. Since triangle ABC is similar to triangle DBE, their sides are proportional. Let $DE = y$.

$$\frac{15}{20} = \frac{y}{8}$$
$$y = \frac{(15)(8)}{20}$$
$$y = 6$$

Therefore, Choice B is correct.

12. **G.** First determine the slope of the given line. Put the equation into slope-intercept form ($y = mx + b$):

$$5x - 2y = -2$$
$$-2y = -5x - 2$$
$$y = \frac{5}{2}x + 1$$

From this equation, you can see that the slope of this line is $\frac{5}{2}$. Perpendicular lines have slopes that are negative reciprocals of each other. So the slope of line m, which is perpendicular to the given line, is $-\frac{2}{5}$.

13. D. First, you need to determine the number of ways to select the two men from the five men in the club. The direct approach would be to count the ways. If the five men were numbered 1, 2, 3, 4, and 5, you see that there are ten ways to select two of them: 12, 13, 14, 15, 23, 24, 25, 34, 35, and 45. (The order of the selection of the committee members does not change the composition of the committee, therefore 12 and 21 are not counted as being different.) If you know the combinations formula (not necessary for this test), you could apply it as follows:

$$_5C_2 = \frac{5!}{2!(5-2)!} = \frac{5 \times 4 \times 3 \times 2 \times 1}{2 \times 1 \times 3 \times 2 \times 1} = 10$$

Next, you need to determine the number of ways to select the two women from the four women in the club. If the women were numbered 1, 2, 3, and 4, you see that there are six ways to select two of them: 12, 13, 14, 23, 24, and 34. To obtain the total number of ways to select the four-member committee, multiply (10)(6) = 60 ways. This is Choice D.

14. G. The percentage of men who are Democrats is $\frac{2}{5} = 40\%$. The percentage of women who are Democrats is $\frac{3}{4} = 75\%$. Now calculate the ratio of these percentages.

$$\frac{40\%}{75\%} = \frac{40}{75} = \frac{8}{15}$$

This is Choice G.

15. D. Since three women are Democrats and nine members total are in the club, the probability would be $\frac{3}{9} = \frac{1}{3} \approx 0.33$.

16. H. If you add angle c to the diagram, you see that $c + z = y$, or $c = y - z$. This follows from the fact that vertical angles are equal in size.

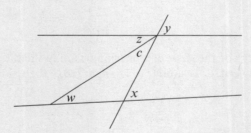

From the external angle theorem, $x = w + c$, or $x = w + y - z$. Solving this equation for y gives $y = x + z - w$, or Choice H.

17. E. The total weight of all ten apples is (10)(210) = 2100 grams. The total weight of the seven red apples is (7)(190) = 1330 grams. Subtracting gives you 2100 – 1330 = 770 grams for the total weight of the three green apples. Dividing by 3 yields $\frac{770}{3} \approx 256.67$. The closest answer choice is 260, Choice E.

18. F. The cotangent is the reciprocal of the tangent and is, therefore, defined as the ratio of the adjacent side to the opposite side. This is $\frac{a}{b}$, or Choice F.

19. C. First, draw in radius $\overline{CO}$. This radius is perpendicular to $\overline{AB}$ at point C.

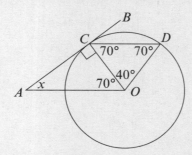

Since triangle CDO has two radii as two of its sides, it is an isosceles triangle, and both its base angles must be equal in value. Therefore $\angle DCO = 70°$. Subtracting from 180°, $\angle COD$ must be 40°. Since $\overline{CD} \parallel \overline{AO}$, $\angle CDO$ and $\angle AOD$ are supplementary and, therefore, $\angle AOC = 70°$. Since the three angles of a triangle must add up to 180°, angle x must be 20°. Another approach would be to consider quadrilateral $ACDO$. The sum of all four angles must be 360°. Since $\angle CDO$ and $\angle AOD$ are supplementary, the other two angles of the quadrilateral must also add up to 180°. Therefore, $x + 90° + 70° = 180°$, or $x = 20°$.

20. J. For the flat rate plan the cost is $(75)(0.11) = \$8.25$. For the flexible rate plan, the cost is $(40)(0.07) + (35)(0.20) = \$2.80 + \$7.00 = \$9.80$. Therefore, the savings is $\$9.80 - \$8.25 = \$1.55$.

21. B. Rewrite the first and third equation into slope-intercept form.

$$3x - 2y = -4 \qquad 2x = 3y - 4$$
$$-2y = -3x - 4 \qquad -3y = -2x - 4$$
$$y = \frac{3}{2}x + 2 \qquad y = \frac{2}{3}x + \frac{4}{3}$$

You see that the first and second equations are the same. Therefore, the first and second equations represent the same line. Since the slope of the third line is different from the slope of the first (and second) line, there is one point of intersection. This is Choice B. If all three lines had the same slope, but different y-intercepts, there would be no points of intersection. If all three lines had different slopes, there would be either one or three points of intersection, depending on where they intersected. For this problem it was not necessary to determine where the point of intersection was, only that there was one.

22. F. One approach would be to multiply through by the common denominator of 3. This would certainly work, but in this case is not necessary. First, subtract $\frac{13}{3}$ from both sides of the equation.

$$4x + \frac{13}{3} = x + \frac{19}{3}$$
$$4x = x + \frac{6}{3}$$
$$4x = x + 2$$
$$3x = 2$$
$$x = \frac{2}{3}$$

Look for shortcuts when solving equations. The test often contains problems that look more difficult than the really are.

23. B. Rewrite the equation such that all the bases are the same. Then, set up an equation in terms of the exponents.

$$\left(2^x\right)\left(8^y\right) = 4^z$$
$$\left(2^x\right)\left(\left(2^3\right)^y\right) = \left(2^2\right)^z$$
$$\left(2^x\right)\left(2^{3y}\right) = 2^{2z}$$
$$x + 3y = 2z$$
$$\frac{x + 3y}{2} = z$$

The correct choice is B.

24. J. Since the sin X is negative, angle X must be located in either the third or fourth quadrant. Since cos Y is positive, angle Y must be located in either the first or fourth quadrant. Therefore, both angle X and angle Y could be located in the fourth quadrant, which is Choice J.

25. D. There are three different ways to select the cake mix. There are six different ways to select the frosting. As far as the toppings are concerned, you need to choose two out of four different toppings. If the toppings are lettered a, b, c, and d, there are six different ways to select two toppings: ab, ac, ad, bc, bd, and cd. (The order of selection of the toppings does not matter, therefore, ab is the same as ba, and is only listed once.) Multiply these three numbers together to obtain the total number of combinations: $(3)(6)(6) = 108$, or Choice D. The combinations formula could also be used, but it is not necessary in this case.

26. H. To find the volume a rectangular solid, multiply the three dimensions. Thus, $(20)(14)(10) = 2800$, or answer choice H.

27. C. The length and width of the suitcase remain the same. Only the height increases. Therefore, the percent increase in volume is percent increase in height.

$$\% \text{ increase} = \frac{\text{increase}}{\text{starting value}} = \frac{2}{10} = 0.20 = 20\%$$

28. J. Since the cubes are 2 inches on each side, ten will fit along the length of the suitcase, and seven will fit along the width of the suitcase. Therefore, each layer consists of $(10)(7) = 70$ cubes. With the expansion zipper open, the inside height is 12. Thus, you can fit six layers of cubes in the suitcase. Therefore, $(70)(6) = 420$. This is Choice J.

29. B. First, multiply the two factors in the numerator and multiply the two factors in the denominator. Then, divide.

$$\frac{\left(4 \times 10^6\right)\left(9 \times 10^4\right)}{\left(2 \times 10^2\right)\left(3 \times 10^5\right)} = \frac{36 \times 10^{10}}{6 \times 10^7} = 6 \times 10^3$$

Remember, when multiplying numbers of the same base, add the exponents. When dividing numbers of the same base, subtract the exponents.

30. F. As you simplify the left side of the equation, be careful of all the negatives.

$$6(2x - 3) - 4(4x - 5) = 7$$
$$12x - 18 - 16x + 20 = 7$$
$$-4x + 2 = 7$$
$$-4x = 5$$
$$x = -\frac{5}{4}$$

The value of x is between -2 and -1. This is Choice F.

31. A. To evaluate a 2×2 determinant, use the following.

$$\begin{vmatrix} a & b \\ c & d \end{vmatrix} = ad - bc$$

$$\begin{vmatrix} -4 & 2 \\ 3 & 5 \end{vmatrix} = (-4)(5) - (2)(3) = -26$$

32. K. You can calculate the degree measure either before or after adding the two angles. If you add the radian measures first, you get

$$\frac{3\pi}{5} + \frac{2\pi}{3} = \frac{9\pi}{15} + \frac{10\pi}{15} = \frac{19\pi}{15}$$

Since 2π radians = $360°$, π radians = $180°$. To convert radians to degrees, multiply the radian measure by $\frac{180}{\pi}$.

$$\frac{19\pi}{15} \text{ radians} = \left(\frac{19\pi}{15}\right)\left(\frac{180}{\pi}\right) \text{ degrees} = 228 \text{ degrees}$$

33. C. The most direct approach to determine the slope of this line is to rewrite its equation in slope-intercept form.

$$\frac{1}{4}x - \frac{1}{3}y = 5$$
$$3x - 4y = 60$$
$$-4y = -3x + 60$$
$$y = \frac{3}{4}x - 15$$

From this form of the equation, it is easy to determine that the slope of the line is $\frac{3}{4}$, or Choice C.

34. G. Use the distance formula to determine the distance between the two points.

$$d = \sqrt{(x_2 - x_1)^2 + (y_2 - y_1)^2}$$
$$= \sqrt{(-8 - (-4))^2 + (-4 - 2)^2}$$
$$= \sqrt{16 + 36}$$
$$= \sqrt{52}$$
$$= 2\sqrt{13}$$

35. E. Starting with the number x, performing the required four operations would yield $\frac{6 \times 3}{3 \times 4}x$. This simplifies to $\frac{6 \times 3}{3 \times 4}x = \frac{6}{4}x = \frac{3}{2}x$. Therefore, the two required operations to accomplish the same thing as the given four operations is to multiply by 3 and then divide by 2. This is Choice E.

36. H. Substitute the values of the trigonometric functions and simplify.

$$\frac{\sin P}{\tan Q \cos P} = \frac{\left(\dfrac{p}{r}\right)}{\left(\dfrac{q}{p}\right)\left(\dfrac{q}{r}\right)} = \frac{\left(\dfrac{p}{r}\right)}{\left(\dfrac{q^2}{pr}\right)} = \left(\frac{p}{r}\right)\left(\frac{pr}{q^2}\right) = \frac{p^2}{q^2}$$

37. **C.** Set up an equation using the given information. Multiply through by y to "clear" the denominators. Then solve for x.

$$xy - \frac{x}{y} = \left(\frac{x}{y} - xy\right) + 2$$

$$xy^2 - x = x - xy^2 + 2y$$

$$2xy^2 - 2x = 2y$$

$$xy^2 - x = y$$

$$x\left(y^2 - 1\right) = y$$

$$x = \frac{y}{y^2 - 1}$$

This is valid for all values of y except -1, 0, and 1. The correct answer is Choice C.

38. **H.** The following diagram can be used to help visualize the given information.

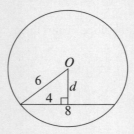

Since the diameter of the circle is 12 cm, the radius is 6 cm. The perpendicular drawn from the center of the circle to the chord bisects the chord. Thus, using the Pythagorean theorem, you can solve for the distance to the chord, d.

$$4^2 + d^2 = 6^2$$

$$16 + d^2 = 36$$

$$d^2 = 20$$

$$d = \sqrt{20}$$

$$d = 2\sqrt{5}$$

39. **D.** Set up an equation in terms of the volume of paint in each can. Let r_1 and r_2 represent the radii of the two cans and let d_1 and d_2 represent the depth of paint in the two cans. The volume of paint can be represented by $\pi r^2 d$. Since the volume of paint is the same in each can, you have the following.

$$\pi r_1^2 d_1 = \pi r_2^2 d_2$$

$$r_1^2 d_1 = r_2^2 d_2$$

$$\left(5^2\right)(5) = \left(4^2\right) d_2$$

$$\frac{\left(5^2\right)(5)}{4^2} = d_2$$

$$\frac{125}{16} = d_2$$

$$7.81 \approx d_2$$

40. F. Solve for y by subtracting 4 from both sides of the inequality and then multiply both sides by -1 which reverses the direction of the inequality symbol.

$$4 - y > 4 > -2$$
$$4 - 4 - y > -2 - 4$$
$$-y > -6$$
$$y < 6$$

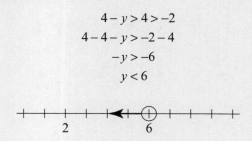

The correct answer choice is F.

41. C. Work from the inside out.

$$f\big(g(x)\big) - g\big(f(x)\big) = \big(2(4x - 2) - 5\big) - \big(4(2x - 5) - 2\big)$$
$$= (8x - 4 - 5) - (8x - 20 - 2)$$
$$= (8x - 9) - (8x - 22)$$
$$= 8x - 9 - 8x + 22$$
$$= 13$$

42. J. The x-coordinate of the midpoint must be the average of the x-coordinates of the endpoints. Therefore, (-2) is the average of 6 and x.

$$-2 = \frac{6 + x}{2}$$
$$(2)(-2) = 6 + x$$
$$(2)(-2) - 6 = x$$
$$-10 = x$$

Thus, $x = -10$. Since $x = 2y$, $y = -5$, or Choice J.

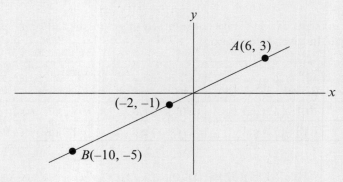

43. D. The defined operation written in general terms is $*x = x^2 + 3x$. Apply the rule twice to the number 5.

$$**5 = *(*5) = *(5^2 + (3)(5)) = *(25 + 15) = *40 = 40^2 + (3)(40) = 1720$$

44. **H.** The perimeter of the figure is made up of two arcs, each of which is a fraction of a complete circumference. If you draw in some radii, you can determine the size on the arcs.

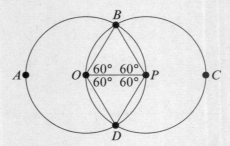

Since the radii of the two circles are the same, the resulting triangles are equilateral triangles, all of whose angles are 60° in size. Looking at circle O, central angle BOD is 120° in size. Since central angles cut off the same size arc, the arc from point B through point P and ending at point D is $\overset{\frown}{120°}$. This is one-third of the circle, leaving two-thirds of the circumference on the perimeter of the figure. This is also true for circle P. Therefore, the perimeter of the figure is

$$(2)\left(\frac{2}{3}\right)(\pi d) = \left(\frac{4}{3}\right)(16\pi) = \frac{64\pi}{3}$$

45. **D.** Set equal to zero and factor.

$$x^3 - 2x^2 = 24x$$
$$x^3 - 2x^2 - 24x = 0$$
$$x(x^2 - 2x - 24) = 0$$
$$x(x - 6)(x + 4) = 0$$

The solutions are, therefore, 0, 6, and (–4). Their sum is 2, or answer choice D.

46. **G.** Point A travels a distance of 4 units (right 3, left 1) for each 2 units it moves to the right. Therefore, to move from (–5) to 17, a distance of 22 units, would require a total distance traveled of 44 units. On the next move of 3 units to the right, point A would arrive at 20. Thus a total of 44 + 3 = 47 units traveled would be required.

47. **C.** Set up an equation in terms of what stays constant. In this case, the salt remains constant. A chart can be used to help organize the given information.

	Start	Add	Totals
Mixture	32 gal	x gal	$32 + x$ gal
Salt	(0.15)(32) gal	(0.00)(x) gal	(0.12)(32 + x)
Water	(0.85)(32) gal	(1.00)(x) gal	(0.85)(32)+ (1.00)(x)

$$(0.15)(32)+(0)(x)=(0.12)(32+x)$$
$$(15)(32)+(0)(x)=(12)(32+x)$$
$$480 = 384 + 12x$$
$$96 = 12x$$
$$8 = x$$

Therefore, 8 gallons of plain (no salt) water must be added to a 15 percent salt solution to obtain a 12 percent salt solution.

48. K. Clearly, you could spend the time adding 13 + 15 + 17 + 19 and so on, but this would take a lot of time. One method is to add them *twice*, and then divide by 2, as follows:

$$13+15+...+59+61$$
$$\underline{61+59+...+15+13}$$
$$74+74+...+74+74$$

Here you get twenty-five sums of 74. This is twice what you want, so divide by 2.

$$\frac{(25)(74)}{2}=(25)(37)=925$$

49. B. In order to find the total surface area of the four faces, you must find the area of each face. Each face is an isosceles triangle with a base length of 10. Your task is to find the height of the triangular face. The following diagram summarizes the information that is given.

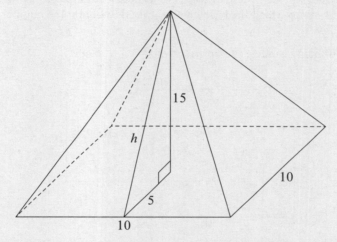

The height of the triangular face, h, is the hypotenuse of a right triangle with legs of 5 and 15.

$$h^2 = 5^2 + 15^2$$
$$h^2 = 25 + 225$$
$$h = \sqrt{250}$$
$$h = 5\sqrt{10}$$

The area of one face is, therefore, $A = \frac{1}{2}bh = \left(\frac{1}{2}\right)(10)\left(5\sqrt{10}\right) = 25\sqrt{10}$. The total area of the four faces is $(4)\left(25\sqrt{10}\right) = 100\sqrt{10}$.

50. G. If you divide the square into four squares, each of which has an inscribed circle, you can determine the correct percentage.

The area of the circle is πr^2 and the area of the square is $(2r)^2 = 4r^2$. To find the percentage, divide the area of the circle by the area of the square.

$$\frac{\text{Area of Circle}}{\text{Area of Square}} = \frac{\pi r^2}{4r^2} = \frac{\pi}{4} \approx \frac{3.14}{4} \approx 0.785 \approx 78\%$$

51. D. Statement III cannot be true. If statement III were true, then $x = -y$, and the quotient of their absolute values would equal 1, which violates the condition of the problem. Both statement I and statement II could be true. For example, to demonstrate that statement I could be true, let $x = 2$ and let $y = -4$. Clearly, $x > y$, but the quotient of their absolute values is less than one. To demonstrate statement II could be true, let $x = 2$ and let $y = 4$. Again, the quotient of their absolute values is less than one. Thus, the correct answer choice is D.

52. J. The definition of the period of a function is the distance required to make one complete cycle. The distance from 0 to $\frac{9\pi}{4}$ covers one and one-half cycles. The period is, therefore, $\frac{3\pi}{2}$, as shown here.

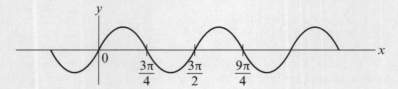

53. A. This follows directly from the definition of logs. For a specific example, let $x = 2$, $y = 10$, and $z = 100$. The log of a number is the power to which the base must be raised to obtain the number. Therefore, $2 = \log_{10} 100$ is equivalent to $10^2 = 100$.

54. F. Drawing a sketch will help visualize the information given.

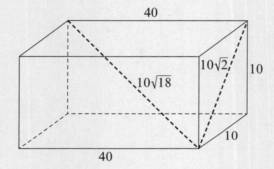

First, find the diagonal of the end of the prism. Since this is an isosceles right triangle, the ratio of the sides is $1 : 1 : \sqrt{2}$. Therefore, the diagonal of the end of the prism is $10\sqrt{2}$. (You could also use the Pythagorean theorem to find the hypotenuse.) The main diagonal of the prism is the hypotenuse of a right triangle with sides of 40 and $10\sqrt{2}$.

$$d^2 = 40^2 + \left(10\sqrt{2}\right)^2$$
$$d^2 = 1600 + 200$$
$$d^2 = 1800$$
$$d = \sqrt{1800}$$
$$d = 10\sqrt{18}$$

This is answer choice F.

55. B. Calculate the slope of the line that contains $\overline{XY}$.

$$m = \frac{y_2 - y_1}{x_2 - x_1}$$

$$= \frac{-10 - 6}{6 - (-2)}$$

$$= \frac{-16}{8}$$

$$= -2$$

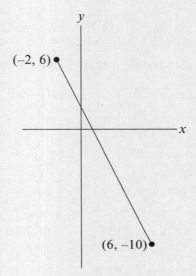

This means that for every drop of two units, move one unit to the right. To move two units to the right would be a drop of four. This line passes through the positive y-axis and also the positive x-axis. Therefore, statements I and II are false. Next, determine the midpoint of the segment.

$$(x, y) = \left(\frac{-2 + 6}{2}, \frac{6 + (-10)}{2} \right) = (2, -2)$$

The distance from $(2, -2)$ to $(0, 0)$ is determined as follows.

$$d = \sqrt{(x_2 - x_1)^2 + (y_2 - y_1)^2}$$

$$= \sqrt{(2 - 0)^2 + (-2 - 0)^2}$$

$$= \sqrt{4 + 4}$$

$$= \sqrt{8}$$

$$= 2\sqrt{2}$$

(This distance is the hypotenuse of a right triangle with legs of length 2.)

Statement III is true. Therefore, the correct answer choice is B.

56. H. Rewrite this equation in the standard form for a circle.

$$\left(\frac{x-2}{2}\right)^2 + \left(\frac{y+2}{2}\right)^2 = 1$$

$$\frac{(x-2)^2}{4} + \frac{(y+2)^2}{4} = 1$$

$$(x-2)^2 + (y+2)^2 = 4$$

$$(x-2)^2 + (y+2)^2 = 2^2$$

This is now in the standard form of $(x-h)^2 + (y-k)^2 = r^2$. In this case, the center is located at the point $(2, -2)$, and the radius is 2. The area of a circle with a radius of 2 is $A = \pi r^2 = 4\pi$, or Choice H.

57. B. You can solve this problem by either using substitution or the addition method.

$$2x - y = 20 \qquad\qquad 2x - y = 20$$
$$y = 16 - x \qquad\qquad\quad y = 16 - x$$

$$2x - (16 - x) = 20 \qquad 2x - y = 20$$
$$2x - 16 + x = 20 \qquad\quad \underline{x + y = 16}$$
$$3x = 36 \qquad\qquad\qquad 3x = 36$$
$$x = 12 \qquad\qquad\qquad x = 12$$
$$y = 16 - 12 \qquad\qquad y = 16 - 12$$
$$y = 4 \qquad\qquad\qquad\quad y = 4$$
$$x - y = 12 - 4 = 8 \qquad x - y = 12 - 4 = 8$$

58. H. The general form for multiplying two 2×2 matrices is the following.

$$\begin{bmatrix} a & b \\ c & d \end{bmatrix}\begin{bmatrix} e & f \\ g & h \end{bmatrix} = \begin{bmatrix} ae+bg & af+bh \\ ce+dg & cf+dh \end{bmatrix}$$

Substitute the given values and simplify.

$$\begin{bmatrix} 3 & 4 \\ -1 & 2 \end{bmatrix}\begin{bmatrix} -2 & 1 \\ 3 & -1 \end{bmatrix} = \begin{bmatrix} (3)(-2)+(4)(3) & (3)(1)+(4)(-1) \\ (-1)(-2)+(2)(3) & (-1)(1)+(2)(-1) \end{bmatrix}$$

$$= \begin{bmatrix} 6 & -1 \\ 8 & -3 \end{bmatrix}$$

59. D. Multiply both the numerator and denominator by the complex conjugate of the denominator. Remember that $i^2 = -1$.

$$\frac{a}{b} = \frac{3-2i}{2-3i}$$

$$= \left(\frac{3-2i}{2-3i}\right)\left(\frac{2+3i}{2+3i}\right)$$

$$= \frac{6-4i+9i-6i^2}{4-6i+6i-9i^2}$$

$$= \frac{6+5i+6}{4+9}$$

$$= \frac{12+5i}{13}$$

60. **G.** Since cot $\angle ABC = \frac{4}{3}$, you can assign a value of 4 for BC and a value of 3 for AC. Since cos $\angle CAD = \frac{3}{4}$, you can assign a value of 4 for AD.

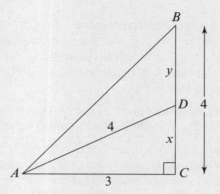

Use the Pythagorean theorem to determine the value of x.

$$3^2 + x^2 = 4^2$$
$$9 + x^2 = 16$$
$$x^2 = 7$$
$$x = \sqrt{7}$$

You now calculate the value of y.

$$y = 4 - x = 4 - \sqrt{7}$$

Dividing and simplifying gives you the required value.

$$\frac{x}{y} = \frac{\sqrt{7}}{4 - \sqrt{7}}$$
$$= \left(\frac{\sqrt{7}}{4 - \sqrt{7}} \right)\left(\frac{4 + \sqrt{7}}{4 + \sqrt{7}} \right)$$
$$= \frac{4\sqrt{7} + 7}{16 - 7}$$
$$= \frac{4\sqrt{7} + 7}{9}$$

Reading Test

Passage I

1. **C.** Line 70 refers to a "continental pension," indicating that such a place had been Lily's previous residence. Notice 'hungry roaming' in line 1 and 'Lily's familiarity with foreign customs' in lines 35–36. Clues as to the type of lodging are in lines 7 and 8. Nothing in Passage I suggests either that Lily's father had deserted them (Choice A) or that Lily and her mother didn't get along (Choice D). Choice B may seem to be the best choice because of Mrs. Bart's focus on Lily's making a brilliant marriage, but to say that this point makes the women fortune-hunters is too strong.

2. **F.** This choice is supported in lines 41–43. Mrs Peniston wants to *appear* unselfish. Choice H might seem to be a good choice, but Lily is Mrs. Peniston's niece, and it is unlikely in context that she would expect Lily to be a maid. There is no suggestion of Choice G in Passage I. That Mrs. Peniston wishes only to *seem* unselfish rules out Choice J.

3. C. Since the Bart relatives have sufficient money, it is more likely that Mrs. Bart (and Lily) regard "dinginess" as not merely a lack of money but also a lack of sophistication and taste. See lines 17–18 and 66–70.

4. G. Lily had been taught to look down on her Bart relatives "for living like pigs," and the author suggests that they may have had an "inkling" of this and, therefore, weren't eager to take her in (lines 18–21). There is no reference to her father or how the Bart relatives viewed him (Choice F). The relatives are not shown as miserly (Choice H). While they "deplored Lily's familiarity with foreign customs," nothing indicates that this is the reason they didn't want to take her in.

5. D. In lines 32–38 the author cites the reasons given by the relatives (choices A and B), but lines 18–21 indicate that the actual reason was that they themselves wouldn't be required to care of Lily.

6. F. Mrs. Bart had hated "dinginess," and "it was her fate to be dingy" (lines 2–3). The conclusion one can come to is that her marriage had been a disappointment. This conclusion is supported by her vision of a "brilliant marriage" for Lily. Lines 11–13 also suggest that her marriage had dragged her down. Another indication is her disdain for her husband's relatives. Choices G, H, and J are not supported by anything in Passage I.

7. B. The phrase "to a more penetrating mind than her aunt's" (lines 55–56) supports this choice. The author suggests that Mrs. Peniston, had she been more perceptive, might have suspected Lily's pliancy as being less honest than "open selfishness." Choice D may be true, but it is not indicated; in fact, Lily is grateful (line 64). Although Mrs. Peniston may have expected Lily to be headstrong, there is no indication that she fears young people (Choice A). Mrs. Peniston wants to appear unselfish and superior to her relatives, but she does not feel inferior to them (Choice C).

8. J. This is the best choice in view of the last paragraph of Passage I. Nothing suggests that Lily resents her aunt's attitude (Choice F), is hypocritical in her actions (Choice G), or disapproves of her aunt's lifestyle. She may see that the "expensive routine" of Mrs. Peniston's life is ultimately "dingy," but she doesn't disapprove of its lavishness.

9. A. The author pokes mild fun at Mrs. Peniston's unselfishness (lines 40–48), but the tone is not strongly critical (Choice B) nor is the author objective (Choice C). (It is clear what the author thinks of Mrs. Peniston.) The picture she paints falls short of stereotyping, however (Choice D).

10. G. As it is used in line 70, the word is clearly "a lodging," not "a monetary pension," which rules out Choice F. Because Lily and her mother were not living in luxury in Europe, choices H and J are also not appropriate.

Passage II

11. C. See line 23 of Passage II. March's point is that groups made up of people with the same skills, education, and background find it difficult to continue learning, and, therefore, diversity brings new knowledge and alternatives to solving problems. Although choices A and B are no doubt important in groups, it is diversity of the members (not individuality, Choice D) that March focuses on.

12. F. The author and March agree that homogenous groups rely too much on what they already know. These groups do not explore other points of view. Passage II doesn't suggest that homogenous groups "resist" ideas or make conservative judgments (Choice G). Nothing indicates that the members "lack a broad education" (Choice H) or are reluctant to challenge each other (Choice J).

13. B. See lines 14–19. The point is that the members of a homogenous group possess the same kind of knowledge, which makes for redundancy. Introducing new members with diverse backgrounds and skills eliminates the problem of redundancy. Choices A, C, and particularly Choice D, may be true in homogenous groups, but these are not points the author makes in Passage II.

14. H. See lines 27–32 of Passage II. The author doubts whether the general belief (or intuition) that the best organization is made of the smartest people is true. His belief is counter to this intuition; he believes that a diverse group of people with "varying degrees of knowledge and insight" makes the best organization. Choice F goes too far; he is not suggesting that those with limited education make the best decisions, only that diversity in an organization is best. He also does not indicate that groups shouldn't have leaders, only that decisions shouldn't be made by one or two people (Choice G). He doesn't say that consulting experts is invalid (Choice J), only that decisions shouldn't be made by "experts" alone.

15. **C.** The importance of this example is that it proves the limitations of experts. See lines 54–61. Passage II recognizes that chess is imprinted on the mind of an expert player, but that does not mean the expert can succeed if the chess pieces are irregularly or haphazardly placed. The author quotes Chase in line 68: expertise is "spectacularly narrow."

16. **J.** This choice underlines the author's thesis that expertise is overrated in some situations. Choice F is not a point that is made in Passage II, and Choice H is contradicted, in that the author comments on the importance of a chess expert's memory. Nothing suggests Choice G; Passage II doesn't imply that amateurs do better than experts when chess pieces are randomly placed.

17. **A.** The second half of the sentence in lines 64–66 makes it clear that Choice A is the best definition of *fungible.*

18. **J.** This is the best choice. See lines 69–71. The author doubts that decision-making and forecasting skills can be taught, which eliminates Choice F. Although he believes that groups make better decisions than individuals, he does not think people with real-life experience are "smarter" than well-educated people (Choice H). He also doesn't "mistrust" experts (Choice G), but he does believe expertise is narrow.

19. **B.** Although the term *heresy* is associated with religious beliefs, it is also used to describe ideas that depart from accepted beliefs in any field. That is the definition that applies in lines 38–44 of Passage II.

20. **F.** Of the choices given, this is the one that the author of Passage II is *least* likely to agree with. He does not imply that advanced education is of "no use" in business organizations, whereas he does agree that bringing in new recruits is a good idea (Choice G), that expertise in one area doesn't guarantee expertise in another (Choice H), and that decisions should be made by more than one or two people (Choice J).

Passage III

21. **C.** See lines 21–27. Vasari, according to Passage III, wanted to be considered as heir to the time of those artists he believed to be the greatest. The concept of "renaissance" was *adopted*, not originated, by Vasari (Choice A). Nothing suggests he wrote the "definitive" book on the period (Choice D). Choice B is the opposite of what Vasari believed about the Renaissance.

22. **F.** This is made clear in the last sentence of the third paragraph and also in the fourth paragraph of Passage III. The fourteenth century is not designated the "golden age" of Italian art (Choice G). Choice H is not implied or stated (nor is it accurate); Martini and Pisano are simply mentioned as artists of the second half of the fourteenth century (Choice J).

23. **D.** Although the authors would see Choice C as true, Vasari himself believed the Renaissance was a return to the splendor of classical art (lines 29–30). Choice A is inaccurate, and Choice B is not addressed in Passage III.

24. **H.** Modern critics, according to the authors, do not see Giotto as an initiator, as Vasari did, but as a precursor to the Renaissance. Nothing suggests that modern critics value Byzantine and Gothic art "more" than early Renaissance art, only that they do not dismiss those periods as Vasari did. Choice G is not indicated, nor is the judgment in Choice J implied.

25. **B.** According to Passage III, Choice B is the best choice, and Choice C is the second best. (It is not as encompassing as Choice B.) Choices A and D may both be considered part of humanism but they are not the definition.

26. **H.** This choice is the explicit point made by the author in lines 69–74 of Passage III.

27. **A.** According to the authors, the reason artists, poets, and writers of this period were revolutionary was that they changed the meaning of art. Rather than seeing art simply as self-expression, they saw it as a mean to accomplish tasks in society. See lines 42–46. Choice B is not inclusive enough; Choice C is not supported; and Choice D, though possibly true, is not implied as the reason these artists were revolutionary.

28. **F.** Of the choices, this is the best definition. The clue is the context, which emphasizes a "clear, precise narration of events" rather than a scholarly (Choice H) or theological (Choice J) interpretation. Choice G is not suggested by the context of the lines or by Passage III as a whole.

29. **D.** Choices A and C are secondary points. Choice B is not addressed in Passage III. Most of Passage III deals with the change that occurred in the artists' view of the world.

30. **G.** The best choice is G. The authors stress that art became more focused on reality and a "clear, precise narration of events" (lines 50–51). Previous periods are described in ways that suggest a more rigid view. See lines 56–59.

Passage IV

31. **D.** Finding spear points and long-extinct large mammals together suggests to archaeologists that the early Americans were big-game hunters.

32. **H.** This is the best choice. See lines 15–17. The Folsom finds did not "prove" that the first humans in America lived in the Southwest (Choice F). The findings showed that humans had existed in America longer than 2,000 years, making Choice J incorrect. Choice G relates to Paul Martin's theories, not to the Folsom findings.

33. **A.** See lines 27–30. Of the choices, this is the only one that proves that the Clovis people preceded the period of the Folsom findings. Choice C may be true, but it doesn't prove that the Clovis people came before the Folsom findings. Choice B would indicate the opposite, that Folsom preceded Clovis.

34. **H.** See lines 53–64. Choice J is contradicted in lines 69–70. Nothing in Passage IV indicates that modern archaeologists question Figgins' dating of the first humans in America (Choice F). There is also no support for the statement in Choice G; Passage IV says that "for years" the Clovis people were the epitome of the first Americans.

35. **D.** Choices A, B, and C are all dramatic expression, whereas "colonized" is not.

36. **G.** See lines 55–57. Choices F, H, and J are not indicated anywhere in Passage IV.

37. **C.** The twelve kill sites that were discovered are "presumed" to be mammoth kill sites, making this the best definition in context. All the sites in Passage IV are "ancient" (Choice A) and have been "discovered" (Choice B), so "putative" would not refer only to the twelve killing sites. All the sites were "identified," ruling out Choice D.

38. **F.** This is the best choice. See line 44–51. Martin believed that the Clovis people were such voracious hunters that they hunted large animals to extinction. This "overkill theory" has been generally discounted by modern archaeology (lines 65–72). Choice J is not supported, although Martin was the person who set forth the theory. Choice H is also not supported, and although modern archaeologists have largely discredited Martin's theory, nothing suggests that they called it the "overkill theory" because they believed it was too extreme (Choice G).

39. **D.** In Choice C, "denounces" is too strong a word. Also, Judge is not "poking fun" at the Clovis people but instead commenting on the lack of evidence that they killed a large number of mammoths (Choice B). Choice A states the opposite of Judge's point.

40. **F.** Passage IV is a brief summary of early archaeological findings and the theories about the Clovis people. The author doesn't "prove" anything (Choice G). He doesn't support Martin's theory but questions it (Choice H). Choice J is covered in Passage IV, but it is not the author's main purpose.

Science Test

Passage I

1. **B.** The repeated sequence, TA, is two base-pairs long. Therefore, if the full length is 60 base-pairs long, the sequence must be repeated 30 times.

2. **H.** In Study 1, the students measured STR-3 alleles that are 15, 20, and 30 base pairs long. Choice H is a sequence that is 25 base-pairs long.

3. **C.** Each chick shares one allele with its mother and one with its father. Where mother and father share the same allele, it may sometimes be impossible to tell which copy came from which parent, but this is not important as long as one can be matched to each parent. The chick, Epsilon, has two STR-1 alleles that match the female at the nest, but none that match the male at the nest; therefore, this male is unlikely to be its father.

4. **G.** The relative number of copies of an allele in a random sample of the population predicts the frequency of that allele in the population as a whole. You can assume this from the general rules of probability and independent assortment. The chicks are not a "random sample" as they receive their alleles from their parents and so will only amplify the frequency of whatever alleles their parents carry. Choices H and J are incorrect because it is informative that some birds have two copies of the 102 base-pair allele; you should count the number of times each allele occurs, not the number of birds in which it occurs.

5. **D.** The chick in question is Epsilon, with the following alleles: STR-1 (54, 56); STR-2 (102, 110). Its mother donated half of her alleles at each locus: STR-1 (54, 56); STR-2 (102, 104). We can assume that the chick got either the 54 OR the 56 base-pair allele at STR-1 from its mother, and the other from its father. We know it got the 102 base-pair allele at STR-2 from its mother, and so we also know that its father must have at least one 110 base-pair allele at STR-2. Because Eta has no 110 base-pair allele at STR-2, it can be eliminated. However both Theta and Iota have the alleles required to donate EITHER the 56 or 54 base-pair allele at STR-1 AND the 110 base-pair allele at STR-2.

6. **H.** In order to increase the certainty of their results, the students need to be able to exclude more potential fathers, until only one reasonable option remains. The only way to exclude fathers is to measure alleles at more loci, thereby revealing which potential fathers lack the correct alleles to match with each chick. Adding data from STR-3 and STR-4 will improve the students' ability to exclude potential males, and will make them more confident they have identified the correct father if they find a male that carries all of the necessary alleles.

Passage II

7. **B.** Scientist 1 states that dark matter is made of baryonic particles; Scientist 2 states that it cannot be made of baryonic particles. Although they have many other differing ideas about the nature of dark matter, the baryonic or non-baryonic nature of dark matter is fundamental to each argument.

8. **J.** Both scientists agree that there are observable gravitational anomalies in the universe that indicate the presence of large quantities of unseen matter. The other choices are mentioned in the passage, but not as points of agreement.

9. **A.** As the name implies, MACHO is a collective term for massive objects, on the order of stars and planets. B and C are not correct because Scientist 1 thinks dark matter is essentially normal matter that we are simply ill-equipped to visualize. D is not correct because it does not correctly define dark matter.

10. **G.** Scientist 2 describes an experiment that attempts to detect dark matter as it passes through the earth. For this same reason, Choice F cannot be correct. Choice H is not correct because although WIMPs are hypothesized to interact with the weak force, this does not mean they are radioactive. If they were, they would be much easier to detect. J is incorrect because we know that the gravitation effect of dark matter is the primary evidence of its existence.

11. **B.** Scientist 2 describes an experiment that attempts to detect dark matter as it passes through the earth.

12. **J.** MACHOs are massive objects; WIMPs, though massive relative to some other particles, are still tiny particles.

13. **A.** One of the key arguments Scientist 1 makes in favor of dark matter being a non-baryonic particle is that the Big Bang is not thought to have resulted in sufficient baryonic matter to account for the quantity of total matter. Therefore, Choice B is impossible; Choice C is not a refutation of Scientist 2's theory, and Choice D is nonsensical.

Passage III

14. F. The fact that argon is a gas means that while volcanic rock is in a liquid state, all of the argon built up over the past eons can escape, essentially "resetting" the clock. Choices G and J are not true; Choice H is not discussed.

15. C. As soon as the lava hardens, any subsequently created ^{40}Ar cannot escape the rock crystals, and so slowly rebuilds over time.

16. G. Plate tectonics leads to sporadic shifts in the earth's crust, so the relationship is not a perfect trend. However, the graph still suggests a clear upward trend as the island age and the distance from Island 1 both increase.

17. D. Given the options, this is the best answer, though the pattern is very rough. The three youngest islands form an upward trend prior to the downward trend of the older islands. Although not discussed, this may be due to the youngest islands still being in the "growth" phase and older islands experiencing erosion.

18. G. The age-geography trend is apparent and can justify an assumption that the underwater mound could be part of the same pattern until further testing can be performed. This hypothesis has significantly less evidence to support it than the ages of the other islands that were measured directly, but is a more reasonable guess than the other options.

Passage IV

19. A. The reduction potential voltage is created by the difference in electron attraction between the two substances. If the same substance is at each electrode, the electrons are not attracted in either direction and create no current. Note, also, that hydrogen is used as the standard against which other electrodes are measured and so its reduction potential is defined as zero. It is not necessary to know that for the purposes of this passage. The other answers are only partial truths that are not relevant to the particular question of reduction potentials.

20. J. Silver has the highest (i.e., most positive) reduction potential of the elements shown and, therefore, has the strongest tendency to accept electrons. The answer is not Choice F because magnesium is strongly negative—it has the lowest tendency to accept electrons. Choices G and H both have intermediate values.

21. A. Whichever element has the higher (more positive or less negative) reduction potential will be the electron acceptor in a redox reaction. Therefore, when hydrogen (reduction potential = 0) reacts with an element with a negative reduction potential, hydrogen is the more positive element.

22. G. Lead (RP = –0.13) has a higher reduction potential than zinc (RP = –0.76); therefore, lead will accept electrons, that is, be reduced. Choices H and J are incorrect because in a redox reaction, there is always one element being reduced and another being oxidized.

23. A. The element with the higher reduction potential will be reduced (Cu = +0.34). As mentioned in the passage, the oxidation potential is the inverse of the reduction potential for a given element. Therefore, the oxidation potential of zinc is +0.76. The sum is, therefore, 0.34 + 0.76 = 1.10 volts (as seen in Table 2).

24. H. This reaction will reduce copper (+0.34) and oxidize lithium (+3.05). The sum is, therefore, 0.34 + 3.05 = 3.39 volts.

Passage V

25. A. Ampicillin and novobiocin are the only antibiotics to which the bacteria were "susceptible," rather than "intermediate" or "resistant."

26. J. The zone of inhibition is 21 millimeters, which is between "resistant" (<13) and susceptible (>23). The answer is not Choice G, because it is important to note that the bacteria are not "resistant."

27. D. The zones of inhibition from the antibiotics in that area inhibited all growth, so there is no way to identify the diameter of the zone created specifically by novobiocin. Choices A and B are not correct because it is reasonable to believe that a portion of the inhibition near the disk is due to novobiocin. Choice C, however, overstates our knowledge.

28. F. The bacteria from all three dogs were "resistant" to penicillin and grew very close to the antibiotic disk.

29. A. The bacteria from Dog 3 are susceptible to six of the eight antibiotics tested.

30. G. The expected size of the zone of inhibition for bacteria susceptible to erythromycin is ≥ 23mm. Dogs 2 and 3 both meet this standard, but Dog 1 does not. This may indicate that erythromycin will not be effective in treating that dog's infection.

Passage VI

31. B. In Figure 1, contaminants such as NO_x are being released from both man-made and non-man-made sources.

32. J. There are two downward-pointing arrows in Figure 1: rain and dry deposition. These imply that the compounds that were released into the atmosphere are returned in these two ways. There is no indication of the deposition processes being specific to sulfur or nitrogen.

33. A. H_2O (water) contains the two hydrogen ions that give acid rain its acidity. The answer is not Choice B because the hydrogen ions begin in H_2SO_4; they do not end there. The answer is not Choice C because although the hydrogen ions do bond with the carbonate briefly, the passage explains that these molecules then break down further into carbon dioxide (CO_2) and water (H_2O).

34. H. The pH of the rainwater measured from Site 3 has not dropped below 5.0—the cutoff for acid rain.

35. B. Site 2 shows the longest period of time with very acidic (low) pH, and, therefore, we expect to see the most damage at that site.

Passage VII

36. H. The empty passenger elevator has a mass of ~3000 kg and a downward acceleration due to gravity of 9.8 m/s². This can be rounded to 10 m/s² for the ease of calculation. F = ma gives us F = 3000 kg × 10 m/s² = 30,000 N.

37. A. It takes 3 seconds for a construction elevator to reach its maximum speed of 1.5 m/s. Therefore, we can assume it accelerates during these 3 seconds at a rate of 0.5 m/s². If you answered Choice B, then you probably forgot to divide the speed by 3 seconds. If you answered Choice C, you may have made an error with decimal places. If you answered Choice D, you included gravity in your calculation, rather than giving the acceleration net of gravity.

38. H. It takes only 1 second for the passenger elevator to reach its maximum speed of 2.5 m/s. It, therefore, accelerates away from the earth at a rate of 2.5 m/s². Incorporating the acceleration due to gravity, the elevator is accelerating at 2.5 + 9.8 m/s² = 12.3 m/s². If you answered Choice F, you forgot to include the effect of gravity. If you answered Choice G, then you subtracted where you should have added the numbers together. If you answered Choice J, then you multiplied the accelerations together instead of adding them.

39. D. It is apparent from Figure 2 that the force exerted by a fully loaded freight elevator at maximum velocity is just shy of 135,000 N. This is more than the tolerances for the 14 millimeter cable (108,000 N) but less than those of the 16 millimeter cable (141,000 N).

40. G. In the current model the maximum acceleration of the freight elevator, net of gravity, is $\frac{2\,m/s}{2\,s} = 1\,m/s^2$. If it reaches 2 m/s in only 1 second, then it will have an acceleration of 2 m/s². Incorporating the acceleration of gravity, this means it will change from 10.8 m/s² to 11.8 m/s², a change of 9.3 percent, or roughly 10 percent. If you answered Choice F, you probably forgot to incorporate gravity and also confused your units. If you answered choices H or J, you likely were misled by the doubling of the acceleration of the elevator and did not incorporate the acceleration due to gravity.

Answer Sheets

English Test

1 Ⓐ Ⓑ Ⓒ Ⓓ	26 Ⓕ Ⓖ Ⓗ Ⓙ	51 Ⓐ Ⓑ Ⓒ Ⓓ
2 Ⓕ Ⓖ Ⓗ Ⓙ	27 Ⓐ Ⓑ Ⓒ Ⓓ	52 Ⓕ Ⓖ Ⓗ Ⓙ
3 Ⓐ Ⓑ Ⓒ Ⓓ	28 Ⓕ Ⓖ Ⓗ Ⓙ	53 Ⓐ Ⓑ Ⓒ Ⓓ
4 Ⓕ Ⓖ Ⓗ Ⓙ	29 Ⓐ Ⓑ Ⓒ Ⓓ	54 Ⓕ Ⓖ Ⓗ Ⓙ
5 Ⓐ Ⓑ Ⓒ Ⓓ	30 Ⓕ Ⓖ Ⓗ Ⓙ	55 Ⓐ Ⓑ Ⓒ Ⓓ
6 Ⓕ Ⓖ Ⓗ Ⓙ	31 Ⓐ Ⓑ Ⓒ Ⓓ	56 Ⓕ Ⓖ Ⓗ Ⓙ
7 Ⓐ Ⓑ Ⓒ Ⓓ	32 Ⓕ Ⓖ Ⓗ Ⓙ	57 Ⓐ Ⓑ Ⓒ Ⓓ
8 Ⓕ Ⓖ Ⓗ Ⓙ	33 Ⓐ Ⓑ Ⓒ Ⓓ	58 Ⓕ Ⓖ Ⓗ Ⓙ
9 Ⓐ Ⓑ Ⓒ Ⓓ	34 Ⓕ Ⓖ Ⓗ Ⓙ	59 Ⓐ Ⓑ Ⓒ Ⓓ
10 Ⓕ Ⓖ Ⓗ Ⓙ	35 Ⓐ Ⓑ Ⓒ Ⓓ	60 Ⓕ Ⓖ Ⓗ Ⓙ
11 Ⓐ Ⓑ Ⓒ Ⓓ	36 Ⓕ Ⓖ Ⓗ Ⓙ	61 Ⓐ Ⓑ Ⓒ Ⓓ
12 Ⓕ Ⓖ Ⓗ Ⓙ	37 Ⓐ Ⓑ Ⓒ Ⓓ	62 Ⓕ Ⓖ Ⓗ Ⓙ
13 Ⓐ Ⓑ Ⓒ Ⓓ	38 Ⓕ Ⓖ Ⓗ Ⓙ	63 Ⓐ Ⓑ Ⓒ Ⓓ
14 Ⓕ Ⓖ Ⓗ Ⓙ	39 Ⓐ Ⓑ Ⓒ Ⓓ	64 Ⓕ Ⓖ Ⓗ Ⓙ
15 Ⓐ Ⓑ Ⓒ Ⓓ	40 Ⓕ Ⓖ Ⓗ Ⓙ	65 Ⓐ Ⓑ Ⓒ Ⓓ
16 Ⓕ Ⓖ Ⓗ Ⓙ	41 Ⓐ Ⓑ Ⓒ Ⓓ	66 Ⓕ Ⓖ Ⓗ Ⓙ
17 Ⓐ Ⓑ Ⓒ Ⓓ	42 Ⓕ Ⓖ Ⓗ Ⓙ	67 Ⓐ Ⓑ Ⓒ Ⓓ
18 Ⓕ Ⓖ Ⓗ Ⓙ	43 Ⓐ Ⓑ Ⓒ Ⓓ	68 Ⓕ Ⓖ Ⓗ Ⓙ
19 Ⓐ Ⓑ Ⓒ Ⓓ	44 Ⓕ Ⓖ Ⓗ Ⓙ	69 Ⓐ Ⓑ Ⓒ Ⓓ
20 Ⓕ Ⓖ Ⓗ Ⓙ	45 Ⓐ Ⓑ Ⓒ Ⓓ	70 Ⓕ Ⓖ Ⓗ Ⓙ
21 Ⓐ Ⓑ Ⓒ Ⓓ	46 Ⓕ Ⓖ Ⓗ Ⓙ	71 Ⓐ Ⓑ Ⓒ Ⓓ
22 Ⓕ Ⓖ Ⓗ Ⓙ	47 Ⓐ Ⓑ Ⓒ Ⓓ	72 Ⓕ Ⓖ Ⓗ Ⓙ
23 Ⓐ Ⓑ Ⓒ Ⓓ	48 Ⓕ Ⓖ Ⓗ Ⓙ	73 Ⓐ Ⓑ Ⓒ Ⓓ
24 Ⓕ Ⓖ Ⓗ Ⓙ	49 Ⓐ Ⓑ Ⓒ Ⓓ	74 Ⓕ Ⓖ Ⓗ Ⓙ
25 Ⓐ Ⓑ Ⓒ Ⓓ	50 Ⓕ Ⓖ Ⓗ Ⓙ	75 Ⓐ Ⓑ Ⓒ Ⓓ

Mathematics Test

1 Ⓐ Ⓑ Ⓒ Ⓓ Ⓔ	21 Ⓐ Ⓑ Ⓒ Ⓓ Ⓔ	41 Ⓐ Ⓑ Ⓒ Ⓓ Ⓔ
2 Ⓕ Ⓖ Ⓗ Ⓙ Ⓚ	22 Ⓕ Ⓖ Ⓗ Ⓙ Ⓚ	42 Ⓕ Ⓖ Ⓗ Ⓙ Ⓚ
3 Ⓐ Ⓑ Ⓒ Ⓓ Ⓔ	23 Ⓐ Ⓑ Ⓒ Ⓓ Ⓔ	43 Ⓐ Ⓑ Ⓒ Ⓓ Ⓔ
4 Ⓕ Ⓖ Ⓗ Ⓙ Ⓚ	24 Ⓕ Ⓖ Ⓗ Ⓙ Ⓚ	44 Ⓕ Ⓖ Ⓗ Ⓙ Ⓚ
5 Ⓐ Ⓑ Ⓒ Ⓓ Ⓔ	25 Ⓐ Ⓑ Ⓒ Ⓓ Ⓔ	45 Ⓐ Ⓑ Ⓒ Ⓓ Ⓔ
6 Ⓕ Ⓖ Ⓗ Ⓙ Ⓚ	26 Ⓕ Ⓖ Ⓗ Ⓙ Ⓚ	46 Ⓕ Ⓖ Ⓗ Ⓙ Ⓚ
7 Ⓐ Ⓑ Ⓒ Ⓓ Ⓔ	27 Ⓐ Ⓑ Ⓒ Ⓓ Ⓔ	47 Ⓐ Ⓑ Ⓒ Ⓓ Ⓔ
8 Ⓕ Ⓖ Ⓗ Ⓙ Ⓚ	28 Ⓕ Ⓖ Ⓗ Ⓙ Ⓚ	48 Ⓕ Ⓖ Ⓗ Ⓙ Ⓚ
9 Ⓐ Ⓑ Ⓒ Ⓓ Ⓔ	29 Ⓐ Ⓑ Ⓒ Ⓓ Ⓔ	49 Ⓐ Ⓑ Ⓒ Ⓓ Ⓔ
10 Ⓕ Ⓖ Ⓗ Ⓙ Ⓚ	30 Ⓕ Ⓖ Ⓗ Ⓙ Ⓚ	50 Ⓕ Ⓖ Ⓗ Ⓙ Ⓚ
11 Ⓐ Ⓑ Ⓒ Ⓓ Ⓔ	31 Ⓐ Ⓑ Ⓒ Ⓓ Ⓔ	51 Ⓐ Ⓑ Ⓒ Ⓓ Ⓔ
12 Ⓕ Ⓖ Ⓗ Ⓙ Ⓚ	32 Ⓕ Ⓖ Ⓗ Ⓙ Ⓚ	52 Ⓕ Ⓖ Ⓗ Ⓙ Ⓚ
13 Ⓐ Ⓑ Ⓒ Ⓓ Ⓔ	33 Ⓐ Ⓑ Ⓒ Ⓓ Ⓔ	53 Ⓐ Ⓑ Ⓒ Ⓓ Ⓔ
14 Ⓕ Ⓖ Ⓗ Ⓙ Ⓚ	34 Ⓕ Ⓖ Ⓗ Ⓙ Ⓚ	54 Ⓕ Ⓖ Ⓗ Ⓙ Ⓚ
15 Ⓐ Ⓑ Ⓒ Ⓓ Ⓔ	35 Ⓐ Ⓑ Ⓒ Ⓓ Ⓔ	55 Ⓐ Ⓑ Ⓒ Ⓓ Ⓔ
16 Ⓕ Ⓖ Ⓗ Ⓙ Ⓚ	36 Ⓕ Ⓖ Ⓗ Ⓙ Ⓚ	56 Ⓕ Ⓖ Ⓗ Ⓙ Ⓚ
17 Ⓐ Ⓑ Ⓒ Ⓓ Ⓔ	37 Ⓐ Ⓑ Ⓒ Ⓓ Ⓔ	57 Ⓐ Ⓑ Ⓒ Ⓓ Ⓔ
18 Ⓕ Ⓖ Ⓗ Ⓙ Ⓚ	38 Ⓕ Ⓖ Ⓗ Ⓙ Ⓚ	58 Ⓕ Ⓖ Ⓗ Ⓙ Ⓚ
19 Ⓐ Ⓑ Ⓒ Ⓓ Ⓔ	39 Ⓐ Ⓑ Ⓒ Ⓓ Ⓔ	59 Ⓐ Ⓑ Ⓒ Ⓓ Ⓔ
20 Ⓕ Ⓖ Ⓗ Ⓙ Ⓚ	40 Ⓕ Ⓖ Ⓗ Ⓙ Ⓚ	60 Ⓕ Ⓖ Ⓗ Ⓙ Ⓚ

CUT HERE

Reading Test

1 Ⓐ Ⓑ Ⓒ Ⓓ	21 Ⓐ Ⓑ Ⓒ Ⓓ
2 Ⓕ Ⓖ Ⓗ Ⓙ	22 Ⓕ Ⓖ Ⓗ Ⓙ
3 Ⓐ Ⓑ Ⓒ Ⓓ	23 Ⓐ Ⓑ Ⓒ Ⓓ
4 Ⓕ Ⓖ Ⓗ Ⓙ	24 Ⓕ Ⓖ Ⓗ Ⓙ
5 Ⓐ Ⓑ Ⓒ Ⓓ	25 Ⓐ Ⓑ Ⓒ Ⓓ
6 Ⓕ Ⓖ Ⓗ Ⓙ	26 Ⓕ Ⓖ Ⓗ Ⓙ
7 Ⓐ Ⓑ Ⓒ Ⓓ	27 Ⓐ Ⓑ Ⓒ Ⓓ
8 Ⓕ Ⓖ Ⓗ Ⓙ	28 Ⓕ Ⓖ Ⓗ Ⓙ
9 Ⓐ Ⓑ Ⓒ Ⓓ	29 Ⓐ Ⓑ Ⓒ Ⓓ
10 Ⓕ Ⓖ Ⓗ Ⓙ	30 Ⓕ Ⓖ Ⓗ Ⓙ
11 Ⓐ Ⓑ Ⓒ Ⓓ	31 Ⓐ Ⓑ Ⓒ Ⓓ
12 Ⓕ Ⓖ Ⓗ Ⓙ	32 Ⓕ Ⓖ Ⓗ Ⓙ
13 Ⓐ Ⓑ Ⓒ Ⓓ	33 Ⓐ Ⓑ Ⓒ Ⓓ
14 Ⓕ Ⓖ Ⓗ Ⓙ	34 Ⓕ Ⓖ Ⓗ Ⓙ
15 Ⓐ Ⓑ Ⓒ Ⓓ	35 Ⓐ Ⓑ Ⓒ Ⓓ
16 Ⓕ Ⓖ Ⓗ Ⓙ	36 Ⓕ Ⓖ Ⓗ Ⓙ
17 Ⓐ Ⓑ Ⓒ Ⓓ	37 Ⓐ Ⓑ Ⓒ Ⓓ
18 Ⓕ Ⓖ Ⓗ Ⓙ	38 Ⓕ Ⓖ Ⓗ Ⓙ
19 Ⓐ Ⓑ Ⓒ Ⓓ	39 Ⓐ Ⓑ Ⓒ Ⓓ
20 Ⓕ Ⓖ Ⓗ Ⓙ	40 Ⓕ Ⓖ Ⓗ Ⓙ

Science Test

1 Ⓐ Ⓑ Ⓒ Ⓓ	21 Ⓐ Ⓑ Ⓒ Ⓓ
2 Ⓕ Ⓖ Ⓗ Ⓙ	22 Ⓕ Ⓖ Ⓗ Ⓙ
3 Ⓐ Ⓑ Ⓒ Ⓓ	23 Ⓐ Ⓑ Ⓒ Ⓓ
4 Ⓕ Ⓖ Ⓗ Ⓙ	24 Ⓕ Ⓖ Ⓗ Ⓙ
5 Ⓐ Ⓑ Ⓒ Ⓓ	25 Ⓐ Ⓑ Ⓒ Ⓓ
6 Ⓕ Ⓖ Ⓗ Ⓙ	26 Ⓕ Ⓖ Ⓗ Ⓙ
7 Ⓐ Ⓑ Ⓒ Ⓓ	27 Ⓐ Ⓑ Ⓒ Ⓓ
8 Ⓕ Ⓖ Ⓗ Ⓙ	28 Ⓕ Ⓖ Ⓗ Ⓙ
9 Ⓐ Ⓑ Ⓒ Ⓓ	29 Ⓐ Ⓑ Ⓒ Ⓓ
10 Ⓕ Ⓖ Ⓗ Ⓙ	30 Ⓕ Ⓖ Ⓗ Ⓙ
11 Ⓐ Ⓑ Ⓒ Ⓓ	31 Ⓐ Ⓑ Ⓒ Ⓓ
12 Ⓕ Ⓖ Ⓗ Ⓙ	32 Ⓕ Ⓖ Ⓗ Ⓙ
13 Ⓐ Ⓑ Ⓒ Ⓓ	33 Ⓐ Ⓑ Ⓒ Ⓓ
14 Ⓕ Ⓖ Ⓗ Ⓙ	34 Ⓕ Ⓖ Ⓗ Ⓙ
15 Ⓐ Ⓑ Ⓒ Ⓓ	35 Ⓐ Ⓑ Ⓒ Ⓓ
16 Ⓕ Ⓖ Ⓗ Ⓙ	36 Ⓕ Ⓖ Ⓗ Ⓙ
17 Ⓐ Ⓑ Ⓒ Ⓓ	37 Ⓐ Ⓑ Ⓒ Ⓓ
18 Ⓕ Ⓖ Ⓗ Ⓙ	38 Ⓕ Ⓖ Ⓗ Ⓙ
19 Ⓐ Ⓑ Ⓒ Ⓓ	39 Ⓐ Ⓑ Ⓒ Ⓓ
20 Ⓕ Ⓖ Ⓗ Ⓙ	40 Ⓕ Ⓖ Ⓗ Ⓙ

CUT HERE

Directions

The practice tests are for assessment purposes only. These tests are designed to measure skills learned in high school that relate to success in college. Try to simulate test conditions and time yourself as you begin each of the following practice tests:

> English Test—45 minutes
>
> Mathematics Test—60 minutes
>
> Reading Test—35 minutes
>
> Science Test—35 minutes

- Calculators may be used on the mathematics test only.

- The numbered questions on each test are followed by lettered answer choices. Make sure to properly mark the answer you have selected next to the corresponding question number on the answer sheet. If you want to change an answer, erase your original answer thoroughly before marking in the new answer.

- On the actual exam, you must use a soft lead pencil and completely blacken the oval of the letter you have selected because your score is based completely on the number of questions you answer and mark correctly on the answer sheet. Do NOT use a ballpoint pen or a mechanical pencil.

- You are allowed to work on only one test at a time. If you complete a test before time is up, you may go back and review questions only in that test. You may NOT go back to previous tests, and you may NOT go forward to another test. On the actual exam day, you will be disqualified from the exam if you work on another test.

- There is no penalty for guessing, so *answer every question*, even if you need to guess.

- On the actual exam, when time is up, be sure to put your pencil down immediately. After time is up, you may NOT for any reason fill in answers. This will disqualify you from the exam.

- Do not fold or tear the pages of your test booklet.

English Test

Time: 45 Minutes
75 Questions

Directions: In the passages that follow, you will find various words and phrases are underlined and numbered. A set of responses corresponding to each underlined portion will follow each passage. If the underlined portion is correct standard written English, is most appropriate to the style and feeling of the passage, and best expresses the intended idea, mark the letter indicating "NO CHANGE." If, however, the underlined portion is not the best choice given, choose the best answer to the question. For these questions, consider only the underlined portions and assume that the rest of the passage is correct as written.

You will also find questions concerning a sentence, several parts of the passage, or the whole passage. These questions do not refer to an underlined portion, but refer to the portion of the passage that is identified with the corresponding question number in a box. Choose the response you feel is best for these questions.

Passage I

Paragraphs are numbered in brackets, and sentences in paragraph 4 are numbered.

Library Meeting

[1]

The city council met on Tuesday to determine the best site for a new library, although a few council members have already spoken out against a new building, believing that <u>a renovation is what should be done of the current library.</u> The debate was heated, and a group in the audience <u>had interrupted</u> the proceedings so often that <u>they</u> had to adjourn before anything could be decided.

[2]

<u>Speaking afterwards, it was made clear by the mayor</u> that the <u>issues, concerning the library,</u> required more investigation by the planning committee, which had submitted <u>their</u> report <u>but without</u> a clear financial statement. "I believe that <u>us council members have rose</u> to our responsibilities, and it is up to the planning committee to spend less time considering details <u>such as paint color or what paintings to hang on the library walls</u> and more time determining the <u>basic fundamentals</u> of the financial impact." He made the comments to a crowd outside the council chambers.

[3]

When a reporter spoke to the chairman of the planning committee after the mayor's statement, <u>he</u> said, "<u>In my opinion, I think</u> the mayor is being unfair when he blames the committee, <u>which has met regular</u> every week for three months so that we could present a viable plan at tonight's meeting. We did not spend our time arguing about paint color. The absence of a detailed financial plan should be blamed on our not receiving sufficient information from the city financial manager in time for the meeting. He is clearly not doing his job." [14]

GO ON TO THE NEXT PAGE

[4]

[1] In an angry response, the financial manager claimed that the chairman of the library committee's request for a plan had not been received early enough for contractors and suppliers to provide the necessary information. [2] At the next city council meeting the mayor apologized to the planning committee for his earlier criticism. [3] Praising the committee's efforts, he asked residents to support the building of a new, improved library. [4] According to the manager, a detailed financial plan would be available within two weeks. 15

1. A. NO CHANGE
   B. to renovate is called for of the current library.
   C. the current library should be renovated.
   D. a renovation is a better idea for the current library.

2. F. NO CHANGE
   G. had been interrupting
   H. has been interrupting
   J. interrupted

3. A. NO CHANGE
   B. the council
   C. the audience
   D. it

4. F. NO CHANGE
   G. Speaking afterwards, the point was made clear by the mayor
   H. It was made clear, by the mayor, speaking afterwards
   J. Speaking afterwards, the mayor made clear

5. A. NO CHANGE
   B. issues concerning the library
   C. issues, which were concerning the library,
   D. issues that were of concern to the library

6. F. NO CHANGE
   G. its
   H. it's
   J. the committees'

7. A. NO CHANGE
   B. however without
   C. without
   D. and without

8. F. NO CHANGE
   G. us council members have risen
   H. we council members have rose
   J. we council members have risen

9. Deleting the underlined section would
   A. improve the flow of the paragraph.
   B. omit important information about the renovation.
   C. soften the tone of the mayor's criticism.
   D. detract from the relevance of the mayor's comment.

10. F. NO CHANGE
    G. fundamentals
    H. basic, fundamentals
    J. primary fundamentals

11. A. NO CHANGE
    B. the mayor
    C. the reporter
    D. the chairman

12. F. NO CHANGE
    G. "It is my opinion that . . .
    H. "I believe, in my opinion, . . .
    J. "I think . . .

13. A. NO CHANGE
    B. which has met regularly
    C. which has had regular meetings
    D. that has met regular

GO ON TO THE NEXT PAGE

14. Of the following choices, which sentence of Passage I, if included as the last sentence in paragraph 3, would lead most logically into paragraph 4?

   F. The members of the library planning committee volunteer their efforts and are considered community leaders.

   G. The mayor appointed the members of the library planning committee last year, but they all serve voluntarily.

   H. The chairman of the library planning committee plans to oppose the town's financial manager at the next election.

   J. From the beginning, the library has met with resistance from a group of irate residents.

15. Which of the following is the most logical sequence of sentences in paragraph 4?

   A. 1, 2, 3, 4
   B. 4, 1, 2, 3
   C. 1, 4, 2, 3
   D. 1, 4, 3, 2

Passage II

Paragraphs are numbered in brackets, and sentences in paragraphs 3 and 4 are numbered.

Leaving Home

[1]

Moving out of my parents' house and into an apartment didn't bring me the uncomplicated <u>joy, that</u>
16
<u>I was expecting it to bring me.</u> First of all, I had to
16
struggle to make the rent every month because although my job wasn't bad, it <u>didn't pay good enough</u>
17
to cover all my expenses. It's no big surprise that my landlord wasn't as understanding as my parents. [18]

[2]

I realized that I also hadn't thought of some little

things. <u>Such as doing my own laundry</u> and, even worse,
19

to clean up the place now and then. What surprised me
20
most of all was finding out I actually cared quite a bit about <u>having clean clothes and a clean place to live.</u> (My
21
mother pretended to be shocked, when she found out.)

[3]

[1] The biggest problem of all<u>, however,</u> was having
22
to fix all my meals. [2] One nice thing about my mother <u>has been</u> that she is an excellent cook. [3] I, on the
23
other hand, started throwing frozen dinners in the microwave<u>, just for the reason that</u> it was <u>more easy</u>
24   25
than cooking <u>from scratch.</u> [4] Both my taste buds and
26
my nutrition suffered from my lack of cooking skills. [5] My mother attended a French cooking school before she married my father and worked as a chef. [27]

[4]

[1] I do like the greater freedom I have in my <u>apartment. No one constantly to ask me what time I'll</u>
28
<u>be home and nagging me about my messy room.</u>
28
[2] And my friends can drop by any time they want without bothering my parents. [3] I spent a whole weekend getting rid of a cockroach infestation in the apartment and doing a huge load of smelly laundry. [4] But I have learned that there's a price to pay for freedom. [5] Who <u>would of thought</u> being on my own
29
meant taking care of myself, even on weekends? [30]

GO ON TO THE NEXT PAGE

16. F.   NO CHANGE
    G.   joy that I expected.
    H.   joy, that I expected.
    J.   joy which I had been expecting to have.

17. A.   NO CHANGE
    B.   didn't pay nearly good enough
    C.   didn't pay well enough
    D.   was a position with a salary not good enough

18. Which choice would most effectively signal the shift from paragraph 1 to paragraph 2?

    F.   He charged a fee if I was just three days late with the rent.
    G.   Money problems, however, were not the only issue in my new apartment.
    H.   I looked for a higher paying job, but nothing was available unless I drove for miles.
    J.   To save money for the rent, I started commuting to work on my bicycle.

19. A.   NO CHANGE
    B.   things: such as doing my own laundry.
    C.   things, such as doing my own laundry
    D.   things; as, for example, doing my own laundry

20. F.   NO CHANGE
    G.   to clean now and then.
    H.   cleaning up the place now and then.
    J.   that I should clean up the place now and then.

21. A.   NO CHANGE
    B.   having clean clothes and in addition having a clean place to live.
    C.   to have clean clothes and to have a clean place to live.
    D.   having clean clothes and also having a clean place to live.

22. F.   NO CHANGE
    G.   , however
    H.   however
    J.   however,

23. A.   NO CHANGE
    B.   is
    C.   will be
    D.   will have been

24. F.   NO CHANGE
    G.   , just on account of that
    H.   because of the reason that
    J.   because

25. A.   NO CHANGE
    B.   easier
    C.   more easily
    D.   easiest

26. F.   NO CHANGE
    G.   with recipes that are written down and contain a plethora of ingredients.
    H.   all the way from the very beginning.
    J.   complicated and byzantine.

27. Which of the following sentences should be omitted from paragraph 3 to improve its unity?

    A.   None of the sentences should be omitted.
    B.   sentence 2
    C.   sentence 4
    D.   sentence 5

28. F.   NO CHANGE
    G.   apartment. No one constantly asks me what time I'll be home and nags me about my messy room.
    H.   apartment. There is no one who is constantly asking what time I'll be home and nags me about my messy room.
    J.   apartment, no one to ask me what time I'll be home or nagging me about my messy room.

29. A.   NO CHANGE
    B.   would ever of thought
    C.   would have thought
    D.   would of ever been thinking

GO ON TO THE NEXT PAGE

30. Which of the following sequences of sentences makes paragraph 4 most logical?

   F.   1, 2, 4, 3, 5

   G.   1, 2, 3, 5, 4

   H.   1, 3, 2, 4, 5

   J.   5, 1, 2, 3, 4

Passage III

Paragraphs are numbered in brackets, and sentences in paragraphs 2 and 5 are numbered.

Plants

[1]

Although different plants have different environmental requirements because <u>of their physiology there are</u>₃₁ <u>certain plant species which are found</u>₃₁ associated with relatively extensive geographical areas. <u>The distribution</u>₃₂ <u>of plants depend</u>₃₂ upon a number of <u>factors. Among</u>₃₃ <u>which are the amount</u>₃₃ of daylight and darkness, temperature averages and extremes, and the types and amounts of precipitation.

[2]

[1] To regulate their cycle, plants <u>are dependent on</u>₃₄ daylight and darkness. [2] <u>How long daylight is appears</u>₃₅ to be a key. [3] A case in point is that many greenhouse plants bloom only in the spring without being influenced by outside conditions other than light. [4] Normally, the plants keyed to daylight and <u>darkness</u>₃₆ <u>phenomena, are restricted to</u>₃₆ particular latitudes. [5] In one way or another, every plant is affected by temperature. 37

[3]

Some plant species are <u>killed by frost; others require</u>₃₈ <u>frost</u>₃₈ and cold conditions to bear fruit. For example, orange blossoms are killed by frost, but<u>, on the other</u>₃₉ <u>hand,</u>₃₉ cherry blossoms will develop only if the buds have been chilled for an appropriate time. <u>The worlds</u>₄₀ <u>great vegetation zones which are aligned</u>₄₀ with temperature belts.

[4]

Various plant species adjust to changes in the seasons, some retarding growth and arresting vital functions during the winter<u>; whereas other plants will</u>₄₁ <u>disappear</u>₄₁ entirely at the end of the growing season. Those that disappear are called annuals and will reappear only through their seeds. The other plants <u>called perennials</u>₄₂ will appear year after year because they "rest" during off-season.

[5]

[1] Plants get their water from precipitation, but different kinds of plants require different amounts of water. [2] Taken in at the roots, some moisture is needed by all plants. [3] Those that are drought resistant have a variety of defenses<u>, which they can use,</u>₄₃ when there are deficiencies of water. [4] But plants<u>, which have</u>₄₄ <u>been adapted to humid environments,</u>₄₄ have hardly any such defenses. 45

GO ON TO THE NEXT PAGE

31. A. NO CHANGE
B. of their physiology, certain plant species are found
C. of their physiology; there are certain plant species
D. of their physiology. Certain plant species

32. F. NO CHANGE
G. Plants depend
H. The distribution of plants depends
J. The distribution of plants depend,

33. A. NO CHANGE
B. factors, among them the amount
C. factors: among which are the amount
D. factors, and among them are the amount

34. F. NO CHANGE
G. are dependent for
H. will be dependent on
J. depend on

35. A. NO CHANGE
B. The length of daylight appears
C. However long the daylight is appears
D. Daylight appears

36. F. NO CHANGE
G. darkness phenomenon have been restricted to
H. darkness phenomena are restricted to
J. darkness phenomena, will be

37. What is the best placement of sentence 5 in paragraph 2 of Passage III?

A. before sentence 2
B. before sentence 3
C. move it to paragraph 3 and make it the last sentence
D. move it to paragraph 3 and make it the first sentence

38. F. NO CHANGE
G. killed by frost. While others require frost and cold conditions
H. killed by frost, while on the other hand others require frost and cold conditions
J. killed by frost, and then frost and cold conditions are required by others

39. A. NO CHANGE
B. Omit the underlined phrase.
C. , but, just the opposite,
D. , however,

40. F. NO CHANGE
G. The world's great vegetation zones, aligned
H. The world's great vegetation zones are aligned
J. The worlds great vegetation zones that are aligned

41. A. NO CHANGE
B. , others disappearing
C. while other plants will be disappearing
D. and other plants will disappear

42. F. NO CHANGE
G. , those that are referred to as perennials,
H. , that are called perennials,
J. , called perennials,

43. A. NO CHANGE
B. , which they will be using
C. to use
D. , and they can be used,

44. F. NO CHANGE
G. , that have been adapted to humid environments,
H. which will have been adapted to humid environments,
J. that have adapted to humid environments

45. The best order of sentences in paragraph 5 of Passage III is

A. 3, 4, 1, 2
B. 1, 2, 3, 4
C. 2, 3, 4, 1
D. 2, 1, 3, 4

GO ON TO THE NEXT PAGE

Passage IV

The following paragraphs may or may not be in the most logical order. Paragraphs are numbered in brackets, and sentences in paragraph 3 are numbered.

Variability Hypothesis

[1]

In the early 19th century, Johann Meckel set forth an idea which came to be referred to as the variability hypothesis. His argument was that <u>men have a greater range of ability especially in intelligence than women.</u>
₄₆ In other words, he believed that most geniuses and most mentally retarded people were <u>men; whereas</u>
₄₇ women had a much smaller range of intelligence. Their greater range of ability made men superior, Meckel believed. It was women's lack of variation that made them <u>more inferior.</u>
₄₈

[2]

Later, when Charles Darwin came along, the variability hypothesis was changed to fit Darwin's emphasis on the important part that variation from the average played <u>in the evolutionary process.</u> The
₄₉ <u>amount of men at opposite ends of the intellectual</u>
₅₀ <u>spectrum was seen</u> as evidence that men had greater
₅₀ innate variability. Women, on the other hand, <u>don't</u>
₅₁ <u>exhibit</u> such range.
₅₁

[3]

[1] The variability hypothesis flourished in the early 20th century. [2] <u>A conclusion that was drawn from it</u>
₅₂ <u>by many people was</u> that women<u>, whom were not to be</u>
₅₂ ₅₃ <u>expected to be of great intelligence,</u> could not be
₅₃ expected to be great achievers. [3] Feminists in the 1960s did not agree that women possess only average intelligence. [4] Two early psychologists<u>, whose names</u>
₅₄ <u>were G. Stanley Hall and Edward Lee Thorndike,</u>
₅₄ <u>made the suggestion</u> in the early part of the century
₅₄ that the school curriculum for women should be adapted so that their studies <u>are preparing them</u> to be
₅₅ wives and <u>mothers, their appropriate roles.</u> 57
₅₆

[4]

In the most recent studies, the variability theory has been found wanting. For example, two professors at the University of Wisconsin in 2011 published analysis of data on math performance from 52 countries. One finding was that the variability range between male and female performance on mathematics tests <u>were essentially equal to each other.</u> Another
₅₈ finding was that the ratio of males' to females' variance differs greatly from one country to the next. According to one of the scientists, the range of variability between men's and women's scores was "all over the place."

GO ON TO THE NEXT PAGE

[5]

Leta Hollingworth, another American psychologist at the time of Hall and Thorndike, had attacked Meckel's variability hypothesis by looking at the case records of 1,000 patients at the Clearing House for Mental Defectives, where she worked. She determined that although men outnumbered women, the ratio of men to women decreased with age, and she believed this to be because men had to face more expectations than women in society. Hollingworth also attacked the hypothesis because it had not been empirically shown that men were innately more variable in <u>either physical traits or in traits that are mental.</u> [60]
⁵⁹

46. F. NO CHANGE
    G. men, not women, have a greater range of ability, in intelligence especially.
    H. men have a greater range of ability than women, especially in intelligence.
    J. men have a greater range of ability than women do, and this is especially true when it comes to intelligence.

47. A. NO CHANGE
    B. men, on the other hand
    C. men. Whereas
    D. men because

48. F. NO CHANGE
    G. inferior.
    H. more inferior than men.
    J. made them most inferior.

49. A. NO CHANGE
    B. to the evolutionary process.
    C. as far as the evolutionary process was concerned.
    D. during the process known as evolution.

50. F. NO CHANGE
    G. number of men at opposite ends of the intellectual spectrum was seen
    H. number of men at opposite ends of the intellectual spectrum were seen
    J. amount of men at opposite ends of the intellectual spectrum were seen

51. A. NO CHANGE
    B. didn't exhibit
    C. could not have exhibited
    D. will not have exhibited

52. F. NO CHANGE
    G. A conclusion that many people drew from it was
    H. From it was concluded by many people
    J. Many people concluded

53. A. NO CHANGE
    B. , who were not intelligent,
    C. , who were not expected to be of great intelligence,
    D. , whom were seen as not possessing above-average intelligence,

54. F. NO CHANGE
    G. whose names were G. Stanley Hall and Edward Lee Thorndike made the suggestion
    H. , G. Stanley Hall and Edward Lee Thorndike, suggested
    J. named G. Stanley Hall and Edward Lee Thorndike made the suggestion

55. A. NO CHANGE
    B. would prepare them
    C. will be preparing them
    D. are to be preparing them

56. F. NO CHANGE
    G. mothers, which will be their appropriate roles.
    H. mothers, and these would be their appropriate roles.
    J. mothers. Since these are their appropriate roles.

GO ON TO THE NEXT PAGE

57. The best location for sentence 3 in paragraph 3 is

    A. where it is now.
    B. after sentence 1.
    C. after sentence 4.
    D. The sentence should be omitted.

58. **F.** NO CHANGE
    G. was essentially equal to each other.
    H. was essentially equal.
    J. were essentially equal.

59. **A.** NO CHANGE
    B. in either traits that are physical or traits that are mental.
    C. in either physical or mental traits.
    D. either in physical traits, or in mental traits.

Question 60 poses a question about Passage IV as a whole.

60. Which of the following sequences of paragraphs will make the structure of Passage IV most logical?

    F. NO CHANGE
    G. 1, 3, 2, 4, 5
    H. 1, 2, 4, 3, 5
    J. 1, 2, 3, 5, 4

Passage V

Paragraphs are numbered in brackets, and sentences in paragraph 3 are numbered.

The Pace of Technology

[1]

Technology in the fields of communications and
                        61
media have been moving at a staggering pace. It seems
     61
as if right after you purchase the latest cell phone or the biggest flat-screen television, companies announce a later version that would have more bells and whistles
            62
than you would have believed would be possible.
                 63

[2]

Walking into a coffee house these days, chances are
                        64
at least half of the people there will be texting or phoning or watching miniature basketball players on miniature screens. Of them remaining, several will be
            65
busy on their laptop computers or tablets. Very few people will simply be conversing or reading magazines and newspapers. Those that are conversing are probably talking about which new gizmo is the best while others commiserate over malfunctions and
                   66
"down time," as well as the price of their wireless
  66
services. The monthly fees for wireless devices vary greatly, depending on what plan you choose, and therefore before you sign a contract, you should be careful to read the small print so that you know not only exactly what it covers but you need to know
                  67
how long the contract is for. 68 69
    67

[3]

[1] Did the introduction of the automobile move this fast? [2] Probably not. [3] It seems like technology
                       70
moved more slowly then. [4] Economic times were
     70
different, too, and advertising hadn't become so constant and aggressive. [5] Now, we consumers are
            71
eager to have the very latest thing, and it has become
  71
harder and harder to keep up the pace. [6] When an exotic new feature comes along in the fields of media

GO ON TO THE NEXT PAGE

or communications, do we think about <u>whether it will really add to our lives.</u> [72] [7] That's another thing we should blame the media for. [8] Current advances in technology are impressive, but sometimes we should stop and think before we spend money trying to keep up with the rapid changes. [9] <u>While watching bad programs</u> [73] on ever more gigantic television screens or texting meaningless chatter on ever more sophisticated phones, our lives—as well as our budgets—may be suffering. 74 75

61. A. NO CHANGE
B. Technology, both in media and in communications, have been moving
C. Media technology and communications technology, they have been moving
D. Media and communications technology has been moving

62. F. NO CHANGE
G. later versions that have
H. a later version, which will have
J. later versions, and they will have

63. A. NO CHANGE
B. you would have believed that could be possible.
C. you would have believed possible.
D. one would of believed possible.

64. F. NO CHANGE
G. When you walk into a coffee shop these days, chances are
H. Chances are walking into a coffee shop these days
J. When walking into a coffee shop these days, it is likely

65. A. NO CHANGE
B. of them who remain
C. of those remaining
D. of those whom are remaining

66. F. NO CHANGE
G. commiserated about malfunctions and "down time,"
H. will have been commiserating about malfunctions and "down time,"
J. are commiserating about malfunctions and "down time,"

67. A. NO CHANGE
B. not only exactly what it covers but also how long it is in effect.
C. not only exactly what it covers, but you also need to know how long it is for.
D. but also you should know for how long the contract will be in effect.

68. The writer is considering deleting the last sentence of paragraph 2. Should the writer delete this sentence?

F. No, because it is a practical warning to consumers shopping for the best wireless service.
G. No, because the paragraph would be too short without it.
H. Yes, because it changes the direction and tone of the paragraph.
J. Yes, because it is the writer's opinion rather than fact.

69. Of the following sentences, which would be the most effective as the first sentence of paragraph 3?

A. In the future, maybe we will see advances that we saw in shows like "Star Trek," such as the ability to "beam" people up.
B. Technological advances have always introduced new problems as well as solutions to everyday problems.
C. The speed of advances in media and communication technology may be what sets the current situation apart from earlier changes in the way we live.
D. The desire to be innovative, to make exciting changes in the world, is a powerful motivation, especially when it can involve becoming a billionaire.

GO ON TO THE NEXT PAGE

70. F. NO CHANGE
G. as if technology moved more slowly then.
H. like technology moved more slow then.
J. as if technology moved at a much slower pace than compared to today.

71. A. NO CHANGE
B. we consumers have become eager to have
C. we, that is, the consumers will be eager to have
D. us consumers are eager to have

72. F. NO CHANGE
G. if really it will add to our lives.
H. if it will really be adding to our lives.
J. whether it will really add to our lives?

73. A. NO CHANGE
B. While we are watching bad programs
C. During the time of watching bad programs
D. Watching bad programs

74. Which of the following sentences in paragraph 3 could be omitted to improve the unity of the paragraph?

F. Sentence 3
G. Sentence 5
H. Sentence 7
J. Sentence 9

Question 75 poses a question about Passage V as a whole.

75. Passage V would be most appropriate in a

A. textbook chapter on communications.
B. research paper on recent technology.
C. local paper opinion piece.
D. news magazine.

IF YOU FINISH BEFORE TIME IS CALLED, CHECK YOUR WORK ON THIS SECTION ONLY. DO NOT WORK ON ANY OTHER SECTION IN THE TEST.

Mathematics Test

Time: 60 Minutes

60 Questions

Directions: After solving each problem, choose the correct answer and fill in the corresponding space on your answer sheet. Do not spend too much time on any one problem. Solve as many problems as you can and return to the others if time permits. You are allowed to use a calculator on this test.

Note: Unless it is otherwise stated, you can assume all of the following:

1. Figures are NOT necessarily drawn to scale.
2. Geometric figures lie in a plane.
3. The word "line" means a straight line.
4. The word "average" refers to the arithmetic mean.

1. Forty-eight students took a test. Eight received a grade of A. Ten received a grade of B. Ten received a grade of D. Two received a grade of F. The rest received a grade of C. What percent of the students received a grade of C?

A. 20%
B. 25%
C. 30%
D. $33\frac{1}{3}\%$
E. $37\frac{1}{2}\%$

2. Tony has taken six out of eight tests in a mathematics class. If each test is worth the same number of points and Tony's average on the first six tests was 78, what would his average have to be on the next two tests so that his overall average on all eight tests would increase to 80?

F. 82
G. 84
H. 86
J. 88
K. 164

3. Twelve students belong to club E, 15 students belong to club F, and 20 students belong to club G. If 12 students belong to exactly two of the clubs and three students belong to all three clubs, then how many students belong to exactly one of the three clubs?

A. 11
B. 14
C. 18
D. 23
E. 32

4. Two cubes have total surface areas in the ratio of 3 to 4. What is the ratio of their volumes?

F. $\dfrac{9\sqrt{3}}{64}$
G. $\dfrac{\sqrt{3}}{4}$
H. $\dfrac{9}{16}$
J. $\dfrac{5\sqrt{2}}{12}$
K. $\dfrac{3\sqrt{3}}{8}$

GO ON TO THE NEXT PAGE

5. What is the least common multiple of 24, 48, and 60?

   A. 120
   B. 240
   C. 480
   D. 960
   E. 1080

6. One of the two roots of $3x^2 + cx - 12 = 0$ is $x = -3$. What is the other root?

   F. $\dfrac{2}{3}$

   G. $\dfrac{3}{4}$

   H. $\dfrac{4}{5}$

   J. $\dfrac{4}{3}$

   K. $\dfrac{5}{3}$

7. If $a = -3$ and $b = -1$ and $c = 3$, then $ab^2c - a^2b^3c + abc = ?$

   A. -27
   B. -9
   C. 9
   D. 27
   E. 45

8. Which of the following is equivalent to $\left(\left(-3x^2 y\right)\left(xy^3\right)\right)^2$?

   F. $-9x^5 y^6$
   G. $-6x^5 y^6$
   H. $6x^6 y^8$
   J. $9x^5 y^6$
   K. $9x^6 y^8$

9. Which of the following is equivalent to $(x + 2)^3$?

   A. $x^3 + 8x^2 + 16x + 8$
   B. $x^3 + 4x^2 + 12x + 8$
   C. $x^3 + 8x^2 + 4x + 8$
   D. $x^3 + 4x^2 + 10x + 8$
   E. $x^3 + 6x^2 + 12x + 8$

10. A rectangular block of wood in the shape of a rectangular prism measures 2 inches by 2 inches by 3 inches. It is painted on all six sides. It is then cut into small cubes along the dotted lines shown in the following figure. What is the ratio of the number of painted surfaces to the number of unpainted surfaces of the small cubes?

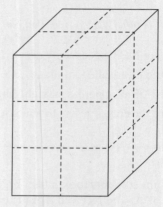

   F. 2:3
   G. 4:5
   H. 1:1
   J. 5:4
   K. 3:2

11. In the standard (x, y) coordinate plane, what is the equation of the line that passes through the point $(-1, -2)$ and is perpendicular to the line $y = \dfrac{1}{4}x + 2$?

   A. $y = 4x + 6$
   B. $y = -4x - 6$
   C. $y = 4x - 6$
   D. $y = -4x + 6$
   E. None of the above

12. A rectangle is twice as long as it is wide. What is the area, in square centimeters, if the perimeter of the rectangle is 42 cm?

   F. 50
   G. 72
   H. 98
   J. 120
   K. 392

GO ON TO THE NEXT PAGE

Use the following information to answer questions 13–15.

Two cars, *A* and *B*, start from the same point and are driven east on a straight road. Car *A* starts out at 9 a.m. and is driven at 40 miles per hour. Car *B* starts out 3 hours later and is driven at 50 miles per hour.

13. After Car *B* has driven for three hours, how many miles apart will the cars be?

    A. 50
    B. 70
    C. 90
    D. 110
    E. 130

14. When Car *A* is 200 miles from the starting point, Car *B* will be how far from the starting point?

    F. 0 miles
    G. 50 miles
    H. 100 miles
    J. 150 miles
    K. 200 miles

15. At approximately what time will Car *B* catch up to Car *A*?

    A. 8 p.m.
    B. 9 p.m.
    C. 10 p.m.
    D. 11 p.m.
    E. 12 midnight

16. A straight line is graphed in the standard (x, y) coordinate plane. Its *x*-intercept is 5, and its *y*-intercept is 3. What is the equation of this line?

    F. $8x + 5y = 15$
    G. $5x - 3y = -15$
    H. $5x + 3y = 15$
    J. $3x - 5y = 15$
    K. $3x + 5y = 15$

17. A rectangular room is 24 feet long and 16 feet wide. The floor of the room is being tiled with 16-inch square tiles. The tiles are slightly undersized to allow for a thin grout joint. Approximately how many linear feet of grout joint will there be between the tiles?

    A. 440
    B. 480
    C. 536
    D. 576
    E. 728

18. The price of a stock decreased in value 10 percent the first month, increased 20 percent the second month and then decreased 10 percent the third month. How did the price of the stock after the three price changes compare to the price of the stock before the three price changes?

    F. Up 2.8%
    G. Up 1.4%
    H. Unchanged
    J. Down 1.4%
    K. Down 2.8%

19. Two of the sides of an isosceles triangle measure 4 cm and 10 cm. What is the area in square centimeters of the triangle?

    A. $2\sqrt{21}$
    B. $4\sqrt{6}$
    C. $4\sqrt{21}$
    D. $8\sqrt{6}$
    E. 20

20. For a club function, adult tickets are sold for $5 each, and child tickets are sold for $2 each. If the ratio of adult to child tickets sold is 4:1, and a total of $682 was taken in from ticket sales, then how many child tickets were sold?

    F. 20
    G. 27
    H. 31
    J. 34
    K. 37

GO ON TO THE NEXT PAGE

21. A car travels at an average speed of 40 miles per hour for 200 miles, then at an average speed of 50 miles per hour for another 200 miles. Approximately what was the average speed for the entire 400-mile trip?

   A. 44 miles per hour

   B. $44\frac{1}{2}$ miles per hour

   C. 45 miles per hour

   D. $45\frac{1}{2}$ miles per hour

   E. 46 miles per hour

22. If θ lies in the third quadrant and $\cos\theta = -\frac{5}{13}$, then what is the value of $\cot\theta$?

   F. $-\frac{12}{5}$

   G. $-\frac{5}{12}$

   H. $\frac{5}{13}$

   J. $\frac{5}{12}$

   K. $\frac{12}{5}$

Use the following information to answer questions 23–25.

Triangle *ABC* is drawn in the (*x, y*) coordinate plane. The three vertices of the triangle are *A*(–6, 2), *B*(8, 4), and *C*(–2, –6).

23. What is the *x*-coordinate of the *x*-intercept of $\overline{AC}$?

   A. –5

   B. –4

   C. –3

   D. 4

   E. 5

24. What is the length of $\overline{AB}$?

   F. $5\sqrt{6}$

   G. $6\sqrt{5}$

   H. $8\sqrt{3}$

   J. $10\sqrt{2}$

   K. 15

25. What is the equation of the perpendicular bisector of $\overline{BC}$?

   A. $x + y = 4$

   B. $x - y = 4$

   C. $x + y = 2$

   D. $x - y = 2$

   E. $x + 2y = 1$

26. The perimeter of the rectangle below is 28 inches. If *AD* = 4 in. and *BE* = 2 in., then what is the perimeter, in inches, of triangle *CDE*?

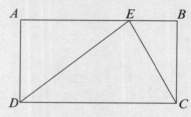

   F. $10 + 8\sqrt{2}$

   G. $16 + 5\sqrt{2}$

   H. $10 + 6\sqrt{5}$

   J. $20 + 2\sqrt{5}$

   K. $16 + 4\sqrt{5}$

27. Points *A*, *B*, *C*, *D*, and *E* are points on the following circle. The length of $\overparen{BD}$ is 25 percent longer than the length of $\overparen{BC}$. If $\angle x = 40°$, then what is the size of $\angle y$?

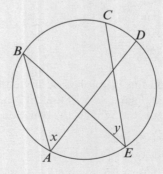

   A. 30°

   B. 32°

   C. 36°

   D. 38°

   E. Cannot be determined from the information given.

GO ON TO THE NEXT PAGE

28. If three pears weigh the same as three oranges plus one apple, and if three apples weigh the same as one pear plus one orange, then how many oranges weigh the same as four pears?

   F. 2

   G. 3

   H. 4

   J. 5

   K. 6

29. Given the following right triangle, what is the value of $\sin X + \tan Y$ in terms of x, y, and z?

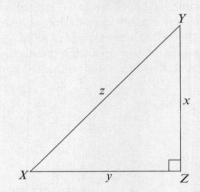

   A. $\dfrac{xy + xz}{yz}$

   B. $\dfrac{y + z}{x}$

   C. $\dfrac{x^2 + yz}{xz}$

   D. $\dfrac{x^2 - yz}{xz}$

   E. $\dfrac{y^2 + xz}{xy}$

30. Solve for x: $\dfrac{10}{x} = \dfrac{12}{x+1}$.

   F. 2

   G. 4

   H. 5

   J. 6

   K. 8

31. If $2w = 3x - \dfrac{y}{2} - z$, and w, x, and y are each increased by 2, then how must the value of z change so that the equation remains valid?

   A. Increase by 2

   B. Increase by 1

   C. Remain the same

   D. Decrease by 1

   E. Decrease by 2

32. What is the greatest common factor of $8x^2y$, $12x^3y^2$, and $16x^4y^2$?

   F. $4x^2y$

   G. $4x^4y^2$

   H. $8xy^2$

   J. $48x^9y^5$

   K. $48x^4y^2$

33. Which of the following statements must be true about the line $y = \dfrac{2}{3}x - 8$ when it is graphed in the standard (x, y) coordinate plane?

   I. The line passes through the negative x-axis.

   II. The line passes through the negative y-axis.

   III. The points $(12, 2)$ and $(6, -5)$ are located on the same side of the line.

   A. I only

   B. II only

   C. III only

   D. Exactly two of the above statements

   E. I, II and III

34. You are given a list of the even integers from 10 through 28, inclusive. How would the median value of this list change if the odd integers from 13 through 23, inclusive, were added to the list?

   F. Decrease by 1

   G. Decrease by $\dfrac{1}{2}$

   H. Remain the same

   J. Increase by $\dfrac{1}{2}$

   K. Increase by 1

35. Which of the following best represents the value of x such that $\sqrt{(4-x)^2} < 6$?

   A. $-2 < x < 2$

   B. $-4 < x < 10$

   C. $-6 < x < 6$

   D. $-2 < x < 10$

   E. $-4 < x < 12$

GO ON TO THE NEXT PAGE

36. Two standard six-sided dice are rolled. Each time they are rolled, the sum of the two top faces of the dice will be an integer from 2 through 12, inclusive. What is the probability that the sum will be a prime number?

F. $\frac{7}{18}$

G. $\frac{5}{12}$

H. $\frac{4}{9}$

J. $\frac{17}{36}$

K. $\frac{1}{2}$

37. In the standard (x, y) coordinate plane, points that satisfy both of the following two inequalities could be located in how many quadrants?

$x + 2y < 8$

$2x - y > 4$

A. One quadrant
B. Two quadrants
C. Three quadrants
D. Four quadrants
E. Cannot be determined from the given information.

38. Given the following right triangle, which of the following statements is false?

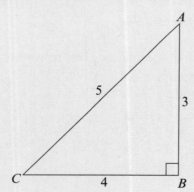

F. $\cos A \sin A = \frac{12}{25}$

G. $\sin^2 A = \frac{16}{25}$

H. $\sin C - \cos C = -\frac{1}{5}$

J. $\tan C \sin A = \frac{3}{5}$

K. $\sin C - \cos^2 A = -\frac{6}{25}$

39. Given quadrilateral $ABCD$ with $BC = CD$ and $AB = AD$, if $\angle BCD = 20°$ and $\angle ADC = 155°$, then what is the size of $\angle BAD$?

A. 15°
B. 27.5°
C. 30°
D. 35°
E. 40°

40. A ball is shot up into the air. The equation that defines its height (h) above the ground t seconds after launch is $h = -4t^2 + 32t$. The ball reaches a maximum height of 64 feet, 4 seconds after launch. How many seconds does it take from the time the ball passes a height of 48 feet above the ground on the way up until it passes a height of 48 feet above the ground on the way back down?

F. 2
G. 4
H. 6
J. 8
K. 10

41. Given isosceles triangle ABC with $AB = BC$ and $\angle A > 70°$, which of the following must be true?

  I. $\angle B < 40°$

  II. $AB > AC$

 III. $2\angle B > \angle C$

A. Exactly one of the above must be true.
B. I and II only
C. II and III only
D. I and III only
E. I, II, and III

42. Given right triangle XYZ with $XY = 26$ and $XZ = 10$, what is the length of side YZ?

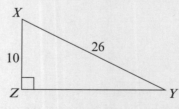

F. 20
G. 21
H. 22
J. 23
K. 24

GO ON TO THE NEXT PAGE

43. Which one of the following shows the relationship between a, b, and c when $(x - 4)^2 - (2x - 1)^2$ is written in the form $ax^2 + bx + c$?

A. $a < b < c$

B. $b < a < c$

C. $a < c < b$

D. $c < a < b$

E. $b < c < a$

44. A flagpole casts a shadow 32 feet long. At the same time of day, a 5-foot pole casts a shadow 6 feet long. What is the approximate height, in feet, of the flagpole?

F. 25

G. 25.5

H. 26.3

J. 26.7

K. 27

45. If $g(x) = 3x^2 - 2x + 8$, then what is the value of $g(-6)$?

A. -88

B. -40

C. 62

D. 84

E. 128

46. If x and y, where $x < y$, are two consecutive odd integers, then which of the following is equal to their product?

I. $(x + 1)^2 - 1$

II. $(x + 2)(y - 2)$

III. $(x - 1)(y + 1) + 3$

F. I only

G. II only

H. III only

J. Exactly two of these

K. I, II, and III

47. Each side of a square is the diameter of a circle, as shown in the following diagram. If the perimeter of the figure is 24π, what is its area?

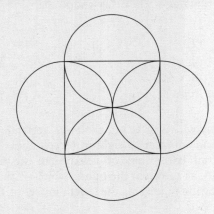

A. $72 + 36\pi$

B. $144 + 36\pi$

C. $36 + 72\pi$

D. $144 + 72\pi$

E. $36 + 144\pi$

48. Given triangle ABC with $\angle A = 45°$, $\angle C = 30°$, and $AB = 10$ inches, what is the length of AC, in inches?

F. $5\sqrt{2}\left(1 + \sqrt{3}\right)$

G. $5\sqrt{2}\left(2 + \sqrt{3}\right)$

H. $5\sqrt{3}\left(1 + \sqrt{2}\right)$

J. $10\sqrt{2}\left(1 + \sqrt{3}\right)$

K. $10\sqrt{3}\left(1 + \sqrt{2}\right)$

49. Which of the following must be true about irrational numbers?

I. The product of two different irrational numbers is irrational.

II. The difference of two different irrational numbers is irrational.

III. The sum of two different irrational numbers is irrational.

A. Exactly one of the above

B. I and II only

C. I and III only

D. II and III only

E. I, II and III

GO ON TO THE NEXT PAGE

Practice Test 2

50. In the standard (x, y) coordinate plane, the midpoint of $\overline{AB}$ is $(-4, 8)$. If one endpoint of $\overline{AB}$ is $(-8, -20)$, then what is the sum of the coordinates of the other endpoint?

    F. 4
    G. 12
    H. 20
    J. 28
    K. 36

51. A guy wire is to be attached to a vertical antenna mast at a height of 65 feet above level ground. If the angle of elevation of the guy wire is 50°, as shown in the figure, which of the following represents the length in feet of the guy wire (x)?

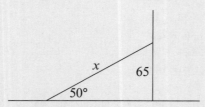

    A. $\dfrac{65}{\cos 50°}$

    B. $65 \cos 50°$

    C. $\dfrac{65}{\tan 50°}$

    D. $65 \sin 50°$

    E. $\dfrac{65}{\sin 50°}$

52. Sixteen years from now Jen will be twice as old as she was 12 years ago. How old in years is Jen now?

    F. 20
    G. 28
    H. 36
    J. 40
    K. 44

53. A triangle is drawn in the standard (x, y) coordinate plane. The vertices of the triangle are $A(-2, 4)$, $B(3, 16)$, and $C(12, 4)$. What is the length of the perimeter of the triangle?

    A. 38
    B. 40
    C. 42
    D. 44
    E. 46

54. If this geometric sequence continues, what will be the next term?

$$w^6 x^3 y^4, \ w^8 x^2 y^5, \ w^{10} x y^6, \ \ldots$$

    F. $w^{12} x^2 y^8$
    G. $w^{10} x^2 y^7$
    H. $w^{12} x^4$
    J. $w^{12} y^7$
    K. $w^{14} x^{-1} y^7$

55. Sphere A has a surface area that is 4 times that of sphere B, and 16 times that of sphere C. What is the ratio of the volume of sphere B to the volume of sphere C?

    A. 2:1
    B. 3:1
    C. 4:1
    D. 8:1
    E. 16:1

56. Simplify: $\dfrac{\left(x^2 - x - 20\right)\left(x^2 - 7x + 12\right)}{\left(x^2 + 3x - 28\right)\left(x^2 - 8x + 15\right)}$

    F. $\dfrac{x - 4}{x + 7}$

    G. $\dfrac{x - 3}{x - 5}$

    H. $\dfrac{x - 5}{x - 4}$

    J. $\dfrac{x + 4}{x - 5}$

    K. $\dfrac{x + 4}{x + 7}$

57. What is the sum of the three numerical real coefficients of the quadratic equation if one of the roots of the equation is $(1 + i)$?

    A. 1
    B. 2
    C. 4
    D. 5
    E. 6

GO ON TO THE NEXT PAGE

58. Which of the following best represents this piece-wise function?

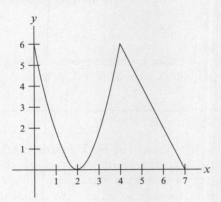

F. $g(x) = \begin{cases} \dfrac{3}{2}x^2 - 3x + 6 & \text{if } 0 \le x < 4 \\ 2x & \text{if } 4 \le x \le 7 \end{cases}$

G. $g(x) = \begin{cases} \dfrac{2}{3}x^2 - 6x - 6 & \text{if } 0 \le x < 4 \\ -2x & \text{if } 4 \le x \le 7 \end{cases}$

H. $g(x) = \begin{cases} \dfrac{3}{2}x^2 - 6x + 6 & \text{if } 0 \le x < 4 \\ -2x & \text{if } 4 \le x \le 7 \end{cases}$

J. $g(x) = \begin{cases} \dfrac{2}{3}x^2 + 6x + 6 & \text{if } 0 \le x < 4 \\ -2x & \text{if } 4 \le x \le 7 \end{cases}$

K. $g(x) = \begin{cases} \dfrac{3}{2}x^2 - 6x + 6 & \text{if } 0 \le x < 4 \\ 2x & \text{if } 4 \le x \le 7 \end{cases}$

59. Given the rhombus $ABCD$ with sides of length x and $\angle A = 40°$, which of the following represents the length of the longer diagonal, $\overline{AC}$?

A. $2x \sin 20°$

B. $2x \cos 20°$

C. $2x \sin 40°$

D. $2x \cos 40°$

E. None of the above

60. What is the value of $(\log_4 16)(\log_{16} 2)(\log_8 4)$?

F. $\dfrac{1}{3}$

G. $\dfrac{1}{4}$

H. $\dfrac{3}{4}$

J. 8

K. 64

IF YOU FINISH BEFORE TIME IS CALLED, CHECK YOUR WORK ON THIS SECTION ONLY. DO NOT WORK ON ANY OTHER SECTION IN THE TEST.

STOP

Reading Test

Time: 35 Minutes

40 Questions

Directions: Each of the four passages in this test is followed by a series of multiple-choice questions. Read the passage and choose the best answer to each question. Return to the passage as often as necessary to answer the questions.

Passage I

PROSE FICTION: This passage is from *The View from Castle Rock: Stories* by Alice Munro (Alfred A. Knopf, a division of Random House, 2006).

All over the countryside, in spring, there was a sound that was soon to disappear. Perhaps it would have disappeared already if it were not for the war. The war meant that the people who had
(5) the money to buy tractors could not find any to buy, and the few who had tractors could not always get the fuel to run them. So the farmers were out on the land with their horses for the spring ploughing, and from time to time, near
(10) and far, you could hear them calling out their commands, in which there would be degrees of encouragement, or impatience, or warning. You couldn't hear the exact words, any more than you could make out what the seagulls on their inland
(15) flights were saying or follow the arguments of crows. From the tone of voice, though, you could generally tell which words were swearing.

With one man it was all swearing. It didn't matter which words he was using. He could have
(20) been saying "butter and eggs" or "afternoon tea," and the spirit that spilled out would have been the same. As if he was boiling over with a scalding rage and loathing.

His name was Bunt Newcombe. He had the
(25) first farm on the county road that curved southwest from town. Bunt was probably a nickname given him at school for going around with his head lowered, ready to bump and shove anybody aside. A boyish name, a holdover, not
(30) really adequate to his behavior, or to his reputation, as a grown man.

People sometimes asked what could be the matter with him. He wasn't poor—he had two hundred acres of decent land, and a banked barn
(35) with a peaked silo, and a drive shed, and a well-built square red-brick house. (Though the house, like the man himself, had a look of bad temper. There were dark-green blinds pulled most of the way, or all of the way down on the
(40) windows, no curtains visible, and a scar along the front wall where the porch had been torn away. The front door which must at one time have opened onto that porch now opened three feet above weeds and rubble.) And he was not a
(45) drunk or a gambler, being too careful of his money for that. He was mean in both senses of the word. He mistreated his horses, and it goes without saying that he mistreated his family.

In the winter he took his milk cans to town on
(50) a sleigh pulled by a team of horses—snowplows for the county roads being in short supply then, just like tractors. This was at the time in the morning when everybody was walking to school, and he never slowed down as other farmers did
(55) to let you jump on the back of the sleigh and catch a ride. He picked up the whip instead.

Mrs. Newcombe was never with him, on the sleigh or in the car. She walked to town, wearing old-fashioned galoshes even when the weather
(60) got warm, and a long drab coat and scarf over her hair. She mumbled hello without ever looking up, or sometimes turned her head away, not speaking at all. I think she was missing some teeth. That was more common than it is now,
(65) and it was more common also for people to make plain a state of mind, in their speech and dress and gestures, so that everything about them said, *I know how I should look and behave and if I don't do it that's my own business,* or, *I don't care, things
(70) have gone too far with me, think what you like.*

Nowadays Mrs. Newcombe might be seen as a serious case, terminally depressed, and her husband with his brutish ways might be looked on with concern and compassion. *These people
(75) need help.* In those days they were just taken as

GO ON TO THE NEXT PAGE

they were and allowed to live out their lives without anyone giving thought to intervention. They were regarded in fact as a source of interest and entertainment. It might be said—it was (80) said—that nobody had any use for him and that you had to feel sorry for her. But there was a feeling that some people were born to make others miserable and some let themselves in for being made miserable. It was simply destiny and (85) there was nothing to be done about it.

1. The sound referred to in the opening sentence of Passage I is the

   A. cries of seagulls.
   B. rumble of tractors.
   C. movements of horses.
   D. voices of farmers.

2. The author implies that the sound will soon disappear because

   F. fuel will be too expensive.
   G. ploughing will stop at the end of spring.
   H. farmlands will be replaced by urban development.
   J. tractors will replace horse-drawn ploughs.

3. From the first paragraph of Passage I all of the following are indicated or stated EXCEPT that the

   A. setting of Passage I is rural.
   B. events take place in springtime.
   C. narrator of Passage I is a child.
   D. country is at war.

4. Bunt Newcombe is first introduced in Passage I through

   F. his swearing.
   G. the actions of the other farmers toward him.
   H. the mistreatment of his horses.
   J. the narrator's anger at him.

5. Which of the following is a fact presented about Bunt Newcombe?

   A. He is older than the other farmers.
   B. His nickname came from his schoolmates.
   C. He is wealthy.
   D. He owned he first farm on the country road.

6. Which of the following is NOT used by the narrator to describe Mr. Newcombe?

   F. Dialogue
   G. Simile
   H. Direct statement
   J. Contrast

7. What does the narrator mean by the statement "He was mean in both senses of the word"?

   A. Newcombe dressed poorly and treated his family with indifference.
   B. Along with being tight with his money, Newcombe was unkind to others.
   C. Newcombe was only an average farmer, but he enjoyed taunting others with his success.
   D. Newcombe beat his wife and children and mistreated his horses.

8. Which of the following best describes the point of view in Passage I?

   F. The description is from an omniscient narrator, that is, one who knows what everyone is thinking.
   G. The point of view is limited to that of an enemy of the Newcombe family.
   H. The point of view is an adult's, describing childhood impressions.
   J. The point of view is that of an adolescent.

9. The italicized sentences (lines 68–70)

   A. describe what Mrs. Newcombe is thinking.
   B. refer to the impression the Newcombes make on their neighbors.
   C. are the narrator's version of Mrs. Newcombe's thoughts.
   D. reflect the author's omniscient picture of the Newcombes.

10. The function of the last paragraph of Passage I is to

   F. question the fairness of the narrator's observations about the Newcombe family.
   G. defend the Newcombes behavior by describing the terrible events of their lives.
   H. emphasize the role of destiny in people's lives.
   J. contrast how the Newcombes were viewed in the past to the way they would probably be viewed today.

GO ON TO THE NEXT PAGE

Passage II

SOCIAL SCIENCE: This passage is from *Guns, Germs, and Steel: The Fates of Human Societies* by Jared Diamond (W.W. Norton and Company, Inc., 1997).

Where do innovations actually come from? For all societies except the few past ones that were completely isolated, much or most new technology is not invented locally but is instead borrowed
(5) from other societies. The relative importance of local invention and of borrowing depends mostly on two factors: the ease of invention of the particular technology, and the proximity of the particular society to other societies.

(10) Some inventions arose straightforwardly from a handling of natural raw materials. Such inventions developed on many independent occasions in world history, at different places and times. One example is plant domestication,
(15) with at least nine independent origins. Another is pottery, which may have arisen from observations of the behavior of clay, a very widespread natural material, when dried or heated. Pottery appeared in Japan around 14,000 years ago, in the Fertile
(20) Crescent and China by around 10,000 years ago, and in Amazonia, Africa's Sahel zone, the U.S. Southeast, and Mexico thereafter.

An example of a much more difficult invention is writing which does not suggest itself by
(25) observation of any natural material. It had only a few independent origins, and the alphabet arose apparently only once in world history. Other difficult inventions include the water wheel, rotary quern (*a primitive hand tool for*
(30) *grinding grain*), tooth gearing, magnetic compass, windmill, and *camera obscura*, all of which were invented only once or twice in the Old World and never in the New World.

Such complex inventions were usually acquired
(35) by borrowing, because they spread more rapidly than they could be independently invented locally. A clear example is the wheel, which is first attested around 3400 B.C. near the Black Sea, and then turns up within the next few centuries
(40) over much of Europe and Asia. All those early Old World wheels are of a peculiar design: a solid wooden circle constructed of three planks fastened together, rather than a rim with spokes. In contrast, the sole wheels of Native American
(45) societies (depicted on Mexican ceramic vessels) consisted of a single piece, suggesting a second independent invention of the wheel—as one would expect from other evidence for the isolation of New World from Old World civilizations.

(50) No one thinks that the same peculiar Old World wheel design appeared repeatedly by chance at many separate sites of the Old World within a few centuries of each other, after 7 million years of wheelless human history.
(55) Instead, the utility of the wheel surely caused it to diffuse rapidly east and west over the Old World from its sole site of invention. Other examples of complex technologies that diffused east and west in the ancient Old World, from a
(60) single Asian source, include door locks, pulleys, rotary querns, windmills—and the alphabet. A New World example of technological diffusion is metallurgy, which spread from the Andes via Panama to Mesoamerica.

(65) When a widely useful invention does crop up in one society, it then tends to spread in either of two ways. One way is that other societies see or learn of the invention, are receptive to it, and adopt it. The second is that societies lacking the
(70) invention find themselves at a disadvantage vis-a-vis the inventing society, and they become overwhelmed and replaced if the disadvantage is sufficiently great. A simple example is the spread of muskets among New Zealand's Maori tribes.
(75) One tribe, the Ngapuhi, adopted muskets from European traders around 1818. Over the course of the next 15 years, New Zealand was convulsed by the so-called Musket Wars, as musketless tribes either acquired muskets or were subjugated
(80) by tribes already armed with them. The outcome was that musket technology had spread throughout the whole of New Zealand by 1833: All surviving Maori tribes now had muskets.

11. Based on information in Passage II, which of the following is most likely to be an example of technology adopted by a society from the society that invented it?

A. Transistors
B. Footwear
C. Knives
D. Digging tools

12. Of the choices, which is the best description of the passage?

F. An imaginative representation of history
G. A theory supported by evidence
H. A description of past events
J. A biased account of history

GO ON TO THE NEXT PAGE

13. According to the author, innovations or inventions that come about in many places at different times are

   A. designed to answer a specific and unique need.
   B. usually short-lived and inefficient.
   C. suggested by handling raw material.
   D. easily transported from one country to another.

14. The invention of the wheel in the Old World

   F. was probably borrowed by the New World.
   G. diffused both east and west over the Old World from its point of origin.
   H. came about through handling various materials.
   J. followed the invention of the wheel by Native Americans.

15. According to the passage, a "borrowed" invention that occurred within the New World is

   A. pottery.
   B. the alphabet.
   C. metallurgy.
   D. water wheel.

16. The best definition of the word *attested* in line 38 is

   F. testified to.
   G. affirmed.
   H. estimated.
   J. described.

17. According to the available evidence, the invention of the alphabet

   A. occurred simultaneously throughout the world.
   B. was not an original innovation.
   C. is considered a recent invention.
   D. probably occurred only once.

18. The author's purpose in Passage II is to

   F. explain and give examples of how innovations come about.
   G. describe the way in which an innovation is diffused within a country.
   H. contrast the value of innovations in the Old World with those in the New World.
   J. explain why "borrowed" innovations are more important than local innovations.

19. According to Passage II, which of the following is evidence that a second independent invention of the wheel took place in the New World?

   A. A replica of the wheel invented in the Old World appears on Mexican pottery.
   B. The design of the wheel in the New World differs from the design in the Old World.
   C. Native Americans claimed to have invented a wheel before the appearance of a wheel in the Old World.
   D. The timeline of the wheel's invention indicates that it couldn't have been borrowed by the New World.

20. The author's main point in using the musket example in the last paragraph of Passage II is to

   F. emphasize that Europeans were the first to introduce muskets to New Zealand.
   G. show how the Maori tribes that adopted European muskets were the tribes that survived.
   H. explain how the Europeans were ultimately defeated by the Ngapuhi.
   J. illustrate the importance of local technology.

GO ON TO THE NEXT PAGE

Practice Test 2

Passage III

HUMANITIES: This passage is from *Dada & Surrealism* by Robert Short (University Press of America, 1980).

Dada's name was its fortune. The pair of sharply repeated, percussive syllables formed "the magic word," as Raoul Hausmann recalled, a catalyst which helped poets, artists and
(5) disaffected intellectuals in a dozen countries during the Great War to focus their hatred and ideals into a programme of cultural action. Like Coca Cola, which had been invented thirty years before, the word Dada became an instantly
(10) recognizable brand image transcending national boundaries. No wonder that after its early demise, Dada's "grey beards" went on quarreling about the paternity of the word until finally silenced by their recent deaths.

(15) Then, as now, everybody thought they knew what Dada meant. Dada's brilliant impresarios, Tristan Tzara, Francis Picabia, and Richard Huelsenbeck, only had to spell out in their manifestos what was already implicit in the
(20) name. A manifesto in itself, it is a word which has stuck. According to the stereotype, it stands for a movement of radical cultural revolt: the disgusted response of artists to the debacle of Western civilization and its values in the First
(25) World War. Dada represents a revolt against art by artists themselves who, appalled by developments in contemporary society, recognized that art was bound to be a product, reflection, and even support of that society and
(30) was therefore criminally implicated. Dada stands for exacerbated individualism, universal doubt and aggressive iconoclasm. Debunking the canons of reason, taste and hierarchy, of order and discipline in society, of rationally controlled
(35) inspiration in imaginative expression, Dada resorted to the arbitrary, to chance, the unconscious, and the primitive, where man is at the behest of nature and gives up pretending to be its master. Dada delighted in the shock effect
(40) of its blasphemies among the right-thinking.

The Dadas themselves energetically promoted such an idea of their action and it is this image which has passed into history. At the same time they insisted that Dada was indefinable, they
(45) stressed its simplicity for the sake of maximum impact. And we too seem to require the presence of a totally nihilistic movement to complete the cast-list of "isms" that played out the drama of modernism in the first half of the twentieth
(50) century. Nevertheless, for all its attractive clarity, this stereotype is incomplete and misleading. It is erroneous not merely because it oversimplifies the extraordinary diversity of Dada and ignores contradictory currents in the movement, but, more
(55) seriously, because it obscures the fundamental and fruitful paradoxes that were inherent in a programme devised by gifted artists to do away with art.

Faced with the Dada phenomenon, a reviewer
(60) in the *Times Literary Supplement* showed understandable perplexity when he asked: "How is one to define, let alone confine, a movement which cannot be identified with any one personality or place, viewpoint or subject, which
(65) affects all the arts, which has a continually shifting focus and is moreover intentionally negative, ephemeral, illogical and inconclusive?" (John Richardson, "The Dada Movement," *Times Literary Supplement,* October 23, 1953)

21. From information in Passage III, which of the following choices best defines Dada?

   A. primarily a political statement against war and international conspiracy.

   B. the precursor of surrealistic art.

   C. a call by young artists for social justice and equality.

   D. an artistic movement against rationality, order, and traditional art.

22. Raoul Hausmann called *Dada* "the magic word" because it

   F. captivated the public's interest in an art movement.

   G was nonsensical and had no linguistic history.

   H. served as a catalyst for disaffected artists and intellectuals.

   J. crossed national boundaries.

23. The Dada movement originated

   A. in the late 19th century.

   B. during World War I.

   C. after World War II.

   D. in the 1920s.

GO ON TO THE NEXT PAGE

24. The author compares the name *Dada* to *Coca Cola* because both

   F. became internationally recognizable "brand" names.

   G. originated at approximately the same time.

   H. were not associated with any particular language.

   J. were made up of nonsense syllables.

25. The term "grey beards" in line 12 refers to

   A. conservative art reviewers.

   B. early Dada artists.

   C. elderly art collectors.

   D. art history professors.

26. According to the author, one reason the stereotype of the Dada artist is misleading is that it

   F. discounts the international impact of the movement.

   G. emphasizes the irrational nature of Dada art.

   H. ignores the movement's diversity and contradictory manifestations.

   J. does not take into account the technical virtuosity of Dada artists.

27. The author sees the basic paradox in the Dada movement as which of the following?

   A. The movement encompassed too many artistic styles to be considered one movement.

   B. The Dada artists rejected artistic tradition while wanting to be part of it.

   C. The Dada artists wanted to do away with art.

   D. Although believing in simplicity, the Dada artists argued among each other and wrote conflicting manifestos.

28. The best definition of *exacerbated* in line 31 is

   F. made harsher or more violent

   G. greatly disappointed

   H. not easily understood

   J. made more justifiable

29. The author includes the quotation from a reviewer of the Dada movement to

   A. show how harshly the Dada artists were treated by the art community.

   B. explain the influences responsible for the Dada movement.

   C. illustrate the negativity of the Dada artists.

   D. emphasize the difficulty of defining a movement like Dada.

30. According to Passage III, all of the following are true about the Dada movement EXCEPT:

   F. It did not last for a long time.

   G. The artists came from many countries.

   H. Most of the works were rejected by the public.

   J. The Dada artists took pleasure in shocking their audience.

Passage IV

NATURAL SCIENCE: This passage is from *A Short History of Nearly Everything* by Bill Bryson (Broadway Books, a division of Random House, 2003).

     It is a remarkable fact that well into the space age most school textbooks divided the world of the living into just two categories—plant and animal. Micro-organisms hardly featured.
(5) Amoebas and similar single-celled organisms were treated as proto-animals and algae as proto-plants. Bacteria were usually lumped in with plants, too, even though everyone knew they didn't belong there. As far back as the late
(10) nineteenth century the German naturalist Ernst Haeckel had suggested that bacteria deserved to be placed in a separate kingdom, which he called Monera, but the idea didn't begin to catch on among biologists until the 1960s, and then only
(15) among some of them. (I note that my trusty *American Heritage* desk dictionary from 1969 doesn't recognize the term.)

     Many organisms in the visible world were also poorly served by the traditional division. Fungi,
(20) the group that includes mushrooms, moulds, mildews, yeast, and puffballs, were nearly always treated as botanical objects, though in fact nothing about them—how they reproduce and respire, how they build themselves—matches
(25) anything in the plant world. Structurally, they

GO ON TO THE NEXT PAGE

Practice Test 2

have more in common with animals in that they build their cells from chitin, a material that gives them their distinctive texture. The same substance is used to make the shells of insects and the claws
(30) of mammals, though it isn't nearly so tasty in a stag beetle as in a Portobello mushroom. Above all, unlike all plants, fungi don't photosynthesize, so they have no chlorophyll and thus are not green. Instead they grow directly on their food
(35) source, which can be almost anything. Fungi will eat the sulphur off a concrete wall or the decaying matter between your toes—two things no plant will do. Almost the only plant-like quality they have is that they root.
(40) Even less comfortably susceptible to categorization was the peculiar group of organisms formally called myxomycetes but more commonly known as slime moulds. The name no doubt has much to do with their
(45) obscurity. An appellation that sounded a little more dynamic—"ambulant self-activating protoplasm," say—and less like the stuff that you find when you reach deep into a clogged drain would have almost certainly earned these
(50) extraordinary entities a more immediate share of the attention they deserve, for slime moulds are, make no mistake, among the most interesting organisms in nature. When times are good, they exist as one-celled individuals, much like
(55) amoebas. But when conditions grow tough, they crawl to a central gathering place and become, almost miraculously, a slug. The slug is not a thing of beauty and it doesn't go terribly far— usually just from the bottom of a pile of leaf
(60) litter to the top, where it is in a slightly more exposed position—but for millions of years this may well have been the niftiest trick in the universe.

And it doesn't stop there. Having hauled itself
(65) up to a more favourable locale, the slime mould transforms itself yet again, taking up the form of a plant. By some curious orderly process the cells reconfigure, like the members of a tiny marching band, to make a stalk atop of which forms a bulb
(70) known as a fruiting body. Inside the fruiting body are millions of spores which, at the appropriate moment, are released to the wind to blow away to become single-celled organisms that can start the process again.

31. In the first paragraph of Passage IV, the author is questioning which of the following?

A. Classifying life as either plant or animal
B. The accuracy of science textbooks in the 19th century
C. Identifying bacteria as proto-animals
D. Haeckel's Monera classification of bacteria

32. Lines 15–17 serve all of the following functions EXCEPT:

F. Indicating how long the term *Monera* wasn't accepted
G. Introducing the author as a first-person narrator
H. Criticizing the *American Heritage* dictionary
J. Humanizing the character of the narrator

33. According to Passage IV, fungi should not be classified as plants primarily because they don't

A. require water.
B. root.
C. reproduce.
D. photosynthesize.

34. *Chitin* can best be described as

F. material found primarily in insects.
G. building material for claws and shells.
H. a spongy surface.
J. a pliable surface.

35. The author of Passage IV suggests that *ambulant self-activating protoplasm* would be a better name for slime mould because it

A. describes the organism in more detail.
B. is less distasteful than the current name.
C. isn't as difficult to pronounce as myxomycetes.
D. is a more dynamic name than "slime mould."

GO ON TO THE NEXT PAGE

36. The author uses the phrase "almost miraculously" in line 57 to

   F. explain how slime moulds are capable of rapid movement.

   G. describe the respiration processes of slime moulds.

   H. characterize how slime moulds are transformed into slugs.

   J. emphasize the distinctive qualities and varieties of slime moulds.

37. Which of the following versions most completely and correctly describes how slime moulds propagate?

   A. Slime mould cells form slugs; slugs move to an exposed position and form a plant. Spores are released from a bulb atop the plant, blown away, and develop into new single-celled organisms.

   B. Slugs move to an exposed position and release millions of spores, some of which become slime moulds.

   C. Drains and similar damp places generate slime moulds.

   D. After becoming slugs, slime mould cells are released by the wind.

38. What is the main point of Passage IV?

   F. Some interesting life forms fall outside traditional categories.

   G. Bacteria have been incorrectly classified because of the limitations of scientific categories.

   H. Slime mould is arguably the most interesting organism in nature.

   J. Fungi and slime mould have been ignored by scientists because of incorrect categorization.

39. Of the choices, which of the following best describes the author's presentation of information?

   A. Obscure and pedantic

   B. Colloquial and humorous

   C. Argumentative and sarcastic

   D. Flippant and ironic

40. With which of the following statements would the author of the passage be most likely to agree?

   F. Both slime moulds and fungi should be classified as animals rather than plants.

   G. Botanists do not fully understand the attributes of fungi.

   H. The traditional categories of life on earth are both wrong and dangerous.

   J. Ernst Haeckel was correct in his suggestion that bacteria should have its own classification.

Practice Test 2

IF YOU FINISH BEFORE TIME IS CALLED, CHECK YOUR WORK ON THIS SECTION ONLY. DO NOT WORK ON ANY OTHER SECTION IN THE TEST.

Science Test

Time: 35 Minutes

40 Questions

Directions: Each of the seven passages in this test is followed by several questions. After you read each passage, select the correct choice for each of the questions that follow the passage. Refer to the passage as often as necessary to answer the questions. You may NOT use a calculator on this test.

Passage I

Figure 1 shows the variation of temperature with altitude in our atmosphere. The four layers of different shades correspond to atmospheric zones, which are named on the right side of the graph.

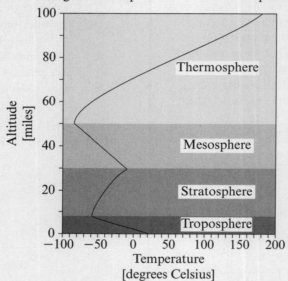

Figure 1: Temperatures in the Atmosphere

1. What is the approximate temperature of the atmosphere at an altitude of 70 miles?

   A. −80°C
   B. −15°C
   C. 27°C
   D. 50°C

2. Which of the four atmospheric zones has the smallest range of temperature?

   F. The mesosphere
   G. The stratosphere
   H. The thermosphere
   J. The troposphere

GO ON TO THE NEXT PAGE

3. Which two atmospheric zones show decreasing temperature with increasing altitude?

   A. The mesosphere and troposphere
   B. The stratosphere and thermosphere
   C. The thermosphere and mesosphere
   D. The troposphere and stratosphere

4. Air pressure at any given altitude is caused by the weight of the air above that level. Which of the atmospheric zones has the highest air pressure?

   F. The mesosphere
   G. The stratosphere
   H. The thermosphere
   J. The troposphere

5. Conditions are most favorable in the stratosphere for the formation of ozone molecules from oxygen. At that altitude, oxygen absorbs ultraviolet radiation and is transformed into ozone. How does ozone formation explain the temperature pattern in the stratosphere?

   A. The absorption of solar energy causes a rise in temperature.
   B. Energy released by ozone formation causes a rise in temperature.
   C. The loss of oxygen molecules causes a fall in temperature.
   D. Ozone molecules absorb energy and cause a fall in temperature.

Passage II

To determine the types of crystals making up a coarse-grained rock, a researcher had only two analytical methods available.

The semiquantitative *X-ray fluorescence unit* could detect the presence of certain chemical elements, but it could not measure their abundances precisely. The chemical compositions for all crystals likely to be found in the rock are given in Table 1.

Table 1

Crystal Varieties	Atomic Percentages							
	Oxygen	Silicon	Aluminum	Iron	Magnesium	Calcium	Sodium	Potassium
Magnetite	57	0	0	43	0	0	0	0
Olivine	57	14	0	13	16	0	0	0
Hypersthene	60	20	0	9	11	0	0	0
Augite	60	20	0	4	6	10	0	0
Hornblende	57	19	5	7	5	5	2	0
Biotite	60	15	5	9	6	0	0	5
Plagioclase	61	19	12	0	0	4	4	0
Quartz	67	33	0	0	0	0	0	0
Orthoclase	61	23	8	0	0	0	0	8

The second apparatus available was a *heavy liquids kit* containing three bottles of organic liquids of known specific gravity, an alternate method of reporting density. The specific gravity of crystals may be estimated by seeing whether they sink or float in each liquid. Table 2 states the specific gravity for each liquid and all crystal varieties suspected to be in the rock.

GO ON TO THE NEXT PAGE

Table 2

	Specific Gravity
Methylene iodide	3.33
Bromoform	2.89
Acetone	0.79
Magnetite	5.18
Olivine	3.65
Hypersthene	3.45
Augite	3.25
Hornblend	3.20
Biotite	3.00
Plagioclase	2.69
Quartz	2.65
Orthoclase	2.57

Experiment 1

The coarse-grained rock was crushed enough to free the crystals from each other. Then 200 grams of the sand-like material was stirred into a beaker containing bromoform. Some of the material floated, while most of the material sank to the bottom of the beaker. The fraction that floated appeared uniform, as if it were only one variety of crystal. An X-ray fluorescence analysis of the floated material detected the presence of silicon and calcium, but not potassium. The other five elements were not checked.

Experiment 2

The fraction of the material that sank in Experiment 1 was then washed free of bromoform and dried. It was stirred into another beaker containing methylene iodide; again the material separated into two fractions. Each fraction appeared to be homogeneous and composed of only one crystal type. The part that had floated in the methylene iodide was analyzed with the X-ray fluorescence unit and found to contain silicon and magnesium, but not sodium. The other five elements were not checked.

Experiment 3

The rock fraction that sank in the previous experiment was quickly analyzed for the presence of silicon. After that element was found to be present, the investigator discontinued her work.

6. The crystals that were analyzed by X-ray fluorescence in Experiment 1 must be

   F. hornblende.
   G. magnetite.
   H. plagioclase.
   J. quartz.

GO ON TO THE NEXT PAGE

7. The three liquids in the kit are mutually *miscible* (capable of being mixed), so by mixing them, a liquid of intermediate specific gravity may be obtained. Which pair of crystals may be separated by using a liquid produced by mixing equal volumes of bromoform and methylene iodide?

    A. Augite and hornblende
    B. Hornblende and biotite
    C. Hypersthene and augite
    D. Olivine and hypersthene

8. To specifically identify the crystals that were analyzed in Experiment 2, the researcher should try to detect any of the following elements EXCEPT:

    F. Aluminum
    G. Calcium
    H. Iron
    J. Potassium

9. The usefulness of the X-ray fluorescence unit could be most improved if it could

    A. analyze two samples at the same time.
    B. detect the presence of oxygen.
    C. measure the amount of each element.
    D. work with wet or dry samples.

10. Why would it be fruitless for the researcher to analyze the material in Experiment 3 for the remaining elements?

    F. The material could not contain any of those elements.
    G. The possible crystals had already been narrowed to only one.
    H. The two likely crystals contain the same elements.
    J. The three possible crystals are all known to contain iron.

11. All rock-forming crystals are denser than the acetone included in the heavy liquids kit. How can that light liquid best be used in crystal separations?

    A. Mix a small amount of it into bromoform to produce a liquid with a specific gravity of less than 2.89.
    B. Mix a small amount of it into bromoform to produce a liquid with a specific gravity of more than 2.89.
    C. Mix a small amount of it into methylene iodide to produce a liquid with a specific gravity of less than 3.33.
    D. Mix a small amount of it into methylene iodide to produce a liquid with a specific gravity of more than 3.33.

GO ON TO THE NEXT PAGE

Practice Test 2

Passage III

Figure 1 shows the feeding relationships in one woodland community. The arrows point toward the dependent organism. For example, frogs eat insects.

Figure 1: Feeding Relationships in a Woodland Community

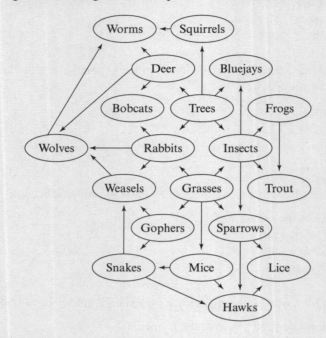

12. According to Figure 1, sparrows feed on

  F. grasses and mice.
  G. insects and grasses.
  H. lice and insects.
  J. mice and trees.

13. The longest food chain in the diagram links six different organisms. That longest chain runs from

  A. grasses to deer.
  B. trees to lice.
  C. grasses to worms.
  D. trees to wolves.

14. Which of the following animals are natural enemies of snakes?

  F. Gophers and mice
  G. Hawks and weasels
  H. Mice and hawks
  J. Weasels and gophers

GO ON TO THE NEXT PAGE

15. At the base of the network of feeding relationships are independent organisms that do not feed on other organisms. In this woodland, which organisms are at the base of the network?

   A. Worms and lice
   B. Frogs and snakes
   C. Grasses and trees
   D. Wolves and bobcats

16. A campaign by chicken farmers to eradicate weasels throughout the area could lead indirectly to

   F. a decrease of hawks.
   G. a decrease of snakes.
   H. an increase of bluejays.
   J. an increase of bobcats.

Passage IV

To investigate the ionization of air by alpha radiation, the apparatus shown in Figure 1 was assembled.

Figure 1: Experimental Setup

A large, round, glass flask was coated with a silver lining so it could conduct electricity. Through a cork at the top, a slender brass rod supported a 10-milligram sample of polonium-210 at the center of the flask. ^{210}Po is strongly radioactive, decaying by emitting alpha particles. The half-life is 138 days; in that period, half of all ^{210}Po atoms decay to nonradioactive lead-206 plus high-velocity alpha particles. As the alpha particles travel through the air in the flask, some of their kinetic energy is dissipated by ionizing some of the nitrogen and oxygen molecules to electrons and positive ions. Normal air is a good electrical insulator, but ionized air allows an electrical current to flow around the circuit: battery/brass/air/silver/battery. The electrometer measures the amount of current flowing, which is directly proportional to the degree of ionization in the air.

The cork is also pierced by a tube to a pump that can lower the air pressure within the flask. The manometer permits reading the pressure at any time. Beginning at 1 atmosphere air pressure, the researcher made nine readings of the electrical current flowing at progressively lower pressures. The prior hypothesis was that as the pressure was lowered, less of the energy of the alpha particles would be spent in ionizing air molecules. The results of the study are shown in Figure 2.

GO ON TO THE NEXT PAGE

Figure 2: Current and Pressure Relationship under Experimental Conditions

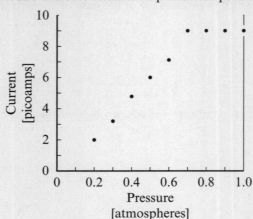

17. The prior hypothesis that the amount of ionization would be proportional to air pressure is supported by readings made over which of the following ranges?

    A.   0.2 to 0.7 atmosphere
    B.   0.3 to 0.8 atmosphere
    C.   0.4 to 0.9 atmosphere
    D.   0.5 to 1.0 atmosphere

18. At the moment when the researcher records one data point to be graphed, which one of the four instruments may be switched off without affecting the measurement?

    F.   The battery
    G.   The electrometer
    H.   The manometer
    J.   The pump

19. The low currents measured at low air pressures may be explained by

    A.   the electrical resistance of a vacuum.
    B.   fewer air molecules to be ionized.
    C.   fewer alpha particles reaching the silver.
    D.   less energetic alpha radiation.

20. The researcher must complete one series of measurements within a day or two. What difference would result if the researcher tried three months later to check the measurements?

    F.   The measured pressure would be higher because of leakage around the cork.
    G.   The measured pressure would be lower because the pump slowly removes the air.
    H.   The measured current would be lower because the radioactive source is weaker.
    J.   The measured current would be higher because the silver lining will have tarnished.

GO ON TO THE NEXT PAGE

21. The nearly constant current measured at high air pressures can be explained only if

- **A.** all the alpha particles reach the silver lining without ionizing air molecules.
- **B.** all the energy of the alpha particles is dissipated in ionizing air molecules.
- **C.** all the nitrogen and oxygen molecules in the flask have been ionized.
- **D.** all the silver atoms have been ionized by alpha particles.

22. Which of the following alterations to the apparatus would NOT significantly alter the measured current?

- **F.** Using aluminum to line the flask
- **G.** Using a larger flask
- **H.** Using a 150-volt battery
- **J.** Using radioactive cerium as the source

Passage V

Are viruses an important cause of some human cancers? Two differing views are presented here.

Scientist 1

A seminal study in 1908 showed that healthy chickens could contract leukemia, a cancer afflicting blood, by being injected with a highly filtered extract from diseased birds. Three years later, another researcher found that a connective-tissue cancer could likewise be transferred among chickens. The latter cancer originally appeared spontaneously in one hen; highly filtered plasma injected into other chickens caused highly malignant tumors of the same kind, called *sarcomas*. Extended investigation showed that the tumor-causing agent in the filtrate was one specific virus. In 1932, a virus causing tumors in a mammal was discovered. Again, cell-free filtrates from a skin tumor in a rabbit induced malignant skin tumors, *carcinomas,* in healthy rabbits. A few years later, the first of many tumor viruses in mice was isolated. The mouse viruses are capable of causing leukemias, sarcomas, and solid tumors (*lymphomas*). Some of these cancer-inducing viruses can be transmitted from a mother mouse to her suckling offspring through the milk. By the 1950s, scientists had found tumor viruses in other mammals, including primates like the Rhesus monkey. Especially disturbing was the discovery that human adenoviruses induced cancers in laboratory mice and rats. It seems highly probable that several human cancers are caused by viral infections. In fact, the human papillomavirus (HPV), the hepatitis virus, and a handful of less common viral agents are strongly correlated with tumor growth. In 2008, the Nobel Prize was awarded to a team that demonstrated that HPV can cause cervical cancer, leading to a wide-spread vaccination effort.

Scientist 2

No virus has been shown to be the sole and direct cause of a human cancer. Eighty years of searching for human viruses that induce cancerous growth have borne limited fruit. Very few human cancers have been shown to be strongly correlated with viral infection. Cancers have been shown to be far more commonly caused by genetic defects, radioactivity, light, X-rays, and numerous chemicals. Modern cancer research techniques are so advanced and sensitive that new mutagenic agents are identified each day, very few of which are viral. In fact, even the causative mechanisms for viral cancer in humans or other animals have not been positively established. Most animals infected with a virus supposed to induce malignancy in that species do not develop any tumors. Therefore, the cause of the tumors in the few cancerous animals is uncertain. The most well-known example of viral cancer in humans—the human papillomavirus (HPV), which is found in almost all cases of cervical cancer—is no exception; the vast majority of women infected with this virus never develop cancer. Possibly some viral infections simply weaken the infected subject's resistance until a cancer is induced by another agent, such as an ingredient of the diet. Therefore, even the viruses known to correlate with cancers could be addressed by studying more common causal agents. The reports of tumor viruses are too frequently from researchers seeking yet another grant. Surely it is time to focus our research budget on more common causes of cancer in humans.

GO ON TO THE NEXT PAGE

23. Which type of animal mentioned by Scientist 1 would be most relevant to human medicine?

    A. Chickens
    B. Mice
    C. Primates
    D. Rabbits

24. The strongest point that Scientist 2 raises against the belief that viral infections directly cause tumors in animals is that

    F. the infections may be bacterial rather than viral.
    G. laboratory animals eat an unnatural diet.
    H. most animal researchers need results to receive grants.
    J. not all infected animals develop cancer.

25. Scientist 1 also refers to a cancer of connective tissues as a

    A. carcinoma.
    B. papilloma.
    C. lymphoma.
    D. sarcoma.

26. All of the following points support the belief of Scientist 2 EXCEPT:

    F. The cause of many human cancers is already known.
    G. New cancer-causing agents are discovered often.
    H. No virus has been shown to be the sole and direct cause of any cancer.
    J. Present techniques should be capable of detecting human viruses.

27. In the rabbit research reported by Scientist 1, why is it important to specify that the injected liquid be cell-free?

    A. The disease was not transmitted as cancerous cells.
    B. Cancer might not develop in the presence of cells.
    C. The liquid must not be contaminated with any virus.
    D. Some cells could kill any viruses in the liquid.

28. The argument presented by Scientist 2 would be considerably weakened if Scientist 1 could prove that

    F. more human tumor viruses will be discovered soon.
    G. no animal is truly resistant to cancer.
    H. research on viruses uses only 10 percent of cancer research grants.
    J. some animal tumors are directly and reliably caused by viruses.

29. The evidence presented by Scientist 1 for animal tumor viruses could be shaken if Scientist 2 showed that

    A. adenoviruses occur in other animals as well as humans.
    B. herpes infections are not associated with any specific type of cancer.
    C. leukemia may be induced in mice by exposure to radioactivity.
    D. some particles besides the viruses passed through the filters.

GO ON TO THE NEXT PAGE

Passage VI

Table 1 gives both the chemical symbols and atomic sizes of six nonmetallic elements. The last four elements are referred to as *halogens* in the questions for this passage.

Table 1

Element	Symbol	Diameter of Atom (angstrom units)
Hydrogen	H	0.74
Oxygen	O	1.21
Fluorine	F	1.42
Chlorine	Cl	1.99
Bromine	Br	2.28
Iodine	I	2.67

Atoms of each of the six elements form chemical bonds to identical atoms and to each of the other five elements. A research project measured the energy required to break those chemical bonds, and the results are given in Table 2. A higher energy corresponds to a greater force of attraction between the two atoms. Note that the chemical symbols are defined in Table 1.

Table 2

Bond	Energy kcal/mole
F–H	135
F–O	45
F–F	37
Cl–H	103
Cl–O	49
Cl–F	61
Cl–Cl	58
Br–H	88
Br–F	57
Br–Cl	52
Br–Br	46
I–H	71
I–Cl	50
I–Br	43
I–I	36

GO ON TO THE NEXT PAGE

30. Which halogen forms the weakest bond to hydrogen?

    F. Bromine
    G. Chlorine
    H. Fluorine
    J. Iodine

31. The pure halogen elements occur as molecules with two identical atoms, such as F_2. Which of these elements would have to be heated to the highest temperature to decompose the molecule into atoms?

    A. Bromine
    B. Chlorine
    C. Fluorine
    D. Iodine

32. Hydrogen and the halogens all react with carbon to form organic compounds with four such atoms bonded to a central carbon atom. Which of these organic compounds has the largest molecules?

    F. Carbon tetrachloride, CCl_4
    G. Methyl bromide, CH_3Br
    H. Methylene fluoride, CH_2F_2
    J. Methyl iodide, CH_3I

33. The bond study did not measure the energy of a bromine-oxygen bond. Based on the information given concerning chlorine bonds to oxygen and fluorine, which of the following is an estimate of that energy?

    A. 25 kcal/mole
    B. 45 kcal/mole
    C. 65 kcal/mole
    D. 85 kcal/mole

34. Which of the following statements best summarizes the relative strengths of bonds between any two halogen atoms?

    F. The bond is always weakest between identical atoms.
    G. The bond is always stronger with hydrogen than with oxygen.
    H. The bond is weakest if iodine is involved.
    J. The bond is stronger between smaller atoms.

Passage VII

    To investigate the possibility of gene transfer between different strains of bacteria, the following series of experiments was performed. In each case, the bacterial culture was carefully plated onto petri dishes containing a sterilized growth medium composed of glucose and various salts. The medium did not contain any amino acids, although it is known that all organisms require amino acids for metabolism.

Experiment 1

    As shown in Figure 1, in the first experiment, a culture of normal bacteria was plated onto the growth medium that lacked any amino acids. The cluster of circular colonies that appeared was the evidence of bacterial growth. The normal bacteria were able to internally synthesize any necessary amino acids.

GO ON TO THE NEXT PAGE

Figure 1: Bacteria Growth under Experiment 1 Conditions

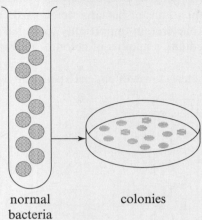

normal   colonies
bacteria

Experiment 2

In the second experiment, the researcher used two mutant strains of the same bacterial species. These mutant bacteria lacked the ability to synthesize certain amino acids, leucine and cystine. One strain (L) could not synthesize leucine, but it could synthesize cystine. The other strain (C) could not synthesize cystine. As shown in Figures 2 and 3, neither strain could grow on the petri medium.

Figure 2: Bacteria Growth under Experiment 2 Conditions

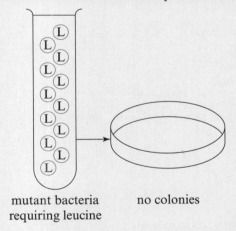

mutant bacteria   no colonies
requiring leucine

Figure 3: Bacteria Growth under Experiment 2 Conditions

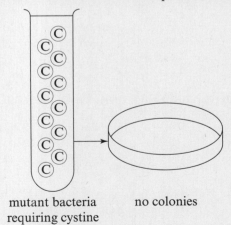

mutant bacteria   no colonies
requiring cystine

GO ON TO THE NEXT PAGE

Experiment 3

In Experiment 3, the two mutant strains of bacteria were mixed. That mixed culture remained in the test tube for three hours to allow the bacteria an opportunity to exchange genes. When the culture was plated onto the nutritionally deficient medium, a number of colonies appeared, as shown in Figure 4.

Figure 4: Bacteria Growth under Experiment 3 Conditions

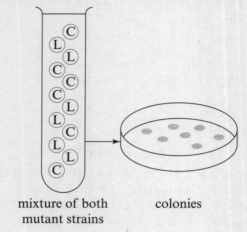

mixture of both   colonies
mutant strains

35. The fundamental assumption of the entire set of experiments is that the ability of bacteria to synthesize specific amino acids is

    A. due to environmental requirements.
    B. governed by specific genes.
    C. inhibited by glucose and salts.
    D. the result of genetic mutations.

36. In the set of experiments, the crucial term "synthesize" must mean

    F. digest.
    G. manufacture.
    H. require.
    J. utilize.

37. The fact that the L strain of bacteria required only leucine in order to grow on the glucose-salts medium shows that it must have a gene to synthesize

    A. cystine.
    B. glucose.
    C. leucine.
    D. all amino acids.

38. If cystine had been added to both petri dishes in Experiment 2, the result would have been growth of

    F. the C strain only.
    G. the L strain only.
    H. both C and L strains.
    J. neither mutant strain.

GO ON TO THE NEXT PAGE

39. The appearance of colonies in Experiment 3 can best be explained by which of these descriptions of genetic exchange?

   A.   The C strain must have received the cystine-synthesizing gene from the L strain.

   B.   The L strain must have received the leucine-synthesizing gene from the C strain.

   C.   Both the L strain received the leucine-synthesizing gene and the C strain received the cystine-synthesizing gene.

   D.   Either the C strain received the cystine-synthesizing gene or the L strain received the leucine-synthesizing gene or both.

40. If no colonies had appeared in Experiment 3, one interpretation would be that no genes were transferred between strains in the test tube. What would be another valid interpretation?

   F.   All bacteria may have starved during the three hours.

   G.   Both strains lacked at least one identical, vital gene.

   H.   One strain had mutated to synthesize all amino acids.

   J.   Some normal bacteria may have contaminated the culture.

IF YOU FINISH BEFORE TIME IS CALLED, CHECK YOUR WORK ON THIS SECTION ONLY. DO NOT WORK ON ANY OTHER SECTION IN THE TEST.

STOP

Scoring the Practice Test

The following section will assist you in scoring and analyzing your practice test results. Use the answer key to score your results, and then carefully review the analysis charts to identify your strengths and weakness. Finally, read through the answer explanations starting in the study guide on page 476 to clarify the solutions to the problems.

Answer Key

English Test

1. C	14. H	27. D	40. H	53. C	66. J
2. J	15. C	28. G	41. B	54. H	67. B
3. B	16. G	29. C	42. J	55. B	68. H
4. J	17. C	30. F	43. C	56. F	69. C
5. B	18. G	31. B	44. J	57. D	70. G
6. G	19. C	32. H	45. D	58. H	71. A
7. C	20. H	33. B	46. H	59. C	72. J
8. J	21. A	34. J	47. D	60. J	73. B
9. C	22. F	35. B	48. G	61. D	74. H
10. G	23. B	36. H	49. A	62. G	75. C
11. D	24. J	37. D	50. G	63. C	
12. J	25. B	38. F	51. B	64. G	
13. B	26. F	39. B	52. J	65. C	

Mathematics Test

1. E	11. B	21. B	31. B	41. B	51. E
2. H	12. H	22. J	32. F	42. K	52. J
3. B	13. C	23. A	33. B	43. B	53. C
4. K	14. H	24. J	34. G	44. J	54. J
5. B	15. E	25. C	35. D	45. E	55. D
6. J	16. K	26. H	36. G	46. K	56. K
7. D	17. C	27. B	37. C	47. D	57. A
8. K	18. K	28. J	38. K	48. F	58. H
9. E	19. D	29. C	39. C	49. D	59. B
10. G	20. H	30. H	40. G	50. K	60. F

Reading Test

1. D	**8.** H	**15.** C	**22.** H	**29.** D	**36.** H
2. J	**9.** C	**16.** G	**23.** B	**30.** H	**37.** A
3. C	**10.** J	**17.** D	**24.** F	**31.** A	**38.** F
4. F	**11.** A	**18.** F	**25.** B	**32.** H	**39.** B
5. D	**12.** G	**19.** B	**26.** H	**33.** D	**40.** J
6. F	**13.** C	**20.** G	**27.** C	**34.** G	
7. B	**14.** G	**21.** D	**28.** F	**35.** D	

Science Test

1. B	**8.** H	**15.** C	**22.** F	**29.** D	**36.** G
2. G	**9.** C	**16.** J	**23.** C	**30.** J	**37.** A
3. A	**10.** H	**17.** A	**24.** J	**31.** B	**38.** F
4. J	**11.** A	**18.** J	**25.** D	**32.** F	**39.** D
5. A	**12.** G	**19.** B	**26.** G	**33.** B	**40.** G
6. H	**13.** C	**20.** H	**27.** A	**34.** J	
7. B	**14.** G	**21.** B	**28.** J	**35.** B	

Charting and Analyzing Your Test Results

The first step in analyzing your test results is to chart your answers. Use the following chart to identify your strengths and areas of improvement. Complete the process of evaluating your strengths and analyzing problems in each area. Re-evaluate your results as you look for trends in the types of errors (repeated errors), and look for low scores in results in *specific* subject areas. This re-examination and analysis is a tremendous asset to help you maximize your best possible score. The answers and explanations following these charts will provide you clarification to help you solve these types of problems in the future.

Practice Test 2 Analysis Sheet

Test	Number Possible	Number Correct	Number Incorrect		
			(A) Simple Mistake	(B) Misread Problem	(C) Lack of Knowledge
English Test	75				
Mathematics Test	60				
Reading Test	40				
Science Test	40				
Total Possible Explanations for Incorrect Answers: Columns A, B, and C					
Total Number of Questions Correct and Incorrect	215	Add the total number of correct questions here: _____	Add columns A, B, and C for total number of incorrect questions here: _____		

Practice Test 2: Answers and Explanations

English Test

Passage I

1. C. This is the most concise version, and it also uses the active rather than the passive voice of the verb. Other things being equal, the active voice is preferable, as are the most economical expressions. The one caution in choosing the most concise expression: don't change the meaning of the original version.

2. J. The simple past tense is appropriate; it is consistent with the tense used in the first clause of the sentence.

3. B. "They" has no clear antecedent. Is it the group in the audience, the nearest possibility? Choice B, "council," is the correct antecedent. Make sure antecedents of pronouns are completely clear.

4. J. This choice avoids the dangling participle ("it" isn't speaking afterwards; "the mayor" is). Choice H is awkward.

5. B. This phrase is necessary to the meaning of the sentence and, therefore, commas shouldn't be used. Necessary phrases are called restrictive.

6. G. "Committee" is a singular noun, and, therefore, it takes a singular possessive pronoun. The correct possessive is "its," not "it's," which is a contraction of "it is." Choice J is repetitious and also uses a plural rather than a singular possessive.

7. C. There is no need to use "but" or "however" here. "Without" is sufficient.

8. J. The correct pronoun is the subjective "we." This will be obvious if "council members" is removed. "Have risen" (not "rose") is the correct past participle of "rise."

9. C. The mayor's tone is conveyed by his use of such details, which imply that the committee's concerns are not only minor but extremely trivial. These details don't interrupt the flow of the paragraph (Choice A) nor would their omission cause valuable information about the renovation to be lost (Choice B). Losing the details would also not affect the relevance of the mayor's remark (Choice D).

10. G. "Fundamentals" *are* basic; it is redundant to use the adjective "basic" with the word.

11. D. Clarify the pronoun by replacing it with the correct noun: "chairman."

12. J. This choice is the most direct and simple way to make the point. The original version is redundant, as are choices G and H. (Note: If the passage is directly quoting the committee member and no editing is allowed—as, for example, by a newspaper reporter—the quote would remain as it was originally. For the purpose of this exercise, however, choosing the best expression is required.)

13. B. This choice correctly uses an adverb ("regularly") rather than an adjective to modify the verb "met." It is less wordy than Choice C.

14. H. This choice is best because it explains the chairman's comment that the financial manager is "clearly not doing his job"—and the angry response of the financial manager in the following paragraph. None of the other choices provides such a logical link between paragraphs 3 and 4.

15. C. This sequence makes most sense in the paragraph because the financial manager's angry response is then followed by his statement that the plan will soon be available. Sentences 2 and 3 interrupt that connection because they deal with the mayor's comments. Sentences 2 and 3 should remain as they are; the mayor's praise is the best concluding sentence.

Passage II

16. G. A comma should not be used before "that" (choices F, H). Choice J corrects this but is wordy. Choice G is succinct and also correctly uses the simple past tense.

17. C. The adverb "well," not the adjective "good," is needed with the verb "pay."

18. G. This sentence signals the shift from the writer's point about paying the rent to his other points about leaving home. Choices F, H, and J, while related to his financial issues and his landlord, do not signal the change to concerns like cleaning his apartment and cooking his meals.

19. C. The phrase beginning with "Such" is a sentence fragment. To correct the fragment, "things" should be followed by a comma, not a semicolon or colon.

20. H. This is the best choice. In a sentence, like items should be structurally parallel: "doing" and "cleaning," not "doing" and "to clean."

21. A. The original version is the best choice. "Having" applies to both "clean clothes" and "a clean place." Choice A is more idiomatic than Choice C and less wordy than choices B and D.

22. F. The original is correct. Interrupters like "however" should be set off with commas in a sentence.

23. B. The assumption should be that Mother is still an excellent cook, so the present tense is best here.

24. J. Of the choices, this one is most concise. Avoid wordy constructions that can be replaced with a single word. A comma shouldn't be used before "because" here.

25. B. The comparative adjective "easier" is correct. Although adverbs usually modify verbs, some verbs are called *linking verbs*, and they are modified by adjectives. Verb forms of "to be" are an example. Other examples are "smell," "taste," "feel," and "seem." This isn't a complete list, however, and sometimes these verbs can be active verbs rather than linking verbs. For example, "The coffee smells good" (linking verb followed by an adjective) or "Ever since his nose injury, the dog doesn't smell as well as he used to" (active verb, taking an adverb).

26. F. The original is slang or colloquial language, and it fits the style and diction of the passage. In this type of essay, there's no need to replace phrases like this with more formal language.

27. D. This sentence should be omitted. Even though the writer has mentioned his/her mother's cooking skill, the paragraph is not about the mother but about the writer. Of the choices, sentence 5 is the one most off the topic.

28. G. This choice is parallel in structure ("asks" and "nags"). It also turns a fragment into a complete sentence.

29. C. The correct verb form here is "would have," not "would of." This error is often made in speech, but the replacement of "have" with "of" is substandard. The correct past participle is "have thought."

30. F. Sentences 1 and 2 are positive points about living in his/her own apartment. Sentence 4 shifts to the negative aspects, one of which is illustrated in sentence 3.

Passage III

31. B. A comma is the correct punctuation after an opening dependent clause: "Although . . . physiology." This choice also eliminates the wordiness ("there are") of the original version. Choice D creates a fragment by using a period rather than a comma.

32. H. The original version, Choice F, uses a plural verb with a singular noun: "distribution depend." Don't be misled by "plants," which is not the subject of the sentence. Choice G, while concise, changes the meaning; it is plants' *distribution* that the sentence is about.

33. B. The original version, Choice A, creates a fragment by using a period rather than a comma after "factors." Choice B corrects the problem. Although Choice D also corrects the problem, it is less concise (and graceful) than Choice B.

34. J. This is a case of choosing the active voice of the verb rather than the passive one. Not only is "depend on" more concise, but active verbs also improve sentence style.

35. B. The original version (Choice A) is not grammatically incorrect, but Choice B is less awkward and more concise. Choice D is even more concise, but changes the meaning. It is the *length* of daylight that appears to be the key.

36. H. The main problem with the original version in Passage III is that a comma separates subject and verb. Subject and verb should not be separated by a comma. Also, "phenomena" is the correct plural of "phenomenon" (Choice G).

37. D. This sentence would be appropriate as a topic sentence in the next paragraph, as that paragraph deals with temperature. In its present position, it is off the topic of daylight and darkness.

38. F. The original version is the best choice. The semicolon is correctly used between two independent clauses, and this version is the most concise.

39. B. "On the other hand" should be omitted. Choice A correctly encloses the phrase in commas, but the phrase itself contributes nothing to meaning. Choice D would create a run-on sentence or comma splice.

40. H. The original version (Choice F) is a sentence fragment. If "which" is deleted, the problem is corrected. Choice G remains a fragment. A second error in the original version is the failure to use an apostrophe to indicate a possessive: "world's," not "worlds."

41. B. The original version (Choice A) is a sentence fragment because "whereas" begins a dependent clause, and a semicolon shouldn't be used to separate it from the main clause. All the choices correct the problem, but the phrase in Choice B is the most effective because it is parallel to "some retarding growth and arresting...."

42. J. The phrase is nonrestrictive; in other words, it is additional information and not required for meaning in the sentence. Nonrestrictive phrases should be set off in commas.

43. C. This choice, which replaces a clause with the infinitive "to use," is the most concise. Commas shouldn't be used to set off the original clause (Choice A) or the revised clause in Choice D. The verb tense in Choice B is incorrect in context.

44. J. Choice J changes the verb to the active voice, which is more concise than the other choices.

45. D. The second sentence is a better introduction to the paragraph than the first. The second sentence states that all plants need moisture, which is a general opening. The next sentence would then explain where the moisture comes from.

Passage IV

46. H. This choice places elements in the most logical order. The "greater than" construction is not interrupted by "especially in intelligence." Choice J is wordy.

47. D. Choice D is concise and correct. The correct punctuation between an independent and dependent clause is a comma, not a semicolon. Both choices A and C create a fragment, and Choice B is a run-on sentence, or comma splice.

48. G. "Inferior" should not be used with a comparative like "more"; it *is* a comparative. The sentence states that women are inferior to men; they can't be *more* inferior to men.

49. A. The original version is best. It is a phrase in common use; "in," not "to" (Choice B), is idiomatic. Choices C and D are wordy.

50. G. "Number" is correct for individual units, "amount" for a single quantity: "a number of men," "an amount of money." "Number" generally takes a singular verb, as it does in Choice G.

51. B. The proper tense here is the past tense, which is consistent with the other verbs.

52. J. With the active voice of the verb, this choice avoids the wordiness of the original version and of Choice H. The sentence order in Choice G, and the use of the noun "conclusion" rather than the verb "concluded," makes this choice less effective than Choice J.

53. C. This is the best choice. The pronoun should be "who," not "whom"; it is the subject of "were." Choice B, although more concise, changes the meaning.

54. H. An appositive is a noun or pronoun that follows another noun or pronoun to describe or identify it. In this case, the two names identify the psychologists. Choice H is the most succinct expression; appositives should be enclosed in commas.

55. B. This is the best choice. It is a conditional form, that is, on the condition that the curriculum is adapted, it *would* prepare . . .

56. F. The original version is best. It is clearer and more concise than choices G and H. Choice J creates a sentence fragment.

57. D. Although the point made in this sentence may be true, the sentence itself does not fit well in this paragraph. Passage IV as a whole is chronological in structure, and this statement interrupts the chronology.

58. H. First of all, "equal to each other" is wordy and unnecessary; Choice H is a better choice than choices F or G. Second, the subject of the verb is singular, not plural: "range was" not "range were." It is important to identify the subject and use the correct number of the verb.

59. C. This choice corrects the faulty parallelism of the original version. It is also more concise than choices B or D.

60. J. Reversing paragraphs 4 and 5 is the best choice. Chronologically, the information about Leta Hollingworth precedes the information about recent studies, which makes the reversal logical.

Passage V

61. D. "Technology" is a singular noun and, therefore, takes a singular verb. "Communication" and "media" are not the subject of the sentence; "technology" is. The other choices, in addition to a subject/verb agreement problem, are wordy.

62. G. Since the sentence deals with both phones and television, the plural "versions" is the best choice. Also, Choice G makes the point more concisely than the other choices.

63. C. "You" is consistent with "you" at the beginning of this sentence. Choices A and B are both wordy. Choice D, in addition to changing "you" to "one," makes the common mistake of changing the construction "would have" to "would of."

64. G. Choice F is dangling participle; adding "you" to the phrase as in Choice G corrects this. Choice J still includes a dangling participle, and in Choice H, a comma should follow the phrase "chances are."

65. C. The original version, Choice A, uses the objective pronoun "them," but here "those" (the subject of "remaining") is correct. Choice D also incorrectly uses an objective pronoun ("whom").

66. J. For consistency and to maintain parallel construction, the present tense is the best choice: "are talking" and "are commiserating."

67. B. The "not only/but also" construction is correctly parallel in Choice B. The other choices are wordy or don't maintain parallel structure.

68. H. The sentence should be deleted because it interferes with the coherence of the paragraph and also because the tone is different from the rest of Passage V. The writer is not giving practical advice in Passage V but commenting on the phenomenon of rapid technological advances.

69. C. This choice is best because it focuses on the speed of technological advance, which is picked up by the following question. It is not necessarily the most elegant or the most interesting sentence, but it is the most logical.

70. G. "As if," not "like," is correct when followed by a clause. "Like" is a preposition that takes an object—for example, "The ice cream tastes like peaches." Choice J is wordy.

71. A. The subjective pronoun "we" is correct. Read the sentence without "consumers," and this is clear. The present tense "are" is also correct.

72. J. This sentence is a question and should be followed by a question mark. Except for that, the original version is correct.

73. B. Choice B is the only one that corrects the dangling participle in the original version. "We," not "our lives," are watching bad television programs.

74. H. Sentence 7 introduces a separate topic, the role of the media in our purchasing habits. This may be a valid subtopic of the essay, but it shouldn't be "stuck into" this paragraph. The other sentences maintain the paragraph's unity.

75. C. Of the choices given, this is best. The style and approach are appropriate for an opinion piece, not for a fact-based textbook, research paper, or news magazine.

Mathematics Test

1. E. The total number of students is 48. Subtract from 48 the number of students earning an A, B, D, or F. This leaves the number that earned a C: $x = 48 - 8 - 10 - 10 - 2 = 18$. You can use a proportion to solve:

$$\frac{\text{part}}{\text{whole}} = \frac{\%}{100} \Rightarrow \frac{18}{48} = \frac{x}{100} \Rightarrow x = 37.5\%$$

2. H. A single equation can be used to calculate the required amount.

$$80 = \frac{(6)(78) + 2x}{8}$$
$$640 = (6)(78) + 2x$$
$$640 = 468 + 2x$$
$$172 = 2x$$
$$86 = x$$

Tony needs to average 86 on the next two tests.

3. B. This type of problems is best solved using a Venn diagram. Start entering values from the inside toward the outside. Since three students belong to all three clubs, place a 3 in the center. Since 12 students belong to exactly two clubs, place three numbers (it does not matter what they are as long as the total within a circle representing a particular club does not exceed the total membership in the club) that add up to 12 into the three regions that are in exactly two circles. Here, 4, 4, and 4 are used for these three numbers. Since there are 12 students in club E, and there are already $4 + 3 + 4 = 11$ students in the E circle, place the number 1 in the remaining region in circle E. Similarly, determine and place the numbers 4 and 9 in the two remaining regions in circle F and G. The total number of students in exactly one club is $1 + 4 + 9 = 14$, or Choice B.

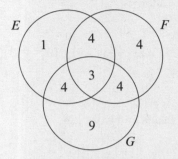

4. K. In similar solid figures, the ratio of the areas is the square of the ratio of the linear measures, and the ratio of the volumes is the cube of the ratios of the linear measures. Since you are given that the ratio of the areas is $\frac{3}{4}$, the ratio of their linear measures must be $\sqrt{\frac{3}{4}} = \frac{\sqrt{3}}{\sqrt{4}} = \frac{\sqrt{3}}{2}$.

Therefore, the ratio of their volumes is $\left(\frac{\sqrt{3}}{2}\right)^3 = \frac{\left(\sqrt{3}\right)^3}{2^3} = \frac{3\sqrt{3}}{8}$.

5. B. The mathematical approach would be to find the prime factorization for each number and then determine what the LCM needs to be.

$24 = 2 \times 2 \times 2 \times 3$
$48 = 2 \times 2 \times 2 \times 2 \times 3$
$60 = 2 \times 2 \times 3 \times 5$

Therefore, the LCM would be $2 \times 2 \times 2 \times 2 \times 3 \times 5 = 240$. This is Choice B. A more direct approach would be to test each answer choice. Start with 120. Although 24 and 60 divide evenly into 120, 48 does not. Therefore, it is not Choice A. Next try 240. Since 24, 48, and 60 all divide evenly into 240, this is the correct answer choice. This method might be a bit faster than the factoring method.

6. J. First, substitute the given root into the equation for x and solve for c.

$$3x^2 + cx - 12 = 0$$
$$3(-3)^2 + c(-3) - 12 = 0$$
$$27 - 3c - 12 = 0$$
$$-3c = -15$$
$$c = 5$$

Next, substitute this value for c into the equation and factor. Remember that one of the factors will need to be $(x + 3)$ since one of the roots is (-3).

$$3x^2 + cx - 12 = 0$$
$$3x^2 + 5x - 12 = 0$$
$$(3x - 4)(x + 3) = 0$$

To determine the other root, set $(3x - 4) = 0$ and solve.

$$3x - 4 = 0$$
$$3x = 4$$
$$x = \frac{4}{3}$$

This is Choice J.

7. D. This is a substitution problem, as follows.

$$ab^2c - a^2b^3c + abc$$
$$= (-3)(-1)^2(3) - (-3)^2(-1)^3(3) + (-3)(-1)(3)$$
$$= -9 - (-27) + 9$$
$$= 27$$

8. K. When simplifying, start from the inside and work out.

$$\left(\left(-3x^2y\right)\left(xy^3\right)\right)^2$$
$$\left(-3x^3y^4\right)^2$$
$$9x^6y^8$$

Remember, when multiplying numbers of the same base, add the exponents. When raising a power to a power, multiply the powers. The correct choice is K.

9. E. Perform the successive multiplications.

$$(x + 2)^3 = (x + 2)(x + 2)(x + 2)$$
$$= (x + 2)\left(x^2 + 4x + 4\right)$$
$$= x^3 + 4x^2 + 4x + 2x^2 + 8x + 8$$
$$= x^3 + 6x^2 + 12x + 8$$

10. G. When cut apart, the total number of painted surfaces (of the small cubes) is $6 + 6 + 6 + 6 + 4 + 4 = 32$. There are a total of 12 small cubes, each with 6 surfaces, for a total $(12)(6) = 72$ total surfaces. Since 32 are painted, $72 - 32 = 40$ surfaces are unpainted. The ratio of 32:40 reduces to 4:5, or Choice G.

11. B. Perpendicular lines have negative reciprocal slopes. Therefore, since the slope of the given line is $\frac{1}{4}$, the slope of the line in question must be $m = -4$. Use the point-slope form to determine the equation of the line.

$$y - y_1 = m(x - x_1)$$
$$y - (-2) = -4(x - (-1))$$
$$y + 2 = -4x - 4$$
$$y = -4x - 6$$

12. H. Since the rectangle is twice as long as it is wide, you can think of the length as $2w$ and the width as w. You know that the perimeter is 42. Therefore, $2w + 2w + w + w = 42$, or $6w = 42$. The width is, therefore, 7, and the length is 14. Thus, the area is the product of 7 and 14, or 98.

13. C. After Car *B* has been driven for 3 hours, Car *A* has been driven for 6 hours. Use the formula $d = rt$ to determine the distance traveled by each car and then subtract to determine the number of miles apart the cars are.

$$d = rt \qquad\qquad d = rt$$
$$d = (6)(40) \qquad d = (3)(50)$$
$$d = 240 \qquad\quad d = 150$$

They are 240 – 150 = 90 miles apart. This is Choice C.

14. H. When Car *A* is 200 miles from the starting point, it means that it has been driven for 5 hours. This implies that Car *B* has been driven for only 2 hours, since Car *B* leaves three hours after Car *A*. Thus, in two hours Car *B* will be 100 miles from the starting point.

15. E. For each car, the distance traveled is the product of the speed of the car and the number of hours driven. When Car *B* catches up to Car *A*, they will have traveled the same distance. Set up an equation to determine the travel time. Let *t* be the number of hours driven by Car *A*.

$$50(t - 3) = 40t$$
$$50t - 150 = 40t$$
$$10t = 150$$
$$t = 15$$

Therefore, Car *A* has been driven for 15 hours. Since Car *A* left the starting point at 9 a.m., Car *B* will catch up to Car *A* 15 hours later, or at 12 midnight.

16. K. The easiest way to solve this problem is to work from the answers. Start with either intercept. For example, start with the *x*-intercept. For the *x*-intercept to be 5, the point (5, 0) must satisfy the equation. Substitute $x = 5$ and $y = 0$ into each answer choice. Choices F, G, and H can be eliminated since (5, 0) does not satisfy the equation. Only choices J and K work with (5, 0). Now try the *y*-intercept. Try (0, 3) in choices J and K. It does not satisfy Choice J, but does satisfy Choice K. Therefore, Choice K is correct.

An alternative, but longer, solution would be to use the two intercepts to determine the slope of the line and then use the slope along with one of the two intercepts to determine the equation. In this case, testing the answer choices is much faster.

17. C. First, determine how many tiles will fit in each direction. Converting 24 feet to inches and dividing by 16 gives 18 tiles along the length of the room. Converting 16 feet to inches and dividing by 16 gives 12 tiles along the width of the room.

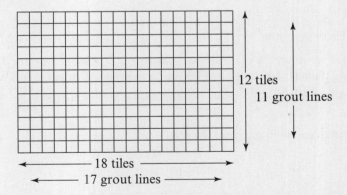

12 tiles
11 grout lines

18 tiles
17 grout lines

Since 18 tiles are along the length of the room, there are 17 grout joints, each 16 feet long. Since 12 tiles are along the width of the room, there are 11 grout joints, each 24 feet long. The total length of grout joints is $(17)(16) + (11)(24) = 536$ feet, or Choice C.

18. K. Using specific stock prices can simplify the process. Start with a stock price of $100.00. After the first 10 percent price decrease, the price will be $100 - (100)(0.10) = 100 - 10 = \$90.00$. After the 20 percent increase the price will be $90 + (90)(0.20) = 90 + 18 = \$108.00$. After the second 10 percent decrease the price of the stock will be $108 - (108)(0.10) = 108 - 10.8 = \$97.20$. This reflects a decrease of $2.80 from the original price of $100.00, or a 2.8 percent decrease. Therefore, the correct choice is K.

19. D. In an isosceles triangle, two of the sides are the same length. This means that the three sides of the triangle must be 10 cm, 10 cm, and 4 cm. It is not possible to have two sides of length 4 cm and one side of length 10 cm since the two shorter sides of a triangle must add up to more than the third side. The height of the triangle can be calculated using the Pythagorean Theorem.

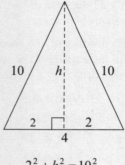

$$2^2 + h^2 = 10^2$$
$$4 + h^2 = 100$$
$$h^2 = 96$$
$$h = \sqrt{96}$$
$$h = 4\sqrt{6}$$

The area of the triangle is $A = \frac{1}{2}bh = \left(\frac{1}{2}\right)(4)\left(4\sqrt{6}\right) = 8\sqrt{6}$ cm^2.

20. H. Since the ratio of adult to child tickets sold is 4:1, let $4x$ represent the number of adult tickets sold and let x represent the number of child tickets sold. Multiply each quantity by the cost of the respective type of ticket. Set up an equation and solve.

$$(5)(4x) + (2)(x) = 682$$
$$20x + 2x = 682$$
$$22x = 682$$
$$x = 31$$

Therefore, 31 child tickets were sold.

21. B. Traveling at 40 miles per hour, the car will travel the first 200 miles in 5 hours. Traveling at 50 miles per hour, the car will travel the next 200 miles in 4 hours. Consequently, it will take $5 + 4 = 9$ hours to travel the entire 400 miles. Therefore, the average speed for the entire 400-mile trip was $\frac{400}{9} = 44\frac{4}{9} \approx 44\frac{1}{2}$ miles per hour, or Choice B.

22. J. Drawing a quick sketch can help organize the data.

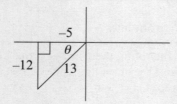

Use the Pythagorean Theorem or your knowledge of Pythagorean Triples to find the third side of the right triangle. The cotangent is the quotient of the adjacent side and the opposite side.

$$\frac{-5}{-12} = \frac{5}{12}$$

23. A. Drawing a sketch of the given information can help you visualize the problem.

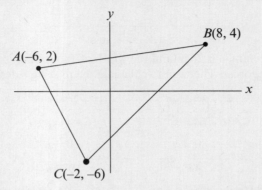

Clearly, from the sketch, $\overline{AC}$ passes through the negative x-axis. Therefore, you can immediately eliminate choices D and E. The slope of $\overline{AC}$ is $\frac{-6-2}{-2-(-6)} = \frac{-8}{4} = -2$. For every two units down, shift one to the right. Thus, the x-intercept must be $(-5, 0)$. The correct choice is A.

24. J. Use the distance formula to determine the distance between two points.

$$\begin{aligned}
d &= \sqrt{(x_2 - x_1)^2 + (y_2 - y_1)^2} \\
&= \sqrt{(8 - (-6))^2 + (4 - 2)^2} \\
&= \sqrt{14^2 + 2^2} \\
&= \sqrt{196 + 4} \\
&= \sqrt{200} \\
&= 10\sqrt{2}
\end{aligned}$$

25. C. To determine the equation, find the midpoint of the segment and the slope of the line that contains the segment.

$$\text{Midpoint} = (x_k, y_k) = \left(\frac{8 + (-2)}{2}, \frac{4 + (-6)}{2}\right) = (3, -1)$$

$$\text{Slope} = \frac{4 - (-6)}{8 - (-2)} = \frac{10}{10} = 1$$

The slope of the perpendicular bisector has a negative reciprocal slope. Therefore, the slope of the line in question is $m = -1$, and it passes through the point $(3, -1)$. Use the point-slope form to find the equation of the bisector.

$$\begin{aligned}
y - y_k &= m(x - x_k) \\
y - (-1) &= (-1)(x - 3) \\
y + 1 &= -x + 3 \\
x + y &= 2
\end{aligned}$$

This is Choice C.

26. H. Redraw the figure, filling in the information given.

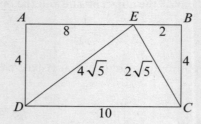

Since the perimeter of the rectangle is 28 in and the width of the rectangle is 4 in, the length of the rectangle must be 10 in. Use the Pythagorean Theorem to calculate the missing sides of the triangle.

$$4^2 + 8^2 = x^2 \qquad\qquad 4^2 + 2^2 = y^2$$
$$16 + 64 = x^2 \qquad\qquad 16 + 4 = y^2$$
$$80 = x^2 \qquad\qquad 20 = y^2$$
$$x = \sqrt{80} \qquad\qquad y = \sqrt{20}$$
$$x = 4\sqrt{5} \qquad\qquad y = 2\sqrt{5}$$

Adding the three sides of the large triangle gives $10 + 6\sqrt{5}$ in, or Choice H.

27. B. Inscribed angles are equal to one-half of their intercepted arcs. Therefore, the sizes of angles x and y are in the same ratio as the lengths of their intercepted arcs. Since $\overparen{BD}$ is 25 percent longer than $\overparen{BC}$, they are in the ratio of 5 to 4. Set up a proportion and solve for y.

$$\frac{\text{Length of } \overparen{BD}}{\text{Length of } \overparen{BC}} = \frac{x}{y}$$
$$\frac{5}{4} = \frac{40°}{y}$$
$$5y = 160°$$
$$y = 32°$$

28. J. This problem requires you to set up two equations that represent the given information and then combine them to eliminate the "apples."

Let a = weight of one apple, p = weight of one pear, and r = weight of one orange. The two equations that represent the given information are as follows:

$3p = 3r + a$
$3a = p + r$

Multiply the first equation by 3 and then substitute for the "$3a$."

$9p = 9r + 3a$
$9p = 9r + p + r$
$8p = 10r$
$4p = 5r$

Therefore, four pears weigh the same as five oranges, or Choice J.

29. C. Since $\sin X = \dfrac{x}{z}$ and $\tan Y = \dfrac{y}{x}$, you have $\sin X + \tan Y = \dfrac{x}{z} + \dfrac{y}{x} = \dfrac{x^2 + yz}{xz}$. This is Choice C.

30. H. The simplest way to solve this problem is to test answer choices to determine which one works. Choice F does not work since $5 \neq 4$. Choice G does not work since $\dfrac{10}{4} \neq \dfrac{12}{5}$. Choice H *does* work since $\dfrac{10}{5} = \dfrac{12}{6}$. It is not necessary to proceed any further since you found an answer choice that works. Another approach is to actually solve for x.

$$\frac{10}{x} = \frac{12}{x+1}$$
$$10(x+1) = 12x$$
$$10x + 10 = 12x$$
$$10 = 2x$$
$$5 = x$$

31. B. First, multiply both sides of the equation by 2 and then isolate the term containing z.

$$2w = 3x - \frac{y}{2} - z$$
$$4w = 6x - y - 2z$$
$$2z = 6x - y - 4w$$

If w, x, and y are each increased by 2, the x-term will increase by 12, the y-term will decrease by 2, and the w-term will decrease by 8. Therefore, the right side of the equation will increase by 2. In order for the left side of the equation to increase by 2, z would have to increase by 1. This is Choice B.

32. F. First, start with the numerical coefficient. The largest integer that divides evenly (no remainder) into 8, 12, and 16 is 4. Knowing this eliminates answer choices H, J, and K. Next, select a variable. The highest power of x that divides evenly into x^2, x^3, and x^4 is x^2. Knowing this eliminates Choice G. So, even without checking the y variable, you know that the answer must be Choice F.

33. B. From the equation, you see that the y-intercept is (-8). Clearly, statement II is true. Since the slope of the line is positive and passes through the negative y-axis, the line must pass through the positive x-axis, so statement I is false. To determine which side of the line the given points are on, substitute the x-coordinates into the equation to determine the y-coordinate. If $x = 12$, then $y = 0$. Clearly, the first point, $(12, 2)$, is above the line. If $x = 6$, then $y = -4$. This second point, $(6, -5)$, is below the line. Therefore, the points are on opposite sides of the line, making statement III false. Thus, only statement II is true, and the correct choice is B.

34. G. There are ten even integers from 10 through 28. Therefore, the median is the average of the two middle integers. The average of 18 and 20 is 19.

10 12 14 16 **18 20** 22 24 26 28

The median is the average of the two **bold** numbers, which is 19.

After the six odd integers from 13 through 23 are added to the list, the median would be the average of the two middle numbers. The average of 18 and 19 is $18\frac{1}{2}$.

10 12 13 14 15 16 17 **18 19** 20 21 22 23 24 26 28

The median is the average of the two **bold** numbers, which is $18\frac{1}{2}$.

This represents a decrease of $\frac{1}{2}$ from the original median. This is Choice G.

35. D. Since $\sqrt{x^2} = \text{abs}(x)$, this problem is solved the same as an absolute value problem.

$-6 < 4 - x < 6$
$-10 < -x < 2$
$10 > x > -2$
$-2 < x < 10$

This is Choice D.

36. G. The following table of the possible outcomes will be helpful.

Die	1	2	3	4	5	6
1	2	3	4	5	6	7
2	3	4	5	6	7	8
3	4	5	6	7	8	9
4	5	6	7	8	9	10
5	6	7	8	9	10	11
6	7	8	9	10	11	12

There are (6)(6) = 36 possible outcomes when two dice are rolled. The prime numbers in this range of sums are 2, 3, 5, 7, and 11. The sum of 2 occurs one time. The sum of 3 occurs two times. The sum of 5 occurs four times. The sum of 7 occurs six times. The sum of 11 occurs two times. Adding gives 1 + 2 + 4 + 6 + 2 = 15. Therefore, 15 out of the 36 possible outcomes are prime numbers. This is a probability of $\frac{15}{36} = \frac{5}{12}$. This is Choice G.

37. C. Rewrite these two inequalities and draw a rough sketch.

$$x + 2y < 8 \quad \text{and} \quad 2x - y > 4$$
$$y < -\frac{1}{2}x + 4 \qquad\qquad y < 2x - 4$$

The first inequality has a *y*-intercept of 4 and a negative slope.

The second inequality has a *y*-intercept of –4 and a positive slope.

Test a sample point, such as the origin (0, 0) to determine which side of the line satisfies the inequality.

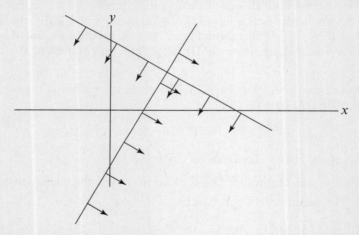

Even with only rough placement, it is clear that points that satisfy the first inequality could be in any of the four quadrants, but the points that satisfy the second inequality, the one with a positive slope, cannot lie in the second quadrant. Therefore, the correct answer is three quadrants, or Choice C.

38. K. Each of the answer choices is a true statement except Choice K, as follows:

$$[\text{Choice F}] \quad \cos A \sin A = \left(\frac{3}{5}\right)\left(\frac{4}{5}\right) = \frac{12}{25}$$

$$[\text{Choice G}] \quad \sin^2 A = \left(\frac{4}{5}\right)^2 = \frac{16}{25}$$

$$[\text{Choice H}] \quad \sin C - \cos C = \frac{3}{5} - \frac{4}{5} = -\frac{1}{5}$$

[Choice J] $\tan C \sin A = \left(\dfrac{3}{4}\right)\left(\dfrac{4}{5}\right) = \dfrac{3}{5}$

[Choice K] $\sin C - \cos^2 A = \dfrac{3}{5} - \left(\dfrac{3}{5}\right)^2 = \dfrac{15}{25} - \dfrac{9}{25} = \dfrac{6}{25} \neq -\dfrac{6}{25}$

For Choice K, the value of the expression is $\dfrac{6}{25}$, not $-\dfrac{6}{25}$. Thus, Choice K represents the false statement.

39. C. Drawing in $\overline{BD}$ you can determine the missing angles.

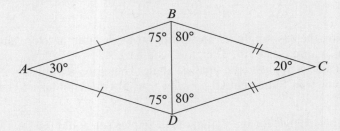

The quadrilateral is now divided into two isosceles triangles. Since $\angle BCD = 20°$, the congruent base angles must add up to 160°. Therefore, each one is 80°. Since $\angle ADC = 155°$, $\angle ADB = 155° - 80° = 75°$. This is one of the congruent base angles of the other isosceles triangle. Therefore, $\angle BAD = 180° - 75° - 75° = 30°$, or Choice C.

40. G. The direct way to solve this problem is to substitute the height of 48 feet into the equation and determine the two values of t that satisfy the equation.

$$h = -4t^2 + 32t$$
$$48 = -4t^2 + 32t$$
$$4t^2 - 32t + 48 = 0$$
$$t^2 - 8t + 12 = 0$$
$$(t-6)(t-2) = 0$$

The ball passes a height of 48 feet at $t = 2$ and $t = 6$. The difference is 4 seconds, or Choice G. Another method you can use to solve this problem is to build a table of values. Calculate the height above the ground for each second of time starting with 0.

Time (t)	Height (h)
0	0
1	28
2	48
3	60
4	64
5	60
6	48
7	28
8	0

You see from the table that the height of the ball will be 48 feet at $t = 2$ and $t = 6$. The difference is 4 seconds, or Choice G. Solving the equation is probably faster than building the table.

41. B. Drawing a figure can help visualize the given information.

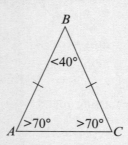

Angle A and angle C are the base angles of an isosceles triangle and, therefore, must be equal in size. Since $\angle A > 70°$, you must also have $\angle C > 70°$. Therefore, you have $\angle B < 40°$. Thus, statement I must be true. In a triangle, the shortest side is opposite the smallest angle. Therefore, $\overline{AC}$ must be the shortest side. Thus, statement II must also be true. Statement III *could* be true, but does not have to be true. Therefore, Choice **B** is correct.

42. K. The three sides of this triangle form a Pythagorean Triple. You could use the Pythagorean Theorem to solve, but being able to recognize some basic Pythagorean Triples can save you time.

In this case, the sides are in the ratio of 5:12:13. The lengths of the sides of this triangle are double the ratio. Therefore, the missing side must have a length of 24. Other basic Pythagorean Triples are 3:4:5 and 8:15:17. Of course, using the Pythagorean Theorem gives the following:

$$10^2 + x^2 = 26^2$$
$$100 + x^2 = 676$$
$$x^2 = 576$$
$$x = \sqrt{576}$$
$$x = 24$$

43. B. Multiply out the expression, combine similar terms, and write in descending order of powers of x.

$(x - 4)^2 - (2x - 1)^2$
$(x^2 - 8x + 16) - (4x^2 - 4x + 1)$
$x^2 - 8x + 16 - 4x^2 + 4x - 1$
$-3x^2 - 4x + 15$

Thus, $a = -3$, $b = -4$, and $c = 15$. Ordered smallest to largest, this is $b < a < c$, or Choice **B**.

44. J. Since specific values are given as answer choices, you must assume that both the flagpole and pole are vertical and that the ground is level.

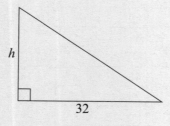

Both triangles are right triangles with equal angles. Therefore, their sides are proportional.

$$\frac{h}{32} = \frac{5}{6}$$
$$6h = 160$$
$$h = \frac{160}{6}$$
$$h \approx 26.7$$

45. E. Simply substitute the value of –6 into the function for x.

$$g(x) = 3x^2 - 2x + 8 = 3(-6)^2 - 2(-6) + 8 = 108 + 12 + 8 = 128$$

46. K. Since x and y are consecutive odd integers, the number between them is an even integer that you can call a. Then $(a-1)$ and $(a+1)$ can represent x and y. Since $(a-1)(a+1) = a^2 - 1$, and $a = x + 1$, statement I is equal to the product of x and y. Statement II is equal to the product of x and y since $y = x + 2$ and $x = y - 2$. Since $(a-2)(a+2) = a^2 - 4$ and $a^2 - 4 + 3 = a^2 - 1$, statement III is also equal to the product of x and y. Therefore, Choice K is correct. If you were running out of time you could choose two arbitrary consecutive odd integers and test to see which of the three statements could work. Although this does not verify all possible replacement values it could help you make the correct choice. For example, use 5 and 7. Their product is 35. I: $(5+1)^2 - 1 = 35$. II: $(5+2)(7-2) = 35$. III: $(5-1)(7+1) + 3 = 35$. All three statements are true.

47. D. The area of the figure is made up of four semi-circles and one square. The perimeter of the figure is equal to the circumference of two circles. Since the perimeter is 24π, the circumference of one circle must be 12π. If the circumference of a circle is 12π, its diameter must be 12, and its radius must be 6. The side of the square is equal to the diameter of the circle, therefore, the area of the square is $12^2 = 144$. Since the radius of the circle is 6, the area of one circle is πr^2, or 36π. The total area of the figure is the area of the square plus the area of two circles, or $144 + 72\pi$.

48. F. The following figure summarizes the given information.

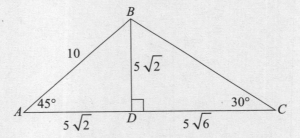

By drawing an additional line in the figure, you can divide the original triangle into two right triangles. The triangle on the left is a 45-45-90 isosceles right triangle. The ratio of its sides is $1:1:\sqrt{2}$. To find the lengths of the missing equal sides, divide 10 by $\sqrt{2}$.

$$\frac{10}{\sqrt{2}} = \frac{10\sqrt{2}}{2} = 5\sqrt{2}$$

The triangle on the right is a 30-60-90 right triangle. The ratio of its sides is $1:2:\sqrt{3}$. To find the length of the missing side, multiply $5\sqrt{2}$ by $\sqrt{3}$. This gives $5\sqrt{6}$. Add the lengths of the two sides and factor to obtain the correct answer.

$$5\sqrt{2} + 5\sqrt{6} = 5\sqrt{2} + 5\sqrt{2}\sqrt{3} = 5\sqrt{2}\left(1 + \sqrt{3}\right)$$

49. D. The sum and difference of irrational numbers are always irrational. This is not true of the product. For example, $\sqrt{18}$ and $\sqrt{2}$ are each irrational numbers, but their product of $\sqrt{18}\sqrt{2} = \sqrt{36} = 6$ is rational. The correct choice is D.

50. K. The coordinates of the midpoint are the averages of the coordinates of the endpoints. If (x, y) are the coordinates of the missing endpoint, solve for x and y and determine their sum.

$$-4 = \frac{-8 + x}{2} \qquad\qquad 8 = \frac{-20 + y}{2}$$
$$-8 = -8 + x \qquad\qquad 16 = -20 + y$$
$$0 = x \qquad\qquad\qquad 36 = y$$

The endpoint is $(0, 36)$. The sum of the coordinates is 36, or Choice K.

51. E. The sine is defined as the opposite side divided by the hypotenuse. Set up an equation and solve for x.

$$\sin 50° = \frac{65}{x}$$
$$x = \frac{65}{\sin 50°}$$

Therefore, Choice E represents the length of the guy wire.

52. J. A chart may be useful in organizing the given information. Let x represent Jen's current age.

Person	Age 12 years ago	Current Age	Age 16 Years from Now
Jen	$x - 12$	x	$x + 16$

Set up an equation using the information given in the chart above and solve for x.

$$2(x - 12) = x + 16$$
$$2x - 24 = x + 16$$
$$x = 40$$

53. C. First, draw a sketch of the triangle using the given information.

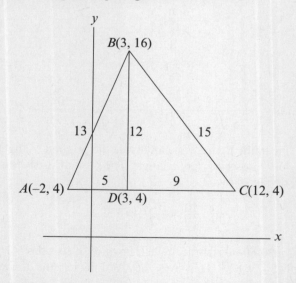

Draw the height of the triangle from point B to point D. This divides this triangle into two right triangles, each of which has sides in the ratio of a Pythagorean Triple. From the drawing you see that $BD = 12$, $AD = 5$, and $CD = 9$. The triangle on the left has sides in the ratio of 5:12:13. The triangle on the right has sides in the ratio of 3:4:5. These are two Pythagorean Triples. The hypotenuses of these two right triangles can be determined directly instead of spending the time using the Pythagorean Theorem. The sum of the three sides is 13 + 14 + 15 = 42, or Choice C. An alternative method of solution would be to use the distance formula to calculate the length of each of the three sides of the large triangle. The process is straight forward since you are given the coordinates of each of the endpoints of the three sides. This method would probably be much more time consuming than the method shown.

54. J. In this sequence, the exponent of w increases by 2, the exponent of x decreases by 1, and the exponent of y increases by 1. Thus, in the fourth term in this sequence the exponent of w will be 12, the exponent of x will be 0, and the exponent of y will be 7. Since any number to the power of zero has a value of 1, the correct choice is J.

55. D. Since the ratio of the surface areas of the spheres $A{:}B{:}C$ is 16:4:1, the ratio of the surface areas of sphere B to sphere C is 4:1. Since the ratio of the areas must be the square of the ratio of the linear measures, the ratio of the linear measures must be 2:1. The ratio of the volumes is the cube of the ratio of the linear measures, or 8:1. This is Choice D.

56. K. Factor and simplify.

$$\frac{\left(x^2 - x - 20\right)\left(x^2 - 7x + 12\right)}{\left(x^2 + 3x - 28\right)\left(x^2 - 8x + 15\right)}$$

$$\frac{(x+4)(x-5)(x-4)(x-3)}{(x-4)(x+7)(x-5)(x-3)}$$

$$\frac{(x+4)\cancel{(x-5)}\cancel{(x-4)}\cancel{(x-3)}}{\cancel{(x-4)}(x+7)\cancel{(x-5)}\cancel{(x-3)}}$$

$$\frac{x+4}{x+7}$$

57. A. Quadratic equations have two roots. If the equation has only real coefficients and one of the roots is a complex number, the other root must be the complex conjugate. Therefore, the two roots of the equation are $(1 + i)$ and $(1 - i)$. If m and n are the roots of a quadratic equation, then the factored form of the equation is $(x - m)(x - n) = 0$. Therefore, you can solve for the needed equation be substituting your complex roots into this general form, multiply, and then add the coefficients.

$(x - 1 - i)(x - 1 + i) = 0$

$x^2 - x + xi - x + 1 - i - xi + i - i^2 = 0$

$x^2 - 2x + 1 + 1 = 0$

$1x^2 - 2x + 2 = 0$

The three numerical coefficients of the equation are 1, –2, and 2. Their sum is 1, or Choice A.

58. H. First, the line segment from (4, 6) to (7, 0) has a negative slope. With this information you can eliminate choices F and K. The parabola has a y-intercept of 6. With this information you can eliminate Choice G. Since the parabola has a line of symmetry that is shifted to the right of the y-axis, the coefficient of the linear term must be negative. This eliminates Choice J. Without doing any more work, you have eliminated four of the five possible answer choices. Thus, the correct choice is H.

Another approach, after eliminating choices F and K, would be to substitute $x = 2$ into choices G, H, and J to determine which one would yield an answer of zero. Only Choice H works. This would clearly take longer than the method outlined.

59. B. In a rhombus, all four sides are the same length, and the diagonals bisect each other at a right angles. Therefore, $\angle CAD = 20°$ and $\angle BAC = 20°$. Calculate the value of y using the cosine.

$$\cos 20° = \frac{y}{x}$$

$$y = x \cos 20°$$

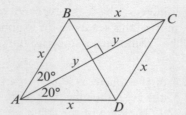

The main diagonal, $\overline{AC}$, is equal to $2y$. Therefore, the length of diagonal $\overline{AC}$ is $2x \cos 20°$, or Choice B.

60. F. Remember that the log of a number is the power that the base of the log must be raised to in order to obtain the number. $(\log_4 16) = 2$ since $4^2 = 16$. $(\log_{16} 2) = \frac{1}{4}$ since $16^{\left(\frac{1}{4}\right)} = 2$. $(\log_8 4) = \frac{2}{3}$ since $8^{\left(\frac{2}{3}\right)} = 4$. Now, multiply these values together. $(2)\left(\frac{1}{4}\right)\left(\frac{2}{3}\right) = \frac{4}{12} = \frac{1}{3}$. This is Choice F.

Reading Test

Passage I

1. D. See lines 7–12. Choice B is incorrect; the tractors are missing because of the war, and although choices A and C are mentioned, the sound referred to in the first sentence is the sound of the farmers' voices as they manage the horses.

2. J. When the war is over, the tractors will return and replace the horse-drawn plows. See lines 2–7.

3. C. Nothing in the first paragraph indicates that the narrator is a child, although it is clear that the narrator is part of the scene. Choices A, B, and D are all made clear in the opening paragraph.

4. F. Line 18 introduces Bunt Newcombe: "With one man it was all swearing." Although the other choices about Newcombe are stated or implied in Passage I, his swearing is the one that occurs first.

5. D. See lines 24–26. A is not stated or implied in Passage I. Although he "wasn't poor" (line 33), nothing indicates Choice C. Choice B is a guess of the narrator's. Notice the word "probably" in line 26.

6. F. The author uses contrast (lines 52–56); simile (lines 37–39); direct statement (lines 47–48). However, Passage I contains no dialogue.

7. B. This is the best choice. The narrator describes both Newcombe's meanness (ill-temper, unkindness) to others and his meanness (stinginess). Choice B is the best selection for describing both senses of the word "mean."

8. H. This is the best choice. The point of view is not omniscient (Choice F); the narrator doesn't describe what everyone is thinking. Also, there is no evidence that the narrator is an enemy of the Newcombes, even if he/she doesn't like Bunt Newcombe (Choice G). Choice J is the second-best choice, but the perceptions and comments of the narrator more accurately characterize those of an adult looking back on childhood. Also, the last paragraph of Passage I makes it clear that the narrator is looking back at an earlier time.

9. C. These lines are the narrator's supposition about Mrs. Newcombe's thoughts, not an omniscient author's description of the woman's thoughts (choices A and D). They are also not the neighbors' thoughts (Choice B).

10. J. The final paragraph contrasts what the reaction to the Newcombes was at the time the narrator is describing with what the reaction might be in today's world. Choice H is part of what the narrator describes as the past reaction, but the main purpose of the paragraph is to contrast past and present beliefs. No judgment of the narrator (Choice F) or defense of the Newcombes (Choice G) is supported by evidence in Passage I.

Passage II

11. A. Transistors are not likely to have been suggested by raw materials, as many original inventions (choices B, C, D) might be, according to Passage II. They are much more like complex inventions, which are adopted by a society from another society. The best analogy in Passage II is the description of the Maori tribes adopting the invention of muskets from Europe.

12. G. Passage II is the author's theory of how inventions and innovations come about. The passage isn't an "imaginative" version (Choice F) nor is it biased (Choice J). But it is more than simply a description of the past (Choice H). The author is clearly presenting a theory about inventions and innovations and supporting the theory with evidence.

13. C. Handling of raw material is often the origin of simple inventions. Plant domestication and pottery are two innovations that the author says were invented in different places at different times. Choices A, B, and D are inaccurate.

14. G. This is the only choice supported by Passage II (lines 55–57). The design did not come from the New World (the wheel there was significantly different, suggesting an second independent invention) and the isolation of the New World from the Old indicates this was not a case of "borrowing" (choices F and J). Nor is there any support for the idea that the wheel came about through handling raw materials (Choice H).

15. C. Of the inventions, metallurgy is the only one that is described as probably having been diffused across the New World (lines 62–64).

16. G. In context, "affirmed" makes the most sense. The wheel would not be "testified to" (Choice F) or "estimated" (Choice H). "Attested" here means "affirmed," which is a better choice than Choice J.

17. D. See lines 26–27. The author says that the alphabet probably occurred only once in human history. In lines 57–61, he says the alphabet was a difficult, original invention that, like some other inventions, diffused from east to west in the Old World. None of the other choices is supported in Passage II.

18. F. This is the best description of the author's purpose. He does not explain the details of how inventions or innovations are diffused (Choice G) nor does he contrast the "value" of innovations in the Old World with those in the New (Choice H). He also does not suggest that a borrowed innovation is "more important" than a local innovation (Choice J).

19. B. According to the author, the very different designs of the two wheels suggest two independent inventions, rather than "borrowing." See lines 44–49. Neither Choice C nor Choice D is considered in Passage II. Choice A is incorrect; it is not the Old World wheel that appears on the pottery.

20. G. The musket example makes the author's point that if a society is at great disadvantage against an enemy with an advanced technology, then if the society without the technology doesn't adopt it, that society may not survive. Choice F is a secondary point; choices H and J are inaccurate.

Passage III

21. D. Passage III refers to several aspects of Dada, but Choice D is the best here. Although the movement was a precursor of surrealism (Choice B), this choice doesn't *define* the movement. Dada was a movement against rationality, order, and traditional art. See lines 30–39. Although the movement may have originated in artists' disgust with contemporary society, World War I, and politics in general, it was not a call to action (Choice C) nor a political statement (Choice A).

22. H. According to Passage III, the word "Dada" itself, with its "sharply repeated, percussive" syllables acted as a catalyst for disaffected artists and intellectuals (lines 4–5). Choices G and J are both accurate, but neither is the reason Hausmann called the word "magic." Choice F isn't supported by Passage III.

23. B. From evidence in the passage (lines 6, 24–25), the movement closely followed World War I. Passage III states that the impetus for the movement was disaffection during World War I.

24. F. The author compares the two names because both became recognizable brand names; people knew immediately what was being referred to when someone said either "Dada" or "Coca Cola." Choices G, H, and J are accurate statements, but the author's comparison of the two names is their status as recognizable brands.

25. B. This is the best choice. The "grey beards" are the older Dada artists who each had a theory of where the word came from. The biggest clue is that they are referred to as "Dada's grey beards," which indicates that they themselves are part of the movement, and are not reviewers, collectors, or professors (choices A, C, and D).

26. H. See lines 50–58. The stereotype doesn't discount the movement's international impact (Choice F). Technical virtuosity is never addressed in Passage III (Choice J). The stereotype emphasizes the irrationality nature of Dada, which *is* accurate and, therefore, not a good choice (Choice G).

27. C. The central paradox of Dada is expressed in lines 55–58. The Dada artists reject art while creating art, which gives rise to the "fundamental and fruitful" paradoxes of the movement. Choice A is not a paradox, and Choice D, although perhaps true, is not a central paradox. Choice B is perhaps the best second choice, but nothing in Passage III indicates that Dada artists really wanted to be part of the existing artistic tradition.

28. F. This choice fits the context best. The movement stood for harsher individualism and aggressive iconoclasm. None of the other choices fits in this sentence.

29. D. The reviewer's perplexity emphasizes that even for someone trained in viewing and understanding art, the movement was difficult to define because not only did it continually shift focus but also it was "negative, ephemeral, illogical, and inconclusive." The comments are not an example of harsh treatment of the artists (Choice A), nor do they explain the influences (Choice B). Although the reviewer does mention the negativity of the movement (Choice C), the author of Passage III includes the quotation from the reviewer primarily to emphasize the perplexity Dada caused.

30. H. Of the choices, this is the only point about Dada not indicated by the author of Passage III. Dada's "early demise" is mentioned in lines 11–12 (Choice F), its international sources in lines 9–11 (Choice G), and its commitment to shocking the audience in lines 39–40 (Choice J).

Passage IV

31. A. In the first paragraph, the author questions the long-standing classification of living things into plant and animal. He also questions the accuracy of textbooks (Choice B), but only because they too recognize only the two classifications. Choice C is not covered in the first paragraph, and although the Monera classification is mentioned, it is not questioned (Choice D).

32. H. The author isn't criticizing the dictionary but is pointing out that even by 1969 the Monera classification wasn't recognized. All the other choices are supported by these lines.

33. D. The most important reason fungi shouldn't be classified as plants, according to the author of Passage IV, is that unlike plants, fungi don't photosynthesize (lines 31–32). They do root (lines 38–39, Choice B), and they do reproduce (line 23, Choice C). There is no indication that they don't require water (Choice A).

34. G. Chitin is a material used to build claws and shells (lines 28–30). Nothing in Passage IV implies that it is "primarily" found in insects (Choice F) or that it is a spongy or pliable surface (choices H, J). (That it is used to build claws suggests that it is not spongy or pliable.)

35. D. The author suggests this name (tongue-in-cheek) because it is more dynamic and might gain slime mould "the attention it deserves." (See lines 46–51.) All the other choices might be accurate, but his reason for suggesting the new name is clearly to make "slime mould" more dynamic and worthy of study than the "stuff that you find when you reach deep into a clogged drain."

36. **H.** The author doesn't (or can't) describe exactly how slime moulds become slugs, and, therefore, he uses the phrase "almost miraculously." The phrase has nothing to do with the movement of slime moulds or their respiration (choices F, G) Also, it doesn't emphasize qualities or varieties of slime moulds (Choice J).

37. **A.** Although an abbreviated version of the process described in lines 55–74, this is the best choice. Choice B doesn't include enough of the process. Choice C does not describe propagation, and Choice D is too abbreviated.

38. **F.** This is the best choice. Most of Passage IV deals with organisms that are both interesting and not easily classified as plant or animal. Choices G and H are secondary points, and Choice J may or may not be true, but it is not the author's main point.

39. **B.** The author uses both colloquial language and humor to present information. A few examples of colloquial language are in line 7 ("lumped in"), lines 15–16 ("trusty . . . dictionary"), and lines 47–48 ("stuff that you find"). The author's humor can also be seen throughout, for example in lines 30–31, lines 35–38, and lines 57–63. Choice A describes the opposite of the author's style, and choices C and D are too harsh and extreme to characterize the author's presentation.

40. **J.** The author agrees with Haeckel that bacteria is a separate classification. Choice F is inaccurate; the author doesn't recommend that the classification of fungi and slime moulds should be animal rather than plant. In his view, neither classification describes these organisms. Choice G is not supported. Choice H may seem to be the best choice—except for the word "dangerous." The author never indicates any "danger" presented by the current classifications.

Science Test

Passage I

1. **B.** Find the mark representing 70 miles on the y-axis, halfway between 60 and 80. Trace rightward to the temperature line and then downward to the x-axis. The temperature at that altitude is approximately $-15°C$.

2. **G.** The stratosphere varies in temperature from $-60°$ at its base to $-10°$ at its top, for a total range of only $50°$. The range of the troposphere is $80°$, the mesosphere $70°$, and the thermosphere at least $270°$.

3. **A.** The mesosphere and troposphere both show lower temperatures as you move upward to higher altitudes. In contrast, the stratosphere and thermosphere both display increasing temperatures with increasing altitudes.

4. **J.** The troposphere has the highest air pressure because it has the most air overlying that level. The variation of air pressure is much simpler than the variation of temperature because the air pressure always decreases with increasing altitude.

5. **A.** The rise in temperature upward through the stratosphere is caused by the solar energy absorbed by oxygen molecules at that height.

Passage II

6. **H.** Since those crystals floated in bromoform, they must have a specific gravity less than 2.89. The detection of calcium proves that they must be plagioclase, not quartz or orthoclase.

7. **B.** The liquid would have a specific gravity of 3.11, which is the average of the values for bromoform and methylene iodide. In such a liquid, biotite (3.00) would float and hornblende (3.20) would sink. To separate any two crystal varieties, it is necessary to have a liquid of intermediate specific gravity.

8. **H.** The crystals must be either augite or biotite, and those crystals could be distinguished by detecting aluminum (biotite), calcium (augite), or potassium (biotite). The absence of sodium in Experiment 2 shows that the crystals could not be hornblende.

9. C. The X-ray fluorescence unit would be much more useful if it could measure the amount of each element detected. For example, a silicon abundance of 20 percent would indicate hypersthene, augite, hornblende, or plagioclase.

10. H. The crystals must be either olivine or hypersthene because they have a specific gravity over 3.33 and contain silicon. Unfortunately, olivine and hypersthene have the same elements present and, therefore, cannot be distinguished with the available apparatus.

11. A. Possessing a liquid of specific gravity less than 2.89 would permit separating light crystals like plagioclase, quartz, and orthoclase. Choice C is not the best choice because such a liquid could be prepared by mixing bromoform and methylene iodide, without any acetone.

Passage III

12. G. Sparrows feed on insects and grasses. Notice the arrows pointing from insects and grasses toward sparrows.

13. C. The longest food chain on the diagram is as follows: grasses to mice (or gophers) to snakes to weasels to wolves to worms.

14. G. According to the diagram, the only animals that eat snakes are hawks and weasels. You must look at the arrows in the diagram to answer the questions dealing with the network of feeding relationships.

15. C. Grasses and trees are the only independent organisms in the diagram. The photosynthesis of green plants derives energy from solar radiation. All the animals in the diagram are dependent on plants or other animals.

16. J. Because weasels eat rabbits, a reduction in the number of weasels would allow an increase in the number of rabbits. Since bobcats eat rabbits, the larger number of rabbits would allow an increase in the number of bobcats. Probably the chicken farmers do not realize that their weasel campaign could lead to more bobcats.

Passage IV

17. A. Within the range 0.2 to 0.7 atmosphere, it is true that lower current accompanied the lower pressure. Since the current is proportional to the amount of ionization, the prior hypothesis holds for that pressure range.

18. J. The battery must be present to produce the current that flows around the circuit. Both meters must be present to measure the current and pressure. However, the vacuum pump could be switched off during one reading; it would have to be switched back on to lower the pressure for the next reading.

19. B. At lower pressures, there are fewer molecules of nitrogen and oxygen in the flask. So the alpha particles encounter fewer molecules to ionize. The lower degree of ionization results in lower currents.

20. H. The polonium-210 loses half of its radioactivity every 138 days. If the researcher tried to repeat the experiment 90 days later, there would be fewer alpha particles emitted from the source and less ionization of the air. The new current readings would be lower than the original readings.

21. B. In the pressure range 0.7 to 1.0 atmosphere, the energy of the alpha particles must be completely dissipated in ionization. This would explain why a change of pressure within that range doesn't affect the degree of ionization.

22. F. The lining of the flask serves only to conduct current. Substituting aluminum—or any other metal—for the silver should not affect the results. Choice G affects the degree of ionization; Choice H affects the current directly; and Choice J affects the number of alpha particles.

Passage V

23. C. The passage mentions Rhesus monkeys as an example of primates. Apes and monkeys are closely related to humans (also classified as primates), so any primate studies would be relevant to human medicine.

24. J. The statement that few of the animals infected with a supposedly carcinogenic virus actually develop cancers certainly suggests that the causal mechanisms of animal tumor viruses are still uncertain.

25. D. In the second sentence, Scientist 1 mentions connective-tissue cancer. The following sentence says that cancers of the same kind are called sarcomas.

26. G. If new cancer-causing agents are discovered frequently, then all causes of cancer are not known. Perhaps viruses are a "new," major cause with several examples yet to be discovered.

27. A. It is accepted that cancer may be spread by injecting cancerous cells into a healthy animal. To show that some other material in the injected liquid causes the cancer, it is necessary to filter out any cancer cells.

28. J. Scientist 2 doesn't accept the evidence that some animal cancers are induced by viruses. If Scientist 1 could prove that point, it would weaken the argument presented by Scientist 2.

29. D. Scientist 1 implies that only minuscule virus particles are small enough to pass through the filters and remain in the liquid to be injected. If some material besides viruses also passes through the filters, that other material could be the cause of the induced cancers.

Passage VI

30. J. Iodine forms the weakest bond with hydrogen. The I–H bond has an energy of 71 kcal/mole, less than the value for F–H, Cl–H, or Br–H. It is important to realize that a high energy means a strong bond, while a low energy means a weak bond.

31. B. The Cl–Cl bond has a higher energy and thus is stronger than the F–F, Br–Br, or I–I bonds. Notice that the question refers to molecules with two identical halogen atoms.

32. F. Carbon tetrachloride would be the largest molecule because the central carbon atom is surrounded by four large chlorine atoms. Look at Table 1 to see the relative sizes of the atoms. Molecules in choices G and J aren't as large as carbon tetrachloride because they have only one large halogen atom.

33. B. In the chlorine bonds, Cl–O is 12 kcal/mole less than Cl–F. By analogy, Br–O should be about 12 kcal/mole less than the value for Br–F, which is 57 kcal/mole. 57 minus 12 equals 45 kcal/mole.

34. J. The best generalization of bond strengths is that the bond is stronger (energy is higher) between smaller atoms. This explains the very strong bonds with the small hydrogen atom and the very weak bonds with the large iodine atom.

Passage VII

35. B. The experiments were performed to explore the possibility of gene exchange. The assumption is that the abilities to synthesize leucine and cystine are governed by different genes.

36. G. Since all organisms need amino acids for metabolism and growth, yet the normal bacteria don't require an external source, they must manufacture the needed amino acids internally.

37. A. Since the L strain needed a supply of leucine to survive, that strain can't manufacture its own leucine. However, the strain didn't require any cystine nutrient, so it must be able to synthesize its own cystine.

38. F. The C strain would have been able to grow if supplied with a source of cystine because it could synthesize all other needed amino acids. The L strain wouldn't have been able to grow under those conditions because it still had no possible means of obtaining the leucine that it needed but couldn't synthesize.

39. D. At least one of the two strains must have received the gene, permitting it to manufacture the one amino acid that it originally couldn't manufacture. However, the mere growth of colonies doesn't reveal whether the growing bacteria come from the C strain, the L strain, or both strains.

40. G. It is possible that the mutant C and L strains lacked more than one gene apiece compared to the normal bacteria. If they each were missing the same gene (plus other missing genes to differentiate the two strains), then even perfect gene exchange in the mixed culture couldn't have reconstructed the normal gene set. This difficult question is best answered by eliminating the other three choices.

Chapter 15

Practice Test 3

Answer Sheets

English Test

1 A B C D	26 F G H J	51 A B C D
2 F G H J	27 A B C D	52 F G H J
3 A B C D	28 F G H J	53 A B C D
4 F G H J	29 A B C D	54 F G H J
5 A B C D	30 F G H J	55 A B C D
6 F G H J	31 A B C D	56 F G H J
7 A B C D	32 F G H J	57 A B C D
8 F G H J	33 A B C D	58 F G H J
9 A B C D	34 F G H J	59 A B C D
10 F G H J	35 A B C D	60 F G H J
11 A B C D	36 F G H J	61 A B C D
12 F G H J	37 A B C D	62 F G H J
13 A B C D	38 F G H J	63 A B C D
14 F G H J	39 A B C D	64 F G H J
15 A B C D	40 F G H J	65 A B C D
16 F G H J	41 A B C D	66 F G H J
17 A B C D	42 F G H J	67 A B C D
18 F G H J	43 A B C D	68 F G H J
19 A B C D	44 F G H J	69 A B C D
20 F G H J	45 A B C D	70 F G H J
21 A B C D	46 F G H J	71 A B C D
22 F G H J	47 A B C D	72 F G H J
23 A B C D	48 F G H J	73 A B C D
24 F G H J	49 A B C D	74 F G H J
25 A B C D	50 F G H J	75 A B C D

Mathematics Test

1 A B C D E	21 A B C D E	41 A B C D E
2 F G H J K	22 F G H J K	42 F G H J K
3 A B C D E	23 A B C D E	43 A B C D E
4 F G H J K	24 F G H J K	44 F G H J K
5 A B C D E	25 A B C D E	45 A B C D E
6 F G H J K	26 F G H J K	46 F G H J K
7 A B C D E	27 A B C D E	47 A B C D E
8 F G H J K	28 F G H J K	48 F G H J K
9 A B C D E	29 A B C D E	49 A B C D E
10 F G H J K	30 F G H J K	50 F G H J K
11 A B C D E	31 A B C D E	51 A B C D E
12 F G H J K	32 F G H J K	52 F G H J K
13 A B C D E	33 A B C D E	53 A B C D E
14 F G H J K	34 F G H J K	54 F G H J K
15 A B C D E	35 A B C D E	55 A B C D E
16 F G H J K	36 F G H J K	56 F G H J K
17 A B C D E	37 A B C D E	57 A B C D E
18 F G H J K	38 F G H J K	58 F G H J K
19 A B C D E	39 A B C D E	59 A B C D E
20 F G H J K	40 F G H J K	60 F G H J K

CUT HERE

Reading Test

1 Ⓐ Ⓑ Ⓒ Ⓓ	21 Ⓐ Ⓑ Ⓒ Ⓓ
2 Ⓕ Ⓖ Ⓗ Ⓙ	22 Ⓕ Ⓖ Ⓗ Ⓙ
3 Ⓐ Ⓑ Ⓒ Ⓓ	23 Ⓐ Ⓑ Ⓒ Ⓓ
4 Ⓕ Ⓖ Ⓗ Ⓙ	24 Ⓕ Ⓖ Ⓗ Ⓙ
5 Ⓐ Ⓑ Ⓒ Ⓓ	25 Ⓐ Ⓑ Ⓒ Ⓓ
6 Ⓕ Ⓖ Ⓗ Ⓙ	26 Ⓕ Ⓖ Ⓗ Ⓙ
7 Ⓐ Ⓑ Ⓒ Ⓓ	27 Ⓐ Ⓑ Ⓒ Ⓓ
8 Ⓕ Ⓖ Ⓗ Ⓙ	28 Ⓕ Ⓖ Ⓗ Ⓙ
9 Ⓐ Ⓑ Ⓒ Ⓓ	29 Ⓐ Ⓑ Ⓒ Ⓓ
10 Ⓕ Ⓖ Ⓗ Ⓙ	30 Ⓕ Ⓖ Ⓗ Ⓙ
11 Ⓐ Ⓑ Ⓒ Ⓓ	31 Ⓐ Ⓑ Ⓒ Ⓓ
12 Ⓕ Ⓖ Ⓗ Ⓙ	32 Ⓕ Ⓖ Ⓗ Ⓙ
13 Ⓐ Ⓑ Ⓒ Ⓓ	33 Ⓐ Ⓑ Ⓒ Ⓓ
14 Ⓕ Ⓖ Ⓗ Ⓙ	34 Ⓕ Ⓖ Ⓗ Ⓙ
15 Ⓐ Ⓑ Ⓒ Ⓓ	35 Ⓐ Ⓑ Ⓒ Ⓓ
16 Ⓕ Ⓖ Ⓗ Ⓙ	36 Ⓕ Ⓖ Ⓗ Ⓙ
17 Ⓐ Ⓑ Ⓒ Ⓓ	37 Ⓐ Ⓑ Ⓒ Ⓓ
18 Ⓕ Ⓖ Ⓗ Ⓙ	38 Ⓕ Ⓖ Ⓗ Ⓙ
19 Ⓐ Ⓑ Ⓒ Ⓓ	39 Ⓐ Ⓑ Ⓒ Ⓓ
20 Ⓕ Ⓖ Ⓗ Ⓙ	40 Ⓕ Ⓖ Ⓗ Ⓙ

Science Test

1 Ⓐ Ⓑ Ⓒ Ⓓ	21 Ⓐ Ⓑ Ⓒ Ⓓ
2 Ⓕ Ⓖ Ⓗ Ⓙ	22 Ⓕ Ⓖ Ⓗ Ⓙ
3 Ⓐ Ⓑ Ⓒ Ⓓ	23 Ⓐ Ⓑ Ⓒ Ⓓ
4 Ⓕ Ⓖ Ⓗ Ⓙ	24 Ⓕ Ⓖ Ⓗ Ⓙ
5 Ⓐ Ⓑ Ⓒ Ⓓ	25 Ⓐ Ⓑ Ⓒ Ⓓ
6 Ⓕ Ⓖ Ⓗ Ⓙ	26 Ⓕ Ⓖ Ⓗ Ⓙ
7 Ⓐ Ⓑ Ⓒ Ⓓ	27 Ⓐ Ⓑ Ⓒ Ⓓ
8 Ⓕ Ⓖ Ⓗ Ⓙ	28 Ⓕ Ⓖ Ⓗ Ⓙ
9 Ⓐ Ⓑ Ⓒ Ⓓ	29 Ⓐ Ⓑ Ⓒ Ⓓ
10 Ⓕ Ⓖ Ⓗ Ⓙ	30 Ⓕ Ⓖ Ⓗ Ⓙ
11 Ⓐ Ⓑ Ⓒ Ⓓ	31 Ⓐ Ⓑ Ⓒ Ⓓ
12 Ⓕ Ⓖ Ⓗ Ⓙ	32 Ⓕ Ⓖ Ⓗ Ⓙ
13 Ⓐ Ⓑ Ⓒ Ⓓ	33 Ⓐ Ⓑ Ⓒ Ⓓ
14 Ⓕ Ⓖ Ⓗ Ⓙ	34 Ⓕ Ⓖ Ⓗ Ⓙ
15 Ⓐ Ⓑ Ⓒ Ⓓ	35 Ⓐ Ⓑ Ⓒ Ⓓ
16 Ⓕ Ⓖ Ⓗ Ⓙ	36 Ⓕ Ⓖ Ⓗ Ⓙ
17 Ⓐ Ⓑ Ⓒ Ⓓ	37 Ⓐ Ⓑ Ⓒ Ⓓ
18 Ⓕ Ⓖ Ⓗ Ⓙ	38 Ⓕ Ⓖ Ⓗ Ⓙ
19 Ⓐ Ⓑ Ⓒ Ⓓ	39 Ⓐ Ⓑ Ⓒ Ⓓ
20 Ⓕ Ⓖ Ⓗ Ⓙ	40 Ⓕ Ⓖ Ⓗ Ⓙ

CUT HERE

Directions

The practice tests are for assessment purposes only. These tests are designed to measure skills learned in high school that relate to success in college. Try to simulate test conditions and time yourself as you begin each of the following practice tests:

> English Test—45 minutes
>
> Mathematics Test—60 minutes
>
> Reading Test—35 minutes
>
> Science Test—35 minutes

- Calculators may be used on the mathematics test only.
- The numbered questions on each test are followed by lettered answer choices. Make sure to properly mark the answer you have selected next to the corresponding question number on the answer sheet. If you want to change an answer, erase your original answer thoroughly before marking the new answer.
- On the actual exam, you must use a soft lead pencil and completely blacken the oval of the letter you have selected because your score is based completely on the number of questions you answer and mark correctly on the answer sheet. Do NOT use a ballpoint pen or a mechanical pencil.
- You are only allowed to work on one test at a time. If you complete a test before time is up, you may go back and review questions only in that test. You may NOT go back to previous tests, and you may NOT go forward to another test. On the actual exam day, you will be disqualified from the exam if you work on another test.
- There is no penalty for guessing, so *answer every question*, even if you need to guess.
- On the actual exam, when time is up, be sure to put your pencil down immediately. After time is up, you may NOT for any reason fill in answers. This will disqualify you from the exam.
- Do not fold or tear the pages of your test booklet.

English Test

Time: 45 Minutes
75 Questions

Directions: In the passages that follow, you will find various words and phrases underlined and numbered. A set of responses corresponding to each underlined portion will follow each passage. If the underlined portion is correct standard written English, is most appropriate to the style and feeling of the passage, and best expresses the intended idea, mark the letter indicating "NO CHANGE." If, however, the underlined portion is not the best choice given, choose the best answer to the question. For these questions, consider only the underlined portions and assume that the rest of the passage is correct as written.

You will also find questions concerning a sentence, several parts of the passage, or the whole passage. These questions do not refer to an underlined portion, but refer to the portion of the passage that is identified with the corresponding question number in a box. Choose the response you feel is best for these questions.

Passage I

The following paragraphs may or may not be in the most logical order. Paragraphs are numbered in brackets, and sentences in paragraph 2 are numbered.

Black Holes

[1]

In 2010, astronomers watched a giant black hole in a galaxy far away dismantle and devour a star. The event itself didn't happen a year or two ago but about two billion years <u>ago; which is how long</u> it took the
₁
radiation <u>signals, that escaped from the catastrophe, to</u>
₂
<u>reach</u> the earth. The viewing was the first time an event
₂
like this <u>from start to finish has been able to be viewed</u>
₃
<u>on earth.</u> <u>The event unfolded slow over 15 months to</u>
₃   ₄
<u>the viewers.</u>
₄

[2]

[1] <u>Star-obliterating events like this one are called</u>
₅
<u>by astronomers "tidal disruptions."</u> [2] Estimates are
₅

that they occur only about once in 10,000 years and are difficult to spot. [3] <u>Astronomers, when they do occur,</u>
₆
<u>are given a chance to study black holes.</u> [4] <u>Normally,</u>
₆   ₇
<u>black holes remain</u> dormant and invisible. [5] When a
₇
tidal disruption occurs, however, black holes interact with the star's <u>gases, and producing intense flares of</u>
₈
<u>radiation.</u> [6] Very briefly, the hole lights up and
₈
becomes visible. ⑨

[3]

<u>To understand the pull, the ocean tides on earth are</u>
₁₀
<u>created by the moon's gravity tugging the earth and its</u>
₁₀
<u>oceans.</u> Of course, the black hole's pull on a nearby
₁₀
star is much more <u>violent, it can entirely and completely</u>
₁₁
<u>dismantle and devour that star.</u>
₁₁

[4]

A black hole can rip apart a star when the star comes too close. In this recent case viewed by astronomers, the

GO ON TO THE NEXT PAGE

star <u>comes as close to the black hole as the planet,</u>
₁₂

<u>Mercury,</u> is to the sun. Astronomers could see the star
₁₂

stretched out and <u>tore apart by the black holes intense</u>
₁₃

<u>gravity</u>. In the words of Johns Hopkins University
₁₃

astronomer <u>Suvi Gezari, the lead author of a paper that</u>
₁₄

<u>was concerned with the observations,</u> the star "turned
₁₄

into this really thin piece of spaghetti." $\boxed{15}$

1. A. NO CHANGE
   B. ago; how long it took
   C. ago, which is the length of time
   D. ago, which is how long

2. F. NO CHANGE
   G. signals that escaped from the catastrophe to reach
   H. signals, those which then escaped from the catastrophe, to reach
   J. signals, which escaped from the catastrophe to reach

3. A. NO CHANGE
   B. was able, from start to finish, to be viewed on earth.
   C. could be viewed on earth from start to finish.
   D. from start to finish, could be viewed on earth.

4. F. NO CHANGE
   G. To the viewers, the event unfolded slowly over 15 months.
   H. The event slowly over 15 months unfolded itself to the viewers.
   J. Unfolding slow over 15 months, the viewers saw the event.

5. A. NO CHANGE
   B. "Tidal disruptions" is the term used to describe star obliterating events like this one by astronomers.
   C. Astronomers use the term "tidal disruptions" to describe star-obliterating events like this one.
   D. Star obliterating events like this, are called "tidal disruptions" by astronomers.

6. F. NO CHANGE
   G. Astronomers when they do occur are given a chance to study black holes.
   H. When they do occur, astronomers will then have a chance to study black holes.
   J. Astronomers are given a chance to study black holes when they do occur.

7. A. NO CHANGE
   B. It is normal for black holes to remain
   C. Black holes have remained in a normal way
   D. Black holes will be remaining normally

8. F. NO CHANGE
   G. gases, and produced intense flares of radiation.
   H. gases, producing intense flares of radiation.
   J. gases that are producing intense flares of radiation.

9. The writer wants to add a sentence to follow sentence 6 in paragraph 2 of Passage I. Which of the following would be the best choice of a sentence to add?

   A. In the past, the theories about black holes have been either misunderstood or denied.
   B. Black holes have been a mystery to both professional and amateur astronomers.
   C. Tidal disruptions therefore are a boon to astronomers studying the phenomenon of black holes.
   D. The term "black hole" was first publicly used by John Wheeler in 1967.

10. F. NO CHANGE
   G. By thinking of the moon's gravity on earth, this pull can be understood.
   H. To understand this pull, think of the moon's gravity creating tides by tugging on the earth and the oceans.
   J. The moon's gravity pulls on the earth and the oceans. Like a black hole's pull on the stars.

11. A. NO CHANGE
   B. violent. Because it can completely devour that star.
   C. violent. It can entirely and completely devour that star.
   D. violent; it can completely devour that star.

GO ON TO THE NEXT PAGE

12. F. NO CHANGE
  G. came as close to the black hole as the planet Mercury
  H. was coming as close to the black hole as the planet Mercury
  J. comes as close to the black hole as the planet, Mercury,

13. A. NO CHANGE
  B. tore apart, by the black hole's intense gravity
  C. torn apart by the black holes intense gravity
  D. torn apart by the black hole's intense gravity

14. F. NO CHANGE
  G. Suvi Gezari who was the lead author of a paper that concerned the observations
  H. Suvi Gezari, the lead author of a paper about the observations,
  J. Suvi Gezari that was the lead author of a paper which was about the observations

Question 15 poses a question about Passage I as a whole.

15. Which of the following is the most logical paragraph sequence in Passage I?

  A. NO CHANGE
  B. 1, 3, 2, 4
  C. 1, 4, 3, 2
  D. 4, 1, 2, 3

Passage II

The following paragraphs may or may not be in the most logical order. Paragraphs are numbered in brackets, and sentences in paragraph 3 are numbered.

Uncle Ed

[1]

My Uncle Ed has had so many adventures in his 52 years that he could write a book. He used to tell my
16
sister Carrie and I tales that might of shocked my
16   17
father (his younger brother) except that he has always
18
admired him. My father calls Uncle Ed the "wild one"
18
and him the "stick in the mud."
19

[2]

Uncle Ed, among other things, climbed half way up Mt. Everest, took a solo trip up the Amazon River, has rode broncos in big rodeos, sailed by himself
20
around the world alone, and still plays the guitar good
21
enough to be in a rock and roll band. I don't know if
21
everything he has told us is true, but one thing is definitely true: Uncle Ed is a very unique person as
22
well as the best storyteller I will have ever known.
22

[3]

[1] One of my favorite stories is about the hippie trail; a term that is used even now to describe the route
23
of journeys taken by hippies and others especially
24
young people in the 1960s and 1970s. [2] The hippie
24
trail went from Europe overland to and from India, Pakistan, and Nepal. [3] In fact, Uncle Ed said that in Katmandu there is still a road nicknamed Freak Street in memory of all the hippies who passed through there. [4]. Many of the hippies were Uncle Ed's friends, backpacking with him along the way. [5] Although he has lost touch with most of them, a few of them still get together now and then. 25

GO ON TO THE NEXT PAGE

[4]

Uncle Ed told us about the joys of backpacking, not only on the hippie trail but also through Europe. He emphasized that <u>it was a great way to meet people and also being inexpensive.</u> <u>Comparing it to conventional vacations, backpacking</u> was more exciting and more rewarding. Sometimes Uncle Ed sounded very nostalgic and even very sad. He said that in the old days when he backpacked, he experienced the "real" destination rather than the packaged version that <u>one might have if you were just a tourist in a group.</u> I know one thing for sure. He made me want to follow in his footsteps, traveling places the way he did and maybe some day hiking the hippie trail.

[5]

When he listens to Uncle Ed's stories, I see on my father's face a mixture of admiration and envy. I think he wishes that he had been <u>more adventurous and not complied to his parents' wishes</u> that he go to law school immediately after college graduation. Instead of hitting the road the way that Uncle Ed did, he got married and settled down. He loves our family and likes being a lawyer, but I think he sometimes wishes he had done even half of the things his younger brother did. 30

16. F. NO CHANGE
    G. be telling my sister Carrie and I
    H. tell my sister Carrie and me
    J. tell my sister, whose name is Carrie, and I

17. A. NO CHANGE
    B. may well of shocked
    C. might be somewhat shocking to
    D. might have shocked

18. F. NO CHANGE
    G. he had always admired him.
    H. he has always admired Ed.
    J. he will always admire him.

19. A. NO CHANGE
    B. himself the "stick in the mud."
    C. he is what he calls a "stick in the mud."
    D. himself the stick in the mud.

20. F. NO CHANGE
    G. rode broncos in big rodeos
    H. have ridden broncos, in big rodeos
    J. had rode broncos in big Rodeos

21. A. NO CHANGE
    B. still plays the guitar well enough
    C. still will have played the guitar good enough
    D. still had played the guitar good enough

22. F. NO CHANGE
    G. very unique person in addition to being the best storyteller I have ever known.
    H. unique person; as well as the best storyteller I knew.
    J. unique person and the best storyteller I have ever known.

23. A. NO CHANGE
    B. trail, a term used even now
    C. trail; a term that is being used, even now,
    D. trail, a term which is even now being used

24. F. NO CHANGE
    G. and others, especially young people
    H. and others, that is, especially young people
    J. and others, especially young people,

GO ON TO THE NEXT PAGE

25. The writer is considering deleting sentence 3 from paragraph 3. Should the sentence be omitted?

    A. Yes, because the meaning of the term "Freak" would be unfamiliar to many people.

    B. Yes, because this sentence adds nothing to the point of the paragraph.

    C. No, because the sentence helps identify the location of Katmandu.

    D. No, because the sentence adds a colorful detail to Uncle Ed's story about the hippie trail.

26. **F.** NO CHANGE

    G. it was a great way to meet people, being inexpensive.

    H. it was a great way to meet people and it was inexpensive as well.

    J. it was both inexpensive and a great way to meet people.

27. **A.** NO CHANGE

    B. Comparing it to other conventional vacations, he thought backpacking

    C. When it was to be compared to other conventional vacations, backpacking was

    D. By comparing it to other conventional vacations, backpacking was

28. **F.** NO CHANGE

    G. one might have if he was just a tourist in a group.

    H. you might have if you were just a tourist in a group.

    J. you might have in the event of your being just a tourist in a group.

29. **A.** NO CHANGE

    B. more inclined to have adventure and not complied to his parents' wishes

    C. more adventurous, not complying to his parents' wishes

    D. more adventurous and had not complied with his parents' wishes

Question 30 poses a question about Passage II as a whole.

30. Which of the following sequences of paragraphs in Passage II is the most logical?

    F. NO CHANGE

    G. 1, 3, 2, 4, 5

    H. 1, 5, 2, 3, 4

    J. 1, 4, 5, 2, 3

Passage III

Paragraphs are numbered in brackets, and sentences in paragraph 2 are numbered.

Recalled Cars

[1]

When something goes wrong with a car—and then with many cars of the same make or model—the car's manufacturer may determine that a recall is necessary and let owners know that <u>their cars will be repaired</u>
<u>and it will be at no cost to them.</u> But there is <u>a problem</u>
₃₁   ₃₂
<u>in which many owners</u> among those who have been
₃₂
notified do not bother to get their cars fixed. One <u>manufacturer who recalled a particular model</u> says
₃₃
that in 2011 only 52.5 percent of the recalled cars were brought in for repair. As a member of an online auto forum noted, <u>there is only so many things a</u>
₃₄
<u>manufacturer can do</u> to reach out to car <u>owners, the</u>
₃₄   ₃₅
<u>responsibility to have had the car repaired lays with</u>
₃₅
<u>the owner.</u>
₃₅

GO ON TO THE NEXT PAGE

[2]

[1] <u>When an owner of a car that has been recalled</u>
₃₆
<u>decides</u> that selling the car rather than <u>to take it in for</u>
₃₆   ₃₇
<u>repairs</u> is the best idea, <u>what is the new owner of the</u>
₃₇   ₃₈
<u>car suppose to do.</u> [2] It isn't easy for used car owners
₃₈
to know <u>whether their vehicles are up to date on recall</u>
₃₉
<u>services.</u> [3] Owners should <u>take it into their own</u>
₃₉   ₄₀
<u>hands.</u> [4] People who buy used cars should register
₄₀
with the automakers to <u>make sure of the fact that</u> they
₄₁
are in the loop for any existing and future recalls.

[5] Buying a used car is risky because the new owner has no way of knowing how the original owner took care of the car, for example, getting it serviced at the proper intervals. [6] Another thing the new owner can do is check a U.S. Transportation Department database to see if the model of the car was included in a recall. [7] A new <u>system, one which would enable a</u>
₄₂
<u>car owner to use his vehicle identification number</u>
₄₂
<u>(VIN) to check whether or not his car has been recalled</u>
₄₂
<u>and whether or not the car has been repaired after the</u>
₄₂
<u>recall</u> is <u>now currently in the process of being</u>
₄₂   ₄₃
<u>developed.</u> [8] No laws at this time require a car's
₄₃
owner to notify potential buyers that the car being sold is the subject of a recall. [44] [45]

31.
- **A.** NO CHANGE
- **B.** their cars will be repaired; and it will be of no cost to them.
- **C.** at no cost to them their cars, will be repaired.
- **D.** their cars will be repaired at no cost to them.

32.
- **F.** NO CHANGE
- **G.** a problem because many owners
- **H.** a problem because of the reason that many owners
- **J.** a problem for the reason that many owners

33.
- **A.** NO CHANGE
- **B.** manufacturer, who recalled a particular model,
- **C.** manufacturer which recalled a particular model,
- **D.** manufacturer, who has recalled a particular model,

34.
- **F.** NO CHANGE
- **G.** there is only so many possibilities for a manufacturer to do
- **H.** a manufacturer can only do so many things
- **J.** there is, in fact, not many things a manufacturer can do

35.
- **A.** NO CHANGE
- **B.** owners. The responsibility to have the car repaired lays with the owner.
- **C.** owners; the responsibility to have had the car repaired, lays with the owner.
- **D.** owners. The responsibility to have the car repaired lies with the owner.

36.
- **F.** NO CHANGE
- **G.** When an owner of a car, that has been recalled, decides
- **H.** When an owner of a car that has been recalled decides,
- **J.** When an owner, of a car that has been recalled, decides

37.
- **A.** NO CHANGE
- **B.** taking it in for repairs
- **C.** to take it in to be repaired
- **D.** to have taken it in to be repaired

GO ON TO THE NEXT PAGE

38. F. NO CHANGE
G. what is the new owner of the car supposed to do.
H. what should the new owner of the car do.
J. what should the new owner of the car do?

39. A. NO CHANGE
B. whether their vehicles, they are up to date on recall services.
C. if their vehicles would be up to date on the recall services.
D. whether or not their vehicles will have received all the service required by the recall.

40. F. NO CHANGE
G. have taken it into their own hands.
H. take it on as one of their responsibilities.
J. take finding out into their own hands.

41. A. NO CHANGE
B. ensure of the fact that
C. make sure that
D. ensure the fact that

42. F. NO CHANGE
G. system, one which would enable a car owner, using his vehicle identification number (VIN), to check his particular car to see if it had been recalled and if it had been repaired,
H. system that would allow a car owner to use his vehicle identification number (VIN) to check the car's recall and repair status
J. system; one which would allow a car owner, using his vehicle identification number (VIN), to check whether or not his particular car has been subjected to a recall and then whether it has been repaired,

43. A. NO CHANGE
B. now being developed.
C. currently in the process of being developed.
D. undergoing development at the current time.

44. To shorten paragraph 2 of Passage III, the writer wants to eliminate a sentence. Which sentence could be eliminated without affecting the logic of the paragraph?

F. sentence 5
G. sentence 3
H. sentence 8
J. sentence 2

45. In paragraph 2 of Passage III, the best position for sentence 8 is

A. its current position.
B. after sentence 5.
C. after sentence 4.
D after sentence 2

Passage IV

Paragraphs are numbered in brackets.

Disgusting

[1]

Why does the idea of eating insects disgust most of us? Its just icky, my brother said when I told him insects
46
are not only abundant but also high in protein. I had
47
been reading a book about making insects a part of our diets, so I thought I'd test the idea on Ricky, who's idea
48
of preparing exotic food is putting mushrooms on a
48
hamburger or to eat sushi. My brother Ricky is only
48
twelve years old, has never traveled outside the United States, in addition to which he has little patience with
49
anything I might suggest. 50

[2]

However, in some cultures insects are a staple of the diet. Even considered a delicacy in some of these. When
51   52
visiting Mexico two years ago, my hosts were polite in
52
offering me a plate of *escamole,* a dish that features ant
52
eggs sauteed in butter and spices. I hesitated for a few
53
seconds; but then took a big bite, not wanting my hosts
53
to think I was rude or just a provincial American. I
54
surprised even myself by finding the dish delicious. The
55

GO ON TO THE NEXT PAGE

experience in Mexico went a long way to convince me that the disgust with such foods <u>are in the mind of the beholder, just as beauty is also.</u>
₅₆

[3]

From an evolutionary standpoint disgust probably once served a <u>purpose; to help us avoid eating food</u>
₅₇
<u>that had been tainted or was containing toxic</u>
₅₇
<u>substances.</u> But what disgusts a person today differs
₅₇
from culture to culture and even from person to <u>person, it isn't related</u> to either the presence of toxins
₅₈
or taint. Our feelings of disgust don't seem to fully develop right away; for example, a toddler may refuse mashed carrots and then the same child may delight in chewing on mud, leaves and sticks off the ground. As I tried to explain to Ricky, what disgusts us in terms of food is largely dependent on our age, our background, our culture, our mood, and even our religion. (For example, an orthodox Jewish man might be revolted by a big plate of ham, whereas my brother Ricky's mouth would water when he saw it.) ⬚59

46. F. NO CHANGE
   G. "Its just icky" my brother said
   H. "It's just icky," my brother said
   J. It's just icky, my brother said

47. A. NO CHANGE
   B. not only in abundance but also they have a lot of protein.
   C. not only abundant but their protein is high.
   D. not only are they abundant but offering high protein.

48. F. NO CHANGE
   G. who's idea of fixing exotic food is to put mushrooms on a hamburger or eating sushi.
   H. whose idea of what constitutes exotic food is mushrooms on a hamburger or sushi.
   J. whose idea of exotic food is putting mushrooms on a hamburger or eating sushi.

49. A. NO CHANGE
   B. and has little patience
   C. and, additionally, he has little patience
   D. also he doesn't have patience,

50. The writer wants to add a sentence to the end of paragraph 1 that would lead into paragraph 2. Which of the following would be the best sentence to add?

   F. I'm sure that many people in the United States would agree with Ricky that the idea of eating insects is just plain "icky."
   G. Ricky accuses me of having as ridiculous ideas about music as I have about food.
   H. Once I prepared a special dinner for the family, and Ricky left the table and made himself a peanut butter and jelly sandwich.
   J. In some countries, children Ricky's age would be grateful to have something to eat and wouldn't complain about the source of the food.

51. Which of the following could replace the underlined phrase without changing the meaning?

   A. NO CHANGE
   B. diet, and insects are even considered to be a delicacy.
   C. diet, even considered a delicacy in some.
   D. diet; even considered, in some cultures, a delicacy.

52. F. NO CHANGE
   G. When I visited Mexico two years ago, my hosts politely offered me a plate of *escamole,*
   H. Visiting in Mexico two years ago, I was offered by my hosts politely a plate of *escamole,*
   J. Two years ago when visiting in Mexico my hosts offered me, politely, a plate of *escamole*

GO ON TO THE NEXT PAGE

53. A. NO CHANGE
B. a few seconds. But then taking a big bite,
C. a few seconds, but would take a big bite then
D. a few seconds but then took a big bite,

54. Which of the following could replace the underlined phrase without changing the meaning?

F. an arrogant American
G. an American of limited intelligence
H. an unsophisticated American
J. a lower-class American

55. A. NO CHANGE
B. even me by finding the dish delicious.
C. even myself when I discovered that the dish was delicious.
D. even me to find the dish delicious.

56. F. NO CHANGE
G. are in the mind of the beholder, like beauty is.
H. is in the mind of the beholder; like beauty is.
J. is in the mind of the beholder, just as beauty is.

57. A. NO CHANGE
B. purpose; to help us avoid food that was tainted and toxic substances.
C. purpose. To help us in avoiding food that had been tainted and substances that had been toxic.
D. purpose: to help us avoid tainted food and toxic substances.

58. F. NO CHANGE
G. person, not having been related to
H. person. Disgust with certain foods
J. person: not related to

59. Which of the following choices would be the best sentence to end paragraph 3 of Passage IV?

A. The fact that we reject certain foods while we find others enticing has more to do with our own circumstances than it does with the foods themselves.
B. Neurologists have identified an area of the brain called the *insula* that seems to control our ability to experience disgust.
C. We should all look forward to trying new and different foods, no matter how strange they may first appear.
D. Ricky would much rather play video games and eat a hamburger than enjoy a gourmet meal.

Passage V

Paragraphs are numbered in brackets, and sentences in paragraph 2 are numbered.

3-D

[1]

Three-dimensional movies are plentiful these days, and movies that weren't originally 3-D are sometimes remade so that viewers can have the 3-D experience. Today's commercial 3-D movie screens, in addition to some new televisions, <u>makes objects, people, and</u>
60
<u>monsters leap out at an audience</u> by showing two over-
60
lapping <u>images. Each capturing a different perspective</u>
61
<u>offset by the space between the viewer's eyes.</u> <u>You need</u>
61   62
special glasses to filter the pictures, which often <u>have</u>
63
<u>slightly different colors or light that bends different.</u>
63
The left eye sees one image and the right eye sees another. <u>The brain puts both these two scenes together</u>
64
<u>in a way that makes the viewer see depth,</u> or at least
64
<u>he will be thinking he would be seeing depth.</u> This trick
65

GO ON TO THE NEXT PAGE

dates back a long way. In the first half of the 19th
66
century, English scientist Sir Charles Wheatstone used
66
mirrors to re-direct side-by-side images. One eye saw
67
one image and the other eye saw the second image.
67

[2]

[1] Research teams are working to create a 3-D
experience for which the viewer will not need special
glasses when he goes to the movies. [2] Combining
some existing technologies with new tricks, the brain is
68
being fooled by the movie makers into thinking the
68
action is right there in the room. [3] Interestingly
enough, human brains actually have a built-in ability
to work out depth from flat images. [4] No special
69
glasses and no special screens required. [5] Even an
69
old-time movie can look sort of three-dimensional on
70
an ordinary television set. [6] If a viewer watches the
71
movie *2001: A Space Odyssey* for example you can see
71
shadows on a bone that is tossed into the air and this
tells him it is a real bone and not a cardboard cut-out.

[7] And when watching a movie chariot race, even on
72
the flat screen, a viewer can tell which chariot is in the
72
lead. [8] This natural ability, of course, is not as dramatic
72
or exciting as seeing a monster that has broke through
73
the screen and is aiming a scaly fist at the audience, but
73

it does show that the brain, and not advanced technology
alone, makes 3-D possible. [9] For full three-dimensional
viewing, holographic displays are the closest to how
viewers see around themselves. 74 75

60. F. NO CHANGE
G. will have made an object, person, or monster
H. makes an object or a person or a monster, leap out at an audience
J. make objects, people, and monsters leap out at an audience

61. A. NO CHANGE
B. images, each capturing a different perspective. The images are offset by the space between the viewer's eyes.
C. images; each capturing a different perspective which is offset by the space between the viewer's eyes.
D. images and they are each capturing a different perspective and the images are offset by the space between the viewer's eyes.

62. F. NO CHANGE
G. You will need
H. A viewer needs
J. One would have needed

63. A. NO CHANGE
B. have colors that differ slightly or light that bends different.
C. have colors and lights that bend differently.
D. have slightly different colors or light that bends differently.

64. F. NO CHANGE
G. The brain puts these two scenes together to make the viewer see depth,
H. These two scenes both are put together by the brain in order to make the viewer see depth,
J. The brain makes the viewer put these two scenes together, and therefore sees depth,

GO ON TO THE NEXT PAGE

65. A. NO CHANGE
   B. he thinks he would be seeing depth.
   C. he would be thinking he would be seeing depth.
   D. he thinks he is seeing depth.

66. F. NO CHANGE
   G. In the first half of the 19th century, the English scientist, Sir Charles Wheatstone
   H. In the first half of the 19th century, Sir Charles Wheatstone who was an English scientist
   J. The English scientist, Sir Charles Wheatstone, in the first half of the 19th century

67. A. NO CHANGE
   B. Only one eye saw one image, and the second image was seen by the other eye.
   C. Both the two images went into two different eyes.
   D. Both eyes saw different images.

68. F. NO CHANGE
   G. the brain can be fooled by the movie makers
   H. the brain allows itself to be fooled by the movie makers
   J. movie makers are able to fool the brain

69. A. NO CHANGE
   B. There is no requirement for special glasses or for special screens.
   C. No special glasses and no special screens are required.
   D. Special glasses, and also special screens, will not be required.

70. F. NO CHANGE
   G. somewhat three-dimensional
   H. a little bit three-dimensional
   J. kind of three-dimensional

71. A. NO CHANGE
   B. If a viewer watches the movie *2001: A Space Odyssey*; for example, you can see
   C. If a viewer watches the movie *2001: A Space Odyssey*, for example, he could have saw
   D. If a viewer watches the movie *2001: A Space Odyssey*, for example, he can see

72. F. NO CHANGE
   G. When a viewer is watching a movie chariot race, that viewer can tell which of the chariots even on the flat screen is in the lead.
   H. When watching a movie chariot race, you even on the flat screen can tell which chariot is in the lead.
   J. On a flat screen, a chariot race in a movie can be viewed and the viewer can tell which chariot is in the lead.

73. A. NO CHANGE
   B. has breaked through the screen
   C. was breaking through the screen
   D. has broken through the screen

74. If the writer were to delete sentence 6 in paragraph 2, Passage V would primarily lose a detail that

   F. interrupts the flow of the paragraph.
   G. illustrates how movies that aren't made in 3-D can still suggest depth.
   H. shows how far 3-D techniques have progressed since the earliest days.
   J. points to the superiority of 3-D movies over traditionally filmed movies

75. Which of the following is the best placement of sentence 9 in paragraph 2?

   A. The sentence should be omitted.
   B. After sentence 4
   C. After sentence 1
   D. After sentence 7

IF YOU FINISH BEFORE TIME IS CALLED, CHECK YOUR WORK ON THIS SECTION ONLY. DO NOT WORK ON ANY OTHER SECTION IN THE TEST.

Mathematics Test

Time: 60 Minutes

60 Questions

Directions: After solving each problem, choose the correct answer and fill in the corresponding space on your answer sheet. Do not spend too much time on any one problem. Solve as many problems as you can and return to the others if time permits. You are allowed to use a calculator on this test.

Note: Unless it is otherwise stated, you can assume all of the following:

1. Figures are NOT necessarily drawn to scale.
2. Geometric figures lie in a plane.
3. The word "line" means a straight line.
4. The word "average" refers to the arithmetic mean.

---

1. Three boxes weigh $1\frac{3}{4}$ ounces, $2\frac{1}{2}$ ounces, and $1\frac{2}{3}$ ounces, respectively. What is the sum of the weights of the three boxes, in ounces?

- **A.** $4\frac{1}{3}$
- **B.** $4\frac{5}{6}$
- **C.** $5\frac{7}{12}$
- **D.** $5\frac{19}{24}$
- **E.** $5\frac{11}{12}$

2. Which of the following is equivalent to $(2x^3)(3x^2)$?

- **F.** $6x^6$
- **G.** $6x^5$
- **H.** $5x^6$
- **J.** $5x^5$
- **K.** $6x^3$

3. If apples cost $6.40 for 14 and pears cost $7.20 for 12, how much money is saved by using three apples instead of three pears?

- **A.** $0.27
- **B.** $0.39
- **C.** $0.43
- **D.** $0.49
- **E.** $0.55

4. If five numbers average 32, then what must a sixth number be so that all six numbers would average 38?

- **F.** 42
- **G.** 48
- **H.** 52
- **J.** 68
- **K.** 72

5. Gee has found that when he uses premium fuel costing $3.50 per gallon his car gets 28 miles per gallon and when he uses regular fuel costing $3.30 per gallon his car gets 26 miles per gallon. Which of the following statements best describes the difference in fuel cost per mile when using these two fuels?

- **A.** Using premium fuel costs 0.2 cent per mile more than when using regular fuel.
- **B.** Using premium fuel costs 0.1 cent per mile more than when using regular fuel.
- **C.** Cost per mile is the same when using premium or regular fuel.
- **D.** Using premium fuel costs 0.1 cent per mile less than when using regular fuel.
- **E.** Using premium fuel costs 0.2 cent per mile less than when using regular fuel.

GO ON TO THE NEXT PAGE

6. In a regular geometric shape, all sides are the same length (congruent) and all angle sizes are the same (congruent). What is the degree measure of each interior angle in a regular pentagon?

    F. 104°

    G. 108°

    H. 112°

    J. 116°

    K. 120°

7. Which of the following is equivalent to $(a - b)(a + b - c)$?

    A. $a(a - b) - b(b - c)$

    B. $b(a - c) - a(b - c)$

    C. $b(a - b) - a(a - c)$

    D. $a(a - c) - b(b - c)$

    E. $a(b - c) - b(a - c)$

8. If $6 - 4x = 2 + 7x$, then what is the value of x?

    F. $\dfrac{11}{4}$

    G. $\dfrac{4}{3}$

    H. $\dfrac{4}{11}$

    J. $\dfrac{3}{4}$

    K. $-\dfrac{4}{3}$

9. Vicki's salary increased 10 percent in January, decreased 10 percent in February, and then increased 10 percent in March. What was the change in salary after the three percent changes?

    A. 8.9% increase

    B. 9.9% increase

    C. 10% increase

    D. 12.1% increase

    E. 13% increase

10. If $x^{\left(\frac{1}{2}\right)} = 4$, then what is the value of $x - \left(\dfrac{x}{2}\right)^2$?

    F. −48

    G. −8

    H. −2

    J. 0

    K. 1

11. Triangle ABC and triangle ADE are similar as shown in the following figure. All measures are in centimeters. If $BC = 9$, $AD = 4$, $DE = 3$, and $AE = 6$, then what is the perimeter of triangle ABC?

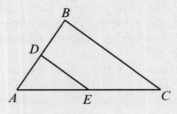

    A. 26

    B. 33

    C. 36

    D. 39

    E. 42

12. Three contestants, A, B, and C, played a game. The order of finish from 1st place through 3rd place was B, A, C. As a prize, 1st place received twice as many apples as 2nd place and 2nd place received twice as many apples as 3rd place. If contestant A received eight apples as a prize, how many total apples were given as prizes to the three contestants?

    F. 56

    G. 28

    H. 24

    J. 18

    K. 14

13. Perform the following matrix multiplication

$$\begin{bmatrix} 40 & 25 \\ 50 & 40 \end{bmatrix} \begin{bmatrix} 5 \\ 10 \end{bmatrix}$$

    A. $\begin{bmatrix} 1100 \end{bmatrix}$

    B. $\begin{bmatrix} 325 \\ 900 \end{bmatrix}$

    C. $\begin{bmatrix} 450 \\ 650 \end{bmatrix}$

    D. $\begin{bmatrix} 200 & 250 \\ 250 & 400 \end{bmatrix}$

    E. $\begin{bmatrix} 200 & 125 \\ 500 & 400 \end{bmatrix}$

GO ON TO THE NEXT PAGE

14. Simplify the following complex fraction: $\dfrac{4+2i}{1-3i}$

- **F.** $\dfrac{-1+7i}{5}$
- **G.** $\dfrac{5-7i}{4}$
- **H.** $1+i$
- **J.** $3-i$
- **K.** $\dfrac{-3+6i}{2}$

15. A bag contains 3 blue, 4 white, and 5 red marbles, identical except for color. Two marbles are randomly selected from the bag without replacement. If b represents the probability that both selected marbles were blue and w represents the probability that both marbles were white, then which of the following represents the relationship between b and w?

- **A.** $b = w$
- **B.** $3b = 4w$
- **C.** $4b = 3w$
- **D.** $w = 2b$
- **E.** $b = 2w$

16. If doubling a number and then doubling the answer gives a result that is 20 larger than the original number, then what was the original number?

- **F.** 5
- **G.** $6\dfrac{2}{3}$
- **H.** 8
- **J.** $8\dfrac{1}{3}$
- **K.** 10

17. In the standard (x, y) coordinate plane, a line passes through the points $(3, -6)$ and $(-3, 12)$. What is the sum of the x-intercept and the y-intercept of the line?

- **A.** −2
- **B.** 0
- **C.** 2
- **D.** 4
- **E.** 6

18. A reverse osmosis system uses 6.5 gallons of water to produce 1.2 gallons of purified water. (The rest is wasted.) How many gallons of water would be required if the system produced 220 gallons of purified water?

- **F.** 41
- **G.** 52
- **H.** 1066
- **J.** 1192
- **K.** 1244

19. A student must select two questions from each of three sections on a test. Each section lists four unique questions. How many unique six-question tests can a student create?

- **A.** 18
- **B.** 27
- **C.** 64
- **D.** 125
- **E.** 216

20. The four angles of a quadrilateral are in the ratio of 2 to 4 to 5 to 7. What is the size of the largest angle?

- **F.** 40°
- **G.** 70°
- **H.** 100°
- **J.** 120°
- **K.** 140°

21. If $wxyz \neq 0$, then which of the following is equivalent to this expression:

$$\dfrac{\dfrac{x}{y}}{\dfrac{w}{z} \cdot \dfrac{y}{w}}$$

- **A.** $\dfrac{x}{z}$
- **B.** $\dfrac{xy}{w^2}$
- **C.** xyz
- **D.** $\dfrac{zy^2}{x}$
- **E.** $\dfrac{xz}{y^2}$

GO ON TO THE NEXT PAGE

22. In the standard (x, y) coordinate plane, the graphs of $y = x^2$ and $x - y = -6$ intersect at two points. What is the sum of the y-coordinates of these two points?

   F.   –6

   G.   1

   H.   8

   J.   13

   K.   15

23. If $\frac{3}{8}y - \frac{3}{4} = \frac{3}{2}$, then what is the value of y?

   A.   2

   B.   4

   C.   6

   D.   8

   E.   12

24. Given the right triangle shown here, $CD = 10$. If $\cos E = \frac{2}{3}$, what is the length of side $\overline{CE}$?

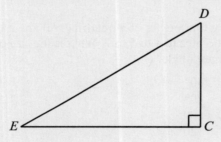

   F. $2\sqrt{5}$

   G. $4\sqrt{5}$

   H. $\frac{20}{3}$

   J. $2\sqrt{13}$

   K. $4\sqrt{13}$

25. One angle of an isosceles triangle measures 30°. Which of the following could be the measure of the largest angle in the triangle?

   I.   75°

   II.   85°

   III.   120°

   IV.   140°

   A.   III only

   B.   I and III only

   C.   I and IV only

   D.   II and III only

   E.   II and IV only

26. What is the sum of the two solutions of the equation $2x^2 + 8x = 0$?

   F.   –8

   G.   –4

   H.   –2

   J.   0

   K.   4

27. Three lines intersect to form the triangle shown in the following figure. What is the value of x?

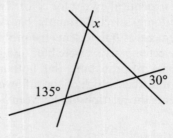

   A.   55°

   B.   65°

   C.   75°

   D.   85°

   E.   Cannot be determined from the information given.

28. If $\cos\theta = -\frac{1}{3}$, then which of the following must be true?

   F. $0 < \theta < \frac{\pi}{2}$ or $\pi < \theta < \frac{3\pi}{2}$

   G. $\frac{\pi}{2} < \theta < \pi$

   H. $\frac{\pi}{2} < \theta < \frac{3\pi}{2}$

   J. $\pi < \theta < \frac{3\pi}{2}$

   K. $\frac{\pi}{2} < \theta < \pi$ or $\frac{3\pi}{2} < \theta < 2\pi$

29. A tank is full of brand A gasoline. After one-fourth of the tank is used, it is filled up with brand B gasoline. After half of the tank is used, it is filled with brand B gasoline. If a full tank holds 32 gallons of gasoline, how many gallons of brand B gasoline are now in the tank?

   A.   12

   B.   14

   C.   16

   D.   18

   E.   20

GO ON TO THE NEXT PAGE

Use the following information to answer questions 30–32.

A triangle is formed by three intersecting lines as shown in the following figure.

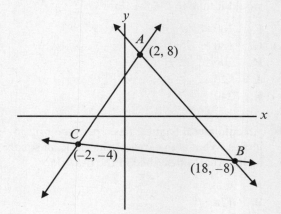

30. What is the length of the side of the triangle between points *A* and *C*?

F. $8\sqrt{2}$
G. $2\sqrt{34}$
H. $4\sqrt{10}$
J. $18\sqrt{2}$
K. $8\sqrt{10}$

31. A fourth line is drawn through point *C* and perpendicular to the line drawn through points *A* and *B*. What is the equation of this fourth line?

A. $x - y = 6$
B. $x + y = 2$
C. $x - y = 4$
D. $x + y = -6$
E. $x - y = 2$

32. A fifth line is drawn through point *B* and intersects segment $\overline{AC}$ between points *A* and *C*. Which of the following cannot be the slope of this fifth line?

I. $-\dfrac{5}{6}$
II. $-\dfrac{2}{3}$
III. $-\dfrac{1}{3}$
IV. $-\dfrac{1}{6}$

F.   None of the above
G.   One of the above
H.   Two of the above
J.   Three of the above
K.   All of the above

33. A circle, centered at *O*, with two radii, two chords, and two angle measures is shown in the following figure. What is the measure of angle *x*?

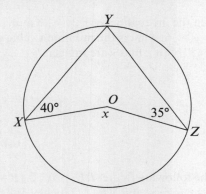

A.   105°
B.   120°
C.   135°
D.   150°
E.   Cannot be determined from the information given.

GO ON TO THE NEXT PAGE

34. Solve the following for y: $x - y = z - 4y$

   F. $z - \dfrac{x}{3}$

   G. $\dfrac{z + x}{5}$

   H. $\dfrac{x - z}{3}$

   J. $\dfrac{z - x}{3}$

   K. $\dfrac{z - x}{5}$

35. Points W, X, Y, and Z are midpoints of the sides of square $RSTU$. What is the perimeter of square $RSTU$, in yards, if the perimeter of square $WXYZ$ is 24 yards?

   A. $12\sqrt{2}$
   B. $24\sqrt{2}$
   C. 36
   D. 48
   E. $36\sqrt{2}$

36. Given the inequalities $x + 2y > -8$ and $2x - y > -6$, what is the minimum value of $x + y$ if both x and y are integers?

   F. -6
   G. -5
   H. -4
   J. -3
   K. -2

37. In the following figure, $DE = BC$, $2AB = 3DE$, $AE = 5$ inches, and $AB = 12$ inches. What is the perimeter, in inches, of pentagon $ABCDE$?

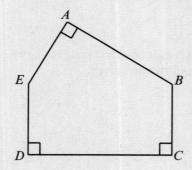

   A. 42
   B. 44
   C. 46
   D. 48
   E. 50

38. In order to tile a 9-foot by 12-foot rectangular floor, a choice between using 6-inch square tiles or 9-inch square tiles must be made. How many more 6-inch square tiles than 9-inch square tiles would it take to tile the floor?

   F. 160
   G. 180
   H. 200
   J. 220
   K. 240

39. An equilateral triangle has a perimeter of 36 inches. What is the area of the circle, in square inches, that is inscribed in the triangle?

   A. $6\sqrt{3}\pi$
   B. 12π
   C. 18π
   D. $12\sqrt{3}\pi$
   E. $18\sqrt{3}\pi$

40. The three sides of a triangle are in the ratio of 3 to 4 to 5. If the perimeter of the triangle is 30 inches, then what is the sum of the lengths, in inches, of the shortest and longest sides?

   F. 15
   G. 17.5
   H. 20
   J. 22.5
   K. 25

41. What is the tenth number in the following list of numbers if the pattern continues?

$$1, -3, 6, -10, 15, -21, 28, \ldots$$

   A. -65
   B. -61
   C. -55
   D. 55
   E. 61

GO ON TO THE NEXT PAGE

42. The LCM of y and z is w. The GCF of y and z is x. If w, x, y, and z are positive even integers and $w = 6x$, then what is the minimum sum of y and z?

  F. 6
  G. 8
  H. 10
  J. 12
  K. 14

43. A suit is discounted 15 percent from its original price. After a sales tax of 8 percent is added to the discounted price, the "out the door" price of the suit is $114.29. What, to the nearest cent, was the original price of the suit, before the discount and before the tax?

  A. $122.75
  B. $123.95
  C. $124.25
  D. $124.50
  E. $124.95

44. Four nuts weighing 18 grams each are combined with eight nuts weighing 12 grams each. What is the average weight of the twelve nuts, in grams?

  F. 13
  G. 14
  H. 15
  J. 16
  K. 17

45. If $a + b = c + 4$, then what is $(c - a) + (b - c)$?

  A. $a - b$
  B. $c - b$
  C. $b - a$
  D. $a - c$
  E. $b - c$

46. Two circles are internally tangent such that the diameter of the smaller circle is the radius of the larger circle. If the circumference of the larger circle is 40, what is the area of the smaller circle?

  F. $\dfrac{50}{\pi}$
  G. 20
  H. $\dfrac{100}{\pi}$
  J. $\dfrac{150}{\pi}$
  K. $\dfrac{200}{\pi}$

47. In the standard (x, y) coordinate plane, line k passes through the point $(-8, -4)$ and is parallel to the line $5x - 6y = 4$. What is the slope of line k?

  A. $-\dfrac{6}{5}$
  B. $-\dfrac{3}{2}$
  C. $-\dfrac{2}{3}$
  D. $\dfrac{4}{5}$
  E. $\dfrac{5}{6}$

48. If $2x + 3y < 8$ and $5z - 2x < -4$, then solve for z in terms of y.

  F. $z > \dfrac{5y - 4}{3}$
  G. $z < \dfrac{4 - 5y}{3}$
  H. $z > \dfrac{3y + 4}{5}$
  J. $z < \dfrac{4 - 3y}{5}$
  K. $z > \dfrac{4 - 3y}{5}$

GO ON TO THE NEXT PAGE

49. If $g(x) = 2x^2 + 1$, then what is the value of $g(a + b) - g(a)$?

   A. $2b^2 + 1$
   B. $2ab + 4b^2 - 2$
   C. $2a^2 + 4ab + 2b^2 - 4$
   D. $4a^2 + 4ab + 2b^2 + 2$
   E. $4ab + 2b^2$

50. Given two numbers, A, and B, where A is six less than one-third of the size of B and B is four more than twice the size of A. What is the size of the smaller number?

   F. -24
   G. -16
   H. -14
   J. -12
   K. -6

51. If $f(x) = 4x + 5$ and $g(x) = x^2 - 3$, then what is the value of $g(f(-2))$?

   A. -3
   B. 0
   C. 6
   D. 9
   E. 12

52. Segments $\overline{BE}$ and $\overline{CE}$ divide triangle ADE into three smaller triangles with $AD = 20$ inches and $BC = 14$ inches as shown in the following figure. If the area of triangle $ADE = 80$ square inches, what is the total area, in square inches, of the shaded triangles?

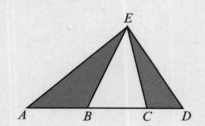

   F. 24
   G. 30
   H. 36
   J. 48
   K. 56

53. Which of the following must be true about the following figure?

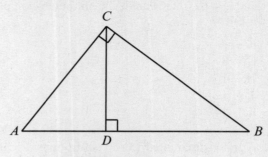

   I. $\triangle ACD \sim \triangle ABC$
   II. $\dfrac{AD}{CD} = \dfrac{CD}{BD}$
   III. $\angle CAD + \angle BCD = \angle ACD + \angle CBD$

   A. Statement I only
   B. Statement II only
   C. Statement I and II only
   D. Statement I and III only
   E. Statement I, II and III

54. Given triangle RST, where R, S, and T are the three angles of the triangle and r, s, and t are the corresponding opposite sides of the triangle, the law of sines states that $\dfrac{\sin R}{r} = \dfrac{\sin S}{s} = \dfrac{\sin T}{t}$. If $s = 6$, $r = 8$, and $\sin S = \dfrac{2}{3}$, then what is the value of $\sin R$?

   F. $\dfrac{3}{4}$
   G. $\dfrac{5}{6}$
   H. $\dfrac{8}{9}$
   J. $\dfrac{6}{5}$
   K. $\dfrac{4}{3}$

55. If $y = \dfrac{3}{16}x^2 - 16x + 20$ is graphed in the standard (x, y) coordinate plane and point $P(a, b)$ is a point on the curve, what is the value of b when $a = 8$?

   A. -116
   B. -96
   C. -84
   D. -48
   E. 24

GO ON TO THE NEXT PAGE

56. If x is an integer such that $x \neq 2$, then which of the following sets of numbers contains values of x, all of which satisfy the inequality $\dfrac{|x+4|}{|x-2|} > 2$?

   F. $\{-2, 0, 2, 4, 6\}$

   G. $\{-1, 4, 6, 8\}$

   H. $\{0, 3, 4, 7\}$

   J. $\{1, 3, 5, 7\}$

   K. $\{1, 3, 6, 8\}$

57. In the standard (x, y) coordinate plane, a parallelogram is drawn with vertices of $(1, 2)$, $(3, 10)$, $(12, 10)$, and $(10, 2)$. A line segment is drawn from $(10, 2)$ to $(6, 10)$, dividing the parallelogram into a trapezoid and a triangle. What is the ratio of the area of the triangle to the area of the trapezoid?

   A. $\dfrac{1}{3}$

   B. $\dfrac{1}{2}$

   C. $\dfrac{2}{3}$

   D. $\dfrac{2}{1}$

   E. $\dfrac{3}{1}$

58. In the standard (x, y) coordinate plane, a circle has a diameter of 8 and its center is located at $(-8, 8)$. Which of the following is the equation of the circle?

   F. $(x + 8)^2 + (y - 8)^2 = 4$

   G. $(x + 8)^2 + (y - 8)^2 = 16$

   H. $(x - 8)^2 + (y + 8)^2 = 8$

   J. $(x - 8)^2 + (y + 8)^2 = 16$

   K. $(x + 8)^2 + (y - 8)^2 = 64$

59. Tiel's age, in years, is 12 more than five times a positive number, x. Bev's age is eight times the number, x. For what values of x will Tiel be older than Bev?

   A. $x < 6$

   B. $x < 4$

   C. $x < 3$

   D. $x > 4$

   E. $x > 6$

60. If $\pi < \alpha < \dfrac{3\pi}{2}$ and $\dfrac{\pi}{2} < \beta < \pi$, then which of the following statements could be true?

   I. $\cos \beta > \dfrac{\tan \alpha}{2}$

   II. $\dfrac{\tan \beta}{\tan \alpha} < 0$

   III. $\cos \alpha < \dfrac{\tan \beta}{2}$

   F.   Statement I only

   G.   Statement II only

   H.   Statement III only

   J.   Statements I and II only

   K.   Statements II and III only

IF YOU FINISH BEFORE TIME IS CALLED, CHECK YOUR WORK ON THIS SECTION ONLY. DO NOT WORK ON ANY OTHER SECTION IN THE TEST.

STOP

Practice Test 3

Reading Test

Time: 35 Minutes

40 Questions

Directions: Each of the four passages in this test is followed by a series of multiple-choice questions. Read the passage and choose the best answer to each question. Return to the passage as often as necessary to answer the questions.

Passage I

PROSE FICTION: This passage is adapted from *Good Girls Don't Wear Trousers* by Lara Cardella. Reprinted by permission of Arcade Publishing, an imprint of Skyhorse Publishing, Inc.

After I had cried for a bit, I fled the house through the window, which luckily was so near the ground that I could use it as a door. I didn't take any of my belongings, since I knew I must (5) offer myself to God just as I was, and anyway the convent was sure to provide me with a pair of trousers and a habit.

It wasn't far, but the stifling Sicilian heat makes even doing nothing tiring. I had to go (10) cross-country to reach the convent, and the scenery on the way was so breathtaking that the sight of it dried my tears more quickly than the sun. In Sicily the seasons do not seem to follow the usual course; it is as if time has stopped. As I (15) made my way along the tracks and over the fields, I breathed the smell of hand-tilled soil, the trees nurtured by manure, and the sweat of men's brows. Everything here is imbued with sweat. Even the horses are never alert and frisky but are (20) weighed down with the burden of work. Beast is indistinguishable from man and man from beast.

I arrived at the convent exhausted, after walking for well over half an hour under that sun, crying all the way. My hair was matted with (25) sweat, and the tiredness had penetrated my very bones. There loomed the great entrance portal, which I could barely see through a haze of tears, but I felt triumphant, like a martyr given up to suffering. And I was the martyr, knocking three (30) times on the door.

A nun appeared on the balcony and looked around but, seeing nobody, went back inside. I sat on a step and fanned myself with the hem of my long skirt, licking my lips from time to time (35) because my mouth was like a furnace. I saw her but she didn't notice me, and I stayed silent as I had no idea what to say. However, after a bit I heard chains being rattled behind me, once, twice, and finally a third time, then more rattling (40) and the jangling of keys. I froze, tucked into a corner, trying to make myself as inconspicuous as possible. Then a face, pale as a ghost, peeked out from behind the door, looked around, and saw me.

(45) "Whatever are you doing here?"

"Um I... I want to be a nun," I stammered.

"But who are you?"

"I'm Annetta... my name is Anna and I'd like to become a nun," I said more resolutely.

(50) "I see... but where are your parents?"

"I... I haven't got any. I'm an orphan and I live alone." And with that I dissolved into tears, mainly at the thought of my father's thrashing, which made me wish I really was an orphan. The (55) nun gave me an odd look, then smiled and beckoned me in.

"All right, orphan Annie, tell me a bit about yourself."

"Well... what do you want to know."

(60) "Well, you can tell me how old you are, how you have lived until now, and whether you go to school."

"I'm thirteen, and I don't go to school because I haven't got any money.... I used to live with my (65) aunt Concetta, but she asked me to leave because she was so poor she couldn't feed me any longer."

"Just a minute. I thought you lived alone."

I felt myself blushing. "Oh, well, yes... I meant I live alone now, and since I haven't got anything (70) to wear... Could I have a glass of water?"

"Of course," she said. "Wait a minute." And she disappeared inside.

I stayed where I was on that threadbare sofa, planning what to invent next and taking stock (75) of my surroundings. There was a small hanging

GO ON TO THE NEXT PAGE

embroidered with the image of the Virgin Mary, and enormous crucifix that took up half the wall, two chairs, a desk, some red carnations in a vase, a large trunk, and the sofa on which I was sitting.

(80)   As soon as the nun returned with a glass of icy water, she resumed her questioning.

"So tell me, why do you want to become a nun?"

"Well, I'd like to be with God forever," I replied.

(85)   "I see, but why did you come here?"

"Because my father... I mean my uncle won't let me wear trousers—"

"Trousers? And what, may I ask, do they have to do with anything?" The nun was visibly amused.

(90)   "But don't you wear them under your habits? Father Domenico wears them under his cassock."

"So he should, my dear, because he's a man. No, believe me, Annetta, we don't."

Then she turned away from me in a valiant (95) attempt to suppress her laughter. I must have been a sorry sight.

"So do I have to become a priest for trousers?"

"No, you don't have to be a priest... but you do need to be a man. Girls don't wear trousers."

(100)   I left, utterly dejected, pursued by the nun's mirth but mulling over a whole new prospect. It was obvious that if only men could wear trousers, then, somehow, a man I must be.

1. Aside from her thirst, which of the following can be reasonably inferred as the main reason Anna asks the nun for a glass of water (line 70)?

A. She wants to find out what is in the large trunk next to the sofa.

B. She fears that the nun may berate her, as her father has previously done.

C. She hopes that the nun will not come back and that a priest will return in her place.

D. She needs to buy some time to get her story straight.

2. As it is used in the passage, the word *dejected* (line 100) means

F. ashamed.

G. defiant.

H. deflated.

J. rejected.

3. From Anna's description of the Sicilian countryside in the second paragraph, it can be reasonably inferred that

A. she does not want to leave the place where she has grown up.

B. she perceives her native place to be beautiful, but backward and stifling.

C. she prefers a life outdoors to the sequestered life of a nun.

D. she understands that life in a big city would ultimately disappoint her.

4. When Anna says "I felt triumphant, like a martyr given up to suffering" (lines 28–29), it can be reasonably inferred that the author is

F. imparting some ironic distance between herself and her narrator.

G. foreshadowing a momentous event that is about to occur.

H. introducing a religious metaphor that will continue to resonate throughout Passage I.

J. setting up a plot twist to take the novel in a previously unimagined direction.

5. When the nun calls her "orphan Annie," this is an early sign in their conversation that she takes Anna

A. for a fool.

B. in jest.

C. far too seriously.

D. as a victim.

6. From their conversation, the nun most likely perceives Anna's religious devotion as

F. committed and passionate.

G. disingenuous and calculating.

H. serious but pedantic.

J. earnest but superficial.

7. In the fourth paragraph, her reaction to the first appearance of the nun reveals that Anna is

A. daunted by her presence.

B. disappointed by her indifference.

C. envious of her station in life.

D. unimpressed by her initial appearance.

GO ON TO THE NEXT PAGE

Practice Test 3

8. As used in Passage I, the word *imbued* (line 18) means

    F. debased.
    G. permeated.
    H. poisoned.
    J. trounced.

9. The nun's final pronouncement that "Girls don't wear trousers" (line 99) contains irony because

    A. in the course of her conversation with the nun, Anna has already concluded that she no longer wishes to wear trousers.
    B. her father has already intimated that he would be proud of Anna if she decided to become a nun in response to a true religious vocation.
    C. Anna has traveled a long distance for the nun to tell her, essentially, what her father has already told her.
    D. as can be plainly seen, nuns do dress in a manner that is entirely different from everyone else in Anna's world.

10. Which of the following reflects the clearest change in Anna's outlook over the course of Passage I?

    F. She no longer intends to be a nun, but instead resolves to be a man.
    G. She no longer wishes to wear trousers, but resigns herself to fitting in with her contemporaries.
    H. She no longer feels anger at her father, but now unleashes this emotion on the church.
    J. She no longer wishes to leave home, but finds a new opportunity there that she hadn't originally perceived.

Passage II

SOCIAL SCIENCE: Passage taken from *Flow: The Psychology of Optimal Experience* by Mihaly Csikszentmihalyi (Harper Collins Publishers, 1990).

At this point in our scientific knowledge we are on the verge of being able to estimate how much information the central nervous system is capable of processing. It seems we can manage at
(5) most seven bits of information—such as differentiated sounds, or visual stimuli, or recognizable nuances of emotion or thought—at any one time, and that the shortest time it takes to discriminate between one set of bits and
(10) another is about 1/18 of a second. By using these figures one concludes that it is possible to process at most 126 bits of information per second, or 7,560 per minute, or almost half a million per hour. Over a lifetime of seventy years, and
(15) counting sixteen hours of waking time each day, this amounts to about 185 billion bits of information. It is out of this total that everything in our life must come—every thought, memory, feeling, or action. It seems like a huge amount,
(20) but in reality it does not go that far.

The limitation of consciousness is demonstrated by the fact that to understand what another person is saying we must process 40 bits of information each second. If we assume
(25) the upper limit of our capacity to be 126 per second, it follows that to understand what three people are saying simultaneously is theoretically possible, but only by managing to keep out of consciousness every other thought or sensation.
(30) We couldn't, for instance, be aware of the speakers' expressions, nor could we wonder about why they are saying what they are saying, or notice what they are wearing.

Of course, these figures are only suggestive at
(35) this point in our knowledge of the way the mind works. It could be argued justifiably that they either underestimate or overestimate the capacity of the mind to process information. The optimists claim that through the course of
(40) evolution the nervous system has become adept at "chunking" bits of information so that processing capacity is constantly expanded. Simple functions like adding a column of numbers or driving a car grow to be automated,
(45) leaving the mind free to deal with more data. We also learn how to compress and streamline information through symbolic means—language, math, abstract concepts, and stylized narratives. Each biblical parable, for instance, tries to encode
(50) the hard-won experience of many individuals over unknown eons of time. Consciousness, the optimists argue, is an "open system"; in effect, it is infinitely expandable, and there is no need to take its limitations into account.

(55) But the ability to compress stimuli does not help as much as one might expect. The requirements of life still dictate that we spend about 8 percent of waking time eating, and almost the same amount taking care of personal
(60) bodily needs such as washing, dressing, shaving,

GO ON TO THE NEXT PAGE

(65) and going to the bathroom. These two activities alone take up 15 percent of consciousness, and while engaged in them we can't do much else that requires serious concentration. But even when there is nothing else pressing occupying their minds, most people fall far below the peak capacity for processing information. In the roughly one-third of the day that is free of obligations, in their precious "leisure" time, most (70) people in fact seem to use their minds as little as possible. The largest part of free time—almost half of it for American adults—is spent in front of the television set.

The plots and characters of the popular shows (75) are so repetitive that although watching TV requires the processing of visual images, very little else in the way of memory, thinking, or volition is required. Not surprisingly, people report some of the lowest levels of concentration, (80) use of skills, clarity of thought, and feelings of potency when watching television. The other leisure activities people usually do at home are only a little more demanding. Reading most newspapers and magazines, talking to other (85) people, and gazing out the window also involve processing very little new information, and thus require little concentration.

So the 185 billion events to be enjoyed over our mortal days might either be an overestimate (90) or an underestimate. If we consider the amount of data the brain could theoretically process, the number might be too low; but if we look at how people actually use their minds, it is definitely much too high. In any case, an individual can (95) experience only so much. Therefore, the information we allow into consciousness becomes extremely important; it is, in fact, what determines the content and quality of life.

11. The main idea of Passage II is to

A. attempt to provide a framework for quantifying the informational capacity of the human brain.

B. argue that the human brain potential is heretofore untapped and, therefore, potentially limitless.

C. lament the fact that so much human intelligence is wasted on mindless, repetitive trivia.

D. suggest ways in which aptitude, which is inherently limited by brain structure, can be psychologically maximized.

12. Which of the following could best replace the word *nuances* in line 7?

F. delineations

G. gradations

H. imitations

J. limitations

13. The author discusses the difficulty of following three different conversations at once in order to

A. explain the relevance of the calculations in the first paragraph to readers who may feel hostile to an argument based solely upon mathematical analysis.

B. provide an example of how the physical limitation on consciousness explains a real-world phenomenon.

C. invite the reader to challenge his purported conclusions, as the author himself does in the paragraph that follows.

D. critique the very notion that a conversation can be understood properly without non-verbal cues such as the facial expressions of the speakers.

14. The contrast between the third and fourth paragraphs is best characterized as

F. physiological versus psychological.

G. theoretical versus practical.

H. radical versus reactionary.

J. religious versus secular.

15. Which of the following is NOT put forth as a factual statement?

A. Consciousness is infinitely expandable and there is no need to take its limitations into account.

B. 40 bits of information per second are required to understand human speech.

C. American adults spend on average about half of their leisure time watching television.

D. The human mind can process about 126 bits of information per second.

GO ON TO THE NEXT PAGE

16. According to the passage, each of the following might reasonably qualify as a bit of information EXCEPT:

    F. noticing the color of a person's shirt.

    G. perceiving that a friend is smiling at you.

    H. observing a sudden feeling of jealousy in yourself.

    J. overhearing a five-second exchange of conversation.

17. Which of the following can be reasonably inferred as what the author believes about how most people spend their time?

    A. We can and should learn to spend less than 15 percent of our time on eating and taking care of personal bodily needs.

    B. Television can be a motivator and a force for positive change.

    C. Reading newspapers and magazines provides vital opportunities for the productive use of the mind.

    D. Many people waste vast quantities of time in leisure activities that are essentially unchallenging.

18. When the author refers to "chunking" (line 41), he means

    F. making decisions based on intuition rather than knowledge.

    G. taking action in response to emotion rather than reason.

    H. the double-edged sword of acting on received wisdom rather than evidence.

    J. learning how to do relatively complex tasks without much conscious thought.

19. The author presents an optimistic outlook of his topic as one arguing that

    A. the processing capacity of the central nervous system can be maximized through symbolic means.

    B. the limitation of 185 billion bits in a lifetime only applies to a life of average duration.

    C. the processing time of 126 bits per second has no factual basis in the physiology of the central nervous system.

    D. when people are presented with information about how much time they are wasting, most naturally choose to make better use of their time.

20. The sixth paragraph (lines 88–98) does all of the following EXCEPT:

    F. sums up the argument of the previous five paragraphs.

    G. acknowledges that there is a limitation on consciousness.

    H. posits that the information that enters consciousness strongly influences the qualitative experience of life.

    J. suggests what a wise use of consciousness might look like.

Passage III

HUMANITIES: This passage is from *A Brief History of Thought* by Luc Ferry. Copyright 2011 by Plon. Translation copyright by Theo Cuffe. (Harper Collins Publishers, 2010).

As one contemporary philosopher, Andre Comte-Sponville, has emphasized, Stoicism here is very close to one of the most subtle tenets of Oriental wisdom, and of Tibetan Buddhism in

(5) particular: contrary to the commonplace idea that one 'cannot live without hope', hope is the greatest of misfortunes. For it is by nature an absence, a lack, a source of tension in our lives. For we live in terms of plans, chasing after

(10) objectives located in a more or less distant future, and believing that our happiness depends upon their accomplishment.

What we forget is that there is no other reality than this one in which we are living here and

(15) now, and that this strange headlong flight from the present can only end in failure. The objective accomplished, we almost invariably experience a puzzling sense of indifference, if not disappointment. Like children who become

(20) bored with their toys the day after Christmas, the possession of things so ardently coveted makes us neither better nor happier than before. The difficulties of life and the tragedy of the human condition are not modified by ownership or

(25) success and, in the famous phrase of Seneca, 'while we wait for life, life passes.'

Perhaps you like imagining what you would do if you were to win the lottery: you would buy this and that; you would give some of it to this friend

(30) or that cousin; you would definitely give some of

GO ON TO THE NEXT PAGE

it to charity; and then you would take off on a trip around the world. And then what? In the end, it is always the gravestone that is silhouetted against the horizon, and you come to realize soon (35) enough that the accumulation of all imaginable worldly goods solves nothing (although let us not be hypocrites: as the saying goes, money certainly does make poverty bearable).

Which is also why, according to a celebrated (40) Buddhist proverb, you must learn to live as if this present moment were the most vital of your whole life, and as if those people in whose company you find yourself were the most important in your life. For nothing else exists, in (45) truth: the past is no longer and the future is not yet. These temporal dimensions are real only to the imagination, which we 'shoulder'—like the 'beasts of burden' mocked by Nietzsche—merely to justify our incapacity to embrace what (50) Nietzsche called (in entirely Stoic mode) *amor fati*: the love of reality for itself. Happiness lost, bliss deferred, and, by the same token, the present receding, consigned to nothingness whereas it is the only true dimension of existence.

(55) It is with this perspective that the *Discourses* of Epictetus aimed to develop one of the more celebrated themes of Stoicism: namely, that the good life is a life stripped of both hopes and fears. In other words, a life reconciled to what (60) is the case, a life which accepts the world as it is. As you can see, this reconciliation cannot sit alongside the conviction that the world is divine, harmonious, and inherently good....

Let us be very clear about this: The God of (65) whom Epictetus speaks is not the personal God of Christianity, but merely an embodying of the *cosmos*, another name for the principle of universal reason which the Greeks named the *Logos*: the true face of destiny that we have no (70) choice but to accept, and should yearn for with our entire soul.

Whereas, in fact, victims as we are of commonplace illusions, we keep thinking that we must oppose it so as to bend it to our purposes. (75) As the master advises his pupil...:

We must bring our own will into harmony with whatever comes to pass so that none of the things which happen may occur against our will, nor those which do not happen be wished for by us. (80) *Those who have settled this as the philosopher's*

task have it in their power never to be disappointed in their desires, or fall prey to what they wish to avoid, but to lead personal lives free from sorrow, fear, and perturbation. (Discourses)

(85) Of course, such advice seems absurd to ordinary mortals: amounting to an especially insipid version of fatalism. This sort of wisdom might pass for folly, because it is based upon a vision of the world which requires a conceptual (90) effort out of the ordinary to be grasped. But this is precisely what distinguishes philosophy from ordinary discussion, and, to me, why it possesses an irreplaceable charm.

21. The main idea of Passage III is to

   A. place Stoicism into a proper historical and philosophical context, especially with regard to other Greek traditions.

   B. correct a basic misconception about Stoicism: that it is essentially an emotionless and overly intellectual philosophy.

   C. clarify how several distinct tenets of Stoicism can be found in a variety of apparently unrelated philosophical works.

   D. illuminate the reader's understanding of one tenet of Stoicism as an overlooked and untapped source of wisdom.

22. The author equates people with children the day after Christmas (lines 19–20) when they

   F. predictably find themselves disappointed by possessions they have obtained.

   G. jealously guard what they have from the grasping hands of other people.

   H. fastidiously find fault with what they have been given, no matter how luxurious.

   J. inexplicably destroy the very thing that they claim to love the most.

GO ON TO THE NEXT PAGE

23. If you suddenly found yourself unemployed, which of the following would reasonably be the best practical example of what Nietzsche calls *amor fati*?

    A. resolving neither to look for a new job nor apply for unemployment benefits

    B. adopting a wise moderation in your spending habits coupled with a rational, step-by-step approach to finding work

    C. remaining optimistic, clear that having found work in the past, you will most likely find another job

    D. accepting your unemployment as a current reality and refusing steadfastly to wallow in regret or worry

24. The author's reference to "commonplace illusions" (line 73) refers to the human propensity for

    F. denying the truth.

    G. excess.

    H. self-pity.

    J. self-aggrandizement.

25. The image of the "gravestone that is silhouetted against the horizon" (lines 33–34) illustrates what the author, elsewhere in Passage III, refers to as

    A. "the tragedy of the human condition" (lines 23–24).

    B. "the 'beasts of burden' mocked by Nietzsche" (lines 47–48).

    C. "a life stripped of both hopes and fears" (lines 58–59).

    D. "an especially insipid version of fatalism" (lines 86–87).

26. When the author says in lines 61–63 "this reconciliation cannot sit alongside the conviction that the world is divine, harmonious, and inherently good," he implies that

    F. the greater good must supersede one's personal desires.

    G. the past must be put aside while the future is embraced.

    H. the Greek and Christian conceptions of deity must not be confused.

    J. the real must be substituted for the ideal.

27. In the last paragraph (lines 85–93), the author's rhetorical intent with regard to Stoicism is to

    A. toss it as ultimately banal and ineffectual, as entrée to what he considers to be a more worthy philosophical approach.

    B. subtly condemn it by appearing to praise it for traits that he knows most readers will find unconvincing.

    C. suggest that what readers may perceive to be its main weakness is precisely what he finds so appealing about it.

    D. lament that so few current thinkers apprehend the ways in which it is fundamentally and fatally flawed.

28. According to Passage III, which of the following ideas is most distinct from the Tibetan Buddhist tenet that hope is "the greatest of misfortunes"?

    F. the Greek principle of *Logos*

    G. Nietzsche's notion of *amor fati*

    H. the Christian conception of a loving deity

    J. the "philosopher's task" set forth in the *Discourses* by Epictetus

29. As used in line 39, the word *celebrated* means

    A. rejoiced.

    B. renowned.

    C. noble.

    D. accurate.

30. The author's acknowledgment that "as the saying goes, money certainly does make poverty bearable" attempts to do all of the following EXCEPT:

    F. inject a touch of humor into an otherwise gloomy passage.

    G. acknowledge that he is no less prone to human temptation than his reader is likely to be.

    H. tip his hand that he is about to reject the philosophical point that he is illustrating.

    J. win the reader to his way of thinking by tempering it just a bit.

GO ON TO THE NEXT PAGE

Passage IV

NATURAL SCIENCE: This passage is taken of *Natural Capitalism* by L. Hunter Lovins, Amory Lovins, and Paul Hawken (Hachette Book Group, a division of Little, Brown and Company, 1999).

Hypercars gain much of their advantage by abandoning nearly a century of materials and manufacturing experience based on steel. This notion might at first appear quixotic. Steel is
(5) ubiquitous and familiar, and its fabrication highly evolved. The modern steel car expertly satisfies often conflicting demands—to be efficient and yet relatively safe, powerful yet relatively clean. Most automakers still believe
(10) that only steel is cheap enough for affordable cars, and that alternatives like carbon fiber are prohibitively costly.

Yet industrial history is filled with examples in which standard materials have been quickly
(15) displaced. U.S. autobodies switched from 85 percent wood in 1920 to over 70 percent steel in 1927. The same Detroit executives who think polymer composites will never gain much of a foothold in automaking may in fact spend their
(20) weekends zooming around in glass-and-polyester-composite boats: Synthetic materials already dominate boatbuilding and are making rapid gains in aerospace construction. Logically, cars are next, because new manufacturing
(25) methods, and new ways of thinking about the economics of producing an entire vehicle, suggest that steel is a cheap material but is costly to make into cars, while carbon fiber is a costly material but is cheap to make into cars.

(30) Carbon fibers are black, shiny, stiff filaments finer than a human hair, and one-fourth as dense as steel but stiffer and stronger. In 1995, structural carbon fiber cost about twenty times as much per pound as did steel. By 2000, the
(35) ratio may fall to about twelve. But if fibers are aligned properly to match stress and interwoven to distribute it, the same strength and stiffness as steel can be achieved with two or three times fewer pounds of carbon fiber, embedded in a
(40) strong polymer "matrix" to form a composite material. Moreover, for many uses, such fibers as glass and Kevlar are as good as or better than carbon and are two to six times cheaper. Combinations of fibers offer vast design
(45) flexibility to match exactly the properties that a given part needs. Composites also make it possible to use the lightest-weight body designs, including truly frameless "monocoques" (like an egg, the body *is* the structure) whose extreme
(50) stiffness improves handling and safety. (If you doubt the strength of a thin, stiff, frameless monocoque, try eating a lobster or a crab claw with no tools.) Such designs economize on the use of costly materials, needing only about one
(55) hundred pounds of fiber per car.

Carbon fiber, even if frugally used, still looks too costly per pound. But cost per pound is the wrong basis for comparison, because cars are sold by the car, not by the pound, and must be
(60) manufactured from their raw materials. Only about 15 percent of the cost of a typical steel car part is for the steel itself; the rest pays for pounding, welding, and finishing it. But composites and other molded synthetics emerge
(65) from a mold *already* shaped and finished. Even very large and complex units can be molded in a single piece. A composite autobody needs only about five to twenty parts instead of a steel unibody's two hundred to four hundred. Each of
(70) those hundreds of steel parts needs an average of four tool-steel dies, each costing an average of $1 million. Polymer composites, in contrast, are molded to the desired shape in a single step, using low-pressure molding dies that can even be
(75) made of coated epoxy, cutting tooling costs by up to 90 percent.

More savings arise in the manufacturing steps after the autobody is formed, where assembly effort and the space to carry it out decrease by
(80) about 90 percent. The lightweight, easy-to-handle parts can be lifted without a hoist. They fit together precisely without rework, and are joined using superstrong glues instead of hundreds of robotized welds. Painting—the costliest, most
(85) difficult, and most polluting step in automaking, which accounts for one-fourth to one-half the total finished cost of painted steel body parts— can be eliminated by lay-in-the-mold color. Together, these features can make carbon-fiber
(90) autobodies competitive with steel ones.

Practice Test 3

31. The main idea of Passage IV is to

A. endorse a change in the basic materials used in automobile manufacturing.

B. extol the potential virtues of new modes of automotive design while lamenting that they are unlikely to occur.

C. place the history of automobile engineering into an explanatory historical framework.

D. predict what the future of the automobile may be if industry leaders fail to take decisive action.

32. In the first paragraph, the authors' rhetorical tack is to

F. describe the key advantages of hypercars in order to advance their thesis.

G. dispel the most prevalent objections to the use of steel in cars in order to bolster their thesis.

H. outline the strongest arguments in opposition to their thesis in order to address them.

J. provide a preview of their overall argument before proceeding to a more detailed analysis.

33. In line 4, the word *quixotic* means

A. innovative.

B. romantic.

C. unfeasible.

D. viable.

34. The first two sentences of the fourth paragraph (lines 56–60) serve to acknowledge that

F. a potential economic argument against hypercars does exist, and there is a better way to assess their fiscal viability.

G. the task of engineers who design hypercars will be to leverage the inherent advantages in the raw materials from which they are made.

H. the path for hypercars from the drawing board to the assembly line and, finally, to the consumer will be challenging at best.

J. the ongoing debate about how hypercar design will actually manifest over time will be resolved only in practice, not in theory.

35. The main idea of the fifth paragraph focuses on

A. the economic advantages of carbon fiber during the manufacturing phase of car production.

B. the ecological advantages of carbon fiber over steel in automotive construction in terms of environmental degradation.

C. the comparative cost of painting in the production of a steel versus carbon fiber autobodies.

D. the implication that carbon fiber autobodies, being lightweight, will create a competitive advantage for consumers in savings at the gas pump.

36. The apparent economic advantages of preferring steel over polymers in automaking include all of the following EXCEPT:

F. The use of steel in auto manufacture has been highly developed and tested over time, while polymers are relatively untried.

G. The steel car provides a balance of demands that are often in conflict with one another—for example, efficiency and safety.

H. Steel is a relatively inexpensive raw material in comparison with polymers.

J. Steel is less expensive to make into cars than polymers are.

37. The reference to "glass-and-polyester-composite boats" (lines 20–21) furthers the authors' case through the use of

A. hyperbole.

B. irony.

C. metaphor.

D. simile.

38. Physical properties of carbon fibers include all of the following EXCEPT:

F. Carbon fibers weigh less than steel.

G. Carbon fibers are stronger than steel.

H. Carbon fibers are more dense than steel.

J. Carbon fibers have a greater stiffness than steel.

GO ON TO THE NEXT PAGE

39. In lines 15–17, the authors mention the auto industry's switch from wood to steel to

   A. caution that change that is ill-advised can wreak havoc on an industry.

   B. predict that what the industry now views as risky and forward-looking will, in retrospect, appear to have been inevitable.

   C. counsel that an industry remaining unresponsive to changing styles can sacrifice long-term market viability for immediate economic security.

   D. illustrate that industry-standard materials have been, and therefore can be, successfully replaced by newer options.

40. The fact that a polymer composite autobody requires far fewer separate parts than a steel unibody results in which of the following advantages for the hypercar?

   F. Fewer workers are required for the assembly of each car.

   G. The design phase is significantly shortened.

   H. The need for high-cost tool-steel dies is eliminated.

   J. The expense of painting steel body parts is drastically reduced.

IF YOU FINISH BEFORE TIME IS CALLED, CHECK YOUR WORK ON THIS SECTION ONLY. DO NOT WORK ON ANY OTHER SECTION IN THE TEST.

Science Test

Time: 35 Minutes

40 Questions

Directions: Each of the seven passages in this test is followed by several questions. After you read each passage, select the correct choice for each of the questions that follow the passage. Refer to the passage as often as necessary to answer the questions. You may NOT use a calculator on this test.

Passage I

Materials exist in and transition between gaseous, liquid, or solid phases under different temperature and pressure conditions. Transitions can occur between any two phases (Figure 1).

Figure 1: Phases and Transitions of Materials

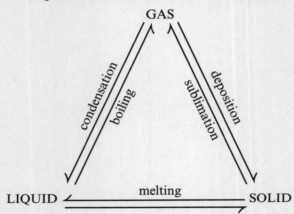

The conditions under which each phase occurs or transitions can be summarized in a phase diagram (Figure 2). A phase diagram succinctly illustrates the phase of any compound at a given pressure and temperature, and the transition points between each phase. Of particular interest are phases and transitions of a compound at 1 atmosphere or atm (normal pressure at sea level); the conditions of the "triple point" where a compound can exist as a gas, a liquid, and a solid (and transition between each) simultaneously; and the "critical point" above which a compound will not condense from a gas to a liquid at any pressure. Figure 2 shows the phase diagram for water.

GO ON TO THE NEXT PAGE

Figure 2: Phase Diagram of Water

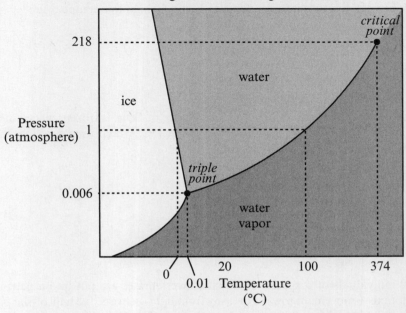

1. According to Figure 1, what is the term for when a compound transitions from a gas to a solid?

   A.   condensation
   B.   deposition
   C.   freezing
   D.   sublimation

2. According to Figure 2, at what temperature can you expect to observe the sublimation of water at 1 atm of pressure?

   F.   0.01°C
   G.   0°C
   H.   100°C
   J.   Water does not sublimate at 1 atm of pressure.

3. According to the passage and Figure 2, what are the temperature and pressure at which water will exist as and transition between being a gas, a liquid, and a solid simultaneously?

   A.   0°C at 1 atm
   B.   0.01°C at 0.006 atm
   C.   0°C at 0.006 atm
   D.   0.01°C at 1 atm

Practice Test 3

GO ON TO THE NEXT PAGE

4. Water is heated in a pressurized container to 400°C. According to the passage and Figure 2, how much pressure must be exerted to cause it to condense to liquid form at that temperature?

  F. 1 atm
  G. 218 atm
  H. 374 atm
  J. It cannot condense into water at that temperature.

5. Freeze drying is a process in which an item, such as a piece of fruit, is frozen, placed in a vacuum to reduce the pressure to about 0.006 atm, and then heated to about 1°C. Which term describes the phase shift of water as it leaves the piece of fruit in this process?

  A. The water sublimates.
  B. The water boils.
  C. The water condenses.
  D. The water melts.

Passage II

Approximately 300 individuals of a species of aquatic invertebrates are put into a petri dish full of water. A student studying phototaxis—movement toward or away from light—covers one half of the petri dish with opaque black plastic and shines a white light on the other side of the dish (Figure 1). She uses an undermounted camera to record the locations of all the invertebrates throughout the experiment.

Figure 1: Experimental Setup

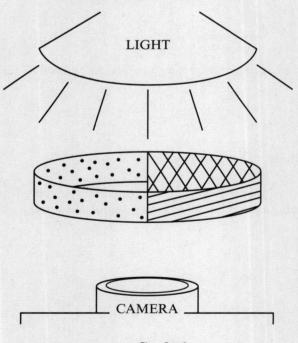

Study 1

The student leaves the petri dish in total darkness for five minutes and then takes a photograph. She turns the light on for five minutes and then takes another photograph. She turns the light off for an additional five minutes and repeats the photograph. Lastly, she switches the side of the dish that is covered with black plastic, turns the light back on, and takes another photograph after a five-minute wait. She repeats this cycle, permitting the animals

GO ON TO THE NEXT PAGE

to rest an hour between cycles, until she has ten photographs each of the fully dark and half-dark petri dish. She counts the number of individuals in each half of the dish and enters the averages into Table 1.

Table 1

Invertebrates	Light On		Light Off	
	Dark Half	Light Half	Covered Half	Uncovered Half
Daphnia magna	55	235	149	141
Aëdes aegypti (larvae)	164	135	156	143
Artemia salina	278	26	154	150

Study 2

The student repeats the experiment four times, replacing the white light with a blue, green, yellow, or red light. She summarizes her results in Figure 2.

Figure 2: Response of Invertebrates to Light

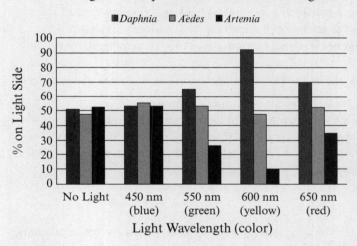

6. According to Table 1, which statement correctly describes how *Daphnia* and *Artemia* respond to white light?

   F. *Daphnia* move toward light; *Artemia* move away from light.
   G. *Daphnia* move away from light; *Artemia* move toward light.
   H. *Daphnia* and *Artemia* both move toward light.
   J. *Daphnia* and *Artemia* both move away from light.

7. Reviewing the experimental design, why does the student switch which side is covered by plastic every other trial?

   A. To keep the invertebrates moving constantly so they will switch sides when the light is turned on.
   B. To ensure the invertebrates cannot guess which side will be light or dark before the light is turned on.
   C. To control for factors other than light exposure that might cause the invertebrates to favor one side of the dish over another.
   D. To make sure the invertebrates do not settle into another activity such as eating or sleeping.

8. Do the results of Study 2 support or conflict with the results of Study 1?

    F. Support, because all of the species were attracted to light in both studies.

    G. Conflict, because the responses of *Daphnia* and *Artemia* shown in Figure 2 are reversed from what is shown in Table 1.

    H. Support, because all three species show the same pattern of response to light in both studies, though they do not all respond to all colors of light.

    J. Conflict, because in Study 1 *Daphnia* and *Artemia* responded to blue light, and in Study 2 they did not.

9. According to Figure 2, to which wavelength of light do the invertebrates respond most strongly?

    A. 450 nanometers

    B. 550 nanometers

    C. 600 nanometers

    D. 650 nanometers

10. Which statement is a potential explanation of the phototactic responses observed in Study 2?

    F. *Daphnia* can sense blue (450 nanometers) light, but *Artemia* cannot.

    G. *Artemia* can sense blue (450 nanometers) light, but *Daphnia* cannot.

    H. Both *Daphnia* and *Artemia* can sense blue (450 nanometers) light.

    J. Neither *Daphnia* nor *Artemia* can sense blue (450 nanometers) light.

11. According to Table 1 and Figure 2, what conclusion can be drawn about the phototactic response of *Aëdes*?

    A. *Aëdes* do not have a consistent phototactic response.

    B. *Aëdes* have a positive (moving toward light) phototactic response.

    C. *Aëdes* have a negative (moving away from light) phototactic response.

    D. About half of *Aëdes* have a positive phototactic response, and the other half have a negative phototactic response.

Passage III

Mass spectrometry is a technique used to identify compounds by the mass-charge ratio of their component molecules or atoms. Compounds to be analyzed are vaporized and then stripped of one or, occasionally, more electrons. These charged particles are propelled down a bent tube, with a strong electromagnet positioned at the bend (Figure 1).

Figure 1: Diagram of a Mass Spectrometer

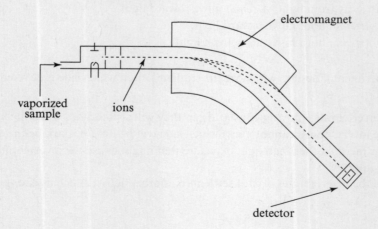

GO ON TO THE NEXT PAGE

Just as the wind can blow a ball to one side as it flies through the air, the electromagnet pushes the charged particles away from it, bending their trajectories. And just as the wind would blow a tennis ball farther than a bowling ball, charged molecules or atoms with smaller masses or stronger charges are pushed further aside than those with larger masses or weaker charges.

$$m/z = \frac{\text{Mass of the particle}}{\text{Charge of the particle}}$$

The amount that a particle's trajectory is bent by the electromagnet can be predicted from its mass-charge ratio (m/z), and the strength of the electromagnet. If a particle is repelled precisely the right amount to navigate the bend in the machine, it will be detected at the end of the tube. The electromagnet, therefore, can be tuned to detect particles of specific mass-charge ratios. The output of a mass spectrometer shows the abundance of particles in the sample that belong to different mass-charge ratios (Figure 2).

Figure 2: Data Output from a Mass Spectrometer

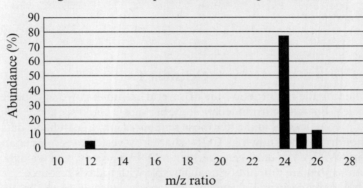

12. Using your knowledge of atomic structure, and the information in the passage, what is the charge of particles being detected in the mass spectrometer?

    F.   Negative, because they have extra electron(s).
    G.   Positive, because they are missing electron(s).
    H.   Neutral, because they lose their charge if they hit the sides of the tube.
    J.   50 percent positive and 50 percent negative, because they are turned into ions.

13. According to the formula given, which has the larger mass/charge ratio—a carbon ion with a mass of 12 and a charge of +1 or a magnesium ion with a mass of 24 and a charge of +2?

    A.   Carbon
    B.   Magnesium
    C.   They are about the same.
    D.   It is impossible to tell.

14. Which of the following statements is a correct conclusion that can be drawn from Figure 2?

    F.   About 80 percent of the particles have a mass-charge ratio of 24.
    G.   Sample 24 has the much larger particles than the other samples.
    H.   This sample is contaminated by small amounts of other particles.
    J.   There are at least four different elements in this sample.

GO ON TO THE NEXT PAGE

Practice Test 3

15. Magnesium normally has a mass of 24, though it has two other common isotopes with masses 25 and 26. If a sample of pure magnesium (Mg) were analyzed, and the output looked like Figure 2, how would you interpret the small signal with an m/z ratio of 12?

   A. It is probably an error or impurity.
   B. It is probably the fraction of ^{24}Mg that lost 2 electrons instead of 1 and, thus, has a charge of 2.
   C. It is probably a small amount of Mg that split in half during analysis.
   D. It is probably a fourth isotope of Mg.

16. Most oxygen has a mass of 16. If a sample of magnesium oxide (MgO) were included in the sample shown in Figure 2, at which m/z ratio would the full MgO molecules missing two electrons be detected?

   F. 16
   G. 20
   H. 24
   J. 40

Passage IV

Scientist 1

Imagine a database containing the full genetic code of several exemplars of every species of organism on earth. That dream is still out of reach, but with current technology, biologists could sequence a single common gene from several hundred thousand different species and enter those sequences into a searchable database. Although no gene will be perfect, the mitochondrial gene known as COI—shared by vertebrates, plants and bacteria alike—is the gene of choice for this effort. With a standard gene, termed a DNA barcode, and a single repository for the data, scientists could study questions that are difficult or unachievable with today's resources.

Using a database of DNA barcodes, small fragments of insects collected from the nose of an airplane or the stomach of a bird could be sequenced and compared for identification and study. Cryptic species—groups of species that all look alike but are actually not the same—could be easily distinguished from each other with minimal specialized knowledge or effort. New species could be named in days, rather than following years of careful comparison. We could monitor and study more environmental, ecological, and evolutionary trends, more quickly and easily than ever before.

A full database of DNA barcodes stands to become one of the most important resources available to biologists today.

Scientist 2

DNA barcoding is a waste of time and money that will lead to spurious and misleading results from scientists with a poor understanding of the limitations and constraints from which the single-gene approach suffers.

It is incorrect to suggest that all species can be identified from a single gene—although there are many instances in which that is the case, the "one gene fits all" approach of barcoding greatly oversimplifies the task of properly differentiating closely related species. The further suggestion that a single-gene sequence could be used as the primary identifier of a new species completely disregards the nuances of modern species concepts, as well as the work of taxonomists who use multiple lines of evidence to identify and distinguish new species.

Although a comprehensive database of a single gene from many thousands of species would be informative and useful to those who understand its limitations, DNA barcoding will not be the shortcut solution its proponents are envisioning.

17. What is Scientist 1 proposing that biologists should do?

   A. Sequence the entire genome of every organism on earth.
   B. Sequence as many genes as possible, from as many organisms as possible, and share the results.
   C. Sequence the same gene across many species and record the results in a single database.
   D. Sequence the unique barcode that exists in the genetic code of all organisms and record the results in a single database.

GO ON TO THE NEXT PAGE

18. How would you characterize Scientist 2's opinion of Scientist 1's proposal?

    F. Scientist 2 opposes Scientist 1's proposal because she thinks it cannot be done.

    G. Scientist 2 supports Scientist 1's proposal because she thinks it will be informative and somewhat useful.

    H. Scientist 2 opposes Scientist 1's proposal because she thinks it will not be as useful as proposed and may lead to incorrect results.

    J. Scientist 2 supports Scientist 1's proposal because she thinks it will improve how species are identified and distinguished.

19. Has Scientist 1 made a new discovery?

    A. Yes, Scientist 1 has discovered a new gene.

    B. No, Scientist 1 is proposing a new use for DNA.

    C. Yes, Scientist 1 has discovered a new species.

    D. No, Scientist 1 is proposing a standardized repository of genetic data.

20. Which of the following compromises is likely to be agreeable to both scientists?

    F. Quantify the accuracy of DNA barcodes for assigning samples to different species and do not rely on barcodes where this technique yields inaccurate results.

    G. Confirm that the mitochondrial gene COI is the single best gene for this effort.

    H. Encourage each scientist to sequence whichever gene is best for the group of organisms with which they are working, rather than standardizing the COI sequence.

    J. Use barcodes only to confirm species identities, not to identify new species.

21. What is Scientist 2's biggest concern with the barcoding effort?

    A. The mitochondrial gene COI is a poor choice for the barcoding effort; a different gene should be selected.

    B. Some people will draw incorrect conclusions from DNA barcode data because they do not understand the limitations of a single-gene approach.

    C. Species cannot be identified from any single gene.

    D. A comprehensive database of a single gene from thousands of species is not a useful tool for biologists.

22. On what point do the two scientists agree?

    F. The mitochondrial gene COI is the perfect choice for the barcoding effort.

    G. Each species has a unique COI gene sequence.

    H. Many species can be identified from a single gene.

    J. Too much time is spent trying to identify new species.

23. If the technology became available to sequence the entire genome (every gene instead of only one) of hundreds of thousands of species on earth, what might Scientist 2's stance be then?

    A. Scientist 2 would fully embrace that approach because it would eliminate her concern about using only a single gene.

    B. Scientist 2 would acknowledge that many of her objections had been addressed, but would still say that we should use multiple lines of evidence (not just genes) to identify new species.

    C. Scientist 2 would still object on the same principle that a many-gene approach is not significantly better than a single-gene approach for identifying species.

    D. Scientist 2 already embraces this barcoding effort and would see this as yet another improvement to the database of genetic information.

GO ON TO THE NEXT PAGE

Passage V

The magnetic field of volcanic rock retains the orientation of the earth's magnetic field at the time the rock solidified. Since the magnetic field of the earth switches polarity on average every half-million years, the magnetic field of some volcanic deposits is reversed relative to the earth's current state.

Study 1

A geologist measures the strength of the magnetic field along the ocean floor over a 100-kilometer stretch in the middle of the Atlantic Ocean (Figure 1). When the underlying ocean floor shares the same polarity as the earth, he knows to expect his measurements to be higher than the earth's field; likewise, when the underlying ocean floor has the opposite polarity to earth, the measured field will be weaker than earth's field.

Figure 1: Variation in the Magnetic Field of the Ocean Crust, Relative to That of the Earth

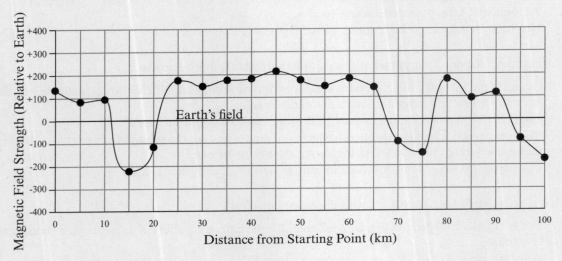

Study 2

During the same expedition, the geologist retrieves samples of the ocean floor every 10 kilometers and calculates the age of the rock using an isotopic technique. He records his results in Figure 2.

Figure 2: Age of the Ocean Across the 100 km Sampling Path

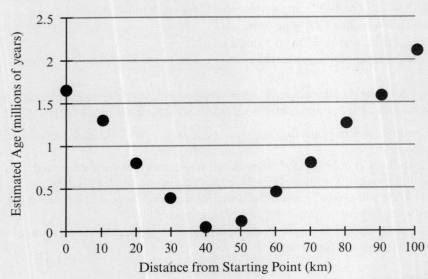

GO ON TO THE NEXT PAGE

24. Referring to Figure 1, which statement is a correct interpretation of the magnetic field data point measured 15 kilometers from the survey's starting point.

    F. The earth's magnetic field is very weak at that location.

    G. The polarity of the magnetic field of ocean floor is opposite to that of earth as a whole at that location.

    H. The strength of the magnetic field of the ocean floor is weaker than that of earth as a whole at that location.

    J. The earth's magnetic field weakened momentarily at the time that measurement was taken.

25. According to Figure 2, approximately how many kilometers from the starting point is newly formed rock likely to be found?

    A. 40–45 kilometers from the starting point

    B. 50–55 kilometers from the starting point

    C. 60–65 kilometers from the starting point

    D. 70–75 kilometers from the starting point

26. Referring to Figures 1 and 2, which of the following statements correctly describes the relationship between the magnetic fields and the ages of the rocks?

    F. Older rock samples have stronger magnetic fields.

    G. Older rock samples have weaker magnetic fields.

    H. Older rock samples' magnetic fields have the opposite polarity compared to current rock samples.

    J. Older rock samples' magnetic fields may have either the same or opposite polarity compared to current rock samples.

27. According to the two figures, approximately how many years ago did earth's magnetic field most recently switch polarity?

    A. 100,000 years ago

    B. 750,000 years ago

    C. 15,000,000 years ago

    D. 45,000,000 million years ago

28. If the pattern in the figures remains consistent, what would you expect the strength of the magnetic field and the age of the rock sample to be at −10 kilometers from the starting point?

    F. The magnetic field would be stronger than earth's normal field, and the rock would be more than 1.6 million years old.

    G. The magnetic field would be weaker than earth's normal field, and the rock would be less than 1.6 million years old.

    H. The magnetic field would be stronger than earth's normal field, and the rock would be less than 1.6 million years old.

    J. The magnetic field would be weaker than earth's normal field, and the rock would be more than 1.6 million years old.

29. The geologist calculates that about 25 kilometers of new ocean crust is being formed every 750,000 years. About how many years does it take for 1 meter of ocean crust to form?

    A. 3 years

    B. 30 years

    C. 3,000 years

    D. 30,000 years

GO ON TO THE NEXT PAGE

Passage VI

The Arctic, at the earth's northern pole, is geographically quite different from the Antarctic on the other side of the earth. Most notably, the Arctic is mostly water, surrounded by land, whereas the Antarctic is mostly land, surrounded by water. This difference, and many other factors, can lead to differences in how the poles respond to climate change.

Satellite photographs and on-the-ground measurements of the amount of polar surface area covered by ice (termed "ice extent") have allowed scientists to track changes to earth's polar ice caps over the past 30 years (Figures 1 and 2).

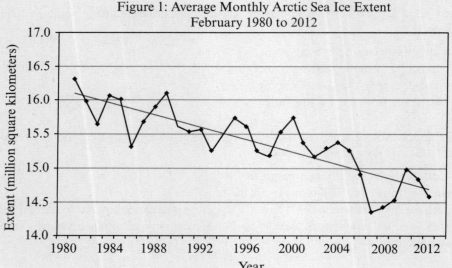

Figure 1: Average Monthly Arctic Sea Ice Extent
February 1980 to 2012

Figure 2: Average Monthly Antarctic Sea Ice Extent

Ice extent is a two-dimensional measure. Ice mass, though more difficult to track, gives a more complete picture of the amount of ice present, because it also accounts for the thickness of the ice. Figure 3 shows measurements of the Antarctic ice mass over the past decade.

GO ON TO THE NEXT PAGE

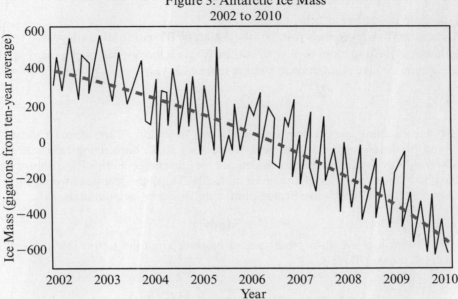

Figure 3: Antarctic Ice Mass
2002 to 2010

30. According to Figure 1, accounting for seasonal and annual fluctuations, how has the average Arctic ice extent changed over the past 30 years?

    F.   The ice extent has decreased, on average.
    G.   The ice extent has increased, on average.
    H.   The ice extent has decreased, and then increased, on average.
    J.   The ice extent has not changed, on average.

31. According to Figure 2, accounting for seasonal and annual fluctuations, how has the average Antarctic ice extent changed over the past 30 years?

    A.   The ice extent has decreased, on average.
    B.   The ice extent has increased, on average.
    C.   The ice extent has increased, and then decreased, on average.
    D.   The ice extent has not changed, on average.

32. According to the Figures 1 and 2, how does ice extent compare between the poles currently?

    F.   The Arctic currently has a greater ice extent, on average.
    G.   The Antarctic currently has a greater ice extent, on average.
    H.   The poles have roughly equal areas covered in ice.
    J.   The ice extent cannot be compared between the figures given.

33. According to Figure 3, which statement accurately describes the changes in the Antarctic ice mass?

    A.   The Antarctic ice mass has increased over the past decade.
    B.   The Antarctic ice mass has decreased over the past decade.
    C.   The Antarctic ice mass increased and then decreased over the past decade.
    D.   The Antarctic ice mass has not changed over the past decade.

GO ON TO THE NEXT PAGE

Practice Test 3

34. According to the figures, what changes in polar ice have occurred in recent decades?

    F.   There has been no change at either pole.

    G.   The Arctic is melting more each year, but the Antarctic is melting less each year.

    H.   The Antarctic is melting more each year, but the Arctic is melting less each year.

    J.   Both the Arctic and the Antarctic are melting more each year.

Passage VII

A dermatologist is researching laser tattoo removal. In this procedure, lasers direct a short blast of photons within a narrow band of wavelengths into the skin, where they strike both living cells and tattoo inks. These photons are absorbed only by molecules able to absorb the specific energy levels of the photons emitted—that is, photons within the absorption spectrum of the given molecule. Thus, an ideal laser would target predominately tattoo ink and not critical bio-molecules like hemoglobin in the blood or melanin in the skin.

Study 1

The dermatologist determines the absorption spectra of three common tattoo inks, as well as melanin and hemoglobin, and records these in Table 1.

Table 1: Absorption Spectra of Three Tattoo Inks

Sample	Maximum Absorption Wavelength (nanometers)	Absorptive Ranges (nanometers)
Black Ink	750	350–1000+ (more absorption toward longer wavelengths)
Red Ink	540	400–650
Green Ink	700	550–900
Hemoglobin (from red blood cells)	420	400–450; 520–580 (second discrete range)
Melanin (brown skin pigment)	380	370–700 (higher at shorter wavelengths)

Study 2

The dermatologist tests the efficacy of two common types of lasers on the tattoos of several patients. She records the wavelength of the laser used, the average amount of tattoo ink removal after five treatments, as well as the level of skin reddening (a sign of damaged hemoglobin) or skin whitening (a sign of damaged melanin) in Table 2.

Table 2: Efficacy of Two Common Laser Types

Laser Wavelength	Ink Color	Ink Reduction	Skin Reddening	Skin Whitening
532	Black	30%	High	High
1064	Black	75%	Low	Low
532	Red	68%	High	High
1064	Red	5%	Low	Low
532	Green	0%	High	High
1064	Green	15%	Low	Low

GO ON TO THE NEXT PAGE

35. According to Table 1, which of the samples tested has the broadest absorption spectrum?

    A. Black ink

    B. Red ink

    C. Green ink

    D. Melanin

36. According to the passage, the dermatologist is seeking a laser that emits a wavelength that can satisfy which of the following criteria?

    F. The laser energy is absorbed by the ink pigments and is also absorbed by melanin or hemoglobin.

    G. The laser energy is absorbed by the ink pigments but is not absorbed by melanin or hemoglobin.

    H. The laser energy is not absorbed by the ink pigments but is absorbed by melanin or hemoglobin.

    J. The laser energy is not absorbed by the ink pigments, nor is it absorbed by melanin or hemoglobin.

37. According to Table 2, which wavelengths are most effective on black and red inks?

    A. The 532 nanometers laser is best for both black ink and red ink.

    B. The 532 nanometers laser is best for black ink, and the 1064 nanometers laser is best for red ink.

    C. The 1064 nanometers laser is best for black ink, and the 532 nanometers laser is best for red ink.

    D. The 1064 nanometers laser is best for both black ink and red ink.

38. According to Table 2, the 532 nanometers laser has a side effect of damaging both hemoglobin and melanin. Referring to Table 1 for additional information, why might this happen?

    F. Hemoglobin and melanin both have absorption peaks below 532 nanometers.

    G. Hemoglobin and melanin are both bio-molecules that occur naturally in the body.

    H. Hemoglobin and melanin both absorb light with a 532 nanometer wavelength.

    J. Hemoglobin and melanin both have broad absorption spectra.

39. According to Table 1, red ink has an absorption spectrum that includes short and medium wavelength colors such as blue and yellow, with a peak at about 540 nanometers, which is a green light. Red light has the longest wavelength of the visible spectrum, at around 650–750 nanometers. According to your knowledge of color and light, explain how the color of the ink relates to its absorption spectrum.

    A. The visible color of a compound is the light that is absorbed by that compound. So to appear red, a compound must absorb the color red.

    B. The visible color of a compound is a mix of the light that is absorbed and reflected by that compound. So to appear red, a compound must absorb and reflect the color red.

    C. The visible color of a compound is the light that is reflected, not absorbed, by that compound. So to appear red, a compound must absorb all colors except red.

    D. The visible color of a compound is not related to the absorption spectrum of that compound.

40. The dermatologist decides to test a third laser that emits light with a 755 nanometer wavelength. What do you predict about the efficacy of this laser when used on green ink?

    F. The laser will be effective at removing the ink and will have minimal side effects.

    G. The laser will be effective at removing the ink but will damage the hemoglobin and melanin.

    H. The laser will not be effective at removing the ink and will damage the hemoglobin and melanin.

    J. The laser will not be effective at removing the ink but will have minimal side effects.

IF YOU FINISH BEFORE TIME IS CALLED, CHECK YOUR WORK ON THIS SECTION ONLY. DO NOT WORK ON ANY OTHER SECTION IN THE TEST.

Practice Test 3

Scoring the Practice Test

The following section will assist you in scoring and analyzing your practice test results. Use the answer key to score your results and then carefully review the analysis charts to identify your strengths and weakness. Finally, read through the answer explanations starting in the study guide on page 550 to clarify the solutions to the problems.

Answer Key

English Test

1. D	14. H	27. B	40. J	53. D	66. F
2. G	15. C	28. H	41. C	54. H	67. A
3. C	16. H	29. D	42. H	55. A	68. J
4. G	17. D	30. H	43. B	56. J	69. C
5. C	18. H	31. D	44. F	57. D	70. G
6. J	19. B	32. G	45. D	58. H	71. D
7. A	20. G	33. A	46. H	59. A	72. F
8. H	21. B	34. H	47. A	60. J	73. D
9. C	22. J	35. D	48. J	61. B	74. G
10. H	23. B	36. F	49. B	62. H	75. A
11. D	24. J	37. B	50. F	63. D	
12. G	25. D	38. J	51. C	64. G	
13. D	26. J	39. A	52. G	65. D	

Mathematics Test

1. E	11. D	21. E	31. E	41. C	51. C
2. G	12. G	22. J	32. G	42. H	52. F
3. C	13. C	23. C	33. D	43. D	53. C
4. J	14. F	24. G	34. J	44. G	54. H
5. E	15. D	25. B	35. B	45. C	55. B
6. G	16. G	26. G	36. G	46. H	56. J
7. D	17. D	27. C	37. C	47. E	57. B
8. H	18. J	28. H	38. K	48. J	58. G
9. A	19. E	29. E	39. B	49. E	59. B
10. F	20. K	30. H	40. H	50. F	60. K

Reading Test

1. D	**8.** G	**15.** A	**22.** F	**29.** B	**36.** J
2. H	**9.** C	**16.** J	**23.** D	**30.** H	**37.** B
3. B	**10.** F	**17.** D	**24.** F	**31.** A	**38.** H
4. F	**11.** A	**18.** J	**25.** A	**32.** H	**39.** D
5. B	**12.** G	**19.** A	**26.** J	**33.** C	**40.** H
6. J	**13.** B	**20.** H	**27.** C	**34.** F	
7. A	**14.** G	**21.** D	**28.** H	**35.** A	

Science Test

1. B	**8.** H	**15.** B	**22.** H	**29.** B	**36.** G
2. J	**9.** C	**16.** G	**23.** B	**30.** F	**37.** C
3. B	**10.** J	**17.** C	**24.** G	**31.** B	**38.** H
4. J	**11.** A	**18.** H	**25.** A	**32.** F	**39.** C
5. A	**12.** G	**19.** D	**26.** J	**33.** B	**40.** F
6. F	**13.** C	**20.** F	**27.** B	**34.** J	
7. C	**14.** F	**21.** B	**28.** J	**35.** A	

Charting and Analyzing Your Test Results

The first step in analyzing your test results is to chart your answers. Use the following chart to identify your strengths and areas of improvement. Complete the process of evaluating your and analyzing problems in each area. Re-evaluate your results as you look for trends in the types of errors (repeated errors), and look for low scores in results in *specific* subject areas. This re-examination and analysis is a tremendous asset to help you maximize your best possible score. The answers and explanations following these charts will provide you clarification to help you solve these types of problems in the future.

Practice Test 3 Analysis Sheet

Test	Number Possible	Number Correct	Number Incorrect		
			(A) Simple Mistake	(B) Misread Problem	(C) Lack of Knowledge
English Test	75				
Mathematics Test	60				
Reading Test	40				
Science Test	40				
Total Possible Explanations for Incorrect Answers: Columns A, B, and C					
Total Number of Questions Correct and Incorrect	215	Add the total number of correct questions here: _____	Add columns A, B, and C for total number of incorrect questions here: _____		

Practice Test 3: Answers and Explanations

English Test

Passage I

1. **D.** The problem here is that a comma, not a semicolon, should precede "which" in the original version. Dependent clauses (Choice A) or phrases (Choice B) are separated from an independent clause with a comma, not a semicolon. Choices C and D both correct the problem, but Choice D is a better choice because it is less wordy than Choice C.

2. **G.** Choice G corrects the problem of Choice F, which is setting off a restrictive phrase with commas. A restrictive phrase is one that is necessary to clarify meaning by identifying the noun (in this case, "signals") it modifies. When a phrase is nonrestrictive, it adds information and can be set off in commas: "The house across the street, a large two-bedroom, took longer to sell than ours."

3. **C.** Choice C is the most economical of all the choices. Using "could" rather than "was able to" is less wordy and more direct. Placing "from start to finish" after "on earth" is smoother than Choice D, which also incorrectly adds a comma after "finish."

4. **G.** The best choice is G. Most importantly, it replaces the adjective "slow" with the adverb "slowly." The adverb modifies the verb "unfolded." Choice J includes a dangling participle, and the sentence order in Choice H is awkward.

5. **C.** Choice C replaces the passive voice of the verb ("are called by astronomers") with the active voice: "Astronomers use." When possible, the active voice is preferred. Also, "star-obliterating" is correctly hyphenated; it acts as a compound adjective describing "events." Choice D also incorrectly separates subject and verb ("events are") with a comma.

6. **J.** Choice J is the only choice that places the clause "when they do occur" next to the noun it modifies: "black holes." The original version and choices G and H place the clause so that it logically appears to modify "astronomers."

7. **A.** The original version is best. There is no reason to replace "normally" with "it is normal" (Choice B). The verb tenses in choices C and D are not called for; the sentence is appropriately in the present tense. Choice C is also wordy.

8. **H.** The participial phrase "producing intense flares of radiation" is the best choice here, but it should not be introduced by "and" as the original is. The phrase is a modifier, not a verb (Choice G), and J unnecessarily adds "that are."

9. **C.** Choice C is the best choice for an added sentence; it refers specifically to tidal disruptions, which are the subject of the paragraph. The other choices, while related to black holes or adding historical information, are not specifically concerned with the importance of tidal disruptions.

10. **H.** Of the choices offered for this sentence, Choice H is best. First, the subject of "think" is an unstated, but understood, "you." This construction avoids the misplaced infinitive phrase; "To understand this pull" refers to you, the reader, not to the ocean tides. Choice G includes a dangling participle and also doesn't cover the meaning of the original version. Choice J includes a sentence fragment: "Like the black hole's pull on stars."

11. **D.** The original version is a run-on sentence or comma splice. A punctuation mark stronger than a comma (a period or a semicolon) is needed to separate two independent clauses.

   Choice C corrects the problem with a period, but uses two words ("entirely and completely") that mean the same thing. Choice B creates a fragment by beginning the second clause with "Because." Choice D is therefore the best choice, using a semicolon to divide the two clauses and avoiding redundancy.

12. **G.** This choice corrects two problems of the original version. First, the verb should be in the past tense. The sentence is describing a completed past event. Second, "Mercury" should not be enclosed in commas. It is necessary to identify the planet being mentioned (restrictive); it does not simply add information that isn't necessary (nonrestrictive). None of the other choices corrects both of these problems.

13. **D.** This choice uses the correct participle of the verb ("torn"). "Tore" is the simple past tense. Also, "holes" should be the possessive "hole's."

14. **H.** In this choice, Suvi Gezari is followed by an appositive, which is a noun or pronoun—often with modifiers—that follows another noun or pronoun to identify it. Appositives of several words should be enclosed in commas. Choice H shortens "that was concerned with" to the more succinct "about."

15. **C.** Paragraph 4 describes how the pull of gravity from the black hole destroyed the star. This paragraph smoothly follows the first paragraph. Paragraph 3 uses the analogy of the moon's gravitational force on the tides to explain gravity's pull in a black hole, and so it logically follows paragraph 4. Paragraph 2 describes the rare opportunity for astronomers to view a black hole. It works well as a final paragraph.

Passage II

16. **H.** The objective case of the pronoun ("me") is correct. It is the object of the infinitive "to tell." Reading the sentence without "my sister Carrie" makes the correct pronoun case obvious. The progressive "be telling" in Choice G is also not appropriate here. In Choice J, the pronoun case is wrong but also the phrase "whose name is Carrie" is wordy.

17. **D.** "Might of" is incorrect in the original version. The phrase is "might have." Sometimes, particularly in speech, "of" replaces "have," but this is incorrect. Choice B makes the same mistake, and changing "might" to "may well" doesn't help. Choice C is not incorrect, but Choice D is more succinct and direct.

18. **H.** Replacing the pronoun "him" with "Ed" is a good idea in this sentence because two men are being discussed. The original is not wrong, but in this case clarification of the second pronoun is a better choice. The verb tense changes in choices G and J are not called for. Using the present tense is consistent with the next sentence.

19. **B.** Using the reflexive pronoun "himself" is correct because the verb is referring back to father, not to Uncle Ed. The use of the quotation marks is also correct; it is consistent with father's calling Ed "the wild one." These are both direct quotes. Choice C is wordy.

20. **G.** The original version uses the wrong past participle of the verb: "ride, rode, has ridden." Choice G uses the simple past tense, which is parallel to the other items in the series. Choice H uses the wrong number in the verb; the subject is singular. In Choice J, the wrong tense and the wrong participle are used, and "rodeo" should not be capitalized because it is not a proper noun.

21. **B.** In this item of the series, the present tense is correct because of the word "still." The two previous items are in the past tense because they are completed actions, but the present tense is used here for an action that is still going on. The adverb "well" replaces the incorrect adjective "good"; "well" modifies the verb "plays."

22. **J.** "Unique" is an absolute term; something is either one-of-a-kind or not. Therefore, the modifier "very" shouldn't be used. Also in Choice J "and" replaces the wordier conjunctive phrases "as well as" and "in addition to." The semicolon in Choice H creates a fragment. Finally, the verb tense in Choice J is correct. In the original version, "will have ever known" is illogical, and the past tense "knew" (Choice H) is inconsistent with the context.

23. **B.** The original creates a fragment by using a semicolon before a dependent clause. Choice B correctly replaces the semicolon with a comma. It also succinctly replaces a "that" clause and a "which" clause (choices C and D).

24. **J.** The phrase adds information that isn't necessary to the meaning of the sentence. It should be enclosed in commas. Choice G uses only one comma, and Choice H adds unnecessary words in addition to leaving out the second comma.

25. **D.** This sentence provides a colorful detail about Katmandu and illustrates Uncle Ed's story-telling ability. It doesn't, however, help identify Katmandu's location, Choice C. There is no advantage to omitting this sentence.

26. **J.** The original version incorrectly includes "being" with "inexpensive." "Being" doesn't correctly parallel the verb "was" in the first part of the sentence. Choice H adds another clause, which makes the sentence seem strung out; Choice J is less awkward. Choice G actually changes the meaning of the sentence.

27. **B.** This choice eliminates a dangling participle by beginning the next clause with "he thought," making it clear that "he" is doing the comparing. Choice C also eliminates the dangling participle by including "it" in the opening clause, but it is awkward and wordy. Choice D does not correct the problem with the original version.

28. **H.** The problem with the original version is that it changes the person of the pronoun in the second part of the sentence: "one . . . you." Choice H corrects this. Choice G, in addition to being inconsistent with the pronoun, uses the wrong verb. After a contrary-to-fact "if" clause, the subjunctive "were" is correct. Choice J is wordy.

29. **D.** The correct idiom is "complied with," not "complied to," as in the original version and the other choices. The contrary-to-fact verb form ("had not complied") is also correct.

30. **H.** The final paragraph more logically follows the first paragraph, which ends with the speaker's comment about his father's view of Uncle Ed and himself. Paragraph 5 expands on the differences and the speaker's father's feelings.

Passage III

31. **D.** In the original version, two independent clauses are joined by "and"; this is correct, but a comma should precede "and." In Choice B, the independent clauses are joined by a semicolon followed by "and"; this is also correct, but both choices are also less concise than Choice D, which is the best selection. In Choice C, subject and verb are separated by a comma, which is incorrect.

32. G. Choice G is the best choice; "because" is all that is necessary to make the point. The phrase "in which" (Choice F) does not logically fit here, and Choice H is awkward: "because" and "of the reason" repeat the same idea. Choice J is not incorrect, but it is wordy.

33. A. The original version is best. The clause "who recalled a particular model" is restrictive, necessary to the meaning. Therefore, it should not be enclosed in commas (Choice B). The change to "which" in Choice C is not a good one; because the manufacturer "says" something, "who" is a better choice than the nonhuman "which." Along with the incorrect use of commas in Choice D, there is also no reason for the tense change.

34. H. This choice eliminates the unnecessary "there is/there are" construction, and by doing so also corrects an agreement problem. "There is" refers to "things," which would make "there are" correct, not "there is."

35. D. The problem with the original version is that it is a run-on sentence, or comma splice. All three choices correct the run-on. However, choices B and C do not change "lays" to "lies," which is the correct verb. ("Lay" takes an object and "lie" does not. "I lay my cell phone on the table," "I lie with my cell phone next to me.")

36. F. The original version is correct. "That has been recalled" is necessary to the meaning and shouldn't be enclosed in commas. All of the other choices use commas incorrectly.

37. B. Choice B is the best choice. "Taking" is parallel in structure to "selling." The other choices add words, but none of them corrects the faulty parallel construction.

38. J. Choice J is the best choice. The sentence is a question and should be followed by a question mark. Choices F, G, and H are also questions that are not followed by question marks.

39. A. The original version is correct, and it is the most succinct choice. The use of "they" in Choice B is incorrect; it simply repeats the subject of the verb. In Choice C, the change of "are" to the conditional "would be" is inconsistent with the meaning of the sentence. Choice D changes tense for no reason, in addition to being wordy.

40. J. The original version seems at first to be best. But the problem is an indefinite "it." The sentence doesn't make clear what "it" refers to. Choice J clarifies the sentence by using the gerund phrase (verbal noun phrase) "finding out." The other choices do not provide a reference for "it."

41. C. Choice C is both correct and simple. "The fact" is unnecessary in all the other choices. "Ensure of" is also not idiomatic.

42. H. This wordy clause is corrected most efficiently in Choice H, which uses a short phrase: "recall and repair status." The other choices, as well as the original, are wordy. Choice J incorrectly follows "system" with a semicolon, which creates a fragment.

43. B. The original version contains both "now" and "currently"; this is redundant. "In the process of" is wordy. Choice B says the same thing much more concisely. Both choices C and D are also wordy.

44. F. Sentence 5 not only could but also should be eliminated. It is off the main topic of recalls and used cars and instead provides advice to anyone buying a used car.

This irrelevant information affects the coherence of the paragraph, and the sentence should be deleted here.

45. D. This sentence most logically precedes the advice that used car owners should take the job of finding out about their car's history "into their own hands." That advice is a logical follow-up to the sentence stating that currently there is no law requiring a car seller to inform a car buyer about a recall or whether repairs have been done on a recalled car.

Passage IV

46. H. Choice H is the correct choice. A direct quotation should be enclosed in quotation marks, and a comma should be within those quotation marks to introduce the speaker of the words being quoted. "It's" (a contraction of "it is") is also correct. Choice G lacks the necessary comma and uses the possessive "its" rather than the contraction.

47. A. The original version is the best. It maintains parallel construction. "Not only" is followed by a modifier ("abundant"), as is "but also" ("high" in protein). None of the other choices is parallel in structure.

48. J. The possessive of "who" is "whose." Choice F is also not parallel in structure; Choice J is—"putting," "eating." Choice H may seem the best choice because it is concise, but the logic of the sentence suggests incorrectly that the word "mushrooms" applies to both a hamburger and sushi.

49. B. This choice is succinct and parallel in structure to the other two items in the series. Choice C is wordy. Choice D creates a run-on sentence.

50. F. The next paragraph begins with the word "However," and the sentence in Choice F leads smoothly into this opening word. The transition is between Ricky's negative reaction to eating insects and the writer's point in the second paragraph that people from other cultures react differently. None of the other choices creates this link.

51. C. This choice avoids the sentence fragment of the original. The second clause of the sentence is dependent and should not be preceded by a period (Choice A) or a semicolon (Choice D). Choice B is wordy and awkward. Choice C is the most direct and concise expression.

52. G. The original version contains a dangling modifier; the "hosts" weren't visiting in Mexico, "I" was. Choice G is the best choice because it corrects that problem and also eliminates unnecessary words. Choice H corrects the problem, but the adverb "politely" is awkwardly placed; it should be closer to the verb "offered." This choice is also less concise. Choice J does not correct the misplaced modifier.

53. D. The error in the original version, Choice A, is that the semicolon creates a fragment. Semicolons divide two independent clauses. The words following "seconds" do not constitute a clause.

54. H. "Provincial" literally means "coming from the provinces," but it also means unsophisticated, lacking urban polish. Choices F, G, and J are not suitable replacements.

55. A. Using the reflexive pronoun "myself" (Choice A) is correct; the remainder of that choice is idiomatic and not as wordy as Choice C.

56. J. In the original version and in Choice G, the subject and verb do not agree in number: "disgust is," not "disgust are." "Foods" is not the subject. Choice H corrects the basic agreement problem, but a semicolon shouldn't be used here. Choice J is the best choice.

57. D. Choice D is the best choice. It is parallel in structure (choices A and B are not), does not create a fragment (choices A, B, and C do), and is concise. A colon is used here to mean "note what follows," and that is an acceptable use.

58. H. Although this choice may seem wordy, it makes the point more clearly than the original "it." More importantly, H corrects the run-on sentence. The verb "having been" in Choice G is incorrect, and a colon (Choice J) is not the correct punctuation in this case.

59. A. A is the best choice because it most clearly provides a conclusion to the paragraph and is clearly connected to the previous sentence. Choice B introduces a new point. In Choice C, the writer is lecturing the reader, which is out of place here. Ricky is included in D, but this sentence has no connection to the previous one.

Passage V

60. J. This choice corrects the problem of subject-verb agreement. The subject is "screens," which requires the plural verb "make." Choice H has the same error as the original version, and it also changes (not for the better) the series "objects, people, and monsters." The comma after "monster" is incorrect; it separates "objects, people, and monsters" from the verb "leap." The tense change in Choice G is incorrect; the context requires present tense.

61. B. This choice is the best of those given. It corrects the sentence fragment created by following "images" with a period or semicolon (choices A, C) and also clarifies the meaning of the phrase "offset by the space. . . ." Choice D, in addition to being a strung-out sentence, doesn't use commas to separate the independent clauses.

62. H. This is the best answer. The word "viewers" is used in the opening sentence and "viewer's eyes" in the sentence preceding this one, and there is no reason to change from third-person to second person ("you"). "One" in Choice J would be acceptable, but the conditional verb is inconsistent in context.

63. D. Choice D is the best choice; it corrects the one problem with the sentence, which is the use of "different" (an adjective) to modify a verb ("bends"). The correct adverb is "differently." Choice B has the same error and is wordier. It might seem that Choice C is the best choice because it is succinct and does use "differently"; however, it changes the meaning of the sentence. The colors themselves differ slightly, but they don't "bend" differently.

64. G. Choice G is the best choice because it is the most concise and direct. It eliminates "both," which is unnecessary, and substitutes "to make" for "in a way that makes." Choice H is the second-best choice, but uses the passive voice. In Choice J, the subject of the verb is "brain" rather than "viewer."

65. D. In Choice D, the verbs are correctly in the present tense. The use of the conditional in the other choices is awkward. The present tense is consistent with "puts" and with the rest of Passage V.

66. F. The original version is the best choice. No commas should be used around "Sir Charles Wheatstone" because the name identifies which English scientist used mirrors. His name is necessary to the meaning; if the name were removed, the sentence would read "The English scientist used mirrors." When an appositive or phrase adds information but is not necessary to the meaning, it is enclosed in commas. For example, "The English scientist who won the Nobel Prize this year, John Doe, lived in the United States last year."

67. A. Of the choices, the original version (Choice A) is the best. Choice B uses both the active and the passive voice and is wordy and awkward. Choices C and D don't convey the meaning clearly, although both are concise. Being concise isn't always possible when it affects meaning.

68. J. This is the only choice that corrects the dangling or misplaced modifier. The original version and the other choices are structured so that it appears that the brain is combining existing technologies with new tricks.

69. C. The original version is a sentence fragment. Choice C easily corrects this by adding the verb "are." Choice B is not incorrect, but "There is no requirement" is wordy. Choice D uses a future tense, but the sentence is saying that *right now* our brains can work out depth from flat images without help from special glasses or screens.

70. G. Choice G is the best choice. In standard usage, avoid "kind of" (Choice J), "sort of" (Choice F), or "a little bit" (Choice H) to mean "somewhat" or "rather." These are colloquial expressions generally not appropriate in writing.

71. D. Choice D corrects the original version, where the third-person "viewer" is followed by the second- person pronoun "you." The original version also fails to enclose the interrupting phrase "for example" in commas. Choice B also uses a second-person pronoun to refer to "viewer" and incorrectly follows the "if" clause with a semicolon. Choice C corrects the problems but makes a different error. The participle of "see" is "have seen," not "have saw."

72. F. The original is the best choice. The participial phrase refers to the viewer. The sentence order in this choice is more logical than choices G and H. Choice J is in the passive voice and is awkward and wordy.

73. D. The past participle of "break" is "broken," not "broke," as in the original version. "Breaked" is not a word, Choice B, and the past progressive tense "was breaking," Choice C, is not appropriate here.

74. G. This sentence concerns how movies that are not 3-D can suggest depth, which is a point made in this paragraph. Therefore, it doesn't interrupt the flow of the paragraph (Choice F) but rather provides a concrete example. The sentence does not indicate the superiority of 3-D movies (choices H and J).

75. A. This sentence should be omitted. It deals with holographic displays, which are not defined or described in Passage V. To maintain paragraph unity and coherence, each sentence should be connected to the next. For example, sentence 2 is connected to sentence 3 by the references to the brain; sentence 6 is an example of the point in sentence 5, and so on.

Mathematics Test

1. **E.** Change all fractions so that they have the same denominator and then add and reduce if necessary.

$$1\frac{3}{4}+2\frac{1}{2}+1\frac{2}{3}=1\frac{9}{12}+2\frac{6}{12}+1\frac{8}{12}=4\frac{23}{12}=5\frac{11}{12}$$

2. **G.** Multiply the numeric coefficients and add the exponents.

$$(2x^3)(3x^2)=(2)(3)(x^3)(x^2)=(6)(xxx)(xx)=6x^5$$

3. **C.** If 12 pears cost $7.20, dividing gives a cost per pear of $0.60. Therefore, three pears would cost $1.80. If 14 apples cost $6.40, dividing gives a cost per apple of about $0.46. Therefore, three apples would cost about $1.38. The difference in cost would be $1.80 – $1.38 = $0.42, thus Choice C would be the best choice. A more accurate answer would result by using $0.457 for the cost of each apple instead of rounding to $0.46.

4. **J.** If five numbers average 32, their total must be (5)(32) = 160. If six numbers average 38, their total must be (6)(38) = 228. Therefore, the sixth number must be 228 – 160 = 68.

5. **E.** Divide to determine the cost per mile when using each type of fuel. For premium fuel: $3.50 divided by 28 gives a cost of 12.5 cents per mile. For regular fuel: $3.30 divided by 26 gives a cost of 12.7 cents per mile. Using premium fuel costs 0.2 cent per mile less than when using regular fuel. Thus, Choice E is correct.

6. **G.** The total number of degrees in the interior angles of a polygon is given by the equation $x = (n-2)180°$. In a regular polygon, all angles have the same measure, therefore, in a regular pentagon (5 sides and 5 angles) each interior angle measures $\frac{(n-2)180}{n}=\frac{(5-2)180}{5}=108$ degrees.

7. **D.** First, multiply out and simplify.

$$(a-b)(a+b-c)=a^2+ab-ac-ab-b^2+bc=a^2-b^2-ac+bc$$

Search the answer choices to see which will give you $a^2 - b^2$. You can eliminate answer choices B and E since neither produces either a^2 or b^2. Choice A gives you $a^2 - b^2$, but also produces the term $(-ab)$, which you do not have, so eliminate Choice A. Choice C produces $(-a^2)$, so eliminate Choice C. This leaves Choice D as the correct one. Of course, another method would be to completely multiply out all the answer choices until you find a match, but that involves unnecessary work.

8. **H.** You should use standard algebraic manipulation to solve for x.

$$6-4x=2+7x$$
$$-11x=-4$$
$$x=\frac{4}{11}$$

9. **A.** Since no actual salary is given in the problem and only specific values are given as answers, it should be clear that the actual salary is not important. Therefore, you can choose a sample salary to make the calculations easier. Suppose Vicki's salary starts at $100. After the 10 percent increase in January, her salary increases to $110. Now, the 10 percent decrease in February is based on this new salary of $110. Ten percent of $110 is $11. Therefore, her salary is now $99. The 10 percent increase in March is based on the salary of $99. Ten percent of $99 is $9.90. Therefore, her ending salary is $108.90. This represents an 8.9 percent increase as follows:

$$\%\text{ increase}=\left(\frac{\text{increase}}{\text{original amount}}\right)(100\%)=\left(\frac{8.90}{100.00}\right)(100\%)=8.9\%$$

10. **F.** When raising a number to a fractional power, the numerator of the fraction represents the power and the denominator of the fraction represents the root. In this case, the root is 2. Therefore, you have $x^{\left(\frac{1}{2}\right)}=\sqrt{x}$.

First, solve for x, then solve for $x - \left(\dfrac{x}{2}\right)^2$.

$$\sqrt{x} = 4$$
$$x = 16$$
$$x - \left(\frac{x}{2}\right)^2 = 16 - \left(\frac{16}{2}\right)^2$$
$$= 16 - 64$$
$$= -48$$

11. D. Filling in the measurements given, you get the following.

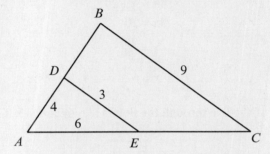

In similar triangles, respective side lengths have the same ratio. Since the ratio of BC to DE is 3 to 1, other respective sides must have that same ratio. Therefore, $AC = 3AE = 18$ and $AB = 3AD = 12$. Therefore, the perimeter of triangle ABC is $12 + 18 + 9 = 39$, or Choice D.

12. G. Remember, contestant A finished in 2nd place. Since 2nd place received twice as many apples as 3rd place, the 3rd place contestant must have received 4 apples. Since the 1st place contestant received twice as many apples as the 2nd place contestant, the 1st place contestant must have received 16 apples. The total number of apples given as prizes is, therefore, $16 + 8 + 4 = 28$ apples, or Choice G.

13. C. When multiplying a 2×2 matrix by a 2×1 matrix, the result will be a 2×1 matrix. This eliminates choices A, D, and E. Perform the multiplication as follows.

$$\begin{bmatrix} a & b \\ c & d \end{bmatrix} \begin{bmatrix} e \\ f \end{bmatrix} = \begin{bmatrix} ae + bf \\ ce + df \end{bmatrix}$$
$$= \begin{bmatrix} (40)(5) + (25)(10) \\ (50)(5) + (40)(10) \end{bmatrix}$$
$$= \begin{bmatrix} 200 + 250 \\ 250 + 400 \end{bmatrix} = \begin{bmatrix} 450 \\ 650 \end{bmatrix}$$

14. F. When simplifying a complex fraction where there is an imaginary number in the denominator, multiply both the numerator and denominator by the complex conjugate of the denominator and simplify.

$$\left(\frac{4 + 2i}{1 - 3i}\right)\left(\frac{1 + 3i}{1 + 3i}\right) = \frac{4 + 2i + 12i + 6i^2}{1 - 3i + 3i - 9i^2} = \frac{4 + 14i - 6}{1 + 9} = \frac{-2 + 14i}{10} = \frac{-1 + 7i}{5}$$

15. D. There are 12 marbles in the bag. First, consider the probability that both selected marbles are blue. Since there are 3 blue marbles in the bag of 12 marbles, the probability that the first selected marble is blue is $\dfrac{3}{12}$. Now, given that the first marble selected is blue, there are 11 marbles left in the bag of which 2 are blue. Therefore, the probability that the second marble selected is also blue is $\dfrac{2}{11}$. Multiply to get the probability that both selected marbles are blue. $\left(\dfrac{3}{12}\right)\left(\dfrac{2}{11}\right) = \dfrac{1}{22}$. Second, consider the probability that both selected marbles are white. Since there are 4 white marbles in the bag of 12 marbles, the probability that the first selected marble is white is $\frac{4}{12}$. Now, given that the first marble selected is white, 11 marbles are left in the bag, 3 of which are white. Therefore, the probability that the second marble selected is also white is $\frac{3}{11}$. Multiply to get the probability that both selected marbles are white. $\left(\frac{4}{12}\right)\left(\frac{3}{11}\right)=\frac{1}{11}$. Therefore, $b=\frac{1}{22}$ and $w=\frac{1}{11}$. Because $\frac{1}{11}$ is 2 times $\frac{1}{22}$, it is twice as likely to randomly choose two white marbles than to choose two blue marbles. Thus $w = 2b$.

16. G. If x represents the original number, then doubling the number would give $2x$ and then doubling again would give $4x$. Now, set up an equation and solve for x.

$$4x = x + 20$$
$$3x = 20$$
$$x = \frac{20}{3}$$
$$x = 6\frac{2}{3}$$

17. D. First, calculate the slope of the line through the points $(3, -6)$ and $(-3, 12)$.

$$m = \frac{y_2 - y_1}{x_2 - x_1}$$
$$= \frac{12 - (-6)}{-3 - 3}$$
$$= \frac{18}{-6}$$
$$= -3$$

Next, use the point-slope form of the equation of the line. Use the calculated slope and either point.

$$y - y_1 = m(x - x_1)$$
$$y - (-6) = -3(x - 3)$$
$$y + 6 = -3x + 9$$
$$3x + y = 3$$

Since the value of y is zero at the x-intercept and the value of x is zero at the y-intercept, substitute zero for each variable in the equation and solve for the other variable.

$$3x + y = 3 \qquad\qquad 3x + y = 3$$
$$3x + 0 = 3 \qquad\qquad 3(0) + y = 3$$
$$x = 1 \qquad\qquad\qquad y = 3$$

Therefore, the sum of the intercepts is $1 + 3 = 4$, or Choice D.

18. J. The following proportion can be used to solve the problem. After the proportion is set up, cross-multiply and then divide to obtain the correct answer.

$$\frac{\text{Purified Water Produced}}{\text{Total Water Used}} = \frac{1.2}{6.5} = \frac{220}{x}$$
$$1.2x = (6.5)(220)$$
$$1.2x = 1430$$
$$x = 1191.7$$

19. E. Look at each section separately. The student must choose two of four unique questions. If the questions were numbered 1, 2, 3, and 4, the student can choose the two questions six ways: 1 and 2, 1 and 3, 1 and 4, 2 and 3, 2 and 4, or 3 and 4. Since the student can choose questions from each of the three sections in six ways, the total number of unique six-question tests is $(6)(6)(6) = 216$, or Choice E. A more mathematical way to determine that there are six ways of choosing the two questions from each section is to use combinations. You want the number of combinations of four things taken two at a time. This is illustrated as follows:

$$_nC_r = \frac{n!}{r!(n-r)!} = {_4C_2} = \frac{4!}{2!(4-2)!} = \frac{4 \times 3 \times 2 \times 1}{2 \times 1 \times 2 \times 1} = 6$$

20. **K.** A quadrilateral has four angles totaling 360°. If x represents the scale factor of the degree measure of each angle, then you can write an expression for the sum of the degree measures of all four angles: $2x + 4x + 5x + 7x = 360°$. Thus, $18x = 360°$, or $x = 20°$. Therefore, substituting 20° for x, the degree measures of the four angles are 40°, 80°, 100°, and 140°. The largest angle is 140°, or Choice K.

21. **E.** Simplify as follows: $\dfrac{\dfrac{x}{y}}{\dfrac{w}{z} \cdot \dfrac{y}{w}} = \dfrac{\dfrac{x}{y}}{\dfrac{y}{z}} = \dfrac{x}{y} \cdot \dfrac{z}{y} = \dfrac{xz}{y^2}$

22. **J.** To solve for the points of intersection, you can use the substitution method. Since $y = x^2$, substitute x^2 for y in the second equation and solve for x.

$$x - y = -6$$
$$x - x^2 = -6$$
$$x^2 - x - 6 = 0$$
$$(x-3)(x+2) = 0$$
$$x = -2 \text{ or } x = 3$$

Therefore, the x-coordinates of the two points of intersection are –2 and 3. Substitute into either equation to determine the y-coordinates.

$$y = x^2 = (-2)^2 = 4 \text{ and } y = x^2 = 3^2 = 9$$

Adding gives a total of 13, or Choice J.

23. **C.** Multiply both sides of the equation by the common denominator of 8 and solve for y.

$$\frac{3}{8}y - \frac{3}{4} = \frac{3}{2}$$
$$8\left(\frac{3}{8}y - \frac{3}{4}\right) = 8\left(\frac{3}{2}\right)$$
$$3y - 6 = 12$$
$$3y = 18$$
$$y = 6$$

24. **G.** Using the fact that $\cos E = \dfrac{2}{3} = \dfrac{2k}{3k}$, where k represents a scale factor, fill in the information in the diagram and calculate the missing side of the right triangle as shown below.

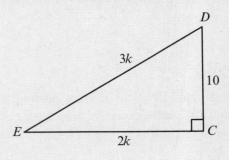

$$(2k)^2 + 10^2 = (3k)^2$$
$$4k^2 + 100 = 9k^2$$
$$100 = 5k^2$$
$$20 = k^2$$
$$k = \sqrt{20} = 2\sqrt{5}$$
$$2k = 4\sqrt{5}$$

The scale factor is $k = 2\sqrt{5}$ and $CE = 2k = 4\sqrt{5}$. This is Choice G.

25. B. In an isosceles triangle, two of the angles have the same measure. Two possible arrangements of angle sizes will work. You are given that one of the angles measures 30°. If this is one of the pair of angles that are the same size, then the second angle is 30° and the third angle is $180 - 30 - 30 = 120°$. If the given 30° angle is different from the other two, subtract 30 from 180, giving 150, and then divide by 2, giving two angles of measure 75°. Therefore, the largest angle in the triangle could be either 120° or 75°. This is I and III, or Choice B.

26. G. Factoring the equation gives $2x(x + 4) = 0$. The two solutions of this equation are 0 and (–4). Therefore, the sum of the solutions is (–4).

27. C. Additional angle sizes can be determined as follows:

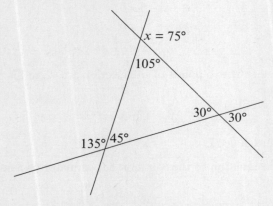

One angle of the triangle is supplementary to 135° and is, therefore, 45°. Another angle of the triangle is a vertical angle to 30° and is, therefore, also 30°. The three angles of the triangle must sum to 180°. Therefore, the third angle of the triangle must be 105°. Thus, you are looking for the supplement of 105°, which is 75°, or Choice C.

28. H. If $\cos\theta = -\frac{1}{3}$, then $\angle\theta$ must lie in the second or third quadrant as shown in the following figure.

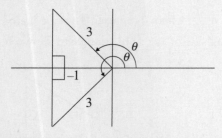

The second quadrant lies between 90° and 180°, and the third quadrant lies between 180° and 270°. The range of degree measure between 90° and 270° can be expressed in radian measure as $\frac{\pi}{2} < \theta < \frac{3\pi}{2}$, or Choice H.

29. E. The tank begins full of brand A gasoline, and then, only brand B gasoline is added. The easiest method to use to solve this problem is to simply keep track of the number of gallons of brand A gasoline in the tank. Then simply subtract from 32 to determine the number of gallons of brand B gasoline in the tank. So, the tank begins with 32 gallons of brand A gasoline. After one-fourth of the tank is used, 24 gallons of brand A gasoline are in the tank. After the tank is filled up with brand B gasoline, half of the tank is used. Therefore, of the 24 gallons of brand A gasoline, half are used, leaving 12 gallons of brand A gasoline in the tank. After the tank is filled up with brand B gasoline, 32 gallons of gasoline are in the tank, 12 of which is brand A gasoline. Thus, 20 gallons of brand B gasoline are now in the tank. You could also approach this problem by keeping track of the fractional part of the tank made up of each brand of gasoline. Begin with $A = 1$ and $B = 0$. After the first use and fill-up, $A = \frac{3}{4}$ and $B = \frac{1}{4}$. After the second use and fill-up, $A = \frac{3}{8}$ and $B = \frac{5}{8}$. Five-eighths of 32 is 20 gallons of brand B gasoline.

30. H. To calculate the length of side $\overline{AC}$, use the distance formula.

$$
\begin{aligned}
d &= \sqrt{\left(x_2 - x_1\right)^2 + \left(y_2 - y_1\right)^2} \\
&= \sqrt{\left(2 - (-2)\right)^2 + \left(8 - (-4)\right)^2} \\
&= \sqrt{4^2 + 12^2} \\
&= \sqrt{160} \\
&= 4\sqrt{10}
\end{aligned}
$$

31. E. First, determine the slope of the line drawn through points A and B.

$$
\begin{aligned}
m &= \frac{y_2 - y_1}{x_2 - x_1} \\
&= \frac{8 - (-8)}{2 - 18} \\
&= \frac{16}{-16} \\
&= -1
\end{aligned}
$$

Since the fourth line is perpendicular to this line, its slope is the negative reciprocal of –1, or a slope of 1. Using the point-slope form of the equation of a line, determine the equation of this fourth line.

$$
\begin{aligned}
y - y_1 &= m\left(x - x_1\right) \\
y - (-4) &= 1\left(x - (-2)\right) \\
y + 4 &= x + 2 \\
x - y &= 2
\end{aligned}
$$

Thus, the answer is Choice E.

32. G. Calculate the slopes of $\overline{AB}$ and $\overline{BC}$. The slope of the fifth line must lie between these two slopes.

$$
\begin{aligned}
m &= \frac{y_2 - y_1}{x_2 - x_1} \\
&= \frac{8 - (-8)}{2 - 18} \\
&= \frac{16}{-16} \\
&= -1
\end{aligned}
\qquad\qquad
\begin{aligned}
m &= \frac{y_2 - y_1}{x_2 - x_1} \\
&= \frac{(-4) - (-8)}{(-2) - 18} \\
&= \frac{4}{-20} \\
&= -\frac{1}{5}
\end{aligned}
$$

The slope of the fifth line must be between –1 and $-\frac{1}{5}$. The only choice that does *not* lie in this range is IV. Therefore, the correct answer choice is G.

33. D. Drawing an additional radius in the figure will allow you to calculate additional angle sizes.

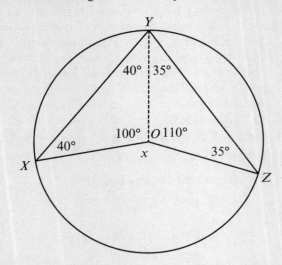

The two resulting small triangles are both isosceles, since two sides of each triangle are radii of the same circle. Therefore, knowing that base angles of isosceles triangles are the same size, and that there are 180° in a triangle, you can calculate the two central angles of 100° and 110°. The total number of degrees in the central angles of a circle is 360°. Subtracting gives you the measure of angle x. You have 360° − 100° − 110° = 150°, or Choice D.

34. J. Solve for y as follows:

$$x - y = z - 4y$$
$$3y = z - x$$
$$y = \frac{z - x}{3}$$

35. B. Draw a sketch and fill in the lengths of the sides as you calculate them.

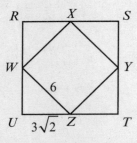

First, since the perimeter of square $WXYZ$ is 24 yards, each of its sides must have a length of 6. This is the hypotenuse of a 45-45-90 right triangle. The ratio of the sides of a 45-45-90 right triangle is 1 to 1 to $\sqrt{2}$. Since the hypotenuse is 6, each leg of the triangle must be $\frac{6}{\sqrt{2}} = \left(\frac{6}{\sqrt{2}}\right)\left(\frac{\sqrt{2}}{\sqrt{2}}\right) = 3\sqrt{2}$. The required perimeter of square $RSTU$ is eight times this length or $24\sqrt{2}$. Thus, the answer is Choice B.

36. G. These two linear inequalities partition the plane into four regions. First, graph the corresponding linear equalities. Rewriting both in y-intercept form will help. Then find the intersection of the lines by solving the system of equations.

$$x + 2y = -8$$
$$2y = -x - 8$$
$$y = -\frac{1}{2}x - 4$$

$$2x - y = -6$$
$$-y = -2x - 6$$
$$y = 2x + 6$$

The first line has a slope of $-\frac{1}{2}$ and a y-intercept of -4. The second line has a slope of 2 and a y-intercept of 6. Since the equations are now in y-intercept form, it is easy to solve for x by substitution.

$$-\frac{1}{2}x - 4 = 2x + 6$$
$$-x - 8 = 4x + 12$$
$$-5x = 20$$
$$x = -4$$

Substituting back into either equation gives $y = -2$. Therefore, the point of intersection is $(-4, -2)$.

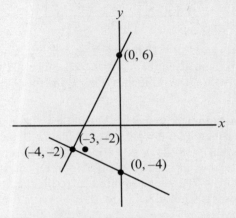

Next, determine which region is represented by the inequalities. If you substitute the origin $(0, 0)$ into both inequalities, you get true statements. This means that the origin is located in the correct region. Since the point in question cannot lie on either line and must lie in the same region with the origin, you must determine which point gives the smallest sum for x and y. By inspection, it is clear that the point $(-3, -2)$ gives the minimum value for $x + y$. Hence, the answer is Choice G.

A more direct, algebraic solution would be to solve the two inequalities simultaneously and eliminate the y variable first.

$$x + 2y > -8$$
$$2x - y > -6$$

Multiply the second inequality by 2 and add

$$x + 2y > -8$$
$$\underline{4x - 2y > -12}$$
$$5x > -20$$
$$x > -4$$

Since x is an integer greater than -4, and you are looking for the minimum value of $x + y$, choose $x = -3$. Now substitute $x = -3$ into the first inequality and solve for y.

$$x + 2y > -8$$
$$-3 + 2y > -8$$
$$2y > -5$$
$$y > -\frac{5}{2}$$

Since y is an integer greater than $-2\frac{1}{2}$, choose -2. Therefore, $x + y = (-3) + (-2) = -5$. Choice G is the correct answer.

Practice Test 3

37. **C.** Redraw the figure, adding the segment between points E and B.

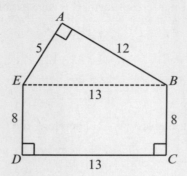

You are given that $AE = 5$ inches and $AB = 12$ inches. Using the Pythagorean Theorem you calculate the hypotenuse, BE, as 13 inches. You are given that $2AB = 3DE$. Since $AB = 12$ inches, $DE = 8$ inches. Since $DE = BC$, $BEDC$ is a rectangle with $CD = 13$ inches. The perimeter of pentagon $ABCDE$ is $5 + 12 + 8 + 13 + 8 = 46$ inches, or Choice C.

38. **K.** Convert the floor dimensions from feet to inches. The floor is 108 inches wide and 144 inches long. First calculate the number of 6-inch square tiles it would take to tile the floor. Divide 108 and 144 by 6, getting 18 and 24, respectively. It would take $(18)(24) = 432$ 6-inch square tiles to tile the floor. Similarly, calculate the number of 9-inch square tiles it would take to tile the floor. Divide 108 and 144 by 9, getting 12 and 16, respectively. It would take $(12)(16) = 192$ 9-inch square tiles to tile the floor. Subtract to find the difference: $432 - 192 = 240$. Hence, the answer is Choice K.

39. **B.** If the perimeter of an equilateral triangle is 36 inches, each of the three sides has a length of 12 inches.

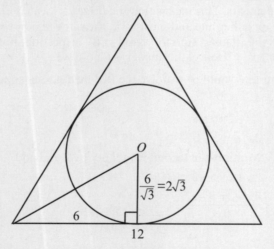

Draw a radius in the circle to the point of tangency. The radius will be perpendicular to the side of the triangle at that point. The point of tangency bisects the side of the equilateral triangle. Draw a segment from the center of the circle to the vertex on the triangle as shown. Since each angle of an equilateral triangle is 60° and this segment bisects the angle of the triangle, the small right triangle shown in the figure is a 30-60-90 right triangle. Remember that the angle bisectors of a triangle intersect at a point, and that point is equidistant from the sides of the triangle, so it is the center of the inscribed circle. The ratio of the three sides of a 30-60-90 right triangle is 1 to 2 to $\sqrt{3}$. This means that the side opposite the 60° angle is equal to the side opposite the 30° angle times $\sqrt{3}$. To find the shortest side of this right triangle divide 6 by $\sqrt{3}$, giving $\dfrac{6}{\sqrt{3}} = 2\sqrt{3}$. This is the radius of the circle. Calculate the area of the circle. $A = \pi r^2 = \left(2\sqrt{3}\right)^2 \pi = 12\pi$. Therefore, Choice B is correct.

40. H. If x is the scale factor for the measures of the sides of the triangle, then $3x + 4x + 5x = 30$. Thus, $12x = 30$, or $x = 2.5$. Therefore, the lengths of the sides of the triangle are $(3)(2.5) = 7.5$, $(4)(2.5) = 10$, and $(5)(2.5) = 12.5$. The sum of the shortest and longest sides is $7.5 + 12.5 = 20$, or Choice H.

41. C. If you look at successive differences between pairs of numbers in the list you get the following: –4, 9, –16, 25, –36, 49. These alternate in sign and their absolute values are the perfect squares of the integers 2, 3, 4, 5, 6, and 7. Continuing this pattern, to get the eighth number in the list, simply subtract $8^2 = 64$. This gives the value of $28 – 64 = –36$. For the ninth number, add $9^2 = 81$. This gives the value of $–36 + 81 = 45$. Finally, for the tenth number, subtract $10^2 = 100$.

This gives the value of $45 – 100 = –55$, or Choice C.

42. H. The product of the two numbers, y and z, must equal the product of their LCM and GCF. Therefore, $yz = wx$. Substituting for w, you have $yz = 6x^2$. Since all four variables are positive even integers, the smallest x can be is 2. Therefore, $yz = (6)(2^2) = 24$. Knowing that the product of y and z must be 24, you can write out the possibilities. Remember, y and z must be even and positive. You have $(2)(12) = 24$ and $(4)(6) = 24$. For each of these pairs, (2 and 12) and (4 and 6), their GCF is 2, and their LCM is 12. Next, check the sums. You have $2 + 12 = 14$ and $4 + 6 = 10$. You are looking for the minimum value for the sum. That is 10, or Choice H.

43. D. If you knew the original price of the suit, you would multiply by 0.85 to get the discounted price and then multiply by 1.08 to get the final price, including tax. Since you know the final price, you must work backward. First divide by 1.08 and then divide by 0.85.

$$\frac{114.29}{1.08} = 105.824 \qquad \frac{105.824}{0.85} = 124.499$$

Therefore, the original price of the suit was \$124.50, or Choice D.

44. G. This problem can be approached several ways. First, the arithmetic method would simply determine the total weight of the twelve nuts and then divide by 12.

$$\frac{(4)(18) + (8)(12)}{12} = \frac{72 + 96}{12} = \frac{168}{12} = 14$$

A second more logical approach would be to look at the problem in terms of ratios. The ratio of the number of each kind of nut must be the inverse of the ratio of the differences between the average weight and the individual weights of the two kinds of nuts. The ratio of the number of 18-gram nuts to the number of 12-gram weights is 4:8 or 1:2. Therefore, the difference in their weights ($18 – 12 = 6$) must be divided into two numbers that are in the ratio of 2:1. To divide 6 into two numbers in the ratio of 2:1, simply set up the equation $2x + 1x = 6$. It is clear that $x = 2$ so the two numbers are 4 and 2. This means that the average (mean) weight must be 4 grams from the 18-gram weight and 2 grams from the 12-gram weight. Thus, the average is 14 grams. If you were running out of time and needed to make a quick guess at the correct answer, you could observe that since there are more 12-gram nuts, the average weight must be closer to 12 than to 18. This eliminates choices H, J, and K. You would then be guessing from either 13 or 14, with 14 being the more obvious choice.

45. C. Simply remove the parentheses and combine terms.

$$(c – a) + (b – c) = c – a + b – c = c – c – a + b = b – a$$

46. H. Since the ratio of the radii of the two circles is 1 to 2, the ratio of their areas must be in the ratio of 1 to 4. The circumference of the larger circle is 40. Since $C = \pi d$, the diameter of the larger circle is $\frac{40}{\pi}$. The radius of the larger circle is half of its diameter, or $\frac{20}{\pi}$. Next, if A represents the area of the larger circle, then $A = \pi r^2 = \pi\left(\frac{20}{\pi}\right)^2 = \frac{400}{\pi}$. The ratio of the area of the smaller circle to the area of the larger circle is 1 to 4. If B represents the area of the smaller circle, you can set up a proportion to solve.

$$\frac{B}{A} = \frac{1}{4}$$

$$\frac{B}{\left(\dfrac{400}{\pi}\right)} = \frac{1}{4}$$

$$4B = \frac{400}{\pi}$$

$$B = \frac{\left(\dfrac{400}{\pi}\right)}{4}$$

$$B = \frac{100}{\pi}$$

47. E. Because line k and the line $5x - 6y = 4$ are parallel, they have the same slope. Rewrite the equation into slope-intercept form.

$$5x - 6y = 4$$

$$-6y = -5x + 4$$

$$\frac{-6y}{-6} = \frac{-5x}{-6} + \frac{4}{-6}$$

$$y = \frac{5}{6}x - \frac{2}{3}$$

Clearly, the slope of this line is $\frac{5}{6}$, and therefore the slope of line k is also $\frac{5}{6}$, which is Choice E.

48. J. Solve both inequalities for $2x$. Subtracting $3y$ from both sides of the first inequality gives $2x < -3y + 8$. Adding $2x + 4$ to both sides of the second inequality gives $5z + 4 < 2x$. Rewriting as a single inequality gives $5z + 4 < 2x < -3y + 8$, or $5z + 4 < -3y + 8$. Subtract 4 from both sides of the inequality and divide both sides by 5.

$$5z + 4 < -3y + 8$$

$$5z < -3y + 4$$

$$z < \frac{4 - 3y}{5}$$

49. E. Substitute $(a + b)$ for x in the function $g(x)$, substitute a for x in the function $g(x)$, and then subtract the results.

$$g(x) = 2x^2 + 1$$

$$g(a + b) - g(a) = \left(2(a + b)^2 + 1\right) - \left(2a^2 + 1\right)$$

$$= \left(2\left(a^2 + 2ab + b^2\right) + 1\right) - \left(2a^2 + 1\right)$$

$$= 2a^2 + 4ab + 2b^2 + 1 - 2a^2 - 1$$

$$= 4ab + 2b^2$$

50. **F.** Set up two equations using the variables A and B. Solve by substitution.

$$A = \frac{1}{3}B - 6$$
$$B = 2A + 4$$
$$A = \left(\frac{1}{3}\right)(2A + 4) - 6$$
$$3A = (2A + 4) - 18$$
$$3A = 2A + 4 - 18$$
$$A = -14$$
$$B = 2A + 4$$
$$B = 2(-14) + 4$$
$$B = -24$$

The smaller number is (-24) and the larger number is (-14).

Thus, the correct choice is F.

51. **C.** Work from the inside out. First evaluate the function f at -2, then evaluate the function g with that answer.

$$f(-2) = (4)(-2) + 5 = -3$$
$$g(-3) = (-3)^2 - 3 = 9 - 3 = 6$$

This is called a composite of functions.

52. **F.** The most direct way to solve this problem is by subtracting the area of the small unshaded triangle from the area of the large triangle. The difference will be the total of the two shaded triangles. First, calculate the height of the large triangle.

$$A = \frac{1}{2}bh$$
$$80 = \left(\frac{1}{2}\right)(20)h$$
$$80 = 10h$$
$$h = 8$$

This is also the height of the small unshaded triangle. Find the area of the unshaded triangle.

$$A = \frac{1}{2}bh = \left(\frac{1}{2}\right)(14)(8) = 56$$

Subtract to find the total area of the shaded triangles as $80 - 56 = 24$, or Choice F.

53. **C.** An altitude drawn in a right triangle creates three similar triangles. In this case, triangle ABC, triangle ACD, and triangle CBD are all similar. Therefore, statement I is true. In similar triangles, corresponding sides are proportional. Therefore, statement II is also true. Since corresponding angles are the same size, not complementary, statement III is not true in general. The only exception is when you have a 45-45-90 right triangle. But since it is not always true, you must say it is false. Therefore, Choice C is correct.

54. H. It should be clear that sin R must be less than 1. Therefore, the answer cannot be J or K. Set up a proportion and solve for sin R.

$$\frac{\sin R}{r} = \frac{\sin S}{s}$$

$$\frac{\sin R}{8} = \frac{\left(\frac{2}{3}\right)}{6}$$

$$\sin R = 8\left(\frac{2}{3}\right)\left(\frac{1}{6}\right)$$

$$= \frac{16}{18} = \frac{8}{9}$$

55. B. Simply substitute the value of 8 for x in the equation.

$$y = \frac{3}{16}x^2 - 16x + 20$$

$$= \left(\frac{3}{16}\right)(8)^2 - 16(8) + 20$$

$$= \left(\frac{3}{16}\right)(64) - 128 + 20$$

$$= 12 - 128 + 20$$

$$= -96$$

Since a represents the x-coordinate and b represents the y-coordinate, the correct answer is Choice B.

56. J. First, if $x > 2$, which will guarantee that both numerator and denominator are positive, you can treat this absolute value inequality like a regular inequality.

$$\frac{x+4}{x-2} > 2$$

$$x + 4 > 2(x - 2)$$

$$x + 4 > 2x - 4$$

$$8 > x$$

$$x < 8$$

Therefore, since $x < 8$, you can eliminate answer choices G and K. Testing $x = 0$, you get $\frac{|0+4|}{|0-2|} = 2$. Thus, $x = 0$ does not satisfy the inequality. Therefore, you can eliminate choices F and H. This leaves Choice J as the correct choice. Alternative methods of solution include graphing the inequality and observing when the graph is greater than 2 in value, or simply testing all the possible choices.

57. B. First, a sketch will help organize the given information.

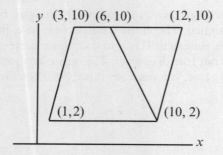

The parallelogram has a base length of $(10 - 1) = 9$ and a height of $(10 - 2) = 8$. Therefore, the area of the parallelogram is $(9)(8) = 72$. The triangle has a base of $(12 - 6) = 6$ and a height (same as the parallelogram) of $(10 - 2) = 8$. Therefore, the area of the triangle is $\frac{1}{2}(6)(8) = 24$. The trapezoid, therefore, has an area equal to the difference between the parallelogram and the triangle, or $72 - 24 = 48$. The ratio of the area of the triangle to the area of the trapezoid is $\frac{24}{48} = \frac{1}{2}$, which is Choice B.

58. G. The equation for a circle is $(x - h)^2 + (y - k)^2 = r^2$, where (h, k) are the coordinates of the center of the circle and the radius is r. Using the information presented in the problem, $h = -8$, $k = 8$, and since the diameter is 8, $r = 4$. Substituting gives Choice G.

59. B. Set up an inequality, and solve.

$$5x + 12 > 8x$$
$$12 > 3x$$
$$4 > x$$
$$x < 4$$

60. K. First, since $\pi < \alpha < \frac{3\pi}{2}$, angle α must lie in the third quadrant. Since $\frac{\pi}{2} < \beta < \pi$, angle β must lie in the second quadrant. The following figure illustrates the placement of the angles and the signs of the respective trigonometric functions.

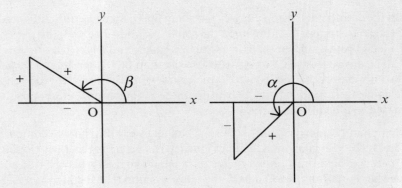

The three statements involve four functions.

$\cos\alpha = \dfrac{\text{adjacent}}{\text{hypotenuse}} = \dfrac{"-"}{"+"} = "-"$ $\cos\beta = \dfrac{\text{adjacent}}{\text{hypotenuse}} = \dfrac{"-"}{"+"} = "-"$

$\tan\alpha = \dfrac{\text{opposite}}{\text{adjacent}} = \dfrac{"-"}{"-"} = "+"$ $\tan\beta = \dfrac{\text{opposite}}{\text{adjacent}} = \dfrac{"+"}{"-"} = "-"$

Statement I *is* false since $\cos\beta$ is negative and $\tan\alpha$ is positive. Statement I says a negative value is greater than a positive value, and that is false. Statement II *is* true since $\tan\beta$ is negative and $\tan\alpha$ is positive. Statement II says the quotient of a negative value and a positive value is negative, which is true. Statement III *could be* true since $\cos\alpha$ is negative and $\tan\beta$ is negative. Statement III says a negative value is less than half of another negative value, which could be true, depending on the sizes of the two angles. For example if $\alpha = 181°$, $\cos\alpha$ would be a negative value very close to -1. If $\beta = 179°$, $\frac{\tan\beta}{2}$ would be a negative value very close to 0. In this case, statement III would be true. Therefore, Choice K is correct.

Reading Test

Passage I

1. **D.** After the nun leaves to get the water, Anna describes herself as "planning what to invent next" (line 74). Additionally, the nun's last statement before Anna's request for a glass of water catches her in a lie, and in response Anna "felt myself blushing." The answer is not Choice A because Anna mentions the trunk only in passing, but neither examines it nor shows any further interest in it. It is not Choice B because Anna shows no sign of fear toward the nun, nor does the nun give her any reason to think that she will berate Anna, even after it is clear that Anna is not telling the truth. It is not Choice C because Anna shows no interest in seeking out a priest, either before or after finding that nuns do not wear trousers but priests do wear them.

2. **H.** "The nun's mirth" (lines 100–101) has dashed the optimism with which Anna arrived at the convent. Anna imagines that the nun sees her as "a sorry sight" (line 96), which causes her previous hopes to feel unwarranted. The answer is not Choice F because Anna's reaction is not shame, but rather disappointment at the nun's reaction. It is not G because Anna does not attempt to contradict or oppose what the nun has told her, but accepts it and incorporates it into her assessment of the situation. It is not Choice J because Anna shows no sign of feeling that the nun has pushed her away or actively discouraged her from becoming a nun, but rather the nun has informed Anna of some facts that now make Anna's entering the convent seem unnecessary.

3. **B.** Anna describes the countryside using phrases revealing life in Sicily as difficult and dominated by hard work: "It is as if time has stopped"; "I breathed the smell of hand-tilled soil, the trees nurtured by manure, and the sweat of men's brows"; "Even the horses are never alert and frisky but are weighed down with the burden of work." The answer is not Choice A because she is, in fact, intending to leave home. It is not Choice C because, although Anna sees beauty in the course of her journey, this does not dissuade her from continuing to the convent. It is not Choice D because there is no mention, either positive or negative, of life in the city as opposed to life in the country.

4. **F.** The words "triumphant," "martyr," and "suffering" are all overly dramatic in comparison with Anna's circumstances. Clearly, 13-year-old Anna feels her journey has been long and her troubles great—a modern-day Joan of Arc, perhaps—but the author's choice of language suggests that she (the author) and her readers will find this somewhat humorous. And, indeed, the nun's reaction that follows is further evidence of this irony. The answer is not Choice G because the event that follows—the conversation with the nun—is not momentous, but merely informs Anna in her discovery. It is not Choice H because, although Anna is preoccupied with religion, the nun quickly puts her feelings of religious martyrdom into perspective. It is not Choice J because, although the conversation with the nun affects Anna, no plot twist follows.

5. **B.** The nun's prevailing attitude toward Anna is one of mirth, as Anna perceives correctly. When she facetiously calls Anna "orphan Annie," we can infer that the nun already has doubts about Anna's story, and certainly doesn't believe that she is all alone in the world. With the seriousness of Anna's predicament in question, the nun finds Anna to be unwittingly amusing. The answer is not Choice A because the nun respects Anna enough to answer her questions with the expectation that she can clear up the girl's misunderstandings. It is not Choice C because the words "orphan Annie" are intended facetiously, indicating that the nun considers Anna's plight to be far from serious. It is not Choice D because the nun shows no indication that she is concerned for Anna's overall well-being, but rather allows Anna to leave after a few minutes, confident that she comes from a relatively loving home.

6. **J.** Anna tells the nun that "I'd like to be with God forever," but then reveals that her main reason for wanting to be a nun is so she can wear trousers. When the nun tells her that nuns don't wear trousers under their habits, Anna loses interest in being a nun. Thus, Anna means well, but her belief does not come from true conviction. The answer is not Choice F because Anna loses interest in being a nun once she discovers that nuns don't wear trousers. It is not Choice G because Anna enters the convent believing that she wishes to be a nun, even though she is soon dissuaded. It is not Choice H because, although Anna takes herself very seriously, her religious devotion is not shown to be meaningful or even very sophisticated.

7. **A.** As Anna describes herself, "I stayed silent as I had no idea what to say" and "I froze, tucked into a corner, trying to make myself as inconspicuous as possible." This reaction indicates that she is initially intimidated by the nun and wants to hide from her. The answer is not Choice B because Anna's first reaction of silence indicates that the nun's presence was not disappointing, but rather more forbidding than Anna had expected. It is not Choice C because there is no evidence in Anna's description that she is envious, but rather that she is unsure how to respond. It is not Choice D because Anna's reaction of intimidation runs counter to the notion that she is unimpressed.

8. **G.** *Imbued* means *filled* or *permeated*. Note that, despite the context, the word *imbued* carries no specifically negative connotation and could, in another context, be used positively. The answer is not Choice F because in this context, sweat is not considered so negatively as to debase the things it touches. It is not Choice H because, again, sweat cannot reasonably be construed as so negative as to poison things. It is not Choice J because the word *trounced* means *conquered*, which is incorrect as a synonym for *imbued*.

9. **C.** Anna has traveled to the convent to escape from the societal strictures of her family, and especially her father. She believes that as a nun she would be free to live as she chooses. But she discovers from her conversation with the nun not only that this is not so, but that the nun and her father share the same judgment about her wearing trousers. Therefore, Anna's journey has been in vain. The irony is that she has traveled "long and hard" to hear that she can't wear trousers—the same response she had received from her father at home.

   The answer is not Choice A because Passage I concludes with Anna's reconfirmation that she wishes to wear trousers, even though she now understands that becoming a nun will not serve this purpose. It is not Choice B because there is no evidence that Anna's father has either wished for her to become a nun or discouraged her from this path. It is not Choice D because Anna has not expressed an interest in wearing a nun's habit, but rather expressed the misunderstanding that they wear trousers under their habits.

10. **F.** The passage ends with Anna's assertion, "It was obvious that if only men could wear trousers, then, somehow, a man I must be." That is, her desire to wear trousers has not changed, but the means to fulfill this desire has. It has become clear that nuns don't wear trousers but men do wear them, so she decides that she must, somehow, become a man. The answer is not Choice G because her resolve to wear trousers has not changed. It is not Choice H because, although she feels embarrassed that the nun has laughed at her, she takes this upon herself rather than blaming the nun. It is not Choice J because, although Anna does find a new opportunity in the prospect of somehow becoming a man, this is not specifically related to remaining at home.

Passage II

11. **A.** The first paragraph begins with estimates of how much information the brain can process at one time and how quickly it can process information. The second paragraph provides an example of how these estimates explain human inability to follow more than two or three conversations at once. The third, fourth, and fifth paragraphs discuss the ways in which the original estimate may be too low or too high. And the sixth paragraph sums up the argument and suggests that the information a person lets in determines what his or her life becomes. Thus, every paragraph discusses and enhances the topic of brain capacity. The answer is not Choice B because only the third paragraph discusses the possibility that brain potential may be unlimited. It is not Choice C because only the fourth and fifth paragraphs discuss how people waste time with trivial activities. It is not Choice D because Passage II does not fully accept the premise that aptitude is limited by brain structure.

12. **G.** The word *gradations* is the best synonym for *nuances* in the given context. This context is the words "differentiated sounds, or visual stimuli, or recognizable *nuances* of emotion or thought." The words "differentiated sounds" indicate that small distinctions are important. The answer is not Choice F because *delineations* is not a good synonym for *nuances* and refers to an outline or explanation of a single thing rather than subtle differences between several things. It is not Choice H because *imitations* is not a synonym for *nuances* and makes no sense in the context of the sentence. It is not Choice J because *limitations* is also not a synonym for *nuances*.

13. B. The author introduces the second paragraph by stating, "The limitation of consciousness is demonstrated by the fact that to understand what another person is saying we must process 40 bits of information each second." He then continues this demonstration, using this information to explain a common human experience: the difficulty of processing three conversations at a time. This example provides the reader with a concrete understanding about the limitation of 140 bits per second. The answer is not Choice A because, although the example is somewhat less mathematical than what precedes it, it is still numerical. Moreover, there is no evidence that the author is anticipating hostility toward numbers and attempting to overcome it. It is not Choice C because the example supports rather than challenges the argument he is making. It is not Choice D because the author only touches briefly and in passing upon the difficulty of processing a conversation without nonverbal cues.

14. G. The third paragraph discusses how the brain may ideally be understood as limitless, while the fourth paragraph focuses on the reality that most people do not, in fact, make full use of their brains. That is, the third paragraph argues for what the brain may theoretically be capable of under the best of circumstances, and the fourth describes the practical use that most people make of their brains. The answer is not Choice F because the author has made a physiological (body-related) argument in the first two paragraphs, but in the third and fourth paragraph has moved on to two different psychological (mind-related) arguments. It is not Choice H because, although the argument in the third paragraph could be construed as less conservative than that in the fourth, the continuum from radical to reactionary is usually intended as political, and there is no particular hint of politics in Passage II. It is not Choice J because the concept of religion versus secularity is absent from Passage II.

15. A. Although the third paragraph explores the possibility that consciousness is infinitely expandable, Passage II does not conclude that this is true. In fact, the fourth paragraph provides an argument that consciousness is more limited by brain usage than brain capacity. And the sixth paragraph reiterates that the limitations on brain capacity proposed in the first paragraph "might either be an overestimate or an underestimate." The answer is not Choice B because lines 22–24 state "the fact that to understand what another person is saying we must process 40 bits of information each second." It is not Choice C because lines 71–73 state "The largest part of free time—almost half of it for American adults—is spent in front of the television set." It is not Choice D because lines 10–12 state "By using these figures one concludes that it is possible to process at most 126 bits of information per second." While this figure is used in a variety of contexts, it is never challenged in the context of Passage II and, therefore, is reasonably construed as a factual statement.

16. J. In lines 5–7, a bit of information is described as a single piece of information "such as differentiated sounds, or visual stimuli, or recognizable nuances of emotion or thought." In contrast, "to understand what another person is saying we must process 40 bits of information each second" (lines 22–24), so a five-second conversation requires 200 bits of information. The answer is not Choice F because the color of a person's shirt is a single visual stimulus, which qualifies as one bit. It is not Choice G because perceiving a friend's smile is a single visual stimulus, which also qualifies as one bit. It is not Choice H because observing a sudden feeling of jealousy in yourself is a recognizable nuance of emotion, which also qualifies as one bit.

17. D. Passage II states that "most people fall far below the peak capacity for processing information" (lines 66–67). It adds that "in their precious 'leisure' time, most people in fact seem to use their minds as little as possible" (lines 69–71). It goes on to discuss how specific activities, such as watching television and reading newspapers and magazines, "also involve processing very little new information" (lines 85–86). The answer is not Choice A because, although line 62 states that eating and taking care of bodily needs "take up 15 percent of consciousness," the author does not discuss the possibility of reducing this percentage. It is not Choice B because the author states that "although watching TV requires the processing of visual images, very little else in the way of memory, thinking, or volition is required" (lines 75–78). It is not Choice C because the author states that "Reading most newspapers and magazines . . . involve(s) processing very little new information, and thus require(s) little concentration" (lines 83–87).

18. J. The term "chunking" is introduced and then explained in the next two sentences: "Simple functions like adding a column of numbers or driving a car grow to be automated, leaving the mind free to deal with more data. We also learn how to compress and streamline information through symbolic means—language, math, abstract concepts, and stylized narratives" (lines 43–48). The answer is not Choice F because intuition is not mentioned in reference to "chunking." It is not Choice G because emotion is also not mentioned in reference to "chunking." It is not Choice H because, although some aspects of "chunking"—such as the use of narrative or parable—can be thought of as received wisdom, many aspects—such as learning how to drive a car without thinking about it—have no such connotation.

19. A. The paragraph mentioning "optimists" twice (in lines 39 and 52) discusses how the mind can "compress and streamline information through symbolic means" (lines 46–47). The answer is not Choice B because, while Passage II does assert that the limitation of 185 billion bits applies to an average life span, it does not use this fact to enhance the optimistic argument of the third paragraph. It is not Choice C because Passage II argues that the 126-bit capacity of the central nervous system does, in fact, have a basis in physiology. It is not Choice D because Passage II does not discuss whether people who are presented with information about how they spend their time tend to change their behavior.

20. H. The sixth paragraph ends with the idea that what the brain focuses on determines the content and the quality of life, but nowhere suggests which content or qualities might be desirable. Hence, Choice H is incorrect and, therefore, the answer. The answer is not Choice F because the first three sentences of the sixth paragraph (lines 88–95) summarize the main points of the argument as discussed in the previous five paragraphs. It is not Choice G because the third sentence of the sixth paragraph states, "In any case, an individual can experience only so much" (lines 94–95). Choice H is the only possible answer.

Passage III

21. D. The first paragraph links Stoicism with the tenet from Oriental philosophy that "hope is the greatest of misfortunes" (lines 6–7). The second paragraph states that "there is no other reality than this one in which we are living here and now" (lines 13–15), clarifying the tenet introduced in the first paragraph. The third paragraph provides a narrative explaining how this tenet might play out in a very hopeful event in a person's life. The fourth reiterates the basic idea that "according to a celebrated Buddhist proverb, you must learn to live as if this present moment were the most vital of your whole life" (lines 39–42). The remaining paragraphs link this tenet back to the Stoic philosopher, Epictetus, and further clarify it. Thus, the main idea of Passage III illuminates a single tenet of Stoicism. The answer is not Choice A because, though the passage discusses Stoicism in terms of Eastern traditions, it fails to mention other Greek traditions. It is not Choice B because, although the last paragraph makes passing reference to the possibility that "ordinary mortals" might view this tenet as an "especially insipid version of fatalism," Passage III makes no other reference to Stoicism as either emotionless or overly-intellectual. It is not Choice C because Passage III focuses on a single tenet of Stoicism, that of attending solely to the present moment, rather than several tenets.

22. F. Passage III states that once people accomplish an objective, "we almost invariably experience a puzzling sense of indifference, if not disappointment." It then uses the example of children the day after Christmas to exemplify this, adding that "the possession of things so ardently coveted makes us neither better nor happier than before." The answer is not Choice G because no mention is made of any tendency for people to jealously guard what they have attained. It is not Choice H because, although part of the disappointment felt after attainment may be linked to finding fault with what has been gained, this is not the key point of the example. It is not Choice J because no mention is made of any tendency for humans to destroy what they have gained.

23. D. *Amor fati* is Nietzsche's term for the Stoic tenet that is being explored in this passage: "the love of reality for itself" (lines 50–51). This tenet is further described as "a life stripped of both hopes and fears . . . reconciled to what is the case . . . which accepts the world as it is" (lines 58–60). Thus, in the case of sudden unemployment, this response would be acceptance of the current reality and unwillingness to dwell in past regret or worrying about the future. The answer is NOT Choice A because resolving not to look for a new job would be a response oriented toward future action (or inaction), which would be counter to the principle of *amor fati*. It is not Choice B because a step-by-step approach to finding work would be future-oriented, which is in contradiction with *amor fati*. It is not Choice C because using the past as the basis for judging the future is entirely removed from the present moment and, therefore, distinct from *amor fati*.

24. F. The "commonplace illusions" spoken of are those in opposition to "the principle of universal reason which the Greeks named the *Logos*: the true face of destiny" (lines 67–69). This is further described as follows: "We must bring our own will into harmony with whatever comes to pass" (lines 76–77). Thus, the "commonplace illusions" referred to are beliefs that are in denial of the truth. The answer is not Choice G because excess is not an important point in the paragraph that discusses "commonplace illusions." It is not Choice H because, while Passage III does make passing reference to the need to avoid self-pity, this is not the principle point it makes in discussing "commonplace illusions." It is not Choice J because the passage does not particularly address self-aggrandizement (self-importance).

25. A. Passage III states "In the end, it is always the gravestone that is silhouetted against the horizon, and you come to realize soon enough that the accumulation of all imaginable worldly goods solves nothing" (lines 32–36). This is a reference to the inevitability of death and the futility of avoiding it by accumulating possessions. This is the same point being made that "the tragedy of the human condition [is] not modified by ownership or success" (lines 23–25). The answer is not Choice B because Nietzsche's reference to the "beasts of burden"—that is, to humans when they become slaves to hope and fear in opposition to reality— is only partially related to the image of the gravestone. It is not Choice C because Passage III tells us that Stoicism advocates, rather than warns against, "a life stripped of hopes and fears." It is not Choice D because "an especially insipid version of fatalism" is a misunderstanding of the tenet of Stoicism that the passage is describing.

26. J. The sentence in question is preceded by "the good life is a life stripped of both hopes and fears. In other words, a life reconciled to what is the case, a life which accepts the world as it is." In other words, an ideal of the world as inherently good must be let go of to make room for the world as it is in reality. The answer is not Choice F because Passage III does not address the choice between the greater good and personal desire. It is not Choice G because the tenet in question rejects the future as well as the past. It is not Choice H because, while Passage III touches upon the distinction between Greek and Christian gods, the sentence in question does not relate to this distinction.

27. C. In the last paragraph, the author acknowledges that the reader may find Stoicism to be "amounting to an especially insipid version of fatalism" (lines 86–87), which is a weakness in this philosophy. He then goes on to say "But this is precisely. . ., to me, why it possesses an irreplaceable charm" (lines 90–93), that is, that the weakness of Stoicism is why it appeals to him. The answer is not Choice A because, while the author acknowledges that Stoicism has its weaknesses, he does not toss it aside but rather embraces it. It is not Choice B because the author's intent in acknowledging Stoicism's weakness is part of a strategy to convince the reader to consider this philosophy despite its weakness. It is not Choice D because the author fully expects that the reader has apprehended the flaw in Stoicism, and discusses a possible response to this flaw.

28. H. Passage III distinguishes between "the personal God of Christianity" (lines 65–66) and the God described in the *Discourses* of Epictetus, which was the "embodying of the cosmos," another name for the principle of universal reason. The answer is not Choice F because the passage describes *Logos* as "the true face of destiny that we have no choice but to accept" (69–70), which is similar to the Buddhist tenet that hope is the greatest of misfortunes. It is not Choice G because Nietzsche's notion of *amor fati* is "the love of reality for itself" (line 51), which is similar to the Buddhist tenet in question. It is not Choice J because the "philosopher's task" described by Epictetus is to "bring our own will into harmony with whatever comes to pass" (lines 76–77), which, again, is similar to the Buddhist tenet in question.

29. B. The word *renowned* is a synonym for *celebrated* that fits well within the context of the sentence in which it appears. The answer is not Choice A because, while *rejoiced* is a synonym of *celebrated*, it is not a good fit in the context of Passage III. It is not Choice C because the word *noble* is not a very good synonym of *celebrated*, with very little overlapping meaning. It is not Choice D because the word *accurate* is not a synonym of *celebrated* in any context.

30. H. The point that the author is making is that accumulating worldly goods cannot change the fact of death. This is not a point that he rejects at any point later in Passage III. The answer is not Choice F because the quote about money making poverty bearable does inject humor at a serious moment in the passage. It is not Choice G because the quote acknowledges the obvious allure of money that virtually all people, including him, are aware of. It is not Choice J because the quote takes the edge off of the point he is making about death, which is likely to make it a bit more palatable to the average reader.

Passage IV

31. A. The first paragraph introduces the fact that the hypercar utilizes materials other than steel. The second paragraph discusses several "examples in which standard materials have been quickly displaced" (lines 13–15). The third paragraph introduces carbon fibers as an alternative to steel in automobile design. The fourth and fifth paragraphs acknowledge some possible arguments against replacing steel with carbon fibers and respond to each. Thus, the main idea of Passage IV is to endorse a change in automaking from steel to carbon fibers. The answer is not Choice B because, although the passage does extol the virtues of certain new modes in auto design, it does not lament that they will probably not occur, but rather argues that these changes are viable. It is not Choice C because, although Passage IV does discuss some history of automobile manufacturing, it does so in service to the larger point it is making about using carbon fibers rather than steel. It is not Choice D because Passage IV does not passively predict what might occur in automaking, but rather actively endorses a change in it.

32. H. The paragraph opens by saying that hypercars abandon "nearly a century of materials and manufacturing experience based on steel" (lines 2–3), acknowledging that "This notion might at first appear quixotic" (lines 3–4). It goes on to describe other apparent advantages of steel in automaking, before proceeding to address these in the paragraphs that follow. The answer is not Choice F because the first paragraph does not address any advantages of hypercars, but rather their apparent drawbacks. It is not Choice G because the first paragraph does not dispel objections to the use of steel in hypercars, but rather acknowledges these objections. It is not Choice J because the first paragraph does not provide a preview of the overall argument presented in Passage IV, but simply lays the groundwork for this argument.

33. C. The word *unfeasible* (impractical) is the best synonym for *quixotic* within the context of the passage. The answer is not Choice A because, while one positive connotation of *quixotic* is *innovative*, the passage is using the word *quixotic* in a strictly negative sense. It is not Choice B because, while *romantic* contains a sense of the word *quixotic*, this is not the sense intended in the context of the paragraph. It is not Choice D because *viable* is not a synonym of *quixotic*, but closer to an antonym.

34. F. The fourth paragraph begins a discussion of carbon fibers—the material from which hypercars are made—from an economic perspective. The first sentence of the fourth paragraph states that carbon fiber "still looks too costly per pound" (lines 56–57), which is an argument against its use. The second sentence counters this argument, arguing that "cost per pound is the wrong basis for comparison" (57–58). The answer is not Choice G because the two sentences in question do not address considerations of engineering, but rather of economics. It is not Choice H because these sentences do not focus on the process of making hypercars a viable product, but rather on the economics behind using carbon fibers rather than steel to make cars. It is not Choice J because, although a discussion of economics is a turn toward the practical rather than the theoretical, this is not the main point of the sentences in question.

35. A. The fifth paragraph continues the discussion of the economics of hypercars begun in the fourth paragraph. Specifically, it focuses on the savings that "arise in the manufacturing steps after the autobody is formed" (lines 77–78)—that is, in the manufacturing phase of car production. The answer is not Choice B because the fifth paragraph does not discuss the ecological advantages of hypercars, but rather their economic advantages. It is not Choice C because, although the paragraph does address the comparative cost of painting to support its argument, this is not its main point. It is not Choice D because the fifth paragraph does not discuss or even imply the idea, even if true, that lightweight cars will provide savings in fuel consumption.

36. J. Passage IV states that "new manufacturing methods . . . suggest that steel is a cheap material but is costly to make into cars, while carbon fiber is a costly material but is cheap to make into cars" (lines 24–29). That is, steel is *more* expensive to make into cars than polymers are. The answer is not Choice F because Passage IV states that after "nearly a century of materials and manufacturing experience based on steel" (lines 2–3), steel is "ubiquitous and familiar, and its fabrication highly evolved" (lines 5–6). It is not Choice G because the passage states that "The modern steel car expertly satisfies often conflicting demands—to be efficient and yet relatively safe" (lines 6–8). It is not Choice H because the passage states that "steel is a cheap material" (line 27) even while acknowledging that it "is costly to make into cars" (lines 27–28).

37. B. Passage IV states that "The same Detroit executives who think polymer composites will never gain much of a foothold in automaking may in fact spend their weekends zooming around in glass-and-polyester-composite boats" (lines 17–21). This is ironic in that the executives who reject modern materials for automaking may already be using them for sailing. The answer is not Choice A because hyperbole is rhetorical exaggeration, which is not used in this reference. It is not Choice C because metaphor is the use of analogy for rhetorical purpose, which is not present here. It is not Choice D because simile is rhetorical comparison, which also is not present here.

38. H. Passage IV states "Carbon fibers are . . . one-fourth as dense as steel" (lines 30–32). The answer is not Choice F because the passage states "Composites also make it possible to use the lightest-weight body designs" (lines 46–47) and "The lightweight, easy-to-handle parts can be lifted without a hoist" (lines 80–81). It is not choices G or J because the passage states "Carbon fibers are . . . one-fourth as dense as steel but stiffer and stronger."

39. D. The best answer is D because Passage IV, paragraph 2 states "industrial history is filled with examples in which standard materials have been quickly displaced." In advocating a change from steel to carbon fibers, the author is citing the fact that steel itself was, at one time, a new material in automobile engineering. The answer is not Choice A because the authors neither believe that change is ill-advised nor do they cite an example that would illustrate this. It is not Choice B because, while they are advocating for a change in materials, they do not imply that this change is inevitable. It is not Choice C because their argument in this part of Passage IV does not touch upon economics.

40. H. Passage IV states of steel unibody technology: "Each of those hundreds of steel parts needs an average of four tool-steel dies, each costing an average of $1 million. Polymer composites, in contrast, . . . [use] low-pressure molding dies . . ., cutting tooling costs by up to 90 percent" (lines 69–76). The answer is not Choice F because Passage IV does not mention the number of workers required for each type of car. It is not Choice G because the length of the design phase is not mentioned and may, in fact, be longer. It is not Choice J because, although the expense of painting steel body parts is reduced, this is not a function of the fact that a polymer-based car has fewer parts.

Science Test

Passage I

1. B. Deposition is the correct term. If you answered Choice D (sublimation) you may have read the direction of the arrows incorrectly. If you selected a different answer, you did not find the arrow with GAS at one end and SOLID at the other.

2. J. In the phase diagram of water (Figure 2), sublimation occurs where the "ice" and "water vapor" areas touch. There is no such point at 1 atm in this phase diagram. If you selected a different answer, you were looking at one of the other important transition points for water, such as the triple point (Choice F), the freezing/melting point (Choice G), or the condensing/boiling point (Choice H).

3. B. This is the "triple point" of water, as labeled on Figure 2. In addition, you can see that all three phases exist here because it is the one point where all three areas touch each other. If you selected a different answer, you either did not know that you were seeking the "triple point" described in the passage, or you did not correctly read the temperature and pressure values on that point in Figure 2.

4. J. 400°C is hotter than the critical point of water (which is 374°C according to Figure 2). Therefore, as described in the passage, there is no pressure at which water will condense into a liquid. If you selected choices F or G, you probably misread the significance of those pressure values. 1 atm is normal room pressure at sea level. 218 atm is the pressure at the critical point—the highest temperature and pressure at which water will condense. If you selected Choice H, then you misread the axes of the figure and gave the temperature of the critical point.

5. A. Water at 0.006 atm and heated from 0°C to 1° C will sublimate, according to Figure 2. Although 1°C is not shown directly, it is certainly to the right of the 0.01°C marker at the triple point, so you know that you are moving directly from a solid (0°C) to a gas (1°C).

Passage II

6. **F.** In Table 1, far more than half the *Daphnia* are on the light side, and far more than half of *Artemia* are on the dark side, when the light is on. They do not favor sides when the light is off.

7. **C.** There are many possible reasons that the invertebrates might be on one side or another that have nothing to do with the light. For example, there may be an unseen food source, oxygen imbalance, temperature gradient, and so on that either species favors. By switching the cover, the student controls for those unknown factors because the only thing changing between trials is the location of the light side.

8. **H.** In both Study 1 and Study 2, *Daphnia* are attracted to light, *Artemia* are repelled by light, and *Aëdes* do not respond either way. However, in Study 2, the invertebrates do not react as strongly (or at all) to some wavelengths.

9. **C.** The strongest reaction in Study 2, which resembles the results of Study 1, happens under 600 nanometers (yellow) light. In this trial, almost 90 percent of *Daphnia* move to the light side and almost 90 percent of *Artemia* move away from the light side.

10. **J.** One possible reason for *Daphnia* and *Artemia* to have no measurable phototactic response to the blue light is that they cannot sense that wavelength of light. In that case, Figure 2 suggests that neither can sense that wavelength of light.

11. **A.** *Aëdes* were not observed to cluster on either the light side or the dark side of the dish. There could be a number of explanations for this, but answer choices B and C are contrary to the data shown in Table 1. Choice D is one of many possible explanations that cannot be ruled out from the data shown, but it is also not specifically supported. Therefore, Choice A is the best answer because it is only as specific as the data can support.

Passage III

12. **G.** According to the passage, the test samples are stripped of one or more electrons. A basic fact of atomic structure is that electrons are negatively charged. Therefore, when an atom or molecule loses an electron, it becomes positively charged. Choice F is incorrect because the passage explains that the test sample loses electrons, not gains them. Choice H is a true statement, in that a sample that hits the wall loses its charge, but those molecules never hit the detector, which is what the question is asking about. Choice J correctly states that the charged particles are ions; however, for the reasons given, they are all positive ions, not half and half.

13. **C.** The formula given for m/z would find the mass/charge ratio of both atoms to be 12. This is because carbon $= \frac{12}{1}$ and magnesium $= \frac{24}{2}$. Although very slight differences might exist between the exact mass or charge of these elements, they are equal according to the formula given.

14. **F.** The output can be read that whatever the sample in Figure 2 is made of, about 80 percent of the constituent particles have a mass/charge ratio of 24. Choice G is a misinterpretation of the axes—there is no "sample 24." Choices H and J assume more information than is provided in the figure.

15. **B.** Remember from the passage that the particles occasionally lose more than one electron. Most of the magnesium in Figure 2 has a mass of 24 and a charge of 1+. A small part of it may have a mass of 24 and a charge of 2+, giving it an m/z ratio of 12 instead of 24. Although the same could happen to the other isotopes, those rare instances are probably not plentiful enough to show in this figure. Choice A, while possible, is unlikely; an impurity is unlikely to also have the same properties of the part of the sample with a charge of 2+. Choices C and D are not consistent with the passage or the general principles of atomic structure.

16. **G.** The MgO molecule has a mass of $24 + 16 = 40$. With two electrons missing, the m/z ratio would be $\frac{40}{2} = 20$.

Passage IV

17. C. Scientist 1 wants to have a single database that records the sequence of the same gene in many species. Scientist 1 recognizes that sequencing the entire genome of every organism (Choice A) is currently beyond our reach; sequencing different genes haphazardly (Choice B) is disorganized and not standardized; and an actual unique-to-species barcode (Choice D) does not exist in organisms.

18. H. The answer to this question is summed up in Scientist 2's opening paragraph. Choice F is not correct as Scientist 2's final paragraph indicates that she thinks the database will be useful (and, therefore, is possible). Choices G and J are not correct because Scientist 2 does not support Scientist 1's proposal.

19. D. Scientist 1 is proposing to collaborate with other scientists to collect and organize a repository for specific genetic data, and not describing a discovery.

20. F. This compromise refines Scientist 1's methodology while it also addresses some of Scientist 2's concerns about data accuracy. Scientist 1 would oppose Choice G because he indicates that there is no single "perfect" gene. He would oppose Choice H because this haphazard data collection eliminates the key idea in barcoding—standardization. He would oppose Choice J because this would greatly and perhaps unnecessarily limit the utility of the barcode database.

21. B. Scientist 2 states her concerns regarding spurious and misleading results in her opening paragraph and continues to elaborate on these in her second paragraph. Scientist 2 does not address the selection of the gene COI (Choice A); she admits that many species can be identified from a single gene sequence (Choice C); and she specifically states that such a tool could be useful (Choice D).

22. H. As stated in the explanation for question 21, Scientist 2 admits that many species can be identified from a single gene sequence.

23. B. Scientist 2 states two main concerns: the single-gene approach is too narrow for reliable results, and new species identification should incorporate multiple lines of evidence.

Passage V

24. G. The passage notes that the magnetic field of the ocean floor combines with that of earth such that where the polarities are opposite, the readings are lower than the background magnetic field of earth. The measured magnetic field at 15 kilometers is lower than that of earth as shown in Figure 1, so that must be a region where the polarity at the ocean floor is reversed from the current polarity of the earth.

25. A. The data in Figure 2 form a clear "V" shape with a point at zero that can be assumed to be just to the right of the 40 kilometers mark. Zero, in this graph, indicates a rock age of zero million years—newly formed rock.

26. J. As shown in the figures and described in the passage, the polarity of the earth has switched several times in its history, and so older rocks may have the same or opposite polarity, depending on the polarity of the earth when they were formed.

27. B. According to Figure 1, the polarity of the ocean floor switches at a point about 20–25 kilometers from the start of the survey. This corresponds in Figure 2 to rocks between roughly 600,000–800,000 years old. Thus, Choice B is the best answer available. If you selected one of the other options, you may have read the graph incorrectly, misidentified the indicator in Figure 1 that showed where the earth's polarity switched, or read the wrong axis.

28. J. The pattern in the figures is of roughly symmetrical rock ages and magnetic field measurements, centered around 40–45 kilometers from the starting point. However, the center point of the data (40–45 km) is not the centerpoint of the graphs—it is shifted such that the 100 kilometers measurements do not have a matching set of data on the left side of the figures. Thus –10 kilometers from the starting point (that is, 10 kilometers before the starting point, off the left side of the graphs) should be similar to the data point on the far right of the graph, at 100 km from the starting point.

29. B. As indicated by the prefix "kilo-," 1 kilometer is 1000 meters; thus, 25 kilometers is 25,000 meters. The calculation is, therefore, $\dfrac{750,000 \text{ years}}{25,000 \text{ meters}}$. Eliminating the thousands, this becomes $\dfrac{750}{25}$. Dividing top and bottom by 25 will yield $\dfrac{30}{1}$, or 30 years per meter of crust formed. If you selected a different answer, you may have either not correctly transformed the units from kilometers, or not correctly divided the two numbers.

Passage VI

30. F. Although there are numerous fluctuations that track both the seasons (more ice in winter) and annual differences, the trend line in Figure 1 is a strong downward one.

31. B. As with the previous question, despite a significant amount of variation, there is a visible upward trend.

32. F. According to the figures, the Arctic currently averages an ice extent of about 14.75 million square kilometers, whereas the Antarctic averages about 13 million square kilometers. These numbers are derived by looking at the rightmost point (most current value) of the central trend line, not the peaks and valleys of the data.

33. B. The central trend line of the Antarctic ice mass graph shows a clear downward trend. As noted in the passage, this reflects the three-dimensional mass of ice (extent as well as thickness).

34. J. Although the ice extent of Antarctica is expanding in surface area, the total mass of ice in the southern hemisphere is declining, as shown in Figure 3. Therefore, based on the information provided so far, there appears to be more melting happening each year in both the Arctic and Antarctic.

Passage VII

35. A. Black ink absorbs wavelengths from 350 nanometers to more than 1000 nanometers. This range of more than 650 nanometers is greater than that of any of the other options.

36. G. In order to effectively remove the tattoo, the laser's energy must be absorbed by the tattoo ink. However, in order to avoid unpleasant side effects, the laser light must not be absorbed by the molecules hemoglobin or melanin.

37. C. Table 2 shows that the 1064 nanometers laser eliminated 75 percent of the black ink after five treatments—more than any other laser. However, it was not effective on red ink (5 percent removed). The 532 nanometers laser was very effective at removing red ink (68 percent removed after five treatments), but was not as effective at removing black ink (only 30 percent removed). The side effects of the 532 nanometers laser are important overall, but not relevant to the question of which laser most effectively removed which ink.

38. H. The absorption spectra of both hemoglobin and melanin include the 532 nanometers wavelength, and thus, both can absorb the energy from this laser. This can be seen in the right column of Table 1, which shows the full range of absorption rather than just the peak. Choices F and G, although true statements, are not good explanations for the side effects. Choice J is not specific enough to explain the side effects for this particular laser.

39. C. This answer is a correct statement of the relationship between the visible color of an object and the light that it reflects and absorbs. The other answers confuse the role of absorption and reflectance in determining the observed color.

40. F. The laser shines a light that is 755 nanometers. Green ink will absorb this light because it is within its absorption spectrum (550–900 nanometers, peaking at 700 nanometers) and, therefore, should be effective at removing the ink. The absorption spectra of hemoglobin and melanin do not include a value at 755 nanometers, and so they are not likely to absorb significant amounts of energy from the laser light. Thus, the hemoglobin and melanin are unlikely to be damaged, resulting in minimal side effects.

Practice Test 3

Final Preparation

One Week before the Exam

- **Clear your schedule** one week before the exam. Try to avoid scheduling events during this week so that you can focus on your preparation.
- **ACT website.** Review the ACT website at www.actstudent.org for updated exam information.
- **Review your notes** from this study guide and make sure you that know the question types, basic skills, strategies, and directions for each section on the test.
- **Practice tests.** Allow yourself enough time to review the practice problems you have already completed from this study guide. If you haven't yet taken all of the practice tests, take the practice tests during this week. Be sure to time yourself as you practice.
- **Testing center.** Make sure that you are familiar with the driving directions and where the parking facilities near to the testing center are located.
- **Relax the night before the exam.** The evening before the exam, try to get a good night's sleep. Trying to cram a year's worth of reading and studying into one night can cause you to feel emotionally and physically exhausted. Save your energy for the exam day.

Exam Day

- **Arrive early.** Arrive at the exam location in plenty of time (at least 30 minutes early).
- **Dress appropriately** to adapt to any room temperature. If you dress in layers, you can always take off clothing to adjust to warmer temperatures.
- **Bring identification.** Remember to bring the required identification documents: valid photo-bearing ID and your authorization voucher.
- **Leave your electronic devices.** Leave all electronic devices at home or in your car (cell phone, smartphone, PDA, calculator, etc.). You may also be asked to remove your watch during the exam.
- **Bring an acceptable calculator** to perform math calculations; also bring extra batteries. For more information about calculator requirements, visit the ACT website www.actstudent.org/faq/calculator.html.
- **Answer easy questions first.** Start off crisply, working the questions you know first, and then go back and try to answer the others within the section. Use the elimination strategy to determine whether a problem is possibly solvable or too difficult to solve.
- **Don't get stuck on any one question.** Never spend more than about one minute on any multiple-choice question.
- **Guess,** if you can narrow down your choices. Remember there is no penalty for guessing.
- **Writing in the test booklet (not answer sheet)** is a test-taking advantage. You can write notes in the margins to perform calculations, redraw diagrams, note eliminated choices, or simply make helpful notes to jog your memory.

Notes

Notes

Notes

WILDLIFE

OF THE WORLD

WILDLIFE

OF THE WORLD

Penguin Random House

First published in Great Britain in 2015 by
Dorling Kindersley Limited 80 Strand, London WC2R 0RL
Copyright © 2015 Dorling Kindersley Limited
A Penguin Random House Company

2 4 6 8 10 9 7 5 3 1

001-259136-October/2015

A CIP catalogue record for this book
is available from the British Library.
ISBN: 978-0-2411-8600-8
Printed in China

A WORLD OF IDEAS:
SEE ALL THERE IS TO KNOW
www.dk.com

Consultants

■ MAMMALS
Professor David Macdonald CBE is a leading world authority on mammals and is founder and director of the Wildlife Conservation Research Unit at Oxford University. Aside from his many scientific publications, he is known for his prize-winning books and films, such as *Meerkats United*.

■ BIRDS
David Burnie studied Zoology at Bristol University and has contributed to nearly 150 books on animals and the environment. He is a Fellow of the Zoological Society of London.

■ REPTILES
Dr Colin McCarthy is a scientific associate of the Life Sciences Department, and formerly collection manager of Reptiles, Amphibians, and Fish, at the Natural History Museum, London.

■ AMPHIBIANS
Professor Tim Halliday retired as professor of biology at the Open University in 2009, but continues to pursue his interest in the reproductive biology of amphibians.

■ INVERTEBRATES
Dr George C McGavin is a zoologist, author, explorer, and television presenter. He is an honorary research associate of the Oxford University Museum of Natural History and a research associate of the Department of Zoology at Oxford University. His TV credits include *Expedition Borneo*, *Lost Land of the Jaguar*, *Lost Land of the Tiger*, and *Monkey Planet*.

■ GENERAL CONSULTANT
Dr Kim Dennis-Bryan is a palaeontologist who worked at the Natural History Museum, London, before becoming an associate lecturer in life and environmental sciences at the Open University. As well as scientific publications, she has contributed to and consulted on many zoology and geology books.

Contributors

Jamie Ambrose is a UK-based American author, editor, and journalist with a special interest in the natural world.

Richard Beatty (glossary writer) is a writer and editor based in Edinburgh, UK.

Dr Amy-Jane Beer is a biologist, nature writer, and editor of the UK charity PTES (People's Trust for Endangered Species) *Wildlife World* magazine.

Ben Hoare is features editor of *BBC Wildlife* magazine, UK.

Rob Hume is a natural history writer and editor with a lifetime interest in wildlife, especially birds. He is author of more than 20 books, including DK's *Bird*, and *Birds of Europe and North America*.

Steve Parker has a zoology degree and has written more than 200 books and websites on nature, ecology, conservation, and evolution.

Dr Katie Parsons has a PhD in animal behaviour and ecology. She is currently a freelance natural history writer and conservation consultant.

Tom Jackson is a zoologist and science writer based in Bristol, UK.

DK LONDON
Senior Art Editor Ina Stradins
Senior Editors Janet Mohun, Peter Frances
Project Editor Gill Pitts
Project Art Editor Francis Wong
Designer Simon Murrell
Editorial Assistant Frankie Piscitelli
Indexer Hilary Bird
Picture Researcher Liz Moore
New Photography Gary Ombler
Cartography Simon Mumford, Ed Merritt
Jacket Designer Mark Cavanagh
Jacket Editor Claire Gell
Jacket Design Development Manager Sophia MTT
Pre-production Producer Francesca Wardell
Producer Rita Sinha
Managing Art Editor Michael Duffy
Managing Editor Angeles Gavira
Art Director Karen Self
Design Director Phil Ormerod
Publisher Liz Wheeler
Publishing Director Jonathan Metcalf

DK INDIA
Senior Art Editor Mahua Mandal
Senior Editor Vineetha Mokkil
Project Editor Dharini Ganesh
Art Editors Divya P R, Anjali Sachar
Editor Susmita Dey
Managing Art Editor Sudakshina Basu
Managing Editor Rohan Sinha
Picture Researchers Deepak Negi, Surya Sankash Sarangi
Jacket Designer Suhita Dharamjit
Managing Jackets Editor Saloni Singh
Production Manager Pankaj Sharma
Pre-production Manager Balwant Singh
Senior DTP Designers Harish Aggarwal, Vishal Bhatia
DTP Designer Vijay Kandwal

DATA PANELS

Summary information is given at the start of each profile. Measurements are for adults of the species and may be a typical range, single-figure average, or maximum, depending on available records.

LENGTH (all groups)
MAMMALS Head and body excluding tail. For dolphins, whales, seals, sea lions, manatees, and dugongs it includes the tail. **BIRDS** Tip of bill to tip of tail (except penguins, ostrich, rhea, and emu, which indicates height from feet to head). **REPTILES** Tip of snout to tip of tail (apart from tortoises and turtles where it is the length of the upper shell). **FISH AND AMPHIBIANS** Head and body, including tail. **INSECTS** Body length; wingspan for butterflies and moths.

WEIGHT (mammals, birds, reptiles, amphibians, and fish only)
Body weight.

DIET All diet listed by commas (apart from caterpillars' diet; butterflies' diet, separated by a semicolon).

BREEDING SEASON (amphibians only) The time of year in which breeding occurs.

STATUS (all groups) *Wildlife of the World* uses the IUCN Red List (see p381) and other threat categories, as follows:
Critically endangered (IUCN) Facing an extremely high risk of extinction in the wild in the immediate future.
Endangered (IUCN) Facing a very high risk of extinction in the wild in the near future.
Vulnerable (IUCN) Facing a high risk of extinction in the wild in the medium-term future.
Near threatened (IUCN) Strong possibility of becoming endangered in the near future.
Common/Locally common (IUCN: Least concern) Low-risk category that includes widespread and common species.
Not known (IUCN: Data deficient, Not evaluated) Not a threat category. Population and distribution data is insufficient for assessment. Data not yet assessed against IUCN criteria.

HABITAT SYMBOLS

Temperate and deciduous forest, open woodland

Evergreen, coniferous, and boreal forest and woodland

Tropical forest and rainforest, dry forest of Madagascar

Mountains, highlands, scree slopes, any habitat considered alpine or subalpine conditions

Desert and semi-desert

Open habitats including grassland, moor, heath, savanna, fields, and scrub

Wetlands and all still bodies of water, including lakes, ponds, pools, marshes, bogs, and swamps

Rivers, streams, and all flowing water

Mangrove swamps, above or below the waterline

Coastal areas including beaches and cliffs, areas just above high tide, in the intertidal zone, and in shallow, offshore waters

Seas and oceans

Coral reefs and waters immediately around them

Polar regions, including tundra and icebergs

Urban areas, including buildings, parks, and gardens

LOCATION MAP

Shows distribution of species in the wild

CONTENTS

ANIMAL HABITATS
10

12 FORESTS

14 GRASSLANDS

16 EXTREME ENVIRONMENTS

18 AQUATIC ENVIRONMENTS

NORTH AMERICA
20

22 PEAKS AND PRAIRIES

24 CANADIAN ARCTIC

34 YELLOWSTONE

44 CENTRAL GREAT PLAINS

52 SIERRA NEVADA

60 MOJAVE DESERT

66 FLORIDA EVERGLADES

CENTRAL AND SOUTH AMERICA
74

76 LAND OF THE JAGUAR

78 COSTA RICAN RAINFOREST

84 ANDEAN YUNGAS

90 AMAZON RAINFOREST

100 THE PANTANAL

108 ANDEAN ALTIPLANO

114 ARGENTINE PAMPAS

122 GALAPAGOS ISLANDS

EUROPE
130

132 PLAINS AND PENINSULAS

134 NORWEGIAN FJORDS

140 SCOTTISH HIGHLANDS

146 THE CAMARGUE

152 TAGUS VALLEY

158 THE ALPS

164 BAVARIAN FOREST

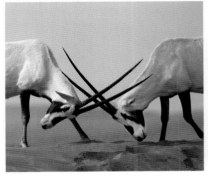

AFRICA
174

176 A SUNBAKED LAND

178 ETHIOPIAN HIGHLANDS

184 GREAT RIFT VALLEY LAKES

192 SERENGETI SAVANNAS

208 CONGO BASIN

218 OKAVANGO DELTA

228 KALAHARI DESERT

236 MADAGASCAN DRY
FORESTS

ASIA
244

246 LAND OF EXTREMES

248 ARABIAN HIGHLANDS

254 TERAI-DUAR SAVANNAS

266 EASTERN HIMALAYAS

272 UPPER YANGTZE FORESTS

278 GOBI DESERT

284 NIHONKAI MONTANE
FOREST

292 BORNEAN RAINFOREST

302 SULU-SULAWESI SEAS

AUSTRALASIA
310

312 THE RED CONTINENT

314 NEW GUINEA MONTANE
FOREST

320 NORTH AUSTRALIA
SAVANNAS

328 GREAT SANDY-TANAMI
DESERT

334 EAST AUSTRALIAN
FORESTS

344 GREAT BARRIER REEF

354 NEW ZEALAND MIXED
FOREST

ANTARCTICA
360

362 LAND OF ICE AND SNOW

364 SOUTHERN OCEAN ISLANDS

370 ANTARCTIC PENINSULA

378 GLOSSARY

382 INDEX

398 ACKNOWLEDGMENTS

FOREWORD

The range, the diversity, and the sheer beauty of life on show in this book is utterly astonishing. It will be almost impossible to read through and come up with a favourite region, the most interesting animal, the most attractive species, or even the most effective survival strategy, because on every page there is a likely contender. It is not all about the most dashing or glamorous of the animals – the tigers, the peregrines, the polar bears – nor the most engaging – the chimpanzees, the pandas, the raccoons. It is also about the pygmy seahorses, the silky anteaters, the giant parrot snakes, and most of all, it is about the sum of all these species.

This book separates wildlife geographically into zones that typify and exemplify the world's notable habitats and ecosystems. Within each, a portfolio of animals portrays the range and types of creatures living there and explains their adaptations and survival strategies. Some species are familiar, others bizarre, some rare, others common, some popular, still others feared, but all are celebrated visually with a superb pictorial depiction and zoologically with some fascinating facts.

For me, the book works on many levels. A brilliant introduction to wildlife for the younger reader, a cover-to-cover read for the enthusiast, a book to dip into when you need a slice of life's riches, or a ready reckoner when you need to satisfy your curiosity on a nagging question about a species or its habits. It is lovely, a treasury, an encyclopaedia, a rich catalogue of knowledge and surprises. It is everything I wanted when I was 10, I would have burst with excitement if I had found this in the local library back then! But the fact that 40 years on I am still as excited by this fabulous book is a testament to the power these pages have on young minds and to the lifelong interest they stir into life. I remember turning from my humble jar of tadpoles to read about armadillos and sharks and tortoises, and other such species. Dreaming about fantastic encounters with such exotic animals was a rich fuel to the mind of the budding naturalist.

We live in an age of instantly available information. Within seconds we can source facts via smartphones, tablets, and computers. But these facts, when seen in isolation, are disconnected and lack context. Knowledge only develops if all relevant facts are joined together to generate a wider understanding – something of altogether greater value. And this is what the book is all about – it is not about random facts on random species, but about relationships, concepts, strategies, and the complex way in which everything is intertwined. It is about the science of life.

Science is the art of understanding truth and beauty. This book is a beautiful work of art filled with truths – what a combination!

CHRIS PACKHAM
NATURALIST AND WILDLIFE PHOTOGRAPHER

ANIMAL HABITATS

Two-thirds of Earth's surface is covered by oceans. It is this abundance of water that enables the planet to support billions of living organisms, both in the seas and on the continents and islands that make up the land. The environment in which an organism lives is its habitat, and the huge range of habitats found on land are home to a vast number of plant species and a spectacular diversity of animals.

Geographers divide the world into ecoregions characterized by broad habitat types such as forest, grassland, wetland, desert, or polar zones. These can in turn be subdivided almost endlessly into more precise habitats, each supporting a unique community of plant and animals.

Climate exerts a powerful influence over each of the world's great ecoregions. Energy input from the Sun is greatest at the tropics, and the transfer of this energy via the atmosphere and oceans generates the currents of air and water that drive the world's weather systems. On land, weathering of rock leads to the formation of soil in which plants grow, forming the basis of ecological communities.

Variety of life

Biodiversity refers to the variety of life in a given habitat or ecoregion. As a rule, biodiversity increases towards the equator, with tropical forests and warm coastal seas registering the greatest numbers of species. Both poles are inhabited by comparatively few animal species, but in the Arctic, many animals live on land whereas in Antarctica, most animal life is found in the ocean.

Plants and animals become better adapted to their particular habitat through natural selection – those most suited to the environmental conditions survive in greater numbers and produce more offspring. This is a continuous process as habitats change slowly over time. Sudden events such as volcanic eruptions, floods, or human development can have catastrophic impacts, especially on species that are specialized to a certain way of life. So-called generalist species cope better with change, such as a fall or rise in temperature, but may be displaced by specialist species when conditions stabilize.

ECOREGION

The Alps comprise one of the world's best-known montane ecoregions. They extend into eight European countries, forming a snow-tipped arc that stretches from France and Italy in the southwest to Austria in the east.

CONTINENT

In southern Europe, the warm waters of the Mediterranean lap the coast and much of the land is covered by Mediterranean woodland and scrub. The soaring mountains of the Alps form a physical barrier, beyond which lies the colder, wetter north.

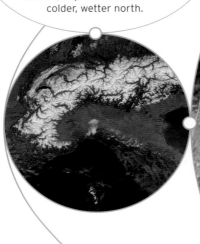

Scientists estimate that only **14 per cent of species** have been identified so far, and of those, **91 per cent live on land**

THE ALPS ECOREGION

If you pick any place on the planet, you will find a unique set of conditions, influenced by geography, latitude, and climate. This means the area, such as the Alps, will be home to a unique community of plants and animals.

HABITATS

The habitats of the Alps are found elsewhere in the world, but here their characteristics are contrasted by large differences in altitude. The grasses and herbs found in a high alpine meadow, for example, are very different to those in a lowland grassland.

FOOD CHAINS

One way all the plants and animals in a habitat interact is via a food chain. Plants convert the Sun's energy into food for growth and reproduction, and are eaten by herbivorous animals. These in turn become food for predatory or scavenging animals.

MOUNTAINS AND SCREE SLOPES

Mountains are effectively inland islands, where unique species can live and evolve in isolation. Slope habitats are heavily influenced by latitude, altitude, incline, aspect, and the underlying rock. Conditions above the tree line (beyond which no trees grow) are harsh.

EAGLE OWL

The Eurasian eagle owl is the top predatory bird in the Alps. It hunts mainly small mammals, but will also target other birds of prey.

MONTANE FOREST

Forests on mountains are banded according to altitude, with broadleaf trees dominating the warmer, lower slopes, and conifers thriving on higher ground up to the tree line. Because sloping, rocky ground is difficult to farm, mountainsides often retain more tree cover than flatter ground.

MARMOT

Alpine marmots spend the summer months feeding on lush grasses and herbs, building up fat to help them survive the long alpine winter.

ALPINE MEADOW

Where flooding or unstable ground prevent trees encroaching, grasses and herbs flourish in spectacular diversity. At high-altitude, there is a sudden burst of growth in spring and summer and the meadows are filled with blooms – an important food source for many animals.

DANDELION

As well as providing food for marmots, alpine dandelions are a welcome source of nectar for butterflies and bees.

FORESTS
The lungs of our planet

Roughly one-third of the world's land area is covered with trees. Some are the largest and longest-living organisms on Earth. Their roots, trunks, branches, and leaves form an uncountable variety of microhabitats, the character of which varies according to location. Dead and decaying leaves and wood also form a vital component of forest ecosystems, providing habitat and food, and releasing nutrients back into forest soils. Clearings left by fallen trees throng with light-loving ground plants and insects until new trees close the gap.

Boreal and temperate forests

The wide range of climates in temperate areas supports coniferous, deciduous, broadleaf evergreen, and mixed forest. In the far northern boreal forests, winters are longer, temperatures lower, and snow fall more frequent – conditions to which coniferous trees are well adapted. Their triangular shape and narrow leaves prevent excess snow settling on their branches and

breaking them. By keeping their dark green leaves all year, they can make food whenever the Sun shines. The resin-filled leaves are distasteful to all but a few insects and so are not eaten even when food is scarce.

Farther south, winters are still cold, but summers are longer and warmer. Forests here are generally deciduous. The trees have broad leaves and spreading branches that maximize their ability to harvest light and get

TEMPERATE BROADLEAF

The seasonal availability of some foods presents a challenge to woodland animals. Some, such as grey squirrels, solve the problem by hoarding nuts and seeds in tree holes and underground caches, to which they return in winter.

TEMPERATE CONIFEROUS

Non-flowering plants, such as conifers, produce their seeds in cones, which are released when dry conditions cause the cones to open. The tiny seeds of western hemlock are eaten by chickadees, pine siskins, and deer mice.

BOREAL

The hardy, evergreen conifers found in northern boreal forests provide less food than other trees due to the harsh climate and short growing season. In winter, when food is scarce, many animals migrate to warmer areas or hibernate.

SEYCHELLES ▷
Tropical rainforest on Silhouette Island, Seychelles, in the Indian Ocean.

energy from the Sun. However, such leaves also pose a risk in strong winds and heavy snow, so temperate broadleaf trees tend to produce thin leaves that are shed in autumn. The trees remain in an almost dormant state all winter and produce new leaves the following spring.

In the most southerly temperate areas, summers are long, hot, and dry, and winters are warm and wet. The broadleaf evergreen forest that grows in these climates ranges from the tall eucalypts of Australia to the shorter, more open woodland of parts of California and the Mediterranean.

Tropical forests

At the equator, the climate is warm and moist all year round, providing ideal conditions for plant growth and creating the most diverse of all terrestrial habitats. Trees and other forest plants grow in profusion forming vast rainforests, cloud forests, and montane forests that are green all year round. In the northern tropics, the forests of Southeast Asia are influenced by heavy monsoon rains, giving the region distinct wet and dry seasons. During the rains the forest is lush and green but in the dry season, many trees shed their leaves, allowing the sunlight to penetrate to the forest floor.

In areas where there is a long dry season, such as Madagascar and the Caribbean, tropical and subtropical dry forests are found. Composed mainly of broadleaved trees that shed their leaves to conserve water during dry spells, these forests are less diverse than other tropical forests. However, they are still home to a diverse community of animals adapted to cope with the demands of living in a hot, dry climate.

MEDITERRANEAN

Broadleaf evergreen forest is also known as Mediterranean forest, and typical trees include cork oaks, some species of pine, and eucalypts. Cork oaks are a particularly important habitat, providing food, shelter, and nesting sites for many species of animal.

TROPICAL DRY

Trees in tropical dry forests survive the long dry season by shedding their leaves, having thick bark, and deep roots that access groundwater. Many species have thorns or spines as a deterrent to animals that might try to feed on them.

TROPICAL MOIST

The dense canopy of the broadleaf trees growing in most tropical forests holds most of the forest's food. This means that many animals are adapted to life in the trees and are rarely seen at ground level. They include scarlet macaws and spider monkeys.

GRASSLANDS
Little shelter, but plenty of food

Where the climate is too dry to support trees, but wet enough for plants to grow, grasses and low-growing herbs dominate the landscape. These plants are highly diverse, and grassland habitats range from the high alpine meadows of Europe to tree-studded African savanna, tall grass prairies of North America, windswept Asian steppes, seas of head-height grass in India, China, and South America, and the dry desert scrublands of Australia. Today, they account for about 40 per cent of the land area.

Temperate grasslands
The relatively flat terrain and scarcity of trees in temperate grassland gives rise to vast expanses of fairly uniform landscape across which strong winds can blow unimpeded. There are fewer habitats than in forests and, as a result, there are fewer animal species in temperate grassland, too. Grass is, however, able to support vast numbers of herbivores because, unusually in plants, its growth point is below ground level. As it is untouched

by the animals that graze on it, grass regrows quickly after it has been cropped. This adaptation also allows grass to survive long periods without rain that kill many other plants.

In the past, grassland covered large tracts of the temperate world, but with the advent of agriculture, much of it has been used for growing crops – often with unforeseen consequences. Grass is unusual in that it channels most of its energy into growing roots rather than leaves. This allows grass to get the water and nutrients it needs and has

TEMPERATE GRASSLAND

Although grasses predominate, many herbaceous plants also grow in temperate grassland. Bright flowers attract insects, which in turn attract insect-eating birds. The grassland also provides food for mammals of all sizes, from bison to hares.

MONTANE GRASSLAND

These high-altitude grasslands occur at all latitudes. The plants and animals that live in these regions must be able to endure low temperatures, intense sunlight, and potentially harmful ultraviolet radiation. They include the guanaco of South America.

CUSTER STATE PARK ▷
The prairie habitat in South Dakota, US, provides a natural refuge for a herd of American bison.

the side-effect of stabilizing the soil it is growing in. When land such as this is ploughed and the grass removed, the soil rapidly deteriorates and is blown away as dust, leaving only bare earth in its place.

Tropical grasslands

Scattered trees and scrub are a feature of tropical savannas, making them more diverse than their temperate counterparts. However, they cannot encroach far because, unlike grass, trees and scrub cannot survive the frequent fires that occur during the dry season. Although these fires appear destructive, the ash created provides soil nutrients that fuel the growth of fresh grass during the wet season that follows.

While some tropical grasses, such as bamboo and elephant grass, grow very tall, most savanna grassland provides little cover, making it difficult for both predators and prey to hide. Predators rely on stealth, speed, and sometimes cooperation to catch their food, whereas prey animals rely on spotting hunters before they get too close and running away. They do this by living in groups, which offers safety in numbers, and by relying on their senses. Prey animals have eyes on the sides of their heads for good all round vision, large swivelling ears, and an excellent sense of smell – hares are a good example.

GRASSLAND DISTRIBUTION

The largest temperate grasslands are the prairies of North America and the Asian steppes, which stretch from the far east of Europe to northern China. Tropical grasslands include those of sub-Saharan Africa and Brazil.

■ Temperate grasslands ■ Tropical grasslands

SCRUB

In areas with long dry summers such as California and the Mediterranean, there is a transition zone between woods and grassland that is dominated by low, woody shrub vegetation. Also called heathland and chaparral, scrub offers more cover for animals.

TROPICAL GRASSLAND

These are usually warm year-round, with a long dry season followed by a short wet season that sees a spurt of plant growth. African savanna elephants help to maintain their habitat by eating woody shrubs and knocking down trees to feed on their leaves.

WETLANDS

Areas of land that are routinely inundated by fresh or salt water are often dominated by grasses, reeds, and sedges, while water hyacinths form free-floating mats of vegetation. Wetlands support many species, particularly birds.

EXTREME ENVIRONMENTS
Survival against the odds

Polar areas and deserts are some of the least hospitable habitats on Earth. The lack of rain and extreme temperatures create difficult conditions for life, and the few humans that live there lead a semi-nomadic existence. Today, several of these fragile, untouched ecoregions are under threat because of the discovery of oil, gas, and other minerals.

Polar regions

Much of the Arctic and Antarctica is effectively a desert gripped by ice. Winters are long and permanently dark and summers are short but, because the Sun never sets, there is a continual source of energy for plant growth. Where rock is exposed, the soil is virtually non-existent, and usually at freezing point or below. Trees cannot survive here, and vegetation is limited to mosses, lichens, fungi, and a handful of flowering plants. This open, rather featureless landscape, called tundra, is found between 60-80 degrees north and south of the equator. It is far more extensive in the northern hemisphere, covering large tracts of northern Canada and Russia. Similar areas on mountains above the tree line are called alpine tundra.

Polar regions may support a number of large land animals, but most are reliant on the sea for their food. This is because despite the icy conditions, sea life is plentiful. The cold waters of the Arctic and Southern oceans are rich in oxygen and the seabed provides

ALPINE TUNDRA

Found at altitudes of around 3,000 m (10,000 ft) with snow above and boreal forest below, alpine tundra is cold and windy and has sparse vegetation. Golden eagles hunt there during the summer as the open ground provides little cover for their prey.

ARCTIC TUNDRA

The Arctic poppy is one of the few flowering plants found on the Arctic tundra. The short growing season means the plant must grow, flower, and produce its seeds rapidly. It is usually pollinated by flies, but can self-pollinate if necessary.

POLAR

Polar regions may seem inhospitable, but their icy waters support several specialist mammal species, including walruses and seals. Small ice floes and broken pack ice are ideal habitat for bearded seals, for example, as they need easy access to the water to feed.

ANTARCTICA ▷
Snow covers the tundra on the northeast tip of the Antarctic Peninsula in winter.

plentiful nutrients. In summer, these oceans provide rich pickings for the many marine mammals and seabirds that migrate to these areas to feed and breed. The tundra also has summer visitors, such as reindeer that spend the winter sheltering from the cold in the taiga forest to the south, but return each summer.

Desert regions

Most of the world's great hot deserts, such as Africa's Sahara, are found in the subtropics, where dry conditions persist for months at a time. Others, such as the Mojave in the US southwest, are found on the dry leeward side of mountains. A few, such as the Atacama Desert in South America, are coastal and lack rain due to cold offshore water inhibiting cloud formation. Cold deserts are found in continental interiors and are very hot in summer and very cold in winter. All of these deserts are dry, receiving less than 15 cm (6 in) rain annually, and most are cloudless. The exception is coastal

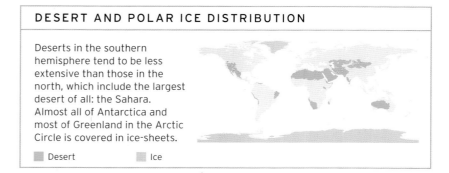

DESERT AND POLAR ICE DISTRIBUTION

Deserts in the southern hemisphere tend to be less extensive than those in the north, which include the largest desert of all: the Sahara. Almost all of Antarctica and most of Greenland in the Arctic Circle is covered in ice-sheets.

■ Desert   ■ Ice

desert, which can benefit from early morning fog drifting in from the ocean. Hot deserts, although hot all year, are cold at night as the lack of cloud cover allows heat to escape freely. Cold deserts also have large daily temperature fluctuations but in winter, temperatures are below freezing and snow is not uncommon.

Plants growing in deserts must cope not only with lack of water and extreme temperatures, but also with soils that have little organic matter and few soil microorganisms. All desert plants and animals tend to restrict their reproductive efforts to periods of rainfall and show a range of adaptations to heat, such as being able to retain or store water, and many animals forage at night.

COLD DESERT

Despite the hostile treeless environment, limited rainfall, and enormous seasonal temperature differences, cold deserts are home to a variety of animals. Small mammals include the dwarf hamster, large ones the critically endangered Gobi bear.

COASTAL DESERT

In the early morning, coastal deserts benefit from moisture carried inland as fog. It is an important source of water for a number of arthropods and reptiles, some of which have adaptations to enhance water collection and storage.

HOT DESERT

Daytime temperatures in hot deserts are so high that even "cold blooded" arthropods, which are reliant on the Sun for warmth, seek shade to avoid the heat. Many animals, such as the deathstalker scorpion, avoid the Sun altogether by being nocturnal.

AQUATIC ENVIRONMENTS
Planet Earth is really planet Ocean

More than 70 per cent of the Earth's surface is covered by water, which in its liquid form is essential for life. Water is continually circulating around the planet, evaporating from its surface and being carried as water vapour in the atmosphere until it falls again as rain. Around 95 per cent of the Earth's water is salt water, which is found in seas, oceans, and coastal lagoons as well a few isolated soda and salt lakes. The other 5 per cent is fresh water, which is seen in rivers and lakes, but also includes the ice held in polar regions and glaciers, and groundwater that is hidden from view. The challenges of life in fresh and salt water are very different and relatively few animal species are able to move from one to the other.

ranging from fast-flowing rivers and swampy wetlands to the relatively calmer but deeper water of many lakes. Organisms living in lakes and rivers must cope with strong currents, survive freezing conditions in winter, and endure summer droughts when some rivers and

Rivers and lakes
Fresh water is vital for life on land – without water plants cannot grow and animals would have nothing to drink. Rivers and lakes create diverse habitats

LAKES

Lakes are often isolated, with little opportunity for new aquatic species to colonize them (unless introduced by humans). As a result they may have large numbers of endemic species or subspecies that have evolved to exploit the available habitats.

MANGROVES

These wetlands provide safe inshore nurseries for various marine animals as well as breeding sites and roosts for many bird species, including the scarlet ibis. These wading birds use their long, curved, sensitive bills to locate food in the soft mud.

RIVERS

The steeper the gradient of a river, the faster the water flows and the stronger the current. More animal species tend to be found downstream, where slower-flowing water allows aquatic plants to grow. This increases the number of habitats.

CALIFORNIA COAST ▷
The sheer power of a breaking wave in Monterey Bay, US, is revealed.

shallow lakes disappear. Plants, including tree species, tend to grow where water flow is slow along stream and river banks or on islands in river channels. However, plants, such as water hyacinth, can cover large areas of fresh water. Animals may be confined to water – fish, for example – while others spend only part of their life there, including frogs, hippopotamuses, and dragonflies. Each species occupies a particular habitat, and together they create a distinct community unique to that particular river or lake.

Mangroves

Restricted to tropical and subtropical regions, mangrove swamps usually develop in intertidal areas on muddy shores, although some extend for some distance inland. Only mangrove trees can grow successfully in the waterlogged, salty mud and survive regular inundation by seawater. The different species have various adaptations that allow them to do this, including having prop roots for additional support in soft sediment, and the ability to filter out salt as it enters their roots, or to store it in their leaves and lose it when the leaves are shed. Mangrove swamp is the most endangered of the world's habitats due to large scale removal in recent years to make way for aquatic farming of fish, crustaceans, and molluscs.

Oceans and seas

Although the world's oceans are interconnected, numerous seas, each with their own distinct characteristics, exist within them. The sunlit upper waters of the ocean have the most organisms, and coral reefs are among the most biodiverse. However, ecoregions also exist much deeper, with food chains based on organic material drifting down from above or on bacteria able to manufacture food using chemical reactions that do not need sunlight. Coastal regions are extremely harsh environments for wildlife as rocks and sandy shores are periodically exposed to the air, and buffeting by waves can damage and dislodge organisms unless they are firmly anchored. Oceans support a huge variety of life, ranging from microscopic algae that underpin oceanic food chains to the planet's largest living animal, the blue whale.

COASTS

Exposure to the air twice a day and buffeting by the waves are just two features of coastlines that make them the most demanding of all habitats to live in. On rocky shores, many animal species have shells for protection and to retain moisture.

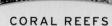

CORAL REEFS

Coral reefs provide plenty of food and hiding places. This means that reef fish are usually colourful and come in a multitude of shapes and sizes as, unlike oceanic fish, they do not need to be streamlined and fast to hunt or escape from predators.

OPEN OCEAN

Most life in the open ocean is found at or just below the surface as this is where most of the food is produced. Despite the vast expanse of this habitat, only around 5 per cent of the world's animal species live here.

British Columbia

A young grizzly bear searches for salmon during a spawning run in a Canadian river. Its mother won't be far as cubs don't become independent until they are more than two years old.

North America

PEAKS AND PRAIRIES

North America

The world's third largest continent is bordered by the Pacific, Arctic, and Atlantic oceans, and the Caribbean Sea. Geographically, Greenland and the islands of the Caribbean are considered part of North America. Most of the continent occupies a single plate, with small parts of Mexico and California lying on the neighbouring Pacific plate, which abuts the North American plate along the infamous San Andreas fault. The mountain ranges of the Western Cordillera have a profound influence on the climate of the west side of the continent. For example, rainshadow deserts form on the mountains' eastern flanks. Smaller, more ancient mountain ranges follow the eastern coast, while much of the interior of North America is low-lying.

The vast north-south extent of the continent means it encompasses a wide range of climate types, from Arctic cold to tropical heat. Dominant ecosystems include tundra, boreal and temperate forest, prairie, desert, and extensive wetlands. These diverse habitats support an impressive range of animals, from the largest mammals – American bison and bears – to alligators living in the swamps and wetlands of the southeast.

KEY DATA

ECOSYSTEMS

- Tropical broadleaf forest
- Tropical dry broadleaf forest
- Tropical coniferous forest
- Temperate broadleaf forest
- Temperate coniferous forest
- Mediterranean woodland, scrub
- Tropical, subtropical grassland
- Temperate grassland
- Wetland
- Desert, scrub
- Boreal forest/taiga
- Tundra
- Ice

AVERAGE TEMPERATURE

°F	°C
86	30
68	20
	10
50	0
32	-10
14	-20
-4	-30
-22	-40
-40	

AVERAGE RAINFALL

IN	MM
394	10,000
295	7,500
197	5,000
98	2,500
0	0

CANADIAN SHIELD

Extending north from the Great Lakes to the Arctic Ocean is one of the world's largest geologic continental shields (exposed Precambrian crystalline rocks). The rocks of the Canadian Shield have remained above sea level for almost 4 billion years. Soils form a thin layer or are absent as the rocks have been scoured by ice during repeated glaciations.

ALEUTIAN ISLANDS

An arc of 69 volcanic islands, largely treeless and fogbound, that support an array of plant life and seabird colonies.

ARCTIC OCEAN

PACIFIC OCEAN

Greenland

Labrador Sea

Labrador

Baffin Bay

Baffin Island

Davis Strait

Hudson Strait

Péninsule d'Ungava

Ellesmere Island

Queen Elizabeth Islands

Hudson Bay

Parry Islands

Reindeer

Victoria Island

Banks Island

Lake Athabasca

Great Bear Lake

Great Slave Lake

Beaufort Sea

Mackenzie

Mackenzie Mountains

Rock

Brooks Range

Mount McKinley (Denali) 6,194m

Yukon

Gulf of Alaska

Queen Charlotte

Bering Strait

Kodiak Island

Bering Sea

Aleutian Islands

ATLANTIC OCEAN

Nova Scotia

St Lawrence

Cape Cod

APPALACHIANS

The oldest mountains in North America include the Great Smoky and Blue Ridge ranges. The region is largely forested and has rivers rich in fish and invertebrates.

Lake Ontario

Niagara Falls

Lake Erie

Lake Huron

Great Lakes

Lake Superior

Lake Michigan

Canadian Shield

Ohio

Illinois

Tennessee

Alabama

Appalachian Mountains

Blue Ridge

Straits of Florida

The Everglades

Lake Okeechobee

Gulf of Mexico

Caribbean Sea

DEAN'S BLUE HOLE

Located in the Bahamas, the world's deepest salt water blue hole plunges to depths of 202 m (663 ft). A blue hole is a water-filled sinkhole formed by rainwater seeping into limestone bedrock. The entrance is now underwater.

BLUE DAMSELFISH

Yucatan Peninsula

Mississippi Delta

Mississippi

Arkansas

NORTH AMERICA

Great Plains

Lake Winnipeg

Lake Manitoba

Missouri

Platte

Kansas

Red River

Rio Grande

Sierra Madre Oriental

Lago de Chapala

Sierra Madre del Sur

South Saskatchewan

Yellowstone

Colorado Plateau

Colorado

Snake

Great Salt Lake

Sierra Madre Occidental

Mountains

Great Basin

Grand Canyon

Mt Whitney 4,141m

Death Valley -86m

Mojave Desert

Sonoran Desert

Gulf of California

Baja California

Mount St Helens 2,549m

Sierra Nevada

Coast Ranges

Vancouver Island

GULF OF CALIFORNIA

Also known as the Sea of Cortés, the Gulf of California lies between the west coast of mainland Mexico and the peninsula of Baja California. Around 800 species of fish are found in the gulf, but they are threatened by overfishing.

WESTERN CORDILLERA

This chain of mountain ranges includes the Coastal Ranges, Rocky Mountains, and Sierra Nevada, and runs southeast from Alaska to western Mexico. Most of it formed millions of years ago as an ancient oceanic plate moved under the North American plate. This ancient plate has now almost completely disappeared.

subducting oceanic plate

continental (North American) plate

mountain range

GRAND CANYON

Carved by the passage of the Colorado River over 17 million years, the Grand Canyon is 446 km (277 mile) long and up to 1.8 km (1 mile) deep.

TORNADO ALLEY

Late spring on the lowlands of the Midwestern prairies, where there are no mountains to block air flow, creates the perfect conditions for tornadoes to form. These are columns of violently rotating air that develop within storm clouds and are in contact with the ground. The most powerful tornadoes occur almost exclusively in North America.

FEATURED ECOREGIONS

Canadian Arctic ≫ p24-33
Tundra, ice

Yellowstone ≫ p34-43
Temperate coniferous forest

Central Great Plains ≫ p44-51
Temperate grassland

Sierra Nevada ≫ p52-59
Temperate coniferous forest

Mojave Desert ≫ p60-65
Desert, scrub

Florida Everglades ≫ p66-73
Wetland: flooded grassland, mangrove

CANADIAN ARCTIC

A far northern place of ice and snow

The Canadian Arctic includes one of the world's largest archipelagos – 36,563 islands, most of which are uninhabited by people. The easternmost islands are mountainous, becoming lower lying in the west. For much of the long, dark winter, land and sea are bound in a vast ice-scape, broken only by rocky island peaks and occasional polynyas – areas of sea that freeze late and thaw early. Polynyas are a vital resource for marine mammals including belugas and bowhead whales, which use them as breathing holes, and for seals and polar bears, which need to access the water from the sea ice. In summer, strong tides sweep the channels between the islands.

Frozen ground

On land, the top metre of soil thaws briefly in summer, but the ground beneath is permanently frozen (permafrost). Plant life is limited to mosses, lichens, and around 200 species of grass, sedge, hardy forbs, and dwarf shrubs. Land mammals able to withstand the cold include reindeer, muskoxen, Arctic foxes, and lemmings. The number of invertebrate species is low, but mites and springtails become superabundant in summer, providing food for breeding migrant birds such as Arctic terns, ivory gulls, common eiders, and red phalaropes.

Melting of the permafrost releases methane and carbon, increasing the rate of global warming

ARCTIC TERN

Of 36 mammal species here, 17 are marine

This is a Land of the Midnight Sun – the Sun never sets in summer

HOODED SEAL MOTHER AND PUP

WOOD FROG

LONG-DISTANCE TRAVELLER
The Arctic tern travels further than any animal on the planet as it migrates between its Arctic breeding areas and the Antarctic. Many Arctic animals head south to avoid the winter – reindeer make a shorter but equally arduous trip to the tundra regions of Canada.

TOUGH START IN LIFE
Newborn hooded seals feed on super-rich milk that enables them to increase their weight from 25 to 45 kg (55–100 lb) in just four days. After that, their mothers return to the sea to mate and feed. Each pup must learn to swim, dive, and hunt before it starves.

WINTER FREEZE
Wood frogs pass the winter dormant, their blood and skin frozen solid. To survive, they pump their cells full of a protective glucose syrup made by the liver. In contrast, Arctic cod have antifreeze proteins that prevent their blood freezing.

BANDED WOOLLY BEAR

Includes one of the world's largest archipelagos

SLOW AND STEADY
The Isabella tiger moth can breed in the High Arctic by having a long life cycle. Its woolly bear caterpillars hatch in summer and feed for a month. In winter, they freeze solid and lie dormant. They repeat the process for up to 14 years before pupating and emerging as adults that live for only a few days.

ARCTIC HARE

Birds come to the Canadian Arctic to breed but leave before winter

WINTER WHITEOUT
Like other Arctic land mammals, the Arctic hare has exceptionally dense fur, which traps warm air close to the skin. In the south of its range in Newfoundland, hares moult into a grey-brown summer coat. Further north, where the thaw is negligible, they stay winter white all year.

FISH OF THE DAY
Arctic cod are not fished commercially, but feature in the diets of other predators. They are targeted from below by seals, belugas, and narwhals, and from above by birds such as guillemots, or murres, which dive to more than 100 m (330 ft), using their wings to "fly" underwater.

ARCTIC COD

LOCATION
The northernmost parts of the Canadian mainland and the islands, comprising part of the Northwest Territories and the mostly Inuit territory of Nunavut.

CLIMATE
Temperatures are very low all year, only rising above 0°C (32°F) for 6–10 weeks in summer. Average annual temperatures are well below freezing, and virtually all precipitation falls as snow.

(Igloolik, Nunavut)

Key — Average temperature ▮ Rainfall

GETTING WARMER
The Arctic is warmer now than at any time in the last 40,000 years, and the extent and duration of sea ice reduces every year. In 2007, the Northwest Passage linking the Atlantic and Pacific remained ice free for the first time in recorded history. This change in conditions can have profound effects on the growth of plankton, on which all marine life ultimately depends. The sea ice is vital to polar bears, which need it for hunting and breeding.

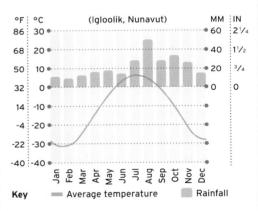

curved horns almost meet in middle of skull

Muskox
Ovibos moschatus

One of the few large mammals to roam the Arctic year round, the muskox is highly adapted to the cold. Its thick undercoat is covered by a coarse cloak of guard hairs over 60 cm (24 in) long, giving the animal its shaggy appearance. Its short, stocky legs and large hoofs provide good traction on snow. The horns are used in defence and in dominance battles among bulls.

Musky males

Muskox herds are usually mixed-sex and can have 10 to more than 100 animals, although some bulls form bachelor herds or remain solitary. Herds are smaller from July to September, when dominant bulls control breeding harems of females. The bulls give off a musky odour during the mating season, giving the animal its name.

Muskox feed in lowland areas in summer, eating flowers in addition to their usual diet. In winter, they move to higher ground for easier foraging.

↔ 1.9–2.3 m (6¼–7½ ft)
⚖ 200–410 kg (440–900 lb)
✖ Locally common
🌾 Sedges, grasses, leaves
🏠 ⛰

N. North America, Greenland

▷ **FACING THE ENEMY**
When threated by predators such as wolves or a polar bear, muskoxen form a circle and face outwards.

Fighting bulls' **collisions can be heard** up to **1.6 km (1 mile) away**

↔ 1.2–2.2 m (4–7¼ ft)
⚖ 120–300 kg (265–660 lb)
✖ Endangered
🌾 Leaves, roots, bark, lichen
🏠 ⛰

N. North America, N. Europe, N. Asia

▽ **COLOUR VARIATION**
High Arctic subspecies, such as the Peary caribou (*R. t. pearyi*), are smaller and lighter coloured than reindeer living at lower latitudes. Both male and female reindeer have antlers that they shed and regrow each year.

branching antlers

outer coat of wool-like hair provides extra insulation

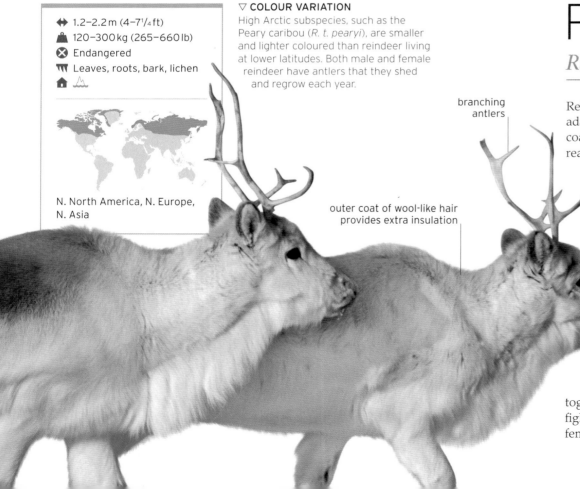

Reindeer
Rangifer tarandus

Reindeer (known as caribou in North America) are well adapted to life in the Arctic tundra. They have a dense coat and a broad muzzle that warms frigid air before it reaches the lungs. Reindeer are strong swimmers, with broad, flat hoofs. These provide stability on soft summer ground and act as snowshoes in winter, becoming harder and sharper-edged – ideal for cutting through snow and ice. Despite their broad hoofs, they can run at up to 80 km/h (50 mph). They can see ultraviolet light, which helps them locate lichens and snow-covered vegetation on dark winter days.

On the move

Reindeer are almost constantly on the move. Some migrate 5,000 km (3,000 miles) in a year – the longest distance any land mammal travels. Herds can be up to half a million strong, with smaller single-sex groups coming together to migrate during spring and autumn. Males fight for control of harems of females in autumn and the females give birth to a single calf the following spring.

muzzle insulated
by fur

stout, rounded body
under thick pelt

Arctic fox

Alopex lagopus

Incredibly well-adapted to its harsh environment in the
Arctic Circle, the Arctic fox can survive temperatures as
low as -50°C (-58°F). Its dense fur is several centimetres
thick during winter, insulating its short ears, muzzle,
and even the soles of its feet, which allows it to walk on
ice without slipping. In winter, most Arctic foxes grow
a white coat (some turn a steely blue) that lets them
blend into the snow.

Varied diet

Although it feeds on smaller mammals such as lemmings,
voles, and Arctic hares in summer, in winter the Arctic
fox may dig out seal pups from their under-ice birth
chambers. It will also follow polar bears and wolves to
feed on carcasses they leave behind. The Arctic fox is the
most common predator of Arctic birds such as snow
geese, but also eats fish, eggs, seaweed, and berries.

Mainly solitary, Arctic foxes may congregate around
carrion or fresh kills, and regularly raid garbage dumps
in northern Alaska. When not hunting, the Arctic fox
curls up in underground burrows during summer, while
in winter it tunnels into snow banks to escape blizzards.
Females give birth in spring to litters of as many as 14
kits, or pups. Both parents raise their young until around
August, when the family group disperses.

The Arctic fox has the **warmest pelt**
of any animal found **in the Arctic**

↔ 53–55 cm (21–22 in)
⚖ 4 kg (8³/₄ lb)
✖ Common
🍖 Small mammals, fish, birds
🏠 〰 ⛰

N. Canada, Alaska, Greenland,
N. Europe, N. Asia

△ **HUNTING IN
THE SNOW**
The Arctic fox listens for
movement below, then
leaps into the air before
plunging head-first to the
ground. This force breaks
through the snow to the
prey beneath.

◁ **SUMMER COAT**
Arctic foxes' white coats
thin and change colour
to grey-brown in
summer to match
surrounding rocks and
low-growing vegetation
of the tundra.

▷ **AT HOME**
Snow dens protect young cubs from the cold. The dens have one entrance and often several chambers, and can be up to 40 degrees warmer than outside temperatures.

▷▷ **STRONG SWIMMER**
A polar bear's broad, partially webbed forepaws make it a superb swimmer, capable of covering up to 100 km (60 miles) at a stretch, at speeds of 10 km/h (6 mph).

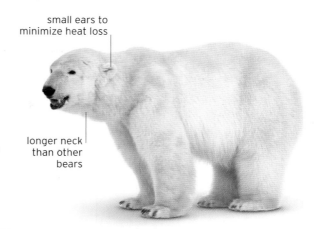

small ears to
minimize heat loss

longer neck
than other
bears

Polar bear

Ursus maritimus

The polar bear vies with the brown bear for the title of the world's largest living land carnivore. It is classified as a marine mammal, and its preferred hunting ground is Arctic pack ice. Superbly adapted to its environment, the polar bear has non-retractable claws and dimpled, partially furred foot pads that provide extra grip, allowing it to walk and run easily on ice.

The polar bear's body is covered in double-layered fur – the thickest of any bear species. The inner layer is a dense undercoat, while the outer fur consists of clear, hollow tubes that trap air for insulation. Since the tubes reflect all visible light, the outer coat makes polar bears seem white, allowing them to blend easily into snowy environments. Their skin is black and rests on a layer of blubber up to 10 cm (4 in) thick.

Feasting and fasting

Polar bears can live up to 25–30 years in the wild. Their lives alternate between feasting and fasting, and their intestines are adapted to process fat, which is easier to digest than meat and has more calories. They can also slow their metabolic rate when food is scarce. Their main diet is seals, but they occasionally hunt belugas or narwhals. When starving, they will also hunt walruses, but the risk of injury is high. They can smell prey up to 1 km (³/₄ mile) away, or up to 1 m (3¹/₄ ft) beneath ice.

Polar bears are generally solitary, except for breeding pairs or mothers with cubs. However, they will congregate around large food supplies such as whale carcasses. In autumn, polar bears also gather together in "transition" areas such as southwestern Hudson Bay and Churchill, Canada to wait for the sea ice to form that allows them access to ringed seals, swimming beneath the ice.

Polar bear territories are vast. Bears nearest the Canadian Arctic Islands have an average range of 50,000–60,000 sq km (19,000–23,000 sq miles), but those closer to the Bering Sea can cover up to 350,000 sq km (135,000 sq miles).

Winter births

Polar bears give birth to cubs every two to three years – one of the lowest reproductive rates of all mammals. Mating occurs from late March through May, but embryos may not start to develop until autumn. Pregnant females must gain about 200 kg (440 lb) extra weight during summer to survive the winter, when they may have to go up to eight months without food. They dig maternity dens mainly in south-facing snowdrifts, where between one and four cubs are born in early winter. Most litters are of twins.

The adult female does not hibernate in the truest sense, but maintains a much warmer body temperature to care for her cubs. Even so, she neither eats, urinates, nor defecates during the months she is in the den. Mother and cubs do not emerge from their den until March or early April, when she leads them towards the sea ice in order to hunt.

Polar bears are capable of running as fast as an Olympic sprinter

↔ 1.8–2.8 m (6–9¹/₄ ft)
🏋 400–680 kg (880–1,500 lb)
⊗ Vulnerable
〰 Seals, fish, birds, vegetation
🏠 ▨ ≈ ⛰

Arctic Ocean, N. Canada,
N. Russia

◁ **MOCK BATTLE**
Young males often engage in playfighting – sparring and trying to push each other over while standing on their hind legs. Some of these males may travel together for weeks or even years.

tusk grows
through
upper lip

Narwhal

Monodon monoceros

Narwhals are unique among whales in having a single long tusk, which is grown mostly by males. The tusk is, in fact, an elongated canine tooth that erupts mainly from the left side of the animal's upper jaw. It grows in a counterclockwise spiral, and is believed to be the reality behind the unicorn legends of medieval Europe.

While scientists once believed that the tusk's function was purely defensive, relating to dominance disputes over mating rights, recent research has revealed millions of nerve endings at the tusk's surface. These nerve endings allow the narwhal to detect changes in water pressure and temperature, as well as degrees of water salinity (saltiness). This discovery suggests that the characteristic rubbing of tusks by males may be a sensation- or information-seeking exercise – not simply "jousting". Tusks can grow to over 2.5 m (8 ft) long and are highly flexible, bending up to 30 cm (1 ft) in any direction without breaking. If a tusk is broken, new growth repairs the damage.

Super pods

Sociable animals, narwhals form small groups that often merge with others to form "super pods" of hundreds of whales. Individuals communicate by clicks, squeaks, and other vocalizations. Pods migrate each year, spending winters in and around the pack ice of the Arctic Ocean, and summers closer inland in bays or deep fjords. Their diet consists mainly of fish, such as halibut and cod, supplemented by squid.

Narwhals can **dive to remarkable depths,** some reaching **1,800 m** (5,900 ft)

△ **TIGHT SQUEEZE**
Restricted space can cause pods of narwhals to merge as they swim along narrow channels that have opened in the sea ice.

▷ **UNICORNS OF THE SEA**
Male narwhals surface with their tusks pointing skywards. The dark staining is caused by algal growth.

- 3.7–5 m (12–16¼ ft)
- 0.7–1.8 tonnes (¾–1¾ tons)
- Near threatened
- Fish, squid

Arctic Ocean

Beluga

Delphinapterus leucas

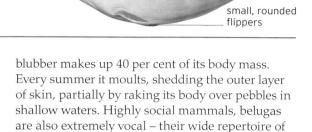

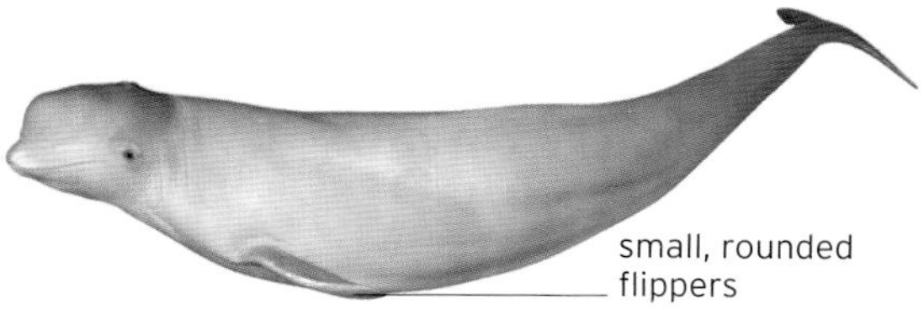
small, rounded flippers

The beluga is the only whale that is white in colour when adult, a feature that helps it to hide from predators among the sea ice. If chased, the absence of a dorsal fin allows the beluga to escape by swimming away beneath the ice. It is also able to move its head up and down and from side to side because its neck vertebrae are unfused. Thick blubber makes up 40 per cent of its body mass. Every summer it moults, shedding the outer layer of skin, partially by raking its body over pebbles in shallow waters. Highly social mammals, belugas are also extremely vocal – their wide repertoire of clicks, whistles, chirps, and squeals has earned them the nickname "canaries of the sea".

▷ **BLOWING BUBBLES**
Belugas amuse themselves by blowing bubble rings and then biting them. They may also produce bubbles if alarmed or surprised.

- 3–4.5 m (10–14¾ ft)
- 0.5–1.6 tonnes (½–1½ tons)
- Near threatened
- Fish, squid, shrimp

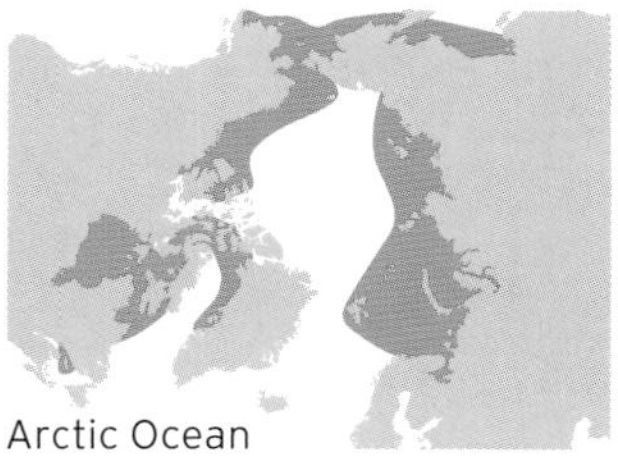

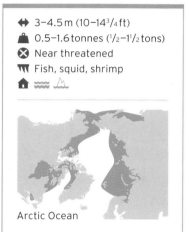

Arctic Ocean

Harp seal

Pagophilus groenlandicus

Named for their markings, harp seals are the most successful of all northern hemisphere seals, with numbers estimated at 8 million. Most inhabit icy northern waters, but some have migrated as far south as Virginia in the US and France. Mating occurs on pack ice in winter, and single pups are born from late February to mid March. Fast-moving on ice, harp seals are also good swimmers. Excellent eyesight and hearing make them formidable hunters, and also alert them to predators such as polar bears.

- 1.7 m (5½ ft)
- 130 kg (286 lb)
- Common
- Fish, krill

Arctic Ocean, North Atlantic

black head markings of adult
backward-directed hind flippers

▽ **HARP-SHAPED MARKINGS**
The dark markings on the sides of this adult seal curve upwards to meet over the shoulders, forming a harp shape.

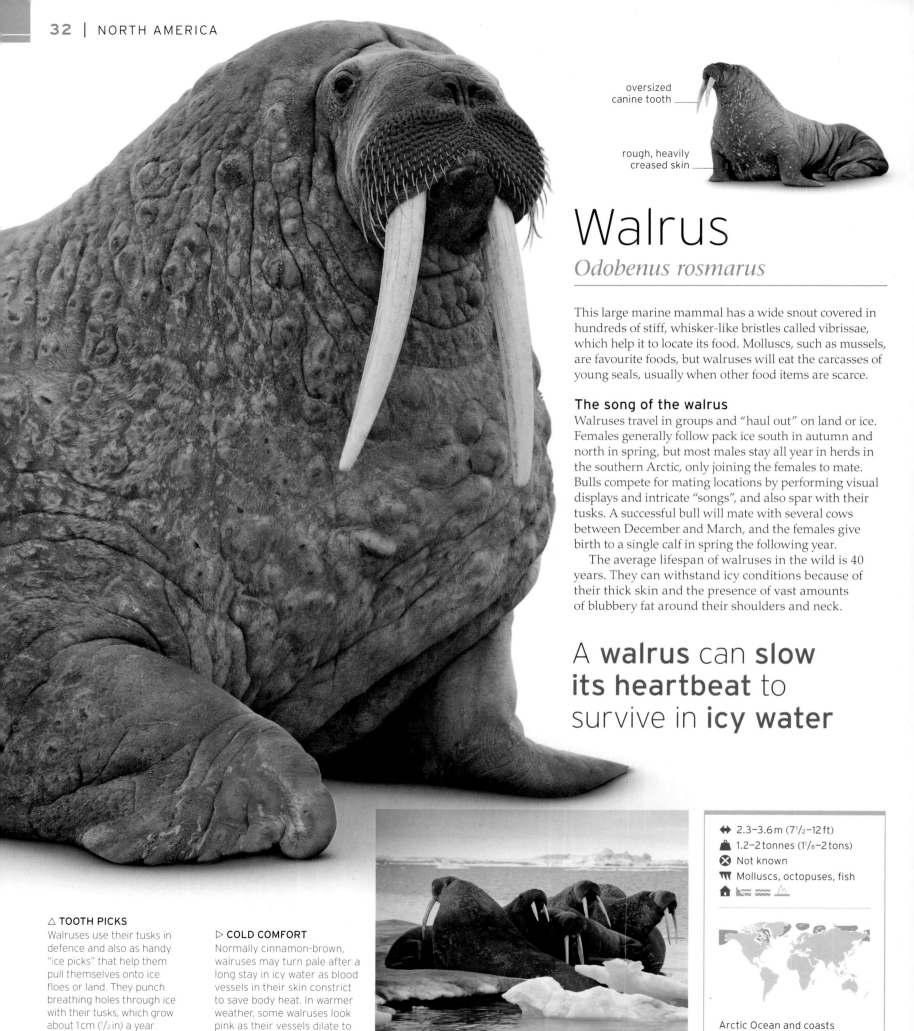

oversized
canine tooth

rough, heavily
creased skin

Walrus
Odobenus rosmarus

This large marine mammal has a wide snout covered in hundreds of stiff, whisker-like bristles called vibrissae, which help it to locate its food. Molluscs, such as mussels, are favourite foods, but walruses will eat the carcasses of young seals, usually when other food items are scarce.

The song of the walrus

Walruses travel in groups and "haul out" on land or ice. Females generally follow pack ice south in autumn and north in spring, but most males stay all year in herds in the southern Arctic, only joining the females to mate. Bulls compete for mating locations by performing visual displays and intricate "songs", and also spar with their tusks. A successful bull will mate with several cows between December and March, and the females give birth to a single calf in spring the following year.

The average lifespan of walruses in the wild is 40 years. They can withstand icy conditions because of their thick skin and the presence of vast amounts of blubbery fat around their shoulders and neck.

A **walrus** can **slow its heartbeat** to survive in **icy water**

△ TOOTH PICKS
Walruses use their tusks in defence and also as handy "ice picks" that help them pull themselves onto ice floes or land. They punch breathing holes through ice with their tusks, which grow about 1 cm (½ in) a year throughout their lives.

▷ COLD COMFORT
Normally cinnamon-brown, walruses may turn pale after a long stay in icy water as blood vessels in their skin constrict to save body heat. In warmer weather, some walruses look pink as their vessels dilate to get rid of excess heat.

- ↔ 2.3–3.6 m (7½–12 ft)
- ⚖ 1.2–2 tonnes (1⅛–2 tons)
- ✖ Not known
- ♛ Molluscs, octopuses, fish
- 🏠 ≋ ⛰

Arctic Ocean and coasts

Snowy owl

Nyctea scandiaca

mature male almost pure white

The snowy owl is a creature of the extremes, living in the High Arctic tundra. It is equipped with exceptionally thick plumage for insulation against the cold, the old males as white as a swan. Unusually among owls, females look different, with more dark spots and bars.

Winter wanderings

Snowy owls mostly feed on lemmings, surviving the long, dark Arctic winter and the extreme cold so long as they have food to eat. If food is scarce, they move south with regular winter migrations into central Canada and Siberia. Hundreds of snowy owls go farther south every few years as the populations of different lemming species boom and bust. Occasionally, they reach as far as Florida. Snowy owls breed every four or five years, with clutches of 3–13 eggs, and have barren years in between, so populations vary enormously.

↔ 52–71cm (20$\frac{1}{2}$–28 in)
⚖ 1–2.5 kg (2$\frac{1}{4}$–5$\frac{1}{2}$ lb)
✕ Common
🔱 Small mammals, birds
🏠 ⛰ 🌾 ⛰

N. North America, NE. Europe, and N. Asia

long wings

▷ **GRACEFUL FLIER**
"Snowies" are huge owls, flying low and silently between regular lookout perches on long, powerful, pointed wings.

heavily feathered legs and toes

Snow goose

Chen caerulescens

Snow geese breed in the extreme north of Arctic North America and migrate through western, central, and eastern states to winter in the far south. Hundreds of thousands of them stop to feed at regular "service stations", with large, noisy flocks making a spectacular sight. Despite the danger of being shot, they thrive on agricultural land, and they are highly sociable.

↔ 69–83cm (27–32$\frac{1}{2}$ in)
⚖ 2.4–3.4 kg (5$\frac{1}{4}$–7$\frac{1}{2}$ lb)
✕ Common
🔱 Grass, roots, seeds
🏠 🌾 ⛰ ≈ ⛰
◉ North America; Wrangel Island, Russia

black-tipped wings

▷ **BRILLIANT WHITE**
Snow geese are found in two colour forms: brilliant white (pictured) and blue-grey with a white head.

Arctic char

Salvelinus alpinus

Adapted to deep water and extreme cold, Arctic char are the most northerly of freshwater fish. A migratory, river-breeding form lives in the sea, and there is also a landlocked lake form. Spawning occurs at 4°C (39.2°F). Females scrape shallow nests, or redds, to lay their eggs in clean gravel.

↔ Up to 96cm (38 in)
⚖ Up to 12 kg (26$\frac{1}{2}$ lb)
✕ Common
🔱 Insects, crustaceans
🏠 🍴 ≈ ≈ ⛰ ≈ ⛰
◉ N. North America, N. Europe, N. Asia, and Arctic Ocean

▷ **FIGHTING MALES**
During breeding season, males become aggressively territorial. They develop hooked jaws and sport brilliant red bellies.

YELLOWSTONE
America's forested geothermal wilderness

Lying within the South Central Rockies ecoregion and dominated by coniferous forest, Yellowstone was home to American Indians for 11,000 years. Eighty per cent of Yellowstone's forests consist of lodgepole pine, a tree so-named because its straight trunk is ideal for use as tipi poles.

Yellowstone was established as a national park in 1872 – the first in the US and the world – and remains one of the largest, with more than 9,000 sq km (3,500 sq miles) of mostly pristine wilderness. The region is one of the last strongholds of American bison, and the reintroduction of the grey wolf in 1995 allows park managers to claim the area as the largest intact ecoregion in the northern temperate zone. The potentially damaging impacts of logging, hunting, and tourism are regulated, but not always successfully.

Hot springs and geysers

Around 1,700 species of plant live in the forests, meadows, and upland grasslands of the park, which also boasts mountains, lakes, rivers, and canyons. Yellowstone is also famous for being the world's largest centre of geothermal activity – it has around half of the known geothermal features on the planet, including the Old Faithful geyser. People also visit the park in the hope of seeing animals such as grizzly and black bears and American beavers, whose tree-felling and stream-damming activities renew habitats such as pools, swamps, and meadows.

On average, **Old Faithful** produces columns of steam and water **every 67 minutes**

MILLER MOTH

THERMAL ACTIVITY
The localized effects of geothermal heat include extended plant-growing periods, thinner snow – allowing bison to graze in winter – and ice-free lakes, where waterfowl feed year round. The hot springs are also home to micro-organisms whose range of heat tolerances cause them to grow in distinctive bands.

MOTH FEAST
In summer, millions of miller moths (also known as army cutworm moths) migrate to Yellowstone to feed in alpine meadows. Their vast numbers attract grizzly bears, which consume up to 40,000 of the nutritious insects a day. The grizzlies often live on little else for up to three months.

THE WHITEBARK ZONE
Open-canopied whitebark pine forests depend on a nutcracker prises open the crow to survive. Clark's cones to harvest the seeds and then caches them. The bird forgets about some of the seeds, which means they can germinate.

HOT SPRINGS

3 million visitors every year

More than 350 major waterfalls and 500 geysers

67 species of mammal

WHITEBARK PINE

The world's first national park, established in 1872

Yellowstone's supervolcano is the only one on land in the world

LANDSCAPE CHANGER

The loss of wolves from Yellowstone in the 1920s meant that within a few years its forests were being damaged by the increasing numbers of wapiti. In particular, quaking aspens failed to regenerate. Today, wolves are helping to control wapiti once more.

WAPITI

FIERY BEGINNINGS

Lodgepole pines are adapted to cope with occasional wildfires. The trees burn rapidly, but their tightly closed cones require the heat of a wildfire to melt the resinous glue that seals them, releasing the seeds to germinate in the newly cleared area.

LODGEPOLE PINE

TOO MUCH COMPETITION

Named for the dramatic slash of scarlet on the lower jaw, cut-throat trout are threatened by habitat loss, disease, and competition from other fish species introduced for sport fishing. Those in Yellowstone are a separate subspecies. They are a key component of the diets of bald eagles and osprey, so the decline of this fish would also lead to a decline in these birds of prey.

YELLOWSTONE CUT-THROAT TROUT

LOCATION

The national park lies primarily within the midwestern US state of Wyoming. It is part of the South Central Rockies ecoregion.

Montana

Wyoming

Idaho

• Rexburg

0 km   50

0 miles   50

CLIMATE

Yellowstone experiences a cool, temperate climate, with cool summers and long, cold winters. Precipitation is evenly spread throughout the year, falling as heavy snow between November and March.

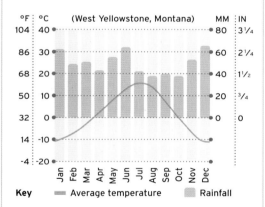

°F	°C	(West Yellowstone, Montana)	MM	IN
104	40		80	3¼
86	30		60	2¼
68	20		40	1½
50	10		20	¾
32	0		0	0
14	-10			
-4	-20			

Jan Feb Mar Apr May Jun Jul Aug Sep Oct Nov Dec

Key — Average temperature   ▮ Rainfall

SUPERVOLCANO

Around 640,000 years ago, a massive volcano erupted, which caused it to collapse and form the giant Yellowstone Caldera. The supervolcano beneath the caldera is still active, and the caldera is closely monitored for signs of increasing activity. Between 1,000 and 2,000 earthquakes and tremors are recorded in the area every year.

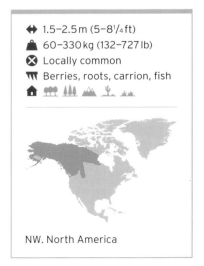

dish-shaped face

long front claws

Grizzly bear

Ursus arctos horribilis

All grizzlies are brown bears, but not all brown bears are grizzlies. This subspecies gets its name from its light-tipped fur, yet not all are "grizzled" – their coats range from whitish-blond to almost black. Their shoulder "hump" consists of muscles that make them efficient diggers and capable of inflicting strong blows with their forepaws.

Despite its often fearsome reputation, the bulk of a grizzly bear's diet comprises nuts, grasses, roots, seeds, and moths. Much of the meat they eat comes from carrion, but they hunt mammals ranging from ground squirrels to moose. Grizzlies prefer coniferous forests broken by fields and meadows with access to rivers. Good swimmers, they are skilled at catching trout, bass, and salmon.

Grizzly threat

Grizzlies mate in late spring to early summer. The female gives birth to up to four cubs, usually while hibernating, nursing them in her den until April or May. Cubs stay with their mothers for two to four years, and the main threat to youngsters is from adult male grizzlies. Once common throughout the western US, grizzlies now occur in small numbers only in Idaho, Montana, Washington state, and Wyoming, with larger populations in Alaska and Canada.

↔ 1.5–2.5 m (5–8¼ ft)
⬛ 60–330 kg (132–727 lb)
✖ Locally common
🍴 Berries, roots, carrion, fish
🏠 🌲 🌳 🏔 🌵 🌿

NW. North America

△ **FOOD FIGHT**
Grizzlies are powerful bears and competition for the best fishing spot can cause a fight to break out. However, most will stop before a serious injury occurs.

◁ **WHO'S THE DADDY?**
Female grizzlies will mate with several males in a breeding season and the cubs in the resulting litter may have different fathers.

large, sensitive ears help detect prey

Grey wolf
Canis lupus

Despite its name, the grey wolf can be black, brown, grey, or almost white. All grey wolves are pack predators, hunting large hoofed mammals such as elk, deer, and caribou, and smaller prey such as rabbits and beavers. They also feed on carrion, particularly in winter.

An average wolf pack has seven to eight adults ruled by an alpha male and female. The alpha pair lead hunts, establish territory, and choose den sites, reinforcing the pack's bonds through vocalizations such as barks and howls. The alphas mate from January to March. After about three months, the female bears a litter of four to seven pups. The entire pack nurtures the pups until they are about 10 months old, when some will leave, travelling up to 800 km (500 miles), in search of other wolves.

Successful reintroduction
The light grey Rocky Mountain wolf subspecies (*C. l. irremotus*) was reintroduced to Yellowstone in 1995. Since the wolves' return, elk and deer are more mobile, letting trees and grassland regenerate.

powerful, long legs

▷ **BUILT FOR STAMINA**
An adult grey wolf may range up to 70 km (45 miles) in a day and can run at top speeds of up to 70 km/h (45 mph).

↔ 1–1.5 m (3¼–5 ft)
⚖ 16–60 kg (35–132 lb)
✖ Common
🐾 Elk, deer, rabbits, carrion

N. North America, Europe, Asia

large feet and claws

Each wolf has its **own signature howl**

↔ 65–110 cm (26–43 in)
⚖ 4–15.5 kg (8¾–34 lb)
✖ Common
🐾 Rabbits, rodents, birds

S. Canada, USA, Mexico

▷ **WINTER FREEZE**
Bobcats are more often seen in daylight hours during winter, when food is scarce. They are ambush predators, with markings that allow them to blend in with their surroundings.

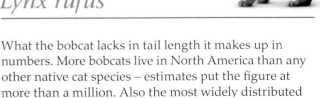

Bobcat
Lynx rufus

What the bobcat lacks in tail length it makes up in numbers. More bobcats live in North America than any other native cat species – estimates put the figure at more than a million. Also the most widely distributed cat, it is found as far north as British Columbia.

Adaptable cat
The secret to this tough little cat's success is adaptability. It prefers dense forests, but can easily survive in swamps, mountains, and deserts. Recently, it has added suburban and urban terrain to its habitats. This often brings it into conflict with humans, as it preys on domestic pets and small livestock. In the wild, rabbits form a large part of a bobcat's diet, but it also hunts rodents, birds, beavers, and small deer, mainly at dawn and dusk. At other times, it rests in dens hidden in thickets, hollow trees, or rocky crevices.

Like most cat species, the bobcat is solitary except during the mating season from December to April. After about a two-month gestation period, females give birth to litters of about three cubs, which remain with their mothers for eight months.

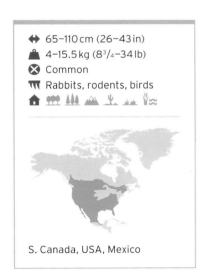

Wolverine

Gulo gulo

Known as the glutton, albeit unfairly, the wolverine satisfies its voracious appetite by killing prey as big as deer. Its strong jaws rip open the toughest hides and crush the biggest bones in search of marrow. Although it is in fact a huge weasel, its heavy fur, sturdy legs, and large feet give the wolverine a bear-like appearance. It can walk on snow with its broad feet, and survive extreme conditions in remote forests, tundra, and mountains encircling the Arctic.

Wolverines store food after a big kill. Reindeer and caribou are dismembered and buried in snow or soil, or pushed into rock crevices and gullies. They mate in summer and two to four cubs are born the following spring.

↔ 65–105 cm (26–41 in)

⚖ 6–18 kg (13–40 lb)

⊗ Common

🦷 Deer, hare, birds, fruit

NW. to N. North America, NE. Europe to N. and E. Asia

▽ **ON THE GO**
Short, powerful legs and a supple, shuffling action help the wolverine cover long distances at a relentless pace in search of food, with minimum expenditure of energy.

◁ **PALMATE ANTLERS**
Male moose grow a new set of their massive antlers every summer. These have a covering of soft skin, or "velvet", which is shed by autumn, the mating season.

▽ **LOSING BATTLE**
This female moose managed to defend her week-old calf from a pack of wolves for 10 minutes, but, despite her superior size and power, they were able to drag the calf away from her.

Moose

Alces alces

pointed hoofs for
digging in snow

The world's largest species of deer, the moose lives below the Arctic Circle, inhabiting coniferous and deciduous woodland, swamps, and lakes. In Europe, the moose is also known as the elk, whereas in North America – to add to the confusion – the elk is an entirely different species.

Solitary nomads

Unlike most other deer species, moose are mostly solitary, although females are accompanied by their calves. They do not defend territories, staying on the move all year around. Male moose select habitats that offer the greatest supply of food, while females choose habitats that provide the most cover for them and their young. Moose are diurnal browsers, and may be found cooling off in water during the hottest days of summer while feeding on lily roots and other aquatic plants.

They use their flexible upper lip to browse the freshest leaves and shoots. In winter, when leafy food is in short supply, they will kick away snow to get at moss and lichens underneath, chew on twigs of trees such as poplar and willow, and strip bark from trunks. Their wide hoofs help them to walk on soft snow as well as wade through soft-bottomed lakes and swamps.

Male moose rut in the autumn, and both sexes bellow to attract a mate. The females choose a mate by sizing up his antlers, which may span 2m (6½ ft) and have up to 20 points each. Rival males frequently joust for mating rights. Female moose give birth to one or two calves the following summer, which are weaned after six months. A healthy adult moose has little to fear from predators other than humans as it can use its antlers or hooves to defend itself, but bears and wolves predate the much smaller calves.

↔ 2.4–3 m (7¾–9¾ ft)
⚖ 280–600 kg (620–1,320 lb)
✖ Common
🍴 Leaves, lichen, water plants, moss, bark

N. North America, N. Europe, N. and E. Asia

White-tailed deer
Odocoileus virginianus

Although widespread and found in large numbers, the white-tailed deer often stays out of sight. For most of the year the deer live alone, occupying small home ranges rarely larger than a square kilometre. They set up home in swamps, woodlands, and scrubland – wherever there are plenty of shrubs to conceal them. They move slowly, constantly on the lookout for predators such as pumas. If danger appears, the deer whistle with alarm and bound away, waving their white tails to startle attackers.

The deer's territory provides all the food they need for the year, even in the northern fringe of their range where winters are long and severe. The deer do not leave when winter comes, but follow well-trodden paths through the snow looking for any greenery they can access. In winter, their coat is grey, but it thins in summer and turns red.

Spotted disguise
The females are ready to breed in autumn, and males deploy their antlers to battle it out for the rights to each mate. Fawns are born in spring and lie hidden under shrubs while the mother is away feeding. They begin to follow their mothers in a month and are weaned when three months old. Their spotty coat, which helps them hide when young, is lost in the first winter.

↔ 1.2–1.9 m (4–6¼ ft)
⚖ 52–140 kg (115–310 lb)
❌ Common
🌾 Buds, leaves, twigs, cacti

S. Canada to N. South America

▷ **MATURE STAG**
Only male white-tailed deer have antlers, growing a fresh set each year. A new point, or tine, is added with each growth.

short, thick fur protects from the cold

American pika
Ochotona princeps

The American pika looks like a cross between a guinea pig – with short legs and a large head – and a rabbit, with round ears and a whiskered face. Its long tail is hidden in fur. Lively in daylight, the animal bounds across scree slopes, pausing to make bird-like "cheeps" that warn of the presence of predators, such as coyotes, weasels, and stoats, or far-carrying "mews" to assert its territory. This consists of a foraging area and a den in a burrow or rock crevice. Pikas live next to a member of the opposite sex, giving a male–female patchwork of territories.

In summer, the pika gathers flowering stems, such as rosebay willowherb, and long grasses. These are stored in a pile near its burrow and left to dry. As winter approaches, the pika drags its hay pile deep into a rock cavity, keeping its food store safe from the snow.

Pikas select plants that will decompose the most slowly to ensure their food store will last them through the winter. This animal is adapted to high, cold places, but climate change has squeezed it into an ever-shrinking range.

↔ 16–22 cm (6¼–8½ in)
⚖ 125–175 g (4–6 oz)
❌ Locally common
🌾 Grasses, herbs

SW. Canada, W. USA

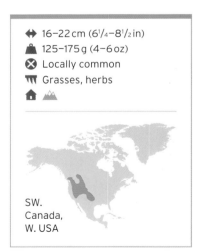

▷ **MAKING HAY**
Pikas forage for grasses and herbs, eating some each day and caching the rest in their winter hay store.

Pikas use their **cheek glands** to **scent-mark their territory**

long whiskers enable beaver to feel its way in the dark

△ CLOSE LIPPED
Beavers close their lips behind their incisor teeth when underwater so they can still nibble and gnaw on branches and stems.

American beaver

Castor canadensis

North America's largest rodent, the American beaver, is a nocturnal "engineer" that alters landscapes throughout the continent, apart from desert areas and northernmost Canada. This stocky, big-skulled aquatic mammal fells trees by gnawing through the trunks, then arranges them into dams across streams or rivers, or uses them to build lodges for shelter. Its flat, scaly tail and webbed hindfeet make it a graceful swimmer, and a waterproof coat protects it from the winter cold.

Woody diet

The beavers' long, orange incisors, which never stop growing, are perfectly suited to their diet of woody bark, twigs, and stems. They also eat cambium, a soft tissue under the bark; favourite sources include birch, alder, and aspen, which they often store as winter food.

They live in small colonies, led by a male and female who mate for life. The female gives birth to three or four fully furred kits between April and June. The kits leave after two years to form their own colonies.

Beavers make their lodges along banks or lake shores, the most impressive being the island lodges in the middle of ponds. With an entrance only accessible underwater, these are the safest refuges from predators such as wolves and coyotes. They tailor their dams to rates of water flow, building straight ones for slow-moving water, and curved ones for faster currents.

▽ MASTER BUILDER
American beavers make their dams and lodges out of logs, branches, grass, and moss, plastered together with mud.

↔ 74–88 cm (29–35 in)
⚖ 11–26 kg (24–57 lb)
✗ Common
Ⓦ Woody bark, twigs, stems
🏠 🌿≈ ≈

North America

▷ **FISHING EXPEDITION**
The bald eagle, like other sea eagles, does not enter the water to catch prey; instead, it swoops down to snatch fish, live or dead, from the surface of a lake.

▷▷ **DOWNY CHICK**
Bald eagle chicks remain in the nest for 10–13 weeks, entirely dependent on their parents for food, protection, and shelter.

pure white hood

△ **BODY RIPPER**
The fiercely hooked bill is not used to kill prey, but to rip it into chunks that can be swallowed, and to tear the hide off the carcass of larger animals.

black-brown body

long talons

Bald eagle

Haliaeetus leucocephalus

The bald eagle is found only in North America, but its image is used as a symbol of power, grace, and durability worldwide. Like many birds of prey, its bold looks suggest a more swashbuckling lifestyle than is really the case, for it spends much of the time doing nothing, and much of its food is carrion. It is doing what big birds of prey do: conserving energy between bouts of hunting and gorging.

Life on the water's edge

There are eight species of giant sea eagles worldwide, including the Eurasian white-tailed eagle, the African fish or river eagle, and the spectacular Steller's sea eagle from far eastern Asia. All these species, including the bald eagle, have a powerful build and broad wings that are "fingered" at the tip when fully spread, a relatively short tail and a long head and neck, creating a cross-like shape in flight. Unlike golden eagles, bald eagles soar with their wings held flat. All sea eagles have bare lower legs and feet, with strong toes and sharp claws to grip and pierce their prey, as well as a strong bill to tear it to pieces.

Fish form a large part of the bald eagle's diet, but it also eats other prey. Bald eagles can catch and kill animals as large as sea otters and birds up to the size of a goose. In summer, many live on seabirds caught in coastal colonies. They are primarily birds of the water's edge, where such prey items – and all kinds of wave-tossed carcasses and scraps – can be easily foraged.

Living along the western seaboard of North America from Alaska to California, bald eagles penetrate far inland along rivers and around lakes. They breed across the far northern parts of Canada and in winter move south as far as Florida and the Gulf of Mexico – to wherever water can be found.

Bald eagles feed in small groups in winter if enough food is available, and nest in small defended territories, covering about 0.2 sq km (³/₄ sq mile). These sites can be grouped quite close together. Nests are built almost anywhere from near-flat ground to small slopes, cliffs, exposed crags, and trees.

Breeding pairs and trios

Each pair of bald eagles usually has several nests – one preferred nest, a huge heap of sticks, grass, and seaweed, can become as large as 4 m (13 ft) deep and 2.5 m (8 ft) across. Although two eggs are the norm, usually only one chick survives to fly. Up to three-quarters of the young die before they are a year old, and only one in ten reaches five years of age. Bald eagles can start breeding when four years old. However, unusually, half the adults are non-breeders and some form trios at one nest. Once grown, adults may go on to live long, productive lives, surviving for almost 50 years in the wild.

long, sharp bill hook

↔ 71–96 cm (28–38 in)
⚖ 3–6.5 kg (6¹/₂–14 lb)
✕ Common
🦃 Fish, birds, mammals
🏠 🌳 🌲 🌾 〜 〜 📡 〜

North America

The **bald eagle** was chosen as the **national bird of the USA** in 1782

CENTRAL GREAT PLAINS
A rolling landscape, once covered in a sea of grass

Forming a broad band through North America almost to Mexico, between the Rocky Mountains and the Missouri River, the Central Great Plains was once an immense, gently rolling prairie landscape that was dominated by mixed grasses for millions of years. Succession by trees and scrub was kept down by wild fires and grazing by native herbivores such as American bison, pronghorn antelope, and prairie dogs. The prairies were also home to a variety of reptiles, birds, and invertebrates, and many of these animals were exploited sustainably by nomadic American Indian tribes.

Conversion to agriculture

As recently as the early 19th century, this vast area was still covered by grassland. Today, most of the fertile land is given over to agriculture. Overexploitation of arable land in the early 20th century led to the environmental and economic catastrophe in the 1930s known as the Dust Bowl, in which the topsoil was entirely lost from vast areas in a series of dust storms caused by drought and wind erosion. The land has mostly recovered sufficiently to support grazing, but the vast herds of bison that once roamed the prairies are largely gone, replaced mainly by domestic cattle.

A few pockets of relatively pristine prairie remain in the US and Canada, and in reserves such as the Wichita Mountains Wildlife Refuge in Oklahoma, surviving bison herds are protected. Even here, trees are few, and large vegetation is limited mainly to mesquite scrub and prickly pear cactus.

BECOMING A PEST
This beetle used to feed on a prairie weed, Solanum rostratum or spiny nightshade. But when settlers planted another Solanum species, the cultivated potato, the beetle changed its diet and became a notorious crop pest.

COLORADO POTATO BEETLE

BOOMING MARVELLOUS
The spring mating rituals of the Greater prairie chicken are a new ecotourism attraction thanks to conservation efforts. Male birds compete at regular "booming grounds", making loud calls amplified by inflated air sacs on the neck.

PRAIRIE CHICKEN

ORNATE BOX TURTLE

> 30 million bison once lived on the Great Plains

Only 1% of the natural grassland survives

LIVING IN A BOX
The ornate box turtle is one of two terrestrial turtles on the Great Plains. They are named for their hinged lower shell, which can be clamped shut to protect the head and limbs from predators. However, many of them are killed trying to cross roads.

Pronghorn
Antilocapra americana

sensitive nose picks up scent of other pronghorns

The pronghorn is the fastest land animal in the Americas, with a top recorded speed of 86 km/h (53½ mph). However, its defining feature is its horns. The forked, antler-like headgear looks like that of a deer, and the pronghorn is also known colloquially as the American antelope. A deer sheds its antlers each year, while an antelope keeps one pair for life; the pronghorn keeps the bony core of the horn for life, shedding the keratin sheath over the bone each winter.

Home on the range

The pronghorn is the sole surviving member of the Antilocaprinae family, which had dozens of species five million years ago. Despite their unique horns, pronghorns share many features with other even-toed ungulates – a herd lifestyle, a diet of leaves and grasses, and long legs. The pronghorn population was devastated by hunting in the 19th century. Today, pronghorn herds survive in the remote parts of the American West, which is appropriate as it is the very beast mentioned in the anthemic western song "Home on the Range".

↔ 1.3–1.4 m (4¼–4½ ft)
⚖ 30–80 kg (66–176 lb)
⊗ Locally common
♈ Forbs, leaves, grasses

W. and C. North America

A pronghorn can **leap 6 m (20 ft)** in a **single bound**

▽ **RACING AWAY FROM DANGER**
Pronghorns live in loose herds, with large males controlling mating territories in summer. They warn each other of danger with snorts and by raising their white rump hairs.

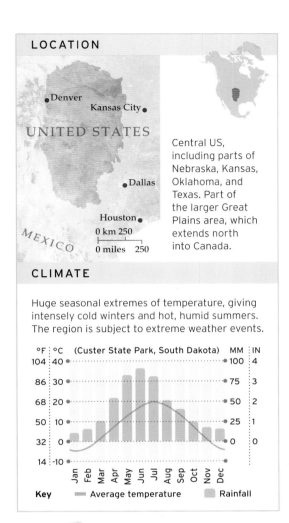

LOCATION

Central US, including parts of Nebraska, Kansas, Oklahoma, and Texas. Part of the larger Great Plains area, which extends north into Canada.

Denver
Kansas City
UNITED STATES
Dallas
Houston
MEXICO
0 km 250
0 miles 250

CLIMATE

Huge seasonal extremes of temperature, giving intensely cold winters and hot, humid summers. The region is subject to extreme weather events.

°F / °C (Custer State Park, South Dakota) MM / IN
104 / 40 — 100 / 4
86 / 30 — 75 / 3
68 / 20 — 50 / 2
50 / 10 — 25 / 1
32 / 0 — 0 / 0
14 / -10

Jan Feb Mar Apr May Jun Jul Aug Sep Oct Nov Dec

Key — Average temperature ▨ Rainfall

RESTORING DIVERSITY
The diminutive swift fox is a short-grass prairie specialist. Its disappearance from 60 per cent of its range reflects wider ecological decline. Projects to restore habitat for this species will benefit others, including ground-nesting birds.

SWIFT FOX

Encompasses Tornado Alley

▷ **STAMPEDING HERD**
When alarmed, bison herds start to stampede and, at top speed, can reach 60 km/h (35 mph).

short, upturned horn

American bison

Bison bison

The American bison is an iconic species of the vast prairies that once stretched from the Rocky Mountains east across central North America, from southern Canada as far south as Texas. Also known as the American buffalo, this massively built animal has a large head, thick neck, and a prominent hump behind the shoulders. Its front-heavy appearance is enhanced by a long beard and a shaggy shawl of fur around the neck and forelegs. Full-grown males weigh 950–1,000 kg (2,100–2,200 lb), which is twice as heavy as females. Despite their huge bulk, bison can run at speeds of up to 60 km/h (35 mph). Both sexes have a pair of short, upturned horns.

Hunted almost to extinction

Bison used to live in huge, nomadic herds that roamed across long distances to graze. The population numbered many millions, with 30 million living on the Great Plains. They had long been hunted by American Indian tribes, but during the 1800s, European settlers moved into the prairies and hunting for meat and hide accelerated. The bison's prairie habitat was converted to farmland, and by the 1880s, as few as 500–1,000 animals were left.

An end to hunting and the creation of national parks have raised the bison population to about 30,000 free-ranging animals, although the species only occupies less than one per cent of its former range. There are about 500,000 domesticated bison on private ranches and farms. However, the domesticated stock have been cross-bred with cattle and have lost many of their wild traits. Wild bison have excellent hearing and sense of smell, which are essential for detecting their chief natural predator, the grey wolf.

Follow the grass

Adult females and young live in groups of 10–60, led by an older cow. The bulls form separate herds or live alone. The breeding season is from July to September, when the bulls rejoin the female-led herds. The bulls fight for mating rights and dominance, clashing heads in spectacular battles. The females give birth to a single calf after a 10-month gestation, usually in April or May when there is a fresh growth of spring grass.

Bison have complex stomachs with four chambers to help them digest large quantities of grass, and they spend long periods chewing the cud. They can paw aside snow to reveal grass below, but in harsh winters, they migrate to lower, snow-free areas.

Wood bison and wisent

Some of the bison found in Canada are a separate subspecies known as wood bison (*B. bison athabascae*). The largest free-ranging herd of this species is found in Wood Buffalo National Park. There is also a population of wild bison in the Bialoweza Forest on the Poland-Belarus border, and these may belong to a second species called the European bison, or wisent (*B. bonasus*).

△ **WINTER TRAVEL**
The bisons' thick coat and heavy mane protect them from the cold. They are so well insulated that even a dusting of snow on their back does not melt.

◁ **YOUNG BISON**
A calf can stand, walk, or run with its mother a couple of hours after it is born. The calves are weaned at about six months.

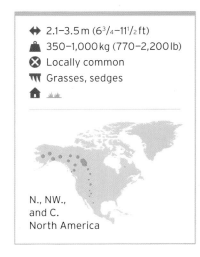

↔ 2.1–3.5 m (6³/₄–11¹/₂ ft)
⚖ 350–1,000 kg (770–2,200 lb)
✖ Locally common
🌾 Grasses, sedges
🏠

N., NW., and C. North America

An adult American bison could **leap over an adult human**

Black-tailed prairie dog
Cynomys ludovicianus

A large species of ground squirrel, black-tailed prairie dogs are highly social rodents. They live in "towns" – extensive networks of underground tunnels and chambers. A town houses hundreds of dogs, all organized into smaller groups called coteries. A coterie, made up of a dozen adults and their offspring, works together to maintain their patch of the tunnel and defend it from intruders. Coterie members share a scent, which marks them out from other groups.

Prairie dogs dig their tunnels deep enough to avoid winter frosts. Any loose earth pushed to the surface forms mounds around the tunnel entrances that are ideal for spotting predators.

▷ **FAMILY UNIT**
Pups emerge from under the ground at the age of six weeks and are looked after by every member of the coterie. Most males leave the group after their first winter.

- ↔ 34–43 cm (13½–17 in)
- ⚖ 0.7–1.5 kg (1½–3¼ lb)
- ✖ Common
- 🌾 Grass, sedge
- 🏠 ⬝⬝⬝

SW. Canada to N. Mexico

Black-footed ferret
Mustela nigripes

This solitary, burrowing hunter is one of North America's rarest mammals. Numbers fell to 18 in the mid-1980s but are now increasing again. About 90 per cent of the black-footed ferret's diet is made up of prairie dogs. The ferrets dig their dens right in the middle of prairie dog communities, even setting up home in unused sections of their tunnel network. They can follow prairie dogs into their burrows, killing and eating them underground.

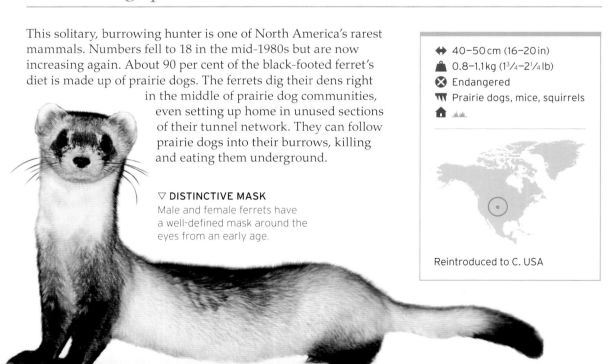

▽ **DISTINCTIVE MASK**
Male and female ferrets have a well-defined mask around the eyes from an early age.

- ↔ 40–50 cm (16–20 in)
- ⚖ 0.8–1.1 kg (1¾–2¼ lb)
- ✖ Endangered
- 🌾 Prairie dogs, mice, squirrels
- 🏠 ⬝⬝⬝

Reintroduced to C. USA

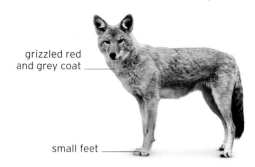

grizzled red and grey coat

small feet

Coyote
Canis latrans

Most wild dog species face enormous pressure from humans encroaching on their wide-ranging habitats. However, the coyote is thriving, even encroaching on human habitats as a proficient poacher of poultry and scavenger of human rubbish.

Somewhere between a fox and wolf in size, the coyote has a highly adaptable lifestyle. Although it may form packs to hunt large animals such as deer, mostly it is a solitary hunter, targeting smaller prey – such as prairie dogs – alone. Coyotes spend the day in an underground den; they may dig their own den, but usually enlarge one abandoned by badgers or ground squirrels.

Involved parenting

When raising offspring, coyotes set out their home ranges by marking bushes and other landmarks with urine and faeces. They assert their claim on the territory with loud yips and howls. Coyotes may form pair bonds that last several years. Mating occurs in late winter, and about six pups are born two months later. Both parents nourish the youngsters with regurgitated food in the den.

Coyotes work with **American badgers** to **hunt burrowing rodents**

◁ **HOWLING COYOTE**
Coyotes are noisy animals, frequently howling to lay claim to a territory or greet a family member.

↔ 74–94 cm (29–37 in)
⬛ 7.7–15.8 kg (17–35 lb)
✖ Common
🐾 Mammals, insects, fruit

North America and N. Central America

Greater sage-grouse

Centrocercus urophasianus

America's largest grouse lacks a muscular gizzard and cannot digest hard seeds and shoots. It relies on various kinds of sagebrush for food and cover. During the breeding season, females watch males display at a lek, a communal display ground. They select the strongest males to mate with. A few dominant males mate with the females and hens lay six to nine eggs. The chicks are fully mobile after six to eight weeks, when families may move to winter ranges at lower altitudes in search of food.

↔ 48–76 cm (19–30 in)
⚖ 1.5–3 kg (3¼–6½ lb)
⊗ Near threatened
▥ Sagebrush, insects
⌂

W. to C. North America

▽ STRUT DISPLAY

When displaying at a lek, male sage-grouse rapidly inflate and deflate their breast air sacs to produce loud, far-carrying, bubbling, popping sounds. They also spread their pointed tail feathers.

Common garter snake

Thamnophis sirtalis

One of North America's most widespread reptiles, the common garter snake frequents all but very dry or very cold habitats. Across its cooler, northern range, individuals gather in burrows, caves, and similar sites to overwinter, conserving energy by slowing their metabolism. In late summer, females have litters of 10–70 babies.

↔ 50–125 cm (20–49 in)
⚖ 140–180 g (5–6½ oz)
⊗ Common
▥ Worms, fish, amphibians
⌂ 🏠 🌲 ⌇ ≈ 🏛
◉ North America

▽ STRIPES OR SPOTS

This species typically has three light stripes running lengthwise, but some garter snakes have rows of spots.

heavily keeled scales

Striped scorpion

Centruroides vittatus

By day, the striped scorpion lurks in damp nooks under rocks and logs, and in thick vegetation. It emerges at sunset to hunt, detecting prey by their smell and movement with the help of comb-like sensory organs between its last set of legs. The scorpion then crushes victims with its pincers and kills them with its stinger.

Females produce young after an estimated gestation of about eight months. The 30–50 offspring are carried on their mother's back until they moult for the first time.

↔ 5.5–7.5 cm (2¼–3 in)
⊗ Not known
▥ Insects, spiders, centipedes
⌂ 🌲 🏛
◉ C. North America to N. Central America

▷ PERFECT CAMOUFLAGE

The scorpion's colouring helps to hide it from predators as well as prey.

two broad stripes along back

black and white markings on wing tips

Monarch butterfly

Danaus plexippus

↔ 9.4–10.5 cm (3³/₄–4¹/₄ in)
✕ Common
Ⅲ Milkweed leaves, nectar
⌂

N. America to
N. South America

The beautiful monarch is a familiar sight in North America. In autumn, monarchs that live west of the Rocky Mountains migrate to coastal California, while those from the east of the Rockies fly south to a small highland area in Michoacán, Mexico. Survivors of the Mexican winter move north to Texas and Oklahoma in March, producing a new generation that spreads northwards once more. Third and fourth generations continue the spread north through the US and Canada, and return south in autumn.

Predators beware

The monarch's bright, contrasted coloration advertises its unpalatability to predators. The caterpillar absorbs steroids from the sap of the milkweed plant that are toxic to predators. However, wasps and various birds can eat the caterpillar: orioles detect the poison and vomit after eating it, while grosbeaks have a degree of immunity and digest butterflies without suffering any harmful effect.

Monarchs are threatened by pesticide use in the US, which kills the milkweed plant, their food, and by logging in Mexico, which reduces their habitat and leaves them susceptible to cold and rain. The Monarch Butterfly Biosphere Reserve in Michoacán, where they overwinter, was declared a a World Heritage Site in 2008.

▽ **MASS MIGRATION**
Millions of monarchs migrate south in autumn. They use stored fat to fuel their flight, and may glide on air currents to save evergy.

▷ **FEEDING ON MILKWEED**
The milkweed plant sustains the monarch butterfly by supplying it with leaves, sap, and nectar.

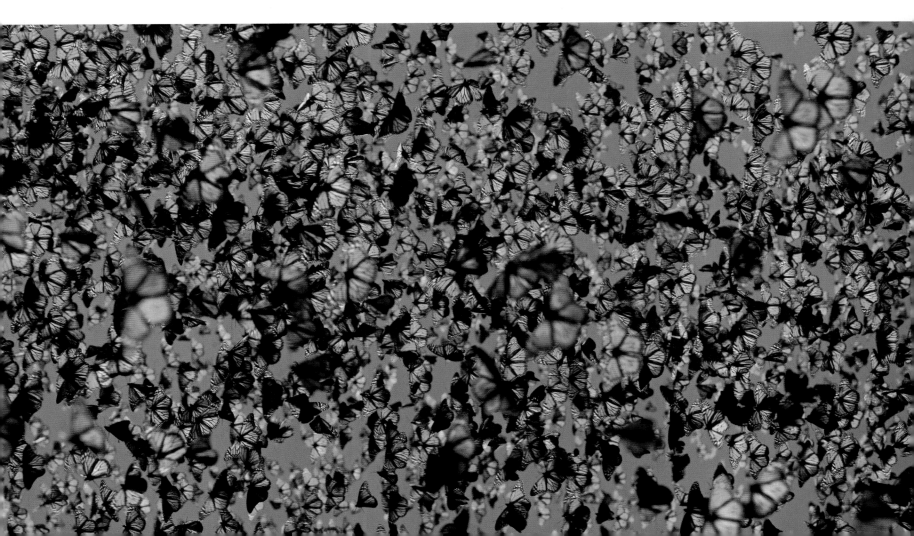

SIERRA NEVADA
California's snowy backbone

At around 4 million years old, the Sierra Nevada is a relatively young range of mountains, forming a dramatic crest 650 km (400 miles) long by 100 km (60 miles) wide along California's eastern edge. At the southern end lies Mount Whitney, the highest US peak outside Alaska at 4,421 m (14,505 ft). The region also boasts the largest alpine lake in North America – the famously clear Lake Tahoe – and three national parks: Yosemite, Sequoia, and Kings Canyon.

Forest and climate zones

The Sierra Nevada's western foothills are cloaked in savanna and deciduous oak woodland, but the rest of the range rising towards the east is dominated by coniferous forest, starting with juniper and Ponderosa and Jeffrey pines at lower altitudes. Giant sequoias start to appear at about 1,000 m (3,280 ft), and higher still, the forests are dominated by lodgepole pines, red and white fir, and eventually, whitebark pine. Finally, the trees give way to hardy alpine plants at about 3,200 m (10,500 ft). The forests are interspersed with rivers and lakes, wet and dry meadows, and extensive areas of brushland.

The wide range of altitudes and climates in the Sierra Nevada is reflected in the diverse wildlife. Animals living at higher altitudes, such as alpine chipmunks and pikas, must be able to tolerate low temperatures and snow for much of the year. The mountains are also home to both black and brown bears, bald eagles, and increasing numbers of American beavers.

PREDATOR IN DECLINE
Once widespread this key forest predator has declined due to trapping. Despite protection, fisher numbers in the Sierra Nevada remain worryingly low. Their loss from the ecosystem would affect the natural balance between predators and prey.

FISHER

SUPERFOOD BONANZA
Sierra Nevada's rivers are important spawning grounds for Chinook salmon, and their spring breeding run provides a feeding bonanza for bears and other predators. However, overexploitation of the region's water resources threatens the species.

CHINOOK SALMON

BLACK-BACKED WOODPECKER

Home to the giant sequoia General Sherman, the second largest living thing

Has North

BURNED FOREST
Black-backed woodpeckers exploit the aftermath of a fire, rapidly colonizing areas where dead wood teems with beetle grubs. As the area regenerates and beetle numbers decline, the birds gradually move on.

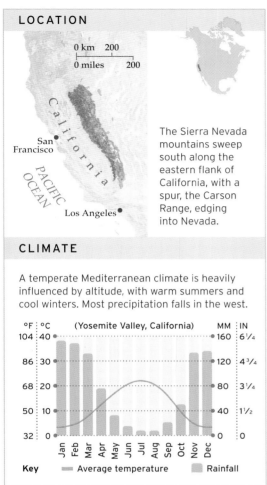
Bighorn sheep

Ovis canadensis

long hairs cover woolly coat

This North American wild sheep is named for the adult male's immense curling horns, which grow to more than 1 m (3 ft) in length. The rams establish a hierarchy based on horn size, with older sheep taking the lead. When it is too close to call, the rivalry is resolved with a head-butting battle. Females grow smaller horns that sweep back from the head. They are mainly defensive, used to deter predators such as eagles and pumas.

↔ 1–1.7 m (3¼–5½ ft)
⚖ 60–145 kg (132–320 lb)
⊗ Vulnerable
🌾 Forbs, grasses, shrubs
🏠 ⛰

C. North America

High living

In summer, bighorn sheep graze in high mountain meadows. They leap from ledge to ledge, never slipping on the steep, rough ground – their forked hoofs split apart as they press down on the ground and grip the rock that fills the gap between them. As winter approaches, the chief ram leads his band of about 10 sheep to lower ground, where they join together to form herds of as many as 100 individuals. The hard outer rim of the bighorn sheep's hoofs cut into snow and ice to provide a better grip. Breeding takes place in the valleys, and lambs are born in spring, a few weeks before the bands trek back up to the peaks.

▽ **CURVED HORNS**
The ram's horns keep growing, and can get so large that the tips impede its field of view. Older rams rub down the tips on a rock to keep them short.

horns of large ram can weigh as much as his skeleton

America's largest alpine lake

LAND OF GIANTS
The largest single trees on Earth depend on two small animals to reproduce. The larvae of a wood-boring beetle and the Douglas squirrel both eat giant sequoia cones, resulting in a steady rain of seeds to the forest floor below.

GIANT SEQUOIA

thick, sleek fur

powerful claws
for digging

Striped skunk

Mephites mephites

About the size of a domestic cat, the striped skunk
is related to badgers, otters, and weasels. Skunks share
features such as a stocky, low-slung body with them,
but have the ability to spray a noxious chemical at
potential predators. This fluid is produced by the
anal scent glands under the tail. The skunk first lifts its
tail in the air like a flag and stamps the ground as a
warning. Should the aggressor stand its ground, the
skunk does a handstand, twists its body, and squirts
the liquid over its head at the attacker's face.

Opportunistic feeder

The striped skunk lives in a wide variety of habitats,
often near water. It will eat virtually anything,
including household rubbish. Mostly solitary and
nocturnal, it can sometimes be spotted in the half-
light of dawn and dusk. Striped skunks breed from
February to March; females give birth in a burrow or a
den underneath a building or fallen tree. The young
become independent at about seven or eight weeks.

▷ **WARNING COLORATION**
The skunk's striking black-and-white coloration
with a bold white "V" running down its back
and tail, and its raised tail, serve as a warning
to potential predators.

△ **NEST RAIDER**
A striped skunk forages in a wild turkey's nest.
Skunks are adept at finding bird eggs, and often
eat an entire clutch at one go.

long,
bushy tail

↔ 55–75 cm (21½–29½ in)
⚖ 2.5–6.5 kg (5½–14 lb)
✖ Common
🍖 Rodents, bird eggs, honey
🏠 🌳🌲🎋

C. Canada to N. Mexico

↔ 1.3–1.9 m (4¼–6¼ ft)
⚖ 55–300 kg (120–660 lb)
✖ Common
🍖 Fruit, nuts, vegetation
🏠 🌳🌲🎋⛰

North America, N. Central
America

powerful
limbs for tree
climbing

American black bear

Ursus americanus

Smaller than grizzlies, black bears also have a straighter profile and are much better climbers. They prefer temperate forests, but can cope with humid Florida swamps as well as subarctic weather in Canada. True omnivores, they mainly feed on wild fruits, nuts, and vegetation, supplemented with insects, grubs, fish, and carrion – occasionally they hunt mammals too. Inquisitive and opportunistic, black bears also exploit rubbish dumps and food left at campsites.

They are solitary except during the mating season, which takes place from mid-May to July. The cubs are born in a den from January to March, while their mothers are hibernating. Litters are usually made up of twins or triplets, but can contain as many as four or five cubs. Cubs remain with their mothers until they are around two years old.

Healthy numbers

American black bear numbers are about twice those of all the world's other bear species combined – despite the fact that it is native to just three countries: Canada, the USA, and Mexico. Of 16 recognized subspecies, only the smallest, the Louisiana black bear (*U.a. luteolus*), is considered threatened under the US Endangered Species Act, due mainly to habitat loss and overhunting. The population of black bears seems stable in areas that are as diverse as their coat colours, which range from cinnamon, light gold, grey-blue, dark brown, and black to British Columbia's white-Kermode or "spirit bear" subspecies (*U.a. kermodei*).

△ SCRATCH MY BACK
Black bears often use trees as scratching posts, but bite and claw marks left on bark may mean certain trees also serve a territorial scent-marking purpose.

△ BATTLE WORN
Black bears are shy and generally avoid humans, but both sexes will fight, kill, and sometimes even eat each other.

◁ TREE CLIMBING
Cubs are taught by their mothers to climb trees to escape danger – including attacks by adult male black bears.

A black bear's **sense of smell** is **seven** times more **acute** than a **bloodhound's**

heavy body

Alpine chipmunk
Tamias alpinus

Chipmunks are small, squirrel-like creatures of open spaces. Alpine chipmunks are found only in California's Sierra Nevada mountains, surviving above 2,500 m (8,000 ft) on broken cliffs and scree with abundant cavities and plentiful seeds of grasses, sedges, and stunted pines. They hibernate from mid-October to June to escape the worst of winter. They store little fat, but cache surplus food in summer and wake often to feed during winter, in between several days of torpor. Alpine chipmunks have no need to find and drink water as they get sufficient moisture from their food.

↔	17–18 cm (6½–7 in)
⚖	27.5–45.5 g (1–1⅝ oz)
⊗	Locally common
ᵜ	Seeds, fruit
⌂ 🌲 ⛰	
◎	SW. USA

◁ **ROCKY PERCH**
Deep, narrow crevices retain heat in high, exposed places, helping this small mammal to survive.

Mountain chickadee
Poecile gambeli

Tits, or titmice, are common worldwide. Several North American species are known as chickadees due to their "chick-a-dee" call. Active, acrobatic, social feeders, mountain chickadees join mixed flocks roaming high coniferous woods in search of food in autumn and winter. A dispersed flock is more likely to find good feeding places than a lone bird, and many pairs of eyes are better at spotting danger.

↔	14 cm (5½ in)
⚖	8–10 g (5/16–3/8 oz)
⊗	Common
ᵜ	Seeds, small insects, spiders
⌂ 🌲 ⛰	
◎	N., W., and S. North America

distinctive white eyebrow

▷ **SOLE TARGET**
Should a predator such as a hawk appear, a lone chickadee would be its only target. It is much safer to be one of many in a flock.

Turkey vulture
Cathartes aura

The turkey vulture is one of seven New World vultures, all of which scavenge dead animals and ride up-currents of warm air over vast areas. They soar on wings raised in a "V" shape for extra stability, their body weight slung low. Their slotted wingtips reduce turbulence – a feature copied by early aircraft designers.

Mutual dependence
While all vultures have excellent sight, few have a keen sense of smell. In forests, other vultures follow turkey vultures to locate carcasses hidden under trees because they can locate food by smell. When large carcasses are found, turkey vultures stand aside as bigger species with stronger beaks open up tough hides. All vultures prefer newly dead animals and avoid putrefying meat.

Turkey vultures that breed in the north migrate to the tropics in winter, but many stay in the southern US all year round. They breed in early spring in the south and in July or August farther north, laying their eggs on a cliff ledge, sometimes in a hollow tree or dense thicket. Two eggs are incubated for up to 40 days, and the chicks are fed in the nest for about 10 weeks.

Turkey vultures can **smell newly dead** animals

64–81 cm (25–32 in)

0.9–2 kg (2–4½ lb)

Common

Carrion

C. North America to S. South America

broad, fingered, two-tone wings

bare head and hooked bill

strong bare legs and feet

◁ **WIDE WINGS**
Turkey vultures spread their wings when perched to allow the sun's heat to warm their body in the morning and to dry wet feathers. This keeps their plumage in good condition.

△ **TOUCHING DOWN**
Tail spread for control, wings beating as brakes, and eyes focused downwards, the vulture thrusts its feet forwards to absorb the shock as it brings its substantial weight in to land.

▷ **EGG TOOTH**
These day-old chicks still have the hard white egg tooth at the end of their beak, which they used to break out of their shell.

thick layer of feathers insulates body

Great grey owl
Strix nebulosa

▽ **WINGED WONDER**
A light body and broad wings allow slow, silent flight, and help the owl to manoeuvre with precision between trees. Special fringes on the wing feathers almost eliminate wing noise.

↔ 59–69 cm (23–27 in)
⚖ 0.8–1.7 kg (1³/₄–3³/₄ lb)
✖ Common
🦷 Voles, mice, birds, frogs
🏠 🌲🌲🌲 ⸬

N. and C. North America, E. Europe, Asia

This owl's thick insulation makes it look large, but its body is actually much smaller and lighter than the eagle owl or great horned owl. A less fearsome predator, the great grey owl focuses on small prey, often in difficult conditions. The disc-like face, more than 50 cm (20 in) wide, suggests astonishingly acute hearing, although the owl's small eyes seem more suited to daylight than night-time activity. Unusually for an owl, it hunts by day and at night. The facial feathers let sound through easily but protect what is hidden behind: an arc of stiff feathers that directs sound right into the assymetrically positioned ears. This helps the owl to locate the source of a sound with pinpoint accuracy.

Great grey owls watch and listen for voles from a perch, often a broken tree stump, and glide down silently to catch them, taking them by surprise. They can hear tunnelling rodents under layers of snow, and penetrate 40–50 cm (16–20 in), plunging headfirst, with a final thrust of their deadly feet. Found mainly in the north, a small population of great grey owls remains in the Sierra Nevada of California.

wide facial disc

broad, fingered wings

short, broad tail

Mountain kingsnake

Lampropeltis zonata

The California Mountain kingsnake has an extensive distribution from Baja California, Mexico, north into Washington state. As its name suggests, the Sierra Mountain subspecies (*L.z. multicincta*) is restricted to that area. Living in uplands and mountains up to altitudes of 3,000 m (10,000 ft), this habitat generalist basks by day in remote gullies or on old logs; rests at night among boulders or tree roots; and shelters in burrows through winter.

False colours

Like most other kingsnakes, this non-venomous constrictor has red or orange, black, and white or cream rings that mimic the coloration of the venomous coral snake to deter predators. A stealthy sight-and-smell predator, it hunts mainly lizards and small snakes. Other prey include birds, especially nestlings of towhees and thrushes, eggs, and less often, small rodents, frogs and other amphibians. It may squeeze a victim in its coils to subdue it before swallowing it whole.

↔ 50–120 cm (20–47 in)
⚖ Up to 1.5kg (up to 3¼ lb)
✖ Locally common
🍴 Small snakes, lizards, birds
🏠 🌲🌲 ⛰

SW. North America

△ **TRICOLOUR SNAKE**
Ready to strike if need be, the Sierra Mountain kingsnake displays its bright warning colours. Not all of the subspecies are alike; some have thinner or even no rings.

The kingsnake **eats other snakes** – even venomous young rattlesnakes

---

Ensatina

Ensatina eschscholtzii

A native of western US mountain forests, the ensatina salamander does not breathe air. This nocturnal amphibian has no lungs – all the oxygen it needs is absorbed directly through its moist skin. The nostrils on the snout are used purely for smelling. Ensatinas have poison glands in their tail, but predators such as raccoons have learned to eat the head then body and discard the tail.

Mating occurs during the cooler seasons, and in summer, pregnant females retreat into a damp nook to lay a dozen eggs. The young hatch out after about four months and have the same body form as an adult, rather than going through a larval tadpole stage. They leave the nest after the first autumn rains.

↔ 6–8 cm (2–3 in)
☁ Spring and summer
✖ Locally common
🍴 Worms, insects, spiders
🏠 🌲🌲
🧭 W. USA

△ **LIVING ON LAND**
Unusually for an amphibian, the ensatina salamander's entire life cycle is based on land.

Yellow-legged frog

Rana sierrae

Found in and around mountain pools and streams, the Sierra Nevada yellow-legged frog lives at altitudes of up to 3,600 m (11,800 ft). It spends winters hibernating at the bottom of frozen lakes. In summer, it hunts by day, rarely straying more than a metre or two from water.

Three species of yellow-legged frogs have now been identified, all with a pale yellow underside. The main difference between the three lies in their distinct mating calls. The breeding season begins after the spring thaw, and after mating the females lay their eggs on aquatic vegetation. The tadpoles take three or four years to reach maturity.

back legs yellow underneath

△ **DEFENSIVE ODOUR**
Yellow-legged frogs exude a pungent garlic-like odour from their skin if they are picked up.

↔ 6–8 cm (2–3 in)
☁ Spring
✖ Endangered
🍴 Insects, spiders, worms
🏠 ⛰ 🌿 ≈
🧭 SW. North America

MOJAVE DESERT
The smallest and driest desert in the US

The Mojave Desert covers 65,000 sq km (25,000 sq miles) of alternating mountain ranges and flat, low-lying basins, mainly in southern California. The Mojave merges almost imperceptibly with the Sonoran Desert to the south and the Great Basin Desert to the north. Its extent is traditionally indicated by the range of an endemic yucca, the Joshua tree (see main photo). This distinctive plant is one of more than 200 found only in the Mojave, which make up a quarter of the desert's plant species.

Land of extremes
The Mojave Desert is dry because it lies in the rain shadow of the Rocky Mountains. It is a high desert, lying mostly at more than 600 m (1,970 ft) above sea level. Daytime temperatures are high, nowhere more so than in Death Valley in the north, where at Furnace Creek on 10 July 1913 the atmospheric temperature reached 56.7°C (134°F), the highest ever recorded on Earth. Death Valley also holds the record for the lowest place in the US: Badwater Basin dips to 86 m (282 ft) below sea level. The name refers to a small spring, whose waters contain high levels of dissolved salts, making them undrinkable for humans. However, the spring does support other life, including pickleweed, a variety of aquatic insects, and the Badwater snail, another Mojave endemic. Other desert specialists living in the Mojave include the kangaroo rat, the desert tortoise, and the deadly Mojave rattlesnake.

BIDING THEIR TIME
Mojave ground squirrels survive droughts by not breeding and extending a form of dormancy known as aestivation to eke out scarce food resources. Even so, populations frequently crash, but their numbers recover rapidly once the rains return.

MOJAVE GROUND SQUIRREL

DESERT BLOOM
Many desert plants are able to remain dormant for years, until sufficient rain falls for them to grow, flower, and set seed. Antelope Valley in the western tip of the desert is famous for the poppies and other flowers that bloom following the winter rains.

CALIFORNIA POPPIE

> The hottest place in North America >

> Average annual

MUTUAL BENEFIT
The yucca moth is named for the plant that depends on it for survival. Females lay eggs in yucca flowers, then pollinate them by forcing pollen into the stigma. When the larvae hatch, they eat some of the developing seeds but the rest is left to grow.

YUCCA MOTH

More than 200 endemic plants >

Kit fox

Vulpes macrotis

black patch on either side of snout

LOCATION

The Mojave Desert lies between the Sonoran and Great Basin deserts, mostly in southeastern California.

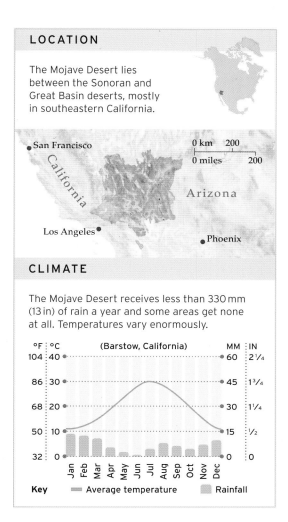

San Francisco

California

Arizona

Los Angeles

Phoenix

0 km 200
0 miles 200

CLIMATE

The Mojave Desert receives less than 330 mm (13 in) of rain a year and some areas get none at all. Temperatures vary enormously.

(Barstow, California)

°F	°C		MM	IN
104	40		60	2¼
86	30		45	1¾
68	20		30	1¼
50	10		15	½
32	0		0	0

Jan Feb Mar Apr May Jun Jul Aug Sep Oct Nov Dec

Key ▬ Average temperature ▢ Rainfall

Thanks to its huge ears, the kit fox has excellent hearing, which helps it locate prey ranging from insects to jackrabbits and lizards. Oversized ears also keep this desert dweller cool by thermoregulation: their huge surface area releases large amounts of heat during the hottest months, keeping the animal's body temperature within comfortable limits.

Survival skills

North America's smallest wild canid has other desert survival skills. The soles of its feet are fur-lined, lending traction but also keeping the pads from burning on hot terrain. Mainly nocturnal, the kit fox avoids the heat as well as predators, such as coyotes, by spending the day inside one of many burrows that it either digs or takes over from animals such as prairie dogs. It also makes dens in manmade structures such as storm drains.

Kit foxes are mainly monogamous, but pairs do not necessarily share the same den and they always hunt alone. A female bears an average of four young per litter, which stay with her for five to six months.

↔ 45–54 cm (18–21½ in)
⚖ 1.6–2.7 kg (3½–6 lb)
✖ Common
▥ Rodents, hares, insects

SW. North America

Kit foxes rarely drink, obtaining **moisture** from their food

▽ CHANGING COAT
The kit fox sports a rusty-tan to buff grey coat in the summer. It takes on a silvery grey hue in the winter.

AVOIDING THE HEAT
Red spotted toads lie dormant underground in dry periods, but after rain falls, they emerge by the thousand in the cool of the night. Females lay their eggs in small, temporary pools. They hatch in three days, and the tadpoles quickly develop into toads.

rainfall of 170 mm (6¾ in)

RED SPOTTED TOAD

round head
with erect ears
buff-coloured,
thick fur

▷ **VOCALIZATIONS**
Small cats cannot roar as the big cats do. Instead, pumas snarl and hiss when annoyed and purr when content.

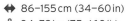

large paws relative
to overall size

Puma

Puma concolor

North America's largest cat has more than 40 common names, including mountain lion and cougar. It is not classified as a big cat, but as the largest of the small cats. Once found across the US, it has now virtually disappeared from eastern and midwestern areas. Pumas farthest from the equator tend to be larger than those nearer to it. Coat colour also varies with geography; the most northern pumas are silver-grey, while those in southerly, humid climates tend to be reddish brown.

Previously elusive and solitary, pumas used to avoid contact with humans whenever possible, although they had been known to kill people when cornered. However, attacks recorded in North America have risen sharply since the 1990s, with hikers, mountain bikers, and skiers particularly at risk.

Flexible feline

Highly adaptable, pumas can live in habitats as diverse as deserts and tropical rainforests. This adaptability also extends to their diet. Although hoofed mammals are preferred – especially by mothers with cubs to feed – pumas hunt rabbits, feral pigs, insects, birds, mice, coyotes, and even other pumas. Although active during the day, they hunt mostly at dawn and dusk.

Female pumas can breed all year round. Males and females stay together for a few days when the female is in season. The male then leaves in search of other potential mates, playing no part in raising his offspring. In about three months, the female gives birth to two or three spotted cubs, which stay with her for up to 18 months. At 12–14 weeks, the cubs' spots begin to fade.

△ **AGILE AND ATHLETIC**
A puma's powerful hind legs allow it to bound up to 12 m (40 ft) when running, and leap up 5.4 m (18 ft) from the ground.

↔ 86–155 cm (34–60 in)
34–72 kg (75–160 lb)
Common
Mammals

W. and S. North America, Central America, South America

Black-tailed jackrabbit

Lepus californicus

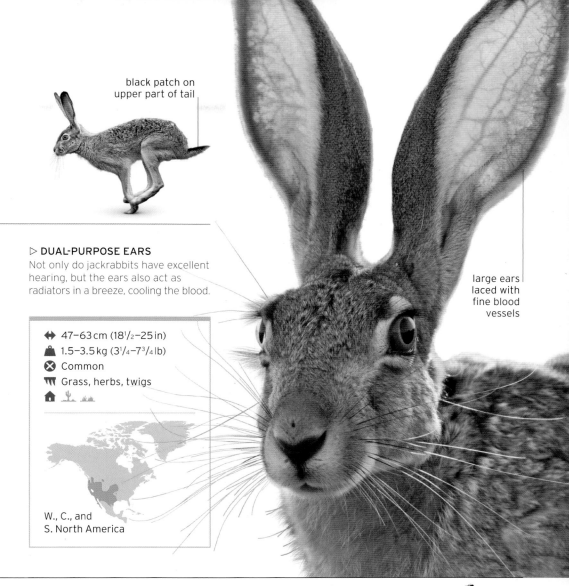

black patch on upper part of tail

Despite their name jackrabbits are in fact hares, not rabbits, with an above-ground lifestyle and a preference for outrunning predators, rather than diving into a burrow. A muscular, flexible body and long, powerful hind legs and feet act as a spring, giving the jackrabbit great speed and acceleration from a standing start.

Black-tailed jackrabbits are widespread in semi-arid regions with sagebrush and creosote bush, and other open shrubland. They avoid searing heat by being active mostly at night. Unusually for hares, they occasionally burrow to escape excessive heat.

Precocious young

Females give birth to three to five fully furred, open-eyed young, called leverets, which are active soon after birth. Females can breed when under a year old, but the rate of predation is high – animals from pumas and coyotes to hawks and rattlesnakes eat jackrabbits. In favourable conditions, their numbers increase rapidly, but they fall again as food becomes scarce.

▷ **DUAL-PURPOSE EARS**
Not only do jackrabbits have excellent hearing, but the ears also act as radiators in a breeze, cooling the blood.

large ears laced with fine blood vessels

↔ 47–63 cm (18$\frac{1}{2}$–25 in)
⬛ 1.5–3.5 kg (3$\frac{1}{4}$–7$\frac{3}{4}$ lb)
✖ Common
🌿 Grass, herbs, twigs

W., C., and S. North America

Greater roadrunner

Geococcyx californianus

lighter throat and chest with dark stripes

Roadrunners are predominantly ground-dwelling birds that belong to the cuckoo family. They have long, strong, bare legs, with two toes facing forwards and two backwards – a feature not seemingly ideal for fast running. Roadrunners favour semi-desert regions with open spaces as well as dry, bushy cover, but have spread into moister, greener habitats with scattered trees. They are weak fliers but can get up onto treetops, wires, or roadside poles. Roadrunners eat lizards and mice, as well as small snakes and birds, snapping them up in their beak. This moisture-rich diet is an advantage when drinking water is scarce. They also conserve moisture by excreting excess salt from a gland near the eye, rather than wasting water in expelling it via the kidneys.

↔ 56 cm (22 in)
⬛ 325 g (11$\frac{1}{2}$ oz)
✖ Common
🌿 Lizards, snakes, mice, birds

S. North America

◁ **DESERT RUN**
The roadrunner is well adapted to life in the fast lane. It walks and runs through the desert, trying to flush out prey.

Gila monster

fat tail stores food and water

Heloderma suspectum

A Gila **bite is painful** but **rarely fatal** to humans

shiny, bead-like scales

Solidly built, strong, slow, solitary, and secretive, the Gila (pronounced "hee-luh") is North America's largest native lizard – and one of very few that are venomous. Toxins from the Gila's modified salivary glands flow into a victim by capillary action along grooved teeth in the lower jaw, aided by its tenaciously chewing grip. As a result, the Gila has few natural predators.

Supersize meal

Gila monsters spend 90 per cent of their time resting in a den in an appropriated old burrow, among roots, or under rocks. They feed on bird and reptile eggs, small mammals, birds (especially nestlings), reptiles such as lizards, and frogs and other amphibians, as well as bugs and worms. Given its energy-saving habits, and the ability to store fat in its tail, a sizeable meal lasts a Gila for weeks. A young Gila can eat one-half its own body weight in a sitting, an adult one-third. As a result, some Gilas eat as few as six times in a year.

Mojave rattlesnake

Crotalus scutulatus

A member of the pit viper family, this rattlesnake has bowl-like pits below the eyes that detect infrared (heat) in warm-blooded animals. Its potent venom is used both to subdue prey, such as rats and mice, and to defend itself. The warning rattle from which its common name is derived increases in size each time the snake sheds its skin.

The Mojave rattlesnake differs from its famous close cousin, the western diamondback rattlesnake, in that the back markings fade earlier towards the tail and its white tail rings are wider than the black ones.

rattle

△ **MOJAVE GREEN**
Some Mojave rattlesnakes have an olive-green tinge – locals call them Mojave greens.

↔ 1–1.3 m (3¼–4¼ ft)
⬛ 2–4 kg (4.4–8.8 lb)
✖ Locally common
🎋 Small mammals, lizards
🏠 🌿
🧭 SW. North America, Central America

Couch's spadefoot

Scaphiopus couchii

skin mottled with dark markings

The spadefoot is named after the hard pads on its hind feet, which it uses to dig burrows in the sand. The toad spends months deep underground to avoid dry conditions. While underground, it retains the toxins that are usually expelled in urine. This creates a high chemical concentration in the toad's body, allowing water to be absorbed from the soil through its permeable skin.

Breeding takes place in the wet season. The toads come to the surface after the first heavy rains, and females lay their eggs in temporary pools. They hatch within 36 hours, and tadpoles mature into toadlets in 40 days.

△ **FEED AND BREED**
As well as breeding, the toads spend the nights above ground hunting for as much prey as they can find.

↔ 5.5–9 cm (2¼–3½ in)
💧 Rainy season
✖ Common
🎋 Insects, spiders
🏠 🌿 🌿
🧭 S. USA, Mexico

▷ **BURYING HER EGGS**
Females lay 5 to 10 eggs in summer and bury them in dry soil. The young, which are about 15 cm (6 in) long, hatch nine months later.

▽ **BEADED BODY**
Gila scales are rounded and slightly domed. The pattern of black with pink, red, or orange patches – unique on each individual – warns potential predators of its toxic bite.

↔ 40–60 cm (16–24 in)
⬛ 1–2 kg (2$\frac{1}{5}$–4$\frac{2}{5}$ lb)
✖ Near threatened
🐾 Eggs, small birds, mammals
🏠 🌵

SW. USA, N. Mexico

Desert blond tarantula

Aphonopelma chalcodes

Lacking good vision, this desert hunter is at great risk of predation during the day. For this reason it remains in its burrow and waits for night to fall. In the dark, touch is the tarantula's main link to its surroundings. It uses its feet and mouthparts to detect vibrations caused by passing animals that touch a network of silk threads radiating from the entrance of its burrow. The spider lies in wait for prey, then rushes out and kills it with a venomous bite.

Mating quest

Tarantulas grow slowly, reaching sexual maturity at 10 years. Males then search for mates, delivering a silk sac of sperm to each female they find. The eggs are laid on a silk sheet at the sun-warmed mouth of the burrow. Spiderlings stay in the burrow for a few days only.

▽ **HAIRY HUNTER**
The tarantula's body hairs are sensory but also have a defensive function. When threatened, the spider uses its back legs to flick barbed, irritating hairs at its attacker.

dark abdomen

pale hairs on legs

↔ 5–7 cm (2–2$\frac{3}{4}$ in)
✖ Not known
🐾 Crickets, grasshoppers, small lizards
🏠 🌵

SW. North America

FLORIDA EVERGLADES
The largest wetland wilderness in the US

The Everglades is a complex of low-lying, densely vegetated wetlands incorporating a mosaic of habitats. The region lacks the scenic grandeur of some other US national parks, but an area in the south was granted protected status in 1934 on account of its unique ecology and biodiversity. The diverse array of interlinking habitats are defined by the depth, quality, and salinity of the water, and the frequency and duration of flooding.

River of grass

The park's coastal ecosystems include estuaries, tidal mangrove swamps, and coastal prairies dominated by salt- and drought-tolerant succulent plants. These give way inland to prairies and sparsely canopied forests of fast-growing slash pine, which are periodically razed by fire. The prairies are interspersed with lower-lying areas almost permanently inundated with water flowing slowly south from Lake Okeechobee towards Florida Bay. These wet sawgrass prairies – known locally as the river of grass – include areas of sluggish open water, or sloughs, and cypress swamps. Small patches of slightly higher ground support hammocks of hardwood forest with trees including tropical mahogany and temperate oak, usually dripping with ferns and airplants (epiphytes).

More than 300 species of fish live in the Everglades, together with the largest breeding populations of tropical waders in North America. The region is also home to 50 species of reptile, including the American alligator and the threatened American crocodile.

SHARK NURSERY
Baby bull sharks are vulnerable to predation, so females enter low-saline rivers to give birth. In doing so, they endure physiological stress that would kill most marine fish. Young bull sharks eventually migrate to warmer offshore waters.

BULL SHARK

CYPRESS SWAMPS
Pond and bald cypresses thrive in swamps, forming dome-shaped clusters, with smaller, less stable trees at their edge. The largest trees in the middle are stabilized by buttress roots. Aerial roots with distinctive "knees" may play a role in respiration.

BALD AND POND

FLORIDA PANTHER

The only place in the world where alligator

North America's only subtropical wetland

PREDATOR IN PERIL
The Florida panther, a subspecies of puma, is the most endangered mammal in the Everglades – fewer than 100 remain. Its dwindling numbers have been boosted by other subspecies of puma introduced from Texas.

LOCATION

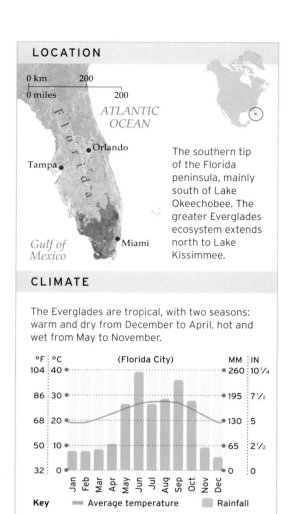

0 km 200
0 miles 200

ATLANTIC OCEAN

Florida

• Orlando

Tampa •

Gulf of Mexico

• Miami

The southern tip of the Florida peninsula, mainly south of Lake Okeechobee. The greater Everglades ecosystem extends north to Lake Kissimmee.

CLIMATE

The Everglades are tropical, with two seasons: warm and dry from December to April, hot and wet from May to November.

°F	°C	(Florida City)	MM	IN
104	40		260	10¼
86	30		195	7½
68	20		130	5
50	10		65	2½
32	0		0	0

Jan Feb Mar Apr May Jun Jul Aug Sep Oct Nov Dec

Key — Average temperature ▮ Rainfall

West Indian manatee
Trichechus manatus

With their bulgy bodies, broad heads, and wide, whiskery muzzles, West Indian manatees resemble walruses, but their closest living relatives are the elephant and the tiny, hoofed, rodent-like hyrax. Gentle and slow-moving, manatees never haul out on land and cannot survive in cold conditions. They graze on salt- and freshwater plants, an activity that, together with their shape and docile nature, has earned them the nickname "sea cow".

↔ 2.5–3.9 m (8¼–13 ft)
⚖ 200–600 kg (440–1,320 lb)
✕ Vulnerable
🌾 Seagrasses, aquatic plants
🏠 🌾 ≈ ≈ ◣

SE. USA to NE. South America, Caribbean

◁ **LANGUID PACE**
Manatees swim slowly, surfacing every three to five minutes to breathe. When resting, they can stay underwater for as long as 20 minutes.

Northern grey fox
Urocyon cinereoargenteus

Slight, quick, and agile, the grey fox is a capable climber, often resting as high as 18 m (59 ft) in trees out of reach of predators such as coyotes and dogs. Mainly nocturnal and a solitary hunter, it preys on rabbits and rodents in the winter, but its diet varies with the season and, like most foxes, it will eat almost anything it comes across. Both parents raise the pups, which are independent by autumn.

↔ 54–66 cm (21½–26 in)
⚖ 2–5.5 kg (4½–12 lb)
✕ Common
🌾 Rodents, birds, insects
🏠 🌲 ⚘ 🏚

North America to N. South America

◁ **BARKING CALL**
The grey fox has a wide range of vocalizations, including yapping barks, screams, and growls.

ESSES

UNWELCOME INVADERS

A quarter of vertebrate species in the Everglades are introduced, posing a major threat to native wildlife. The huge Burmese python has no natural predators and so its numbers are increasing. It is devastating local raccoon and rabbit populations.

and crocodiles coexist

BURMESE PYTHON

↔ 60–95 cm (23¹/₂–37 in)

⚖ 2.7–10.4 kg (5¹/₂–23 lb)

✖ Common

🐾 Small animals, berries, eggs

S. Canada to
Central America

▷ **MASKED BANDIT**
The black "bandit" mask
around a raccoon's eyes
reflects its opportunistic
behaviour. It can climb,
dig, and manipulate
doors and latches
with its forepaws.

pale grey to
almost black fur

Northern raccoon

Procyon lotor

Dexterous, intelligent, and adaptable, the northern raccoon is found in practically every North American environment, from swamp to mountains, urban streets to farmland. Once a tropical animal that foraged mainly along riverbanks, it has changed into a pan-continental species. Raccoons are now found in a variety of habitats, including deserts and mountains where they were previously rare, but they prefer watercourses.

Adapt and thrive

"Flexible" describes this extremely successful omnivore best. Raccoons are optimal survivors, locating food in ponds and streams, in trees, and on the ground in the wild, as well as in gutters, rubbish bins, and rooftops in cities. Insects, frogs, rodents, eggs, nuts, and berries make up their diet in the wild. In urban areas, they consume almost anything edible they come across – they even raid birdfeeders and outdoor feeding stations of domestic animals. Raccoons generally make their dens in hollow trees or burrows in the wild, where they hole up during the day and emerge to hunt at dusk. They are just as willing to live in barns, crawl spaces under houses, and attics. Raccoons thrive in towns and cities due to a plentiful supply of food and the absence of natural predators such as coyotes, bobcats, and pumas.

Master manipulator

Raccoons are exceedingly dexterous. The five toes on their forepaws function in the same way as human fingers, allowing them to grasp and manipulate food, as well as turn doorknobs and release latches. They are strong swimmers, relying heavily on their sense of touch – the sensitivity of which may increase underwater – when feeling about for prey such as frogs and shellfish. Even though its hindlegs are longer than its forelegs – giving it a hunched appearance – the raccoon can run at speeds up to 24 km/h (15 mph).

Females give birth to a litter of three or four young, from multiple fathers, called kits, in spring. The kits begin to follow their mother on her nocturnal forays when they are 8–10 weeks old, and remain with her until they are 13–14 months old.

An adult raccoon is **strong enough to hold a dog's head underwater**

△ **FEELING FOR FOOD**
With their agile, sensitive fingers, raccoons are adept at finding food underwater. Crayfish is a favourite food source.

◁ **TIGHT GRIP**
An adult raccoon can catch prey as large as trout. The raccoon keeps a tight grip on its slippery meal with its sharp claws.

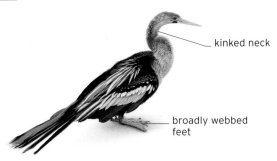

kinked neck

broadly webbed feet

Anhinga
Anhinga anhinga

Found commonly in swamps and waterways, the anhinga is the Americas' equivalent of the similar African darter. It roosts on trees and mangroves, but leaves to feed soon after sunrise, flying to open water. It swims low in the water, head and neck raised, earning the alternative name "snakebird".

Spearfishing
With unusually dense bones and plumage that quickly absorbs water, the anhinga sinks easily and swims underwater for up to a minute. It does not have the powerful legs of the cormorants for active pursuit, but feeds more like an underwater heron, waiting for a chance to spear a passing fish. Special vertebrae and neck musculature give its neck a permanent kink, and an instant, rapid forward stab. The anhinga then rises to the surface, shakes the fish free, and swallows it.

Anhingas nest in mixed colonies with other tree-nesting birds. The female builds the nest from twigs and reeds collected by the male. Up to six eggs are incubated for three to four weeks. The chicks are fed at first with pre-digested fish from the parents' throats and then whole fish. They leave the nest after six weeks, but remain dependent on their parents for a few more weeks.

slender head

silver-white markings on upperparts of wings

long, dagger-like bill

▽ OUTSTRETCHED WINGS
Anhingas display with one or both wings outstretched. They also regularly perch with open wings to help dry saturated feathers and to regulate their body temperature.

Great blue heron
Ardea herodias

black shoulder patches

long, narrow toes

The great blue heron is the largest wading bird in North America. Herons worldwide have a similar long neck, curled back between the shoulders in flight or when the bird is resting, but stretched out to grab a passing fish with a lightning strike of the long, sharp bill. Great blue herons are masters of "wait-and-watch" predation and patient stalking, standing like shadowy statues in the shallows for hours. They can be surprisingly aerobatic around their treetop colonies, where up to six eggs are incubated for 27 days. The chicks are fed by both parents for up to 80 days before they can fly. One subspecies, *A. h. occidentalis*, occurs in a pure white form in Florida.

◁ **PIERCED PREY**
Most fish-eating birds grasp prey in their bills, but anhingas are spear-fishers, piercing small fish with the upper mandible, and larger ones with both.

↔ 85–89 cm (33½–35 in)
⬛ 1.2 kg (2½ lb)
✖ Common
🦅 Fish
🏠 🌿 〰 🏭

S. North America to C. South America

↔ 0.9–1.4 m (3–4½ ft)
⬛ 2.1–2.5 kg (4½–5½ lb)
✖ Common
🦅 Fish, frogs, birds
🏠 🌿 〰 🍄

North America to N. South America

◁ **HIGH LIFE**
Great blue herons build their nests high on trees, safe from ground predators. They must be substantial enough for several chicks to grow to full size.

Purple gallinule
Porphyrio martinica

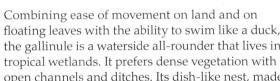

long, yellow legs and toes

Combining ease of movement on land and on floating leaves with the ability to swim like a duck, the gallinule is a waterside all-rounder that lives in tropical wetlands. It prefers dense vegetation with open channels and ditches. Its dish-like nest, made of grasses on a floating mat of weed or attached to reed stems, contains up to 10 eggs, which hatch after 20 days. The chicks feed themselves after a week, become independent three weeks later, and fly when five to seven weeks old.

▷ **QUICK STEPPER**
The gallinule spreads its weight through its elongated toes and steps quickly and rhythmically across floating vegetation. It also often clambers up more awkwardly through dense twigs.

↔ 27–36 cm (10½–14 in)
⬛ 200–275 g (7–9½ oz)
✖ Common
🦅 Seeds, fruit, invertebrates
🏠 🌾 〰 🍄

S. North America to South America

keeled scales on tail

alligators have a more rounded snout than crocodiles

American alligator

Alligator mississippiensis

This fearsome predator is restricted to wetlands and swamps of the southeastern US, and propels itself through water with its muscular, laterally flattened tail. On land, the American alligator can crawl on its belly or lift its body off the ground in a slow, waddling walk. If it draws its legs fully below its body it can gallop for short distances, charging faster than many humans can run. Mostly a night hunter, it drifts or swims stealthily, then lunges at its prey.

Courtship and mating begin in April and May, with the males roaring and bellowing as low as they can to attract females. In August, 30–50 babies hatch in a nest mound of warm decomposing vegetation gathered by the mother. She listens for the hatching babies' chirps, helps them out of the nest, and carries them in her mouth down to the water. Size, power, and a thick skin mean an adult alligator has little to fear, but the young are vulnerable to predators and are protected by their mother for up to three years.

↔ 3–4 m (10–13 ft)
⚖ Up to 300 kg (660 lb)
✖ Locally common
🐟 Fish, waterbirds, mammals
🏠 🌾≈ ≈

SE. USA

▷ **POWERFUL JAWS**
The alligator grabs its prey with about 80 conical teeth set in powerful jaws. A characteristic large tooth in the lower jaw fits into a socket in the upper jaw.

Common snapping turtle

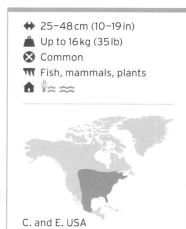

Chelydra serpentina

Ranging as far north as Alberta, Canada, and as far south as the US Gulf Coast, some snapping turtles have even been seen in the Rocky Mountains – no mean feat for an animal that prefers to spend most of its time in muddy freshwater lakes and rivers.

As the name suggests, the snapping turtle bites. Highly aggressive on land, it is prone to snapping the heads off other turtles or taking a bite out of anything it comes across. The shells of older snapping turtles are usually covered in algae, enhancing their camouflage as they hide in wait for prey. Adults sometimes travel long distances overland and can end up as traffic fatalities, whereas hatchlings are vulnerable to attack by raccoons, herons, and skunks, as well as other turtles.

brown or olive to black upper shell

△ **FEROCIOUS SNAPPER**
Given their pugnacious temperament and tough carapace, adult "snappers" have few enemies and can live up to 40 years.

↔ 25–48 cm (10–19 in)
⚖ Up to 16 kg (35 lb)
✖ Common
🐟 Fish, mammals, plants
🏠 🌾≈ ≈

C. and E. USA

Golden silk orbweaver

Nephila clavipes

The golden silk orbweaver is one of the largest American web-spinning spiders. It builds a strong, semi-permanent web between trees in swamps and woodlands. The web of a mature female may be 1 m (3 ft) wide, not including the anchoring strands. The species is named after the yellow-tinged silk of the web, which may transmit the green light reflecting off surrounding plants, making it harder to see when in the shade. When lit by the sun, the silk's gold colour may attract flower-seeking insects, such as butterflies and bees, which become the spider's victims.

↔ 1.25–7.5 cm (½–3 in)
⊗ Not known
ᴍ Insects
🏠 🌳 🌾≈

S. North America to South America

◁ **LITTLE AND LARGE**
The male golden silk orbweaver, seen here next to a potential mate, is a fraction of the female's size.

Costa Rica
Flying high above the tropical rainforest a scarlet macaw spies some brightly coloured flowers in the canopy. These large parrots only breed in tree cavities..

Central and South America

LAND OF THE JAGUAR

Central and South America

Collectively, Central and South America constitute more than 18 million sq km (7 million sq miles) of incredibly varied terrain and climate. Forming South America's backbone is the world's longest mountain range, the Andes, which at its highest point reaches almost 7,000 m (23,000ft) above sea level. The massive lowland drainage basin of the Amazon River and its tributaries is filled with lush rainforest, and at the continent's centre is the world's largest tropical wetland, the Pantanal. The south and east of South America tend to be drier and feature highland plateaus covered with wooded savanna and wide, grassy plains. This range of habitats has resulted in a huge diversity of plant and animal species, many of them found nowhere else.

Historically, the Central American isthmus has been an important bridge for the exchange of land animals between North and South America. It is also a vital flightpath for birds migrating along the Pacific Flyway between Alaska, in North America, and Patagonia, in South America.

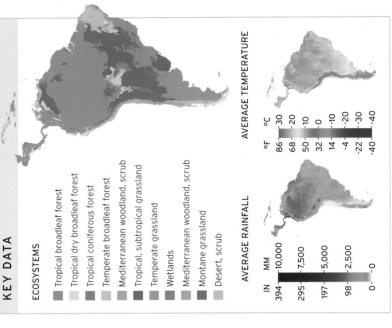

KEY DATA

ECOSYSTEMS

- Tropical broadleaf forest
- Tropical dry broadleaf forest
- Tropical coniferous forest
- Temperate broadleaf forest
- Mediterranean woodland, scrub
- Tropical, subtropical grassland
- Temperate grassland
- Wetlands
- Mediterranean woodland, scrub
- Montane grassland
- Desert, scrub

AVERAGE TEMPERATURE

°F	°C
86	30
68	20
50	10
32	0
14	-10
-4	-20
-22	-30
-40	-40

AVERAGE RAINFALL

IN	MM
394	10,000
295	7,500
197	5,000
98	2,500
0	0

AMAZON RAINFOREST

The largest rainforest on Earth dominates the northern half of South America. Estimated to be at least 55 million years old, the Amazon is home to a dazzling diversity of animal and plant life. It contains around 10 per cent of the world's known species and is a refuge for jaguars, harpy eagles, and pink dolphins, as well as thousands of bird and butterfly species.

CARIBBEAN ISLANDS

The Caribbean has more than 7,000 islands and around 9% of the world's coral reefs.

LAND LINK TO NORTH AMERICA

Formed around 3 million years ago, the isthmus allows movement of land animals between the continents.

COSTA RICAN RAINFOREST

Ecotourists flock to view the beautiful jungles and their wildlife.

GALAPAGOS ISLANDS

These volcanic islands are formed by a mantle plume – columns of molten rock rising from deep within the Earth

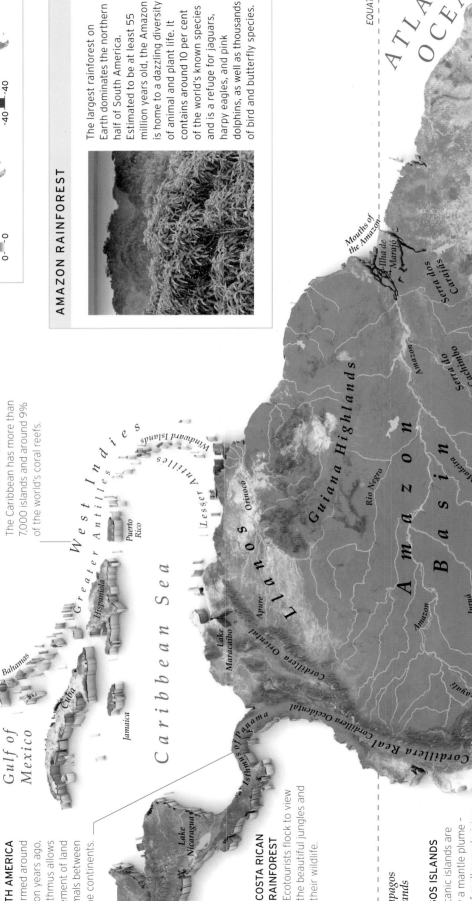

ATLANTIC OCEAN

EQUATOR

Galapagos Islands

Gulf of Mexico

Caribbean Sea

West Indies

Greater Antilles

Lesser Antilles

Windward Islands

Bahamas

Cuba

Jamaica

Hispaniola

Puerto Rico

Lake Nicaragua

Isthmus of Panama

Lake Maracaibo

Cordillera Occidental

Cordillera Oriental

Cordillera Real

Llanos

Orinoco

Apure

Guiana Highlands

Rio Negro

Amazon Basin

Amazon

Madeira

Juruá

Ucayali

Mouths of the Amazon

Ilha de Marajó

Serra dos Carajás

Serra do Cachimbo

Planalto da

PHYSICAL BARRIERS

Geographic barriers such as rivers separate animal populations, limiting their distribution and encouraging separate species to develop. Two capuchin species are separated by the Paraná and Araguaia rivers. Genetic evidence indicates that these populations separated 2 million years ago.

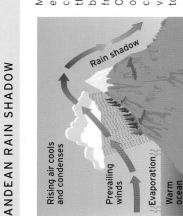

AZURA'S CAPUCHIN

ANDEAN RAIN SHADOW

Much of the south-eastern part of the continent is dry due to the rain shadow cast by the Andes. Winds from the Pacific Ocean rise and cool over the mountains, causing the water vapour they contain to fall as rain on the windward (west) side of the mountain range.

Rain shadow

Rising air cools and condenses

Prevailing winds

Evaporation

Warm ocean

FERTILE GRASSLANDS

The rich temperate grasslands of the Argentine pampas are home to many unique animals.

STRAIT OF MAGELLAN

Fish move through this sea passage between the Pacific and Atlantic oceans.

ATACAMA DESERT

The Atacama is the driest desert in the world – in some parts of the desert, no rainfall has ever been recorded. Nevertheless, around 500 species of plants and a few arthropods, amphibians, reptiles, birds, and mammals have adapted to survive here. These include scorpions, salt flat lizards, Humboldt penguins, and Andean flamingos.

VALLE DE LA LUNA

FEATURED ECOREGIONS

- Costa Rican Rainforest ›› **p78–83**
  Tropical, subtropical moist broadleaf forest
- Andean Yungas ›› **p84–89**
  Tropical, subtropical moist broadleaf forest
- Amazon Rainforest ›› **p90–99**
  Tropical, subtropical moist broadleaf forest
- The Pantanal ›› **p100–07**
  Wetland, flooded grassland
- Andean Altiplano ›› **p108–13**
  Montane grassland, shrub
- Argentine Pampas ›› **p114–21**
  Temperate grassland
- Galapagos Islands ›› **p122–29**
  Desert, scrub

ATLANTIC OCEAN

PACIFIC OCEAN

AMERICA

Brazilian Highlands

Serra do Espinhaço

São Francisco

Serra da Mantiqueira

Serra Dourada

Serra do Roncador

Planalto de Mato Grosso

Serra de Maracaju

Serra do Caiapó

Serra do Mar

Serra Geral

Paraná

Paraná

Pantanal

Gran Chaco

Paraguay

Paraguay

Uruguay

Uruguay

Paraná

Mesopotamia

Lagoa dos Patos

Mirim Lagoon

Río de la Plata

Pampas

Río Grande

Lago Poopó

Altiplano

Salar de Uyuni

Lake Titicaca

Cerro Ojos del Saldo 6.880m

Sierras de Córdoba

Cerro Aconcagua 6.959m

Atacama Desert

Andes

Patagonia

Falkland Islands

Tierra del Fuego

Cape Horn

COSTA RICAN RAINFOREST
A tropical eco-paradise

Costa Rica may be small, but it punches above its size in terms of biodiversity – it contains 5 per cent of all species on just 0.3 per cent of the world's land mass. The Costa Rican rainforest is a lush tropical jungle, with verdant foliage, rivers, and waterfalls, and teems with an exotic array of animal life. Many of this rainforest's inhabitants are dazzlingly beautiful – butterflies and hummingbirds flit among trees that are adorned with glorious blooms. A diverse array of orchid species are found here, considering the ecoregion's comparably small size.

This bountiful biodiversity is due to Costa Rica's location on the land bridge between North and South America, which gives it representatives from both continents. There is also a range of ecological niches in the country – as well as the rainforest, there are damp cloud forests at higher altitudes, dry forests, and mangrove swamps.

Conservation leader

Costa Rica leads the world in terms of protecting its wild heritage. Around a quarter of the country is designated as national parks or protected areas, and Costa Rica has been praised as a model of responsible ecotourism as people flock here to see the region's myriad of monkey species and unique mammals like sloths. The rate of deforestation has dramatically decreased since the 1960s and some areas have been successfully reforested. Costa Rica has also pioneered payments to landowners for environmental services to support conservation measures and to keep the rainforest intact.

HIGH RISER
Trees that emerge high above the main rainforest, such as kapok, benefit from sunlight that doesn't reach lower parts of the rainforest. Nectar-feeding bats pollinate its flowers and fluffy seeds are blown on the wind to new areas.

KAPOK TREE

IF THE BILL FITS
The flowers of heliconia plants are almost exclusively pollinated by hummingbirds that visit to drink the flowers' rich nectar. The two have co-evolved so that heliconias with deeper flower tubes are only pollinated by the species that has a long enough bill.

HUMMINGBIRDS

HARPY EAGLE

More than 50 species of hummingbird

Home to more than 5% of the world's species

HUGE HUNTER
The harpy eagle hunts monkeys and sloths amongst the rainforest canopy. Its short, broad wings make it easier for a bird of its size to manoeuvre, and its long talons and powerful feet allow it to catch and lift large prey.

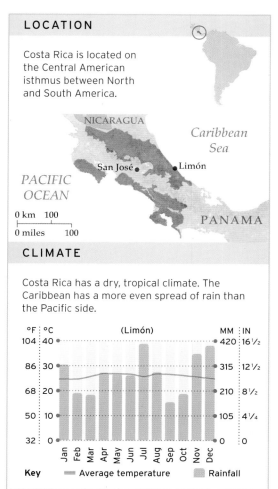

NICARAGUA

Caribbean Sea

San José • Limón

PACIFIC OCEAN

PANAMA

0 km 100
0 miles 100

CLIMATE

Costa Rica has a dry, tropical climate. The Caribbean has a more even spread of rain than the Pacific side.

°F	°C	(Limón)	MM	IN
104	40		420	16½
86	30		315	12½
68	20		210	8½
50	10		105	4¼
32	0		0	0

Jan Feb Mar Apr May Jun Jul Aug Sep Oct Nov Dec

Key — Average temperature ▪ Rainfall

UMBRELLA SPECIES
The black-headed bushmaster viper preys on small mammals, such as spiny rats and marsupials, and lays its eggs in burrows made by other animals. Conservation of this species would benefit many others.

750,000 species of insect

BUSHMASTER VIPER

Honduran white bat
Ectophylla alba

This tiny white bat lives in rainforests where large-leafed heliconia plants are plentiful. Feeding on fruit at night, they roost during the day in tents that they construct by nibbling either side of a leaf's midrib so that the sides collapse, forming an inverted V that protects them from rain and sun. Their snow-white fur is tinted green as sunlight filters through the bright green leaves, thus camouflaging them from potential predators.

↔ 3.5–4.8 cm (1½–2 in)
⬛ 7.5 g (¼ oz)
✖ Near threatened
🌾 Fruit pulp, fig seeds
🏠 🌳

Central America

◁ **LEAF TENT**
Honduran white bats roost in groups of 4–10, usually a single male and his harem of females, underneath a leaf 2 m (6 ft) off the ground.

Hoffmann's two-toed sloth
Choloepus hoffmanni

Sloths live in slow motion to conserve energy. Their metabolism is about 50 per cent slower than that of other similarly sized mammals. Their intestine is shorter than a carnivore's – a trait usually associated with a fast-acting digestion – yet the plant-based diet takes 6–21 days to be digested. This, however, allows sloths to extract the maximum nutrition from low-energy food and may also help neutralize toxins. Awkward and vulnerable on the ground, where the sloth descends once a week to defecate, the algae in its fur conceals it in the trees from predators such as harpy eagles and jaguars.

↔ 55–75 cm (21½–29½ in)
⬛ 4–8.5 kg (8¾–19 lb)
✖ Common
🌾 Leaves, buds, fruit, sap
🏠 🌳 🌴 🌿

Central America, N. and W. South America

▷ **HANGING AROUND**
Sloths spend most of their lives in trees, where they eat, sleep, mate, and give birth – all while dangling upside down from their huge, hooked claws.

distinctive chain-like rosettes

Ocelot

Leopardus pardalis

Ocelots are **good swimmers** and will **catch fish, turtles, and frogs**

short, dense fur

The ocelot is the largest of three small, spotted cats native to Central and South American forests. Its patterned coat and stealthy, mainly nocturnal, habits ensure that the cat is rarely seen. Much of what we know about the species comes from analysing its droppings, and radio-tracking. Ocelots have been tracked travelling long distances at night, with adult females ranging up to 4 km (3 miles) and males 7.5 km (5 miles).

Lone ranger

Ocelots become active in the late afternoon, and hunt by patrolling areas of thick cover. They prefer to feed on small ground-dwelling rodents, particularly rats, but can take young deer, wild pigs, and sloths. More unusual prey include lizards, land crabs, birds, fish, and frogs. Ocelots are agile climbers, often resting in trees during the day. Like most cats, they are solitary – adults socialize only during the breeding season. An adult male's home range overlaps with that of several females. The females breed once every two years and usually give birth to just one cub after 80 days.

◁ **AMBITIOUS HUNTER**
Ocelots will catch prey half their weight, such as green iguanas. To avoid the reptile's claws and lashing tail, a hunting ocelot will aim for the fleshy throat for a quick dispatch.

front paws larger than rear paws

▷ **DAPPLED FUR**
The ocelot's spotted coat provides excellent camouflage among foliage. In the past, this species was heavily hunted to supply the fur trade.

- ↔ 50–100 cm (19¹/₂–39 in)
- 🏋 11.5–16 kg (25–35 lb)
- ✖ Common
- 🐾 Mammals
- 🏠 🌳 🌾 〰 🍄

S. North America to S. South America

Resplendent quetzal
Pharomachrus mocinno

Quetzals are a group of glossy birds found in tropical forests. The resplendent quetzal is the most extravagantly plumed, but when perched, upright, still, and silent, its long, green back makes it inconspicuous in the forest. It mostly eats fruit, especially wild avocados, but will occasionally feed on insects, small frogs, lizards, and snails.

Pairs are territorial, and they carve out a nest hole in a rotting tree. The female lays one or two eggs, which are incubated by both parents for 18 days. The male and female also take turns feeding the chicks; however, often only the male continues to do so for the last few days before the chicks can fly.

- ↔ 35–65 cm (14–25¹/₂ in)
- 🏋 200–225 g (7–8 oz)
- ✖ Near threatened
- 🐾 Fruit, insects
- 🏠 🌳 ⛰

Central America

▷ **SPLENDID PLUMES**
Resplendent quetzals are aptly named after the vibrant tail feathers of breeding males.

Common morpho
Morpho peleides

When viewed at rest with its wings folded up, the common morpho's wings are brown with several large eyespots. However, in flight, the upper wings produce a startling display of iridescent blues and turquoises. Visible even in the thick foliage, the shimmering wings allow the butterflies to spot one another – males keep their distance, while females seek out mates.

- ↔ 9.5–12 cm (3³/₄–4³/₄ in)
- ✖ Not known
- 🐾 Juices of ripe fruits
- 🏠 🌳 🏛 ▭

Central America to N. South America

white marks on dark fringe

◁ **VARIOUS FORMS**
Common morphos vary greatly in colour and form, with different markings on the wing margins and fringes, and there are several subspecies.

black-and-yellow-ringed eyespots

Red-eyed tree frog

Agalychnis callidryas

bright green upper body
provides camouflage

orange feet hidden
when at rest

The red-eyed tree frog is an iconic rainforest amphibian. As its name suggests, it has striking red eyes, although these are usually hidden from view. To camouflage itself against leaves, it makes itself look small by tucking its legs against the body so that only the green upper surfaces are in view. The eyes are shut to conceal the telltale red irises. When a predator gets too close, the frog flashes its eyes wide open, startling it momentarily. As it leaps to safety, extending its legs to a full stretch, it reveals yet more hidden colour on its flanks and thighs.

Agile climber

The red-eyed tree frog is a nocturnal insect hunter. The vertical diamond shape of its iris shows that it is focused on tracking the vertical movements of insects marching up and down tree trunks. Like all frogs, the tree frog is a good jumper, but it also climbs up trees, gripping branches with the suction cups at the tips of its fingers and toes. Unlike most frogs, the red-eyed tree frog can swim, although the adult spends most of its life in trees. It visits water regularly – often just the puddles formed on leaves – to absorb water through the thin skin on its belly.

Show of strength

Mating takes place in the rainy season. Males, who adopt prominent perches, initiate courtship through a croaking call. They also quiver their body so much that the surrounding leaves begin to shake. This show of strength attracts females, and when one gets near, all the males in the area fight to mate with her. The winner fertilizes her egg clutches as she lays them on leaves in several batches.

distinctive blue
and yellow markings
on sides

▷ **FLASH COLOURING**
The bright blue and yellow flanks of the red-eyed tree frog are only visible when the frog is on the move. The flash of colour startles predators as the frog makes a hasty escape.

◁ **MATING PAIR**
The male clambers on to the female's back to mate. Mating takes several hours, with the smaller male clinging to the female as she searches for places to lay her eggs.

△ **FROGSPAWN**
The red-eyed tree frog's eggs are laid on a leaf hanging over a pond or a stream. When the tadpoles emerge, they fall into the water below.

vertical pupil

pads on toes help with grip

4–7 cm (1¹/₂–2³/₄ in)
Summer
Locally common
Insects

Central America

Red-eyed tree frogs can **lighten and darken their skin colour** for camouflage or to **signal a change in mood**

ANDEAN YUNGAS
A species-rich forest reaching into the clouds

The Andean yungas ecoregion covers the eastern slope of the Andes mountain range, from 1,000–3,500 m (3,280–11,480 ft). It is sandwiched between the lowlands of the Amazon basin and Gran Chaco grasslands to the east and the high plateau of the Andean altiplano to the west. The yungas features dramatically varied topography with high ridges and steep-sided valleys created by mountain rivers. The range in altitude produces different climatic zones, which in turn create various habitat types, including moist lowland forest, deciduous and evergreen upland forests, and subtropical cloud forests.

A hotspot for diversity

Among the more than 3,000 species of plants are tree ferns, bamboo, Peruvian pepper trees, and the coca bush. Coca leaves have been chewed or brewed as a tea for centuries by the people of the Andes to counter the

effects of altitude sickness. In addition to the vast array of plants, around 200 species of vertebrate live here. The Andean yungas is known as a biological hotspot because it is home to many endemic species and because species from neighbouring ecoregions – such as the Amazon rainforest – also live here.

Native species are often restricted to "altitudinal belts", which means they are only found at certain altitudes, either because they cannot physically cross certain geographic barriers such as rivers or mountains, or they only eat vegetation that grows at certain altitudes.

RECENT DISCOVERY
New species are still being discovered in the yungas. This dead-leaf toad is so-called because its body shape and coloration is perfectly camouflaged against dead leaves on the forest floor. It was described and named in 2014.

DEAD-LEAF TOAD

ORCHID HAVEN
The yungas contains 200 species of orchid, with a high level of endemism. They are particularly numerous in cloud forests as damp conditions allow epiphytes to thrive on tree trunks and branches. There are also lithophytes that grow on rocky cliffs.

MONKEY ORCHID

LONG-WHISKERED OWLET

3,000 plant species > New species still being foun

Many species unique to the region

SMALL STRANGER
With a population of around 350–1,000, the long-whiskered owlet was discovered in 1976 in Peru. It measures just 14 cm (5½ in) in height. Its whiskery face inspired the Latin name of its genus, *Xenoglaux*, which means strange owl.

LOCATION

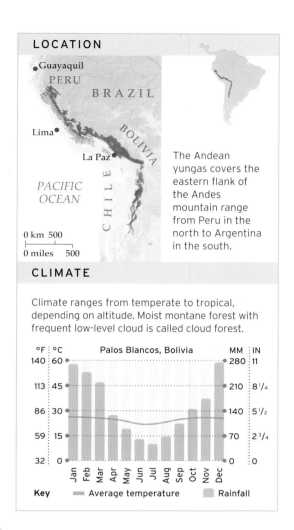

The Andean yungas covers the eastern flank of the Andes mountain range from Peru in the north to Argentina in the south.

0 km 500
0 miles 500

CLIMATE

Climate ranges from temperate to tropical, depending on altitude. Moist montane forest with frequent low-level cloud is called cloud forest.

Palos Blancos, Bolivia

°F	°C		MM	IN
140	60		280	11
113	45		210	8¹/₄
86	30		140	5¹/₂
59	15		70	2³/₄
32	0		0	0

Jan Feb Mar Apr May Jun Jul Aug Sep Oct Nov Dec

Key — Average temperature ■ Rainfall

Mountain tapir

Tapirus pinchaque

short, extensible trunk

The mountain tapir is the smallest, most endangered of all four tapir species – fewer than 2,500 are thought to survive in the wild. It makes its home high in the Andes, where its fur, which grows to 3-4 cm (1¹/₄-1¹/₂ in) thick, has earned it the nickname "woolly tapir".

Snorkelling for safety

Short, stocky legs and splayed toes make the mountain tapir sure-footed and agile, capable of negotiating steep slopes and dense undergrowth. Like other tapirs, it hides in thickets by day, feeding mainly at dawn and dusk. It has a keen sense of hearing and smell, and flees when threatened, often hiding underwater and using its trunk like a snorkel to breathe until danger passes. Tapirs call to each other with shrill, high-pitched whistles that are often mistaken for birdsong.

↔ 1.8–2 m (6–6¹/₂ ft)
🏋 150–200 kg (330–440 lb)
✖ Endangered
🌾 Leaves, herbs, grasses, fruit

NW. South America

◁ **LONG STRIPES**
Young tapirs are often called "watermelons on legs" due to their camouflage markings, which allow them to blend in with dappled sunlight.

▷ **GRIPPING SNOUT**
The mountain tapir feeds using its flexible nose to grasp vegetation, dispersing up to 86 species of plant seeds in the process of eating and digestion.

distinctive white lips

soles of feet are soft and sensitive

SMALLEST DEER
The tiny pudu is the world's smallest deer, standing at the 38 cm (15 in) tall at the shoulder. It relies on a network of tunnels and well-trodden paths through the yungas vegetation to give it protection from predators.

Most areas are protected

NORTHERN PUDU

fine, dense fur

Silky anteater
Cyclopes didactylus

The world's smallest anteater is not much longer than a human hand. Seldom seen, silky anteaters live on trees, feed from sunset to sunrise on as many as 5,000 ants each night, and rest through the day. While the nocturnal habit protects them from humans, these anteaters are preyed upon by harpy eagles, hawks, and spectacled owls.

Silken disguise

Silky anteaters live in silk floss trees, which provide the perfect camouflage for the anteater with its long, fine, smoky-grey fur. Each front foot of the anteater has two enlarged claws, which are perfect for climbing and digging into tree-ant nests but must be turned inwards for it to move on the ground. Although the silky anteater rarely comes to ground, it walks well on flat surfaces and has been seen crossing roads. It also has a prehensile tail and specially adapted hindfeet that wrap firmly around branches, allowing it to move through the canopy.

After mating, a single baby anteater is born in a leaf-lined nest usually situated in a tree hollow. Both parents raise the baby, feeding it regurgitated ants. Males carry the babies on their backs.

↔ 16–21 cm (6½–8½ in)
⚖ 175–357 g (6–12½ oz)
✖ Common
🐜 Ants, termites, ladybirds

Central America to N. South America

◁ **FAST ASLEEP**
The silky anteater spends its daylight hours sleeping high in the safety of trees, often simply hanging from its hook-like front claws, prehensile tail, and wraparound hindfeet.

Coati
Nasua nasua

Coatis move easily between different environments. Although terrestrial, coatis mate, give birth, and sleep in trees. Good climbers with powerful forelegs, they rotate their ankle joints to descend headfirst from trees, but easily jump from branch to branch, using their long tails for balance. They are also good swimmers. Strong claws and a flexible nose make them expert foragers.

Female coatis form bands of up to 65 animals. During the mating season, each band is joined by a male, which mates with all receptive females, then departs. Litters of one to seven young are born in spring and early summer. The females rejoin their band once the youngsters can walk and climb.

▽ **HEALTHY APPETITE**
Active and inquisitive members of the raccoon family, coatis feed on everything from small mammals, birds, and insects to fruit and leaves.

↔ 43–58 cm (17–22¾ in)

⚖ 2–7.2 kg (4½–15¾ lb)
✖ Common
🐜 Fungi, berries, insects, mice

W. South America

banded tail

Spectacled bear

Tremarctos ornatus

South America's only bear is also one of its largest land mammals. Just 60–90 cm (2–3 ft) high at the shoulder, they make their homes in a variety of Andean habitats, ranging from cloud forests to high-level grasslands bordering rainforests. Spectacled bears spend much of their time in trees, where they build a platform of sticks to sleep on and forage from. They eat fruit, flowers, and succulent plants. They also sometimes hunt insects, birds, and small rodents.

The bears are solitary except during the mating season, from April to June, when a male and female stay together for up to two weeks. Cubs are born from December to February. Males do not play any part in raising the young, and may even kill cubs. While pumas and jaguars prey upon the cubs, the greatest threat to the species comes from habitat loss and hunting by humans.

▷ **DISTINCTIVE MARKINGS**
The spectacled bear gets its name from the cream or yellow markings around its eyes. These markings often extend down to its chest.

creamy white markings

↔ 1.3–1.9 m (4¼–6¼ ft)
⚖ 60–175 kg (132–390 lb)
✖ Vulnerable
🦷 Fruit, succulent plants, birds

W. South America

long, needle-like bill for
reaching deep into flowers

slender, tiltable wings

Booted racket-tail hummingbird

Ocreatus underwoodii

Tiny clumps of loose white feathers on
the thighs make the booted racket-tail a member of a
group of hummingbirds called pufflegs. It is a common
species in humid forests. Hummingbirds hover by
flapping their wings in a figure-eight pattern. These
remarkable birds can fly sideways and even backwards.

Hummingbirds feed on nectar from scented, sugar-
rich flowers, often red blossoms, hovering while licking
up fluid with their long, slender tongue. They snap up
small insects, too, and females capture thousands to
provide growing chicks with vital protein.

Polygamous parents

Male booted racket-tails demonstrate their fitness to
females in rapid, swooping display flights. The showiest
males mate with several females, and each female may
mate with a number of males, but she alone makes the
nest and rears her brood of two chicks. The nest of
fibres and moss is a tiny cup, placed on a bare,
horizontal twig. It has a strong, elastic binding of
cobwebs that expands as the chicks grow.

shiny green
plumage

△ **MID-AIR HOSTILITY**
Males defend feeding
territories around fresh
blossoms, chasing off
other males and even
bumblebees, with aerial
displays and rapid
darting flights.

↔ 17–23 cm (6½–9 in)

⚖ 3 g (⅛ oz)

✕ Common

Ⓜ Nectar, insects, spiders

🏠 🌳 ⛰

NW. to W.
South
America

long tail adornment
of male

Booted racket-tails **beat their
wings 60 times per second**
when hovering

Andean cock-of-the-rock
Rupicola peruvianus

In sheltered, moist ravines and river valleys high in the cloud forests of the Andes, male Andean cock-of-the-rocks gather to display for the benefit of the watching females. A chorus of squawks accompanies the rather awkward performance, drawing attention even to birds deep within the forest canopy. The males are at risk of predation during courtship, with various forest cats, birds of prey, and snakes likely to attack them. At other times, they are quiet and inconspicuous.

Mud nests
Females, which are not as colourful as the males and have less exaggerated crests, make a cup-shaped nest of mud and saliva, plastered against a rock or inside a small cave. They incubate two eggs for up to a month and feed the hatchlings on their own. The cock-of-the-rock's main diet consists of a range of fruits, supplemented with a supply of insects.

↔ 30–32 cm (12–12 1/2 in)
⚖ 200–275 g (7–9 1/2 oz)
❌ Locally common
🍽 Fruit, insects

N. to W. South America

◁ **DISPLAYING MALE**
Males compete in communal displays in a tree, bowing, flapping their wings, and calling discordantly. Their actions and sounds intensify if a female appears.

Trueb's cochran frog
Nymphargus truebae

Trueb's cochran frog is a species of glass frog, so-called because its skin is translucent on the underside, making it possible to see its bones and internal organs. This tiny native of the Andean cloud forest is nocturnal, sleeping through the day on leaves in the treetops. The green of the leaves shows through the frog's skin, helping it to blend in easily and stay hidden.

Females lay eggs on leaves above pools of water, and the males guard them until they hatch. The tadpoles plummet into the water below, where they feed among the detritus at the bottom.

yellow-spotted green skin

△ **LONG LIMBS**
Trueb's cochran frog is wide-skulled and long-limbed. Its eyes are placed at the top of the head.

↔ 22.5–25 mm (7/8–1 in)
⚖ Not known
❌ Not known
🍽 Insects
📍 S. Peru

Crimson longwing
Heliconius erato

Known for its wide, rounded black wings with flashes of red on the upper surface, the crimson-patched longwing is a highly variable butterfly with no fewer than 29 subspecies. Each subspecies has a unique wing pattern, some without any red markings. The species as a whole is found all over Central and South America.

To complicate things further, every subspecies mimics the colouring of the subspecies of another equally variable longwing called the common postman, or *Heliconius melpomene*, that lives in the same habitat.

↔ 5.5–8 cm (2 1/4–3 1/4 in)
❌ Common
🍽 Pollen and nectar
📍 Central and South America

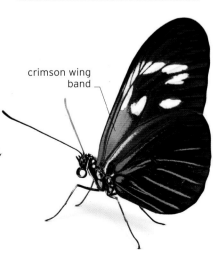

crimson wing band

▷ **PERUVIAN NATIVE**
The crimson longwing subspecies pictured lives in the lowland forests of Peru.

AMAZON RAINFOREST

One of the most productive ecosystems on Earth

The Amazon is the world's largest tropical rainforest, covering 5.5 million sq km (2.1 million sq miles) of the drainage basin fed by the long and winding river that shares its name. The rainforest is among the most productive and biodiverse ecosystems on the planet, containing around 10 per cent of all the world's known species and potentially many more that have yet to be discovered. The enormous variety of plants provides a multitude of habitats and food for a myriad of different animal species. It is also important because it stores large amounts of carbon – 100–140 billion tonnes (110–154 billion tons) – that would otherwise be in the atmosphere.

Life among the layers

Overwhelmingly green to look at, with bright flashes of colour from flowers, fruit, monkeys, and birds, the rainforest consists of several different layers. The tallest trees project above the main rainforest canopy, which itself forms the middle layer. This layer is the most diverse, and beneath it lie the understorey and then ground level, where much less light – and moisture – penetrates. The lush jungle foliage slows the speed of rain falling to the forest floor, where deep soil and decaying plant matter act like a sponge, holding water and slowly releasing it to streams and rivers.

Vegetation can be **so thick, rain** may take **10 minutes to reach the ground**

FIRE ANTS

LIVING RAFT
Many parts of the Amazon rainforest flood periodically, presenting a problem for creatures that nest underground such as fire ants. During floods, members of the ant colony form a raft out of their own bodies on which eggs, larvae, and queen are kept safe and dry.

Been in existence for 55 million years

AGOUTI

The world's largest tropical rainforest

SEED DISPERSER
The agouti is one of the few animals able to gnaw through the tough fruit of the Brazil nut to release its seeds. When fruits are abundant it hoards surplus seeds for later, often far from the parent tree, where they may be forgotten about and grow into new trees.

Covers 40% of South America

PARA RUBBER TREE

RUBBER BOOM
The bark of the Para rubber tree is cut to release milky latex sap. This sap is used to make products such as rubber boots and latex gloves, or is chemically treated to produce tougher items such as tyres.

NATURAL HABITAT

In its native Amazon, the cane toad is regulated by many predators. As an introduced species in Hawaii and Australia, however, this poisonous amphibian breeds out of control.

CANE TOAD

Contains around 390 billion trees of 16,000 different species

CLAMBERING ABOUT

Colourful and pheasant-sized as adult birds, with an impressive head-crest of feathers, as chicks hoatzins have two claws on each wing, which they use to climb through waterside vegetation until they are able to fly. They lose the claws before adulthood.

HOATZIN CHICK

ENVIRONMENTAL MONITOR

Two species of Amazon river dolphin, the pink river dolphin and the tucuxi, are good indicators of the health of the freshwater ecosystems they inhabit. Fewer dolphins are found where there is existing river degradation, such as poor water quality and overfishing by large human populations.

An estimated 2.5 million species of insects live here

PINK RIVER DOLPHIN

LOCATION

The Amazon rainforest stretches across nine South American countries: Brazil, French Guiana, Suriname, Guyana, Venezuela, Colombia, Ecuador, Peru, and Bolivia.

CLIMATE

The Amazon rainforest's climate is tropical and humid. Although all months are wet, rainfall is greatest between December and April, when more than 200 mm (8 in) of rain falls on average each month in Manaus, the region's largest city.

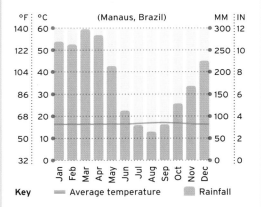

(Manaus, Brazil)

Key — Average temperature ▪ Rainfall

DEFORESTATION

The Amazon rainforest is being felled at such a rate that an estimated 135 plant and animal species become extinct daily. The sustainable harvest of rubber and other wild products, such as Brazil nuts, helps to protect the rainforest from the devastating effects of total land clearance for projects such as soy plantations.

Emperor tamarin
Saguinus imperator

tail twice as long as
head and body

Tamarins are small monkeys with silky fur, and many species also have elaborate facial patterns, crests, beards, or moustaches. Notable, too, for its long orange-red tail, the emperor tamarin lives in small families in the lower and middle levels of rainforests, and these families often forage together with saddleback tamarins. Emperor tamarins eat a variety of plant food, particularly berries and other fruit, and flowers, nectar, tree sap, and leaves. They also hunt insects, snails, frogs, and small lizards, snatching prey off foliage with their dextrous hands. The female usually bears twins, which the father carries except when they are being suckled.

↔ 23–26 cm (9–10 in)
🏋 450 g (16 oz)
⊗ Common
🍴 Fruit, nectar, insects
🏠 🏯

W. South
America

◁ DROOPING
MOUSTACHE
Both adult male and
female emperor
tamarins have a flowing
white moustache.
The long white curls
reach down as far as
their forearms.

Pygmy marmoset
Cebuella pygmaea

This minuscule, hyperactive primate is the world's smallest monkey – a curled-up adult pygmy marmoset would fit into a human palm. Pygmy marmosets keep to dense thickets and tangles of vegetation in the lower levels of forests, hiding from predators such as other monkeys, forest cats, hawks, and snakes. They are exceptionally agile and, despite their tiny size, can leap up to 5 m (16 ft).

Pygmy marmosets live in small family groups, usually consisting of a breeding pair and up to seven or eight young of varying ages, and most births are twins. Unlike other marmosets, they don't move around their home range in a group when feeding during the day, but they spend the night sleeping together in a huddle. They feed mainly on the sugary gum or sap of trees, by gouging the bark with their sharp lower incisors and then lapping up the liquid that flows out.

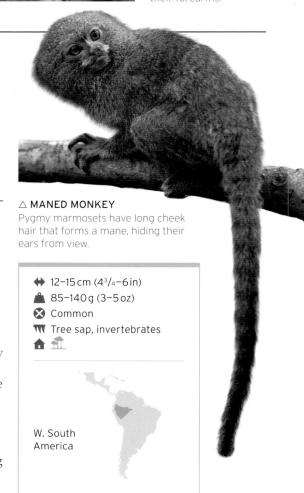

△ MANED MONKEY
Pygmy marmosets have long cheek
hair that forms a mane, hiding their
ears from view.

↔ 12–15 cm (4³/₄–6 in)
🏋 85–140 g (3–5 oz)
⊗ Common
🍴 Tree sap, invertebrates
🏠 🏯

W. South
America

↔ 50–63 cm (20–25 in)
🏋 5–9 kg (11–20 lb)
⊗ Common
🍴 Fruit, leaves
🏠 🌳 🏯 🌲

NW. South
America

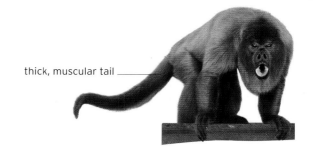

thick, muscular tail

Red howler monkey

Alouatta seniculus

The growling roars of red howler monkeys are among the most distinctive sounds of the Amazonian rainforest. Just before dawn, each troop starts to call from the treetops to announce ownership of their home range, and other groups in the area may reply. Adapted hyoid bones in the monkeys' throat amplify the sounds, which can be heard up to 5km (3 miles) away. Both sexes roar. Male howlers react most to the calls of males in neighbouring troops, while females respond most to the roars of other females, which are higher pitched.

Chunky monkeys

Red howlers are big, solid monkeys that move more slowly than many other monkeys. They typically spend most of their waking hours resting or digesting food in the forest canopy. Their prehensile tails have a bald patch near the underside of the tip to help grip branches. They feed on leaves and fruit – especially figs – and when they find a large fruiting tree, will guard it against rival groups. Red howlers periodically go to the ground to eat clay, which contains salts and minerals that help to neutralize toxins in the leaves they eat.

A red howler monkey troop usually has from three to a dozen members, led by an adult male that remains dominant for several years. Females mate for the first time when around five years old, giving birth to a single young after a seven-month gestation. Babies cling to their mother's belly for the first month, then ride piggyback, and are independent at six months old. Despite their large size, red howler monkeys are preyed on by harpy eagles. On spotting danger, they quickly grunt warnings to alert the rest of the group.

△ **BEARDED MALE**
Adult male howler monkeys, which are much heavier than females, have a long, full beard.

▷ **URSINE HOWLERS**
Many howler monkeys are named after their predominant fur colour. There are brown and black species as well as ones with red fur, such as the ursine howler (*A. arctoidea*).

Howler monkeys are the **loudest land animals** – their calls reach 90 decibels

↔ 1.1–1.7 m (3$\frac{1}{2}$–5$\frac{1}{2}$ ft)

⚖ 32–122 kg (70–270 lb)

✖ Near threatened

🍴 Mammals, reptiles, birds

🏠 🌳🌳 🌴 🌾 〰 🍄

Central America
to N. and C.
South America

▷ **ON THE PROWL**
A jaguar's broad, fur-soled paws make
no sound as it moves through dense
vegetation, and its dappled coat helps
it blend into the surroundings, making
this cat the ultimate stealth hunter.

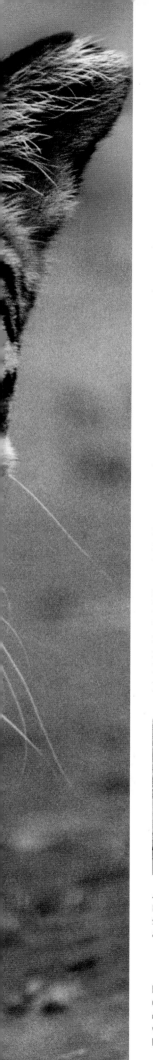

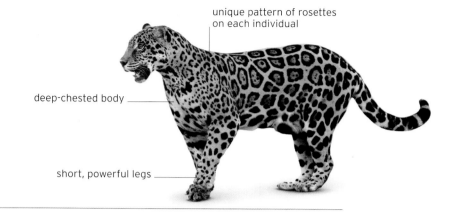

unique pattern of rosettes on each individual

deep-chested body

short, powerful legs

Jaguar
Panthera onca

The western hemisphere's largest feline is the least well-studied – scientists have no idea how many jaguars are left in the wild. This secretive cat once roamed forests from the southwestern US to Argentina, but it now occupies only about 45 per cent of its original range, due to human intervention. Today, it is confined to 19 Latin American countries.

Formidable predator

The epitome of the opportunistic hunter, jaguars feed on a range of mammals, from deer and peccaries to coatis and monkeys. They also eat insects, fish, birds, caimans, anacondas, and eggs. There has been just one, recent, instance of a jaguar eating a human; however, when faced with habitat loss due to human encroachment, they will prey on livestock and domestic pets.

An efficient predator, the jaguar's immense jaw strength allows it to pierce the skull of its victims. It usually hunts at dusk or dawn, when its dappled coat provides maximum camouflage, but is more nocturnal where people are present. An adult male needs about 260 sq km (100 sq miles) of territory to hunt – this can range from humid rainforest, dry pine woods, swamp, scrubland, savanna, to desert.

Adult male jaguars can **break through bone and turtle shell** in a **single bite**

Like lions and tigers, jaguars can roar, but they communicate more frequently using coughs, growls, grunts, "huffs", and low moans.

Jaguars are solitary animals that only pair up to breed. Females give birth to one to four cubs, which are born with sky-blue eyes that turn green-gold in a few weeks. Their head and paws grow more quickly than the rest of their bodies. Cubs are independent at 15 months but may remain in their mother's territory until they are about two years old.

An estimated six per cent of jaguars have a genetic mutation that gives them a "dark phase" coat colour. Dark coated jaguars and leopards are called panthers, although the characteristic rosettes are still visible.

△ **SKILFUL SWIMMER**
Powerfully muscled legs make jaguars strong swimmers – one was seen crossing a river to attack a caiman basking on a sandbank.

▷ **AT THE WATER'S EDGE**
Generally considered a jungle creature, the jaguar can adapt to almost any habitat, provided there is water and prey nearby. In the wild, the jaguar's lifespan is 10–12 years.

oversized yet
lightweight bill

white bib on
black body

Toco toucan
Ramphastos toco

Few birds worldwide are as instantly recognizable as the toco toucan, with its huge, colourful bill. The long bill is useful for reaching fruit on the ends of branches that are too thin to support the toucan's weight. It can also be used to grab small reptiles, eggs and nestlings, and large insects, if fruit is scarce. The bill's bright colour must act as a visual stimulus in social situations, although it is identical in both sexes. It also serves as a striking warning to predators.

Cool discovery

Scientists have recently discovered another use for the toco toucan's enormous bill: it has an important function as a radiator. When temperatures are high, the toucan can lose up to 60 per cent of its body heat through the bill, which has a network of blood vessels

The toco toucan has the **largest bill of any bird**, relative to body size

that controls the flow of blood to its surface. In cool spells, the blood flow is restricted, allowing the toucan to conserve its body heat. During the night, it sleeps with the bill under a wing, to maintain heat.

Tocos are weak fliers. They flutter through the forest canopy, usually in pairs, to find fruiting trees. Tree cavities are often enlarged for the nest, in which two to four eggs are incubated by both parents. They defend the chicks from predators, such as snakes, as it takes several months for a chick's bill to be fully formed.

▽ **PROMINENT BILL**
Despite its size, the toco toucan's bill is comparatively light because it is mostly hollow, with a supporting framework of bony struts.

↔ 55–61cm (21½–24in)
⬛ 500–850g (18–30oz)
✖ Common
〰 Fruit, eggs, insects, frogs
🏠 🏞 🌾

NE. to
C. South
America

bare white
skin on face

△ STRONG FLIGHT
Long, wide wings and powerful chest
muscles help the scarlet macaw speed
through the air, aided by its flexible tail.

Scarlet macaw
Ara macao

Macaws are huge parrots with long tails and massive
bills. The scarlet macaw – one of the largest members of
this group – is a native of humid tropical forests. It lives
in the dense tree canopy and communicates with
far-carrying, ear-splitting screeches.

Scarlet macaws typically live in pairs – they pair for
life – but often assemble in noisy groups, resting in tall
trees. They eat nuts and seeds, cracking open tough
shells with their
powerful bills, as
well as fruit, flowers,
and leaves. Large
flocks gather at
vertical clay cliffs,
where they scrape
up the soil with
their tongues. The
minerals help to
neutralize toxins in
their food that
would be fatal to
most birds. In the
wild, scarlet macaws
can live for 50 years.

↔ 84–89cm (33–35in)
⬛ 0.9–1.5kg (2–3¼lb)
✖ Common
〰 Nuts, seeds, fruit
🏠 🏞 🌾

Central
America to
N. South
America

Emerald
tree boa
Corallus caninus

Well camouflaged among fresh green
foliage, this non-venomous tree boa has a
wide head, powerful jaws, and very long,
curved teeth. These are used to grab
passing prey such as bats, arboreal rodents,
lizards, and birds, while the snake remains
securely anchored to a branch by its strong
prehensile tail. Small victims are quickly
swallowed whole, whereas more substantial
prey is first suffocated by constriction.

Male emerald tree boas mature when
three or four years old. They are slightly
smaller and slimmer than females, which
mature a year later. Mating occurs between
May and July, and the female gives birth to
5–20 live young six months later. The baby
boas are red or orange in colour, changing
to green after about a year. There is no
parental care.

△ READY TO STRIKE
The emerald tree boa
strikes out at airborne
prey or hangs from a
low branch to snatch its
victim from the ground.

↔ 1.5–1.8m (5–6ft)
⬛ Up to 3kg (6½lb)
✖ Not known
〰 Bats, rats, birds
🏠 🏞

N. South
America

Dyeing poison frog
Dendrobates tinctorius

Dyeing poison frogs live on or near the forest floor and are mostly active by day. Males set up breeding territories and call for females, which may fight to win courtship rights. The winning female initiates mating by stroking the male's snout with her back feet. Six eggs are laid on a leaf and the male keeps them moist. The tadpoles hatch after about 14 days and both parents carry them on their backs to a bromeliad pool.

↔ 3–5 cm (1¼–2 in)
🌡 February, March
✖ Common
🌿 Ants, termites, spiders
🏠 🌳
◎ NE. South America

▷ **COLOUR VARIETIES**
This pattern is typical of the species, with blue legs and belly, and broad yellow and black stripes on the back. Many other varieties exist using the same colours in different proportions.

Electric eel
Electrophorus electricus

long, cylindrical body

The electric eel is one of the largest freshwater fish in South America. It uses weak electrical pulses to find its way around and locate food in murky inland waters, such as rivers and ponds. It also produces larger electric shocks of around 600 volts that can kill other fish and even stun a human. The pulses are generated by organs of electrogenesis, which have about 5,000 to 6,000 modified muscle cells called electroplaques, running along almost the entire length of the fish's body.

↔ 2–2.5 m (6½–8¼ ft)
⚖ 20 kg (44 lb)
✖ Common
🌿 Fish, shrimp, crabs
🏠 ≈
◎ N. South America

▷ **DECEPTIVE APPEARANCE**
Although it looks like an eel, the electric eel is a type of knifefish that shares a common ancestor with catfish.

Leaf-cutter ant
Atta cephalotes

↔ 2–22 mm (¹⁄₁₆–¾ in)
✖ Common
🌿 Fungus
🏠 🌳 🌲

Central America to N. South America

Leaf-cutter ants live in extensive underground nests, with each colony consisting of millions of individuals. To feed the colony, small worker ants called "minimas" tend a fungus that grows on a mulch of cut leaves. This fungus can only survive inside the ants' nest, and needs their help to propagate. The pieces of leaf are cut and carried back to the nest by medium-sized "media" workers. The largest workers are called "maximas"; they act as soldiers and guard the colony against intruders. The colony's single queen lays thousands of eggs every day.

▽ **HARD AT WORK**
A media worker can carry 50 times its own body weight. Leaf-cutters are also known as "parasol" ants because of the way they hold the leaves.

Goliath birdeater

Theraphosa blondi

Regarded as the largest spider in the world, this tarantula has a leg span that could cover a dinner plate, and a mass of about 170 g (6 oz), which far outweighs any of its rivals. Only Asia's giant huntsman spider has a larger leg span. Goliath birdeater females are much larger than the males. The name "birdeater" is based on a 1705 engraving by German naturalist Maria Sibylla Merian, which showed a Goliath birdeater devouring a hummingbird. The tarantula has 2-cm- (³/4-in-) long fangs, so it may be possible for it to prey on small birds, but its preferred diet is large insects and frogs and mice.

The Goliath birdeater lives in deep burrows on the forest floor and seldom climbs far off the ground. The males only live for three or four years, dying soon after mating for the first and only time, whereas the females can survive for 15 years or more. Each female lays 100–200 eggs and guards the brood constantly for about two months until the spiderlings hatch. If threatened, Goliath birdeaters can flick irritant hairs from their abdomen using their hind legs.

front legs and pedipalps raised in threat posture

◆ Up to 28 cm (11 in)
✖ Not known
🐾 Insects, frogs, mice

🏠 ⩜ ⛰

NE. South America

◁ **DEFENCE STANCE**
When threatened, the spider raises up its front legs and shows off its hooked fangs. Defensive bites are "dry", saving venom.

fangs inject venom

The goliath birdeater detects its prey by **sensing vibrations** in the ground

THE PANTANAL
The world's largest wetland

The Pantanal is a vast area of tropical wetland, or swamp, making up 3 per cent of the world's wetlands and spreading across 180,000 sq km (approximately 70,000 sq miles). It receives water from the Brazilian highlands and drains into the Paraguay River. Rich, silty soils support a broad complex of plants from the different ecoregions that surround the Pantanal, including the Amazon rainforest to the north and the Cerrado savanna to the east.

Wet and dry

Plant diversity in the Pantanal is particularly great because higher areas remain dry all year round and so maintain drought-tolerant trees, while lower-lying areas host plants that can cope with seasonal flooding, and some parts of the Pantanal are permanently underwater and so contain many aquatic plants. This diversity of plant life presents great opportunities for animals in the region. However, there are few endemic species in the Pantanal, meaning that many of the animals are also found in neighbouring ecoregions. This includes the Yacare caiman, although the Pantanal is its stronghold.

Wetlands act as natural water treatment systems, filtering and removing chemicals from the water, but they are susceptible to pollution from excessive run-off from agriculture and mining activities. Deforestation, infrastructure development, and cattle ranching also risk changing the Pantanal's water resources and so could alter its ecological balance.

MUTUALLY BENEFICIAL
Scented white flowers of the waterlily attract scarab beetles, which are trapped inside when the flower closes. They pollinate the flower, which then loses its scent, turns pink, covers the beetles in pollen, then opens to release them.

GIANT WATERLILY

SUCCESS STORY
By the late 1980s, hyacinth macaws had declined to fewer than 1,500 individuals due to habitat loss and illegal capture of wild birds for the pet trade. Following stringent conservation measures, the population in the Pantanal has risen to more than 5,000.

HYACINTH MACAW

LOWLAND TAPIR

80% of land is submerged during the rainy season 〉 159 species of mammal, 565 species o

KEYSTONE SPECIES
The lowland tapir is a keystone species in the Pantanal ecoregion. It plays a crucial role by dispersing seeds of many large fruiting plants, and by browsing, it clears areas in which the seeds can germinate.

LOCATION

The Pantanal is located to the south of the Amazon river basin in central South America. Around 80% of it is in Brazil.

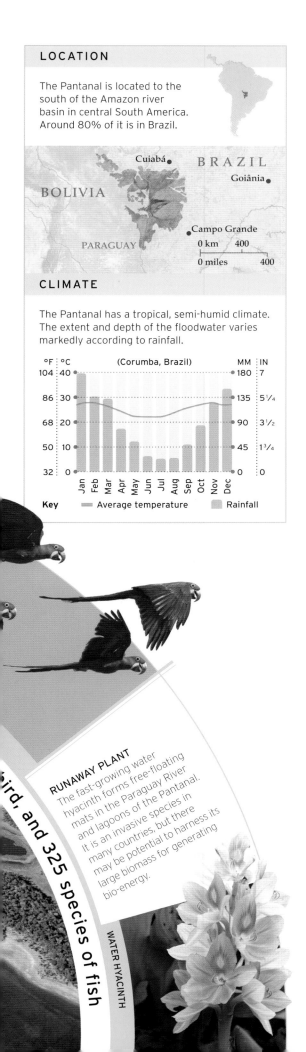

CLIMATE

The Pantanal has a tropical, semi-humid climate. The extent and depth of the floodwater varies markedly according to rainfall.

(Corumba, Brazil)

| Key | — Average temperature | ▮ Rainfall |

RUNAWAY PLANT
The fast-growing water hyacinth forms free-floating mats in the Paraguay River and lagoons of the Pantanal. It is an invasive species in many countries, but there may be potential to harness its large biomass for generating bio-energy.

bird, and 325 species of fish

WATER HYACINTH

White-lipped peccary
Tayassu pecari

large, sharp, interlocking canine teeth

One of the most social mammals, white-lipped peccaries move, feed, and rest together in herds ranging from five to hundreds of individuals. With jaws capable of cracking palm nuts, a group of peccaries can fend off natural predators such as jaguars. Human hunters, however, prey on herds, killing large numbers at a time, which has had a devastating impact on the species.

↔ 75–100 cm (29½–39 in)
⚖ 25–40 kg (55–88 lb)
✖ Vulnerable
🍽 Fruit, nuts, small vertebrates

Central to South America

◁ **GROUP IDENTITY**
Peccaries spread rump scent-gland secretions among members to create a musky herd odour.

Capybara
Hydrochoerus hydrochaeris

↔ 1.1–1.3 m (3½–4¼ ft)
⚖ 35–66 kg (77–145 lb)
✖ Common
🍽 Aquatic plants, bark, grasses

Related to guinea pigs, the capybara is the world's largest living rodent, closer in size to a large domestic dog. It is heavy bodied, with short but sturdy limbs, and almost no tail. This placid, sociable mammal spends much of its time in rivers and lakes, partly to avoid predators such as wild dogs, pumas, and jaguars. Partially webbed, hoof-like toes make it an excellent swimmer, and its eyes, nose, and ears sit high on its head, allowing it to see and breathe while its body remains underwater.

N. and E. South America

coarse but sparse hair

◁ **PRECOCIOUS YOUNG**
Capybara pups can follow their mothers into water shortly after birth and are able to graze within a week.

Giant otter

Pteronura brasiliensis

The world's largest otter is also one of the rarest – only a few thousand are thought to remain in the wild. Nicknamed the "river wolf", this sinuous, web-footed, muscular member of the weasel family is one of South America's largest predators. It is fiercely territorial – which it has to be – in order to protect itself and its family from caimans, jaguars, pumas, and other threats in and around the river systems it calls home.

Scent warning

Giant otters live in groups of up to 20 animals: a male and female – which mate for life – and their offspring. The parents dig a den in riverbanks or under fallen logs and trample a section of the bank around it. All of the group scent-mark the perimeter of their territory with their anal glands to deter intruders. They fish in and patrol a section of the river around their den.

Giant otters are sociable – grooming, hunting, playing, and sleeping together. They have up to nine different vocalizations, from intense territorial screeches to chirrups and whistles. Most cubs are born during the dry season, in litters of one to six, and are cared for by both parents and older siblings. Young otters stay with their families until they are at least two and a half years old.

↔ 1–1.4 m (3¼–4½ ft)
⚖ 22–32 kg (48–70 lb)
✖ Endangered
🍴 Fish, frogs, small caimans

N. to C. South America

stout whiskers detect prey movements in water

well-webbed toes

▷ **SINUOUS BODY**
The giant otter's long, sinuous body, webbed feet, and flattened, wide-based tail mean it is well-adapted for diving and swimming, but its short limbs make it ungainly on land.

Hooded capuchin

Sapajus cay

distinctive black cap

Hooded capuchins are medium-sized, highly sociable monkeys, common in the tropical forests of the Amazon basin in South America. They get their name from the distinctive cap of dark fur at the top of their head, which resembles the hairstyle of a Capuchin monk.

Forest acrobats

These energetic and acrobatic monkeys move quickly through the lower and middle layers of the forest in groups of about 10–20, staying in touch with each other using a variety of bird-like, high-pitched calls.

Capuchins are highly intelligent and use a variety of tools to obtain food. In the lush swamps of the Pantanal, there is no shortage of palm nuts, which make up part of their diet. In northern populations, capuchins have been observed to crack open tough palm nuts by knocking one rock against another, but this behaviour has yet to be confirmed in the south.

↔ 40–45 cm (15¾–17¾ in)
⚖ 3–3.5 kg (6½–7¾ lb)
✖ Common
🍴 Fruit, leaves, small animals

N. South America

◁ **FEEDING ON FRUIT**
Clasping a prized piece of fruit, this hooded capuchin will eat it in the company of its troop.

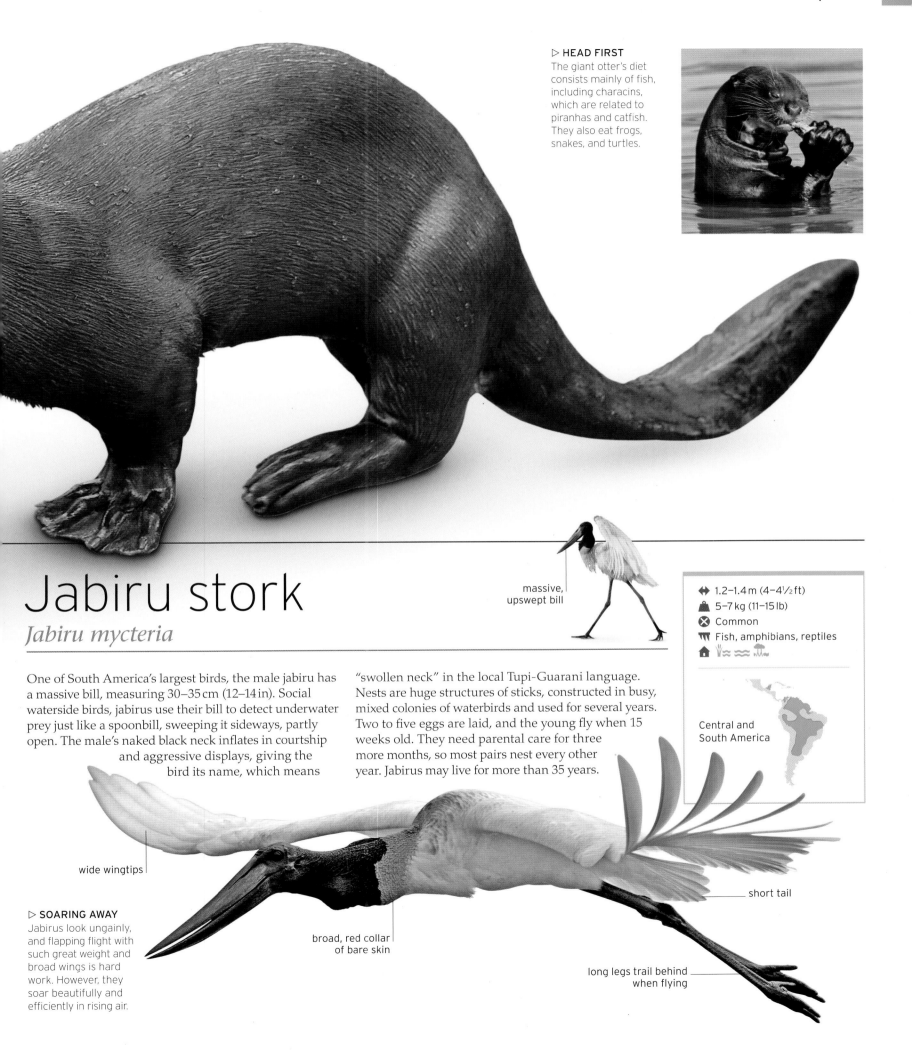

▷ **HEAD FIRST**
The giant otter's diet consists mainly of fish, including characins, which are related to piranhas and catfish. They also eat frogs, snakes, and turtles.

massive, upswept bill

Jabiru stork
Jabiru mycteria

↔ 1.2–1.4 m (4–4½ ft)
⚖ 5–7 kg (11–15 lb)
⊗ Common
🍴 Fish, amphibians, reptiles
🏠 🌾 〰 🍄

Central and South America

One of South America's largest birds, the male jabiru has a massive bill, measuring 30–35 cm (12–14 in). Social waterside birds, jabirus use their bill to detect underwater prey just like a spoonbill, sweeping it sideways, partly open. The male's naked black neck inflates in courtship and aggressive displays, giving the bird its name, which means "swollen neck" in the local Tupi-Guarani language. Nests are huge structures of sticks, constructed in busy, mixed colonies of waterbirds and used for several years. Two to five eggs are laid, and the young fly when 15 weeks old. They need parental care for three more months, so most pairs nest every other year. Jabirus may live for more than 35 years.

wide wingtips

short tail

▷ **SOARING AWAY**
Jabirus look ungainly, and flapping flight with such great weight and broad wings is hard work. However, they soar beautifully and efficiently in rising air.

broad, red collar of bare skin

long legs trail behind when flying

grey spatulate bill

Roseate spoonbill

Platalea ajaja

The only spoonbill in the Americas, of six species worldwide, the roseate is also the world's only pink spoonbill. It has the hallmark long, thick, flattened bill that broadens out into a round tip or "spoon". When feeding, the spoonbill sweeps its bill, partly open, from side to side through shallow water; the bill snaps shut when small fish, water beetles, shrimps, or snails touch the sensitive nerve endings inside the spoon. Nostrils located at the base of the bill help the bird breathe with its bill immersed. Roseate spoonbills feed in rivermouths, mangrove swamps, and freshwater marshes inland, often with other wading birds.

Colonial nesters

Breeding pairs nest in mixed-species colonies in nearby mangroves, trees, or reeds. Both sexes incubate between one and five eggs, which hatch after 22–24 days. The chicks' bills are initially short, straight, and soft, only becoming spoon-shaped after nine days. Both parents feed and protect the chicks, which are never left alone. They beg noisily and reach inside the parent's open bill to take regurgitated food. The young take off on their first flight at six weeks old, and can fly well at seven or eight weeks.

colour varies with diet

white neck stays outstretched in flight

↔ 70–85 cm (28–33 in)
⚖ 1.4 kg (3 lb)
✖ Common
🍴 Fish, crustaceans, molluscs

S. North America, Caribbean, South America

△ **COURTSHIP RITUAL**
Waving their wings and grasping bill tips, roseate spoonbills perform a courtship dance on the ground, in water, or even high in a tree.

long legs ideal for wading

▷ **STUNNING COLOURS**
Certain crustaceans in the roseate spoonbill's diet feed on algae that have carotenoid pigments, giving the bird its striking pink colour.

Golden tegu
Tupinambis teguixin

A flexible diet of insects, spiders, and worms, and also vertebrates from fish to mice, eggs, fruits, and shoots allows this large lizard to colonize many habitats. The female lays 20–30 eggs in a foliage-lined burrow and may stay with them for the cold season until they hatch up to five months later.

↔ 100 cm (40 in)
⚖ 4 kg (8³⁄₄ lb)
✗ Not known
🍴 Insects, birds, mammals
🏠 🏞 🌱≈ 🏘 🏔
◉ N. to C. South America

long toes, sharp claws

tail forms half the length of body

▷ **KILLER BITE**
Strong and often aggressive, the golden tegu has a bite that can even crush bone.

Green anaconda
Eunectes murinus

The world's bulkiest and most powerful snake, the green anaconda is a non-venomous member of the boa constrictor family. It often lies in shallow water waiting to ambush animals that come to the water's edge to drink. The snake grabs its prey with sharp, back-curved teeth, and quickly wraps it into the muscular coils. Each time the victim breathes out, the coils tighten, and death is usually from suffocation or heart failure. Almost any vertebrate prey is taken. Mating occurs in the dry season. The female may eat her much smaller male partner to nourish her pregnancy.

↔ 6–10 m (20–33 ft)
⚖ Up to 250 kg (550 lb)
✗ Vulnerable
🍴 Reptiles, fish, mammals
🏠 🏞 🌱 ≈
◉ N. to C. South America

▷ **AMBUSH CAMOUFLAGE**
Patterned for swampy vegetation and forest undergrowth, the anaconda slides silently after quarry, or strikes from the water's edge.

Giant parrot snake
Leptophis ahaetulla

whip-like tail

Also called the lora or giant lora, this snake is only mildly venomous. It is active during the day and rests at night. Well-camouflaged among dense undergrowth, it ambushes prey, or pursues them with great speed. It also explores crevices, caves, and vegetation for food.

If confronted it rears up, gapes its mouth, hisses, and makes mock strikes. The female lays and leaves three to five eggs in a safe place, usually in a tree hole or mossy branch fork.

↔ 1.5–2 m (5–6¹⁄₂ ft)
⚖ 1–1.5 kg (2¹⁄₄–3¹⁄₄ lb)
✗ Common
🍴 Geckos, tree frogs, birds
🏠 🏞 🌿 ≈ 🏔

Central America to South America

◁ **BRIGHT HUES**
The parrot snake gets its name because of its bright colouring: vivid green on the upper side and yellow underneath.

yellow underside

▷ **COMMUNAL FISHING**
Yacare caimans are often tolerant of others of their kind, crowding together at areas rich in sources of food, such as shoals of fish, or at favoured resting sites.

scales reinforced with bony plates

eyes and nostrils on top of head allow caiman to float low in water yet still see and breathe

broad snout

long, muscular tail

Yacare caiman

Caiman yacare

△ **TOOTHY GRIN**
The Yacare caiman has an average of 74 teeth. As the older ones fall out and leave gaps before replacement, the number may vary from 70 to 82.

▽ **BODY ARMOUR**
Caiman have plates of bone, called osteoderms, that are embedded in the skin. These are smallest and most flexible on the head and underside of the body.

fourth tooth in lower jaw fits into socket in upper jaw when mouth closed

A close relative of the more northerly distributed common or spectacled caiman (*C. crocodilus*), the Yacare caiman is one of the major predators across much of its range. Its stronghold is the swampy wetlands of the Pantanal, where it is locally abundant, hauling out in large groups to bask on mats of floating plants or on banks. Its numbers here are counted in the millions – this may well be the largest crocodilian population on Earth.

Piranha prey

All five species of caiman are broad-snouted, Central and South American cousins of the North American alligator. The medium-sized Yacare caiman hunts mainly in water for snakes, amphibians, fish, and molluscs – in particular large water snails, called apple snails, that are crunched and swallowed in their shells. The local name "piranha caiman" may have arisen because the piranha makes up a considerable proportion of the Yacare caiman's diet. The name could also reflect its toothy appearance, similar to that of the piranha. It has sharp, conical teeth, and some of the larger teeth are still visible when its mouth is closed.

Finding new habitats

Before the global ban on the trade of wild crocodile skins in 1992, millions of Yacare caiman were killed during the 1970s and 1980s. This severe hunting pressure forced some Yacare caiman to move out of the wetlands and adapt to other habitats. These include drier grasslands, scrub, and even farmland, usually with an aquatic retreat such as a pool, ditch, or creek nearby. On land they lie in wait for passing lizards, birds, and mammals up to the size of capybara. In turn, younger Yacare caiman in particular fall prey to jaguars and anacondas.

Nesting on dry ground

The caimans' breeding peaks during the wet season when water levels are high. After mating, the female chooses a drier site, where she constructs a mound of heat-producing rotting vegetation in which to lay her eggs. The clutch size typically varies from 20–35. Incubation takes several weeks and the female usually guards the nest from raiders such as snakes, lizards, and hawks, but not so tenaciously as some crocodilians – the American alligator, for example. In some cases, the mother has left by the time the hatchlings emerge – which occurs mostly in March – so the young caiman must fend for themselves.

↔ 1.5–3 m (5–10 ft)
⚖ 25–55 kg (55–120 lb)
✖ Common
🍴 Fish, birds, mammals
🏠 ⚘ ≈ ≈

C. to S. South America

A caiman will get through up to **40 sets of teeth** in its **lifetime**

ANDEAN ALTIPLANO
Silver salt flats hidden in the mountains

The Andean altiplano – literally, high plain – is the second largest mountainous plateau in the world after the Tibetan plateau in Asia. It is a landscape of extremes, surrounded by the mountains and volcanos of the central Andes. It has the world's highest navigable lake, Lake Titicaca, and the world's largest salt flat, the Salar de Uyuni. At an average altitude of 3,750 m (12,400 ft) above sea level, the air is thin, the sun is strong, winds can be fierce, and temperatures can fluctuate, making the altiplano a harsh place to live.

Harsh but fair
Despite the unforgiving conditions, the altiplano is also a land of strange beauty. The flat white expanse of the salt flats is, in places, adorned with metre-wide polygonal shapes created by the salt crystals, and incredible rock formations are sculpted by wind-blown sand. The mineral-rich lakes support flocks of flamingos numbering in the thousands, and the plains and slopes are home to herds of vicuñas, which are bred by Andean peoples for their wool, and llamas, bred for their wool, skin, and meat.

The Andean altiplano's vegetation, known as puna grassland, is dominated by grasses and shrubs, many of which form tussocks or cushions. Low-growing, mat-forming yareta plants and tall, branching cacti grow in the stony soils. The puna ecoregion is divided into wet, dry, and desert areas depending on the amount of rainfall they receive annually. One region in the centre of the Andes receives a meagre 400 mm (16 in) of rainfull a year and experiences an eight-month long dry season.

STARTLING SPECIALIST
This frog has evolved to survive in the most oxygen-impoverished lakes on Earth. Large folds of extra skin give it an extra-large body surface area. This allows it to maximize absorption of oxygen from the water and the atmosphere.

TITICACA WATER FROG

HARDY CROPS
Quinoa is well-adapted to the dry sandy soils of the altiplano and has been grown as a food crop by Andean peoples for thousands of years. The altiplano is one of few places where agriculture is practised 3,500 m (11,500 ft) above sea level.

QUINOA

Lake Titicaca is the highest navigable lake

Uyuni is the largest salt flat on Earth

ANDEAN FLAMINGOS

THREE FLAMINGOS
Three of the world's six flamingo species live in the altiplano. James and Andean flamingos are found in the region year-round, staying warm near hot springs during winter. In the summer, they are joined by flocks of Chilean flamingos.

LOCATION

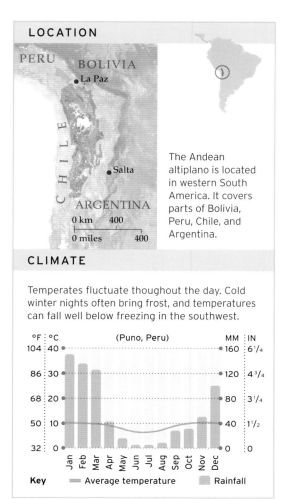

The Andean altiplano is located in western South America. It covers parts of Bolivia, Peru, Chile, and Argentina.

0 km 400
0 miles 400

CLIMATE

Temperates fluctuate throughout the day. Cold winter nights often bring frost, and temperatures can fall well below freezing in the southwest.

°F	°C	(Puno, Peru)	MM	IN
104	40		160	6¹/₄
86	30		120	4³/₄
68	20		80	3¹/₄
50	10		40	1¹/₂
32	0		0	0

Jan Feb Mar Apr May Jun Jul Aug Sep Oct Nov Dec

Key — Average temperature ▮ Rainfall

Culpeo
Pseudalopex culpaeus

reddish brown legs

The second largest wild canid in South America, the culpeo is also known as the Andean fox, a name that reflects many of its characteristics. Like most fox species, it is an opportunistic hunter, feeding on wild berries as well as rodents and introduced European hares and rabbits. It also takes young domestic livestock such as lambs occasionally, which brings it into conflict with farmers.

↔ 0.6–1.2 m (2–4 ft)
⚖ 5–13.5 kg (11–30 lb)
✖ Locally common
🐾 Rodents, hares, fruit, insects
🏠 🌳 ⛰ 🌵

W. to S. South America

◁ HOME IN THE ROCKS
Culpeos are usually solitary, but mated pairs stay together for up to five months, making dens in caves, which both parents guard from predators.

Northern viscacha
Lagidium peruanum

The northern viscacha resembles a long-tailed rabbit, but this high-altitude rodent is more closely related to chinchillas. Its soft, ultra-dense coat protects it from frigid temperatures, while thin-walled arteries help it to survive in the oxygen-depleted conditions of the high Andes.

↔ 30–45 cm (12–18 in)
⚖ 0.9–1.6 kg (2–3¹/₂ lb)
✖ Locally common
🐾 Grass, lichen, moss
🏠 ⛰

W. South America

whiskers around 15 cm (6 in) long

▷ CLIFF DWELLER
Viscacha colonies are often located on steep cliffs, which provide protection from predators – as well as being prime spots for basking.

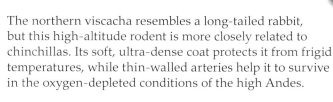

COVETED FUR
The long-tailed chinchilla's ultra-dense fur keeps it warm in the freezing temperatures of the high plateau. However, its fur became its downfall because chinchillas were trapped by hunters for the pet and fur trade. They are now critically endangered.

v season lasts eight months

CHINCHILLA

Vicuña

Vicugna vicugna

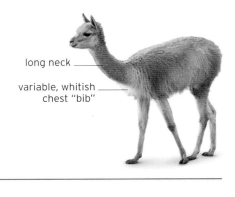

long neck

variable, whitish chest "bib"

A small, slender relative of the llama and the alpaca, the vicuña is well adapted to life in the high Andes. It lives in small family groups in arid meadows above 3,500 m (11,500 ft) and sometimes as high as 5,750 m (18,850 ft), but always below the snow line. In this environment, days are frequently sunny and warm, so tough thickets of grass can grow. At night, the thin air chills rapidly and temperatures plunge below freezing. The vicuña has a thick fleece of fine-layered hairs, which traps warm air around its body and keeps the cold out.

Unique teeth

The vicuña has unique teeth for a hoofed mammal. The front teeth (incisors) in its lower jaw grow constantly, like those of a rodent, and have enamel only on the front. The incisors are kept sharp by constant contact with the hard dental pad in the upper jaw as the vicuña relentlessly uses its molars to chew the tough grass. Vulnerable to attack on open grassland, vicuñas are always on the lookout for predators, such as foxes. They have excellent hearing and vision and when a predator is spotted, they give a warning whistle.

Families, led by a single male, consist of about five females and their young. The groups stay small, with only about 10 members, because the chief male drives away the young at the age of 10 months. Young vicuñas live alone or form single-sex herds until they start their own families at about the age of two. Unusually, vicuñas have separate feeding and sleeping territories, which are mostly marked out with dung. Vicuñas need to drink water every day so their feeding territory has to have a source of fresh water.

↔ 1.5–1.6 m (5–5¼ ft)
⬤ 40–55 kg (88–120 lb)
✕ Locally common
🌾 Grass
🏠 ⛰ 🌵 ☘

W. South America

△ PLAY FIGHTING
Young male vicuñas often play fight and bite each other. The fights become more serious as they reach sexual maturity, and the victor will join a female-only herd to start his own family.

▽ DAILY MIGRATION
Vicuña families spend the night in the relative safety of steeper slopes. They climb back down to graze in the high plains by day.

Titicaca grebe
Rollandia microptera

So adapted to life in water that it cannot fly and can barely stand, this flightless grebe is found only on lakes in the Lake Titicaca basin. Populations on separate freshwater lakes have lived in isolation for a very long time and are vulnerable to habitat change. A few thousand pairs live on reed-fringed lakes, with areas of open water, 3,000 m (9,850 ft) above sea level. The Titicaca grebe dives skilfully for fish – it mostly eats pupfish – and skitters across the water with raised wings. It can breed in any month of the year, making a platform of damp vegetation in which the female lays two eggs and can have several broods each year.

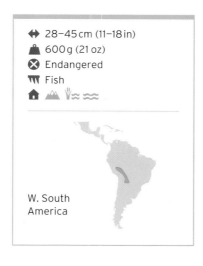

↔ 28–45 cm (11–18 in)
⚖ 600 g (21 oz)
✗ Endangered
🍴 Fish
🏠 ⛰ 〰 ≈

W. South America

◁ DAGGER-LIKE BILL
Grebes have sharply pointed bills. The Titicaca grebe's bill has a red upper and yellow lower mandible.

Andean flicker
Colaptes rupicola

Flickers are New World woodpeckers, noted for their terrestrial feeding behaviour, and the Andean flicker is the most terrestrial of them all. It is widespread in bushy habitats and open grassland at altitudes of 2,000–5,000 m (6,500–16,500 ft).

Barbed tongue
Andean flickers feed in groups on the ground, digging or scraping around grass tussocks with their large bills to reveal ants or beetle and moth larvae. They seize their prey with the barbed tip of their long, extendable tongue. Sociable even when nesting, they build a dozen or more burrows in road cuttings or sandy or earth cliffs. The 1–1.5 m (3–5 ft) long burrows lead to a 30 cm (12 in) nesting chamber that holds up to four chicks.

↔ 32 cm (12½ in)
⚖ 140–200 g (5–7 oz)
✗ Locally common
🍴 Insect larvae
🏠 ⛰ 草

NW. to SW. South America

◁ FEMALE FLICKER
The striking black moustache combined with the red patch on the back of the neck identifies this flicker as female.

long, barred tail

bold, white ruff

Andean condor

Vultur gryphus

The Andean condor has the largest wing area of any bird, and its wingspan is more than 3 m (10 ft). Condors rely entirely on constant winds and rising thermal air currents to fly. They can glide great distances using gravity alone – energetic flapping is not an option for such a heavy bird. Fortunately, perpetual winds allow condors to search beaches, plateaus, and valleys, confident they can regain height easily.

Condors feed on carrion, using their strong bills to tear the hides and flesh. Unlike eagles and hawks, the condors' long legs are used simply for standing, not for killing prey. In the past, Andean condors mainly fed on vicuñas, guanacos, and seals, but nowadays they more often eat dead domestic livestock. Although no longer common, in their core range flocks of 30 or 40 condors still gather around large carcasses.

On the wane

Andean condors breed only once every two years and miss a year if food is short. The whole reproduction cycle is long and slow: females lay just one egg, which hatches after 56 to 58 days, and then it is six months before the chick can fly. Chicks rely on their parents for several months more. Young birds do not breed for six years, often more. Condors balance this low "output" with very low natural mortality – they can live for 70 years – but whole populations are extremely vulnerable to human persecution. They are simply unable to make up lost numbers quickly, if at all.

△ **COMMUNAL ROOSTING**
Groups of condors roost in remote caves and on sheltered ledges. In the morning, they leave their perch and rise effortlessly on thermal currents.

↔ 1–1.3 m (3¼–4¼ ft)
⚖ 11–15 kg (24–33 lb)
✕ Near threatened
🔱 Dead mammals
🏠 ⛰ 🌵

NW. to SW. South America

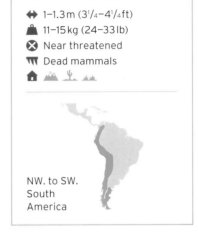

outspread flight
feathers

Fabian's lizard
Liolaemus fabiani

First identified as a distinct species in 1983, Fabian's lizard (also called Yañez's iguana) is endemic to the largest saltflat in Chile, Salar de Atacama. This lizard scampers around by day among the salty lumps and hypersaline shallows, even when surface temperatures exceed 45°C (113°F). It copes with drinking salty water by excreting excess salt from parts on its snout called lateral nasal glands – similar to its large cousin, the marine iguana. The lizard hunts flies, grabbing them in midair, but also takes beetles and other small prey.

Bars and stripes
Fabian's lizard has a big, strong head, a wide-gaping mouth, and robust limbs. Its "beaded" scales – small, smooth, shiny, and rounded – form 11 to 13 untidy, variable stripes or bars of black and sulphur-yellow to orange-red, on a speckly background along the flanks. This colouration fades on the underside.

Particularly aggressive about territory as well as mating partners, males display their striking side patterns to rivals. They also flick their limbs and tail, and clack their jaws at each other.

↔ 15 cm (6 in)

⚖ 30–50 g (1–1¾ oz)

✕ Not known

♨ Flies, beetles, other insects

🏠 ⛰

Chile (Salar de Atacama)

▽ **AT HOME ON SALT**
Fabian's lizard is active by day among the salty accretions and saline pools. It snaps with lightning speed at passing flies.

△ **NOT FOR SHARING**
Males will deliver vicious bites when disputes over territory or females arise. Their jaws are even strong enough to draw blood through their tough scales.

△ **PERFECT FLIGHT**
Gliding at speeds of up to 200 km/h (125 mph), the Andean condor covers extensive distances.

ARGENTINE PAMPAS
One of the richest grazing areas in the world

The term pampas describes the wide, flat, grassy plains of southern South America, covering an area of more than 750,000 sq km (300,000 sq miles). It was named after a Quechua Indian word meaning flat surface. In North America, this sort of habitat is referred to as prairie and in Eurasia as steppe. The dominant vegetation comprises perennial grasses, such as stipas, and herbs.

Grasses are able to regenerate after the frequent wildfires, but few trees can survive them and so they are seldom found on the pampas. The scarcity of trees for shade and roosting has led to many animals burrowing underground for shelter.

Gauchos – cowboys – have herded cows, horses, and sheep on the grasslands for at least 200 years. The temperate climate and rich, fertile soils of the pampas also make it very good for cultivating crops such as soybeans, wheat, maize, and grape vines.

Over-grazing, habitat loss, and fertilizer use has diminished and degraded the natural pampas environment, making it less suitable for its native species. The Argentine pampas ecosystem is classified as an endangered ecoregion by the World Wide Fund for Nature (WWF) because none of the natural pampas is protected, despite plans by the Argentine government to create a national park.

Endangered ecosystem
Very little of the pampas remains pristine and undisturbed by human activity, and the original vegetation of coarse grasses has been greatly reduced.

BLOWING IN THE WIND The iconic plant species of the pampas, this coarse grass grows up to 3m (10ft) in height in large tussocks. Pampas grass leaves are razor sharp, and the feathery flower plumes can each produce 100,000 seeds that are blown on the wind.

PAMPAS GRASS

ENDANGERED DEER This small, shy deer was once numerous in the pampas but was hunted to near extinction during the 1800s. More recently, the pampas deer has suffered loss of its natural habitat to agriculture. Now there are fewer than 3,000 individuals left.

PAMPAS DEER

TINY RECYCLERS Termites are colonial insects that benefit the grassland environment by recycling plant matter and aerating the soil. They are a valuable source of food for pampas animals, including giant anteaters and armadillos.

TERMITES AND MOUND

15 mammal species and 20 bird species at risk of extinction > Just one plume of pampas

Vampire bat
Desmodus rotundus

elongated finger bones
support wing membrane

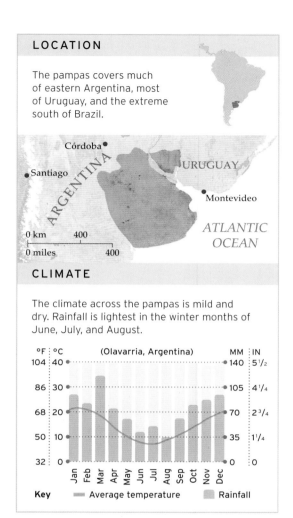
As its name suggests, the common vampire bat feeds on blood, mainly of mammals such as tapirs, peccaries, agoutis, and sea lions along with domesticated species such as cattle and horses. Two other species of vampire bat, also living in Central and South America, feed predominantly on bird blood. The common vampire bat can scuttle over the ground with amazing speed and agility, propped on its forearms and back legs. It usually lands close to a resting animal and uses its heat-sensitive nose pad to seek areas of warm blood vessels close to the skin. Once bitten, the anticoagulant properties of the bat's saliva help to keep the victim's blood flowing freely.

Reciprocal regurgitation

The common vampire bat has a communal roost in a hollow tree, cave, mine, or old building, which it shares with hundreds of others. Not only will adult females regurgitate blood to their offspring, they also share blood with hungry roost mates. Bats are more likely to help one another if they are related or have roosted together for a substantial amount of time. To judge whether a fellow bat is hungry, they engage in mutual grooming sessions that allow them to feel how distended each others' stomachs are before regurgitating.

↔ 7–9.5 cm (2³⁄₄–3³⁄₄ in)
⚖ 19–45 g (⁵⁄₈–1⁵⁄₈ oz)
✕ Common
▥ Blood

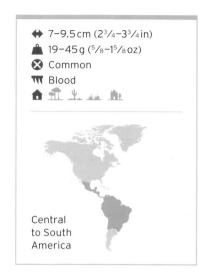

Central to South America

▽ **BLOOD LICKER**
The vampire bat's razor sharp teeth, long tongue, grooved chin, and short nose are all adaptations for getting access to and lapping up blood.

A vampire bat can **drink 50 per cent of its body weight** in 30 minutes

black stripe with a white
or cream border

Giant anteater

Myrmecophaga tridactyla

The giant anteater has a large, tube-shaped skull but a small brain. It has poor eyesight, yet its sense of smell is 40 times greater than that of a human. The tiny mouth at the end of its snout contains no teeth, but its 60-cm- (2-ft-) long tongue is covered in microscopic spines and sticky saliva, which can lap up as many as 35,000 termites per day. The anteater shuffles when walking, yet runs quickly and swims well.

Ripping claws

Ants, termites, and their eggs make up most of the giant anteater's diet. It uses its powerful foreclaws to rip into anthills and termite mounds, and also against predators such as jaguars, pumas, or humans. A giant anteater is not aggressive but can defend itself well as it stands on its hindlegs – balancing its body on its massive tail – and lashes out with its clawed forelimbs.
Solitary except when seeking mates, giant anteaters adapt their behaviour according to their proximity

to humans. Those living near populated areas are generally nocturnal (the species is threatened by hunting), whereas animals in remote regions feed during the day. They sleep in the shelter of a bush or hollow, with their extremely bushy tail draped over their head and body for warmth.

Once they have mated, female giant anteaters give birth to one offspring after a gestation of about six months. The baby clings to its mother's back for much of its first year, and will stay with her until it is about two years old.

Giant anteaters **flick their tongues** in and out about **150 times per minute**

↔ 1–2 m (3¼–6½ ft)
⚖ 18–40 kg (49–86 lb)
✕ Vulnerable
🐜 Ants, termites
🏠 🌳 🏜 🌿

S. Central
America to S.
South America

long, tube-like
snout

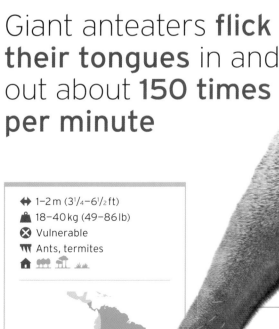

△ ANT FEAST
A giant anteater feeds from one anthill only for a few moments before moving on to the next to ensure it does not exhaust its food supply.

◁ KNUCKLE-WALKER
Giant anteaters have a shuffling gait. They walk on the knuckles of their forelimbs whereas they keep the heels of their hindlimbs on the ground.

Patagonian mara
Dolichotis patagonum

A mara looks like a small deer, when on the move. When seated on its haunches, it could be mistaken for a giant rabbit. It is, however, a large, long-legged relative of the cavy, or guinea pig. Maras live in arid grasslands, where they spend the day grazing on sparse shoots and herbs. As temperatures drop at night, they retreat to burrows, which they dig using the sharp claws on their forefeet. While foraging, maras are preyed upon by foxes, pampas cats, and birds of prey. In defence, they operate in pairs – a male and female that stay together for life. While one feeds, the other keeps watch. If a threat is spotted, they gallop away, reaching a top speed of 45 km/h (28 mph).

⟷ 69–75 cm (27–29½ in)
🏋 9–16 kg (20–35 lb)
✖ Near threatened
🌾 Grasses, herbs, seeds
🏠 🌳 🌵 🌿

S. South America

◁ LIFE IN A COMMUNE
Maras give birth in summer, which is also the rainy season. Pups are born in communal burrows occupied by several breeding pairs.

Six-banded armadillo
Euphractus sexcinctus

This native of the savannas digs out most of its food, such as roots, with its large forefeet. It also eats fallen fruit and licks up ants with its long, feathery tongue. The six-banded armadillo lives alone in burrows it digs about a metre into the ground. Marking territory with scent from a gland under the tail, it bites and scratches other armadillos that stray inside. The armadillo is a good swimmer, and swallows air before entering water to aid its bouyancy.

⟷ 40–50 cm (16–20 in)
🏋 3.2–6.5 kg (7–14 lb)
✖ Common
🌾 Roots, fruit, insects, carrion
🏠 🌳 🌿 🌿

C. to E. South America

▽ BODY ARMOUR
The armadillo buries itself when it spots predators. The armoured body plates protect any exposed upper body part, while the armadillo wedges itself into its burrow.

six-banded armadillos have six, seven, or eight bands

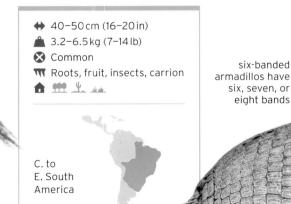

long, bushy, brown tail

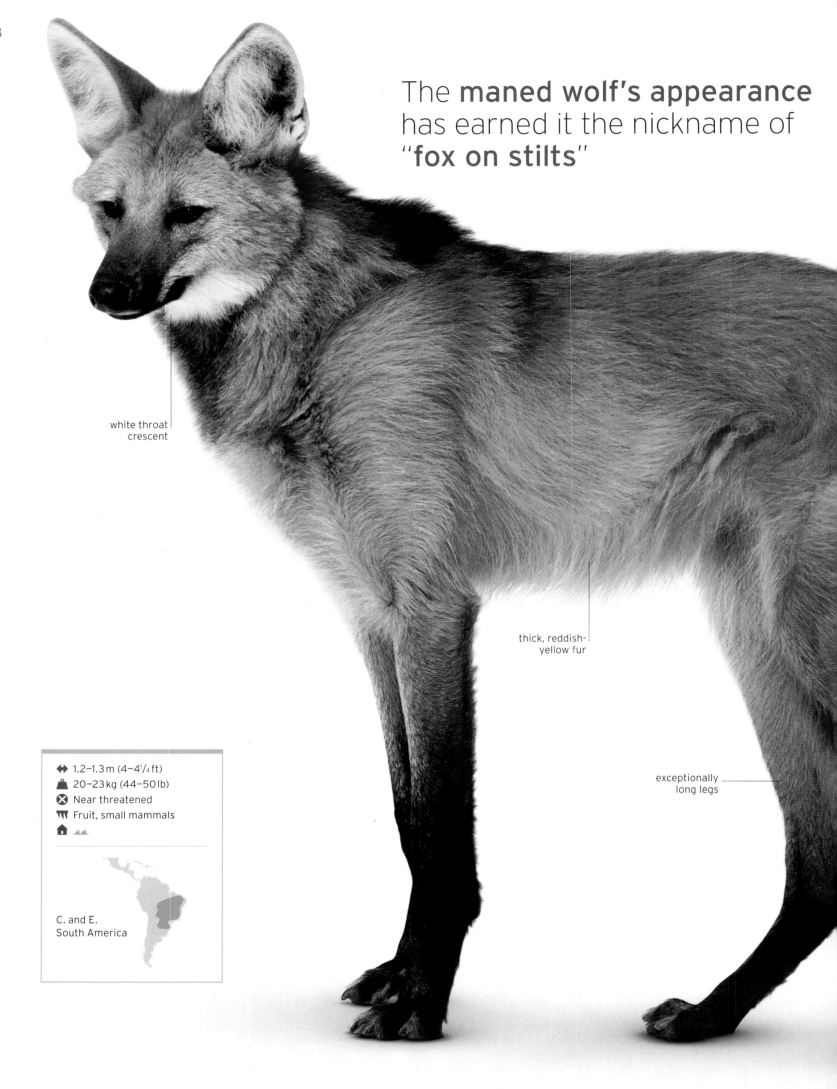

The **maned wolf's appearance** has earned it the nickname of **"fox on stilts"**

white throat crescent

thick, reddish-yellow fur

exceptionally long legs

↔ 1.2–1.3 m (4–4¼ ft)
⚖ 20–23 kg (44–50 lb)
⊗ Near threatened
🍴 Fruit, small mammals
🏠 🌲

C. and E. South America

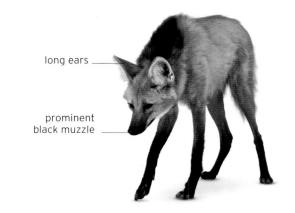

long ears

prominent
black muzzle

Maned wolf
Chrysocyon brachyurus

A slender fox- or wolf-like animal, the maned wolf has a different evolutionary lineage from both groups. This little-studied animal is probably an ancient relic that became an isolated species in South America thousands of years ago.

Superficially fox-like
Although not related, a resting maned wolf looks remarkably like a red fox. Large, whitish, triangular, and very mobile ears, and a white throat crescent beneath a prominent black muzzle, give it a distinctly fox-like look. Once it stands up and moves, however, it looks quite different with its high stance and long-striding walk.

The wolf has a long, black crest or rippling mane between the shoulders, and a striking white-tipped tail. Long legs allow it to move easily and see greater distances in the tall, dense grass in which it lives. It has a slightly awkward, undulating gait in open spaces, but in the long grass, it forces its way through with a slower, forward-reaching stride and short leaps.

Lone hunter
The maned wolf is a loner – more like a fox than a wolf – although several may gather where food is abundant. It uses its excellent hearing to locate, stalk, and pounce on prey, killing it by biting on or around the neck or spine. The wolf prefers mammals, mainly pacas – large rodents – and will eat armadillos and birds, even fish. However, the maned wolf is remarkable for the large proportion of vegetable matter in its diet. It is fond of the tomato-like wolf apple, the fruit of the lobeira plant, and regularly eats various other fruits and roots. This fruit-rich diet is essential to the animals' health; when captive maned wolves were given a pure meat diet they developed kidney and bladder stones.

Nightly patrols
Maned wolves create tracks through grassland by using regular routes in their night-time patrols. They defend territories based on these paths, using strongly scented urine as a marker. Females give birth to between two and six pups, which are dependent on their parents for up to a year. The males may help feed the young.

Maned wolves are threatened by habitat loss, and are vulnerable to road traffic. They are sometimes killed by domestic dogs and are susceptible to their diseases, and myths about the medicinal value of their body parts sometimes lead to persecution by humans. Maned wolves require large areas of open ground, and are difficult to keep and even harder to breed in zoos. Their conservation relies on the protection of large areas of suitable habitat.

◁ **LONG-LEGGED ROAMER**
The maned wolf uses its long legs in an efficient, loping gait, covering long distances each night through its 30–55 sq km (12–20 sq mile) territory.

▷ **YOUNG PUP**
This pup, almost five weeks old and becoming increasingly inquisitive, will stay with the family group for up to a year.

△ **SOCIAL ENCOUNTER**
Prominent ears help maned wolves communicate: one lays them flat, in fear or submission, the other raises them, showing dominance.

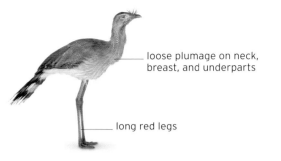

loose plumage on neck, breast, and underparts

long red legs

Red-legged seriema

Cariama cristata

Tall, long-legged, and gangly, seriemas share much of the same range and habitat as the larger rheas. They use the abundant termite mounds in grassy, savanna-like scrub and bush as lookouts and song posts. The territorial males make the air ring with long series of loud yelps, with abrupt changes of pitch. These extraordinary sounds are audible over several kilometres. The head is flung back, bill wide open, almost touching the back at the loudest moments.

Short sprints

The red-legged seriema's short-toed feet are adapted for running – in short bursts of up to 40 km/h (25 mph) – to escape predators, and for pursuing and stamping on tough and lively prey. The seriema clambers about in the lower branches of trees or flies up higher to roost. The nest is built within reach of a short series of fluttering leaps. Otherwise, flight is infrequent and short-lived, with quick flaps of the wings followed by long glides.

Seriemas kill prey such as snakes by beating them on the ground with their bill. They are sometimes kept as "watchdogs" among chickens to keep them safe. Seriemas prefer open and bushy areas, so are not threatened by loss of habitat and, at times, may even benefit from deforestation.

↔ 75–90 cm (29½–35½ in)
⬛ 1.5 kg (3¼ lb)
✕ Common
🍴 Lizards, birds, rodents
🏠 ⸏

E. South America

permanently raised crest of feathers at base of bill

△ **THREAT DISPLAY**
Males sing loud duets to reinforce territorial claims. If they still chance to meet, they use ritual postures to settle differences without resorting to fighting.

◁ **DISTINCTIVE BILL**
A seriema's broad, hooked bill is its main tool, grabbing, manipulating, and breaking apart large prey such as lizards, snakes, and tough beetles.

finely barred body plumage

Burrowing owl

Athene cunicularia

white speckles on brown body

Short-grass prairies, sagebrush, and semi-desert are the preferred habitats of the burrowing owl, but it will make do with cultivated ground, even golf courses and airfields. Roosting and nesting in holes, the owls may take over empty mammal burrows. They hunt by day and night, watching for prey such as small rodents from low mounds, bobbing and turning their heads to fix their victim's precise position. Viscachas and prairie dogs keep the grass short, giving the owls a better view.

↔ 19–25 cm (7½–10 in)
⚖ 125–250 g (4½–9 oz)
✖ Common
🪶 Insects, reptiles, birds
🏠 🌵

North America, Central America, and South America

Nests are **lined with dried dung**, perhaps to mask the owls' scent from predators

△ **IN THE BURROW**
Several pairs nest close together, each in a 1-m- (3-ft-) long burrow in soft ground containing between two and 12 eggs.

Greater rhea

Rhea americana

Open grassland is typical greater rhea habitat, where South America's largest bird hunts for large insects, reptiles, and seeds. Each male makes a nest and displays to attract six or seven females in succession. The females lay eggs in the nests, before moving on to mate with other males. Each male incubates 20–30 eggs and cares for the young by itself, or with a subordinate male "helper". Male rheas are very protective about their young, charging even at females during this period.

↔ 0.9–1.5 m (3–5 ft)
⚖ 15–30 kg (33–66 lb)
✖ Near threatened
🪶 Seeds, fruit, insects
🏠 🌳 🌾
◉ E. and SE. South America

◁ **GROUNDED**
One of the world's large flightless birds, the rhea is more like Australia's emu than Africa's ostrich.

Argentine horned frog

Ceratophrys ornata

horn-like projection

This burly ground frog is also known as the Argentine wide-mouthed frog or the Pac-Man frog because of its tendency to gobble up anything that will fit in its immense mouth. The Argentine horned frog employs a sit-and-wait strategy to capture prey, lying hidden among fallen leaves with just its eyes and mouth showing. The frog's "horns" are small projections above the eyes, which disrupt the animal's body shape and help with camouflage. When suitable-sized prey comes within striking distance, the frog lunges forward and engulfs it within its cavernous mouth.

△ **FEARLESS DEFENDER**
The aggressively territorial Argentine horned frog will take on larger and more powerful encroachers fearlessly.

↔ 10–12 cm (4–4¾ in)
🌱 Spring
✖ Near threatened
🪶 Frogs, songbirds, snakes
🏠 🌾 〰
◉ SE. South America

GALAPAGOS ISLANDS
The island group that inspired the theory of evolution

The Galapagos is a remote archipelago of volcanic islands in the vast blue of the Pacific Ocean. These islands formed when the Earth's crust moved over a hot spot in the mantle (a warmer layer of semi-solid rock below the crust), causing it to melt and form a sequence of volcanoes. Many erupting volcanoes reached the sea's surface before becoming extinct, and the cooled lava created the Galapagos Islands. Due to their remoteness from other land masses, these islands have unique endemic species found nowhere else on Earth.

The story of evolution

Charles Darwin, a British naturalist, travelled to the Galapagos Islands in 1835. What he saw there helped him develop his theory of evolution by natural selection, whereby species change as generations pass. Darwin saw fascinating examples of divergence – where animals on different islands had developed sufficient differences to become separate species. As a result, the Galapagos Islands have many unique animals, such as the various finches and giant tortoises.

Three major currents converge here, bringing nutrients and plankton that support fish, marine mammals, and seabirds. The islands are periodically affected by El Niño, which causes warmer and wetter conditions that can benefit plants and land animals but is devastating to marine life.

DIFFICULT TO ESCAPE
Historically there were no land-based predators on the Galapagos Islands and so this cormorant lost the ability to fly. Since the arrival of humans its numbers have decreased because of introduced predators such as cats, dogs, and pigs.

FLIGHTLESS CORMORANT

PIONEER SPECIES
The lava cactus is quick to colonize the bare rock of lava fields. Its fleshy stems store water and are a valuable source of moisture for wildlife including land iguanas and tortoises. Cactus finches assist in populating new areas by distributing its seeds.

LAVA CACTUS

Approximately 127 islands and islets in total

SALLY LIGHTFOOT CRAB

A World Heritage Site since 1978

CLEANER CRABS
Bright red Sally Lightfoot crabs have a mutually beneficial relationship with marine iguanas. They keep the resting iguanas clean by picking ticks and algae off their skin. The crabs eat what they find and so receive a reward for their work.

CLIMATE

The average temperature varies by a mere 0.7°C (1.26°F) throughout a year, whereas the rainfall varies drastically, especially during El Niño years.

°F	°C	(Galapagos Islands)	MM	IN
104	40		320	12½
86	30		240	9½
68	20		160	6¼
50	10		80	3¼
32	0		0	0

Jan Feb Mar Apr May Jun Jul Aug Sep Oct Nov Dec

Key ▬ Average temperature ▬ Rainfall

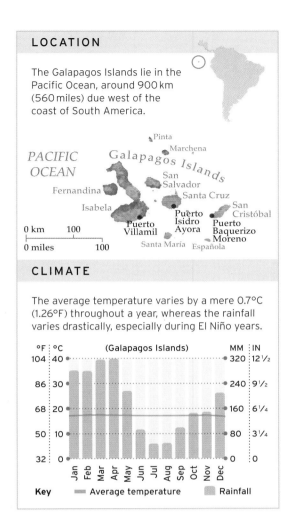

COMMON ANCESTOR
Seven species of colourful lava lizard live in the Galapagos; one species occurs on several islands, but the others are found on only one island each. Like the Galapagos finches, all the lava lizard species evolved from a single ancestor.

9 endemic species identified

LAVA LIZARD

Galapagos sea lion
Zalophus wollebaeki

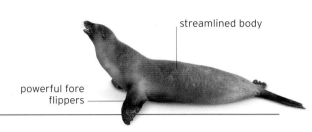

streamlined body

powerful fore flippers

Unlike its relatives, the true seals and walruses, the Galapagos sea lion is an otarid or eared seal. External ear flaps are one difference between otarids and true seals; another is the ability to work their hind flippers independently, which, together with stronger fore flippers, allows sea lions to move more easily on land. Like most sea lions, they can move rapidly due to their rotatable pelvis.

Colonies of curiosity

Highly social, sea lions are coastal mammals, feeding in ocean shallows before returning to the shore to sleep, rest, and nurse their young in colonies ruled by an adult male. Their inquisitive nature, particularly that of younger sea lions, brings them into contact with human activities such as fishing – often with fatal consequences. In addition, they are severely impacted by El Niño weather events: climatic changes that affect Pacific winds, ocean currents, and temperature patterns every few years, leading to a sudden depletion of fish in the area. During the El Niños of 1997–98, sea lion numbers in the Galapagos Islands fell by almost 50 per cent.

↔ 1.2–1.5 m (4–5 ft)
⚖ 50–250 kg (110–550 lb)
✕ Endangered
🍴 Fish, squid, crustaceans
🏠 ≋ ≋ ≋

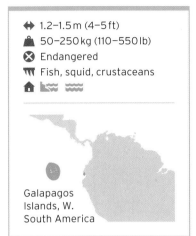

Galapagos Islands, W. South America

▽ **STRONG SWIMMERS**
Unlike true seals, which swim mainly by moving their rear flippers, sea lions use powerful, elongated front flippers to pull themselves along.

Sea lion **pups** start to develop **swimming skills** at **one to two weeks**

▽ **ATTENTION SEEKER**
The male's throat pouch expands into a red balloon as he sits on a treetop nest, displaying to female frigatebirds flying overhead.

long tail used as rudder when flying

Great frigatebird
Fregata minor

The great frigatebird looks almost prehistoric, with its long beak, forked tail, and huge, pointed, angular wings set in an inverted "W". It has the largest wing area to body mass, or the lowest wing-loading, of any bird. This, together with the large tail spread wide or closed to a single point, makes the frigatebird extremely stable as it soars effortlessly for hours, as well as supremely agile while dashing to grab flying fish or chase other birds. It also steals food from seabirds, especially boobies, harassing them until they regurgitate. The frigatebird flies over the sea, but avoids landing on water because it lacks fully waterproof plumage. It nests in trees on remote tropical islands in the Pacific, Indian, and South Atlantic oceans. Pairs take turns to incubate one egg for a period of 55 days.

↔ 85–105 cm (34–41 in)
⚖ 1–1.5 kg (2¼–3¼ lb)
✖ Common
🍴 Fish, squid, seabird chicks

Tropical Pacific, South Atlantic, and Indian Oceans

inflated pouch

Frigatebirds **rarely land during the day,** except when breeding

Galapagos penguin
Spheniscus mendiculus

The only penguin that lives north of the Equator, the Galapagos penguin breeds mostly on the Fernandina and Isabela islands of the Galapagos archipelago. Swimming in the Cromwell Current by day, they exploit small shoaling fish such as mullets and sardines – the cold ocean current provides a higher nutrient content than warm, tropical waters. The penguins visit land at night, when it is both cooler and safer for flightless birds. Like Antarctic penguins, they can flap their tiny wings to lose excess body heat.

↔ 53 cm (21 in)
⚖ 1.7–2.1 kg (3¾–4½ lb)
✖ Endangered
🍴 Mullets, sardines

Galapagos Islands

Rare bird
The Galapagos penguin is one of the world's rarest penguins, with fewer than 1,000 breeding pairs. Their breeding season is regulated by the availability of food. Climatic events such as El Niño cycles warm the waters around the islands, reducing fish numbers as they depart for cooler waters. The resulting food shortage makes the penguins skip an entire breeding season.

Galapagos penguins are also threatened by pollution, intensive fishing, and predators such as cats and dogs that human settlers have brought to the islands.

▷ **PARTNERS FOR LIFE**
Galapagos penguins mate for life. The female lays one or two eggs in deep rock crevices to keep them cool. Both parents take turns incubating them for a period of 38-40 days.

Blue-footed booby
Sula nebouxii

large feet fully
webbed across
four toes

The male blue-footed booby relies on his colourful feet to impress potential mates. The blue colour is enhanced by pigments that come from a regular supply of fresh fish. The brighter the feet, the better nourished the male is, showing how good a provider he will be for offspring. Females tend to mate with younger males, as the brightness declines with age. Closely related to gannets, and more loosely to pelicans and cormorants, boobies have broad webbing across all four toes.

Survival of the fittest

About half of the world's blue-footed booby population is centred in the Galapagos Islands, although few young have been reared there recently. This is mainly due to a drop in the sardine population on which the booby feeds almost exclusively. The breeding season is short and the female lays two or three eggs, which hatch several days apart.

When there is enough food, the different sizes of chicks allow them all to be fed without much rivalry. Should food be scarce, the older, bigger chick kills its siblings and is more likely to survive. If more than one survives, the smaller chick will have as good a chance of becoming a productive adult.

↔ 75–90 cm (30–35 in)
🏋 1.3–1.8 kg (2³/₄–4 lb)
⊗ Common
🐟 Sardines, other fish
🏠 ~~~~ ~~~~

W. Mexico
to NW. South
America,
Galapagos
Islands

▷ **COURTSHIP DANCE**
Courting blue-footed boobies show off the brilliance of their webbed feet, lifting them alternately in a ritualized, waddling dance.

Waved albatross
Phoebastria irrorata

dull yellow bill

chestnut-brown plumage

The only tropical albatross, the waved albatross, breeds on the Galapagos Islands and feeds off the coast of Ecuador and Peru. It forages up to 100 km (60 miles) from its nest, where fish are found close to the surface. Waved albatrosses use their long, slender wings to exploit air currents to travel far with little effort.

↔ 85–93 cm (33¹/₂–36¹/₂ in)
🏋 3–4 kg (6¹/₂–8³/₄ lb)
⊗ Critically endangered
🐟 Fish, squid, crustaceans
🏠 ~~~~
📍 Galapagos Islands

△ **CALLING OUT FOR A MATE**
Albatrosses mate for life after an elaborate courtship ritual involving a precise sequence of moves, such as circling and bowing their bills.

Woodpecker finch
Camarhynchus pallidus

Finches in the Galapagos Islands have evolved into 15 distinct species, each with a different feeding strategy. In wet periods, the woodpecker finch feeds on abundant insects. However, in the hot, dry season it finds half its food by using a special tool – one of very few birds to do so. It wields a fine twig or cactus spine to remove grubs from crevices in bark or from tunnels bored into wood. The finch tests several tools and chooses the right one for the task, at times even snapping a twig to shorten it and make it more effective. It then goes on to use its favourite tool at several sites.

△ **BILL EXTENDER**
The woodpecker finch can use its bill to find grubs but using a long spine means it can probe more deeply.

↔ 15 cm (6 in)
🏋 20–31 g (¹¹/₁₆–1¹/₁₆ oz)
⊗ Locally common
🐟 Insects, larvae
🏠 🌳 🌲
📍 Galapagos Islands

Galapagos tortoise

Chelonoidis nigra

five-toed
forefoot

The Galapagos tortoise is famous both for its enormous size and for being one of the world's longest-lived animals. Six of the Galapagos Islands are home to 14 different kinds of this giant land reptile. Some experts regard them as subspecies or races; others class them as separate species in view of genetic studies. However, the Galapagos tortoise can be split into two types based on the shape of the shell. These are the large "domed" type, which have big, round shells, and the slightly smaller "saddleback", with an arched or saddle-like flare in the shell above the neck. This arch may be an adaptation to feeding in more arid habitats, where vegetation – such as the prickly pear cactus, a favourite food – is higher off the ground and can only be reached by craning the head and neck.

Partial migrators

On some islands, when the dry season begins, older males and some adult females leave the lowlands for the more humid highlands. It takes them two to three weeks to migrate about 6 km (4 miles), and they remain in the highlands until the rains return. The rest of the tortoises stay in the lowlands all year. The Galapagos tortoise's unhurried lifestyle, slow metabolism, and ability to store food energy and water mean it can survive for a whole year without eating or drinking if it has to.

Traditional nesting sites

Mating peaks from February to May – the rainy season – when the male becomes territorial and starts to sniff, pursue, nip, and ram the female. Female tortoises usually choose a traditional site near the coast and dig a hole in loose soil or sand to lay the eggs. She lays up to four clutches of between five and 18 eggs (the average is eight to 10 per clutch), then fills in the hole. The eggs take from four to eight months to hatch, depending on the temperature, and the babies may spend several days, even weeks, digging their way up to the surface. The eggs and hatchlings are threatened by introduced predators such as cats and black rats.

Galapagos tortoises are **exceptionally long-lived**, with **one female** living more than **170 years**

◁ **SADDLEBACK SHELL**
Galapagos tortoises have long, flexible necks. The above-neck flare of the shells of tortoises on the drier Española Island allows them to reach taller plants.

▷ **DOMED SHELL**
Domed-shelled tortoises are generally less territorial and more social. They often rest in groups or herds, in earthen scrapes called pallets.

↔ Up to 1.2 m (4 ft)
⚖ Up to 300 kg (660 lb)
✖ Vulnerable
🌾 Cacti, grass, leaves, berries
🏠 ⛰

Galapagos
Islands

△ **SYMBIOTIC RELATIONSHIP**
Like other Galapagos reptiles, such as the giant tortoise, the marine iguana has a symbiotic relationship with the small ground finch, which cleans parasites from its skin.

high dorsal crest
in older males

blunt snout

Marine iguana

Amblyrhynchus cristatus

The remote Galápagos Islands, straddling the Equator in the Pacific Ocean, are famed for their unique animals. The islands' marine iguanas are especially interesting, being the only marine lizard that feeds exclusively on seaweed.

Agile in water

Marine iguanas do not live in the sea but gather in colonies on rocky shorelines. They spend the early hours of daylight basking in the sun so that their bodies are warmed enough for a busy day of swimming and feeding. When ready, the lizards plunge into the deep water, diving to depths of 10 m (33 ft) to graze on the short seaweeds that grow on the sunlit rocks of the seabed. An iguana can stay under for an hour if it has to, but most feeding dives last a few minutes before the animal surfaces to breathe. With its plump body and short legs, the marine iguana is ungainly on land but very agile in the water. It has partially webbed feet but swims mainly with the help of its flattened, oar-shaped tail, while the crest of spines along its back provides stability.

Warm on land

A marine iguana cannot remain in the sea for long. The chilly water begins to make it lethargic, and so it must get out of the water regularly to warm up in the sunshine. After eating it clambers back up the slippery rocks, gripping on with long, hooked claws. Its dark leathery skin helps it to absorb heat more quickly.

As it dries out, the body colour becomes a paler grey, with blotches of orange, green, and other colours appearing. These are most pronounced in adult males, which develop vibrant colouring to attract mates. The colours are derived from the pigments in the seaweed they eat and, therefore, vary from island to island. The faces of male and female marine iguanas are also streaked with white. This is the excess salt consumed in their food, which is excreted through glands in the nose.

Along with boosting body temperature, the time spent on land is an opportunity for the iguanas to digest the tough seaweed. This is done with the aid of gut bacteria inside a bulbous fermentation chamber, hence the iguana's large and rotund figure.

Big not always best

Males can grow to twice the size of females, and they will guard a harem of mates from rivals during the breeding season. Conflicts are generally a show of bluff and bluster, with a dominant male bobbing his head at a rival, who normally withdraws. If he bobs back, however, the rivals will fight, each trying to shove the other away with his head. Large size helps with this, but is a hindrance in other ways. Bigger lizards take longer to warm up between foraging dives, and when seaweed cover in the water is low due to climatic events – such as El Niño – they cannot feed as often as their smaller counterparts.

△ **MARINE IGUANA COLONY**
Iguanas bask in the sunshine in colonies, their dark bodies helping them to both absorb the sun's warmth and blend in among the volcanic rocks and sand.

◁ **UNDERWATER MEAL**
The marine iguana gets all of its food from the seabed. It uses its hard, horny lips to scrape away the sea lettuce that grows on rocks.

↔ 50–100 cm (20–40 in)
🏋 1–11 kg (2¼–24 lb)
✖ Vulnerable
🌿 Seaweed
🏠 🏞 〰

Galapagos Islands

When **food is scarce,** the marine iguana can **reduce its body size**, including **shrinking its skeleton** by 10 per cent

Central Apennines

A grey wolf cautiously approaches a small herd of red deer, but they are alert to the predator's presence. Fewer than 1,000 wolves live in Italy and only in the Apennine mountains.

Europe

LAND OF ICE AND FIRE

Iceland lies on the volcanic seam of the mid-Atlantic ridge, where two tectonic plates are gradually growing and being forced apart. The land is dotted with active volcanoes, geysers, and glaciers.

AGRICULTURAL IMPACT

In Europe, ecological damage associated with human development is significant, with extensive urbanization, deforestation, and the conversion of land for agriculture.

FEATURED ECOREGIONS

■ Norwegian Fjords **»p134-39**
Coastal marine, alpine tundra

■ Scottish Highlands **»p140-45**
Temperate coniferous forest, moorland

■ The Camargue **»p146-51**
Wetland: river delta

■ Tagus Valley **»p152-57**
Mediterranean woodland, scrub

■ The Alps **»p158-63**
Temperate coniferous forest, alpine meadow

■ Bavarian Forest **»p164-73**
Temperate coniferous forest, broadleaf and mixed forest

ARCTIC OCEAN

Iceland

NORWEGIAN FJORDS
The landforms of the Norwegian coast, including flooded U-shaped valleys known as fjords, are among the most dramatic clues to northern Europe's glacial history.

Norwegian Sea

Scandinavia

Gulf of Bothnia

Faroe Islands

Norwegian Fjords

Shetland Islands

Orkney Islands

Vänern

Gotland

British Isles

Grampian Mountains

North Sea

Baltic Sea

Jutland

North Europe

Elbe

Vistula

Severn

Thames

Rhine

E U R O P E

English Channel

Seine

Ardennes

Bavarian Forest

Carpathia

WARMING CURRENT
A warm Atlantic current – an extension of the Gulf Stream – bathes the European coast, bringing a fairly stable climate, frequent rain, and mild temperatures to northern latitudes.

Brittany

Loire

Black Forest

Danube

Tisza

Bay of Biscay

Massif Central

Lake Geneva

Alps

Mt Blanc 4,807m △

Rhône

Po

Drava

Great Hungarian Plain

Cordillera Cantábrica

Pyrenees

Camargue

Apennines

Dinaric Alps

Adriatic Sea

Douro

Ebro

Tagus

Iberian Peninsula

Balearic Islands

Corsica

Sardinia

Ionian Sea

Sierra Nevada

M e d i t e r r a n e a n

Sicily

Etna 3,263m △

Pelopon

MEDITERRANEAN SEA
Warm, salty, and almost landlocked, this sea has been adversely affected by fisheries and shipping, but still supports diverse underwater life.

Malta

S e a

Barents Sea

Kola Peninsula

White Sea

Lake Onega

Lake Ladoga

Ural Mountains

Volga

Central Russian Upland

Don

Volga Uplands

Dnieper

Volga

Caspian Sea

Caucasus
El'brus
▲ 5,642m

Black Sea

Mountains

egean Sea

Crete

URAL MOUNTAINS
Forming a natural boundary between Europe and Asia, the Urals run from the Arctic Circle to the dry temperate steppes of Kazakhstan.

PLAINS AND PENINSULAS
Europe

Europe is the western portion of the supercontinent of Eurasia, separated from Asia by the Black and Caspian seas, and the Ural and Caucasus mountains. It is a geologically and ecologically complex continent, with ancient glaciated uplands to the north and west, a vast plain sweeping east from southern England to Russia, and central uplands preceding the steep rocky terrain of the Alps – the longest mountain chain in Europe. Roughly half of the landmass comprises major peninsulas – Scandinavia, Jutland, Brittany, Iberia, Italy, and the Balkans – or large islands such as Great Britain, Ireland, and Iceland. The influence of the surrounding oceans and seas on climate is considerable.

Natural habitats and their plant and animal life occur in zones according to latitude. Tundra and coniferous forests dominate the north, giving way to deciduous forests, agricultural landscapes, mountains, and Mediterranean habitats in the south. Many species of bird and insect migrate annually between Asian breeding grounds and European wintering areas.

LIMESTONE CAVES

Karst landscapes, such as the Kras region of Slovenia and Italy, consist of thin, dry, alkaline soils above limestone bedrock with caves and underground rivers. Some are home to the cave salamander, or olm.

MANITA PEC CAVE

OLM

KEY DATA

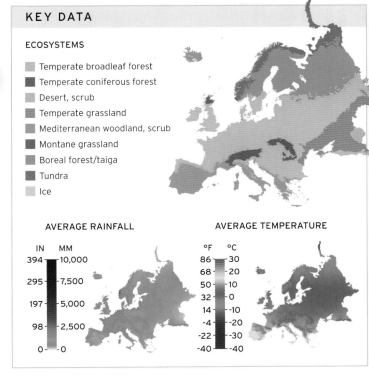

ECOSYSTEMS

- Temperate broadleaf forest
- Temperate coniferous forest
- Desert, scrub
- Temperate grassland
- Mediterranean woodland, scrub
- Montane grassland
- Boreal forest/taiga
- Tundra
- Ice

AVERAGE RAINFALL

IN	MM
394	10,000
295	7,500
197	5,000
98	2,500
0	0

AVERAGE TEMPERATURE

°F	°C
86	30
68	20
50	10
32	0
14	-10
-4	-20
-22	-30
-40	-40

NORWEGIAN FJORDS
Sheltered havens of a convoluted coast

The coast of Norway is dominated by steep-sided valleys gouged out by glaciers over several ice ages. These were then flooded by the sea, forming long, narrow inlets with vertiginous rock walls known as fjords. The waters are fully marine, but sheltered, largely inaccessible from land, and often extremely deep. Despite their high latitude, the fjords usually remain ice-free all year thanks to the warming influence of the Gulf Stream. They support an abundance of resident and migratory fish, seals and porpoises, and sea birds, and the world's largest accumulation of deep-water coral reefs.

Cold-water corals
Deep-water corals were first discovered in 1869, but it took more than a century for their size and extent to be revealed. The main reef-forming coral in the Atlantic is *Lophelia pertusa*, and lophelia reefs more than 13 km

(8 miles) long and 30m (100 ft) high have been found off the coast of Norway. Some of the reefs are thousands of years old. The reefs in the more shallow, but still cold waters of the fjords were discovered in 2000. They greatly enhance the ecological value of the fjords, giving shelter to a wide range of marine invertebrates and providing nursery and feeding areas for fish.

The mountainous land adjacent to and between the fjords is cloaked in coniferous and deciduous forests, dotted with glacial lakes and summer-grazing pastures in high valleys. Above 1,700 m (5,600 ft), the trees and meadows give way to alpine plants and snowy peaks.

SPAWNING GROUNDS
The Atlantic herring migrates to Norwegian fjords to spawn when it reaches five years. It is a key food item for several other fish, seals, cetaceans, and sea birds, and so all these animals suffer from overfishing of herring stocks by humans.

ATLANTIC HERRING

BOOM AND BUST
Norway lemmings can breed very quickly. When good conditions prevail, populations boom, leading to large-scale dispersal and the myth that lemmings hurl themselves into fjords to escape overcrowding. Populations crash due to limited food.

NORWAY LEMMING

The largest lophelia reefs are more

WHITE-BACKED WOODPECKER

Sognefjord is the longest ice-free fjord in the world

HAMMERED HOME
The relatively undisturbed coastal forests of Norway support dense populations of the white-backed woodpecker. Considered an indicator of healthy and mature ecosystems, its excavations provide nest holes for many other species.

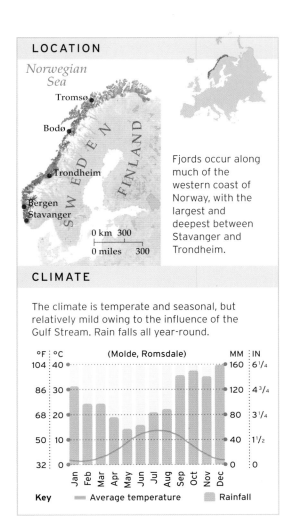

Norwegian Sea

Tromsø

Bodø

S W E D E N

FINLAND

Trondheim

Bergen
Stavanger

0 km 300
0 miles 300

Fjords occur along much of the western coast of Norway, with the largest and deepest between Stavanger and Trondheim.

CLIMATE

The climate is temperate and seasonal, but relatively mild owing to the influence of the Gulf Stream. Rain falls all year-round.

(Molde, Romsdale)

°F	°C		MM	IN
104	40		160	6 1/4
86	30		120	4 3/4
68	20		80	3 1/4
50	10		40	1 1/2
32	0		0	0

Jan Feb Mar Apr May Jun Jul Aug Sep Oct Nov Dec

Key ▬ Average temperature ▬ Rainfall

Grey seal
Halichoerus grypus

long, sharp claws on front flippers

The grey seal is perfectly adapted to its cold-water environment. Up to 6 cm (2½ in) of blubber gives this marine mammal excellent insulation, but it also diverts blood from the skin to vital organs. It hunts at depths of 60–300 m (200–985 ft), even in zero visibility, exhaling to collapse its lungs, then using its super-sensitive whiskers to track wakes left by sand eels and other prey.

↔ 1.7–2.3 m (5½–7½ ft)
⚖ 100–310 kg (220–680 lb)
✖ Common
🦷 Sand eels, squid, octopus
🏠 🏞 〰

N. Atlantic

◁ **SURFING ASHORE**
Found in large colonies, grey seals haul out on beaches, ice, and rocky outcrops to rest, breed, moult, and give birth.

Harbour porpoise
Phocoena phocoena

Harbour porpoises frequent coastal areas, particularly cold-water shallow bays, where they search for food along the sea floor. Although often confused with dolphins, when viewed from a distance, porpoises have small dorsal fins, are more rotund, and lack a distinct beak. They also avoid boats, and seldom bow-ride.

↔ 1.3–2 m (4¼–6½ ft)
⚖ 45–75 kg (99–165 lb)
✖ Common
🦷 Fish, squid, octopus
🏠 🏞 〰

△ **LOUD EXHALER**
Due to the sneeze-like sound made when they breathe through their blowholes, harbour porpoises were once known as "puffing pigs".

N. Pacific, N. Atlantic, Black Sea

tail has two partially separated flukes

DEEP, DARK REEFS
Lophelia pertusa is an unusual coral, able to live at depth in cold water. It grows exceptionally slowly, feeding on dead plankton that drifts down from the sunlit waters above. Norway's coast hosts the greatest known density of lophelia reefs in the world.

than 8,000 years old

LOPHELIA CORAL

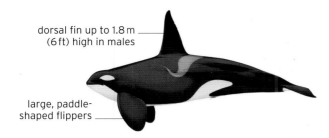

dorsal fin up to 1.8 m (6 ft) high in males

large, paddle-shaped flippers

Killer whale
Orcinus orca

The killer whale, or orca, is not a true whale but the largest member of the dolphin family. Living up to 90 years, it is the only cetacean that regularly eats other marine mammals, including other dolphins.

Intelligent hunters

There are three types of killer whales: resident, transient, and offshore; each group has a different diet and lives in different areas. Resident orcas form the largest groups, or pods, and primarily hunt fish, squid, and octopuses. Transient orcas are the world's biggest predators of warm-blooded animals, feeding almost exclusively on marine mammals, including large whales, as well as seabirds such as penguins. The offshore orcas eat fish, especially sharks.

All types of orca are highly intelligent. Adults teach juveniles how to hunt: herding, stunning prey with tail strikes, and "wave-washing" seals off sea ice.

Orca pods range from just a few to 50 or more. An average pod generally includes smaller groups comprising a mature female and its female offspring. They communicate using a shared vocabulary of clicks, whistles, and pulsed calls (which sound like screams to human ears). Different populations have distinctive calls.

Orcas mate throughout the year, but most often in late spring and summer. After a 15- to 18-month gestation period – the longest of all cetaceans – females bear a single calf, usually born tail-first.

◁ **SURFACE BREACH**
Breaching, tail and flipper slaps, and "spy-hopping" - pushing only the head above water - are known forms of communication among orcas.

- ↔ 7.5–10 m (24½–33 ft)
- ⚖ 2.6–6.6 tonnes
- ⊗ Not known
- ᛘ Fish, mammals, seabirds
- ⌂ ▰▰▰ ≈≈≈

Worldwide

King eider
Somateria spectabilis

This sea-going duck winters mostly north of the Arctic Circle and breeds on small lakes or rivers in coastal tundra and bogs. The king eider dives as deep as 35 m (115 ft) for food, but also tips forwards to forage in the shallows. Courtship displays are ritualized, with the male's rump raised, tail depressed, and head and bill pushed forwards.

- ↔ 47–63 cm (18½–25 in)
- ⚖ 1.5–2 kg (3¼–4½ lb)
- ⊗ Common
- ᛘ Molluscs, crabs
- ⌂ ⛰ 〰 ≈≈≈ ▰▰▰
- ◉ Arctic Ocean, N. Pacific, N. North America, N. Europe, N. Asia

▽ **DIRECT FLIGHT**
King eiders have a swift, direct flight pattern with rapid wing beats. Large flocks tend to fly abreast, rather than one bird behind the other.

bright red bill and enormous yellow frontal shield of breeding male

Atlantic salmon
Salmo salar

Young Atlantic salmon spend a year, or more, in the upper reaches of clear-running rivers before swimming out to sea. Once at sea, the salmon follows coastal currents in search of food, and matures rapidly. After three or four years at sea, it locates its birth river by the unique smell of its water and journeys back to breed.

- ↔ 0.7–1.5 m (2¼–5 ft)
- ⚖ 2.3–9.1 kg (5–20 lb)
- ⊗ Common
- ᛘ Fish, insect larvae,
- ⌂ 〰 ≈≈≈ ▰▰▰
- ◉ NE. North America, W. and N. Europe, N. Atlantic

◁ **HEADING UPSTREAM**
Many salmon die on the tough journey upstream, but survivors may make the trip three or four times.

↔ 28–30 cm (11–12 in)
⬆ 400 g (14 oz)
✖ Common
〜 Sand eels, capelins, herring
🏠 ⬛ 〜 ⛰

North Atlantic, Arctic Ocean

pale face darkens
in winter

▷ **FRESH CATCH**
Tiny sand eels hang in a row, held
in place by the puffin's muscular,
grooved tongue and inward-facing
serrations on the edges of its bill.

bill has bright
sheath in summer

webbed feet

Atlantic puffin

Fratercula arctica

Puffins are probably one of the most easily recognizable birds – particularly the Atlantic puffin, with its large, brightly coloured, triangular bill. They are small, upright seabirds that come to land only to breed. They are less like penguins than their cousins the guillemots, which stand upright on their heels and tails, their legs set right at the back of the body. Puffins have more centrally placed legs and walk more easily.

Temporary finery

In spring, the puffin's bill sheath expands and gains its bright red summer colours. The number of yellow grooves in the red tip indicate the bird's age. By autumn, the sheath is shed and the bill becomes smaller and duller for the winter. Without the need for the visual communication required at a breeding colony, the bill transforms into a practical tool for catching fish. Puffins dive deep for food, "flying" through the water with ease. They usually catch several small fish in a single dive, especially when collecting food for their chick.

Cliff-top colonies

Puffin colonies, some consisting of hundreds of thousands of pairs, spread over clifftop slopes and broken, rocky screes. Puffins from a colony often fly out over the sea in magnificent, swirling flocks to keep predators at bay and reduce the chances of individual puffins being killed. On land, they are noisy, at times aggressive, showing off their bright beaks and feet.

Puffins have a lifespan of 10–20 years, and they will often return to the same nest burrow year after year. If a new breeding pair cannot find an old burrow to occupy, they dig one with their feet, kicking out the soft soil until it is about 1m (3ft) deep. The female lays a single egg, which is held by either parent against a bare, hot "brood patch" under one drooped wing. The chick hatches after 36–45 days and both parents feed it for up to 60 days. The young puffin is then left alone and stands at the end of the burrow for several nights until it flies off to the sea. The synchronized timing of breeding leads to almost all adults leaving the colony together, so busy colonies become silent within a few days.

The **record number of sand eels** seen in an **Atlantic puffin's bill is 83**

◁ **UP IN THE AIR**
Atlantic puffins are capable of flapping their wings 400 times a minute, giving them a top speed of 90 km/h (55 mph).

△ **PUFFIN COLONY**
Adults fly up to 100 km (60 miles) out to sea in search of fish for their chick, usually returning to the colony in groups.

SCOTTISH HIGHLANDS
Britain's last wilderness

The Highlands of Scotland are both culturally and ecologically distinct. The region encompasses ancient rocky mountains with highly complex geology, grassy plateaux, peat bogs, abundant small rivers and lochs, and remnants of native forest, as well as extensive plantations and vast swathes of heather moorland. Some authorities also classify the Hebridean islands as Highland areas, though most of these are relatively low-lying. The relative wildness of the region is due to the limited opportunities for intensive agriculture and a sparse human population.

Restoring native forest

The highest summits are well above the treeline, and include Britain's highest peak, Ben Nevis, at 1,344 m (4,409 ft), and the Cairngorm plateau resembles subarctic tundra in terms of plant and animal diversity. Meanwhile the lowlands bear the hallmarks of glaciation, with broad valleys, large meandering rivers, and extensive bogs. Most of the forest in the region is coniferous plantation containing non-native Norway and sitka spruce and Douglas fir, but forest managers are increasingly looking to restore more natural assemblages similar to the ancient Caledonian forest that once cloaked lower slopes in Scots pine, juniper, birch, willow, rowan, and aspen.

Other attempts to rebalance the region's ecology include the reintroduction of Eurasian beavers, extinct for 400 years, and a high-profile rewilding experiment on the private Alladale Wilderness Reserve, where the aim is to have grey wolves and brown bears living free within a substantial fenced area.

GROUSE MOORS
Vast areas of moorland are intensively managed to ensure an abundance of red grouse for shooting. Ruthless predator control and burning of heather to promote tender new growth for the grouse to eat are controversial practices.

RED GROUSE

BLANKET BOGS
Scotland holds a significant proportion of the world's blanket bogs, where peat is formed from dead moss, especially sphagnum. The amount of atmospheric carbon bound up in peat plays a key role in moderating climate change.

SPHAGNUM MOSS

WOOD ANT

Only 1.2% of ancient Caledonian forest remains, split across 84 sites

Ben Nevis is the

SMALL WONDERS
Wood ants perform vital ecological roles: aerating soil, dispersing seeds, controlling problem insects, and providing food for many other species. Their nests are also home to the tiny shining guest ant, woodlice, and chafer beetle grubs.

long, slender legs

Western red deer

Cervus elaphus

LOCATION

The Highlands occupy the northern and western half of Scotland.

ATLANTIC OCEAN

North Sea

Inverness

Aberdeen

Dundee

0 km   100
0 miles   100

CLIMATE

Cool temperate, heavily influenced by Atlantic weather systems bringing frequent precipitation and high winds, and by altitude.

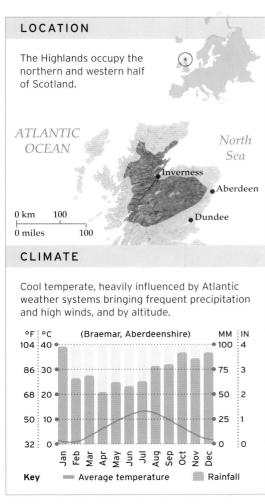

(Braemar, Aberdeenshire)

°F	°C		MM	IN
104	40		100	4
86	30		75	3
68	20		50	2
50	10		25	1
32	0		0	0

Jan Feb Mar Apr May Jun Jul Aug Sep Oct Nov Dec

Key — Average temperature ▯ Rainfall

The largest animal in Scotland (and in many other European countries), the red deer is named after the colour of its fur during the summer. At this time, the deer have a short coat, and small herds can be seen browsing in open habitats. In winter, the coat grows thick and grey as the deer retreat into woodlands that offer more shelter in bad weather.

Red deer live in single sex herds, but mixing is tolerated in winter. As spring arrives the males start to grow antlers, and the females give birth to spotted fawns. The rut begins in late summer. Dominant males control a harem of females, using a bellowing roar to keep them together. The weaker stags, the young and the old, harass the females at the edge of the group, driving them towards the protection of the stronger males. The rut lasts until the arrival of winter, when the males shed their antlers, and the deer prepare for cold conditions once more.

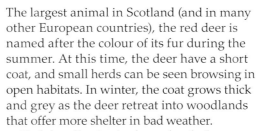

↔ 1.7–2.1 m (5½–7 ft)
⚖ 75–220 kg (165–485 lb)
✖ Common
🌾 Leaves, grasses, sedges
🏠

Europe to W. Asia, N. Africa

mature stag has several points on each antler

antler bone grows 2.5 cm (1 in) per day

▷ **STANDING PROUD**
Females judge males by their antlers. Younger stags have fewer points, or tines, while the antlers of ageing males are less symmetrical.

△ **HEADS DOWN**
Rutting stags try to avoid all-out combat. They walk side by side to size each other up and will only fight if neither backs down.

ASSISTED RECOVERY
Water voles saw a huge decline in the UK in the late 20th century, partly due to heavy predation by introduced American mink. But because Highland river catchments are too exposed for mink, the voles have a refuge here.

WATER VOLE

highest mountain in Britain

↔ 20–25 cm (8–10 in)
⚖ 200–475 g (7–17 oz)
⊗ Common
⋔ Conifer seeds, nuts

W. Europe to W. Asia

fluffy tail, moults annually

▷ TUFTED EARS
Unlike grey squirrels, red squirrels have tufts on their ears, which are particularly long in winter.

Eurasian red squirrel
Sciurus vulgaris

Eurasian red squirrels have remarkably varied coat colours, with the upper coats ranging from very light red to black. However, only the red form occurs in the UK. Agile climbers, these rodents can leap distances of up to 4 m (13 ft) and have great vision, hearing, and sense of smell.

Focus on food
Red squirrels spend most of the day feeding or caching food, such as seeds and nuts. In the warmest hours of summer, they retire to a drey, or nest. They do not hibernate, relying on their food stores to survive winter, but they stay in their drey in harsh weather. Males compete for females, but play no role in caring for young, and, apart from mating, these rodents live mainly independent lives. Although found across most of Europe, they are restricted to a few mixed woodlands in areas where they have to compete with the larger, more successful grey squirrel introduced from North America.

△ EYES OPEN
Squirrel kits spend their first weeks in a drey, lined with soft moss and grass, opening their eyes at around five weeks old.

Wildcat
Felis silvestris

thick coat with distinct dark stripes

At first glance, any of the 19 subspecies of wildcat could be mistaken for a domestic tabby – not surprisingly, as the African subspecies, *F. s. lybica*, is its ancestor. Look closely and differences emerge. European wildcats, for example, are generally larger than domestic cats, with longer, thicker coats, broader heads, and flatter faces. Their dark-ringed tails are also shorter, with blunt, black-tipped ends. In Europe, wildcats inhabit mainly mixed forests or broadleaved woods, but in other parts of the world their habitats range from desert to alpine meadows.

Passing on hunting skills

Wildcats have excellent night vision and mainly hunt small mammals, although some subspecies occasionally hunt young deer. They are solitary and highly territorial, except when mating and rearing kittens – two to five is the usual litter size. As weaning begins, the mother brings live food to the den, often an old rabbit burrow or fox den, to teach the kittens to hunt. They become independent at five to six months. Hybridization is considered the main threat to this species as domestic cats readily breed with wildcats.

▷ **STAY AWAY**
Wildcats use urine and faeces to mark their territories, but also communicate vocally, yowling and snarling to warn off intruders.

↔ 40–75 cm (15³/₄–29¹/₂ in)
⚖ 2–7.25 kg (4¹/₂–16 lb)
✕ Common
🐾 Rodents, birds, reptiles

Europe, W. and C. Asia, Africa

Scottish crossbill
Loxia scotica

green plumage of female

crossed bill tips

The Scottish crossbill is the only bird endemic to Scotland. A member of the finch family, it lives in the Scots pine forests of the Highlands, where it feeds almost exclusively on ripe cones, using its specialist bill to pry apart the scales so it can reach the seeds with its tongue.

Courtship begins in late winter or early spring, with flocks of males competing to see who can sing the loudest. Once a female selects a male, he touches his bill to hers, then feeds her. They build a nest of twigs high up in a pine tree and two to six eggs are laid, usually in March or April. Incubation lasts around two weeks, the male feeding the female all this time, and then both birds feed the chicks. They leave the nest after three weeks, but the parents have to feed them for 10 more days – until their bills are crossed.

Tough call

Two other species of crossbill also breed in the UK: the common crossbill, which feeds on spruce cones, and the slightly larger parrot crossbill, which specializes in tough pine seeds. Telling them apart is difficult, but they can be distinguished by their distinct calls.

↔ 16–17 cm (6¹/₄–6¹/₂ in)
⚖ 36.5–49 g (1¹/₄–1³/₄ oz)
✕ Locally common
🐾 Conifer seeds, buds

NW. Europe (UK)

◁ **SCOTTISH MALE**
The male is red like the common and parrot crossbill males, but its muscular neck and large bill are intermediate between those two species.

broad,
muscular body

Peregrine falcon
Falco peregrinus

Renowned for its skill in the air, the peregrine chases down prey, rising above and diving, or rolling over underneath to grasp the bird in its claws. Its spectacular "stoop" is a long, angled dive with wings folded in a teardrop shape, reaching speeds of 200–240 km/h (125–150 mph). In level flight, while sometimes outflown by a desperate pigeon, the peregrine puts on a burst of speed that few birds can match.

Formidable hunter
Hunting success is around 50–60 per cent, but peregrines often chase birds without attacking them. They catch birds up to the size of a pigeon, and occasionally ducks

and larger species. The decline of peregrines in the 1960s drew attention to the catastrophic effect of pesticides such as DDT, which is more concentrated further up the food chain. Birds of prey died or laid infertile or thin-shelled eggs. Peregrines have since recovered and often nest in towns, exploiting pigeon populations. They traditionally nested on cliffs, but high buildings are now used too.

tapered,
pointed wing

↔ 34–50 cm (13½–20 in)
⚖ 0.6–1.5 kg (1¼–3¼ lb)
✖ Common
🦅 Birds

Worldwide

△ **BRACED TO LAND**
Landing peregrines swoop upwards to lose speed, spread their wings and tail as air brakes, then thrust out their feet to take the shock of landing and to grasp the perch.

◁ **TINY PORTIONS**
Like most birds of prey, peregrines bring freshly killed animals back to the nest. They tear off a small piece of food and delicately offer it to a chick.

Western capercaillie

Tetrao urogallus

short, rounded wings

The capercaillie is the world's largest grouse. It survives mostly in old pine forests with an abundance of shoots and berries beneath the trees and in clearings close by. In summer, the birds look for food on the ground, but in winter, they often feed on shoots high up in trees. Male capercaillies gather and display in a lek to attract and impress the females, which then move away to nest.

Increasing deer, declining capercaillies

Capercaillie populations have declined almost everywhere, disappearing entirely from some forests. Climate change may play a role, but deterioration in capercaillie habitat is sometimes related to an increase in the deer population.

Capercaillies need a healthy growth of low shrubs, which provide essential cover and a rich diet. With too many deer browsing on these shrubs, capercaillies face a food shortage. High fences pose another problem. Because these birds can only fly low, many collide with fences intended to keep out deer and are killed.

↔ 60–85 cm (23½–34 in)
⚖ 1.8–4.1 kg (4–9 lb)
✕ Common
🌾 Seeds, berries, shoots

N., W., and S. Europe, W. to C. Asia

▷ **VYING FOR ATTENTION**
A male capercaillie displays to impress females, while making croaking, gurgling, and cork-popping sounds.

Common adder

Vipera berus

The common adder is the most widely distributed member of the viper family and is the only venomous snake in northwest Europe. Its front upper fangs, usually folded back along the jaws, tilt down in an instant to strike immobilizing venom into prey. The adder's diet includes frogs, lizards, birds, voles, and other small mammals. It is not an aggressive snake, but it will bite a human if trodden on or handled. The bite is painful, and may cause some swelling, but is rarely fatal.

Winter retreat

In their southern ranges, common adders remain above the ground and active all year. Further north, however, they spend the long cold winters together in large groups in a cave, burrow, or similar hideaway. They emerge from late spring to summer to mate. Females breed only once every two or three years and may mate with several males. The female gives birth to 10–15 live young who have to fend for themselves within hours of birth.

▷ **HOSTILE DANCE**
Male adders wrestle with each other to establish dominance. They raise up the front part of their body and attempt to push their opponent to the ground.

↔ 60–90 cm (24–35 in)
⚖ Up to 180 g (6⅜ oz)
✕ Common
🌾 Small mammals, reptiles

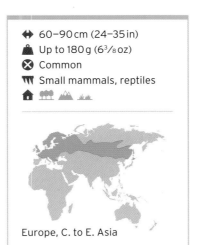

Europe, C. to E. Asia

flat head

distinctive dark zigzag line running down back

THE CAMARGUE
Europe's most famous coastal wetland

The largest river delta in Western Europe forms where the River Rhône splits to enclose more than 930 sq km (360 sq miles) of salt marsh, low-lying islands and sand bars, saltwater lagoons, and reed beds. In 1986, the Camargue was officially designated as a wetland of international importance. It is also a UNESCO World Heritage Site.

Shifting landscape

The landforms of the Camargue shift continually, and the gradual accumulation of silt and sand means the delta is gradually growing. The coastal flats are stabilized by salt-tolerant sea lavender and glasswort. Further inland are juniper woodlands, and the north of the delta is stable enough to support agriculture including seasonal grazing for horses and cattle, rice paddies, and vineyards. Aside from the greater flamingos and semi-wild horses

for which the region is famous, the most conspicuous wildlife of the Camargue in summer is often the mosquitoes – reputed to be the most voracious in France. These deeply unpopular bloodsucking insects are nevertheless an important food resource for birds such as house martins, swallows, and alpine swifts. Other insect life includes more than 30 species of dragonfly, but it is birds for which the wetlands are best known. More than 400 species live in or visit the Camargue, and egrets, herons, and harriers that would turn heads elsewhere are almost ubiquitous.

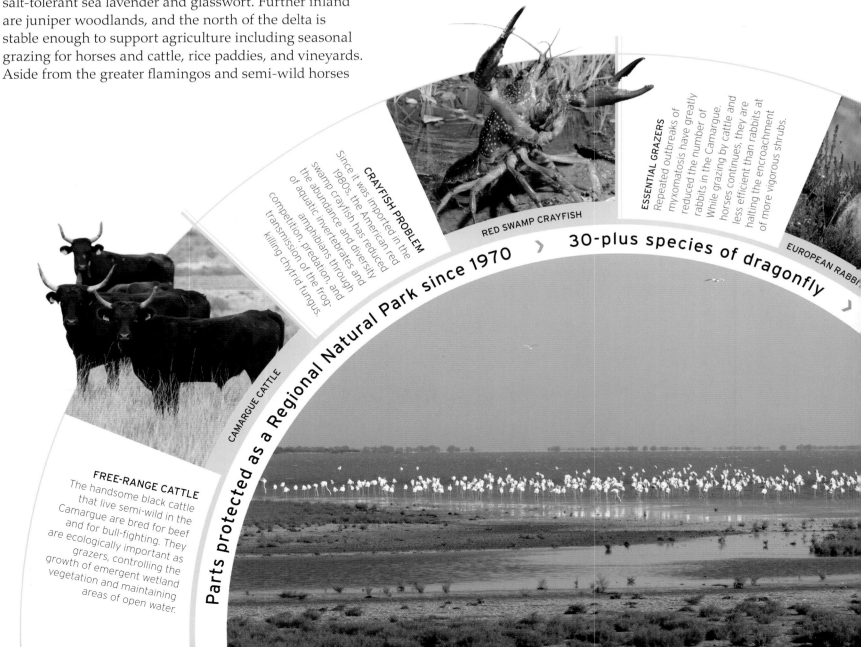

CRAYFISH PROBLEM
Since it was imported in the 1980s, the American red swamp crayfish has reduced the abundance and diversity of aquatic invertebrates and amphibians through competition, predation, and transmission of the frog-killing chytrid fungus.

RED SWAMP CRAYFISH

ESSENTIAL GRAZERS
Repeated outbreaks of myxomatosis have greatly reduced the number of rabbits in the Camargue. While grazing by cattle and horses continues, they are less efficient than rabbits at halting the encroachment of more vigorous shrubs.

EUROPEAN RABBIT

CAMARGUE CATTLE

30-plus species of dragonfly

Parts protected as a Regional Natural Park since 1970

FREE-RANGE CATTLE
The handsome black cattle that live semi-wild in the Camargue are bred for beef and for bull-fighting. They are ecologically important as grazers, controlling the growth of emergent wetland vegetation and maintaining areas of open water.

LOCATION

The Camargue lies within the Rhône Delta, on the Mediterranean coast of southeastern France.

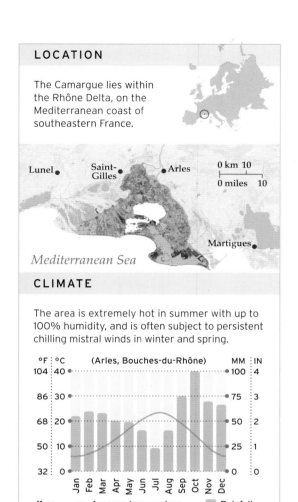

Lunel Saint-Gilles Arles

0 km 10
0 miles 10

Mediterranean Sea

Martigues

CLIMATE

The area is extremely hot in summer with up to 100% humidity, and is often subject to persistent chilling mistral winds in winter and spring.

°F	°C	(Arles, Bouches-du-Rhône)	MM	IN
104	40		100	4
86	30		75	3
68	20		50	2
50	10		25	1
32	0		0	0

Jan Feb Mar Apr May Jun Jul Aug Sep Oct Nov Dec

Key — Average temperature ▪ Rainfall

Camargue horse
Equus caballus

compact stature

Although their exact origin is unknown, horses have lived in the salty marshlands of southern France, particularly around the Rhône Delta, for thousands of years. Today, Camargue horses live a semi-wild existence as a protected breed. If described in horse-breeding terms, these small, compact horses are technically "grey" not white. When born, the foals are black or brown – the horses only turn grey at around four years old.

Water horses
Rugged and sturdy, Camargue horses are never stabled, nor are their hard hoofs ever shod. They survive extreme weather conditions partly by grazing on plants too tough for other herbivores. However, their even temperament and agility lead many to be tamed and ridden, and they are used to help manage the feral black Camargue cattle that also live in the wetlands.

↔ 2.1m (6¾ ft)
⬤ 300–400 kg (660–880 lb)
✖ Endangered
♈ Grass, leaves, herbs

S. Europe (Camargue)

Camargues are known in France as **"horses of the sea"**

▽ **RUNNING FREE**
Camargue horses naturally live in small herds, with the mares and foals usually led by a single dominant stallion.

THREATENED FISH
Eels were once the most common predatory fish in the Camargue, but they have declined here as elsewhere. This is due to a combination of pollution, the damming of their migration routes, and a parasitic nematode.

EUROPEAN EEL

More than 400 species of bird

adult has orange
bill with black
knob at base

large webbed feet
helps swan "run"
across water

Mute swan

Cygnus olor

While by no means silent – they make a snakelike hiss
when threatened, for example – mute swans are the least
vocal of all swans. Other swans make loud, bugling calls
when flying, but mute swans stay in touch in flight with
a different sound: their wings create a far-carrying,
deep, rhythmic, throbbing noise.

Mute swans are powerful enough to have few
predators as adults. Although an occasional fox or otter
may attack an unwary bird, swans have little need for
camouflage. Nor is there much demand for territorial
display because their huge size and white colour stand
out. However, aggressive encounters are frequent. Mute
swans will allow younger swans into their territory but
chase away competitors. They arch their wing feathers,
curve back their necks, and thrust out their chests.
A charge towards another swan on water, powered by
thrusts of their big webbed feet, is fast and impressive.

Summer flocks

Large flocks of mute swans gather to moult and often to
feed in shallow, sheltered water or on open fields. Some
of these flocks persist through the summer with many
swans, even seemingly fully mature ones, not breeding.

Nesting pairs separate off and defend a territory in
spring, building a massive nest of reed stems and other
waterside vegetation. The young "ugly ducklings", or
cygnets, are drab grey-brown. It takes two to three years
for them to turn all-white and develop the bright orange
and black bill colours of the adults. Adult males have the
thickest necks and biggest bills, with a large basal knob.

↔ 1.2–1.6 m (4–5¼ ft)
⚖ 9.5–12 kg (21–26½ lb)
✕ Common
〰 Vegetation, snails
🏠 ⛰ 🌾 〰 〰 🏛

Europe, W. and E. Asia

The mute swan is one
of the **heaviest flying**
birds in the world

△ **TAKE OFF AND LANDING**
Getting airborne from water or land requires a run to gather speed, before the swan's wings can generate sufficient lift. When coming in to land on water, the large webbed feet and wings act as brakes.

◁ **GOING FOR A RIDE**
Cygnets accompany their parents for several weeks, sometimes taking a ride on one of their backs while they are still small.

Greater flamingo
Phoenicopterus roseus

Flamingos feed unlike any other bird. The angled bill, held upside down and swept sideways, works like a sieve, gathering tiny invertebrates and algae from the salty water. If disturbed, flamingos run to take flight. The slim body, long neck, and trailing legs form a cross with the crimson-and-black wings.

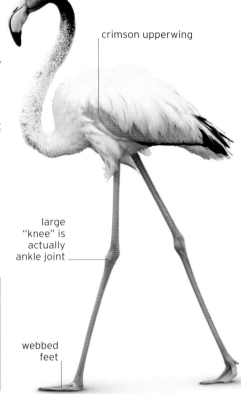

crimson upperwing

large "knee" is actually ankle joint

webbed feet

▷ **WALKING ON STILTS**
Long legs mean the greater flamingo can wade in deep water with its long, sinuous neck reaching down to its toes to feed.

↔	1.2–1.45 m (4–4³⁄₄ ft)
⚖	Up to 4 kg (8³⁄₄ lb)
✖	Common
🦐	Krill, shrimps, algae
🏠	🌱 ≈ ≈≈
◉	SW. Europe, Asia, Africa

Pied avocet
Recurvirostra avosetta

The pied avocet has the most upcurved bill of any European bird. The delicate, sensitive, slightly flat tip is swept horizontally through soft, saline mud, and tiny shrimps and other creatures are located by touch.

Few suitable natural nesting sites of the pied avocet remain in Europe, but many colonies have formed on artificially created lagoons and salt pans, most of which are nature reserves. In winter, the avocets collect in flocks, hundreds strong, on suitably mild, wet, muddy estuaries.

↔	42–46 cm (16¹⁄₂–18 in)
⚖	225–400 g (8–14 oz)
✖	Common
🦐	Crustaceans, insects
🏠	🌱 ≈ ≈≈ ≋
◉	Europe, Asia, Africa

▷ **OPEN NEST**
Avocets lay their eggs almost directly on dried mud. Colonies are vulnerable to predation despite the combined defensive efforts of the adults.

turquoise patch on breast

long, triangular wing

European bee-eater

Merops apiaster

European bee-eaters live up to their name – their food largely comprises bees and wasps with minor variations according to location and season. The birds are partially immune to the insects' venom, but take care to remove the stings before swallowing the bees. They show a preference for the non-venomous drones, particularly selecting such harmless food for their young.

Chorus singers

European bee-eaters can be seen roosting in rows on telephone wires, or in small groups on dead trees. Flying out to catch prey, they glide on flat, fully-stretched wings with bursts of quick beats. Even their calls draw attention – the chorus of rich, chirruping notes is a familiar sound in much of southern Europe. Migrating flocks sometimes number more than 100 birds, held together by almost constant calling.

Bee-eaters nest in colonies that range from a handful of nests up to hundreds, and large colonies are busy places bustling with noise and activity. Initially, the birds tend to fight while defending their nest hole and nearby perch. Breeding pairs may last for life, and their

behaviour is often interchangeable. It is only when the male feeds the female – helping to cement the pair bond and also to build up nutrients before egg-laying – that the sexes can be told apart. Four to seven eggs hatch after 20 days, and the chicks are fed in the nest for a month. The chicks continue to roost in the nest hole for a while after fledging, and families often migrate together in autumn, spending the winter in Africa.

curved, dagger-shaped bill

▷ **CONTROLLED LANDING**
Bee-eaters have sleek and streamlined bodies. Their long, triangular wings and long tails allow them to manoeuvre with ease as they accelerate, twist, and turn to catch flying insects in mid-air.

wide tail with central spike

A bee-eater must **eat** about **225 bee-sized insects every day**

△ **MANIPULATING PREY**
A bee-eater turns bees and wasps in its bill, then rubs them against a branch to remove the sting or squeeze out their venom.

△ **NESTING HOLE**
Bee-eaters dig metre-long holes in earth banks or sandy ground, digging with their bills and kicking out spoil with their feet.

↔ 28 cm (11 in)
⚖ 45–80 g (1⅝–2⅞ oz)
✖ Common
𝍬 Bees, wasps

Europe, Africa, W., C., and S. Asia

softly rounded head

TAGUS VALLEY
The great natural artery of Iberia

The principal river of Spain and Portugal passes through some of the most biodiverse landscapes in Europe, with a mixture of both European and North African plants and animals. The Tagus river begins its course in Spain's forested Alto Tajo Natural Park, cutting a series of dramatic limestone gorges. It winds past cereal fields, olive groves, and world-renowned vineyards and cork oak forests, and powers more than 60 hydroelectric dams. Then it cleaves its way through the spectacular canyons of the Monfragüe National Park, where birds of prey including the Iberian imperial eagle, black and griffon vultures, and European eagle owls are found.

in 2000. Roughly 100 km (60 miles) from the sea, the valley opens out onto a broad floodplain, and emerges into one of the largest and most important wetlands in Europe. Here, extensive saltmarsh and creeks provide prime habitats for birds including the greater flamingo, little egret, purple heron, booted eagle, and Montagu's harrier. They also provide a major stopover point for birds migrating between Europe and Africa.

Commercial forestry is banned in most of the national parks that the river passes through, and work to eradicate introduced trees in Monfragüe National Park, especially eucalypts, is ongoing.

Protected river

The river and its adjacent habitats remain protected as it passes into Portugal within the boundaries of the International Tagus Natural Park, which was created

DECLINING AMPHIBIAN
The European tree frog favours the open-canopied forests and meadows that flank sections of the Tagus. It uses pools and swamps to breed and so is affected by drainage and water pollution. Another factor in its decline is collection for the pet trade.

ENDEMIC EAGLE
The Iberian imperial eagle population fell to just 30 pairs in the 1970s as a result of habitat loss and collisions with powerlines. Thousands of pylons have since been modified and the population now numbers more than 600 adult birds.

EUROPEAN TREE FROG

IMPERIAL EAGLE

45% of Tagus fish species

Longest river in Iberia at more than 1,000 km (620 miles)

MEDITERRANEAN POND TURTLE

REPTILE REFUGE
The Mediterranean pond turtle is widely threatened by wetland drainage and pollution. It is protected under national and European law, and the Tagus Valley is considered an important stronghold for the species.

Western roe deer
Capreolus capreolus

narrow hoofs

The smallest deer native to Europe, this species was the original Bambi – Walt Disney changed his character to the US white-tailed deer for the animated film. Roe deer spend most of their time in woodlands, but may occasionally move into open ground, especially around dawn or dusk when they are most active.

Mostly alone

Solitary for most of the year, roe deer gather for the rut in late summer. After establishing territories, males chase the females around the woodland, and their hoofs flatten the underbrush, forming distinctive roe rings. Fawns are born 10 months later. The newborns lie hidden on leaf-littered ground, camouflaged in the dappled light by their white spots.

- ↔ 0.9–1 m (3–3¼ ft)
- ⚖ 11–15.5 kg (24–34 lb)
- ⊗ Common
- 🌾 Grasses, sedges, forbs
- 🏠 🌳 🌲 🌿

Europe, W. Asia

▷ **ANTLER GROWTH**
Males shed their antlers in October and start to regrow them in November. By next year's rut, the last of the velvet skin is replaced by the hard bone beneath.

Iberian ibex
Capra pyrenaica

sturdy legs

This wild goat lives in the sparse oak woodlands that grow on rocky mountain slopes. With short legs giving a low centre of gravity and wide, flexible hoofs that navigate tiny footholds, the Iberian ibex can climb out of the reach of predators. In spring, the females and their young form a separate herd from the older males.

- ↔ 97–155 cm (38–61 in)
- ⚖ 31–90 kg (69–198 lb)
- ⊗ Locally common
- 🌾 Grasses, forbs
- 🏠 ⛰ 🌿

SW. Europe

△ **PLACE OF SAFETY**
Iberian ibex climb a sheer cliff to escape predators. The herd is led to safety by an older individual that knows the best routes in the steep landscape.

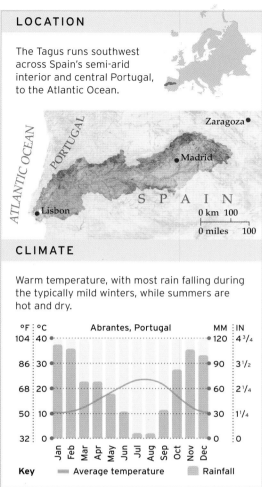
DEMAND FOR CORK
Cork oak forests have been carefully managed for centuries and comprise one of the most biodiverse habitats on earth. These unique ecosystems are vulnerable to a fall in global demand for cork.

are found nowhere else

CORK OAK

Iberian lynx
Lynx pardinus

tufts of black hair
on tip of ears

distinctive beard
around face

The Iberian lynx is the most endangered cat on Earth. Once found throughout Spain and Portugal, as well as in southern France, fewer than 250 breeding adults are left in the wild, mostly confined to two tiny areas of southern Spain. This is largely due to human impact, but the lynx's highly specialized diet and habitat requirements have also contributed to its decline.

Reliant upon rabbits

This muscular, spotted wild cat has evolved to feed mainly on one animal – the European rabbit. In summer, rabbits make up as much as 93 per cent of the lynx's diet, which means that if rabbit populations fall due to hunting or diseases, so do lynx numbers. If it has no other choice, the Iberian lynx will hunt rodents, hares, ducks, or even small deer, but it has become so specialized in its tastes that, without rabbits, its numbers inevitably decline.

Added to this is the increasing destruction of the lynx's habitat due to the rise in human population. The Iberian lynx prefers large areas of dense scrubland, such as heather interspersed with open pasture. Since lynxes are highly territorial and solitary as adults, maturing juveniles that leave their birth zones in search of their own territories face a high risk of being hit by traffic,

which in recent decades has increased dramatically in southern Spain. Even when they make it to adulthood, female lynxes will breed only after they establish their own territories.

Lynxes mate mainly during January and February, and before giving birth, a pregnant female will establish a den in a hollow tree, cave, or other sheltered spot, such as underneath dense bushes. Up to four cubs are born about two months later, although rarely more than two survive to weaning stage. Caring for her offspring puts an extra strain on the mother in many ways; a female lynx with cubs to feed needs to catch at least three rabbits a day, as opposed to the one she requires for herself. In addition, the female changes den sites frequently in order to keep the cubs safe. Like many species of wild cat, Iberian lynxes are primarily nocturnal, and spend the day resting away from the heat of the sun.

Future imperfect

Captive breeding programmes and stricter hunting and development restrictions have led to a slight increase in Iberian lynx numbers, but conservationists are uncertain whether it will survive in the wild.

↔ 85–110 cm (34–43 in)
⚖ 10–13 kg (22–29 lb)
✖ Critically endangered
⚟ Rabbits
🏠 🌲 ⛰ ≈

SW. Europe

▷ **BEARDED CAT**
Tufts of long, mainly black fur around the face give adult lynxes a bearded appearance, which makes their narrow jawline seem broader.

▷ **KILLING BITE**
Unlike larger cats, Iberian lynxes kill with a single bite, puncturing the rabbit's neck and severing its spinal cord.

▷ **MOTHER AND CUB**
Lynx cubs are weaned at 10 weeks and become independent at seven or eight months old, although they may remain with their mother for longer.

coat of stiff,
sharp spines

European hedgehog

Erinaceus europaeus

With a coat of around 8,000 spines, the European hedgehog is one of the most recognizable – and most surprising – mammals. Earthworms, slugs, and snails feature in its diet, but its preferred food is insects, preferably ants and beetles. Stinging insects have little effect on it, and so it can even eat wasps and bees. A natural but variable resistance to venomous snakes allows it to eat adders as well. Hedgehogs spend daylight hours resting in shallow nests of leaves and twigs. At night they are highly active, covering up to 2 km (1 mile) as they forage for food.

Handle with care

Mating is tricky. A male circles a female, which hisses and snorts, initially. However, if the female flattens her spines by relaxing a special muscle, the male will mate with her several times before leaving in search of other females. Each year female hedgehogs have one or two litters of two to seven hoglets, born with white spines encased in fluid-filled skin. Once the fluid dissipates, the spines are revealed and are replaced by a darker set two to three days later. The banded adult spines appear when they are two to three weeks old. When threatened, hedgehogs roll up into a tight ball. They also cover their spines with foamy saliva in a practice known as "self-anointing" – but the reason for this is uncertain.

↔ 22–27 cm (8³/₄–10¹/₂ in)
⬛ 0.9–1 kg (2–2¹/₄ lb)
✖ Common
🐛 Insects, slugs, bird eggs
🏠 🌳 🌾 🏡

Europe

△ **BUNDLED UP**
Piles of leaves, fallen logs or twigs, or garden compost heaps are favourite hibernation locations for hedgehogs in winter.

◁ **BLIND AT BIRTH**
Hoglets are born blind and remain blind, like these two youngsters, for between 11 and 14 days, at which time they begin to open their eyes.

Great crested grebe

Podiceps cristatus

Great crested grebes are renowned for their courtship rituals. One bird swims with the head and bill extended low on the water, then dives suddenly to reappear almost beneath its partner. The two perform "weed ceremonies" and dances. The nest is a mass of damp weed, which covers the eggs if a parent leaves the nest unattended. The stripey-headed chicks whistle to beg their parents for fish.

↔ 46–51 cm (18–20 in)
⬤ 0.6–1.5 kg (1¼–3¼ lb)
✖ Common
♒ Fish
🏠 🌿 ≋ ≋
◉ Europe, Asia, Africa, Australia, New Zealand

▽ **MALE AGGRESSION**
Male great crested grebes may fight over territorial boundaries during the breeding season.

Hoopoe

Upupa epops

fan-shaped crest with black tips

Hoopoes spend most of their time foraging quietly on the ground, picking and probing with their bill in search of insects. Singing hoopoes spread their crests vertically, like a fan, giving low, far-carrying "hoop-hoop-hoop" calls from a tree or rooftop. They nest in tree cavities, which quickly become foul with the chicks' droppings and rotten food waste.

↔ 28 cm (11 in)
⬤ 75 g (2½ oz)
✖ Common
♒ Insects, earthworms, snails
🏠 🌳 🌿 🏚
◉ Europe, Asia, Africa

△ **SWIRL OF COLOURS**
A hoopoe returning to its nest catches the eye in a flurry of black and white feathers.

Jewelled lizard

Timon lepidus

↔ 50–80 cm (20–32 in)
⬤ Up to 0.5 kg (1.1 lb)
✖ Near threatened
♒ Insects, frogs, mammals
🏠 🌳 ⛰ 🌿 🏚

SW. Europe

Europe's largest lizard – the jewelled, eyed, or ocillated lizard – gets its name from the blue "eyes" or rosette-like markings on its flanks. Its head and body are stocky, while the tapering tail makes up three-fifths of its length. The lizard hunts by day in mainly open, drier habitats. It hibernates in an old burrow or tree root for two to three midwinter months, and breeds in early summer. The female hides her clutch of 8–25 eggs in loose soil or undergrowth. If threatened by a predator, the jewelled lizard defends itself by opening its mouth and hissing. It also bites very hard and can be difficult to dislodge.

▽ **COLOURFUL MALE**
The male jewelled lizard is larger and heavier, and more colourful, than the female.

blue eye-shaped markings

THE ALPS
The mountainous heart of Europe

With an area of just under 200,000 sq km (77,000 sq miles), and 82 summits higher than 4,000 m (13,120 ft), the Alps form a natural climate barrier, dividing Europe into a cool, wet north and a warm, drier south. The mountains arc from France and Italy in the southwest to Austria in the east, and extend into eight countries. They rise from sea level to a peak of 4,807 m (15,771 ft) – the top of Mont Blanc, which straddles the French-Italian border.

Bountiful valleys

The Alps have several habitats, including glacial lakes, valleys, forests, high alpine meadows, and the slopes above the tree line. The meadows were created by specialist alpine plants colonizing rocky soil exposed by retreating glaciers. The region has been populated since prehistoric times, and a long history of mainly subsistence agriculture has changed the nature of the valleys and mountainsides to quite high levels. However, the steepness of the terrain and the need for trees to block avalanches means that large areas remain in a natural state. The Alps, therefore, support a rich diversity of plant and animal life, which, because of their location, are well studied. Of 13,000 plant species, 388 are endemic, and the Alps are also home to around 30,000 animal species.

Changing attitudes to wild carnivores and increasing forest cover are reflected in the gradual expansion of tiny remnant populations of grey wolf, European brown bear, and Eurasian lynx. However, these recoveries are not without problems – livestock, without protection, are easy prey for predators.

SMALL AND WHITE...
A symbol of the Alps, Edelweiss grows from 1,800 m (5,900 ft) to the snow line. The star-like pale leaves are covered in white hairs that insulate the plant from the cold and offer protection from drying winds and ultraviolet radiation.

EDELWEISS

MAKING A COMEBACK
Grey wolves were hunted to the brink of extinction across western Europe. However changes in land use, habitat improvement, and legal protection in recent decades have allowed wolves to recolonize parts of their former range.

GREY WOLF

WOODLAND BEAUTY
The spectacular Rosalia longicorn beetle has declined severely due to changes in forest management, which reduce the availability of dry dead wood in which the grubs develop. Unscrupulous collectors also take a toll.

ROSALIA LONGICORN BEETLE

Home to 75% of Europe's plant diversity > Covers 11% of Europe > More than 20%

LOCATION

The Alps cover 11 per cent of Europe's land area, including most of Austria and Switzerland.

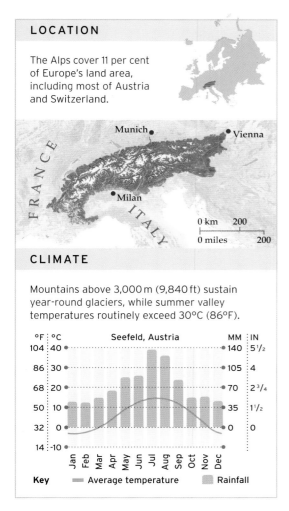

FRANCE

Munich

Vienna

ITALY

Milan

| 0 km | 200 |
| 0 miles | 200 |

CLIMATE

Mountains above 3,000 m (9,840 ft) sustain year-round glaciers, while summer valley temperatures routinely exceed 30°C (86°F).

Seefeld, Austria

°F	°C		MM	IN
104	40		140	5½
86	30		105	4
68	20		70	2¾
50	10		35	1½
32	0		0	0
14	-10			

Jan Feb Mar Apr May Jun Jul Aug Sep Oct Nov Dec

Key — Average temperature ▬ Rainfall

Alpine chamois

Rupicapra rupicapra

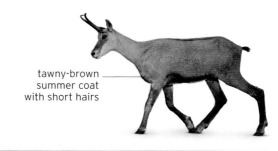

tawny-brown summer coat with short hairs

Agility is the trademark of the Alpine chamois – an adaptation to its rugged mountainous environment and a crucial survival skill when pursued by predators such as lynxes and wolves. A chamois' hoofs provide maximum traction on slippery rocks, and even in snow-covered terrain it can run, sure-footed, at speeds of up to 50 km/h (30 mph), leap upwards of 2 m (6½ ft), and span 6 m (19½ ft) in a single bound.

Lethal headgear

Both sexes have vertical horns ending in a sharp, hook-like curve, although the horns are slightly thicker in males. As well as wielding these against predators, males use their horns to fight each other for access to females. Unlike other hoofed mammals that engage in head-to-head combat, male chamois attack each other's bellies and flanks, often with fatal consequences.

↔ 1.1–1.3 m (3½–4¼ ft)
⚖ 25–60 kg (55–132 lb)
✖ Common
🌾 Grasses, forbs, leaves

C. to S. Europe

A **newborn** chamois can **stand minutes after birth**, ready to follow its mother

◁ **MOUNTAINEERING EXPERT**
The chamois' thick winter coat provides excellent insulation. Their hoofs have a thin, hard edge and softer, more pliable soles for grip, so they can negotiate the steepest, iciest terrain.

LOSS OF VARIETY
The alpine lakes are home to several subspecies of whitefish, which spawn in different levels of the lakes. Because fertilizer run-off has led to algal blooms, some of the subspecies have interbred and the whitefish diversity has declined.

of the Alps is protected

WHITEFISH

sharp claws used
to scrape earth

Alpine marmot
Marmota marmota

▷ **SPARRING MALES**
Alpine marmots will defend their territory against intruders and to maintain their dominance in the group.

Alpine marmots are large ground-dwelling members of the squirrel family. They are of a sturdier build than their tree-dwelling cousins, with powerful legs for digging into hard, rocky ground. Most of their digits have sharp claws except the thumb, which has a nail.

Burrowing down

Alpine marmots live at altitudes of 600–3,200 m (2,000–10,500 ft), but more commonly over 1,200 m (4,000 ft). They create extensive deep burrow systems in alpine meadows and high-altitude pastures above the tree line. In the summer months, they feed during the day on lush grasses and herbs, accumulating fat that will see them through the long winter hibernation. Alpine marmots spend as many as nine months in a year hibernating, sealed in their hay-lined burrows for insulation as well as safety. Adults and older offspring cuddle up to younger animals to help maintain their body temperature, which drops as low as 5°C (41°F). While hibernating, alpine marmots breathe only one to two times each minute and their heartbeat drops to 28–38 beats per minute. They emerge in April when the mountains are still covered in snow. Dominant pairs mate soon after, and the young are born a month later.

Traditionally, alpine marmots were killed because their fat was thought to help with rheumatism. They are still hunted for sport today.

▽ **MOTHER AND YOUNG**
Alpine marmots breed once a year, with litter sizes of one to seven. Mothers take on the main role of looking after the young.

↔ 45–68 cm (17³⁄₄–26³⁄₄ in)
⚖ 2.2–6.5 kg (4³⁄₄–14 lb)
✕ Common
Grass, shrubs, herbs

C. Europe

Yellow-billed chough

Pyrrhocorax graculus

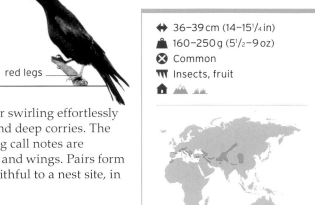

red legs

- ↔ 36–39 cm (14–15¼ in)
- ⚖ 160–250 g (5½–9 oz)
- ✖ Common
- 🍴 Insects, fruit

Europe, NW. Africa, W. to C. Asia

Skiers and climbers in the high Alps are familiar with this elegant member of the crow family, but flocks of yellow-billed choughs are sometimes seen at much lower elevations, especially in the Balkans. These choughs often visit tourist sites in search of extra scraps of food. They form flocks that are hundreds strong when feeding in green pastures or swirling effortlessly in a whirlwind over high peaks and deep corries. The yellow-billed chough's soft, lisping call notes are distinctive, as are its rounded tail and wings. Pairs form lifelong bonds and also remain faithful to a nest site, in a cave or rock crevice.

◁ **ON TOP OF THE WORLD**
Flocks of yellow-billed choughs settle on high ridges and forage on alpine pastures. In the Himalayas they can reach altitudes as high as 8,000 m (26,250 ft).

Ptarmigan

Lagopus muta

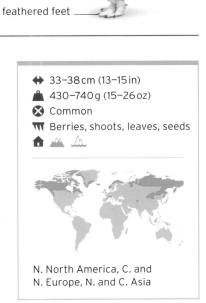

feathered feet

Unusually for a gamebird, the ptarmigan is monogamous. Pairs stay together to protect their growing chicks, although sexes often separate when they form winter flocks. A high-altitude bird in most of Europe, the ptarmigan lives much lower in the far north and northwest, commonly at sea level in Iceland. It is feared that climate change may wipe out southern populations on lower ranges, as their habitat and climate "envelope" rises above the available peaks.

Ptarmigans moult through a sequence of white, salt-and-pepper, grey-and-white, and beautiful mottled plumages, keeping pace with the change from white-out snow to the rich colours of rock, gravel, moss, and lichen in summer. Throughout the seasons they show white wings in flight, catching the light against blue skies – a vital clue for predators such as eagles.

- ↔ 33–38 cm (13–15 in)
- ⚖ 430–740 g (15–26 oz)
- ✖ Common
- 🍴 Berries, shoots, leaves, seeds

N. North America, C. and N. Europe, N. and C. Asia

▷ **SUMMER PLUMAGE**
The ptarmigan's mottled summer plumage offers camouflage, hiding it from golden eagles and Arctic foxes.

Golden eagle

Aquila chrysaetos

heavily feathered thighs

Golden eagles fly with incomparable skill and grace over mountain peaks and cliffs, and are often seen merely as dots over a distant high skyline. Their subtly curved wings are held in a shallow "V" as they soar high in the sky. They have excellent sight, several times more acute than a human's, and can see prey such as a mountain hare from 2–3 km (1¼–2 miles) away. They feed on whatever they can catch up to the size of a goose. In winter, they often eat dead sheep and deer, tearing the carcasses apart with their heavy, hooked bill. Golden eagles fare better on rich moors with plentiful prey than on colder, wetter peaks and forests.

Favourite eyrie

Pairing up for life, golden eagles have several nest sites, but one favoured nest, or eyrie, in a tree or on a cliff ledge may become up to 4 m (13 ft) deep as sticks are added to the structure each breeding season. Courtship displays include high soaring, deep switchback undulations, and stunning stoops. In these long plunges with closed wings, the eagles reach extremely high speeds. The female usually lays two eggs, but the first-hatched chick often attacks its younger sibling, and frequently only the stronger, bigger chick survives.

Golden eagles can live for up to 38 years in the wild. However, in some parts of their range they are persecuted by humans and are under threat from activities such as illegal shooting, trapping, and the use of poisoned bait.

broad wings for soaring and braking

↔ 75–90 cm (29½–35½ in)
⚖ 3–6.5 kg (6½–14 lb)
✖ Common
🍖 Hares, grouse, carrion
🏠 ⛰ 🌵 🌾

North America, Europe, Asia, N. Africa

△ **IN FOR THE KILL**
With its wings, tail, and talons stretched wide, this golden eagle swoops down onto its prey, attacking the animal from behind.

Midwife toad

Alytes obstetricans

Looking much like a common European toad at first glance, the midwife toad has a more pointed snout and vertical pupils. The toad's name refers to the way this small amphibian carries around fertilized eggs to keep them out of harm's way while they develop. However, the name is slightly misleading in that it is the male, not the female, that looks after the next generation. During mating, the male glues the string of eggs to his rump and then delivers them to a pond a few weeks later in time for the tadpoles to hatch.

▷ **PATERNAL CARE**
The male midwife toad may carry the eggs of more than one mate. It secretes antibiotic mucus to protect the developing young.

↔ 3–5 cm (1¼–2 in)
☁ Spring and summer
✖ Locally common
🍖 Insects
🏠 🌳 🌾 ≈ ≈ 🏚

W. to C. Europe

upcurved
wingtips

powerful feet
for killing

▽ **SEEING OFF A FOX**
This immature golden eagle is
still big and strong enough to
chase away a red fox that has
tried to steal its meal.

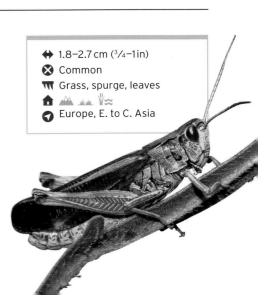

Apollo butterfly

Parnassius apollo

red eyespot
on hind wing

△ **NECTAR OF THE GODS**
Adult Apollos can be seen drinking
nectar from flowers in mountain
meadows at the height of summer.

Although widespread across
Europe's mountainous regions,
this unusual member of the
swallowtail family is an
endangered species. Its colour
pattern of pale wings dotted
with black and red spots is
so variable that dozens of
subspecies have been identified,
some of which are restricted to a
single alpine valley. Females lay
their eggs close to plants such as
stonecrop; the caterpillars eat
the leaves when they hatch.

↔ 5–10 cm (2–4 in)
✖ Vulnerable
🌱 Leaves; nectar
🏠 ⛰
◉ Europe, W. Asia

Large mountain grasshopper

Stauroderus scalaris

This is the largest species of
grasshopper in Europe, and in
late summer, alpine meadows
resound with its whirring
stridulations, or "songs".
The bright green males sing
to attract the larger, drab
brown females.

↔ 1.8–2.7 cm (³⁄₄–1 in)
✖ Common
🌱 Grass, spurge, leaves
🏠 ⛰ 🌾 〰
◉ Europe, E. to C. Asia

▷ **PREPARED TO JUMP**
Grasshoppers have long wings,
but instead of flying away from
danger they usually jump, using
their large, powerful hind legs.

BAVARIAN FOREST
Europe's original deep dark wood

Germany's Bavarian Forest National Park and the Czech Republic's Bohemian forest combine to form the largest area of forest remaining in central Europe. The forest cloaks rolling mountains that, despite being relatively low, constitute a continental divide from which the headwaters of the Danube, Vlatva, and Elbe rivers drain in different directions. The mountains, gentle hills, curved valleys, and pockets of hard granite rock are evidence of a land carved by glaciers during the last ice age.

Ancient woodland
Much of the Bavarian forest is old-growth and undisturbed by humans, and conservation work in Germany's first national park aims to keep it untouched. Its plants and animals include several ice age relict species, such as the boreal owl, three-toed woodpecker, Norwegian wolf spider, and quillwort, a scarce semi-aquatic fern.

The Bavarian forest has acidic soil and water. This is partly due to its cool, wet climate, but also to the overwhelming dominance of trees such as spruce, fir, and beech, which form closed canopies that block sunlight and warmth. These conditions limit opportunities for ground plants and some insect species to thrive, but fungi, mosses, and invertebrates associated with dead wood abound. Indeed, the forest boasts more than 1,300 species of mushroom, bracket fungus, and puffball. The ancient forest is also home to several large animals, including brown bears, grey wolves, lynxes, wild cats, roe deer, wild boar, capercaillies, and eagle owls.

DORMOUSE DUO
Two native dormice share the forest, using different zones to avoid competition. The tiny, golden-furred hazel dormouse favours a complex matrix of low shrubs, while the much larger, silver-grey edible dormouse lives in the forest canopy.

HAZEL DORMOUSE

LINKED FORTUNES
The cyclic boom and bust of roe deer populations has a dramatic effect on the reintroduced Eurasian lynx. Severe winters reduce deer numbers so the lynx lose out to the larger wolves, which work cooperatively to drive out competitors.

EURASIAN LYNX

PORCELAIN FUNGUS

Germany's first national park, created in 1970 > **95% forest cover** > **3,693 invertebrat**

CLEVER COMPETITOR
The porcelain fungus is a beechwood specialist. Its pale fruiting bodies appear in autumn on dead wood, into which it secretes a chemical known as strobilurin. This inhibits the growth of other fungi, thus reducing competition.

LOCATION

The Bavarian forest straddles the border between Germany and the Czech Republic, and becomes the Bohemian forest.

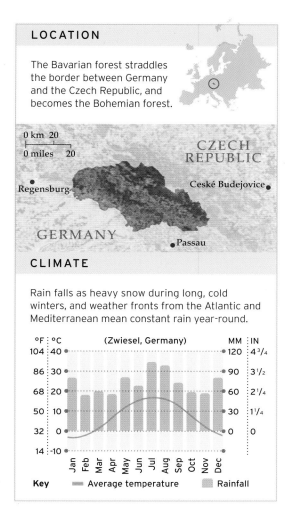

0 km 20
0 miles 20

CZECH REPUBLIC

Regensburg

Ceské Budejovice

GERMANY

Passau

CLIMATE

Rain falls as heavy snow during long, cold winters, and weather fronts from the Atlantic and Mediterranean mean constant rain year-round.

°F	°C	(Zwiesel, Germany)	MM	IN
104	40		120	4³/₄
86	30		90	3¹/₂
68	20		60	2¹/₄
50	10		30	1¹/₄
32	0		0	0
14	-10			

Jan Feb Mar Apr May Jun Jul Aug Sep Oct Nov Dec

Key — Average temperature ▢ Rainfall

European pine marten
Martes martes

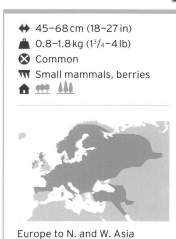

long, slender body

Pine martens can live in any tree-filled environment. Powerful forelimbs and strong claws allow them to leap from tree to tree in pursuit of small animals such as squirrels. Most of their hunting occurs on the ground, however, where they forage between dusk and dawn.

↔ 45–68 cm (18–27 in)
⚖ 0.8–1.8 kg (1³/₄–4 lb)
✖ Common
🍴 Small mammals, berries
🏠 🌳 🌲

Europe to N. and W. Asia

◁ **SNOW PATROL**
In winter, pads on the marten's soles are covered with fur, which insulates its feet and provides traction in the snow.

European badger
Meles meles

Badgers live in groups of six or more members, sharing the same sett – a system of underground tunnels, chambers, and toilet areas. Setts may evolve into huge networks over time. A sett is ruled by a dominant male, or boar, and one breeding female. The pair mate throughout the year, but a litter of one to five cubs is not born until February.

↔ 56–90 cm (22–35 in)
⚖ 10–16 kg (22–35¹/₂ lb)
✖ Common
🍴 Earthworms, fruit, birds
🏠 🌳 🌲 ⛰ 🌾

Europe to W. Asia

◁ **WHITE-STRIPED IDENTITY**
The badger's black-and-white striped face makes it instantly recognizable, but ginger-coated and albino (all-white) badgers have also been found.

short, powerful legs

MOSS SANCTUARY
Compared to flowering plants and ferns, the diversity of mosses in the national park is extraordinary. At around 490 species, this is 42 per cent of mosses in Germany. They thrive because of the minimal human disturbance.

species recorded here

HAIRCAP MOSS

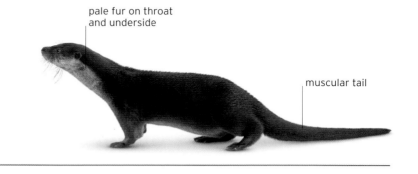

pale fur on throat
and underside

muscular tail

Eurasian otter

Lutra lutra

Webbed feet and the ability to close their ears and noses underwater may mark them out as a semi-aquatic member of the weasel family, but oddly enough, Eurasian or common otter cubs are not naturally drawn to water. In fact, female otters often have to drag their protesting cubs in for their first swim at around 16 weeks of age. However, once the initial shock has worn off, they quickly learn to love the water, spending hours play-fighting together in the shallows near the holt, or den, where they were born.

Staying dry

Once grown, their double-layered coats trap air bubbles for insulation in frigid waters, and the waterproof outer layer keeps them dry. Slender bodies and thick, tapered tails make them exteremely graceful swimmers, highly skilled at catching fish. They eat shellfish (particularly crabs), amphibians, and even water birds such as ducks. The year that the cubs spend with their mother is the longest time Eurasian otters live in a group. Otherwise, apart from mating, when a male and female may spend a week or so together, these highly vocal mammals lead solitary lives, staking out territories of 1.6–6.4 km (1–4 miles) along rivers, estuaries, lakes, streams, and ocean shores. Otters mark their territories with spraints, or droppings, usually on top of rocks, driftwood, or other debris near the water's edge.

On the lookout

Spraints and tracks are often the only signs of these highly vocal carnivores, because acute hearing, smell, and sight mean otters are more likely to be alert to a human being's presence and duck out of sight before the latter is aware they were ever nearby. The positioning of their eyes, ears, and noses towards the top of the head also means they can keep their bodies hidden from view underwater while they watch, until the coast is clear.

↔ 57–70 cm (22½–28 in)

🏋 7–10 kg (15–22 lb)

✗ Near threatened

🐾 Fish, ducks, water voles

🏠 🌾 〰 ▬

Europe, Asia

Otters that **hunt in coastal waters** need fresh water to **remove salt from their coat**

◁ **CLEAR VIEW**
Thick, double-layered fur keeps otters warm in icy conditions, and their long whiskers, called vibrissae, help them to locate prey in murky water.

△ **FRESH CATCH**
Fish make up about 80 per cent of a Eurasian otter's diet. Adults eat up to 15 per cent of their body weight in fish per day.

◁ **UNDERWATER DIVE**
Although the Eurasian otter is an exceptionally agile swimmer, it cannot hold its breath for long. Average dives last no more than 30 seconds.

Red fox
Vulpes vulpes

back of ear often black

long, bushy tail, or brush

Found throughout the northern hemisphere from sea level to 4,500 m (14,750 ft), in deserts, mountains, forests, farmland, and city centres, red foxes are the most widespread wild canines on the planet. They tailor their behaviour and diets to suit highly diverse habitats. Small mammals make up a large part of the red fox's diet, but if rabbits, voles, and mice are scarce, it will eats birds, eggs, earthworms, beetles, and wild fruit such as blackberries.

Opportunistic hunters

Intelligent and territorial, these solitary hunters search for food from dusk until dawn. They are always ready to exploit landfill sites, compost heaps, dustbins, bird feeders, and other easy sources of food. Excellent vision and a keen sense of smell give all 44 subspecies of red foxes an edge when it comes to survival, as does a cooperative lifestyle when raising their young.

Once a dominant pair establishes a territory, mating occurs in early winter. The vixen digs out a den, or earth, in which she gives birth to four to six cubs around two months later. For the first three weeks, she stays with the cubs, relying on the male to bring her food.

▽ **MATED PAIR**
A vixen (left) and dog fox (right) race each other through deep snow in early winter, having spotted a potential meal.

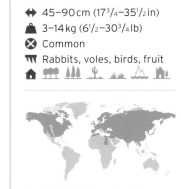

↔ 45–90 cm (17³/₄–35¹/₂ in)

⬛ 3–14 kg (6¹/₂–30³/₄ lb)

✖ Common

🐾 Rabbits, voles, birds, fruit

Arctic, North America, Europe, Asia, and N. Africa

Wild boar
Sus scrofa

↔ 0.9–1.8 m (3–6 ft)
⚖ 44–200 kg (97–440 lb)
✗ Common
🍴 Plant matter, eggs, rodents

Europe, Asia, N. Africa

The ancestor of most domestic pigs, the wild boar is an example of extreme species success. Now found on every continent except Antarctica, the highly adaptable wild boar is so prolific that it is often considered a pest, largely due to its impact on agricultural landscapes.

Sounders and solitary boars

Whether wild boar are solitary or social depends on their sex. Sows live in herds or "sounders" made up mainly of other females and their offspring. Sows only leave a sounder to give birth, returning as soon as their piglets – litter sizes vary from three to 12 – are large enough to travel with the sounder. Sows may have two litters a year, and will protect all piglets in the sounder. Males only come into contact with other boar to mate, although they sometimes join sounders to feed.

coat of thick, coarse hair

▷ **BRISTLY PIG**
Many wild boar have longer bristles on their backs that raise when they are threatened. Hence they are often called razorbacks in North America.

▷ **STRIPED PIGLETS**
Sows give birth to striped piglets that live in the sounder and are protected by the mother. Males leave their birth sounder at one or two years of age.

Black woodpecker
Dryocopus martius

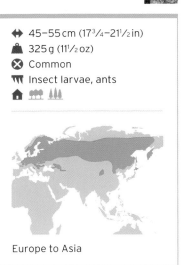

stiff tail used to maintain balance

Large woodpeckers have dagger-like beaks, crested heads, and stiff tails. A long outer toe turns outwards or back, rather than the usual three-toes-forward, one-back shape of other perching birds, giving a better grip for climbing trees. Black woodpeckers need big trees – pine, oak, beech, or mixed forests are all occupied. In winter, they prefer wooded parks and gardens. They chisel a new nesting cavity at the start of each breeding season. The eggs hatch in 12–14 days and the young can fledge after 24–28 days.

Noisy neighbours

Black woodpecker calls are loud and frequent, with strident, discordant laughing notes and high, long calls. They proclaim their ownership of a territory by "drumming" – a loud, deep, staccato sound produced by a rapid drumroll beat of the billtip against a branch.

△ **HARD AT WORK**
A female black woodpecker, with a smaller red cap than the male, chips away bark and living wood to get at the beetle larvae and carpenter ants inside.

↔ 45–55 cm (17³⁄₄–21¹⁄₂ in)
⚖ 325 g (11¹⁄₂ oz)
✗ Common
🍴 Insect larvae, ants

Europe to Asia

Great crested newt

Triturus cristatus

This is the largest newt species in northern Europe. In summer, great crested newts hunt on land by night. In winter, they hibernate in sheltered spots or at the bottom of their breeding pools. Males court by arching their bodies and wafting their paddle-shaped tails. Females lay their eggs on submerged plants, each egg wrapped in a leaf for protection. The larvae hatch after three weeks and transform into the air-breathing form after about four months.

- ↔ 10–14 cm (4–5½ in)
- ☁ Spring
- ✖ Common
- 〰 Larvae, worms
- 🏠 〜
- ◉ Europe, C. Asia

▽ **BREEDING CREST**
Females are larger than males, but only males grow a crest during the spring breeding season.

distinctive black markings

Pale tussock

Calliteara pudibunda

heavily feathered antennae of male

crescent-shaped marking

This chunky moth is one of the most widespread moth species. It lives in the woodlands of Europe, where the adults (which do not feed) can be seen flying at night in late spring and early summer. Males use their antennae to sweep the air for the scent of mates. Eggs are laid on trees and hatch the following spring.

- ↔ 5–7 cm (2–2¾ in)
- ✖ Common
- 〰 Tree foliage
- 🏠 🌳 🏞
- ◉ Europe

▷ **TUFTED CATERPILLAR**
Some of the bristles are bunched into four distinct tufts.

- ↔ Average 12 mm (½ in)
- ✖ Common
- 〰 Pollen, nectar, honey
- 🏠 🌳 🌵 🏞

Europe, W., C., and SW. Asia, W., E., and S. Africa

△ **HARD AT WORK**
During construction of a new honeycomb, honeybee workers use their bodies to form a bridge across the gap.

▷ **PACKING POLLEN**
A forager bee packs pollen into her pollen baskets – a hollow section of each hind leg caged in by bristles.

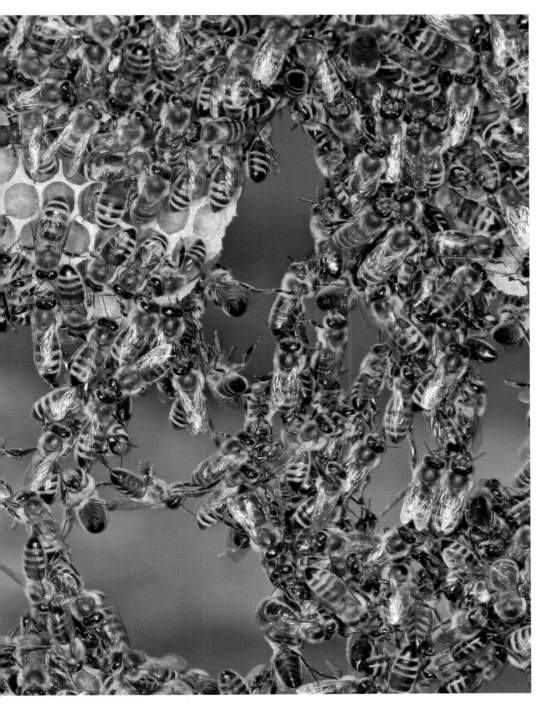

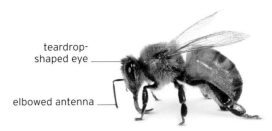

teardrop-
shaped eye

elbowed antenna

European honey bee

Apis mellifera

Honeybees pollinate many flowering plants, including dozens of human food plants. They are social insects that live in wild colonies and in commercial hives, which are kept for honey production. Their natural range includes Africa, Europe, and the Middle East, but they have been introduced commercially into most parts of the world. Each colony is founded by a single queen, who rears her infertile daughters as workers. The workers extend and maintain the nest, raise more sisters, and make foraging trips to collect nectar and pollen from flowers.

Division of labour

A nest is typically built in a tree hollow. It consists of honeycomb – sheets of hexagonal cells made from wax. The cells are used as nurseries for larvae (and later, pupae) and for storing nectar and pollen. Honey is produced by workers regurgitating nectar and then fanning it until it dries out. Pollen is stored separately and provides food for the developing larvae. Honey is the main source of food for the rest of the colony.

Worker bees are infertile females that live for around four to five weeks. As they age, they graduate from duties in the nest to taking off on nectar-gathering flights to flowers. Foragers communicate the location of flowers to other workers back at the colony by a figure of eight "dance". In winter, numbers fall to 5,000, with the workers surviving on honey stores.

When a colony reaches a certain size, the queen flies off, taking half the workers with her. She leaves behind a new queen who flies off and mates with several males, collecting enough sperm to sustain her through a life that can be as long as five years, before flying back and taking over the colony.

△ **WORKER BEE PUPAE**
It takes 11 days for a worker bee egg to transform into a larva and then a pupa. The adult emerges at 21 days.

80,000 bees live in a **colony** in summer

enlarged, pronged mandibles of male

Stag beetle

Lucanus cervus

This large forest insect is famed for the enormous mandibles of the male, which are used in jousting fights. They resemble the antlers used by male deer in battles of strength over potential mates, hence the name stag beetle. Females are smaller than males, and although their mandibles are more discreet, they can grip more strongly than the males. Like all beetles, both sexes have a hard, armoured shell for protection.

Fuelled by fat reserves

Adult stag beetles do not feed. Instead, they rely on their fat reserves built up while they were larvae living underground. They will, however, occasionally sip tree sap or juices from decomposing fruit using their smaller hairy mouthparts. Otherwise, the adults devote themselves to mating.

The males dig their way out of the ground in May or June, a week or so before the females. They establish a mating territory and use their "antlers" to fight off any late arrivals hoping to muscle in. The females walk from territory to territory, during which time they mate with several males. Adult life rarely lasts more than three months. The last thing a female does before she dies is find a suitable piece of rotting wood – usually decaying tree stumps or roots – where she lays about 20 eggs. Sometimes, females return to the site where they were larvae to lay their eggs.

Growing up underground

In total, a stag beetle lives for about six years. Most of this time is spent as a larva, eating wood rotting underground. The eggs hatch in August, and the tiny orange-headed grubs begin a five-year feeding session. It takes this long for a grub to reach full size and build up the crucial fat supply for the adult phase. When ready, the grub builds a cocoon chamber out of chewed wood fibres and turns into a pupa. In this form, it remains immobile for at least two months as its larval body is broken down and rebuilt as an adult. The pupa is protected by a hard case and the sex of the beetle can be identified – the large mandibles of a male are already visible. Pupation occurs in autumn, but once emerged, the adult stays underground for the ensuing winter, readying itself to emerge the following summer.

The stag beetle population across the world is rapidly declining for many reasons, including changes in forest management that has led to the removal of dead timber. Increased urbanization is also a threat.

Stag beetles spend almost **their entire lives underground** as larvae

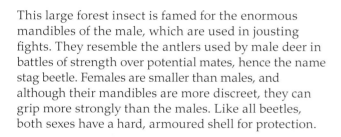

- ↔ 7.5 cm (3 in)
- ⊗ Near threatened
- 𝕎 Dead wood, sap, fruit juices
- 🏠 🌲 🌲

Europe, Asia

▷ JOUSTING MALES

The stag beetle fights to overturn the opposition. The mandibles have a series of prongs that give a good grip as the fighters try to flip their rival. However, injuries are rare.

◁ FREQUENT FLIER

Despite their large size and cumbersome appearance, stag beetles are frequent fliers. The males fly more often than the females, as they patrol their territories.

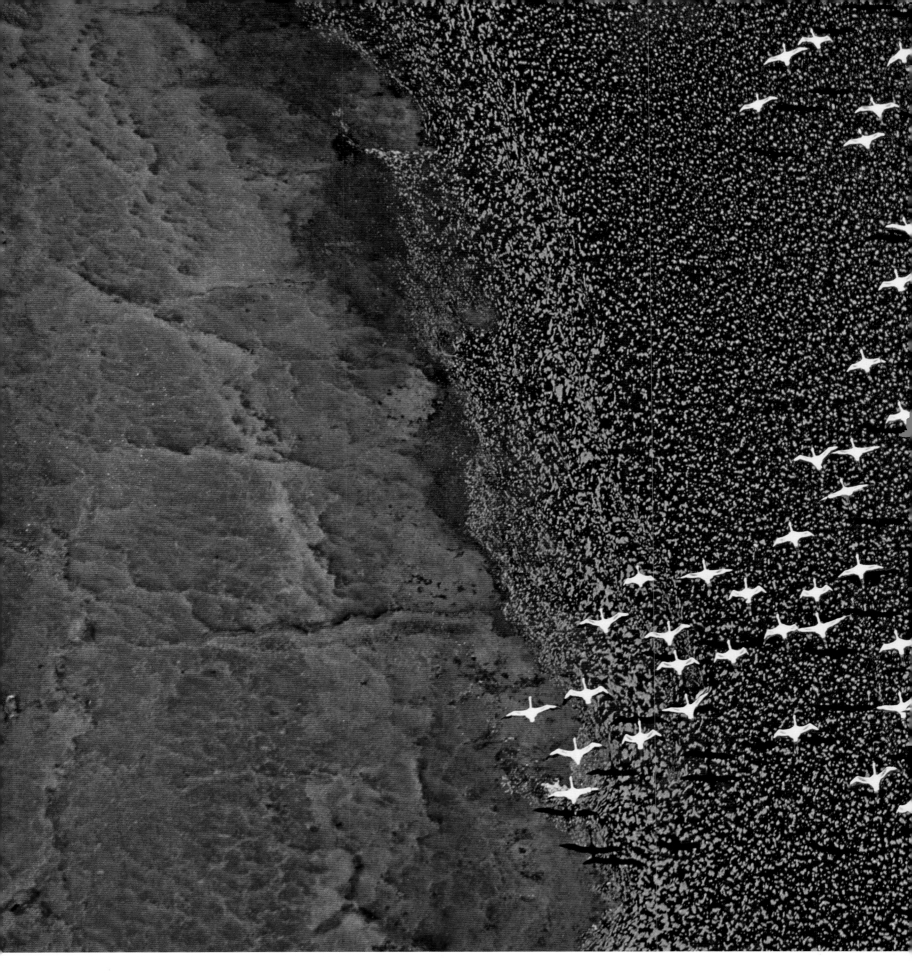

Great Rift Valley
Millions of lesser flamingos feed and breed around the edges of alkaline lakes in East Africa's Great Rift Valley. Flocks of adults fly in formation every day in search of fresh water to drink.

Africa

A SUNBAKED LAND
Africa

The second-largest continent, Africa covers 30 million sq km (12 million sq miles), and accounts for more than 20 per cent of the world's land area. Dominated by sunbaked landscapes and tropical forest, Africa is famous for its wildlife. Even the rift valley lakes boast a spectacular diversity of cichlid fish that is every bit as impressive to zoologists as the large mammals of the Serengeti savannas are to tourists. Africa's habitats are some of the planet's most productive and biodiverse and include wetlands, uplands, and several major deserts as well as the forests and grasslands.

The eastern mountain ranges are part of the East African Rift, where the African plate is slowly splitting into two parts called the Somali and Nubian plates. The Great Rift Valley is one of its main arms. The Drakensberg range in South Africa marks the edge of a plateau that covers most of the south and east.

The continent is drained by several great rivers, including the Nile, Niger, Congo, Zambezi, Limpopo, and Orange. Some rivers never reach the sea. The Okavango feeds a vast inland wetland, while the Chari drains into Lake Chad in the Sahel from which the water evaporates or seeps into the ground.

ATLAS MOUNTAINS

The Atlas Mountains formed in a region where the African plate is colliding with the Eurasian plate to the north. The highest point is Mount Toubkal in Morocco.

KEY DATA

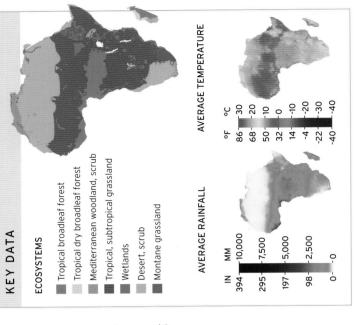

ECOSYSTEMS

- Tropical broadleaf forest
- Tropical dry broadleaf forest
- Mediterranean woodland, scrub
- Tropical, subtropical grassland
- Wetlands
- Desert, scrub
- Montane grassland

AVERAGE TEMPERATURE

°F	°C
86	30
68	20
50	10
32	0
14	-10
-4	-20
-22	-30
-40	-40

AVERAGE RAINFALL

IN	MM
394	10,000
295	7,500
197	5,000
98	2,500
0	0

SAHARA DESERT

The world's largest desert began to form 7 million years ago and is still growing. It covers about 30 per cent of Africa's land area, limiting the north–south distribution of many species. Animals specially adapted to the dry conditions include the jerboa and fennec fox.

NILE DELTA

The vast Nile Delta fans out along 240 km (150 miles) of Egypt's Mediterranean coast. Its deep alluvial soils have been farmed for thousands of years.

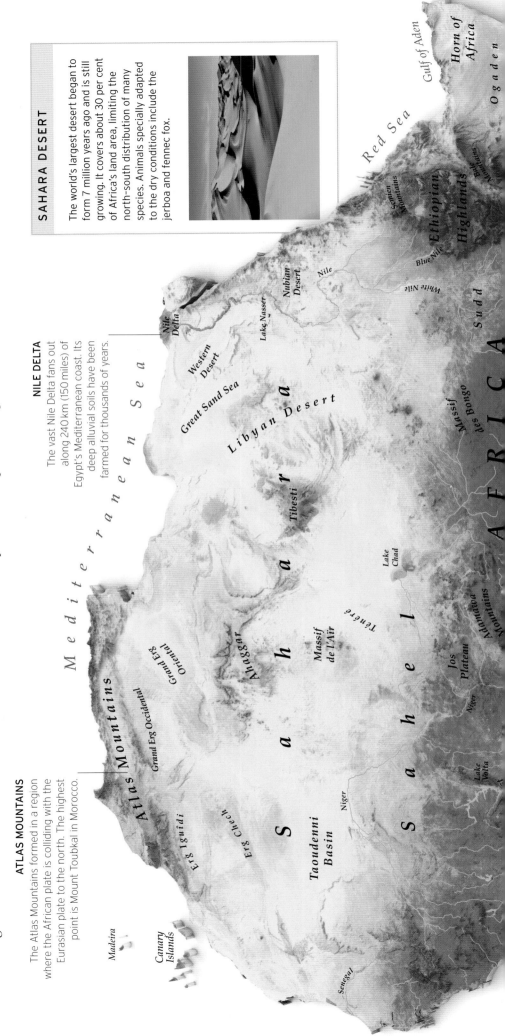

Gulf of Aden

Horn of Africa

Ogaden

Red Sea

Semien Mountains

Ethiopian Highlands

Blue Nile Mountains

Blue Nile

Nile

White Nile

Sudd

Nubian Desert

Lake Nasser

AFRICA

Nile Delta

Western Desert

Great Sand Sea

Libyan Desert

Mediterranean Sea

Tibesti

Massif des Bongo

Lake Chad

Adamawa Mountains

Ténéré

Ahaggar

Massif de l'Aïr

Jos Plateau

Niger

Lake Volta

Sahel

Grand Erg Oriental

Grand Erg Occidental

Atlas Mountains

Erg Iguidi

Erg Chech

Taoudenni Basin

Niger

Madeira

Canary Islands

Senegal

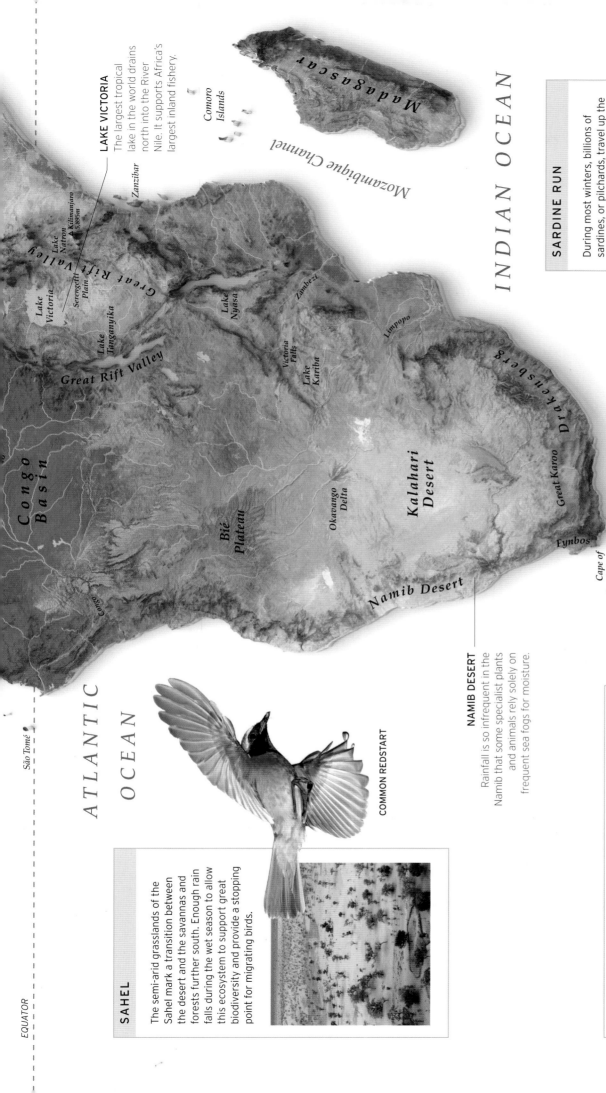

São Tomé

ATLANTIC OCEAN

Congo Basin

Congo

Bié Plateau

Great Rift Valley

Lake Victoria

Lake Tanganyika

Serengeti Plain

Lake Natron

▲ Kilimanjaro 5,895m

Zanzibar

Lake Nyasa

Zambezi

Victoria Falls

Lake Kariba

Okavango Delta

Kalahari Desert

Namib Desert

Limpopo

Drakensberg

Great Karoo

Fynbos

Cape of Good Hope

LAKE VICTORIA
The largest tropical lake in the world drains north into the River Nile. It supports Africa's largest inland fishery.

Comoro Islands

Mozambique Channel

Madagascar

INDIAN OCEAN

SARDINE RUN
During most winters, billions of sardines, or pilchards, travel up the east coast of South Africa. Single shoals stretch for miles, and are the target of spectacular feeding frenzies attracting predators such as sharks, dolphins, and birds.

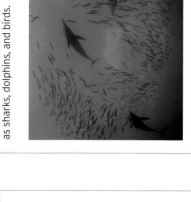

FYNBOS
This band of coastal and upland heath, flourishing in the Mediterranean climate of the Western Cape of South Africa, is a central component of the Cape Floristic Region. This tiny ecoregion is unmatched in biodiversity and endemic plants per square kilometre. Of 9,000 plant species known in the area, a staggering 6,200 occur nowhere else.

NAMIB DESERT
Rainfall is so infrequent in the Namib that some specialist plants and animals rely solely on frequent sea fogs for moisture.

SAHEL
The semi-arid grasslands of the Sahel mark a transition between the desert and the savannas and forests further south. Enough rain falls during the wet season to allow this ecosystem to support great biodiversity and provide a stopping point for migrating birds.

COMMON REDSTART

FEATURED ECOREGIONS
- Ethiopian Highlands ›› **p178-83**
  Montane grassland, woodland
- Great Rift Valley Lakes ›› **p184-91**
  Freshwater lakes, soda lakes
- Serengeti Savannas ›› **p192-207**
  Tropical grassland
- Congo Basin ›› **p208-17**
  Tropical, subtropical moist broadleaf forests
- Okavango Delta ›› **p218-27**
  Wetland; inland river delta
- Kalahari Desert ›› **p228-35**
  Desert, scrub
- Madagascan Dry Forest ›› **p236-43**
  Tropical dry broadleaf forest

ETHIOPIAN HIGHLANDS
A hotspot of unique species in the roof of Africa

The largest area of land above 1,500 m (4,920 ft) in the whole of Africa, the Ethiopian Highlands rise to about 4,550 m (nearly 15,000 ft) in the northeast of the continent. The region contains the Semien Mountains in the northwest and the Bale Mountains in the southeast, with part of the Great Rift Valley separating the two.

Loss of habitat
The area contains three distinct regions, differentiated by altitude. Up to about 1,800 m (5,900 ft) is dense montane forest, where the natural vegetation is dominated by evergreen trees, including myrrh, acacia, and juniper, and other conifers, with a shrub layer that includes wild coffee. Between 1,800 and 3,000 m (5,900 and 9,840 ft) is a region of montane grassland and woodland, which comprises a mosaic of forest, thicket, grassland, and brushlands and is home to ibex and gelada baboons.

Above the treeline, from 3,000 m (9,840 ft) upwards, is montane moorland. The natural vegetation of this area is dominated by alpine shrubs and herbs. The densest collection of endemic wildlife, including mountain nyala and the world's rarest dog species, the Ethiopian wolf, is found here. All three regions have been severely impacted by human population increase and activities, mainly farming and unsustainable use of natural resources. As a result, an estimated 97 per cent of the area's original habitat has been lost. Therefore, many of the plants and animals are being intensively studied and protected.

ARBOREAL BIRD
The colourful Prince Ruspoli's turaco feeds largely on figs and juniper berries. It is endemic to the Ethiopian Highlands, and its close association with the now fragmented montane forests of lower altitudes make it vulnerable to extinction.

PRINCE RUSPOLI'S TURACO

WINGED DRAGON
The Ethiopian highlander dragonfly is found only by clear mountain streams surrounded by forest, but its habitat is disappearing as a result of forest clearance and water pollution, and this endemic species is in danger of disappearing.

ETHIOPIAN HIGHLAN

Only 3% of the

Has 20 species of endemic mammals and 30 species of endemic birds

GIANT LOBELIA

ALL TOGETHER NOW
The giant *Lobelia* can grow to about 9 m (30 ft) high when flowering. Groups of *Lobelia* flower simultaneously after several years' growth, all producing a single flowering spike. They shed millions of seeds, then the plants die.

LOCATION

Northeastern Africa, within the Tigray, Amhara, and Oromia regions of Ethiopia, reaching into Eritrea in the north.

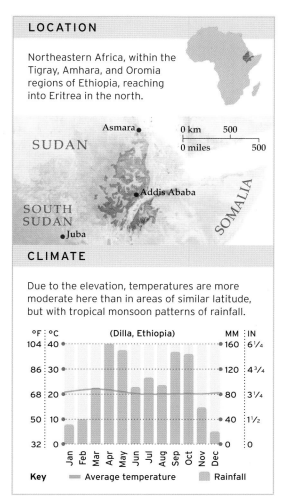

Asmara

0 km 500

0 miles 500

SUDAN

SOUTH SUDAN

Addis Ababa

Juba

SOMALIA

CLIMATE

Due to the elevation, temperatures are more moderate here than in areas of similar latitude, but with tropical monsoon patterns of rainfall.

°F	°C	(Dilla, Ethiopia)	MM	IN
104	40		160	6¼
86	30		120	4¾
68	20		80	3¼
50	10		40	1½
32	0		0	0

Jan Feb Mar Apr May Jun Jul Aug Sep Oct Nov Dec

Key — Average temperature — Rainfall

UNDERGROUND GIANT
The giant mole rat lives alone, but in densities of up to 6,000 per sq km (15,000 per sq mile), so each burrow system overlaps many others. Insects and worms disturbed by the mole rats are eaten by alpine chats, which, in return, warn if Ethiopian wolves approach.

Original vegetation remains

GIANT MOLE RAT

Ethiopian klipspringer

Oreotragus saltatrixoides

Unlike many other antelope species, where horns are either absent or smaller in females, Ethiopian klipspringer females grow the same spiked horns as the males. Klipspringers do not form herds, but move around their rock-strewn habitat in breeding pairs, marking territory with dung. The young are kept in hiding for two months and then follow the parents on feeding forays.

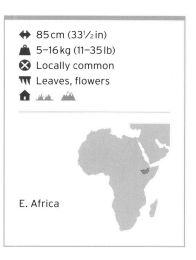

↔ 85 cm (33½ in)
⚖ 5–16 kg (11–35 lb)
⊗ Locally common
🌿 Leaves, flowers

E. Africa

speckled coat blends with rocks

▷ **AGILE AND STURDY**
The klipspringer's "high-heeled" hoofs allow it to perch all four feet in the smallest rocks as it moves around its rugged habitat.

short legs and narrow hoofs

Mountain nyala

Tragelaphus buxtoni

spiralled horns

A relative of the kudu, not the lowland nyala, the mountain nyala migrates to higher altitudes in the dry season, but descends again when heavy rains arrive. Births peak after the end of the rains, with calves staying with their mother's herd until they are around two years old. Only males grow the tall "lyrate" horns.

↔ 1.9–2 m (6¼–6½ ft)
⚖ 150–320 kg (330–705 lb)
⊗ Endangered
🌿 Leaves, grasses, ferns, lichen

E. Africa

◁ **RELATED FEMALES**
Mountain nyalas live in small herds made up of females and their young. Mature males join them for the breeding season.

Gelada

Theropithecus gelada

adult males have long, thick mane

Geladas are cousins of the more common savanna baboons, which are found throughout much of sub-Saharan Africa. Geladas were widespread in Africa 50,000 years ago, but have gradually been squeezed out by competing subspecies of savanna baboon as well as human pressure. Today, geladas survive only in their remote highland refuge. They can forage on grasses – including roots – more efficiently than other baboons, surviving almost entirely on the grass of high-altitude meadows in the mountains of Ethiopia. A garnish of bulbs, seeds, fruit, and insects supplements this diet.

Signal patches

Most baboons have colourful patches of bare skin on their rears, which help to communicate mood, dominance, and breeding condition. Geladas spend most of their time sitting down, with their rumps hidden, while foraging on grasses within reach of their long arms. Perhaps this is why they have developed bare red patches on their chests. The male's patch mimics the female's, which mimics her own sexual skin and genitals with remarkable accuracy. This colourful area is used in both sexual and social interaction. "Social presenting" – a quick hind-end flash – among primates is a frequent peaceable signal, reducing aggression. Mimicry by males and non-oestrous females helps enhance the message. Unless you are a gelada, however, it is hard to glean from a signal that a female is ready to mate.

Bachelor boys and bands

Geladas form herds several hundreds strong. Many males live in bachelor groups around the fringes of the herd until they are old enough to compete for dominance. The herd is comprised of several reproductive groups, or bands, each of which consists of an older male and his harem of females. They communicate using subtle facial signals and not-so-subtle "lip flicks" (see far right).

Geladas are also called **bleeding-heart baboons** after the **red patch on their chest**

△ **MOTHER AND INFANT**
Born helpless, baby geladas clamber over and ride on their mothers about a month after birth. Gelada families spend much time grooming.

▷ **ON TOP OF THE WORLD**
Geladas feed in meadows in Ethiopia, above 1,700 m (5,600 ft). They sleep in high rocky cliffs close by.

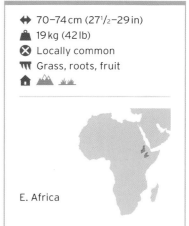

↔ 70–74 cm (27½–29 in)
⚖ 19 kg (42 lb)
❌ Locally common
〿 Grass, roots, fruit
🏠 ⛰ 〰

E. Africa

△ **STRIKING A POSE**
A male curls his lip in a "lip flick", exposing his gums and impressive teeth. This warns off rivals and reduces the need for physical aggression.

◁ **IMPRESSIVE MANE**
An adaptation to high-altitude cold, geladas are very heavily furred, especially around the head and upper body. The thick mane also increases the apparent size of a charging male.

Ethiopian wolf

Canis simensis

long, slender legs

A pack animal that mainly hunts alone, Africa's only wolf species is also the continent's rarest predator, and the world's most threatened canine: fewer than 500 adults are thought to remain in the wild. With its distinctive red coat and pointed muzzle, the Ethiopian wolf more closely resembles a fox. While on rare occasions a pack will work together to hunt a hare, this wolf is a specialist rat-catcher – up to 95 per cent of its diet consists of small rats that live in the high African heathlands.

↔ 84–100 cm (33–39¼ in)
⚖ 14–30 kg (31–66 lb)
⊗ Endangered
⫿⫿⫿ Rodents
🏠 ⷍ

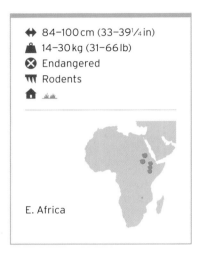

E. Africa

◁ **PACK LUNCH**
Pups mob adults until food is regurgitated for them to eat. All the adults in a pack care for the pups, although only the alpha female breeds.

↔ 1–1.2 m (3¼–4 ft)
⚖ 4.5–7 kg (10–15½ lb)
⊗ Near threatened
⫿⫿⫿ Bones, carrion, tortoises
🏠 ⛰ ⷍ 🏠

Europe, Asia, N., E., and Southern Africa

▽ **CLAIMING SUPERIORITY**
An adult lammergeier (right), although moulting and unusually scruffy, reminds a juvenile who the boss is. The young bird shows the characteristic diamond-shaped tail.

Rufous sengi

Elephantulus rufescens

flexible snout to sniff out food

This sengi lives its life in literal "fast lanes" – it creates a network of trails that allow it to navigate its territory at high speed. Speed is essential; their metabolism is so rapid that sengis are constantly searching for food, and known pathways allow them to find prey in the most efficient manner possible. Trails also provide a handy escape route from predators such as owls, hawks, and lizards. Adult sengis are adept at choosing paths that lead danger away from their single offspring, which spends its first few days in the nest, often an abandoned burrow. Sengis have a keen sense of smell that is enhanced by a flexible snout, which gives them their other name: elephant-shrew.

↔ 12–12.5 cm (4¾–5 in)
⚖ 50–60 g (1¾–2⅛ oz)
⊗ Common
⫿⫿⫿ Insects
🏠 ⷍ ⷍ

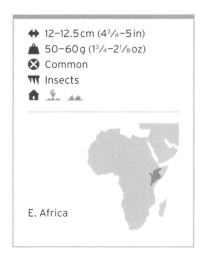

E. Africa

◁ **READY TO RUN**
Long hindlegs give sengis added power and manoeuvrability when attempting to outrun predators on their network of trails.

black bristles either side of bill give alternative name of bearded vulture

feathers stained orange

Lammergeier

Gypaetus barbatus

An ancient Greek playwright, Aeschylus, was allegedly killed when an eagle dropped a tortoise, mistaking his bald head for a stone. Myth turned the eagle into a lammergeier: the enormous vulture that carries bones (and sometimes tortoises) and drops them onto rocks to break open, exposing the marrow or flesh. Lammergeiers can swallow and digest shards of broken bone and eat gristly, bony scraps that other vultures leave behind, although flesh and skin of live prey such as tortoises and hares are preferred. With their huge wings and long tails, lammergeiers have a truly dramatic presence. This is often enhanced by a deep orange colour brought about by iron oxide staining – they rub their feathers in red soil and rock dust and debris.

Highs and lows

Lammergeiers reach the summits of Africa's highest mountains and inhabit the most remote gorges, yet they frequently forage at town refuse tips, where they are astonishingly agile at flying in congested spaces.

△ **EASY GLIDING**

A huge wingspan allows lammergeiers to glide almost endlessly with no effort. Occasionally they use a single, deep, emphatic wingbeat to adjust their course.

GREAT RIFT VALLEY LAKES
A global hotspot for freshwater diversity

The Great Rift Valley is part of a huge set of fissures in the Earth's crust that are expanding at a rate of about 7 mm (¼ in) a year and may eventually split Africa in two. The result is a sweep of low-lying land running from Jordan to Mozambique, which is flanked by some of the highest mountains in Africa. This land is dotted with lakes that include several of the oldest, largest, and deepest bodies of freshwater in the world. The rift valley splits into two branches in Kenya and Tanzania, between which lies Lake Victoria – the largest lake in Africa and the second largest freshwater lake in the world.

Fresh water, soda water
The Great Rift Valley lakes are generally stretched along the vertical axis of the rift. They differ widely in character, ranging from large, deep, and freshwater – like Malawi (also known as Nyasa), Tanganyika, and Turkana – to

shallow and intensely mineralized and alkaline in the so-called soda lakes. Having been isolated from each other for millions of years, each lake has its own unique collection of aquatic animals. The deep waters of Lake Malawi, for example, which encompass a wide variety of habitats, are home to as many as 3,000 species of fish – more than any other lake in the world. The Great Rift Valley lakes also support large numbers of land-based animals and birds, such as pelicans and waders. The soda lakes – Natron, Bogoria, Nakuru, and Elementalia – are famous for their huge flocks of lesser flamingos.

UNDER THREAT
The lakes are home to the African clawless otter and the smaller spotted-necked otter. Both are declining as a result of hunting for bushmeat, water pollution, and the introduced Nile perch, which eat the smaller fish on which the otters depend.

SPOTTED-NECKED OTTER

LONG-DISTANCE VISITORS
Huge numbers of migrant birds arrive at the lakes in autumn, including familiar European species such as swifts, swallows, and wigeon. Some remain until March, feasting in and around the lakes; others pass through to wintering areas further south.

WIGEON

COMMON CARP

Home to 10% of the world's fish species – 3,000 in Lake Malawi alone ❯ Tanganyika is the

DOMINANT INTRODUCTION
The common carp was accidentally introduced to Lake Naivasha in 2001. It increased so rapidly that by 2010 it accounted for 90% of the lake's harvest, displacing a previously dominant introduction, the American red swamp crayfish.

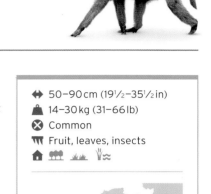

long dog-like muzzle

Olive baboon
Papio anubis

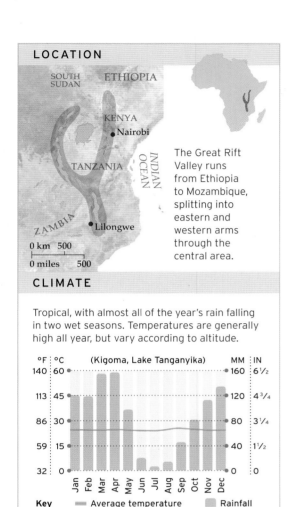
Ever the opportunists, these intelligent, adaptable monkeys eat virtually anything they can get their hands on, from grasses to small animals and human refuse. They are also at home in many different habitats – even where there are few trees, such as rocky hills, semi-desert, and open savanna.

Baboon society

Olive baboons live in large groups of up to 120 and spend most of their time foraging on the ground, often moving in columns. Adult males weigh twice as much as females, and have longer canine teeth and an impressive neck ruff, or mane. They fight for access to sexually receptive females, but usually only a few dominant males in each group manage to mate. Females can breed throughout the year, giving birth to a single baby after a gestation of around six months. It is carried by the mother, clinging to her belly, until it is around six weeks old and strong enough to ride on her back. Infants have black fur, which changes to greyish brown within a few months.

Because of their frequent crop-raiding, olive baboons are seen as pests and are widely persecuted by farmers. Their chief natural predators are leopards.

↔ 50–90 cm (19½–35½ in)
⚖ 14–30 kg (31–66 lb)
✖ Common
🍃 Fruit, leaves, insects

W. to E. Africa

▽ **MONKEYING AROUND**
Baboons are among the most playful of animals. They have an extended juvenile phase, during which they must learn the rules of their society.

Adult male baboons are **efficient hunters** – they can catch hares, baby antelopes, **even other monkeys**

2.7 m (8³/₄ft)

1.4–1.5 tonnes (1³/₈–1¹/₂ tons)

Vulnerable

Grass, aquatic plants

Africa

△ **COMMUNAL POOL**

Highly social, hippopotamuses live in groups or pods of 10–100 members, usually presided over by a dominant male. Other males are tolerated, provided they are submissive.

▷ **STAYING COOL**

Along with regulating its body temperature in the hot African sun, water keeps a hippopotamus's skin from drying out and cracking.

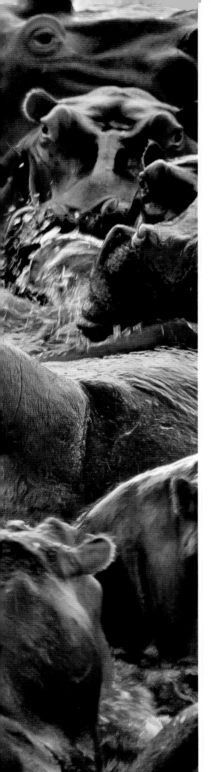

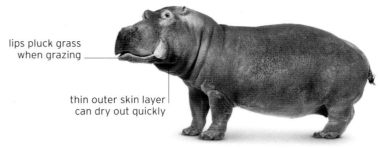

lips pluck grass
when grazing

thin outer skin layer
can dry out quickly

Hippopotamus

Hippopotamus amphibius

Although its name means "river horse", the hippopotamus, or hippo, more closely resembles the pig. In addition to similar teeth patterns, the two animals belong to the order artiodactyls – even-toed hoofed mammals. However, the hippopotamus's closest living relatives are not land mammals but whales and dolphins, with which it shared a common ancestor millions of years ago.

The hippopotamus is nearly hairless, and has an enormous mouth with teeth to match. Its bulky, barrel-shaped body makes it the Earth's third largest land animal, after elephants and rhinoceroses. Adult males weigh an average of 1,500 kg (3,300 lb) while females average 1,300 kg (2,900 lb). Despite its size and short, stocky legs, a hippo can sprint up to 30 km/h (18 mph). Speed, natural aggression, and 40–50-cm- (16–20-in-) long canine and incisor teeth that grow and sharpen themselves continuously make hippos one of Africa's most unpredictably dangerous species. They kill more people in Africa each year than any other mammal.

Walking underwater

As a semiaquatic animal, the hippopotamus spends its days in rivers, lakes, and swamps, where water and mud keep it cool and cover its skin in vital moisture. Water also supports its weight, and the animal can easily trundle or even leap along a lake bottom at speeds of up to 8 km/h (5 mph). However, even though a hippopotamus has webbed feet, it is not a strong swimmer; it cannot even float, so it stays in the shallows, closing its nostrils as it submerges, surfacing every 3–5 minutes to breathe.

Night grazer

Hippos feed at dusk, moving inland up to 10 km (6 miles) in search of the short grass that makes up the bulk of their diet. Adults consume as much as 70 kg (150 lb) of grass each night, pulling it up with their lips before crushing it with their large, grinding molars. The massive canines and incisors are only used in fighting and defence. Hippos "yawn" when threatened to show these teeth to their best advantage, opening their mouths nearly 180 degrees. Males defend territories by day, and it is thought that "dung-spinning" – performed mainly by males wagging their tails when defecating – is done partially as a territorial marking activity.

Mother and calf

Females can breed all year round but most mating occurs in the dry season. Mating takes place in the water, with the female staying submerged for most of the process. A single calf, weighing up to 50 kg (110 lb), is born underwater and has to swim or be helped to the surface for its first breath. Baby hippopotamuses have sterile intestines, and must eat their mother's dung in order to obtain the bacteria they need for digesting grass. Juveniles are vulnerable to attacks by crocodiles, lions, and spotted hyenas.

△ **BABY HIPPO**
Calves are born and suckle underwater.
They often ride on their mother's back
if the water is too deep.

Hippo calls can reach up to **115 decibels** – as loud as **close-range thunder**

angled bill

extremely
long legs

Lesser flamingo
Phoenicopterus minor

The lesser flamingo is an iconic bird of the African Rift Valley. Flocks hundreds of thousands strong turn whole landscapes pink at the steaming fringes of inhospitable alkaline lakes. In East Africa there are 3–4 million lesser flamingos; smaller populations live in southern Africa, including the Etosha Pan, and in India.

Incredible colonies

These monogamous birds breed in huge colonies on remote, caustic alkaline mudflats, exposed to searing heat, which are almost impossible for mammalian predators to reach. Their nests are small cones of mud and soda crystals, holding a single egg that hatches after 28 days. When two weeks old, chicks form herds of hundreds of thousands, attended by just one or two adults, leaving the parents free to find food. Chicks form lines up to 30 km (20 miles) long, and the crèches are driven up to 50 km (30 miles) across burning mud to reach shallow freshwater lagoons.

Although a million or more flamingos may gather, only a small proportion breed each year. Of East Africa's 1.5 million pairs, an average of 319,000 breed, rearing 140,000 young. Half of them die before reaching breeding age, so to maintain the population, lesser flamingos require an adult lifespan of more than 20 years.

Natural mortality of full-grown birds, mainly from eagles and marabou storks, is low, but disturbance caused by tourism, including low-flying aircraft, may be more damaging, and there are increasing threats from pollution and industrial development.

↔ 80–90 cm (31½–35½ in)
⚖ Up to 2 kg (4½ lb)
✖ Common
🦅 Algae
🏠 ⫷ ≈ ⤙

W., E., and
S. Africa,
S. Asia

△ **TAKING OFF**
Short daily flights take flamingos to fresh water, for drinking, but longer nocturnal journeys between strings of alkaline lakes may lead them to fly hundreds of kilometres.

▽ **DIFFERENT DIETS**
Constant begging by flamingo chicks stimulates adults to produce a rich "crop milk", which is regurgitated to feed their young. The brilliant pink colours of the adult plumage are derived from the diet of algae.

Great white pelican
Pelecanus onocrotalus

Great white pelicans feed in flocks, herding fish into shallow water inside a tightening arc. Billfulls of water and fish are scooped up – the water spills out, but the fish rarely escape and are swallowed whole. Pelicans are massive birds but buoyant on water, and they are surprisingly elegant in the air, where they fly in synchronized lines, V-shapes, and huge flocks. In Africa, they will breed at any time of the year if the conditions are briefly favourable, nesting in colonies.

△ **FISH SCOOP**
A pelican's large, sensitive bill detects fish by touch. It then scoops up to 11 litres (3 gallons) of water, complete with prey, in its elastic pouch.

↔ 1.4–1.8 m (4½–6 ft)
⚖ 10–11 kg (22–24 lb)
✖ Common
🍴 Fish
🏠 🌿 ≋ ≈

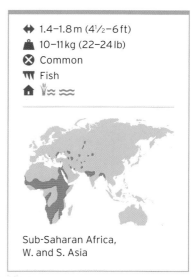

Sub-Saharan Africa, W. and S. Asia

Grey crowned crane
Balearica regulorum

This spectacular crane used to be a common sight in East Africa's savannas and farmland. It strides majestically, picking seedheads and taking grasshoppers, locusts, worms, frogs, and lizards when it can. It has the typical crane dancing displays involving deep, rhythmic bowing movements with outspread wings, leading to dramatic leaps up to 2.5 m (8 ft) high.

Grey crowned crane pairs stay together for life and have large breeding territories. They nest in marshy places, clearing a large space by stamping on vegetation and gathering it into a huge central mound with a shallow cup to hold up to four eggs. These hatch after a month and the chicks quickly leave the nest. By the time they are three months old, the young are half the weight of an adult, but well grown and able to fly.

◁ **ELEGANT DESIGN**
The crown of stiff golden feathers is shared only with the closely related black crowned crane (*B. pavonina*).

pearl-grey feathers on neck ⎯⎯⎯

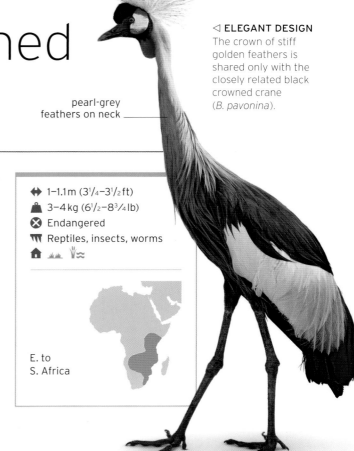

↔ 1–1.1 m (3¼–3½ ft)
⚖ 3–4 kg (6½–8¾ lb)
✖ Endangered
🍴 Reptiles, insects, worms
🏠 ⛰ 🌿 ≈

E. to S. Africa

↔ 3–6 m (10–20 ft)
⚖ 400–800 kg (880–1,760 lb)
✖ Common
🍴 Fish, mammals, birds
🏠 🌾 ≈ ≋

Africa, W. Madagascar

Nile crocodiles often roll their eggs gently in their mouths to help hatching babies emerge

dorsal scales reinforced by underlying bony plates (scutes)

◁ **RESTING CROCODILE**
When basking in the sun, crocodiles open their mouth to lose excess heat from its lining and their tongue.

long, keeled, powerful tail for propulsion

Shoebill
Balaeniceps rex

clog-shaped bill gives rise to name

Pointed, hooked, saw-edged, and spoon-shaped beaks, even pelicans' flexible pouches, are all used to catch fish. However, only one other bird has such a broad, deep, hook-tipped bill as the shoebill. The boat-billed heron's smaller bill helps it to fish by touch at night, whereas the shoebill fishes by sight during the day.

The shoebill moves remarkably delicately for a bird of its size, walking through waterside vegetation, bill tilted down so it can look for fish. The bill is also used to cool overheating eggs and chicks in the nest by pouring water over them. The nest is a huge, flat mound of wet vegetation in shallow water, among reeds or papyrus. The female usually lays two eggs. The chicks have to feed themselves on regurgitated fish dropped into the nest because of the adults' unusual bill structure.

▷ **HOOK-TIPPED BILL**
The broad, deep bill is adapted to grab fish, underwater vegetation, and mud in a swift open-mouthed lunge. Unwanted debris is then discarded.

long, bare legs

↔ 1.1–1.4 m (3¹⁄₂–4¹⁄₂ ft)
⚖ 4.5–6.5 kg (10–14 lb)
✖ Vulnerable
🍴 Lungfish, frogs
🏠 🌾 ≈ ≋

C. Africa

Nile crocodile
Crocodylus niloticus

Among reptiles, only the saltwater crocodile (*C. porosus*) exceeds the Nile crocodile in bulk, but perhaps not in ferocity and size of prey taken. With a range extending to most wetland habitats south of the Sahara, the Nile crocodile is reputed to kill buffaloes, giraffes, hippos, rhinos, and elephants. Typically, the Nile crocodile floats log-like close to animals at the water's edge, then it suddenly rears and lunges towards its victim, seizes the animal in its jaws, and pulls it under to drown. It may spin in a "death roll" to dismember a struggling animal or large carcass. Land attacks also occur. The crocodile bursts from bushy cover in a "high walk" and may even "gallop" for short distances, reaching 15 km/h (9 mph) with its body held high off the ground.

Nile crocodiles form large groups at sunny basking sites or regular kill locations such as river crossings. Large males are dominant, while juveniles rank the lowest.

fourth tooth in lower jaw can be seen even when mouth closed

five toes (three-clawed) on front foot

△ **FORMIDABLE PREDATOR**
The Nile crocodile's eyes, ears, and nostrils are located high on the head, allowing it to float almost submerged in water, yet see, hear, and breathe.

Zebra mbuna
Maylandia zebra

This striped fish grazes on the thick algal mats that grow in the shallower areas in Lake Malawi. It feeds with its head held perpendicular to the rock, scraping away with its teeth to scoop up the algae and any tiny animals that live in it. Like many species of lake cichlid, the zebra mbuna is a mouth brooder, with the female carrying her eggs in her mouth for three weeks. She is unable to feed during this time, and once the fry have hatched, she will spit them out.

↔ 11 cm (4¼ in)
🏋 Not known
✖ Locally common
🍴 Algae, zooplankton
🏠 🌿 ≈ ≈

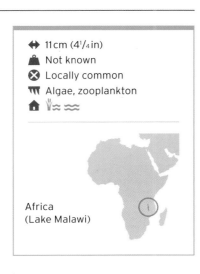

Africa
(Lake Malawi)

△ **FISH OF MANY COLOURS**
Light and dark male morphs are found in different parts of the lake. Females also vary in colour, from pale orange to dark brown, but these variations are not restricted by location.

SERENGETI SAVANNAS
Home of the world's most famous migration

Grassland systems depend on natural or artificial factors that prevent natural succession to scrub and then forest. In the Serengeti, these factors are fire and grazing. This is a highly seasonal ecoregion, where the rain-induced growth of grasses such as red oat and couch grass supports vast herds of herbivores, which travel as the seasons progress, following the best grazing opportunities. When zebras, wildebeest, and Thompson's gazelles gather to migrate, their numbers seem uncountable and their movement unstoppable. Other significant species include elephant, giraffe, impala, and Cape buffalo. The herbivorous hordes support abundant predators and scavengers including big cats, hyenas, wild dogs, birds of prey, and vultures.

Changing but the same

The wildlife seen today is a fraction of that which existed 100 years ago. Human encroachment, mainly for agriculture, has greatly reduced the area of habitat available and this, together with hunting, has drastically reduced populations. Even so, the character of this ancient landscape and the cycles of life it shapes have changed little in millions of years. The land would be recognizable to the early humans whose remains have been discovered at sites such as Olduvai Gorge, which today lies within the Serengeti National Park.

The Serengeti is the **only ecoregion** in the world **still dominated by large mammals**

WILDEBEEST IN THE MASAI MARA

One of the seven natural wonders of the world

CIRCULAR MIGRATION
More than 1 million wildebeest travel in search of fresh pasture each year. Late in the rainy season, they calve in the south of the Serengeti, where the grass is rich in phosphorus, a vital nutrient for lactating mothers. They then circle back towards the north and do not return for 10 months.

LIVINGSTONE'S TURACO

predators that hunt them

BIRDS, BEETLES, AND TREES
Bruchid beetles eat fallen seeds of trees in riverside forests, but not seeds that have first been eaten by birds and passed in their droppings. Thus, fruit-eaters such as Livingstone's turaco help preserve the forests; if they decline, the trees decline.

CREMATOGASTER ANTS

Famed for its profusion of grazing animals and

RECIPROCAL BEHAVIOUR
A species of Crematogaster ant lives in the swollen thorn bases of whistling acacias. The ants feed on nectar produced near leaf bases and are safer from predation among the thorns. They defend the tree by biting any browser that tries to eat its leaves.

DUNG REMOVAL

Dung beetles are vital to the health of this ecosystem. They clear dung, recycle nutrients, and improve soil. As well as eating fresh dung, they roll it into balls and take it underground.

DUNG BEETLE AT WORK

Home to 7,500 elephants in 2014

Occupies 14% of Tanzania's land area

STRATIFIED GRAZING

To avoid competing for food, grazing and browsing animals specialize in eating different plants or parts of plants. Zebras, for example, feed on older, tougher grasses than wildebeest, while giraffes browse from branches of acacia trees that no other animal can reach.

GIRAFFE FEEDING ON ACACIA BRANCHES

One of the oldest terrestrial ecosystems

THE ROLE OF FIRE

Lightening striking dry vegetation can cause fire. This does not kill grasses because their growing points are safe in the soil, but it can kill trees, thereby preventing woodland from forming. White storks hunt insects fleeing the fire.

WHITE STORK HUNTING

LOCATION

The Serengeti region covers 31,000 sq km (12,000 sq miles) of Kenya and Tanzania. The name is derived from a Masai term meaning endless plain.

KENYA

• Musoma

• Mwanza

TANZANIA

0 km 50
0 miles 50

CLIMATE

The climate is warm and dry, with two wet seasons: the short rains in November and December, and the long rains from March to May. The highest rainfall is in the west, near Lake Victoria, and lowest in the rain shadow of the Ngorongoro uplands to the southeast.

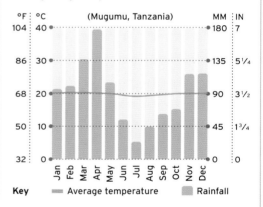

(Mugumu, Tanzania)

°F	°C		MM	IN
104	40		180	7
86	30		135	5¼
68	20		90	3½
50	10		45	1¾
32	0		0	0

Jan Feb Mar Apr May Jun Jul Aug Sep Oct Nov Dec

Key ▬ Average temperature ▬ Rainfall

THE FAMOUS FIVE

Big game hunters used to visit the Serengeti with the aim of shooting and killing the "Big Five" - a lion, leopard, elephant, rhinoceros, and Cape buffalo. Today, most tourists want to see and photograph the wildlife, and the cheetah has replaced the buffalo in the top five.

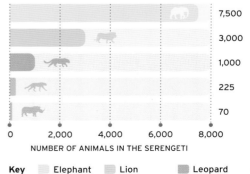

7,500
3,000
1,000
225
70

0   2,000   4,000   6,000   8,000

NUMBER OF ANIMALS IN THE SERENGETI

Key Elephant Lion Leopard
 Cheetah Black rhinoceros

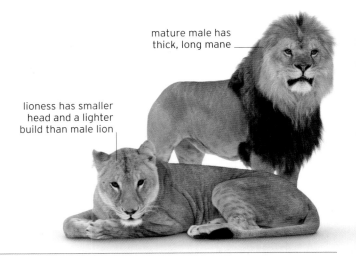

mature male has thick, long mane

lioness has smaller head and a lighter build than male lion

Lion

Panthera leo

Lions are the most social species of cat. They form units called prides, consisting of a group of adult females that share a home range with their young and up to three adult males. Prides have just four or five members where food is scarce, such as the Namibian semi-desert, and at least a dozen in East Africa's prey-rich savannas – the record is 39. Prides often split into subgroups to search for food or explore their range.

Hunting as a team

Lions are the only big cats to hunt cooperatively. In larger prides, most kills are made by the faster, lighter females. Lions stalk grazing mammals in teams, leaping onto the back of prey or seizing its legs and rear, and delivering a suffocating bite to its throat when it is grounded. Kills are shared between pride members, and an adult consumes 15–20 kg (33–44 lb) of meat at a sitting. Because lions hunt mostly at night, they doze in the shade during the day. They also scavenge the carcasses of dead animals.

Synchronized litters

The lionesses in a pride become sexually receptive at the same time, resulting in synchronized births, after an average gestation of 110 days. Each female has up to

six cubs in a litter, although two or three is usual. Male lions leave the pride that they were born into at 2–4 years old and form a coalition with several other males. These coalitions roam in search of prides to take over and lead, sometimes fighting a bloody battle to oust resident males. After a takeover, the new males kill any existing cubs in the pride so the lionesses come back into oestrus and so are ready to mate again.

The population of lions in Africa has gone down from 100,000 just 50 years ago to fewer than 30,000 today. This is due to hunting, a decline in their prey, and persecution by local people in retaliation for attacks on their livestock. Lions have long since vanished from North Africa and the Middle East. In Asia, they now survive only in the Gir Forest area of northwest India.

> ## Lions can be **recognized** by their **whisker-spot patterns**, which are as **unique as human fingerprints**

▷ **KING OF THE SAVANNA**
Adult males develop a long, shaggy mane around their head and neck. Their territorial roar can be heard up to 5 km (3 miles) away.

△ **LIONESS WITH CUBS**
Cubs stay with their mother for 20-30 months, but they may suckle from several adult females in the pride until they are weaned.

▷ **HUNTING IMPALA**
When chasing prey, lionesses may accelerate to a speed of 45 km/h (28 mph). Such sprints are short; rarely more than 200 m (650 ft).

↔ 1.6–2.5 m (5¼– 8¼ ft)
🏋 150–250 kg (330–550 lb)
✕ Vulnerable
🐾 Mammals, carrion
🏠 ⛰ 🌵 🌿

Sub-Saharan Africa (excluding Congo Rainforest), NW. India

black face line

ringed tail

hard foot pads and exposed claws

Cheetah

Acinonyx jubatus

The cheetah is built for speed. Its light, slender body and highly flexible spine help it to turn without losing its balance. Long muscular legs enable it to quickly reach strides of up to 7m (23ft). A small, short-muzzled head adds to its aerodynamics, and wide nostrils and large lungs enhance its breathing capacity. A large heart pumps blood to an optimal degree. Yet the cheetah is the least successful hunter among African cats – precisely because the adaptations that give it speed also restrict it in other ways. A short muzzle and small head lessen jaw strength. Its quick sprints can be sustained only for short distances, so it often fails to make a kill. High-speed bursts leave it overheated and in need of rest, so kills are easily stolen by other animals. For these reasons, cheetahs hunt mainly during the day to avoid stronger nocturnal predators.

Band of brothers

The cheetah's slight frame also makes it vulnerable to larger predators such as lions and hyenas; so solitary females with cubs are constantly on the lookout for danger. Males often band together for life, forming "coalitions" of 2 to 5 animals – sometimes related – which offers them greater protection. Once found throughout Asia and Africa, this species is now confined mainly to 25 African countries, with a critically endangered population of Asiatic cheetahs in Iran.

horns present
only in males

reddish fawn coat

short, rounded ears

Impala

Aepyceros melampus

A medium-sized antelope, the impala is distinguished by its black-tipped ears, rump and tail stripes, and black tufts above its rear hoofs. Male impala grow beautiful ridged, lyre-shaped horns that are up to 90 cm (36 in) long. These superbly agile mammals can change direction almost instantly and leap long and high over shrubs, bushes, and even other impala.

Impala rest and graze during the day and night. They eat grass in the wet season and feed on shrubs, bushes, fruit, and acacia pods during drier periods.

Spring and autumn ruts

Mating takes place in a twice-yearly "rut," when males fight each other for access to females. They become noisier than usual, snorting and bellowing to advertise and defend territories. Successful males mate with several females in spring and autumn, and the young are born about seven months later.

Outside the mating season, impala divide into smaller herds of bachelor males and larger herds of females and calves. The herd provides protection from predators, such as lions, hyenas, and leopards – an alert impala "barks" a warning that sets the entire herd fleeing.

↔ 1.1–1.5 m (3½–5 ft)
⬛ 40–65 kg (88–143 lb)
✖ Locally common
▥ Grass, leaves, bark
🏠 ⚘

E. and
S. Africa

↔ 1.2–1.5 m (4–5 ft)
⬛ 21–72 kg (46–160 lb)
✖ Vulnerable
▥ Gazelles, antelopes
🏠 ⚘ ⚘

Africa and
SW. Asia

▽ **LEAPING TO SAFETY**
Impala flee from predators into dense vegetation. They can leap as far as 9 m (30 ft) and as high as 2.5 m (8 ft).

△ **BORN TO RUN**
The "greyhound of cats" is the fastest mammal on land. The cheetah can reach speeds of more than 115 km/h (70 mph) in three seconds. An average sprint lasts about 20 seconds.

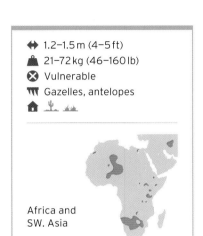

◁ **TEAR LINES**
The distinctive black lines on a cheetah's face may protect its eyes from the sun's glare and also help it to focus on prey.

Impala **release scent signals** as they **kick and leap**, which are thought to **lay trails** for other **herd members**

sharp, curved horns

long white beard

Wildebeest
Connochaetes mearnsi

▷ **BLUE WILDEBEEST**
All wildebeest males bellow and snort to retain mating rights, but will fight each other if required. These blue wildebeest (*C. taurinus*) in South Africa have locked horns.

The Serengeti white-bearded wildebeest is on its feet within three to seven minutes of birth, can run at 65 km/h (40 mph) and migrates up to 1,600 km (1,000 miles) annually. This is enabled by several physical adaptations. High shoulders, a thick neck, and a large head place the bulk of its weight towards the front, while its back slopes to narrow, muscular hips. Mount this arrangement on long, thin legs and you get a bearded antelope that can lope along effortlessly, sharing a similar build with that of a key predator, the spotted hyena.

Super herd formation
The broad mouth, wide row of incisors, and flexible lips are adapted to grazing on the Serengeti short grass, which is rich in phosphorus. This diet compels the wildebeest to follow short grass growth, which depends on seasonal rains, leading to spectacular migrations across the Serengeti plains of Kenya and Tanzania. The wildebeest merge with other grazers such as zebra to form a "super herd" of 1.25 million animals – the vast number keeps individuals relatively safe from predators.

At the end of the rainy season, all females become sexually receptive for two to three weeks – but each is fertile for just one day. Males set up small mating territories within the super herd. Most calves are born about eight months later, within a two- to three-week period, and can keep up with the herd within two days.

▽ **MASS CROSSING**
As many as 5,000 to 10,000 wildebeest may make the perilous crossing of the Mara river in Kenya at a time, but hundreds of Nile crocodiles lie in wait for them.

↔ 1.5–2.4 m (5–7³/₄ ft)
⚖ 120–275 kg (265–606 lb)
❌ Locally common
🌾 Grass
🏠 🏞

E. Africa

△ **RITUALIZED "NECKING"**
Male giraffes reach sexual maturity at three to four years. To establish dominance, rivals engage in a ritual battle that involves slamming their necks against each other.

Giraffe
Giraffa camelopardalis

Giraffes are the world's tallest living animals, with adult males reaching 5–6 m (16–20 ft) and adult females growing to 4.5–5 m (15–16 ft). Even the calves are 1.5–1.8 m (5–6 ft) tall at birth. Much of this height comes from the giraffe's massively elongated neck and legs. It has thick blood vessels, high blood pressure, and a powerful heart to pump blood all the way to its brain.

Despite their size, giraffes are threatened by predators. A pride of lions can bring down an adult, and young calves are vulnerable to hyenas and leopards. If alarmed, giraffes can gallop at speeds of up to 55 km/h (35 mph).

Unique markings

The Masai giraffe (*G. c. tippelskirchi*) is one of nine subspecies, each of which has a different pattern of red-brown or almost black markings, with straight or fuzzy edges, on a white or yellow background. It lives in small herds in the Serengeti savanna and open woodland, and can browse leaves from trees that are out of reach of antelopes and other browsers. Giraffes have a prehensile upper lip and an extremely long, tough, and mobile tongue, which enables them to strip leaves from thorny acacia trees with ease.

Both sexes have a pair of blunt, skin-covered horns, called ossicones, which are larger in males. The females mate with the dominant bull in their home range, giving birth to a single calf after 16 months, usually in the dry season. She will have weaned the calf by the time it is 13 months old.

prehensile upper lip

distinctive skin pattern of Masai giraffe

long black tail tuft for whisking away flies

markings fade towards feet

↔ 3.8–4.7 m (12½–15½ ft)
⬛ 0.6–1.9 tonnes
✖ Common
🌿 Tree leaves
🏠 ⋯

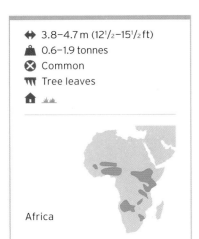

Africa

▷ **STANDING TALL**
As well as their great height, giraffes are distinguished by their large eyes and ears, short body, and a back that slopes steeply from shoulder to rump.

stripe pattern unique
to each individual

Grant's zebra

Equus quagga boehmi

Grant's zebras migrate to find food, travelling up to 3,000 km (1,800 miles) in search of the coarse long grass that they are best-adapted to eat. The smallest of the plains zebras, they are highly adaptable, able to survive in harsh conditions on the plains and in woodland at sea-level and on the slopes of Mount Kenya at heights of up to 4,000 m (13,000 ft).

Easily recognized by their black-and-white striped bodies (the function of which is not known for certain), zebras are social animals. They form close-knit family units that graze in large herds across East and Southern Africa. They are often joined by wildebeest, giraffes, and Thomson's gazelles, which benefit from the zebras' warning "bray-bark" when a predator is spotted. Zebras can also maintain a top speed of 55–65 km/h (35–40 mph), outlasting short-burst predators such as lions.

A family unit consists of a dominant stallion and several mares – the harem – and their foals. Males leave to join bachelor herds at between one and three years of age. Adult males try to lure females away, or take over a harem, resulting in violent fights. Most foals are born during the rainy season, after a year-long gestation.

△ **CHAPMAN'S ZEBRA**
A less-common subspecies of the plains zebra, *E. q. chapmani* has dark stripes alternating with fainter shadow stripes.

↔ 2.2–2.5 m (7$^{1}/_{4}$–8$^{1}/_{4}$ ft)
🏋 175–385 kg (385–850 lb)
✖ Common
🌾 Grass
🏠 ᨆ

E. Africa

◁ **DEADLY DUEL**
Fighting between stallions over mating rights is fierce, involving bites, powerful kicks, and strikes that frequently cause damage – and sometimes kill.

◁ **SAFETY IN NUMBERS**
Zebras have superb eyesight, hearing, and a sharp sense of smell, which help detect predators. Living in a herd means more senses at work, making it safer for members.

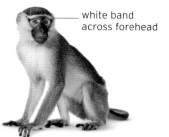

white band
across forehead

Vervet monkey

Chlorocebus pygerythrus

Africa's most widespread monkey, vervets thrive in a variety of environments. They prefer scrub forests bordering rivers, but are found in habitats as diverse as semi-desert and swamp, from sea level to altitudes up to 4,500 m (14,750 ft). Vervets eat all plant parts, from root to fruit, but also feed on insects, lizards, eggs, and small mammals. However, their appetite for sweet potatoes and bananas often brings them into conflict with farmers.

United we stand

A highly social species, vervets travel, feed, drink, groom, and rest in troops of as few as seven or as many as 75 individuals. Adult females rule the troop, which includes a smaller number of males (with their own hierarchy), juveniles, and offspring. While females stay with their troops for life, males leave at around age five, often in twos or threes to avoid an attack by a high-status female. They transfer mainly during the mating season (April to June), when dominant females are less prone to attack them.

Vervet monkeys have **specific vocal warnings** for **specific predators**

↔ 35–66 cm (14–26 in)

⬛ 3.2–7.7 kg (7–17 lb)

✖ Common

🌿 Plants, insects, lizards

🏠 🌳 🌵 🌾 〜 🏜

E. and
S. Africa

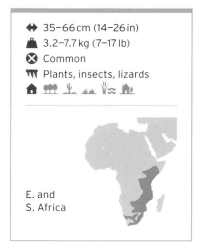

△ **SHARP AS A KNIFE**
Adult male vervets have longer canines than females. They reveal them in dominance displays and will use them as a weapon.

◁ **INHERITED RANK**
High-status females receive the best of everything, from food to sleeping trees, and their offspring inherit this status.

forward-curving tusks

trunk ends in two finger-like tips

African savanna elephant

Loxodonta africana

The world's largest land animal, African savanna elephants are capable of carving paths through dense undergrowth, clearing shrubs, and excavating waterholes. They also help to replant forests because they excrete the seeds of fruit that they eat – many species of tree depend on African elephants for survival.

The elephant's range is shrinking rapidly due to expanding human population. As many as 3–5 million elephants roamed Africa less than a century ago, but today an estimated 470,000–690,000 are confined to fragmented areas south of the Sahara. More elephants die annually from hunting and ivory poaching than are born.

Complex anatomy

The African elephant's head weighs up to half a tonne and its brain is larger than any other land animal's – about four times the size of the human brain. Its trunk – a fusion between upper lip and nose – contains a staggering 40,000 muscle bundles. The trunk is so adaptable that the elephant can pluck a grape-sized fruit without damaging it or throw a 30-cm- (12-in-) thick tree limb. Besides breathing, the elephant uses its trunk to smell, touch, and caress its family members, as well as to feed and drink. Its enormous ears are full of blood

Elephants **care for and aid** wounded relatives

vessels that radiate excess heat, while its tusks are used for tearing the bark and limbs of trees as well as for defence. Both male and female African elephants have tusks, although the female's tusks are shorter.

Females rule elephant society, which is highly social and family-based, with a matriarch leading related females and calves. The young are dependent on their mother for 8–10 years, learning how to behave, where to find water, and what to eat. Females remain with their birth herd, while most males leave at around 14 years old, joining other bulls in loose-knit bachelor herds and only coming into contact with females to mate.

Elephants are highly vocal communicators, with calls ranging from high-pitched squeaks to low-frequency "infrasound" rumbles. The deep rumbles can travel more than 3 km (2 miles) in the air and three times that distance through the ground, and elephants detect these vibrations through their feet and trunk.

▷ **REFRESHING SHOWER**
Bathing after drinking is a common activity. Elephants frequently use their trunks to spray themselves and each other with water.

◁ **MIGHTY TUSKER**
A fully grown bull African elephant with enormous tusks is a formidable opponent, capable of charges up to 40 km/h (25 mph).

↔ 4–5 m (13–16½ ft)
🏋 4–7 tonnes
✖ Vulnerable
🌾 Grass, fruit, flowers

Sub-Saharan Africa

Black-capped social weaver

Pseudonigrita cabanisi

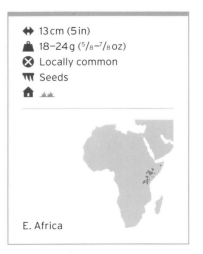

distinctive white beak

black tail

Its name says a lot about this small, neat, handsome bird. The black cap, red eye, and pale beak give the black-capped social weaver a unique look. It shares the nest-building habit of all weavers, although the nests that this social weaver builds have a rough, unfinished appearance as compared to some weavers' more precise constructions. Like other weavers, this is a gregarious bird, living in flocks, nomadic when not breeding, and nesting in colonies that are a few to 60 pairs strong. The need for social stimulation seems to be strong among them. Perching birds often squeeze together shoulder to shoulder and occasionally even preen each other.

Restricted range

The black-capped social weaver is a very localized bird found only in a small part of East Africa, very nearly restricted to Kenya and Tanzania, where it inhabits low-lying dry thorn bush plains. In this limited range, it is common in suitable habitats. Flocks of birds feed on the ground, foraging for seeds and a few grasshoppers; however, they frequently dash up to perch on treetops if disturbed. They should be a familiar bird to many safari-goers, but are often overlooked in parks and reserves where more glamorous big game claim most of the attention.

Expert builders

Breeding males create an insignificant, buzzy chattering from nesting trees, often flapping their wings; however, courtship is generally undistinguished. Nests often hang from tips of long, pendulous branches in a spreading acacia. A pair adds material all year round, using nests as roosts when not breeding. A new nest is built up above a slender twig in an arch and extended into a tube-like structure, with an entrance at the bottom. Eventually, the weight pulls the twig downwards and the upper end of the tube is closed off. Up to four eggs are laid, but little is known about the chicks.

Large nests may contain more than
9,000 grass stems

▷ **AT HOME**
Black-capped social weavers use prickly grass stems to make an unlined, conical nest. When used for roosting it has two entrances; one is sealed off for breeding.

◁ **NESTING TREE**
Often, the largest tree in a wide area forms the basis for a breeding colony, holding up to 60 nests.

↔ 13 cm (5 in)
⚖ 18–24 g (⅝–⅞ oz)
✕ Locally common
⫿⫿⫿ Seeds
⌂ 🌾

E. Africa

Red-billed hornbill

Tockus erythrorhynchus

bright beak used to impress mates

long tail

Groups of red-billed hornbills, sometimes numbering hundreds, wander through thorn bush and grasslands looking for food, which is mostly taken on the ground.

They build their nests in tree-holes or hollow logs. The female seals herself inside with mud up to 24 days before laying eggs, which take about the same time to hatch. All this time, the male brings her food. She breaks out 21 days later, when the oldest chick is ready to fly.

↔	40–48 cm (15¹/₂–19 in)
⚖	100–225 g (3¹/₂–8 oz)
✖	Common
♈	Dung beetles, seeds
🏠 🌳	
➤	Sub-Saharan Africa

◁ **FLAP-AND-GLIDE FLIGHT**
Hornbills hunt prey on the ground during the day, but they fly back to trees to roost at night.

Helmeted guineafowl

Numida meleagris

tiny head

large, rounded body

Abundant in bushy savannas, helmeted guineafowl are named for the bony casque on their head. They need drinking water, thick cover to escape into if threatened, and trees to roost in at night. They eat seeds and shoots, but prefer grasshoppers and termites when abundant.

↔	53–63 cm (21–25 in)
⚖	1–1.5 kg (2¹/₄–3¹/₄ lb)
✖	Common
♈	Seeds, shoots, insects
🏠	
➤	Sub-Saharan Africa

▷ **BOLTING AWAY**
Guineafowl live in busy, noisy groups on the ground. They run rather than fly from danger, unless sorely pressed.

Secretary bird

Sagittarius serpentarius

The secretary bird strides along elegantly on extraordinarily long legs in grassy plains, its head bobbing back and forth. It feeds mainly on grasshoppers, mice, and voles, but will eat anything it can kill. Long, bare legs help protect it from snakes, even deadly cobras, which it kills by stamping.

Each breeding pair needs about 50 sq km (20 sq miles) of "home range" for nesting. They drive out rival birds from their territories, jumping and kicking if they catch an intruder.

↔	1.3–1.5 m (4¹/₄–5 ft)
⚖	4 kg (8³/₄ lb)
✖	Vulnerable
♈	Grasshoppers, mice, voles
🏠 🌵	

Sub-Saharan Africa

quill-like crest

long, powerful legs

△ **SNAKE SNACK**
Secretary birds stalk determinedly across open grassland in search of prey, which even includes venomous snakes.

Lilac-breasted roller

Coracias caudatus

Several similar kinds of rollers occupy Africa at various times of the year, distinguished by their tail shapes and minor colour differences. The lilac chest is the identifying feature of the lilac-breasted roller, but it shares elongated tail streamers with the Abyssinian roller. It prefers bushy savanna and dry, open woodland, and perches prominently on trees. It is a very territorial and pugnacious bird.

Disperse after breeding

Lilac-breasted rollers build their nest in a cavity in a decaying stump or termite mound, which is left unlined. Both parents incubate the eggs for 18 days, and the chicks fly when they are 35 days old. Although lilac-breasted rollers do not migrate as such, they disperse widely after breeding, finding feeding territories that they defend individually or in pairs. Rollers are generalist and opportunistic feeders. They swoop to the ground to catch big insects, scorpions, centipedes, small reptiles, and occasionally, a small bird.

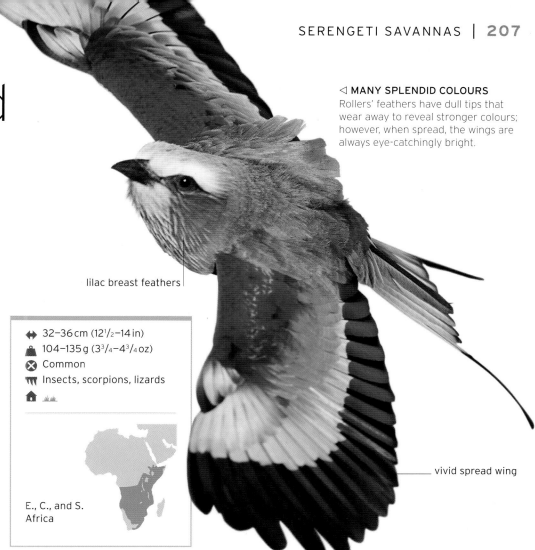

↔ 32–36 cm (12½–14 in)
⚖ 104–135 g (3¾–4¾ oz)
✖ Common
🍴 Insects, scorpions, lizards
🏠 🌾

E., C., and S. Africa

lilac breast feathers

vivid spread wing

◁ **MANY SPLENDID COLOURS**
Rollers' feathers have dull tips that wear away to reveal stronger colours; however, when spread, the wings are always eye-catchingly bright.

Black mamba

Dendroaspis polylepis

Strong, fast, agile, and deadly, the black mamba is Africa's longest venomous snake, and second only to the king cobra worldwide. Its "racing slither" – usually used to escape danger rather than to pursue prey – has been timed at 14 km/h (9 mph) and it may exceed 20 km/h (12 mph). Its somewhat drab olive, green, grey, or brown coloration has subdued, if any, markings.

Africa's deadliest snake

The black mamba is found in varied habitats, from rocky hills to coastal scrub. It rests at night in a home lair in a termite mound, small mammal burrow, tree root hollow, or rocky crevice. By day, the snake lurks in cover to strike out at passing victims. Its two fixed, hollow upper fangs inject exceptionally toxic venom – it can kill a human in 30 minutes. The black mamba holds smaller prey for a few minutes until lifeless, but bites larger ones and withdraws, following them until the venom acts. The black mamba climbs well to hunt for nesting birds and squirrels. If threatened, it rears up, spreads its small "hood" cobra-fashion, opens its mouth, and hisses.

streamlined body with smooth scales

↔ 2.5–3.5 m (8¼–11½ ft)
⚖ Up to 2 kg (4½ lb)
✖ Common
🍴 Small mammals, birds
🏠 🌳 🌾

E. and S. Africa

◁ **BLACK BITE**
Hissing, gaping, tongue erect, upper fang tips visible – it is the dark interior of the mouth that gives the "black" mamba its name.

CONGO BASIN
The dark green heart of Africa

The Congo Basin was carved by glaciers into a vast depression about the size of Europe. Much of the 2,000 mm (78 in) of rain that falls over the area each year ultimately drains into the Congo River, the second largest in the world. The river defines the character of the entire region, but it also represents an ecological barrier, with many groups of species found only on one side or the other – for example, chimpanzees live to the north of the river, while bonobos, or pygmy chimpanzees, occur only to the south.

Abundance under threat

Up to 10,000 plant species grow in the Congo Basin, about a third of which are found nowhere else. More than 1,000 bird species live here, as well as 700 known species of freshwater fish. New species of mammal are being discovered regularly in the basin, including fairly large animals that had remained unknown until relatively recently. The okapi was first described in 1901, followed by the bonobo in 1929, yet the forest elephant was not discovered until 2001.

In addition to its vast amounts of wildlife, the Congo Basin has been inhabited by humans for more than 20,000 years and is currently home to or supports more than 75 million people. Although new flora and fauna species undoubtedly exist in large areas of rainforest that remain unexplored, as the human population continues to grow, many are likely to become extinct before discovery. This is due to exploitation of land for agriculture, mining, fossil fuels, logging, and hunting for the bushmeat trade.

The forest in the Congo Basin is **so dense, only 1% of sunlight** reaches the ground

SITATUNGA

Contains the second-largest block of rainforest in the world

ADAPTABLE ANTELOPE
Sitatunga emerge from forests to graze in wet grasslands and swamps at night. Their long, splayed hoofs and flexible foot joints allow them to walk on waterlogged ground without sinking. They are excellent swimmers and use the water to escape predators.

BONOBO

GUTS OF THE MATTER
Bonobos, or pygmy chimpanzees, are highly social, fruit-eating apes endangered by habitat loss and hunting. Threats to bonobos affect the entire ecosystem: the seeds of many tree species cannot germinate unless they pass through the apes' guts.

Home to around half of Africa's elephant population

AFRICAN CHERRY

THE MEDICINE TREE
The African cherry grows widely in the Congo Basin's mountain forests. Its bark is used in African medicine to treat everything from chest pains to mental illness, and it shows promising cancer-fighting properties.

BLACK COLOBUS MONKEY

More than 900 butterfly species live here

SALT OF THE EARTH
Occasional natural clearings in the forest are usually filled with wet grassland and swamp. They often contain important minerals, which attract a variety of wildlife. Forest elephants dig or even dive underwater to find the richest salt deposits.

FOREST ELEPHANT

Congo trees store an estimated 8% of the Earth's forest-trapped carbon

WATERS OF LIFE
The Congo is richer in fish than any other African river, with around 700 known species, many found nowhere else on earth. These include elephantfish, which use electric fields to sense surroundings, Goliath tigerfish, whose teeth grow up to 2.5 cm (1 in) long, and the planet's largest freshwater pufferfish.

FRESHWATER PUFFERFISH

LOCATION

Central Africa, between the Gulf of Guinea and the African Great Lakes; mostly within the Democratic Republic of Congo (DRC) and neighbouring countries.

NIGERIA
CHAD
SOUTH SUDAN
Yaoundé
Bangui
ATLANTIC OCEAN
Kinshasa
TANZANIA
ANGOLA

0 km 500
0 miles 500

CLIMATE

The Congo Basin is unrelentingly hot and humid, with average daytime temperatures reaching 21–27°C (70–80°F) year round. The humidity rarely drops below 80 per cent, thanks to frequent rainfall, which peaks in spring and particularly autumn.

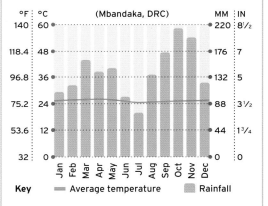

(Mbandaka, DRC)

°F	°C		MM	IN
140	60		220	8½
118.4	48		176	7
96.8	36		132	5
75.2	24		88	3½
53.6	12		44	1¾
32	0		0	0

Jan Feb Mar Apr May Jun Jul Aug Sep Oct Nov Dec

Key — Average temperature ▬ Rainfall

HUMANS IN THE CONGO

The Congo is home to more than 250 ethnic groups. The lifestyle of modern hunter-gatherer peoples such as the semi-nomadic Bayaka and Bagyeli (formerly known as "pygmies") requires small groups of people to live sustainably on the land. They exchange forest goods for farmed produce grown in more settled communities.

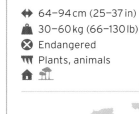

bare skin on face
darkens with age

arms longer than legs

grasping feet
and hands

Chimpanzee

Pan troglodytes

Our closest living relatives, chimpanzees are great apes that share numerous features with humans, such as large brains, expressive faces, a prominent "brow ridge" over the eyes, and dextrous hands with opposable thumbs. They also share some human biology – they go bald and get arthritis with old age, and suffer many human diseases. They display some aspects of human behaviour, too, such as an ability to walk upright and play.

Making and using tools

Chimpanzees live in communities of about 35 members, although exceptionally large groups may have up to 150. Active by day, they spend half of it foraging in the forest for plants and animals. Some groups are known to eat as many as 200 types of food. Each evening, they construct sleeping nests in treetops.

British primatologist Jane Goodall's study at Gombe Stream, Tanzania, found that chimpanzees band together to hunt other primates, mainly colobus monkeys. Males do most of the hunting, and share the meat with the group. Goodall was also the first to record tool use in chimpanzees – they deploy stone anvils to crack nuts, hold up leaves as umbrellas, and use sticks to fish termites out of tree trunks or extract honey from bees' nests.

Chimpanzees share more than 98.5 per cent of their DNA with humans

Females are sexually mature at between seven and eight years old, but only bear their first single infant at 13–14 years, after a gestation of about eight months. Babies are dependent on their mothers, sharing the maternal nest at night, and are weaned when four or five years old. Juveniles learn tool-use and other complex behaviour by watching older relatives. If food is plentiful, chimpanzees can breed all year round.

Fragmented range

Up to the early 1900s, chimpanzees occurred throughout the tropical forests of West and Central Africa. Today their range is highly fragmented due to decades of deforestation, capture for zoos, circuses, and medical research, and hunting for the bushmeat trade. About 200,000–300,000 remain in the wild, and populations continue to fall.

▷ **HIGHLY INTELLIGENT**
After humans, chimpanzees are the most intelligent primate, with a sophisticated language of facial expressions, gestures, and vocalizations. They may live more than 50 years in the wild.

△ **BONOBO**
Bonobos, or pygmy chimpanzees (*P. paniscus*), are more agile than chimpanzees, and spend more time walking upright. They are rarer, confined to the Congo Basin, where about 30,000 may survive.

▷ **BABY CHIMPANZEE**
Young chimps are inquisitive and playful, engaging in frequent games of rough and tumble with playmates of their age.

↔ 64–94 cm (25–37 in)
⚖ 30–60 kg (66–130 lb)
✕ Endangered
🌿 Plants, animals
🏠 🏛

W. and
C. Africa

grasping hand with
semi-opposable thumb

Western gorilla

Gorilla gorilla

In the past, gorillas were often portrayed as brutish and dangerous, a reputation not helped by the early King Kong films, but they are, in fact, highly intelligent, peaceful, and almost entirely vegetarian. Western gorillas live in lowland forests and swamps in Central Africa and feed mainly on ripe fruit, together with some plant shoots and leaves. Their grinding teeth and massive jaw muscles are adapted for chewing vegetation. The only animals they eat are ants and termites.

Non-aggressive displays

Although the western gorilla is the heaviest and most powerfully built of all the great apes, the huge mature males rely on ritual displays rather than aggression to assert their dominance. They take 18 years to reach their full size and are known as silverbacks after the pale patches of fur on their backs. Adult females are only around half the size.

A typical gorilla family group consists of a single silverback and up to 12 adult females and their offspring of various ages. The bonds between the family members are very strong, and many group members stay together for life.

Western gorillas are threatened by deforestation, illegal poaching for the bushmeat trade, and some human diseases such as the ebola virus, which affects apes as well as humans.

△ **DEPENDENT YOUNG**
Young gorillas depend on their mothers for three to five years, suckling throughout. This is one of the longest nursing periods of any mammal.

△ **RITUAL DISPLAY**
Dominant male gorillas advertise their status by standing upright, baring their long canine teeth, thrashing vegetation, and beating their broad chests with their hands.

◁ **ON THE MOVE**
Gorillas travel mainly on foot, covering an average of 2 km (1 mile) a day in search of food. The young ride piggyback on their mothers, or cling to their bellies.

subordinate male has paler muzzle

Mandrill
Mandrillus sphinx

Mandrills live in large groups in tropical forest and forest-savanna mosaic habitats. They spend time on the ground and in trees where they feed mainly on fruit and insects, but will also eat small vertebrates. Groups number several hundred and even more than a thousand adult females and their young. Adult males may be solitary except during the mating season.

Size and colour

Mandrills exhibit marked differences between the sexes: in addition to their colourful faces and yellow beards, the genital region and rump of the dominant males are a kaleidoscope of blue, red, pink, and purple. The dominant males are also roughly twice the size of the females, which are plain in comparison. When the females are ready to mate, the skin around their genitalia becomes swollen and red.

↔ 55–110 cm (1³/₄–3¹/₂ ft)
🏋 11–33 kg (24–73 lb)
❌ Vulnerable
🍽 Fruit, eggs, small animals
🏠 🎋

W. Central Africa

thick, olive-grey fur

▷ **A FACE TO REMEMBER**
Dominant male mandrills are the most colourful monkeys in the world. Their striking faces have a red stripe down the nose with blue ridges on either side. The long canine teeth may be displayed.

↔ 1.3–1.7 m (4¹/₄–5¹/₂ ft)
🏋 57–190 kg (125–420 lb)
❌ Critically endangered
🍽 Fruit, leaves, seeds, termites
🏠 🎋

C. Africa

Western gorillas feed on the fruit of more than **100 plant species**

paler background
colour on underparts

Leopard
Panthera pardus

↔ 0.9–1.9 m (3–6¹/₄ ft)
⚖ 37–90 kg (82–200 lb)
✕ Near threatened
🐾 Deer, baboons, fish, birds

Africa, S. Asia

Leopards can catch prey up to **10 times their own weight**

One of the smallest and strongest climbers of the big cats, leopards are famed for their spots or "rosettes", but not all have the same type. Some are solid, others have light patches in the centre, but all spots camouflage this hunter in habitats ranging from rainforest to desert, from Africa to the Himalayas.

Night hunter
Solitary except during the mating season, leopards are mainly nocturnal. Like all cats, they have a membrane called the tapetum lucidum at the back of their eyes that reflects twice as much light through their retinas, giving them superb night vision. They eat fish, birds, reptiles, hoofed mammals such as antelope as well as wild pigs and baboons, and carrion. Long-bodied and powerfully built, leopards hunt by stealth, pouncing on their prey and quickly suffocating it. They can pull 125 kg (275 lb) giraffe carcasses up into trees.

Each leopard has a home territory, and its boundaries overlap with those of nearby leopards. Females give birth to two or three smoky-grey cubs, keeping them in a variety of den sites to protect them from predators. By the age of six to eight weeks, cubs regularly leave their den site and begin to eat solid food. They remain with their mother for the first two years of their lives.

△ **AT EASE**
Leopards are very comfortable in trees, often hauling their kills into branches to keep them safe from lions and scavengers such as hyenas.

▷ **OPEN WIDE**
The leopard's long canines are used for stabbing and gripping. The rough tongue is used to lick scraps of meat from bones and for grooming.

Red river hog

Potamochoerus porcus

Tufted ears, a fox-red coat, and a white spinal stripe make Africa's smallest wild pig a striking animal. What the red river hog lacks in size, it makes up for in strength. Its muscular, stocky body and wedge-shaped head are designed to dig up the hardest ground for roots, tubers, and other food.

Nocturnal foragers

Mostly active at night, red river hogs are strong swimmers, and can forage in water as well as on land. Small family groups are usually found resting in a burrow or undergrowth during the day. Unfortunately, their fondness for agricultural crops brings them into conflict with humans, their main persecutors.

↔ 1–1.5m (3¼–5 ft)
⚖ 46–130 kg (100–290 lb)
✖ Common
🌾 Grass, roots, tubers, snails
🏠 🍄 🏚

W. to
C. Africa

long, pointed ears with prominent white tufts

facial hair fluffed out when threatened, making hog appear larger and more intimidating

▷ **DOMINANT BOAR**
Only male red river hogs have large warts in front of their eyes, whereas both sexes have tusks.

Common pangolin

Manis tricuspis

↔ 25–43 cm (10–17 in)
⚖ 1.6–3 kg (3½–6½ lb)
✖ Vulnerable
🌾 Termites, ants
🏠 🍄 🌱 ≈

W. to
C. Africa

Pangolins are covered in overlapping scales made of keratin, a material found in hair and fingernails. When threatened, these burrowing mammals roll themselves up into a ball to protect their underparts – the only area of their body that is not covered in tough scales.

The common African pangolin feeds mainly on termites and, to a lesser extent, ants, gathering the insects with its long, sticky, muscular tongue. It is able to seal its nostrils and ears shut to protect them from stings and bites as it feeds. The pangolin has no teeth, and special muscles in its mouth keep insects in place once sucked inside. Its muscular stomach contains keratin spines, and the pangolin also swallows stones to help crush its food, ready for digestion.

◁ **FIFTH LIMB**
The common pangolin uses its long, strong, prehensile tail to manoeuvre around in trees.

Okapi

Okapia johnstoni

The closest relative of the giraffe, the okapi lives a solitary life, following well-trodden paths through dense forests. Like the giraffe, it uses its long, prehensile tongue to strip leaves from twigs. Okapis gather to mate at the end of the spring rainy season. Although silent at other times, adults make soft coughing calls to attract mates. Gestation lasts for 14 months, and a single calf is born between August and October.

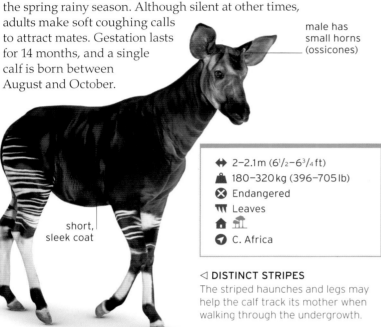

male has small horns (ossicones)

short, sleek coat

↔	2–2.1 m (6½–6¾ ft)
📐	180–320 kg (396–705 lb)
⊗	Endangered
🌾	Leaves
🏠 🏛	
◉	C. Africa

◁ **DISTINCT STRIPES**
The striped haunches and legs may help the calf track its mother when walking through the undergrowth.

Collared sunbird

Anthreptes collaris

This sunbird darts between flowers growing on tangled creepers and bushes at the forest edge. Acrobatically searching through cobwebs, dead leaves, and foliage, it gleans whatever it can eat. It suspends a tiny purse of plant fibres, leaf mould, and moss, knitted together with cobwebs, to hold two eggs, which hatch after 12 days.

▷ **VARIED DIET**
Its small, spiky bill makes the collared sunbird a generalist feeder. Although it feeds at flowers, it takes small insects, spiders, and snails more than nectar.

iridescent green plumage

↔	10 cm (4 in)
📐	6–10 g (¼–³⁄₈ oz)
⊗	Common
🌾	Insects, nectar
🏠 🏛 🌿 ≋	
◉	Africa

Emperor scorpion

Pandinus imperator

Aptly named, this fearsome-looking creature is the world's biggest scorpion, although at least one more slender species is longer. Its front end is dominated by immense clawed pincers while, at the back, the tail-like telson is frequently curled menacingly forwards over the body to display the curved stinger. However, the large size does not make this scorpion more deadly – its venom is not as potent as some other, smaller scorpions. A sting is painful to humans, but has few further ill effects. The emperor scorpion reserves its venom for self-defence or to incapacitate prey, and uses the crushing power of its pincers to kill it.

Feeling its way

Emperor scorpions are nocturnal and have poor eyesight. Touch-sensitive hairs are especially thick on the pincers and legs. These are used to detect prey in the dark, along with help from the comb-like pectines under the body that are used to sense vibrations running through the ground.

Mating involves an elaborate dance, where the male leads the female by her pincers to a patch of flat ground where sperm can be transferred. After seven to nine months, she gives birth to between nine and 32 live young, which are white in colour.

upper claw fixed; lower claw moves to grip

↔	20 cm (8 in)
⊗	Not known
🌾	Arthropods, mice, lizards
🏠 🏛	

W. to C. Africa

◁ **SAFE JOURNEY**
Baby scorpions ride on their mother's back, and remain under her protection until their first moult gives them a darker, waterproof exoskeleton.

▽ **LIQUID FEEDER**
A scorpion's mouthparts cannot chew, so it uses its chelicerae to tear off small bits of prey. Digestive enzymes are regurgitated onto the food in a special cavity and the resultant liquid then enters the mouth.

rear walking leg

chelicerae (pair of pincer-like appendages in front of mouth)

massive pedipalps (pincers)

The emperor scorpion's **courtship dance** may last for **several hours**

OKAVANGO DELTA

The wetland jewel of southern Africa

River deltas are so called due to their triangular shape, which resembles the Greek letter Δ, or delta. Most form where rivers deposit vast amounts of silt and sand close to the point at which they meet the sea, but the Okavango River in Botswana never finds the coast. Instead, it drains into a depression in the Kalahari Desert, fanning out to create the greatest oasis in Africa – a vast complex of permanent and seasonal swamps, reed beds, forests, and grasslands. The precise pattern of its waterways changes constantly from year to year as channels become blocked by sand, silt, and vegetation, and the slow-moving water backs up and is forced to find an alternative route.

Breathing space

Much of the water in the Okavango Delta's permanent swamps is oxygen-poor, so the fish and aquatic invertebrates that live there are adapted to extract oxygen from the air. The waters support an estimated 35 million fish of 80 species, while the greatest abundance and diversity of terrestrial life is found in marginal areas, where swamps populated byhippopotamus and crocodiles are fringed with forest. This, in turn, gives way to open savannas, where huge herds of grazing animals attract top predators such as cheetahs, lions, hyenas, leopards, and wild dogs.

One of the **world's largest inland river deltas,** it swells to three **times its size** during winter

GIANT TERMITE MOUND

An estimated 482 bird species live here ❯

MASTER BUILDERS
In low-lying deltas, slight variations create land high enough to support plants and animals. Many such mounds owe their existence to termites, whose nests rise several feet above ground, often sprouting trees, which contribute the organic material needed to form soil.

COMMON WARTHOG

into the delta evaporates or seeps away ❯

GLORIOUS MUD
Warthogs roll in mud to cool off and gain a protective skin covering, creating hollows in the process that may be enlarged by elephants. Old wallows quickly fill with water when the rains return, often transforming into permanent water holes.

PAPYRUS

More than 97% of water flowing into the delta ❮

FLOOD CONTROL
Papyrus grows in flooded areas, filling channels so that water moves elsewhere, fixing carbon, and reducing evaporation. Its submerged stems provide nurseries for fish, while birds roost on its flower heads.

FISH SNATCHER
Forest-fringed swamps are perfect habitats for Pel's fishing owl, a huge bird capable of grabbing fish weighing 1–2 kg (2–4½ lb) in its talons.

PEL'S FISHING OWL

Swamps make up 27% of the delta

Highly endangered black and white rhinoceros have adapted to wetland life here

FRIEND OR FOE?
Often seen on the backs of hoofed grazers, oxpeckers are small perching birds that specialize in feeding on ticks and other skin parasites that afflict mammals. Their services may not be entirely benign: they also peck at wounds as a source of blood.

RED-BILLED OXPECKER

BORN SURVIVOR
A lungfish thrives in oxygen-poor waters due to a lung-like offshoot of the gut that extracts oxygen as the fish gulps air. During droughts, the fish squirms into mud and forms a slime cocoon to hold air and moisture that keep it alive until water returns.

WEST AFRICAN LUNGFISH

LOCATION

The Okavango River rises in the highlands of Angola, and flows southeast into Botswana, where it spreads out to form the vast delta landscape.

ANGOLA

Katima Mulilo

Shakawe

NAMIBIA

BOTSWANA

Maun

0 km 100
0 miles 100

CLIMATE

Most of the rain reaching the delta falls in the Angolan part of the Okavango river catchment area during the hot, humid summer months (December–February). Winters are dry and mainly mild, though night-time temperatures may approach freezing.

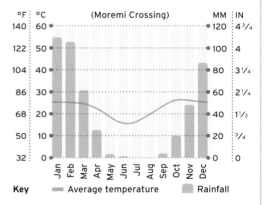

°F	°C	(Moremi Crossing)	MM	IN
140	60		120	4¾
122	50		100	4
104	40		80	3¼
86	30		60	2¼
68	20		40	1½
50	10		20	¾
32	0		0	0

Jan Feb Mar Apr May Jun Jul Aug Sep Oct Nov Dec

Key ── Average temperature ▇ Rainfall

NO WAY OUT

The Okavango Delta is an endorheic basin: a closed water system that does not involve the sea. Rain falling over such an area drains via rivers into a low point, forming a lake, inland sea (such as the Caspian), or a swamp. There is no route by which water can flow to the ocean, and all water flowing in is lost through evaporation or gradual seepage into the ground.

Cape buffalo

large, curved horns

relatively short legs

Syncerus caffer

The Cape buffalo is a massively built, ox-like hoofed mammal, and one of Africa's largest herbivores. Adult males mature at about five years of age, and weigh two-thirds more than females. Both sexes have a pair of formidable, curved horns, which in bulls almost meet across the top of the forehead, spanning up to 1.3 m (4 ft) in length. Bulls establish their dominance by displaying their horns in various threat positions and rarely fight.

Cape buffaloes have poor eyesight, and largely rely on their keen hearing to detect lions – their chief predators. Mixed herds comprise cows, their calves, and males of various ages. At certain times of the year, their numbers may reach hundreds or even thousands of animals. Bachelor herds contain five to 10 bulls.

↔ 2.4–3.4 m (7³/₄–11 ft)
⬛ 500–900 kg (1,100–1,985 lb)
✖ Common
▦ Grass, leaves

E. to S. Africa

▽ **QUENCHING THEIR THIRST**
Cape buffaloes eat huge quantities of grass. Their diet is thirst-inducing and they travel long distances to drink at rivers or waterholes They also rest for many hours, digesting their food.

△ **ON THE RUN**
Red lechwes have water-repellant hairs on their lower legs that prevent the legs becoming waterlogged as they run further into the swamp away from predators, giving them an advantage.

↔ 1.3–1.8 m (4¹/₄–6 ft)
⬛ 52–135 kg (115–298 lb)
✖ Locally common
▦ Aquatic plants, grasses

C. Africa

▷ **BATTLE FOR SUPREMACY**
Two mature males fight to take possession of a prime breeding territory. A couple of male onlookers await the outcome with interest, while the females keep their heads down and carry on grazing.

male has long, swept-back, deeply ringed horns

Red lechwe
Kobus leche

This medium-sized antelope seldom moves far from water. In the rainy season, the red lechwe often feeds in the water, grazing on plants breaching the surface. If its shallow swampy habitat is heavily flooded, it will retreat to higher ground as it waits for the water to recede. When the water levels drop further in the dry season, the red lechwe is forced out again to forage on land. However, it has to drink regularly in hot weather and always stays within running distance of water.

Water crossing

The water is the red lechwe's primary defence. The lechwe has long, flattened hoofs which provide a firm footing on the soft waterlogged ground, and it runs with a bounding gait that carries it over the shallow water. Although this way of running makes it ungainly on land, it is very effective for crossing shallow water quickly to escape attack from predators such as lions, African wild dogs, spotted hyenas, and leopards. The females and young tend to stay closer to the water than the usually solitary males.

Red lechwes breed during the rainy season between December and May. At this point, each mature male takes up a breeding territory, or lek. Male lechwes mature at five years or older, but females do so at 18 months, and so outnumber the mature males. Driven into the centre of the lek – sometimes by harassing, immature males – where the dominant males hold court, the females are safe from attack as predators target the males left at the edge. Calves are born eight months later, towards the end of the dry season.

85 per cent of the wild population **lives in the Okavango Delta**

growing horn
of young rhino

three-toed feet

White rhinoceros

Ceratotherium simum

↔ 3.7–4 m (12–13 ft)
⚖ 2,300 kg (5,000 lb)
✖ Near threatened
🍴 Grasses
🏠 ⋀⋀⋀ ⋎≈

E. and S. Africa

The white rhinoceros is one of the biggest mammals on earth, outweighed only by elephants and the semi-aquatic hippopotamus. White rhinos are paler than their fellow African black rhinoceros, but still a dull lead grey. "White" is probably a misinterpretation of the Dutch/Boer term *wijd*, which means wide, referring to the animal's broad mouth unlike the black rhino's narrow, pointed lip. White rhinos graze with their heads held low, whereas black rhinos are browsers, grasping and twisting foliage from thorny scrub. Their large size as well as a process of hind-gut fermentation allows them to extract sufficient nutrition from a high-volume yet low-quality grass diet.

Both African rhinos have two horns. The one in front can be exceptionally long, especially in females. Rhino horn, which is made of a hair-like material, is used in traditional medicine in some Asian countries. In an attempt to save the rhino, conservationists in some reserves remove the horn under anaesthetic, thereby giving poachers no reason to kill the animal.

◁ BLACK RHINOCEROS
Slightly smaller and rounder than the white rhino, the black rhino (*Diceros bicornis*) is identified by its narrow, pointed lip.

More than **1,000 rhinos were killed** by poachers in South Africa in 2014

Group dynamics

White rhinos follow a complex system of social organization. Females and calves live in groups of five or six. Although the ranges of adult females overlap, there is little contact between the groups. The female gives birth to a single calf after a gestation of 16 months and the young stay with their mothers for two to three years. Adolescents form "friendships" or accompany cows that are without calves. Adult bulls, however, are solitary unless on the lookout for a breeding female.

They may tolerate one or two subordinate males close by – so long as they do not pose a challenge. Bulls mark their territories vigorously and stand horn-to-horn with intruding males, screaming defiance. It is safer for the weaker ones to back off than to turn tail, which invites a chase and heavy, damaging strikes from the fearsome horn. Adult white rhinos are effectively immune from attack by predators because of their huge size – humans are their only enemy – and healthy animals can live for around 45 years.

▽ LITTLE AND LARGE
Females are aggressively protective of their young, vulnerable calves, but chase them away after two to three years, before breeding again.

uniquely patterned
coat gives alternative
name of painted dog

African wild dog

Lycaon pictus

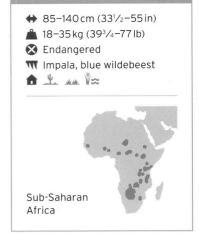

⟷ 85–140 cm (33½–55 in)
⚖ 18–35 kg (39¾–77 lb)
✗ Endangered
🏹 Impala, blue wildebeest
🏠 🌵 🌾 🌱 ≈

Sub-Saharan
Africa

Highly adaptable, African wild dogs live in a variety
of habitats across sub-Saharan Africa. Like many
members of the dog family, African wild dogs live in
packs and hunt cooperatively. A pack consists of four
to nine adults with one dominant breeding pair and
their pups. New packs usually form when siblings
of the same sex leave their birth pack and join with
a group of the opposite sex from another pack – a
behaviour that reduces inbreeding.

Wild dog packs require large home ranges – typically
around 750 sq km (290 sq miles). Medium-sized
antelope such as impala and Thomson's gazelles make
up the majority of their prey. However, some packs
have developed specialized skills for hunting different
savanna animals such as zebras and ostriches. Wild
dogs are threatened by habitat loss, human persecution,
traffic, and diseases such as rabies and canine distemper;
the latter is caught from domestic dogs.

△ **FACE OFF**
Notoriously tough-skinned and
aggressive in defence, a pair of honey
badgers fight off an attack by a pack
of wild dogs despite their inferior size.

▷ **RARE AGGRESSION**
Fights, either for dominance or for
food, are rare within a pack. African
wild dogs rely on cooperation for
their survival.

African jacana

Actophilornis africanus

⟷ 30 cm (12 in)
⚖ 150–250 g (5–9 oz)
✗ Common
🏹 Insects, molluscs
🏠 🌱 ≈
🧭 Sub-Saharan Africa

Equipped with long toes and sharp claws, jacanas move
elegantly over floating leaves, but are as likely to perch
on top of a swimming hippopotamus. The jacana eats
whatever it can reach in the water and on submerged
stems and leaves. It snatches bees from lily flowers,
dipping them into the water before swallowing. Typically,
several jacanas feed on a marsh, but keep their distance,
calling and chasing should another venture too near.

Female jacanas mate with several males and lay about
four eggs in each of their nests. The male incubates them
over 21–26 days. He also cares for the chicks, often
carrying his brood beneath his wings, which are
specially adapted for this purpose.

◁ **LILY TROTTER**
As one leaf gradually sinks beneath
it, the lily-trotting jacana steps to the
next, curling over leaf edges with its
beak to find snails and beetles.

Red-billed quelea

Quelea quelea

Known as Africa's "feathered locust", the red-billed quelea is perhaps the world's most abundant bird. It is nomadic, descending on areas covered with tall seeding grasses or, if they cannot be found, cultivated cereal crops. Although individual birds only eat about 18 g (⁵/₈ oz) of seed a day, a flock of 2 million birds can consume around 36 tonnes (40 tons). In South Africa alone, more than 180 million queleas are killed each year in pest control operations.

Flocks of red-billed queleas, millions strong, look like billowing clouds of smoke. The birds at the rear constantly leapfrog forwards, to take a turn at the front, as the feeding flock forges ahead. Breeding birds weave a ball-shaped nest out of grass when the seasonal rains arrive.

↔	12 cm (4³/₄ in)
⚖	15–30 g (¹/₂–1 oz)
✖	Common
♏	Seeds, insects
🏠	
◉	Sub-Saharan Africa

thick red beak of breeding male

▷ **SEED CRACKER**
The quelea's thick beak is ideal for cracking and peeling seeds held by the tongue. Its red colour is simply to impress a potential mate.

African skimmer

Rynchops flavirostris

Although it looks "broken" at first glance, the African skimmer's bill is a specialized tool, used for fishing at the surface of calm water. Fine, parallel grooves on each side reduce friction, so that the bird can fly with the elongated tip of the lower mandible dipped in the water without tipping forwards. Skimmers nest on remote, exposed sandbanks, often in temperatures above 35°C (95°F).

↔ 36–42 cm (14–16½ in)
⚖ 100–200 g (3½–7 oz)
✖ Near threatened
🍴 Fish
🏠 ⫯≈ ≈
◉ Sub-Saharan Africa

▽ **SNATCHING FISH**
When the African skimmer's lower mandible touches a fish it triggers a reflex mechanism to snatch the prey.

Leopard tortoise

Stigmochelys pardalis

This large tortoise prefers drier habitats, where it eats grassy plants, herbs, flowers, seeds, and berries. Males compete for females by butting one another until one is overturned. The female lays up to six clutches of between five and 25 eggs in a season, burying each clutch in a burrow. The eggs hatch after about nine to 14 months, depending on temperature, rainfall, and location, and the young mature in five to six years. The maximum lifespan of the leopard tortoise is more than 100 years.

↔ 30–70cm (12–27½ in)
⚖ 20 kg (44 lb)
✖ Not known
🍴 Grasses, fruit, seeds
🏠 ⫯ ⩫ ⩯
◉ E. to Southern Africa

▷ **HIGHLY PATTERNED**
The scutes of the shell have rosettes similar to those of a leopard: straw yellow or tan-brown with black.

high-domed shell with raised scutes

powerful front legs used for digging

whip-like tail used for swimming and defence

Nile monitor

Varanus niloticus

Fiercely defiant, the powerful Nile monitor readily defends its meal against crocodiles and big cats. Food can be almost any meat from insects, snails, and crabs to fish, amphibians, turtles, snakes, small mammals, and bird and reptile eggs as well as carrion. This huge lizard – the largest in Africa – stalks prey quietly and then strikes in a flash. It bites hard with its peg-like teeth set in crushing jaws, writhes its muscular body, whips its long tail, and slashes violently with its sharp-clawed feet.

Generally found in or near slow-moving rivers and lakes, the semi-aquatic Nile monitor can swim as fast and expertly as it runs and climbs. They bask in the sun on exposed sections of a bank or on nearby rocks or tree stumps. In cooler parts of their range, Nile monitors hibernate in communal dens.

Sealed in for safety

After the August–September rains, male Nile monitors wrestle and grapple for the right to mate. The female digs a hole in a damp termite mound and lays up to 60 eggs – the largest number of any lizard in a single clutch. The termites repair the mound, sealing in the eggs so they incubate in stable conditions. The eggs hatch in six to nine months, but the hatchlings, which are about 30 cm (12 in) long, remain in the nest until fresh rains soften the soil enough for them to dig their way out.

A **threatened** Nile monitor will **squirt fetid material** from its **cloaca**

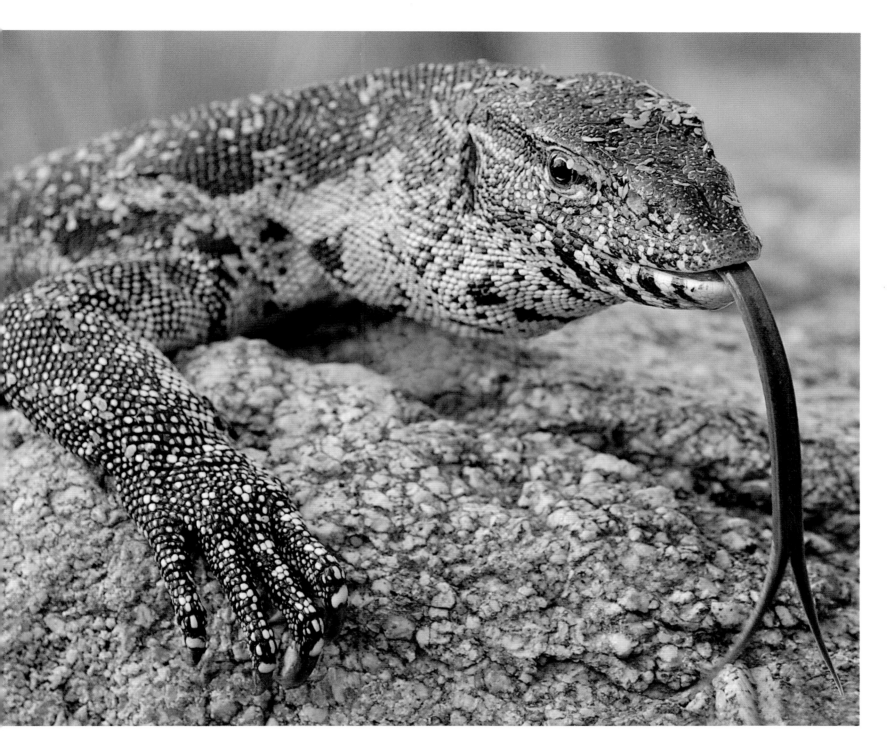

1.8–2.3 m (6–7¹/₂ ft)
Up to 15 kg (33 lb)
Common
Amphibians, birds, mammals

Sub-Saharan
Africa

△ FORKED TONGUE

Monitor lizards have a long, forked tongue, which they use to test their surroundings and to detect prey or carrion or the presence of predators such as crocodiles and pythons.

◁ AT HOME IN WATER

Nile monitors spend much of their time in water. They are reputed to be able to stay submerged underwater for up to one hour.

KALAHARI DESERT
A thirsty land where life finds a way

Covering an area of about 900,000 sq km (350,000 sq miles) in southern Africa, the Kalahari comprises a mixture of dry savanna and extensive areas of sand dunes. In summer, daytime temperatures can exceed 40°C (104°F), but the heat is moderated by altitude, with most of the region lying above 800 m (2,630 ft). The name Kalahari comes from the local Tswana language: *Kgalagadi* means waterless place. However, although it is commonly called a desert on account of its aridity, the Kalahari supports a far greater range of plant and animal life than a true desert.

Temporary greening
The Kalahari has a summer rainy season, when 100–500 mm (4–20 in) of rain may fall and parts of the region may become relatively green. However, the rains may fail completely in some years and as a result, the plants and animals have numerous adaptations to periodic drought.

For example, the plants of the dry savanna conserve water by producing tough, succulent or needle-like leaves and they take advantage of the rains to store water in roots, tubers, stems, and large, watery fruits such as melons and cucumbers.

The area has a diverse range of animals, including large herbivores such as antelopes and elephants, as well as predators such as lions, cheetahs, leopards, hyenas, wild dogs, and birds of prey. Other notable animals include aardvarks, ostriches, and meerkats. In recent years, the movement of larger herbivores has been restricted by cattle fencing, and wild predators have been persecuted by livestock farmers.

SURVIVAL FOOD
The deep roots of the camel thorn acacia help it to survive droughts, when its flowers and large seed pods become vital survival food for many of the Kalahari's herbivores. The leaves are protected by thorns, which deter browsers.

CAMEL THORN ACACIA

SAFE REFUGE
Colonies of 100 or more pairs of sociable weavers breed in a huge, multi-chambered nest, usually woven around the branches of a tree. Parent birds are aided by unrelated adults and older offspring, allowing them to raise up to four broods in succession.

SOCIABLE WEAVER

GEMSBOK

Contains the world's largest unbroken expanse of sand

More than 400 species of plants

KEEPING A COOL HEAD
Among a variety of adaptations to the heat, the gemsbok pants through its nose to cool blood in the fine capillaries in the nostrils. Blood entering the brain is cooled by a close-knit network of vessels below it.

LOCATION

The Kalahari semi-arid zone of Namibia, Botswana, and the northern Cape of South Africa is part of the larger Kalahari Basin.

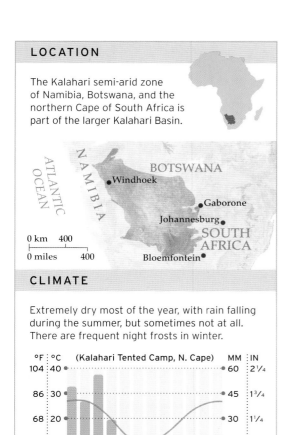

ATLANTIC OCEAN

NAMIBIA

BOTSWANA

Windhoek

Gaborone

Johannesburg

SOUTH AFRICA

Bloemfontein

0 km 400
0 miles 400

CLIMATE

Extremely dry most of the year, with rain falling during the summer, but sometimes not at all. There are frequent night frosts in winter.

°F	°C	(Kalahari Tented Camp, N. Cape)	MM	IN
104	40		60	2¼
86	30		45	1¾
68	20		30	1¼
50	10		15	½
32	0		0	0

Jan Feb Mar Apr May Jun Jul Aug Sep Oct Nov Dec

Key ▬ Average temperature ▮ Rainfall

DESERT SLEEPER
African bullfrogs survive droughts in a dormant state known as aestivation. They seal themselves underground inside a watertight cocoon made of shed skin. Here, they can survive for up to 10 months until roused by fresh rainfall.

Too wet to be a true desert

AFRICAN BULLFROG

Caracal
Caracal caracal

short forelegs

Africa's second-largest small cat, the caracal can bring down prey up to three times its own size. Speed and agility allow it to run down faster animals such as hares and small antelopes, while powerful muscles in its long hind legs enable it to leap up to 3 m (10 ft) in the air to grab flying birds with its large front paws. The caracal's hunting skills so impressed Persian and Indian royalty that many were trained to hunt gamebirds for royal families.

↔ 0.6–1.1 m (2–3½ ft)
⚖ 6–20 kg (13–44 lb)
⊗ Common
♛ Birds, mammals
🏠 🏘 ⛰ 🌵 🌾

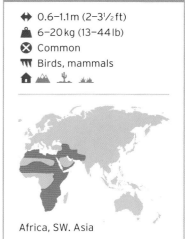

Africa, SW. Asia

◁ **EAR TUFTS**
The long, black ear tufts may be used as protection against flies, camouflage in long grass, or even as a tool for communication.

Aardvark
Orycteropus afer

Short, stocky legs and a flattened snout inspired South Africa's Dutch settlers to give this mammal a name that means "earth pig". Yet the solitary, night-foraging aardvark is not related to pigs or even anteaters, though it feeds mainly on ants, using its long, sharp claws to tear into their mounds. It extracts the ants with its 30-cm (12-in) long, sticky tongue, and an adult can eat up to 50,000 in one night. The food is ground up by a muscular area of the aardvark's stomach.

↔ 0.9–1.4 m (3–4½ ft)
⚖ 40–65 kg (88–143 lb)
⊗ Common
♛ Ants, termites
🏠 🏘 🌴 🏜 ⛰ 🌵 🌿 🌾

Sub-Saharan Africa

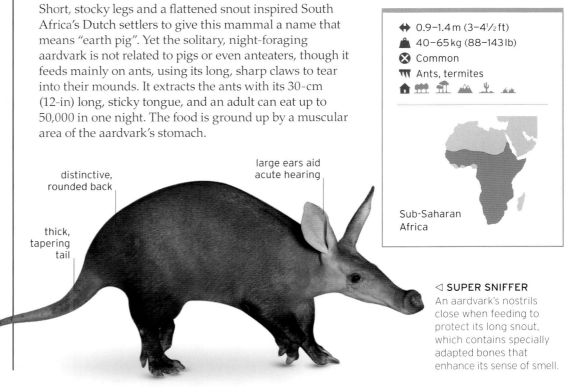

large ears aid acute hearing

distinctive, rounded back

thick, tapering tail

◁ **SUPER SNIFFER**
An aardvark's nostrils close when feeding to protect its long snout, which contains specially adapted bones that enhance its sense of smell.

Common warthog
Phacochoerus africanus

protective warty pad on cheek

Despite its rugged appearance, the common warthog is more likely to flee than fight if threatened, reaching speeds of up to 55 km/h (35 mph) on its long legs. If cornered, however, it uses its two sets of tusks to defend itself. Warthogs have reason to run – besides being hunted by humans for bushmeat, their natural predators include lions, leopards, hyenas, and crocodiles. The warthog is the only pig adapted for grazing. It "kneels" when eating grass or rooting with its tough snout, developing calluses on its wrists.

Facial armour

The warthog's facial "warts" are lumps of tissue that provide protection during fights. The warts are larger in adult males, which compete for mating rights. Females live in family groups called "sounders", with one or more litters of piglets, and individuals communicate using squeaks, grunts, and squeals.

↔ 1–1.5 m (3¼–5 ft)
⚖ 50–150 kg (110–330 lb)
⊗ Common
⁞⁞⁞ Grass, roots, small animals
🏠 🌵 🌾

Sub-Saharan Africa

◁ **SOLITARY BOAR**
Males leave their birth group after about two years and join a bachelor herd. Adult males, however, are solitary and mix with female-dominated sounders mainly to mate.

Kalahari springbok
Antidorcas hofmeyri

The name springbok refers to the way this antelope makes high, stiff-legged leaps when excited or threatened by predators, which include leopards, cheetahs, hyenas, and lions. It can leap 4 m (13 ft) through the air and reach speeds of 100 km/h (60 mph) when running away. The Kalahari springbok looks and lives very like the common springbok found to the east and south. However, this species is slightly larger and is a pale brown compared to its cousin's chestnut-red, and the band on its flank is nearer to black. These are presumably adaptations to help it blend in among the arid sands and sparse vegetation of the Kalahari.

Kalahari springbok breed throughout the year. Females leave their herd when ready to give birth, usually to a single calf. They leave the calf hidden under a bush when feeding, and rejoin the herd when the calf is three or four weeks old. Calves are weaned when five or six months old, but usually stay with their mother until she next gives birth.

↔ 1.4–1.6 m (4½–5¼ ft)
⚖ 30.5–47.5 kg (67–105 lb)
⊗ Common
⁞⁞⁞ Grass, roots, tubers
🏠 🌵 🌾

Southern Africa

▷ **RACING AHEAD**
Springboks spend most of the year in single-sex herds. This male herd is on the move; any stragglers will be more at risk from predators.

Cape porcupine

Hystrix africaeaustralis

porcupine raises quills to make itself look bigger

This impressive rodent has taken defence to the extreme. All along its back are sharp spines called quills, which are modified hairs up to 30 cm (12 in) long. If threatened, the Cape porcupine flicks these out to form a black-and-white crest, while stamping its feet and shaking its hollow tail quills like a rattle. This dramatic display is enough to deter most predators. Porcupines are born with soft quills and stay in the family burrow for around two months until their quills have hardened. Adults live in pairs and form a close bond.

- 63–80 cm (25–31½ in)
- 10–24 kg (22–53 lb)
- Common
- Roots, bulbs, tubers, fruit

C. to Southern Africa

◁ **WATCH OUT!**
If an inexperienced predator such as a leopard or lion cub attacks a porcupine, it risks a paw- or face-full of quills. If the wounds become infected, it may even die.

Meerkat
Suricata suricatta

dark bands on back

Small enough to sit in the palm of a human hand, meerkats are feisty, highly territorial mongooses that live in complex groups, known as mobs, clans, or gangs, of up to 50 animals. Each clan consists of a dominant male and female, with subordinate "helpers" of both sexes. In smaller clans, the alpha female gives birth to most litters, while the male tries to prevent other males from mating. The female also releases pheromones that stop young females from coming into season. If this fails, she attacks ovulating or pregnant females, often killing their pups. During late pregnancy, she drives off other females to safeguard her young. They rejoin the clan later.

Mob mentality
Meerkat society relies on cooperation, and helpers play a crucial role in raising pups to adulthood. Some young females produce milk to help feed the dominant female's pups, while helpers of both sexes alert them to predators, teach them to forage, protect them, and bring them food during the weaning process.

Meerkats depend on their clan in many vital ways. A gang digs a series of multi-level tunnel-and-room burrows in its territory – usually with many entrances – where all its members sleep at night and rest during the hottest part of the day. In the morning, they emerge to warm up in the sun. They spend the day foraging and taking turns on lookout duty. While the clan searches for beetles, lizards, and scorpions, or digs for tubers and roots that supply much-needed water, sentry meerkats keep watch for predators such as jackals, snakes, and, especially, birds of prey. When alerted to danger by an alarm call, clan members retreat to a nearby bolthole or mob together to ward off the predator. If an adult is surprised, it may use its own body to shield nearby pups.

A meerkat clan may have as many as **1,000 boltholes** in its territory

△ GROUP ATTACK
A meerkat mob acts as a single unit to ward off predators. All members arch their backs, raise their tails, and growl and hiss to intimidate the enemy.

▷ OLD AND YOUNG
Meerkats are highly social and the father may take an active role in guarding their pups. Non-breeding members of the clan also look after the young.

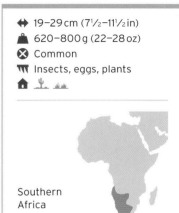

↔ 19–29 cm (7½–11½ in)
⚖ 620–800 g (22–28 oz)
✖ Common
🦷 Insects, eggs, plants

Southern
Africa

◁ ON GUARD
While its clan forages, a
sentry meerkat finds
a good vantage point
and keeps watch for
predators, often staying
at its post for hours,
and squeaking to alert
the group to danger.

long legs and two-toed
feet adapted for sprinting

Ostrich
Struthio camelus

The largest living bird, the
ostrich is immensely heavy and
unable to fly. Standing more than
2 m (6½ ft) tall, ostriches are
the tallest keen-sighted plains
animals, except for giraffes. A
bolting ostrich – reaching speeds
of 70 km/h (45 mph) – alerts all
prey species to danger.

Males attract females and
repel rivals by making a deep
boom. Akin to the roar of a lion,
the "ohh-oooh-ooooooooo" can
be heard 3 km (2 miles) away.

↔ 1.7–2.7 m (5½–8¾ ft)
⚖ 100–160 kg (220–353 lb)
✖ Common
🦷 Plants, insects
🏠 🌵 🌾

W., E., and
Southern Africa

△ **CHOOSING HER MATE**
In the breeding season, a female ostrich bends her
neck forwards, flaps her wings backwards, and makes
a clapping noise when she selects a displaying male.

▽ **DEFENSIVE MEASURES**
Body arched, mouth holding tail but
ready to bite, scale edges sharp and
forbidding, and foot claws ready to
scratch – all these form the armadillo
lizard's excellent defence mechanism.

tail gripped in
powerful jaws to form
protective hoop

Cape cobra
Naja nivea

The Cape cobra prefers dry,
scrubby habitats, where it hunts
by day for small prey, such as
colonial weaver bird eggs and
nestlings. Like other cobras, it
has fixed (not tilting) front fangs
that inject nerve-disabling
venom. After mating in early
spring, the female lays 10–20
eggs in midsummer, usually in
a rodent burrow or termite nest.
Young Cape cobras have a
characteristic dark throat patch
that fades with age.

◁ **STANDING ITS GROUND**
A threatened Cape cobra rears up,
spreads its hood, gapes, and hisses.
Predators include meerkats, snake
eagles, and secretary birds.

↔ 1.2–1.4 m (4–4½ ft)
⚖ 2–3 kg (4½–6½ lb)
✖ Not known
🦷 Rodents, reptiles, birds
🏠 🌱
➤ Southern Africa

thick, hard head shield

broad, triangular head

Armadillo lizard

Ouroborus cataphractus

Large, thick, sharp-edged scales around the body and a habit of curling up when threatened give this distinctive reptile its common name. The armadillo lizard is a type of girdled lizard. Its hard scales, reinforced with bony plates, form bands or rings that encircle its body. With such defences the armadillo lizard usually lives an unhurried life. It basks in the sun or ambles around its dry scrub habitat in search of small prey, especially termites, then rests in a rocky crevice, empty burrow, or among tree roots by night.

Social lizards

Armadillo lizards are unusual in both their social and breeding habits. Extended family groups numbering three or four to occasionally 50 or more, of all ages and both sexes rest together in crevices. The territorial males within a group generally defend their small areas peaceably, but are extremely aggressive to unrelated intruding males. Also unusually for a reptile, the female gives birth to just one or two large young. Mating occurs in early spring and the offspring are born six to seven months later.

spines protect soft belly

↔ 16–21 cm (6^1/$_4$–8^1/$_4$ in)

🏋 70–100 g (2^1/$_2$–3^1/$_2$ oz)

✖ Vulnerable

🗡 Insects, millipedes, plants

🏠 🌵

Southern Africa

MADAGASCAN DRY FOREST
Evolution in isolation

Madagascar is the world's fourth largest island. In the 135 million years since it separated from the continent of Africa, its plants and animals have diversified, producing a unique collection. The natural vegetation in the drier, western part of this tropical island is dominated by dry deciduous forests interspersed with wetlands. The geology of the area is mostly karst, a type of limestone, which means that surface water rapidly drains into underground rivers.

Baobabs, lemurs, and chameleons

Madagascar's trees include the gigantic baobabs – six species of which are endemic – and the spiny, succulent pachypodiums. The dry forests once extended from the coastal plain to about 800 m (2,600 ft) of altitude, but have been widely replaced by grazing pasture. Today, only three per cent of the original forests remain, and they are of global ecological importance because of the hundreds of endemic plants and animals they support. These include lemurs – a group of primates found only in Madagascar. The forests are also home to a range of specialist insectivores and carnivores, and the world's most endangered tortoise, the ploughshare tortoise – and two-thirds of the world's chameleon species.

Some of the more unusual wildlife is partly protected from persecution by traditional beliefs that place a *fady*, or taboo, on certain species. However, this has not protected the animals from the indirect threat of forest clearance for firewood and charcoal production, and some are still collected for the pet trade.

WORLD'S RAREST TORTOISE
This critically endangered tortoise has a wild population of just 200 adults, living in scraps of rocky scrub where they feed on grasses. Eggs and young are predated by introduced bush pigs, and individuals are still poached for the pet trade.

PLOUGHSHARE TORTOISE

MINIATURE MARVEL
With a total length of 45 mm (1¾ in), it is no surprise the dwarf chameleon escaped scientific attention until as recently as 1996. One of the world's smallest reptiles, it hunts in the leaf litter at night and climbs into low leafy branches to hide by day.

DWARF CHAMELEO

Baobabs can store up to 100,000 litres (26,400 gallons) of water in their trunk

95% o

BAOBABS

THE MAGNIFICENT SEVEN
Madagascar's seven species of baobab are a symbol of the island. During wet periods, the fibrous wood swells with stored water, causing the trunk to bloat. Baobabs are deciduous, and shed their leaves in the dry season to reduce water loss.

LOCATION

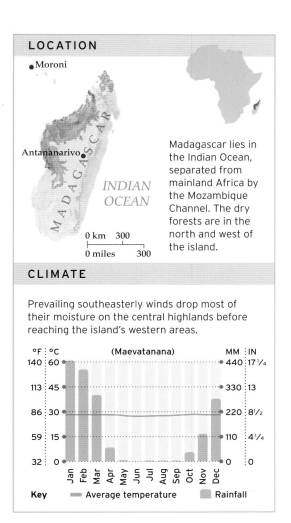

- Moroni
- Antananarivo

INDIAN OCEAN

MADAGASCAR

0 km 300
0 miles 300

Madagascar lies in the Indian Ocean, separated from mainland Africa by the Mozambique Channel. The dry forests are in the north and west of the island.

CLIMATE

Prevailing southeasterly winds drop most of their moisture on the central highlands before reaching the island's western areas.

°F	°C	(Maevatanana)	MM	IN
140	60		440	17¼
113	45		330	13
86	30		220	8½
59	15		110	4¼
32	0		0	0

Jan Feb Mar Apr May Jun Jul Aug Sep Oct Nov Dec

Key — Average temperature — Rainfall

BURROWING RAT
The Malagasy giant jumping rat occupies a similar burrowing niche to rabbits, which are absent from Madagascar. This endemic rodent's feeding and burrowing behaviours are important in seed dispersal and soil aeration.

Reptile species are endemic

GIANT JUMPING RAT

Fosa
Cryptoprocta ferox

Although they look like cats, fosas belong to a group of mammals thought to have evolved from a prehistoric mongoose-like ancestor. Madagascar's largest predator, the fosa is active both day and night, and is able to hunt small mammals, birds, and reptiles in trees as well as on the ground. Because they occasionally take domestic poultry, fosas are targeted by local farmers as a pest.

↔ 70–80 cm (27½–31½ in)
⚖ 5.5–8.5 kg (12–19 lb)
✖ Vulnerable
🦙 Lemurs, tenrecs, birds

Madagascar

▷ **UNIQUE FEATURES**
The fosa's cat-like head ends in a dog-like snout, and when walking slowly it keeps its heels on the ground like a bear - or a human.

semi-retractable claws provide good grip in trees

Berthe's mouse lemur
Microcebus berthae

The smallest living primate, this solitary nocturnal mammal spends its life in trees, searching for food around 10 m (33 ft) off the ground. Berthe's mouse lemurs enter a state of torpor during the day, lowering their metabolism and temperature to conserve energy.

▽ **TINY PRIMATE**
Berthe's mouse lemurs use all four limbs to run quickly along branches, leaping to flee from predators such as owls or fosas.

↔ 9–9.5 cm (3½–3¾ in)
⚖ 30 g (1¹⁄₁₆ oz)
✖ Endangered
🦙 Fruit, gum, honeydew

Madagascar

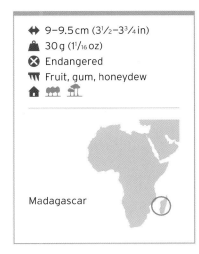

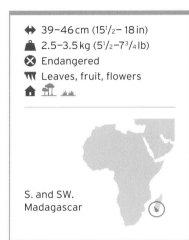

- 39–46 cm (15$^1/_2$– 18 in)
- 2.5–3.5 kg (5$^1/_2$–7$^3/_4$ lb)
- Endangered
- Leaves, fruit, flowers

S. and SW.
Madagascar

▷ **ON THE MOVE**
Ring-tailed lemur troops cover 6 km
(3$^3/_4$ miles) a day in search of food.
When travelling, ringtails raise their
tails like flags to ensure the troop
stays together.

Ring-tailed lemur

Lemur catta

dark, triangular eye patch

tail used for signalling

With their distinctive black-and-white faces and long, striped tails, ring-tailed lemurs are the most recognizable of all the lemur species. Covered in thick, grey-brown fur, they move so easily both on the ground and in trees that they seem like a cross between a cat and a raccoon. In fact, ring-tailed lemurs belong to the primates – the order that includes monkeys, apes, and humans. This means that, just like humans, lemurs have fingerprints and vision is their prime sense, although smell is also important to them.

Girl power

Native only to Madagascar, ring-tailed lemurs are found mainly in bush and dry forests, where these highly sociable animals live in groups of several males and females. Females rule the troop, winning fights with males, getting the best food, and ultimately deciding which males to mate with. During the mating season, males have "stink fights" – rubbing their tails over scent glands in their genitals and wrists, then flicking them at each other. Mating occurs between mid-April and June. In August or September, females give birth to one or two babies, weighing less than 100 g (3^{1}/$_{2}$ oz) each. Females tend to raise their young jointly, often caring for groups of infants and carrying each other's offspring.

Sunshine and socializing

Unlike most other lemurs, ring-tails sunbathe in the morning, socializing at these times with a wide range of vocalizations and facial expressions. Ringtails are mainly plant eaters, including flowers and even bark and sap, but the fruit of the tamarind tree is a favourite. Sometimes they eat insects or small vertebrates such as lizards and, rarely, birds.

The main predators of ringtails are fossas – cat-like carnivores also native to Madagascar – and large birds of prey, but devastation of habitat by humans is the chief threat to these and all other lemur species. On average, ring-tails live for 16–19 years in the wild, but they have been known to survive to the age of 27 in captivity.

△ **BLACK-AND-WHITE RUFFED LEMUR**
Unlike ring-tails, which spend much of their time on the ground, black-and-white ruffed lemurs (*Varecia variegata*) prefer to live high up in the tree canopy.

◁ **EARLY MORNING RITUAL**
Ring-tailed lemurs sit upright and expose their bellies to the warmth of the sun before beginning the search for their first meal of the day.

long tail used for balance when leaping

Verreaux's sifaka

Propithecus verreauxi

One of the largest members of the lemur family, the Verreaux's sifaka lives in the dry and spiny forests of south and southwest Madagascar. Sifakas are active during the daytime, feeding in trees – mainly on leaves, flowers, and fruit. They extract moisture from the leaves of succulent plants or by licking water droplets that have condensed on their woolly fur.

In leaps and bounds

Sifakas venture to the ground to cross open spaces in their distinctive bipedal leaping gait. In the trees, they move by clinging vertically and leaping with their long, strong hindlegs, covering gaps of up to 10 m (33 ft). Although their large hands and feet can be used for grasping, sifakas rarely use them in feeding. Instead they lean the whole body forwards and pick up food directly with the mouth. Females are dominant in sifaka social groups. Groups of sifakas tend to spread out while travelling and searching for food, but come together in the same tree to rest.

Sifakas live in small groups of a few females and two or three males, one of which may be a "stain-chested" male, so-called because it produces scent from a gland in its throat which it uses in marking. All sifakas scent-mark their territories with urine and use it to signal to members of their own social group. They also communicate through calls, including a bark-like "shi-fak" call which gave them their name.

Like many lemurs, the Verreaux's sifaka is at risk from destruction of its habitat due to slash-and-burn agriculture and timber felling.

About **30 per cent** of Verraux's sifakas are **killed by fosas** in their **first year**

△ **COQUEREL'S SIFAKA**
Like all sifakas, Coquerel's sifakas
(*P. coquereli*) have one young at a time.
At first, it is carried across the mother's
belly, then later rides on her back.

◁ **DANCING MALE**
When crossing open ground, a
Verreaux's sifaka gracefully "dances"
sideways on its strong hindlegs with
its forearms held out for balance. Its
tail is almost as long as its body.

↔	40–48 cm (15³⁄₄–19 in)
⚖	3–5 kg (6¹⁄₂–11 lb)
✕	Endangered
🌿	Leaves, fruit, flowers, bark
🏠	

SW. and S.
Madagascar

Aye-aye
Daubentonia madagascariensis

The world's largest nocturnal primate, the aye-aye is
superbly adapted to locating insect larvae, in particular
beetle grubs, beneath the bark of trees. It taps the tree
trunk with its elongated middle finger and listens for the
echo of a larva tunnel before chiselling away at the wood
with its incisors and extracting the grub. The aye-aye's
teeth and fingers are also useful when opening nuts and
hard-shelled fruit. Aye-ayes are mainly solitary and
spend the day in treetop nests made of twigs.

↔	30–37 cm (12–14¹⁄₂ in)
⚖	2.4–2.6 kg (5¹⁄₄–5³⁄₄ lb)
✕	Endangered
🌿	Grubs, fruit, nuts, fungi
🏠	
◉	NW. and E. Madagascar

▷ **NOCTURNAL PROWLER**
Large eyes and ears help the aye-aye
to see and hear in the gloom of the
forest at night.

Greater hedgehog tenrec
Setifer setosus

Greater hedgehog tenrecs rely on their long whiskers as
well as smell and sound to find prey at night. These expert
climbers nest in tree hollows or on the ground. They
lower their body temperature during the day and for
weeks at a time during cooler times to conserve energy.

↔	15–22 cm (6–8³⁄₄ in)
⚖	180–270 g (6¹⁄₄–9¹⁄₂ oz)
✕	Locally common
🌿	Earthworms, insects, fruit
🏠	
◉	Madagascar

▽ **SHIELD OF SPINES**
Like true hedgehogs, greater
hedgehog tenrecs can roll into a prickly
ball for protection when threatened.

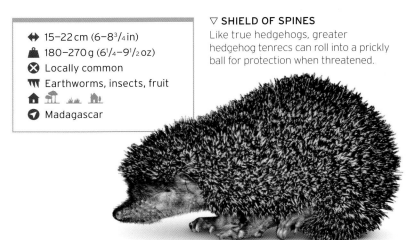

opposing fused
toes give feet
pincer-like grip

Panther chameleon

Furcifer pardalis

independently
moving eyes
give almost
360° view

△ **DAZZLING DISPLAY**
Male panther chameleons are more colourful than females. They are at their brightest when competing with another male or courting a female, and least colourful when hunting.

The panther chameleon's impressive colour changes are affected by its mood, such as when it is being aggressively territorial, dealing with a threat, or courting a mate. Temperature, humidity, light levels, and – to a lesser extent than popularly believed – matching the colours of its surroundings as a means of camouflage are also influencing factors.

An aid to recognizing coloration changes in other individuals is excellent eyesight, which is also important for capturing prey. The two turret-like eyes move independently to look in different directions simultaneously, or are both aimed at prey to judge its distance and motion. Then, the muscular, catapult-like tongue – which is longer than the chameleon's body – flicks out and back with the prey in just 0.007 seconds. Panther chameleons feed mostly on insects, such as crickets and beetles, and spiders, but they will also eat small vertebrates such as frogs, baby lizards (including other chameleons), and rodents. They are active during the day, spending most of their time in low trees or bushes hunting for prey. At night, they sleep with their tail coiled tight around a thin branch.

Ducking and bobbing

Panther chameleons live mostly alone and the males will display to, and even physically fight, others that intrude into their territory. However, during the breeding season (January–May), the aroused males – which are up to twice the size of the females – duck and bob to impress potential partners. The female lays up to six clutches of 10–50 eggs buried in moist soil, and the young hatch six to 12 months later.

△ **ON TARGET**
The chameleon shoots out its elastic tongue onto the prey, which adheres to the sticky cup-like end before the tongue springs back into the mouth.

thick, muscular tail base typical of males

↔ 40–52 cm (15³/₄–20¹/₂ in)
⚖ 140–220 g (5–7³/₄ oz)
✗ Locally common
🗡 Insects, small vertebrates
🏠 🌳 🏛 🌱

N. and E. Madagascar, Reunion Island

prehensile tail acts as fifth limb when climbing

Henkel's leaf-tailed gecko
Uroplatus henkeli

large, triangular head

Henkel's leaf-tailed gecko's remarkable camouflage is heightened by the "frill" of skin along the sides of its head – giving it a "beard" – and part of its body. When resting during the day, lying flat on a mossy, lichen-covered rock or tree trunk, these features break up the otherwise recognizable lizard-shaped outline. It hunts at night, mainly for insects, usually just a few metres above ground.

↔ 27 cm (11 in)
⚖ 40–50 g (1¹/₂–1³/₄ oz)
✗ Vulnerable
🗡 Insects, snails
🏠 🌳 🏛

○ N. and W. Madagascar

△ **STICKY TOES**
Henkel's gecko's large, adhesive toe pads, typical of the gecko family, stick even to glossy leaves and crumbly bark and so help in climbing trees.

Tomato frog
Dyscophus antongilii

The tomato frog's bright orange-red skin is a warning to predators, such as snakes. When threatened, its first line of defence is to puff itself up to look larger, and this also makes it difficult to swallow. If taken into a predator's jaws, the frog exudes a sticky liquid from its skin that clogs up the attacker's mouth and inflames its skin. The liquid can cause swellings and rashes in humans.

↔ 6–10.5 cm (2¹/₄–4¹/₄ in)
🌧 Rainy season
✗ Near threatened
🗡 Insects
🏠 🌳 🌱 🏘
○ N. and E. Madagascar

plump body

▷ **RED ALERT**
Female tomato frogs, such as the one shown here, are larger and more brightly coloured than males.

Northern Thailand
Two Asian elephants wander into a jungle
clearing as the sun rises. Elephants are highly
social mammals – females stay with their
families, headed by a matriarch, for life.

Asia

LAND OF EXTREMES

Asia

Asia is the world's largest continent, covering around 30 per cent of the Earth's land area. It extends nearly 6,500 km (4,000 miles) from the polar regions in the north of Siberian Russia, through the subtropics and tropics to the islands of Southeast Asia, which lie on and below the equator. Due to its vast size, parts of Central Asia experience a continental climate with extremes of heat in the summer and cold in the winter.

To the south of the Siberian plateau lies a sparsely populated landscape of mountain and plateau, desert, and steppe. The southern parts of Asia are geologically much younger. Tectonic activity to the east and southeast has created numerous volcanic island arcs that form the western side of the Pacific Ring of Fire. The Himalayas isolate the Indian subcontinent from the rest of Asia, and have a profound effect on the climate of Asia as a whole. More than 100 mountains have summits higher than 7,200 m (23,600 ft), and little moisture is left in the air flowing over them into Central Asia during the summer.

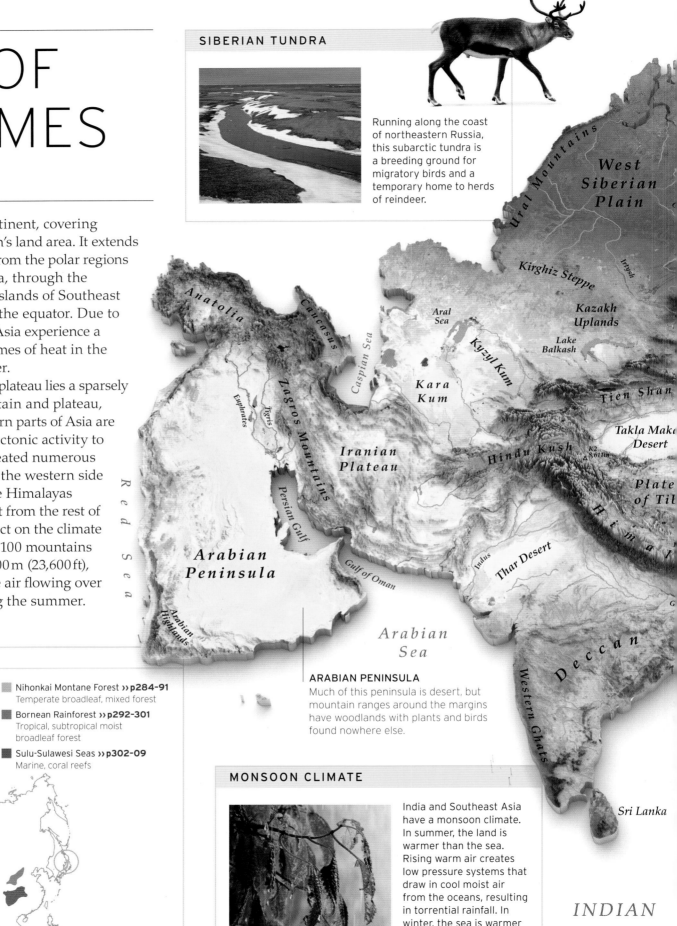

SIBERIAN TUNDRA

Running along the coast of northeastern Russia, this subarctic tundra is a breeding ground for migratory birds and a temporary home to herds of reindeer.

Ural Mountains
West Siberian Plain
Irtysh
Kirghiz Steppe
Kazakh Uplands
Lake Balkash
Aral Sea
Kyzyl Kum
Kara Kum
Caspian Sea
Caucasus
Anatolia
Euphrates
Tigris
Zagros Mountains
Iranian Plateau
Persian Gulf
Red Sea
Arabian Peninsula
Arabian Highlands
Gulf of Oman
Arabian Sea
Indus
Thar Desert
Hindu Kush
K2 8,611m
Tien Shan
Deccan
Western Ghats
Sri Lanka
INDIAN OCEAN

ARABIAN PENINSULA
Much of this peninsula is desert, but mountain ranges around the margins have woodlands with plants and birds found nowhere else.

FEATURED ECOREGIONS

- Arabian Highlands ›› p248-53
  Montane woodland, desert scrub
- Terai-Duar Savanna ›› p254-65
  Subtropical grassland
- Eastern Himalayas ›› p266-71
  Temperate broadleaf, mixed forest
- Upper Yangtze Forests ›› p272-77
  Temperate broadleaf, mixed forest
- Gobi Desert ›› p278-83
  Desert, scrub
- Nihonkai Montane Forest ›› p284-91
  Temperate broadleaf, mixed forest
- Bornean Rainforest ›› p292-301
  Tropical, subtropical moist broadleaf forest
- Sulu-Sulawesi Seas ›› p302-09
  Marine, coral reefs

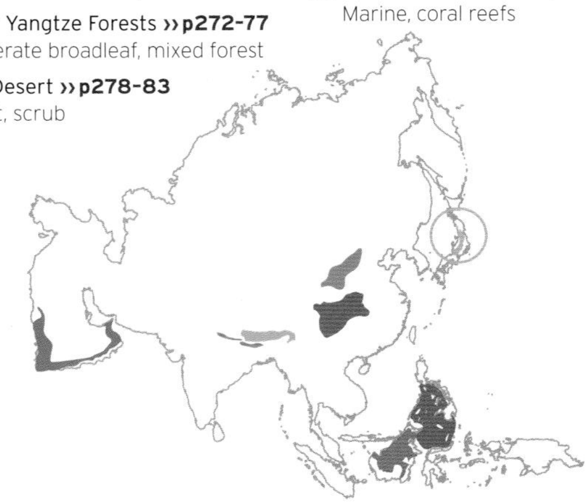

MONSOON CLIMATE

India and Southeast Asia have a monsoon climate. In summer, the land is warmer than the sea. Rising warm air creates low pressure systems that draw in cool moist air from the oceans, resulting in torrential rainfall. In winter, the sea is warmer than the land and so the air flow reverses, causing the dry season.

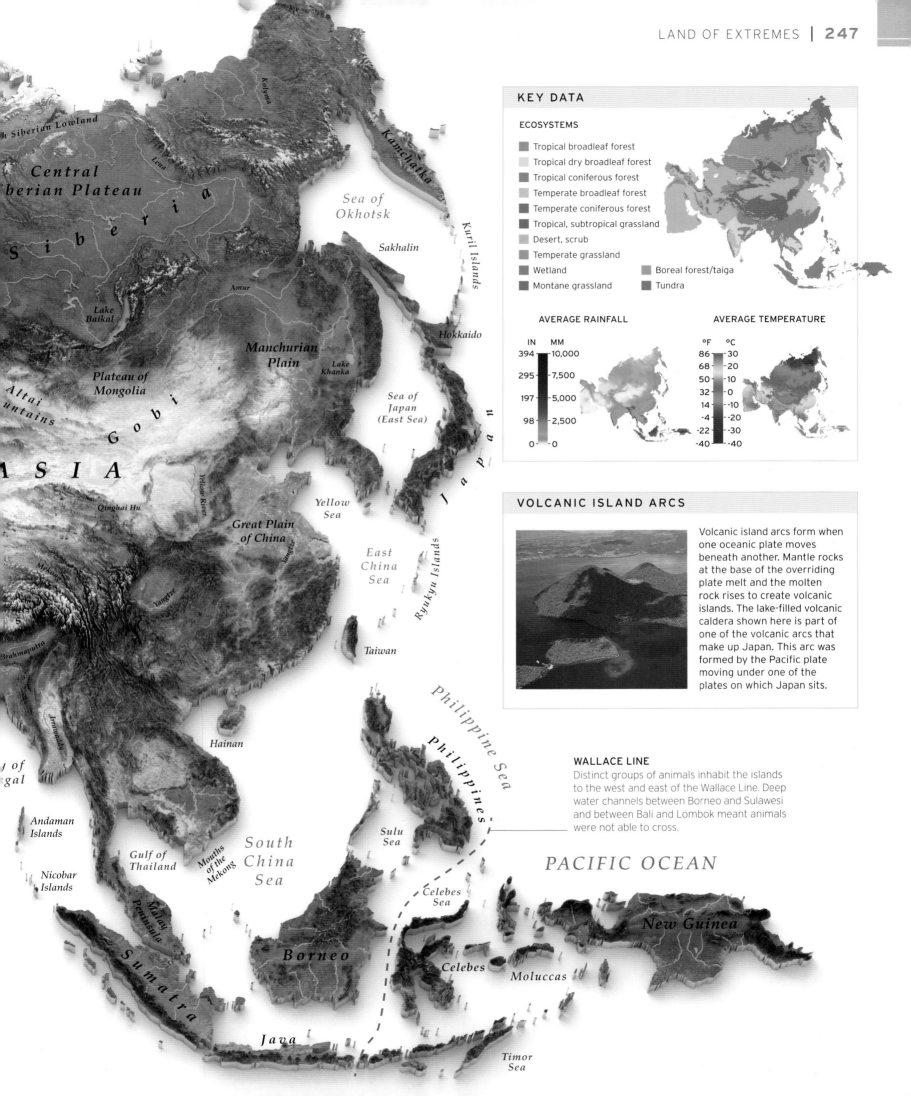

Central
~~Siberian~~ Plateau

~~h~~ Siberian Lowland

Siberia

Lena

Kolyma

Kamchatka

Sea of
Okhotsk

Sakhalin

Kuril Islands

Amur

Hokkaido

Lake
Baikal

Manchurian
Plain

Lake
Khanka

Altai
~~untains~~

Plateau of
Mongolia

Gobi

Sea of
Japan
(East Sea)

A S I A

Japan

Qinghai Hu

Yellow River

Great Plain
of China

Yellow
Sea

Yangtze

Mekong

Yangtze

East
China
Sea

Ryukyu Islands

S

Taiwan

Brahmaputra

Irrawaddy

Hainan

Philippine Sea

Philippines

~~y~~ of
~~gal~~

Andaman
Islands

Gulf of
Thailand

Mouths
of the
Mekong

South
China
Sea

Sulu
Sea

Nicobar
Islands

Malay Peninsula

Sumatra

Borneo

Celebes
Sea

Celebes

Moluccas

New Guinea

PACIFIC OCEAN

Java

Timor
Sea

KEY DATA

ECOSYSTEMS

- Tropical broadleaf forest
- Tropical dry broadleaf forest
- Tropical coniferous forest
- Temperate broadleaf forest
- Temperate coniferous forest
- Tropical, subtropical grassland
- Desert, scrub
- Temperate grassland
- Wetland
- Montane grassland
- Boreal forest/taiga
- Tundra

AVERAGE RAINFALL

IN	MM
394	10,000
295	7,500
197	5,000
98	2,500
0	0

AVERAGE TEMPERATURE

°F	°C
86	30
68	20
50	10
32	0
14	-10
-4	-20
-22	-30
-40	-40

VOLCANIC ISLAND ARCS

Volcanic island arcs form when one oceanic plate moves beneath another. Mantle rocks at the base of the overriding plate melt and the molten rock rises to create volcanic islands. The lake-filled volcanic caldera shown here is part of one of the volcanic arcs that make up Japan. This arc was formed by the Pacific plate moving under one of the plates on which Japan sits.

WALLACE LINE

Distinct groups of animals inhabit the islands to the west and east of the Wallace Line. Deep water channels between Borneo and Sulawesi and between Bali and Lombok meant animals were not able to cross.

ARABIAN HIGHLANDS
A moisture-laden haven for wildlife and plant species

The Arabian Highlands are a collection of mountain ranges, ridges, and plateaus rising around the fringes of the Arabian Peninsula. They stretch inland from the coastal "fog desert" and surround the Empty Quarter, the peninsula's vast sandy desert. Due to their altitude, the highlands are cooler and damper than the nearby deserts and are able to support a greater diversity of plant and animal life. Moisture-laden oceanic winds are forced up and over the mountains, producing seasonal rainfall, and low night-time temperatures cause fog and dew formation.

Vital juniper woodland

Unusually, it is the highest areas of this ecoregion that are covered with woodland. Here juniper trees are particularly abundant and provide vital cover and food for several bird species. Drier, south-facing slopes are home to more succulent plants, such as aloe and euphorbia,

while the foothills are covered with shrubland and savanna. Many of the area's plant and bird species are found nowhere else in the world, but the peninsula also serves as an important land bridge between Africa and Eurasia for migrating birds, many of which follow the ridge of the Asir Mountains that run parallel to the Red Sea coast. In terms of mammal species, the Arabian Highlands are home to several large carnivores, including the caracal, the rare Arabian wolf, and the striped hyena. They also form one of the last strongholds of the critically endangered Arabian leopard.

SPIKY SUCCULENT
Reaching up to 10 m (33 ft) in height, *Euphorbia ammak* resembles a cactus, but is actually a succulent tree-like plant from the spurge family. Its thick, spiny stems contain an unpleasant-tasting sap that discourages herbivores from browsing on it.

EUPHORBIA AMMAK

Home to more than 2,000 plant species >

ACACIA EATER
The slender mountain gazelle lives throughout the Arabian Highlands, especially where its main food plant, the acacia, is found. As well as leaves and seed pods, it eats succulent plants and digs for bulbs and corms, especially when water is scarce.

MOUNTAIN GAZELLE

41 reptile species live here >

CLIMBING SERPENT
The Arabian cat snake is an agile, stealthy predator, able to climb trees and rock faces in search of prey such as rodents, lizards, fledgling birds, and bats. This nocturnal species kills with its venomous fangs and is widespread in the region.

ARABIAN CAT SNA

Arabian oryx

Around the southern edge of the Arabian Peninsula, crossing the United Arab Emirates, Oman, Yemen, and Saudi Arabia.

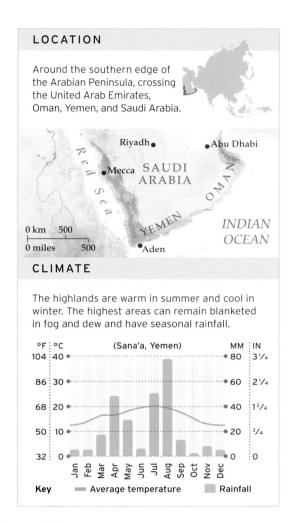

CLIMATE

The highlands are warm in summer and cool in winter. The highest areas can remain blanketed in fog and dew and have seasonal rainfall.

Key — Average temperature ▢ Rainfall

Hamadryas baboon

Papio hamadryas

dog-like muzzle

Full-grown male Hamadryas baboons are among the world's most impressive monkeys, with a muscular build, sharp canine teeth, and a magnificent cape of silvery fur that contrasts with their bright pink faces. Both sexes have pads of bare reddish skin on their buttocks, which swell in females to advertise when they are sexually receptive.

↔ 50–95 cm (19½–37½ in)
⬤ 9–21.5 kg (20–47 lb)
✖ Common
🌾 Grass, fruit, insects

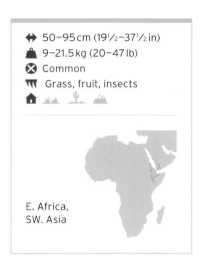

E. Africa, SW. Asia

Harems and bands

Hamadryas baboons were well known to the ancient Egyptians, who featured them in religious hieroglyphic carvings and paintings – they are also called sacred baboons. Like other baboon species, they spend most of their time on the ground and forage widely, eating grass, crops, and almost any small animals they find. At night many harems band together and climb cliffs for safety – in some places, a few hundred Hamadryas baboons may sleep on the same rock face.

The big dominant males jealously guard their females from rival males. They use visual threats such as yawning to reveal their large canine teeth and aggressive displays such as neck bites.

Dominant male baboons **lip-smack to reassure** their females

▽ GROOMING IN PROGRESS
Two female baboons groom a resplendent adult male as an act of loyalty and submission. Each adult male rules over a harem of several smaller, olive-brown females.

KEEPING COOL
Although relatively small compared to other grey wolf subspecies, the Arabian wolf has proportionately larger ears to disperse heat and help keep it cool during hot summers. In winter, its coat thickens to withstand freezing conditions.

were reintroduced in 1980

ARABIAN WOLF

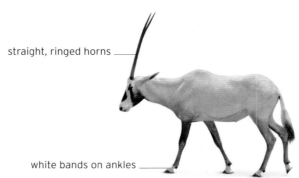

straight, ringed horns

white bands on ankles

Arabian oryx

Oryx leucoryx

Few large mammals are so well adapted to survive in the extreme heat and drought of the desert as the Arabian oryx. It has wide shovel-shaped hooves for plodding great distances over loose sand. The oryx is not a great runner – its only natural predators, wolves and striped hyenas, are few in number.

The bright, almost luminous white coat helps reflect away the sun's heat but also makes the Arabian oryx stand out against the barren landscape, even in the dark. The benefit to the antelopes of seeing their herd mates easily outweighs any risk of attracting the attention of predators. If a predator does appear on the horizon, the oryx has nowhere to hide. It takes the threat side-on, showing its full size in an attempt to deter attack.

Following the leader
An oryx herd is led by an older female and contains a few other females and their young, the dominant male, and some subordinate males. When food is plentiful after rainfall, the herd can swell into hundreds, and males defend small territories, mating with any female that comes along. In favourable conditions, females can give birth to a single calf once a year, after about 34 weeks of gestation. However, births are rare in years with low rainfall. Outside of the breeding season, herd members are tolerant of each other, with both sexes adopting a simple hierarchy based on horn length. The lack of rivalries lets a small herd cluster in the shade of a tree during the warmest part of the day. When it is cooler, members spread out to graze, always staying within sight of each other. When it is time to move on, the lead female sets off, but stops regularly to ensure the others in her herd are following close behind.

The Arabian oryx can smell rain falling up to 80 km (50 miles) away. The herd follows the scent, covering 30 km (20 miles) in one go, mostly during the night. When they arrive, the oryxes graze on the newly sprouting desert plants. Oryxes also dig up roots and tubers using their shovel-like hooves. They can go for weeks without water, extracting the moisture they need from their food.

Operation oryx
The Arabian oryx was one of international conservation's earliest success stories. By 1972, trophy hunters had made the species extinct in the wild. By the following decade, a captive-born herd was reintroduced to a protected reserve in Oman, and they eventually spread into the wild. Today, the wild population numbers more than 1,000.

Arabian oryx can **smell rain** more than **two days' walk away**

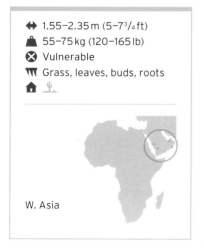

- ↔ 1.55–2.35 m (5–7³/₄ ft)
- 🏋 55–75 kg (120–165 lb)
- ⊗ Vulnerable
- 🌾 Grass, leaves, buds, roots
- 🏠 🌵

W. Asia

▷ **LOCKING HORNS**
Dominance is established with visual displays by individuals showing off their impressive horns. However, when the males are establishing territories, all-out fights do take place.

◁ **KEEPING COOL**
Young oryxes often rest near a shrub. They make a shallow pit to lie in, scraping away the hot surface sand to expose the cooler layer below.

dark brown or
black throat patch

Striped hyena
Hyaena hyaena

▷ **SPOTTED HYENAS**
Spotted hyenas
(*Crocuta crocuta*) are
the largest and most
powerful members
of the hyena family.
They are native to
sub-Saharan Africa.

Found from Africa to Central Asia and India, the striped hyena has the largest range of the world's four hyena species and frequents the widest variety of habitats. However, it is now extinct in many areas and populations are declining in most places. Like other hyenas, the striped hyena resembles a lanky, big-eared dog. Its front legs are longer than those at the back, giving it a front-heavy profile with a sloping back.

Bone cruncher

The striped hyena is primarily a scavenger, using its massively powerful jaw muscles to tear into carcasses, rip apart tough sinews, and crunch up bones. It also hunts small prey and forages for dates, melons, and other fresh fruit. Usually found alone or in small groups, striped hyenas are strictly nocturnal and roam large distances in search of food.

The female gives birth to one to four young in a rocky den or a burrow. The cubs start eating meat when they are around 30 days old. They may suckle for as long as a year while learning important foraging skills from their mother. Most striped hyenas are killed by lions or humans.

forelegs longer
than hindlegs

↔ 1–1.2 m (3¼–4ft)
🏋 26–41kg (57–90lb)
✖ Near threatened
🍴 Carrion, hares, insects, fruit
🏠 ⛰ 🌵 🌾

W., N., and E. Africa, W. to S. Asia

▷ **AGGRESSIVE STANCE**
Striped hyenas have extremely
shaggy fur, creating a mane along
the back. This is raised during
aggressive encounters with other
hyenas or predators such as lions.

Rock hyrax
Procavia capensis

dense coat

The tiny, tail-less rock hyrax makes its den in crevices and cavities in rocky outcrops or cliffs, which offer protection from predators such as leopards, snakes, and eagles. Rocks also help hyraxes to regulate their body temperature by providing basking places in cold weather and shade in hot conditions. The moist, rubber-like soles of their feet enable hyraxes to climb with ease. Despite their thick coats, hyraxes are sensitive to temperature extremes, avoiding cold winds and rain as well as midday heat.

A typical day begins with an hour or two of sunbathing, followed by an hour's foraging, then resting before feeding again in the afternoon.

↔ 30–58 cm (12–23 in)
⚖ 3–5 kg (6½–11 lb)
✖ Common
🌾 All vegetation
🏠 ⛰ 🌵 🌿

W., S., and E. Africa, W. Asia

◁ **GROUP HUDDLE**
Young hyraxes stay close to their mother. After resting together in the sun, this family is getting ready to resume feeding.

pale brown coat with vertical flank bars

Arabian partridge
Alectoris melanocephala

This is a bird of vegetated wadis, valleys, high slopes, and cultivated desert fringe, especially scrubby juniper forest. Currently common, the Arabian partridge is threatened by droughts and changes in its habitat caused by cultivation and overgrazing. It escapes predators by running rather than flying. Most feeding and drinking takes place in the cooler morning and evening. Females lay five to eight eggs in a nest hidden in low vegetation.

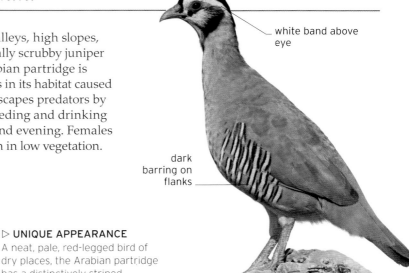

white band above eye

dark barring on flanks

↔ 39–43 cm (15½–17 in)
⚖ 500–550 g (17½–19½ oz)
✖ Common
🌾 Seeds, grass, small insects
🏠 🌿
🧭 SW. Asia

▷ **UNIQUE APPEARANCE**
A neat, pale, red-legged bird of dry places, the Arabian partridge has a distinctively striped head and neck.

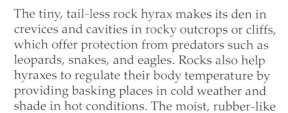

TERAI-DUAR SAVANNAS

Home to the world's tallest grasslands

This narrow region at the base of the Himalayas comprises a mosaic of river grassland, savannas, and forests. Much of the grassland is unusually high, which provides excellent cover for both predators and their prey. The Terai-Duar is home to numerous species of hoofed mammals, including at least five different deer species, the endangered Asiatic wild buffalo, and the Indian rhinoceros. At the top of the Terai food chain is the tiger, populations of which are increasing here, especially in established national parks such as Chitwan and Bardia in Nepal. Leopards and the rare clouded leopard are also resident. Three bird species – the spiny babbler, the grey-crowned prinia, and the Manipur bush-quail – have ranges that are restricted to the Terai-Duar and neighbouring regions.

Fertile floodplain

Alluvial or floodplain grasslands are submerged during monsoon rains and replenished with fertile silt, prompting rapid grass growth once the waters retreat. However, the moist, nutrient-rich soil is ideal for cultivation, and much of the land has been converted to agriculture. The survival of the Terai-Duar's wildlife depends on an extensive network of protected areas connected by wildlife corridors so that species such as tigers, elephants, and rhinoceros can move freely between reserves, with as little interaction with humans as possible.

The Terai-Duar is one of Earth's most **biologically outstanding habitats**

EGYPTIAN VULTURE

Has Asia's highest populations of tigers and rhinos

Manipur bush-quail was thought extinct until found here in 2006

SWAMP DEER

MUGGER CROCODILE

PLIGHT OF THE VULTURES
India's vulture populations crashed spectacularly in the 1990s after veterinary drugs used to treat cattle were ingested by birds that fed on livestock carcasses. Although one drug has since been banned, it will take time for the slow-breeding species to recover.

ENDANGERED DEER
Terai grasslands are home to the barasingha, or swamp deer, which has large, splayed hooves that can cope with its swampy habitat. A vital prey species for tigers and leopards, barasingha numbers are threatened by habitat loss and hunting.

ENDANGERED REPTILE
Mugger crocodile populations declined in the 1950s and 60s mainly due to hunting for their skin. Despite improved protection and captive breeding programmes, the mugger still suffers because of habitat loss.

SMALL AND RARE

Standing just 25cm (10in) at the shoulder, the critically endangered pygmy hog is the smallest member of the pig family. Its range is restricted to a national park in northwest Assam, and as few as 150 animals survive.

Home to mugger crocodiles and rare gharials

PYGMY HOG

ICONIC GRASSES

The dominant grasses of the Terai-Duar are actually members of the sugarcane family. Kans grass grows up to 3m (10ft) high; baruwa grass is smaller, but both are important food for animals, including the Indian rhinoceros and pygmy hog. The grasses grow quickly after the monsoon rains.

KANS GRASS

Six of India's nine species of vulture live in the Terai-Duar grasslands

REJUVENATING NEWT

The Himalayan newt inhabits streams and paddy fields in the region. It possesses a remarkable ability to regrow lost limbs. Its wounds heal quickly thanks to a peptide called tylotoin that scientists have isolated from its skin, leading to speculation about its future use in speeding up human wound treatment.

HIMALAYAN NEWT

The Terai-Duar savannas are situated in a narrow belt of lowland in front of the Himalayas of southern Asia, where India borders Nepal, Bhutan, and Bangladesh.

CHINA

NEPAL

New Delhi

Kathmandu

Lucknow

Patna

INDIA

0 km 200
0 miles 200

CLIMATE

The Terai-Duar has a humid, subtropical climate with year-round warm temperatures averaging 22°C (72°F). Most of the rainfall takes place during the monsoon season, which occurs between June and September.

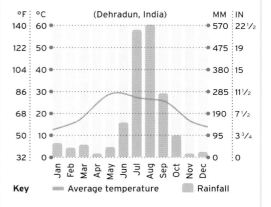

(Dehradun, India)

°F	°C		MM	IN
140	60		570	22½
122	50		475	19
104	40		380	15
86	30		285	11½
68	20		190	7½
50	10		95	3¾
32	0		0	0

Jan Feb Mar Apr May Jun Jul Aug Sep Oct Nov Dec

Key — Average temperature ▬ Rainfall

CULTIVATING CLIMATE CHANGE

Rice is cultivated in the Terai in flooded paddy fields. Microscopic soil organisms in the paddies are a major source of the greenhouse gas methane. Because methane levels increase with rising atmospheric carbon dioxide and warmer temperatures, rice cultivation is likely to fuel global warming. Seasonal drainage of the paddies helps to reduce their methane production.

single horn averages 25 cm (10 in) in both sexes

Indian rhinoceros

Rhinoceros unicornis

Of all five rhinoceros species, the Indian rhino is second in size only to Africa's white rhino. It is also the one most at home in water – a trait seemingly at odds with its appearance. Its skin is 4 cm (1½ in) thick and develops deep folds speckled with lumps, giving it an armour-plated look. Nevertheless, Indian rhinos are good swimmers and like to wallow. They are also surprisingly agile on land, able to turn quickly and charge at high speed. Since they have relatively poor eyesight, Indian rhinos rely on keen hearing and an excellent sense of smell to navigate their surroundings. A semi-prehensile upper lip makes them adept at grasping grass stems.

Still at risk

Due to stricter protection laws, Indian rhino numbers have recovered from fewer than 200 in the early 20th century to more than 3,000 in the wild. Poaching, however, is still a problem, despite the fact that the Indian rhino's horn – which it uses mainly for foraging – is relatively small.

- 3.4–3.5 m (11 ft)
- 2,000 kg (4,400 lb)
- Vulnerable
- Grasses, shrubs, fruit

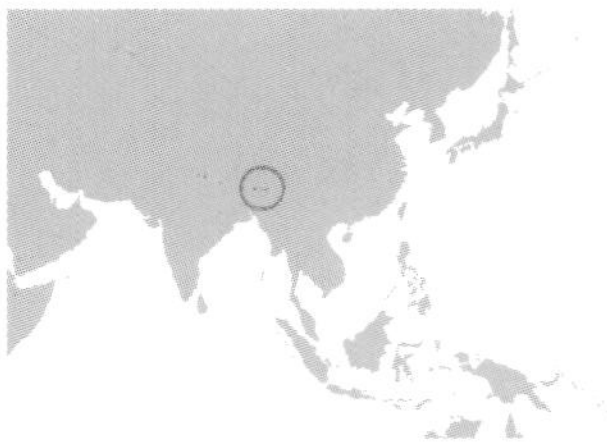

S. Asia (Terai and Brahmaputra basins)

Blackbuck
Antilope cervicapra

pointed hoof

△ **AT PEACE**
Although generally solitary, several Indian rhinos may wallow or graze near each other without fighting if food is plentiful in the area.

▽ **STAY CLOSE**
A rhino calf is vulnerable to predators such as tigers, and remains with its mother for up to two years

hair only on rims of ears, tip of tail, and as eyelashes

heavy neck folds provide protection

Once India's most numerous hoofed mammal, the blackbuck has become extinct in many areas due to habitat loss and hunting. However, it is recovering in protected areas, and introduced populations thrive in Argentina and Texas, USA. Males are larger and darker than females, and have spiralled horns. Herds may contain both sexes, only females with young, or just bachelors.

↔ 1.2–1.3 m (4–4¼ ft)
⚖ 25–35 kg (55–77 lb)
⊗ Near threatened
🌾 Grass, seed pods
🏠
◉ S. Asia

▽ **WARNING LEAP**
A high leap is a danger alert; smaller leaps follow before the herd gallops away at up to 80 km/h (50 mph).

Gaur
Bos gaurus

dewlap under chin extends to forelegs

One of the largest, most heavy-set of wild cattle, gaurs mostly live in herds of between five and 12 animals, led by a single bull. Usually active during the day, when humans encroach on their habitat gaurs become nocturnal to avoid hunters.

↔ 2.5–3.3 m (8¼–11 ft)
⚖ 650–1,000 kg (1,430–2,200 lb)
⊗ Vulnerable
🌾 Grasses, fruit, twigs, bark
🏠
◉ S. and SE. Asia

◁ **HAZARDOUS HORNS**
Both male and female gaurs have curved horns that grow up to 60 cm (24 in) long. Unfortunately, these are prized by hunters.

Red muntjac
Munitiacus muntjak

↔ 0.9–1.2 m (3–4 ft)
⚖ 20–28 kg (44–62 lb)
⊗ Common
🌿 Leaves, fruit, eggs, carrion

S. to SE. Asia

▷ **SIMPLE ANTLERS**
The short, simple antlers are seen only in males. The males also have long upper canine teeth and a scent gland under each eye.

The red muntjac is one of few deer that are habitually omnivorous. A solitary animal, the deer supplements its diet of shoots, seeds, and fruit with the occasional bird egg, rodent, or a meal of carrion.

Breeding occurs at all times of the year, with males scent-marking to attract a harem of receptive females. Fights between rutting males involve both butting and biting, leading to frequent injury. Gestation lasts seven months, and the single offspring is weaned early for deer at just ten weeks after birth. Sexual maturity is reached at the age of two.

long, flexible trunk used like a fifth limb

Asian elephant

Elephas maximus

Asia's largest land mammal, the Asian elephant spends most of the day eating up to 150 kg (330 lb) of plant material, including grass and fruit. It also eats cultivated crops such as bananas, causing conflict with humans. About 20 per cent of the world's human population lives either in or near the Asian elephant's habitat, forcing these animals into increasingly fragmented areas. Poaching is also a threat, although, unlike African elephants, only male Asian elephants grow tusks, and some males lack them altogether. Females and some males grow "tushes" – small tusks that rarely extend beyond their mouths. Asian elephants also differ from African elephants in that they have arched backs, double-domed heads, and smaller ears.

Males leave their birth group when they are six or seven years old, living alone or in loose groups with other bulls. Females stay with their families, headed by a matriarch, who leads the herd to water and browsing areas. Females stay bonded to family members for life, using their trunks to greet and caress each other.

◁ **HEAVY DRINKERS**
Adult Asian elephants need to drink 70–90 litres (18–24 gallons) of water daily, spraying it into their mouth with their trunk.

▷ **MALES AT PLAY**
Young elephants, particularly bull calves, spend much of their time at play, often charging, sparring, or trunk-wrestling with one another.

- ↔ 2–3.6 m (6½–12 ft)
- ⬛ 2–5 tonnes
- ✖ Endangered
- 🌾 Grass, fruit, bark, roots
- 🏠 🌳 🌲 🌲

S. and SE. Asia

Terai sacred langur

Semnopithecus hector

Like other species of langur and the related leaf monkeys, the Terai sacred langur (also called the Hanuman langur) feeds mainly on leaves. Its large stomach is separated into two chambers: an upper one, where the leaves are fermented by bacteria, and a lower acidic chamber. This system, like that found in cows and sheep, helps to break down the tough cellulose found in leaves. Because leaves are low in nutrients, langurs have to spend much of their day feeding in trees. However, they can eat many types of leaves and fruit that would be toxic to other species.

long, slender limbs

▷ **BLACK FACE**
According to Hindu mythology, the langur's face was scorched as punishment for stealing a mango.

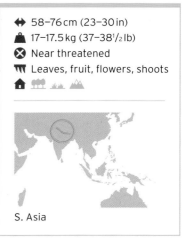

- ↔ 58–76 cm (23–30 in)
- ⬛ 17–17.5 kg (37–38½ lb)
- ✖ Near threatened
- 🌾 Leaves, fruit, flowers, shoots
- 🏠 🌳 🌿 ⛰️

S. Asia

↔ 1.4–2.8 m (4¹/₂–9¹/₄ ft)

⚱ 125–240 kg (275–530 lb)

✖ Endangered

🐾 Deer, wild pigs, ground birds

S. and E. Asia

▷ **WATER FIGHT**
Tigers are usually solitary, so if a stranger ignores the boundary scent marks and wanders into another tiger's territory a fierce fight often ensues.

no two tigers have the same markings

tail used for balance when chasing prey or climbing

powerful forelegs, big feet, and large claws enable tiger to grip prey securely

Bengal tiger

Panthera tigris tigris

The tiger is the largest of all the big cats. Five subspecies remain alive today, of which the Bengal tiger is the most common. It is found in a wide range of forest and mangrove habitats in India and Bangladesh. The Bengal tiger's distinctive coat is a deep orange with white undersides, chest, throat and parts of its face, and dark stripes. The Amur tiger (*P. t. altaica*), which lives to the north in the coniferous forests of Siberia, Russia, is the largest of the five. It is the lightest in colour and has the longest, thickest coat to cope with the freezing winters. The southernmost subspecies, the Sumatran tiger (*P. t. sumatrae*), is also the smallest, being a good 30 per cent smaller and weighing about 50 per cent less than its massive cousins to the north.

Ambush attacker

Tigers are chiefly nocturnal but will hunt by day in places where they are undisturbed by daytime human activities. The tiger uses its sense of smell and hearing to detect and track prey. Its great strength and speed mean it can bring down prey that is at least as large as it is, sometimes more so. The Bengal tiger typically hunts hoofed animals, such as gaur, sambar, chital, and wild boar, and stalks them while hidden by the undergrowth. Once the tiger is near enough, it will launch a lightning strike, surging out of cover and using its weight to knock the prey to the ground. The tiger then delivers a deadly bite to the throat, which crushes the windpipe, leading to death by strangulation, or breaks the neck. Small prey are often killed with a bite to the neck. The tiger then hauls the carcass back into the undergrowth to eat. Despite the tiger's great killing potential, only one in 20 ambushes is a success.

Solitary cat

An adult tiger lives alone. It marks out a territory by scratching marks on tree trunks and rocks with its claws and leaving piles of faeces in prominent places. The tiger also scent marks by spraying squirts of urine mixed with oils from a scent gland under the tail, and it gives out roars that can be heard 2 km (1 mile) away.

A tigress breeds every two or three years, and changes in her scent will attract a nearby male. The pair roar to each other as they get near and will live together for a few days, mating around 20 times before going their separate ways. Tigresses give birth to litters of up to six cubs, but half of them will not reach two years. Surviving cubs stay with their mother for up to two years, learning to hunt alongside her from the age of six months. They may breed when four or five years old.

△ SUMATRAN TIGRESS AND CUB
The smaller size of the Sumatran tiger (*P. t. sumatrae*) is an adaptation to life in the dense undergrowth of the swamp forests of Sumatra.

Tiger **cubs often have practice fights**, gaining the **speed and agility** they will need as **territorial adults**

short, rounded ears closed in dusty places

Indian grey mongoose

Herpestes edwardsii

The Indian grey mongoose is a dietary opportunist – eating lizards, eggs, and fruit as well as larger mammals such as hares and venomous cobras. Mongooses are so adept at preying on rodents and snakes that they are used as a form of pest control in some areas.

Head clamp

While its molars are used to crush insects, its strong jaws and sharp, protruding canines give the mongoose an edge when fighting snakes, allowing it to clamp onto a snake's head and puncture its skull. Although not immune to snake venom, highly reactive reflexes help them avoid being bitten. Mongooses are solitary except during mating season. Females bear litters of two to four pups up to three times a year.

Mongooses **crack large eggs by throwing** them between their hindlegs **against a hard surface**

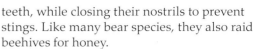

Sloth bear
Melursus ursinus

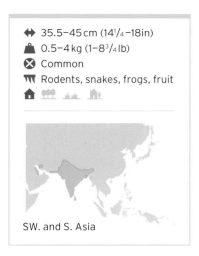

↔ 35.5–45 cm (14¼–18 in)
⚖ 0.5–4 kg (1–8¾ lb)
✕ Common
🍴 Rodents, snakes, frogs, fruit

SW. and S. Asia

The sloth bear is a solitary, elusive forest dweller, but the slurping sounds it makes when feeding can be heard up to 200 m (650 ft) away. These shaggy-looking members of the bear family use their long, curved claws to dig out ants, termites, and other insects, sucking them up through flexible lips and a special gap in their teeth, while closing their nostrils to prevent stings. Like many bear species, they also raid beehives for honey.

Sloth bears mate during the summer months. Females bear one or two cubs, which stay with their mother for up to four and a half years. They are the only bears known to carry cubs on their backs.

long, rough fur

↔ 1.4–1.9 m (4½–6 ft)
⚖ 50–145 kg (110–320 lb)
✕ Vulnerable
🍴 Ants, termites, fruit, honey

S. Asia

▷ **LONG, MOBILE SNOUT**
Sloth bears use their nostrils to blow dust and earth out of the way before sucking up insects to eat.

▽ **STRATEGIC COMBAT**
Mongooses defeat cobras by agility and endurance – dodging away each time a snake strikes, then biting into its skull once it tires.

Sarus crane
Grus antigone

At 1.8 m (6 ft), the sarus crane is the tallest flying bird on earth. It has dramatic displays: rhythmic bowing leading into two-footed leaps, with head extended and wings half open, while making loud trumpeting calls.

The sarus crane is a declining bird, being confined to wet paddy fields and reservoir edges as marshlands are drained and rice cultivation becomes more intensive. Breeding pairs occupy territories and forage for aquatic plants, insects, and frogs, mainly in natural vegetation, but occasionally in cultivated fields.

mainly grey plumage in adults

↔ 1.5 m (5 ft)
⚖ 6.5 kg (14 lb)
✕ Vulnerable
🍴 Roots, tubers, insects, frogs

S. and SE. Asia, N. Australia

long, trailing legs

△ **TAKING OFF**
Although long legs and broad wings power its take off, the sarus crane uses a steady, efficient action once airborne.

Great Indian hornbill
Buceros bicornis

This large hornbill relies on forest fruit for food and essential moisture. Fruiting trees attract scores of birds whose droppings, in turn, help disperse seeds throughout the forest. The function of the angular casque is uncertain, but the larger bones in the bill have networks of hollow cavities, combining lightness with strength.

sickle-shaped bill

casque

▷ **LIGHT AND SHADE**
Horizontal bands create effective camouflage in the light and shade of a forest canopy.

↔ 95–120 cm (37½–47 in)
⚖ 3 kg (6½ lb)
✖ Near threatened
🍴 Figs, lizards, frogs, rodents
🏠 🌳 🌿 ⛰
🧭 S. and SE. Asia

Indian cobra
Naja naja

Found in habitats from remote uplands to urban sprawl, the Indian cobra's diet ranges from tiny frogs to large rats. Females lay 12–20 eggs in a tree hollow, rodent burrow, or termite mound, and guard them. Hatchlings can immediately spread their hood and strike with venom.

↔ 1.8–2.2 m (6–7¼ ft)
⚖ 2–3 kg (4½–6½ lb)
✖ Not known
🍴 Frogs, rats, lizards, birds
🏠 🌿 🌾 🏘
🧭 S. Asia

◁ **SPECTACLED HOOD**
This classic "snake charmer" species is also called the spectacled cobra from the markings on the rear of the hood and often on the front as well.

△ **SAFETY ISLAND**
Parents care for the young for the first few weeks, escorting them on their first swims. However, many other crocodilians nurture their offspring for longer periods.

▷ **FISH TRAP**
The gharial's 100–110 teeth are small and sharp – ideal for snagging fish, which are bitten several times to subdue them, then tossed around to be swallowed head first.

Gharial

Gavialis gangeticus

male has bulbous tip on long, narrow snout

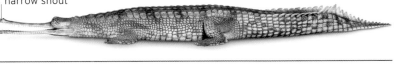

The gharial's unique long, narrow jaws – designed to make sudden sideways snaps at passing fish – make it instantly recognizable. It is more aquatic than its robust crocodile cousins and is highly adapted to move in water. Its rear feet are well webbed and the long tail has fin-like keel scales along the top for powerful propulsion. On land, its limbs are not strong enough to lift its body in a high walk, so it pushes forward on its belly instead.

Females mature at eight to 10 years and are around 3.5 m (11½ ft) long; males take another three to five years to mature and grow longer. At mating time, territorial male gharials intimidate rivals and display to females with much noise and thrashing. The male's bulbous snout – locally known as the "ghara", a type of pot – helps to make enticing bubbles to attract a mate.

Still on the brink

The gharial was on the verge of extinction in the 1970s due to habitat loss, poaching, and falling fish stocks. Captive breeding programmes have led to more than 3,000 animals being released back into the wild since 1981, but the species is still critically endangered.

↔ 3.5–7 m (11½–23 ft)
🏋 160–180 kg (353–397 lb)
✖ Critically endangered
🍴 Fish, waterbirds
🏠 🌿 ≈ ≈

S. Asia

EASTERN HIMALAYAS
Earth's highest mountains support a variety of rare species

The peaks and steep-sided valleys of the world's highest mountain range are home to varied but vulnerable plants and animals. The lower and middle elevations of the Eastern Himalayas are covered with various types of forest. Depending on latitude and altitude they might be subtropical or temperate, evergreen, or deciduous. Oaks and rhododendrons dominate the forests, which support a diverse array of wildlife. Even above the treeline, seemingly inhospitable rocky slopes are home to such elusive creatures as the snow leopard and blue sheep.

Vital water regulators

The mountains and their forests are also important for the region's water supply. They catch and gradually release rainwater to tributaries of some of Asia's most iconic rivers, including the Ganges and the Brahmaputra. The plants and animals of the high Himalayas are likely to experience great challenges due to climate change, as the melting of glaciers accelerates and they are forced to adapt to warmer temperatures, if they can.

There are 163 globally threatened species in the Eastern Himalayas, and a quarter of their original habitat remains intact. The challenge for conservationists is to protect sufficiently large areas and corridors between them to sustain animals that range over large areas. The main threat to the forests and their wildlife comes from poaching, collection of wood for fires and charcoal, and habitat loss or damage resulting from agricultural practices.

NATURAL CAMOUFLAGE
The Himalayan blue sheep's grey-blue coat provides superb camouflage against its rocky environment. This agile animal is able to scamper up steep cliffs when trying to escape predators such as the snow leopard.

HIMALAYAN BLUE SHEEP

BLOOMING PARTNERSHIP
The higher elevations of the Himalayas feature a diversity of rhododendron species. More than 50 flourish in the Indian state of Sikkim and 60 in Bhutan. Rhododendron forests support insects and birds that pollinate the flowers when feeding on nectar.

RHODODENDRON

WILD YAK

Home to 10,000 plant species and nearly 1,000

Boasts 9 of the world's 10 highest peaks

ADAPTED TO THE COLD
The wild yak conserves body heat in the cold mountain climate – generating it uses valuable energy. It stores fat beneath its skin, and its thick, dark fleece has a layer of soft insulating down and another of coarse outer hair.

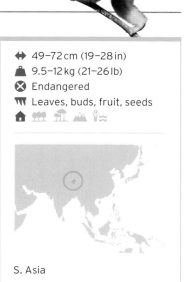

LOCATION

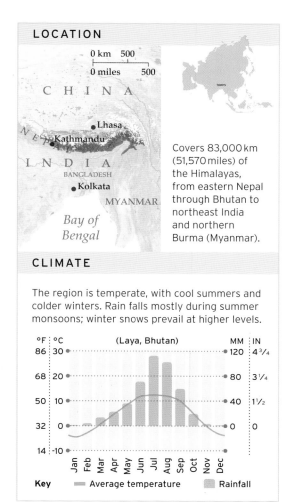

0 km 500
0 miles 500

CHINA

Lhasa
Kathmandu

INDIA
BANGLADESH
Kolkata
MYANMAR

Bay of
Bengal

Covers 83,000 km
(51,570 miles) of
the Himalayas,
from eastern Nepal
through Bhutan to
northeast India
and northern
Burma (Myanmar).

CLIMATE

The region is temperate, with cool summers and
colder winters. Rain falls mostly during summer
monsoons; winter snows prevail at higher levels.

°F	°C	(Laya, Bhutan)	MM	IN
86	30		120	4¾
68	20		80	3¼
50	10		40	1½
32	0		0	0
14	-10			

Jan Feb Mar Apr May Jun Jul Aug Sep Oct Nov Dec

Key — Average temperature ▪ Rainfall

CHANGING ALTITUDES

Many species migrate up and
down the Himalayas to avoid
the worst of the winter
weather and exploit summer
food sources. One example
is the satyr tragopan, a
pheasant that moves to
low-altitude forests in winter
and high areas in summer.

...rd and 300 mammal species

SATYR TRAGOPAN

Golden langur
Trachypithecus geei

The golden langur's coat varies from cream-coloured in
summer to burnished gold in winter. This elusive, long-
tailed monkey was not recognized as a species until the
1950s, and very little is known about it even today. Golden
langurs live in groups of 3–40, and rarely come to the
ground, a strategy that helps them avoid predators such
as tigers. They are severely threatened by habitat loss.

↔ 49–72 cm (19–28 in)
⚖ 9.5–12 kg (21–26 lb)
✗ Endangered
♨ Leaves, buds, fruit, seeds

S. Asia

◁ **TREETOP DWELLER**
Golden langurs spend most of their
time high in the forest canopy, only
rarely descending to the ground to
drink or lick up mineral salts.

Bhutan takin

Budorcas whitei

barrel-shaped
body covered
in shaggy hair

During spring, large mixed herds of takin – robust relatives
of wild goats – congregate in sunny clearings high up in
bamboo forests. As winter approaches, they fragment into
fours and fives and head for lower areas. If threatened, they
retreat into dense bamboo thickets and lie down.

↔ 1.7–2.2 m (5½–7¼ ft)
⚖ 150–350 kg (330–772 lb)
✗ Vulnerable
♨ Forbs, shrubs, trees

both sexes
have short,
thick horns

S. Asia

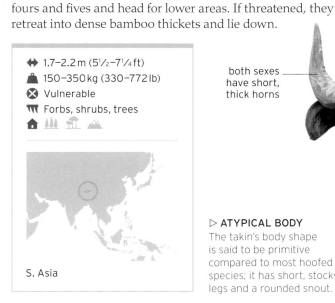

▷ **ATYPICAL BODY**
The takin's body shape
is said to be primitive
compared to most hoofed
species; it has short, stocky
legs and a rounded snout.

◆ 0.9–1.2 m (3–4 ft)
⚖ 25–75 kg (55–165 lb)
✖ Endangered
🐑 Wild sheep, wild goats
🏠 ⛰

C. Asia

▷ **MOUNTAIN GHOST**
Snow leopards are nomadic
creatures, constantly on the move in
search of food. In territory where prey
is scarcest, one leopard may patrol as
much as 1,000 sq km (400 sq miles).

thick fur coat

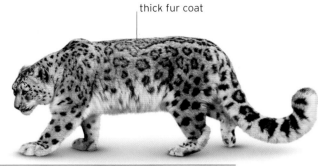

Snow leopard

Panthera uncia

To local people, snow leopards are "mountain ghosts" because they are so well camouflaged that they are as good as invisible even at close range. They are the most elusive, most secretive, and smallest of the big cats – and the only one that cannot roar. Snow leopards are among the planet's most endangered species. The estimated 4,000–7,000 remaining in the wild live mainly in the harsh mountain ranges of Central Asia, at elevations of 3,000–5,000 m (10,000–16,400 ft). They are still hunted illegally in "retribution" for killing livestock or for use in traditional medicine and for their pelts.

Fighting the cold

The snow leopard's thick, creamy grey coat dotted with brown and grey-black spots blends in seamlessly with a rocky or scrub-filled landscape, while its dense, white belly hair merges into the snow. Even the pads of its feet are covered with fur, as is the long, thick tail, which serves both as a balancing aid and a furry scarf, wrapping around its body and face when the animal is at rest. Short, rounded ears, also covered in dense fur, minimize heat loss, and a wider-than-average nasal cavity warms incoming air before it reaches the lungs. Short forelimbs and huge, snowshoe-like forepaws give

The snow leopard is the **only big cat that cannot roar**

snow leopards extra traction in the snow. The longer, powerful hind legs let it leap as far as 15 m (50 ft) while chasing after prey such as wild sheep (argali and bharal) or wild goats such as ibex.

Lone hunters

Apart from the mating season and mothers raising cubs, snow leopards live and hunt alone, travelling far in search of food. Due to the harsh nature of their environment, which stretches across the Himalayas to the Hindu Kush mountains, a snow leopard will patrol an average home range of 260 sq km (100 sq miles), marking the landscape with urine and faeces that act as scent signals to other snow leopards. Females have litters of two or three cubs, which stay with their mother until they are 18–22 months old.

△ **ATTRACTING A MATE**
When a female snow leopard is ready to mate, she may climb to a ridge or peak and make long, wailing cries to attract nearby males.

◁ **MISSED OPPORTUNITY**
Although wild sheep and goats are preferred prey, snow leopards eat small mammals such as lemmings and hares - and birds when they can catch them.

Red panda
Ailurus fulgens

soft, dense fur

alternating light and dark rings on tail

Once thought to be related to giant pandas, the red panda has closer genetic links to weasels and raccoons. Also called the firefox in China, this slow-moving mammal spends most of its life in trees in Asia's mountain forests, where its striking reddish brown fur allows it to blend in with the moss-covered branches of its arboreal home.

Red pandas move slowly to conserve energy as the bamboo shoots and leaves that make up most of their diet are so indigestible. They eat up to 30 per cent of their body weight daily, but use only about a quarter of bamboo's available nutrients; yet, they rely on the plant to survive when other food is scarce. In winter, red pandas can lose up to 15 per cent of their body weight due to lack of food, so they slow down their metabolism to compensate as temperatures fall.

Red pandas mate on the ground, but females return to their nest to give birth to between one and four cubs, which stay with their mother for a year or more.

↔ 51–73 cm (20–28¾ in)
⚖ 3–6 kg (6½–13 lb)
⊗ Vulnerable
🍴 Bamboo, fruit, insects, eggs

S. to SE. Asia

◁ **WATCHFUL GAZE**
Although they regularly use scent marking, red pandas also communicate with each other using "stare downs" accompanied by head bobbing and vocalizations.

red-and-white markings provide camouflage

△ **MOVING A CUB**
Female red pandas move their cubs to different nests to avoid discovery by predators such as martens and snow leopards.

fanned crest

iridescent eyespots

Indian peafowl

Pavo cristatus

Peafowl have been collected for ornamental purposes for more than 3,000 years. This, combined with artificial introductions into other parts of the world, has made the peacock's display familiar to millions who have never visited its Asian homeland. Here, peafowl live in open or riverside woodland and close to human habitation, in orchards and cultivated land. Drawing attention with their loud, off-key calls, they may be seen flying into trees at dusk to find a safe roost for the night.

Ground nesters

By day, peafowl forage on the ground. Females visit several displaying males at a lek before choosing the one with most eyespots on its tail. Males play no part in nesting or caring for the young. The nests are made on the ground in dense vegetation. Up to six eggs hatch after four weeks, and the chicks quickly learn to find food for themselves.

Peacock blue is one of the most intense blues in the world

↔ 1.8–2.3 m (6–7¹/₂ ft)
⚖ 4–6 kg (8³/₄–13 lb)
✖ Common
🍃 Seeds, fruit, plants, insects
🏠 🌳 🏞 ⛰

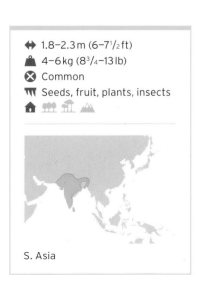

S. Asia

▷ **IRIDESCENT TRAIN**
The peacock's "tail" is actually a train of elongated feathers supported by a short, stiff tail beneath.

UPPER YANGTZE FORESTS
Home to China's national treasure, the giant panda

The Upper Yangtze Forests ecoregion comprises three areas: the Qinling Mountains, the Daba Mountains, and the Sichuan Basin. All three form a watershed between the drainage basins of the Yellow River to the north and the Yangtze River to the south. The climate is cooler and more temperate in the north of the region, where the forests are predominantly made up of deciduous trees. To the south are subtropical evergreen forests that flourish in this area's warmer temperatures and plentiful rain.

Rare lowland species

The lowlands of the Sichuan Basin are the most heavily populated. Here most of the land has been turned over to agriculture, but fragments of evergreen and broadleaf forest remain, particularly on the steeper hillsides and on any mountains considered sacred by local people. This area is home to the dawn redwood, an unusual deciduous conifer that was known only from fossil records until the 1940s, when groups of the trees were discovered growing in Sichuan province.

The Upper Yangtze Forests' most famous inhabitant is the giant panda, and the Wolong Nature Reserve near Chengdu is dedicated to the preservation of this iconic yet rare black-and-white bear. The middle elevations of the Qinling forests in Shaanxi province have a dense bamboo understorey, which provides a home and food to a distinctive type of giant panda that has dark- and light-brown fur. The smaller, tree-dwelling red panda also lives in the Upper Yangtze Forests.

HIDDEN FORAGER
The common but elusive Chinese bamboo partridge inhabits hillside forests, feeding on seeds, shoots, leaves, and insects. If it cannot remain hidden from predators, it flies uphill, but is much more often heard than seen.

CHINESE BAMBOO PARTRIDGE

SEX-LINKED STRIPES
The Chinese green tree viper is a venomous snake endemic to Asia. Males and females can be distinguished from one another by a stripe that runs along the side of their bodies. In males, it is orange or brown and white; females' stripes are just white.

GREEN TREE VIPER

Home to the world's largest amphibian, the Chinese giant salamander › Contains one-fift

YELLOW-THROATED MARTIN

GROUP THREAT
The large, brightly coloured yellow-throated marten eats eggs and fruit as well as small prey, such as rodents, reptiles, and ground-nesting birds. Sometimes hunting in small groups, it also kills deer fawns, wild boar piglets, and even giant panda cubs.

short, stumpy nose

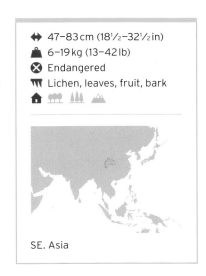

Golden snub-nosed monkey

Rhinopithecus roxellana

LOCATION

Cover 390,000 sq km (150,600 sq miles) in the provinces of Shaanxi and Sichuan in south-central China.

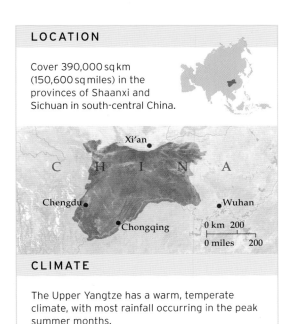

CLIMATE

The Upper Yangtze has a warm, temperate climate, with most rainfall occurring in the peak summer months.

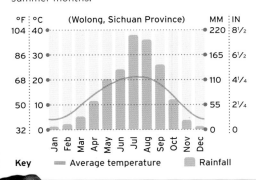

Key   ▬ Average temperature   ▬ Rainfall

This Chinese monkey lives its entire life in a series of groups, the size of which waxes and wanes depending upon the season. During the warmer months, a single group's numbers can swell to 200 or even 600 individuals. In winter, this splits into several groups of 60–70 monkeys, which are further divided into small family troops of a single male, several females, and their offspring or all-male groups.

Startling appearance

With vertical nostrils and dark, almond-shaped eyes set in a striking blue face framed by blazing red-gold fur, golden snub-nosed monkeys look more like alien elves than primates. Yet for all their unique features, because they live in high mountainous forests and spend over 95 per cent of their time in trees snub-nosed monkeys are heard more than they are seen. Their calls are eerily human-like, and frequently compared to the cries of young children or babies. Highly prized by hunters, their fur is so long across the back and shoulders that when they leap from one branch to another it gives the appearance of wings.

↔ 47–83 cm (18½–32½ in)
⚖ 6–19 kg (13–42 lb)
⊗ Endangered
🍃 Lichen, leaves, fruit, bark

SE. Asia

▽ **GROOMING SESSION**
Golden snub-nosed monkeys regularly check each other for parasites, a practice usually accompanied by whining and squealing.

FAST-GROWING GRASS
Among the world's fastest-growing plants, bamboo is a member of the grass family. More than 500 species grow in China alone. Bamboo is unusual in exhibiting mass flowering, where all plants in one stand flower together, set seed, and then die.

BAMBOO

of China's mammal species

Snub-nosed monkeys can **vocalize without moving their faces** or bodies

↔ 1.6–1.9 m (5¼–6¼ ft)
⚖ 70–125 kg (155–275 lb)
⊗ Endangered
🎋 Bamboo
🏠 🌲🌲🌲 🌲🌲 ⛰

E. Asia

△ **JUVENILE PANDAS**
Panda cubs don't move much until they are three months old. By five to six months, they are able to climb trees, and may sit there for hours.

▷ **FEEDING TIME**
Large molars and strong jaw muscles help giant pandas cope with even the toughest bamboo stems. Giant pandas also occasionally eat rodents, eggs, and birds.

distinctive
rounded face ____

front limbs more
muscled than rear
limbs, for climbing ____

Giant panda

Ailuropoda melanoleuca

The giant panda – one of the most endangered and rarest mammals – is found only in six small, densely forested regions of central China. Estimates place the number of giant pandas remaining in the wild at 1,000–2,500. Once common in lowland areas, human activity has fragmented their habitat and pushed them up into the mountains.

The giant panda has the most distinctive coat of all bear species, but for decades its unique black and white markings, rounded face, and largely vegetarian diet led many scientists to conclude it was not a bear at all, until genetic testing settled the debate.

Slower than the average bear

The giant panda's diet continues to be a puzzle. It has the canine teeth and short digestive tract of a carnivore (meat-eater), but 99 per cent of its food is bamboo, which, for pandas, is nutritionally poor. Carnivores, including giant pandas, lack special gut bacteria that would allow them to process grasses such as bamboo. This means that giant pandas get only about 20 per cent of a meal's energy; if they ate meat, this would shoot up to 60–90 per cent. It is not surprising, then, that the giant panda is slow-moving, spends most of the day eating up to

Giant pandas spend up to **16 hours a day** eating bamboo

18kg (40lb) of bamboo, then rests for 8–12 hours. Its diet also prevents it from sleeping through the winter as it cannot put on enough fat to go without food for long. However, adults are truly bear-sized, and they are agile climbers and good swimmers as well.

Milk for two?

Giant pandas reach sexual maturity when they are between five and six years old. Although generally solitary, males and females spend two to four days together during the mating season from March to May. One or two tiny cubs are born around five months later, but the mother will abandon one cub if she cannot produce enough milk for both. A cub is fully dependent on its mother for the first few months, and may stay with her for up to three years.

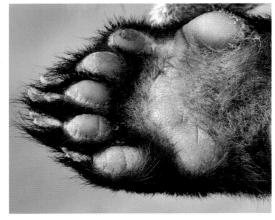

◁ **MOTHER AND CUB**
Born hairless and blind, a newborn weighs just a few grams. New reserves and conservation work in China and zoos abroad are helping to boost the giant panda population.

△ **PSEUDO-THUMB**
An enlarged wrist bone in the giant panda's forepaw acts like a human thumb and helps it to manipulate bamboo stems.

long tail
helps balance

long face compared
to other, smaller cats

Indochinese clouded leopard

Neofelis nebulosa

While they share a name and markings that allow them to blend in with their environment, clouded leopards and other leopards are not directly related. In fact, the Indochinese clouded leopard is unique in many ways. Relative to its size, this solitary cat has the longest upper canine teeth of any living felid – around 4 cm (1½ in). It also has an impressive gape of almost 100 degrees, whereas a lion's mouth, for example, only opens to an average of 65 degrees.

Short, powerful legs, broad paws, and a thick, densely furred tail that is often as long as its body make the clouded leopard an excellent climber. It is able to move along the underside of branches, run headfirst down trees, and hang upside down by its hind feet, which rotate backwards courtesy of flexible ankle joints. Clouded leopards are also superb swimmers.

Secretive cat

Since they are such experts at blending into their dense forest habitat, little is known about clouded leopard behaviour, although males show a high degree of aggression towards females in captivity. Once believed to be nocturnal hunters, recent evidence suggests that they may hunt during the day as well, taking prey on the ground despite being such good climbers.

↔ 70–110 cm (27½–43 in)
⚖ 11–23 kg (24–51 lb)
⊗ Vulnerable
♛ Mammals
🏠 🌳 🌲 ⛰ 🌿 〰

S. and SE. Asia

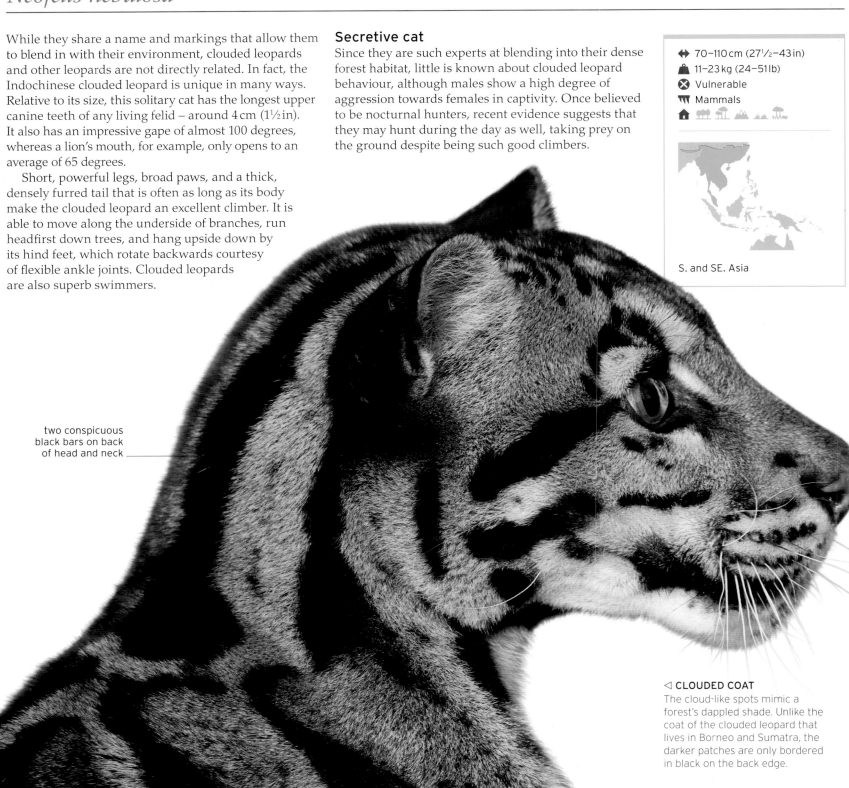

two conspicuous
black bars on back
of head and neck

◁ **CLOUDED COAT**
The cloud-like spots mimic a forest's dappled shade. Unlike the coat of the clouded leopard that lives in Borneo and Sumatra, the darker patches are only bordered in black on the back edge.

dholes living at higher
altitudes have thicker coats

Dhole
Cuon alpinus

With fewer than 2,500 individuals thought to exist in
the wild, the dhole is one of the world's rarest canids.
Also called the Asian red dog because of its tawny or
dark red coat, it differs from other canids in having a
much shorter jaw and two fewer molar teeth. Like
wolf-like dogs and foxes, however, the dhole has been
persecuted as a pest, and is now found in just 40 per
cent of its former range.

Strength in numbers
Dholes are extremely social mammals, forming
territorial, day-active packs of 5–10 individuals
(occasionally up to 30), usually with just one breeding
female. Group members readily cooperate to hunt, often
chasing deer, but also killing animals up to 10 times
their own body weight and aggressive species such as
wild boar. Good swimmers, dholes frequently drive deer
into water to gain an advantage. They also scavenge
from Asian elephant and wild cattle carcasses.
   As well as a high-pitched whistle used to call pack
mates, dholes use a remarkable range of vocalizations,
including mews and screams.

Dholes are nicknamed "whistling hunters"

- ↔ 90 cm (35 in)
- ⚖ 15–20 kg (33–44 lb)
- ⊗ Endangered
- 🍖 Deer, insects, lizards, grass

E., SE., and S. Asia

◁ **PLAY FIGHTING**
Social rank within a dhole pack is not
established by using aggression –
instead it is achieved by pushing or
restraining another pack member.

Golden pheasant
Chrysolophus pictus

Few birds are as showy as the male golden pheasant,
but ironically, when these gamebirds were brought to
Europe for their bright colours they proved very hard
to see in dense conifer forest.
   Golden pheasants feed on the ground, picking up
food with a precise, chicken-like action. Although
tending to run rather than fly if approached, they seek
safety and shelter in treetops at night. Males have loud,
crowing calls and use ritualized, rhythmic posturing to
impress the mottled-brown females. They repeatedly
run to "corner" a hen, stretching up on tiptoe and
spreading the colourful ruff, or cape, over their head
to produce a shiny orange semicircle
with concentric blue-black rings.

- ↔ 60–110 cm (23½–43 in)
- ⚖ 550–700 g (19½–25 oz)
- ⊗ Common
- 🍖 Green shoots, insects

S. to SE. Asia

tail roughly
twice as long
as female's

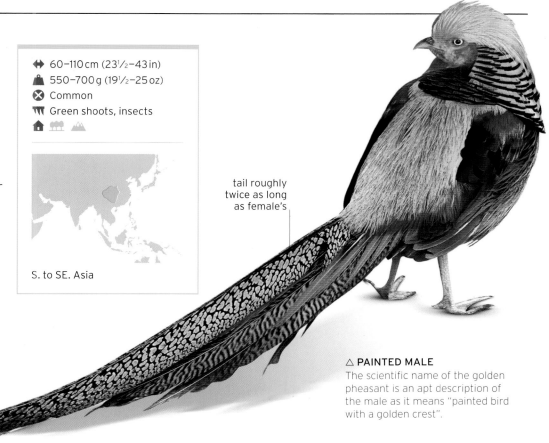

△ **PAINTED MALE**
The scientific name of the golden
pheasant is an apt description of
the male as it means "painted bird
with a golden crest".

GOBI DESERT
A high, mainly rocky desert that is the largest in Asia

Stretching across part of northern China and into southern Mongolia, the Gobi is the largest desert in Asia and the fifth largest in the world, with an area of around 1.3 million sq km (500,000 sq miles). It is located on a high-altitude plateau, which means that temperatures can fluctuate wildly: in summer they may reach 50°C (122°F) and in winter may fall as low as -40°C (-40°F). Most rain falls during the summer, but annual rainfall diminishes across the region, ranging from around 250 mm (10 in) in the east to just 10 mm (³⁄₈ in) in the west.

Rocky and harsh

The land is primarily rocky rather than sandy. The stony ground supports sparse vegetation in the form of hardy, drought-adapted shrubs and grasses. Despite the scanty plant life and harsh climate, many animals make the desert their home. Smaller mammals, such as the dwarf hamster and midday gerbil, burrow into sandy ground to escape the searing daytime heat in summer and to hibernate during winter. They benefit the environment by aerating the soil and recycling plant nutrients. Larger animals, such as the Bactrian camel, Mongolian saiga, and Przewalski's wild horse range far and wide over the desert plains to find sufficient food and water.

The Gobi Desert is expanding by around 3,600 sq km (1,400 sq miles) a year, with the result that devastating dust storms are becoming increasingly frequent. This desertification is also being accelerated by human activities, including deforestation and overgrazing.

VITAL MARMOTS
The Mongolian marmot is a key species in the Gobi. Not only is it a food source for predators, it also provides shelter to corsac foxes, which use their old burrows. The two species are closely connected: when marmot numbers decline, so do foxes.

MONGOLIAN MARMOTS

HARASSED HERDS
Herds of khulan, or Mongolian wild ass, roam across the southern Mongolian part of the Gobi Desert. Populations are at risk from poaching and damage to their habitat from grazing livestock. Khulan dig holes in dry riverbeds to obtain water.

KHULAN

STABILIZING TREE
One of the few trees able to grow in the Gobi Desert, the saxaul has thick bark that stores water. Its network of horizontal roots helps to stabilize sandy soil, so it is planted by people in an effort to fix sand dunes and slow down desertification.

SAXAUL

Temperatures vary by more than 35°C (63°F) in a day

Dinosaur eggs first found here

Gobi bear
Ursus arctos gobiensis

limbs longer
than grizzly's

Smaller and lighter than other brown bears, Gobi bears have short, golden coats and proportionally longer limbs. They mainly eat plants, such as wild rhubarb, roots, and berries. The species is threatened by droughts, climate change, habitat destruction, and cubs being killed by wolves – fewer than 30 Gobi bears are thought to survive today.

▽ **GENETIC MYSTERY**
DNA hair analysis indicates that Gobi bears are related to but distinct from other brown bears. No other brown bear could survive the Gobi Desert's harsh environment.

↔ 1.5–2.2 m (5–7¼ ft)
⚖ 50–160 kg (110–350 lb)
✖ Critically endangered
Ⅲ Plants, rodents, insects
🏠 🌵

C. Asia

LOCATION

Lying in northern China and southern Mongolia, the Gobi is bordered by the Tibetan Plateau to the southwest.

Ulan Bator
Ürümqi
Beijing
C H I N A

0 km 500
0 miles 500

CLIMATE

The Gobi is a cold, dry desert, and temperatures fluctuate wildly on both a daily and a seasonal basis.

(Mandalgovi, Mongolia)

°F °C | MM IN
86 30 | 60 2¼
68 20 | 40 1½
50 10 | 20 ¾
32 0 | 0 0
14 -10
-4 -20

Jan Feb Mar Apr May Jun Jul Aug Sep Oct Nov Dec

Key ▬ Average temperature ▬ Rainfall

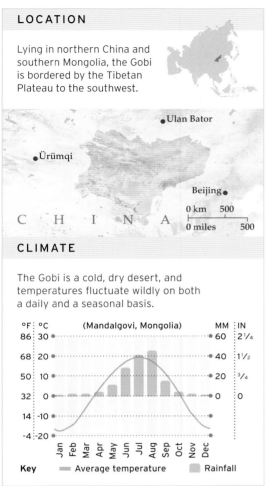

95% of the desert is rocky

BIG EARS
The tiny long-eared jerboa has one of the largest ear-to-body ratios of any mammal. It spends the day in tunnels, emerging at night to hunt insects. Small hairs on its feet help it move on sand, hopping like a kangaroo.

LONG-EARED JERBOA

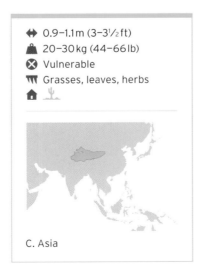

Yarkand gazelle
Gazella yarkandensis

This antelope is one of three "goitered" species, named after the way males develop a swollen larynx for making loud bellows in the breeding season. Female Yarkand gazelles have tiny horns compared to males.

▽ **RACING AHEAD**
Unlike other gazelles, this species does not use a prancing running style to confuse chasing predators. It escapes threats with a flat-out sprint.

↔ 0.9–1.1 m (3–3½ ft)
⚖ 20–30 kg (44–66 lb)
✖ Vulnerable
Ⅲ Grasses, leaves, herbs
🏠 🌵

C. Asia

Mongolian saiga

Saiga mongolica

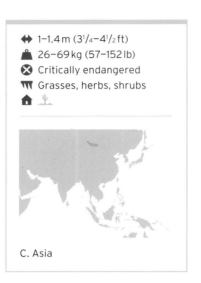

coat becomes thicker and paler in winter

The saiga is unmistakable. The males of this "goat-antelope" have pointed, ringed horns that are waxy and translucent. Both sexes sport long, drooping nostrils. The fleshy proboscis contains convoluted air passages lined with hairs. In summer, the hairs filter out dust that blows across the steppes. In winter, the long nasal passages warm the air before it reaches the lungs.

Saiga gather in huge herds and spend the winter – which is also the mating season – in the south of their range to avoid the worst of the weather.

↔ 1–1.4 m (3¼–4½ ft)
⚖ 26–69 kg (57–152 lb)
✗ Critically endangered
▥ Grasses, herbs, shrubs
⌂

C. Asia

Due to **human activity,** only **750 Mongolian saigas remain** in the wild

▷ GRAZING MALE
Saiga graze in the morning and afternoon – often travelling up to 80 km (50 miles) a day – and spend the middle of the day resting to aid digestion. As night falls, they scrape a shallow hollow to sleep in.

◁ POINTED HUMPS
Bactrian camels have erect humps that are much more pointed than those of feral and domesticated camels.

▽ DESERT CROSSING
Domesticated Bactrian camels are used for transport in cold regions from northern China to Turkey. They are shorter and more well-built than the wild camels.

two toes on each
foot cushioned
by fatty pads

Bactrian camel
Camelus bactrianus

The Bactrian camel roams the dry, rocky plains and hills of Central Asia, especially the Gobi Desert of China and Mongolia, where vegetation is scarce. The two humps on its back store fat, which is converted to water and energy to sustain the camel during droughts. The humps shrink as the fat is used up.

Little is known about the Bactrian camel's behaviour as it is difficult to study due to its nomadic lifestyle and remote habitat. It does not defend a territory, but lives in small herds that travel long distances in search of food. Mature breeding males spit at, bite, and kick rivals in battles. The strongest males gather a harem of females around them to mate with.

The Bactrian camel obtains most of the water it needs from its diet of leaves. It seldom sweats, to help conserve fluids during hot desert summers. However, after a drought, when it finally reaches water it can drink up to 135 litres (36 gallons) of water in just 15 minutes. It can also tolerate drinking much saltier water than domesticated camels can. The desert winters are bitterly cold, so the Bactrian camel grows a long, thick, woolly coat. The two broad toes on each foot spread out to prevent it from sinking in snow or sand.

Tamed existence

Fewer than 1,400 Bactrian camels remain in the wild and the population continutes to decline, but the species is widely domesticated as a hardy transport animal. Its relative, the one-humped dromedary, is now an entirely domesticated species found in North Africa, the Middle East, and Central Asia, and has been introduced to Australia.

↔ 3.2–3.5 m (10¹/₂–11¹/₂ ft)
⚖ 400–500 kg (880–1,100 lb)
✖ Critically endangered
♈ Herbs, shrubs
⌂

C. Asia

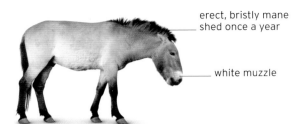

erect, bristly mane
shed once a year

white muzzle

Przewalski's wild horse

Equus przewalskii

For centuries, these stocky mammals grazed grassy plains ranging from Germany to China and Mongolia, but due to severe winters, habitat loss, and excessive hunting, their numbers fell during the 18th century. In 1969, the species was declared extinct in the wild. Thanks to cooperative captive breeding programmes in Europe, the US, and Australia, since 1985 small herds have been reintroduced to China, Mongolia, Kazakhstan, and Ukraine. Today, more than 300 Przewalski's wild horses roam their historic range in Mongolia.

Dangerous union

Although closely related, Przewalski's differ from domestic horses at a genetic level: they have 66 chromosomes in each body cell, while domestic horses have 64. The two species can interbreed, producing fertile offspring, and interbreeding is considered a major threat to the remaining Przewalski's wild horses. Physical differences from domestic horses include a smaller, more compact body; a shorter, thicker neck; a short, erect mane; and all individuals being the same colour.

In the wild, Przewalski's horses constantly roam in search of water and the short grasses that form the bulk of their diet. Herds consist of a dominant stallion, a harem of one to three females, and their offspring, which stay with the family group for two to three years.

△ **FIGHTING FOR DOMINANCE**
If ritualized signalling fails to deter a bachelor challenger, the dominant stallion will defend his right to lead a harem by fighting, often resulting in severe injuries.

All **pure Przewalski's wild horses** alive today are **descended from just 12 individuals**

▷ **MOTHER AND FOALS**
Foals stay close to their mothers for food, warmth, and protection against predators such as wolves. Sometimes, herds join forces in search of food.

Przewalski's wonder gecko

Teratoscincus przewalskii

Sheltering in a burrow by day, this gecko emerges at night to hunt. Its toes have fringes rather than the expanded pads seen in other geckos to help it dig and move easily over loose sand.

↔ 10–15 cm (4–6 in)
⚖ 15–30 g (½–1 oz)
✕ Common
🍴 Insects, arachnids, worms
🏠 🌵 🌿

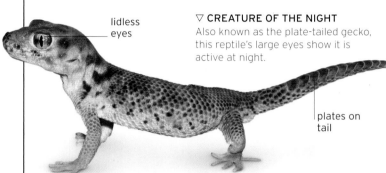

lidless eyes

▽ **CREATURE OF THE NIGHT**
Also known as the plate-tailed gecko, this reptile's large eyes show it is active at night.

plates on tail

C. Asia

Great bustard

Otis tarda

↔ 75–100 cm (29½–39¼ in)
⚖ 3.3–18 kg (7¼–39½ lb)
✕ Vulnerable
🍴 Seeds, insects, frogs, beetles
🏠 🌵 🌿

With the heaviest males reaching 21 kg (46 lb), the great bustard can be the world's heaviest flying bird, but many are leaner and lighter and females smaller still. All are big birds, but size can be deceptive in the wide open spaces they inhabit. Great bustards have a slow, stately walk and tend to run, not fly, when disturbed, but they are strong flyers with powerful wingbeats. Although extensive cereal fields are now their preferred habitat, they are disturbed by human activity and agricultural improvement. Asian populations migrate south and west to avoid bitter winters.

Males gather at leks to display and find a mate. Dominant males mate with several females, each of which lays two eggs in a scrape on the ground.

Europe, Asia

▽ **SPARRING MALES**
Before raising their tails and wings to become big balls of white in full display, males fight to establish dominance.

↔ 2.2–2.8 m (7¼–9 ft)
⚖ 200–300 kg (440–660 lb)
✕ Endangered
🍴 Grass, leaves, buds
🏠 🌵 🌿

C. Asia

NIHONKAI MONTANE FOREST

A hilly ecoregion that experiences harsh winters

This deciduous forest ecoregion covers 82,300 sq km (31,800 sq miles) of the mountainous backbone of Japan's main island, Honshu, and a small portion of the more northerly island of Hokkaido. Two-thirds of Japan is covered with forest, although only a quarter is original, or primary, natural forest; the rest is secondary forest or plantations. Japan has a total of seven different natural forest ecoregions, including several evergreen and deciduous types and subtropical moist forest.

Wet summers, snowy winters

The Nihonkai montane forest is characterized by trees, shrubs, and grasses that flourish in warm, wet summers and then shed their leaves to survive throughout cold, snowy winters. The most numerous deciduous tree in the Nihonkai ecoregion is the Japanese cherry, which is now widely cultivated as an ornamental in parks and gardens

around the world. Other trees typically found in the forests include Japanese beech, katsura, and Japanese hornbeam. Many forest animals feed on the nuts and fruits produced by the trees, and so play an important role in dispersing their seeds.

In addition to the montane forest's canopy of mature full-sized trees, there is a lower layer of trees that are yet to reach full size, a shrub layer, and an understorey of grasses and herbs. Biodiversity is greatest near the forest floor, unlike in tropical rainforests, where the number of species is highest in the canopy. The most iconic animal of the Nihonkai forest is the Japanese macaque.

POPULATION BOOM
More than 100,000 sika deer are estimated to live in Japan. Their numbers have boomed since the extinction of their main predator, the grey wolf, around a century ago. They are now considered a pest in their natural forest habitat and on farmland.

SIKA DEER

TRANSIENT BEAUTY
The Japanese cherry, or sakura, has profuse but short-lived displays of white or pink blossoms in spring. To the Japanese, their temporary beauty symbolizes the ephemeral nature of life and is celebrated in the hanami, or flower viewing, festival.

CHERRY BLOSSOM

Japanese cherry is the most common deciduou

One of seven forest ecoregions in Japan

JAPANESE WHITE-EYE

SEASONAL DIET
One of the most widespread and abundant birds in Japan, the white-eye is seldom seen on the ground. It forages in trees and shrubs, searching for insects in summer and berries in autumn, and feeding on blossoms, particularly cherry, in spring.

LOCATION

Extends from Hiroshima in the west of the island of Honshu, eastwards and northwards to the most southerly tip of Hokkaido.

CHINA

Sapporo

Sea of Japan

JAPAN

PACIFIC OCEAN

Tokyo

Osaka

0 km 400
0 miles 400

CLIMATE

The region's climate is seasonal and temperate. Temperatures can drop below freezing during winter, but may reach 30°C (86°F) in summer.

°F	°C	(Okaya, Nagano)	MM	IN
104	40		200	8
86	30		150	6
68	20		100	4
50	10		50	2
32	0		0	0
14	-10			

Jan Feb Mar Apr May Jun Jul Aug Sep Oct Nov Dec

Key — Average temperature — Rainfall

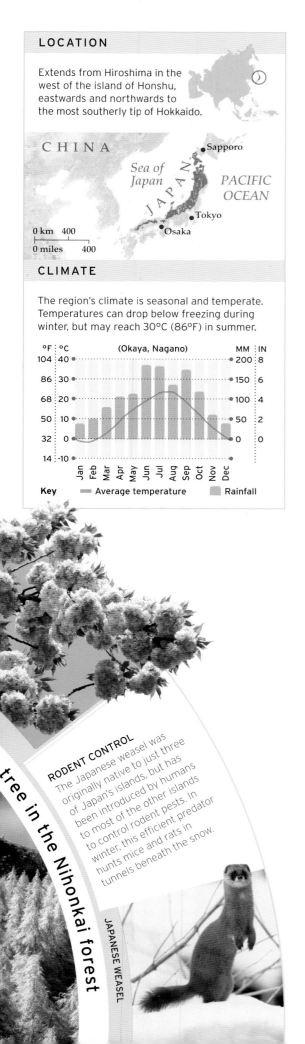

RODENT CONTROL
The Japanese weasel was originally native to just three of Japan's islands, but has been introduced by humans to most of the other islands to control rodent pests. In winter, this efficient predator hunts mice and rats in tunnels beneath the snow.

tree in the Nihonkai forest

JAPANESE WEASEL

Siberian flying squirrel
Pteromys volans

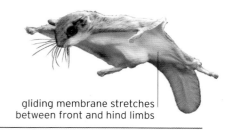

gliding membrane stretches between front and hind limbs

Using its sail-like gliding membrane and flattened tail for lift, the flying squirrel is capable of gliding 75 m (245 ft) or more between trees. Old-growth forests are this nocturnal mammal's preferred habitat, as the trees provide food as well as woodpecker holes, which it uses as a nest site.

↔ 12–23 cm (4³/₄–9 in)
⚖ 90–170 g (3¹/₄–5³/₄ oz)
✖ Common
▥ Nuts, buds, leaves

E. Europe to E. Asia

◁ **SEASONAL EATER**
In summer, the Siberian flying squirrel feeds mainly on fresh aspen, birch, and alder leaves.

Japanese serow
Capricornis crispus

white woolly ruff around neck

A small relative of goats, both male and female serows have short horns, and a long, woolly coat to withstand harsh winters. Diurnal browsers, they often retreat to a cave at night. They mark their territory with scent, chosen so they can exploit a wide range of plant food sources.

↔ 1.3 m (4¹/₄ ft)
⚖ 31–48 kg (68–106 lb)
✖ Locally common
▥ Grass, leaves, acorns

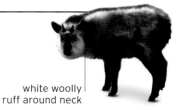

E. Asia (Japan)

◁ **GOING SOLO**
In winter, serows adopt a solitary lifestyle to make the most of the scarce food resources in their territory.

△ **IN THE SNOW**
Just like human children, young Japanese macaques play with snowballs, and are often seen rolling them or carrying them around.

face darker
red during
mating season

◁ **WARMING UP**
Japanese macaques
regularly exploit hot
springs to keep warm
and rid themselves of
parasites. High-ranking
individuals within a
troop are allowed
greater privileges at
the springs.

Japanese macaque

Macaca fuscata

Native to the Japanese islands, the Japanese macaque is also known as the snow monkey – with good reason. This short-tailed monkey lives in snowy regions farther north than any other non-human primate species on the planet. Northern Honshu in particular can be snow-covered for a third of the year, and the Japanese macaque's dense grey-brown coat, which covers its entire body except the face and rump, grows thicker as the temperature falls. This allows it to survive temperatures as low as - 20°C (- 4°F).

Its habitat ranges from subtropical forests in southern Japan to subarctic woods in the north. The females spend more time in trees, while males prefer to stay on the ground; however, all Japanese macaques sleep in trees whenever possible to avoid predators such as feral dogs. They are true omnivores, although they eat more plants than animals. Their preferred diet consists of seasonal fruit, nuts, seeds, and leaves, but they will eat fungi, insects, shellfish, fish, roots, and even soil, for minerals, when necessary.

Inherited rank

The males are slightly larger and heavier than females, and social groups, known as troops, are made up of both sexes. However, the rank, or standing, in a troop passes from mothers to daughters. One troop may have several of these "matrilines" arranged in a hierarchy, with members of one matriline outranking all lower-ranking matrilines. Males within a troop also follow a dominance system, led by an alpha male. Females stay in their troops for life, but males join different ones when they reach sexual maturity.

Female Japanese macaques decide which males to mate with, and will not necessarily choose an alpha male. Mating takes place on the ground or in trees, and a single infant (or twins in rare cases) is born five to six months later. Infants begin foraging for themselves at around seven weeks, but they depend on their mothers for about 18 months. Grandmothers sometimes raise their abandoned grandchildren – the first non-human primate known to do so.

Versatile communicator

An intelligent species, Japanese macaques use a number of sounds and calls to communicate, as well as to alert troop members to danger. They also learn behavioural techniques from each other, such as bathing in hot springs, rolling snowballs, and washing food in fresh water before dipping it in salt water to enhance the taste.

Japanese macaque troops in **different locations have different accents,** just like humans do

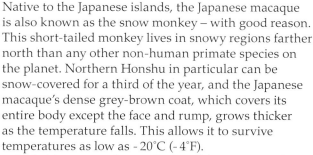

◁ **WINTER FORAGING**
The diet of Japanese macaques
changes with the seasons – in
winter they eat mainly tree bark
and buds.

↔ 47–72 cm (18¹/₂–28 in)
⬛ 8–11 kg (18–24 lb)
❌ Common
🍴 Plants, insects, shellfish

Japan

△ ICE HOUSE
Hollow trees or ground burrows provide shelter and sleeping dens for the primarily nocturnal Japanese marten, as well as protection from predators such as feral dogs.

▷ STEPPING STONES
Powerful leg muscles enable Japanese martens to leap several times their own body length, while sharp claws give them excellent traction. This means crossing thawing rivers poses no problem.

cream-coloured neck patch

face has black "mask" like a raccoon

Japanese marten

Martes melampus

Although they belong to the weasel family, whose members are known for catching small mammals, Japanese martens are opportunists when it comes to food, adapting their diets to the seasons and whatever is available where they live. In spring, for example, birds may feature as prey of some populations, while insects make up a large part of their diet in summer.

Dispersal agents

Martens do eat small mammals such as field mice, as well as birds, eggs, fish, frogs, and crustaceans. However, their droppings, or scat, contain a wider variety of whole plant and fruit seeds than other native flesh-eating mammals, making the martens vital seed dispersers, particularly for plants producing flesh-rich fruits.

Japanese martens were once bred for their fur, which varies from yellowish to dark brown among the three subspecies, but very little is known about these agile and elusive mammals in the wild. They regularly mark their boundaries with scat, are thought to be highly territorial, and prefer broadleaf woodland to conifers due to the wider array of food choices the former offers.

Males are larger than females, which bear one to five kits per litter. Other than females with kits, Japanese martens live and hunt alone. They are threatened by the rise in the number of conifer plantations, increased use of agrochemicals, and over-hunting for the fur trade.

In **Japanese folklore, martens** are said to have **shapeshifting abilities**

↔ 47–55 cm (18½–21½ in)
⚖ 1–1.5 kg (2¼–3¼ lb)
✖ Locally common
🍴 Mammals, birds, plants
🏠 🌲 🏠

E. Asia

Raccoon dog

Nyctereutes procyonoides

Native to East Asia, the raccoon dog is so adaptable that it is now widespread in eastern and northern Europe, where it was initially introduced by the fur trade. This member of the canid (dog) family is a distant cousin of wolves and dogs, but several characteristics set it apart. It is the only canid to semi-hibernate in winter, going into a state of lethargy unless its fat reserves are too low. It does not bark, but whines, mews, or growls. Raccoon dogs have smaller teeth and longer intestines than other canids – traits found in animals that consume plant matter. During autumn in their native range, fruit and berries make up a large part of their diet.

↔ 50–71 cm (19½–28 in)
⚖ 3–12.5 kg (6½–27½ lb)
✖ Common
🍴 Birds, rodents, frogs, fruit
🏠 🌲 🌲 🏔 🌾 ≈ 🏠

long winter coat with thick fur undercoat

E. Asia

◁ **READY FOR WINTER**
Due to their relatively poor eyesight, raccoon dogs rely on their sense of smell to find enough food in autumn to fatten up for winter.

Mandarin duck

Aix galericulata

female
much less
colourful

male has
spiky ruff

triangular orange
sails

Like many brightly patterned birds, mandarin ducks are surprisingly inconspicuous in the wild. They usually keep well out of sight beneath overhanging lakeside vegetation, or perch high up in trees. In spring, they nest in cavities in old trees. Males defend occupied nests at first, but do not incubate the eggs and leave the area before they hatch. Mandarins feed on small invertebrates, seeds, acorns, and other vegetable matter, taken from shallow water or while grazing on nearby short grass. They fly quickly through trees and across open water, making high-pitched, squeaky, quacking calls.

Numbers game

Habitat loss and exploitation have caused a dramatic decline in the mandarin's natural range, but, being an ornamental bird, it has been introduced into parts of Europe. Some mandarins escaped from collections to establish wild populations in North America. Normally, such out-of-range introductions turn out to be ecologically damaging, but in the mandarin's case, they may prove to be the species' salvation in the long term.

↔ 41–49 cm (16–19½ in)
⚖ 625 g (22 oz)
✕ Common
〰 Seeds, nuts, insects, snails

E. Asia

broad white
crescent of male

◁ **MAGNIFICENT MALE**
Few birds look quite so singular. While the male is unique, the female looks like a female American wood duck.

Mandarin ducks **symbolize lifelong fidelity and affection** in Chinese culture

Asian tiger keelback

Rhabdophis tigrinus

The Asian tiger keelback is a very unusual snake. It is both venomous (from its rear-fanged bite) and poisonous. Known as *yamakagashi* in Japan, the keelback absorbs toxins from its poisonous toad prey and stores it in its neck glands. When threatened, the snake arches its neck and oozes the poison as a deterrent. The female lays two to 40 eggs (average 10–14), which hatch after 30–45 days.

↔ 0.7–1.2 m (2¼–4 ft)
⚖ 60–800 g (2–28¼ oz)
✖ Not known
🍴 Amphibians
🏠
📍 E. and SE. Asia

▽ TRANSFERRING TOXINS
The black-banded keelback can pass on the toxins derived from toads to its offspring via the egg yolk.

Alpine black swallowtail

Papilio maackii

This large butterfly lives along forest edges and in grasslands where there are plentiful bushes. There are two broods per year, one hatching in late spring and the other in late summer. The adults survive for two weeks, feeding on nectar and gathering in crowds to mate. Eggs are laid on prickly ash and cork oak leaves – the preferred food of the caterpillars.

iridescent scales

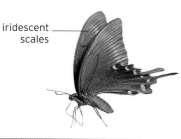

↔ 12–14 cm (4¾–5½ in)
✖ Not known
🍴 Prickly ash leaves, nectar
🏠
📍 E. Asia

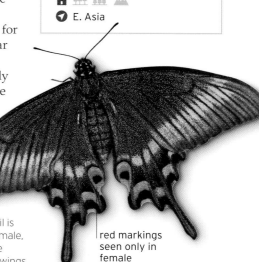

△ FANCY FEMALE
The female alpine black swallowtail is more vibrantly coloured than the male, with red and blue spots behind the green band that runs across both wings.

red markings seen only in female

Japanese giant salamander

Andrias japonicus

↔ 1–1.4 m (3¼–4½ ft)
🌢 Late summer
✖ Near threatened
🍴 Fish, insects, crustaceans
🏠

E. Asia (Japan)

This freshwater monster is the second largest amphibian on earth after the Chinese giant salamander. It breathes exclusively through its skin, which restricts it to living in cold, fast-flowing, oxygen-rich rivers. Between August and September, adults congregate at underwater nest sites to spawn. Females lay their eggs in burrows in riverbanks. These are fertilized and guarded by males until they hatch. The young remain as larvae for four to five years, and mature 10 years later.

bulbous head

wrinkled skin exudes milky fluid when salamander is threatened

forelimbs same length as hind limbs

△ SENSITIVE SKIN
The salamander's tiny eyes are no use in finding prey. Instead, it uses its sense of smell and sensors in its skin that pick up water currents produced by passing prey.

BORNEAN RAINFOREST
Southeast Asia's treasure trove of rare species

At around 140 million years of age, Borneo's lowland rainforest is one of the oldest and most biodiverse in the world. But the forest's diversity is also what makes it attractive to commercial exploitation. The lowland forests boast 267 species of large hardwood trees, 60 per cent of which are endemic to Borneo. Estimates put forest loss in the region at 30 per cent since 1970, due mainly to the logging of hardwoods for the global timber market and the conversion of land to agricultural use. Increasing fragmentation of the rainforest presents difficulties for endangered wide-ranging species such as orangutans, which require large, continuous tracts of forest for survival. Also, there is a staggering 99 per cent drop in species diversity just a couple of metres into a plantation compared to the untouched rainforest.

High, green island heart
Currently just over half of the island retains its forest cover, with the majority consisting of lowland rainforest below 1,000 m (3,300 ft). The cooler, higher-altitude centre of the island – now known internationally as the Heart of Borneo – is covered with unbroken mountainous rainforest, which has so far suffered less from logging and the encroachment of agriculture, mainly because the terrain is less suitable. Other important habitats for wildlife in Borneo include swamp forests and mangroves.

18 mammal species in Borneo's mountain rainforest exist nowhere else on Earth

SHRUB FROG

IMMUNE TO DANGER
Pitcher plants use bright colours and sweet smells to attract insects to their sticky, fluid-filled "pitchers". Prey that drowns in the liquid is digested by the plant. Shrub frogs are unaffected by the fluid, and lay their eggs in the pitchers, where they develop safely from predators.

SUN BEAR

HONEY HUNTER
The Borneo sun bear is found only in the island's rainforests. It uses its large claws to rip open beehives and termite nests in search of honey and insects to eat. It also consumes fruit from various rainforest trees and plays an important role in seed dispersal.

The third-largest island on Earth

44 of which are found nowhere else in the world

221 mammal species live here, 44

SLIPPER ORCHID

WONDERFUL ORCHIDS
Borneo has 2,500–3,000 orchid species; 51 new kinds were discovered between 2007 and 2010. The region is home to rare flowers, such as the Rothschild's slipper orchid – beautiful and endangered.

USELESS SCALES

Sunda pangolins have declined more than 50% in the last 15 years due to poaching. Their scales are illegally sold to buyers in China, and the medicines they are used in are useless.

SUNDA PANGOLIN

Called "Kalimantan" in Indonesian, or "burning-weather island" Home to about 15,000 species of flowering plants

FOREST GIANT

The titan arum's 3 m (10 ft)-tall inflorescence is actually a collection of small flowers on a fleshy stem, surrounded by a single petal-like structure called a spathe. The blooms give off an odour of rotting flesh that attracts flies to pollinate it.

TITAN ARUM

SEED DISPERSER

Eight species of hornbill live in Borneo. Like the sun bear, bushy-crested, helmeted, and great rhinoceros hornbills are important dispersers of seeds. In addition to facing habitat loss, the birds are hunted for their feathers and meat.

RHINOCEROS HORNBILL

LOCATION

Borneo is located in Southeast Asia, southwest of the Philippines and north of Java. Politically the island is divided among three countries: Indonesia, Malaysia, and Brunei.

South China Sea

Bandar Seri Begawan

Sulawesi Sea

Kuching

Banjarmasin

0 km 250
0 miles 250

CLIMATE

Borneo's rainforest has a severely hot, tropical climate, with warm temperatures and significant rainfall occurring year round. The island's average annual rainfall is 2,992 mm (118 in), with an average temperature of 26.7°C (80°F).

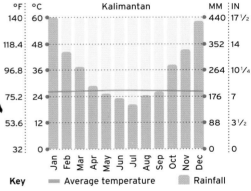

Kalimantan

°F	°C		MM	IN
140	60		440	17½
118.4	48		352	14
96.8	36		264	10¼
75.2	24		176	7
53.6	12		88	3½
32	0		0	0

Jan Feb Mar Apr May Jun Jul Aug Sep Oct Nov Dec

Key — Average temperature ▬ Rainfall

THE PROBLEM WITH PALM OIL

Vast tracts of Borneo's forests have been destroyed to make way for oil-palm plantations. Palm oil, extracted from the fruit and seed kernels of the palms, is used globally in the food and cosmetics industries. Demand for cheap vegetable oils is expected to increase as human population grows.

Large flying fox
Pteropus vampyrus

Unlike the smaller microbats, flying foxes do not echolocate to find their way around in the dark. Instead, they use their big eyes and sensitive noses to find fruit and flowers to eat in the rainforest. This diet gives them their other common name: fruit bat. Flying foxes spend the day roosting upside down in large, noisy groups in trees. They can move around by using the thumbs on the edges of their wings to cling onto branches. At night they fly to feeding trees, which may be many kilometres away from their roost.

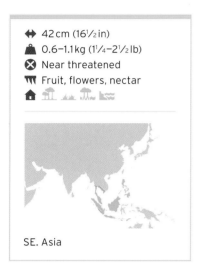

↔ 42 cm (16½ in)
⚖ 0.6–1.1 kg (1¼–2½ lb)
✖ Near threatened
🍽 Fruit, flowers, nectar

SE. Asia

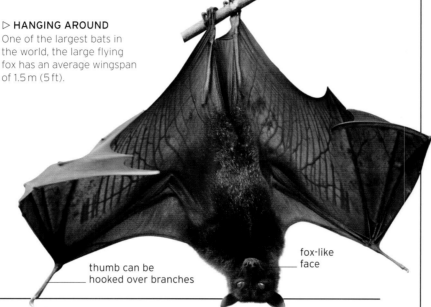

▷ **HANGING AROUND**
One of the largest bats in the world, the large flying fox has an average wingspan of 1.5 m (5 ft).

thumb can be hooked over branches

fox-like face

Western tarsier
Cephalopachus bancanus

Relative to its size, the western tarsier has the largest eyes of any mammal – each is slightly heavier than its brain. The eyes cannot move, but this nocturnal primate can turn its head to look backwards for possible predators or prey. It also locates prey with its keen hearing, grabbing or leaping on its victim.

Leaping is the tarsier's main form of locomotion – it can jump across distances almost 40 times its body length. Mainly tree-dwelling, it has slender fingers and its toes have pads, nails, and sharp claws, for gripping branches.

Females have one offspring at a time. At first, the baby is carried by the mother, but it soon learns to cling to her fur.

↔ 11.5–13 cm (4½–5 in)
⚖ 100–140 g (3½–5 oz)
✖ Vulnerable
🍽 Insects, bats, snakes, birds

SE. Asia

▷ **CLINGING ON**
The agile western tarsier easily holds on to vertical trunks, using its long tail as a support.

↔ 61–76 cm (24–30 in)
⚖ 10–24 kg (22–53 lb)
✖ Endangered
🍽 Leaves, unripe fruit, seeds

SE. Asia

adult male has orange face and enormous nose

Proboscis monkey

Nasalis larvatus

Proboscis monkeys are as complex as their facial features are unusual. Both sexes have exceptional noses. The females' and juveniles' noses are long for primates but upturned, while adult males sport the clown-like, pendulous proboscis that gives the species its common name. Its purpose is still uncertain, but it may function as an "echo chamber", amplifying the males' calls and helping them attract mates.

Deceptive appearance

Males are much larger than females. Due to the high volume of leaves they consume coupled with a very slow digestive rate, both sexes have large, swollen stomachs that make them look perpetually pregnant.

A mature male heads a harem of several females and their young. Unusually for primates, females in a harem compete with each other for mating opportunities with the male, and may join several harems during their lifetimes. As they mature, males form bachelor groups before vying for harems of their own. Although rival males engage in noisy displays, they are not fiercely territorial. Several groups often come together at dusk, sleeping high up in the trees for safety.

Proboscis monkeys are never far from water and they are remarkable swimmers, aided by their partially webbed feet.

△ MIGHTY LEAP
Leaping from trees and belly flopping into water is a common activity. Proboscis monkeys can swim up to 20 m (65 ft) underwater when threatened.

◁ BABY FACE
Both sexes are born with a "normal" monkey nose, and black fur and blue faces. The nose grows and the coloration changes with age.

△ ADOLESCENT SQUABBLE
Bonds are forged and broken as juveniles grow in size, get stronger, and learn new skills.

An adult male's **nose is often so long** it has to be **pushed aside** to allow its owner **to eat**

Bornean orangutan

Pongo pygmaeus

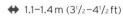

arms twice as long as legs

The orangutan is the only great ape to live in Asia. Its name means "man of the forest" in Malay. This shaggy, red-haired ape is found in the forests of Borneo and Sumatra. The Bornean species outnumbers the Sumatran orangutan (*P. abelii*) by almost 10 to one. However, with a population of around 55,000, Bornean orangutans are still highly endangered.

Life in the trees

Orangutans spend the day climbing up branches in search of food and sleep in trees at night. Their arm span is considerably longer than their height – an adult male's arms can span up to 2.2 m (7¼ ft) – so they can reach for branches and swing across precipitous drops with relative ease. Weighing about the same as an adult human, although six times stronger, orangutans cannot reach the very top of trees safely and so spend most of their time in the lower 40 m (130 ft) of the forest. Older males are too heavy to climb that high, and in Borneo, where there are no large predators to speak of, the males spend long periods on the ground. Females and younger males, by contrast, may not touch the ground for weeks on end.

Orangutans feed primarily on fruit, using their dextrous hands and their teeth to remove the peel and expose the flesh. They also eat leaves, bark, and flowers, as well as honey, birds' eggs, insects, and fish.

Solitary ape

Adult male orangutans stay out of each other's way, using a series of calls to advertise their presence and warn off neighbours. Some male Bornean orangutans do not develop facial flaps when mature. They are less vocal and use stealth tactics to approach and mate with a female while the other males are vying with each other for mating rights. Female orangutans may spend short periods feeding in small groups, letting their young play together. A female orangutan cares for her young for about seven years, and will not have another until the previous offspring has become independent.

↔ 1.1–1.4 m (3½–4½ ft)
🏋 40–80 kg (88–176 lb)
✖ Endangered
🍽 Plants, eggs, insects
🏠 🌳

SE. Asia (Borneo)

◁ **MATURE MALE**
There is considerable physical difference between male and female orangs. Most males develop wide facial flaps at the age of 14, and grow a thin moustache and beard.

△ **NIGHT NEST**
Orangutans sleep in nests made of folded branches. They make a fresh one every night.

◁ **A SIP OF RAIN**
A young orangutan drinks rainwater dripping from forest leaves. Orangutans often use a leafy branch as an umbrella in heavy downpours.

Müller's gibbon

Hylobates muelleri

arms one-and-a-half times as long as legs

The smallest members of the ape family, gibbons are among the most acrobatic primates, able to bridge gaps of more than 10 m (33 ft) between trees by flinging themselves across with their long arms. Müller's gibbon is one of four gibbon species native to Borneo, where it inhabits tall rainforest and tropical forest canopies. Since it rarely comes down to the ground, this species is mainly threatened by loss of habitat due to forest clearance.

While touch and grooming play vital roles in other ape species, gibbons bond and communicate largely by vocalizing, or "singing", and each species has its own unique song. Adults are serial monogamists, and mated pairs defend their territory with morning duets. The male begins singing shortly before dawn and is joined by the female after sunrise for an average of 15 minutes, before the daily search for food begins.

Gibbons use the same **vocalization techniques as operatic sopranos**

◁ **KING OF THE SWINGERS**
Gibbons are highly agile and move by brachiation, or arm-swinging, travelling through trees at speeds of up to 55 km/h (34 mph).

- 41–64 cm (16–25 in)
- 4.6–7 kg (10–15½ lb)
- Endangered
- Ripe fruit, leaves, flowers

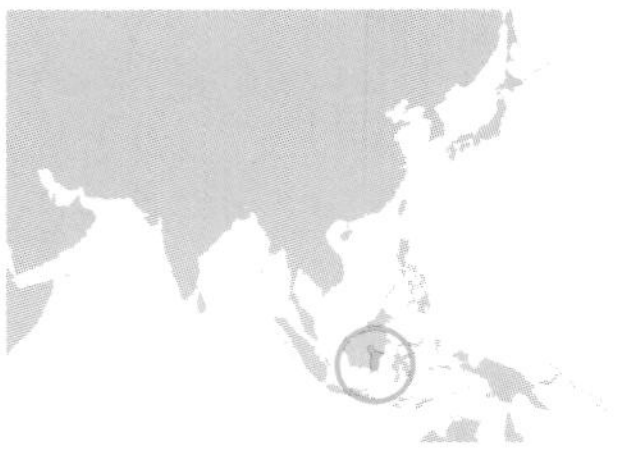

SE. Asia (Borneo)

Common flying dragon

Draco volans

▷ **CONTROLLED GLIDE**
As it glides, the dragon's chest muscles extend and tilt the ribs to curve the wings for lift, if air currents allow, and for directional control, aided by the tail and feet.

Rather than flying like its mythical namesake, this lizard glides between tree trunks to find food or mates, or to avoid territorial conflicts or predators. Its wings consist of stretchy skin supported by elongated ribs. Common flying dragon glides have been measured at more than 10 m (33 ft), with anecdotal records exceeding 50 m (165 ft). When not airborne, the wings are folded along the sides of the body for protection. They also aid camouflage, both with their coloration and by disrupting the typical body shape of a lizard. The dragon's favourite foods are tree ants and termites, usually caught morning and evening.

Mating displays

At breeding time the territorial male head-bobs, unfurls his wings, and fans out his bright yellow dewlap (chin flap) to repel rival males and attract females. After mating, the female climbs down to the ground and digs a shallow hole with her snout for her eggs.

- 15–20 cm (6–8 in)
- 5–10 g (3/16–3/8 oz)
- Common
- Ants, termites, small insects

SE. Asia

Black-and-red broadbill

Cymbirhynchus macrorhynchos

Named for the wide, flattened bill designed to scoop up insects and other prey, this strikingly coloured broadbill is surprisingly inconspicuous in thick foliage. It is often silent, but has a distinctive low song. Perched upright, taut and slim, with its tail pointing down, the male peers around, twisting his large head, then stretches and partially opens his bill to produce a brief phrase of buzzing notes.

↔ 25 cm (10 in)
🏋 50–76 g (1³⁄₄–2⁵⁄₈ oz)
✖ Common
🦗 Insects, fruit, crabs, fish
🏠 🎋 🌱 〰 🍄
🧭 SE. Asia

△ **MATCHED PAIR**
Black-and-red broadbills nest in tree stumps near water. The males help incubate the eggs and feed the chicks.

Stork-billed kingfisher

Pelargopsis capensis

Although it dives for fish, this kingfisher hunts in drier, wooded places, too, for a variety of prey. It is usually located by its loud, fast cackle of alarm and a regularly repeated low, three-note call. Aggressively territorial, it chases other birds, even birds of prey, from its patch.

▷ **TOP HEAVY**
With the largest bill vof any kingfisher, the stork-billed kingfisher can handle prey almost as big as itself.

large head compared to body

↔ 35 cm (14 in)
🏋 150–200 g (5¼–7 oz)
✖ Common
🦗 Fish, frogs, crabs, rodents
🏠 🎋 🌱 〰 〰 🍄
🧭 S. to SE. Asia

Wallace's flying frog

Rhacophorus nigropalmatus

▷ **GROUNDED FROGLET**
Juvenile froglets have brown granular skin more suited to life among mud and soil than the smooth green skin of the tree-living adult.

Named after its discoverer A.R. Wallace, the English naturalist who developed the theory of evolution with Charles Darwin, the flying frog is a perfect example of how species can adapt to their environments. The webbed feet used for swimming by the frog's ancestors are repurposed as parachutes, allowing it to leap long distances between trees. Adults need never come down to the ground – they can leap away from predators or towards new feeding areas. During the rainy season, eggs are laid inside a foam nest whipped up on a branch from the female's mucus secretions. When the tadpoles hatch, they fall into a pond or waterhole below.

↔ 7–10 cm (2³⁄₄–4 in)
☁ Rainy season
✖ Locally common
🦗 Insects, spiders

SE. Asia

◁ **PARACHUTING ADULT**
The splayed webbed feet allow Wallace's flying frogs to make leaps up to 15 m (50 ft). Large toe pads provide a strong grip on landing.

Atlas moth

Attacus atlas

feathery antennae of male

Named after the Greek demigod who carried the world on his shoulders, this species once held the title of the largest living moth; however, the Hercules moth of New Guinea and Australia has the biggest wing area of all. Nevertheless, the female Atlas moth can cover a dinner plate (the males are smaller).

Adult Atlas moths do not feed, and they live for a week at most, so they need to breed as soon as possible; males can track the scent of females several miles away with their feathery antennae. The females lay around 250 tiny eggs on the underside of leaves, particularly of citrus and other fruit trees.

↔ 16–30 cm (6¹⁄₄–12 in)
✖ Not known
🦗 Leaves

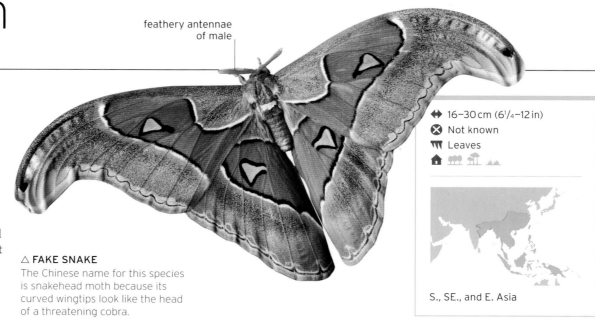

△ **FAKE SNAKE**
The Chinese name for this species is snakehead moth because its curved wingtips look like the head of a threatening cobra.

S., SE., and E. Asia

Malaysian orchid mantis

Hymenopus coronatus

With its fine pink and cream shading, this mantis is a master of disguise. It resembles a forest orchid, with the back legs flattened to look like petals, and the plump abdomen resembling a ripening bud. The trick this insect plays not only keeps it hidden from predators that might snatch it from plants, but also fools its prey, which fly straight to it thinking it is a nectar-filled bloom.

Killer mimic

This strategy is known as aggressive mimicry. The Malaysian orchid mantis clambers around a plant until it finds a cluster of flowers. It can fine-tune its colour from pink to brown to match its location, making it indistinguishable even when viewed in the ultraviolet spectrum by its insect prey. The mantis sways with the flimsy blooms, making it even harder to spot. Pollinating insects appear to approach the mantis as frequently as they do the real flowers – and are snatched up with lightning speed.

↔ 3–6 cm (1¼–2¼ in)
✖ Not known
♒ Insects
⌂ 🏚

SE. Asia

▷ **GRABBING FORELIMBS**
The mantis catches prey with its raptorial forelegs – sometimes snatching them from midair. The legs are lined with spikes to grip its victims.

fleshy, budlike abdomen

horn-like eyes

The orchid mantis can **match the colours of 13 flowers** that live in its habitat

SULU-SULAWESI SEAS
The world's most biodiverse marine ecoregion

The Sulu-Sulawesi marine ecoregion covers around 900,000 sq km (660,000 sq miles) of the Sulu and Sulawesi seas and the inland seas of the Philippines. It sits at the top of the Coral Triangle of Southeast Asia. Its complex mix of marine habitats includes seagrass plains, coral reefs, deep sea trenches, seamounts, active volcanic islands, and mangrove forests. The diverse habitats support astonishing underwater biodiversity with more than 2,000 species of marine fish and 400 species of coral represented. The seas are also home to five of the world's seven sea turtle species, and the dugong and Irrawaddy dolphin – both vulnerable marine mammals.

Threatened paradise

The water is predominantly warm and clear thanks to the tropical climate. Such bountiful and beautiful waters draw crowds of tourists that come to experience the coral reefs and islands. Many of the reefs are popular dive sites, and the Tubbata Reefs in the Sulu Sea were declared UNESCO World Heritage Site in 1993. Fishermen exploit the large populations of commercial fish, such as tuna.

Tourism and growing local populations put pressure on the marine environment through the development of coastlines and the use of coral for building. There is also increased pollution from untreated sewage and industrial and agricultural run-off into the sea. Efforts are being made by conservationists to curb harmful fishing techniques that use dynamite or cyanide, which damage the coral reefs and kill marine life indiscriminately.

OVERFISHING
Along with commercial fishing for the international food market, local people catch fish for their own consumption, and coral reef fish are sought for the aquarium trade. The sardine population is approaching collapse.

SARDINES

LIVING FOSSIL
Discovered in 1997, the Sulawesi coelacanth is one of two survivors of a group of fish that was thought to be extinct. It has become a flagship species for the better management and protection of the Bunaken National Park where it is found.

COELACANTH

LOCH'S CHROMODORIS

TOXIC SEA SLUG
The colourful Loch's chromodoris is a sea slug that lives on coral reefs. It feeds on sponges and is able to ingest their toxins into its own body, making it inedible to potential predators. Its bright coloration serves as a warning that it is poisonous.

More than 400 species of coral ❯ Home to around 2,000 species of fish ❯ Five species of

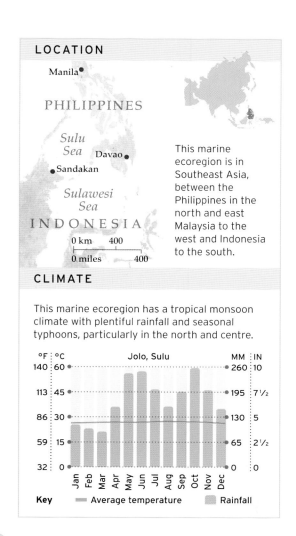
Spinner dolphin

Stenella longirostris

triangular dorsal fin

pointed flippers

Spinner dolphins get their name from their ability to twirl several times in mid-air as they leap clear of the sea. Like most dolphin species, spinners are highly social, grouping together in schools that may range from under 200 to 1,000 or more individuals. They often swim with other dolphins and whales as well as fish such as yellowfin and skipjack tuna – a habit that results in many of these mammals dying in commercial tuna nets as bycatch.

Shallow sleepers, deep feeders

Although they are deep-water feeders, spinner dolphins retreat to areas safe from predators to rest during the day, usually frequenting the same area such as an inlet, bay, or shallow water. Hunting and feeding occur mainly at night, which is also when they do most of their leaping. Spinner dolphins use touch, such as nudges or flipper rubbing, whistles, and also echolocation to keep in contact with members of their group. They mate year round, and females give birth to a single calf, which stays with its mother for around seven years.

↔ 1.3–2.8 m (4¼–9¼ ft)
⚖ 45–80 kg (99–175 lb)
✕ Not known
〰 Fish, squid, shrimp
🏠 〰 ≋

Tropical waters worldwide

Spinner dolphins make a **series of leaps**, often as many as **14 in a row**

▽ **AQUATIC ACROBAT**
Theories for the reason behind the spinner's trademark leaps include communication with other dolphins, parasite-removal, or sheer joy.

MULTIFACETED GRASS

Seagrass beds are vital to the marine ecosystem. They are a food source for dugongs and turtles and a nursery habitat for young fish. They also clean the water of chemicals, recycle nutrients, and help stabilize sandy sediments on the seafloor.

a turtle live in these waters

SEAGRASS

Dugong
Dugong dugon

thick bristles on snout used to detect food

The dugong, a close relative of the elephant, is often called the sea cow, because it feeds almost exclusively on seagrass in shallow coastal tropical waters. Dugongs have torpedo-shaped bodies, broad heads, stubby flippers, and fleshy, bristled lips.

When dugongs dive, their valved nostrils seal themselves off. However, these large mammals can stay underwater only for about three minutes. Adult dugongs have few natural enemies because of their size and dense bones, though crocodiles, sharks, and killer whales attack calves and juveniles. Dugongs do not

mate until they are at least six years old, and only one calf is produced every three to seven years. Born in shallow water, after a 14-month gestation, the calf is immediately helped to the surface for its first breath by its mother.

Dugongs can live up to 70 years. However, their low reproductive rate, the loss of seagrass due to human activity, collisions with boats, drownings from fish net entanglements, and hunting mean that dugong populations are in decline. Today the largest numbers are concentrated around Australia's Great Barrier Reef.

↔ 2–3.3 m (6½–10¾ ft)
⚖ 250–570 kg (550–1,257 lb)
✗ Vulnerable
🌱 Seagrass, algae
🏠 〰 ⌁

E. Africa, W., S., and SE. Asia, Australia, Pacific Islands

◁ **KEEPING COMPANY**
Dugongs are often flanked by golden trevallies. These brightly coloured fish feed on the creatures dugongs disturb when grazing.

▷ **MOTHER AND CALF**
Dugongs communicate with each other using trills, whistles, barks, and chirps, each at a different frequency and amplitude.

Ribbontail stingray
Taeniura lymma

↔ Up to 70 cm (28 in)
⚖ Not known
✗ Near threatened
🌱 Fish, crustaceans
🏠 ⌁ ⌁

Indo-Pacific Oceans

Viewed from below, a ribbontail stingray's white underside disappears into sunlit waters; from above, its speckled back blends into coral reefs. During low tide, stingrays seek shelter in reefs, moving into shallower water to feed as the tide rises.

A ribbontail stingray's mouth contains numerous tooth rows arranged in plates, ideal for crushing crustacean shells. Rays can sense food by detecting the prey's electrical field. They have few natural predators; only the hammerhead shark is known to eat them. They breed in late spring and summer. A female delivers up to seven live pups that hatch from eggs inside her body.

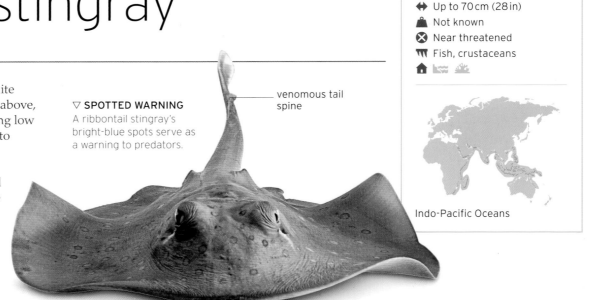

▽ **SPOTTED WARNING**
A ribbontail stingray's bright-blue spots serve as a warning to predators.

venomous tail spine

Mandarinfish

Synchiropus splendidus

↔	6 cm (2½ in)
⚖	Not known
✖	Not known
🦐	Crustaceans, worms, snails
🏠 🪸	

Indonesian Ocean

The small, colourful mandarinfish lives on shallow lagoons and inshore reefs. It hides among dead coral during the day, but small groups gather to forage at night. A weak swimmer, it often "walks" along the bottom on its large pectoral fins. A small mouth limits its diet to small prey, such as tiny crustaceans.

The skin cells of the mandarinfish contain a blue pigment. This and one closely related species are the only fish known to produce this coloured chemical. The colour pattern is also a warning to predators. Its skin is coated in a protective layer of mucus. Filled with noxious chemicals, the mucus smells – and tastes – unpleasant. The slime also keeps off external parasites, which might exploit a sleeping fish.

▷ **PREPARING TO SPAWN**
The fish remain in bodily contact as they swim up from the reef, releasing eggs and sperm into the open water.

skin mottled with
pale spots

Whale shark

Rhincodon typus

Possibly the most misnamed aquatic creature in the world, the whale shark is not a whale, but a fish, although it resembles whales in terms of size. It belongs to the same class as sharks, skates, and rays. The word "shark" brings to mind a toothy, prey-crunching predator that could be a threat to humans, but the whale shark is in fact a gentle giant. This docile, slow-swimming filter feeder allows divers to grasp its large dorsal fin without displaying any signs of aggression. Ironically, the largest living fish in the world survives on a diet made up entirely of the ocean's smallest organisms – tiny algae and animals known as phytoplankton and zooplankton.

Filter feeding

Relatively little is known about the whale shark's life and behaviour. The average adult can be up to 12 m (39 ft) in length – although there are unverified reports of specimens as long as 23 m (75 ft) – and weighs around 10 tonnes. The whale shark's huge, flat head ends in a mouth that is almost as wide as its body and contains hundreds of minuscule teeth, the function of which is unknown. It has specialized, sieve-like filter pads lining the gill arches, which separate food from seawater. Unusually for a shark, its mouth is at the end of its snout rather than underneath. As well as non- or slow-moving microscopic organisms, whale sharks also eat small fish, tiny squid, fish eggs, and larvae – in short, anything small enough to flow in with water but large enough to be trapped by their filter pads. Mostly solitary, whale sharks are occasionally seen in loosely organized schools of up to 100 individuals where food is plentiful.

Whale sharks migrate thousands of kilometres through the world's oceans. Individuals can be tracked using satellite tags and can be identified by the pattern of spots on their bodies – no two patterns are alike, just like human fingerprints. Adult males can be distinguished from females by the presence of "claspers" – external protrusions on their bellies that channel sperm into the female during mating. Little is known about when and how whale sharks breed, but a female retains up to 300 eggs inside her body until they hatch – a characteristic known as ovoviviparity. She then gives birth to live young or "pups", although it is believed that not all the pups are born at the same time.

Uncertain future

Once it has reached sexual maturity, which is estimated at about 30 years of age, the whale shark's primary predator is man. They are hunted for food supplements, such as shark liver oil; their fins, which are made into soup; their meat; and their skin, which is made into leather. However, many adult whale sharks carry scars that suggest they were attacked, possibly by killer whales (orcas) or other sharks, at some point in their lives. It is believed that whale sharks are capable of living up to 70–100 years in the wild.

△ **SPECIALIZED GILLS**
Cartilage rods support the spongy filter pads, which trap food such as plankton and tiny fish and squid.

△ KEEPING COMPANY
Schools of small fish often swim around the heads of whale sharks, possibly for protection.

↔ 12 m (39 ft)
⚖ Over 12 tonnes
⊗ Vulnerable
🦐 Phytoplankton, zooplankton
🏠 〰 🌊

Tropical and temperate waters worldwide

◁ SUCTION FEEDING
A whale shark often holds its mouth close to the surface during suction feeding, opening and closing it to suck in water as well as food.

When feeding, a whale shark **filters enough water to fill an Olympic-sized swimming pool** every 100 minutes

Great barracuda
Sphyraena barracuda

flat-topped, elongated skull

adult has stiff front dorsal fin

This long, torpedo-shaped fish hunts alone or in packs. By day, great barracudas gather in large schools that patrol the periphery of warm-water coral reefs, opting for safety in numbers over the chance to make a kill. By night, the school fragments, and lone adults glide over the reef to ambush fish at close quarters, while juveniles maraud in smaller groups that harass shoals of fish.

Toothy jaw

The great barracuda's long, streamlined body, along with short, stiff fins that provide stability, make it capable of many modes of swimming, from a steady cruise to a lightning fast surge – all powered by the large, triangular tail fins. The barracuda's jaw has a distinctive underbite with the lower jaw poking out in front of its head. This gives the fish a wide gape and exposes needle-like teeth, which are embedded in the jaw bones and the roof of the mouth. The long, toothy jaw is ideal for gripping small, struggling fish, but is also capable of delivering a powerful bite that can cut through larger prey. Occasionally, a lone barracuda will give a diver a nasty bite if it mistakes a hand or shiny diving watch for a small, silvery fish.

Great barracudas spawn in open water, and the eggs are left to drift unattended. The fry shelter in estuaries until they are 8 cm (3 in) long, then they head out to sea.

The **flesh of large barracudas** contains **lethal toxins**

↔ Up to 2 m (6½ ft)
⚖ Up to 50 kg (110 lb)
✖ Not known
🍴 Fish
🏠 🌿 🐚 〰 🪸

Tropical and subtropical waters worldwide

Boxer crab
Lybia tessellata

walking legs covered
in short hairs

The boxer crab's slender pincer-bearing legs are of no use for attack or defence. Instead, it uses a pair of sea anemones as bodyguards. It grips them in its front pincers and thrusts their stinging tentacles at anything threatening. This relationship also benefits the anemones as they are carried through the water, allowing them to collect food particles suspended in it. The crab cannot catch its own food and so uses its long mouthparts to collect some of the food scraps snared by the anemones.

↔ 1–2.5 cm (³/₈–1 in)
✖ Not known
🌾 Plankton
🏠

W. Indian Ocean, W. and
S. Pacific Ocean

△ **STINGING GLOVES**
Without the anemones, the crab is more or less defenceless, with little more than a picket of spines around the edge of its carapace.

Green humphead parrotfish
Bolbometopon muricatum

The largest of all parrotfish, the green humphead is one of the most social – feeding, sleeping, and spawning in large groups. This makes it an easy target for spearfishers, and overfishing has led to a decline in numbers. Like all parrotfish, green humpheads eat live coral; they use their forehead bulge to ram reefs, breaking the coral down into small pieces, which they crush with their beak-like front teeth.

↔ Up to 1.3 m (4¹/₄ ft)
⚖ Up to 46 kg (101 lb)
✖ Vulnerable
🌾 Coral, algae
🏠

▷ **REEF CRUNCHER**
An adult parrotfish consumes around 5-6 tonnes (5¹/₂-6¹/₂ tons) of coral each year. Any hard, undigested material is passed out in the fish's faeces, adding sediment back to the reef ecosystem.

Indian Ocean, S. Pacific Ocean

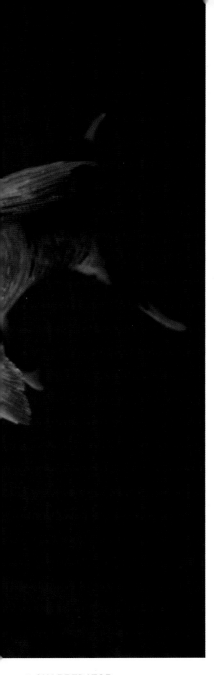

△ **SLY PREDATOR**
The barracuda's silver scales reflect the water, helping it blend into the background, and the narrow head gives prey little chance of seeing it coming.

△ **HERDING SCHOOL**
Groups of barracudas will work together to herd shoals of smaller fish into shallow waters, where they are easier to catch.

Vatuira, Fiji Islands
The warm, clear waters of coral reefs support an
incredible variety of life. The bright coloration of
fish that live in reefs helps them recognize
members of their species.

Australasia

FEATURED ECOREGIONS

- New Guinea Montane Forest **›› p314-19**
  Tropical moist broadleaf, mixed forest
- North Australia Savannas **›› p320-27**
  Tropical grassland, scrub
- Great Sandy-Tanami Desert **›› p328-33**
  Desert, scrub
- East Australian Forests **›› p334-43**
  Temperate broadleaf, mixed forest
- Great Barrier Reef **›› p344-53**
  Marine, coral reef
- New Zealand Mixed Forest **›› p354-59**
  Temperate broadleaf, mixed forest

ARNHEM LAND

Within 1,500 km (930 miles) of the equator, this north-central region has a fiercely seasonal, monsoon tropical climate. Its intricate mix of coastal landscapes and hills harbours dozens of unique species, from rock rats to snakes. It also provides an important conservation habitat for dugongs, nesting turtles, and migratory birds.

Timor Sea

Arafura Sea

Melville Island

INDIAN OCEAN

Arnhem Land

Barkly Tableland

Kimberley Plateau

Great Sandy Desert

Tanami Desert

A U S T R

Macdonnell Ranges

WESTERN COASTAL DESERTS
Starved from rain due to cold ocean currents and prevailing offshore winds, there is little coastal vegetation and arid conditions extend throughout.

Hamersley Range

Gibson Desert

△ *Uluru (Ayers Rock) 867m*

Simpson Desert

Great Victoria Desert

Nullarbor Plain

Darling Range

NULLARBOR PLAIN
This vast plain, with much bare rock, has no permanent water. Life is sparse and restricted to a narrow coastal strip.

Kangaroo Island

KEY DATA

ECOSYSTEMS

- Tropical broadleaf forest
- Temperate broadleaf forest
- Mediterranean woodland, scrub
- Tropical, subtropical grassland
- Temperate grassland
- Desert, scrub
- Montane grassland

AVERAGE RAINFALL

IN	MM
394	10,000
295	7,500
197	5,000
98	2,500
0	0

AVERAGE TEMPERATURE

°F	°C
86	30
68	20
50	10
32	0
14	-10
-4	-20
-22	-30
-40	-40

SHARK BAY

The shallow, sheltered conditions in Shark Bay encourage the formation of curious concretions called stromatolites. These mounds of layered sediment with surface films of cyanobacteria are almost identical to ones that formed more than 3 billion years ago. The cyanobacteria were among the first organisms to inhabit Earth.

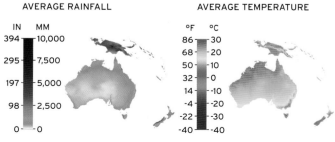

THE RED CONTINENT
Australasia

Australasia consists of the mainland, or large island, of Australia, together with Tasmania, New Zealand, the huge tropical island of New Guinea, and a few other nearby islands. All of these, apart from New Zealand, make up the Australian continent. It is the smallest of the continents and also, on average, the driest inhabited continent: about one-third has a desert-like climate and another third is semi-arid. On the mainland of Australia, appreciable rain falls only around the eastern margins, while the great interior, or outback, is often parched.

The Australian continent has a unique evolutionary history. It split from the rest of the southern supercontinent of Gondwana more than 80 million years ago, taking with it plants and animals common at the time, especially marsupial mammals. What are now the Australian mainland and New Guinea remained linked by land bridges until 6,000 years ago, when sea levels rose after the last ice age. Consequently, they share much of their wildlife, a high proportion of which consists of endemic species – most of the continent's plants and mammals and a high proportion of its birds are found nowhere else.

Much more isolated, lying more than 2,100 km (1,300 miles) to the southeast of the Australian mainland, is New Zealand. It, too, boasts many unique plants and animals, including kiwis and other flightless birds.

GONDWANA RAINFOREST

Only remnants of these southern supercontinent forests survive, with prehistoric ferns and conifers and ancient flowering plants. Among birds, the lyrebird, bowerbird, and catbird lineages stretch back more than 60 million years.

GREAT MOUNTAIN RANGE

More than 3,500 km (2,200 miles) long, the continent's only major uplands moisten the climate to the east, while aridity increases westwards.

MURRAY-DARLING BASIN

Named for its two major rivers, the wetlands here are seasonal and ephemeral.

TASMANIA

Australia's southern island state has dense rainforest and cool deciduous woodlands. They provide refuges for species once also on the mainland, such as the Tasmanian devil.

NEW ZEALAND ALPS

Forming the backbone of New Zealand's South Island, the Southern Alps' rugged high terrain is glaciated, with deep valleys, pockets of forest, and plunging cliffs. Iconic species include the rock wren, kea, and great spotted kiwi. It is the highest mountain range in Australasia.

New Guinea

Solomon Islands

Torres   Strait

Great Barrier Reef

Cape York Peninsula

Coral Sea

Great Dividing Range

A L I A

Fraser Island

Great Dividing Range

e Eyre asin

ers

nges

Darling

Murray

△ Mount Kosciuszko 2,228m

Bass   Strait

Flinders Island

Tasmania

North Island

New Zealand

Aoraki (Mt Cook) 3,744m △

Southern Alps

South Island

NEW GUINEA MONTANE FOREST
Remote tropical highlands form a biodiversity stronghold

Situated almost on the equator, New Guinea is the world's second-largest island. Politically it is divided into two halves: Indonesia in the west and Papua New Guinea in the east. The island's biodiversity, among the richest in the world, is a blend of Australian and Asian wildlife, which arrived here hundreds of thousands of years ago before the continents and New Guinea diverged.

Protected by terrain

Despite two centuries of encroachment by logging, agriculture, livestock, and mineral exploitation – which is persistently increasing – around two-thirds of New Guinea is still cloaked in forest, due mainly to the island's inaccessibly mountainous terrain. The upland forests are broadly organized into the Vogelkop (Bird's Head) montane rainforests in the northwest Doberai Peninsula, the Central Ranges rainforests along the backbone of the

island, and the Huon Peninsula rainforests in the northwest. The moist, tropical climate encourages riotous growth. Populations of plants and animals, isolated in steep, remote valleys and on scattered peaks, have evolved into thousands of species found nowhere else on the planet.

Active volcanoes and earthquakes continue to create new land forms, encouraging further diversity. So does altitude; lower hills are hot and steamy, while taller peaks are cooler and cloud-shrouded. These forests harbour more than 6,000 plant species and dozens of unique birds and mammals, including egg-laying echidnas and marsupials such as tree-kangaroos.

BOWER BUILDER
The Vogelkop bowerbird assembles a highly designed structure, or bower of twigs, stems, and leaves decorated with flowers, shells, and other bright items. All his effort is aimed at one thing: to impress females enough to attract a mate.

VOGELKOP BOWERBIRD

POCKET PREDATOR
Dasyures are Australasian carnivorous marsupials, such as the quoll and Tasmanian devil. One of the smallest is New Guinea's speckled dasyure, a Central Ranges inhabitant that hunts various species of insects, worms, and grubs.

SPECKLED DASYUR

Home to all four echidna species

Dozens of new species found here each year

HOODED PITOHUI

POISONOUS BIRD
Tests in the late 1980s showed that the hooded pitohui's skin and feathers exude the nerve poison homobatrachotoxin, which causes numbness and tingling if touched by humans. Furthermore, the toxin has since been found in other pitohui species.

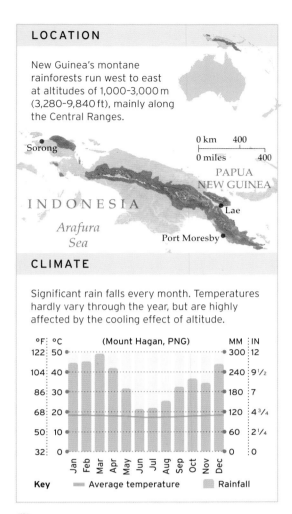
Common spotted cuscus

Spilocuscus maculatus

male's coat more spotted and patched than female's

A mainly nocturnal, tree-living marsupial, the common spotted cuscus has a woolly pelt that is prized by hunters, who also kill it for its meat. The cuscus sleeps on branches with its head tucked between its legs, often pulling large leaves around itself to hide from predators.

↔ 35–44 cm (14–17½ in)
⚖ 1.5–3.5 kg (3¼–7¾ lb)
✖ Common
🌾 Fruit, flowers, leaves

▷ **TELLING TAIL**
As well as its five-toed feet, the cuscus climbs with its prehensile tail – the lower half is naked on the inside to better grip branches.

Papua New Guinea, N. Australia

Long-beaked echidna

Zaglossus bartoni

Protective white spines cover the eastern long-beaked echidna's head, back, and sides, but are almost hidden beneath its coarse, dark fur. This species is the largest of the monotremes, the group of egg-laying mammals that also includes the duck-billed platypus. Males have hind ankle spurs, and both female and male long-beaked echidnas use the electroreceptors in their snout to detect their prey's electric fields.

▽ **WORM HUNTER**
When foraging for earthworms, echidnas probe the soil with their long snout. They grasp the worms with their tongue, which has a spine-like structure at the back.

↔ 60–100 cm (23½–39 in)
⚖ 5–10 kg (11–22 lb)
✖ Critically endangered
🌾 Earthworms

New Guinea

RARE BUTTERFLY
New Guinea has a diverse array of birdwings, or large swallowtail butterflies. The rare Rothschild's birdwing, which has a wingspan of 15–18 cm (6–7 in), is found only at 2,500 m (8,200 ft) in the Doberai Peninsula.

World's highest island

ROTHSCHILD'S BIRDWING

ears swivel to
detect prey

Sugar glider
Petaurus breviceps

large eyes adapted
for night vision

The most widespread of all
glider species, this highly
social marsupial's most
striking characteristic is
its method of locomotion. The
sugar glider launches itself from one tree
and coasts to the next in a lengthy, controlled
glide, courtesy of two furry wing-like membranes.
Just before it reaches its target, it swoops upwards
to land, clinging to the bark with strong claws.
Sugar gliders rarely venture to the ground.

The importance of scent
Smell is a complex communication tool for these
nocturnal possums. Dominant males use the scent
glands on their foreheads, throats, chests, and tail
region to mark territory – defended aggressively against
intruders – as well as members of their colony. Up to
seven adults and the season's young sleep together in
leaf-lined tree hollows by day, partly for warmth. In
cold or wet weather or times of drought, sugar gliders
can enter a daily semi-hibernative state called torpor,
lasting for up to 13 hours, to conserve energy.

furry membrane
stretched wide
when gliding

The sugar glider's **scientific name** means **short-headed rope dancer**

long rudder-like tail
helps control
direction of glide

◁ **HITCHING A RIDE**
Young sugar gliders, called
joeys, frequently cling to
their mother's back as she
goes in search of food.

△ **LICKING SAP**
Sugar gliders use large incisors
to chisel into tree bark, exposing
the sap that makes up a large
part of their diet.

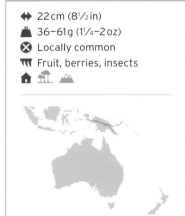

Goodfellow's tree kangaroo
Dendrolagus goodfellowi

With its broad face, short muzzle, and rounded ears, Goodfellow's tree kangaroo's head resembles that of a bear more than that of a ground-dwelling kangaroo. Shorter, independently moving hindlegs, powerful shoulders, and longer, muscular front legs are other differences – as is the fact that it spends much of its time in trees, feeding mainly on leaves, as well as fruit and flowers. It is largely nocturnal and solitary except when breeding, which occurs year-round.

Flexible climber

Goodfellow's tree kangaroo climbs by grasping a trunk or branch with its strong front claws, then "walking" up or along it with its hindlegs. Flexible ankle joints and greater dexterity allow easy movement among branches, and it has a larger brain in proportion to body size than many marsupials. It also descends to the ground to find food, where it both walks and hops.

Like most tree kangaroos, Goodfellow's is most at risk from habitat loss due to logging and other forms of forest clearance. It is also hunted for meat.

▷ **BALANCING ACT**
Broad, padded hindfeet give tree kangaroos excellent grip, while a long tail aids stability on branches.

↔ 52–80 cm (20¹⁄₂–31¹⁄₂ in)
⚖ 6.5–14.5 kg (14–32 lb)
✗ Endangered
🍴 Leaves, fruit, flowers, grass
🏠 🌳 ⛰

New Guinea

◁ **GLIDING AROUND**
The gliding membrane stretches from wrist to ankle, allowing the sugar glider to parachute between trees up to 90 m (295 ft) apart.

↔ 15–21 cm (6–8¹⁄₂ in)
⚖ 80–160 g (2⁷⁄₈–5⁵⁄₈ oz)
✗ Common
🍴 Sap, flowers, insects, spiders
🏠 🌳 🌳 🏞

SE. Asia, New Guinea, N. to W. Australia

Crested berrypecker
Paramythia montium

As is typical of animal species living at varying altitudes, crested berrypeckers in high forests are bigger than those lower down. Groups join mixed flocks to roam the forest canopy or gather in fruiting trees.

Crested berrypecker pairs are monogamous, building open, cup-shaped nests of moss and other plant materials. The female incubates the eggs alone, but both parents care for the chicks, which fledge after 15 days.

▷ **COURTING APPEAL**
Normally slim and sleek, the male stretches upright, puffs out his plumage, and raises his crest to maximize his appeal when courting.

↔ 22 cm (8¹⁄₂ in)
⚖ 36–61 g (1¹⁄₄–2 oz)
✗ Locally common
🍴 Fruit, berries, insects
🏠 🌳 ⛰

New Guinea

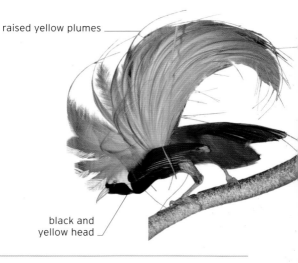

raised yellow plumes

black and
yellow head

Greater bird-of-paradise

Paradisaea apoda

More than 40 species of birds-of-paradise survive today, almost all in the dense forests of New Guinea, although a few extend into Indonesia and northern Australia. The greater bird-of-paradise is the largest in its family, and is roughly the size and shape of a crow, with strong, scaly legs and feet and a pointed beak. It is chiefly vegetarian, eating fruit and seeds as well as a few small insects.

Some species are relatively drab and form stable breeding pairs. Others are polygynous, with the more ornate males mating with several females. The males of these species boast beautiful feathers that have evolved into many kinds of plumes and spring-like shafts, loops, spirals, and extensive iridescent shawls. Male greater birds-of-paradise have spectacular plumes that extend back from their flank but which can be raised and spread, giving the impression that their whole body is adorned with long, wide sickles of maroon, white, and golden yellow. The females are dark maroon-brown and free of such eye-catching adornments.

Display perches
The males of polygynous species display at special sites called leks, where females assess their remarkable courtship dances and choose only the brightest, fittest males to mate with. A greater bird-of-paradise lek consists of large horizontal branches just below the canopy of a tall tree or trees. Adult males remove leaves from branches in the immediate area of the display perches, and the same site may be used for several years. Between eight and as many as 20 males use the same lek, and some leks may be shared with male raggiana birds-of-paradise (*P. raggiana*), which are similar in appearance.

Frenetic performance
Lekking male greater birds-of-paradise wave their wings and raise their long plumes, then briefly pose with spread plumes and arched, half-open wings. Competing males leap around each other, bouncing on a branch, flapping their wings and shaking their plumes. When they lean over and hang upside down, it is sometimes hard to tell which end is which. They keep up a chorus of loud, echoing *wa-wa-wa-wa-wah* sounds, while the females watch quietly then pick a favoured male to mate with.

As with all the polygynous species, the male plays no part in nesting or the raising of young. The female builds a basin-shaped nest out of leaves and vine tendrils and lays one or two eggs.

Rumours of **"visitors from paradise"** reached Europe before these birds were first **described by naturalists**

- ↔ 42–45 cm (16½–18 in)
- 🏋 170 g (6 oz)
- ✖ Locally common
- 🌾 Fruit, seeds, insects

SE. Asia, New Guinea

◁ **DAWN DISPLAY**
During courtship, the male curves his yellow flank plumes over drooped wings and builds up to a trembling, shuddering performance designed to win a female's favours.

NORTH AUSTRALIA SAVANNAS
Unique tropical grasslands where insects rule

In most regions, grasslands tend to be dominated by a few species of grasses and large grazing mammals. In Australia's tropical north, these savannas stretch roughly 1.5 million sq km (0.6 million sq miles) and harbour a more mixed range of plants and animals, and a greater variety of scenery, from typical rolling plains to rocky gorges hiding secret, almost rainforest-like thickets.

The Wet and the Dry

The scattered trees that dot the savanna and clumps of sparse woodland are mostly eucalypts, or gums. "The Wet", or rainy season, is reliable, with evergreen trees and shubs thriving where there are occasional floods and temporary lakes, and acacias grow in the drier south. During six to eight months of "the Dry", grasses shrivel to grey-brown and some trees shed leaves to curtail water loss.

This seasonality, along with generally poor soils, and Australia's distinctive wildlife due to its prehistoric isolation, mean that large native mammals, chiefly kangaroos, wallaroos, and wallabies, are relatively few in variety. Instead, most plant consumption and recycling is carried out by insects, especially termites. Their mounds, the tallest sometimes reaching 5 m (16 ft), dot the landscape in thousands, and their underground lifestyles and foraging for dead wood and plant matter allow them to survive the Dry. In addition, a rich variety of reptiles, such as the inimitable frilled lizard, and small marsupials, also live here.

POINTING NORTH
So-called "magnetic termites" build 2m (6½ ft) tall mounds, facing north-south - not to do with Earth's magnetic field, but to control temperature. The Sun's heat is side-on at dawn and dusk, and end-on at midday, so the mound stays cool.

TERMITE MOUNDS

COMPETING CATS
With so many smaller marsupial mammals in the rich hunting ground for tropical savannas, these are a introduced cats. In particular, feral cats compete with a native "marsupial cat", the northern quoll, whose numbers are declining.

NORTHERN QUOLL

More th

Temperatures often exceed 50°C (122°F)

Six times the size of the UK

JARRAH

LIFE AFTER FIRE
Like many local trees, the jarrah (a eucalypt tree) is adapted to occasional lightning-sparked fires - its underground part, or lignotuber, grows back. More frequent, extensive burns by livestock farmers threaten it and other vegetation species.

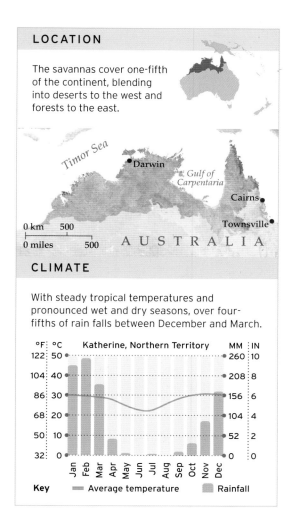

Timor Sea
• Darwin
Gulf of Carpentaria
Cairns •
Townsville •
AUSTRALIA

0 km 500
0 miles 500

CLIMATE

With steady tropical temperatures and pronounced wet and dry seasons, over four-fifths of rain falls between December and March.

Katherine, Northern Territory

°F	°C		MM	IN
122	50		260	10
104	40		208	8
86	30		156	6
68	20		104	4
50	10		52	2
32	0		0	0

Jan Feb Mar Apr May Jun Jul Aug Sep Oct Nov Dec

Key — Average temperature ▮ Rainfall

SEED EATERS
More than half of Australia's 90-plus species of seed-eating birds such as the Gouldian finch frequent the tropical savanna, flying extensively between productive areas. Like so much wildlife, they are at risk from new burning regimes.

bird species live here

GOULDIAN FINCH

Dingo
Canis lupus dingo

irregular white patches on feet

Dingoes originated thousands of years ago in mainland Asia, where populations still remain. However, interbreeding with domestic dogs has made genetically pure numbers impossible to estimate. Persecuted as a pest, this species is vital to Australia's biodiversity, helping to keep introduced animals such as feral cats, European rabbits, and red foxes under control, which devastate indigenous wildlife.

↔ 0.9–1m (3–3¼ft)
⚖ 9.5–19.5 kg (21–43 lb)
✖ Vulnerable
♒ Rabbits, mice, wallabies, birds

SE. Asia, Australia

◁ **WATCHING OVER THE PUPS**
Only the dominant female in a dingo pack breeds and gives birth, and her pups are cared for by all pack members.

Spectacled hare wallaby
Lagorchestes conspicillatus

A spectacled hare wallaby is built to conserve water. It has the most efficient kidneys of all mammal species, allowing this nocturnal marsupial to extract moisture from food, and then produces concentrated urine. It also recycles its own breath moisture straight to its stomach. During the day, when temperatures soar, hare wallabies shelter under thick clumps of grass, which also hide them from predators such as non-native cats and foxes.

↔ 40–48 cm (16–19 in)
⚖ 1.5–4.5 kg (3¼–10 lb)
✖ Common
♒ Grass, herbs, fruit

SW. Australia

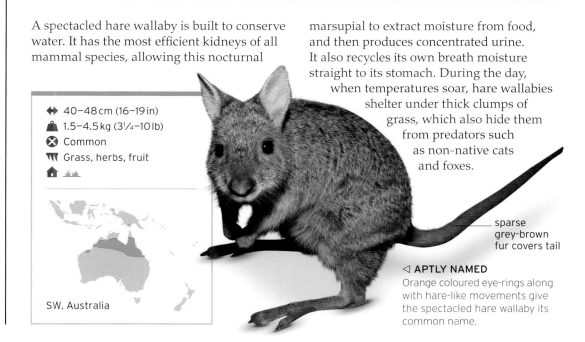

sparse grey-brown fur covers tail

◁ **APTLY NAMED**
Orange coloured eye-rings along with hare-like movements give the spectacled hare wallaby its common name.

male has pale neck;
female's is black

Emu
Dromaius novaehollandiae

Australia's largest bird, the emu has thin, double-shafted feathers, like its equally flightless relatives, cassowaries. Unlike the rounder feathers of Africa's ostrich and South America's rheas, the emu's plumage is more like coarse hair, with a parting along the back.

Emus form large flocks only when forced to move in search of food or water. The female initiates pair formation, circling a male and making low drumming sounds. Later, booming calls, amplified by an inflatable sac, can be heard 2 km (1.2 miles) away. Females fight fiercely for access to males, or to repel potential competitors. Pairs stay together for several months before egg laying. Incubating males do not eat or drink for eight weeks, but females play no part in caring for the chicks, unlike the "major hen" in ostrich groups, and may move on to mate with another male.

Problems and solutions

In 1932, cereal farmers in Western Australia asked the army to exterminate the state's emus because they were damaging crops, but the initiative failed. Today, many of the birds are fenced into "emu refuges", but these enclosures can prove lethal during a drought as the emus are not free to find water. Their natural predators include dingoes and wedge-tailed eagles, as well as reptiles, which try to take the eggs.

powerful joints

▷ **DESIGNED TO RUN**
Emus have calf muscles and three-toed feet designed for running. They can cover long distances with a trotting speed of around 7 km/h (4½ mph). They can also bolt at up to 48 km/h (30 mph) with 2.7 m (8¾ ft) strides.

◁ **WATCHFUL FATHER**
The male emu incubates the eggs and protects growing chicks, even chasing off the female.

↔ 1.7–2.1 m (5½–7 ft)
⚖ 30–60 kg (66–132 lb)
✖ Common
🌾 Seeds, berries

Australia

Blue-winged kookaburra

Dacelo leachii

Kookaburras, famous for their rising and falling "jackass" braying calls, are "tree kingfishers"of Australia and New Guinea. They perch conspicuously in trees, looking around from side to side, and drop to the ground to catch their prey. They concentrate especially on big insects, small reptiles, and frogs, although anything from worms to small birds and rodents are dealt with by the wide, heavy beak. The blue-winged kookaburra is slightly smaller than the more familiar laughing kookaburra, and has a particularly prolonged, manic laughing and cackling call.

Helpful big brother

Kookaburras pair for life and are assisted in defending their nest and raising their young by one or two male "helpers" from earlier broods, an uncommon system in birds. The female incubates her eggs in a hollow in a high tree branch, where they are vulnerable to snakes. Usually two or three chicks survive and fly after 36 days, but it takes 10 weeks before they are fully independent.

↔ 38–42 cm (15–16½ in)
⚖ 310 g (11 oz)
✖ Common
🍴 Insects, reptiles, frogs, fish

S. Papua New Guinea, NW. to NE. Australia

◁ **BEGGING FOR FOOD**
Chicks compete with each other for food, and two or three older chicks may kill the weakest, youngest one while they are still in the nest.

Plumed whistling-duck

Dendrocygna eytoni

Although whistling-ducks often graze on dry land, they require easy access to water. They feed mainly at night and may fly up to 30 km (20 miles) to reach favoured feeding places. Their nests are lined with soft grass, not with down plucked from the female's own body.

long neck

↔ 40–60 cm (16–23½ in)
⚖ 0.5–1.5 kg (1–3¾ lb)
✖ Common
🍴 Grass
🧭 N. and E. Australia

▷ **LOOKING SHARP**
Petite heads and sociable behaviour characterize the whistling-ducks. This species has distinctive pale, scimitar-like flank feathers.

Purple-crowned fairy wren

Malurus coronatus

One of 14 species of fairy wrens that forage in dense low growth, the purple-crowned fairy wren is found in long grass close to a river. Males have brilliant blue patterns. A male and female form a pair to raise the young, but each mates with other birds and helps raise the chicks from those pairings too, creating a complex social structure.

↔ 14 cm (5½ in)
⚖ 9–13 g (⁵⁄₁₆–⁷⁄₁₆ oz)
✖ Common
🍴 Insects
🧭 N. Australia

◁ **UPRIGHT TAIL**
The cocked tail seemed familiar when Europeans first reached Australia, but fairy wrens are not related to Northern Hemisphere wrens.

A **frilled lizard** can give a **painful bite** with two long, **fang-like teeth** in its lower jaw

△ ESCAPE MODE
When fleeing, this mainly tree-living lizard runs on two legs. As it picks up speed, its front end lifts off the ground so it is propelled only by its hindlegs.

mouth held open when frill erected to intimidate predators

long tail raised
when threatened

Frilled lizard

Chlamydosaurus kingii

This iconic member of the agamid or "dragon" family – which also includes Australia's moloch or thorny devil – is famous for its remarkable self-defence display. When threatened, the frilled lizard erects and flutters its highly coloured throat-and-neck ruff of elastic skin, using muscles attached to its jaws, tongue, and the rods of cartilage that support the frill. It opens its large mouth wide to show the pale inner lining, raises and flicks its tail or swipes it against the ground, and hisses loudly. The lizard may also stand almost erect on its hindlegs, or hop from one leg to the other, while waving its front limbs to scare off predators, such as snakes, lizards, eagles, feral cats, and quolls (cat-like marsupials).

Designed to startle

The sudden, intimidating threat display startles many of the lizard's enemies into pausing. This gives it time to run away, usually up a nearby trunk – trees are its main home and hunting place – or among rocks. At these times, the umbrella-like frill lies furled almost flat over the upper back and shoulders.

The frilled lizard uses its frill-erecting display for other reasons as well as defence: males repel intruders from their territory with it, and at breeding time it helps to deter rival males. Both sexes display to impress potential mates. The neck frill also plays an important role in controlling body temperature, acting at times as a sunshade, absorber of the sun's warmth, or radiator of excess body heat.

Temperature dependence

Breeding usually occurs from September to November, as the rains promise an abundance of food, especially insects such as ants, termites, cicadas, and caterpillars. After mating, the female digs a nest hole in loose soil and lays 5–20 soft-shelled eggs, then leaves – there is no maternal care. The eggs take around 10 weeks to hatch. The sex of the young is partially dependent on temperature. Both sexes develop from eggs incubated at temperatures of 29–35°C (84–95°F), but at temperatures above and below this range, the young produced are exclusively female. When the babies dig their way out of the nest, they are capable of putting on a full-frontal frill display straight away.

◁ **THREAT DISPLAY**
When in danger, the lizard may display its frilled neck and simply stand its ground, or it may lunge at the adversary in mock attack, snapping its jaws, and scratching with its claws.

▷ **ARBOREAL LIFESTYLE**
A frilled lizard spends up to 90 per cent of its time on trees. When lying still, or resting, it is very well camouflaged as bark. The lizard can be speedy and agile when it is in search of ants and bugs.

↔ 70–90 cm (27½–35½ in)
⚖ 500–800 g (17½–28 oz)
✖ Common
🍴 Insects, spiders, amphibians

S. New Guinea,
N. Australia

Green tree frog

Litoria caerulea

The large, docile green tree frog is a common sight in the tropical regions of Australia. It spends the day hiding from the sun in damp crevices and emerges at night to hunt. Green tree frogs call all year, but only do so from the ground during the late summer breeding season. Eggs are glued to vegetation in still waters, and the tadpoles transform into adults in six weeks.

- ↔ 5–10 cm (2–4 in)
- ☁ Spring and summer
- ✖ Common
- 🦗 Insects, mice
- 🏠 🌳 🌲 🌾 🌱 ≈ 🏘
- ◉ S. New Guinea, N. and E. Australia

◁ **CLINGING ON**
This frog usually lives in woodland trees close to water sources, but is often found in outside toilets.

Redback spider

Latrodectus hasseltii

This small but potentially deadly species is one of the highly venomous widow spiders, so named because the female often eats the male after mating. The male is less than a third the size of the female and lurks cautiously on the periphery of her untidy web hoping to steal leftover scraps from the insects she snares.

- ↔ 0.3–1 cm (⅛–⅜ in)
- ✖ Common
- 🦗 Insects
- 🏠 🌳 🌾 🏘
- ◉ Australia

▽ **KILLER BITE**
The female kills prey with a venom that is powerful enough to endanger humans unless an antivenin is taken.

front pair of legs longer than other three

distinctive marks on female's abdomen give species its name

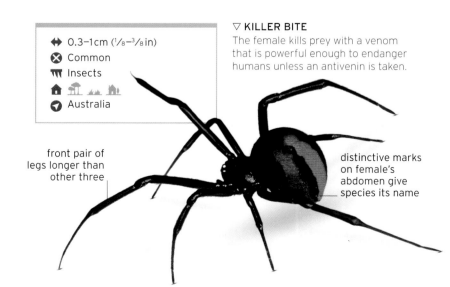

Green jumping spider

Mopsus mormon

female has dark red and white face mask

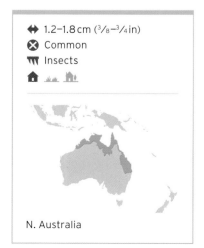

This is the largest jumping spider in Australia. Generally, a jumping spider's fangs are too tiny to pierce human skin, but this species can manage it and delivers a painful, although ultimately harmless, bite. The green jumping spider hunts on leaves and stalks for insect prey, ambushing them with a long jump that can be several times the spider's body length. Wherever it goes, the spider lets out a safety line of silk in case it loses its footing. However, jumps are seldom off target thanks to the acute vision afforded by two huge forward-facing eyes, supported by six others elsewhere on the head.

Long courtship

Jumping spiders are cautious of each other, and males must spend a lot of time earning their mate's trust. The male begins by plucking love messages on the female's nest and silk lines and by stroking her abdomen. This courtship generally occurs while the female is still a non-breeding subadult. The male sets up home next to the female's nest and waits for her to moult into a fully mature form and is ready to mate.

The nest is a crudely woven sheet of silk made on the concave side of long, narrow leaves. It has three sections. The female lives at one end and guards the middle section that will house the eggs. The male builds the far end.

- ↔ 1.2–1.8 cm (⅜–¾ in)
- ✖ Common
- 🦗 Insects
- 🏠 🌾 🏘

N. Australia

▷ **SNATCHING A BITE**
A large but delicate damselfly succumbs to the swift strike of a green jumping spider camouflaged on a green patch of leaf.

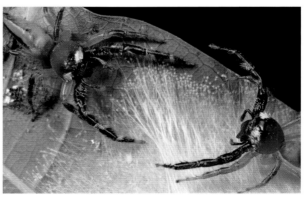

△ **BY A WHISKER**
Males sport side whiskers and a hairy top knot not seen in females. This sexual difference allows males to identify rivals easily.

◁ **BATTLE FORMATION**
Two male green jumping spiders size each other up before a fight. Interactions between members of this species are frequently aggressive.

GREAT SANDY-TANAMI DESERT
Australia's vast northwestern deserts are rich in wildlife

The Great Sandy and Tanami deserts sport a range of semi-arid to arid habitats, from shifting dunes of loose sand to windswept bare rock to low rolling plains dominated by shrubby hummocks of Australia's endemic dryland grass known as spinifex. In various forms, spinifex covers almost one-fifth of the entire continent. In the far southeast of the ecoregion squats the glowing sandstone mound of Uluru, formerly known as Ayers Rock.

Grass-based food chain

Spinifex's sharp, silica-rich, abrasive leaves deter many large grazing animals, yet the soft new shoots and plentiful seeds produced after rain feed a myriad of small creatures. These range from ants, termites, beetles, and cicadas to small parrots such as the budgerigar, as well as the painted firetail and the omnivorous dusky grass wren. Tiny native mice, including the spinifex hopping mouse

and sandy inland mouse, also depend on it. Grass-dwelling insects feed reptiles such as thorny devils and knob-tailed geckoes, and also the smallest marsupial: the shrew-like long-tailed planigale. Farther up the food chains are larger hunters such as the desert death adder, grey falcon, and Australia's largest bird of prey, the wedge-tailed eagle.

This web of life is diverse but sporadic, thriving after downpours, then struggling to survive for months, even years, if the summer rains fail. In recent decades the desert ecology has been unbalanced by introduced grazing animals that can survive on spinifex, especially feral donkeys and camels.

DESERTED WALLABIES
The black-footed rock wallaby feeds during darker, cooler, and damper hours and gains what water it needs from food. Increasing numbers of introduced grazing animals have fragmented its dwindling populations.

BLACK-FOOTED ROCK WALLABY

ELUSIVE HUNTER
The grey falcon is a keen hunter of small birds and some small mammals. Because it has a large range and is difficult to identify in the wild, estimated numbers are problematic. Due to habitat loss, however, they are thought to be declining.

GREY FALCON

One of Australia's least populated areas 〉 Has dune ridges up to 50 km (30 miles) long

NOMADIC FLOCKS
More familiar as a caged bird, the budgerigar is a native of Australian deserts. Large, colourful, chattering flocks fly between seed-rich areas and oases in the wild, and livestock water supplies have helped to extend their range.

BUDGERIGARS

LOCATION

The Great Sandy is north of the Gibson Desert. The Tanami slopes east into the Davenport Murchison Ranges.

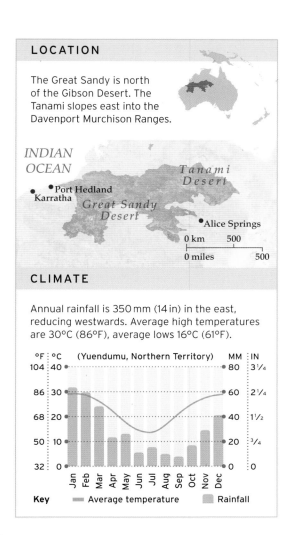

INDIAN OCEAN

Port Hedland
Karratha
Great Sandy Desert

Tanami Desert

Alice Springs

0 km 500
0 miles 500

CLIMATE

Annual rainfall is 350 mm (14 in) in the east, reducing westwards. Average high temperatures are 30°C (86°F), average lows 16°C (61°F).

(Yuendumu, Northern Territory)

°F	°C		MM	IN
104	40		80	3¼
86	30		60	2¼
68	20		40	1½
50	10		20	¾
32	0		0	0

Jan Feb Mar Apr May Jun Jul Aug Sep Oct Nov Dec

Key — Average temperature ▇ Rainfall

Fat-tailed dunnart
Sminthopsis crassicaudata

Despite its mouse-like appearance, the fat-tailed dunnart is a marsupial that mainly feeds on insects, but also eats small lizards. Found in habitats ranging from open woodland and grassland to desert, these nocturnal mammals conserve energy by huddling in communal nests built under logs or rocks during colder weather; they can also enter a state of torpor for up to a few days when food is short.

↔ 6–9 cm (2¼–3½ in)
⚖ 10–20 g (³⁄₈– ¾ oz)
✖ Common
▥ Moths, beetles, lizards

Australia

pointed snout

◁ **FAT STORE**
A dunnart's tail holds excess fat, which supplies it with energy when food is scarce.

Southern marsupial mole
Notoryctes typhlops

creamy yellow to golden fur

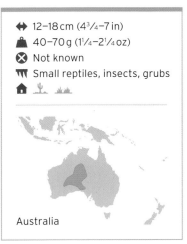

Southern marsupial moles resemble true moles, but belong to a separate order, Notoryctemorphia. These underground dwellers are effectively blind, with vestigial eyes, and also lack external ears. They do not use tunnels; instead, the soil collapses behind them as they move forwards.

↔ 12–18 cm (4¾–7 in)
⚖ 40–70 g (1¼–2¼ oz)
✖ Not known
▥ Small reptiles, insects, grubs

Australia

◁ **DIGGING FOR DINNER**
A horny nose-shield, rigid neck, and huge, spade-like foreclaws allow southern marsupial moles to power through sandy soil in search of food.

SPIKY SHELTERS
Hugely important for so many arid Australian habitats, spinifex sends roots down 2 m (6½ ft) or more for moisture. In doing so, it stabilizes wind-whipped sand and provides food and shelter for a myriad of small creatures.

A rich haven for lizards

SPINIFEX GRASS

large, sensitive ears

long, strong tail

Red kangaroo

Macropus rufus

Standing up to 2 m (7 ft) tall, the red kangaroo is the world's largest marsupial and the largest land animal in Australia. Its huge, muscular hindlegs enable it to hop along at speeds of up to 60 km/h (35 mph) for several minutes, covering several metres in a single bound, with its metre-long tail held out behind as a counterbalance.

Australia's sandy plains, semi-deserts, savanna, and scrubland are extremely harsh environments, but the red kangaroo is well adapted to these hot, dry, and largely barren landscapes. Mostly active at dawn and dusk, it retreats to the shade of trees or rocks during the hottest part of the day. It repeatedly licks its forelegs to regulate its body temperature – as the saliva evaporates, the blood flowing just under the skin is cooled.

Boomers and mobs

A highly nomadic species, the red kangaroo has no fixed home range. It roams large distances in search of fresh grass and leaves. The kangaroo lives in small groups of up to 10 animals that usually consist of one large adult male, known as a boomer, and several smaller females, which are only about half as heavy, plus a few young. If food is plentiful several groups may join together to form a larger unit known as a mob.

Arrested development

Breeding is determined by the availability of food – red kangaroos may not breed at all during droughts. However, a reproductive system in which a female can have three offspring at the same time all at different stages of development allows maximum production of young when times are favourable. A female gives birth to a single baby following a short gestation of 32–34 days. This tiny joey climbs into its mother's pouch, attaches to a teat, and continues to develop. The female then mates again within days of giving birth, but development of this new embryo is suspended until the female's existing joey leaves the pouch at about eight months old. It will still be suckling from its mother when the next baby is born – the female's teats are able to produce milk independently of one another, allowing her to provide milk specific to the needs of each offspring.

More than **11.5 million red kangaroos live** in Australia's **hot, arid landscapes**

◁ **SWIFT HOPPER**
Hopping is very energy-efficient especially at higher speeds. The hindlegs act like springs and so the thrust delivered when leaping uses little energy.

▷ **POUCHED JOEY**
The joey first pokes its head out of the pouch when it is about five months old. It leaves the pouch at eight months, but suckles milk for another four months.

↔ 1–1.6 m (3¼–5¼ ft)
⚖ 25–90 kg (55–200 lb)
✖ Common
🌾 Grasses, leaves
🏠 🌵 🌿

Australia

Thorny devil
Moloch horridus

Secure in its all-over prickly protection, the thorny devil moves with a characteristic slow, swaying, stiff-legged gait. If it senses danger, it stands still, relying on its superb camouflage. Faced with a predator such as a bird of prey or a goanna (a type of monitor lizard), this spiky lizard puffs up its body with air to make itself look bigger – and even harder to swallow. If attacked, it dips its head between its front legs to present the "false head" on its neck; this fat-filled hump recovers quickly from any minor injury.

Trail meal
The thorny devil eats ants almost exclusively, feeding during the day, when ants are on the move. A favourite tactic is to locate a trail of foraging worker ants, stand next to it, then lick up each ant in turn, which it chews with its strong, shearing rear teeth. Solitary except when mating, the thorny devil shelters in a burrow or secluded place at night and also for several weeks during midsummer and midwinter. This desert-dweller obtains most of the water that it needs from fog that condenses on its scales when it emerges in the cool hours of early morning.

Thorny devils mate in late winter to early summer, with the smaller males approaching females to see if they are receptive. Females dig a burrow up to 20 cm (8 in) deep, lay 5–10 eggs, and fill it with sand. The hatchlings emerge three to four months later and take up to five years to grow to full size.

↔ 15–18 cm (6–7 in)
⚖ 25–50 g (7/8–1¾ oz)
✖ Not known
🐜 Ants, other insects
🏠

W. to C. Australia

tail held upright when walking

▷ **SPINY EXTERIOR**
The thorny devil's overall body coloration darkens in cooler temperatures or when alarmed, and pales when it is warmer or at rest.

◁ **WATER CHANNELS**
Grooves between the spines collect moisture and channel the water to the corners of the devil's mouth.

Greater bilby
Macrotis lagotis

The only survivor of Australia's six native bandicoot species, the greater bilby inhabited 70 per cent of the country before European settlement. Today, mainly due to habitat loss and predation by introduced species such as the domestic cat, it occurs in less than 20 per cent of its original range.

A nocturnal marsupial, the bilby uses its strong, three-clawed forelimbs to dig long, spiralling burrows where it sleeps during the day and shelters from dust storms. Huge ears, which give it the alternative name of rabbit-eared bandicoot, help it detect predators and prey, such as termites and ants, which it digs out with its claws. One of its favourite foods is the yalka, or bush onion, a bulb that only germinates in desert soil after fires.

↔ 30–55 cm (12–21½ in)
⚖ 0.6–2.5 kg (1¼–5½ lb)
✖ Vulnerable
🐜 Seeds, insects, fruit
🏠

W. to C. Australia

◁ **SNIFFING THE AIR**
A long, tapering snout and keen sense of smell make up for the bilby's poor eyesight, while long whiskers help bilbies navigate their environment.

A hungry devil can **lick up more than 1,000 ants** in one feeding session

false head

spiky horns above eyes

brown, tan, and yellow coloration mimics sandy habitat

Woma python

Aspidites ramsayi

The nocturnal Woma python consumes mainly other reptiles, but its specialty is killing rodents in their burrows by crushing them against the wall. After winter mating, like most pythons, the female coils around her eggs to protect them and keep them warm by "shivering" until they hatch in spring.

- ↔ 1.5 m (5 ft)
- ⚖ 3–5 kg (6½–11 lb)
- ✖ Endangered
- 🍖 Reptiles, birds, mammals
- 🏠 🌿 🌾
- ➤ Australia

muscular coils

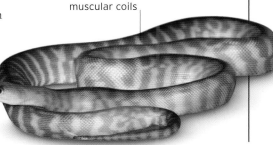

▷ **MARKED BANDING**
The Woma python has a slim head, distinctive banding along the powerful body, and a short, thin tail.

Blistered grasshopper

Monistria pustulifera

Also known as the arid painted pyrgomorph, this flightless, locust-like insect specializes in defoliating strong-scented emu, poverty, and turkey bushes. Blistered grasshoppers are cone-headed and have short antennae, known as horns. Females, which are almost twice as large as the males, lay eggs in soil and only hatch after a cold snap.

- ↔ Up to 6.5 cm (2½ in)
- ✖ Not known
- 🍃 Leaves, shoots
- 🏠 🌿
- ➤ Australia

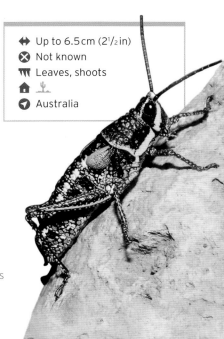

▷ **SPOTTED WARNING**
The "blisters" are yellow patches that warn potential predators of this grasshopper's foul-tasting flesh.

EAST AUSTRALIAN FORESTS

A damp corner of the drought continent

As moisture-laden winds from the Pacific Ocean rise over Australia's southeastern and eastern coast towards the Great Dividing Range, water vapour condenses into rain. This is especially true in the Australian Alps, where rainfall may exceed 2,300 mm (90 in) yearly, and in the Blue Mountains, near Sydney. Tasmania's hills commonly have winter snows, while 2,000 km (1,240 miles) north in southern Queensland, the climate is subtropical.

Eucalypt patchwork

Within this moist, warm mosaic are patches of temperate forest, dominated by more than 120 kinds of eucalypts, or gum trees. Upland eucalypts, especially the tall mountain ash gum, cloak rocky crags and steep gorges. More gum forests and acacia woods, including the golden wattle, grow on lower slopes, as well as ferns, banksias, and grevilleas. This ecoregion is home to some of Australia's most famous animals, including the Tasmanian devil, koala, duck-billed platypus, short-beaked echidna, laughing kookaburra, and Albert's lyrebird. However, human expansion has meant felling and conversion of forest to farmland, while introduced pests such as rabbits, foxes, and cats ravage the native wildlife.

LITTLE RED FLYING FOX

POLLINATING BAT
The little red flying fox visits eucalypt blossoms to lap up nectar and pollen and transfers the latter between trees in the process. This balances out the damage sometimes caused by its dense roosting habit, where dozens of the bats crowd on a few boughs of a tree..

WOLLEMI PINE

LIVING FOSSIL
The Wollemi pine caused a sensation when it was discovered by a Blue Mountains field officer in 1994. The sole survivor of a group dating from the dinosaur era, it grows only in a few locations.

Volatile eucalyptus oils give the Blue Mountains a colourful haze

Total area exceeds 500,000 sq km (193,000 sq miles)

EUCALYPTUS

THREATENED TREES
Eucalypt species range from the ice-hardy snow gum to frost-tender tallow-wood. Food for many animals, including koalas and possums, these forests are now heavily harvested and rarely regrow once felled.

More than **a fifth of Australia's eucalypts grow here,** but are threatened by **climate change**

NECTAR FACTORIES
Many banksias have large, colourful flower spikes with hundreds of nectar-producing blooms. This energy-packed liquid is vital food for marsupials such as honey and pygmy possums, and gliders, as well as bats.

HONEY POSSUM

The world's second-tallest tree, the mountain ash gum, grows here

COOPERATIVE FEEDERS
More than 20 honeyeater species coexist in the Blue Mountains, lapping up honey (nectar) with their brush-tipped tongues. They avoid competition by living at different altitudes, breeding at different times of year, and migration; regent honeyeaters, for example, prefer wetter, lowland sites..

REGENT HONEYEATER

Home to the endangered Leadbeater's possum

FOREST MAINTENANCE
One of the first marsupials to be described by European settlers, the long-nosed potoroo eats mycorrhizal fungi. These truffle-like underground fungi provide minerals to tree roots, receiving carbohydrates in return. The potoroo excretes fungal spores in its faeces, thus spreading them to new trees.

LONG-NOSED POTOROO

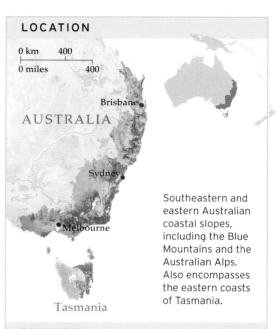

LOCATION

0 km   400
0 miles   400

AUSTRALIA

Brisbane

Sydney

Melbourne

Tasmania

Southeastern and eastern Australian coastal slopes, including the Blue Mountains and the Australian Alps. Also encompasses the eastern coasts of Tasmania.

CLIMATE

Southeastern Australia is generally warm and temperate, with plenty of rainfall throughout the year. Temperatures range from the subtropical in southern Queensland to low enough for snowfall accumulation in Tasmania's hills. Higher altitudes have the most rainfall.

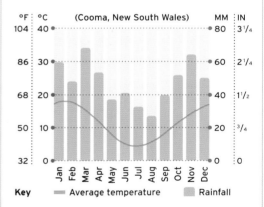

°F	°C	(Cooma, New South Wales)	MM	IN
104	40		80	3 1/4
86	30		60	2 1/4
68	20		40	1 1/2
50	10		20	3/4
32	0		0	0

Jan Feb Mar Apr May Jun Jul Aug Sep Oct Nov Dec

Key — Average temperature   Rainfall

RABBIT PLAGUE

Perhaps Australia's worst invasive species, the European rabbit has devastated huge areas of vegetation, killed trees by bark-ringing, and outcompeted many herbivores. Even if 90 per cent are destroyed in an area, the remainder restore the original population in 12–18 months because of the rabbits' rapid rate of reproduction.

Duck-billed platypus

Ornithorhynchus anatinus

With its duck-like bill, thick fur, and webbed feet, the platypus is one of Earth's most unusual animals, yet it possesses even more distinctive traits. One of just two living monotremes, or egg-laying mammals (the other is the echidna), the average body temperature of the platypus is 32°C (89.6°F), which is lower than most mammals, and its legs extend out, not down. These features are more common in reptiles. Males have a horny spur on the inside of each hind ankle that delivers a venomous sting to rivals vying for their breeding territory. Extremely painful to humans, the venom is strong enough to kill a domestic dog.

Sensory perception

A duck-billed platypus spends most of the day in its burrow, which it digs into an earth bank using its strong front claws. On land, the paddle-like webbing of the front feet folds beneath them, allowing the platypus to walk. It emerges to feed at night, rootling through the muddy bottom of shallow pools, where it detects prey with its bill's highly sensitive electroreceptors. These are capable of spotting the tail-flick of a crayfish from 15–20 cm (6–8 in) away. The platypus stores all the food it catches in its cheek pouches, at the back of the jaw. When it surfaces to breathe, the platypus uses the horny pads and ridges in its mouth to grind up the food before swallowing.

Platypuses mate during spring, and the female lays up to three eggs in a nesting burrow about three weeks later. She incubates them until they hatch, then feeds the young with milk, although not from nipples like other mammals. Female platypuses ooze milk directly through the skin on either side of their belly; the milk is sucked up by their young.

↔ 40–55 cm (16–21½ in)
⚖ 0.7–2.2 kg (1½–5 lb)
✖ Common
🍴 Insect larvae, crayfish
🏠 🌿 ≈ ≈

E. Australia, Tasmania

waterproof coat
with dense underfur

▽ **SOME HOAX**
Aboriginal legend says the platypus was born after a female duck mated with a water rat. When the first platypus skin arrived in Britain in 1799, it was thought to be a hoax.

smooth,
suede-like
skin covering

The **bill** of a platypus is **soft and rubbery**, not hard like a duck's

△ **GRACEFUL SWIMMER**
A platypus moves easily through water using its heavily webbed front feet, while the hindfeet and tail help it change direction.

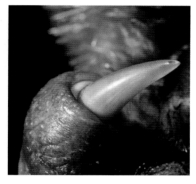

△ **UNIQUE STINGER**
Of all mammals, only male platypuses can deliver a venomous sting. Male echidnas also have horny ankle spurs but lack functional venom glands.

broad tail acts as rudder when swimming

Common wombat
Vombatus ursinus

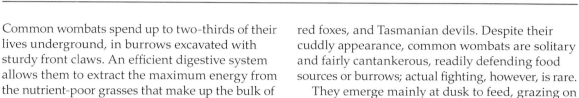

Common wombats spend up to two-thirds of their lives underground, in burrows excavated with sturdy front claws. An efficient digestive system allows them to extract the maximum energy from the nutrient-poor grasses that make up the bulk of their diet. Thick fur and a high tolerance for low-oxygen environments help them to survive underground, avoiding predators such as dingoes, red foxes, and Tasmanian devils. Despite their cuddly appearance, common wombats are solitary and fairly cantankerous, readily defending food sources or burrows; actual fighting, however, is rare.

They emerge mainly at dusk to feed, grazing on short grasses and other plants thanks to a split in their upper lip. Their rootless teeth keep growing throughout their lifetime.

↔ 70–120 cm (27½–47 in)
⚖ 25–40 kg (55–88 lb)
✖ Common
🌾 Grass, sedges, roots, tubers
🏠

E. Australia, Tasmania

◁ **MOTHER AND JOEY**
Born the size of a jellybean, common wombat joeys remain with their mothers until they are around 17-20 months old.

Parma wallaby
Macropus parma

small, thin forelimbs

The "parma" in this marsupial's name comes from an Aboriginal word for the species, rather than the city of Parma, Italy. Once thought to have been hunted to extinction, parma wallabies were rediscovered in New South Wales in 1967.

Mainly nocturnal, wallabies prefer forests with a dense, grassy understorey that shields them from predators such as dingoes, red foxes, and some birds of prey. In addition to the grasses and herbs that make up the bulk of its diet, the parma wallaby also eats truffle-like fungi, the spores of which it helps to spread – and fertilize – via its faeces.

↔ 45–53 cm (18–21 in)
⚖ 3.2–6 kg (7–13 lb)
✖ Near threatened
🌾 Grass, herbs, leaves, bark
🏠

E. Australia

◁ **WEIGHED DOWN**
A parma wallaby joey leaves the maternal pouch permanently only around the age of seven months.

▷ **EMBRYONIC BOND**
A baby koala spends six to seven months in its mother's pouch, which has a strong muscle at the entrance to keep the small joey from falling out.

rounded, white-tufted ears

short, powerful limbs

Koala

Phascolarctos cinereus

Koalas are marsupials that have evolved the unique ability to eat a plant that would poison other animals. They feed almost exclusively on eucalyptus leaves, but not just any eucalyptus will do. Koalas are choosy eaters, feeding only on a few of the 600-plus eucalyptus species found in Australia. They also avoid eating leaves from trees growing in poor soil because these are the most toxic.

Special adaptations

A fibre-digesting organ known as the caecum helps koalas to feed on eucalyptus without ill effects. In humans, this small pouch at the beginning of the large intestine is about 6.25 cm (2½ in) long, but in koalas, it reaches 200 cm (80 in). The caecum contains millions of bacteria that break down the leaf fibre and toxic oils and enable absorption of nitrogen. A slow metabolic rate keeps food within the digestive system for extended periods. Even so, a koala absorbs only about 25 per cent of what it consumes – so one animal must eat 200–500 g (about ½ –1 lb) of eucalyptus leaves a day in order to survive.

Fortunately, the koala's teeth are made for the job. Sharp front incisors cut leaves from stems, while molars shear and crush, breaking the food down before it reaches the caecum. While it chews, a koala stays safely anchored in a tree to avoid ground predators such as dogs. As well as sharp, curved claws, its paws have rough pads that grasp bark and branches. The front paws have two digits that oppose the other three to give the animal a firm, fist-like grip. The koala's dense, thick coat varies from light grey in northern animals to dark-brown in southern ones. The soft, long, fur protects the koala from extreme temperatures as well as rain.

Mainly nocturnal, koalas are highly territorial animals; each adult maintains a home range within a breeding group, marking the trees it visits regularly with scratches. The males also scent-mark from a brown gland in the middle of their chests, which they rub on the base of trees.

Joey in a pouch

The breeding season lasts from August to February, punctuated by frequent bellowing from males. Females give birth to a single hairless, embryonic joey, roughly 2 cm (³/₄ in) long and weighing less than a gram. The tiny joey clambers from the birth canal to its mother's pouch and once inside, latches on to one of her two teats. It stays there and develops, for about 22–30 weeks, when it begins to feed on "pap" as well as milk. Pap, a special type of dropping the mother produces, contains the microbes needed to digest eucalyptus leaves. Once large enough to leave the pouch, the joey rides on its mother's back, and stays with her until her next joey is born.

The main threats koalas face today are habitat loss and fragmentation due to logging and increasing urbanization – an estimated 4,000 koalas a year are killed by dogs and car accidents.

△ **TIME TO REST**
Eucalyptus leaves provide little energy, so when koalas are not sleeping up to 18 hours a day, they rest between bouts of feeding, cushioned on a dense pad of rump fur, to conserve energy.

◁ **FAVOURITE FOOD**
A koala's diet is made up almost entirely of eucalyptus leaves, but it occasionally eats tea tree and wattle leaves as well.

↔ 65–82 cm (26–32 in)
🏋 4–15 kg (8³/₄–33 lb)
✕ Common
🌿 Eucalyptus leaves
🏠 🌲

E. Australia

Koalas eat such large quantities of **eucalyptus leaves** that their body oil **smells like cough drops**

white patches on chest, sides, and rump

Tasmanian devil

Sarcophilus harrisii

The world's largest living carnivorous marsupial gets its name from the screeches and growls it produces during hunts for food. Tasmanian devils are predominantly scavengers, using their strong, wide jaws to devour the flesh, fur, and bone of often rotting animal carcasses. However, they will eat whatever is available, from insects to mammals, including "imps": young Tasmanian devils. Devils are equally unfussy about their habitat, provided they can find shelter during the day and food by night.

Uncertain future

Once common throughout Australia, today the species exists only in Tasmania, where it is critically endangered in the wild due to a contagious cancer called devil facial tumour disease (DFTD), spread from animal to animal through biting – a common occurrence when devils meet. To preserve the species, a national conservation programme has established a DFTD-free captive "insurance population".

△ **HIDING OUT**
Young Tasmanian devils shelter in caves, hollow logs, or burrows to avoid predators such as eagles or other devils.

most powerful bite relative to body size of any animal

Tasmanian devils can **eat 40 per cent of their body weight** in half an hour

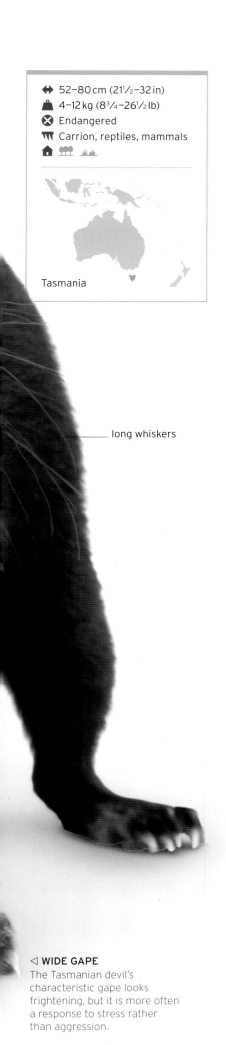

↔ 52–80 cm (21½–32 in)
⚖ 4–12 kg (8¾–26½ lb)
✖ Endangered
🗡 Carrion, reptiles, mammals
🏠 🌳 🌾

Tasmania

— long whiskers

Tiger quoll

Dasyurus maculatus

markings give alternative name of spotted-tailed quoll

The largest of six quoll species, the tiger quoll is a fierce nocturnal hunter that is as at home in trees as it is on the ground. This carnivorous marsupial prefers woodland habitats, and will venture into cleared farmland in search of food, despatching small mammals such as bandicoots and gliders with a powerful bite to the head or neck. Forest clearance is a major threat.

△ **HOLDING HER OWN**
Although much smaller than males, female tiger quolls are no less aggressive and have been seen chasing Tasmanian devils away from carcasses.

↔ 40–76 cm (16–30 in)
⚖ 1.8–3.5 kg (4–7¾ lb)
✖ Near threatened
🗡 Small mammals, reptiles
🏠 🌳 🌳 🌾

E. Australia, Tasmania

Sulphur-crested cockatoo

Cacatua galerita

Sulphur-crested cockatoos have excellent foot-eye-bill co-ordination as they feed on seeds and fruits. They form large flocks in parts of Australia, and are sometimes dealt with as pests on cereal crops. The distinctive crest is usually held flat, but is raised in a fan up to 14 cm (6 in) high when the birds are excited, such as when mating.

↔ 50 cm (20 in)
⚖ 950 g (33½ oz)
✖ Common
🗡 Seeds, nuts, fruit, crops
🏠 🌳 🌳 🌾 🏠

New Guinea, Australia, Tasmania

◁ **WIDE GAPE**
The Tasmanian devil's characteristic gape looks frightening, but it is more often a response to stress rather than aggression.

▷ **AIMING HIGH**
Cockatoos are so familiar as pets that their high, soaring flight far above forested slopes comes as a surprise in the wild.

primrose yellow underwing

long, narrow tail
aids swimming

long legs and claws
for climbing

Australian water dragon

Intellagama lesueurii

True to its name, this large lizard frequents many flowing freshwater habitats, from cool upland streams to city rivers, and even occasional estuaries. It is a proficient swimmer and also a capable climber.

Basking then hunting

The water dragon basks on rocks (or a road or patio) until it is warm enough to hunt – in trees, on the ground, and along the water's edge. It searches for snails and crabs as well as small vertebrates such as frogs and chicks. In some locations, however, fruit and vegetation comprise up to half of its diet. To avoid danger, the water dragon races up a tree or dives underwater, where it can stay submerged for more than an hour. In winter, water dragons living to the south of their range hide in a burrow, or among roots or rocks, and brumate (similar to hibernation); in the north, they remain active all year. In spring, territorial males display to rivals and to attract females with much head-bobbing, tail-flicking, and leg-flourishing. Hatchlings mainly eat insects until they are about half grown.

↔ 1m (3¼ ft)
⚖ 1–1.3 kg (2¼–2¾ lb)
✗ Not known
🍴 Small animals, fruit, plants
🏠 🌾≈≈ 🏚

E. Australia

large tympanum
(external eardrum)

◁ **SNUB-NOSED PROFILE**
The short, deep snout and angular head is accentuated by a central crest of scales that runs from head to tail, enlarging considerably from the neck rearwards.

Sydney funnelweb spider
Atrax robustus

This funnelweb is a member of the mygalomorph spider group, whose prominent fangs point straight down rather than diagonally as in other spiders. It spins its tube-shaped web in a cool, moist, shady site, under a rock or log – or an outhouse. Repeated bites quickly subdue its small prey; untreated, the venom may be fatal to humans.

In late summer, the smaller, longer-legged, wider-roaming male mates with the more sedentary female. She keeps the 100–150 eggs in a silken egg sac safe in her burrow. They hatch in three to four weeks and the spiderlings remain for a few more months.

▷ **GOOD VIBRATIONS**
Silk thread trip-lines fan out from the web entrance and alert the funnelweb spider to passing prey.

↔ 2.5–4 cm (1–1½ in)
✖ Not known
🦷 Insects, snails, frogs, mice
🏠 🌳🌳 🏚️ 🪨

SE. Australia

Macleay's spectre
Extatosoma tiaratum

spiny legs kick in defence

Also known as the giant prickly stick insect, Macleay's spectre is well camouflaged by the twigs of its favourite food trees: eucalyptus. Females are longer, twice as heavy, and spinier than males, and their small wing buds mean they cannot fly. The slimmer, winged males fly readily, especially to find a mate. The female flicks her abdomen when releasing her eggs so they reach the forest floor. The eggs are gathered by spider ants, which carry them to their colony, then eat the outer layer but leave the rest of the egg intact. Hatching nymphs mimic the colours of their hosts, protecting them until they leave the colony in search of food trees.

◁ **GREEN LICHEN FORM**
Among the coloured forms of this species, *E. t. tiaratum* is hard to spot amid green leaves, lichens, and mosses.

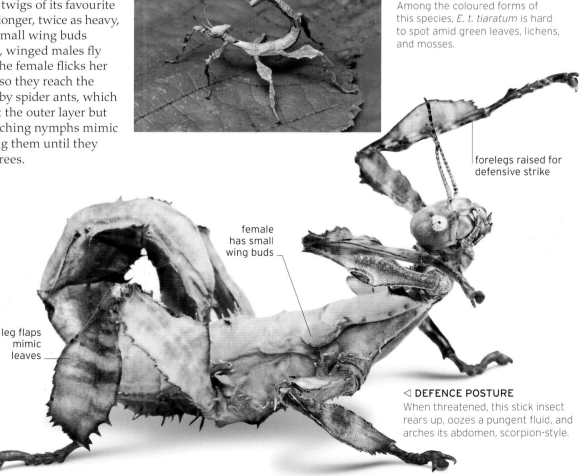

forelegs raised for defensive strike

female has small wing buds

leg flaps mimic leaves

↔ 7.5–16 cm (3–6½ in)
✖ Not known
🦷 Leaves, especially eucalyptus
🏠 🌳🌳 🏛️

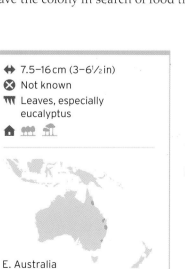

E. Australia

◁ **DEFENCE POSTURE**
When threatened, this stick insect rears up, oozes a pungent fluid, and arches its abdomen, scorpion-style.

GREAT BARRIER REEF

The world's most famous reef system

Possibly Earth's most massive single ecoregion, the Great Barrier Reef – actually 3,000 interlinked reefs – is 2,300 km (1,430 miles) long, more than 100 km (62 miles) wide in parts, and covers 345,000 sq km (133,200 sq miles). More than 400 species of coral polyps (small anemone-like creatures) constructed the reef system among 900 islands. Its waters are warm, sunlit, clear, and bathed by mild currents. Dazzling reef fish, shrimp, starfish, sea slugs, and other sea creatures hide, feed, and claim territories here, while more than 100 species of shark and ray hunt among them. Around 200 species of bird also live here all year round.

Complex ecosystems

Along the reef, temperatures climb several degrees from south to north, and the seabed profile continually changes. Mingling with the reefs themselves are inshore waters averaging 35 m (115 ft) deep, sandy cays, seagrass meadows, sponge gardens, and mangrove stands, all giving way to continental slopes plunging down 2,000 m (6,560 ft). As one of the planet's most complex and biodiverse ecoregions, the Great Barrier Reef is carefully managed and conserved in some respects, but industrial and agricultural pollution, while declining, are still large-scale problems. In addition, rising water temperature and acidity linked to climate change, which causes environmental upheaval, are intensifying threats.

The Great Barrier Reef receives more than **2 million tourists** every year

CROWN-OF-THORNS STARFISH

The Great Barrier Reef is the largest living structure on the planet

SPINY ENEMY
Crown-of-thorns starfish periodically plague the reef. By eating polyps, the have destroyed up to one-quarter of its coral cover. Land nutrient run-off aids their increase in numbers, because it increases plankton, which in turn feeds larval starfish.

BLACK NODDY

BIRD BREEDING HUB
The Great Barrier Reef supports over one-quarter of Australia's tropical breeding birds, and more than half the population of one species, the black noddy. Noddy nests are made of leaves, twigs, and debris cemented with their own droppings.

Declared a UNESCO World Heritage Site in 1981

BRAIN CORAL

CORAL DIVERSITY
The reef's builders are 450-plus species of stony or hard corals. Their polyps construct limestone cups and calcareous skeletons around their soft bodies. Coral colonies grow into patterns that resemble antlers and even brains.

HELPFUL PARTNERS

Guard crabs scavenge debris, defend their cauliflower coral hosts against intruders, and occasionally help catch prey. The corals provide shelter and the crabs share meals.

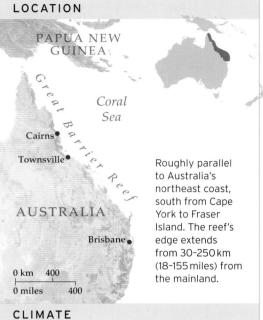

GUARD CRAB

Can be seen from outer space

SEA SNAKE HOTSPOT

Sea snakes are aquatic and give birth in the water to live young. They are venomous, hunting fish and similar prey. Around 17 species dwell on the reef, but their survival is threatened by habitat change and declining water quality.

Covers roughly the same area as Japan

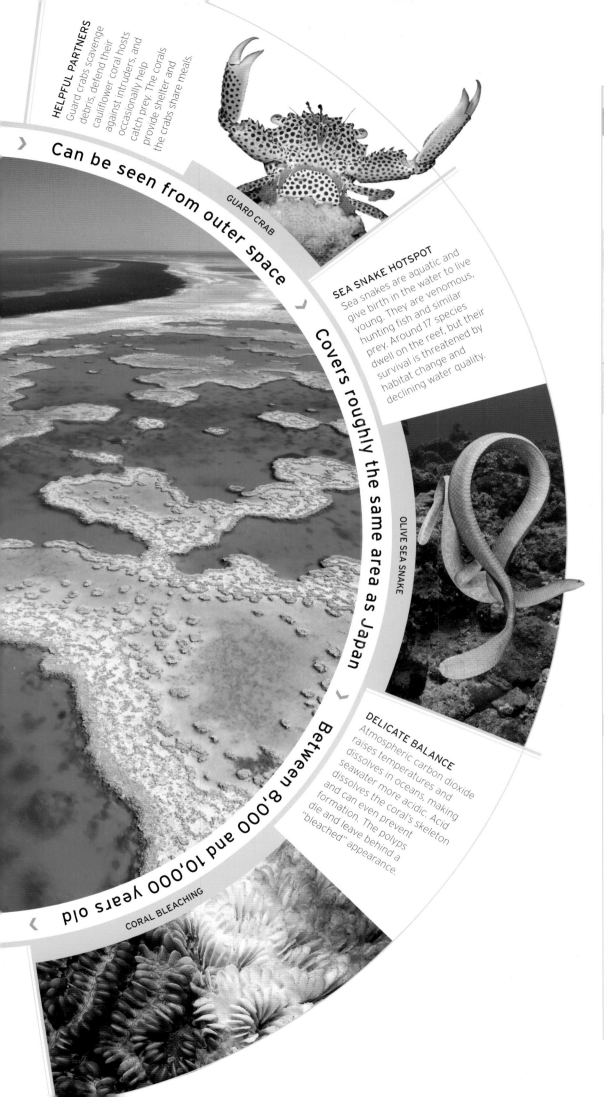

OLIVE SEA SNAKE

DELICATE BALANCE

Atmospheric carbon dioxide raises temperatures and dissolves in oceans, making seawater more acidic. Acid dissolves the coral's skeleton and can even prevent formation. The polyps die and leave behind a "bleached" appearance.

Between 8,000 and 10,000 years old

CORAL BLEACHING

LOCATION

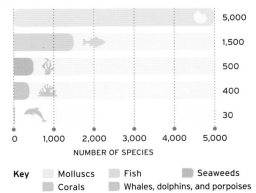

PAPUA NEW GUINEA

Coral Sea

Cairns

Townsville

AUSTRALIA

Brisbane

0 km   400
0 miles   400

Roughly parallel to Australia's northeast coast, south from Cape York to Fraser Island. The reef's edge extends from 30–250 km (18–155 miles) from the mainland.

CLIMATE

Almost entirely within the tropic zone, the climate is moist and warm to hot most of the year, averaging 23–26°C (73–79°F), and rarely below 17°C (63°F) or above 32°C (90°F). In the wettest months of December to April, rain reduces the salinity of the more isolated lagoons.

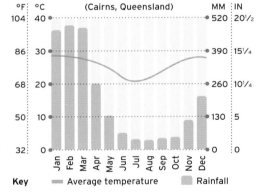

(Cairns, Queensland)

°F	°C		MM	IN
104	40		520	20½
86	30		390	15¼
68	20		260	10¼
50	10		130	5
32	0		0	0

Jan Feb Mar Apr May Jun Jul Aug Sep Oct Nov Dec

Key   — Average temperature   ▬ Rainfall

LIFE ON THE REEF

Thousands of species live on the reef year-round, their numbers boosted by annual visitors such as humpback and dwarf minke whales. The smallest fish include permanent residents such as pygmy seahorses and gobies; the largest would be a passing whale shark.

5,000
1,500
500
400
30

0   1,000   2,000   3,000   4,000   5,000

NUMBER OF SPECIES

Key   Molluscs   Fish   Seaweeds
   Corals   Whales, dolphins, and porpoises

Green sea turtle
Chelonia mydas

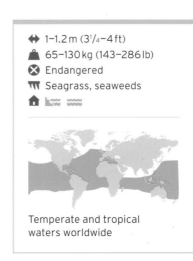

elongated
front limbs
modified
into flippers

The world's second largest turtle (after the leatherback), the green sea turtle is mostly solitary, swimming from one feeding area to another. Adult sea turtles graze inshore on marine plants using their toothless, horny, sharp-edged beaks, which have serrations on the lower jaw. When young, they are partly carnivorous, eating jellyfish, crustaceans, worms, and sponges.

Green sea turtles have a streamlined, teardrop-shaped carapace (upper shell). The common name comes from the layer of green fat between their shell and organs. The turtles swim using a flap-twist motion of the front flippers, with the shorter rear flippers acting as rudders. Their cruising speed is 2–3 km/h (1–2 mph) – in mid-migration they can cover 80 km (50 miles) daily – but can reach 30 km/h (20 mph) if threatened. Sea turtles can hold their breath for more than five hours when resting underwater, although they surface every three to five minutes when feeding and travelling, and often sleep under a ledge or on the sea floor.

Distinct populations

Two green sea turtle populations occur in the Pacific and Atlantic oceans. Individuals roam widely, some covering more than 8,000 km (5,000 miles) yearly between their traditional feeding and mating-nesting areas. When mature, they return to their natal (hatching) beach. Many males arrive every year, females every two to three years. Hundreds gather 1–2 km (½–1 mile) offshore to mate. The female crawls onto the sandy beach at night, digs a hole with her flippers, deposits 100–200 eggs, fills the pit, and returns to sea. Depending on the temperature, hatching occurs 45–70 days later.

↔ 1–1.2 m (3¼–4 ft)
⚖ 65–130 kg (143–286 lb)
⊗ Endangered
🍴 Seagrass, seaweeds
🏠 〰 〰

Temperate and tropical waters worldwide

Turtle-headed seasnake

Emydocephalus annulatus

This fully aquatic snake's high-snouted, blunt-nosed head and sharp-edged jaw scales are adapted to scrape up its specialized food: fish eggs, laid in seabed nests. Unlike almost all other seasnakes, it has no need to disable prey, so its venom glands are reduced and its fangs are less than 1 mm (1/25 in) long. Each individual lives in a small area, where it seems to memorize which eggs are laid where and in which season.

↔	60–120 cm (23½–47 in)
⚖	Up to 1.5 kg (3¼ lb)
✗	Common
𝍬	Fish eggs
🏠	🪸
◎	Philippines, Timor Sea, Coral Sea

△ **REEF COURTSHIP**
Male and female green sea turtles are similar-sized, although males have longer tails. Rival males bite and flipper-slap, then the winner shadows the female before grasping her shell with his flipper claws to mate.

▽ **LONG LUNG**
A single lung that runs almost the length of their body lets seasnakes stay submerged for up to two hours.

Ocean sunfish

Mola mola

After a deep feeding dive, the world's heaviest bony fish basks at the surface to warm up with its disc-like body lying side-on. The sunfish's fused jaw teeth form a "beak", which it uses to seize its main prey, jellyfish, and to break up its food. The female releases more eggs than almost any other animal – up to 300 million.

↔	Up to 4 m (13 ft)
⚖	Up to 2 tonnes
✗	Not known
𝍬	Jellyfish
🏠	〰
◎	Philippines, Timor Sea, Coral Sea

△ **SCULLING ACTION**
The sunfish's tail is reduced to just a fleshy frill. It swims by moving its elongated dorsal and anal fins from side to side.

◁ **RACE FOR LIFE**
Hatchlings flailing to the sea are feasted on by crabs, lizards, snakes, gulls, and other predators. In the sea lie more perils including sharks, kingfish, and dolphins.

▷ **DAY SCHOOL**
Female scalloped hammerheads spend the day in large schools that gather along the edges of coral reefs. At night the sharks disperse to hunt alone.

▽ **SHELL HEAD**
The scalloped hammerhead is named for the notches in the leading edge of its hammer. This, combined with grooves running down to the mouth, give the hammerhead's underside the look of a scallop shell.

pointed upper
tail lobe

eye on side of
hammer-shaped head

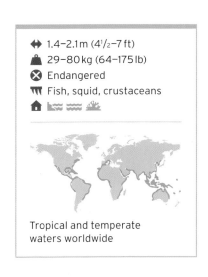

Scalloped hammerhead shark

Sphyrna lewini

There are few fish as iconic as a hammerhead shark, and the scalloped hammerhead is one of the most widespread. Contrary to their reputations as lone killers, these sharks are highly social – at least the females are. Groups develop around older, dominant females, with the lowest ranked individuals out on the edge. Hammerhead sharks display dominance by swimming in a corkscrew or ramming each other. Weaker individuals submit with a shake of the head.

Love bite

Male scalloped hammerheads reach maturity at the age of six – a full 10 years before the females, which are normally 2 m (7 ft) long before they are ready to breed. A mature male swims into the school of females, sweeping towards the centre in an S-shaped path. When he meets a likely mate, he secures himself to her by biting on one of her pectoral fins. Scalloped hammerheads give birth to live young and about 25 pups are born after an 8–12 month gestation.

At birth, the pups are only 40 cm (16 in) long, but fully formed with the distinctive hammerhead. They receive no parental care and have to fend for themselves. Most hunting takes place at night, with younger scalloped hammerheads feeding in shallow water, while the older ones move further out to sea.

The hammer feature has benefits in both habitats. The wide head acts like a hydrofoil – an underwater wing that creates lift, keeping the shark afloat. The head also acts as a communication dish, allowing the shark's senses to work better.

Prey detector

Hammerheads, like other sharks, have an excellent sense of smell. They can detect tiny quantities of chemicals in the water with two nostril-like slots called nares, which are located towards the ends of the hammer just in front of the eyes. The large distance between the nares means that a scent coming from a particular direction arrives at each nare at different times. This allows the hammerhead to zero in on the exact source of the scent.

Tiny pits arrayed along the underside of the hammerhead are filled with electrical sensors called the ampullae of Lorenzini. The large scanning surface provided by the head greatly enhances the sensitivity of these sensors, which can detect very tiny electrical currents produced by the nerves and muscles of all animals. By sweeping its head over the seabed like a metal detector, the hammerhead locates prey buried in the sand and takes hold of it, sometimes pinning it down with its head.

Scalloped hammerheads' **teeth** are more **suited to seize prey** than to rip it apart

↔ 1.4–2.1 m (4½–7 ft)
⬛ 29–80 kg (64–175 lb)
✖ Endangered
〿 Fish, squid, crustaceans
🏠 〜 〜 🐚

Tropical and temperate waters worldwide

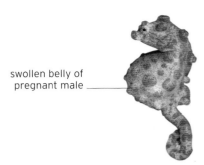

swollen belly of
pregnant male

Bargibant's pygmy seahorse

Hippocampus bargibanti

Found on coral reefs at depths of 16–40 m (53–130 ft), Bargibant's pygmy seahorse is so adept at mimicry that it was only discovered by chance in the late 1960s, when a laboratory researcher examining a gorgonian – a piece of soft, fan-like coral – realized that this tiny fish was attached to it. In addition to their much shorter, flattened snouts, pygmy seahorses differ from larger seahorse species in that the male's downward-facing brood pouch, in which he nurtures the fertilized eggs after mating, is located on his body cavity and not at the base of the tail. Their fleshier bodies lack easily distinguished segments, and they cling only to gorgonians, or sea fans, of the *Muricella* genus.

Little is known about the Bargibant's behaviour, but like many other seahorse species, it anchors itself to corals with its prehensile tail, feeding on tiny crustaceans that float past.

↔ 2.5 cm (1 in)
⚖ Not known
✖ Not known
🦐 Microscopic crustaceans
🏠 🪸

Indo-Pacific oceans

△ **DENISE'S PYGMY SEAHORSE**
At first believed to be a juvenile Bargibant's, Denise's pygmy seahorse (*H. denise*) is, at just 1.6 cm (½ in) in length, the smallest known seahorse species – and an equally effective camouflage artist.

▷ **MASTER OF DISGUISE**
Bargibant's pygmy seahorses are covered in wart-like tubercles that resemble the colour and polyp texture of their host gorgonians so closely as to make them almost invisible.

Barrier Reef anemonefish

Amphiprion akindynos

two black-edged white bands encircle body

Also known as clownfish, Barrier Reef anemonefish live in groups among anemones in reef waters up to 25 m (80 ft) deep. All anemonefish are born male, but some change to females as required. The largest fish in a group becomes the dominant female and the second-largest, her mate. When the female dies, the dominant male changes sex to take her place.

↔ 4.5–13 cm (1³⁄₄–5 in)
🏋 28 g (1 oz)
✕ Not known
🍴 Algae, zooplankton
🏠 🪸

SW. Pacific Ocean (Coral Sea)

◁ **SAFE SHELTER**
By blending anemone mucus into their skin's own mucus coating, anemonefish avoid stings – and predators.

Peacock mantis shrimp

Odontodactylus scyllarus

↔ 3–18 cm (1¹⁄₈–7 in)
✕ Not known
🍴 Crabs, gastropods, fish
🏠 🪸

Indo-Pacific oceans

Peacock mantis shrimp are as complex as their colours. Their compound eyes have 12 different colour photoreceptors (humans have three), which process infrared, ultraviolet, and polarized light, and they communicate using muscle-generated vibrations. Their "smasher" claws generate underwater explosions that can crack aquarium glass.

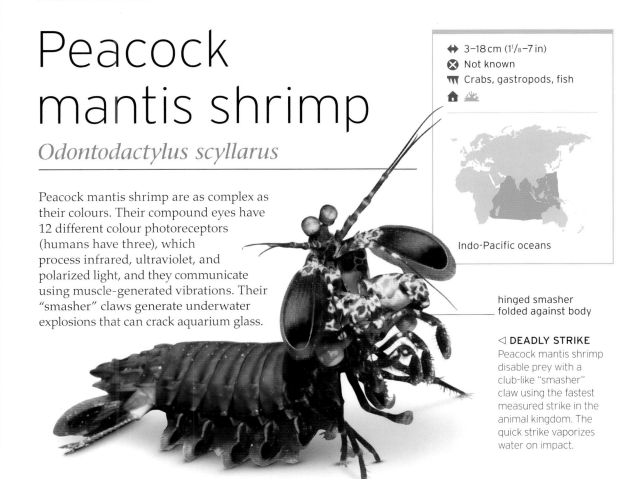

hinged smasher folded against body

◁ **DEADLY STRIKE**
Peacock mantis shrimp disable prey with a club-like "smasher" claw using the fastest measured strike in the animal kingdom. The quick strike vaporizes water on impact.

Greater blue-ringed octopus

Hapalochlaena lunulata

swims by jet propulsion

Although small enough to fit in a teacup, this species poses the greatest danger to humans of any octopus. It rests by day in rocky crevices close to the shore, piling up a wall of stones for extra privacy. If disturbed, the octopus can give a deadly bite. Fatalities are rare, but its saliva contains tetrodotoxin, a poison 10,000 times more toxic than cyanide. It hunts on the seabed, catching prey with its beak or paralyzing it by releasing poison into the water.

↔ 15–20 cm (6–8 in)
✕ Not known
♈ Fish, crabs, shrimps
🏠 🌊 〰
◉ Indo-Pacific, S. Australia coasts

▷ **BLUE ALERT**
If the octopus is alarmed, its rings turn electric blue, warning that a deadly bite will follow.

Giant clam

Tridacna gigas

ridged shell covered in seaweed

The giant clam is the largest living mollusc. Its immense shell is opened and closed by a powerful muscle, and animals sometimes get trapped, although the giant clam is not carnivorous. It feeds by filtering suspended food items from seawater. Adult giant clams also get nutrients from algae that live inside their fleshy tissues. These single-celled plants need light to photosynthesize, which restricts the clams to shallow, sunlit areas.

△ **SPAWNING**
Giant clams start life as males and later become hermaphrodites. However, they only release either eggs or sperm during a spawning session to avoid self-fertilization.

↔ 1–1.4 m (3¼–4½ ft)
✕ Vulnerable
♈ Algae, plankton
🏠 🌊
◉ Pacific, Indo-Pacific oceans

Portuguese man o' war

Physalia physalis

This relative of jellyfish floats on the surface of the ocean, snaring fish in its stinging tentacles that trail for 10 m (33 ft) or more below the surface. It is named after a passing resemblance between its gas-filled float and the distinctive curved sails of an 18th-century fighting ship. The Portuguese man o' war is unable to power its own movements, and the float, or pneumatophore, is also a sail of sorts, intended to catch the wind, which takes the organism wherever it may.

Colonial creature

A man o' war looks like a single animal but is actually a colony of several individual polyps, all of which connect beneath the float. There are three polyp types, each adapted for a particular job. The dactylozooids develop the long blue-green tentacles. These are lined with stinging cells, which are primed to fire barbed venomous darts into anything that touches them. The tentacles are used in defence and can inflict thousands of painful stings on anyone who tangles with them. The stingers also gather food, which is slowly hoisted up the tentacle to the gastrozooids, the feeding polyps. These engulf prey of all sizes and secrete enzymes to digest them.

The third polyp type – the reproductive gonozooid – has male and female parts, which produce new larval individuals that bud off from the main body to start life on their own.

↔ 10–50 m (33–165 ft)
✕ Not known
♈ Small fish, plankton
🏠 〰

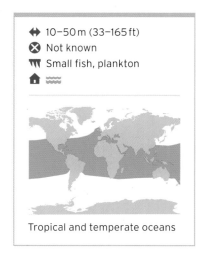

Tropical and temperate oceans

▷ **DRIFTING DANGER**
The float is mostly air, topped up with carbon monoxide. If attacked at the surface, the gas is released so the man o' war can sink safely underwater.

NEW ZEALAND MIXED FOREST
Remnants of vast tree cover provide evergreen oases

Aligned almost south-north, and 1,600 km (1,000 miles) long, New Zealand straddles considerable latitude and experiences a wide temperature range as a consequence. The annual average is below 10°C (50°F) in the far south, yet nearly double this at the northern tip. Since the country's greatest width is 400 km (250 miles), nowhere is far from the Pacific Ocean. The result is a cool-to-warm, generally moist climate where temperate forests thrive.

Main forested regions
On South Island, the Richmond temperate forests cloak the northeast. The damper west becomes more rugged southwards, through the Westland temperate forest ecoregion to the Fjordland National Park alpine zone in the far southwest. In the far north of North Island is the flatter, milder Northland temperate kauri forests. These mixed forests are home to many kinds of indigenous conifers, such as the totara, rimu, and giant kauri – all in the pine group – as well as silver, red, black, and hard beeches. The majority of these trees are evergreen, so the forest floor remains in shade all year, with a dense understorey of mosses, ferns, and small shrubs.

Much unique New Zealand wildlife thrives in these forests, from grasshopper-like wetas, to the bold kea and flightless kakapo parrots and ground-based kiwis. Before humans arrived, mixed temperate forests covered more than three-quarters of New Zealand. Burning, logging, and conversion to agriculture mean that today only a quarter remains.

SEED STIMULATION
Certain trees, such as the rimu, depend on a few native animal species, including New Zealand pigeons, to distribute their seeds. The seeds must pass through the birds' gut and be expelled in droppings before they can germinate.

NEW ZEALAND PIGEON

SNAILS IN PERIL
Unique to New Zealand forests, fist-sized amber snails – a type of land snail – are carnivores, feeding on earthworms. However, introduced possums, rats, hedgehogs, and other animals have devastated their numbers.

AMBER SNAIL

New Zealand is home to more species of flightless bird

BRUSHTAIL POSSUM

Kauris may live for 1,500 years

PLAGUE POSSUMS
To launch a fur trade in the 1830s, brushtail possums were introduced from Australia. These omnivorous marsupials have been a disaster for New Zealand's native ecology, damaging trees and eating eggs, insects, snails, and even bats.

LOCATION

Most mixed forest cover is found on South Island, apart from the drier east, and the north of North Island.

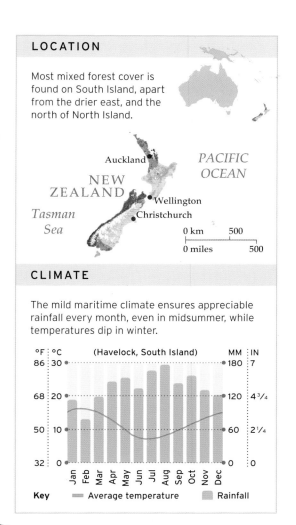

PACIFIC OCEAN

NEW ZEALAND

Auckland
Wellington
Christchurch

Tasman Sea

0 km 500
0 miles 500

CLIMATE

The mild maritime climate ensures appreciable rainfall every month, even in midsummer, while temperatures dip in winter.

(Havelock, South Island)

°F	°C		MM	IN
86	30		180	7
68	20		120	4¾
50	10		60	2¼
32	0		0	0

Jan Feb Mar Apr May Jun Jul Aug Sep Oct Nov Dec

Key ▬ Average temperature ▮ Rainfall

Lesser short-tailed bat
Mystacina tuberculata

The lesser short-tailed bat spends about 30 per cent of its feeding time foraging among deep leaf litter on the forest floor. The talons on the claws of its thumbs and feet aid its agility on the ground.

▽ **GROUND FEEDER**
The short-tailed bat's folded wings are protected from damage by a leathery sheath when it moves on the ground.

↔ 6–8 cm (2¼–3¼ in)
⚖ 24 g (⅞ oz)
✖ Vulnerable
🍴 Fruit, nectar, pollen, insects
🏠🌳

New Zealand

talon on side of claw gives extra grip

tubular nostrils

Welcome swallow
Hirundo neoxena

Australia's familiar rural and suburban swallow remains all year in most of its range. Unlike swifts, it perches on wires and bare branches, but it is a harvester of airborne insects, swerving elegantly at low level in pursuit of flies, and rising higher in humid conditions.

↔ 15 cm (6 in)
⚖ 12–17 g (⁷⁄₁₆–⅝ oz)
✖ Vulnerable
🍴 Insects
🏠

Australia, New Zealand

◁ **FEEDING TIME**
Chicks from nests in sheds and car ports line up on wires, and call out to be fed whenever a parent appears.

KAURI MAJESTY
In Northland, giant kauri conifers, which have survived from Jurassic times, reach heights of 50 m (165 ft) with diameters up to 20 m (66 ft). Their numbers have been so ravaged by logging that only five per cent remain.

than any other country

KAURI CONES

Kea

Nestor notabilis

"scaly" body feathers

The only alpine parrot, the kea is a great tourist attraction – investigating cars, bags, and clothing with its hooked bill – but many locals deem it a pest. Keas eat roots, berries, and insects, but came under scrutiny in the 1860s because of suspicions that they attacked sheep. Bounties were offered and more than 150,000 were killed between 1870 and 1970. By then there were only 5,000 keas left and protective measures were taken, but their numbers still declined and have yet to recover.

- ↔ 48 cm (19 in)
- 825 g (29 oz)
- Vulnerable
- Fruit, insects, grubs, carrion
- New Zealand

◁ **ALPINE SURVIVOR**
The kea is exceptionally intelligent – a quality that is vital to its survival in its harsh mountain habitat.

Kakapo

Strigops habroptila

blunt, round, owl-like head

The biggest, heaviest, and only flightless parrot, the kakapo is one of the world's longest-lived birds – averaging 95 years and reaching 120. Males compete for females in a lek, digging shallow bowls in the ground, perhaps to help amplify their calls, which continue for up to eight hours a night for several months.

- ↔ 64 cm (25 in)
- 2 kg (4½ lb)
- Critically endangered
- Plants
- New Zealand

◁ **RARE BIRD**
Just 126 kakapos were known in 2014, with only six chicks having hatched since 2011. The best chance of the species' survival rests on the birds having been moved to offshore islands free from predators.

Kiwis are the **only birds** in the world with **external nostrils** at the **tip of the bill**

soft, fur-like plumage

△ **LITTLE SPOTTED KIWI**
The little spotted kiwi (*A. owenii*) often lays two eggs, three weeks apart, on a bed of moss. Each egg is a quarter of the female's weight.

North Island brown kiwi

Apteryx mantelli

Nothing else looks remotely like a kiwi, but they share their origins with other flightless birds and are most closely related to emus and cassowaries. Kiwis prefer rainforest, but habitat loss has forced them into scrub and pine plantations, from coasts to alpine regions. They need high humidity, well-drained soil for digging nesting burrows and daytime dens, and moist leaf litter in which to find food such as worms and grubs at night. They detect prey by sound, smell, and touch, leaving a trail of holes where they have probed with their bill.

Extraordinary eggs
Kiwis form life-long pairs in fixed territories, digging burrows months or years before using them for nesting, so new growth disguises the entrance. Females are bigger than males, and produce eggs four times as large as might be expected for the bird's size. The North Island brown kiwi's egg may be 20 per cent of the body weight, its yolk an exceptional 60 per cent of the egg's volume. The egg takes a month to develop, and in this time the grossly distended female stops feeding. Incubation is by the male, using a temporary brood patch on his belly to keep the egg warm, and may last 90 days.

large feet with fleshy pads and long, sharp claws

long, slender bill

△ **NATIONAL ICON**
New Zealand's national bird, the kiwi's big round body, small head, and long, slim bill make it instantly recognizable around the world.

↔ 50–65 cm (19½–25½ in)
⚖ 2.8–3.5 kg (6–7¾ lb)
✕ Endangered
Ⅲ Insects, worms, millipedes
🏠 🌳 🌿

N. New Zealand

Tuatara

Sphenodon punctatus

Although it looks like a fairly standard if rather chunky lizard, the tuatara belongs to an ancient order of reptiles of which it is the sole survivor. Differences in its teeth, skull bones, and other anatomy – little changed from its group's origins some 200 million years ago – set it apart from lizards and snakes.

Island strongholds

Tuataras inhabit around 30 New Zealand offshore islands, chiefly those without invasive pests such as rats that eat their eggs and young. Breeding tuataras have recently been discovered at a release site on the mainland, where they are protected by a mammal-proof fence.

The tuatara is better adapted than any other reptile to a cool, damp climate, remaining active at just 5°C (41°C) and showing heat stress above 25°C (77°C). In winter, it lies torpid in its home burrow – self-dug or usurped from a seabird – sometimes for several weeks. Tuataras have a lengthy breeding cycle, reaching sexual maturity at 10–20 years. Females lay eggs only once every three to four years, which take at least a year to hatch. Juveniles are at risk of being cannibalized by adults, otherwise tuataras may live for more than 100 years.

light-sensitive organ, or "third eye", covered by scales

△ **POWERFUL BUILD**
Clawed toes, strong legs, a muscular build, and a crushing, tenacious bite make tuataras formidable adversaries.

Auckland tree weta

Hemideina thoracica

This chunky cricket is a common sight in gardens and scrublands. Mostly nocturnal, it spends the day inside burrows – known as galleries – in branches and trunks. Each gallery contains up to 10 wetas, with a single male living with a harem of females and juveniles. The insects enlarge a natural hollow or burrows vacated by a beetle grub, using their powerful biting mouthparts to snip away the bark. Tree wetas are mostly wingless, although a few grow small wings unsuited to flight. The female has what looks like a large stinger on her abdomen. This is actually the ovipositor, which is used to lay eggs into rotting wood or soil. Both sexes readily hiss and may bite when threatened, often flicking forwards their spiky back legs to scratch attackers.

↔ 4 cm (1½ in)
✖ Not known
🌾 Leaves, fruit, seeds, insects
🏠 🌳

N. New Zealand

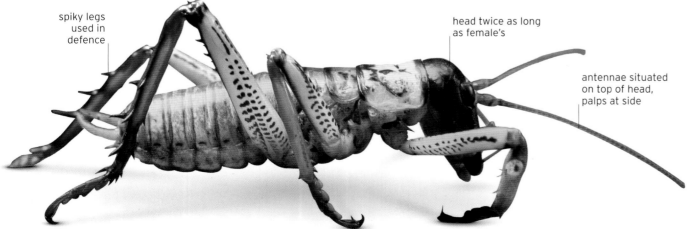

spiky legs used in defence

head twice as long as female's

antennae situated on top of head, palps at side

◁ **MALE TREE WETA**
The male Auckland tree weta has a much larger head and mouthparts than the female, which it uses to defend its harem and gallery from interloping males.

soft, jagged crest
along back and tail,
larger in male

stout limbs and
sharp-clawed
toes for
burrowing

↔ 50–60 cm (20–23½ in)
⚖ 0.4–1 kg (⅞–2¼ lb)
✖ Locally common
🐛 Spiders, insects, worms
🏠 🌳 〰

New Zealand
(coastal islands)

The tuatara's
closest **relatives
died out** more
than **60 million
years ago**

△ **BONY TEETH**
The sharp teeth are fused to the jaw
bone and are not shed and regrown
as in most other reptiles.

---

wings point backwards at rest

Blue damselfly

Austrolestes colensonis

The largest damselfly in New Zealand, the blue damselfly
can be seen fluttering around reeds and rushes in areas
of still water. Frequently confused with dragonflies,
damselflies are less powerful fliers and hold their wings
along the body, rather than out sideways, when at rest.
The blue damselfly can change colour to control its
temperature – the blue males and greener females turn
darker when the weather is cold in order to absorb more
heat from their surroundings.

Aerial hunters

Adult damselflies live only for a couple of weeks. They
are aerial hunters, snatching smaller insects, using their
enormous round eyes to track moving targets. Mating
couples can be seen flying in tandem over still water – the
male guards the female as she lays her eggs, ensuring
no other mate is able to copulate with her. The emerging
nymphs spend the winter underwater, breathing with
gills that are located on the tip of their abdomen. They
hunt on the bottom using a specialized mouthpart to
skewer prey. In spring, the wingless nymphs climb out
of the water to moult into the adult form.

↔ 4–4.8 cm (1½–2 in)
✖ Common
🐛 Water fleas
🏠 🌳 🌾 〰 ≈

New Zealand

◁ **LOVER'S EMBRACE**
During mating the male clasps the
female just behind her head and
she then reaches around with her
flexible abdomen to accept a packet
of sperm from him.

Southern Ocean
Chinstrap penguins spend winter out at sea
hunting for krill, fish, and squid. Their main
predator is the leopard seal, from which they
take refuge on large icebergs.

Antarctica

SNOW ALGAE

Some species of single-celled algae can survive in snow and ice. Some produce red pigments that mask green chlorophyll and resist frost and deadly ultraviolet rays that penetrate snow. Barely visible in winter, algae rise to the surface in summer, creating algal blooms that colour whole snowbanks red, pink, orange, green, or grey.

ANTARCTIC PLANTS

The coastal fringe of the peninsula is the only area free of permanent ice. Mosses and lichens dominate the tundra vegetation. Swards of Antarctic hair grass and cushions of Antarctic pearlwort are the only flowering plants.

ROARING WINDS

Westerly winds sweep unimpeded around the Southern Ocean. The Roaring Forties is the area between 40° and 50° latitude south. Now, due to a shift in weather patterns caused by climate change, these winds appear to be moving south, becoming stronger, and merging with the Furious Fifties.

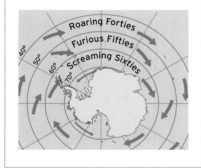

CIRCULAR OCEAN MOVEMENT

The winds around Antarctica drive the Antarctic Circumpolar Current, sealing off the Southern Ocean and creating the world's roughest seas.

FEATURED ECOREGIONS

■ Southern Ocean Islands **p364-69**
Tundra, ice

■ Antarctic Peninsula **p370-75**
Tundra, ice

ROSS SEA AND ICE SHELF

The vast Ross Ice Shelf shelters an abundance of invertebrate life below. Winds driving away sea-ice next to the ice shelf can create ice-free areas of water called polynyas. The summer sun brings forth blooms of phytoplankton and the Ross Sea bursts into life, supporting whales, seals, penguins, petrels, fish, and more than 1,000 species of invertebrate.

LAND OF ICE AND SNOW
Antarctica

The Antarctic ice-sheet, which covers most of the continent, is the largest mass of ice on Earth. It is 4.5 km (2¾ miles) thick in places, its volume is more than 30 million cubic km (7.2 million cubic miles), and it holds more than 70 per cent of Earth's fresh water. The ice-sheet is separated into two parts by the Transantarctic Mountains, most of which are hidden, but several peaks more than 4,000 m (13,000 ft) high emerge from the ice. How the mountains formed is debated, but an active rift on the West Antarctica side of the range is thought to have played a part. The rift may be causing a plate to be pushed under East Antarctica, causing uplift. West Antarctica is low-lying; East Antarctica is a larger, higher region of ancient rocks overlain in places by sandstones, shales, limestones, and coal laid down during warmer times.

Plant, dinosaur, and marsupial fossils provide further evidence of Antarctica's warm past, before it broke from the Gondwana supercontinent and moved south. Now it is typically below freezing all year round and recorded temperatures have plunged to -89 °C (-129 °F). Small wonder that, with the exception of a few researchers, Antarctica is uninhabited.

LAKES UNDER THE ICE
Vast lakes deep within the ice, sealed from the atmosphere for thousands of years, retain complex communities of thousands of microbes.

TRANSANTARCTIC MOUNTAINS
The curved belt of mountains separates East and West Antarctica.

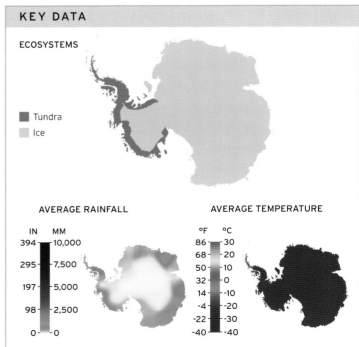

KEY DATA

ECOSYSTEMS

Tundra
Ice

AVERAGE RAINFALL

AVERAGE TEMPERATURE

SOUTHERN OCEAN ISLANDS
Inhospitable to man, last refuges for threatened species

Remote, mostly uninhabited volcanic islands, many with glaciers, ice caps, and snow fields year round, are dotted north of the 60 degrees south latitude line that marks the boundary of the Southern Ocean. They include South Georgia, South Sandwich, Bouvet, Prince Edward, and Kerguelen islands, and Heard Island. Situated close to the Antarctic Convergence, where cold Antarctic waters sink under warmer seas, these islands are home to a great variety and number of fish, birds, and mammals.

Lynchpin of the food chain
The food chain for the survival of all these creatures is based on tiny plankton and vast numbers of krill – small, shrimp-like crustaceans. Krill form the staple diet of petrels and albatrosses, crabeater seals, and humpback, right, blue, fin, sei, and minke whales arriving from tropical seas for the Antarctic summer. Ironically,

whales were hunted from these islands until they were declared commercially extinct by 1965. This created a surplus of Antarctic krill, so other marine species subsequently increased. For example, fur seals, once thought extinct, now breed here in their millions. Yet even a krill surplus may not help slow-breeding whales. Human exploitation has now shifted to the krill itself, threatening the basis of all Antarctic sea life.

VULNERABLE TO RATS
The South Georgia pintail is found only on the South Georgia and South Sandwich islands, preferring freshwater areas with tussock grass, and coastal bogs but often feeding offshore. Introduced rats threaten this duck as they eat eggs and chicks.

SIEVING THE SEA
The most abundant seal species in the world, crabeater seals eat krill by taking in seawater and squeezing it out between interlocking teeth, which act like sieves to retain the prey. When not feeding, they rest on floating sea ice.

SOUTH GEORGIA PINTAIL

CRABEATER SEAL

The total weight of Antarctic krill is more than that

Home to millions of crabeater seals

SPERM WHALE

DIVING FOR DINNER
Earth's deepest-diving mammal, the sperm whale can hold its breath for up to an hour or more as it dives in search of squid, a main food source. Its lungs collapse to cope with crushing water pressure at depths of up to 3,000 m (almost 2 miles).

LOCATION

Island groups situated between Antarctica to the south and New Zealand, South Africa, and South America to the north.

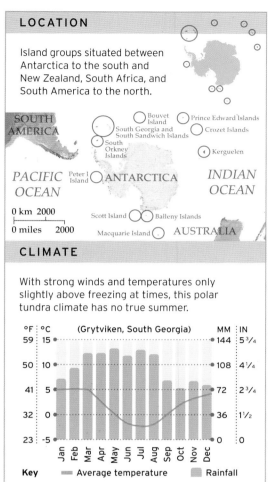

CLIMATE

With strong winds and temperatures only slightly above freezing at times, this polar tundra climate has no true summer.

°F	°C	(Grytviken, South Georgia)	MM	IN
59	15		144	5¾
50	10		108	4¼
41	5		72	2¾
32	0		36	1½
23	-5		0	0

Jan Feb Mar Apr May Jun Jul Aug Sep Oct Nov Dec

Key — Average temperature ▮ Rainfall

Southern elephant seal

Mirounga leonina

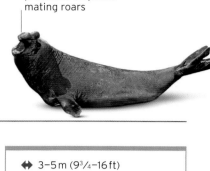

proboscis amplifies mating roars

The largest of the pinnipeds, or flipper-footed marine mammals, the southern elephant seal shows the greatest sex-related size difference of all mammals. Males weigh up to 10 times as much as females, and only mature bulls bear the trunk-like inflatable proboscis that gives the species its common name.

↔ 3–5 m (9¾–16 ft)
⚖ 0.6–3 tonnes
✖ Common
🍴 Fish and squid
🏠 ▧ ≈ ⩗

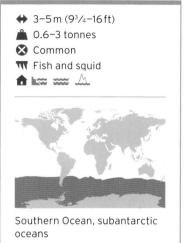

Southern Ocean, subantarctic oceans

Fighting to breed

Southern elephant seals may reach depths of up to 2,000 m (6,550 ft) in search of food, aided partly by their special, oxygen-rich red blood cells. They spend up to 90 per cent of their lives at sea, often sleeping underwater, but like all seals they haul out on land to moult, breed, and give birth. Adult males fight for mating rights to groups of females, but only 2–3 per cent are successful. The largest harems are controlled by a single dominant bull known as a "beachmaster". While females and pups can be injured or even killed during these fights, the breeding season is tough on both sexes: males lose an average of 12 kg (26 lb) a day – more than 40 per cent of their body weight.

Southern elephant seals are able to **stay underwater for up to two hours** at a time

▽ **DUELLING FOR DOMINANCE**
Male elephant seals fight for breeding rights early in the mating season. They raise more than half of their body off the ground and inflict wounds to an opponent's neck and face with their teeth.

COLOURFUL SWARM
The sea often turns orange-red as vast swarms of Antarctic krill gather in summer. Just 5 cm (2 in) long, krill are shrimp-like creatures that feed on phytoplankton (microscopic plants), but they can go up to 200 days without food.

of all the humans on Earth

KRILL

Wandering albatross

Diomedea exulans

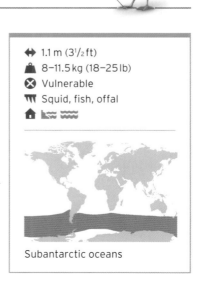

stands upright on
large webbed feet

With a wingspan of up to 3.5 m (12 ft), the wandering albatross is the largest flying bird in the world. Old males become so white they have been called "snowy albatrosses", but the bird's scientific name comes from the Latin term for "living as an exile". This refers to the fact that wandering albatrosses spend months at a time on the wing in the world's southern oceans.

Male wandering albatrosses are 20 per cent heavier than females but with only slightly larger wings. They forage farther south than females and their 12 per cent greater wing loading (body weight related to wing area) seems to help them deal with stronger winds. Immature birds circle the southern hemisphere before becoming old enough to breed at 10 years. Wandering albatrosses form large breeding colonies on remote islands, creating nest mounds out of mud and vegetation. Pairs mate for life, then breed every two years, incubating one egg for around 80 days and sharing parental duties.

Longline fishing threat

Albatrosses have a very good sense of smell thanks to their large, tubular external nostrils, and most of their diet is fish and squid taken at the ocean's surface or in shallow dives. Scavenging around fishing boats for fish and other unwanted sea creatures that are thrown aside gives these seabirds an easy feeding option but has increased risk. With just 8,000 pairs nesting in any year and a slow reproductive rate, wandering albatrosses, in particular, are extremely vulnerable to threats such as drowning when caught on baited hooks from long-line trawlers.

↔ 1.1 m (3¹/₂ ft)
🏋 8–11.5 kg (18–25 lb)
✕ Vulnerable
🦑 Squid, fish, offal
🏠 〰 〰

Subantarctic oceans

△ **DYNAMIC SOARING**
Instead of beating their wings, albatrosses hold them out stiffly and fly by dynamic soaring, exploiting air currents rising over ocean waves. Getting airborne, however, relies on a headwind.

△ **INFREQUENT MEAL**
Chicks are fed every two to four days at first, less often as they grow. They remain at the nest for as long as 9–11 months.

◁ **COURTSHIP RITUAL**
An elaborate ritual involving spread wings, clapping bill, and moaning calls is much the same for all large albatross species.

Rockhopper penguin
Eudyptes chrysocome

strong webbed feet
with sharp claws
give good grip

After six months at sea, chasing shrimp-like krill and fish, rockhopper penguins must begin nesting promptly once melting sea ice allows them access to firm land. Of around 3.5 million pairs, some 2.5 million breed in the Falkland Islands. Males return first, to begin building nests of stones, grass, and fish bones. Courtship is short, but caressing, billing, and other rituals reaffirm past pair-bonds and establish new ones – vital if pairs are to act in concert to rear their chick.

Each parent incubates two eggs while the other is away feeding at sea for 7–17 days. They may forage up to 250 km (155 miles) from the colony. With such long periods between meals, only the stronger chick survives. Unusually among birds, the second egg, laid several days after the first, can be 70 per cent heavier and hatches first. Scientists speculate whether the species is still evolving a single-egg clutch. The chick is brooded constantly for three weeks before being moved into a crèche, where "aunties" strive to protect vast numbers of chicks from giant petrels, skuas, and gulls. Only the parents feed their chick, and the first few days between parental guarding and establishment in the crèche expose it to the greatest risk of predation.

distinctive black
and yellow crest and
yellow eyebrow

↔ 50 cm (19¹⁄₂ in)

⚖ 2.5 kg (5¹⁄₂ lb)

✖ Vulnerable

♒ Fish, crabs, squid

⌂

S. South America;
S. Pacific, S. Atlantic,
S. Indian, Southern Oceans

▷ **HURRYING HOME**
Having escaped predatory
leopard seals lurking inshore,
these rockhoppers are heading back
to the colony with a belly full of fish.

△ **GOING FISHING**
These stocky little penguins use their short, strong legs to make double-footed kangaroo hops across rocks when going to and from the ocean.

Imperial shag
Phalacrocorax atriceps

old brown feathers replaced by new black ones during moult

The imperial shag nests on rocky headlands and islands and mostly feeds quite close to the shore. Like other shags and cormorants, it has relatively heavy bones and little body fat – this reduces buoyancy and makes it a more efficient underwater forager. Unlike terns and gannets, which locate fish from the air by sight, the shag dives deep and searches systematically for prey.

↔ 68–76 cm (27–30 in)
⚖ 2.5–3.5 kg (5¹/₂–7³/₄ lb)
✖ Common
🍴 Fish
🏠 ▬ 〜

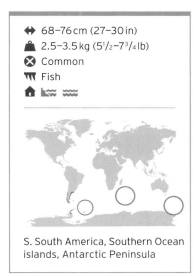

S. South America, Southern Ocean islands, Antarctic Peninsula

△ **EGG CUPS**
Each nest is a mound of seaweed, grass, and mud liberally mixed with white excrement, with a shallow bowl for two or three eggs.

Antarctic tern
Sterna vittata

The southern equivalent of the Arctic tern, the Antarctic tern does not undertake vast migrations from north to south. It breeds in November and December when the northern species is "wintering" at sea. Some birds remain close to nesting colonies, while others move far out to sea, feeding along the edges of the pack ice and often resting on ice floes.

↔ 35–40 cm (14–15¹/₂ in)
⚖ 150–175 g (5–6 oz)
✖ Common
🍴 Fish
🏠 ▬ 〜 ⛰

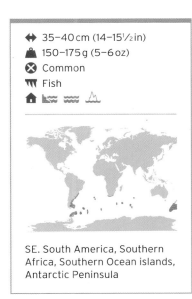

SE. South America, Southern Africa, Southern Ocean islands, Antarctic Peninsula

◁ **BREEDING ADULT**
In its summer plumage, the Antarctic tern looks very similar to its Arctic cousin. It breeds on rocky islands in the Southern Ocean.

ANTARCTIC PENINSULA
The coldest, most remote continent is ruled by ice

More than 99 per cent of Antarctica – Earth's driest, coldest, windiest continent – is covered by ice. Only the 2,000-km (1,240-mile) long Antarctic Peninsula reaches beyond the Antarctic Circle, pointing north towards Cape Horn. Life here is shaped by extremes. Antarctica's interior is elevated, with air so cold it cannot hold moisture, yet the coastal belt is damp. Cold air falls from the interior in blistering gales. Rain, fog, and blizzards alternate with sunny days when temperatures reach 5°C (41°F). Months of darkness give way to summers of 24-hour daylight, but even the best summer conditions are still challenging.

Life among the ice
The waxing and waning of sea ice is the driving force for most Antarctic life. Pack ice expands by up to 4 km (2½ miles) per day, thickening to 2 m (6½ ft), with fallen snow on top. For much of the year, ice locks away feeding areas and breeding sites for many creatures. Most seals and penguins, skuas, and other birds only breed when the ice melts to reveal solid rock, so they move away from land as the ice expands. Emperor penguins, however, head south, where the males endure the worst winter conditions as they incubate eggs and fast for 65 days while the females go back to the ocean to feed. Weddell seals remain, using breathing holes so they can live under the ice all winter.

While approximately 300 species of algae, 200 lichens, 85 mosses, and 25 liverworts are known to exist in this icy landscape, only two flowering plant species are considered to be native to the Antarctic.

LOYAL MATE
Snow petrels nest farther south than any other bird, with many colonies along the peninsula. Mated pairs remain faithful for life, and lay one egg per year in a rock crevice. Their pure white plumage camouflages them against snow and ice.

SNOW PETREL

WHITE-BLOODED FISH
Blackfin icefish survive in temperatures that would freeze most other fish solid. Glycoproteins prevent their body fluids from freezing, and although their blood lacks haemoglobin (red blood cells), it is more fluid and so uses less energy to circulate.

BLACKFIN ICEFISH

ANTARCTIC PEARLWORT

Antarctica holds 90% of the planet's ice and more

So dry it is classified as a cold desert

EXPANDING BLOOMS
One of only two flowering plants on the entire continent, Antarctic pearlwort forms green cushions, seen more and more frequently on the Antarctic fringe. This white-blossomed plant is widening its range due to a warming climate.

LOCATION

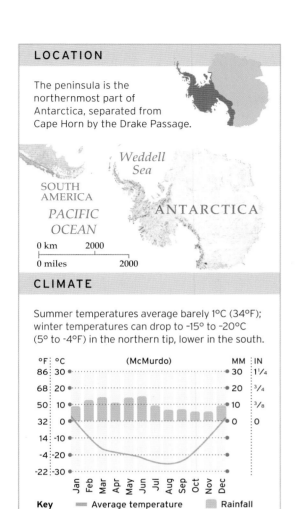

The peninsula is the northernmost part of Antarctica, separated from Cape Horn by the Drake Passage.

Weddell Sea

SOUTH AMERICA
PACIFIC OCEAN
ANTARCTICA

0 km — 2000
0 miles — 2000

CLIMATE

Summer temperatures average barely 1°C (34°F); winter temperatures can drop to -15° to -20°C (5° to -4°F) in the northern tip, lower in the south.

°F	°C	(McMurdo)	MM	IN
86	30		30	1¼
68	20		20	¾
50	10		10	⅜
32	0		0	0
14	-10			
-4	-20			
-22	-30			

Jan Feb Mar Apr May Jun Jul Aug Sep Oct Nov Dec

Key —— Average temperature   ▢ Rainfall

Leopard seal
Hydrurga leptonyx

head has no forehead

Named for its spotted coat, this aquatic mammal is an expert hunter, thanks to its almost snake-like head and wide, powerful jaws with long canine teeth. Although it is the only true seal that feeds on other seals, up to half of a leopard seal's diet consists of tiny, shrimp-like krill, and it has a set of specially adapted cheek teeth that serve as a sieve for feeding on them.

Different strokes

Unlike other true seals, the leopard seal swims not by propelling itself solely with its hindquarters, but by strong, simultaneous strokes of its large, elongated front flippers. This technique gives the seal increased speed and agility in the water, but makes it difficult for the animal to move about on land. Females are slightly larger than males – the opposite of size differences in most true seals. Females give birth on pack ice to single pups, which are suckled for three to four weeks.

Although they are the most formidable carnivores in their ecoregion, leopard seals are occasionally hunted by killer whales. Seals are protected from commercial hunting, but juveniles, which depend largely on krill to survive, may also be threatened by a decrease in krill numbers due to commercial overfishing.

↔ 2.5–3.5 m (8¼–11½ ft)
⚖ 200–455 kg (440–1,003 lb)
✖ Common
🍴 Krill, squid, seals, penguins
🏠 〜 ≈ ⛰

Southern Ocean and subantarctic waters

▽ **OPPORTUNISTIC PREDATOR**
Leopard seals patrol penguin rookeries in search of young, newly fledged penguins, which are more vulnerable to attacks.

Leopard seals **vocalize underwater**, making **long-lasting calls**, some of which can be **felt through ice**

FLIGHTLESS INSECT
Antarctica's only insect is flightless and so avoids the constant buffeting winds. It tolerates high salinity and loss of body water, and its black colour absorbs heat. By living in shallow burrows, the midge survives temperatures just below freezing.

...than 70% of its fresh water

ANTARCTIC MIDGE

55-68 throat grooves

Blue whale
Balaenoptera musculus

Apart from the tiny, shrimp-like krill it eats, everything about the blue whale is supersized. The largest animal on Earth, the blue whale is roughly the size of a jumbo jet. It weighs twice as much as the biggest dinosaurs; even its tongue weighs 4 tonnes (4⅜ tons). A human could easily swim through its blood vessels, which carry 10 tonnes of blood, circulated by a heart that weighs up to 900 kg (2,000 lb) – about the size of a small car.

Despite their huge size, blue whales are almost perfectly hydrodynamic – the long, streamlined body moves through seawater with minimal resistance, propelled by the strong tail. They travel either alone or in small groups, but occasionally up to 60 animals may come together to feed. Blue whales produce the loudest vocalizations on the planet – up to 188 decibels – via a series of low-frequency calls that can be heard underwater for hundreds of kilometres.

Back from the brink

Their massive proportions kept blue whales safe from human threats until the mid-19th century, when the invention of the exploding harpoon focused the whaling industry's attention on the species. Thousands of blue whales were slaughtered, and despite a 1966 global ban on hunting them, today's population has decreased by an estimated minimum of 70 per cent, possibly as much as 90 per cent. There have, however, been signs of very slow recovery in recent years, and current blue whale numbers are thought to be around 10,000–25,000.

◁ **HIGHEST SPOUT**
At 9-12 m (30-40 ft), blue whales have the highest "blow" or spout of any whale. It happens when the whale expels air through the two blowholes.

↔ 32–33 m (105–108 ft)
⚖ 113–150 tonnes (111–148 tons)
⊗ Endangered
🦐 Krill, copepods
🏠 〜〜 ⏝

Oceans worldwide, except Arctic

Hourglass dolphin
Lagenorhyncus cruciger

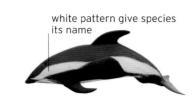

white pattern give species its name

Usually seen far out at sea, hourglass dolphins live in colder, deeper Antarctic and subantarctic waters. They are often found in groups of seven or eight, although schools of 60 to 100 dolphins have also been sighted. They excel at bow-wave riding and frequently approach boats, as well as larger cetaceans such as fin whales, to "catch a ride". Although little is known about its behaviour, research has revealed that this species' echolocation clicks allow it to find prey at over twice the distance of other dolphins.

↔ 1.4–1.9 m (4½–6¼ ft)
⚖ Up to 94 kg (207 lb)
⊗ Common
🦐 Fish, squid, crustaceans
🏠 〜〜 ⏝
◉ S. Pacific, S. Atlantic, S. Indian, Southern oceans

▷ **PORPOISING**
Hourglass dolphins swim at speeds of up to 22 km/h (14 mph), leaping out of the water when riding a bow wave.

Adelie penguin
Pygoscelis adeliae

white ring around eyes

Adelie penguins nest on large ice-free areas of rock, often far from shore, in colonies up to 280,000 pairs strong. Although new scientific bases and tourism cause disturbance, more than 2 million pairs breed around Antarctica. Their insulation is so good that falling snow does not melt but simply covers them.

↔ 46–61 cm (18–24 in)
⚖ 4–5.5 kg (8¾–12 lb)
⊗ Near threatened
🦐 Krill, small fish
🏠 〜〜 ⏝
◉ Circumpolar around Antarctica

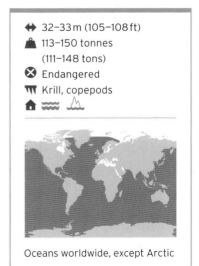

△ **FEEDING IN SHIFTS**
Both parents take turns to feed their chick for 16–19 days until it is ready to join a crèche of juveniles.

golden cheek patch

white front and dark back
help camouflage penguins
when swimming

Emperor penguin

Aptenodytes forsteri

Adapted to some of the most challenging conditions on Earth, the emperor penguin is the only bird that breeds during the severe Antarctic winter. It is the largest of the penguins but has the same upright pose, short legs, waddling walk, and stiff wings held like arms at its sides, as well as an incurably inquisitive nature.

Built for survival

When moving from ice-cold water into the warmth of the sun, penguins may wave their wings to dissipate heat and they also pant to keep cool. In cold conditions, emperor penguins tilt back onto their heels and tails, avoiding contact between the ice and their feet. The dark plumage absorbs heat from the sun and beneath the dense feathers is a trapped layer of insulating warm air. Beneath this they have a thick layer of fat – creating the familiar rotund, streamlined shape – that is indispensable for survival in temperatures as low as -60°C (-76°F).

Emperor penguins live in a narrow band of ice floes and frozen bays surrounding the Antarctic continent. The rookeries get further from the open sea as it freezes, forcing these flightless birds to undertake annual treks to establish their colonies in March or April, and then make repeated and even longer marches – up to 60 km (37 miles) each way – to bring food back to their chick.

Teamwork

The female lays a single egg, which she transfers to the male before heading to the open ocean on a feeding trip that lasts about two months. The male incubates the egg in his brood pouch, a fold of featherless skin just above his feet. Emperor penguin colonies may be several thousand strong, with the incubating males huddling together over large open areas. They stand almost motionless for days in low temperatures and raging blizzards. When the female returns, care of the newly hatched chick transfers to her and the near-starving male goes off to feed.

After 45 days, when it is well grown and covered in down, the chick joins a crèche, but it is still fed by its parents. The crèche breaks up after five months, when the parents abandon their chick and leave for the open sea. The chicks eventually follow and, having acquired adult plumage, take to the water.

Emperor penguins **dive deeper than any other bird** to find food

◁ BUBBLE POWER

Penguin feathers release a stream of air bubbles when the birds head back to the surface from a deep dive. This increases their speed of ascent sufficiently for them to clear the water and land safely on the ice.

▷ KEEPING WARM

The solitary emperor penguin chick is hatched almost naked. It is kept warm by a parent until it is covered with down and big enough to join a crèche.

↔ 1.1 m (3½ ft)
⚖ 30–40 kg (66–88 lb)
⊗ Near threatened
♟ Krill, fish, squid
⌂ ▬ ⛰

Circumpolar around Antarctica

Glossary and Index

GLOSSARY

A

ACID RAIN Most rain (and snow) is slightly acidic due to dissolved carbon dioxide. More strongly acidic rain results from atmospheric pollution or sometimes from gases released by volcanoes.

ACIDIFICATION Becoming more acid. The term is used especially in the context of the Earth's oceans and fresh waters.

ADAPTATION Any feature that helps an organism survive in its habitat or the process that allows it to do so.

AESTIVATION A state similar to hibernation but occurring in hot, dry seasons.

ALGAE Any of a variety of plant-like life forms. They include single-celled species as well as larger forms such as seaweeds, and are especially important in the oceans.

ALTIPLANO The huge high-plateau region in the central Andes mountains of South America.

AMBUSH PREDATOR Any predator whose main feeding strategy is to stay in one place and wait for suitable prey to approach; also called a "sit-and-wait" predator.

AMPULLA (plural Ampullae) The enlarged end of a tube or duct.

ANTENNA (plural Antennae) The paired sensory "feeler" of insects, crustaceans, and some other invertebrates.

ANTLERS Paired bony structures, often branched, on the heads of most members of the deer family. Except for reindeer, only male deer have antlers. They are shed and regrown every year. See also *Horns*.

APEX PREDATOR A predator at the top of its food chain, hunted by no other animal (except humans).

ARACHNIDS The group of arthropods that includes spiders, scorpions, mites, and relatives. See also *Arthropods*.

ARCHIPELAGO A group of islands.

ARTHROPODS A major group of invertebrate animals having jointed legs and a hard outer skeleton. Arthropods include insects, crustaceans, and arachnids. See also *Exoskeleton*.

AXIL In plants, the upper angle between a leaf stalk and a stem, or between a side shoot and a main stem.

B

BACHELOR GROUP A group formed by immature males or males of the same species that have no sexual partners.

BILL The jaws of a bird, consisting of bone with a horny outer covering, also known as a beak. Also a similar structure in other animals, such as turtles.

BINOCULAR VISION The ability to see in 3D, which allows animals to judge distances.

BIODIVERSITY A general term for the variety of living things, either on the Earth as a whole or in a particular region. Frequently it refers to the number of different species, but it can also be applied to genetic variety, ecological variety, and so on.

BIOMASS The total mass or weight of living organisms in a given area.

BIOME A large-scale ecosystem or set of ecosystems with characteristics determined by environmental factors, such as climate and geography. Deserts and tropical rainforests are examples of biomes.

BLOWHOLE The nostril(s) of cetaceans, situated on top of their heads.

BOG A mossy wetland, common in cooler regions, composed mainly of rotting plant material. It receives most of its water from rain and snow. Soils are nutrient-poor and acidic. See also *Fen*.

BOREAL Relating to or coming from the colder parts of the northern hemisphere, between the Arctic and temperate zones.

BOREAL FOREST The huge region of forest dominated by coniferous trees that circles the cooler regions of the northern hemisphere, between the tundra to the north and temperate broadleaved forests to the south. See also *Taiga*.

C

BRACKET FUNGUS Any of a variety of fungi that are relatives of toadstools and have spore-producing fruiting bodies that resemble shelves or brackets.

BROMELIAD A plant with numerous species, some of which grow in rainforests, using trees and shrubs for support. Typically they have rosettes of tough, waxy leaves in which rainwater collects. See also *Epiphyte*.

BROOD PARASITE An animal, such as the cuckoo, that makes use of other species to raise its young rather than raising its own young.

BRUMATION A state similar to hibernation that occurs in reptiles and other cold-blooded animals.

CAECUM A blind-ended part of the digestive tract, at the junction of the small and large intestines. See also *Hind-gut digestion*.

CAMOUFLAGE A means of being undetected used by predators, prey, and plants. It may involve colour and/or pattern, shape, or even using a disguise. See also *Mimicry*.

CANID A member of the dog family, which includes foxes, wolves, and relatives.

CANINE (TOOTH) In mammals there is one canine tooth in each side of the upper and lower jaws. In carnivores it is enlarged and used for holding and/or stabbing prey.

CANOPY The part of the forest formed by the crowns of trees. It is also the name given to that part of a forest ecosystem.

CARAPACE A hard shield on the back of an animal's body – for example, in crabs and turtles.

CARNIVORE (1) A member of the Carnivora, the group of mammals that includes cats, dogs, bears, seals, and relatives. (2) Any flesh-eating animal.

CARRION Dead, decaying flesh.

CETACEANS The group of mammals comprising whales, dolphins, and porpoises.

D

CHORDATE An animal that has a notochord, a rod support that runs the length of the body, for at least part of its life. See also *Notochord*.

CLASPERS In sharks and relatives, modified parts of the males' pelvic fins used to channel sperm to the female. In insects, claspers are structures used to hold the female during mating.

CLOVEN-HOOFED Having a hoof split into two halves, each containing one toe of the foot. This is a characteristic of two-toed herbivores, such as cattle and deer.

COALITION A cooperative alliance between individuals of the same species for defending or winning a territory or gaining access to females. Coalitions may be long or short term.

COLONY In zoology, any group of animals living together or in close association with one another, including birds such as emperor penguins in their breeding season; swarms of bees; and reef-forming coral polyps.

CONFLUENCE A place where two rivers, streams, or glaciers meet.

CONIFERS Predominantly evergreen trees and shrubs that produce seed-bearing cones and have needle- or scale-like leaves. The most numerous of the non-flowering plants, including pines, firs, and spruces.

CORAL (1) Simple animals related to sea anemones and jellyfish. (2) The hard skeleton left behind by some coral polyps that can form large reefs.

CROP MILK A milk-like substance rich in nutrients secreted by some birds in their lower throat (crop) and used to feed their nestlings.

CRUSTACEANS The dominant group of arthropods in the oceans, though they also live in fresh water and on land. Crustaceans include crabs, lobsters, shrimp, and krill. See also *Arthropods*, *Zooplankton*.

CURRENT A flow of water or air. In the oceans, large-scale currents exist on the surface and also at depth, driven either by the wind or by differences in temperature and salinity.

D

DECIDUOUS Of trees and shrubs: having leaves that fall at a particular time of the year, such as winter or a dry season.

DELTA An often fan-shaped area at the mouth of a river that is built up by deposited sediment.

DIURNAL Active by day.

DIVERSITY See *Biodiversity*.

DREY A squirrel's nest.

DRY FOREST A forest growing in a region that has a long dry season.

E

ECHOLOCATION A method of detecting surrounding objects and prey, used by dolphins, bats, and some other animals, that involves emitting high-pitched sounds and interpreting their echoes.

ECOREGION Any geographical region defined on the basis of the particular ecosystems and distinctive flora and fauna that it contains.

ECOSYSTEM Any community of organisms considered together with the interactions between them and their associated physical environment.

EL NIÑO Phenomenon involving the waters of the eastern Pacific off South America that become warmer than usual every few years. It is part of a larger climatic cycle that seriously affects marine life and global weather patterns.

EMERGENT (1) In tropical forests, an emergent is a tall tree that grows higher than the surrounding tree canopy. (2) In freshwater ecosystems, emergent plants, such as the bulrush, grow out of the water into the air above. See also *Canopy*.

ENDEMIC A living species native to a particular region and only found in that region.

ENDOSKELETON An internal skeleton, such as the bony skeleton of vertebrates.

EPIPHYTE A plant that grows on another plant as a means of support.

EROSION The processes by which rocks or soil are loosened and transported to another location.

EVERGREEN Having some green leaves all the year round.

EVOLUTION Cumulative change over time brought about mainly by natural selection. Organisms with characteristics that not only enhance survival but can also be inherited pass them on to their offspring. The genetic makeup of the population changes as these advantageous features spread through the population. See also *Adaptation*.

EXOSKELETON A skeleton situated on the outside of an animal, such as is found in insects and other arthropods. See also *Arthropod*.

EXOTIC In ecology, a term for any non-native species.

F

FEN A type of wetland, formed when glaciers retreat, that receives its water supply mainly through groundwater seepage. Typically, it does not have standing water in the growing season, and is less nutrient-poor than a bog. See also *Bog*.

FERAL Term applied to an animal, or population of animals, living successfully in the wild but descended from a domestic species or breed.

FJORD A narrow, steep-sided, deep inlet of the sea, once occupied by a glacier.

FOOD CHAIN A food pathway that can be followed from its creation by plants to the apex predators.

FORAGING Activities concerned with seeking and obtaining food.

FORB Any herbaceous (non-woody) plant other than grass, and especially such a plant growing naturally in grassland.

FRUGIVORE A fruit-eating animal.

FUMAROLE In volcanic regions, a small opening in the ground from which hot gases can escape.

G

GASTROPODS The group of invertebrate animals that includes snails and slugs.

GENUS The first level of traditional biological classification above species. A genus may contain one or more species. For example, lions belong to the genus *Panthera*.

GESTATION Pregnancy. In animals that produce live young, the gestation period is the time between fertilization and birth of the young.

GEYSER A jet of boiling water and steam that rises at intervals from the ground. It is powered by hot rocks heating groundwater.

GROOMING Behaviours that keep body coverings (fur, feathers, etc.) in good condition. In some species individuals may groom each other for social reasons.

H

HABITAT Any area that can support a group or community of living things.

HELICONIA A genus of plants mainly found in the American tropics, often having flower clusters with distinctive red bracts that are pollinated by hummingbirds.

HERBIVORE An animal that eats plants.

HERMAPHRODITE An animal that is both male and female at some point in its life. Species that are both sexes at once are called "simultaneous hermaphrodites"; those that change from one sex to the other are "sequential hermaphrodites".

HIBERNATION A state in which the bodily processes of an animal are drastically slowed down in winter, with the animal becoming completely inactive. The term is mainly applied to "warm-blooded" animals that drastically reduce their heart rate and let their body temperatures fall close to those of their surroundings. See also *Aestivation, Brumation*.

HIND-GUT DIGESTION A type of digestion found in animals such as horses and elephants, in which tough plant food is fermented in the hind part of the gut, often in an enlarged caecum. See also *Caecum*.

HORNS Paired, permanent structures with a core of bone sheathed by a hard outer layer of keratin, found on the heads of cloven-hoofed animals such as antelope and cattle. Rhinoceros horns are not paired or attached to the skull, and they are sited on the nasal bones rather than the top of the head. Consisting only of keratin, there may be one or two depending on species. See also *Antlers, Keratin*.

HOTSPOT (1) In ecology, a region or location with a very high biodiversity, especially one that contains many endemic species and is under threat. (2) In geology, hotspots are fixed points that are unusually hot due to molten rock rising from deep within the Earth.

They are sites of volcanic activity; examples include Hawaii and the Galapagos Islands.

HYBRIDIZATION Cross-breeding between different species or strains of organisms.

I

INDICATOR SPECIES A species whose presence or absence may define an ecoregion or indicate some significant feature, such as the presence of pollution.

INSECTIVORE An animal, especially a land vertebrate, that eats mainly insects.

INTRODUCED SPECIES A species introduced by humans to a particular region and now living successfully in the wild there. See also *Exotic*.

INVERTEBRATE Any animal without a backbone. Of the 30 or so major groups into which animals are classified, vertebrates (back-boned animals) form only part of one single group (see *Chordate*): all other animals are invertebrates.

ISLET A small island.

J

JET STREAM High-altitude strong winds that are confined to a relatively narrow band within the atmosphere. Such winds blow in a winding course from west to east in both hemispheres, and their position influences the pattern of weather systems nearer the ground.

K

KARST A type of landscape that develops in regions where the underlying rock, most commonly limestone, is water soluble. Karst landscapes are characterized by deep gorges, underground rivers, and caves.

KERATIN A tough structural protein found in hair, claws, feathers, and horns.

KEYSTONE SPECIES Any species native to a particular ecosystem whose presence or absence has a major impact on the functioning of that ecosystem.

KINGDOM The second highest level in traditional biological classification. Originally there were just the animal and plant kingdoms, but later other kingdoms were introduced to cover fungi and various types of microorganisms.

KIT Name for the young of various mammals, such as mink and muskrat.

L

LARVA (plural Larvae) A young stage of an animal when it is completely different in form from the adult. Caterpillars and tadpoles are examples.

LEKKING Mating system found in some species that involves males gathering at traditional locations (leks) and competing for the attention of females by performing ritualized displays, building mounds, or undertaking other "show-off" activities.

LIGNOTUBER A swollen woody base of a stem or trunk that occurs in some plants.

LITHOPHYTE A plant adapted to grow on rock surfaces.

LIVE-BEARER An animal species where the females give birth to live young, rather than laying or releasing eggs.

M

MANDIBLE A jaw or jawbone. In mammals it usually refers to the lower jaw, while in birds both the upper and lower parts of the bill are referred to as mandibles. Mandibles are also the chewing mouthparts of insects and other arthropods.

MANTLE (1) In geology, the layer lying between the Earth's crust and its core. The mantle is subject to high temperatures and pressures, and can slowly move. (2) In zoology, a protective skin layer in snails and relatives that secretes the shell.

MARSUPIALS The group of mammals that includes kangaroos, opossums, wombats, and relatives. Unlike most other mammals including humans, marsupials give birth to offspring in a relatively undeveloped state, and the young then typically continue their growth within an external pouch on the mother's body.

MEDITERRANEAN WOODLAND AND SCRUB A type of habitat found in warm temperate regions with hot dry summers and cool wet winters. As well as the Mediterranean area itself, this habitat is found in California, US, parts of Australia, and elsewhere.

METABOLISM The sum total of the biochemical processes taking place in the body.

METAMORPHOSIS Phenomenon in which an animal's body undergoes a major change in structure between the young and the adult form as in butterflies, or transforms more gradually, as in frogs. Metamorphosis occurs in many types of animals including crabs, starfish, frogs, and butterflies.

MID-OCEAN RIDGE A submerged range of mountains running along the deep-ocean floor. It is caused when tectonic plates move away from one another and new crust is created by upwelling of molten rocks from the Earth's mantle. See also *Mantle*.

MIGRATION Movements undertaken by an animal species on a regular seasonal or diurnal basis. Some migrations cover huge distances.

MIMICRY Phenomenon in which one species of animal has evolved to look very similar to another unrelated animal.

MIXED FORESTS Temperate forests in which a mixture of broadleaf and coniferous tree species grow.

MONOGAMY Situation where a male and female of a given species mate only with one other and not with other partners. The pairs thus formed may last for life or for a single season, depending on the species.

MONOTREMES The egg-laying mammals, comprising the platypus and the echidnas (spiny anteaters).

MONTANE Relating to or found in mountainous regions.

MONTANE GRASSLANDS Grassland habitats occurring high on mountains, in both tropical and temperate regions.

MORPH A physical variant of a species. Some species have several clearly defined morphs, which may differ in colour or patterning but can interbreed.

MOULTING Shedding or renewing the body covering, such as periodically replacing the feathers in birds, or shedding the exoskeleton to allow for growth in insects. A moult is any period when this happens.

MUTUALISM A close relationship between two different species in which both benefit.

N

NICHE The ecological "role" that an animal or other living thing plays. Ecological theory states that no two species can occupy exactly the same niche, because one should outcompete the other.

NOCTURNAL Active by night.

NOTOCHORD A reinforcing rod that runs the length of the body, it is the defining feature of chordates. It is present in embryonic vertebrates but later becomes incorporated into the backbone.

NYMPH An immature insect that looks similar to its parents except that it does not have functioning wings or reproductive organs. See also *Larva*.

O

OLD-GROWTH Term applied, especially in North America, to natural forests that have not been significantly altered by human activity. In Britain the equivalent term is ancient woodland.

OMNIVORE An animal whose natural diet includes a wide variety of animal and vegetable food.

OPERCULUM A cover or lid. In many snails, an operculum on the back of the foot is used to seal the shell when the animal has withdrawn inside. In bony fish and larval amphibians, there is an operculum on each side of the body to protect the gill chamber.

P

PARASITE Any organism that lives on or in the body of another organism and feeds off it for an extended period. The relationship is beneficial to the parasite but not to its host.

PECTORAL FIN One of two sets of paired fins positioned on either side towards the front of a fish's body, often just behind its head. Pectoral fins are usually highly mobile and are normally used for manoeuvring and braking.

PECTORAL MUSCLES Large, paired muscles that pull the forelimbs towards the chest. In birds they are the main flight muscles.

PEDIPALPS A pair of jointed structures found near the front of the body in spiders and relatives. They have various functions including sensing the environment and as aids in reproduction, depending on the species. The large "pincers" of scorpions are pedipalps.

PENINSULA An area of land jutting out into the sea or a lake.

PERMAFROST Permanently frozen ground (technically, ground that has remained frozen for at least two years). It is characteristic of polar regions. See also *Tundra*.

PHOTOSYNTHESIS The process by which green plants and algae utilize the sun's energy, carbon dioxide, and water to produce energy-containing sugars. Oxygen is a by-product.

PHYTOPLANKTON Plant-like life-forms of the plankton that produce their own food by photosynthesis. They are mainly microscopic algae. See also *Algae, Plankton, Zooplankton*.

PLANKTON Mainly microscopic floating life-forms living in open water that cannot swim strongly (or at all) and so drift with the currents.

PLATE TECTONICS A concept that explains how the plates that make up the Earth's crust move. They are created at mid-ocean ridges and destroyed where plates collide or slide by each other.

PNEUMATOPHORE (1) An aerial root produced by some trees living in waterlogged conditions to take in the air their roots need. (2) The large gas-filled float of the Portuguese man o' war (a relative of jellyfish).

POLYGAMY The situation where members of a species (male, female, or both sexes) have multiple sexual partners.

PREDATOR An animal that hunts and eats other animals.

PREHENSILE Capable of grasping, such as the tails of some monkeys.

PREY Any animal hunted for food by another animal or trapped by a carnivorous plant.

PROBOSCIS In mammals, an elongated nose or snout, such as that of an elephant, or an elongated mouthpart for sipping liquids as seen in many butterflies.

PUFFBALLS Fungi that produce globular fruiting bodies, which release spores in a dust-like cloud when they rupture.

PUNA GRASSLAND An ecoregion of the montane grasslands in the Andes mountains of South America.

PUP A name for the young of many animals, including sharks and seals as well as (more obviously) dogs.

PUPA In many insects such as flies and moths, a stage in which the larval body is broken down and rebuilt as an adult. See also *Larva*.

R

RANGE (1) The geographical distribution of a particular species. (2) The "home range" of an individual animal is the area within which it normally forages, which may or may not also be a territory. See also *Territory*. (3) In geology, a term applied to a mountain belt.

RAPTOR A bird of prey.

RUMINANT Cloven-hoofed mammals, such as antelope and sheep, that have a specialized digestive system with a compartmented stomach. The first compartment, the rumen, contains microorganisms that help break down tough plant food. It is also regurgitated and rechewed, a process called ruminating or "chewing the cud".

RUT The breeding season of deer. Also called the rutting season, it is marked by intense rivalry between males for mates. It often involves roaring ("rut" is an old word for roar) and displaying. Equally matched males fight.

S

SALINE Of water, springs, or lakes: having a high concentration of dissolved salts.

SAVANNA A general term for all tropical grasslands. Most savannas also have scattered trees.

SCUTES Shield-like plates or scales that form a hard covering on some animals.

SEAMOUNT An undersea mountain, usually formed from an extinct volcano.

SEXUAL DIMORPHISM Condition in which the males and females of a species differ obviously in appearance (for example, in colour pattern, shape, or size).

SHIELD In geology, any large stable region of ancient rocks that has not been altered by mountain-building in recent geological history. Shield regions are usually relatively flat and form the central parts of most continents.

SPAWN The eggs of fish, amphibians, and marine invertebrates, especially when laid as a large mass. "To spawn" is to lay such eggs.

SPECIATION The formation of new species.

SPECIES A species is the basic unit of biological classification. It is a group of organisms that are similar in appearance and behaviour, usually breed only with each other, and differ in some way from other similar species.

SPERMATOPHORE A packet of sperm that is transferred either directly from the male to the female, or indirectly – for example, by being left on the ground. Spermatophores are produced by a range of animals, including squid, salamanders, and some insects.

STOOP Of a bird of prey: to swoop down swiftly on its target prey.

STRATIFIED GRAZING The different feeding levels (grasses, bushes, trees) and different parts and ages of plants (new shoots, older plants) eaten by various grazers and browsers in the same area.

STRIDULATE Of insects such as grasshoppers: to make a shrill or grating noise by rubbing modified parts of the body against one another. Some tarantula spiders and venomous snakes also stridulate.

STROBILURIN Any of several related chemical compounds used in agriculture to kill fungi.

SUBDUCTION The sinking of one tectonic plate beneath another when the two plates collide. See *Plate tectonics* and *Mid-ocean ridge*.

SUBTROPICAL DRY BROADLEAF FORESTS Forests in warm subtropical regions where frost is still occasionally possible and where there is a long dry season, during which trees may shed their leaves.

SYMBIOTIC RELATIONSHIP A close living, relatively long-term relationship between two species. See also *Mutualism, Parasite*.

T

TAIGA Another term for boreal forest, though sometimes used just for the northern part of this, nearest the tundra.

TECTONIC PLATE Any of the large, rigid sections into which the Earth's surface is divided, such as the Pacific Plate.

TEMPERATE Relating to the regions of the Earth between the tropics and the polar regions.

TEMPERATE BROADLEAF FORESTS Forests in temperate regions that are dominated by broadleaf tree species.

TEMPERATE CONIFEROUS FORESTS Evergreen forests, often dominated by conifers, that occur in temperate regions with warm summers, cold winters, and typically plentiful rainfall.

TERRITORY A particular area or section of habitat defended by an animal or group of animals against rivals, usually of the same species. See also *Range*.

TROPICAL Relating to the warm regions of the Earth that lie between the Equator and the tropics of Cancer (to the north) and Capricorn (to the south).

TROPICAL DRY BROADLEAF FORESTS Tropical broadleaf forests growing in regions with a long dry season.

TROPICAL MOIST BROADLEAF FORESTS Tropical forests dominated by broadleaved trees and characterized by high rainfall and no long dry season.

TUNDRA A treeless habitat of low-growing, cold-tolerant plants widespread in the far north of North America, Russia, and the Antarctic peninsula. A similar habitat (alpine tundra) is found high on some mountain ranges as well.

TUSK In mammals, an enlarged modified tooth that often projects outside the mouth.

TYPHOON A tropical cyclone, especially in Pacific regions (equivalent to a hurricane in the Atlantic).

U

ULTRAVIOLET RADIATION Radiation of shorter wavelength than the light visible to humans, which other animals may be able to see.

UMBRELLA SPECIES A species whose protection and conservation has the side effect of protecting threatened habitats where it lives, and the other animals and plants that live there.

UNGULATE A hoofed mammal.

V

VASCULAR PLANT Any plant with specialized tissues for transporting water and nutrients between its different parts. Most land plants except for mosses and their relatives are vascular plants.

VENOM Any toxic fluid produced by an animal that is actively transferred into the body of another. Venomous animals commonly deliver their venom via fangs, stings, or similar structures.

VENTRAL Relating to the lower surface or belly of an animal.

VERTEBRATE Any animal with a backbone (fish, amphibians, reptiles, birds, and mammals). See also *Chordate, Invertebrate*.

VIVIPAROUS Giving birth to live young, rather than laying eggs.

W

WARNING COLORATION Striking colours on an animal designed to warn potential predators that it is poisonous or otherwise dangerous.

WEANING The period of adjustment in young mammals' lives when they start taking solid food rather than relying on their mother's milk.

WORLD HERITAGE SITE A site designated by the United Nations Educational, Scientific, and Cultural Organization (UNESCO) as being of world importance either for cultural reasons (such as historic city centres) or for aspects of its natural heritage, such as its natural beauty, conservation value, or geological interest.

Y

YUNGAS The varied and biodiverse warm, moist broadleaf forests on the eastern side of the Andes mountains.

Z

ZOOPLANKTON Animals such as krill that are part of the plankton. See *Plankton*.

ZYGOMATIC ARCH Bony arch under the eye socket on each side of the face.

The IUCN (International Union for the Conservation of Nature) is the leading source of information on the conservation and status of animal and plant species. Scientists and organizations collect data on a species' population size, rate of habitat fragmentation and decline, and the IUCN assess the risk for each species using this information.

INDEX

Page numbers in **bold** refer to
main entries.

A

aardvark 228, **229**
Abyssinian roller 207
acacia 178, 193, 320, 334
    camel thorn 228
    whistling 192
Acinonyx jubatus **196–97**
Actophilornis africanus **224**
adders
    common **145**
    desert death 328
Adelie penguin **372**
Aepyceros melampus **197**
Africa 14, **174–243**
    Congo Basin **208–17**
    Ethiopian Highlands **178–83**
    Great Rift Valley lakes **184–91**
    Kalahari Desert **228–35**
    Madagascan dry forest **236–43**
    Okavango Delta **218–27**
    Serengeti savannas **192–207**
African bullfrog 229
African cherry 208
African clawless otter 184
African darter 70
African jacana **224**
African plate 176
African Rift Valley 188
African savanna elephant 15, **202–03**
African skimmer **226**
African wild dog 192, **224–25**
Agalychnis callidryas **82–83**
aggressive mimicry 301
agouti 90
Ailuropoda melanoleuca **274–75**
Ailurus fulgens **270**
Aix galericulata **290**
Alaska 76
    Arctic fox 27
    bald eagle 43
    grizzly bear 36
albatrosses 364
    wandering **366–67**
    waved **125**
Alberta 72
Albert's lyrebird 334
Alces alces **38–39**
Alectoris melanocephala **253**
Aleutian Islands 22
algae 19
    Antarctica 362, 370
Alladale Wilderness Reserve 140
alligator, American 66, **72–73**, 107
Alligator mississippiensis **72–73**
Alopex lagopus **27**
Alouatta arctoidea 92
Alouatta seniculus **92–93**
alpha males
    grey wolf 37
    Japanese macaque 287
alpine black swallowtail **291**

alpine chamois **159**
alpine chipmunk 52, **56**
alpine marmot **160**
alpine meadow 11, 14
    Alps **158–59**
    Eastern Himalayas **266–67**
    Yellowstone **34–35**
alpine swift 146
alpine tundra 17
Alps, Australian 334
Alps, European 10, 11, 132, 133, **158–63**
Alps, New Zealand 313
altiplano, Andean **108–13**
altitude 11, 14, 18
    Andean altiplano 108
    Andean yungas 84
    Arabian Highlands 248
    Bornean rainforest 292
    Ethiopian Highlands 178
    Kalahari Desert 228
    New Guinea montane forest
        314
    Sierra Nevada 52
Alto Tajo Natural Park 152
Alytes obstetricans **162**
Amazon rainforest 76, 84, **90–99**, 102
amber snail 354–55
Amblyrhynchus cristatus **128–29**
American alligator 66, **72–73**, 107
American beaver 34, **41**, 52
American bison 34, 44, **46–47**
American black bear 34, 52, **54–55**
American buffalo **46–47**
American crocodile 66
American pika **40**, 52
American red swamp crayfish 146, 184
amphibians *see* frogs; newts; salamanders;
    toads
Amphiprion akindynos **351**
Amur tiger 261
anaconda, green **105**
Andean cock-of-the-rock **89**
Andean condor **112–13**
Andean flamingo 77, 108
Andean flicker **111**
Andean fox 109
Andes 76, 87, 110
    Andean altiplano **108–13**
    Andean yungas **84–89**
Andrias japonicus **291**
anemonefish, Barrier Reef **351**
anhinga **70–71**
Anhinga anhinga **70–71**
Antarctic Circumpolar Current 362
Antarctic Convergence 364
Antarctic hair grass 362
Antarctic ice-sheet 363
Antarctic midge 371
Antarctic pearlwort 362, 370
Antarctica 10, 18, **360–75**
    Antarctic Peninsula 363, **370–75**
    Southern Ocean islands **364–69**
anteaters
    giant **116–17**
    silky **86**
Antelope Valley 60–61
antelopes
    Arabian oryx **250–251**

blackbuck **257**
    common springbok 230
    Ethiopian klipspringer **179**
    impala **197**
    Kalahari springbok **230–31**
    pronghorn 44, **45**
    red lechwe **220–21**
    sitatunga 208
    Yarkand gazelle **279**
Anthodiaeta collaris **216**
Antidorcas hofmeyri **230–31**
Antilocapra americana **45**
Antilope cervicapra **257**
antlers
    moose 38, 39
    red muntjac 258
    reindeer 26
    western red deer 141
    western roe deer 153
    white-tailed deer 40
    see also horns
ants 229, 263, 328, 332
    Crematogaster 192
    fire 90
    leaf-cutter **98**
    spider 343
    wood 140
apes *see* primates
Aphonopelma chalcodes **65**
Apis mellifera **170–71**
Apollo butterfly **163**
Appalachians 23
apple snail 107
Aptenodytes forsteri **374–75**
Apteryx mantelli **356**
Apteryx owenii 356
aquatic environments **18–19**
    Antarctic Peninsula **370–71**
    Camargue **146–47**
    Canadian Arctic **24–25**
    Florida Everglades **66–67**
    Galapagos Islands **122–23**
    Great Barrier Reef **344–45**
    Great Rift Valley lakes **184–85**
    Norwegian Fjords **134–35**
    Okavango Delta **218–19**
    Pantanal **100–01**
    Southern Ocean islands **364–65**
    Sulu-Sulawesi Seas **302–03**
Aquila chrysaetos **162–63**
Ara macao **97**
Arabian cat snake 248–49
Arabian Highlands **248–53**
Arabian leopard 248
Arabian oryx **250–51**
Arabian partridge **253**
Arabian Peninsula 246
Arabian wolf 248, 249
Araguaia River 77
Arctic 10, 18, 22, **24–33**, 38, 137
Arctic char 33
Arctic cod 24, 25, 30
Arctic fox 24, **27**
Arctic hare 25
Arctic Ocean 16
Arctic tern 24, 369
Arctic tundra 17
    Canadian Arctic **24–25**

Ardea herodias **71**
Ardea herodias occidentalis 71
Argentina 257
    pampas **114–21**
Argentine horned frog **121**
arid painted pyrgomorph 333
armadillo, six-banded **117**
armadillo lizard **234–35**
army cutworm moth 34
Arnhem Land 312
arum, titan 293
Asia 14, **244–309**
    Arabian Highlands **248–53**
    Bornean rainforest **292–301**
    Eastern Himalayas **266–71**
    Gobi Desert **278–83**
    Nihonkai montane forest **284–91**
    Sulu-Sulawesi Seas **302–09**
    Terai-Duar savannas **254–65**
    Upper Yangtze Forests **272–77**
Asian elephant **258–59**
Asian red dog 277
Asian tiger keelback **291**
Asiatic wild buffalo 254
Asir Mountains 248
aspen 140
    quaking 35
Aspidites ramsayi **333**
ass, Mongolian wild 278–79
Atacama Desert 17, 77
Athene cunicularia **121**
Atlantic herring 134
Atlantic Ocean 22, 25, 77, 124, 346
Atlantic puffin **138–39**
Atlantic salmon **137**
Atlas moth **300**
Atlas Mountains 176
Atrax robustus **343**
Atta cephalotes **98**
Attacus atlas **300**
Auckland tree weta **359**
Australasia 263, 281, 300, 304–05,
    310–59
    East Australian forests **334–43**
    Great Barrier Reef **344–53**
    Great Sandy-Tanami Desert **328–33**
    New Guinea montane forest **314–19**
    New Zealand mixed forest **354–59**
    North Australia savannas **320–27**
Australia 13, 14
Australian Alps 334
Australian water dragon **342**
Austria 10
avocet, pied **149**
aye-aye **241**
Azura's capuchin 77

B

babbler, spiny 254
baboons
    gelada 178, **180–81**
    hamadryas **249**
    olive **185**
    savanna 180
baby animals *see* chicks; cubs; litters;

pups; young animals
bachelor herds
  Cape buffalo 220
  gelada 180
  Grant's zebra 200
  impala 197
  muskox 26
Bactrian camel 278, **280–81**
badgers
  European **165**
  honey 224
Badwater Basin 60
Badwater snail 60
Bagyeli people 209
Bahamas 23
Baja California 59
Balaeniceps rex **190**
Balaenoptera musculus **372–73**
bald cypress 66–67
bald eagle **42–43**, 52
Bale Mountains 178
Balearica pavonia 189
Balearica regulorum **189**
Bali 247
Balkans 133, 161
Bambi 153
bamboo 15, 272, 273, 275
bamboo partridge, Chinese 272
bandicoots
  greater bilby **332**
Bangladesh 261
banksia 334, 335
baobab 236
barasingha 254
Bardia National Park 254
Bargibant's pygmy seahorse **350–51**
barracuda, great **308–09**
Barrier Reef *see* Great Barrier Reef
Barrier Reef anemonefish **351**
baruwa grass 255
bats
  Honduran white **79**
  large flying fox **294**
  lesser short-tailed **355**
  little red flying fox 334
  vampire **115**
Bavarian Forest **164–73**
Bayaka people 209
beaks *see* bills and beaks
bears
  American black 34, 52, **54–55**
  brown 29, 36, 52, 279
  European brown 158
  Gobi **279**
  grizzly 34, **36**
  Kermode 55
  Louisiana black 55
  polar 24, 25, 27, **28–29**, 31
  sloth **263**
  spectacled **87**
  sun 292
beavers
  American 34, **41**, 52
  Eurasian 140
bee-eater, European **150–51**
beech trees 354
  Japanese 284
bees, European honey **170–71**
beetles 328
  Bruchid 192
  dung 193
  rosalia longicorn 158
  scarab 100
  stag **172–73**
Belarus 47

beluga 24, 29, **31**
Ben Nevis 140–41
Bengal tiger **260–61**
Bering Sea 29
berrypecker, crested **317**
Berthe's mouse lemur **237**
Bhutan 266
Bhutan takin **267**
Bialoweza Forest 47
bighorn sheep **53**
bilby, greater **332**
bills
  African skimmer 226
  Atlantic puffin 139
  bald eagle 42
  black-and-red broadbill 299
  black woodpecker 169
  duck-billed platypus 336
  flightless grebe 111
  great Indian hornbill 264
  great white pelican 189
  greater flamingo 149
  jabiru stork 103
  pied avocet 149
  red-billed quelea 225
  red-legged seriema 120
  roseate spoonbill 104
  Scottish crossbill 143
  shoebill 190
  toco toucan 96–97
biodiversity
  Australia 321
  Bornean rainforest 292
  Costa Rican rainforest 78
  Great Barrier Reef 344
  New Guinea 314
  Nihonkai montane forest 284
  Sulu-Sulawesi Seas 302
birch trees 140
birdeater, Goliath **99**
birds
  Adelie penguin **373**
  African jacana **224**
  African skimmer **226**
  Andean cock-of-the-rock **89**
  Andean condor **112–13**
  Andean flicker **111**
  anhinga **70–71**
  Antarctic tern **369**
  Arabian partridge **253**
  Atlantic puffin **138–39**
  bald eagle **42–43**, 52
  black-and-red broadbill **299**
  black-capped social weaver **204–05**
  black woodpecker **169**
  blue-footed booby **125**
  blue-winged kookaburra **323**
  booted racket-tail humming bird **88**
  burrowing owl **121**
  collared sunbird **216**
  crested berrypecker **317**
  emperor penguin 370, **374–75**
  emu **322**, 356
  European bee-eater **150–51**
  flightless grebe **111**
  Galapagos penguin **124**
  golden eagle **162–63**
  golden pheasant **277**
  great blue heron **71**
  great bustard **283**
  great crested grebe **157**
  great frigatebird **124**
  great grey owl **58**
  great Indian hornbill **264**
  great white pelican **189**

greater bird-of-paradise **318–19**
greater flamingo **149**, 152
greater rhea **121**
greater roadrunner **63**
greater sage-grouse **50**
grey crowned crane **189**
helmeted guineafowl **206**
hoopoe **157**
imperial shag **369**
Indian peafowl **271**
jabiru stork **103**
kakapo 354, **356**
kea 354, **356**
king eider **137**
lammergeier **182–83**
lesser flamingo 184, **188–89**
lilac-breasted roller **207**
mandarin duck **290**
migration 76, 152, 248
mountain chickadee **56**
mute swan **148–49**
North Island brown kiwi **356**
ostrich **234**, 322
peregrine falcon **144**
pied avocet **149**
plumed whistling-duck **323**
ptarmigan **161**
purple-crowned fairy wren **323**
purple gallinule **71**
red-billed hornbill **206**
red-billed quelea **225**
red-legged seriema **120**
resplendent quetzal **81**
rockhopper penguin **368–69**
roseate spoonbill **104**
sarus crane **263**
scarlet macaw **97**
Scottish crossbill **143**
secretary bird **206**
shoebill **190**
snow goose **33**
snowy owl **33**
stork-billed kingfisher **299**
sulphur-crested cockatoo **341**
toco toucan **96–97**
turkey vulture **56–57**
wandering albatross **366–67**
waved albatross **125**
welcome swallow **355**
western capercaillie **145**
woodpecker finch **125**
yellow-billed chough **161**
birds-of-paradise
  greater **318–19**
  raggiana 319
birdwing, Rothschild's 315
birth *see* calves; chicks; cubs; eggs;
    gestation; young animals
bison
  American 34, 44, **46–47**
  European 47
  wood 47
Bison bison **46–47**
Bison bison athabascae 47
Bison bonasus 47
black-and-red broadbill **299**
black-and-white ruffed lemur 239
black-backed woodpecker 52
black bears
  American 34, 52, **54–55**
  Louisiana 55
black-capped social weaver **204–05**
black colobus 209
black crowned crane 189
black-footed ferret **48**

black-footed rock wallaby 328
black-headed bullmaster viper 79
black mamba **207**
black noddy 344
black rhinoceros 193, 222, 223
Black Sea 135
black swallowtail, Alpine **291**
black-tailed jackrabbit **63**
black-tailed prairie dog **48**
black vulture 152
black woodpecker **169**
blackbuck **257**
blackfin icefish 370–371
blanket bogs 140
blazing star 14
blistered grasshopper **333**
blood suckers, vampire bat 115
blood vessels, blue whale 372
blubber
  beluga 31
  grey seal 135
  walrus 32
blue damselfly **359**
blue-footed booby **125**
Blue Mountains 334
Blue Ridge Mountains 23
blue-ringed octopus, greater **352**
blue sheep, Himalayan 266
blue whale 19, 364, **372–73**
blue-winged kookaburra **323**
boar, wild 164, **169**, 261
boas
  emerald tree **97**
  green anaconda **105**
bobcat **37**, 69
Bogoria, Lake 184
bogs, blanket 140
Bohemian Forest 164
Bolbometopon muricatum **309**
bonobo 208, 210
boobies 124
  blue-footed **125**
booted eagle 152
booted racket-tail humming bird **88**
boreal forest 12, 16
  North America 22
boreal owl 164
Bornean orangutan **296–97**
Bornean rainforest **292–301**
Borneo 247, 298
Bos gaurus **257**
Botswana
  Okavango Delta **218–27**
Bouvet Island 364
bowerbirds 313
  Vogelkop 314
bowhead whale 24
box turtle, ornate 44
boxer crab **309**
Brahmaputra River 266
brain *see* intelligence
brain coral 344
Brazil
  Pantanal **100–07**
breaching, killer whale 137
breathing
  Alpine marmot 160
  ensatina 59
  green sea turtle 346
  Japanese giant salamander 291
breeding *see* captive breeding; courtship;
    eggs; gestation; mating; young animals
Britain 133
  Scottish Highlands **140–45**
British Columbia 37

Brittany 133
broadbill, black-and-red **299**
broadleaf evergreen forest 12, 13
   Upper Yangtze Forests **272–73**
brown bears 29, 36, 52, 158, 279
Bruchid beetle 192
brushtail possum 354
bubble rings, beluga 31
Buceros bicornis **264**
budgerigars 328–29
Budorcas whitei **267**
buffalos
   American **46–47**
   Asiatic wild 254
   Cape 192, 193, **220**
bull shark 66
bullfrog, African 229
bullmaster viper, black-headed 79
Bunaken National Park 302
Burmese python 67
burrowing owl **121**
burrows and tunnels
   Alpine marmot 160
   Andean flicker 111
   Arctic fox 27
   Auckland tree weta 358
   black-footed ferret 48
   black-tailed prairie dog 48
   burrowing owl 121
   common wombat 337
   Couch's spadefoot 64
   desert blond tarantula 65
   duck-billed platypus 336
   greater bilby 332
   kit fox 61
   meerkat 232
   North Island brown kiwi 356
   Patagonian mara 117
   six-banded armadillo 117
   thorny devil 332
   tuatara 358
bush-quail, Manipur 254
bushy-crested hornbill 293
bustard, great **283**
butterflies 78, 315
   Alpine black swallowtail **291**
   Apollo **163**
   common morpho **81**
   crimson longwing **89**
   monarch **51**
   see also moths

C

Cacatua galerita **341**
cactus
   lava 122–23
   prickly pear 44
   saguaro 17
cactus finch 122
caecum, koala 339
Caiman crocodilus 107
Caiman yacare **106–07**
caimans
   spectacled 107
   Yacare **106–07**
Cairngorms 140
California 13, 15, 22, 51
   Mojave Desert **60–65**
   Sierra Nevada **52–59**
Calliteara pudibunda **170**
calls *see* communication
calves

Arabian oryx 250
   giraffe 199
   Kalahari springbok 230
   moose 39
   red lechwe 221
   wildebeest 198
Camargue **146–51**
Camargue horse **147**
Camarhynchus pallidus **125**
camel thorn acacia 228
camels 328
   Bactrian 278, **280–81**
   dromedary 281
Camelus bactrianus **280–81**
camouflage
   Argentine horned frog 121
   Bargibant's pygmy seahorse 350
   bobcat 37
   common flying dragon 298
   common snapping turtle 72
   Denise's pygmy seahorse 350
   emerald tree boa 97
   frilled lizard 325
   green anaconda 105
   Henkel's leaf-tailed gecko 243
   Himalayan blue sheep 266
   jaguar 95
   Macleay's spectre 343
   Malaysian orchid mantis 301
   mountain tapir 85
   ocelot 80
   panther chameleon 242
   ptarmigan 161
   red-eyed tree frog 82
   snow leopard 269
   striped scorpion 50
   thorny devil 332
Canada
   Canadian Arctic **24–33**
Canadian Shield 22
"canaries of the sea" 31
cane toad 91
Canis latrans **49**
Canis lupus **37**
Canis lupus dingo **321**
Canis lupus irremotus 37
Canis simensis **182**
cannibalism, tuatara 358
Cape buffalo 192, 193, **220**
Cape cobra **234**
Cape Floristic Region, South Africa 177
Cape porcupine **231**
capercaillie 164
   western **145**
Capra pyrenaica **153**
Capreolus capreolus **153**
Capricornis crispus **285**
captive breeding
   Arabian oryx 250
   gharial 265
   Iberian lynx 154
   Przewalski's wild horse 282
capuchins
   Azura's 77
   hooded **102**
capybara **101**
caracal **229**, 248
Caracal caracal **229**
Cariama cristata **120**
Caribbean 13, 22, 76
caribou 38
   Peary 26
   see also reindeer
carnivorous plants 292
carp, common 184

Caspian Sea 133
cassowary 322, 356
Castor canadensis **41**
cat snake, Arabian 248–49
catbird 313
caterpillars
   Apollo butterfly 163
   monarch butterfly 51
   pale tussock 170
Cathartes aura **56–57**
cats
   Bengal tiger **260–61**
   caracal **229**
   cheetah 193, **196–97**
   feral 320
   Iberian lynx **154–55**
   Indochinese clouded leopard 254, **276**
   jaguar 87, **94–95**, 107
   leopard 95, 193, 199, **214**, 254
   lion 15, 193, **194–95**, 199
   ocelot **80–81**
   panther 95
   puma 62, 66, 69, 87
   snow leopard 266, **268–69**
   wildcat **143**, 164
cattle
   Camargue 146, 147
   gaur **257**
Caucasus Mountains 133
cave salamander 133
caves, limestone 133
cavy 117
Cebuella pygmaea **92**
Central and South America **74–129**
   Amazon rainforest **90–99**
   Andean altiplano **108–13**
   Andean yungas **84–89**
   Argentine pampas **114–21**
   Costa Rican rainforest **78–83**
   Galapagos Islands **122–29**
   Pantanal **100–07**
Central Great Plains **44–51**
Centrocercus urophasianus **50**
Centruroides vittatus **50**
Cephalopachus bancanus **294**
Ceratophrys ornata **121**
Ceratotherium simum **222–23**
Cervus elaphus **141**
Chad, Lake 176
chameleons 236
   dwarf 236–37
   panther **242–43**
chamois, Alpine **159**
chaparral 15
   see also scrub
Chapman's zebra 200
char, Arctic **33**
characin 103
Chari River 176
cheetah 193, **196–97**
Chelonia mydas **346–47**
Chelonoidis nigra **126–27**
Chelydra serpentina **72**
Chen caerulescens **33**
Chengdu 272
cherry trees
   African 208
   Japanese 284–85
chickadee, mountain **56**
chicks
   African jacana 224
   Andean condor 112
   anhinga 70
   Atlantic puffin 139
   bald eagle 42

blue-footed booby 125
blue-winged kookaburra 323
crested berrypecker 317
emperor penguin 375
European bee-eater 150
golden eagle 162
great blue heron 71
greater sage-grouse 50
grey crowned crane 189
lesser flamingo 188
purple gallinule 71
rockhopper penguin 368
roseate spoonbill 104
Scottish crossbill 143
toco toucan 96
turkey vulture 56
Chile 113
Chilean flamingo 108
chimpanzees 208, **210–11**
   pygmy 208, 210
China 247
   Gobi Desert **272–83**
   Upper Yangtze Forests **272–77**
chinchilla, long-tailed 109
Chinese bamboo partridge 272
Chinese giant salamander 291
Chinese green tree viper 272–73
Chinook salmon 52–53
chipmunk, Alpine 52, **56**
chital 261
Chitwan National Park 254
Chlamydosaurus kingii **324–25**
Chlorocebus pygerythrus **201**
Choloepus hoffmanni **79**
chough, yellow-billed **161**
chromodoris, Loch's 302
Chrysocyon brachyurus **118–19**
Chrysolophus pictus **277**
Churchill, Canada 29
cicadas 328
cichlids 176, 185
   zebra mbuna 191
clam, giant **352**
clans, meerkat 232
Clark's nutcracker 34
clawless otter, African 184
claws
   giant anteater 116
   peacock mantis shrimp 351
   silky anteater 86
   see also pincers
climate 10, 14
   Alps 159
   Amazon rainforest 91
   Andean altiplano 109
   Andean yungas 84, 85
   Antarctica 363, 370, 371
   Arabian Highlands 248, 249
   Argentine pampas 115
   Asia 246
   Australasia 313
   Bavarian Forest 164, 165
   Bornean rainforest 293
   Camargue 147
   Canadian Arctic 25
   Central Great Plains 45
   Congo Basin 209
   East Australian forests 334, 335
   Ethiopian Highlands 179
   Europe 133
   Florida Everglades 67
   forests 12-13
   Galapagos Islands 123
   Gobi Desert 278, 279
   Great Barrier Reef 345

Great Rift Valley lakes 185
Great Sandy-Tanami Desert 329
Kalahari Desert 228, 229
Madagascan dry forest 237
Mojave Desert 60
monsoon 246
New Guinea montane forest 314, 315
New Zealand mixed forest 354, 355
Nihonkai montane forest 285
North America 22
North Australia savannas 321
Norwegian fjords 135
Okavango Delta 219
Pantanal 101
Serengeti savannas 193
Sierra Nevada 52, 53
Southern Ocean islands 365
Sulu-Sulawesi Seas 302, 303
Tagus Valley 153
Terai-Duar savannas 254
Upper Yangtze Forests 272
Yellowstone 35
climate change
    Arctic 25
    Eastern Himalayas 266
    Great Barrier Reef 344, 345
    paddy fields 255
climbing
    American black bear 55
    Bornean orangutan 297
    coati 86
    Goodfellow's tree kangaroo 317
    Iberian ibex 153
    Indochinese clouded leopard 276
    ocelot 80
    silky anteater 86
cloud forests 13
    Andean yungas **84–85**
    Costa Rican rainforest 78
clouded leopard, Indochinese 254, **276**
clownfish 351
coastal desert 17
coat
    Alpine chamois 159
    American bison 47
    Amur tiger 261
    Arctic fox 27
    Bactrian camel 281
    Bengal tiger 261
    Eurasian otter 167
    Eurasian red squirrel 142
    giant panda 275
    giraffe 199
    golden langur 267
    grizzly bear 36
    Indochinese clouded leopard 276
    jaguar 95
    Japanese macaque 287
    Japanese serow 285
    kit fox 61
    koala 339
    leopard 214
    muskox 26
    polar bear 29
    puma 62
    snow leopard 269
    vicuña 110
    western red deer 141
    wild yak 266
    see also fur
coati **86**
cobras 206, 262–63
    Cape **234**
    Indian **264**
    king 207

coca bush 84
cock-of-the-rock, Andean **89**
cockatoo, sulphur-crested **341**
cocoons, stag beetle 172
cod
    Arctic 24, 25, 30
    polar 30
coelacanth, Sulawesi 302–03
Colaptes rupicola **111**
cold conditions
    Amur tiger 261
    Arctic fox 27
    emperor penguin 375
    see also Antarctica; Arctic
cold desert 17
    Gobi Desert **278–79**
collared sunbird **216**
colobus, black 209
colonies
    American beaver 41
    anhinga 70
    Atlantic puffin 139
    black-capped social weaver 204–05
    emperor penguin 375
    European bee-eater 150
    European honey bee 171
    Galapagos sea lion 123
    great blue heron 71
    great white pelican 189
    grey seal 135
    leaf-cutter ant 98
    lesser flamingo 188
    marine iguana 128–29
    pied avocet 149
    Portuguese man o' war 352
    roseate spoonbill 104
    sugar glider 316
    wandering albatross 366
    see also social groups
colour
    blue damselfly 359
    common morpho 81
    lesser flamingo 188
    marine iguana 129
    mountain kingsnake 59
    striped skunk 54
communication
    African savanna elephant 203
    American pika 40
    beluga 31
    black woodpecker 169
    blue whale 372
    blue-winged kookaburra 323
    coyote 49
    dhole 277
    emu 322
    European bee-eater 150
    gelada 180, 181
    giant otter 102
    golden snub-nosed monkey 273
    hippopotamus 187
    hooded capuchin 102
    impala 197
    jaguar 95
    Japanese macaque 287
    kakapo 356
    killer whale 137
    large mountain grasshopper 163
    leopard seal 372
    maned wolf 119
    mountain tapir 85
    Müller's gibbon 298
    narwhal 30
    northern grey fox 67
    okapi 216

ostrich 234
peacock mantis shrimp 351
raccoon dog 289
red howler monkey 93
red-legged seriema 120
red panda 270
scarlet macaw 97
spinner dolphin 303
stork-billed kingfisher 299
Verreaux's sifaka 240
vervet monkey 201
walrus 32
condor, Andean **112–13**
Congo Basin **208–17**
Congo River 176, 208, 209
coniferous forests 12
    Europe 133
    New Zealand mixed forest 354
    Sierra Nevada 52
    Yellowstone 34
Connochaetes mearnsi **198**
conservation see endangered species
Coquerel's sifaka 241
coral, brain 344
coral reefs 19, 309, 350
    Great Barrier Reef **344–53**
    Norwegian fjords 134, 135
    Sulu-Sulawesi Seas 302
Coral Sea 347, 351
Coral Triangle 302
Corallus caninus **97**
cork oak 13, 153
cormorants 70, 125, 369
    flightless 122
Costa Rican rainforest 76, **78–83**
coteries, black-tailed prairie dog 48
couch grass 192
Couch's spadefoot **64**
cougar **62**
courtship
    American alligator 72
    black-capped social weaver 204–05
    blue-footed booby 125
    golden eagle 162
    golden pheasant 277
    great crested grebe 157
    great crested newt 170
    greater bird-of-paradise 319
    green jumping spider 326
    king eider 137
    red-eyed tree frog 82
    rockhopper penguin 368
    roseate spoonbill 104
    Scottish crossbill 143
    waved albatross 125
coyote 40, **49**, 69
crabeater seal 364–65
crabs
    boxer **309**
    guard 345
    Sally Lightfoot 122
cranes
    black crowned 189
    grey crowned **189**
    sarus **263**
crayfish, American red swamp
    146, 184
crèches
    lesser flamingo 188
    rockhopper penguin 368
Crematogaster ants 192
crested berrypecker **317**
crickets
    Auckland tree weta **358**
    see also grasshoppers

crimson longwing **89**
crocodiles
    American 66
    Nile **190–91**, 198
    saltwater 191
Crocodylus niloticus **190–91**
Crocodylus porosus 191
Crocuta crocuta 253
Cromwell Current 124
"crop milk", lesser flamingo
    188
crossbills
    common 143
    parrot 143
    Scottish **143**
Crotalus scutulatus **64**
crown-of-thorns starfish 344
crows
    Clark's nutcracker 34
    yellow-billed chough **161**
Cryptoprocta ferox **237**
cubs
    American black bear 55
    Bengal tiger 261
    bobcat 37
    giant panda 275
    grizzly bear 36
    Iberian lynx 154
    jaguar 95
    leopard 214
    ocelot 80
    polar bear 29
    puma 62
    red fox 168
    sloth bear 263
    spectacled bear 87
    striped hyena 252
cuckoo family
    greater roadrunner **63**
culpeo **109**
Cuon alpinus **277**
cuscus, common spotted **315**
cutthroat trout 35
cutworm moth, army 34
Cyclopes didactylus **86**
cygnets, mute swan 148, 149
Cygnus olor **148–49**
Cymbirhynchus macrorhynchos
    299
Cynomys ludovicianus **48**
cypress swamps 66–67
Czech Republic 164

D

Daba Mountains 272
Dacelo leachii **323**
dams, American beaver 41
damselfly, blue **359**
Danaus plexippus **51**
dances
    blue-footed booby 125
    emperor scorpion 216, 217
    European honey bee 171
    great crested grebe 157
    greater bird-of-paradise 319
    roseate spoonbill 104
    Verreaux's sifaka 241
    see also displays
Danube, River 164
darter, African 70
Darwin, Charles 122, 300
dasyure, speckled 314–15

Dasyurus maculatus **341**
Daubentonia madagascariensis **241**
dawn redwood 272
DDT 144
dead-leaf toad 84
Dean's Blue Hole 23
desert death adder 328
Death Valley 60
deciduous forest 12
　Bavarian Forest **164–165**
　Nihonkai montane forest **284–85**
deciduous trees 133, 284
deer 145, 254
　barasingha 254
　moose **38–39**
　northern pudu 85
　pampas 114
　red muntjac **258**
　sika 284
　western red **141**
　western roe **153**, 164
　white-tailed **40**, 153
defences
　armadillo lizard 234–35
　boxer crab 309
　Cape cobra 234
　Cape porcupine 231
　common pangolin 215
　Goliath birdeater 99
　jewelled lizard 157
　Macleay's spectre 343
　mandarinfish 305
　meerkat 232, 233
　monarch butterfly 51
　Nile monitor 227
　Portuguese man o' war 352
　striped skunk 54
　thorny devil 332
　tomato frog 243
　yellow-legged frog 59
Delphinapterus leucas **31**
deltas
　Camargue **146–47**
　Nile 176
　Okavango **218–19**
Dendroaspis polylepis **207**
Dendrobates tinctorius **98**
Dendrocygna eytoni **323**
Dendrolagus goodfellowi **317**
Denise's pygmy seahorse 350
dens
　coyote 49
　Gila monster 64
　grizzly bear 36
　Iberian lynx 154
　northern raccoon 69
　polar bear 28, 29
desert blond tarantula **65**
desert tortoise 60
deserts 10
　Australia 312
　Gobi Desert **278–79**
　Great Sandy-Tanami Desert
　　328–33
　Kalahari Desert **228–29**
　Mojave Desert **60–61**
　North America 22
Desmodus rotundus **115**
dexterity
　Bornean orangutan 297
　northern raccoon 69
　see also tool users
dhole **277**
Diceros bicornis **223**
digestive system

American bison 47
　giant panda 275
　koala 339
　sloths 79
　Terai sacred langur 259
dingo **321**, 322, 337
Diomedea exulans **366–67**
Disney, Walt 153
displays
　Andean cock-of-the-rock 89
　anhinga 70
　Australian water dragon 342
　booted racket-tail humming bird 88
　common flying dragon 298
　Fabian's lizard 113
　frilled lizard 324–25
　gharial 265
　golden eagle 162
　golden pheasant 277
　great bustard 283
　great frigatebird 124
　greater bird-of-paradise 319
　greater sage-grouse 50
　grey crowned crane 189
　Indian peafowl 271
　jabiru stork 103
　king eider 137
　ostrich 234
　panther chameleon 242
　red-legged seriema 120
　roseate spoonbill 104
　sarus crane 263
　wandering albatross 367
　western capercaillie 145
　western gorilla 212, 213
　see also dances
diving
　Atlantic puffin 139
　dugong 304
　emperor penguin 375
　Eurasian otter 167
　grey seal 135
　imperial shag 369
　king eider 137
　marine iguana 129
　narwhal 30
　southern elephant seal 365
Doberai Peninsula 314, 315
Dolichotis patagonum **117**
dolphins 187
　hourglass **372**
　Irrawaddy 302
　killer whale **136–37**, 372
　pink river 91
　spinner **303**
　tucuxi 91
domestication, American bison 47
donkeys, feral 328
dormouse, hazel 164
Douglas fir 140
Douglas squirrel 53
Draco volans **298–99**
dragonflies 19, 146
　blue damselfly **359**
　Ethiopian highlander 178–79
Drakensburg Mountains 176
dreys, Eurasian red squirrel 142
Dromaius novaehollandiae **322**
dromedary 281
droughts
　Gobi Desert 278
　Great Sandy-Tanami Desert 328
　Kalahari Desert 228
　Mojave Desert 60
dry desert 17

Arabian Highlands **248–49**
　Great Sandy-Tanami Desert **328–29**
　Kalahari Desert **228–29**
　Mojave Desert **60–61**
dry forest, Madagascan **236–37**
Dryocopus martius **169**
duck-billed platypus 334, **336–37**
ducks
　king eider **137**
　mandarin **290**
　plumed whistling-duck **323**
dugong 302, 303, **304–05**, 312
Dugong dugon **304–05**
dung beetle 193
"dung-spinning", hippopotamus 187
dunnart, fat-tailed **329**
dusky grass wren 328
Dust Bowl, North America 44
dwarf chameleon 236–37
dwarf hamster 278
dwarf minke whale 345
dyeing poison frog **98**
Dyscophus antongilii **243**

E

eagle owl 58, 152, 164
eagles 188
　bald **42–43**, 52
　booted 152
　fish 43
　golden **162–63**
　harpy 76, 78, 86, 93
　Iberian imperial 152–53
　Steller's sea 43
　wedge-tailed 322, 328
　white-tailed 43
eared seals 123
ears and hearing 15
　African savanna elephant 203
　black-tailed jackrabbit 63
　caracal 229
　Galapagos sea lion 123
　great grey owl 58
　greater bilby 332
　Iberian lynx 154
　kit fox 61
earthquakes, New Guinea 314
East African Rift 176
East Australian forests **334–43**
Eastern Himalayas **266–71**
echidnas 314, 336
　long-beaked **315**
　short-beaked 334
echolocation
　bats 294
　hourglass dolphin 372
　spinner dolphin 303
ecoregions
　Alps **158–59**
　Amazon rainforest **90–91**
　Andean altiplano **108–09**
　Andean yungas **84–85**
　Antarctic Peninsula **370–71**
　Antarctica **362–63**
　aquatic **18–19**
　Arabian Highlands **248–49**
　Argentine pampas **114–15**
　Bavarian Forest **164–65**
　Bornean rainforest **292–93**
　Camargue **146–47**
　Canadian Arctic **24–25**
　Central Great Plains **44–45**

Congo Basin **208–09**
　Costa Rican rainforest **78–79**
　East Australian forests **334–35**
　Eastern Himalayas **266–67**
　Ethiopian Highlands **178–79**
　Florida Everglades **66–67**
　Galapagos Islands **122–23**
　Gobi Desert **278–79**
　Great Barrier Reef **344–45**
　Great Rift Valley lakes **184–85**
　Great Sandy-Tanami Desert **328–29**
　Kalahari Desert **228–29**
　Madagascan dry forest **236–37**
　Mojave Desert **60–61**
　New Guinea montane forest **314–15**
　New Zealand mixed forest **354–55**
　Nihonkai montane forest **284–85**
　North Australia savannas **320–21**
　Norwegian fjords **134–35**
　Okavango Delta **218–19**
　Pantanal **100–01**
　Scottish Highlands **140–41**
　Serengeti savannas **192–93**
　Sierra Nevada **52–53**
　Southern Ocean islands **364–65**
　Sulu-Sulawesi Seas **302–03**
　Tagus Valley **152–53**
　Terai-Duar savannas **254–55**
　Upper Yangtze Forests **272–73**
　Yellowstone **34–35**
Ectophylla alba **79**
Ecuador 125
edelweiss 11, 158
eel, European 147
egg tooth, great grey owl 58
eggs
　African jacana 224
　Andean condor 112
　anhinga 70
　Atlantic puffin 139
　Couch's spadefoot 64
　desert blond tarantula 65
　duck-billed platypus 336
　dyeing poison frog 98
　emperor penguin 375
　ensatina 59
　European bee-eater 150
　frilled lizard 325
　Galapagos penguin 124
　Galapagos tortoise 127
　Gila monster 65
　golden tegu 105
　greater rhea 121
　green sea turtle 346
　Indian cobra 264
　Japanese giant salamander 291
　leopard tortoise 226
　lesser flamingo 188
　Macleay's spectre 343
　midwife toad 162
　Nile monitor 226
　North Island brown kiwi 356
　ocean sunfish 347
　panther chameleon 242
　red-eyed tree frog 83
　resplendent quetzal 81
　rockhopper penguin 368
　Sydney funnelweb spider 343
　tuatara 358
　whale shark 306
　Yacare caiman 107
　zebra mbuna 191
egrets 146
　little 152
Egyptian vulture 254

eider
common 24
king **137**
Elbe, River 164
electroreceptors
duck-billed platypus 336
long-beaked echidna 315
ribbontail stingray 304
scalloped hammerhead shark 349
Elementalia, Lake 184
elephants 67, 192, 193, 304
African savanna 15, **202–03**
Asian **258–59**
forest 208, 209
elephant grass 15
elephant seal, southern **365**
elephant shrew 182
elephantfish 209
Elephantulus rufescens **182**
Elephas maximus **258–59**
elk 39
emerald tree boa **97**
emperor penguin 370, **374–75**
emperor scorpion **216–17**
emperor tamarin **92**
Empty Quarter, Arabian Peninsula 248
emu **322**, 356
Emydocephalus annulatus **347**
endangered species
Arabian oryx 250
barasingha 254
Bornean orangutan 297
Eurasian beaver 140
fisher 52
gharial 265
giant panda 275
Gobi bear 279
golden langur 267
grey crowned crane 189
Iberian lynx 154
Indian rhinoceros 256
koala 339
Louisiana black bear 55
mountain tapir 85
pampas deer 114
Przewalski's wild horse 282
Sunda pangolin 293
Endangered Species Act (US) 55
ensatina **59**
Ensatina eschscholtzii **59**
Equus caballus **147**
Equus przewalskii **282–83**
Equus quagga boehmi **200**
Equus quagga chapmani 200
Erinaceus europaeus **156**
Ethiopia 180
Ethiopian highlander **178–79**
Ethiopian Highlands **178–83**
Ethiopian klipspringer **179**
Ethiopian wolf 178, **182**
Etosha Pan 188
eucalypts 13, 152, 306, 320, 334, 339
Eudyptes chrysocome **368–69**
Eunectes murinus **105**
Euphorbia ammak 248
Euphractus sexcinctus **117**
Eurasia 43, 114
Eurasian beaver 140
Eurasian eagle owl 11
Eurasian lynx 158, 164–65
Eurasian otter **166–67**
Eurasian plate 176, 247
Eurasian red squirrel **142**
Europe 10, 14, **130–73**
Alps **158–63**

Bavarian Forest **164–73**
Camargue **146–51**
Norwegian fjords **134–39**
Scottish Highlands **140–45**
Tagus Valley **152–57**
European badger **165**
European bee-eater **150–51**
European bison 47
European brown bear 158
European eel 147
European hedgehog **156**
European honey bee **170–71**
European pine marten **165**
European tree frog 152
European whitefish 159
Everglades, Florida **66–73**
evolution, theory of 122
Extatosoma tiaratum **343**
Extatosoma tiaratum tiaratum 343
extreme environments **16–17**
Andean Altiplano **108–09**
Antarctic Peninsula **370–71**
Canadian Arctic **24–25**
Gobi Desert **378–79**
Great Sandy-Tanami Desert **328–29**
Kalahari Desert **228–29**
Mojave Desert **60–61**
eyes
golden eagle 162
green jumping spider 326
jaguar 95
leopard 214
panther chameleon 242
peacock mantis shrimp 351
red-eyed tree frog 82
scalloped hammerhead shark 349
southern marsupial mole 329
western tarsier 294
Yacare caiman 106

F

Fabian's lizard **113**
facial flaps, Bornean orangutan 297
fairy wren, purple-crowned **323**
Falco peregrinus **144**
falcon
grey 328
peregrine **144**
Falkland Islands 368
fangs
black mamba 207
Cape cobra 234
common adder 145
Sydney funnelweb spider 343
turtle-headed sea snake 347
see also teeth
fat-tailed dunnart **329**
feathers
booted racket-tail humming bird 88
emperor penguin 375
emu 322
golden pheasant 277
great grey owl 58
greater bird-of-paradise 319
grey crowned crane 189
Indian peafowl 271
lilac-breasted roller 207
ptarmigan 161
resplendent quetzal 81
snowy owl 33
feet
Bactrian camel 281

blue-footed booby 125
capybara 101
European pine marten 165
giant otter 103
giant panda 275
kit fox 61
koala 339
mountain tapir 85
northern raccoon 69
southern marsupial mole 329
see also hoofs
Felis silvestris 143
Felis silvestris lybica 143
feral cats 320
Fernandina Islands 124
ferns 165
ferret, black-footed **48**
fights
African wild dog 225
Alpine chamois 159
bighorn sheep 53
common adder 145
common warthog 230
emu 322
Grant's zebra 200
great bustard 283
moose 39
muskox 26
olive baboon 185
polar bear 28
Przewalski's wild horse 282
red lechwe 220
red muntjac 258
reindeer 26
southern elephant seal 365
stag beetle 172–73
vicuña 111
western red deer 141
filter feeders, whale shark 306
fin whale 364, 372
finches
cactus 122
Galapagos 123
Gouldian 321
ground 128
Scottish crossbill **143**
woodpecker **125**
fir trees
Douglas 140
red 52
white 52
fire ant 90
firefox 270
fires 35
Central Great Plains 44
Florida Everglades 66
Serengeti savannas 192, 193
firetail, painted 328
fish
Arctic char **33**
Atlantic salmon **137**
Barrier Reef anemonefish **351**
Congo Basin 208
electric eel **98**
Florida Everglades 66
great barracuda **308–09**
Great Barrier Reef 344
Great Rift Valley lakes 184
green humphead parrotfish **309**
mandarinfish **305**
ocean sunfish **347**
Okavango Delta 218
ribbontail stingray **304**
sardine 177, 302
whale shark **306–07**

zebra mbuna **191**
see also sharks
fish eagle 43
fisher 52
fishing owl, Pel's 219
Fjordland National Park, New Zealand 354
fjords, Norwegian 132, **134–39**
flamingos
Andean 108
Chilean 108
greater 146, **149**, 152
James 108
lesser 184, **188–89**
flicker, Andean **111**
flight
Andean condor 112
golden eagle 162
great bustard 283
great frigatebird 124
great white pelican 189
humming birds 88
jabiru stork 103
king eider 137
lammergeier 183
lesser flamingo 189
monarch butterfly 51
mute swan 149
peregrine falcon 144
red-legged seriema 120
scarlet macaw 97
stag beetle 172
wandering albatross 366, 367
flightless cormorant 122
flightless grebe **111**
flippers
Galapagos sea lion 123
harp seal 31
leopard seal 372
flocks
black-capped social weaver 204–05
emu 322
great white pelican 189
lesser flamingo 188
mountain chickadee 56
mute swan 148
pied avocet 149
ptarmigan 161
red-billed hornbill 206
red-billed quelea 225
scarlet macaw 97
sulphur-crested cockatoo 341
yellow-billed chough 161
see also colonies; herds; social groups
floods 10, 11
Amazon rainforest 90
Terai-Duar savannas 255
Florida 33, 43, 55, 71
Florida Bay 66
Florida Everglades **66–73**
Florida panther 66
flying dragon, common **298–99**
flying foxes
large **294**
little red 334
flying squirrel, Siberian **285**
forbs, hardy 24
forest elephant 208, 209
forests 10, **12-13**
Amazon rainforest 76, **90–91**
Andean yungas **84–85**
Bavarian Forest **164–65**
Bohemian Forest 164

boreal 12
Bornean rainforest **292–93**
broadleaf evergreen 12, 13
Congo Basin **208–09**
Costa Rican rainforest **78–79**
cloud 13
East Australian forests **334–35**
Eastern Himalayas 266
Ethiopian Highlands 178
Europe 133
Gondwana rainforest 313
Madagascan dry forest **236–37**
Mediterranean 13
montane 11, 13
New Guinea montane forest **314–15**
New Zealand mixed forest **354–55**
Nihonkai montane forest **284–85**
North America 22
Sierra Nevada 52
temperate broadleaf 12
temperate coniferous 12
tropical dry 13
tropical moist 13
Upper Yangtze Forests **272–73**
Yellowstone 34
fossa **237**, 239, 240
foxes
Andean 109
Arctic 24, **27**
culpeo **109**
kit 61
northern grey 67
red 119, 163, **168**, 321, 337
swift 45
France 10, 31, 154
Camargue **146–51**
Fratercula arctica **138–39**
Fregata minor **124**
freshwater pufferfish 209
frigatebird, great **124**
frilled lizard 320, **324–25**
frogs
African bullfrog 229
Argentine horned **121**
dyeing poison **98**
European tree 152
green tree **326**
red-eyed tree **82–83**
shrub 292
Titicaca water 108
tomato **243**
Trueb's cochran **89**
Wallace's flying **300**
wood 24
yellow-legged **59**
funnelweb spider, Sydney **343**
fur
Arctic hare 25
common spotted cuscus 315
emperor tamarin 92
golden snub-nosed monkey 273
hamadryas baboon 249
Honduran white bat 79
Iberian lynx 155
Japanese marten 289
mountain tapir 85
northern viscacha 109
ocelot 80
olive baboon 185
red panda 270
sloths 79
striped hyena 252
wolverine 38
see also coat
fur seal 364

Furcifer pardalis **242–43**
Furnace Creek 60
fynbos 177

G

Galapagos finch 123
Galapagos Islands 76, **122–29**
Galapagos penguin **124**
Galapagos tortoise **126–27**
Galapagos penguin **124**
Galapagos sea lion **123**
gallinule, purple **71**
Ganges River 266
gannet 125, 369
garter snake, common **50**
gaur **257**, 261
Gavialis gangeticus **264–65**
Gazella yarkandensis **279**
gazelles
mountain 248
Thomson's 192, 200, 224
Yarkand **279**
geckoes
Henkel's leaf-tailed **243**
knob-tailed **328**
Przewalski's wonder **283**
gelada 178, **180–81**
gemsbok 228
Geococcyx californianus **63**
geothermal features 34
gerbil, midday 278
Germany
Bavarian Forest **164–73**
gestation
American bison 47
Arabian oryx 250
bobcat 37
lion 194
olive baboon 185
polar bear 29
red howler monkey 93
red kangaroo 331
red muntjac 258
scalloped hammerhead shark 349
striped scorpion 50
geysers 34, 132
gharial **264–65**
giant anteater **116–17**
giant clam **352**
giant huntsman spider 99
giant kauri 354, 355
giant lobelia 178
giant mole rat 179
giant otter **102–03**
giant panda 272, **274–75**
giant parrot snake **105**
gibbon, Müller's **298**
Gila monster **64–65**
gills, whale shark 306
Gir Forest 194
Giraffa camelopardalis **199**
Giraffa camelopardalis tippelskirchii **199**
giraffes 192, 193, **199**, 200, 216
Masai 199
glass frogs 89
glasswort 146
gliding
common flying dragon **298–99**
Siberian flying squirrel 285
squirrel glider 335
sugar glider **316–17**, 335

Wallace's flying frog 300
glutton 38
goanna 332
goats
Iberian ibex 153
Gobi bear **279**
Gobi Desert **278–83**
goby 345
golden eagle **162–63**
golden langur **267**
golden pheasant **277**
golden silk orbweaver **73**
golden snub-nosed monkey **273**
golden tegu **105**
golden wattle 334
Goliath birdeater **99**
Goliath tigerfish 209
Gombe Stream, Tanzania 210
Gondwana rainforest 313
Gondwana 313, 363
Goodall, Jane 210
Goodfellow's tree kangaroo **317**
goose, snow **33**
gorilla, western **212–13**
Gorilla gorilla **212–13**
Gouldian finch 321
Grand Canyon 23
Grant's zebra **200**
grass wren, dusky 328
grasshoppers
blistered **333**
large mountain **163**
grasslands 10, **14–15**
Argentine pampas 114
Central Great Plains **44–45**
lowland grassland 11
montane grassland 15, 178
North Australia savannas **320–21**
Serengeti savannas **192–93**
spinifex 328, 329
stratified grazing 193
temperate grassland 15
Terai-Duar savannas **254–55**
tropical grassland 15
great barracuda **308–09**
Great Barrier Reef 304, **344–53**
Great Basin Desert 60
great blue heron **71**
Great Britain 133
Scottish Highlands **140–45**
great bustard **283**
great crested grebe **157**
great crested newt **170**
Great Dividing Range, Australia 334
great frigatebird **124**
great grey owl **58**
great horned owl 58
great Indian hornbill **264**
Great Plains **44–51**
great rhinoceros hornbill 293
Great Rift Valley 178
lakes **184–91**
Great Sandy-Tanami Desert **328–33**
Great Smoky Mountains 23
great white pelican **189**
greater bilby **332**
greater bird-of-paradise **318–19**
greater blue-ringed octopus **352**
greater flamingo 146, **149**, 152
greater hedgehog tenrec **241**
greater prairie chicken **44–45**
greater rhea **121**
greater roadrunner **63**
greater sage-grouse **50**
grebes

flightless **111**
great crested **157**
green anaconda **105**
green humphead parrotfish **309**
green iguana 80
green jumping spider **326–27**
green sea turtle **346–47**
green tree frog **326**
green tree viper, Chinese **272–73**
Greenland 22
Greenland halibut 30
grey crowned crane **189**
grey-crowned prinia 254
grey falcon 328
grey fox, northern **67**
grey owl, great **58**
grey seal **135**
grey squirrel 13
grey wolf 34, 35, **37**, 47, 158–59
griffon vulture 152
grizzly bear 34, **36**
grooming
golden snub-nosed monkey 273
hamadryas baboon 249
vampire bat 115
grosbeak 51
ground finch 128
ground squirrels
black-tailed prairie dog **48**
Mojave 60
grouse 140
greater prairie chicken **44–45**
western capercaillie **145**
Grus antigone **263**
guard crab 345
guillemot 139
guinea pig 101, 117
guineafowl, helmeted **206**
Gulf Stream 132, 134
gull, ivory 24
Gulo gulo **38**
gum trees *see* eucalypts
Gypaetus barbatus **182–83**

H

hair grass, Antarctic 362
haircap moss 165
Haliaeetus leucocephalus **42–43**
halibut, Greenland 30
Halichoerus grypus **135**
hamadryas baboon **249**
hammerhead shark 304
scalloped **348–49**
hamster, dwarf 278
Hanuman langur 259
Hapalochlaena lunulata **352**
harbour porpoise 135
hares
Arctic 25
black-tailed jackrabbit **63**
hare wallaby, spectacled **321**
harems
Auckland tree weta 358
hamadryas baboon 249
marine iguana 129
proboscis monkey 295
Przewalski's wild horse 282
red muntjac 258
southern elephant seal 365
western red deer 141
harp seal **31**
harpy eagle 76, 78, 86, 93

harriers 146
  Montagu's 152
hazel dormouse 164
Heard Island 364
hearing *see* ears and hearing
heart
  blue whale 372
  giraffe 199
Heart of Borneo 292
heath, fynbos 177
heathland 15
  see also scrub
Hebridean islands 140
hedgehog, European **156**
hedgehog tenrec, greater **241**
Heliconia plants 78–79
Heliconius erato **89**
Heliconius melpomene 89
helmeted guineafowl **206**
helmeted hornbill 293
Heloderma suspectum **64–65**
Henkel's leaf-tailed gecko **243**
Hercules moth 300
herds
  African savanna elephant 203
  American bison 46, 47
  Arabian oryx 250
  Bactrian camel 281
  Bhutan takin 267
  bighorn sheep 53
  Camargue horse 147
  Cape buffalo 220
  gaur 257
  gelada 180
  Grant's zebra 200
  impala 197
  Kalahari springbok 230–31
  Masai giraffe 199
  Mongolian saiga 280
  mountain nyala 179
  muskox 26
  pronghorn 45
  Przewalski's wild horse 282
  reindeer 26
  Serengeti savannas 192
  walrus 32
  western red deer 141
  white-lipped peccary 101
  wild boar 169
  wildebeest 198
  see also bachelor herds; flocks;
    harems; packs; prides; social
    groups; troops
herons 146
  great blue **71**
  purple 152
Herpestes edwardsii **262–63**
herring, Atlantic 134
hibernation
  Alpine chipmunk 56
  Alpine marmot 160
  American black bear 55
  common adder 145
  European hedgehog 156
  forests 12
  great crested newt 170
  grizzly bear 36
  jewelled lizard 157
  Nile monitor 226
  polar bear 29
  raccoon dog 289
  yellow-legged frog 59
Highlands
  Arabian **248-9**
  Ethiopian **178–83**

Scottish **140–45**
Himalayan blue sheep 266
Himalayan newt 254, 255
Himalayas 176, 246, 254
  Eastern Himalayas **266–71**
Hindu Kush 269
Hindu mythology 259
Hippocampus bargibanti **350–51**
Hippocampus denise 350
hippopotamus 19, **186–87**, 224
Hippopotamus amphibius
  186–87
Hirundo neoxena **355**
hoatzin 91
Hoffmann's two-toed sloth **79**
hogs
  pygmy 255
  red river **215**
Hokkaido
  Nihonkai montane forest
    284–91
Honduran white bat **79**
honey badger 224
honey bee, European **170–71**
honey possum 335
honeycomb 171
honeyeaters 335
  regent 335
  yellow-faced 335
Honshu
  Nihonkai montane forest
    284–91
hooded capuchin **102**
hooded pitohui 314
hooded seal 24
hoofs
  Alpine chamois 159
  Arabian oryx 250
  bighorn sheep 53
  Ethiopian klipspringer 179
  Iberian ibex 153
  moose 39
  red lechwe 221
  reindeer 26
hoopoe **157**
hornbean, Japanese 284
hornbills
  bushy-crested 293
  great Indian **264**
  great rhinoceros 293
  helmeted 293
  red-billed **206**
horns
  Alpine chamois 159
  American bison 47
  Arabian oryx 250
  bighorn sheep 53
  blackbuck 257
  Cape buffalo 220
  Ethiopian klipspringer 179
  gaur 257
  giraffe 199
  impala 197
  Indian rhinoceros 256
  Japanese serow 285
  Mongolian saiga 280
  mountain nyala 179
  muskox 26
  pronghorn 45
  white rhinoceros 222
  Yarkand gazelle 279
  see also antlers
horses
  Camargue **147**
  domestic 282

Przewalski's wild 278, **282–3**
  semi-wild 146
hot conditions
  black-tailed jackrabbit 63
  red kangaroo 331
  see also deserts
hot desert 19
  Mojave Desert **60–61**
  Kalahari Desert **228–29**
  Arabian Highlands **248–49**
  Great Sandy-Tanami Desert **328–329**
hot springs 34
hourglass dolphin **372**
house martin 146
hovering, humming birds 88
howling
  coyote 49
  grey wolf 37
Hudson Bay 29
humans
  ancient 192, 208
  ethnic groups 209
hummingbirds 78–79
  booted racket-tail **88**
humpback whale 345, 364
humphead parrotfish, green **309**
hunting
  anhinga 70, 71
  Arctic fox 27
  Bengal tiger 261
  blue damselfly 359
  bobcat 37
  caracal 229
  cheetah 196
  chimpanzee 210
  coyote 49
  dhole 277
  fossa 237
  great barracuda 308
  great blue heron 71
  great grey owl 58
  grey wolf 37
  grizzly bear 36
  harp seal 31
  Iberian lynx 154
  jaguar 95
  killer whale 137
  leopard 214
  leopard seal 372
  lion 194
  maned wolf 119
  Nile crocodile 191
  ocelot 80
  olive baboon 185
  peregrine falcon 144
  puma 62
  red fox 168
  striped scorpion 50
  wildcat 143
  Yacare caiman 107
  see also poaching
Huon Peninsula 314
hyacinth macaw 100–01
Hyaena hyaena **252–53**
Hydrochoerus hydrochaeris **101**
Hydrurga leptonyx **371**
hyenas 192, 199
  spotted 198, 253
  striped 248, 250, **252–53**
Hylobates muelleri **298**
Hymenopus coronatus **301**
hyrax, rock 67, **253**
Hystrix africaeaustralis **231**

I

Iberian ibex **153**
Iberian imperial eagle 152–53
Iberian lynx **154–55**
Iberian peninsula 133
ibex 178
  Iberian **153**
icefish, blackfin 370–71
Iceland 132, 133, 161
Idaho 36
iguanas
  green 80
  marine 113, 122, **128–29**
  Yañez's 113
impala 192, **197**, 224
imperial eagle, Iberian 152–53
imperial shag **369**
incubation
  African jacana 224
  blue-winged kookaburra 323
  crested berrypecker 317
  Yacare caiman 107
India 246
  Bengal tiger 261
  blackbuck 257
  lesser flamingo 188
  lion 194
Indian cobra **264**
Indian grey mongoose **262–63**
Indian Ocean 12
Indian peafowl **271**
Indian rhinoceros 254, 255, **256–57**
Indochinese clouded leopard 254, **276**
Indonesia 314, 318–19
infrared sensing, green anaconda 105
insects
  Auckland tree weta **358**
  blue damselfly **359**
  dragonfly 146
  European honey bee **170–71**
  giant prickly stick insect 343
  Macleay's spectre **343**
  Malaysian orchid mantis **301**
  mosquitoes 146
  see also beetles; butterflies;
    grasshoppers; moths
Intellagama lesuerii **342**
intelligence
  African savanna elephant 203
  chimpanzee 210
  Japanese macaque 287
  killer whale 137
  see also tool users
Iran 196
Ireland 133
Irrawaddy dolphin 302
Isabela islands 124
Isabella tiger moth 25
islands
  Canadian Arctic 24
  Caribbean 76
  Europe 133
  Galapagos Islands **122–23**
  island arcs 247
  Southern Ocean **364–65**
Italy 10, 133
ivory gull 24

J

Jabiru mycteria **103**
jabiru stork **103**

jacana, African **224**
jackrabbit, black-tailed **63**
jaguar 76, 87, **94–95**, 107
James flamingo 108
Japan
　Nihonkai montane forest **284–91**
　volcanic islands 247
Japanese beech 284
Japanese cherry 284–85
Japanese giant salamander **291**
Japanese hornbean 284
Japanese macaque 284, **286–87**
Japanese marten **288–89**
Japanese serow **285**
Japanese weasel 285
Japanese white-eye 284
jarrah 320
jaws
　Fabian's lizard 113
　gharial 265
　golden tegu 105
　great barracuda 308
　jaguar 95
　wolverine 38
　see also teeth
Jeffrey pine 52
jerboa, long-eared 279
jewelled lizard **157**
Joshua tree 60
jumping rat, Malagasy giant 237
jumping spider, green **326–27**
jungle *see* rainforest
juniper 52, 140, 146, 178, 248
Jutland 133

K

kakapo 354, **356**
Kalahari Desert 218, **228–35**
Kalahari springbok **230–31**
kangaroo rat 60
kangaroos 320
　Goodfellow's tree **317**
　red **330–31**
kans grass 255
kapok 78
karst landscapes 133, 236
katsura 284
kauri, giant 354, 355
Kazakhstan 282
kea 354, **356**
keelback, Asian tiger **291**
Kenya
　black-capped social weaver **204–05**
　Grant's zebra 200
　Great Rift Valley lakes 184
　wildebeest 198
Kenya, Mount 200
Kerguelen Islands 364
Kermode bear 55
khulan 278–79
killer whale **136–37**, 306, 372
king cobra 207
king eider **137**
kingfisher, stork-billed **299**
Kings Canyon National Park 52
kingsnake, mountain **59**
kit fox **61**
kiwis 313, 354
　little spotted 356
　North Island brown **356**
klipspringer, Ethiopian **179**
knob-tailed gecko 328

koala 334, **338–39**
Kobus leche **220–21**
kookaburras
　blue-winged **323**
　laughing 334
Kras region, Slovenia 133
krill 364, 365, 371
kudu 179

L

Lagenorhynchus cruciger **372**
Lagidium peruanum **109**
Lagopus muta **161**
Lagorchestes conspicillatus **321**
lakes
　Alps 159
　Great Rift Valley **184–91**
lammergeier **182–83**
Lampropeltis zonata **59**
Lampropeltis zonata multicincta
　59
langurs
　golden **267**
　Terai sacred **259**
large flying fox **294**
large mountain grasshopper **163**
larvae
　Japanese giant salamander 291
　stag beetle 172
Latrodectus hasseltii **326**
laughing kookaburra 334
lava cactus 122–23
lava lizard 123
leaf-cutter ant **98**
leaf monkeys 259
leaf-tailed gecko, fantastic 13
leatherback turtle 346
leathery moonwort 165
lechwe, red **220–21**
leks
　great bustard 283
　greater bird-of-paradise 319
　greater sage-grouse 50
　Indian peafowl 271
　kakapo 356
　red lechwe 221
　western capercaillie 145
lemmings 24, 27, 33
　Norway 134–35
Lemur catta **238–39**
lemurs 236
　Berthe's mouse **237**
　black-and-white ruffed 239
　Coquerel's sifaka 241
　ring-tailed **238–39**
　Verreaux's sifaka **240–41**
leopards 95, 193, 199, **214**, 254
　Arabian 248
　Indochinese clouded 254, **276**
　snow 266, **268–69**
leopard seal **371**
leopard tortoise **226**
Leopardus pardalis **80–81**
Leptophis ahaetulla **105**
Lepus californicus **63**
lesser flamingo 184, **188–89**
lesser short-tailed bat **355**
Letoptilus crumenifer **207**
leverets, black-tailed jackrabbit 63
lichens 24, 362, 370
lifespans
　African savanna elephant 203

Andean condor 112
Atlantic puffin 139
bald eagle 43
blue damselfly 359
common snapping turtle 72
dugong 304
golden eagle 162
Goliath birdeater 99
jabiru stork 103
leopard tortoise 226
lesser flamingo 188
ring-tailed lemur 239
scarlet macaw 97
snow leopard 269
walrus 32
whale shark 306
light, ultraviolet 26
lilac-breasted roller **207**
limestone caves 133
limestone karst 236
Limpopo River 176
Liolaemus fabiani **113**
lion 193, **194–95**, 199
Litoria caerulea **326**
litters
　American black bear 55
　Bengal tiger 261
　bobcat 37
　European hedgehog 156
　grey wolf 37
　kit fox 61
　lion 194
　maned wolf 119
　northern raccoon 69
　polar bear 29
　red fox 168
　wild boar 169
　see also young animals
little egret 152
little red flying fox 334
little spotted kiwi 356
liverworts 370
Livingstone's turaco 192
lizards
　armadillo **234–35**
　Australian water dragon **342**
　common flying dragon **298–99**
　Fabian's **113**
　frilled 320, **324–25**
　Gila monster **64–65**
　golden tegu **105**
　jewelled **157**
　lava 123
　Nile monitor **226–27**
　thorny devil **332–33**
lobelia, giant 178
Loch's chromodoris 302
lodgepole pine 34, 35, 52
lodges
　American beaver 41
Lombok 247
long-beaked echidna **315**
long-eared jerboa 279
long-nosed potoroo 335
long-tailed chinchilla 109
long-tailed planigale 328
long-whiskered owlet 84
longicorn beetle, rosalia 158
longwing, crimson **89**
Lophelia pertusa 134, 135
lora 105
Louisiana black bear 55
lowland nyala 179
lowland tapir 100
Loxia scotica **143**

Loxodonta africana **202–03**
Lucanus cervus **172–73**
lungfish 219
Lutra lutra **166–67**
Lybia tessellata **309**
Lycaon pictus **224–25**
lynxes
　Eurasian 158, 164–65
　Iberian **154–55**
Lynx pardinus **154–55**
Lynx rufus **37**
lyrebirds 313
　Albert's 334

M

Macaca fuscata **286–87**
macaque, Japanese 284, **286–87**
macaws
　hyacinth 100–01
　scarlet 13, **97**
　see also parrots
Macleay's spectre **343**
Macropus parma **337**
Macropus rufus **330–31**
Macrotis lagotis **332**
Madagascar 13
　Madagascan dry forest **236–43**
Magellan, Strait of 77
mahogany 66
Malagasy giant jumping rat 237
Malawi, Lake 184, 185, 191
Malaysian orchid mantis **301**
Malurus coronatus **323**
mamba, black **207**
man o' war, Portuguese **352–53**
manatee, West Indian **67**
mandarin duck **290**
mandarinfish **305**
mandibles, stag beetle 172
mandrill **213**
Mandrillus sphinx **213**
maned wolf **118–19**
manes
　gelada 181
　lion 194–95
mangrove swamps 19
　Bornean rainforest 292
　Costa Rican rainforest 78
　Florida Everglades 66
Manipur bush-quail 254
Manis tricuspis **215**
mantis, Malaysian orchid **301**
mantis shrimp, peacock **351**
mara, Patagonian **117**
Mara River 198
marabou stork 188
marine ecosystems *see* seas
marine iguana 113, 122, **128–29**
marmoset, pygmy **92**
Marmota marmota **160**
marmots
　Alpine 11, **160**
　Mongolian 278
marsupial mole, southern **329**
marsupials 313, **314–15**, 363
　brushtail possum 354
　common spotted cuscus **315**
　common wombat **337**
　fat-tailed dunnart **329**
　Goodfellow's tree kangaroo **317**
　greater bilby **332**
　koala **338–39**

long-nosed potoroo 335
parma wallaby **337**
red kangaroo **330–31**
southern marsupial mole **329**
spectacled hare wallaby **321**
sugar glider **316–17**
Tasmanian devil **340–41**
tiger quoll **341**
martens
European pine **165**
Japanese **288–89**
yellow-throated 272
Martes martes **165**
Martes melampus **288–89**
martin, house 146
Masai giraffe 199
mating
American bison 47
Arabian oryx 250
Bengal tiger 261
blue damselfly 359
bobcat 37
Bornean orangutan 297
common adder 145
coyote 49
dyeing poison frog 98
emerald tree boa 97
emperor scorpion 216
European hedgehog 156
greater sage-grouse 50
grey wolf 37
hippopotamus 187
Iberian lynx 154
impala 197
Japanese macaque 287
leopard seal 372
meerkat 232
moose 39
red-eyed tree frog 82, 83
red fox 168
red howler monkey 93
red kangaroo 331
ring-tailed lemur 239
scalloped hammerhead shark 349
southern elephant seal 365
whale shark 306
wildebeest 198
matrilines, Japanese macaque 287
Maylandia zebra **191**
mbuna, zebra **191**
meadow, alpine 11, 14
Alps **158–59**
Eastern Himalayas **266–67**
Yellowstone **34–35**
Mediterranean 10, 13, 15
Mediterranean forest 10, 13
Tagus Valley **152–153**
Mediterranean pond turtle 152
Mediterranean scrub 10
Mediterranean Sea 132
meerkat 228, **232–33**
Meles meles **165**
Melursus ursinus **263**
Mephites mephites **54**
Merian, Maria Sibylla 99
Merops apiaster **150–51**
mesquite scrub 44
metabolism
Berthe's mouse lemur 237
polar bear 29
red panda 270
sloths 79
methane, climate change 255
Mexico 22
American black bear 55

bald eagle 43
deserts 23
monarch butterfly 51
mountain kingsnake 59
mice
sandy inland 328
spinifex hopping 328
Microcebus berthae **237**
midday gerbil 278
Middle East
dromedary 281
lion 194
midge, Antarctic 371
midwife toad **162**
migration 16
American bison 47
Arctic char 33
Arctic tern 24
Asia 246
birds 76, 152, 248, 312
European bee-eater 150
Galapagos tortoise 127
Grant's zebra 200
great bustard 283
green sea turtle 346
harp seal 31
monarch butterfly 51
mountain nyala 179
narwhal 30
reindeer 26
Serengeti savannas 192
snow goose 33
snowy owl 33
turkey vulture 56
whale shark 306
wildebeest 198
Mihoacán, Mexico 51
milk
duck-billed platypus 336
hooded seal 24
koala 339
red kangaroo 331
milkweed 51
miller moth 34
mimicry
Bargibant's pygmy seahorse 350
crimson longwing 89
gelada 180
Malaysian orchid mantis 301
mountain kingsnake 59
mink, American 141
minke whale 364
Mirounga leonina **365**
Missouri River 44
mites 24
Mojave Desert 16, **60–65**
Mojave ground squirrel 60
Mojave rattlesnake 60, **64**
Mola mola **347**
mole rat, giant 179
molluscs
giant clam **352**
moloch 325
Moloch horridus **332–33**
monarch butterfly **51**
Monarch Butterfly Biosphere Reserve,
Mihoacán 51
Monfragüe National Park 152
Mongolia 278–83
Mongolian marmot 278
Mongolian saiga 278, **280**
Mongolian wild ass 278–79
mongooses
Indian grey **262–63**
meerkat **232–33**

Monistria pustulifera **333**
monitor, Nile **226–27**
monkey orchid 84–85
monkeys 78
Azura's capuchin 77
black colobus 20, 209
emperor tamarin **92**
gelada 178, **180–81**
golden langur **267**
golden snub-nosed **273**
hamadryas baboon **249**
hooded capuchin **102**
Japanese macaque **286–87**
leaf monkeys 259
mandrill **213**
olive baboon **185**
proboscis **294–95**
pygmy marmoset **92**
red howler **92–93**
savanna baboon 180
spider 13
Terai sacred langur **259**
vervet **201**
Monodon monoceros **30–31**
monotremes
duck-billed platypus **336–37**
long-beaked echidna **315**
monsoon 246
Montagu's harrier 152
Montana 36
montane forests 11, 13
Ethiopian Highlands 178
New Guinea **314–15**
Nihonkai **284–85**
montane grassland 14, 178
montane moorland 178
moonwort, leathery 165
moorland, montane 178
moose **38–39**
Mopsus mormon **326–27**
morpho, common **81**
Morpho peleides **81**
mosquitoes 146
mosses 24, 362
Antarctic Peninsula 370
haircap 165
sphagnum **140–41**
moths
Atlas **300**
Hercules 300
Isabella tiger 25
miller 34
pale tussock **170**
yucca 60
see also butterflies
moulting
beluga 31
ptarmigan 161
mounds, termite 320
mountain ash gum 334
mountain chickadee **56**
mountain gazelle 248
mountain kingsnake **59**
mountain lion **62**
mountain nyala 178, **179**
mountain tapir **85**
mountains 11
Alps 133, **158–59**, 176
Andes 76, 363
Arabian Highlands
248–49
Atlas Mountains 176
Australia 313
Ethiopian Highlands **178–79**
Himalayas 176, 246, **266–67**

Scottish Highlands **140–41**
Sierra Nevada **52–53**
Upper Yangtze Forests **272–73**
mouse lemur, Berthe's **237**
mouth brooders, zebra mbuna 191
mouths
Indochinese clouded leopard 276
lion 276
ribbontail stingray 304
whale shark 306, 307
see also jaws; teeth
Müller's gibbon **298**
Muntiacus muntjak **258**
muntjac, red **258**
Murray-Darling Basin 313
muskox 24, **26**
Mustela nigripes **48**
mute swan **148–49**
mygalomorph 343
Myrmecophaga tridactyla **116–17**
myrrh 178
Mystacina tuberculata **355**

N

Naivasha, Lake 184
Naja naja **264**
Naja nivea **234**
Nakuru, Lake 184
Namib Desert 177
Namibia 194
narwhal 29, **30–31**
Nasalis larvatus **294–95**
Nasua nasua **86**
Natron, Lake 184
neck
beluga 31
giraffe 199
"necking", giraffe 199
Neofelis nebulosa **276**
Nepal 254, 255
Nephila clavipes **73**
Nestor notabilis **356**
nests 15
African jacana 224
African skimmer 226
Andean cock-of-the-rock 89
anhinga 70
Atlantic puffin 139
bald eagle 43
black-capped social weaver 204–05
booted racket-tail humming bird 88
Bornean orangutan 297
chimpanzee 210
collared sunbird 216
crested berrypecker 317
European bee-eater 150, 151
European honey bee 171
fat-tailed dunnart 329
frilled lizard 325
golden eagle 162
great blue heron 71
great crested grebe 157
great frigatebird 124
greater bird-of-paradise 319
greater rhea 121
green jumping spider 326
grey crowned crane 189
imperial shag 369
Indian peafowl 271
jabiru stork 103
lesser flamingo 188
lilac-breasted roller 207

mandarin duck 290
mute swan 148
peregrine falcon 144
pied avocet 149
plumed whistling-duck 323
purple gallinule 71
red-billed hornbill 206
resplendent quetzal 81
shoebill 190
termites 218
toco toucan 96
see also dreys
New Guinea 300, 313, 323, 325–26, 341
  montane forest **314–19**
New South Wales 337
New Zealand 313
  mixed forests **354–59**
New Zealand Alps 313
New Zealand pigeon 354
Newfoundland 25
newts
  great crested **170**
  Himalayan 254, 255
Niger, River 176
nightshade, spiny 44
Nihonkai montane forest **284–91**
Nile, River 176
Nile crocodile **190–91**, 198
Nile Delta 176
Nile monitor **226–27**
Nile perch 184
El Niño 122, 123, 124, 129
nocturnal animals
  aardvark 229
  Auckland tree weta 358
  aye-aye 241
  Bengal tiger 261
  Berthe's mouse lemur 237
  black-tailed jackrabbit 63
  desert blond tarantula 65
  duck-billed platypus 336
  emperor scorpion 216
  European hedgehog 156
  fat-tailed dunnart 329
  giant anteater 116
  greater bilby 332
  kit fox 61
  koala 339
  leopard 214
  maned wolf 119
  northern grey fox 67
  ocelot **80–81**
  parma wallaby 337
  red-eyed tree frog 82–83
  red river hog 215
  Siberian flying squirrel 285
  silky anteater 86
  spectacled hare wallaby 321
  striped hyena 252
  tiger quoll 341
  Trueb's cochran frog 89
  western tarsier 294
  Woma python 333
noddy, black 344
North Africa
  dromedary 281
  lion 194
North America **22–73**
  Canadian Arctic **24–33**
  Central Great Plains **44–51**
  Florida Everglades **66–73**
  Mojave Desert **60–65**
  Sierra Nevada **52–59**
  Yellowstone **34–43**
North American plate 22

North Australia savannas
    320–27
North Island brown kiwi **356**
northern grey fox **67**
northern pudu 85
northern quoll 320–21
northern raccoon **68–69**
northern viscacha **109**
Northland temperate forest,
    New Zealand 354
Northwest Passage 25
Norway lemming 134–35
Norway spruce 140
Norwegian fjords 132, **134–39**
Norwegian wolf spider 164
noses
  proboscis monkey 295
  Yacare caiman 106
Notoryctes typhlops **329**
Nubian plate 176
Nullarbor Plain 312
Numida meleagris **206**
nutcracker, Clark's 34
nyalas
  lowland 179
  mountain 178, **179**
Nyasa, Lake 184
Nyctea scandiaca **33**
Nyctereutes procyonoides
    289
Nymphargus truebae **89**
nymphs, blue damselfly 359

O

oak trees 52, 66, 266
  cork 153
oases
  Okavango Delta **218–19**
ocean sunfish **347**
oceans *see* seas
ocelot **80–81**
Ochotona princeps **40**
Ocreatus underwoodii **88**
octopus, greater blue-ringed **352**
Odobenus rosmarus **32**
Odocoileus virginianus **40**
Odontodactylus scyllarus **351**
oil, palm 293
okapi 208, **216**
Okapia johnstoni **216**
Okavango Delta **218–27**
Okavango River 176
Okeechobee, Lake 66
Oklahoma 44, 51
Old Faithful geyser 34
Olduvai Gorge 192
olive baboon **185**
olive sea snake 345
olm 133
Ombu tree 115
Orange River 176
orangutans 292
  Bornean **296–97**
  Sumatran 297
orbweaver, golden silk 73
orca (killer whale) **136–37**, 306
orchid mantis, Malaysian **301**
orchids 78
  monkey 84–85
  Rothschild's slipper 292
Orcinus orca **136–37**
Oreotragus saltatrixoides **179**

oriole 51
ornate box turtle 44
Ornithorhynchus anatinus **336–37**
Orycteropus afer **229**
oryx, Arabian **250–51**
Oryx leucoryx **250–51**
osteoderms, Yacare caiman 107
ostrich 228, **234**, 322
otarids 123
Otis tarda **283**
otters
  African clawless 184
  Eurasian **166–67**
  giant **102–03**
  sea 43
  spotted-necked 184
Ouroborus cataphractus **234–35**
Ovibos moschatus **26**
ovipostors, Auckland tree weta
    358
Ovis canadensis **53**
owls
  boreal 164
  burrowing **121**
  eagle 58, 152, 164
  eurasian eagle 11
  great grey **58**
  great horned 58
  Pel's fishing 219
  snowy **33**
  spectacled 86
owlet, long-whiskered 84
oxpecker 219

P

Pac-Man frog 121
Pachypodiums 236
Pacific Flyway 76
Pacific Ocean 22, 25, 77, 334, 354
  Galapagos Islands **122–23**
  El Niño 122, 123, 124, 129
Pacific plate 22, 247
Pacific Ring of Fire 246
packs
  African wild dog 224
  coyote 49
  dhole 277
  Ethiopian wolf 182
  grey wolf 37
Pagophilus groenlandicus **31**
painted firetail 328
pale tussock **170**
palm oil 293
pampas, Argentine 77, **114–21**
pampas deer 114
pampas grass 114–15
Pan paniscus 210
Pan troglodytes **210–11**
pandas
  giant 272, **274–75**
  red **270**, 272
Pandinus imperator **216–17**
pangolins
  common **215**
  Sunda 293
Pantanal 76, **100–07**
panther chameleon **242–43**
panthers 95
  Florida 66
Panthera leo **194–95**
Panthera onca **94–95**
Panthera pardus **214**

Panthera tigris altaica 261
Panthera tigris sumatra 261
Panthera tigris tigris **260–61**
Panthera uncia **268–69**
Papilio maackii **291**
Papio anubis **185**
Papio hamadryas **249**
Papua New Guinea 314
papyrus 218
Para rubber tree 90
Paradisaea apoda **318–19**
Paradisaea raggiana 319
Paraguay River 100, 101
Paramythia montium **317**
Parana River 77
parma wallaby **337**
Parnassius apollo **163**
parrot crossbill 143
parrot snake, giant **105**
parrotfish, green humphead
    309
parrots
  budgerigars 328–29
  kakapo 354, **356**
  kea **356**
  scarlet macaw **97**
partridges
  Arabian **253**
  Chinese bamboo 272
Patagonia 76
Patagonian mara **117**
Pavo cristatus **271**
paws *see* feet
peacock mantis shrimp **351**
peafowl, Indian **271**
pearlwort, Antarctic 362, 370
Peary caribou 26
peat swamps 292
peccary, white-lipped **101**
Pelargopsis capensis **299**
Pelecanus onocrotalus **189**
pelicans 125
  great white **189**
Pel's fishing owl 219
penguins 370, 371
  Adelie **372**
  emperor 370, **374–75**
  Galapagos **124**
  rockhopper **368–69**
peninsulas, Europe 133
perch, Nile 184
peregrine falcon **144**
permafrost 24
Peru 89, 125
pesticides 51, 144
Petaurus breviceps **316–17**
petrels 364
  snow 370
Phacochoerus africanus **230**
Phalacrocorax atriceps **369**
phalarope, red 24
Pharomachrus mocinno **81**
Phascolarctos cinereus **338–39**
pheasant, golden **277**
pheromones 232
Philippine plate 247
Philippines
  Sulu-Sulawesi Seas **302–09**
Phocoena phocoena 135
Phoebastria irrorata **125**
Phoenicopterus minor **188–89**
Phoenicopterus roseus **149**
Physalia physalis **352–53**
phytoplankton 306
pickleweed 60

pied avocet **149**
pigeon, New Zealand 354
pigs 187
  common warthog **230**
  pygmy hog 255
  red river hog **215**
  wild boar 164, **169**, 261
pikas, American **40**, 52
pilchard 177
pincers
  emperor scorpion 216
  see also claws
pine trees 13
  Jeffrey 52
  lodgepole 34, 35, 52
  New Zealand mixed forest 354
  Ponderosa 52
  Scots 140
  whitebark 34
  Wollemi 334
pine marten, European **165**
pink river dolphin 76, 91
pintail, South Georgia 364
piranha 107
pit vipers
  Mojave rattlesnake **64**
pitcher plants 292
pitohui, hooded 314
planigale, long-tailed 328
plankton 306, 364, 365
plantations, palm oil 293
plants
  Alps 158
  Amazon rainforest 90
  Andean altiplano 108
  Andean yungas 84
  Antarctica 362, 370
  Arabian Highlands 248
  Argentine pampas 114
  Australasia 313
  Bavarian Forest 164
  Camargue 146
  Canadian Arctic 24
  carnivorous 292
  Congo Basin 208
  Costa Rican rainforest 78
  East Australian forests 334–35
  Eastern Himalayas 266–67
  Ethiopian Highlands 178
  Florida Everglades 66
  forests 12-13
  Galapagos Islands 122–23
  Kalahari Desert 228
  Madagascan dry forest 236
  Mojave Desert 60–61
  New Guinea montane forest 314
  Nihonkai montane forest 284–85
  North Australia savannas 320
  Norwegian fjords 134
  Pantanal 100–01
  Scottish Highlands 140
  Serengeti savannas 192
  Upper Yangtze Forests 272
  Yellowstone 34
Platalea ajaja **104**
plate-tailed gecko 283
platypus, duck-billed 334, **336–37**
ploughshare tortoise 236
plumage see feathers
plumed whistling-duck **323**
poaching
  African savanna elephant 203

Arabian oryx 250
Asian elephant 259
Indian rhinoceros 256
white rhinoceros 222
Podiceps cristatus **157**
pods
  killer whale 137
  see also schools
Poecile gambeli **56**
poisons
  Asian tiger keelback 291
  black mamba 207
  Cape cobra 234
  common adder 145
  desert blond tarantula 65
  duck-billed platypus 336
  emperor scorpion 216
  ensatina 59
  Gila monster 64
  great barracuda 308
  greater blue-ringed octopus 352
  hooded pitohui 314
  Indian cobra 264
  Mojave rattlesnake 64
  monarch butterfly 51
  Portuguese man o' war 352
  redback spider 326
  ribbontail stingray 304
  Sydney funnelweb spider 343
  tomato frog 243
Poland 47
polar bear 24, 25, 27, **28–29**, 31
polar cod 30
polar regions 17
  Antarctic Peninsula **370–71**
  Canadian Arctic **24–25**
pollination 17
  honey bee 171
polynyas 24
polyps, Portuguese man o' war 352
pond cypress 66–67
pond turtle, Mediterranean 152
Ponderosa pine 52
Pongo abelii 297
Pongo pygmaeus **296–97**
poppies 60–61
porcelain fungus 164
porcupine, Cape **231**
Porphyrio martinica **71**
porpoises
  harbour **135**
Portugal
  Tagus Valley **152–57**
Portuguese man o' war **352–53**
possums
  brushtail 354
  honey 335
  pygmy 335
postman, common 89
Potamochoerus porcus **215**
potoroo, long-nosed 335
prairie chicken, greater 44–45
prairie dogs 44, 49, 61, 121
  black-tailed **48**
prairies 14, 114
  Central Great Plains **44–45**
  Florida Everglades 66
  North America 22
pregnancy see gestation
prides, lions 194
primates
  aye-aye **241**
  Berthe's mouse lemur **237**

Bornean orangutan **296–97**
chimpanzee 208, **210–11**
lemurs 236
Müller's gibbon **298**
pygmy chimpanzee 208, 210
western gorilla **212–13**
western tarsier **294**
  see also monkeys
Prince Edward Island 364
Prince Ruspoli's turaco 178
prinia, grey-crowned 254
proboscis monkey **294–95**
proboscises
  Mongolian saiga 280
  proboscis monkey 295
  southern elephant seal 365
Procavia capensis **253**
Procyon lotor **68–69**
pronghorn 44, **45**
Propithecus coquereli 241
Propithecus verreauxi **240–41**
Przewalski's wild horse 278, **282–83**
Przewalski's wonder gecko **283**
Pseudalopex culpaeus **109**
Pseudonigrita cabanisi **204–05**
ptarmigan **161**
Pteromys volans **285**
Pteronura brasiliensis **102–03**
Pteropus vampyrus **294**
pudu, northern 85
pufferfish, freshwater 209
puffin, Atlantic **138–39**
puma 62, 66, 69, 87
Puma concolor **62**
pupas, stag beetle 172
pups
  coyote 49
  grey wolf 37
  maned wolf 119
  see also cubs; young animals
purple-crowned fairy wren **323**
purple gallinule **71**
purple heron 152
pygmy chimpanzee 208, 210
pygmy hog 255
pygmy marmoset **92**
pygmy possum 335
pygmy seahorses 345
  Bargibant's **350–51**
  Denise's 350
Pygoscelis adeliae **372**
pyrgomorph, arid painted 333
Pyrrhocorax graculus **161**
pythons
  Burmese 67
  Woma **333**

Qinling Mountains 272
quaking aspen 35
queens
  European honey bee 171
  leaf-cutter ant 98
Queensland 334
quelea, red-billed **225**
Quelea quelea **225**
quetzal, resplendent **81**
quills, Cape porcupine 231
quillwort 164

quinoa 108–09
quolls 314, 325
  northern 320–21
  tiger **341**

R
rabbit 14, 146–47, 154, 321, 335
rabbit-eared bandicoot 332
raccoons 59
  coati 86
  northern **68–69**
raccoon dog 284, **289**
raggiana bird-of-paradise 319
rainfall
  Andean altiplano 108
  Antarctica 363
  Arabian Highlands 248
  Australasia 313
  Congo Basin 208
  East Australian forests 334
  Europe 133
  Gobi Desert 278
  Kalahari Desert 228
  monsoon 246
rainforests 13
  Amazon 76, **90–91**
  Bornean **292–93**
  Congo Basin **208–09**
  Costa Rican 76, **78–79**
  Gondwana 313
Ramphastos toco **96–97**
Ramsar convention 146
Rana sierrae **59**
Rangifer tarandus **26**
Rangifer tarandus pearyi 26
rats
  kangaroo 60
  Malagasy giant jumping 237
  rock rat 312
rattlesnakes
  Mojave 60, **64**
  western diamondback 64
rays 344
  ribbontail stingray **304**
Recurvirostra avosetta **149**
red-billed hornbill **206**
red-billed quelea **225**
red deer, western **141**
red dog, Asian 277
red-eyed tree frog **82–83**
red fir 52
red flying fox 334
red fox 119, 163, **168**, 321, 337
red howler monkey **92–93**
red kangaroo **330–31**
red lechwe **220–21**
red-legged seriema **120**
red muntjac **258**
red oat grass 192
red panda **270**, 272
red phalarope 24
red river hog **215**
Red Sea 248
red spotted toad 60–61
red swamp crayfish, American 146, 184
redback spider **326**
redstart, common 177
redwood, dawn 272
reefs see coral reefs
regent honeyeater 335
reindeer 16, 24, **26**, 38, 246

reproduction *see* captive breeding; courtship; eggs; gestation; mating
reptiles
American alligator 66, **72–73**, 107
American crocodile 66
Nile crocodile **190–91**, 198
panther chameleon **242–43**
Przewalski's wonder gecko **283**
saltwater crocodile 191
thorny devil 325, 328, **332–33**
tuatara **358–59**
Yacare caiman **106–07**
see also lizards; iguanas; snakes; tortoises, turtles
resplendent quetzal **81**
Reunion Island 242–43
Rhabdophis tigrinus **291**
Rhacophorus nigropalmatus **300**
Rhea americana **121**
rheas 120, 322
greater **121**
Rhincodon typhus **306–07**
rhinoceros
black 193, 222, 223
Indian 254, 255, **256–57**
white **222–23**, 256
rhinoceros hornbill, great 293
Rhinoceros unicornis **256–57**
Rhinopithecus roxellana **273**
rhododendrons 266–67
Rhône Delta 146–47
ribbontail stingray **304**
rice cultivation 255
Richmond temperate forest, New Zealand 354
right whale 364
rimu 354
ring-tailed lemur **238–39**
river deltas
Camargue **146–47**
Nile 176
Okavango Delta **218–19**
river dolphin, pink 91
river eagle 43
"river wolf" 102
roadrunner, greater **63**
rock hyrax 67, **253**
rock wallaby, black-footed 328
rock rat 312
rockhopper penguin **368–69**
Rocky Mountain wolf 37
Rocky Mountains 34, 44, 47, 51, 60, 72
rodents
Cape porcupine **231**
capybara 101
Eurasian red squirrel **142**
northern viscacha **109**
roe deer 164
western **153**
Rollandia microptera **111**
rollers
Abyssinian 207
lilac-breasted **207**
rookeries
emperor penguin 375
see also colonies
roosts 15
Andean condor 112
Honduran white bat 79
large flying fox 294
vampire bat 115
rosalia longicorn beetle 158
roseate spoonbill **104**
Ross Sea ice shelf 362
Rothschild's birdwing 315

Rothschild's slipper orchid 292
rowan trees 140
rubber trees 90
rufous sengi 182
Rupicapra rupicapra **159**
Rupicola peruvianus **89**
Russia 261
rut
impala 197
moose 39
red muntjac 258
western red deer 141
western roe deer 153
Rynchops flavirostris **226**

S

sacred baboon 249
sacred langur, Terai 259
saddleback tamarin 92
sage-grouse, greater **50**
Sagittarius serpentarius **206**
saguaro cactus 17
Saguinus imperator **92**
Sahara Desert 17, 176
Sahel 176, 177
saiga, Mongolian 278, **280**
Saiga mongolica **280**
salamanders
cave 133
Chinese giant 291
ensatina **59**
Japanese giant **291**
Salar de Atacama 113
Salar de Uyuni 108
Sally Lightfoot crab 122
Salmo salar **137**
salmon
Atlantic **137**
Chinook 52–53
salt
Andean altiplano 108
Congo Basin 209
Fabian's lizard 113
saltwater crocodile 191
Salvelinus alpinus **33**
sambar 261
San Andreas fault 22
sand eel 138, 139
sandy inland mouse 328
Sapajus cay **102**
Sarcophilus harrisii **340–41**
sardine 177, 302
sarus crane **263**
satyr tragopan 267
savanna baboon 180
savannas
Arabian Highlands 248
Kalahari Desert 228
North Australia savannas **320–27**
Serengeti savannas **192–207**
Sierra Nevada 52
Terai-Duar **254–55**
sawgrass prairies 66
saxaul 278
scales
armadillo lizard 235
Australian water dragon 342
common pangolin 215
Fabian's lizard 113
Gila monster 64
scalloped hammerhead shark **348–49**
Scandinavia 133

Norwegian fjords 132, **134–39**
Scaphiopus couchii **64**
scarab beetle 100
scarlet macaw **97**
scavengers
lammergeier 183
northern raccoon 69
red fox 168
striped hyena 252
Tasmanian devil 340
turkey vulture 56–57
scent glands
striped skunk 54
yellow-legged frog 59
scent marking
American pika 40
giant otter 102
Japanese marten 289
Japanese serow 285
koala 339
red muntjac 258
six-banded armadillo 117
snow leopard 269
sugar glider 316
Verreaux's sifaka 240
white-lipped peccary 101
schools
great barracuda 308
hourglass dolphin 372
scalloped hammerhead shark 348, 349
spinner dolphin 303
whale shark 306
Sciurus vulgaris **142**
scorpions
emperor **216–17**
striped **50**
Scotland **140–45**
Scots pine 140
Scottish crossbill **143**
Scottish Highlands **140–45**
scrub 15
sea anemones 309, 351
sea cow 67, 304–05
sea ice 24
sea lavender 146
sea lion, Galapagos **123**
sea otter 43
sea slugs, Loch's chromodoris 302
sea snakes 345
turtle-headed **347**
sea turtles 302
seagrass 303
seahorses
Bargibant's pygmy **350–51**
Denise's pygmy 350
seals 24, 27, 29, 370
crabeater 364–65
eared 123
fur 364
grey **135**
harp **31**
hooded 24
leopard **371**
southern elephant **365**
Weddell 370
seas
polynyas 24
Sulu-Sulawesi Seas **302–09**
see also individual seas and oceans
seaweed, marine iguana 129
secretary bird **206**
sedges 24
sei whale 364
Semien Mountains 178
Semnopithecus hector **259**

sengi, rufous **182**
sequoia 52, 53
Sequoia National Park 52
Serengeti savannas **192–207**
seriema, red-legged **120**
serow, Japanese **285**
Setifer setosus **241**
setts, European badger 165
Seychelles 12
Shaanxi province 272
shag, imperial **369**
sharks 344
bull 66
hammerhead 304
scalloped hammerhead **348–49**
whale **306–07**, 345
Shark Bay 312
sheep
bighorn **53**
Himalayan blue 266
shells
common snapping turtle 72
Galapagos tortoise 127
giant clam 352
green sea turtle 346
leopard tortoise 226
shoebill **190**
short-beaked echidna 334
short-tailed bat, lesser **355**
shrimp, peacock mantis **351**
shrub frog 292
Siberia 33, 246, 261
Siberian flying squirrel **285**
Sichuan Basin 272
Sierra Mountain kingsnake 59
Sierra Nevada **52–59**
sifakas
Coquerel's **241**
Verreaux's **240–41**
sika deer 284
Sikkim 266
Silhouette Island 12
silky anteater **86**
sitatunga 208
sitka spruce 140
six-banded armadillo **117**
skimmer, African **226**
skin
Indian rhinoceros 256
mandarinfish 305
Trueb's cochran frog 89
Wallace's flying frog 300
skipjack tuna 303
skua 370
skunk, striped **54**
sleep
Japanese macaque 287
koala 339
slipper orchid, Rothschild's 292
sloth 76
Hoffmann's two-toed **79**
sloth bear **263**
Slovenia 133
smell, sense of 15
aardvark 229
American black bear 55
Arabian oryx 250
giant anteater 116
polar bear 29
raccoon dog 289
rufous sengi 182
scalloped hammerhead shark 349
turkey vulture 56
wandering albatross 366
Sminthopsis crassicaudata **329**

snails
  amber 354–55
  apple 107
  Badwater 60
"snakebird" 70
snakehead moth 300
snakes
  Arabian cat snake 248–49
  Asian tiger keelback **291**
  black-headed bullmaster viper 79
  black mamba **207**
  Burmese python 67
  Cape cobra **234**
  common adder **145**
  common garter snake **50**
  emerald tree boa **97**
  giant parrot snake **105**
  green anaconda **105**
  Indian cobra **264**
  king cobra 207
  Mojave rattlesnake 60, **64**
  mountain kingsnake **59**
  olive sea snake 345
  sea snakes 345
  turtle-headed sea snake **347**
  western diamondback rattlesnake **64**
  Woma python **333**
snapping turtle, common **72**
snouts
  aardvark 229
  long-beaked echidna 315
  mountain tapir 85
snow 10, 11, 16
  algae 362
  forests 12, 13
  Japanese macaque 286, 287
snow goose **33**
snow leopard 266, **268–69**
snow petrel 370
snowy owl **33**
snub-nosed monkey, golden **273**
sociable weaver 228–29
social groups
  armadillo lizard 235
  Asian elephant 259
  Barrier Reef anemonefish 351
  blue whale 372
  cheetah 196
  coati 86
  common warthog 230
  fat-tailed dunnart 329
  giant otter 102
  mandrill 213
  meerkat 232
  narwhal 30
  Nile crocodile 191
  proboscis monkey 295
  pygmy marmoset 92
  Verreaux's sifaka 240
  vicuña 110
  western gorilla 212
  white rhinoceros 223
  see also colonies; flocks; harems;
    herds; prides; schools
soda lakes 18
  Great Rift Valley 184
Solanum rostratum 44
Somali plate 176
Somateria spectabilis **137**
Sonoran Desert 60
South Africa 176, 177, 225
South America 14
  see Central and South America
South Georgia 364

South Georgia pintail 364
South Sandwich Island 364
southern elephant seal **365**
southern marsupial mole **329**
Southern Ocean 16, 362
  Southern Ocean islands **364–69**
Southern Ocean winds 362
  roaring forties 362
  furious fifties 362
  screaming sixties 362
spadefoot, Couch's **64**
Spain
  Tagus Valley **152–57**
speckled dasyure 314–15
spectacled bear **87**
spectacled caiman 107
spectacled cobra 264
spectacled hare wallaby **321**
spectacled owl 86
speed
  Alpine chamois 159
  American alligator 72
  American bison 46, 47
  Atlantic puffin 139
  black mamba 207
  caracal **229**
  cheetah 196, 197
  common warthog 230
  emu 322
  frilled lizard 324
  giraffe 199
  Grant's zebra 200
  green sea turtle 346
  grey wolf 37
  hippopotamus 187
  Kalahari springbok 230
  lion 194
  Nile crocodile 191
  northern raccoon 69
  ostrich 234
  Patagonian mara 117
  peregrine falcon 144
  pronghorn 45
  red kangaroo 331
  red-legged seriema 120
  reindeer 26
  rufous sengi 182
  wildebeest 198
sperm whale 364
sphagnum moss 140–41
Spheniscus mendiculus **124**
Sphenodon punctatus **358–59**
Sphyraena barracuda **308–09**
Sphyrna lewini **348–49**
spider ant 343
spiders
  desert blond tarantula **65**
  giant huntsman 99
  golden silk orbweaver 73
  Goliath birdeater **99**
  green jumping **326–27**
  Norwegian wolf 164
  redback **326**
  Sydney funnelweb **343**
Spilocuscus maculatus **315**
spines
  Cape porcupine 231
  European hedgehog 156
  greater hedgehog tenrec 241
spinifex 328, 329
spinifex hopping mouse 328
spinner dolphin **303**
spiny babbler 254
spiny nightshade 44
spoonbill, roseate **104**

spotted cuscus, common **315**
spotted hyena 198, 253
spotted-necked otter 184
spotted toad, red 60–61
springboks
  common 230
  Kalahari **230–31**
springtails 24
spruce trees
  Norway 140
  sitka 140
"spy-hopping", killer whale 137
squid 30
squirrel glider 335
squirrels
  Douglas 53
  Eurasian red **142**
  grey 12
  Siberian flying **285**
  see also ground squirrels
stag beetle **172–73**
starfish, crown-of-thorns 344
Stauroderus scalaris **163**
Steller's sea eagle 43
Stenella longirostris **303**
steppes 14, 114
Sterna vittata **369**
stick insect, giant prickly 343
Stigmochelys pardalis **226**
stingray, ribbontail **304**
stoat 40
stomach
  American bison 47
  Terai sacred langur 259
stoop 144
stork-billed kingfisher **299**
storks
  jabiru **103**
  marabou 188
  white 193
stratified grazing 193
Strigops habroptila **356**
striped hyena 248, 250, **252–53**
striped scorpion **50**
striped skunk **54**
Strix nebulosa **58**
stromatolites 312
Struthio camelis **234**
succulent plants 66
sugar glider **316–17**, 335
sugarcane 255
Sula nebouxii **125**
Sulawesi 247
Sulawesi coelacanth 302–03
sulphur-crested cockatoo **341**
Sulu-Sulawesi Seas **302–09**
Sumatran orangutan 297
Sumatran tiger 261
sun bear 292
sunbird, collared **216**
Sunda pangolin 293
sunfish, ocean **347**
super pods 30
supervolcano 35
Suricata suricatta **232–33**
Sus scrofa **169**
swallows 146, 184
  welcome **355**
swallowtail butterflies 315
  Alpine black **291**
  Apollo **163**
swamp crayfish, American red 146, 184
swamp deer 254
swamps
  Florida Everglades 66–67

Okavango Delta **218–19**
Pantanal **100–01**
peat 292
swan, mute **148–49**
swift fox 45
swifts 184
  Alpine 146
swimming
  Eurasian otter 167
  Galapagos sea lion 123
  great barracuda 308
  grizzly bear 36
  hourglass dolphin 372
  Indian rhinoceros 256
  jaguar 95
  leopard seal 372
  marine iguana 129
  northern raccoon 69
  polar bear 28
  proboscis monkey 295
  reindeer 26
  six-banded armadillo 117
  West Indian manatee 67
Sydney funnelweb spider **343**
symbiosis, marine iguana 128
Syncerus caffer **220**
Synchiropus splendidus **305**

T

tadpoles
  Couch's spadefoot 64
  dyeing poison frog 98
  green tree frog 326
  Trueb's cochran frog 89
  Wallace's flying frog 300
  yellow-legged frog 59
Taeniura lymma **304**
Tagus Valley **152–57**
Tahoe, Lake 52
takin, Bhutan **267**
tamarins
  emperor **92**
  saddleback 92
Tamias alpinus **56**
Tanami Desert **328–33**
Tanganyika, Lake 184–85
Tanzania 184, 198, 204–05, 210
tapirs
  lowland 100
  mountain **85**
Tapirus pinchaque **85**
tarantulas
  desert blond tarantula **65**
  Goliath birdeater **99**
tarsier, western **294**
Tasmania 313, 334, 336–37, 340–41
Tasmanian devil 314, 334, 337, **340–41**
Tayassu pecari **101**
tectonic plates, island arcs 247
teeth
  African savanna elephant 203
  American alligator 72
  American beaver 41
  aye-aye 241
  common wombat 337
  dhole 277
  egg teeth 58
  gharial 264
  great barracuda 308
  hamadryas baboon 249
  hippopotamus 187

Indian grey mongoose 262
Indochinese clouded leopard 276
koala 339
leopard 214
leopard seal 372
mandrill 213
Nile crocodile 190, 191
Nile monitor 226
ocean sunfish 347
tuatara 359
vampire bat 115
vervet monkey 201
vicuña 110
whale shark 306
Yacare caiman 107
see also fangs; tusks
tegu, golden **105**
temperate broadleaf forest 12, 13
Bavarian Forest **164–165**
Nihonkai montane forest **284–85**
New Zealand mixed forest **354–55**
temperate coniferous forest 12
Alps **158–59**
Nihonkai montane forest **284–85**
Scottish Highlands **140–41**
Sierra Nevada **52–53**
Yellowstone **34–35**
temperate forests
East Australia forests **334–35**
New Zealand mixed forest
354–55
North America 22
temperate grassland 14
Argentine pampas **114–15**
Central Great Plains **44–45**
temperature regulation
anhinga 70
black-tailed jackrabbit 63
frilled lizard 325
Galapagos penguin 124
greater hedgehog tenrec 241
kit fox 61
Nile crocodile 190
red kangaroo 331
rock hyrax 253
shoebill 190
toco toucan 96
temperatures 10, 12, 14
Antarctica 363
Arabian Highlands 248
Europe 133
Gobi Desert 278
Great Barrier Reef 344
Kalahari Desert 228
Mojave Desert 60
New Zealand mixed forest 354
tenrec, greater hedgehog **241**
tentacles, Portuguese man o' war 352
Terai-Duar savannas **254–65**
Terai sacred langur **259**
Teratoscincus przewalskii **283**
termites 114, 116, 218, 226, 263,
320, 328, 332
terns
Antarctic **369**
Arctic 24, 369
territory
American black bear 54
American pika 40
Arabian oryx 250
armadillo lizard 235
Bengal tiger 261
black woodpecker 169
booted racket-tail humming bird 88
coyote 49

Ethiopian klipspringer 179
Eurasian otter 167
Fabian's lizard 113
giant otter 102
hippopotamus 187
Iberian lynx 154
jaguar 95
Japanese marten 289
Japanese serow 285
koala 339
leopard 214
lilac-breasted roller 207
maned wolf 119
meerkat 232
polar bear 29
red lechwe 220, 221
secretary bird 206
six-banded armadillo 117
snow leopard 269
stag beetle 172
stork-billed kingfisher 299
sugar glider 316
Verreaux's sifaka 240
vicuña 110
white rhinoceros 223
wildcat 143
Tetrao urogallus **145**
Texas 47, 51, 257
Thamnophis sirtalis **50**
Theraphosa blondii **99**
Theropithecus gelada **180–81**
Thomson's gazelle 192, 200, 224
thorny devil 325, 328, **332–33**
three-toed woodpecker 164
thumb, pseudo 275
Tierra del Fuego 77
tiger keelback, Asian **291**
tiger moth, Isabella 25
tiger quoll **341**
tigerfish, Goliath 209
tigers 254
Amur 261
Bengal **260–61**
Sumatran 261
Timon lepidus **157**
Timor Sea 347
titan arum 293
Titicaca, Lake 108, 111
Titicaca water frog 108
tits (titmice) 56
toads
cane 91
Couch's spadefoot **64**
dead-leaf 84
midwife **162**
red spotted 60–61
Tockus erythrorhynchus **206**
toco toucan **96–97**
tomato frog **243**
tongues
Andean flicker 111
giant anteater 116
giraffe 199
long-beaked echidna 315
Nile monitor 227
okapi 216
panther chameleon 242, 243
tool users
chimpanzee 210
hooded capuchin 102
woodpecker finch 125
see also intelligence
tornadoes 23
torpor
Berthe's mouse lemur 237

fat-tailed dunnart 329
sugar glider 316
tuatara 358
see also hibernation
tortoises 183
desert 60
Galapagos **126–27**
leopard **226**
ploughshare 236
toucan, toco **96–97**
touch, sense of
northern raccoon 69
spinner dolphin 303
"towns", black-tailed prairie dog 48
Trachypithecus geei **267**
Tragelaphus buxtoni **179**
tragopan, satyr 267
trails, rufous sengi 182
tree dwellers
American black bear 54, 55
aye-aye 241
Bornean orangutan 297
coati 86
emperor tamarin 92
European pine marten 165
golden langur 267
golden snub-nosed monkey 273
Goodfellow's tree kangaroo 317
Hoffmann's two-toed sloth 79
Müller's gibbon 298
pygmy marmoset 92
silky anteater 86
spectacled bear 87
Terai sacred langur 259
Verreaux's sifaka 240
western tarsier 294
tree frogs
European 152
green **326**
red-eyed 82–83
tree kangaroos 314
Goodfellow's **317**
tree viper, Chinese green 272–73
trees
acacia 178, 193, 320, 334
African cherry 208
Amazon rainforest 90–91
baobab 236
broadleaf 11
conifers 11
cork oak 13, 153
deciduous 284
Ethiopian Highlands 178
eucalypts 152, 306, 320, 334, 339
forests 12–13
giant kauri 354, 355
Japanese cherry 284–85
jarrah 320
Jeffrey pine 52
Joshua tree 60
juniper 52, 140, 146, 178, 248
kapok 78
lodgepole pine 34, 35, 52
Madagascan dry forest **236–37**
mahogany 66
oak 52, 66, 266
ombu 115
pine 13
Ponderosa pine 52
quaking aspen 35
red fir 52
rimu 354
saxaul 278
Scottish Highlands 140
sequoia 52, 53

white fir 52
Wollemi pine 334
see also forests; rainforests
Tremarctos ornatus **87**
Trichechus manatus **67**
Tridacna gigas **352**
Triturus cristatus **170**
troops
golden snub-nosed monkey 273
Japanese macaque 287
red howler monkey 93
ring-tailed lemur 239
vervet monkey 201
see also social groups
tropical dry forest 13
Madagascan dry forest **236–37**
tropical grassland 15
North Australian savannas **320–321**
Serengeti savannas **192–93**
Terai-Duar savannas **254–55**
tropical moist forest 13
see also tropical rainforest
tropical rainforests 90–91
Amazonian rainforest **90–91**
Andean yungas **86–87**
Bornean rainforest **292–293**
Congo Basin **208–209**
Costa Rican rainforest **80–81**
New Guinea montane forest **314–315**
trout, cutthroat 35
Trueb's cochran frog 89
trunk, African savanna elephant 203
tuatara **358–59**
tucuxi 91
tuna
skipjack 303
yellowfin 303
tundra 362
Antarctica 362
Arctic 22, 33
Europe 133
Siberia 246
Tupinambis teguixin **105**
turaco
Livingstone's 192
Prince Ruspoli's 178
Turkana, Lake 184
turkey vulture **56–57**
turtle-headed sea snake **347**
turtles 312
common snapping **72**
green sea **346–47**
leatherback 346
Mediterranean pond 152
ornate box 44
sea 302
tusks
African savanna elephant 203
Asian elephant 259
common warthog 230
narwhals 30
walrus 32
tussock, pale **170**
two-toed sloth, Hoffmann's **79**

U

Ukraine 282
ultraviolet light 26
underground living
Arctic fox 27
black-footed ferret 48
black-tailed prairie dog 48

common garter snake 50
Couch's spadefoot 64
coyote 49
European badger 165
southern marsupial mole 329
stag beetle 172
see also burrows and tunnels
unicorn 30
United Kingdom
Scottish Highlands 140-141
United States of America
Central Great Plains 44–51
Florida Everglades 66–73
Mojave Desert 60-5
Sierra Nevada 52-9
Yellowstone 34–43
Upper Yangtze Forests 272–77
Upupa epops 157
Ural Mountains 133
Urocyon cinereoargenteus 67
Uroplatus henkeli 243
Ursus americanus 54–55
Ursus americanus kermodei 55
Ursus americanus luteolus 55
Ursus arctos gobiensis 279
Ursus arctos horribilis 36
Ursus maritimus 28–89

V

vampire bat 115
Varanus niloticus 226–27
Varecia variegata 239
venom *see* poisons
Verreaux's sifaka 240–41
vertebrae
anhinga 70
beluga 31
vervet monkey 201
Victoria, Lake 177, 184
Vicugna vicugna 110–11
vicuña 110–11
vipers
black-headed bullmaster 79
Chinese green tree 272–73
common adder 145
Vipera berus 145
Virginia 31
viscachas 121
northern 109
Vltava, River 164
Vogelkop bowerbird 314
Vogelkop montane rainforests 314
volcanoes
Antarctica 363
Galapagos Islands 122
Iceland 132
island arcs 247
New Guinea 314
Pacific Ring of Fire 246
Yellowstone Caldera 35
voles 27, 58
water 141
Vombatus ursinus 337
Vulpes macrotis 61
Vulpes vulpes 168
Vultur gryphus 112–13
vultures 192
black 152
Egyptian 254
griffon 152
lammergeier 182–83
turkey 56–57

W

wallabies 320
black-footed rock 328
parma 337
Wallace, A.R. 300
Wallace line 247
Wallace's flying frog 300
wallaroo 320
walrus 32
wandering albatross 366–67
warning signs
mountain kingsnake 59
striped skunk 54
warthog, common 218, 230
Washington state 36, 59
wasps 51
water conservation, spectacled hare
wallaby 321
water cycle, Okavango Delta 219
water dragon, Australian 342
water hyacinth 19, 101
water snail 107
water vole 141
waterlily 100
wattle, golden 334
waved albatross 125
weasels 40
Eurasian otter 166–67
giant otter 102–03
Japanese 285
Japanese marten 288–89
wolverine 38
weavers
black-capped social 204–05
sociable 228–29
webbed feet, capybara 101
webs
golden silk orbweaver 73
Sydney funnelweb spider 343
Weddell Sea 363
wedge-tailed eagle 322, 328
welcome swallow 355
West Indian manatee 67
western capercaillie 145
Western Cordillera 22, 23
western diamondback rattlesnake 64
western gorilla 212–13
western red deer 141
western roe deer 153
western tarsier 294
Westland temperate forest, New Zealand
354
weta 354
Auckland tree weta 359
wetlands 10, 15
Camargue 146–47
Florida Everglades 66–67
Murray-Darling Basin 313
North America 22
Okavango Delta 218–19
Pantanal 76, 100–01
Tagus Valley 152
whale shark 306–07, 345
whales 187
beluga 24, 31
blue 19, 364, 372–73
bowhead 24
dwarf minke 345
fin 364, 372
humpback 364, 345
minke 364
narwhal 30–31
right 364

sei 364
sperm 364
whiskers
greater hedgehog tenrec 241
grey seal 135
whistling acacia 192
whistling-duck, plumed 323
white-backed woodpecker 134
white bat, Honduran 79
white-eye, Japanese 284
white fir 52
white-lipped peccary 101
white rhinoceros 222–23, 256
white stork 193
white-tailed deer 40, 153
white-tailed eagle 43
whitebark pine 34
whitefish, European 159
Whitney, Mount 52
Wichita Mountains Wildlife Refuge 44
widow spiders, redback 326
wigeon 184
wild boar 164, 169, 261
wild dogs
African 192, 224–25
coyote 49
wildcat 143, 164
wildebeest 192, 193, 198, 200
willow trees 140
winds, Antarctica 362
wings
Andean condor 112
common flying dragon 298–99
common morpho 81
great frigatebird 124
lammergeier 183
mute swan 148
turkey vulture 56, 57
wandering albatross 366
wisent 47
wolf spider, Norwegian 164
Wollemi pine 334
Wolong Nature Reserve 272
wolverine 38
wolves 27, 38, 164
Arabian 248, 249
Ethiopian 178, 182
grey 34, 35, 37, 47, 158–59
maned 118–19
Rocky Mountain 37
Woma python 333
wombat, common 337
wonder gecko, Przewalski's 283
wood ant 140
wood bison 47
Wood Buffalo National Park 47
wood frog 24
woodchuck 14
woodpecker finch 125
woodpeckers
Andean flicker 111
black 169
black-backed 52
three-toed 164
white-backed 134
woolly bear caterpillar 25
World Heritage Sites 51
World Wildlife Fund 114
wrens
dusky grass 328
purple-crowned fairy 323
Wyoming 36

Y

Yacare caiman 106–07
yak, wild 266
Yañez's iguana 113
Yangtze Forests 272–77
Yangtze River 272
Yarkand gazelle 279
yellow-billed chough 161
yellow-faced honeyeater 335
yellow-legged frog 59
Yellow River 272
yellow-throated marten 272
yellowfin tuna 303
Yellowstone 34–43
Yellowstone Caldera 35
Yosemite National Park 52
young animals
American alligator 72
armadillo lizard 235
black-tailed jackrabbit 63
Bornean orangutan 297
common adder 145
duck-billed platypus 336
emerald tree boa 97
emperor scorpion 216
ensatina 59
European hedgehog 156
giant anteater 116
Japanese macaque 287
koala 339
northern raccoon 69
olive baboon 185
red howler monkey 93
red kangaroo 331
ring-tailed lemur 239
scalloped hammerhead shark 349
striped scorpion 50
striped skunk 54
western roe deer 153
wild boar 169
Yacare caiman 107
see also calves; chicks; cubs; pups;
tadpoles
yucca 60
yucca moth 60
yungas, Andean 84–89

Z

Zaglossus bartoni 315
Zalophus wollebaeki 123
Zambezi River 176
zebra mbuna 191
zebras 192, 193, 198
Chapman's 200
Grant's 200
zooplankton 306

ACKNOWLEDGMENTS

DK would like to thank:

Robert Dinwiddie for consultancy on main continent feature pages; Christopher Bryan for additional research; Sanjay Chauhan, Parul Gambhir, Alison Gardner, Meenal Goel, Konica Juneja, Roshni Kapur, Alexander Lloyd, Upasana Sharma, Riti Sodhi, and Priyansha Tuli for additional design assistance; Suefa Lee, Vibha Malhotra, and Ira Pundeer for editorial assistance; Katie John for proofreading, and the following people and organizations for allowing us to carry out photography:

British Wildlife Centre, Lingfield, Surrey, UK

The British Wildlife Centre is home to more than 40 species of native British wildlife, all housed in large natural enclosures that mimic their wild habitats. The centre actively manages or participates in several conservation programmes for British wildlife, and focuses on education in all aspects of their work. The British Wildlife Centre is an excellent place to see Britain's wonderful wildlife up close and personal.
(Liza Lipscombe, Marketing and Information Officer; Matt Binstead, Head Keeper); Izzy Coomber (Senior Keeper)

Liberty's Owl Raptor and Reptile Centre, Hampshire, UK

Liberty's Owl, Raptor and Reptile Centre is located near Hampshire's New Forest National Park. It is named after Liberty, the Alaskan bald eagle who lives there. Liberty's houses a large collection of birds of prey including owls, hawks, falcons, and vultures, as well as a collection of reptiles and other small animals. The centre also offers falconry experience days, photographic experience days, and hawking days.
(Lynda Bridges and all the staff)

Wildlife Heritage Foundation, Kent, UK

Wildlife Heritage Foundation (WHF) is a centre of excellence dedicated to the captive breeding of endangered big cats within European Endangered Species Programmes with the eventual aim of providing animals for scientifically based re-introduction projects. WHF is also a sanctuary for older big cats.
(The trustees, management, staff, and volunteers)

Blackpool Zoo, UK

Blackpool Zoo is a medium-sized collection of more than 1,000 animals that has been open for over 40 years on its current site. Species vary from those critically endangered such as Amur tigers, Bactrian camels, and Bornean orangutans to western lowland gorillas, Asian elephants, giraffes, and many other favourites. A growing and varied collection of birds includes the only Magellanic penguins in the UK, and Californian sea lions offer an educational display daily throughout the year.
(Judith Rothwell, Marketing & PR Coordinator; Laura Stevenson, Digital Marketing Executive; all the keepers)

Cotswolds Wildlife Park, Oxfordshire, UK

The Cotswold Wildlife Park was opened in 1970. It covers 65 hectares (160 acres) and is home to 254 species. Highlights include a breeding group of white rhinos and a collection of lemurs. The gardens are also highly regarded among the horticultural community. The park has its own charity that funds conservation work all over the world and also directly manages the Sifaka Conservation Project in Madagascar.
(Jamie Craig, Curator; Hayley Rothwell, Activities Coordinator)

Picture credits
The publisher would like to thank the following for their kind permission to reproduce their photographs:

(Key: a-above; b-below/bottom; c-centre; f-far; l-left; r-right; t-top)

1 FLPA: Frans Lanting. **2-3 FLPA:** Minden Pictures / Tui De Roy. **4 Alamy Images:** Matthijs Kuijpers (cl); Life On White (fcr). **Corbis:** Joe McDonald (fcl). **Dorling Kindersley:** Thomas Marent (c). **Getty Images:** Tim Flach (ffcr). **SuperStock:** Animals Animals (cr). **5 FLPA:** ImageBroker (fcl); Minden Pictures / Chris van Rijswijk (fcr). **6 Corbis:** AlaskaPhotoGraphics / Patrick J. Endres (fcl); AlaskaStock (cr). **FLPA:** Minden Pictures / Ingo Arndt (cl). **Getty Images:** Gail Shumway (c). **7 Corbis:** Anup Shah (cl); Staffan Widstrand (c). **Getty Images:** Digital Vision / David Tipling (fcr). **National Geographic Creative:** Tim Laman (cr). **8 Carl Chapman:** (cl). **FLPA:** Frans Lanting (cb); Albert Visage (tl); Ben Sadd (tr); Minden Pictures / Thomas Marent (cla). **Getty Images:** Grambo Grambo (bl); Gail Shumway (tc). **naturepl.com:** Aflo (clb). **stevebloom.com:** (br). **9 Corbis:** Design Pics / Natural Selection William Banaszewski (cl); All Canada Photos / Wayne Lynch (cla). **FLPA:** Frans Lanting (bc); Minden Pictures / Steve Gettle (tl); Minden Pictures / Konrad Wothe (clb). **Tom & Pat Leeson Photography:** Thomas Kitchin & Victoria Hurst (c). **SuperStock:** Mark Newman (cb). **10 Alamy Images:** Bernd Schmidt (cr). **Getty Images:** Stocktrek Images (c). **11 Corbis:** Tim Graham (bl). **Dreamstime.com:** Viophotography (br). **FLPA:** Minden Pictures / Ingo Arndt (cra). **Getty Images:** Ascent Xmedia (ca). **iStockphoto.com:** Anita Stizzoli (cr). **12 FLPA:** Minden Pictures / Tim Fitzharris (cr); Minden Pictures / Konrad Wothe (clb). **12-13 Corbis:** Minden Pictures / Buiten-beeld / Wil Meinderts (b). **13 Alamy Images:** MShieldsPhotos (crb). **Dreamstime.com:** Isselee (cra). **FLPA:** ImageBroker (c). **naturepl.com:** Nick Upton (cl). **14 Dreamstime.com:** Iakov Filimonov (cla). **FLPA:** Imagebroker / Herbert Kratky (crb); Minden Pictures / Michael Durham (ca). **naturepl.com:** Onne van der Wal (clb). **14-15 Alamy Images:** Blaine Harrington III (b). **15 123RF.com:** Tatiana Belova (cr). **FLPA:** Bob Gibbons (cl); Minden Pictures / Richard Du Toit (c). **16 Dorling Kindersley:** Liberty's Owl, Raptor and Reptile Centre, Hampshire, UK (cra). **FLPA:** Dickie Duckett (c); Imagebroker / Peter Giovannini (crb). **Getty Images:** DC Productions (clb). **16-17 FLPA:** ImageBroker (b). **17 Dreamstime.com:** Subhrajyoti Parida (cla). **FLPA:** ImageBroker (cra); Minden Pictures / Michael & Patricia Fogden (c). **Getty Images:** Imagemore Co., Ltd. (crb). **18 Dreamstime.com:** Fabio Lotti (clb); Welcomia (c). **FLPA:** Minden Pictures / Kevin Schafer (cr). **18-19 Getty Images:** Design Pics / Vince Cavataio (bc). **19 FLPA:** Imagebroker / Alfred & Annaliese T (cl); Minden Pictures / Konrad Wothe (cr). **OceanwideImages.com:** Gary Bell (c). **20-21 SuperStock:** age fotostock / Don Johnston. **22 Alamy Images:** Charline Xia Ontario Canada Collection (cb). **23 123RF.com:** David Schliepp (bc). **Ardea:** (cra). **Getty Images:** Jad Davenport (tr). **24 Alamy Images:** Gary Tack (tr). **FLPA:** Biosphoto / Sylvain Cordier (c). **naturepl.com:** MYN / Carl Battreall (bc). **24-25 FLPA:** Minden Pictures / Jim Brandenburg (c). **25 Alamy Images:** Wildscotphotos (ca). **Corbis:** Tim Davis (br). **FLPA:** Minden Pictures / Jim Brandenburg (c). **Peter Leopold, University of Norway:** (bl). **naturepl.com:** MYN / Les Meade (tl). **26 Corbis:** All Canada Photos / Wayne Lynch (tr). **FLPA:** Minden Pictures / Jim Brandenburg (b). **27 Corbis:** AlaskaStock (tr); Tom Brakefield (tl). **Getty Images:** Photodisc / Paul Souders (b). **28 Corbis:** Cultura (tr); Jenny E. Ross (tc). **stevebloom.com:** (b). **30-31 National Geographic Creative:** Paul Nicklen (t). **30 FLPA:** Minden Pictures / Flip Nicklin (tl). **Getty Images:** National Geographic / Paul Nicklen (b). **31 Alamy Images:** Andrey Nekrasov (tr). **Corbis:** All Canada Photos / Wayne Lynch (bc). **Getty Images:** AFP / Kazuhiro Nogi (ca). **32 Corbis:** All Canada Photos / Wayne Lynch (b). **Dreamstime.com:** Vladimir Melnik (l). **FLPA:** Minden Pictures / Flip Nicklin (tr). **33 123RF.com:** Vasiliy Vishnevskiy (cra). **Alamy Images:** Blickwinkel (br). **Dorling Kindersley:** Liberty's Owl, Raptor and Reptile Centre, Hampshire, UK (tc). **Getty Images:** Universal Images Group (bl). **34 Margarethe Brummermann Ph.D.:** (c). **Corbis:** Joe McDonald (cb). **naturepl.com:** Ben Cranke (tr). **34-35 Alamy Images:** Nature Picture Library (c). **35 Corbis:** Jeff Vanuga (br). **FLPA:** Minden Pictures / Donald M. Jones (ca); Minden Pictures / Michael Quinton (bl); Fritz Polking (c). **36 FLPA:** Frans Lanting (b). **naturepl.com:** Andy Rouse (tr). **37 Corbis:** Charles Krebs (bc). **Dorling Kindersley:** Jerry Young (tl, tr). **38-39 Alaskaphotographics.com:** Patrick J. Endres (Moose). **38 Alamy Images:** Danita Delimont (tc). **Getty Images:** Robert Postma (bl). **39 Corbis:** Minden Pictures / Mark Raycroft (tr). **40 FLPA:** Minden Pictures / Donald M. Jones (tr). **naturepl.com:** Shattil & Rozinski (bl). **Robert Harding Picture Library:** James Hager (cr). **41 Ardea:** Tom & Pat Leeson (tr, b). **Dreamstime.com:** Musat Christian (tl). **42 Alamy Images:** franzfoto.com (tc). **Corbis:** Arthur Morris (b). **43 FLPA:** Frans Lanting (tr). **Getty Images:** Tom Murphy / National Geographic (tl). **44 FLPA:** ImageBroker (c); Photo Researchers (cl). **Getty Images:** Jake Rajs (b). **45 Alamy Images:** (bl, br). **Dreamstime.com:** Izanbar (tr). **naturepl.com:** Gerrit Vyn (clb). **46 FLPA:** Minden Pictures / Ingo Arndt (bl). **Ben Forbes:** (t). **National Geographic Creative:** Tom Murphy (br). **48 FLPA:** Minden Pictures / Donald M. Jones (b). **48-49 FLPA:** Paul Sawer. **49 123RF.com:** Steve Byland (tr). **50 123RF.com:** Melinda Fawver (cr); Benjamin King (br). **FLPA:** Minden Pictures / Donald M. Jones (bl). **SuperStock:** Animals Animals (tc). **51 Dreamstime.com:** Janice Mccafferty | (cr). **FLPA:** Minden Pictures / Ingo Arndt (b). **52 Corbis:** All Canada Photos / Glenn Bartley (clb). **naturepl.com:** Tom Vezo (cb). **Photoshot:** NHPA (bc). **53 123RF.com:** (tr). **Corbis:** Imagebroker / Michael Rucker (bl). **FLPA:** Minden Pictures / Donald M. Jones (br). **naturepl.com:** (clb). **54 Corbis:** First Light / Thomas Kitchin & Victoria Hurst (b). **FLPA:** S & D & K Maslowski (tc). **Getty Images:** Fuse (tl). **54-55 Alamy Images:** Melody Watson (t). **55 Ardea:** M. Watson (bc). **FLPA:** Minden Pictures / Donald M. Jones (tr); Minden Pictures / Konrad Wothe (bl). **56 Corbis:** 167 / Ralph Lee Hopkins / Ocean (bl). **FLPA:** Frans Lanting (br). **Paul Whalen:** (cl). **57 Getty Images:** mallardg500. **58 FLPA:** Jules Cox (b); Minden Pictures / Michael Quinton (tc). **Robert Royse:** (tr). **59 123RF.com:** Tom Grundy (crb). **Alamy Images:** Design Pics Inc (tr). **FLPA:** Minden Pictures / Sebastian Kennerknecht (bl). **60 Christopher Talbot Frank:** (bc). **Robert A. Klips, Ph.D.:** (clb). **Wikipedia:** Ryan Kaldari (cb). **61 FLPA:** Minden Pictures / Tim Fitzharris (clb); Minden Pictures / Kevin Schafer (br). **Getty Images:** Joel Sartore (tr). **Warren E. Savary:** (bc). **62 123RF.com:** Eric Isselee (l). **Corbis:** George H H Huey (br). **63 Alamy Images:** Jaymi Heimbuch (tc). **Corbis:** Minden Pictures / Alan Murphy / BIA (cr). **Getty Images:** Danita Delimont (tr). **Rick Poley Photography:** (b). **64 Dorling Kindersley:** Jerry Young (tc). **FLPA:** Photo Researchers (crb). **naturepl.com:** Daniel Heuclin (clb). **64-65 Dorling Kindersley:** Jerry Young (c). **65 Corbis:** Visuals Unlimited / Jim Merli (tr). **National Geographic Creative:** Joel Sartore (b). **66 4Corners:** Susanne Kremer (bc). **Alamy Images:** WaterFrame (cb). **FLPA:** Frans Lanting (clb). **67 Alamy Images:** F1online digitale Bildagentur GmbH (bl). **Corbis:** Design Pics / Natural Selection William Banaszewski (bc). **FLPA:** Mark Newman (clb). **Photoshot:** Franco Banfi (c). **68-69 Getty Images:** Life on White. **69 Alamy Images:** Arco Images GmbH (br). **Getty Images:** Craftvision (tr); Joe McDonald (bl). **70 123RF.com:** Tania and Jim Thomson (tr). **FLPA:** Imagebroker / Christian Hutter (tl). **70-71 FLPA:** Minden Pictures / Donald M. Jones (b). **71 123RF.com:** John Bailey (tr). **Alamy Images:** Blickwinkel (cr). **Getty Images:** Russell Burden (ca). **naturepl.com:** George Sanker (bc). **72-73 Alamy Images:** Jeff Mondragon (t). **72 Corbis:** Biosphoto / Michel Gunther (bc). **Dorling Kindersley:** Jerry Young (tl, crb). **73 Science Photo Library:** MH Sharp (br). **74-75 Corbis:** Jim Zuckerman. **76 Corbis:** Galen Rowell (cra). **77 Corbis:** Novarc / Nico Stengert (bc). **Oscar Fernandes Junior:** (tr). **Getty Images:** Pasieka (tc). **78-79 Photo Bee1, LLC / Myer Bornstein. . Photo Bee1, LLC / Myer Bornstein:** (cb). **78 FLPA:** Minden Pictures / Michael & Patricia Fogden (bc). **Paul Latham :** (cb). **naturepl.com:** Nick Garbutt (clb). **79 Lucas M. Bustamante / Tropical Herping:** (bl). **FLPA:** Minden Pictures / Konrad Wothe (ca); Minden Pictures / Suzi Eszterhas (br). **80 Corbis:** E & P Bauer (bl). **81 Corbis:** Minden Pictures / Stephen Dalton (br). **FLPA:** Minden Pictures / Juan Carlos Vindas (tr). **82-83 Dorling Kindersley:** Thomas Marent. **83 FLPA:** Minden Pictures / Michael & Patricia Fogden (tl); Minden Pictures / Ingo Arndt (tr). **84 Alamy Images:** All Canada Photos (clb). **Corbis:** Image Source / Gary Latham (bc). **National Geographic Creative:** Christian Ziegler (cb). **85 Ardea:** Kenneth W. Fink (cb, tr). **Flickr.com:** diabola62 / www.flickr.com / photos / bilder_heinzg / 11874681244 (clb). **Getty Images:** Joel Sartore (br). **Science Photo Library:** James H. Robinson (bl). **86 Corbis:** Kevin Schafer (ca). **FLPA:** Chris Brignell (b).

Photoshot: Jany Sauvanet (tr). **87 Robert Harding Picture Library:** C. Huetter (br). **88 Dreamstime.com:** Suebmtl (tl). **Getty Images:** Mark J Thomas (r). **89 Alamy Images:** Wildlife GmbH (ca). **FLPA:** Minden Pictures / James Christensen (cb). **Getty Images:** Kim Schandorff (br). **90 Corbis:** JAI / Gavin Hellier (cb). **FLPA:** Robin Chittenden (c). **Keith Newton:** (tr). **90-91 Getty Images:** Elena Kalistratova (c). **91 FLPA:** Minden Pictures / Flip de Nooyer (c); Minden Pictures / Kevin Schafer (bl); Silvestre Silva (br). **92 Alamy Images:** Wildlife GmbH (cb). **Dorling Kindersley:** Gary Ombler, Courtesy of Cotswold Wildlife Park (tc, ca). **92-93 Ardea:** Thomas Marent (c). **93 FLPA:** Minden Pictures / Piotr Naskrecki (bc). **94 FLPA:** Frans Lanting. **95 123RF.com:** Anan Kaewkhammul (tr). **Corbis:** Minden / Foto Natura / SA Team (clb). **FLPA:** Frans Lanting (br). **96-97 Alamy Images:** Steve Bloom Images (b). **97 Corbis:** Joe McDonald (crb). **FLPA:** Minden Pictures / Chris van Rijswijk (tc). **98 Dorling Kindersley:** Thomas Marent (cl). **Getty Images:** Gail Shumway (b). **SuperStock:** Mark Newman (cra). **99 123RF.com:** Mirosław Kijewski (tl). **Getty Images:** Tim Flach (c). **100 FLPA:** Mike Lane (clb); Malcolm Schuyl (c); Minden Pictures / Luciano Candisani (bc). **101 123RF.com:** Noppharat Manakul (bl). **Ardea:** François Grohier (tr). **Dorling Kindersley:** Courtesy of Blackpool Zoo, Lancashire, UK (bc). **FLPA:** Biosphoto / Sylvain Cordier (clb); Minden Pictures / Pete Oxford (c). **102-103 FLPA:** Minden Pictures / Pete Oxford (t). **102 Alamy Images:** DPA Picture Alliance (bc). **naturepl.com:** Angelo Gandolfi (crb). **103 Corbis:** Jami Tarris (cr). **FLPA:** ImageBroker (b); Frans Lanting (tr). **104 FLPA:** Minden Pictures / Steve Gettle (bc). **Getty Images:** Dickson Images / Photolibrary (r). **105 FLPA:** Minden Pictures / Pete Oxford (ca). **Getty Images:** Suebg1 Photography (br). **Andrew M. Snyder:** (cr). **John White:** (cl). **106-107 Corbis:** SuperStock / Nick Garbutt (b). **106 Corbis:** Minden Pictures / Tui De Roy (tr). **107 Corbis:** SuperStock / Nick Garbutt (tl). **FLPA:** Minden Pictures / Luciano Candisani (tr). **108 Ignacio De La Riva:** (cb). **FLPA:** Biosphoto / Denis Bringard (cr); Biosphoto / Alain Pons (clb); Imagebroker / GTW (cl); ImageBroker (bc). **109 Flickr.com:** Fernando Rosselot (br). **FLPA:** Biosphoto / Antoni Agelet (ca). **Pablo Omar Palmeiro:** (tr). **110-111 Getty Images:** Padmanaba01 (b). **111 Corbis:** All Canada Photos / Glenn Bartley (bc). **FLPA:** Minden Pictures / Tui De Roy (tl). **Paul B Jones:** (ca). **112 Getty Images:** Joel Sartore (tr). **naturepl.com:** Daniel Gomez (ca). **112-113 Alamy Images:** Blickwinkel. **113 Manuel Francisco Gana Eguiguren:** (c). **María de la Luz Vial Bascuñán www.fotonaturaleza.cl:** (br/FabianLizard). **114 FLPA:** Carr Clifton (bc); Minden Pictures / Luciano Candisani (c). **naturepl.com:** Luiz Claudio Marigo (cl, clb). **115 Dreamstime.com:** Lunamarina (clb). **Flickr.com:** Yeagov C / www.flickr.com / photos / yeagovc / 15252486009 (bl). **FLPA:** Minden Pictures / Michael & Patricia Fogden (br). **naturepl.com:** Barry Mansell (tr). **116-117 Alamy Images:** Life On White. **117 Ardea:** (ca). **Corbis:** Tom Brakefield (tl). **Dreamstime.com:** Poeticpenguin (tr). **119 Dorling Kindersley:** Jerry Young (tr). **FLPA:** Minden Pictures / Tui De Roy (bc); Minden Pictures / Pete Oxford (br). **120 123RF.com:** Eric Isselee (tl). **FLPA:** Minden Pictures / Pete Oxford (tr). **Photoshot:** Picture Alliance (br). **121 FLPA:** Minden Pictures / Jim Brandenburg (bl). **Photoshot:** Juniors Tierbildarchiv (cra). **122-123 FLPA:** Frans Lanting (cb). **122 FLPA:** Frans Lanting (bc); Minden Pictures / Pete Oxford (clb); Minden Pictures / Tui De Roy (c). **123 FLPA:** Minden Pictures / Tui De Roy (tr, br); Minden Pictures / Pete Oxford (bl). **124 Corbis:** Kevin Schafer (tl). **FLPA:** Frans Lanting (br). **Dan Heller Photography:** (tr). **125 123RF.com:** Keith Levit (tr). **FLPA:** Minden Pictures / Tui De Roy (cra, bc). **126-127 SuperStock:** Mark Jones. **127 123RF.com:** Smileus (cra). **FLPA:** Minden Pictures / Tui De Roy (bc). **128-129 FLPA:** Frans Lanting (t). **128 FLPA:** Minden Pictures / Tui De Roy (bl, br). **129 FLPA:** Imagebroker / Ingo Schultz (tr). **130-131 naturepl.com:** Bruno D'Amicis. **132 FLPA:** Imagebroker / Hans Blossey (cl). **Getty Images:** Traumlichtfabrik (tl). **133 Corbis:** Imagebroker / Günter Lenz (bl). **FLPA:** Minden Pictures / Karl Van Ginderdeuren (bc). **134 Corbis:** imagebroker / Olaf Krüger (bc). **naturepl.com:** Espen Bergersen (cb). **Markus Varesvuo:** (bl). **135 Corbis:** Andrew Parkinson (ca). **FLPA:** Minden Pictures / Peter Verhoog (br). **naturepl.com:** Geomar / Solvin Zankl (bl). **136-137 Corbis:** AlaskaStock. **137 FLPA:** Harri Taavetti (cr). **National Geographic Creative:** Paul Nicklen (bc). **138 FLPA:** Minden Pictures / Luc Hoogenstein. **139 Fotolia:** Lux / Stefan Zeitz (tr). **Tomi Muukkonen:** (bc). **naturepl.com:** Asgeir Helgestad (br). **140 Corbis:** Fortunato Gatto / PhotoFVG (bc). **naturepl.com:** Arco / Meul (clb); Paul Hobson (cb). **141 Alamy Images:** (cb). **Corbis:** Niall Benvie (clb). **Dorling Kindersley:** British Wildlife Centre, Surrey, UK (tr, br). **FLPA:** Terry Whittaker (bl). **142 123RF.com:** Eric Isselee (tr). **FLPA:** Albert Visage (br). **Fotolia:** Eric Isselée (l). **143 Dorling Kindersley:** British Wildlife Centre, Surrey, UK (tc, cra). **FLPA:** Paul Hobson (bc). **144 Photoshot:** Picture Alliance (cr); Dave Watts (bc). **145 Alamy Images:** Christoph Bosch (tc). **Matt Binstead, British Wildlife Centre:** (br). **FLPA:** Desmond Dugan (tr). **146 123RF.com:** Wouter Tolenaars (bc). **Alamy Images:** Tim Moore (clb). **FLPA:** Fabio Pupin (cb). **147 Corbis:** JAI / Nadia Isakova (br). **FLPA:** Minden Pictures / Wim Weenink (clb); Minden Pictures / Wil Meinderts (bl). **148-149 naturepl.com:** 2020VISION / Fergus Gill (t). **148 FLPA:** Minden Pictures / Flip de Nooyer (br). **149 FLPA:** Imagebroker / Winfried Schäfer (tr); Minden Pictures / Ramon Navarro (br). **150 Dreamstime.com:** Geanina Bechea (tl). **150-151 FLPA:** Imagebroker / Franz Christoph Robi. **151 FLPA:** Rebecca Nason (tl). **Getty Images:** Joe Petersburger (tc). **152 Corbis:** JAI / Mauricio Abreu (bc). **Dorling Kindersley:** Thomas Marent (cb). **FLPA:** Minden Pictures / Lars Soerink (clb). **153 123RF.com:** Eric Isselee (tr). **Ardea:** Stefan Meyers (crb). **FLPA:** Bob Gibbons (bl); Minden Pictures / Willi Rolfes (cr). **naturepl.com:** Juan Carlos Munoz (clb). **Wild-Wonders of Europe, Staffan Widstrand:** (br). **154 FLPA:** Biosphoto / Jorge Sierra (tr). **Iberian Lynx Ex-situ Conservation Programme. www.lynxexsitu.es:** (bc). **naturepl.com:** Wild Wonders of Europe \ Pete Oxford (bl). **155 Marina Cano www.marinacano.com:** (r/lynx). **156 FLPA:** Paul Hobson (tr); Minden Pictures / Ingo Arndt (bc). **157 Corbis:** Biosphoto / Michel Gunther (b). **FLPA:** Gianpiero Ferrari (cl); Imagebroker / Bernd Zoller (tr). **158 FLPA:** Imagebroker / Bernd Zoller (clb); ImageBroker (cb). **Getty Images:** Look-foto / Andreas Strauss (bc). **159 FLPA:** Biosphoto / Remi Masson (bl); Imagebroker / Stefan Huwiler (tr). **naturepl.com:** Angelo Gandolfi (clb). **Wild-Wonders of Europe, Staffan Widstrand:** (bc). **160 123RF.com:** Eric Isselee (tl). **FLPA:** Minden Pictures / Misja Smits, Buiten-beeld (tr). **naturepl.com:** Alex Hyde (b). **161 Corbis:** Minden Pictures / BIA / Patrick Donini (cb). **FLPA:** Jurgen & Christine Sohns (cl). **naturepl.com:** Radomir Jakubowski (br). **162 Dreamstime.com:** Outdoorsman (tr). **FLPA:** Minden Pictures / Jelger Herder (bc). **162-163 age fotostock:** Blickwinkel / P Cairns (c). **163 Ettore Balocchi:** (br). **naturepl.com:** Stefan Huwiler (cr); Alex Hyde (cb). **164 Corbis:** Novarc / NA / Martin Apelt (bc). **FLPA:** Imagebroker / Christian Hütter (clb); Gerard Lacz (cb). **165 Alamy Images:** Blickwinkel (ca); imagebroker (bl). **Dorling Kindersley:** British Wildlife Centre, Surrey, UK (tr). **FLPA:** ImageBroker (clb). **166 FLPA:** Minden Pictures / Ernst Dirksen. **167 123RF.com:** Eric Isselee (tr). **Alamy Images:** AGE Fotostock (bc, br). **168 James Kruger:** (b). **169 Ardea:** Duncan Usher (ca). **Dreamstime.com:** Isselee (tr). **FLPA:** Duncan Usher (br). **Photoshot:** Niko Pekonen (crb). **170-171 Heidi & Hans-Jürgen Koch:** (t). **170 Dorling Kindersley:** Frank Greenaway / Courtesy of the Natural History Museum, London (cb). **FLPA:** Minden Pictures / Jelger Herder (cla); Minden Pictures / Thomas Marent (bc). **171 Getty Images:** Bill Beatty (bl); Oxford Scientific (OSF) (bc). **172 Dom Greves:** (bc). **172-173 FLPA:** Minden Pictures / Thomas Marent. **174-175 Corbis:** Minden Pictures / Tim Fitzharris. **176 FLPA:** Imagebroker / Egmont Strigl (tr). **177 Alamy Images:** Steve Bloom Images (tr). **naturepl.com:** Rhonda Klevansky (bl, cr); Poinsignon & Hackel (clb). **178 Corbis:** Robert Harding World Imagery / Gavin Hellier (bc). **FLPA:** Imagebroker / Stefan Auth (clb). **Fran Trabalon:** (c). **179 Africa Image Library:** (crb). **Alamy Images:** Papillo (bc). **© Dr Viola Clausnitzer. :** (clb). **FLPA:** Ignacio Yufera (bl). **Rene Mantei www.zootierliste.de:** (cra). **180 Dorling Kindersley:** Andy and Gill Swash (tc). **FLPA:** Imagebroker / GTW (bc). **Getty Images:** Anup Shah (bl). **180-181 FLPA:** Ignacio Yufera. **181 FLPA:** Imagebroker / Christian Hütter (crb). **182 Corbis:** Biosphoto / Michel Gunther (ca). **Dorling Kindersley:** Andy and Gill Swash (tc). **FLPA:** Martin B Withers (cb). **Getty Images:** John Downer (bc). **182-183 Mitchell Krog www.mitchellkrog.com:** (b). **183 Photoshot:** Jordi Bas Casas (tl, tr). **184 Ardea:** Ian Beames (c). **FLPA:** Frans Lanting (bc); Jack Perks (clb). **185 FLPA:** Dickie Duckett (clb); ImageBroker (tr); Frans Lanting (crb). **Magdalena Kwolek-Mirek. :** (bl). **186 FLPA:** Frans Lanting (t). **186-187 FLPA:** Frans Lanting (b). **187 Corbis:** Minden Pictures / ZSSD (bc). **Fotolia:** Eric Isselée (tr). **188-189 Corbis:** Anup Shah (b). **FLPA:** Elliott Neep (t). **189 Getty Images:** Grambo Grambo (ca). **190 Alamy Images:** Sue O'Connor (bc). **FLPA:** Frans Lanting (tl). **191 Ardea:** Leesonphoto / Thomas Kitchin & Victoria Hurst (br). **192 123RF.com:** Mike Price (c). **Getty Images:** Claudia Uribe (tr). **naturepl.com:** Visuals Unlimited (bc, crb, cb). **192-193 FLPA:** Frans Lanting (c). **193 Corbis:** (cb); Anup Shah (bl). **Getty Images:** Joel Sartore (c). **Kimball Stock:** HPH Image Library (tc). **194 Ardea:** Chris Harvey (br). **FLPA:** Frans Lanting (bl). **195 Alamy Images:** Chris Weston. **196 Dorling Kindersley:** Wildlife Heritage Foundation, Kent, UK (tl). **FLPA:** Frans Lanting (c). **197 Dorling Kindersley:** Greg & Yvonne Dean (tr). **FLPA:** Minden Pictures / Stephen Belcher (cl); Minden Pictures / Richard Du Toit (crb). **198 123RF.com:** mhgallery (tl). **FLPA:** Minden Pictures / Tui De Roy (tr). **Photoshot:** Andy Rouse (b). **199 123RF.com:** Fabio Lotti (c). **Corbis:** Hemis / Denis-Huot (tr). **200 FLPA:** Biosphoto / Mathieu Pujol (cl). **Cain Maddern / wildfocusimages.com:** (tr). **201 Getty Images:** Angelika Stern (bc); Pal Teravagimov Photography (tr). **202-203 stevebloom.com. 203 FLPA:** Frans Lanting (tr). **Getty Images:** Danita Delimont (bc). **204-205 FLPA:** Bernd Rohrschneider. **205 FLPA:** Minden Pictures / Tui De Roy (cra, bc). **206 123RF.com:** Gerrit De Vries (cb). **Dorling Kindersley:** Frank Greenaway, Courtesy of the National Birds of Prey Centre, Gloucestershire (br). **FLPA:** Frans Lanting (bc). **naturepl.com:** Charlie Summers (cla). **207 Corbis:** Richard du Toit (tr). **naturepl.com:** Michael D. Kern (bc). **SuperStock:** Animals Animals (cr). **208 Ardea:** Chris Harvey (tr). **FLPA:** Frans Lanting (c). **Witbos Indigenous Nursery:** (br). **208-209 Getty Images:** Cultura Travel / Philip Lee Harvey (c). **209 Alamy Images:** Blickwinkel (bl). **FLPA:** Phil Ward (br). **naturepl.com:** Tim Laman (tc); Mark MacEwen (c). **210 FLPA:** Frans Lanting (bl); Minden Pictures / Konrad Wothe (bc). **211 FLPA:** Frans Lanting. **212-213 FLPA:** Minden Pictures / Cyril Ruoso (t). **212 Alamy Images:** Terry Whittaker (bc). **OceanwideImages.com:** Mark Carwardine (bl). **Thinkstock:** Matt Gibson (tl). **214 Corbis:** Jami Tarris (br). **Dorling Kindersley:** Jerry Young (tl). **naturepl.com:** TJ Rich (bl). **215 123RF.com:** Jatesada Natayo (tr). **FLPA:** Frans Lanting (bc). **216 FLPA:** Neil Bowman (bc). **Getty Images:** Joel Sartore (cla). **217 San Diego Zoo Global:** (tl/EmperorScorpion). **218 FLPA:** Biosphoto / Sergio Pitamitz (tr); Biosphoto / David Santiago Garcia (c); David Hosking (br). **218-219 FLPA:** Frans Lanting (c). **219 FLPA:** Wendy Dennis (tc). **naturepl.com:** (c). **Science Photo Library:** Tom McHugh (bl); NASA (br). **220 123RF.com:** Nico Smit (tc). **Ardea:** Ferrero-Labat (bl). **220-221 FLPA:** Frans Lanting (t). **221 Alamy Images:** David Hosking (bl). **FLPA:** Imagebroker / Andreas Pollok (tr). **222-223 FLPA:** Minden Pictures / Tui De Roy (b). **223 Kevin Linforth:** (tc). **224 Corbis:** Minden Pictures / Suzi Eszterhas (c). **Dorling Kindersley:** Jerry Young (tl). **FLPA:** Minden Pictures / Martin Willis (bc). **225 123RF.com:** Alta Oosthuizen (br). **naturepl.com:** Tony Heald (t). **226 Dorling Kindersley:** Jerry Young (cra). **FLPA:** Chris Mattison (bc); Minden Pictures / Winfried Wisniewski (tc). **Chris Van Rooyen:** (cla). **227 naturepl.com:** Francois Savigny (b). **Shannon Wild:** (t). **228 FLPA:** Imagebroker / Winfried Schäfer (clb); Minden Pictures / Vincent Grafhorst (bc). **naturepl.com:** Philippe Clement (cb). **228-229 naturepl.com:** Ingo Arndt (c). **229 123RF.com:** Anan Kaewkhammul (tr). **Dorling Kindersley:** Courtesy of Blackpool Zoo, Lancashire, UK (bc). **Getty Images:** Heinrich van den Berg (ca). **Sharifa Jinnah:** (clb). **Photoshot:** Karl Switak (bl). **230 Corbis:** Imagebroker / Erich Schmidt (tc). **FLPA:** Frans Lanting (ca). **231 FLPA:** Minden Pictures / Richard Du Toit (b). **Getty Images:** Tim Jackson (ca). **232 FLPA:** Minden Pictures / Pete Oxford (tc). **naturepl.com:** Will Burrard-Lucas (bc); Charlie Summers (clb). **233 FLPA:** Ben Sadd. **234 Corbis:** Nature Picture Library / Tony Heald (ca); Ocean / 2 / Martin Harvey (bl). **234-235 Alamy Images:** Matthijs Kuijpers. **235 Corbis:** Biosphoto / Michel Gunther (tr). **236 FLPA:** Minden Pictures / Thomas Marent (clb). **naturepl.com:** Brent Stephenson (cb). **Photoshot:** Nick Garbutt (bc). **237 Dr. Melanie Dammhahn:** (br). **Dr. Jörn Köhler:** (clb). **naturepl.com:** Alex Hyde (tr). **238 FLPA:** Minden Pictures / Cyril Ruoso. **239 Corbis:** Nature Picture Library / Inaki Relanzon (bc). **Dorling Kindersley:** Courtesy of Blackpool Zoo, Lancashire, UK (tr). **FLPA:** Minden Pictures / Konrad Wothe (bc). **240 FLPA:** Frans Lanting (tl). **240-241 naturepl.com:** Nick Garbutt. **241 FLPA:** Frans Lanting (cb). **naturepl.com:** Nick Garbutt (cra, br). **242-243 FLPA:** Jurgen & Christine Sohns (c). **243 Corbis:** Biosphoto / Michel Gunther (tr); Visuals Unlimited / Simone Sbaraglia (tl).

Dorling Kindersley: Thomas Marent (br). **Tom & Pat Leeson Photography:** Thomas Kitchin & Victoria Hurst (cra). **244-245 4Corners:** Andy Callan. **246 Dreamstime.com:** Horia Vlad Bogdan (tr). **FLPA:** Minden Pictures / Hiroya Minakuchi (bc); Winfried Wisniewski (tc). **247 Getty Images:** Datacraft Co Ltd (cr). **248 FLPA:** Imagebroker / Winfried Schäfer (bc). **Svein Erik Larsen www.selarsen.no:** (clb). **naturepl.com:** Hanne & Jens Eriksen (cb). **249 Dreamstime.com:** Lawrence Weslowski Jr (tr). **FLPA:** Biosphoto / Xavier Eichaker (bl); ImageBroker (br). **naturepl.com:** Michael D. Kern (clb). **250 123RF.com:** Sirylok (tc). **FLPA:** Biosphoto / Michel Gunther (bc). **250-251 Corbis:** Staffan Widstrand. **252-253 Ardea:** Jean Michel Labat (t). **Dreamstime.com:** Isselee (b). **253 Alamy Images:** Blickwinkel (bl). **FLPA:** Minden Pictures / Ingo Arndt (tr); Jurgen & Christine Sohns (c). **254 FLPA:** Bernd Rohrschneider (c). **naturepl.com:** Hanne & Jens Eriksen (tr); Axel Gomille (cb). **254-255 iStockphoto.com:** Danielrao (c). **255 Christopher Casilli:** (c). **Getty Images:** EyeEm / Damara Dhanakrishna (br). **naturepl.com:** Sandesh Kadur (tc). **256 123RF.com:** Carlos Caetano (tl). **256-257 FLPA:** John Zimmermann (b). **257 Dreamstime.com:** Shailesh Nanal (crb). **FLPA:** Biosphoto / Patrice Correia (tl); Minden Pictures / ZSSD (bc). **naturepl.com:** Bernard Castelein (cra). **258-259 FLPA:** Biosphoto / Stéphanie Meng (t). **258 Alamy Images:** Blickwinkel (bc). **259 Dreamstime.com:** (tr, bc). **FLPA:** Minden Pictures / Cyril Ruoso (c). **260-261 Dreamstime.com:** Happystock. **261 FLPA:** ImageBroker (bc). **262 Alamy Images:** Papillo (tr). **262-263 FLPA:** Biosphoto / Daniel Heuclin (b). **263 FLPA:** Harri Taavetti (br). **Gunnar Pettersson:** (tr). **Dyrk Daniels - Woodinville, WA:** (cra). **264 Alamy Images:** Arco Images GmbH (ca). **Corbis:** Yannick Tylle (br). **Photoshot:** Bruce Coleman (bl). **264-265 Udayan Rao Pawar:** (t). **265 Dreamstime.com:** Lukas Blazek (cb). **266 Corbis:** Radius Images (bc). **naturepl.com:** Wim van den Heever (cb); Xi Zhinong (clb). **267 Alamy Images:** Luis Dafos (clb); Petra Wegner (bl); Kevin Schafer (tr). **James Cargin:** (crb). **Scott Klender:** (br). **naturepl.com:** Bernard Castelein (ca). **268-269 FLPA:** Paul Sawer. **269 Alamy Images:** Nature Picture Library (crb). **Dorling Kindersley:** Wildlife Heritage Foundation, Kent, UK (tr). **naturepl.com:** Jeff Wilson (bc). **270 Alamy Images:** Wildlife GmbH (br). **Dorling Kindersley:** Gary Ombler, Courtesy of Cotswold Wildlife Park (tr, b). **271 FLPA:** Frans Lanting (r). **272 Alamy Images:** Fuyu Liu (bc). **FLPA:** F1online (clb). **Natalia Paklina:** (cb). **273 FLPA:** Biosphoto / Emmanuel Lattes (bl); Minden Pictures / Cyril Ruoso (tr); Minden Pictures / Thomas Marent (br). **naturepl.com:** Michael D. Kern (clb). **274 FLPA:** Biosphoto / Juan-Carlos Munoz (clb). **274-275 FLPA:** Minden Pictures / Konrad Wothe. **275 FLPA:** Minden Pictures / Katherine Feng (bc); Minden Pictures / Thomas Marent (br). **Fotolia:** Eric Isselée (tr). **276 Dorling Kindersley:** Gary Ombler / Wildlife Heritage Foundation, Kent, UK (t, b). **277 123RF.com:** Iakov Filimonov (tr). **naturepl.com:** Mary McDonald (ca). **278 Alamy Images:** Cultura RM (cb). **FLPA:** Imagebroker / Stefan Auth (clb). **Getty Images:** Wan Ru Chen (bc). **279 FLPA:** Biosphoto / Eric Dragesco (clb, br). **naturepl.com:** Eric Dragesco (tr); Roland Seitre (bl). **Jenny E. Ross:** (cra). **280 FLPA:** Biosphoto / Eric Dragesco (tr). **naturepl.com:** Igor Shpilenok (bc). **Science Photo Library:** Anthony Mercieca (tc). **280-281 Corbis:** Yi Lu (b). **282 FLPA:** Imagebroker / Dieter Hopf (tr); Minden Pictures / ZSSD (br). **283 Alamy Images:** AGE Fotostock (br). **Vladimír Motyčka. Vladimir Motycka:** (ca). **284 Ardea:** Chris Knights (cb). **Corbis:** Amanaimages / Satoru Imai (bc). **FLPA:** Imagebroker / Klaus-Werner Friedri (clb). **285 Alamy Images:** Yuriy Brykaylo (clb); Interfoto (crb). **FLPA:** Imagebroker / Stefan Huwiler (bc). **naturepl.com:** Jussi Murtosaari (ca); Nature Production (bl, tr). **286 Corbis:** Nature Picture Library / Yukihiro Fukuda (b); T.Tak (tr). **FLPA:** Minden Pictures / Hiroya Minakuchi (tl). **287 Dreamstime.com:** Mikelane45 (tr). **288-289 naturepl.com:** Aflo (t). **288 naturepl.com:** Nature Production (b). **289 Alamy Images:** Prisma Bildagentur AG (br). **Ardea:** Stefan Meyers (tr). **Asian Nature Vision:** Masahiro Iijima (tc). **290 Alamy Images:** Bildagentur-online / McPhoto-Rolfes (tr). **FLPA:** ImageBroker (b). **291 Alamy Images:** Survivalphotos (cra). **Dreamstime.com:** Valeriy Kirsanov | (tr). **Getty Images:** Joel Sartore (b). **Kevin Messenger:** (cla). **292 FLPA:** Biosphoto / Berndt Fischer (crb); Minden Pictures / Chien Lee (tr). **naturepl.com:** Nick Garbutt (c). **292-293 FLPA:** Frans Lanting (c). **293 FLPA:** Biosphoto / Alain Compost (tc); Minden Pictures / Sebastian Kennerknecht (br). **naturepl.com:** Tim Laman (bl); Neil Lucas (c). **294 FLPA:** Frans Lanting (bc). **Getty Images:** Lucia Terui (ca). **294-295 FLPA:** Minden Pictures / Suzi Eszterhas (t). **295 FLPA:** Minden Pictures / Sebastian Kennerknecht (tr); Minden Pictures / Suzi Eszterhas (bl). **naturepl.com:** Anup Shah (bc). **296 FLPA:** Frans Lanting. **297 FLPA:** Biosphoto / Theo Allofs (tr); Frans Lanting (bc); Minden Pictures / Konrad Wothe (br). **298-299 FLPA:** Photo Researchers (b). **298 Johannes Pfleiderer www.zootierliste.de/en:** (tr). **SuperStock:** age fotostock (ca). **299 123RF.com:** Kajornyot (cr). **Alamy Images:** Panu Ruangjan (ca). **300 Corbis:** Minden Pictures / Stephen Dalton (cl). **FLPA:** Minden Pictures / Thomas Marent (bc). **Kurt (Hock Ping Guek) :** (tr). **301 FLPA:** Minden Pictures / Thomas Marent. **302 Alamy Images:** Steve Bloom Images (clb). **Didi Lotze, roundshot360.de:** Location: Wakatobi Dive Resort, Indonesia (bc). **Kar Seng Sim:** (c). **303 Corbis:** Robert Harding World Imagery / Michael Nolan (br). **Dreamstime.com:** Caan2gobelow (tr). **naturepl.com:** Constantinos Petrinos (bl). **SeaPics.com:** Mark V. Erdmann (clb). **304 FLPA:** Imagebroker / Fotoatelier, Berlin (tc); Imagebroker / Norbert Probst (c). **304-305 naturepl.com:** Doug Perrine (t). **305 FLPA:** Colin Marshall (br). **306 Dreamstime.com:** Torsten Velden (tl). **FLPA:** Reinhard Dirscherl (br). **Science Photo Library:** Alexis Rosenfeld (bl). **306-307 National Geographic Creative:** Brian J. Skerry. **308 FLPA:** Biosphoto / Tobias Bernhard Raff (t). **naturepl.com:** Pascal Kobeh (crb). **309 Alamy Images:** WaterFrame (tr). **Ardea:** Valerie Taylor (bl). **Dreamstime.com:** Teguh Tirtaputra (cra). **Photoshot:** Linda Pitkin (bc). **310-311 National Geographic Creative:** Tim Laman. **312 Corbis:** Nature Connect (tc). **FLPA:** Minden Pictures / Mitsuaki Iwago (br). **313 Alamy Images:** Clint Farlinger (c). **FLPA:** Imagebroker / FB-Fischer (bc). **314 FLPA:** Biosphoto / Daniel Heuclin (clb); Minden Pictures / Piotr Naskrecki (bc). **naturepl.com:** Richard Kirby (cb). **315 Alamy Images:** AGE Fotostock (bl). **FLPA:** Minden Pictures / Gerry Ellis (tr); Minden Pictures / Konrad Wothe (ca). **Markus Lilje:** (clb). **National Geographic Creative:** Tim Laman (br). **316 Corbis:** Nature Connect (bl). **Getty Images:** David Garry (bc); Imagemore Co., Ltd. (tl). **316-317 Getty Images:** Joe McDonald. **317 FLPA:** Minden Pictures / Otto Plantema (bc). **naturepl.com:** Roland Seitre (tr). **318-319 National Geographic Creative:** Tim Laman. **319 FLPA:** Biosphoto / Alain Compost (tr). **320 Dreamstime.com:** Metriognome | (clb). **FLPA:** Minden Pictures / Ingo Arndt (cb). **Getty Images:** UIG / Auscape (bc). **321 123RF.com:** Christian Musat (tr). **Ardea:** Hans & Judy Beste (clb). **Michael J Barritt:** (bc). **Photoshot:** Picture Alliance / I. Bartussek (ca). **322 FLPA:** Biosphoto / Jami Tarris (bl). **323 FLPA:** Minden Pictures / Martin Willis (tr). **Steve Murray:** (br). **324 Ardea:** Auscape (tl). **FLPA:** Biosphoto / Sylvain Cordier (c). **325 FLPA:** Malcolm Schuyl (bc). **326 123RF.com:** Christopher Ison (cl). **OceanwideImages.com:** Gary Bell (bl). **Steve and Alison Pearson Airlie Beach Queensland Australia:** (tr). **327 Michael Doe:** (t). **FLPA:** Minden Pictures / Mark Moffett (bl, br). **328 David Cook:** (ca). **Getty Images:** UIG / Auscape (bc). **Nathan Litjens:** (clb). **329 Alamy Images:** Auscape International Pty Ltd (bc). **Ardea:** Jean Michel Labat (cl). **FLPA:** ImageBroker (bl); Jurgen & Christine Sohns (clb). **OceanwideImages.com:** Gary Bell (ca). **Photoshot:** NHPA (crb). **330-331 Getty Images:** Tier Und Naturfotographie J & C Sohns. **331 Corbis:** Jami Tarris (bc). **332 Getty Images:** Theo Allofs (ca). **naturepl.com:** Roland Seitre (bc). **332-333 naturepl.com:** Steven David Miller (t). **333 Bill & Mark Bell. :** (br). **Stephen Mahony:** (bc). **334 Corbis:** Minden Pictures / Roland Seitre (tr). **Dreamstime.com:** Jeremy Wee (c). **FLPA:** Keith Rushforth (bc). **334-335 123RF.com:** Tim Hester. **335 Corbis:** Minden Pictures / BIA / Jan Wegener (c). **Dorling Kindersley:** Courtesy of Blackpool Zoo, Lancashire, UK (bl). **FLPA:** Martin B Withers (tc). **Getty Images:** Mike Powles (br). **338-339 FLPA:** Jurgen & Christine Sohns (t). **338 Alamy Images:** AGE Fotostock (br). **FLPA:** Minden Pictures / Suzi Eszterhas (bc). **339 Fotolia:** Eric Isselée (tr). **340 Corbis:** Laurie Chamberlain (clb). **National Geographic Creative:** Joel Sartore (tl). **Science Photo Library:** Gerry Pearce (r). **341 123RF.com:** Eric Isselee (cb). **Alamy Images:** Gerry Pearce (tr); David Sewell (ca). **Photoshot:** NHPA (br). **342 123RF.com:** Peter Zaharov (b). **343 Alamy Images:** Redbrickstock.com (tr). **Getty Images:** Oktay Ortakcioglu (cr). **Minibeast Wildlife:** Alan Henderson (ca). **naturepl.com:** Chris Mattison (b). **Koen van Dijken:** (cb). **344 Corbis:** Ocean / 167 / Jason Edwards (br). **FLPA:** Imagebroker / Norbert Probst (tr). **naturepl.com:** Dave Watts (c). **344-345 naturepl.com:** Inaki Relanzon (c). **345 naturepl.com:** Brandon Cole (c). **OceanwideImages.com:** Gary Bell (tc). **346-347 naturepl.com:** David Fleetham (t). **346 FLPA:** Minden Pictures / Pete Oxford (crb). **347 FLPA:** Minden Pictures / Tui De Roy (bl); Minden Pictures / Richard Herrmann (br). **SeaPics.com:** Gary Bell (cra). **348 Alamy Images:** Martin Strmiska (t). **348-349 OceanwideImages.com:** David Fleetham (b). **349 Robert Harding Picture Library:** David Fleetham (tr). **350 OceanwideImages.com:** Gary Bell (tc, cl). **350-351 Vickie Coker**. **351 Carl Chapman:** (ca). **Ecoscene:** Phillip Colla (tr). **FLPA:** (br). **352 Alamy Images:** Natural History Museum, London (tc). **Ardea:** D. Parer & E. Parer-Cook (bc). **353 Corbis:** Stephen Frink. **354 FLPA:** Minden Pictures / Sebastian Kennerknecht (cb). **Wim Kok, Vlaardingen:** (bc). **Photoshot:** Dave Watts (clb). **355 Tom Ballinger:** (bl). **FLPA:** Minden Pictures / Martin Willis (crb); Geoff Moon (ca). **naturepl.com:** Brent Stephenson (bc). **www.rodmorris.co.nz:** (clb). **356 123RF.com:** Eric Isselee (tc). **Alamy Images:** Frans Lanting Studio (cb). **FLPA:** Minden Pictures / Tui De Roy (cla). **Photoshot:** (bl). **356-357 123RF.com:** Eric Isselee. **357 Alamy Images:** Prisma Bildagentur AG (tc). **358 Jérôme Albre:** (b). **359 Alamy Images:** Bruce Coleman (cra). **Grahame Bell (www.grahamenz.com):** (bc). **Alastair Stewart www.flickr.com/photos/alstewartnz:** (crb). **360-361 Corbis:** Maria Stenzel. **362 Corbis:** Wolfgang Kaehler (bc). **Getty Images:** Ralph Lee Hopkins (cla); Henryk Sadura (tc). **364 Xavier Desmier:** (bc). **Linda Martin Photography:** (c). **naturepl.com:** Doug Perrine (bl). **365 FLPA:** Minden Pictures / Konrad Wothe (clb). **naturepl.com:** Charlie Summers (br); David Tipling (bl). **Rex Features:** Gerard Lacz (tr). **366-367 Corbis:** Ocean / 145 / Mike Hill (t). **366 FLPA:** Frans Lanting (cr). **367 Corbis:** National Geographic Creative / Paul Nicklen (crb). **FLPA:** Frans Lanting (bl). **368 FLPA:** Minden Pictures / Tui De Roy (tr). **368-369 Corbis:** Minden Pictures / Otto Plantema / Buiten-beeld (b). **369 Alamy Images:** Cultura RM (tl). **FLPA:** Bill Coster (bc); James Lowen (tr); Malcolm Schuyl (cra). **370 Corbis:** Ocean / 167 / Keenpress (bc). **Getty Images:** Daisy Gilardini (c). **Dr Roger S. Key:** (clb). **371 Corbis:** Momatiuk - Eastcott (tr); Nature Picture Library / Doug Allan (clb); Paul Souders (br). **Richard E. Lee:** (bl). **372 Phillip Colla www.oceanlight.com**. **373 Dreamstime.com:** Freezingpictures / Jan Martin Will (crb). **Graham Ekins:** (cra). **FLPA:** Minden Pictures / Hiroya Minakuchi (br). **Robert Harding Picture Library:** Anthony Pierce (tr). **374-375 National Geographic Creative:** Paul Nicklen. **375 FLPA:** Biosphoto / Samuel Blanc (bc). **PunchStock:** Photodisc / Paul Souders (tr). **376-377 Corbis:** Imagebroker / Christian Handl. **381 Dreamstime.com:** Farinoza (tc)

Jacket images: *Front:* **Getty Images:** Paul Souders; *Back:* **4Corners:** Reinhard Schmid cra; **Alamy Images:** Chris Weston clb; **Corbis:** Jon Hicks cb; **FLPA:** Frans Lanting cr; **Getty Images:** Tim Flach ca, Narvikk cla, Alexander Safonov crb, Mark J Thomas cl; *Spine:* **Getty Images:** Paul Souders t

All other images © Dorling Kindersley
For further information see: www.dkimages.com